CW00968185

# ALCOHOL & ENTERTAINMENT LICENSING LAW

## Second Edition

This comprehensive and authoritative guide to licensing law is co-authored by the UK's only Professor of Licensing Law and two eminent licensing practitioners. It provides a detailed exposition and contextual analysis of the legal provisions governing the licensing of alcohol and entertainment under the Licensing Act 2003, encompassing both the legislative and decision-making framework of the Act as well as its implications for human rights.

Fully updated and revised, it covers the various forms of authorisation for licensable activities and licence and certificate conditions that might be attached as well as the enforcement and appeal provisions of the Act. This new edition, building on the highly acclaimed original work published in 2005, includes subsequent legislative changes and case law decisions.

New additions to this edition include:

- expanded coverage of enforcement provisions and police powers
- a revised and extended chapter on Appeals, in light of the practical and procedural developments that have evolved in the appeal process
- amendments to existing regulations and the revised Statutory Guidance issued in 2007.

This book is essential reading for all local authorities, legal advisers, licensing policy advisors, operators and the police, as well as those applying for licences.

**Colin Manchester** is Professor of Licensing Law at the University of Warwick and a Consultant to Poppleston Allen, Licensing Solicitors, Nottingham. **Susanna Poppleston**, Solicitor, and **Jeremy Allen**, Solicitor, are Founding Partners of Poppleston Allen, Licensing Solicitors, Nottingham.

# ALCOHOL & ENTERTAINMENT LICENSING LAW

## Second Edition

Colin Manchester, Susanna Poppleston,
Jeremy Allen

Routledge·Cavendish
Taylor & Francis Group
LONDON AND NEW YORK

First published in Great Britain 2005
by Cavendish Publishing Limited,
The Glass House, Wharton Street, London WC1X 9PX

Second Edition published 2008
by Routledge-Cavendish
2 Park Square, Milton Park, Abingdon, Oxon OX14 4RN

Simultaneously published in the USA and Canada
by Routledge-Cavendish
270 Madison Ave, New York, NY 10016

*Routledge-Cavendish is an imprint of the Taylor & Francis Group,*
*an informa business*

© 2005, 2008 Colin Manchester

Typeset in Palatino by
RefineCatch Limited, Bungay, Suffolk
Printed and bound in Great Britain by
Antony Rowe Ltd, Chippenham, Wiltshire

All rights reserved. No part of this book may be reprinted or reproduced
or utilized in any form or by any electronic, mechanical, or other means,
now known or hereafter invented, including photocopying and recording,
or in any information storage or retrieval system, without permission in
writing from the publishers.

*British Library Cataloguing in Publication Data*
A catalogue record for this book is available from the British Library

*Library of Congress Cataloging in Publication Data*
Manchester, Colin, 1952– .
Alcohol and entertainment licensing law / Colin Manchester,
Susanna Poppleston, Jeremy Allen. — 2nd ed.
p.   cm.
1. Liquor laws—Great Britain.   2. Bars (Drinking establishments)—Licenses—
Great Britain.   3. Nightclubs—Licenses—Great Britain.   4. Amusements—
Law and legislation—Great Britain.   I. Poppleston, Susanna, 1948–   .
II. Allen, Jeremy, 1944–   .   III. Title.
KD3474.M36  2008
344.4105'41–dc22
2007039119

ISBN 13: 978–0–415–42290–1
ISBN 10: 1–415–42290–6

# PREFACE

When the first edition of this work appeared in May 2005, transitional arrangements for the new licensing scheme contained in the Licensing Act 2003 were in place and operational, but 24 November 2005, when the scheme was to come fully into force, was some months away. There was a good deal of uncertainty and anxiety as to how the new scheme would function after that date and the impact that it would have. Over the course of the last two years, however, the scheme has bedded in as all involved in the licensing process have become familiar with the changes introduced by the 2003 Act and the requirements contained in its legislative scheme. Over this two-year period, there have been a number of important developments, both legislative and case law, which have shaped both the substantive law itself and the underlying focus of the 2003 Act.

Legislative developments, contained principally in the Violent Crime Reduction Act 2006, have included provision for Alcohol Disorder Zones (in which, as a last resort, holders of premises licences and clubs with club premises certificates within the zone can be required to contribute to the cost of the disorder); creation of a new offence of persistently selling alcohol to children, liability for which can result in police and trading standards officers giving closure notices prohibiting alcohol sales at the licensed premises for up to 48 hours; and an expedited review of premises licences which authorise the sale of alcohol in cases where the premises are associated with serious crime and disorder. These developments, coupled with others such as Penalty Notices for Disorder for some licensing offences, have reflected a significant shift in the focus of the 2003 legislation. Initially perceived primarily as a deregulatory measure aimed at developing and promoting the leisure industry, with targeted enforcement against 'problem' premises, the primary focus has shifted significantly, with the Act becoming an important mechanism for preventing crime and disorder and delivering the Government's alcohol harm reduction strategy.

Case law developments have, as expected, clarified several aspects of the new scheme, although inevitably judicial clarification is lacking in a number of areas and here uncertainty continues to prevail. These legislative and case law developments are covered in detail in this new edition, along with substantive changes to the Secretary of State's Guidance, which was revised and reissued in June 2007. Unlike the first edition of the book, the full text of the Guidance is reproduced in an Appendix to this edition, so that, along with the provisions in the 2003 Act and its accompanying regulations and other secondary legislation, there is comprehensive inclusion of all primary source materials.

The format of the book remains largely unchanged, although some chapters have undergone major revision or amendment and the opening chapter has been completely rewritten. This chapter seeks to provide: an introduction to the 2003 Act, which includes an overview of the legislative scheme; an exposition of its nature and underlying themes; a section on converted licences and certificates during transition (which in our view is important in order for readers to appreciate the different terms and conditions that may be attached to them compared to those granted under the 2003 Act); and an account of post-2003 Act developments. Chapters substantially revised include: Chapter 2 on Procedural and Decision-Making Framework, where there has been a restructuring of the chapter's contents; Chapter 11 on Enforcement, to which several sections have been added; and Chapter 12 on Appeals, which has been substantially expanded in the light of developments in magistrates' court practices in hearing appeals under the 2003 Act.

As with the first edition, the book seeks to combine detailed academic analysis of the legislative provisions, in the context of their practical application, so as to provide a comprehensive and (it is hoped) an authoritative exposition of the legal position. The approach, as previously, has been for the writing of the book to be done by Colin Manchester, initially with chapter revisions in draft and subsequently progressing through to final format, as practical aspects were incorporated and our collective views on particular matters were refined. Our feedback from the first edition has been overwhelmingly positive and we have been heartened by the favourable reviews that the book has received in legal periodicals. We hope that the second edition proves to be a valuable aid to understanding the 2003 Act now that it has become fully operational, and that it stimulates debate and discussion on areas that are controversial or where the legal position remains uncertain. We are grateful to everyone who has given us assistance in the preparation of this edition, with particular thanks due to our publishers, Routledge-Cavendish, especially Fiona Kinnear and Maddy Langford, with whom we have worked closely on this edition, and to our families who have put up with our continuing preoccupation with work on the book.

We have attempted to state the law, or at least the law as we understand it, as at 1 January 2008.

*Colin Manchester*
*Susanna Poppleston*
*Jeremy Allen*

# CONTENTS

# TABLE OF CASES

# TABLE OF STATUTES

# TABLE OF INTERNATIONAL LEGISLATION

# TABLE OF SECONDARY LEGISLATION

# GLOSSARY OF ACRONYMS AND ABBREVIATIONS

In the interests of economy of space, where expressions have been commonly used throughout the book, acronyms and abbreviations have been employed. The expressions will have been set out in full on first reference followed by the acronym or abbreviation in parenthesis and thereafter the acronym or abbreviation will have been used. For convenience, however, a list of these acronyms and abbreviations (in alphabetical order) is set out below.

| | |
|---|---|
| ADZ | Alcohol Disorder Zone |
| ADZ Guidance | Guidance on Alcohol Disorder Zones issued under s 19 Violent Crime Reduction Act 2006 |
| AHRSE | Alcohol Harm Reduction Strategy for England |
| ASBO | Anti-Social Behaviour Order |
| AWP | Amusement with Prizes |
| BRTF | Better Regulation Task Force |
| CCTV | closed circuit television camera |
| Convention | European Convention on Human Rights and Fundamental Freedoms |
| CPC | club premises certificate |
| CPR 2005 | Criminal Procedure Rules 2005 |
| DCMS | Department of Culture, Media and Sport |
| DPP | Director of Public Prosecutions |
| DPS | designated premises supervisor |
| ECtHR | European Court of Human Rights |
| ESLR Guidance | Expedited/Summary Licence Reviews Guidance |
| Guidance | Guidance issued by the Secretary of State for Culture, Media and Sport under s 182 Licensing Act 2003 |
| IAN | interim authority notice |
| JCHR | Joint Committee on Human Rights |
| LA 2003 (Fees) Regs 2005 | Licensing Act 2003 (Fees) Regulations 2005, SI 2005/79 |
| LA 2003 (Fees) (Amendment) Regs 2005 | Licensing Act 2003 (Fees) (Amendment) Regulations 2005, SI 2005/357 |
| LA 2003 (Hearings) Regs 2005 | Licensing Act 2003 (Hearings) Regulations 2005, SI 2005/44 |

| | |
|---|---|
| LA 2003 (Hearings) (Amendment) Regs 2005 | Licensing Act 2003 (Hearings) (Amendment) Regulations 2005, SI 2005/78 |
| LA 2003 (Personal Licences) Regs 2005 | Licensing Act 2003 (Personal licences) Regulations 2005, SI 2005/41 |
| LA 2003 (PL and CPC) Regs 2005 | Licensing Act 2003 (Premises licences and club premises certificates) Regulations 2005, SI 2005/42 |
| LA 2003 (PTA) (Notices) Regs 2005 | Licensing Act 2003 (Permitted Temporary Activities) (Notices) Regulations 2005, SI 2005/2918 |
| LA 2003 (SRPL) Regs 2007 | Licensing Act 2003 (Summary Review of Premises Licences) Regulations 2007, SI 2007/2502 |
| LACORS | Local Authority Co-ordinators of Regulatory Services |
| LAI conditions | licensing authority imposed conditions |
| LDN | Licence Dispensation Notice |
| LPA | local planning authority |
| LNR | late night refreshment |
| MCA | Marine Coastguard Agency |
| MCA 1980 | Magistrates' Courts Act 1980 |
| NDRV | non-domestic rateable value |
| Police Guidance | *Police Powers to Close Premises under the Licensing Act 2003*, DCMS, June 2007 |
| Police and TS Guidance | *Interpreting and implementing sections 23 and 24 of the Violent Crime Reduction Act 2006 – Persistently selling to children* |
| PND | penalty notice for disorder |
| SHC | special hours certificate |
| SIA | Security Industry Authority |
| SOE | special order of exemption |
| SOP | Statement of Licensing Policy (Licensing Statement) |
| TEN | temporary event notice |
| White Paper | *Time for Reform: Proposals for the Modernisation of Our Licensing Laws* (2000) Cm 4696 |
| 1964 Act | Licensing Act 1964 |
| 1982 Act | Local Government (Miscellaneous Provisions) Act 1982 |
| 1998 Act | Human Rights Act 1998 |
| 2001 Act | Private Security Industry Act 2001 |
| 2003 Act | Licensing Act 2003 |

# CHAPTER 1

# INTRODUCTION TO THE LICENSING ACT 2003

## 1.1  THE LICENSING SCHEME

### 1.1.1  Introduction

1.1.2    The Licensing Act 2003 (the 2003 Act) introduced a modernised and integrated scheme covering the sale by retail of alcohol or the supply of alcohol by a club to a club member, the provision of various forms of entertainment (principally music and dancing, indoor sports entertainments, films and plays) and the provision of late night refreshment (LNR), which is the provision of hot food or hot drinks at times falling within the period from 11.00 pm to 5.00 am.[1] Various forms of authorisation for these 'licensable activities' can be obtained from licensing authorities, which generally are local authorities (see 1.1.10 below). The forms of authorisation include premises licences, club premises certificates (CPCs) and temporary event notices (TENs), which can authorise any of the above activities, and personal licences that authorise the retail sale of alcohol under a premises licence. Licensing authorities are required to issue these authorisations and discharge their numerous other licensing functions under the 2003 Act with a view to the promotion of specified licensing objectives. These objectives, which are set out in s 4(2) of the 2003 Act, are: (a) the prevention of crime and disorder; (b) public safety; (c) the prevention of public nuisance; and (d) the protection of children from harm.

1.1.3    Prior to the 2003 Act, there were a number of separate licensing schemes for the above-mentioned activities. Licences for the sale or supply of alcohol (or 'intoxicating liquor' as it was termed under the Licensing Act 1964) were issued by licensing justices and there were separate statutory schemes for the licensing by local authorities of public entertainments (which included music, dancing and indoor sports entertainments), films, plays and LNR.[2] None of these schemes had any specified licensing objectives set out in the relevant legislative provisions; rather, the licensing authorities were given a broad, largely unfettered, discretion to determine whether or not licences should be granted in accordance with their perception of the public interest. There was no coherent rationale or purpose underlying the licensing controls and the broad discretion conferred inevitably led to wide inconsistencies, a lack of transparency and, at times, overintrusive regulation. When the Better Regulation Task Force (BRTF) – a body set up by the incoming Labour Government in 1997 to improve the quality of government regulation – measured the areas of liquor and entertainment licensing against its principles of transparency, accountability, targeting, consistency and proportionality, the system, particularly in relation to alcohol, was found wanting on several counts.[3] This led the Government to introduce in April 2000 a White Paper, *Time for Reform:Proposals for the Modernisation of Our Licensing Laws* ((2000) Cm 4696), which proposed reform not only of alcohol and entertainment licensing, but also the licensing of late night refreshment services. A new licensing scheme integrating these three areas of activity was duly implemented by the 2003 Act.

### 1.1.4   The licensable activities

1.1.5    Section 1(1) of the Act defines 'licensable activities' as:

(a)  the sale by retail of alcohol,

(b)  the supply of alcohol by or on behalf of a club to or to the order of a member of the club,

(c)  the provision of regulated entertainment, and

(d)  the provision of late night refreshment.[4]

A single premises licence can be obtained under which a person can provide any or all of these activites and any or all of them can similarly be provided under the authority of a TEN as temporary activities for a period of time not exceeding 96 hours (see s 100(5)(b) and 9.2.3 below), provided certain requirements are met. Section 2(1) provides:

A licensable activity may be carried on–

(a)  under and in accordance with a premises licence (see Part 3), or

(b)  in circumstances where the activity is a permitted temporary activity by virtue of Part 5.

1.1.6    Certain licensable activities are also 'qualifying club activities' and s 1(2) provides:

The following licensable activities are also qualifying club activities–

(a)  the supply of alcohol by or on behalf of a club to or to the order of a member of the club,

(b)  the sale by retail of alcohol by or on behalf of a club to a guest of a member of the club for consumption on the premises where the sale takes place, and

(c)  the provision of regulated entertainment where that provision is by or on behalf of a club for members of the club or members of the club and their guests.

The provision of a CPC for the above activities continues the special arrangements that had previously been applied to the consumption of alcohol on the premises of non-profit-making clubs and extends the arrangements to the provision of entertainment in clubs. As regards the provision of LNR in clubs, these are 'exempt supplies' and do not constitute licensable activities for which an authorisation is required (see Sched 2, para 3(2)(a) and 5.4.6 below).

1.1.7    In most cases, however, authorisation for licensable activities will be provided by a premises licence. Such a licence can authorise licensable activities either indoors or outdoors,[5] but on its own will be insufficient where the licensable activities include the sale of alcohol for consumption on or off the premises. In this instance, a personal licence, held by an individual, will also be needed to enable him to sell or authorise the sale of alcohol. The rationale for this was set out in the White Paper as follows:

The argument for licensing people as well as premises is that there needs to be a reasonable assurance that anyone responsible for the sale of alcohol is aware of his or her obligations and is capable of fulfilling them. In addition, a great many public houses are these days managed by people on behalf of large pub operating companies and the normal transfer of managers from one set of premises to another is unnecessarily inhibited by the current law which ties the licence holder and the venue together. A split licensing system therefore offers much greater flexibility to the industry in terms of human resources. The licence would be held by the person running the premises on a day to day basis (Cm 4696, 2000, para 39)

1.1.8   Whilst a personal licence is needed for the provision of alcohol under a premises licence, one is not needed for provision of alcohol under a CPC or TEN, nor is one required for the provision of entertainment or LNR under any form of authorisation. No personal licence is needed for the provision of alcohol under a CPC since non-profit-making clubs holding a CPC are essentially private premises where alcohol is not sold to the public and there are unlikely to be the problems of disorder or underage sales that might occur in licensed premises open to the public.[6] Nor is a personal licence required for the provision of alcohol under a TEN. Here there might be provision of alcohol to the public but the Act restricts the number of TENs that a person not holding a personal licence can give in any one year to five, compared to 50 that can be given by a personal licence holder (see s 107(1)–(3) and 9.7.1 below). The limitation on numbers clearly minimises, but does not eliminate, the risk of any unsuitable person selling alcohol at a temporary event. The risk might, of course, be eliminated if the police issue an objection notice on the ground that holding the event might undermine the crime prevention objective and this is upheld by the licensing authority (see 9.5 below). Otherwise, the risk remains a present one if the event goes ahead, although as Lord McIntosh stated during the course of the legislation's passage, the police have the power to close down for up to 24 hours premises for which a TEN has been given 'where they are a source of noise, nuisance and disorder likely to threaten public safety' (HL Deb, vol 643, cols 385–86, 17 January 2003). That a personal licence is not required for entertainment or LNR reflects the Government's view, expressed by Lord Davies in Parliament, that 'the risks associated with the provision of public entertainment or late-night refreshment without alcohol are not so great that a system of personal vetting is needed' (HL Deb, vol 643, col 395, 16 January 2003).

1.1.9   In addition to the need for a personal licence where alcohol is sold under a premises licence, there needs to be a 'designated premises supervisor' (DPS) for the premises. The DPS can, but need not be, the premises licence holder (see s 15(2) and 6.4.2 below) and the purpose of this requirement is to ensure that, in the case of premises selling alcohol to the public, there is someone with overall responsibility for the sale of alcohol on the premises, who can be readily identified by enforcement officers. The Government considered it essential that police officers, fire officers or officers of the licensing authority be able to identify immediately the person at any premises selling alcohol in a position of authority. Whilst this is an important consideration, it clearly detracts from the 'portability' concept of the personal licence and undermines the split between premises and personal licences, since the DPS holding the personal licence is 'tied' to the licensed premises for which he is the premises supervisor.

## 1.1.10 The licensing authorities

The licensing authorites administering the scheme are, for the most part, local authorites in England and Wales. In England, licences are granted by district or county councils, except in London where they are granted by borough councils or the Common Council of the City of London, and in Wales they are granted by county or county borough councils. Licensing authorities do, however, include three additional bodies: the Sub-Treasurer of the Inner Temple, the Under-Treasurer of the Middle Temple, and the Council of the Isles of Scilly. Section 3(1) and (2) provides:

(1) In this Act 'licensing authority' means–
  (a) the council of a district in England,
  (b) the council of a county in England in which there are no district councils,
  (c) the council of a county or county borough in Wales,
  (d) the council of a London borough,
  (e) the Common Council of the City of London,
  (f) the Sub-Treasurer of the Inner Temple,
  (g) the Under-Treasurer of the Middle Temple, or
  (h) the Council of the Isles of Scilly.
(2) For the purposes of this Act, a licensing authority's area is the area for which the authority acts.

## 1.1.11 Discharging the licensing functions

1.1.12  As indicated (see 1.1.2 above), a licensing authority is required to issue the various authorisations for licensable activities and discharge its numerous other licensing functions under the 2003 Act with a view to promotion of the licensing objectives. Further, in order to discharge its licensing functions, it is required to draw up a 'Licensing Statement', that is, a Statement of Licensing Policy (SOP), to which it must, under s 4(3)(a), have regard when carrying out its licensing functions. Section 5 provides that an authority must, for each three-year period, determine its policy with respect to the exercise of its licensing functions, and publish a statement of that policy. There are also requirements for consultation before determining the policy, for keeping statements under review and for making revisions as appropriate (see 4.3.3–4.3.5 below). In addition, a licensing authority must, under s 4(3)(b), have regard to any Guidance issued by the Secretary of State under s 182 of the 2003 Act when carrying out its licensing functions.

1.1.13  The requirement in s 4(1) for a licensing authority to discharge its licensing functions with a view to promotion of the licensing objectives focuses the authority's attention on the aims and purposes of licensing control and seeks to ensure that decisions are directed towards achieving them. The requirement in s 4(3)(a) seeks to ensure transparency in the discharge by the authority of its licensing functions by requiring it to set out in its SOP how it will discharge those functions. The requirement in s 4(3)(b) seeks to ensure that, whilst the discharge of licensing functions remains a matter determined primarily at local level, there will be an element of central 'direction' through the the Secretary of State's Guidance with a view to achieving a greater degree of consistency. This element of central 'direction' will feed into the authority's formulation of its SOP, since drawing up the SOP (and keeping it under review) is a licensing function and the authority must therefore have regard to the Guidance when discharging this function. The interrelationship between licensing objectives, the SOP and the Guidance is, however, a complex one and is examined in detail in Chapter 4.

## 1.2    NATURE OF THE LICENSING SCHEME

### 1.2.1   Deregulatory measure

1.2.2    The 2003 Act is first and foremost intended to be a deregulatory measure, aimed at promoting greater freedom of choice for the consumer and encouraging development of the leisure industry, whilst at the same time endeavouring to reduce crime, disorder and public nuisance, and ensuring that there are adequate safeguards provided for residents. Deregulation came in the form of a substantial legislative package, for on its passage the 2003 Act comprised some 200 sections and eight Schedules and was duly supplemented by several tranches of secondary legislation in the form of regulations and orders, along with 178 pages of statutory Guidance. The Act is not, however, simply concerned with eliminating historical anomalies, streamlining bureaucratic requirements and relaxing opening hours. More fundamentally, it seeks to readjust the boundaries between freedom and flexibility on the one hand and public interest regulation of the licensable activities on the other. As such, it can be seen as a flagship or exemplar of core elements of 'Third Way' politics[7] pursued by the Labour Government that introduced it and under which government does:

> all it can to support enterprise but never believes it is a substitute for enterprise. The essential function of markets must be complemented and improved by political action, not hampered by it. We support a market economy, not a market society. The belief that the state should address damaging market failures [has] all too often led to a disproportionate expansion of the government's reach and the bureaucracy that went with it. The balance between the individual and the collective was distorted. Values that are important to citizens, such as personal achievement and success, entrepreneurial spirit, individual responsibility and community spirit, were too often subordinated to universal social safeguards.[8]

The new scheme, the Secretary of State for Culture, Media and Sport, Tessa Jowell, stated during the course of the legislation's passage, represented an attempt to 'walk the tightrope between liberalisation and laissez-faire' (HC Deb, vol 402, col 52, 24 Mar 2003). This was to be achieved by keeping 'red tape' to a minimum, increasing 'choice' for consumers and avoiding 'well meaning interferences' in people's lives, whilst at the same time ensuring that the 'peace of residents and communities' was safeguarded, and that 'the vulnerable, the young and the wider public interest' were protected. The Secretary of State went on to say in her Foreword to the statutory Guidance published in July 2004:

> The Act ensures that premises which are causing problems within our communities can be dealt with appropriately but provides a much lighter touch for those businesses and community activities which benefit and enhance people's lives by providing important opportunities for the enjoyment of leisure time. This modernisation of the licensing laws provides industry with greater freedom and flexibility to meet the needs of consumers but balances that with clear responsibilities for the industry and strong powers for the police to control any disorderly premises and for licensing authorities to protect residents from disturbance.

In some areas this 'lighter touch' approach, however, has been more evident than others. On the one hand, in relation to temporary events, for example, the issuing of temporary event notices (TENs) has generally been a relatively simple and straightforward process (see ss 98–110 and Chapter 9). This is as the 2003 Act intended it to be, although it nevertheless remains more complicated and lengthy than the previous procedure under which temporary events might take place under a special order of exemption. On the other hand, in relation to variations of premises licences, for example, the specified procedure for variation contained in ss 34–36 of the 2003 Act, under which applications have to be publicised by a notice on or at the application premises and a newspaper advertisement (see 2.4.2 below), has not facilitated a 'lighter touch' in respect of alterations to the premises which are of a relatively minor nature, although it is understood that changes are planned for 2008. Further, the application forms contained in the secondary legislation have proved to be not only detailed and complex, but also far from easy to complete or comprehend. So, it has only proved to be in part the case that there has been a general 'lighter touch' deregulatory approach, with greater freedom and flexibility tempered only by the need to regulate where problems arise or are likely to arise, such as in the instances of disorder and disturbance mentioned by the Secretary of State.

1.2.3    Prevention of disorder on or around premises and prevention of disturbance to residents had been identified as key objectives of licensing regulation, both in the BRTF Report and the White Paper, along with the need for public safety and the protection of children from harm, and these became specified licensing objectives under the 2003 Act, which authorities are under a duty to promote. The 2003 Act thus addressed the criticisms of lack of coherent rationale or purpose under the previous law (see 1.1.3 above) by express provision of clear statutory criteria, in the form of licensing objectives, which were to govern the exercise of regulatory control. A focus on the licensing objectives also sought to preclude overintrusive regulation through licensing authorities straying into and duplicating requirements imposed by other statutory provisions governing other areas such as food and health and safety. Wide inconsistencies under the previous schemes were addressed through various regulations contained in secondary legislation (which, for example, introduced centralised forms and fees) and through the Secretary of State's Guidance. Lack of transparency and uncertainty amongst operators as to how authorities might carry out their licensing responsibilities was addressed by requiring authorities to draw up, following wide consultation, a SOP, to which they are required by s 4(3)(a) to have regard when discharging their licensing functions (see 1.1.12 above). These changes sought to ensure that the regulatory burden on operators was reduced and that the regulation of activities was brought into much sharper focus.

### 1.2.4    Underlying market-based philosophy

1.2.5    The deregulatory nature of the 2003 Act is reflected in the underlying market-based philosophy, which establishes an expectation that 'decisions' about licensable activities will be taken initially by operators of premises (for example, public houses or nightclubs) based on their perception of what the market (that is, the consumer) wants, subject to intervention only in respect of specific criteria (namely, the licensing objectives), which bear upon the social impact of individual licensed premises. The fundamental premise, therefore, on which the 2003 Act is based is that, in the first instance, operators should make market-based decisions about how they wish to undertake licensable activities at their premises. These are to be set out in an 'operating schedule' to accompany premises licence applications (and CPC applications) where, for instance, operators of public houses will indicate what parts of their premises they propose to use for the licensable activity of sale of alcohol and the hours at which they propose to do so. Further, responsibility is upon operators to explain in their operating schedule the steps which they propose to take to promote the licensing objectives. The underlying assumption is that operators, rather than the licensing authority, are best able to judge how their businesses will impact upon the licensing objectives and that they should first consider and address these issues.

Others able to judge the likely effect on the licensing objectives of granting a licence are those with expertise in particular fields, such as the police (who have expertise in crime and disorder) and those who live or work in the vicinity of the premises, and the capacity to make 'relevant representations' in respect of an application is confined to such persons. Thus only 'interested parties', essentially residents and businesses in the vicinity of the premises, and 'responsible authorities', such as the police and fire authority, can make 'relevant representations' as to the likely effect on the licensing objectives of the grant of a licence. As Baroness Blackstone explained during the course of the legislation's passage (at HL Deb, vol 645, col 400, 27 February 2003):

> Judgment of the merit of an application against the licensing objectives should be left to the experts. The experts on crime and disorder, and the protection of children from harm are the police, and so the police have a voice. The experts on public safety are the health and safety and fire authorities, and so they have a voice too. The experts on public nuisance are the local environmental health authority. It follows that they should have a voice too, and the Bill provides them with one. The experts in what it is like to live and do business in a particular area are local residents and businesses . . .

If the experts do not raise any concerns, then the operator's market-based decision on how to conduct licensable activities at his premises prevails, the licence must be granted under s 18(2) and matters set out in the operating schedule included as conditions on the licence, along with any mandatory conditions that must be imposed.[9] As Baroness Blackstone went on to state:

> What we are not doing, however, is allowing the licensing authority to make representations in its own right. One of the fundamental principles of the Bill is that applications should be granted administratively where the experts have not raised any concerns about them. Where those circumstances apply, there is no reason for the licensing authority as regulatory authority to give a second opinion to those experts, and it would be wrong to give it that opportunity.

The role of the licensing authority is thus effectively confined to that of a 'referee' or 'umpire' adjudicating between the applicant and those who have made 'relevant representations'. The licensing authority is not, as it might do in other areas of licensing control,[10] able to participate as a 'player' in the licensing process and raise concerns or objections on its own initiative. This is a marked departure from traditional approaches to licensing control, which tend to be characterised by 'command control' style regulation, with central government providing a broad framework within which local authorities seek to control and direct the activities in question in accordance with what, in their view, the public interest requires. However, although the licensing authority cannot participate *qua* licensing authority, the local authority in most cases is the licensing authority (see 1.1.10 above), some of the functions of responsible authorities which can make relevant representations, such as planning and environmental health, are discharged by the local authority (see 6.4.18 below) and the authority is therefore, at least indirectly, able to have an input into the licensing process.

1.2.6    There is, then, available to the licensing authority a much-reduced level of discretion, which becomes operative only if 'concerns' in the form of 'relevant representations' are raised in respect of the application. In such cases, the authority is required to hold a hearing to consider the representations and have regard to them when deciding what steps are necessary to promote the licensing objectives (see s 18(3) and 6.5.1 below). Whilst the discretion of the authority is engaged here, its exercise is subject to various constraints, for under s 4 it must reach its decision with a view to promoting the licensing objectives and must have regard both to the SOP, which it has drawn up, and to the Secretary of State's Guidance (see 1.1.12 above). Steps to promote the licensing objectives include the attachment of conditions, however, and here the underlying market-based philosophy has been tempered in that it has not been uncommon for premises operating under a premises licence to have a range of conditions attached to the licence, although they may have operated without such conditions under the previous law. A relevant representation may well be made by the police, for example, about the need for CCTV to assist in countering crime and disorder, and a condition requiring this is unlikely to be resisted by licensing authorities. The underlying market-based philosophy has been less apparent here and has been less in keeping with the practical reality.

    In addition, the market-based philosophy of the Act is reinforced by the fact that there should, at least in theory, no longer be a restrictive approach taken to the granting of licences for alcohol in cases where licensing authorities are able to exercise discretion. Restricting the number of outlets had, historically, always been regarded as an essential part of the functions of justices when exercising their licensing responsibilities for the provision of alcohol. It was regarded as implicit in the justices' discretion that regard could be had to the 'need' or 'demand' for additional outlets for alcohol and applications for the grant of new licences could be refused merely on the ground that there was no need or demand for a new licence in the area. In the period preceding the passage of the 2003 Act, Government opinion had swung decisively against 'need' and it was no surprise to find that this restrictive concept did not feature in the licensing scheme under the 2003 Act. Indeed, para 13.23 of the Guidance emphasises that 'need' is 'a matter for planning committees and for the market' and not for licensing authorities when discharging their licensing functions under the Act. Nevertheless, the concentration of premises in a particular area may be such that they have a 'cumulative impact' on crime and disorder and/or public nuisance in the area, and policy restrictions on the number and type of premises there may be considered necessary to promote the licensing objectives of prevention of crime and disorder and public nuisance. Although cumulative impact is not a statutory concept within the 2003 Act, the application of cumulative impact policies within certain parameters is recognised in the Secretary of State's Guidance and in judicial decisions on the 2003 Act (see 4.3.7–4.3.9 below). Whilst different from 'need', which operated independently of any concentration of premises in a particular area, cumulative impact policies do represent a restrictive approach to the granting of licences and a departure from a market-oriented strategy.

1.2.7    The reduced level of discretion under the 2003 Act's more market-based approach is part of a wider change to the framework underpinning licensing control in the areas of alcohol, entertainment and LNR. Traditionally, a 'discretion' based model has been employed but this has changed to a model which, at least in part, is 'rule' based, in which discretion plays a much more restricted role. These changes are reflected in the 2003 Act's provisions, which require that licences and other authorisations must be granted by the licensing authority where various criteria are met and there is an absence of any 'relevant representations' about the licensing objectives on premises licence or CPC applications. Thus, s 18(2) provides that the authority must grant a premises licence where an application has been made in accordance with statutory requirements set out in s 17 (for example, that the application is accompanied by an operating schedule giving details of matters such as the licensable activities that will take place and their times), subject only to such conditions as are consistent with the operating schedule and to any mandatory conditions that must be imposed on the licence (see 1.2.5 above). Section 72(2) makes comparable provision in respect of CPCs (see 8.4.2 below). The position is similar in the absence of an objection notice from the police to a personal licence application or a TEN on the ground that granting the licence or permitting the event would undermine the crime prevention objective. Thus, s 120(2) provides that the authority must grant a personal licence if it appears to it that: (a) the applicant is aged 18 or over; (b) he possesses a licensing qualification or is a person of a prescribed description; (c) no personal licence held by him has been forfeited in the period of five years ending with the day the application was made; and (d) he has not been convicted of any relevant offence or any foreign offence.[11] For TENs, there is not even a requirement for authorisation or permission to be granted, but simply for notice, which complies with certain requirements, to be given to licensing authorities (see ss 98–110 and Chapter 9). Thus it is only if there are 'relevant representations' to premises licence or CPC applications, or an objection notice from the police to a personal licence application or a temporary event, that discretion comes into play.

## 1.2.8    Partnership working

1.2.9    There was particular emphasis in the Secretary of State's Guidance when it was issued in July 2004 on the importance of partnership working to promote the licensing objectives. This included partnership working in the wider sense of licensing authorities working with other bodies and organisations outside the licensing process, since it was recognised that promotion of the licensing objectives could not be achieved solely through licensing authorities discharging licensing functions under the 2003 Act. The Act was seen as simply one means of promoting and delivering the licensing objectives under the 2003 Act, along with various other initiatives that are directed towards this end, such as Crime and Disorder Reduction Partnerships (CDRPs) and the Government's *Alcohol Harm Reduction Strategy for England* (AHRSE).[12] Thus, para 2.7 of the 2004 Guidance stated:

> Licensing functions under the 2003 Act are only one means of promoting the delivery of the objectives . . . They can make a substantial contribution in respect of the premises affected but cannot be regarded as a panacea for all community problems. Delivery should therefore involve working in partnership for licensing authorities, planning authorities, environmental health and safety authorities, the police, the fire authority, Crime and Disorder Reduction Partnerships, town centre managers, local business,

performers and their representatives, local people, local transport authorities, transport operators and those involved in child protection working towards the promotion of the ... objectives ... In particular, it is stressed that the private sector and local residents and community groups have an equally vital role to play in partnership with public bodies to promote the licensing objectives. The Secretary of State considers that there is value in the formation of liaison groups that bring together all the interested parties on a regular basis to monitor developments in the area and where problems have arisen, to discuss these and propose possible solutions.

1.2.10 Within the licensing process, there is a similar expectation that all those with an interest or involvement in the process ('stakeholders') will work together in partnership towards a mutually acceptable outcome. Thus para 5.103 of the 2004 Guidance (now para 11.8 of the 2007 Guidance) stated:

It is important to recognise that the promotion of the licensing objectives relies heavily on a partnership between licence holders, authorised persons,[13] interested parties and responsible authorities in pursuit of common aims

whilst para 7.3 (now para 10.3) similarly went on to provide:

All interests – licensing authorities, licence and certificate holders, authorised persons, the police, other responsible authorities and local residents and businesses – should be working together in partnership to ensure collectively that the licensing objectives are promoted.

This is reflected in provisions both in the 2003 Act, for example, the requirement for licensing authorities to consult widely when formulating their SOP (see s 5(3) and 4.3.3 below) and in its accompanying secondary legislation, for example, the requirement for licensing hearings to 'take the form of a discussion led by the authority' (see reg 23 of the Licensing Act 2003 (Hearings) Regulations 2005, SI 2005/42, and 2.3.11 below), which suggests a less formal, less adversarial process with those having an interest in the outcome of the application all working together towards a consensual outcome.

The focus under the Act is thus on facilitating stakeholders to find 'solutions to problems' and the Act seeks to provide a framework for stakeholders to arrive at decisions about issues rather than directing outcomes. As the Secretary of State for Culture, Media and Sport, Tessa Jowell has observed (see 'Grown-up Politics for an Adult World', *The Observer*, 21 Nov 2004):

'Better regulation' is not about Whitehall nannies claiming to know best. Credible and workable regulation only comes about through government and the people it serves negotiating a sensible framework within which choices can be made.

The extent to which partnership working may lead to promotion of the licensing objectives will, however, inevitably depend on the closeness or otherwise of the working relationships between the different parties involved in the licensing process and this may well differ significantly both between particular parties in the process as well as from one licensing authority area to another. Nevertheless, the Secretary of State felt able to say in the Foreword to the revised version of the Guidance published in June 2007 (hereafter 'Guidance'):

There is widespread evidence of good and effective partnership working. In many areas, local authorities have set up licensing forums that bring together residents, licensees, responsible authorities such as the police and others to discuss and try to resolve licensing issues. Enforcement has also benefited from this partnership approach with improved targeting of problem premises and better co-ordination and cooperation to clamp down on the irresponsible minority of retailers.

## 1.2.11 Focused and directed enforcement

The 2003 Act's approach to enforcement and sanctions reflects a philosophy of giving greater freedom to premises not giving rise to problems and applying stronger sanctions where they do. Interested parties and responsible authorities can apply for review of a premises licence where there are problems and the authority can take such steps as it considers necessary for the promotion of the licensing objectives (see ss 51–52 and 6.12 below). The position in respect of CPCs is similar (see ss 87–88 and 8.10 below). Thus a range of 'graded' sanctions depending on the seriousness of the case can be applied, including modification of conditions and exclusion of a licensable activity from the scope of the licence or certificate, with revocation of the licence or certificate as the ultimate sanction. In cases of urgent difficulties with premises operating under a premises licence or a TEN, the police may make a closure order where this is reasonably believed necessary for public safety on account of disorder or to prevent public nuisance because of noise (see s 161 and 11.14 below). This provides for more focused and directed enforcement of licensing control, as the Secretary of State explained in her Foreward to the Guidance published in July 2004, such that 'premises which are causing problems within our communities can be dealt with appropriately' whilst there is 'a much lighter touch for those businesses and community activities which benefit and enhance people's lives by providing important opportunities for the enjoyment of leisure time.' The 2003 Act thereby seeks to avoid a 'a disproportionate expansion of the government's reach and the bureaucracy that went with it' in accordance with 'Third Way' political thinking, as indicated earlier (see 1.2.2 above). However, as also indicated (see 1.2.3 above), the 'lighter touch' has been more evident in some areas than others, whilst at the same time the Act has become increasingly focused on combating alcohol-related crime and antisocial behaviour, with additional powers provided to deal with premises causing problems (see 1.4.2 below).

## 1.2.12 Summary

1.2.13   The 2003 Act is primarily intended to be a deregulatory measure, promoting a market-based approach, and providing support for enterprise and development of the leisure industry. It seeks to regulate only where there are concerns or where problems arise in respect of promotion of the licensing objectives. There has, however, been an increased emphasis, in particular, on the prevention of crime and disorder licensing objective, as the focus has shifted significantly in this direction at the expense of the legislation's original *raison d'etre* of deregulation and promotion of the leisure industry. Nevertheless, the four licensing objectives are, and remain, the touchstone for regulatory control and in this respect regulation departs fundamentally from the traditional regulatory approach under which licensing authorities themselves decide the ground rules for operators to carry out licensable activities and have a broad, unfettered discretion when exercising their licensing responsibilities. Further, the Act is not primarily concerned with directing outcomes, but rather with establishing a framework which encourages stakeholders to work together collectively to promote the licensing objectives with a view to addressing local needs and concerns. Whilst this provides the opportunity for communities to make choices where there are conflicting interests, it is often difficult to strike a balance between such interests and achieve any consensus about what steps are necessary to promote the licensing objectives. Inevitably, therefore, licensing authorities may have to make 'all-things-considered' judgments leading to defensible decisions, notwithstanding that all stakeholders may not be happy with the outcome. In this respect, licensing authorities do retain a significant measure of discretion to ultimately influence the outcome. In contrast, at the practical level, the ability to exercise discretion is, at least in some respects, singularly lacking. There is, for example, a specified procedure for variation of premises licences, which seems to take no account of the nature of variations and whether they are major or minor (see 6.9.2 below). On a strict view, no discretion exists to depart from this procedure and to permit the making informally of minor variations. Similarly, there are a number of specified periods of time within which particular matters or developments must take place, such as the giving of notices, but no provision is made for a 'slip rule', whereby the licensing authority might exercise some discretion in the event that parties are not prejudiced by a failure to comply with the relevant requirements.

1.2.14   In the longer term, it remains to be seen whether licensing authorities' exercise of their discretion to influence the outcome of applications will deliver the Government's intentions in respect of the legislation which, as indicated above, initially consisted of a deregulatory agenda and a market-based philosophy, but more recently have focused on combating alcohol-related crime and antisocial behaviour. The licensing scheme devolves power and influence to a network of stakeholders in conjunction with licensing authorities and decisions made locally, when working together, may well have the effect of undermining these intentions. Where this occurs this will necessarily give rise to tension, but the continuing influence of central government in the licensing process should not be underestimated. The Government retains the capacity continually to influence through detailed statutory guidance, giving it greater influence over licensing matters than it previously had, and, if the more recent focus is maintained, it might be expected that the Government will seek to 'guide' licensing authorities towards combating alcohol-related crime and antisocial behaviour if it feels that they are not moving sufficiently in this direction.

## 1.3   CONVERTED LICENCES AND CERTIFICATES

### 1.3.1   Transition to the 2003 Act

The provisions of the 2003 Act did not have immediate effect and there was a period of transition up until 24 November 2005 before the Act came fully into force. During the transition period, holders of existing licences or certificates could apply to convert them into new licences or certificates under the 2003 Act (and, if they wished, to simultaneously vary them). Although the period of transition has passed, converted licences and certificates remain of enduring importance because they essentially incorporated 'grandfather' rights, that is, existing holders were able in large measure to retain the existing terms and conditions under which they had been operating, and continued to be subject to the same restrictions, and these were replicated in the new licence or certificate which they obtained on conversion. This was so even though the terms, conditions and restrictions might not be in keeping with the licensing objectives under the 2003 Act and might not be ones which could be imposed, had an application been made for a new licence or certificate rather than for conversion of an existing one. Converted licences and certificates may well differ significantly therefore from new licences and certificates and it is important to have some understanding of the 'grandfather' rights that were retained in converted licences and certificates.

## 1.3.2   Conversion of existing licences

1.3.3    When existing licences were converted, the existing licensable activities under the licence(s) were carried across onto the new licence, which, under Sched 8, para 6(3), is to be treated as if it were a premises licence under s 11 of the 2003 Act. 'Existing licensable activities' are defined in Sched 8, para 1(1) to include not only those activities that were authorised by the licence, but also those that could be carried on by virtue of the existence of the licence. The latter, which may be described as an 'embedded benefit', included, for example, the retail sale of alcohol at premises with an existing theatre licence where notice had been given under s 199(c) of the Licensing Act 1964 to the justices' chief executive of an intention to make such sales (see Sched 8, para 1(2)(b)). Although the theatre licence did not authorise the sale of alcohol, sales could be made by virtue of the existence of the licence if notice of intention to make sales had been given to the justices' chief executive. In cases where notice had been given, when the theatre licence was converted to a new licence authorisation for the sale of alcohol as well as for the provision of plays was carried across onto the new licence.

1.3.4    There was one specific 'embedded benefit' excluded by Sched 8, para 1(2)(a) of the 2003 Act, which was provision of public entertainment consisting of music and singing provided by not more than two performers on premises for which there was a justices' licence for the sale of alcohol. This exemption from the need to obtain a public entertainment licence (the so-called 'two in a bar' rule), contained in s 182 of the Licensing Act 1964, was excluded from the 'existing licensable activities', although exclusion applied only where the public entertainment under s 182 took the form of music and singing provided by not more than two performers. Public entertainment consisting of music and singing provided solely by the reproduction of recorded sound, which was also covered by the s 182 exemption, was not excluded and was carried across on conversion onto the new licence. Since the s 182 exemption applied at all times of the day and was not confined in its application to the 'permitted hours' at which alcohol could be sold,[14] authorisation for the reproduction of recorded sound (essentially recorded music), when carried across onto the new licence, would be without any limitations on time. If a licence under the 2003 Act makes provision for recorded music without any time limitation, the licence may well have been one converted from an existing licence under the pre-Act law. If an application was to be made for a new premises licence to include provision for recorded music, grant of the licence is likely to include some limitation on hours as being necessary for the promotion of the licensing objective of prevention of public nuisance, at least if the premises are in a residential area.

## 1.3.5 Conditions on the new licence

1.3.6 All of the conditions attached to the existing licence or licences, including both standard conditions and any special conditions, were attached to the new licence on conversion. The new licence thus replicated the terms under which an applicant was operating prior to obtaining it. When it came to attaching the conditions, there was some measure of discretion available to the authority, for it was required by Sched 8, para 6(6) to 'reproduce the effect' of the conditions rather than simply transfer them verbatim to the new licence. This enabled duplication to be avoided where existing licences contained similar conditions. All the conditions were attached to the new licence, irrespective of whether or not they were necessary for the promotion of the licensing objectives and inevitably in some cases some of the conditions carried across would be ones which could not have been imposed had a new premises licence application been made. The new licence did not, however, replicate completely the 'grandfather rights' under which existing operators traded, for at least some of their trading rights were not contained in licence conditions. This was the case for New Year's Eve, when it was possible for operators to remain open for the sale of alcohol beyond the general 'permitted hours' (see 1.3.4 above) and to provide public music and dancing beyond the hours specified in their public entertainment licence. The right to remain open on New Year's Eve was contained in the Regulatory Reform (Special Occasions Licensing) Order 2002, SI 2002/3205, an order made under s 1 of the Regulatory Reform Act 2001. Not being a condition on the licence but an automatic entitlement to remain open by virtue of this Order, New Year's Eve opening hours were not carried across when, on conversion, conditions on existing licences were attached to the new licence. Such hours were attached to the new licence only if an application for variation to include them was made and some applicants omitted to seek a variation. Where this was the case, either a subsequent application for variation might be made or, alternatively, a TEN might be issued on an annual basis to cover the New Year's Eve period.

Further, conditions carried across included not only ones that regulated the use of the premises, but also ones that imposed a restriction on the use of the premises for any licensable activity under an existing licence. The case of restaurant licences as they were popularly known, which were justices' on-licences granted under Pt IV of the Licensing Act 1964, provides an illustration. Such licences were granted, subject to conditions that required use of the premises for the purpose of habitually providing the customary main meal at midday or in the evening and alcohol being sold or supplied only to persons taking table meals and for consumption by them as an ancillary to the meal (see s 94(1) of the 1964 Act). A person running a restaurant who applies for a new premises licence for the sale of alcohol may well be granted a licence without any or all such conditions being attached. Again, therefore, the existence of any such conditions on a licence under the 2003 Act will probably indicate that the licence was a converted justices' Pt IV on-licence.

1.3.7 It was not only conditions on existing licences that were carried across to the new licence, but also any restrictions imposed on the use of the premises for the existing licensable activities under the existing licence(s) were reproduced as a condition. The purpose of this provision was to carry across into the new licence any 'embedded restrictions' that applied in respect of the existing licence(s). Under Sched 8, para 6(8), all embedded restrictions needed to be reproduced as conditions in cases where the restrictions were contained in any enactment specified by the Secretary of State, and there were four such enactments specified: the Children and Young Persons Act 1933, the Cinematograph (Safety) Regulations 1955, the Licensing Act 1964 and the Sporting Events (Control of Alcohol Etc) Act 1985 (see Art 4 of the LA 2003 (Transitional Provisions) Order 2005, SI 2005/40). Most of the restrictions were contained in the Licensing Act 1964 and many had application in respect of permitted hours at which the sale of alcohol could take place. The normal permitted hours under the 1964 Act for the sale or supply of alcohol in licensed premises were not attached as conditions to justices' licences, but were a restriction (in Pt III of the Act) imposed on the times at which the licensable activity of sale or supply of alcohol could take place on the premises. Under para 6(8), therefore, they were carried across on conversion and reproduced as a condition on the new licence. This was also the case with extensions in hours – 'supper hour' certificates under s 68, extended hours' orders under s 70 and special hours certificates under s 77 of the 1964 Act – which extended the permitted hours under the previous law beyond the normal 11.00 pm closing time. These extensions required the sale of alcohol to be ancillary to other activities, that is, the provision of 'substantial refreshment' (s 68), 'substantial refreshment' and musical or other entertainment (s 70), or 'substantial refreshment' and gaming facilities in the case of casino premises or music and dancing in the case of any other premises (s 77). The position was similar if there were restrictions on hours under s 67A of the 1964 Act, which provided for restriction orders to restrict the permitted hours to avoid or reduce disturbance or annoyance or disorderly conduct. In all the above instances, these were restrictions on the licensable activity of the sale of alcohol under the justices' licence and they were reproduced as conditions on the new licence on conversion. Again, therefore, the existence of any such conditions on a licence under the 2003 Act will probably indicate that the licence was a converted justices' licence. In cases where an application is made for a new premises licence, it is unlikely that any such restrictions would be imposed.

1.3.8    Whilst restrictions on hours for the sale of alcohol were reproduced as conditions, whether the period of 'drinking up' time for the consumption of alcohol on licensed premises after the end of permitted hours (specified in s 63(1) of the 1964 Act) was considered to be a restriction on hours that required it to be carried across and reproduced as a condition on the new licence was less clear (see 13.3.4 of the first edition of this book). Perhaps inevitably where the legal postion was uncertain, some authorities took the view that it was a restriction and should be carried across, whereas others took the view that it was not and should not be reproduced as a condition. Accordingly, some licences under the 2003 Act may contain as a condition a 'drinking up' period for the consumption of alcohol and, where this is the case, these are likely to be converted justices' licences.

### 1.3.9    Conversion of existing club certificates

In much the same way as holders of existing licences could convert them to new licences that were then treated as premises licences, it was open to holders of existing club certificates to convert them to new certificates, which were then treated as CPCs (see Sched 8, para 18(1)). When application was made, the 'existing qualifying club activities' under the existing club certificate were carried across onto the new certificate. Existing club certificates provided authorisation under s 39 of the

Licensing Act 1964 for the supply of alcohol to club members and guests and, under s 49, if the rules of the club provided for the admission of persons other than club members and guests, sale of alcohol to such persons for consumption by them on the premises. Supply of alcohol to club members and guests was certainly an existing qualifying club activity (see s 1(2) of the 2003 Act) and this was carried across on conversion. Sale to persons other than club members and guests, however, was not and would (or should) not have been carried across onto the new certificate. Supply of alcohol to club members and guests should have been the only qualifying club activity carried across on conversion, since the only authorisation that existing club certificates provided was for supply of alcohol. They provided no authorisation for any entertainment. Entertainment was not therefore included within the 'existing qualifying club activities' and could not be carried across onto the new certificate. If clubs applying for conversion wished to provide entertainment under the new certificate, a variation application was needed along with the conversion application.

### 1.3.10 Conditions on the new certificate

Conditions were attached to the new certificate that 'reproduce the effect' of the conditions attached to the existing certificate (see Sched 8, para 18(4)). In fact, the only conditions that were attached to the existing certificate were ones restricting sales of alcohol (to non-members), including conditions prohibiting an alteration to club rules to authorise sales not authorised at the time of application for the certificate. Apart from these conditions, which could be imposed under s 49(3) of the Licensing Act 1964, there was no general power to attach conditions to a certificate. In addition, any restriction imposed on the use of the premises for the existing qualifying club activities under the existing certificate was also reproduced as a condition (see Sched 8, para 18(5)). As in the case of existing licences, the purpose of this was to carry across any 'embedded restrictions' contained in any enactment specified by the Secretary of State and the same enactments were specified as for existing licences (see 1.3.7 above). As the enactments specified included the Licensing Act 1964, restrictions imposed by the 1964 Act in relation to matters such as qualification for a registration certificate (for example, management of the club in relation to the purchase and supply of alcohol through an elective committee) were reproduced as conditions. Similarly, if a club had obtained a special hours certificate (SHC) under s 78 of the Licensing Act 1964 enabling it to supply alcohol after the normal permitted hour of 11.00 pm, the restriction on the supply of alcohol under the SHC, which was that it had to be ancillary to the provision of music and dancing and substantial refreshment, was reproduced as a condition on the new certificate. The existence of any such conditions on a certificate under the 2003 Act will, in all probability, indicate that the certificate was a converted club certificate.

### 1.3.11 Issue of personal licences to holders of justices' licences

For a six months' period during transition (from 7 February 2005 until 6 August 2005), the holder of a justices' licence granted under the Licensing Act 1964 could apply for the grant to him of a personal licence without having to possess the licensing qualification ordinarily required under Pt 6 of the 2003 Act, provided that certain requirements were met.[15] This entitlement to a licence was provided because holders of an existing justices' licence would have been considered fit and proper to retail alcohol by the licensing justices. Only where the holder of a justices' licence had been convicted of a relevant or foreign offence (see 10.5.4–10.5.13 below) since the grant, last renewal or transfer to him of the justices' licence, might grant of a personal licence have been refused if the licensing authority was satisfied, following a police objection, that there were excepional circumstances such that grant would undermine prevention of crime and disorder. There may, accordingly, be holders of personal licences under the 2003 Act not possessing an accredited licensing qualification who nevertheless hold a valid personal licence. These will be persons who, during the relevant transition period, have applied for, and have obtained, a personal licence.

## 1.4   POST-2003 ACT DEVELOPMENTS

### 1.4.1   Reviews and initiatives

The transition period proved to be a fraught time for all involved in the licensing process, with licensing authorities having to handle large numbers of applications in a relatively short period of time and with difficulties exacerbated by delays in the publication of Regulations and Guidance. Further, there have been a number of matters of continuing concern, such as fee levels and structures, the complexity of application forms and advertising requirements, and the strictness of rules over plans. The Government has recognised that there have been a number of problems with the legislation and several reviews have been set up and initiatives taken with a view to improving matters. These have included:

- an Independent Licensing Fees Review Panel, set up in June 2005 under the chairmanship of Sir Les Elton, which produced an interim report in November 2005 and a final report in January 2007;
- a report on the Implementation of the Licensing Act 2003 by the Better Regulation Commission published in April 2006;
- a Scrutiny Council Initiative set up in November 2005 and comprising an advisory group of 10 licensing authorities, which reported in July 2006 and highlighted various practical difficulties;
- two reviews by the DCMS of the Guidance, an interim one addressing the less complex issues, which resulted in the publication of revised Guidance in July 2006, and a more formal review, leading to a further revised version published in June 2007; and
- a report on Violent Crime, Disorder and Criminal Damage since the Introduction of the Licensing Act 2003, published in July 2007, which compared data for recorded crime for a 12-month period immediately preceding the implementation of the 2003 Act (December 2004–November 2005) with the 12-month period immediately following (December 2005–November 2006), and which concluded that there was an increase, albeit a slight one, for each group of offence monitored between 3.00 am and 6.00 am, although the total offences in this time period increased by only four per cent.[16]

In addition, there have been other matters that have impacted on the licensing process, notably the smoking ban under the Health Act 2006 in all enclosed or substantially enclosed premises, which came into effect in Wales in April 2007 and in

England in July 2007. The ban, which does not apply to outdoor areas or premises that are not substantially enclosed, has led to numerous variation applications for premises licences as those operating premises such as public houses and nightclubs have sought to provide outdoor 'smoking shelter' facilities in gardens and other areas within the curtilage of the premises for customers visiting the premises.[17]

### 1.4.2  Supplementary legislation

In addition, there have been legislative developments that have sought to increase the powers available for dealing with alcohol-fuelled disorder. The 2003 Act has become a key part of the Government's strategy for combating alcohol-related crime and antisocial behaviour, but the powers introduced by the Act for preventing crime and disorder have not been seen as sufficient in themselves to control and reduce the level of such disorder. Accordingly, other measures have been introduced, notably the extension of Penalty Notices for Disorder (PND) to various offences under the 2003 Act[18] and the introduction of various provisions in the Violent Crime Reduction Act 2006, which seek to tackle alcohol-related violence and disorder. These include:

- the introduction of a new civil order, a Drinking Banning Order, which will impose restrictions on those who commit offences under the influence of alcohol for up to two years, including banning them from licensed premises;
- the introduction of Alcohol Disorder Zones (ADZs) to give local authorities and police powers to designate areas blighted by serious alcohol-related crime and disorder, as a last resort, to ensure those holding licences within the zone contribute to the cost of the disorder (see 11.18 below);
- the creation of a new offence of persistently selling alcohol to children, for which a premises licence holder may be liable, liability for which can result in police and trading standards exercising powers to close the licensed premises for up to 48 hours (see 11.7.13–11.7.15); and
- the creation of a new power to allow police to ban those who represent a risk to alcohol-related crime or disorder arising or taking place from a particular locality for up to 48 hours.

### 1.4.3  Adjusting the freedom and prevention of harm balance

1.4.4    Provision of increased penalties and sanctions in the event that disturbance is caused to others has always been an integral part of the licensing scheme under the 2003 Act, although it was not the primary focus of the legislation as originally conceived. The Act was seen essentially as a deregulatory and liberalising measure, seeking to promote greater freedom and flexibility for the leisure industry to meet the needs of its customers, without putting any unnecessary obstacles in the way of the industry's further development. At the same time, it did seek to promote social responsibility, with the White Paper that preceded the Act indicating that there would be 'tough and uncompromising powers for the police, the courts and licensing authorities to deal with any individuals and businesses failing to be socially responsible and abusing these freedoms' (Cm 4696, 2000, p 5).[19] These powers, which included ones for the police to control disorderly premises and for licensing authorities to protect residents from disturbance, have in the post-Act period been further supplemented by the additional powers mentioned above.

1.4.5    That further legislative developments have been focused on controls and safeguards reflects the fact that these have come to be seen as of increasing importance, a
view that emerged initially during the latter stages of the Act's passage and which has
subsequently been reinforced in the period following. Indeed, the focus has changed
from what might have been described, when the Bill was introduced in Parliament,
as cultivation of a continental-style café culture to keeping in check the social consequences caused by the increased number of premises selling alcohol (following
regeneration of town and city centres), coupled with increased consumption
occasioned by drinks promotions and the fostering of a 'binge drinking' culture. A
number of other developments have taken place, in addition to the legislative changes
introduced, which reflect this change of emphasis. Alcohol harm reduction, in particular, has been given a much greater priority. This was evident when the Government in March 2004 revealed its AHRSE (an updated version of which, *Safe, Sensible
and Social – next steps for the National Alcohol Strategy*, appeared in June 2007 – see 4.3.4
and 4.3.14 below) and in November 2004 when it published its Public Health White
Paper, *Choosing Health: Making Healthier Choices Easier* (Cm 6374, 2004), both of which
focused on tackling alcohol misuse. More recently, added impetus has been given by
reports published in July 2007 suggesting that, following implementation of the 2003
Act changes, there has been an increase in violent offences (see 1.4.1 above) and that
overnight visits to hospital accident and emergency units have trebled (based on a
study at London's St Thomas Hospital, which was felt by the authors of the report to
be representative of the problems in inner city areas across the country).[20] In the wake
of these reports, the Chief Medical Officer for England, Sir Liam Donaldson, stated
that he would 'strongly commend' the use of tax as a deterrent to excessive drinking
to reduce the damage being caused to health and indicated that he would welcome a
review of 24-hour licensing (*Daily Telegraph*, 21 July 2007). Shortly afterwards, Gordon
Brown, in his first monthly press conference as Prime Minister, announced that the
Government was 'preparing to look at the impact of the relaxation in November 2005
of the licensing laws', was 'ready to look at the 24-hour drinking issue with an open
mind' and 'examine in an objective way all the evidence' (*The Times*, 24 July 2007). The
review was being undertaken by the Home Office, suggesting that crime and disorder
rather than the regulatory system itself were likely to be the primary focus, and it was
expected that the review would be completed by the end of 2007.

There has undoubtedly been a reappraisal of the balance at central government
level between greater freedom and prevention of harm in the post-2003 Act period,
with a significant adjustment in the latter's favour. This reappraisal has to a greater or
lesser extent been evident at the local level, as authorities have to varying degrees
sought to reflect this readjusted balance when discharging their licensing functions.
Striking the right balance is never an easy task – there are, as the Home Secretary
acknowledged in his Foreword to the White Paper, 'many difficult balances to be
struck' (Cm 4696, 2000, p 6) – and it remains to be seen whether there will be further
adjustments to the balance, one way or the other, both centrally and locally in due
course.

## NOTES

1  The Act's provisions extend only to England and Wales (s 201(3)), except for s 155(1),
   which also extends to Northern Ireland (s 201(4)). For the provision in s 155(1), see 11.7.36

below. The Act also applies to the Crown, to Crown property and to land of the Duchies of Lancaster and Cornwall (except to the extent that they are occupied by the Queen or the Prince of Wales) – see s 195.

2 The relevant legislative provisions were Sched 1 to the Local Government (Miscellaneous Provisions) Act 1982 (and, in London, Sched 12 to the London Government Act 1963) for public entertainment; the Cinemas Act 1985 for films, the Theatres Act 1968 for plays; and the Late Night Refreshment Houses Act 1969 for LNR (and, in London, there were additional provisions for night cafés under the Greater London Council (General Powers) Act 1968 and the London Local Authorities Act 1990).

3 See *BRTF Review of Licensing Legislation*, Cabinet Office, 1997. The BRTF's terms of reference were 'to advise the Government on action which improves the effectiveness and credibility of government regulation by ensuring that it is necessary, fair and affordable, and simple to understand and administer, taking particular account of the needs of small businesses and ordinary people': *Principles of Good Regulation*, Cabinet Office, 1998.

4 The meaning of 'licensable activities' is considered in detail in Chapter 5.

5 Section 193 provides: ' "premises" means any place'.

6 As the White Paper recognised, 'private premises, to which public access is restricted and where alcohol is supplied other than for profit, give rise to different issues for licensing law from commercial enterprises selling direct to the public' (Cm 4696, 2000, para 102).

7 Giddens, A, *The Third Way: The Renewal of Social Democracy*, 1998, Cambridge, Polity Press.

8 Blair, T, and Schroeder, G, *Europe: The Third Way/Die Neue Mitte*, joint statement 8 June 1999 – www.socialdemocrats.org/blairandschroeder6–8–99.html On the 2003 Act and 'Third Way' politics, see further Hunt, A, and Manchester, C, 'The Licensing Act and its implementation: Nanny knows the "Third Way" is best' [1997] *Web Journal of Current Legal Issues*, Issue 1.

9 See 6.4.1 below. The mandatory conditions, contained in ss 19–21, relate to the supply of alcohol (s 19); exhibition of films (s 20); and door supervisors being licensed (or exempt from licensing) by the Security Industry Authority (s 21) – see 6.4.2–6.4.5 below.

10 See *R v Howard ex p Farnham Licensing Justices* [1902] 2 KB 363 (considered at 12.8.5 below), which established that licensing justices could raise objections themselves to renewal of licences for the sale of alcohol and which was regarded as having application to other areas of licensing, including licensing by local authorities.

11 For details, see 10.5.6–10.5.12 below. The meaning of 'licensing qualification' is contained in s 120(8), 'relevant offence' in s 113(1) and Sched 4, and 'foreign offence' in s 113(3).

12 An acronym used in the relevant document (and surely one of the best used by any Government department!) – see Cabinet Office, Prime Minister's Strategy Unit, March 2004. An updated version, *Safe, Sensible and Social – next steps for the National Alcohol Strategy*, has since been published (see 1.4.5 below) and in Wales the Welsh Assembly published *Tackling Substance Misuse in Wales: A Partnership Approach* in September 2000, which is currently being further developed. For these initiatives, see 4.3.4 (CDRPs) and 4.3.14 (AHRSE) below.

13 'Authorised persons' are those authorised to carry out various functions under the Act, eg inspection of premises – see s 13(2) and 6.14.2 below.

14 Under s 60 of the Licensing Act 1964, the general 'permitted hours' on weekdays were 11.00 am to 11.00 pm for on-licences (12.00 pm to 10.30 pm on Sundays) and 8.00 am to 11.00 pm for off-licences (10.00 am to 11.00 pm on Sundays). For details of extensions and variations, see Chapter 1 of the first edition of this work.

15 See Sched 8, para 23. Persons holding licences granted by the University of Cambridge and by the Board of the Green Cloth could also do so (see reg 4 of the LA2003 (Personal Licence) Regs 2005, SI 2005/41).

16 The report (see www.homeoffice.gov.uk/rds/pdfs07/rdsolr1607.pdf) concluded that the degree to which patterns had resulted directly from the licensing changes could not be

assessed, due to a combination of various factors, eg changes in recording practices and policing activities, increased and proactive policing, and the use of Penalty Notices for Disorder (see 1.4.2 below).

17 In order for smoking to be permitted, the shelters need to fall outside the definition of 'substantially enclosed premises' in the Smoke-free (Premises and Enforcement) Regulations 2006, SI 2006/3368. Premises are 'substantially enclosed' if they have a ceiling or roof, but there are openings in the walls which are less than half the total areas of the walls, including other structures that serve the purpose of walls and constitute the perimeter of the premises (reg 2(2)). When determining the area of an opening, no account is taken of openings in which doors, windows or other fittings can be open or shut (reg 2(3)).

18 Penalty Notices for Disorder were introduced by the Criminal Justice and Police Act 2001 and the offences under the 2003 Act to which they are extended are those contained in ss 146, 149, 150 and 151 – see 11.7 below.

19 Described by the Home Secretary in his Foreword to the White Paper (Cm 4696, 2000, at p 5) as a 'radically new system which carefully balances rights and responsibilities', the scheme is very firmly rooted in the liberal tradition espoused by the nineteenth century philosopher John Stuart Mill, under which legal restrictions are justified only if harm will be caused to individual interests. As Mill stated in his essay *On Liberty* (3rd edn, 1864, London: Longman, pp 21–22): 'The sole end for which mankind are warranted, individually or collectively, in interfering with the liberty of action of any of their number, is self-protection. That the only purpose for which power can be rightfully exercised over any member of a civilised community against his will is to prevent harm to others.'

20 Newton, A *et al.*, 'Impact of the new UK licensing law on emergency hospital attendances: a cohort study' (2007) 24 *Emergency Medicine Journal* 532–534.

# CHAPTER 2

# PROCEDURAL AND DECISION-MAKING FRAMEWORK

## 2.1 APPLICATION PROCEDURE AND ACCOMPANYING DOCUMENTATION

### 2.1.1 Introduction

The 2003 Act itself contains some requirements for the making of applications and for accompanying documentation, for example, applications for premises licence and CPC must be accompanied by an operating schedule and a plan of the premises.[1] For all forms of authorisation, however, it enables further provision to be made through regulations issued by the Secretary of State. These can be in respect of a number of matters, including the form of any application or notice, the manner in which it is to be made or given, and information and documents that must accompany it, and various regulations have been made under the Act covering these matters. Thus the Licensing Act 2003 (Premises Licences and Club Premises Certificates) Regulations 2005, SI 2005/42 (LA 2003 (PL and CPC) Regs 2005) regulate premises licences and CPCs, which are for the most part treated in similar fashion; the Licensing Act 2003 (Personal Licences) Regulations 2005, SI 2005/41 (LA 2003 (Personal Licences) Regs 2005) regulate personal licences; and the Licensing Act 2003 (Permitted Temporary Activities) (Notices) Regulations 2005, SI 2005/2198 (LA 2003 (PTA) (Notices) Regs 2005) regulate TENs.

### 2.1.2 Premises licences and CPCs

### 2.1.3 Prescribed matters

The LA 2003 (PL and CPC) Regs 2005 prescribe the form the applications shall take and the information that they must contain. Where the application forms 'contain obvious and minor factual errors that can easily be amended', the Guidance, para 8.24, recommends amendment by the licensing authority and 'forms should not be returned'. The Regulations also prescribe the scale and content of the plan (reg 23) and the form of consent for the premises supervisor (reg 24 and Pt A of Sched 11). The LA 2003 (PL and CPC) Regs 2005 make provision for:

- the form in which applications are made;
- the giving of notices and the making of representations;
- the periods of time within which representations must be made;
- the scale of and matters to be delineated in plans of premises; and
- the advertising of applications.

### 2.1.4 Form in which applications are made, giving of notices and making of representations

2.1.5 Not surprisingly, there is a requirement for applications, along with notices and representations, to be in writing, but provision is made for transmission by electronic means, provided certain requirements, which include subsequent written communication, are met. Regulation 21 provides:

(1) An application, a notice or a representation shall be in writing.

(2) Notwithstanding the requirement in paragraph (1) and subject to paragraph (3), that requirement shall be satisfied in a case where–

  (a) the text of the application, notice or representation–

    (i)  is transmitted by electronic means;

    (ii)  is capable of being accessed by the recipient;

    (iii) is legible in all material respects;[2] and

    (iv) is capable of being read and reproduced in written form and used for subsequent reference;

  (b) the person to whom the application or notice is to be given or the representations are to be made has agreed in advance that an application or a notice may be given or representations may be made by electronic means; and

  (c) forthwith on sending the text of the application, notice or representations by electronic means, the application, notice or representations is given or made, as applicable, to the recipient in writing.[3]

(3) Where the text of the application, notice or representations is or are transmitted by electronic means, the giving of the application or notice or the making of the representation shall be effected at the time the requirements of paragraph 2(a) are satisfied, provided that where any application or notice is required to be accompanied by a fee, plan or other document or information that application or notice shall not be treated as given until the fee, plan or other document or information has been received by the relevant licensing authority.

2.1.6    The effect of reg 21(3) is that in cases where additional documentation is required the electronic transmission is not effective until that documentation is received by the licensing authority. While this may not give rise to difficulties in many cases, there may be some instances where this might prove problematic, notably in respect of applications under s 37 by the premises licence holder to vary the designated premises supervisor (DPS) for the premises following a request by the incumbent DPS under s 41 to be removed as the premises supervisor (see 6.9.7 and 6.9.14 below). The request for removal requires no additional documentation and is effective when notice is transmitted electronically to the licensing authority. If the request becomes effective outside office hours, when the licensing authority's offices are closed, an application by the premises licence holder to vary the DPS, if transmitted electronically, does not have immediate effect. This is because, under s 37(2)(b), it needs to be accompanied by a fee and the application is not to be treated as given under reg 21(3), until the fee has been received by the licensing authority. This may mean that there is a period when there is no DPS for the premises, during which it will not be possible for sales of alcohol to take place as this is one of the mandatory conditions for the sale of alcohol (see 6.4.2 below), and premises licence holders need to be alert to the possibility of this occurring. While provision for electronic transmission may prove advantageous in some circumstances, the requirement for accompaniment by the fee (or plan or other doccument) for the electronic transmission to be effective may limit to some degree the application of this procedure.

With regard to the giving of notices, the applicant must give notice of his application to each responsible authority by giving a copy of the application, along with any accompanying documentation, on the same day as the day the application is given to the licensing authority. Regulation 27 provides:

> In the case of an application for a premises licence under section 17, a provisional statement under section 29, a variation of a premises licence under section 34, a review under section 51, a club premises certificate under section 71, a review under section 87 or a variation of a club premises certificate under section 84, the person making the application shall give notice of his application to each responsible authority by giving to each authority a copy of the application together with its accompanying documents, if any, on the same day as the day on which the application is given to the relevant licensing authority.

### 2.1.7    Periods of time within which representations must be made

Under reg 22(b), representations must generally be made within a period of 28 consecutive days after the day on which the application to which it relates was given to the authority by the applicant.[4]

### 2.1.8    Scale of and matters to be delineated in plans of premises

2.1.9    The plans, unless the applicant has requested an alternative scale plan and the authority has given written confirmation that is acceptable, must be to a scale of 1:100 centimetres and must show: the location of the boundary and any external and internal walls of the building and perimeter of the premises; exits, escape routes and any fixed structures that might impact on the ability to use these without impediment; where the licensable activities take place if there is more than one; any stage or raised area, including height; the location of any steps, stairs, elevators or lifts; the location of any public conveniences; fire safety and other safety equipment, including the type; and any kitchen. Inclusion of these details is important to make it clear which premises or parts of premises have been licensed if the application is granted, and to enable responsible authorities and interested parties to better consider the adequacy of any operating schedule.[5] In order to show the location of these items, symbols may be used. Regulation 23 provides:

(1)  An application for a premises licence under section 17, or a club premises certificate under section 71, shall be accompanied by a plan of the premises to which the application relates and which shall comply with the following paragraphs of this regulation.

(2)  Unless the relevant licensing authority has previously agreed in writing with the applicant following a request by the applicant that an alternative scale plan is acceptable to it, in which case the plan shall be drawn in that alternative scale, the plan shall be drawn in standard scale.[6]

(3)  The plan shall show–

    (a)  the extent of the boundary of the building, if relevant, and any external and internal walls of the building and, if different, the perimeter of the premises;

    (b)  the location of points of access to and egress from the premises;

    (c)  if different from sub-paragraph (3)(b), the location of escape routes from the premises;

    (d)  in a case where the premises is to be used for more than one licensable activity, the area within the premises used for each activity;

(e)   fixed structures (including furniture) or similar objects temporarily in a fixed location (but not furniture) which may impact on the ability of individuals on the premises to use exits or escape routes without impediment;

(f)   in a case where the premises includes a stage or raised area, the location and height of each stage or area relative to the floor;

(g)   in a case where the premises includes any steps, stairs, elevators or lifts, the location of the steps, stairs, elevators or lifts;

(h)   in the case where the premises includes any room or rooms containing public conveniences, the location of the room or rooms;

(i)   the location and type of any fire safety and any other safety equipment[7] including, if applicable, marine safety equipment; and

(j)   the location of a kitchen, if any, on the premises.

(4)   The plan may include a legend through which the matters mentioned or referred to in paragraph (3) are sufficiently illustrated by the use of symbols on the plan.

There is, however, no requirement for plans to be professionally drawn as long as they clearly show all the prescribed information (Guidance, para 8.27).

2.1.10   It seems that the plan itself may well form part of the licence. Section 24(1) provides that the premises licence must be in a prescribed form and s 24(2) provides: 'Regulations under subsection (1) must, in particular, provide for the licence to . . . (b) include a plan of the premises to which the licence relates . . .' (see 6.6.3 below). Regulation 33 and Pt A of Sched 12 to the LA 2003 (PL and CPC) Regs 2005 prescribe the format of the premises licence and the Schedule contains four annexes, the first three of which relate to conditions (Annex 1 – Mandatory Conditions; Annex 2 – Conditions Consistent with the Operating Schedule; and Annex 3 – Conditions Attached after a Hearing by the Licensing Authority) and the fourth relates to the plan (Annex 4 – Plans). Section 78(1)(2), along with reg 35 and Pt A of Sched 13 to the Regulations, makes similar provision in respect of a club premises certificate (CPC). If conditions attached as an Annex to the licence or CPC are a part of the licence or CPC, and they undoubtedly are, it is difficult to resist the conclusion that plans are also part of the licence or CPC. Further, this is reinforced by the fact that in the *Consultation on Draft Regulations and Order to be made under the Licensing Act 2003*, para 5.45 stated: 'The plans submitted with the application would form part of the licence', and para 5.51 stated: 'The plans submitted with the application would form part of the certificate.' This may mean that where changes are made to the plans, even if a relatively minor nature, for example, removal or movement of fire equipment, an application for variation of the premises licence or CPC might be needed under s 34 or s 84 (see 6.9 and 8.9 below). Where there are relatively minor changes to the plan, this seems unduly onerous, given the advertisement requirements for variation applications. However, it may be that a s 34 or s 84 application is not needed for all variations and a number of authorities have followed an informal minor variation procedure in such cases (see 6.9.2 below).

Regulation 23(3) prescribes the matters that the plan must show but there may be other matters included on it, for example, location of the bar, in addition to those specified in reg 23(3) as necessary. While location of the bar is a 'fixed structure' under reg 23(3)(e), it is not one that necessarily impacts on the ability of individuals on the premises to use exits or escape routes without impediment and therefore its inclusion on the plan may not be required. If its location is included on the plan, this raises the question of whether this forms part of the plan and, as such, part of the licence itself. If it does, then an application for variation is needed if its location is to be altered. If it does not, then no such application is needed. It is not clear whether the plan constitutes only those matters that must, under reg 23(3), be included on it or whether the plan comprises all of the contents that are included. It may be that, if matters are detailed on the plan other than those required by reg 23(3), they will not be treated as part of the plan if accompanied by a statement that they are not to be regarded as forming part of the plan, but are included for information and a better understanding of the nature and layout of the premises.

## 2.1.11 Advertising of applications

2.1.12   Applications for the grant or variation of premises licences and CPCs, and for the issuing of a provisional statement, must be advertised in two ways. First, the applicant must display a notice of at least A4 size on pale blue paper with black type or legible printing, to a size of at least 16 point font, at or on the application premises where it can conveniently be read from the exterior of the premises for not less than 28 consecutive days, starting on the day following the giving of the application to the licensing authority.[8] In cases where the premises are over 50 square metres, similar notices must be placed every 50 metres along the external perimeter of the premises abutting any highway. Secondly, the applicant must publish a notice on at least one occasion during the period of 10 working days, starting on the day following the giving of the application, in a local newspaper, or local newsletter, circular or similar document where none exists, circulating in the vicinity of the premises (which in the case of a vessel not permanently moored or berthed will only be the vicinity of where it is usually moored or berthed, with no requirement to advertise in other areas through which the vessel might journey: Guidance, para 8.49, and see s 189 and 6.1.5 below). Regulation 25 provides:

> In the case of an application for a premises licence under section 17, for a provisional statement under section 29, to vary a premises licence under section 34, for a club premises certificate under section 71 or to vary a club premises certificate under section 84, the person making the application shall advertise the application, in both cases containing the appropriate information set out in regulation 26–
>
> (a)  for a period of no less than 28 consecutive days starting on the day after the day on which the application was given to the relevant licensing authority, by displaying a notice,
>
>   (i)   which is–
>
>     (aa)  of a size equal or larger than A4,
>
>     (bb)  of a pale blue colour,
>
>     (cc)  printed legibly in black ink or typed in black in a font of a size equal to or larger than 16;
>
>   (ii)  in all cases, prominently at or on the premises to which the application relates where it can be conveniently read from the exterior of the premises and in the case of a premises covering an area of more than fifty metres square, a further notice in the same form and subject to the same requirements every fifty metres along the external perimeter of the premises abutting any highway; and

(b) by publishing a notice –
　　(i)　in a local newspaper or, if there is none, in a local newsletter, circular or similar document, circulating in the vicinity of the premises;
　　(ii)　on at least one occasion during the period of ten working days starting on the day after the day on which the application was given to the relevant licensing authority.

The advertising requirements are clearly intended to draw applications to the attention of interested parties to afford them the opportunity to make relevant representations and it is important therefore that notices on the premises are properly displayed and contain the relevant information (see 2.1.13 below). To this end, the Guidance, para 8.51 indicates that licensing authorities 'may wish to conduct random and unannounced visits to premises to confirm that notices have been clearly displayed and include relevant and accurate information'. The advertising requirements are ones with which the applicant must comply and there is no requirement for the licensing authority to provide any further notification of applications. However, the licensing authority is not precluded from doing so and the Guidance, para 8.52 provides that it is 'open to licensing authorities to notify residents living in the vicinity of premises by circular of premises making an application'.

2.1.13　The information that the premises and newspaper notices must contain includes: the name and postal address of the applicant; the postal address and any website address of the licensing authority where the register of the relevant licensing authority is kept and where the record of the application may be inspected; the dates within which relevant representations in writing can be made; and a statement of the offence and maximum fine for knowingly or recklessly making a false statement in connection with an application. The notices must also: state the relevant licensable or qualifying club activities that it is proposed to carry on; briefly describe the proposed variation in the case of a variation application (for example, 'details of extra hours applied for, hours varied from/to': Guidance, para 8.47); and, in the case of a provisional statement application, state that representations are restricted after the issue of a provisional statement. Regulation 26 provides:

(1)　In the case of an application for a premises licence or a club premises certificate, the notices referred to in regulation 25 shall contain a statement of the relevant licensable activities or relevant qualifying club activities as the case may require which it is proposed will be carried on on or from the premises.

(2)　In the case of an application for a provisional statement the notices referred to in regulation 25–
　　(a)　shall state that representations are restricted after the issue of a provisional statement; and
　　(b)　where known, may state, the relevant licensable activities which it is proposed will be carried on on or from the premises.

(3)　In the case of an application to vary a premises licence or a club premises certificate, the notices referred to in regulation 25 shall briefly describe the proposed variation.

(4)　In all cases, the notices referred to in regulation 25 shall state–
　　(a)　the name of the applicant or club;
　　(b)　the postal address of the premises or club premises, if any, or if there is no postal address for the premises a description of those premises sufficient to enable the location and extent of the premises or club premises to be identified;

(c) the postal address and, where applicable, the worldwide web address where the register of the relevant licensing authority is kept and where the record of the application may be inspected;

(d) the date by which an interested party and responsible authority may make representations to the relevant licensing authority;

(e) that representations shall be made in writing; and

(f) that it is an offence knowingly or recklessly to make a false statement in connection with an application and the maximum fine for which a person is liable on summary conviction for the offence.

The Regulations contain no requirement for advertisements in Wales to be in both English and Welsh, although the Guidance exhorts licensing authorities in Wales to encourage applicants to provide details in both languages of where the application may be viewed. Paragraph 8.46 provides:

> Licensing authorities in Wales should consider encouraging applicants to provide details in the alternative language (Welsh or English) to that of the main advertisement itself where the application may be viewed. Therefore, if an applicant publishes a notice in English they should be encouraged to provide a statement in Welsh as to where the application may be viewed, and vice versa. This would allow the reader of the notice to make enquiries to the licensing authority and find out the nature of the application.

## 2.1.14 Personal licences

For a personal licence application, s 133(1) provides that regulations can prescribe its form, the manner in which it is to be made, and the information and documents that must accompany it. This is similar to the provisions in ss 54 and 91 for premises licences and CPCs, although the Act does not in other respects make specific provision for personal licence applications. Regulation 4(1) and Sched 1 to the LA 2003 (Personal Licences) Regs 2005, SI 2005/41 specify the form the application shall take and the information that it must contain. They also require it to be accompanied by: two photographs of the applicant, one of which is to be endorsed as a true likeness of the applicant by a solicitor, notary, a 'person of standing in the community' or any individual with a professional qualification; a copy of the applicant's licensing qualification; and a criminal conviction or criminal record certificate or a Police National Computer check no earlier than one calendar month before the application, coupled with a declaration as to any convictions for a relevant offence or foreign offence (see 10.4.2 below for details).

## 2.1.15 Temporary event notices

For giving a TEN, regulations can prescribe its form, and the information or matters it must contain (see 9.2.3 below for details). Regulation 3(1) and Sched 1 to the LA 2003 (PTA) (Notices) Regs 2005, SI 2005/2918 specify the form the application shall take and the information that it must contain, which includes: the name and address of the relevant licensing authority; the premises user's personal and contact details, including National Insurance number; the address or description of the premises, the area where it is proposed to carry on licensable activities and the nature of the event; the dates and times of the licensable activities, the maximum numbers attending when these are taking place and whether alcohol is being supplied; information concerning the premises user's personal licence (where he holds one); whether the event period falls within part of the preceding 24-hour period of any TEN given for the same premises by the premises user or any associates or business colleagues; and the number of TENs previously given by any such persons.

The form of acknowledgement of receipt of a TEN is prescribed by reg 4, which requires the TEN or a copy of it to be signed in a section headed 'Acknowledgement' by a person authorised to acknowledge receipt on the authority's behalf; the form of a counter-notice to a TEN is prescribed by reg 5 and Sched 2, which require a person authorised by the authority to issue the counter-notice to indicate the particular permitted limit that would be exceeded if the event were to go ahead and sign the counter-notice; and the manner of giving a counter-notice is prescribed by reg 6, which can be by personal delivery to the premises user, leaving it at his address, or sending to him by post or email (see 9.3.1 and 9.7.5 below for details).

## 2.2    DETERMINING APPLICATIONS AND DISCHARGING OTHER LICENSING FUNCTIONS

### 2.2.1    Introduction

When determining licence applications and discharging other licensing functions, local authorities for the most part carry out these activities in accordance with the general law governing the discharge by them of their statutory responsibilities. Thus authorities might, under s 101 of the Local Government Act 1972, 'arrange for the discharge of any of their functions . . . by a committee or sub-committee or an officer of the authority' and, in making such arrangements, the power of decision-making may or may not be delegated to the committee, subcommittee or officer hearing the application. The 2003 Act, however, contains separate arrangements for the discharge of licensing functions under the Act. Section 6 requires the establishing of a licensing committee, s 7 makes provision for the exercise and delegation by a licensing authority of (most of) its licensing functions through the licensing committee, s 9 provides for the establishing of subcommittees and for various aspects of proceedings of the licensing committee and subcommittees to be prescribed by regulations, and s 10 makes provision for the subdelegation by the licensing committee of its functions to subcommittees and officers.[9] Although the licensing functions must be discharged by the committee, a subcommittee or officers, the authority is not precluded from developing collective working practices with other parts of the authority or other licensing authorities for work of a purely administrative nature, such as mail-outs, or contracting out such administrative tasks to private businesses (Guidance, para 13.77).

### 2.2.2    Establishing the licensing committee and its discharge of licensing functions

### 2.2.3    *Composition and political balance of licensing committee*

2.2.4    Section 6(1) provides: 'Each authority must establish a licensing committee consisting of at least ten, but not more than fifteen, members of the authority', and s 7 provides for the exercise and delegation of licensing functions through the licensing committee.[10] There is no provision in the 2003 Act that licensing committees need to be politically balanced so that membership reflects the balance of different political groups having seats on the authority. Although there are provisions in the Local Government and Housing Act 1989 requiring political balance on local authority committees,[11] it seems unlikely that these will have application to licensing committees established under s 6 of the 2003 Act. This is because the provisions in the 1989 Act are not expressed to be of general application to local authority committees. Instead, s 15(7) provides that Sched 1 to the 1989 Act shall have effect for determining the bodies to which the provisions on political balance are to have application, and under para 1 of Sched 1 there are three categories:

(a)  any ordinary committee or sub-committee of the authority (defined respectively in para 4(1) to mean "the authority's education committee, their social services committee or any other committee of the authority appointed under s 102(1)(a) of the Local Government Act 1972" and "any subcommittee of the authority's education committee or social services committee or any other sub-committee of that authority appointed under s 102(1)(c) of the Local Government Act 1972");

(b)  any advisory committee of the authority (which will be a committee appointed by the authority under s 102(4) Local Government Act 1972) and any sub-committee appointed by such an advisory committee; and

(c)  any such body falling within para 2 of Sched 1 (eg a local fisheries committee for any sea fisheries district or a National Parks Committee) to which at least three seats fall to be filled by appointments by the authority or committee.

2.2.5   Licensing committees are established under s 6 of the 2003 Act (and sub-committees, to which the discharge of licensing functions can be delegated, are established under s 9 – see 2.2.16 below) and do not fall within any of these categories in Sched 1. Most local authorities arrange for the discharge of their functions under s 101 of the Local Government Act 1972 by committees and subcommittees that are appointed under s 102 of that Act, but para 58 of Sched 6 to the 2003 Act specifically provides for their exclusion in relation to the discharge of licensing functions under the 2003 Act by adding to s 101 a new sub-s (15), which provides: 'Nothing in this section applies in relation to any function under the Licensing Act 2003 of a licensing authority (within the meaning of that Act).' It would seem therefore that the requirement for political balance under the 1989 Act will not have application.

The effect of this will be that most local authority committees and subcommittees will need to be politically balanced, but licensing committees and subcommittees discharging licensing functions will not. The rationale for this is not apparent. If political balance is thought to be desirable and applies in most cases (and this seems to be the general legislative intent underlying the 1989 Act), it is not obvious why this should not equally apply to licensing committees. Further, where a matter relates to a licensing function under the 2003 Act and to a function of the authority that is not a licensing function, the authority can, under s 7(5), arrange for the discharge of that function either by the licensing committee or by another of its committees (see 2.2.13 below). If it arranges for discharge by another committee, that committee will need to be politically balanced, but this will not be the case if it arranges for discharge by the licensing committee. A requirement for political balance in one case, but not the other, seems difficult to defend. Nevertheless, this seems to be the legal position although, as a matter of practice, local authorities, when setting up their licensing committee, may well have decided that it should in any event be politically balanced.

## 2.2.6   Quorum for licensing committee

2.2.7    As to whether all members of the licensing committee need to be present for the committee to be quorate, the position is unclear. The Act contains no express provision in this respect, although s 7(9) does provide:

> Where a licensing committee is unable to discharge any function delegated to it in accordance with this section because of the number of its members who are unable to take part in the consideration or discussion of any matter or vote on any question with respect to it, the committee must refer the matter back to the licensing authority and the authority must discharge that function.

This begs the question of when the committee will be unable to discharge any delegated function because of the numbers of members who cannot participate, which may be for a number of reasons, including where members have a 'prejudicial interest' in a matter that requires them to withdraw when that matter is being considered.[12] However, s 7(9) gives no clear steer on the answer. There seems to be three possible answers. First, all members of the licensing committee may have to be present for the committee to be quorate and, whenever any member cannot be present, there is no quorum and the matter must be referred back to the licensing authority for it to discharge the function. If this is the meaning of s 7(9), it is neither sensible nor practical.[13] Secondly, whatever number at which the composition of the committee is fixed between 10 and 15, the number present must never fall below 10 for the committee to be quorate. This is more sensible and practical, but may still present problems for small authorities. Thirdly, while the committee must have between 10 and 15 members appointed to it (so as to comply with s 6(1)), it can still meet and discharge licensing functions delegated to it when fewer than 10 members are present, without having to refer the matter back to the licensing authority, provided some specified quorum for meetings is complied with.[14] This is the most sensible and practical answer, since it allows for diversification and differences in size between different licensing authorities.

2.2.8    While the Act makes provision in s 9(2)(a) for the Secretary of State to set quorum limits through secondary legislation (see 2.2.16 below), the Secretary of State has not done so and it would seem that in the absence of any regulations the quorum may well be a matter for the licensing committee to determine. Support for this view can be found from the following statement by Lord Davies, a government spokesman, at the Report Stage of the Bill in the House of Lords:

> ... the Bill gives the Secretary of State power to make regulations setting out, among other matters, the quorum for meetings of the licensing committee and its sub-committees ... If the Secretary of State does not make such regulations ... each licensing authority can choose to regulate its own procedure and that of its sub-committees. So if the Secretary of State does not make regulations, then the responsibility will be devolved to the licensing committee. (HL Deb, vol 645, cols 382–83, 27 February 2003)

There remains an element of doubt about this, however, since these remarks were preceded by an earlier statement of his Lordship, during the Committee Stage, that: 'all members of the licensing committee will have to be present for the committee to be quorate' (HL Deb, vol 642, col 835, 19 December 2002), and when the Bill was subsequently considered in the House of Commons no clear statement could be discerned from the debates there on the matter of when committees will be quorate.

2.2.9    A further matter affecting whether the licensing committee is quorate and, in turn, whether matters delegated to it need to be referred back to the licensing authority under s 7(9) because there is an insufficient number of members who can participate, is whether members precluded from participating by a 'prejudicial interest' might obtain a dispensation to do so. Under s 81(4) of the Local Government Act 2000, a member is able to participate if a dispensation from the prohibition on being present is granted by the authority's standards committee and it seems that, if one were to be granted and this would make the committee quorate, the matter should not be referred back to the licensing authority. It is unlikely that s 7(9) was intended to prevent a member obtaining a dispensation. It is clearly established under s 81(4) that members can obtain dispensations and there would seem to be no good reason why s 7(9) should be regarded as overriding this. Certainly, on the wording of s 7(9), if a dispensation is granted, it will not prevent the member from taking part in the consideration or discussion of the matter in question or voting on it. The matter will not therefore need to be referred back to the licensing authority under s 7(9) because the committee will be able to discharge the function delegated to it. Section 7(9) should therefore be regarded as confined to cases where a dispensation cannot be granted and, as a result, there is an insufficient number of members for the committee to be quorate. It is only then that the matter should be referred back to the licensing authority.

### 2.2.10  *Licensing functions discharged by the licensing committee*

2.2.11    As a general rule, all matters relating to the discharge by a licensing authority of its licensing functions must be exercised by the licensing committee. One exception is under s 7(9) if the licensing committee is unable to discharge any function because of an insufficient number of members (see 2.2.8 above). Other exceptions are the formulation and publication of the Statement of Licensing Policy (SOP), where arrangements have been made for discharge of licensing functions by another committee, or any matters relating to either of these cases. Section 7(1) and (2) provides:

(1)  All matters relating to the discharge by a licensing authority of its licensing functions are, by virtue of this subsection, referred to its licensing committee and, accordingly, that committee must discharge those functions on behalf of the authority.

(2)  Subsection (1) does not apply to–

(a)  any function conferred on the licensing authority by section 5 (statement of licensing policy), or

(b)  any function discharged under subsection (5)(a) below by a committee (other than a licensing committee),[15]

or any matter relating to the discharge of any such function.

2.2.12    In the case of arrangements made for discharge of licensing functions by another committee (s 7(2)(b)), it is self-evident that the other committee will discharge those functions, but it is not self-evident which body will discharge the functions of formulation and publication of the SOP (s 7(2)(a)). The 2003 Act itself gives no indication whether this function should be discharged by the full council or by its executive, but secondary legislation made under the Local Government Act 2000 indicates how this function should be exercised. In England, amendments to the Local Authorities (Functions and Responsibilities) (England) Regulations 2000, SI 2000/2853 make it clear that the function should not be discharged by an authority's executive. Part 1 of Sched 1 to these regulations specifies various functions that are not to be the responsibility of an authority's executive and the Local Authorities (Functions and Responsibilities) (Amendment No 3) (England) Regulations 2004, SI 2004/2748, reg 2 and para 1(1) of Sched 1, include within these functions those relating to licensing under ss 5–8 of the 2003 Act. Accordingly, where the licensing authority is a local authority, formulation and publication of the SOP should be determined by the full council of the authority. The position is, however, different in Wales. Under The Local Authorities (Executive Arrangements) (Wales) Regulations 2007, SI 2007/399, reg 3 and Sched 1B, para 43, functions in respect of the establishment under s 6 of the 2003 Act of an authority's licensing committee are not to be the responsibility of an authority's executive, but reg 4 and Sched 2, para 23 provide that licensing functions under Pt 2 of the 2003 Act, except s 6, may, but need not, be the responsibility of an authority's executive. Thus formulation and publication of the SOP might be determined by the full council, but equally might be determined by an authority's executive. It is difficult to see why the position should be any different in Wales, but the effect of the regulations seems to be that, unlike in England, whether responsibility for formulation and publication of the SOP should rest with the full council or with the executive is a matter for the authority to decide.

## 2.2.13 Discharge of licensing-related functions

A licensing authority may also arrange for the discharge by its licensing committee of additional functions of the authority that are related to its licensing functions, for s 7(3) provides:

> A licensing authority may arrange for the discharge by its licensing committee of any function of the authority which–
> (a) relates to a matter referred to that committee by virtue of subsection (1), but
> (b) is not a licensing function.

No criteria are provided to determine whether a function is 'related' to a licensing function, so this will be a matter of interpretation and a question of fact in the circumstances. Instances of where a function might be related could perhaps include planning requirements concerning licensed premises[16] or promotion of tourism in connection with entertainments licensable under the 2003 Act. They might also include activities for which a licence is needed under other legislation, for example, a dog track at which bets can be placed and which is licensed for the sale of alcohol will also require a betting premises licence under s 179 of the Gambling Act 2005.

If the authority chooses to discharge such related functions itself, it must before doing so, except in urgent cases, consider any relevant report prepared by the licensing committee. This ensures that the licensing committee will have an input into any matter relating to the authority's licensing functions. In cases where a matter relates to both a licensing function and a function that is not a licensing function, a licensing authority may choose to refer the matter either to the licensing committee or to another committee. Where it opts for the former committee, it must consult the licensing committee and, where it opts for the latter, the other committee must, when considering the matter, take account of any relevant report prepared by the licensing committee. Section 7(4)–(8) provides:

(4) Where the licensing authority does not make arrangements under subsection (3) in respect of any such function, it must (unless the matter is urgent) consider a report of its licensing committee with respect to the matter before discharging the function.

(5) Where a matter relates to a licensing function of a licensing authority and to a function of the authority which is not a licensing function ("the other function"), the authority may–

(a) refer the matter to another of its committees and arrange for the discharge of the licensing function by that committee, or

(b) refer the matter to its licensing committee (to the extent it is not already so referred under subsection (1)) and arrange for the discharge of the other function by the licensing committee.

(6) In a case where an authority exercises its power under subsection (5)(a), the committee to which the matter is referred must (unless the matter is urgent) consider a report of the authority's licensing committee with respect to the matter before discharging the function concerned.

(7) Before exercising its power under subsection (5)(b), an authority must consult its licensing committee.

(8) In a case where an authority exercises its power under subsection (5)(b), its licensing committee must (unless the matter is urgent) consider any report of any of the authority's other committees with respect to the matter before discharging the function concerned.

## 2.2.14 Licensing subcommittees and officers and their discharge of licensing functions

### 2.2.15 *Delegation to subcommittees and officers*

2.2.16 Section 9 provides that a licensing committee can establish one or more sub-committees consisting of three members of the committee, and that regulations made by the Secretary of State may make provision about the proceedings of licensing committees and their subcommittees. The regulations may also extend to other matters, including public access to meetings, publicity to be given to those meetings, agendas and records to be produced in respect of those meetings and public access to such agendas, and records and other information about those meetings.[17] In other respects, however, each licensing committee may regulate its own procedure and that of its subcommittees.[18] Section 9 provides:

(1) A licensing committee may establish one or more sub-committees consisting of three members of the committee.

(2) Regulations may make provision about–

(a) the proceedings of licensing committees and their sub-committees (including provision about the validity of proceedings and the quorum for meetings),

(b) public access to the meetings of those committees and sub-committees,

(c) the publicity to be given to those meetings,

(d)  the agendas and records to be produced in respect of those meetings, and

(e)  public access to such agendas and records and other information about those meetings.[19]

(3)  Subject to any such regulations, each licensing committee may regulate its own procedure and that of its sub-committees.

Regarding a quorum for subcommittees, this is not specified in any regulations under the 2003 Act, but it seems to have been the Government's intention that the quorum should be three members, for there is a clear statement to this effect during the committee stage of the Bill in the House of Commons.[20] However, in the absence of any specified quorum, local authorities appear free to set their own. While they are perhaps most likely to adopt a quorum of three, they are not obliged to do so nor, as with the licensing committee, would there seem to be a need for political balance (see 2.2.3 above). Less clear is whether the three members need to be identified individuals from the licensing committee, with only those three members able to sit on the sub-committee, or whether any three members from the licensing committee might sit whenever the subcommittee is convened. Either view seems a permissible interpretation on the wording of s 9(1). Since the latter approach incorporates a greater degree of flexibility, this is most likely to have been the one adopted by licensing authorities.

2.2.17  Section 10 enables the licensing committee to arrange for the discharge of any functions exercisable by it by a subcommittee established by it, and, in certain circumstances (essentially where an application is uncontested), the subcommittee can arrange for discharge by an officer of the licensing authority. More than one subcommittee can be established[21] and the same function can be discharged concurrently by more than one subcommittee or officer. Section 10(1)–(3) provides:

(1)  A licensing committee may arrange for the discharge of any functions exercisable by it–

(a)  by a sub-committee established by it, or

(b)  subject to subsection (4), by an officer of the licensing authority.

(2)  Where arrangements are made under subsection (1)(a), then, subject to subsections (4) and (5), the sub-committee may in turn arrange for the discharge of the function concerned by an officer of the licensing authority.[22]

(3)  Arrangements under subsection (1) or (2) may provide for more than one subcommittee or officer to discharge the same function concurrently.

Arrangements for discharge by an officer are effectively confined to uncontested cases by s 10(4), which provides:

Arrangements may not be made under subsection (1) or (2) for the discharge by an officer of–

(a)  any function under

(i)  section 18(3) (determination of application for premises licence where representations have been made),

(ii)  section 31(3) (determination of application for provisional statement where representations have been made),

(iii)  section 35(3) (determination of application for variation of premises licence where representations have been made),

(iv)  section 39(3) (determination of application to vary designated premises supervisor following police objection),

    (v)   section 44(5) (determination of application for transfer of premises licence following police objection),

    (vi)  section 48(3) (consideration of police objection made to interim authority notice),

    (via) section 53A(2)(a) or 53B (determination of interim steps pending summary review),

    (vii) section 72(3) (determination of application for club premises certificate where representations have been made),

    (viii) section 85(3) (determination of application to vary club premises certificate where representations have been made),

    (ix)  section 105(2) (decision to give counter notice following police objection to temporary event notice),

    (x)   section 120(7) (determination of application for grant of personal licence following police objection),

    (xi)  section 121(6) (determination of application for renewal of personal licence following police objection),

    (xii) section 124(4) (revocation of licence where convictions come to light after grant etc),

(b)  any function under section 52(2) or (3) (determination of application for review of premises licence) in a case where relevant representations (within the meaning of section 52(7)) have been made,

(ba) any function under section 53C (review following review notice), in a case where relevant representations within the meaning of section 53C(7) have been made,

(c)  any function under section 88(2) or (3) (determination of application for review of club premises certificate) in a case where relevant representations (within the meaning of section 88(7)) have been made, or

(d)  any function under section 167(5) (review following closure order) in a case where relevant representations (within the meaning of section 167(9)) have been made.

## 2.2.18 Recommended delegations

2.2.19 Although the extent to which decisions might be determined by a committee or subcommittee essentially remains a decision for the local authority, the Guidance neverthess contains a 'Recommended delegation of functions' in para 13.79, as follows:

### RECOMMENDED DELEGATION OF FUNCTIONS

| Matter to be dealt with | Full Committee | Subcommittee | Officers |
| --- | --- | --- | --- |
| Application for personal licence | | If a police objection | If no objection made |
| Application for personal licence with unspent convictions | | All cases | |
| Application for premises licence/club premises certificate | | If a relevant representation made | If no relevant representation made |
| Application for provisional statement | | If a relevant representation made | If no relevant representation made |

| Matter to be dealt with | Full Committee | Subcommittee | Officers |
| --- | --- | --- | --- |
| Application to vary premises licence/club premises certificate | | If a relevant representation made | If no relevant representation made |
| Application to vary designated premises supervisor | | If a police objection | All other cases |
| Request to be removed as designated premises supervisor | | | All cases |
| Application for transfer of premises licence | | If a police objection | All other cases |
| Applications for interim authorities | | If a police objection | All other cases |
| Application to review premises licence/club premises certificate | | All cases | |
| Decision on whether a complaint is irrelevant frivolous vexatious etc | | | All cases |
| Decision to object when local authority is a consultee and not the relevant authority considering the application | | All cases | |
| Determination of a police objection to a temporary event notice | | All cases | |

2.2.20   It can be seen that the recommended delegation is for all functions (insofar as they are not dealt with by officers) to be dealt with by a subcommittee, with none of the above functions being discharged by the licensing committee itself. This does not, however, mean that the licensing committee has no effective role, since it can exercise an overseeing role, monitoring and receiving reports from subcommittees on decisions taken by them, and can in appropriate instances (for example, particularly contentious, high-profile or large-scale event cases) determine applications itself. Although under s 4(3)(b) local authorities must have regard to the recommendations in the Guidance, they are not bound by them and can depart from them where there are good reasons for doing so (see 4.5.4 below). Involvement of the licensing committee to obtain a wider spread of views and a fuller consideration of the application in the instances mentioned above may be a good reason for departing from the recommendation that subcommittees should determine applications. Similarly, given the difficulties that might be involved in determining whether representations are frivolous or vexatious and the potentially contentious nature of any such decision which effectively precludes the representations being considered, having the matter determined by a subcommittee of three persons, rather than an individual licensing officer, may be a good reason for departing from the recommendation that an officer should determine such matters.

## 2.3 LICENSING HEARINGS

### 2.3.1 Introduction

Hearings need to be held in contested cases, except where the parties agree that a hearing is unnecessary, and there is a general provision contained in the 2003 Act for the Secretary of State to issue regulations prescribing the procedure to be followed at hearings, while at the same time indicating particular aspects that the regulations might encompass. These are the giving of notice of hearings, expedited procedures in urgent cases, the rules of evidence to be applied and legal representation at hearings. Section 183(1) provides:

> Regulations may prescribe the procedure to be followed in relation to a hearing held by a licensing authority under this Act and, in particular, may–
>
> (a) require a licensing authority to give notice of hearings to such persons as may be prescribed;
> (b) make provision for expedited procedures in urgent cases;
> (c) make provision about the rules of evidence which are to apply to hearings;
> (d) make provision about the legal representation at hearings of the parties to it;
> (e) prescribe the period within which an application, in relation to which a hearing has been held, must be determined or any other step in the procedure must be taken.

The procedure for hearings has been prescribed by the Secretary of State in the Licensing Act 2003 (Hearings) Regulations 2005, SI 2005/44 (LA 2003 (Hearings) Regs 2005). However, where matters arise which are not covered by the Regulations, licensing authorities may make arrangements as they see fit as long as they are lawful (Guidance, para 9.22).

The position in respect of costs is that these are not recoverable and no award can be made by the licensing authority. Section 183(2) provides:

> But the licensing authority may not make any order as to the costs incurred by a party in connection with a hearing under this Act.

### 2.3.2 Notice of hearings

The Regulations contain a number of detailed prescriptive requirements in respect of notice and holding of hearings. First, under reg 5 and Sched 1, there is a prescribed period of time within which hearings must be held, which in general is 20 working days.[23] Secondly, under reg 6(1) and Sched 2, a 'notice of hearing' must be given to various persons; and the notice must set out the date, time and place at which the hearing is to be held, be given within a specified period before the hearing and contain certain information. The persons to whom notice must be given will vary according to the particular provision in question, but will generally include applicants and licence holders, persons who have made relevant representations and the police in cases where only they have a right to object (see Sched 2 to the Regulations for details). Under reg 6(4), the period of notice that must be given is, in general, 10 working days[24] and the information that the notice must contain, under reg 7(1), is:

- the rights of the party in relation to the hearing;[25]
- the consequences of non-attendance or lack of representation at the hearing;
- the procedure to be followed at the hearing; and
- any matters about which the licensing authority wants clarification from a party at the hearing.

Further, under reg 7(2), additional documents must be given with the notice of hearing in certain cases to particular parties (for example, relevant representations made by responsible authorities and interested parties must be given to applicants for premises licences).[26] Thirdly, reg 8(1) requires persons given a notice of hearing to give the licensing authority a notice indicating whether they intend to attend or be represented at the hearing and whether a hearing is considered unnecessary.[27] Where a party wishes a person (other than someone representing him at the hearing) to appear at the hearing, under reg 8(2), the notice he gives that he will be attending the hearing must also contain a request for permission for that person to appear, along with that person's name and a brief description of the point(s) on which that person may be able to assist the authority. Under reg 8(5), such a notice must, in general, be given within five working days before the day or the first day on which the hearing is to be held.[28] Fourthly, reg 10 makes provision for the withdrawal of representations, permitting a party to withdraw them either by giving notice to the authority no later than 24 hours before the day or the first day on which the hearing is to be held, or orally at the hearing. If representations are withdrawn after this time, the hearing must proceed. However, where discussions between an applicant and those making representations are taking place and it is likely that all parties are on the point of reaching agreement, the licensing authority may wish to use its power to extend time limits under reg 11(1), if it considers this to be in the public interest (Guidance, para 9.21). If all representations are withdrawn, the position will be the same as if no representations had been received and the authority in this instance is obliged to grant the application, subject only to such conditions as are consistent with the operating schedule and to any mandatory conditions that must be imposed on the licence (see 1.2.5 above). Fifthly, where the giving of notice is required by the Regulations, reg 34(1) provides that the notice must be given in writing, although reg 34(2) goes on to provide that this is satisfied where the text of the notice is transmitted by electronic means, provided certain requirements are met.[29] Nevertheless, a measure of discretion is conferred on an authority in respect of the above requirements under regs 11 and 12 in that it can extend time limits where it considers this to be necessary in the public interest and can adjourn hearings or arrange additional hearing dates.[30]

### 2.3.3   Hearings in public

Under reg 14(1) hearings are held in public,[31] although under reg 14(2) a discretion is given to the licensing authority to exclude the public from all or part of a hearing where it considers that the public interest in so doing outweighs the public interest in the hearing, or that part of the hearing, taking place in public.[32] It is not clear how this 'public interest' test should be applied and, where the licensing authority is a local authority (which will be the case in most instances), there is an apparent conflict between the power to exclude the public under this provision and the power to exclude the public under the provisions of the Local Government Act 1972. Section 100A(1) of the 1972 Act requires meetings of local authorities to be held in public and provides for exclusion of the public if it is likely that confidential information would be disclosed to them in breach of the obligation of confidence (s 100A(2)) or, following the passing of a resolution, if it is likely that certain categories of 'exempt information' would be disclosed to them (s 100A(4)). There are a number of examples of what constitutes 'exempt information' and these are specified in Sched 12A to the 1972 Act. Whether a 'public interest' test would include some or all of these examples, or might extend beyond them, is uncertain and, further, with competing provisions, it is unclear which should be applied.

### 2.3.4  Supporting documentation

2.3.5    Under reg 15, parties to the hearing have the right to attend,[33] with or without legal or other assistance or representation, and under reg 16 have the right to produce supporting information in response to any point on which the authority has given notice that it requires clarification, to question any party if given permission by the authority, and to address the authority.[34] Under reg 18, any supporting documentary evidence or other evidence produced by a party to the hearing can be taken into account by the licensing authority, either before the hearing or, with the consent of all the other parties, at the hearing. The evidence, it seems, can be produced at the hearing only with the consent of the parties and the authority appears not to have any discretion to admit it in the absence of consent (other than by way of seeking clarification under reg 16). Regarding evidence produced before the hearing, no time limit is specified within which such evidence should be given to the authority. If given immediately prior to the hearing, this may prejudice other interested parties by not providing them with a proper opportunity to consider it, although the authority in such a case might, in the interests of fairness, delay the hearing to enable the evidence to be considered or perhaps exclude the evidence. Further, the authority can, under reg 19, disregard any information or evidence that is not relevant to the party's case and to the promotion of the licensing objectives.[35] Regulation 19 provides:

> The authority shall disregard any information given by a party or any person to whom permission to appear at the hearing is given by the authority which is not relevant to–
>
> (a)  their application, representations or notice (as applicable) or in the case of another person, the application representations or notice of the party requesting their appearance, and
>
> (b)  the promotion of the licensing objectives or, in relation to a hearing to consider a notice given by a chief officer of police, the crime prevention objective.

Regulation 19(b) is no more than declaratory of the position under the 2003 Act. Section 4(2) requires an authority, when discharging its licensing functions, to promote the licensing objectives and it would be *ultra vires* for the authority to have regard to any information not relevant to the promotion of the objectives as such information falls outside the scope of its statutory powers under the Act. Regulation 19(a) requires the authority to disregard any information given by a party or a person whose appearance the party has requested, which is 'not relevant to' the application, representation or notice. If interpreted literally, this may prevent a party from either raising at the hearing, or commenting on, any matter that is not contained in the application, representation or notice. This might mean that an interested party or responsible authority has relevant matters to put before the licensing authority, but the licensing authority has to disregard anything that is said or put forward if not contained in the original representation made. This could be a particular problem for residents living in the vicinity of the premises who, on seeing a notice displayed at or on the premises or when applying for a review of a premises licence or CPC, do not include in their representations everything upon which they subsequently wish to rely. Similarly, it may prevent an applicant from raising matters which promote the wider, social, cultural and economic benefits for the community that might be derived from licensable activities taking place (see 4.2.17 below).

2.3.6    Further, information contained in an applicant's operating schedule, of which residents may be unaware, may impact on their representations, but may not relate specifically to a matter addressed by them in their representations. If the applicant at the hearing were to address the authority in respect of this information, reg 19(b) might prevent residents from cross-examining him on this, even if the authority were willing to grant them permission to do so under reg 23 (see 2.3.11 below). It can be seen that a literal interpretation might have the effect of requiring the authority to disregard information that is relevant to the promotion of the licensing objectives and may preclude a party from addressing a matter that has been raised by another party to the proceedings. If this were the case, there would be a conflict with the obligation on the licensing authority under s 4(2) to promote the licensing objectives when discharging its licensing functions and also to afford a party the right to a fair hearing under the common law and Art 6(1) of the European Convention on Human Rights (see 3.5 below). These, it is submitted, are overriding obligations on a licensing authority and should be regarded as paramount. A literal interpretation therefore seems to be inappropriate and compliance with these obligations might be achieved by giving a broad purposive interpretation to reg 19(b). The aim or purpose of the provision should be seen as preventing parties from, in effect, introducing new grounds or raising completely different matters at the hearing to those contained in their representations, rather than requiring the authority to disregard anything that is not specifically addressed in the representations.

## 2.3.7    Procedure at hearings

### 2.3.8    *Determination generally by the authority*

To a large extent, the Regulations leave it to the licensing authority itself to determine the procedure, with reg 21 providing: 'Subject to the provisions of these Regulations, the authority shall determine the procedure to be followed at the hearing.' In this respect, the position is not dissimilar to that in other areas of local authority licensing, where procedure in relation to local authority hearings is largely a matter for individual authorities, the only constraint being the need to comply with the rules of natural justice. In other areas of local authority licensing, either the applicant or objectors can be heard first; evidence may, but need not, be on oath and cross-examination may, but need not, be allowed, provided the parties have an opportunity to comment on and refute what is put forward; the strict rules of evidence that apply in court proceedings need not be observed; and any evidence that is logically probative, which goes to proving a relevant issue, can be admitted. In addition, licensing authorities might take into account their own local knowledge (see

12.8.5 below). In some of these respects, the Regulations do make provision, for example, cross-examination (see 2.3.11 below), but in others, including the order in which parties appear, the rules of evidence which are to apply and the use of local knowledge, they do not do so and here it may be assumed that authorities are free to determine their own procedure on these matters. The Regulations in fact go on to make only minimal provision in respect of the procedure at the hearing, regulating the procedure in only four respects.

## 2.3.9   Specific provisions in Regulations

2.3.10   First, under reg 22, the authority must explain to parties to the hearing the procedure which the authority proposes to follow at the hearing. Parties to the hearing will be those persons to whom the notice of hearing is to be given in accordance with reg 6(1) and this will essentially comprise applicants and those making relevant representations (see 2.3.2 above). It will not necessarily be the case that all those making relevant representations will appear at the hearing and there is no requirement in the Act for responsible authorities or interested parties that have made representations to attend. However, the Guidance, para 9.23 recommends that attendance 'is generally good practice and assists committees to reach more informed decisions'. In cases where several responsible authorities within a local authority have made representations on an application, the Guidance goes on to indicate that 'a single local authority officer may represent them at the hearing if the responsible authorities and the licensing authority agree'. Explaining the procedure to the parties attending is something that has traditionally been done, as a matter of good practice, in licensing hearings generally, even in the absence of a formal legal requirement to do so, so the requirement in reg 22 is unlikely to have real practical significance. In addition, under reg 22, the authority must consider any request made by a party for permission, which must not be unreasonably withheld, for another person to appear at the hearing.[36] In licensing hearings generally, parties have been able, at least as a matter of practice, to call any witnesses in support of their application without the need to obtain any permission from the authority,[37] although for hearings under the 2003 Act, reg 22 imposes a requirement to request permission for another party to appear. Since a refusal to allow a party to appear may well result in an appeal and there is no requirement on appeals to request permission for a party to appear – this is because the Regulations do not apply to appeals, which are governed by the Criminal Procedure Rules 2005 (see 12.8.1 below) – authorities might perhaps be reluctant to invoke the provision in reg 22 to prevent someone appearing to give evidence as a witness before them. Circumstances in which an authority might perhaps refuse permission for a person to appear as a witness might, however, include where the evidence will not assist the hearing, either because it is in respect of a matter that is not in dispute or because it duplicates other evidence, or perhaps where it is particularly prejudicial in some way that outweighs its probative value.

2.3.11   Secondly, under reg 23, the hearing must take the form of a discussion led by the authority, with cross-examination not permitted unless the authority considers that cross-examination is required to enable the authority to consider the representations, application or notice. This is a substantial change from the practice in hearings in other areas of local authority licensing, which generally follow a court-like procedure with an opportunity for cross-examination. However, this provision reflects the emphasis under the 2003 Act on partnership working to promote the licensing objectives, with all those having an interest or involvement in the licensing process ('stakeholders') working together in partnership towards a mutually acceptable outcome (see 1.2.8–1.2.10 above). Discussion is likely to be led by the chair of the subcommittee (or committee) hearing the application, although there would seem to be no reason why this might not be undertaken by others, such as another subcommittee (or committee) member or a licensing officer, acting under the chair's direction. On the face of it, exclusion of cross-examination might enable a licensing authority to adopt a very cursory approach to dealing with the hearing. However, the risk of the decision being reversed on appeal by the magistrates' court, which might find lack of cross-examination a persuasive factor and might award costs against the authority, should preclude such an approach. Further, there might, if such an approach was adopted, be the risk of contravening Art 6(1) of the European Convention on Human Rights (see 3.5.9 below).

2.3.12   Thirdly, under reg 24, the parties must be allowed an equal maximum period of time in which to present their case. While the sentiments underlying this provision are admirable to ensure fairness and parity of treatment, the provision may prove problematic in application. All persons making relevant representations are 'parties' and, in the case of 'interested parties' living in the vicinity, there may be a considerable number of them. If the provision in reg 24 is given a literal interpretation, each 'interested party' is entitled to the same period of time as any other interested party, even if making a substantially similar point. A pragmatic approach may be to require persons making substantially similar points to elect a spokesperson to present the case, with that person being allowed an equal maximum time to other parties (for example, the applicant, a responsible authority).[38] This might (perhaps) be justified if a purposive interpretation is given to reg 24 and the underlying aim or objective is seen as ensuring that equal time is afforded to competing viewpoints or arguments.

2.3.13   Fourthly, under reg 25, any person attending the hearing who, in the opinion of the authority, is behaving in a disruptive manner may be required to leave the hearing. Where a person who is disruptive is required to leave, the authority may refuse to permit him to return or permit him to return only on such conditions as the authority may specify, but such a person may, before the end of the hearing, submit to the authority in writing any information which he would have been entitled to give orally had he not been required to leave.

## 2.3.14 *Role of the licensing officer*

2.3.15   No reference is made in the Regulations to the role of the licensing officer in hearings. In local authority licensing hearings generally, it is common as a matter of general practice for a report to be produced by a licensing officer prior to the hearing, to which parties have access. The report deals with issues relevant to the hearing (for example, a summary of the application and objections) and the officer is normally present at the hearing to provide professional expertise and assistance to the committee or subcommittee (hereafter 'committee') to enable it to come to a balanced and informed decision on the merits of the application. The report may or may not include recommendations (dependent on findings of fact made by the committee), for practice among authorities differs on whether licensing officers' reports should include recommendations. Given that the Regulations are silent on this matter, there is no reason why this general practice of the licensing officer producing a report should not be followed and, indeed, adoption of this practice has been widespread under the 2003 Act (with reports drawing committees' attention to the relevant parts of the authority's Statement of Licensing Policy and the Secretary of State's Guidance).

2.3.16  The Regulations are similarly silent on whether a licensing officer might be present at the hearing and whether he might assist the committee. An officer, not being a party to the hearing as defined in reg 2 (see 2.3.10 above), has none of the rights afforded to parties under the Regulations, for example, the right to notice of the hearing under reg 6 and the right to attend under reg 15, but his presence at the hearing (at the committee's request) is not precluded by the Regulations. The committee is entitled under reg 21 to determine the procedure to be followed at the hearing and under reg 17 members 'may ask any question of any party or other person appearing at the hearing'. These provisions in combination seem wide enough to enable the committee to determine that a licensing officer (and other persons who are not parties, for example, a legal officer) may be present if it thinks that their presence may be of assistance. The reference in reg 17 to 'other person appearing' is wide enough to cover not only persons who a party has requested permission for them to appear (on his behalf) in accordance with reg 22 (see 2.3.10 above), but also other persons who the committee may wish to appear to assist it with its deliberations.

## 2.3.17 Determination of applications

2.3.18  Under reg 26(2), an authority must normally make its determination[39] of the application within five working days, beginning with the day or the last day on which the hearing was held, although under reg 26(1), in cases where there is a greater degree or urgency attached to the outcome, the authority must make its determination at the conclusion of the hearing.[40] In cases where the parties have agreed to dispense with a hearing, the authority must, under reg 27, make its determination within 10 working days, beginning with the day the authority gave notice that the hearing was dispensed with. Regarding notifying parties of its determination, the 2003 Act sometimes makes provision for the period within which the authority must notify a party of its determination, often requiring that notification be given 'forthwith' (for example, under s 23 where a premises licence application is granted or rejected), but it does not do so in all cases (for example, under s 52 for review of a premises licence). Where no provision is made, however, reg 28 provides that notification must be forthwith.[41] When parties are notified of the authority's determination, reg 29 requires that the notice given must also be accompanied by information regarding the right of a party to appeal against the determination. Once notified of the determination, a party then has 21 days within which to appeal (see 12.4.1 below). Finally, under reg 30, a record of the hearing 'in a permanent and intelligible form' must be taken and kept for a period of six years from the date of determination, or where an appeal is made, the disposal of the appeal.

2.3.19  It can be seen that the Regulations provide a prescriptive framework within which hearings must be conducted and applications determined, albeit with some measure of discretion available to authorities in respect of the requirements (for example, to extend time limits where it is necessary in the public interest). There is also a measure of discretion available where irregularities or clerical errors occur.

Where an authority considers that any person may have been prejudiced by any irregularity resulting from any failure to comply with a requirement before a determination is made, it must, under reg 32, take such steps as it thinks fit to cure the irregularity before reaching its determination.[42] Although expressed in mandatory terms, there is a significant element of discretion in respect of taking steps that the authority thinks fit. When a determination has been made, reg 33 provides that clerical mistakes in any document recording the determination or errors arising in the document from an accidental slip or omission may be corrected by the authority. Nevertheless, a strict application of the provisions in the Regulations is capable of causing injustice and a broad, purposive interpretation may be needed to ensure that hearings overall are conducted in accordance with the normal, established rules of fairness.

## 2.3.20 Hearings appertaining to licensing-related functions

2.3.21   Section 183(1) provides that the Regulations can prescribe the procedure to be followed in relation to 'a hearing held by a licensing authority under this Act' and this will most obviously include hearings held in contested cases where the licensing authority has received relevant representations (for example, on applications for a premises licence or CPC) or a police objection notice (for example, on applications for a personal licence or on the issuing of a TEN) when it is discharging its licensing functions under the Act. Less clear is whether the hearing procedure specified by the Regulations applies when the licensing authority is discharging a licensing-related function under s 7(3)–(4) or dealing with a matter that relates to both a licensing function and another function under s 7(5)–(8) (see 2.2.13 above). In the case of a licensing-related function, the licensing authority can arrange for this to be dealt with by the licensing committee or discharge it itself. In either instance this could be said to be 'a hearing held by a licensing authority under this Act', in which case the hearing procedure specified by the Regulations might apply. In the case of a matter that relates to both a licensing function and another function, the licensing authority can arrange for this to be dealt with by the licensing committee or by another of its committees. Again, where this is dealt with by the licensing committee and (perhaps) where it is dealt with by another committee (since this might nevertheless be seen as dealt with by the licensing authority, albeit through one of its committees), this could be said to be 'a hearing held by a licensing authority under this Act'.

2.3.22   However, it may be that these cases do not fall within the scope of the Regulations that have been prescribed under s 183(1). Regulation 3 of the LA 2003 (Hearings) Regs 2005 provides: 'These Regulations are to make provision for the procedure to be followed in relation to hearings held under the Act by an authority.' By reg 2, '"authority" means, in relation to a hearing, the relevant licensing authority which has the duty under the Act to hold the hearing which expression includes the licensing committee or licensing sub-committee discharging the function of holding the hearing' and '"hearing" means the hearing referred to in column 1 of the table in Schedule 1 as the case may require'. The reference here is to the authority having the 'duty' to hold the hearing, but no duty is expressed to arise under s 7 where licensing-related functions are discharged or a matter that relates to both a licensing function and another function is dealt with. Further, the hearings to which reference is made in Sched 1 comprise contested cases where there is an express statutory obligation under the Act to hold a hearing. In light of this, it seems that the hearing procedure specified by the Regulations may well not apply to cases determined under s 7.

## 2.4 KEEPING A LICENSING REGISTER

### 2.4.1 Record of authorisations and interests

2.4.2 Section 8 requires an authority to keep a record of all premises and personal licences and CPCs issued by it, any TENs received by its various matters specified in Sched 3 (see 2.4.3 below), and any other information prescribed in regulations issued by the Secretary of State (see 2.4.4 below). Regulations may, in addition, prescribe the form or manner in which the register is kept. Section 8(1) and (2) provides:

(1) Each licensing authority must keep a register containing–
   (a) a record of each premises licence, club premises certificate and personal licence issued by it,
   (b) a record of each temporary event notice received by it,
   (c) the matters mentioned in Schedule 3, and
   (d) such other information as may be prescribed.
(2) Regulations may require a register kept under this section to be in a prescribed form and kept in a prescribed manner.

2.4.3 The matters mentioned in Sched 3 comprise the keeping of a record of any applications, notices or requests received under the Act, whether in respect of premises licences, CPCs, TENs or personal licences. Schedule 3 prescribes inclusion in the Register of the following information:

The licensing register kept by a licensing authority under section 8 must contain a record of the following matters–

(a) any application made to the licensing authority under section 18 (grant of premises licence licence or summary),
(b) any application made to it under section 25 (theft etc. of premises licence or summary),
(c) any notice given to it under section 28 (surrender of premises licence),
(d) any application made to it under section 29 (provisional notice in respect of premises),
(e) any notice given to it under section 33 (change of name, etc. of holder of premises licence),
(f) any application made to it under section 34 (variation of premises licence),
(g) any application made to it under section 37 (variation of licence to specify individual as premises supervisor),
(h) any notice given to it under section 41 (request from designated premises supervisor for removal from premises licence),
(i) any application made to it under section 42 (transfer of premises licence),
(j) any notice given to it under section 47 (interim authority notice),
(k) any application made to it under section 51 (review of premises licence),
(l) any application made to it under section 71 (application for club premises certificate),
(m) any application made to it under section 79 (theft, loss, etc. of certificate or summary),

(n)  any notice given to it under section 81 (surrender of club premises certificate),

(o)  any notice given to it under section 82 or 83 (notification of change of name etc.),

(p)  any application made to it under section 84 (application to vary club premises certificate),

(q)  any application made to it under section 87 (application for review of club premises certificate),

(r)  any notice given to it under section 103 (withdrawal of temporary event notice),

(s)  any counter notice given by it under section 105 (counter notice following police objection to temporary event notice),

(t)  any copy of a temporary event notice given to it under section 106 (notice given following the making of modifications to a temporary event notice with police consent),

(u)  any application made to it under section 110 (theft etc. of temporary event notice),

(v)  any notice given to it under section 116 (surrender of personal licence),

(w) any application made to it under section 117 (grant or renewal of personal licence),

(x)  any application made to it under section 126 (theft, loss or destruction of personal licence),

(y)  any notice given to it under section 127 (change of name, etc. of personal licence holder),

(z)  any notice given to it under section 165(4) (magistrates' court to notify any determination made after closure order),

(zi) any application under paragraph 2 of Schedule 8 (application for conversion of old licences into premises licence),

(zii) any application under paragraph 14 of that Schedule (application for conversion of club certificate into club premises certificate).

It seems that there is some measure of discretion available to the licensing authority as to what information is recorded on the register and that not all information in respect of the above matters need be recorded. Thus para 7.24 of the Guidance provides:

> Licensing authorities should be aware that there is no requirement to record all the personal information given on a temporary event notice, and should avoid recording certain details, such as national insurance numbers, which may give rise to identity fraud.

2.4.4   The Licensing Act 2003 (Licensing Authority's Register) (Other Information) Regulations 2005, SI 2005/43 made under s 8(1)(d) prescribe additional information for certain types of application. First, this information includes operating schedules and plans where applications are made for premises licences, provisional statements and CPCs, and revised operating schedules where applications for variation are made. Regulation 2(2) provides:

> In the case of an application under the following provisions of the Act–
>
> (a)  section 17 (application for premises licence), the accompanying operating schedule (provided that the name and address of the premises supervisor, if any, shall be removed from the schedule before it is recorded) and plan of the premises to which the application relates;
>
> (b)  section 29 (application for a provisional statement where premises being built, etc), the accompanying schedule of works and plans of the work being or about to be done at the premises;

    (c)  section 34 (application to vary premises licence), the accompanying revised operating schedule (provided that the name and address of the premises supervisor, if any, shall be removed from the schedule before it is recorded), if any;

    (d)  section 71 (application for club premises certificate), the accompanying club operating schedule and plan of the premises to which the application relates; and

    (e)  section 84 (application to vary club premises certificate), the accompanying revised club operating schedule, if any.

Secondly, under reg 2(3) the information includes, in the case of an application for review of a premises licence under s 51 or a CPC under s 87 or a premises licence review under s 167 following a closure order, the ground(s) of review. Thirdly, under reg 2(3A), added by reg 4 of the Licensing Act 2003 (Summary Review of Premises Licences) Regulations 2007, SI 2007/2502, in the case of an application for summary review of a premises licence under s 53A, the information includes the fact that the application has been made on the basis of the opinion of a senior police officer that the premises are associated with serious crime or serious disorder or both.

### 2.4.5  Inspection and copies

Facilities must be made available for inspection of the register by any person during office hours and without payment, and a copy of information contained in any entry must be supplied on request, for which a reasonable fee can be charged. Section 8(3)–(5) provides:

    (3)  Each licensing authority must provide facilities for making the information contained in the entries in its register available for inspection (in a legible form) by any person during office hours and without payment.

    (4)  If requested to do so by any person, a licensing authority must supply him with a copy of the information contained in any entry in its register in legible form.

    (5)  A licensing authority may charge such reasonable fee as it may determine in respect of any copy supplied under subsection (4).

### 2.4.6  Central registers

The Secretary of State may arrange for any duties imposed under s 8 to be discharged by means of one or more central registers kept by a person appointed pursuant to the arrangements, and licensing authorities may be required to participate in and contribute towards the cost of any such arrangements. Section 8(6) and (7) provides:

    (6)  The Secretary of State may arrange for the duties conferred on licensing authorities by this section to be discharged by means of one or more central registers kept by a person appointed pursuant to the arrangements.

    (7)  The Secretary of State may require licensing authorities to participate in and contribute towards the cost of any arrangements made under subsection (6).

It appears that the Government's intention is to set up a central licensing register to record, *inter alia*, details of personal licence holders, for the Guidance, para 4.17 provides: 'The Government, supported by licensing authorities, aims to develop a central licensing register which will, among other things, include details of all personal licence holders. Future developments relating to the creation of a central licensing register will be reported on the DCMS website.' So watch this space (but do not hold your breath . . .).

### 2.4.7   Notification of persons with an interest in premises of changes relating to the premises in the register

2.4.8    Since persons other than those holding an authorisation (for example, a premises licence) for licensable activities to take place at premises may be affected by licensing matters relating to the premises, provision is made in s 178 for persons having a 'property interest' in the premises to be notified of any changes in the licensing register concerning the premises. Persons having such an interest are freeholders, leaseholders, legal mortgagees, occupiers and those with a prescribed interest. Section 178(4) provides:

> For the purposes of this section a person has a property interest in premises if–
> (a) he has a legal interest in the premises as freeholder or leaseholder,
> (b) he is a legal mortgagee (within the meaning of the Law of Property Act 1925 (c.20)) in respect of the premises,
> (c) he is in occupation of the premises, or
> (d) he has a prescribed interest in the premises.[43]

Notification is not automatic and it is necessary for persons with such an interest to give notice of their interest to the licensing authority. It is entirely at the discretion of such persons whether they choose to register or not and there is no legal requirement to do so (Guidance, para 8.77). Notification must be in the form prescribed under reg 9 and Sched 1 to the LA 2003 (PL and CPC) Regs 2005 and be accompanied by a prescribed fee, which under reg 8 and Sched 6 to the Licensing Act 2003 (Fees) Regulations 2005, SI 2005/79, is £21. Notification lasts for a period of 12 months from the day it is received by the authority. Effectively, therefore, annual renewal is required – and a new notice can be given every year (Guidance, para 8.77) – if persons with the necessary interest are to continue receiving notification of any changes made in the register relating to the premises. Section 178(1) and (2) provides:

> (1) This section applies where–
>      (a) a person with a property interest in any premises situated in the area of a licensing authority[44] gives notice of his interest to that authority, and
>      (b) the notice is in the prescribed form and accompanied by the prescribed fee.
> (2) The notice has effect for a period of 12 months beginning with the day it is received by the licensing authority.

2.4.9    Where a change is made to the register for premises in respect of which a notice of interest has been given and has effect, the licensing authority must forthwith notify the person who gave the notice of the change and his right to obtain a copy of the information contained in any entry in the register. Section 178(3) provides:

> If a change relating to the premises to which the notice relates is made to the register at a time when the notice has effect, the licensing authority must forthwith notify the person who gave the notice–
> (a) of the application, notice or other matter to which the change relates, and
> (b) of his right under section 8 to request a copy of the information contained in any entry in the register.[45]

While the authority is required to give notice of the change 'forthwith', this requirement applies only once the change has been made to the register and making the change in the register may not be done immediately. The ordinary meaning of 'forthwith' is 'at once, without delay', but this does not mean necessarily that notice must be given immediately, for the courts have equated 'forthwith' with as soon as is reasonably practicable and 'what is practicable must depend on the circumstances of each case,' *per* Lord Dilhorne LC in *Sameen v Abeyewickrema* [1963] AC 597, 609 (see 6.6.2 below). This seems to be reinforced by the fact that reg 42 of the LA 2003 (PL and CPC) Regs 2005 provides that an authority 'shall as soon as reasonably practicable on receipt of a notification to it under section 178 acknowledge its receipt by returning a copy of the notification to the notifier duly endorsed'. In this instance, however, once a change is made to the register, it should be possible for more or less immediate notification to be given to a person who has given notice of his interest in the premises. This will certainly be the case if use is made of the optional facility for inclusion of an email address on the form for notification of an interest (in Sched 1 to the LA 2003 (PL and CPC) Regs 2005). Notification by email may be particularly important in some cases, such as where a premises licence has been surrendered by its holder under s 28 and another person (for example, the freeholder of the premises) wishes to apply for transfer to him of the premises licence. Although the premises licence lapses on surrender, s 50 provides for its reinstatement if application for transfer is made within seven days of surrender. Speedy communication, to the person who has given notification of an interest, that there has been a change to the register will be particularly important in such cases, otherwise the opportunity for reinstatement through a transfer application may be lost.[46] In the absence of email notification, how soon notification is received will depend on the method by which notification is given. This is governed by s 184, which is considered below.

## 2.5   NOTIFICATION PROCEDURES

### 2.5.1   Delivery of documents

In cases where statements of reasons or notices need to be given, the 2003 Act sets out rules for delivery of documents.[47] Whenever delivery is required under the Act, it must be in accordance with the rules set out in s 184. Section 184(1) provides:

> This section has effect in relation to any document required or authorised by or under this Act to be given to any person ("relevant document").

### 2.5.2   Delivery to the licensing authority

In cases where delivery to the licensing authority is required the document must be addressed to the authority and left at or posted to its principal office or any other office at which it accept such documents. Section 184(2) provides:

> Where that person is a licensing authority, the relevant document must be given by addressing it to the authority and leaving it at or sending it by post to–
> (a)  the principal office of the authority, or
> (b)  any other office of the authority specified by it as one at which it will accept documents of the same description as that document.

### 2.5.3   Delivery in other cases

2.5.4    In any other case, such as documents sent by the authority or the police to applicants, interested parties, etc, the document may be personally delivered or left at or sent through the post to a person at his proper address. Section 184(3) provides:

> In any other case the relevant document may be given to the person in question by delivering it to him, or by leaving it at his proper address, or by sending it by post to him at that address.

As a general rule, a person's proper address will be his last known address, but the position is different in two instances. One is where documents are given (by any of the means specified in s 184(3)) to a body corporate, partnership or unincorporated association. In the case of such organisations, provision is made for the documents to be given to individuals within the organisations (as an alternative to delivery to the organisation's principal office in the UK or, in the case of a body corporate, at its registered office). The particular individuals are, in the case of a body corporate, its secretary or clerk; in the case of a partnership, a partner or person having control or management of the partnership business; and, in the case of an unincorporated association, an officer of the association. Section 184(4) and (5) provides:

> (4)   A relevant document may–
>
>   (a)   in the case of a body corporate (other than a licensing authority), be given to the secretary or clerk of that body;
>
>   (b)   in the case of a partnership, be given to a partner or a person having the control or management of the partnership business;
>
>   (c)   in the case of an unincorporated association (other than a partnership), be given to an officer of the association.
>
> (5)   For the purposes of this section and section 7 of the Interpretation Act 1978 (c.30) (service of documents by post) in its application to this section, the proper address of any person to whom a relevant document is to be given is his last known address, except that–
>
>   (a)   in the case of a body corporate or its secretary or clerk, it is the address of the registered office of that body or its principal office in the United Kingdom;
>
>   (b)   in the case of a partnership, a partner or a person having control or management of the partnership business, it is that of the principal office of the partnership in the United Kingdom; and
>
>   (c)   in the case of an unincorporated association (other than a partnership) or any officer of the association, it is that of its principal office in the United Kingdom.

2.5.5    The other instance where a person's proper address will not be his last known address is where the person is given the document in his capacity as the holder of a licence or certificate or as a designated premises supervisor. Here the address will be that given for the person in the record of licence contained in the licensing register (see 2.4 above). Section 184(6) and (7) provides:

> (6)   But if a relevant document is given to a person in his capacity as the holder of a premises licence, club premises certificate or personal licence, or as the designated premises supervisor under a premises licence, his relevant registered address is also to be treated, for the purposes of this section and section 7 of the Interpretation Act 1978, as his proper address.

(7) In subsection (6) "relevant registered address", in relation to such a person, means the address given for that person in the record for the licence or certificate (as the case may be) which is contained in the register kept under section 8 by the licensing authority which granted the licence or certificate.

Since s 184(6) provides that such a person's relevant registered address 'is *also* to be treated . . . as his proper address' (emphasis supplied), this suggests that the normal meaning of 'proper address', that is the person's last known address under s 184(5), can nevertheless still apply and that delivery to either address might suffice. Thus the 'proper address' under s 148(3) might be the premises address, if this is the address recorded in the register for the licence or certificate holder or the DPS for the premises, or it might be the last-known (private) address of the individual concerned.

## NOTES

1   Sections 17(3)(a)(b) and 71(4)(a)(b). The Act also requires, in the case of premises licence applications where the licensable activities include the sale or supply of alcohol, a form of consent of the individual whom the applicant wishes to have specified in the premises licence as the premises supervisor (s 17(3)(c)); and, for CPC applications, a copy of the club rules (s 71(3)(c)).
2   Under reg 2, ' "legible in all material respects" means that the information contained in the application, notice or representations is available to the recipient to no lesser extent than it would be if given by means of a document in written form'.
3   For the meaning of 'forthwith', see 6.6.2 below.
4   An exception is provided by reg 22(a) in relation to review of a premises licence following a closure order, where the period is seven working days – see 11.14.21 below.
5   DCMS, *Consultation on Draft Regulations and Order to be Made under the Licensing Act 2003,* 2004, para 5.28.
6   Regulation 2 provides: ' "standard scale" means that 1 millimetre represents 100 milli-metres' and ' "alternative scale plan" means a plan in a scale other than the standard scale'.
7   Regulation 2 provides: ' "fire and other safety equipment" includes fire extinguishers, fire doors, fire alarms, marine safety equipment, marine evacuation equipment and other similar equipment.'
8   In the case of applications for premises licences involving internet or mail-order sales of alcohol, notices should be displayed at the place where the alcohol is appropriated to the contract, ie the premises where the alcohol is specifically and physically selected for the particular purchaser (Guidance, para 8.48, and see 6.1.3 below).
9   Section 8 makes provision for the keeping of a register and is considered below – see 2.4 below.
10  The requirements for establishing a licensing committee and for the exercise and delega-tion of licensing functions through the licensing committee do not apply in cases where the licensing authority is the Sub-Treasurer of the Inner Temple or the Under-Treasurer of the Middle Temple – see s 6(2) and s 7(10).
11  See ss 15–17 and Local Government (Committees and Political Groups) Regulations 1990, SI 1990/1553. There does not appear to be any provision in the 2003 Act for co-opting of members, or outside representatives, so it must be assumed that there can be no additional persons co-opted onto the committee.
12  Where a member has a 'personal interest' in any business of the authority (which includes a decision in relation to that business that might reasonably be regarded as affecting him to a greater extent than the majority of other council taxpayers) and attends a meeting of the authority at which the business is considered, he must disclose to that meeting the existence and nature of that interest at the commencement of that consideration, or when

the interest becomes apparent: Local Authorities (Model Code of Conduct) (England) Order 2007, SI 2007/1159, Sch, Pt 2, arts 8–9. Although he can still take part in the meeting and vote, if the 'personal interest' is also a 'prejudicial interest' then he cannot participate and must withdraw from the meeting at the point when it becomes apparent that the business is being considered (art 12(1)(a)(ii)). This is except where he attends only for the purpose of making representations, answering questions or giving evidence relating to the business, provided that the public are also allowed to attend the meeting for the same purpose, in which case he must withdraw immediately after making representations, answering questions or giving evidence (art 12(1)(a)(i)). Further, under art 12(1), he need not withdraw if he has obtained a dispensation from the authority's standards committee. Under art 10(1), a member has a prejudicial interest in business where the interest is one which a member of the public with knowledge of the relevant facts would reasonably regard as so significant that it is likely to prejudice the member's judgment of the public interest. For the Model Code of Conduct in Wales, see the Conduct of Members (Model Code of Conduct) (Wales) Order 2001, SI 2001/2289. An instance of where a number of members may be required to withdraw and be unable to participate might be where an application is made by a football club where the members are season ticket holders (cf *R v Local Commissioner for Administration in North and North East England ex p Liverpool City Council* [2001] 1 All ER 462, a case concerning a planning application by Liverpool FC, where the Court of Appeal held that Liverpool FC season ticket holders and other regular attenders should have declared their interest).

13  That the Act contains a specified number of members for the licensing committee and for subcommittees should not be seen as indicative of the quorum. If it was intended that the number specified in the Act was to be the quorum, s 9(2)(a) would not have made provision for regulations to extend to the quorum for meetings.

14  The local authority can make general provision as to the quorum in its standing orders and, subject to the standing orders, this is a matter for the committee or subcommittee. Section 106 of the Local Government Act 1972 provides:

> Standing orders may be made as respects any committee of a local authority by that authority or as respects a joint committee of two or more local authorities, whether appointed or established under this Part of this Act or any other enactment, by those authorities with respect to the quorum, proceedings and place of meeting of the committee or joint committee (including any sub-committee) but, subject to any such standing orders, the quorum, proceedings and place of meeting shall be such as the committee, joint committee or sub-committee may determine.

A quorum of one quarter of members is commonly adopted.

15  See 2.2.13 below.

16  Planning requirements might include the hours during which premises may operate and the hours specified in any planning permission might, but need not necessarily, be the same as hours specified in any premises licence or CPC. This is because in each case the hours are determined by reference to different considerations – planning in the one instance and promotion of the licensing objectives in the other. If, for instance, the hours are longer under the premises licence or CPC than under the planning permission, it will be perfectly permissible under the 2003 Act to keep the premises open to the hour specified in the premises licence or CPC but, in doing so, there will be a breach of planning control for which enforcement action and criminal proceedings may be taken under planning legislation. If, however, hours of operation have been specified in the planning permission prior to an application under the 2003 Act, the view may be taken that promotion of the licensing objective of prevention of crime and disorder might require that longer hours are not specified under the premises licence or CPC, since if they are this might encourage a (criminal) breach of planning control. The interrelationship between planning and licensing regarding hours of operation has been considered by the High Court in *R (on the application of Blackwood) v Birmingham Magistrates and Birmingham*

*City Council, Mitchells and Butler Leisure Retail Ltd (Interested Party)* (2006) 170 JP 613 – see 4.2.16 below.

17  The relevant regulations are the Licensing Act 2003 (Hearings) Regulations 2005 – see 2.3.1 below.

18  This is, however, subject to the provision in s 183(1), under which regulations may prescribe the procedure to be followed in relation to a hearing held by a licensing authority – see 2.3.1 below.

19  Regulations made under s 9(2) may differ in content from any provision specified in other legislation (eg the Local Government Act 1972) as having general application to local authorities in respect of the matters mentioned in s 9(2). Where regulations under s 9(2) have application to licensing committees discharging licensing functions under the 2003 Act, there seems little doubt that the regulations will fall within the scope of the enabling legislation (ie the 2003 Act). Less clear is whether, when licensing committees are discharging other functions, eg determining licence applications under other legislation (as they can do – see 2.2.13 above), the regulations might be seen as outside the powers of the enabling legislation and in conflict with rights granted by other legislation.

20  'The sub-committee must have three members to be quorate.' HC Standing Committee D, col 179, 8 April 2003 (Dr Kim Howells).

21  It seems sensible for there to be more than one subcommittee in order to enable sittings of subcommittees to be held simultaneously. If only one subcommittee were established, although any three members of the licensing committee might sit on it, only three members could sit at any one time. This can be avoided if there are several subcommittees with their membership of three drawn from any of the 10 to 15 members of the licensing committee.

22  Section 10(5) provides: 'The power exercisable under subsection (2) by a sub-committee established by a licensing committee is also subject to any direction given by that committee to the sub-committee.'

23  Exceptions are 10 working days for reviews of premises licences following closure orders (s 167(5)(a)); seven working days where a counter-notice is given following a police objection to a TEN (s 105(2)); and five working days where an interim authority notice (IAN) is cancelled following police objections (s 48(3)(a)).

24  Regulation 6(4) was added by the Licensing Act 2003 (Hearings) (Amendment) Regulations 2005, SI 2005/78 after this provision, which appeared in the draft of the Regulations, was omitted from the final version of SI 2005/44. Exceptions, under reg 6(3), are five working days for review of a premises licence following a closure order (s 167(5)(a)) or a review notice (s 53c) and, under reg 6(2), two working days where an IAN is cancelled following police objections (s 48(3)(a)) and where a counter-notice is given following a police objection to a TEN (s 105(2)).

25  See regs 15 and 16. The rights are to attend and be assisted or represented by any person, whether or not that person is legally qualified (reg 15), and to produce supporting information in response to any point on which the authority has given notice that it requires clarification, to question any party if given permission by the authority, and to address the authority (reg 16).

26  The relevant hearings, the parties to whom the additional documentation must be given and the documents to be given are listed in cols 1–3, respectively, in Sched 3 to the Regulations.

27  Where all parties give notice that they consider a hearing is unnecessary, the licensing authority, if it agrees a hearing is unnecessary, must forthwith give notice to the parties that the hearing has been dispensed with: reg 9. For the meaning of 'forthwith', see 6.6.2 below.

28  Exceptions, under reg 8(4), are two working days for reviews of premises licences following closure orders (s 167(5)(a)) or review notices (s 53c); and, under reg 8(3), one working day where an IAN is cancelled following police objections (s 48(3)(a)) and where a counter-notice is given following a police objection to a TEN (s 105(2)).

29  These requirements are that the text is capable of being accessed by the recipient, is legible in all material respects, and is capable of being reproduced in written form and used for subsequent reference (reg 34(2)(a)); the person to whom the notice is to be given has agreed in advance that such a notice may be given to them by those electronic means (reg 34(2)(b)); and forthwith on sending the text of the notice by electronic means, the notice is given to the recipient in writing (reg 34(2)(c)). For the meaning of 'forthwith', see 6.6.2 below. Where the text of the notice is transmitted by electronic means, the giving of the notice is effected at the time the recipient receives the transmission of the text in accordance with reg 34(2)(a): reg 34(3).

30  An authority may not, however, exercise these powers in such a way that the effect will be that it would fail to reach a determination on a review of a premises licence following a closure order under s 167 within the period specified in s 167(3) (reg 13(b)) or fail to reach a determination on a summary review on application of a senior police officer within the period specified in s 53A(2)(b) (reg 13(c)).

31  In this respect the Regulations have been made under the power conferred by s 9(2) rather than s 183(1) – see 2.2.16 above.

32  The power to exclude extends to a party or any person assisting or representing him, for reg 14(3) provides: 'For the purposes of paragraph (2), a party and any person assisting or representing a party may be treated as a member of the public.'

33  Where an authority has not been informed that the party does not intend to attend, it may adjourn the hearing to a specified date if it considers it necessary in the public interest (reg 20(2)(a)), although it must forthwith notify the parties to the hearing of the date, time and place to which the hearing has been adjourned (reg 20(4)). For the meaning of 'forthwith', see 6.6.2 below. It might in general be expected that parties will attend the hearing, but reg 20 provides that a failure by a party to attend need not prevent the hearing from proceeding. However, where a party does not attend and a hearing is held, the authority must still consider that party's case.

34  Regulation 17 also provides that 'members of the authority may ask any question of any party or other person appearing at the hearing', although the scope of this provision is unclear. The wording is wide enough to include any member of the authority, even though not a member of the licensing committee, although it might be doubted whether the entitlement should extend this far. Even if confined to members of the licensing committee, it is nevertheless uncertain whether it would extend only to the members sitting on the subcommittee at the hearing or whether it might also include other members of the licensing committee who were not sitting on the subcommittee.

35  In the case of hearings to consider a notice given by a chief officer of police, it will be information that is not relevant to the crime prevention objective. Information that might be disregarded will include not only that put forward by a party, but also information by another person who, having been given permission by the authority to appear, has appeared at the party's request.

36  The request for permission is made in accordance with reg 8(2), which requires a brief description of the point(s) on which that person may be able to assist the authority.

37  It is doubtful that there is any right as a matter of law to call witnesses in hearings before local authorities, since authorities are considered to have an inherent discretion as to how they regulate their proceedings. The following remarks of Lord Denning MR in the Court of Appeal, in *TA Miller Ltd v Minister of Housing and Local Government* [1968] 1 WLR 992, 995, made in respect of a town planning inquiry conducted by an inspector, are regarded as having general application to tribunals: 'a tribunal of this kind is master of its own procedure, provided that the rules of natural justice are applied.'

38  This does, however, sit rather uneasily with reg 16(c), which provides: 'At the hearing a party shall be entitled . . . to address the authority.'

39  'Determination' is the outcome of the authority's consideration of relevant representations or police notices of objection, as appropriate – see Sched 4 to the Regulations.

40  These cases, excluding ones in the transitional period which no longer have application, are where interim steps are taken pending a premises licence review under s 53B (reg 26(1)(aa); a premises licence review following a review notice under s 53C (reg 26(1)(ab)); a counter-notice given following a police objection to a TEN under s 105(2)(a) (reg 26(1)(c)); and a review of a premises licence following a closure order under s 167(5)(a) (reg 26(1)(d)).

41  Similarly, in cases where the Act provides for the police to be notified of the determination of an authority, but the police are not a party to the hearing (eg under s 31(4) for determination of applications for provisional statements), the police must be notified forthwith of the determination: reg 28(2). For the meaning of 'forthwith', see 6.6.2 below.

42  The irregularity does not of itself render the proceedings void: reg 31.

43  At the time of writing, no interests have been prescribed by the Secretary of State under this provision.

44  Section 178(5) provides: 'In this section–

(a)  a reference to premises situated in the area of a licensing authority includes a reference to premises partly so situated . . .'

45  Section 178(5) provides: 'In this section–

(b)  "register" means the register kept under section 8 by the licensing authority mentioned in subsection (1)(a).'

46  The position is similar for interim authority notices (see 6.11 below) and for these notices the Guidance, para 8.78 states 'it is important that such communications are dealt with promptly'.

47  Although the section refers to 'documents' and not 'notices', it is apparent from the heading to the section ('Giving of notices etc.') that it is intended to cover the latter.

# CHAPTER 3

# LICENSING AND HUMAN RIGHTS

## 3.1 INTRODUCTION

When the Human Rights Act 1998 (the 1998 Act) came into force on 2 October 2000, it 'incorporated' into English law much of the European Convention on Human Rights and Fundamental Freedoms (the Convention), which had been adopted in 1950, following widespread concern in Europe about atrocities associated with the Second World War. The Act was concerned with giving 'further effect' (as the long title to the Act indicates) to rights and freedoms guaranteed by the Convention or what the Act describes as 'Convention rights'.[1]

## 3.2 THE HUMAN RIGHTS ACT 1998 AND GIVING 'FURTHER EFFECT' TO CONVENTION RIGHTS

3.2.1 The Act seeks to give 'further effect' in two ways. First, existing and future legislation has to be interpreted in conformity with Convention rights, although where a compatible interpretation is not possible, legislation continues to have effect despite incompatibility. Section 3(1) and (2) provides:

(1) So far as it is possible to do so, primary legislation and subordinate legislation must be read and given effect in a way which is compatible with the Convention rights.

(2) This section–
   (a) applies to primary and subordinate legislation whenever enacted;
   (b) does not affect the validity, continuing operation or enforcement of any incompatible primary legislation; and
   (c) does not affect the validity, continuing operation or enforcement of any incompatible subordinate legislation if (disregarding any possibility of revocation) primary legislation prevents removal of the incompatibility.

In cases of incompatibility, however, certain courts have a discretion to make a 'declaration on incompatibility' under s 4.[2] Where such a declaration is made in a case, it has no legal effect since s 4(6) provides that it does not affect the validity, continuing operation or enforcement of the legislation and it is not binding on the parties. Rather, it is a mechanism for putting pressure on the Government to take action to remove the incompatibility.[3]

Secondly, under s 6(1), it is 'unlawful for any public authority to act in a way which is incompatible with a Convention right'. A 'public authority' will include: (a) a court or tribunal; and (b) any person certain of whose functions are functions of a public nature (s 6(3)). This broadly defined latter category will clearly include local authorities who act as licensing authorities under the 2003 Act.[4] However, it will not be unlawful, under s 6(2), if the public authority is prevented from acting compatibly either by primary legislation or by provisions made under primary legislation that cannot be read or given effect in a way that is compatible with the Convention. When a public authority has acted (or proposes to act) unlawfully under s 6, s 7 provides a remedy for persons affected by the actions of the authority, which is in addition to any other remedies that such persons may have, for example judicial review. A person affected may, by s 7(1), bring proceedings against the authority (these will be civil proceedings for breach of the statutory duty under s 6) or rely on the Convention right or rights concerned in any legal proceedings, provided he is (or would be) a 'victim' of the unlawful act.[5] Where a court finds the act (or proposed act) of a public authority is (or would be) unlawful, it may, under s 8, grant to the victim such relief or remedy or make such order as it considers just and appropriate.

3.2.2    When seeking to give further effect to Convention rights in accordance with s 3 (interpreting legislation compatibly) and s 6 (public authority acting incompatibly and unlawfully), s 2(1) requires that rulings of various Strasbourg institutions be considered. It provides that a court or tribunal, when determining a question that has arisen under the 1998 Act in connection with a Convention right, must take into account such rulings, whenever made or given, so far as they are relevant to the proceedings in which that question has arisen. The requirement in s 2 is only to take rulings into account. Rulings are not binding and courts are free to decide the extent to which they are relevant on particular issues and the extent to which they shall be taken into account.[6] The rulings that must be taken into account include any judgment, decision, declaration or advisory opinion of the European Court of Human Rights (ECtHR) (s 2(1)(a)), together with opinions and decisions from other bodies that, prior to reorganisation of the Convention's institutional framework in 1998,[7] exercised judicial or quasi-judicial functions. The latter include opinions of the (now defunct) European Commission on Human Rights given in a report (to the Committee of Ministers) adopted under Art 31, that is, whether there has been a violation of Convention rights (s 2(1)(b)); decisions of the Commission in connection with Arts 26 or 27(2), that is, the admissibility of petitions claiming a violation of Convention rights (s 2(1)(c)); and decisions of the Committee of Ministers taken under Art 46, that is, whether there has been compliance with a judgment of the ECtHR (s 2(1)(d)).

## 3.3    CONVENTION RIGHTS

3.3.1    The Convention rights to which the 1998 Act seeks to give further effect are identified in s 1(1), which provides:

> In this Act, "the Convention rights" means the rights and fundamental freedoms set out in–
> (a)   Articles 2 to 12 and 14 of the Convention,
> (b)   Articles 1 to 3 of the First Protocol, and
> (c)   Articles 1 and 2 of the Sixth Protocol,
> as read with Articles 16 to 18.[8]

The Articles are set out in Sched 1 to the Act (s 1(3)) and are as follows:

(a)   Articles 2–12 and 14 of the Convention:
- the right to life (Art 2);
- prohibition of torture (Art 3);
- prohibition of slavery and forced labour (Art 4);
- right to liberty and security (Art 5);

- right to a fair trial (Art 6);
- no punishment without law (Art 7);
- right to respect for private and family life (Art 8);
- freedom of thought, conscience and religion (Art 9);
- freedom of expression (Art 10);
- freedom of assembly and association (Art 11);
- right to marry (Art 12);
- prohibition of discrimination (Art 14).

(b) Articles 1–3 of Protocol 1:[9]
  - the protection of property;
  - right to education;
  - right to free elections.

(c) Articles 1 and 2 of Protocol 6:
  - the abolition of the death penalty;
  - death penalty in time of war.

3.3.2    Articles 1 and 13, although ratified by the UK Government and binding upon it, are excluded from 'the Convention rights' set out in the Act. Article 1, which requires parties to the Convention to 'secure to everyone within their jurisdiction' the rights under the Convention, was excluded because the 1998 Act itself was regarded as meeting this requirement. Article 13, which provides that everyone shall have 'an effective remedy before a national authority' for violation of their Convention rights, was excluded because the remedial provisions contained in the Act, particularly s 8 (under which a court can grant 'such relief or remedy, or make such order, within its powers as it considers just and appropriate'), were regarded as meeting this requirement. Other Convention rights also excluded, obviously, are those not ratified by the UK Government and not binding on it, for example rights under Protocol 4, such as the right (under Art 1) not to be imprisoned for debt. These rights do not fall within the scope of the 1998 Act.

## 3.4    ACCERTAINING COMPATIBILITY WITH CONVENTION RIGHTS

### 3.4.1   Convention right(s) having application and their interpretation

3.4.2    When seeking to ascertain whether legislation is compatible with Convention rights, or whether public authorities are acting incompatibly with Convention rights, it will be necessary first to look at whether there is any Article containing a Convention right that has application. There may be more than one right and rights perhaps most likely to have particular application to licensing are the right to a fair trial (Art 6), protection of property (Protocol 1 of Art 1), freedom of expression (Art 10) and protection of private and family life (Art 8). There may be others, however, that have application, for example prohibition of discrimination (Art 14).[10]

When looking at Convention Articles to see whether they have application (and, in turn, whether there is compatibility), some appreciation is needed of the meaning attributed to terms used in the Convention and in domestic legislation, and the interpretation adopted by the ECtHR in respect of Convention provisions. As regards terms used, these are generally given their ordinary meaning (under Art 31 of the Vienna Convention on the Law of Treaties 1969), but the meaning given will be an autonomous one, that is, it will be independent of any particular meaning that the terms might have in domestic law.[11] Thus, for example, when Article 6 refers to 'the determination of his civil rights and obligations' and a hearing before an independent and impartial tribunal, the reference to 'rights' will include benefits granted as a matter of discretion, rather than as a matter of right.[12] It is not decisive whether a certain benefit, or possible claim that a person may make, is characterised as a 'right' under the domestic legal system, for the term will be given an autonomous meaning. Licences granted at the discretion of licensing authorities, where an applicant has no right to the licence, might therefore be characterised as 'rights' and fall within the scope of Art 6.[13]

3.4.3   As regards interpretation, the general approach adopted by the ECtHR (usually referred to as a teleological approach) has been to interpret the Convention's provisions in the light of its object and purpose, which is to protect human rights. In *Wemhoff v Federal Republic of Germany* (1968) 1 EHRR 55, 75, the ECtHR stated that it was necessary 'to seek the interpretation that is most appropriate in order to realise the aim and achieve the object of the treaty, and not that which would restrict to the greatest possible degree the obligations undertaken by the Parties'.[14] Thus, for example, the right to a fair trial under Art 6, although expressed in terms of every-one being 'entitled to a fair and public hearing within a reasonable time by an independent and impartial tribunal established by law', is not confined to the hearing of a case and conduct of court proceedings. It extends to cases where obstacles are placed in the way of commencing court proceedings[15] and also includes the giving of reasons for judicial decisions.[16]

A further consequence of focusing on the object and purpose of the Convention is that, when identifying the scope of particular provisions, they should not be con-sidered in isolation and should be interpreted having regard to the Convention as a whole.[17] The ECtHR has also demonstrated a commitment to what may be described as an 'evolutionary approach' to interpretation, that is, that the Convention must be interpreted in the light of current social mores. Thus in *Tyrer v UK* (1978) 2 EHRR 1, para 31, the court stated that 'the Convention is a living instrument which . . . must be interpreted in the light of present-day conditions' and, when interpreting the Convention, judges should be influenced by 'the developments and commonly accepted standards in the penal policy of the member States and of the Council of Europe in this field'.[18] Consequently, older decisions may afford less guidance than more recent ones when a contemporary construction of Convention rights is sought and may be less likely to be followed.[19]

### 3.4.4   Compatibility with Convention right(s): balancing competing interests and the principle of proportionality

3.4.5   Once a particular Convention right is considered to have application, it will then be necessary to determine whether there is compatibility of either legislation itself, or its use and application in particular circumstances, with that Convention right or whether there is a violation of it. The ordinary meaning of compatibility is 'consistent with' and there would seem to be consistency with the Convention if there is no conflict in principle and there is compliance with the underlying aims. Deciding whether legislation or the actions of public authorities when using legislative powers comply with the underlying aims of the Convention may well require a teleological approach to be adopted when interpreting legislative provisions. Any differences in language between the Convention and legislative provisions may need to be disregarded and the principle that words should be regarded as having an autonomous meaning applied. Techniques similar to those employed by the ECtHR when interpreting the Convention may therefore need to be employed, in order to ascertain whether compatibility might be achieved.

3.4.6    In determining whether there is compatibility or violation of a Convention right, there will be a 'margin of appreciation', that is, a considerable measure of discretion available as to how compliance with a Convention provision is achieved. No one uniform method need be employed, for, as Lord Hope stated in *R v Director of Public Prosecutions ex p Kebilene* [2000] 2 AC 326, 380–81 (*Kebilene*), 'the Convention should be seen as an expression of fundamental principles rather than as a mere set of rules'. There may therefore be more than one means of complying with the fundamental principles and licensing authorities may well be able to do so provided they exercise their statutory powers rationally and in accordance with statutory purpose. As Lord Hoffman stated in *Belfast City Council v Miss Behavin' Ltd* [2007] UKHL 19, para 16 (*Miss Behavin'*), a sex establishment licensing case:

> This is an area of social control in which the Strasbourg court has always accorded a wide margin of appreciation to member States, which in terms of the domestic constitution translates into the broad power of judgment entrusted to local authorities by the legislature. If the local authority exercises that power rationally and in accordance with the purposes of the statute, it would require very unusual facts for it to amount to a disproportionate restriction on Convention rights.[20]

The questions which the courts will have to decide in the application of the principles contained in the Convention, as Lord Hope went on to state in *Kebilene*, 'will involve questions of balance between competing interests and issues of proportionality'. Balancing competing interests is inherent in many of the Convention rights, which are qualified, rather than absolute ones. Whilst some rights are absolute (for example, the prohibition against torture), most are qualified to the extent that restrictions on the rights are permissible (for example, where these are necessary in a democratic society in the interests of national security, public safety, for the prevention of crime and disorder, for the protection of health or morals or for the protection of the rights and freedoms of others). In striking a balance between competing interests, the principle of proportionality is particularly important.

Under this principle, measures taken (whether to protect rights or impose legitimate restrictions) or penalties imposed need to bear a reasonable and proportionate relationship to their intended objectives. Thus, if an objective can be achieved by means which interfere either not at all or to a lesser extent with a person's Convention rights, those means should be used. Similarly, if in achieving the objective there is only a marginal social gain, but an excessive and disproportionate effect on an individual's rights, the measures should not be taken. In other words, the disadvantages caused must not be disproportionate to the aims pursued. Put simply, and in popular parlance, a sledgehammer should not be used to crack a nut. An example is provided by the offence of unauthorised licensable activities in s 136 of the 2003 Act. As originally drafted (as cl 134), all unlicensed regulated entertainment was criminalised and this included the actions of performers who participated in it. The Joint Committee on Human Rights (JCHR) in its Fourth Report on the Licensing Bill questioned whether this could be justified in terms of the rights to freedom of expression under Art 10 and concluded that clause 134 would give rise to 'a significant risk of disproportionality, and hence incompatibility under Article 10'.[21] An amendment was consequently introduced, the effect of which was that a person did not commit an offence if his only involvement in the provision of the entertainment was as a performer.[22] This still enables the objective of ensuring that a venue is properly licensed to be achieved, firmly placing responsibility on the occupier of the premises where the entertainment is to take place and on the organiser of the entertainment. It does so without interference with performers' rights and the JCHR was accordingly able to reach the following conclusion in its Seventh Report:

> By avoiding the criminalisation of performers, the amendment to clause 134 seems to us to re-balance the rights and interests affected so as to prevent any interference with the performers' right to freedom of expression being disproportionate.[23]

Whilst the principle of proportionality requires that means which interfere to a lesser extent with a person's Convention rights should be used where possible, this does not necessarily mean that the least intrusive means should be adopted and an interference can still be proportionate even if such means are not pursued. In *Smith, Reilly and Reilly v Secretary of State for Trade & Industry and London Development Agency* [2007] EWHC 1013 (Admin), the High Court held that a compulsory purchase order made by the London Development Agency for traveller caravan sites required as part of the site for the 2012 Olympic and Paralympic Games, which was confirmed by the Secretary of State even though no alternative relocation sites had been identified at the time of confirmation, was a proportionate response. The Secretary of State's decision was held not to violate the applicants' Art 8 rights (see 3.8 below) and it was not necessary to demonstrate that the measure he proposed to take was the least intrusive available: 'Realistically, the only way of ensuring that a substantial proportion of the land for the 2012 Games was under the control of the interested party by the necessary date was to make the order, and no other measure achieved that objective'.

3.4.7    Whether the actions of licensing authorities, when exercising their licensing functions under the 2003 Act and seeking to balance competing interests, are justified and proportionate will need to be determined by reference to the time at which the events to which the legislative provisions are being applied take place. Whilst the appropriate balance may be the same as at the time the legislation was passed, it need not necessarily be, since circumstances and the justification (or absence of it) for an authority's actions may change over time. As Lord Hobhouse observed in the House of Lords' decision in *Wilson v First County Trust (No 2)* [2004] 1 AC 816 (at 866):

> Those who are seeking to justify the use of the statutory provision have to do so as at the time of that use. If they cannot justify it at that time, their use of it is a breach of the victim's 'Convention rights'. That is how the European Court would decide the question and it is also how the municipal court is required to look at it. In most cases the difference will probably be academic . . . . But as circumstances change so the justification or the absence of it may change. Merely to examine the situation at the time the Act in question was passed and treat that as decisive is wrong in principle . . . . [J]ust as the current state of the legislation at that time is what has to be the subject matter of the decision so also the circumstances and social needs existing at that time are what is relevant, not those existing at some earlier or different time.

With regard to compatibility of an authority's actions, in some instances this may be governed by compatibility of the legislation itself, so that the authority's actions will not be incompatible unless it can be shown that the legislation itself is in some way incompatible, but it seems this does not have application in licensing cases. In *Miss Behavin'*, a sex establishment licensing case, the House of Lords distinguished its earlier decision in *Kay v Lambeth London Borough Council* [2006] 2 AC 465 where the House, by a 4–3 majority, had decided that, if domestic law (concerning the right of a public authority landlord to enforce a claim for possession of land) struck the proper balance for the competing interests and was compatible with Convention rights, no challenge based on a person's individual circumstances was permissible. In other words, if the legislation was compatible, a person could not seek to demonstrate that the authority had acted incompatibly in his particular case. In *Miss Behavin'* the House held that the legislation itself did not seek to strike a proper balance, but left it to the local authority to strike the balance in each particular case and therefore it was open to a person to demonstrate that, in the individual circumstances of his case, the authority had acted incompatibly. Lord Neuberger stated (at para 87):

> In my judgment, the present case is very different [from *Kay*]. It is not concerned with the property rights of a local authority, but with the exercise of a licensing jurisdiction which has been delegated by the legislature, through the medium of the 1985 [Local Government (Miscellaneous Provisions)] Order, to a local authority which decides to adopt the provisions of Sch 2. In other words, when exercising its functions under Sch 2, a council is carrying out what may be characterised as a public administrative function; in that capacity, a council should carry out its functions in a manner, and to achieve a result, which is compatible with the Convention. That seems to me to follow from the provisions of s 6 of the Human Rights Act 1998, which renders it "unlawful for a public authority to act in a way which is incompatible with a Convention right".

These remarks seem to have general application to local authority licensing cases and should apply to decisions made under the 2003 Act.

When local authorities are seeking to strike the balance in the individual case, a careful weighing of the competing considerations, followed by a finding that either there is no interference with a Convention right or any interference is justified, will make it inherently less likely that a court will find that there has been a contravention of Convention rights if the authority's decision is challenged. The fact that there has been a careful examination of Convention rights will not, however, in itself preclude a successful challenge, since whether there has been a contravention of Convention rights is determined by the outcome of the authority's actions, not its decision-making process. Although procedural rights in respect of decision-making are protected by the Convention, notably the right to a fair trial in Article 6 (see 3.5 below), where a decision is challenged, the court's real concern is not whether the decision has been reached in the correct manner. Whilst this may well be the main focus in judicial review proceedings (see 12.12.1 below), it is not in cases where it is alleged that a person's Convention rights have been infringed. Here the court is more concerned with whether or not there has been an infringement. As Lord Bingham stated in *R (on the application of Begum) v Head Teacher and Governors of Denbigh High School* [2007] 1 AC 100 (at paras 29–31):

29 . . . the focus at Strasbourg is not and has never been on whether a challenged decision or action is the product of a defective decision-making process, but on whether, in the case under consideration, the applicant's convention rights have been violated . . .

30 . . . the court's approach to an issue of proportionality under the convention must go beyond that traditionally adopted to judicial review in a domestic setting . . . There is no shift to a merits review, but the intensity of review is greater than was previously appropriate . . . The domestic court must now make a value judgment, an evaluation, by reference to the circumstances prevailing at the relevant time . . . Proportionality must be judged objectively, by the court . . .

31 . . . If, in such a case, it appears that such a body has conscientiously paid attention to all human rights considerations, no doubt a challenger's task will be the harder. But what matters in any case is the practical outcome, not the quality of the decision-making process that led to it.

## 3.5 ARTICLE 6: RIGHT TO A FAIR TRIAL

### 3.5.1 Article 6(1)

3.5.2    Article 6(1) is concerned with fairness in respect of civil rights and criminal charges and provides:

> In the determination of his civil rights and obligations or of any criminal charge against him, everyone is entitled to a fair and public hearing within a reasonable time by an independent and impartial tribunal established by law. Judgment shall be pronounced publicly . . .[24]

### 3.5.3 Determination of civil rights and obligations

3.5.4    The first issue that will arise in a case concerning Art 6(1) will be whether there is a 'determination' of a civil right (or criminal charge). This will be so only where there is a dispute over a civil right and where the proceedings are determinative of a civil right.[25] This aspect of Art 6(1) was explained by the ECtHR, in *James v UK* (1986) 8 EHRR 123, para 81, as follows:

> Article 6(1) extends only to "contestations" (disputes) over (civil) "rights and obligations" which can be said, at least on arguable grounds, to be recognised under domestic law: it does not in itself guarantee any particular content for (civil) "rights and obligations" in the substantive law of the Contracting States.

It is necessary therefore to identify at least an arguable claim under English law to put before a national tribunal on a matter arising under national law, otherwise there can be no dispute. Contested licensing cases might give rise to such a claim, based on a dispute between the licence applicant or licence holder and other persons such as objectors.

The applicable principles for determining whether there is a 'dispute' were laid down by the ECtHR in *Benthem v Netherlands* (1985) 8 EHRR 1, para 32, where it was stated:

> (a) Conformity with the spirit of the Convention requires that the word "contestation" (dispute) should not be construed too technically and should be given a substantive

rather than a technical meaning . . . (b) The "contestation" (dispute) may relate not only to the existence of a right but also to its scope or the manner in which it may be exercised. It may concern both questions of facts and questions of law. (c) It must be genuine and of serious nature. (d) The expression . . . disputes over civil rights and obligations covers all proceedings the result of which is decisive for such rights and obligations . . . civil rights must be the object, or one of the objects, of the . . . dispute; the result of the proceedings must be directly decisive for such a right.

This last-mentioned principle means that Art 6(1) will apply through all the stages of determination of the dispute, from pre-hearing stages through to cost proceedings.[26]

3.5.5    Secondly, the dispute will have to concern a 'right' that is 'civil' in character. A 'right' can, as seen, include a benefit granted as a matter of discretion, as well as one to which a person is entitled as of right.[27] The ECtHR has held that a licence, which is granted as a matter of discretion, confers a 'right' in the form of an authorisation to carry out the licensed activity. In *Tre Traktörer Aktiebolag v Sweden* (1989) 13 EHRR 309, where the applicants ran a restaurant that had a licence to sell alcohol, it was stated that 'subject to the possibility of its being revoked, the licence conferred a "right" on the applicant company in the form of an authorisation to sell alcoholic beverages in the restaurant Le Cardinal in accordance with the conditions set out in the licence'.[28] Thus, in *R (on the application of Alconbury Developments Ltd) v Secretary of State for the Environment, Transport and the Regions* [2003] 2 AC 295, Lord Clyde stated (at para 150):

> It is . . . clear that article 6(1) is engaged where the decision which is to be given is of an administrative character, that is to say one given in an exercise of a discretionary power, as well as a dispute in a court of law regarding the private rights of the citizen, provided that it directly affects civil rights and obligations and is of a genuine and serious nature.

As to whether a right is 'civil' in character, the term 'civil' will be given an autonomous meaning, so how the right might be classified in domestic law will not be decisive (see 3.4.2 above).[29] In determining whether a right is 'civil', the ECtHR has drawn a distinction, not only between civil rights and criminal charges, but also between public and private law rights. It has interpreted 'civil' to mean, in effect, 'private law', so that in relation to a public law right or obligation Art 6 will not apply (*König v Federal Republic of Germany* (1978) 2 EHRR 170, para 95). It will therefore be necessary to determine whether a right is private or public and, according to *König*, this will depend on the 'character' of the right. In some areas, the character of a right will obviously be private (for example, contract, tort, succession), but in other areas, and this will include licensing, there may be aspects of both public and private rights. In licensing, there are private law rights (for example, the provision of services by licence holders as a commercial activity carried on with the object of earning profits and based on a contractual relationship between the licence holder and his customers) and there are public law rights (for example, licence holders being properly regulated in the public interest to prevent public disorder and to ensure public safety).

3.5.6    It seems, however, clear from ECtHR case law that the public law aspects or features of licensing are not sufficient to exclude it from being a 'civil' private law right and from Art 6(1) having application. In *Pudas v Sweden* (1987) 10 EHRR 380, which concerned revocation of a taxi licence issued by the County Administrative Board of a district in Sweden, the ECtHR stated (at para 37) that, although taxi licensing had certain public law features,[30] these did not suffice to exclude from the category of civil rights under Art 6(1) the rights conferred on the licence holder by virtue of the licence:

> The maintenance of the licence to which the applicant claimed to be entitled was one of the conditions for the exercise of his business activities. Furthermore, public transport services in Sweden are not ensured by a State monopoly but both by public bodies and private persons . . . At least in the latter event, the provision of such services takes the form of a commercial activity. It is carried out with the object of earning profits and is based on a contractual relationship between the licence-holder and the customers.

Similarly, in *Tre Traktörer Aktiebolag v Sweden* (1989) 13 EHRR 309, it was held, in respect of a licence for the sale in a restaurant of alcoholic beverages, that 'subject to the possibility of its being revoked, the licence conferred a "right" on the applicant company in the form of an authorisation to sell alcoholic beverages in the restaurant . . . in accordance with the conditions set out in the licence' (para 39). Further, this right was 'civil' in character, since 'it is enough that the outcome of the proceedings should be decisive for private rights and obligations . . . the serving of alcoholic beverages in restaurants and bars is entrusted mainly to private persons and companies through the issuing of licences . . . [and] the persons and companies concerned carry on a private commercial activity' (paras 41 and 43).[31] Revocation or withdrawal of a licence, as had occurred in this case, was not, however, regarded as 'the determination of a criminal charge' for the purposes of Art 6(1). This was because 'it cannot be characterised as a penal sanction; even if it was linked with the licensee's behaviour, what was decisive was suitability to sell alcoholic beverages'.[32]

The rights of those involved in or affected by licensable activities under the 2003 Act will thus be 'civil' rights for the purposes of Art 6(1). This is consistent with the approach taken by the House of Lords in *R (on the application of Alconbury Developments Ltd) v Secretary of State for the Environment, Transport and the Regions* [2003] 2 AC 295, where the House regarded a dispute under planning law as involving the determination of civil rights and expressed the view (at para 41) that: 'planning, compulsory purchase and other related decisions do affect civil rights even if the procedures and decisions are of an administrative law nature rather than strictly civil law in nature' (*per* Lord Slynn). Indeed, the matter seems not to have been regarded as in doubt by the JCHR which, in its Fourth Report on the Licensing Bill, stated (at para 7):

> As the rights of those in possession of property, and perhaps those entertainers whose freedom of expression would be limited, are civil rights within the meaning of ECHR Article 6.1, the licensing procedures would have to be compatible with the right to a fair hearing by an independent and impartial tribunal under that Article.

### 3.5.7 Fair and public hearing within a reasonable time

3.5.8    Where there is a 'determination of a civil right', as in the above cases, it will be necessary that there is a 'fair and public hearing' by 'an independent and impartial tribunal established by law'. The requirements of a fair hearing have not been specifically laid down by the ECtHR, but the overriding obligation is one of ensuring that proceedings are fair. Therefore, a person must have an opportunity to present his case; submissions, arguments and evidence must be properly examined; and a reasoned decision must be given. Of particular importance is the concept of 'equality of arms', introduced in *Neumeister v Austria* (1968) 1 EHRR 91, which requires a fair balance to be maintained between the opportunities afforded to parties involved in civil litigation. As the ECtHR stated in *Dombo Beheer BV v Netherlands* (1993) 18 EHRR 213, para 33:

> as regards [civil] litigation involving opposing private interests, 'equality of arms' implies that each party must be afforded a reasonable opportunity to present his case – including his evidence – under conditions that do not place him at a substantial disadvantage vis-à-vis his opponent.[33]

Although this statement was made in respect of civil litigation, it should have equal application to civil proceedings generally and should therefore extend to licensing hearings.

3.5.9    Other elements that may be inherent in a fair hearing are the opportunity to call witnesses and to cross-examine witnesses, and to have reasons for a tribunal's decision. As regards witnesses, Art 6(3)(d) specifically provides that everyone charged with a criminal offence has the right 'to examine or have examined witnesses against him and to obtain the attendance and examination of witnesses on his behalf and under the same condition as witnesses against him', although there is no equivalent provision in Art 6(1) in respect of determinations of civil rights. However, in *X v Federal Republic of Germany*, Application No 852/60, 19 September 1961, the European Commission stated:

> it is nevertheless conceivable that, in certain types of cases or in certain circumstances, the refusal by a court to allow the witness or witnesses called by the plaintiff to testify, could involve a violation of Article 6, paragraph (I), which recognises the right of everyone to a fair hearing by an impartial tribunal that will determine his civil rights.[34]

The applicant was found in this case to have 'failed to adduce the slightest *prima facie* evidence' of his allegation that he had been refused permission to call one of his witnesses and the application was duly dismissed. In *X v Austria*, Application No 5362/72; (1972) 42 CD 145, where the applicant was both refused permission to call a witness and to cross-examine another witness, the European Commission referred with approval to the above statement and regarded it as having application to a refusal for a person 'to call a witness or to examine a witness against him'. Again, it did not find that in the circumstances the court's refusal was inconsistent with Art 6(1) because it did not find the witness's evidence or the cross-examination to be relevant. Nevertheless, in *Elsholz v Germany*, Application No 25377/94, 13 July 2000, the ECtHR held that, in proceedings for child access, a failure of the court to seek psychological expert evidence as to the child's views, which was requested by the child's father and supported by the Youth Office, constituted a violation of Art 6(1). Although these decisions concern court proceedings, the same principle should have application to licensing and similar hearings. For licensing hearings under the 2003 Act, reg 8(2) of the Licensing Act 2003 (Hearings) Regulations 2005, SI 2005/44 (LA 2003 (Hearings) Regs 2005) requires a party to the hearing to request permission for any other person, other than someone representing him, to appear (as a witness), with an indication of how that person will assist the authority and reg 23 requires the hearing to take the form of a discussion led by the authority, with cross-examination not permitted unless the authority considers it to be necessary to consider the application or any relevant representations made or notice given (see 2.3.11 above). A refusal of permission will not necessarily infringe Art 6(1), although in the light of the above decisions it is certainly possible that it might do.

Where a licensing committee or subcommittee receives legal advice on a particular matter in private, as where it has retired in order to make a decision, it seems that the legal advice should be regarded as provisional and the matter referred to the parties to afford them an opportunity to comment upon this advice before any action is taken on it. The Privy Council so held in *Clark v Kelly* [2004] 1 AC 681, a case where advice was given by a clerk to the justice in a case where the accused had been charged with theft, and where Lord Hope stated (at para 69):

> Any advice which the clerk gives to the justice in private on matters of law, practice or procedure should be regarded by them as provisional until the substance of that advice has been repeated in open court and an opportunity has been given to the parties to comment on it. The clerk should then state in open court whether that advice is confirmed or is varied, and if it is varied in what respect, before the justice decides to act upon it.

Although these remarks were made in the context of a criminal case, they would seem to have equal application to advice given by legal advisors to licensing committees or subcommittees hearing cases, or to magistrates' courts hearing licensing appeals, under the 2003 Act.

As regards the right to reasons, this is important because both the parties and the public as a whole have a legitimate interest in knowing the basis for any judgment and, further, without reasons, a party cannot effectively exercise any right of appeal. As the ECtHR stated in *Hadjianastassiou v Greece* (1992) 16 EHRR 219, para 33:

> The national courts . . . must indicate with sufficient clarity the grounds on which they base their decision. It is this, *inter alia*, which makes it possible for the accused to exercise usefully the rights of appeal available to him.[35]

The extent to which this requirement applies, however, and when there will be compliance with it, depends on the circumstances. As the ECtHR stated in *Hiro Balani v Spain* (1994) 19 EHRR 565, para 27:

> Article 6(1) obliges the courts to give reasons for their judgments, but cannot be understood as requiring a detailed answer to every argument. The extent to which this duty to give reasons applies may vary according to the nature of the decision.

This means that every point does not have to be covered, but obviously crucial submissions need to be addressed. In *Hiro Balani*, the plaintiff in a trademark case contested removal of her trademark from the register, but the court did not address her argument that she had priority over a competing trademark registered by someone else because of an earlier trademark that she had registered. This was a submission affecting the plaintiff's argument contesting removal and the failure to give reasons for not accepting the argument was held to be a violation of Art 6(1).

Under the 2003 Act, in several instances where licensing authorities are making decisions there is a statutory duty to give reasons (for example, under s 18(8), where an authority determines that representations are frivolous or vexatious and under s 23(3), where an application for a premises licence is rejected). To the extent that there may be no statutory duty, however, authorities will still be required to give reasons in order to comply with Art 6(1).

3.5.10  Article 6(1) requires that the hearing be conducted generally in public ('everyone is entitled to a fair and public hearing') and that judgment be pronounced publicly, although the Article does go on, as follows, to provide for the exclusion of the press and public in certain circumstances:

> judgment shall be pronounced publicly but the press and public may be excluded from all or any part of the trial in the interests of morals, public order or national security in a democratic society, where the interests of juveniles or the protection of the private life of the parties so require, or to the extent strictly necessary in the opinion of the court in special circumstances where publicity would prejudice the interest of justice.

Regulation 14(1) of the LA 2003 (Hearings) Regs 2005 provides for licensing hearings to be held in public, although under reg 14(2), the licensing authority has a discretion to exclude the public from all or part of a hearing where it considers that the public interest in so doing outweighs the public interest in the hearing, or that part of the hearing, taking place in public (see 2.3.3 above). This is a more general test than that specified in Art 6(1), although it is difficult to think of instances where there might be exclusion of the public under this test, which might not be justified under Art 6(1). As to a hearing within a reasonable time, what is a reasonable time will depend on the circumstances, which could include the complexity of factual or legal issues, the conduct of the parties and what was at stake for the applicant.[36] There is no absolute period for what is unreasonable, although significant delays are likely to be needed for a violation of Art 6(1), as in *Robins v UK* (1998) 26 EHRR 527 (see 3.5.4 above). With regard to licensing hearings, the periods of time within which hearings must be held are prescribed under the above-mentioned Regulations (see 2.3.2 above) and compliance with these will undoubtedly meet the Art 6 requirement of a hearing within a reasonable time.

## 3.5.11 Independent and impartial tribunal established by law

3.5.12   It is necessary that the decision-making body is a 'tribunal' for the purposes of Art 6 and this means that it must exercise a judicial function and its decisions must have the force of law.[37] A body that carries out functions other than judicial ones, such as administrative functions, may nevertheless be a 'tribunal' for the purposes of Art 6(1).[38] Local authorities, as licensing authorities under the 2003 Act, may therefore be a 'tribunal' since they will be exercising administrative functions, along with a quasi-judicial function (in contested cases), when determining applications for licences or their review. However, a tribunal must be 'established by law', as opposed to depending on the discretion of the executive, and be 'independent', in the sense that it is independent of the executive and of the parties.[39] This is not the case with local authorities, since they are part of the executive and not therefore independent of it. Nevertheless, where the decision-making body itself is not an 'independent tribunal' for the purposes of Art 6(1), there will be no violation of the right to a fair hearing under the Article if there is available a right of appeal to a body that is an independent tribunal. In other words, if there is access to an independent judicial body, which is able to hear the complaint that the applicant wishes to bring and which satisfies the Art 6 requirements, this will suffice, even though in the case of the decision-making body one (or more) of the elements required by Art 6(1) is lacking. In *Albert and Le Compte v Belgium* (1983) 5 EHRR 533, the ECtHR held that there would be no violation of the Convention if the proceedings before a body are 'subject to subsequent control by a judicial body that has full jurisdiction and does provide the guarantees of Article 6'. The focus is on whether the decision-making process as a whole complies with Art 6 and not simply the original proceedings before the initial tribunal.

In the case of local authority decisions it is therefore important that an appeal can be made to a court which has 'full jurisdiction' as to both law and fact in order to satisfy the requirement of an 'independent tribunal'. As the ECtHR stated in *Le Compte, Van Leuven and de Meyere v Belgium* (1981) 4 EHRR 1, para 51:

> Article 6(1) draws no distinction between questions of fact and questions of law. Both categories of question are equally crucial for the outcome of proceedings relating to 'civil rights and obligations'. Hence the 'right to a court' and the right to a judicial determination of the dispute cover questions of fact as much as questions of law.

Under the 2003 Act the requirement is satisfied by a right of appeal to the magistrates' court where the appeal takes the form of a re-hearing (see 12.7 below) and where the court can hear any complaint that the applicant wishes to bring.

3.5.13   The requirement for 'full jurisdiction' may be met by the availability of appeal to the High Court for judicial review of a decision,[40] even if under the 2003 Act a right of appeal to a court for a re-hearing is unavailable, as appears to be the case in respect of a determination that a representation by an interested party is frivolous or vexatious and accordingly does not constitute a 'relevant representation' (see 6.4.22 below). The availability of judicial review is governed by the principles laid down by the Court of Appeal in *Associated Provincial Picture Houses Ltd v Wednesbury Corporation* [1948] 1 KB 223, a case concerning a challenge to the exercise of a local authority's powers to licence cinematograph exhibitions, where Lord Greene MR stated (at 233–34):

> The court is entitled to investigate the action of the local authority with a view to seeing whether they have taken into account matters which they ought not to take into account, or, conversely, have refused to take into account or neglected to take into account matters which they ought to take into account. Once that question is answered in favour of the local authority, it may still be possible to say that although the local authority have kept within the four corners of the matters which they ought to consider, they have nevertheless come to a conclusion so unreasonable that no reasonable authority could ever have come to it.[41]

These principles were subsequently reformulated by the House of Lords in *Council of Civil Service Unions v Minister of State for the Civil Service* [1985] AC 374, so that the grounds for seeking judicial review fell under three heads: illegality, irrationality and procedural impropriety. Whilst judicial review will be available in principle in respect of all licensing decisions, it may not be able to address all points that are in contention in a dispute concerning a civil right. Disputes on points of law are likely to fall within the three heads recognised and the third heading of procedural impropriety might allow disputes on some factual issues to be addressed. However, it is conceivable that there might be other contested factual issues (for example, the veracity of evidence on a particular matter, the weight to be given to evidence or inferences to be drawn from facts) that cannot be considered, in which case there may be a violation of Art 6(1).

When considering the sufficiency of judicial review in respect of factual matters, the ECtHR, in *Bryan v UK* (1996) 21 EHRR 342, para 45, stated that: 'in assessing the sufficiency . . . it is necessary to have regard to matters such as the subject matter of the decision appealed against, the manner in which that decision was arrived at, and the content of the dispute, including the desired and actual grounds of appeal'. Where the matters concerned are administrative ones of a relatively technical nature, a restricted review of decisions is common amongst States where the Convention applies and in *Zumtobel v Austria* (1994) 17 EHRR 116, the ECtHR recognised that courts may legitimately restrict judicial review on expediency grounds. It was also recognised in *Bryan* that, where the subject matter of the decision was of a specialised character (planning in the case itself), which required the exercise of discretion in the regulation of citizens' conduct, a restricted review as regards the factual application of this discretion was permissible. Factual issues in such cases were established in a quasi-judicial procedure that in many respects was compliant with Art 6(1) safe-guards and a limited review was therefore justified. In the House of Lords in *Runa Begum v Tower Hamlets London Borough Council* [2003] 2 AC 430, a housing case, Lord Hoffmann, having regard to the decision in *Bryan*, stated (at para 53): 'In my opinion the Strasbourg court has accepted, on the basis of general state practice and for . . . reasons of good administration . . . that in such cases a limited right of review on questions of fact is sufficient.'[42] In the light of this, a restricted right of judicial review by the High Court under the 2003 Act may be regarded as permissible and as satisfy-ing the requirement for 'full jurisdiction' as set out in *Albert and Le Compte v Belgium* (1983) 5 EHRR 533.

3.5.14   The requirement that the tribunal is 'impartial', although clearly linked with the independence of the tribunal, extends beyond independence to include an absence of prejudice or bias. There are two aspects to this requirement. First, the tribunal must be subjectively free of personal prejudice or bias. Secondly, it must also be impartial from an objective point of view, that is, it must offer sufficient guarantees to exclude any legitimate doubt as to impartiality. In *Huaschildt v Denmark* (1989) 12 EHRR 266, para 46, the ECtHR stated:

> The existence of impartiality for the purposes of Article 6(1) must be determined according to a subjective test, that is on the basis of the personal conviction of a particu-lar judge in a given case, and also according to an objective test, that is ascertaining whether the judge offered guarantees sufficient to exclude any legitimate doubt in this respect.

Impartiality is presumed, as stated by the ECtHR in *Le Compte, Van Leuven and De Meyere v Belgium* (1981) 4 EHRR 1, para 58, until there is proof to the contrary. The burden of proving subjective bias is obviously difficult to surmount and it is much easier to establish a violation of Art 6 on the basis of an appearance of bias through the objective test of 'legitimate doubt'.[43]

   In the context of the 2003 Act, an appearance of bias may arise in a licensing subcommittee hearing, for instance, if a member of a subcommittee that was to hear an application had previously sat on another committee (for example, the planning committee) that had made a decision that involved passing some judgment on the merits of the application. If planning permission had been granted by the planning committee and an application were made for a premises licence, there may be, to objectors to the application, an appearance of bias in that the member had previously voted in favour of the application. In order to avoid this, it would be advisable for the member not to sit on the licensing subcommittee to hear the premises licence application.[44] Similarly, if the member is a ward councillor for the area in which the application premises are situated, the member should not sit if he wishes to make representations on behalf of his constituents.[45] Again, any expression of views by a member in respect of particular applications ahead of the hearing of the case might give rise to an appearance of bias and the member should not sit.[46]

3.5.15 Finally, the tribunal will have to be 'established by law', which means that it must not depend on the discretion of the executive. Local authority committees and subcommittees might meet this requirement, as local authorities have a general power by statute under s 101 of the Local Government Act 1972 to arrange for the discharge of any of their functions by a committee or subcommittee, to which the power of decision may or may not be delegated. Further, and more particularly, under s 6(1) of the 2003 Act, local authorities are required by statute to establish a licensing committee which, under s 7(1), must discharge the authority's licensing functions. This committee is 'established by law', as are subcommittees, which the committee may establish under s 9(1) and through which it may under s 10(1) arrange for the discharge of any of its licensing functions (see 2.2.1 above).

3.5.16 In conclusion, licensing decisions made by local authorities in contested cases may fall within the scope of Art 6(1) as constituting a determination by the authority of civil rights and obligations. The fact that licensing decisions are made by local authorities, which themselves are not an 'independent' tribunal for the purposes of Art 6(1), does not constitute a violation of the Article, provided the complaint can be addressed on appeal by an independent tribunal, that is a court having 'full jurisdiction'. This might be either the magistrates' court in a re-hearing of the case under the 2003 Act or the High Court on judicial review. Whether there will be violation will depend on whether authorities, when making licensing decisions under the 2003 Act, comply with the requirements outlined above.

### 3.5.17 Article 6(2)

3.5.18 Article 6(2) provides:

> Everyone charged with a criminal offence shall be presumed innocent until proved guilty according to law.

The general principle applying in respect of this provision is set out in *Barberà, Messegué and Jabardo v Spain* (1988) 11 EHRR 360, para 77, where the ECtHR stated:

> Paragraph 2 embodies the principle of the presumption of innocence. It requires, *inter alia*, that when carrying out their duties, the members of the court should not start with the preconceived idea that the accused has committed the offence charged; the burden of proof is on the prosecution, and any doubt should benefit the accused. It also follows that it is for the prosecution to inform the accused of the case that will be made against him, so that he may prepare and present his defence accordingly, and to adduce evidence sufficient to convict him.

This accords with the common-law approach whereby the legal (or persuasive) burden of proof rests with the prosecution, which must prove the existence of the conduct (*actus reus*) and mental (*mens rea*) elements of the criminal offence(s) in question and must do so to a standard of beyond reasonable doubt.[47]

3.5.19 This principle is, however, subject to any statutory exception and it has not been uncommon for statute to modify the normal burden of proof, either in relation to a definitional element of the offence or (more usually) a statutory defence that is provided. In these cases, often referred to as 'reverse onus clauses', the legal burden is placed upon the accused and the standard of proof required of the accused is the normal civil standard of a balance of probabilities, that is the existence of that which has to be established is more likely than not.[48] There is clearly a potential conflict with Art 6(2) where the legal burden is placed on the accused and there may, but not necessarily will, be a violation of Art 6(2). According to the leading ECtHR decision of *Salabiaku v France* (1988) 13 EHRR 379, para 28:

> Presumptions of fact or law operate in every legal system. Clearly, the Convention does not prohibit such presumptions in principle. It does, however, require the contracting states to remain within certain limits in this respect as regards criminal law ... Article 6(2) does not therefore regard presumptions of fact or law provided for in the criminal law with indifference. It requires states to confine them within reasonable limits which take into account the importance of what is at stake and maintain the rights of the defence.

In essence, Art 6 requires only a fair trial and the presumption of innocence in Art 6(2) is merely one aspect of that requirement and not a freestanding obligation, which is why there can be departure in certain circumstances from the principle that the prosecution must prove beyond reasonable doubt all the matters at issue.

3.5.20  Departure is permissible, as can be seen from the last-mentioned sentence in *Salabiaku*, where this is reasonable or proportionate. As Lord Bingham, delivering the leading judgment of the House of Lords in *Sheldrake v Director of Public Prosecutions, Attorney General's Reference (No 4 of 2002)* [2005] 1 All ER 237 (a case which concerned two appeals being heard simultaneously) stated (at para 21) when considering *Salabiaku* and subsequent ECtHR case law:

> The overriding concern is that a trial should be fair, and the presumption of innocence is a fundamental right directed to that end. The convention does not outlaw presumptions of fact or law but requires that these should be kept within reasonable limits and should not be arbitrary. It is open to states to define the constituent elements of a criminal offence, excluding the requirement of *mens rea*. But the substance and effect of any presumption adverse to a defendant must be examined, and must be reasonable. Relevant to any judgment on reasonableness or proportionality will be the opportunity given to the defendant to rebut the presumption, maintenance of the rights of the defence, flexibility in application of the presumption, retention by the court of a power to assess the evidence, the importance of what is at stake and the difficulty which a prosecutor may face in the absence of a presumption ... The justifiability of any infringement of the presumption of innocence cannot be resolved by any rule of thumb, but on examination of all the facts and circumstances of the particular provision as applied in the particular case.

His Lordship went on to state (at para 31): 'The task of the court is never to decide whether a reverse burden should be imposed on a defendant, but always to assess whether a burden enacted by Parliament unjustifiably infringes the presumption of innocence.' In the first instance, therefore, it needs to be established whether a burden enacted by Parliament is in fact a legal burden of proof placed on the defendant and this will be determined according to ordinary principles of statutory interpretation. Once it has been decided that it has, it then needs to be ascertained whether it is fair and reasonable in the achievement of a proper statutory objective for the State to deprive the defendant of the protection normally guaranteed by Art 6(2), that is, whether it is a justifiable response. As Lord Bingham went on to remark (at para 1):

'Thus the first question for consideration in each case is whether the provision in question does, unjustifiably, infringe the presumption of innocence.'

3.5.21 If it does, as Lord Bingham went on to say (at para 1), it is possible that the court may, under s 3(1) of the 1998 Act, interpret the legislation in a way that is compatible with Convention rights (see 3.2.1 above) by 'reading down' the legal burden imposed by the statute so that it is an evidential burden:

> If it does the further question arises whether the provision can and should be read down in accordance with the courts' interpretative obligation under s 3 of the 1998 Act so as to impose an evidential and not a legal burden on the defendant. An evidential burden is not a burden of proof. It is a burden of raising, on the evidence in the case, an issue as to the matter in question fit for consideration by the tribunal of fact.[49]

If the provision is thus 'read down' to impose only an evidential burden, the legal burden will be on the prosecution. If, on the other hand, it is a justifiable response, it then needs to be determined whether the exception is proportionate, that is, whether it goes no further than is reasonably necessary to achieve the statutory objective. If it goes no further than necessary, it will be possible to say, to use the words of Lord Bingham (at para 50), that 'imposition of a legal burden on a defendant in this particular situation is a proportionate and justifiable legislative response'.

3.5.22 There are a number of instances under the 2003 Act of criminal offences to which a defence is provided, where the courts may be required to determine on whom the legal burden of proof lies. There is a defence of 'due diligence' in s 139, which applies in respect of the offences of carrying on an unauthorised licensable activity under s 136(1)(a), exposing alcohol for unauthorised sale under s 137 and keeping alcohol on the premises for unauthorised sale under s 138 (see 11.2.10 below). There is a similar defence in s 156(3) in respect of the offence under that section of selling by retail alcohol from a vehicle when it is not permanently or temporarily parked, that is when the vehicle is moving (see 11.8.2 below). Although these provisions refer to a 'defence', they do not use the term 'to prove' and are thus 'neutral' as far as the burden of proof is concerned.[50] Nevertheless, given the reference to 'defence', it seems likely that, applying ordinary principles of statutory construction to these provisions, the legal burden of proof will be on the defence.

It seems likely that placing such a burden, in these cases, on the defence, thereby depriving the defendant of Art 6(2) protection, is fair and reasonable in the achievement of a proper statutory objective, the effective regulation of licensable activities. Even if it does infringe the presumption of innocence, the infringement may well be regarded as justified and proportionate. Taking into account the essentially regulatory nature of the offences and making reference to factors to which Lord Bingham (at para 21) refers (see 3.5.20 above), the importance of what is at stake is not especially high,[51] there is an opportunity given to the defendant to rebut the presumption and the difficulty which a prosecutor may face in the absence of a presumption is significant. Matters appertaining to 'due diligence' are likely to be within the defendant's knowledge (or means of knowledge) and not especially difficult for him to prove, although they may be for the prosecution. Thus placing the legal burden of proof on the defence for these offences may be justified and not disproportionate, in which case there will be no violation of Art 6(2).

3.5.23  Support for this view can be found in the decision of the Administrative Court in *R (Grundy and Co Excavations Ltd and Parry) v Halton Division Magistrates' Court and the Forestry Commission* [2003] LLR 335. In this case a prosecution was instituted for the felling of some trees on a farmer's land without a licence, contrary to s 17 of the Forestry Act 1967, and an application was made for judicial review of the trial judge's ruling that the legal burden of proof was on the accused to prove on the balance of probabilities that a licence was not required under one of the exceptions in s 9 of the Act. It was accepted that there was an evidential burden on the accused to show that one of the exceptions applied, but it was contended that the burden was not a legal one and the legal burden remained on the prosecution. It was held, applying the provisions of s 101 of the Magistrates' Courts Act 1980 and the principles in *R v Edwards* [1975] 1 QB 27 and *R v Hunt* [1987] AC 352 (see 3.5.19 above), that there was a reverse burden on the accused to show that one of the exceptions in s 9 applied and that this was a legal burden. It was recognised that the reverse burden of proof provisions in ss 9 and 17 of the 1967 Act derogated from the presumption of innocence in Art 6(2), but the derogation was regarded as justified, because it was impossible to negative all defences in advance, and it was proportionate. The legislative scheme, it was felt, would only really work if the burden was on the accused. Much the same may well be said of the legislative scheme in the 2003 Act.[52] Indeed, this view might be reinforced by the fact that the defence of due diligence to under-age sales of alcohol in s 71 of the Licensing (Scotland) Act 1976 has not been regarded as incompatible with Art 6(2) by the High Court of Justiciary in *McLean v Steel Carnegie* [2005] LLR 448.[53]

## 3.6    PROTOCOL 1 OF ARTICLE 1: PROTECTION OF PROPERTY

3.6.1    Protocol 1 of Article 1 is concerned with the protection of property and provides:

> Every natural or legal person is entitled to the peaceful enjoyment of his possessions. No one shall be deprived of his possessions except in the public interest and subject to the conditions provided for by law and by the general principles of international law.
>
> The preceding provisions shall not, however, in any way impair the right of a State to enforce such laws as it deems necessary to control the use of property in accordance with the general interest or to secure the payment of taxes or other contributions or penalties.[54]

The right under Art 1 is a qualified one, for many other rights and interests can only be satisfactorily protected if the State is permitted to override individual claims to enjoyment of property, and Art 1 is restricted to the circumstances in which interference might take place.

3.6.2    The first issue that will arise is what constitutes 'possessions'. As with other provisions in the Convention, this term will be given an autonomous meaning (see 3.4.2 above). It can cover a wide range of property interests, although there must be a right in national law to the property interest and the entitlement to enjoy it.[55] It can include not only tangible property, but also intangible property and economic interests in property. Such an interest can include a person's right to enjoyment of property in respect of which a licence is held. In *Tre Traktörer Aktiebolag v Sweden* (1991)

13 EHRR 309, the ECtHR rejected an argument that a licence was not a 'possession' because it conferred no rights in national law and stated (at para 53):

> The Government argued that a licence to serve alcoholic beverages could not be considered to be a "possession" within the meaning of Article 1 of the Protocol (P1–1). The provision was therefore, in their opinion, not applicable to the case. Like the Commission, however, the Court takes the view that the economic interests connected with the running of Le Cardinal [restaurant] were "possessions" for the purposes of Article 1 of the Protocol (P1–1). Indeed, the Court has already found that the maintenance of the licence was one of the principal conditions for the carrying on of the applicant's company business, and that its withdrawal had adverse effects on the goodwill and value of the restaurant. Such withdrawal thus constitutes, in the circumstances of the case, an interference with . . . [the applicant's] right to the "peaceful enjoyment of [its] possessions".

This case does not decide that a licence is (or is not) a 'possession', but rather that economic interests in property in respect of which the licence is held can be 'possessions'. Whether a licence can be a 'possession' is a matter of some uncertainty. It might well be if it were a licence that could be assigned or transferred (as of right) to another, since the licence would then be an asset, much the same as any other item of property, that a person possesses. As Kenneth Parker QC, sitting as a Deputy High Court judge observed in R *(on the application of Nicholds and others) v Security Industry Authority* [2007] 1 WLR 2067 (at para 74):

> It seems to me that certain licences or permissions are "assets", that is, they have a monetary value and can be marketed for consideration, either through outright sale, "leasing", or sub-licensing. Milk quotas would fall within this category as well as certain spectrum licences which Ofcom allows to be assigned or sub-licensed for consideration.

However, as Kenneth Parker QC went on to remark (at para 75), there are other licences and permissions which are not marketable and are not 'assets' having monetary value. This is the case with licences (and certificates) under the 2003 Act, which take the form of a permission or authorisation. Even if granted on an indefinite basis, as with premises licences (see 6.7.1 below), provision is made for their revocation in certain circumstances and applications are needed to transfer a licence to another person. Where this is the case, it seems that the licence will not be regarded as a possession. Thus in *X v Federal Republic of Germany* (1982) 26 DR 255, where a driving licence was confiscated following motoring convictions, the European Commission stated (at 256): 'As regards the alleged violation of Article 1 of the First Protocol, the Commission finds that the position of the holder of a driving licence does not amount to a property right.'[56]

3.6.3      If the principle in *Tre Traktörer* is applied where licensable activities[57] are carried on under and in accordance with a premises licence granted under the 2003 Act, and account is taken of Strasbourg case law under s 2 of the 1998 Act, then economic interests connected with the running of the premises under a premises licence should be regarded as 'possessions'. Similarly, where qualifying club activities[58] are carried on under and in accordance with a club premises certificate (CPC), then economic interests connected with the running of the club premises ought to be regarded as 'possessions'. Less clear is whether the principle will extend to licensable activities in premises carried on under and in accordance with a temporary event notice (TEN). TENs operate only for a limited period (up to 96 hours) and there is an annual restriction on numbers at 12 per premises (see ss 100(1) and 107(4), and 9.2.1 and 9.7.1 below, respectively). Whilst maintenance of the licence in *Tre Traktörer* was one of the principal conditions for the carrying on of the applicant's company business, the same may not be true where a limited number of activities are held under TENs. The economic interests connected with the running of the premises may in such instances not be sufficient to constitute 'possessions'. The same may be true where a person holding a personal licence is the designated premises supervisor (DPS) under a premises licence.[59] Whilst under s 15(2) the DPS may be the same person who holds the premises licence, he need not be and, where he is not, may well not have any economic interest connected with the running of the business except to the extent that those running it employ him. The position of a DPS here would seem to be analogous to that of a person holding a driving licence, as in *X v Federal Republic of Germany*.

3.6.4    To constitute 'possessions', there must be some existing interest in property or at least a legitimate expectation of obtaining effective enjoyment of a property right. In *Kopecky v Slovakia*, Application No 44912/98, 28 September 2004, the ECtHR stated (at para 35): ' "Possessions" can be either "existing possessions" or assets, including claims, in respect of which the applicant can argue that he or she has at least a "legitimate expectation" of obtaining effective enjoyment of a property right.' It will not, however, suffice if there is simply a hope of recognition of a property right to which a person may become entitled, for a person has no right or legitimate expectation to the property in such a case.

Where a premises licence or a CPC is held, there will be an existing economic interest connected with and arising from the running of the premises under the licence or certificate (hereafter 'licence'), so this will constitute a property right and there will be an interference with that right where the licence is varied or revoked. It seems that this is provided that any conditions attached to the licence are complied with, for the European Commission in *JS and Others v Netherlands* (1995) 20 EHRR CD 41, 51 stated:

> the question whether a licence to conduct economic activities amounts to a "possession" within the meaning of Article 1 of Protocol No. 1 depends, *inter alia*, on whether it gives rise to a reasonable and legitimate expectation of continuing benefits. A licence holder cannot be considered to have such an expectation where the conditions attached to the licence are not or no longer fulfilled.

Where, however, an application is made for the grant of a licence for existing premises and this is refused, there is no economic interest connected with or arising from the running of the premises under a licence, since there is no existing licence or any legitimate expectation to a licence. There may be some existing economic interest in the premises and this may be affected by whether or not the licence is granted, but these interests are neither connected with nor derived from the licence. It seems unlikely therefore that refusal to grant will give rise to any actionable interference.

The position seems to be the same if application is made for a provisional statement under s 29 of the 2003 Act in respect of premises that have not yet been built (or extended or otherwise altered) and this is refused (see 6.8 below). Here there may simply be a right to acquire property rather than the actual existence of property in respect of which there is any existing economic interest. This view might be supported by the decision of the European Commission in *Linde v Sweden* (1986)

47 DR 270, where it was held that, where the applicant was intending to acquire further gaming machines for which an authorisation for use was required and his application for authorisation was refused, this did not constitute an interference with 'possessions' under Art 1. The Commission stated (at 271–72):

> the applicant had not at that time [when a request for authorisation was made] acquired the gambling machines to which his request for authorisation related. The Commission considers therefore that the present application only concerns the right to acquire property, a right which is not covered by Article 1 of Protocol 1.

3.6.5   Secondly, there will have to be an interference with the peaceful enjoyment of possessions. According to the ECtHR, in *Sporring and Lonnroth v Sweden* (1983) 5 EHRR 35, para 61, the provision in Art 1 comprises three distinct rules:

> The first rule, set out in the first sentence of the first paragraph, is of a general nature and enunciates the principle of peaceful enjoyment of property; the second rule, contained in the second sentence of the same paragraph, covers deprivation of possessions and makes it subject to certain conditions; and the third rule, stated in the second paragraph, recognises that contracting states are entitled, amongst other things, to control the use of property in accordance with the general interest. The three rules are not 'distinct' in the sense of being unconnected: the second and third rules are concerned with particular instances of interference with the right to peaceful enjoyment of property and should therefore be construed in the light of the general principle enunciated in the first rule . . .

3.6.6   The first rule, peaceful enjoyment, is wider than the second and third, which cover only particular forms of interference (deprivation and control of use), and can extend to cases outside these instances.[60] In applying this rule, the court, in *Sporring and Lonnroth*, went on to state (at para 69):

> the Court must determine whether a fair balance was struck between the demands of the general interest of the community and the requirements of the protection of the individual's fundamental rights. The search for this balance is inherent in the whole of the Convention and is also reflected in the structure of Article 1.[61]

This principle of 'fair balance', which was devised to assess compliance with the first rule, has subsequently been applied to the second and third rules as well and will determine whether there is a deprivation of property in the public interest under the second rule or a control of use in accordance with the general interest under the third rule. All cases have accordingly tended to be decided by reference to 'fair balance', irrespective of which of the three rules is identified as having application.[62]

3.6.7   The second rule of deprivation of property has been construed rather narrowly and requires that all legal rights in property be extinguished. If ownership of property remains and there is some ability to use of it, a finding of deprivation is unlikely and the third rule, control of the use of property, will be considered to apply. Revocation of a licence has thus been regarded as a control of use rather than a deprivation (and the same may be true for nonrenewal), since the licence holder will still retain rights in the property in respect of which the licence is held.[63] In *Tre Traktörer Aktiebolag v Sweden* (1989) 13 EHRR 309, the ECtHR stated (at para 55):

> Severe though it may have been, the interference at issue [revocation] did not fall within the ambit of the second sentence of the first paragraph [of Article 1]. The applicant company, although it could no longer operate Le Cardinal as a restaurant business, kept some economic interests represented by the leasing of the premises and

the property assets contained therein, which it finally sold in June 1984 . . . There was accordingly no deprivation of property in terms of Article 1 of the Protocol (P1–1).

If the court, in *Tre Traktörer*, had chosen to regard the licence as a 'possession', it would perhaps have been difficult not to regard revocation of the licence as a deprivation of property since all rights would have been extinguished in respect of the licence. Had there been a deprivation, the question of payment of compensation would then have arisen, for the ECtHR has taken the view that a 'fair balance' requires the payment of *some* compensation for deprivation in all but the exceptional case (for example, time of war).[64] There is no such expectation of compensation in the case of control of use; the payment of compensation (or lack if it) may be a relevant factor in such a case, but there can be a fair balance between the community interest and protection of an individual's rights, even where no compensation is payable.[65] Although a justified licence revocation may have been considered an exceptional case, the compensation issue could be avoided if, as in *Tre Traktörer*, economic interests in the licensed premises were regarded as 'possessions' (rather than the licence being regarded as a 'possession') and revocation was seen as a control of use. It may perhaps have been for this reason that the court in *Tre Traktörer* formulated its decision the way that it did.

3.6.8   The third rule enables States to control the use of property if this is necessary 'in accordance with the general interest', and establishing a violation of Art 1 is therefore dependent on showing that controlling the use of property is *not* in the general interest. In determining this in accordance with the 'fair balance' test, the need for controlling the use of property in the general interest for advancing the public good (the purpose of the interference) will have to be balanced against the burden on the individual of the interference and whether the measures taken are proportionate to the aims to be achieved (impact on property rights).

It cannot seriously be disputed that controlling the use of property through licensing the sale of alcohol, the provision of regulated entertainment and late night refreshment facilities does advance the public good and this might be justified on a number of grounds. In *Tre Trakötrer*, for example, the Swedish Government's claim was that its liquor licensing legislation was to implement the long-standing Swedish policy of restricting the consumption and abuse of alcohol (para 56) and the applicants did not contest this.[66] In respect of the licensing provisions under the 2003 Act, the justification is to be found in the four licensing objectives contained in s 4(2), that is, prevention of crime and disorder, public safety, prevention of public nuisance and protection of children from harm (see 4.2 below).[67]

Whilst the use of property might be controlled in accordance with these objectives in the general interest, there might nevertheless be a violation of Art 1 if an excessive burden is imposed on the individual and/or the measures taken are disproportionate. In such a case a fair balance would not be struck and factors particularly relevant in determining this would include the terms and conditions under which the use of property is controlled and whether the purpose could be achieved in some other way without interference (or with less interference) with the rights of the individual, that is, whether the control of use is proportionate (see 3.4.6 above). Thus, for example, on reviews of premises licences, the licensing authority, under s 52(4), can take various steps depending on what it considers necessary to promote the licensing objectives. These include modifying the conditions of the licence, excluding a licensable activity from the scope of the licence, removing the designated premises supervisor, suspending the licence for a period not exceeding three months or revoking the licence (see 6.12.8 below). Promotion of the objectives might well be achieved without recourse to the ultimate sanction of revocation of the licence; for example, curtailment of excessive noise during the early hours of the morning to prevent public nuisance might be achieved by modifying licence conditions to provide for earlier closure or better soundproofing and would not be a disproportionate interference, whereas revocation might be. Similarly, suspension of the licence for a period of time where sales of alcohol have been made to children might promote the licensing objective of prevention of harm to children by indicating to the premises licence holder that greater vigilance and more effective measures are required for preventing such sales. In *Tesco Express v Birmingham City Council and Chief Constable of West Midlands Police* [2007] 70 *Licensing Review* 34, Birmingham Magistrates' Court held that suspension of the appellants' premises licence, following two instances of sales of alcohol to a person under 18 within a six-day period, did not constitute a violation of Art 1 as it was 'in the public interest to do so and in doing so prevented the store from selling to children' (para 16). Even if the ultimate sanction of revocation is used, however, this does not necessarily mean that there will be violation of Art 1 since revocation can be justified in circumstances where this is considered to be in accordance with the general interest. Thus, in *Fredin v Sweden* [1991] ECHR 12033/86, the ECtHR held that revocation of the applicant's existing licence to extract gravel from his land did not infringe his Art 1 rights, even though he suffered a substantial financial loss as a result of the revocation and received no compensation, since this could be justified on environmental grounds and was within the wide margin of appreciation afforded to the State under the third rule.

## 3.7    ARTICLE 10: FREEDOM OF EXPRESSION

3.7.1    Article 10 is concerned with freedom of expression and provides:

(1) Everyone has the right to freedom of expression. This right shall include freedom to hold opinions and to receive and impart information and ideas without interference by public authority and regardless of frontiers. This article shall not prevent states from requiring the licensing of broadcasting, television or cinema.

(2) The exercise of these freedoms, since it carries with it duties and responsibilities, may be subject to such formalities, conditions, restrictions or penalties as are prescribed by law and are necessary in a democratic society, in the interests of national security, territorial integrity or public safety, for the prevention of disorder or crime, for the protection of health or morals, for the protection of the reputation of others, for preventing the disclosure of information received in confidence, or for maintaining the authority and impartiality of the judiciary.

There are, in essence, three rights falling within Art 10(1), the freedoms of expression, of holding opinions, and of receiving and imparting information. These rights are protected from interference, although they are qualified rights because interference is permissible in certain circumstances under Art 10(2). Particular provision is made in respect of these rights by s 12 of the 1998 Act, of which requires, *inter alia*, that courts must have 'particular regard to the importance of the Convention right to freedom of expression'.

## 3.7.2 The rights

### 3.7.3 *Expression*

3.7.4 'Expression' for the most part is concerned with the dissemination of information and ideas, irrespective of whether or not they are valueless, useless or offensive.[68] It most obviously includes words, either spoken or written, but can extend beyond this to include, for example, artistic expression,[69] actions that are expressive and have communicative potential,[70] and also the 'means/medium' of communication of forms of expression.[71] Further, 'expression' can take several different forms and might be conveyed through a variety of media, including print, radio, television, stage play, film or video. Various forms of regulated entertainment falling within the 2003 Act might therefore fall within the scope of Art 10, notably the performance of plays and exhibitions of films, and perhaps the performance or playing of music.[72]

3.7.5 The right to freedom of expression in respect of these forms of entertainment is qualified by the third sentence in Art 10(1), which provides: 'This Article shall not prevent states from requiring the licensing of broadcasting, television or cinema.' This has, however, been regarded as a very limited qualification, applying only in respect of the imposition of a licensing system. Imposition will not, in itself, constitute a violation of Art 10(1) by virtue of this provision, but licensing requirements themselves and decisions made by licensing authorities in accordance with those requirements do not fall within this qualification. They remain subject to the restrictions in Art 10(2) and will have to be justified under that provision; they cannot be justified because of the provision in the third sentence in Art 10(1). As the ECtHR stated in *Groppera Radio AG v Switzerland* (1990) 12 EHRR 321 (at para 61):

> the third sentence of Article 10 § 1 (art 10–1) of the Convention is to make it clear that States are permitted to control by a licensing system the way in which broadcasting is organised in their territories, particularly in its technical aspects. It does not, however, provide that licensing measures shall not otherwise be subject to the requirements of paragraph 2 (art 10–2), for that would lead to a result contrary to the object and purpose of Article 10 (art 10) taken as a whole.

### 3.7.6 *Opinions*

Article 10(1) provides that the right to freedom of expression includes 'freedom to hold opinions'. Thus, action by the State that in some way penalises people for 'holding opinions', as distinct from 'expressing' them, engages Art 10.[73]

### 3.7.7 *Receive and impart information*

Article 10(1) also includes the right to 'receive and impart information'. The ECtHR has indicated in several cases, for example *Sunday Times v UK* (1979) 2 EHRR 245, that there is separate protection both for the right to receive and for the right to impart information. A person's right to receive information does not, however, equate to a right of access to all information generally, but rather it applies in respect of information that others may wish to impart to him. In *Leander v Sweden* (1987) 9 EHRR 433, para 74, the ECtHR stated:

The Court observes that the right to freedom to receive information basically prohibits a Government from restricting a person from receiving information that others wish or may be willing to impart to him. Article 10 (art 10) does not, in circumstances such as those of the present case, confer on the individual a right of access to a register containing information on his personal position, nor does it embody an obligation on the Government to impart such information to the individual.[74]

## 3.7.8  Interference

In deciding whether there is an interference with the above rights much will depend on the nature of the interference and, in particular, whether there is prepublication interference (that is 'prior restraint') or post-publication interference, and whether the interference is 'direct' or 'indirect'.

### 3.7.9  Prior restraint or post-publication interference

3.7.10  Prior restraint is more likely to give rise to a violation of Art 10(1) – as the ECtHR observed in *Wingrove v UK* (1997) 24 EHRR 1, para 58, 'prior restraint calls for special scrutiny by the Court' – since it deprives a person entirely of any opportunity to air his views and deprives society of the opportunity of judging for itself whether the expression merits condemnation. It is generally thought to be more serious than penalising expression after the event, certainly where prior restraint prevents publication permanently as distinct from deferring it for a short time, for example pending trial of an action. Prior restraint operates in respect of some, but not all, forms of media. Generally, it is the visual media that is subject to prior restraint and the print media that is subject to post-publication interference. Thus, broadcasts, films, videos and DVDs are subject to licensing and/or classification regimes, which restrict what can be shown, whereas books, magazines and newspapers are not. The rationale seems to be that something that has a visual impact is more likely to cause harm and therefore a stricter regime is justified. The theatre proves an exception to this generalisation since it is a visual media, but not subject to prior restraint in respect of what can be shown.[75] Although licensing control over stage plays has been exercised by local authorities since it was vested in them by the Theatres Act 1968, s 1(2) of that Act made it clear that authorities could not impose conditions as to the nature of the plays or the manner of performance (except insofar as conditions were necessary in the interests of matters such as safety). This continues to be the position under the 2003 Act.[76]

3.7.11  Films, also subject to licensing control by local authorities, can, however, be subject to prior restraint in respect of what can be shown. This might be prior restraint by the British Board of Film Classification (BBFC) or by the local authority. The Board, a self-censoring body established by the film industry in 1912, issues age-related classification certificates ('U' for universal; 'PG' for parental guidance; '12'; '12A', for viewing by unaccompanied persons aged 12 years or older or younger persons accompanied by an adult; '15'; '18'; and 'R18' for restricted viewing) and was set up when local authorities were given the power by the Cinematograph Act 1909 to licence films shown in their area.[77] Since the Board's establishment, local authorities, when granting licences for film exhibitions, have usually imposed a condition to the effect that films exhibited must have a certificate from the Board. The courts have upheld the validity of such a condition, provided authorities use the Board only as an advisory body and retain the power to reject the Board's views when considering licence applications.[78] Thus local authorities themselves might restrict what can be shown, by refusing to issue a licence for films granted a certificate, and some authorities on occasions have done so.[79] The position is essentially unchanged under the 2003 Act and films continue to be subject to prior restraint by the Board and by the licensing authority.[80]

Since the exhibition of films involves prior restraint, any restrictions imposed are more likely to be regarded as constituting an interference with freedom of expression, not least since films are more heavily censored in England and Wales than in other European jurisdictions. This is due, at least in part, to the nature and composition of the Board as a classification authority. As a film industry body, the Board's decisions are influenced more by commercial considerations – the need to find the widest audience, which may require cuts to a film to secure a '15' classification – than by artistic ones. This may mean that decisions by the Board, and by local authorities whose licensing decisions follow the Board's classification, impinge on the creative freedom of film-makers and might thereby involve an interference with their Art 10 rights.

## 3.7.12 Direct or indirect interference

3.7.13 The most obvious form of interference with expression under Art 10(1) is direct interference, where some action is taken that expressly affects a person's rights. However, interference is not restricted to such circumstances. It can be indirect and this might arise in one of two ways. First, the interference may be a consequence of some other action taken. This could occur under the 2003 Act, where, for example, a licensing authority imposes a condition on a premises licence, which has the indirect effect of restricting a person's ability to carry on an artistic or musical performance at the premises to which the licence relates.[81] Whether this will constitute an interference will, it seems, depend on the extent of the impact resulting from the other action taken and the intention with which the action is pursued.[82] Secondly, there may be inaction of some sort that either itself affects a person's freedom of expression or results in a third party doing something that affects a person's freedom of expression. The use of the words 'without interference by public authority' in Art 10(1) seems to suggest that the public authority must *do something* in order to interfere and that interference can only be *by a public authority*. However the ECtHR has taken the view that Art 10 is not so restricted in scope and has held that 'positive obligations' can be imposed to take action to protect freedom of expression. Thus, Art 10 is seen as concerned not only with negative prohibitions, that is with precluding the doing of anything that interferes with expression, but also as encompassing positive duties to take action to protect expression.[83]

3.7.14 The extent to which action may need to be taken, however, is difficult to state with any degree of precision. It may be that the requirement extends only to taking action to prevent interference that would 'strike at the very substance' of the freedom and that there is no responsibility for actions of other persons that only indirectly affect or only partly affect expression. This seems to follow from the European Commission's decision in *Rommelfanger v Germany* (1989) 62 DR 151, a case involving a doctor's dismissal from employment in a Catholic hospital for expressing in the press an opinion on abortion that was not in conformity with the position of the Church.

When considering a claim by the doctor that there had been indirect State interference in that the German courts had failed to protect his freedom of expression against the sanction of dismissal, the Commission stated (at 160–61):

> It is true that under Article 1 of the Convention the State is required to "secure" the Convention rights to everyone within its jurisdiction. In certain cases it may therefore be necessary for the State to take positive action with a view to effectively securing these rights . . . [however] German law takes account of the necessity to secure an employee's freedom of expression against unreasonable demands of his employer, even if they should result from a valid employment contract . . . As regards employers such as the Catholic foundation which employed the applicant in its hospital, the law in any event ensures that there is a reasonable relationship between the measures affecting freedom of expression and the nature of the employment as well as the importance of the issue for the employer. In this way it protects an employee against compulsion in matters of freedom of expression which would strike at the very substance of this freedom . . . The Commission considers that Article 10 of the Convention does not, in cases like the present one, impose a positive obligation on the State to provide protection beyond this standard.

The Commission accordingly held that there had not been interference with the applicant's right to freedom of expression under Art 10 nor a failure to comply with positive obligations resulting from that provision.

### 3.7.15 Permissible interference

Once it is established (or accepted) that there has been an interference with the right in Art 10(1) to freedom of expression, there is then an obligation to justify that interference by reference to the tests set out in Art 10(2):

> The exercise of these freedoms, since it carries with it duties and responsibilities, may be subject to such formalities, conditions, restrictions or penalties as are prescribed by law and are necessary in a democratic society, in the interests of national security, territorial integrity or public safety, for the prevention of disorder or crime, for the protection of health or morals, for the protection of the reputation of others, for preventing the disclosure of information received in confidence, or for maintaining the authority and impartiality of the judiciary.

In order to justify the interference, it must first be established that the interference is 'prescribed by law', secondly that it is 'necessary in a democratic society', and thirdly that it is necessary in accordance with one of the various interests specified in Art 10(2) (national security, territorial integrity, etc).

### 3.7.16 *Prescribed by law*

3.7.17 As regards the 'prescribed by law' requirement, there will have to be a legal basis, whether at common law or by statute, for constraints on freedom and the legal constraints will have to be both accessible and sufficiently precise.[84] There may not be accessibility, for example, if there are unpublished guidelines to which a person does not have access[85] and there may be a lack of precision in the relevant law if it allows, or leads to, arbitrary interferences with the right to freedom of expression that are not capable of being subject to effective control or restraint. However, the fact that the law is ambiguous, or to some degree indeterminate, will not necessarily mean that it breaches the 'prescribed by law' requirement. All laws are to some extent vague and subject to interpretation, more so in some areas than others, and this has been acknowledged by the ECtHR. 'The Court recognises', it was stated in *Wingrove v UK* (1997) 24 EHRR 1, para 42, 'that the offence of blasphemy cannot by its very nature lend itself to precise legal definition' and similarly in *Müller v Switzerland* (1988) 13 EHRR 212, para 29, the court observed that it was not possible, in the case of obscenity laws, for them to be framed with 'absolute precision'.

3.7.18   The precise nature of the legal action or legal consequences need not be known and, provided it is foreseeable that legal action of some kind may be taken, this will meet the 'prescribed by law' requirement. Thus in *Open Door Counselling and Dublin Well Woman v Ireland* (1992) 15 EHRR 244, the provision of abortion advice was prohibited by injunctions by the State issued pursuant to a recently included constitutional amendment that provided:

> The state acknowledges the right to life of the unborn and, with due regard to the equal right to life of the mother, guarantees in its laws to respect, and, as far as practicable, by its laws to defend and vindicate that right.

No such injunction had been issued before, and the meaning and legal consequences of this provision had not previously been the subject of interpretation by the Irish courts. It was not therefore known how the State might, through its laws, guarantee respect for the right to life of the unborn. However, the ECtHR held that the applicants could foresee, from the general high threshold of protection afforded by the Irish Constitution to the 'unborn', that their actions might have given rise to official action on the State's part to stop the provision of abortion advice, even if they could not foresee exactly the form (that is, State injunctions) that action would take.

3.7.19   The licensing provisions in the 2003 Act, as enacted, seem likely to meet the 'prescribed by law' test. Under s 4(1), licensing authorities must carry out their functions under the Act with a view to promoting the licensing objectives specified in s 4(2) and this should preclude arbitrary interferences with the right to freedom of expression. In carrying out their functions, licensing authorities must, under s 4(3), have regard to their Statement of Licensing Policy, which under s 5 they are required to draw up and publish, and to any guidance issued by the Secretary of State under s 182. Since the Statement of Licensing Policy and the Guidance will both be publicly available, this should ensure compliance with the requirement of accessibility. Less clear is whether such Statements and Guidance, to which licensing authorities will have regard when determining applications, will preclude arbitrary interferences with the right to freedom of expression. Much will depend upon their nature and content and the manner in which it is taken into account.

### 3.7.20 *Necessary in a democratic society*

Secondly, it must be established that the interference is 'necessary in a democratic society', which will be the case if there is a 'pressing social need' for the interference. This involves examining the nature and impact of the particular interference in question, in the light of the (legitimate) aim that, it is claimed, necessitates interfering with the right to freedom of expression. This will be a question of fact in the circumstances of each individual case. In determining what is necessary in a democratic society, the question is not one of balancing competing interests, but rather regarding freedom of expression as paramount, with only compelling arguments sufficient to justify the interference. As the ECtHR observed in *Sunday Times v UK* (1979) 2 EHRR 245, para 65:

> The Court is faced not with a choice between two conflicting principles but with a principle of freedom of expression that is subject to a number of exceptions which must be narrowly interpreted.

As regards the 2003 Act, the Joint Committee on Human Rights (JCHR) has accepted that there is a pressing social need for regulation:

> The licensing regime serves legitimate aims, namely the protection of public safety, the protection of the rights of others, and the prevention of crime and disorder. It is legitimate to say that there is a pressing social need for regulation.[86]

Nevertheless, the JCHR had reservations about whether extending the licensing regime to performances of live music at all venues could be justified under Art 10(2):

> we consider that the proposed blanket requirement for all premises to be licensed before any live performance takes place in them, regardless of whether there is a real risk of noise or nuisance, the nature of the performance, the nature of the premises, or the number of performers and spectators, is somewhat heavy-handed . . . Because the licensing regime would apply generally to live performances, without regard to the circumstances in particular cases, we are not satisfied that the proposed system of entertainment licensing as a whole is a proportionate response to a pressing social need to regulate public performances, as ECHR Article 10.2 requires.[87]

The Government's response of making exemptions from the need to obtain a licence (see 5.3.33–5.3.43 below) and for fee exemptions for premises such as parish or community halls (see 6.3.1 below) went some way towards making the licensing regime more responsive to the requirements of Art 10, although not to the satisfaction of the JCHR, which stated in its Twelfth Report:

> We take the view that there is a significant risk that the proposed system of exemptions from the licensing requirements and from the applicable fees as currently set out in the Licensing Bill might . . . leave a patchwork of different licensing requirements without a coherent rationale, calling in question the existence of a pressing social need for the restriction on freedom of expression through a licensing regime for public entertainment, and so undermining the Government's claim that such a licensing regime is a justifiable interference with the right to freedom of expression under ECHR Article 10.2.[88]

The Government's response was to sidestep the issue of an incoherent patchwork of different licensing requirements in favour of emphasising increased protection for Art 10 rights on account of the deregulatory nature of the legislation:

> far from being more restrictive than the current system of regulation, the Bill will generally lead to a greater promotion of Article 10 rights. When compared with the current system of regulation, the new system is streamlined, coherent, cheap and simple and, if industry makes full use of the reforms, should encourage a significant opening up of the opportunities for performing a huge variety of regulated entertainment.
>
> This is not an area of law where we are moving from non-regulation to regulation and, generally speaking, what the Bill requires to be licensed in any event already requires a licence under current law. In terms of its general impact, the Bill will therefore not present increased regulation . . .[89]

Indeed, during the latter stages of the legislation's passage, the patchwork became more pronounced as further exemptions and restrictions, for example for morris dancing and for small premises, were introduced.[90] Whilst doubts may remain as to the compatibility of the legislation with Art 10, it is nevertheless open to Parliament to enact legislation that is incompatible with Convention rights, a point remarked upon by the JCHR,[91] and it may be that it has done so in this case.

### 3.7.21 Necessary in accordance with a specified interest

3.7.22 Thirdly, the interference has to be necessary in accordance with one of the specified interests in Art 10(2) and the exceptions will need to relate to one or other of these interests. Some of these will have application in respect of licensing decisions under the 2003 Act. As was recognised in the Explanatory Notes accompanying the Licensing Bill when it was published, a condition imposed on a premises licence that may involve a restriction on a person's ability to carry on an artistic or musical performance at the licensed premises would be an interference with his freedom of expression, but this may be justified as necessary in accordance with various interests under Art 10(2):

> given that a licensing authority may act only so far as is necessary to promote any of the licensable activities, it is considered that any such restriction will be justified under Article 10(2) as necessary in a democratic society in the interests of public safety, for the prevention of disorder or crime, or for the protection of health and morals or for the protection of the rights of others.[92]

Whether a particular interference will be justified in the light of these interests will involve an examination of various matters including, first, the 'expression' in question, secondly, the form of the interference, and thirdly, the reasons offered and evidence adduced in support of the interference.

### 3.7.23 The expression

On the first matter, although protection is afforded to a wide range of expression (see 3.7.4 above), not all types of expression are considered to be of the same value or worth. Therefore, a decision as to whether interference with expression in any given instance is justified by reference to being necessary in a democratic society will often involve arriving at a view about the importance of the particular type of expression in question, considering at whom it is aimed, and considering its impact or effect. Different types of expression might be accorded different weight or value and in this respect the ECtHR has, in broad terms, drawn a distinction between three categories of expression – political expression, artistic expression and commercial expression. Political expression, especially the freedom of the press to impart information and ideas on political issues, is highly regarded and seen as essential to the proper working of democracy.[93] Such expression has been robustly protected by the ECtHR and interference with it has proved difficult to justify under Art 10(2). Artistic or commercial expression, in contrast, is less important in the democratic process – it is supported more by the values of individual autonomy and self-development than self-government – and seems to have been accorded a lesser level of protection. In *X and Church of Scientology v Sweden* (1979) 16 DR 68, the European Commission found that commercial speech was protected by Art 10, but that a lower level of protection should be afforded than for the expression of political ideas. The Commission stated (at 73):

> It emerges from the case law of the Convention organs that the "necessity" test cannot be applied in absolute terms, but required the assessment of various factors. Such factors include the nature of the right involved, the degree of interference ie whether it was proportionate to the legitimate aim pursued, the nature of the public interest and the degree to which it required protection in the circumstances of the case.
>
> In considering this question the Commission again attaches significance to the fact that the "ideas" were expressed in a commercial advertisement. Although the Commission is not of the opinion that commercial "speech" as such is outside the protection conferred by Article 10(1) it considers that the level of protection must be less than that accorded to the expression of "political" ideas in the broadest sense, with which the values underpinning the concept of freedom of expression in the Convention are chiefly concerned . . .
>
> Moreover the Commission has had regard to the fact that most European countries that have ratified the Convention have legislation which restricts the free flow of commercial "ideas" in the interests of protecting consumers from misleading or deceptive practices. Taking both these observations into account the Commission considers that the test of "necessity" in the second paragraph of Article 10 should therefore be a less strict one when applied to restraints imposed on commercial "ideas".

This less strict test has been evident by the fact that the ECtHR seems to have been more willing to find interferences with artistic or commercial expression to be justified[94] and English courts have followed a similar approach.[95]

The same type of interference thus may or may not be justified, depending on the form of expression involved. Where film exhibitions are authorised under a premises licence or club premises certificate under the 2003 Act, a mandatory condition is attached to the licence or certificate requiring that the admission of children be restricted (see 6.4.4 and 8.4.2 below). In preventing children of certain ages being admitted to the exhibition, this might interfere with the freedom of expression of the film-maker. If the film is of a political nature and involves interference with political expression, this may well be seen as not justified under Art 10(2). If, on the other hand, the film is sexually explicit and interference is only with artistic or commercial expression, this may perhaps be justified, or at least more easily justified, under Art 10(2).

### 3.7.24 Form of the interference

On the second matter, the form of the interference, it will need to be shown that this is proportionate to the legitimate aim that it is claimed necessitates the interference. It is not sufficient that there is a 'pressing social need' for the interference, for it needs to be shown that the interference is proportionate to that need. This will involve an examination of the extent of the interference and the consequences of it. Therefore, if the interference goes too far and its extent is greater than necessary, it may be considered disproportionate. Thus, for example, in *Sunday Times v UK* (1979) 2 EHRR 245, an injunction issued pursuant to a rule of law banning any discussion at all of an ongoing case was regarded as going too far because it failed to leave room for discussion to take place when issues of public importance arose. In contrast, in *Ahmed and Others v UK* (1998) 29 EHRR 1, a restriction on political expression of local government employees, which was specifically confined to the top three levels of local

authority employees, who were engaged in political sensitive roles, and where provision was made in respect of levels two and three for exemption from the rule in
individual cases was considered proportionate. Under the 2003 Act, although there is
a 'pressing social need' for interference (see 3.7.20 above), doubts may arise as to
whether interference is proportionate in relation to the provision of regulated entertainment, given that there is an exemption under para 9 of Sched 1 where this is
provided in places of worship, but not in secular venues (see 5.3.39 below). If interference is not necessary in respect of places of public worship, and the exemption
indicates that it is not, it may not be necessary in respect of secular venues, so the
extent of the interference may be greater than necessary. This might give rise to a
violation of Art 10(1), as the restriction may not be justified under Art 10(2), and also
to a violation of Art 14 on the basis of discrimination on the ground of religion (see
3.9 below).

Similarly, if the consequences of the interference are particularly serious and less
onerous means are available to achieve the same objective, it may be considered
disproportionate. In *Castells v Spain* (1992) 14 EHRR 445, for example, the Government
could have used the media and press to defend itself against allegations made against
it without having to resort to criminal sanctions. Such a situation might arise in a
licensing context if, for instance, premises were frequented by children and an applicant for a premises licence wished to provide adult entertainment in a part of the
premises. If representations were received and the application rejected, this may be
disproportionate, as the legitimate aim of the interference, protection of children from
(moral) harm, might be achieved by granting the application and imposing conditions
that would prevent children being exposed to such activities.[96]

### 3.7.25 Reasons offered and evidence adduced in support of interference

On the third matter, the reasons offered and evidence adduced in support of the
interference will have to be 'relevant and sufficient' in the particular case. If this is not
the case, then the interference will not be justified under Art 10(2). Thus, in *Autronic
AG v Switzerland* (1990) 12 EHRR 485, for example, the State argued that a satellite
dish could pick up uncoded confidential messages, but failed to demonstrate that it
could do so. Similarly, in *Observer & Guardian Newspapers v UK* (1992) 14 EHRR 153,
the State failed to sustain its argument for the need to suppress a particular publication (*Spycatcher*) dealing with the Security Services and written by a former employee
(Peter Wright) when the material had already been published elsewhere and was
available in the public domain. In the context of the 2003 Act, this means that evidence
will be needed to substantiate restrictions imposed in accordance with the licensing
objectives and reasons given as to why the restrictions were necessary to promote the
particular objective(s).

### 3.7.26 'Particular regard' to the Convention right of freedom of expression

3.7.27  Section 12 of the 1998 Act provides:

> (1) This section applies if a court is considering whether to grant any relief which,
> if granted, might affect the exercise of the Convention right to freedom of
> expression.

(2) If the person against whom the application for relief is made ("the respondent") is neither present nor represented, no such relief is to be granted unless the court is satisfied–

    (a) that the applicant has taken all practicable steps to notify the respondent; or

    (b) that there are compelling reasons why the respondent should not be notified.

(3) No such relief is to be granted so as to restrain publication before trial unless the court is satisfied that the applicant is likely to establish that publication should not be allowed.

(4) The court must have particular regard to the importance of the Convention right to freedom of expression and, where the proceedings relate to material which the respondent claims, or which appears to the court, to be journalistic, literary or artistic material (or to conduct connected with such material), to–

    (a) the extent to which–

        (i) the material has, or is about to, become available to the public; or

        (ii) it is, or would be, in the public interest for the material to be published;

    (b) any relevant privacy code.

(5) In this section–

    (a) "court" includes a tribunal; and

    (b) "relief" includes any remedy or order (other than in criminal proceedings).

3.7.28 The meaning or impact of this provision is presently unclear. One view is that this provision does no more than merely give effect to the positive obligations required by Art 10. First, it makes provision for a regulated process, overseen by a court, to ensure that, where some sort of prior restraint is sought in respect of a publication, the right to freedom of expression is given proper and due consideration, as is required by the Convention. Secondly, it recognises and makes explicit the importance of particular media of expression, for example, journalistic material, which accords with ECtHR case law. A different view is that this provision, particularly s 12(4), attempts to give freedom of expression an exalted status compared to other Convention rights, so that it may (perhaps) take priority or be given prominence over competing rights such as the right to private and family life under Art 8 (see 3.8 below). The courts have not yet decided between these competing interpretations of s 12, although to the extent that the matter has been considered judicial opinion seems to be in favour of the former view. Thus in *Ashdown v Telegraph Group Ltd* [2001] Ch 685, para 34, Sir Andrew Morritt VC stated:

> It is submitted that the phrase "must have particular regard to" indicates that the court should place extra weight on the matters to which the subsection refers. I do not so read it. Rather it points to the need for the court to consider the matters to which the subsection refers specifically and separately from other relevant considerations.

On this view, it would seem that s 12 is simply concerned with providing a procedure in order to comply with the obligations set out in Art 10 of the Convention. If this is correct, then licensing authorities, when discharging their functions under the 2003 Act, should pay no greater regard to the right to freedom of expression than to any other Convention right.

## 3.8    ARTICLE 8: PROTECTION OF PRIVATE AND FAMILY LIFE

3.8.1    Article 8 is concerned with protection of private and family life and provides:

(1) Everyone has the right to respect for his private and family life, his home and his correspondence.

(2) There shall be no interference by a public authority with the exercise of this right except such as is in accordance with the law and is necessary in a democratic society for public safety or the economic well being of the country, for the prevention of disorder or crime, for the protection of health and morals or for the protection of the rights and freedoms of others.

3.8.2    The primary importance and object of Art 8 is to afford protection from arbitrary interference and direct intrusions into private and family life by State agencies, for example through searches, seizures and surveillance. Such interference could arise in respect of the exercise of inspection and search powers under the 2003 Act. Constables and authorised persons, for example licensing officers, have the power under s 59 to enter and inspect premises, before determination of an application for a premises licence, to assess the likely effect of the grant of the application on the promotion of the licensing objectives (see 6.15 below) and under s 179, if they have reason to believe that premises are being, or are about to be, used for a licensable activity, to see whether the activity is being, or is to be, carried on under and in accordance with an authorisation (see 11.19.1 below). Further, constables have a power, under s 180, to enter and search premises, and to use reasonable force if necessary, where they have reason to believe an offence under the Act has been, is being or is about to be committed (see 11.19.1 below). Powers might be exercised in respect of premises in which licensable activities are provided, but which also constitute a person's home, as in the case of premises where there is live-in accommodation, and in such a case the right to respect for private and family life under Art 8 will arise.

Lack of respect for private and family life is not confined to such cases and Art 8 protection also extends to a person's enjoyment of amenities and the quality of life in respect of his home. The general principles applied by the ECtHR have been set out in *Moreno Gómez v Spain* (2005) 41 EHRR 40 (at para 35):

Article 8 of the Convention protects the individual's right to respect for his private and family life, his home and his correspondence. A home will usually be the place, the physically defined area, where private and family life develops. The individual has a right to respect for his home, meaning not just the right to the actual physical area, but also to the quiet enjoyment of that area. Breaches of the right to respect of the home are not confined to concrete or physical breaches, such as unauthorised entry into a person's home, but also include those that are not concrete or physical, such as noise, emissions, smells or other forms of interference. A serious breach may result in the breach of a person's right to respect for his home if it prevents him from enjoying the amenities of his home.

There will undoubtedly be a measure of interference with private and family life from licensable activities taking place under authorisations (premises licences, CPCs and TENs) under the 2003 Act. Interference may take a variety of forms, prominent amongst which will be noise. Whilst this may engage Art 8 protection, proper regulation by the authorities will not involve a violation of the right. This will either be because respect has been shown for the right under Art 8(1) or because interference can be justified as necessary in a democratic society on one of the grounds mentioned in Art 8(2), for example the protection of the rights and freedoms of others, namely, those who wish to attend the licensable activities. Determining whether respect has been shown or whether interference might be justified will involve balancing competing interests – a fair balance has to be struck between the competing interests of the individual and of the community as a whole. If the balance is in favour of protection of the individual, the fact that interference may result from the actions of other individuals rather than from any direct interference by the licensing authority itself will not prevent an Art 8 claim from succeeding. The ECtHR, in *Moreno Gómez*, rejected the Spanish Government's contention that noise from discotheques and nightclubs came from private activities and consequently there had not been direct interference by the public authority in the right to respect for the home and private and family life. The ECtHR stated (at para 55):

> Although the object of Article 8 is essentially that of protecting the individual against arbitrary interference by the public authorities, it may involve the authorities' adopting measures designed to secure respect for private life even in the sphere of the relations of individuals between themselves . . . Whether the case is analysed in terms of a positive duty on the State to take reasonable and appropriate measures to secure the applicants' rights under paragraph 1 of Article 8 or in terms of an interference by a public authority to be justified in accordance with paragraph 2, the applicable principles are broadly similar. In both contexts regard must be had to the fair balance that has to be struck between the competing interests of the individual and of the community as a whole.

3.8.3     It can be seen, from the first quotation from *Moreno Gómez* in the previous paragraph, that a 'serious breach' is needed if there is to be a violation of Art 8 and the court in that case was of the view that there had been. In this case the applicant lived in a flat in a residential quarter of Valencia and over a number of years the City Council allowed an increasing number of licensed premises, such as bars, pubs and discotheques, to open in the vicinity of her home, making it impossible for people living in the area to sleep. Various attempts were made by the City Council to deal with the problem of noise, including passing a resolution in 1983 not to permit any more nightclubs to open in the area (although the resolution was never implemented and new licences were granted) and designating the area under a bylaw introduced in 1996 as an 'acoustically saturated zone'.[97] In such zones there was a limit on external noise levels and a ban on new activities, such as nightclubs and discotheques, that had led to the acoustic saturation but, notwithstanding this, the City Council almost immediately granted a licence (subsequently declared by a court to be invalid) for a discotheque to be opened in the building in which the applicant lived. After unsuccessful court proceedings for violation of her constitutional rights to life, physical and mental integrity, privacy and the inviolability of the home,[98] the applicant alleged a breach of her right to respect for her home contrary to Art 8 of the Convention.

In upholding the applicant's claim, the ECtHR rejected the Spanish Government's contention that the noise came from private activities and there had been no direct interference by the public authority in the right to respect for private and family life (see 3.8.2 above), indicating (at para 56) that the case 'does not concern interference by public authorities with the right to respect for the home, but their failure to take action to put a stop to third-party breaches of the right relied on by the applicant'. Further contentions that the applicant had failed to establish that she had been exposed to noise inside her home emanating from night-time disturbances and that, in any event,

Art 8 protection was restricted to the home and could not apply when the subject matter of the complaint was a nuisance outside the home were also rejected.

With regard to the contention that the applicant had failed to establish noise levels inside her home, the ECtHR stated (at para 59):

> The Court considers that it would be unduly formalistic to require such evidence in the instant case, as the City authorities have already designated the area in which the applicant lives an acoustically saturated zone, which . . . means an area in which local residents are exposed to high noise levels which cause them serious disturbance . . . In the present case, the fact that the maximum permitted noise levels have been exceeded has been confirmed on a number of occasions by council staff . . . Consequently, there appears to be no need to require a person from an acoustically saturated zone such as the one in which the applicant lives to adduce evidence of a fact of which the municipal authority is already officially aware.

With regard to the contention that Art 8 protection was restricted to the home, the ECtHR stated (at para 53):

> The individual has a right to respect for his home, meaning not just the right to the actual physical area, but also to the quiet enjoyment of that area. Breaches of the right to respect of the home are not confined to concrete or physical breaches, such as unauthorised entry into a person's home, but also include those that are not concrete or physical, such as noise, emissions, smells or other forms of interference.

The applicant was consequently entitled to the protection of Art 8 and the court found that there had been a breach of the rights protected in view of the volume of noise, which was at night and beyond permitted levels, and the fact that it continued over a number of years. The ECtHR stated (at para 61):

> Although the Valencia City Council has used its powers in this sphere to adopt measures (such as the bylaw concerning noise and vibrations) which should in principle have been adequate to secure respect for the guaranteed rights, it tolerated, and thus contributed to, the repeated flouting of the rules which it itself had established during the period concerned. Regulations to protect guaranteed rights serve little purpose if they are not duly enforced and the Court must reiterate that the Convention is intended to protect effective rights, not illusory ones. The facts show that the applicant suffered a serious infringement of her right to respect for her home as a result of the authorities' failure to take action to deal with the night-time disturbances.

There was clearly protracted inaction on the part of the City Council in the *Moreno Gómez* case and a 'serious breach' that prevented the applicant from enjoying the amenities of her home. In many cases, the breach will be less substantial than in this case and it may be less easy to ascertain whether there has been a violation of Art 8.

## 3.9    ARTICLE 14: FREEDOM FROM DISCRIMINATION

Article 14 provides:

> The enjoyment of the rights and freedoms set forth in this Convention shall be secured without discrimination on any ground such as sex, race, colour, language, religion, political or other opinion, national or social origin, association with a national minority, property, birth or other status.

It can be seen that Art 14 does not confer any right not to be discriminated against, but rather that there should be no discrimination in respect of the enjoyment of other rights and freedoms under the Convention. It is not therefore an independent right under the Convention in respect of which any claim can be made and an alleged violation of Art 14 needs to be coupled with an interference with another Convention right. Discrimination can be on a wide range of grounds, which cover most, if not all, of the forms that discrimination might take.

One particular provision in the 2003 Act may give rise to difficulties in respect of its discriminatory nature. This is the exemption in para 9 of Sched 1 for the provision of entertainment or entertainment facilities: (a) for the purposes of, or for purposes incidental to, a religious meeting or service; or (b) at a place of public religious worship. Concerns were expressed about this exemption by the JCHR in its Fourth, Seventh and Twelfth Reports on the Licensing Bill, with the JCHR stating in its last-mentioned report that:

> We take the view that there is a significant risk that the proposed system of exemptions from the licensing requirements . . . set out in the Licensing Bill might:
>
> – give rise to an incompatibility with the right to be free of discrimination in respect of the enjoyment of the right to freedom of conscience, religion and belief under ECHR Articles 9 and 14, in so far as the exemption is given to premises used principally for the purposes of religion, or occupied by people or organizations on account of their religious beliefs or practices, and is denied to premises used principally for secular purposes, or occupied by people or organizations without a religious affiliation . . . [99]

The Government's response to this was to emphasise that 'attendance at entertainment held at such premises is in no way confined to, nor in any way distinguishes between, those of any religious belief' and 'there is no requirement for the entertainment to have any religious content'.[100] Further, whilst it was acknowledged that the exemption is not afforded to secular venues

> the creation of this exemption was prompted by a recognition, after discussion with representatives from various faiths, of the distinct pastoral role in the community played by many of the faiths and the wider responsibility that, for example, the church has in bringing the community together. By way of contrast, secular venues are run solely for commercial purposes and have no equivalent pastoral role in our society. Further, churches have a central role to the development of music in this country, particularly because the premises are large enough to stage performances, particularly classical pieces. For these reasons, it would not appear to me as though either Article 9 or 14 are engaged. However, if I am wrong about this, it is my view that there is an objective and reasonable justification for this exemption and that its existence in no way calls into question the pressing social need for the general regulation of public entertainment.[101]

It remains to be seen whether, on either count, this view is right.

## 3.10  CONCLUSION

The provisions in the 2003 Act are, in the Government's view, compatible with the Convention rights, although, as has been seen, doubts remain in respect of some of the provisions. Prior to the Second Reading of the Bill, a 'statement of compatibility' was made by the Minister of the Crown in charge of the Bill in the House of Lords,

Baroness Blackstone, in accordance with s 19(1)(a) of the 1998 Act.[102] It remains to be seen whether this view will be shared by the courts when interpreting the legislation and how 'creative' the courts will need to be to comply with the requirement in s 3 of the 1998 Act that legislation 'must be read and given effect to in a way which is compatible with the Convention rights'. Perhaps of greater practical importance will be the question of whether the licensing authorities themselves, when exercising their functions under the Act, will be acting in a way that is compatible with Convention rights. A licensing authority is a 'public authority' for the purposes of the 1998 Act[103] and s 6 provides that it is 'unlawful for a public authority to act in a way which is incompatible with a Convention right'. The possibility of acting in a way that is incompatible may arise at various stages when a licensing authority is exercising its functions under the Act, from drawing up a Statement of Licensing Policy to reviewing premises licences and club premises certificates once they have been in force for a number of years. Authorities will need to be vigilant and alert to the possibilities of acting incompatibly with Convention rights at all stages when they are discharging their responsibilities under the Act.

## NOTES

1  'Convention rights' are defined in s 1(1) of the Act as the rights and fundamental freedoms set out in: (a) Arts 2–12 and 14 of the Convention; (b) Arts 1–3 of the First Protocol to the Convention; and (c) Arts 1–2 of the Sixth Protocol to the Convention – see 3.3.1 below.

2  These include the House of Lords, Privy Council, Court of Appeal and High Court (s 4(5)), but do not include the Crown Court or magistrates' courts.

3  Under s 10 and Sched 2, ministers are empowered in certain cases to amend legislation by a 'remedial order'.

4  Less clear is whether it will include the Sub-Treasurer of the Inner Temple and the Under-Treasurer of the Middle Temple, who are licensing authorities under s 3(1)(f) and (g) of the 2003 Act – see 1.1.10 above. Given that, when acting in their capacity as a licensing authority, they are acting in a similar manner to local authorities, they may well be regarded as a 'public authority' for the purposes of the Act when exercising their licensing functions.

5  A person can, under s 7(7), make a claim only if he would be a 'victim' for the purpose of Art 34 of the Convention if proceedings were brought in the European Court of Human Rights at Strasbourg (ECtHR) in respect of that act. Thus a person can make a claim under s 7 only if entitled to bring proceedings before the ECtHR for violation of Convention rights. Normally, this will mean a person will need to show that the act has had some personal effect on him and he has been directly affected by it (*Amuur v France* (1996) 22 EHRR 533). However, there are exceptions where a reasonable likelihood or sufficient risk of being affected has sufficed, eg *Campbell and Cosans v UK* (1982) 4 EHRR 293 (pupils' attendance in school where corporal punishment was used held to be a sufficient risk of degrading treatment violating Art 3 of the Convention). Section 7(1) seems to anticipate that a sufficient risk of being affected might suffice, since it permits proceedings to be brought, not only in respect of actual unlawful acts, but also proposed acts, and a proposed act will not have had a personal effect on a person. Thus, for example, if a licensing authority were to include in its Statement of Licensing Policy drawn up under s 5 of the 2003 Act a matter that violated Convention rights, a person not affected by the matter (but who might be) could be regarded as a 'victim' and this could enable him to challenge the authority's inclusion of the matter.

6 If case law is not considered relevant by a court, or is considered relevant and is taken into account, but not applied, reasons may need to be given by the court for the decision that it has reached in this respect. Article 6(1) of the Convention provides that 'everyone is entitled to a fair and public hearing ... by an independent and impartial tribunal' and this right to a fair hearing requires courts to give reasons for their judgments, which have to be sufficient so that a party can effectively exercise any right of appeal: *Hadjianastassiou v Greece* (1992) 16 EHRR 219 – see 3.5.9 below.

7 Since 1998, the ECtHR has been the only Strasbourg institution exercising judicial functions or quasi-judicial functions. Previously, such functions were exercised by the European Commission on Human Rights, which could investigate alleged breaches of the Convention and give a decision on its findings as to the admissibility of the case for consideration by the ECtHR. The Commission could also submit reports on cases to the Committee of Ministers, giving an opinion as to whether there had been a violation of Convention rights, in cases decided by the Committee rather than the ECtHR (eg, cases not involving any new issue, which were not referred to the ECtHR). Although no judicial or quasi-judicial functions were exercised by the Committee of Ministers nor any reasoned judgments given when reaching its decisions, opinions of the Commission, like ECtHR judgments, were sophisticated, generally well reasoned and contributed to the general jurisprudence surrounding the Convention. Although judicial or quasi-judicial functions are now exercised only by the ECtHR, decisions, reports and opinions of the Commission nevertheless continue to be an important source of Convention law.

8 Articles 16–18 are concerned with interpretation of other Convention provisions. Article 16 permits parties to the Convention to impose restrictions on the political activity of aliens, notwithstanding the provisions in Arts 10, 11 and 14. Article 17 provides that nothing in the Convention may be interpreted as implying for any State, group or individual, a right of action aimed at destroying or restricting any right set out in the Convention to a greater extent than is provided for in the Convention. This is to prevent persons (extremists) using Convention provisions to destroy the Convention rights of others. Article 18 is concerned with preventing restrictions of rights permitted under the Convention being applied for purposes other than those for which they have been prescribed. This is to prevent legitimate restrictions being used for ulterior purposes, ie, being subverted and used as a pretext for measures that have other, improper purposes.

9 Protocols are amendments to the Convention, which have extended its original scope.

10 Article 14 is not an independent right under the Convention in respect of which any claim can be made and there needs, in addition, to be interference with another Convention right – see 3.9 below.

11 *Adolf v Austria* (1982) 4 EHRR 313, para 30.

12 *W v UK*, Commission Report, 15 October 1985, para 115.

13 The point has not been judicially determined, but support might be found in the House of Lords' decision in *R (on the application of Alconbury Developments and Others) v Secretary of State for the Environment* [2003] 2 AC 295, where a decision to grant planning permission was held to be a determination of civil rights, ie the right to develop one's own land.

14 See also *Soering v UK* (1989) 11 EHRR 439, para 87, where the ECtHR stated: 'the object and purpose of the Convention as an instrument for the protection of individual human beings require that its provisions be interpreted and applied so as to make its safeguards practical and effective'.

15 *Golder v UK* (1975) 1 EHRR 524 (serving prisoner, refused permission to correspond with a solicitor about instituting a defamation action against a prison officer, held to be denied the right of access, through his solicitor, to a court).

16 *Hadjianastassiou v Greece* (1992) 16 EHRR 219, para 33 (the decision-maker must 'indicate with sufficient clarity the grounds on which they base their decision' in order that an individual can determine whether or not to exercise any right of appeal).

17 See, eg the *Belgian Linguistic Case (No 2)* (1968) 1 EHRR 252, para I B 1, where it was stated that 'the provisions of the Convention and Protocol [1] must be read as a whole'.

18 The reference to penal policy related to the facts of the case, which concerned whether the practice of birching (ie corporal punishment by beating) as a criminal punishment in the Isle of Man was a breach of the prohibition under Art 3 against 'degrading treatment or punishment'. The court held that it was.

19 Although the ECtHR is not bound by its previous decisions, they are usually followed, but (older) decisions may be departed from where it is necessary to 'ensure that the interpretation of the Convention reflects societal changes and remains in line with present day conditions' (*Cossey v UK* (1990) 13 EHRR 622, para 35).

20 See also the remark of Goldring J in *Davies and Atkins v Crawley BC* [2002] LLR 68, para 136, a case concerning street trading and, *inter alia*, whether there was a violation of the right to protection of property under Protocol 1 Article 1: 'In my view, Article 1 itself bestows a very wide margin of appreciation.'

21 JCHR, Fourth Report of 2002–03, *Scrutiny of Bills: Further Progress Report*, HL Paper 50, HC 397 (Fourth Report), para 19.

22 The amendment became s 136(2) – see 11.2.1 below.

23 JCHR, Seventh Report of 2002–03, *Scrutiny of Bills: Further Progress Report*, HL Paper 74, HC 547 (Seventh Report), para 34.

24 The press and public may be excluded in certain instances (see 3.5.10 below). Article 6 clearly overlaps with the rules of natural justice that the courts have developed at common law, ie the *audi alteram partem* (hear the other side) rule, under which both sides should be heard before a decision is given, and the rule against bias, under which the decision-maker must not have an interest in the outcome of the proceedings, must not actually be biased nor must there be an appearance of bias (for which the test laid down in *Magill v Porter* [2001] 1 All ER 4653, para 103, 'is whether the fair-minded and informed observer, having considered the facts, would conclude that there was a real possibility that the tribunal was biased'). For bias under Art 6, see 3.5.14 below.

25 The requirement for a dispute is clearer from the French text of the Convention, which refers to '*une contestation*'.

26 For application to pre-hearing stages, see *Golder v UK* (1975) 1 EHRR 524 (3.4.3 above), and for application to costs, see *Robins v UK* (1998) 26 EHRR 527 (resolution of costs proceedings took over four years, with responsibility on the part of the authorities for about half that period, which was held to have constituted a violation of the right to a hearing within a reasonable time under Art 6(1)).

27 See *W v UK*, Commission Report, 15.10.85, para 115; and 3.4.2 above.

28 Even where the discretion to grant a licence is very wide, this will still constitute a 'right'. It has been argued, but unsuccessfully, that where there is a very wide discretion to grant a licence, applicants could not be said to have a 'right' under Art 6(1). In *Axelsson v Sweden* (1989) 65 DR 99, taxi drivers could obtain a reserve taxi licence for a reserve car; the reserve licence could be granted provided the applicant was suitable and the taxi service in question was deemed necessary and otherwise appropriate, without any more precise criteria specified in the legislation. The European Commission held that nevertheless there was a 'right' under Swedish law to obtain reserve taxi licences, stating (at paras 49–50):

> the discretion at issue in the present case was wide but not unlimited and had to be exercised in the framework of the applicable law ... the authorities did not have an unfettered discretion ... [and were] obliged, when examining the applicants' request, to take all the different public and private interests involved into account as well as the general purposes of the applicable transportation legislation.

There will therefore be a 'right' to licences under the 2003 Act, not only in cases where the licensing authority must grant the licence, but also in cases where it has a discretion whether or not to do so.

29 *Feldebrugge v Netherlands* (1986) 8 EHRR 425.

30 These included the fact that taxi drivers were required to perform a service regulated in

considerable detail by public authorities, as part of public authorities' provision of public transport services, with a substantial part of the licence holder's costs of running the business being covered by public funds: (1988) 10 EHRR 380, para 36.

31  The court rejected the Swedish government's claim that the licence was concerned not with civil rights, but with aspects of public law, eg it was the means of implementing the government's social policy of limiting total consumption and counteracting abuse and resultant damage to health. The ECtHR has shown an increasing willingness to find a 'civil right' within, or alongside, a public law right, especially where economic interests are involved.

32  (1989) 13 EHRR 309, para 46.

33  In this case, it was held that there been a failure to comply with this requirement where one side had been allowed to call one of the parties to an agreement, but the other side had not been permitted to call the other party to the agreement.

34  Details of the case can be found in the 1961 Yearbook of the European Convention on Human Rights at 346–54.

35  Although this statement is expressed with reference to national courts and in relation to the accused person in a criminal case (the case in question involved disclosure of military secrets of minor importance for reward), the requirement to give reasons will apply to decision-makers generally and to civil cases.

36  *Zimmermann and Steiner v Switzerland* (1983) 6 EHRR 17. In civil proceedings, time generally runs from commencement of the proceedings and will continue until enforcement.

37  *Benthem v Netherlands* (1985) 8 EHRR 1, para 40 ('a power of decision is inherent in the very notion of a "tribunal" within the meaning of the Convention').

38  *Campbell and Fell v UK* (1984) 7 EHRR 165, paras 33 and 81 (Board of Visitors in prisons).

39  'Only an institution that has full jurisdiction and satisfies a number of requirements, such as independence of the executive and also of the parties, merits the design "tribunal" within the meaning of Article 6(1)': *Beaumartin v France* (1994) 19 EHRR 485, para 38.

40  See *R (on the application of Alconbury Developments Ltd) v Secretary of State for the Environment, Transport and the Regions* [2003] 2 AC 295, where the House of Lords held that this was the case where the Secretary of State, who was not himself an independent tribunal, had called in a planning application under s 77 of the Town and Country Planning Act 1990 for his own determination.

41  The weight to be attached to particular considerations, if they are relevant, is a matter for the authority to decide. As Lord Keith observed in *Tesco Stores Ltd v Secretary for State for the Environment* [1995] 1WLR 759 at 765, 'it is entirely for the decision maker to attribute to the relevant considerations such weight as he thinks fit, and the courts will not interfere unless he has acted unreasonably in the *Wednesbury* sense'.

42  His Lordship also found support for his opinion in the following statement in *Kingsley v UK* (2002) 35 EHRR 177, para 32, a case where the Gaming Board had decided the applicant was not a fit and proper person to hold a management position in the gaming industry, a decision from which there was no right of appeal:

> The subject matter of the decision appealed against was . . . a classic exercise of administrative discretion, and to this extent the current case is analogous to the case of *Bryan*, where planning matters were initially determined by the local authority and then by an inspector . . . The Court does not accept the applicant's contentions that, because of what was at stake for him, he should have had the benefit of a full court hearing on both the facts and the law.

43  It is uncertain whether the objective test of 'legitimate doubt' differs in substance from the common-law test of a 'real possibility of bias' in *Magill v Porter* [2001] 1 All ER 4653, para 103 (see 3.5.2 above), but the ECtHR, in *Gregory v UK* (1997) 25 EHRR 577, made no adverse comment on the common-law test.

44 It is thought that there would be an appearance of bias only if the member were to sit on the subcommittee hearing the application and not simply if he were a member of the licensing committee, since as a member who did not sit he would take no part in the decision-making process.

45 See 6.4.17 below where the involvement of ward councillors is considered in more detail.

46 Mere expression of views on subjects, however, does not in itself disqualify a member from sitting on a committee – see *Darker Enterprises v Dacorum Borough Council* [1992] COD 465 (a case involving views expressed about sex shops, which was decided under the common-law rule against bias).

47 *Woolmington v DPP* [1935] AC 462 ('Throughout the web of the English Criminal Law one golden thread is always to be seen, that it is the duty of the prosecution to prove the prisoner's guilt subject to . . . the defence of insanity and subject also to any statutory exception. If, at the end of and on the whole of the case, there is a reasonable doubt, created by the evidence given by either the prosecution or the prisoner, as to whether the prisoner killed the deceased with a malicious intention, the prosecution has not made out the case and the prisoner is entitled to an acquittal. No matter what the charge or where the trial, the principle that the prosecution must prove the guilt of the prisoner is part of the common law of England and no attempt to whittle it down can be entertained', *per* Viscount Sankey LC at 481). The burden of proof on the prosecution may also extend to disproving beyond reasonable doubt the existence of various 'defences' raised by the defendant, eg self-defence, duress. Where such defences are raised, the defendant will have merely an evidential burden, ie adducing some evidence to raise the issue and the legal burden will then be on the prosecution to disprove its existence.

48 It was recognised by the House of Lords, in the leading case of *R v Hunt* [1987] AC 352, that placing the legal burden on the accused might be done 'either expressly or by necessary implication'. The former might arise where a statute uses words such as 'it shall be a defence for the defendant to prove'. The latter might arise by virtue of the provision in s 101 of the Magistrates' Courts Act 1980, which provides that:

> Where the defendant to an information or complaint relies for his defence on any exception, exemption, proviso, excuse or qualification, whether or not it accompanies the description of the offence or matter of complaint in the enactment creating the offence or on which the complaint is founded, the burden of proving the exception, exemption, proviso, excuse or qualification shall be on him; and this notwithstanding that the information or complaint contains an allegation negativing the exception, exemption, proviso, excuse or qualification.

This applies to all summary trials (ie before magistrates) and, although there is no corresponding statutory rule for trials on indictment (ie before a judge and jury), the courts have held that s 101 restates an earlier common-law rule that applied to all criminal trials, including those on indictment – see *R v Edwards* [1975] QB 27 (a liquor licensing case where, for the offence of selling liquor without a licence, the Court of Appeal held that the burden of proof was on the defendant to prove that he had a licence) and *R v Hunt* [1987] AC 352, where *Edwards* was approved by the House of Lords.

For a detailed examination of the area of reverse onus clauses, see Dennis, I, "Reverse Onuses and the Presumption of Innocence: In Search of Principle" [2005] *Criminal Law Review* 901.

49 As his Lordship stated later in his judgment (at para 53), 'reading down . . . so as to impose an evidential instead of a legal burden falls well within the interpretative principles'.

50 No indication as to the burden of proof is given in Explanatory Note 223 to s 139 or Explanatory Note 245 to s 156 of the 2003 Act.

51 This is in contrast to the position in the *Attorney General's Reference (No 4 of 2002)*, which concerned offences in s 11(1) of the Terrorism Act 2000 of being a member of a proscribed organisation and professing to be a member of such an organisation, to which s 11(2)

provided a defence for a person to prove that the organisation was not proscribed and that he had not taken part in the activities of the organisation at any time while it was proscribed. The case of *Sheldrake* concerned being in charge of a motor vehicle in a public place, having consumed an excess amount of alcohol contrary to s 5(1)(b) of the Road Traffic Act 1988, to which s 5(2) provided a defence for a person to prove that there was no likelihood of his driving the vehicle whilst the level of alcohol remained likely to exceed the prescribed limit. In both cases, the maximum sentence for these offences includes imprisonment (10 years in the case of s 11(1) and three months in the case of s 5(1)(b)).

52  This decision, although cited in *Attorney General's Reference (No 4 of 2002)*, was not referred to by the House of Lords in its judgments. However, the decision was considered when the case was heard in the Court of Appeal (see [2004] 1 All ER 1) where the fact that the legislative scheme in *Halton* was a regulatory one seems to have been regarded as a matter of some significance. Reference was made to this by Latham LJ (at para 40) when comparing the case to the one that was before the court: 'That type of statutory provision [in *Halton*] is clearly different from the one under consideration in this case. In particular the context of those cases was that the statutory provisions were regulatory in nature'.

53  That a person may be deprived of the opportunity of raising the due diligence defence if criminal proceedings are not instituted does not constitute a contravention of Art 6, according to *Tesco Express v Birmingham City Council and Chief Constable of West Midlands Police* (2007) 70 *Licensing Review* 34, para 20: 'there is no fundamental principle to say that Tesco should have been prosecuted [under s 146] and have a right to be prosecuted' (Birmingham Magistrates' Court).

54  The Convention did not originally include any guarantee of respect for property, but Art 1 of Protocol 1, drawn up in 1952, subsequently afforded protection for property. A desire to avoid obstruction of economic and social programmes perhaps accounted for the original exclusion and this anxiety has influenced the formulation of Art 1, under which there is a strong presumption of government entitlement to interfere with property interests.

55  *S v UK* (1986) 47 DR 274, 279 (occupation of property without a legal right held to be not 'possession').

56  The case, involving a driving ban, was decided primarily on the ground of an alleged violation of Art 6(1) and the European Commission confined its remarks to the quoted statement when considering the alleged violation of Art 1. There are other European Commission decisions that follow a similar approach – see *Batelaan and Huiges v Netherlands* (1984) 41 DR 170 (licence for doctor to dispense medicines); *M v Federal Republic of Germany* (1985) 44 DR 203 (authorisation to practice medicines under a health insurance scheme); and *Størksen v Norway* (1994) 78 DR 88 (fishing licence).

57  These are the sale or supply of alcohol, provision of regulated entertainment and provision of late night refreshment – see s 1(1) and 5.1.2 below.

58  These are the sale or supply of alcohol and provision of regulated entertainment (the provision of late night refreshment being an 'exempt supply' for which authorisation is not required) – see s 1(2) and 5.1.3 below.

59  This will be where the licensable activities include the supply of alcohol. Where a premises licence authorises the supply of alcohol, the licence must include a condition that supply is made only when there is a designated premises supervisor in respect of the premises licence (ie an individual, who holds a personal licence, specified in the premises licence as the premises supervisor) and the supply is made or authorised by a person who holds a personal licence: s 19; and see 6.4.3–6.4.4 below.

60  See, eg the *Sporring and Lonnroth* case itself, where there was a long delay – 23 and 25 years in one case and 8 and 12 in the other – between an initial decision that property was likely to be expropriated for redeveloping the city centre in Stockholm and the execution of the decision. This was held to be an interference with peaceful enjoyment of property, even though there was no deprivation of or measure of control over the property.

61  This reference to the search for balance being inherent in the whole of the Convention needs to be treated with caution, since there are some Convention rights that are absolute. They take the form of a prohibition and no balancing of interests is needed – see, eg the prohibition on torture in Art 3, mentioned in 3.3.1 above.

62  See *James v UK* (1986) 8 EHRR 123, para 37.

63  Deprivation of possessions might occur in other instances, however, eg where there are powers of forfeiture available in relation to property used in connection with licensing offences. A constable has the power to require the surrender of alcohol from persons under the age of 18, under s 1 of the Confiscation of Alcohol (Young Persons) Act 1997. This provision has been amended by s 155(1) of the 2003 Act so that the power is exercisable in respect of sealed containers, if the constable reasonably believes that the person is, or has been, consuming, or intends to consume, alcohol in any relevant place, ie any public place, other than licensed premises, or any place, other than a public place, to which the person has unlawfully gained access – see 11.7.36 below.

64  *James v UK* (1986) 8 EHRR 123, para 54 ('the taking of property in the public interest without payment of compensation is treated as justifiable only in exceptional circumstances').

65  See, eg *Davies and Atkins v Crawley Borough Council* [2002] LLR 68, where Goldring J held that the local authority's designation of a street as a prohibited street under Sched 4 to the Local Government (Miscellaneous Provisions) Act 1982, which precluded the claimants from continuing to trade there from their mobile catering vans, did not require the payment of compensation for a fair balance to be struck:

> Mr Masters [counsel for the Claimants] submits that in deciding whether the use of the 1982 Act was proportionate, the Court should regard the absence of compensation as highly material. He submits it is a highly relevant factor in determining whether a fair balance has been struck . . . I have no doubt at all that the use of the 1982 Act on the facts of this case was proportionate: that it struck a fair balance and was well within the proper exercise of the Council's discretion . . . Fair balance does not require compensation in any case. In this case, where there was no question of the Claimants being required to cease trading, I am clear it does not. All that happened was that in the public good, and in common with others, they were required to move to a different position in the same general location (paras 138–39).

66  The court took the view that revocation of the licence where persons were unfit pursued this general interest because unfit persons might hamper implementation of the policy. It referred to the 'great social responsibility' involved in selling alcoholic beverages and in this instance found unfitness because of a lack of careful handling of the alcoholic beverages and some very serious discrepancies in bookkeeping.

67  Different justifications might apply to different activities, eg public nuisance for the playing of music and prevention of crime and disorder for the sale of alcohol. When commenting on the human rights' implications of the Licensing Bill, the Joint Committee on Human Rights (Fourth Report, para 8) stated, in relation to Protocol 1 Article 1: 'In view of the potentially damaging effects of alcohol on individual health and safety and on public order, there is a clear public interest in regulating the sale and public consumption of alcohol . . .'

68  *Handyside v UK* (1979) EHRR 737, para 49 ('Freedom of expressions constitutes one of the essential foundations of a [democratic] society, one of the basic conditions for its progress and for the development of [e]very man. Subject to paragraph 2 of the Article 10, it is applicable not only to "information" and "ideas" which are favourably received or regarded as inoffensive but also to those that offend, shock, or disturb the state or any sector of the population. Such are the demands of that pluralism, tolerance and broadmindedness without which there is no "democratic society".'). See also *Belfast City Council v Miss Behavin' Ltd* [2007] UKHL 19, para 10, where the House of Lords was 'prepared to assume, without deciding, that freedom of expression includes the right to

use particular premises to distribute pornographic books, videos and other articles' (per Lord Hoffmann). Freedom of expression is thus seen as the bedrock of the liberal–democratic form of society that the Convention is concerned with safeguarding, a society in which there is both respect and tolerance for divergent views and where disagreement, even on fundamental issues, is regarded as healthy and meriting protection.

69  *Müller v Switzerland* (1988) 13 EHRR 212, para 27 (where it was stated that artistic expression 'affords the opportunity to take part in the public exchange of cultural, political and social information and ideas of all kinds').

70  *Steel v UK* (1999) 28 EHRR 603, para 92 ('It is true that these [anti-road building] protests took the form of physically impeding the activities of which the applicants disapproved, but the court considers nonetheless that they constituted expressions of opinion within the meaning of Article 10.'). Acts such as those in this case are expressive in the sense that they allow people to identify themselves with a set of views or values.

71  *Autronic AG v Switzerland* (1990) 12 EHRR 485, para 47 ('Article 10 (art 10) applies not only to the content of information but also to the means of transmission or reception since any restriction imposed on the means necessarily interferes with the right to receive and impart information.').

72  It seems not to have decided whether 'expression' includes music, although it is thought that it will do so.

73  *Vogt v Germany* (1995) 21 EHRR 205 (teacher dismissed from post because of membership of, and acting as prospective parliamentary candidate for, the German Communist Party).

74  There may, however, be circumstances where the court is willing to find that a person is entitled to information in certain situations, eg to protect Art 8 rights of privacy, as in *Gaskin v UK* (1989) 12 EHRR 36 (access to files relating to childhood in care).

75  Historically, the theatre was subject to prior restraint, since a licence for stage plays was required from the Lord Chamberlain, who exercised powers of censorship over plays. The Lord Chamberlain's powers of censorship were abolished by the Theatres Act 1968 and plays were thereafter subject to post-publication control via the criminal law, eg the Act provided an offence of presenting or directing performances that were obscene (s 1) or which used threatening, abusive or insulting words or behaviour, with intent to or likelihood of occasioning a breach of the peace (s 6). A possible explanation of why the theatre may not be subject to prior restraint is that theatre audiences are regarded as more sophisticated and less likely to be affected by what they have seen than cinema audiences.

76  See s 22 for premises licences and s 76 for club premises certificates, and 6.4.6 and 8.4.3 below. The provision of 'regulated entertainment' is one of the licensable activities under the 2003 Act and the performance of a play falls within the meaning of this term – see Sched 1, para 2(1)(a); and 5.3.19 and 5.3.21 below.

77  The aim seems to have been to achieve a degree of uniformity in decision-making by the licensing authorities. The Board can require cuts to be made in films before issuing a certificate or can refuse a certificate.

78  *Ellis v Dubowksi* [1921] 3 KB 621.

79  Notable examples of films banned by some authorities include *A Clockwork Orange, The Life of Brian* and *Crash*. Conversely, authorities might grant a licence for films even though they have no certificate, eg the Greater London Council granted a licence for *More about the Language of Love*, although the film had been refused a certificate by the Board (see *R v Greater London Council ex p Blackburn* [1976] 1 WLR 550).

80  The power of licensing authorities, under the 2003 Act, to restrict what can be shown is, however, more limited than under previous law contained in the Cinemas Act 1985. Section 4(1) of the 2003 Act requires authorities, when carrying out their functions under the act, to do so with a view to promoting the licensing objectives, but there was no such

requirement under the 1985 Act. The imposition of age-related classifications of films will fall within the licensing objectives, since one of these is the protection of children from harm (s 4(2)(d)), but restrictions on adults through the banning of films, as in the case of those mentioned in the preceding footnote, may not fall within the objectives.

81  This example was given in Note 49 of the Explanatory Notes accompanying the Licensing Bill when it was published.

82  *Piermont v France* (1995) 20 EHRR 301 (A German MEP, following exclusion from one French overseas territory, French Polynesia, after participation in a pro-independence and antinuclear demonstration, was subsequently admitted to another French overseas territory, New Caledonia, but detained at the airport following a demonstration and was issued with an exclusion order. A consequence of the detention was that she was unable to express her views and this was held to constitute an interference with her freedom of expression: 'The exclusion order . . . amounted to an interference with the exercise of the right secured by Article 10 as, having been detained at the airport, the applicant had not been able to come into contact with the politicians who had invited her or to express her ideas on the spot' (para 81). There was accordingly an interference and, on the facts of the case, this was held not to be justified.).

83  For a statement to this effect in relation to freedom of assembly under Art 11, which it is generally accepted will have equal application in respect of Art 10, see *Plattform 'Artze für das Leben' v Austria* (1988) 13 EHRR 204 ('Genuine, effective freedom of peaceful assembly cannot, therefore, be reduced to a mere duty on the part of the State not to interfere: a purely negative conception would not be compatible with the object and purpose of Article 11 (art 11) . . . Article 11 (art 11) sometimes requires positive measures to be taken, even in the sphere of relations between individuals, if need be.').

84  See *Sunday Times v UK* (1979) 2 EHRR 245, para 49 of the majority judgment: ('(1) the law must be adequately accessible: the citizen must be able to have an indication that is adequate in the circumstances of the legal rules applicable to a given case; (2) a norm cannot be regarded as law unless it is formulated with sufficient precision to enable the citizen to regulate his conduct: he must be able – if need be with appropriate advice – to foresee, to a degree that is reasonable in the circumstances, the consequences which a given action may entail').

85  See *Khan v UK* (2001) 31 EHRR 45 (an Art 8 right to privacy case concerning Home Office Guidelines on the use of covert listening devices, which were not legally binding nor directly publicly accessible).

86  JCHR, Seventh Report of 2002–03, *Scrutiny of Bills: Further Progress Report*, HL Paper 74, HC 547 (Seventh Report), para 34.

87  JCHR, Fourth Report of 2002–03, *Scrutiny of Bills: Further Progress Report*, HL Paper 50, HC 397 (Fourth Report), para 18.

88  Op. cit., JCHR, Seventh Report, fn 86, para 3.4.

89  JCHR, Fifteenth Report of 2002–03, *Scrutiny of Bills: Further Progress Report*, HL Paper 149, HC 1005 (Fifteenth Report), App 2 (Letter to the Committee's Chairman from Richard Caborn, Minister for Sport, Department of Culture, Media and Sport).

90  See Sched 1, para 11 and s 177; and 5.3.41 and 7.5 below, respectively. The JCHR made no comment on these exemptions, noting only that the morris dancing exemption was one 'which, some correspondents feared, was discriminatory and did not accord with the principles underlying the Bill as a whole' (Fifteenth Report, para 5.5, note 40).

91  'A large number of correspondents wrote to us just prior to the Commons' consideration of Lords Amendments to the Licensing Bill on 8 July, arguing the case for further inter-vention before the Bill became law . . . A number of these were under the misappre-hension that the Government would be required to make a "section 19 statement" on the face of the Act, guaranteeing compliance with Convention rights. In fact, of course, the Human Rights Act expressly preserves the right of Parliament to legislate as it thinks fit, having due regard to Convention rights, and to the opinion of the Minister on these

matters, which is stated only when a Bill is first introduced into either House. In the case of the Licensing Act, Parliament has now legislated' (Fifteenth Report, para 5.5).

92 Explanatory Note 49. The reference to protection of health or morals would seem to be confined to children, as far as the 2003 Act is concerned, in order to fall within the licensing objectives – see s 4(1) and 4.1.1 below. The reference to protection of the rights of others will include the licensing objective of prevention of public nuisance.

93 *Lingens v Austria* (1986) 8 EHRR 103, para 41 ('These principles [of freedom of expression] are of particular importance as far as the press is concerned. Whilst the press must not overstep the bounds set, *inter alia*, for the "protection of the reputation of others", it is nevertheless incumbent on it to impart information and ideas on political issues just as on those in other areas of public interest. Not only does the press have the task of imparting such information and ideas: the public also has a right to receive them . . .'). As Lord Steyn has stated, in *R v Secretary of State for the Home Department ex p Simms* [1999] 3 All ER 400, 408, 'freedom of speech is the lifeblood of democracy'.

94 See, eg, *Müller v Switzerland* (1988) 13 EHRR 212 (paintings containing sexual material) and *Otto-Preminger Institut v Austria* (1994) 19 EHRR 34 (blasphemous film), where no violation of Art 10(1) was found and where the ECtHR placed particular emphasis on the Art 10(2) justifications. Conditions imposed on a premises licence may interfere with artistic expression by restricting a person's ability to carry on an artistic or musical performance at the licensed premises – see 3.7.22 above – but such interference may be found to be justified under Art 10(2).

95 See, eg the remarks of Lord Hoffmann in *Belfast City Council v Miss Behavin' Ltd* [2007] UKHL 19, para 16 ('The right to vend pornography is not the most important right of free expression in a democratic society and the licensing system does not prohibit anyone from exercising it. It only prevents him from using unlicensed premises for that purpose.') and the remarks of Baroness Hale at para 38 ('My Lords, there are far more important human rights in this world than the right to sell pornographic literature and images in the backstreets of Belfast City Centre. Pornography comes well below celebrity gossip in the hierarchy of speech which deserves the protection of the law.').

96 Article 10(2) refers to the protection of morals as justifying restriction (see 3.7.15 above) and protection of the morals of children may accord with promoting the licensing objective of protection of children from harm under s 4(2) of the 2003 Act, since, according to para 2.41 of the Guidance, 'harm' includes moral harm – see 4.2.14 below.

97 These are defined by Art 30 of the bylaw as 'areas in which the large number of establishments, activity of the people frequenting them and passing traffic expose local residents to high noise levels and cause them serious disturbance' – see para 15 of the court's judgment.

98 The applicant's case was dismissed because she had failed to satisfy the test that 'the level of acoustic saturation to which a person is exposed as a result of an act or omission of a public authority causes serious and immediate damage to his or her health' and she was held not to have established a direct link between the noise and the damage she had sustained – see paras 20–40 of the court's judgment.

99 JCHR, Twelfth Report, para 3.4. See also JCHR, Fourth Report, para 18 ('exemptions from the need to obtain a licence for places of religious worship where secular entertainment takes place . . . could engage other human rights issues by appearing to discriminate against occupiers and users of non-religious premises'), and JCHR, Seventh Report, para 35 ('exempting . . . places of worship but not secular venues from the licensing regime might give rise to discrimination and threaten a violation of the right to be free from discrimination under ECHR Article 14 taken together with Article 9 (the right to freedom of thought, conscience and religion) and Article 10 (freedom of expression)').

100 JCHR, Fifteenth Report, App 2 (letter to the Committee's Chairman from Dr Kim

Howells, Minister for Tourism, Film and Broadcasting, Department of Culture, Media and Sport).

101 Ibid.

102 Section 19 provides:

(1) A Minister of the Crown in charge of a Bill in either House of Parliament must, before the Second Reading of the Bill–

(a) make a statement to the effect that in his view the provisions of the Bill are compatible with the Convention rights (a "statement of compatibility"); or

(b) make a statement to the effect that although he is unable to make a statement of compatibility the government nevertheless wishes the House to proceed with the Bill.

(2) The statement must be in writing and be published in such manner as the Minister making it considers appropriate.

103 See s 6(3)(b), which provides that 'public authority' includes 'any person certain of whose functions are functions of a public nature'.

# CHAPTER 4

# LICENSING OBJECTIVES, STATEMENTS OF POLICY AND THE SECRETARY OF STATE'S GUIDANCE

## 4.1 INTRODUCTION

4.1.1 When discharging its functions under the Act, a licensing authority is required by s 4(1) to do so with a view to promoting the licensing objectives, which, under s 4(2), are:

(a) the prevention of crime and disorder;[1]

(b) public safety;

(c) the prevention of public nuisance; and

(d) the protection of children from harm.

However, these are not the only criteria when carrying out licensing functions, for s 4(3) provides that the authority 'in carrying out its licensing functions . . . must have regard to (a) its licensing statement published under section 5, and (b) any guidance issued by the Secretary of State under section 182'.

These provisions in s 4 represent an attempt to set the parameters for the discharge of licensing functions under the Act, by specifying what objectives or purposes licensing control is seeking to achieve and ensuring that decisions are directed towards achieving these ends. They also seek to ensure transparency in decision-making, by requiring a licensing authority to publish a 'Licensing Statement' setting out its policy in respect of the discharge of licensing functions. Since each authority needs to draw up its own policy, this ensures that the discharge of licensing functions remains a matter determined at local level. However, there is the introduction of an element of central control through the issue of Guidance by the Secretary of State, to which a licensing authority must have regard when discharging licensing functions, and this will include the drawing up of and keeping under review its Licensing Statement.

4.1.2 The three factors – licensing objectives, Licensing Statements and Guidance – in principle provide an attractive formulation for the discharge of licensing functions under the Act. There are express criteria against which decision-making can be measured, decisions can be made at the local level to take account of local circumstances, and a measure of consistency can be achieved by requiring decision-makers to have regard to the Guidance. However, the interrelationship between these three factors is a complex one. Thus decisions may seek to promote one licensing objective whilst at the same time impeding the promotion of another,[2] having regard to a particular aspect of the Licensing Statement may promote one licensing objective, but at the expense of another, and, although both the Licensing Statement and the Guidance may be seeking to promote the licensing objectives, having regard to the one may suggest a different decision from having regard to the other. In short, each of the licensing objectives themselves may prove to be competing criteria, as may the Licensing Statement and the Guidance, and the question of balancing these competing criteria will necessarily arise in a number of circumstances. Further, there will be the question of balancing promotion of the licensing objectives when discharging licensing functions with other objectives and considerations that may need to be taken into account in the decision-making process. The three factors, their interrelationship and their relationship with other objectives and considerations, are examined in further detail in the following sections.

## 4.2   LICENSING OBJECTIVES

### 4.2.1   Promoting the licensing objectives

The licensing authority is required to discharge its functions only 'with a view to *promoting* the licensing objectives' (emphasis supplied), so it is not necessary that the licensing authority achieves the licensing objectives or even that it discharges its functions with a view to achieving them. It is sufficient if the authority is acting with the purpose or intention of attaining the objectives. Although the licensing authority will presumably be seeking to achieve the licensing objectives as far as possible, the objectives seem to be more aspirational aims and criteria against which the actions and decisions of the authority will be judged when it is exercising its functions under the Act. It is unrealistic to expect attainment of the objectives, for if an authority grants a licence for a large-scale event at which alcohol is sold, some measure of crime and disorder is inevitable. When granting the licence the authority cannot prevent crime and disorder, but it can seek to do so by taking measures to minimise its occurrence. In doing so, it is likely that the licensing authority can properly be said to be promoting the licensing objectives, albeit with a recognition that the objectives cannot be wholly achieved. Judicial support for this might be found in the High Court's decision in *R (on the application of Murray) v Derbyshire County Council* [2001] Env LR 26, a case in which the local planning authority when granting planning permission was required to have regard, *inter alia*, to statutory 'relevant objectives' in relation to waste disposal contained in para 4(1) of Sched 4 to the Waste Management Licensing Regulations 1994, and where Kay J (at para [13]) approved the following statement of Richards J in *R v Leicester County Council, ex p Blackfordby & Boothorpe Action Group Ltd* [2001] Env LR 2, para 48:

> What matters is that the objectives should be taken into consideration (or had regard to) as *objectives*, as ends at which to aim. If a local planning authority understands their status as objectives and takes them into account as such when reaching its decision, then it seems to me that the authority can properly be said to have reached the decision "with" those objectives. The decision does not cease to have been reached with those objectives merely because a large number of other considerations have also been taken into account in reaching the decision and some of those considerations militate against the achievement of the objectives.[3]

Whilst the requirement in this case was to 'have regard' to the objectives, the principle seems to have equal application where there is a requirement to 'promote' objectives, as there is under s 4(1) of the 2003 Act.

When promoting and seeking to achieve the licensing objectives, it seems that the licensing authority is concerned not only with their direct promotion, but also with indirect promotion through encouragement and adoption of other objectives and strategies that indirectly impact upon the licensing objectives (see Guidance, para 13.55). This matter is further considered below (see 4.2.17).

## 4.2.2   Prevention of crime and disorder

### 4.2.3   *Meaning of crime and disorder*

The term 'crime' is reasonably precise and certain, encompassing conduct that comprises a criminal offence either by virtue of a statute or under the common law, but 'disorder' is less clear. The expression 'crime and disorder' is a commonly used one – indeed, it features as the title of a particular statute, the Crime and Disorder Act 1998 – but 'disorder' is not a clearly defined concept. It must be something that is not itself a criminal offence, otherwise it would have been sufficient simply to have referred to the 'prevention of crime'. The ordinary meaning of 'disorderly', according to the *Shorter Oxford English Dictionary*, includes 'contrary to public order or morality' and it seems to have largely acquired this meaning at common law for the offence of keeping a disorderly house. Thus in *R v Tan* [1983] 1 QB 1053, the Court of Appeal held that a house was disorderly where provision of services by a prostitute in private premises open to the public was of such a character and was conducted in such a manner as to amount to an outrage of public decency or was otherwise calculated to injure the public interest to such an extent as to call for condemnation and punishment. However, in the licensing context, a focus on morality seems inappropriate and it is instructive to consider meanings that have been attributed to 'disorderly' in other jurisdictions. The meaning of the expression was considered in some detail by the New Zealand Court of Appeal in *Mesler v Police* [1967] NZLR 437, where the President of the court, North P, stated (at 443):

> I agree that a person may be guilty of disorderly conduct which does not reach the stage that it is calculated to provoke a breach of the peace, but I am of opinion that not only must the behaviour seriously offend against those values which are recognised by right-thinking members of the public but it must at least be of a character which is likely to cause annoyance to others who are present.

Similar sentiments were expressed by Turner J (at 444):

> Disorderly conduct is conduct which is disorderly; it is conduct which, while sufficiently ill-mannered, or in bad taste, to meet with the disapproval of well-conducted and reasonable men and women, is also something more – it must, in my opinion, tend to annoy or insult such persons as are faced with it – and sufficiently deeply or seriously to warrant the interference of the criminal law.

McCarthy J also expressed a similar view (at 446):

> I agree that an offence against good manners, a failure of good taste, a breach of morality, even though these may be contrary to the general order of public opinion, is not enough . . . There must be conduct which not only can fairly be characterised as disorderly, but also is likely to cause a disturbance or to annoy others considerably.

The essential characteristic seems to be conduct that seriously offends against values generally recognised by society as being of a character likely to cause annoyance to others who are present, although not having reached the stage that it is calculated to provoke a breach of the peace (since, if it has reached this stage, it will constitute a criminal offence).[4] This seems a more appropriate meaning for disorder in the licensing context.

## 4.2.4   Promoting prevention of crime and disorder

The discharge of licensing functions will need to relate to the prevention of crime and disorder in the particular premises themselves or in the immediate neighbourhood of those premises. A contention that the premises will contribute in a general sense to crime and disorder will not suffice, nor will one that persons causing crime and disorder some distance away from the premises might have been at the particular premises. This is apparent from various statements in the Guidance, for example, para 11.6 states:

> After a licence or certificate has been granted or varied, a complaint relating to a general (crime and disorder) situation in a town centre should generally not be regarded as relevant unless it can be positively tied or linked by a causal connection to particular premises, which would allow for a proper review of the licence or certificate. For instance, a geographic cluster of complaints, including along transport routes related to an individual public house and its closing time could give grounds for a review of an existing licence as well as direct incidents of crime and disorder around a particular public house.

On the other hand, para 2.4 provides:

> conditions attached to licences cannot seek to manage the behaviour of customers once they are beyond the direct management of the licence holder and their staff or agents, but can directly impact on the behaviour of customers on, or in the immediate vicinity of, the premises as they seek to enter or leave.

At what point the behaviour of customers is considered to be beyond the direct management of the licensee once they have left the premises will clearly depend on the circumstances, but the further the customers are away from the premises the less likely that the licensing authority, when discharging its licensing functions, will be regarded as acting for the prevention of crime and disorder.[5]

### 4.2.5   Public safety

## 4.2.6   Meaning of public safety

The term 'public' will need to be read in a broad sense, since the licensing controls extend beyond circumstances when the public will be on the premises. In the case of premises operating under a club premises certificate (CPC), the premises will be open only to members of the club and their bona fide guests, and neither the members nor the guests will be members of the public.[6] Similarly, where entertainment or entertainment facilities are provided other than for the public (or a section of it) or for club members and guests, this constitutes a licensable activity if done for consideration and with a view to profit (see Sched 1, para 1(2)(c) and 5.3.3 below). 'Public safety' will need to read as 'safety of those on the premises' if this objective is to have any proper application in such situations. It will surely be given this meaning, since it would be absurd if the objective of promotion of safety could be discounted simply because those on the premises happened not to be there as members of the public.

Safety will include not only the physical safety of the people using the relevant premises or place (Guidance, para 2.19), but also the safety of any performers appearing there (Guidance, para 2.31). Safety will include both general safety and safety from fire, although the latter is now regulated in nondomestic premises by the

Regulatory Reform (Fire Safety) Order 2005, SI 2005/1541. This Order, made under s 1 of the Regulatory Reform Act 2001, has replaced the system of fire certificates under the Fire Precautions Act 1971 (which is repealed) with a general duty to ensure, so far as is reasonably practicable, the safety of employees; a general duty, in relation to non-employees, to take such fire precautions as may reasonably be required in the circumstances to ensure that premises are safe; and a duty to carry out a risk assessment.[7] The public safety objective is not, however, concerned with public health, which is dealt with in other legislation.[8] Similarly, the public safety objective is not concerned with physical safety insofar as this might be covered by other legislative provisions. Thus para 2.26 of the Guidance provides:

> Where there is a requirement in other legislation for premises open to the public or for employers to possess certificates attesting to the safety or satisfactory nature of certain equipment or fixtures on the premises, it would be unnecessary for a licensing condition to require possession of such a certificate.[9]

### 4.2.7  Promoting public safety

The safety of persons using the premises or place will relate not only to safety in respect of the physical state of the premises, which will include their curtilage and means of entry and exit, but also safety in respect of activities taking place on them, for example foam parties or the use of pyrotechnics or other special effects. Further, safety may also relate to the numbers of persons attending activities on the premises, since overcrowding poses a threat to public safety and a capacity limit in respect of the premises might therefore be justified. In addition, as para 2.27 of the Guidance recognises, 'capacity limits may be necessary in preventing disorder, as overcrowded venues can increase the risks of crowds becoming frustrated and hostile'. Under the previous system of fire certificates under the Fire Precautions Act 1971 a capacity limit may well have been included as a condition in a fire certificate for the premises and in such a case its duplication as a condition on a premises licence or CPC would not have been necessary to promote the licensing objective of public safety,[10] except perhaps if the fire certificate had been granted for premises when their future use for a licensable activity was not known. The Regulatory Reform (Fire Safety) Order 2005 similarly seeks to avoid duplication between conditions on premises licences or CPCs, whether relating to capacity limits or more generally, and obligations under the Order, with art 43(2) providing:

> At any time when this Order applies in relation to the premises, any term, condition or restriction imposed by the licensing authority has no effect in so far as it relates to any matter in relation to which requirements or prohibitions are or could be imposed by or under this Order.

This makes it clear that conditions only take effect subject to provisions of the Order, so that any conditions imposed by the licensing authority that relate to any requirements or prohibitions that are or could be imposed by the Order automatically cease to have effect, without the need to vary the licence (Guidance, para 2.20). Licensing authorities are thus precluded from imposing fire safety conditions where the Order applies[11] and, potentially, on its wording, art 43(2) is particularly restrictive. It seems to preclude conditions having effect where requirements or prohibitions *could* be imposed by or *under* the Order (emphasis supplied). If interpreted literally, this might mean licence conditions frequently will not have any effect, since it is likely in many instances that an enforcement notice under Art 30 or a prohibition notice under Art 31 could be served under the Order. Clearly Art 43(2) envisages the Order to be the principal form of regulatory control over fire safety, but it may be doubted whether Parliament intended that the role of licence conditions in relation to fire safety should be reduced to one of little or no significance. If, however, a purposive interpretation is given to Art 43(2) so as to extend it only to requirements or prohibitions imposed by the Order and not to ones which could be imposed under it by way of enforcement, licence conditions relating to fire safety might thereby retain some significance.

If a capacity condition is attached, in the interests of clarity and certainty it should specify whether the number includes or excludes staff and/or performers, although little indication is given in the Guidance as to the types of premises in respect of which capacity conditions should or should not be imposed.[12]

## 4.2.8  Prevention of public nuisance

### 4.2.9  Meaning of public nuisance

Specifying this as a separate objective is in a sense unnecessary, since public nuisance is a criminal offence at common law and therefore this falls within the scope of the first licensing objective of prevention of crime and disorder.[13] However, given the importance of the public nuisance aspect, no doubt the view was taken that this merited inclusion as an objective in its own right. The meaning of public nuisance was recently considered by the House of Lords in *R v Rimmington, R v Goldstein*, where the House approved the following definition contained in Archbold *Criminal Pleading, Evidence and Practice* (Sweet & Maxwell, 54th edn, 2005), paras 31–40, except for its reference to morals:

> A person is guilty of a public nuisance (also known as common nuisance), who (a) does an act not warranted by law, or (b) omits to discharge a legal duty, if the effect of the act or omission is to endanger the life, health, property, morals, or comfort of the public, or to obstruct the public in the exercise or enjoyment of rights common to all Her Majesty's subjects.[14]

Whilst the acts or omissions might be particularly serious, if they endanger life, health or property, they need not be and it will suffice if they endanger the comfort of the public or, to use the words of Romer LJ in *Attorney-General v PYA Quarries Ltd*, if they 'materially affect the reasonable comfort and convenience of life'.[15] Whether this is so will be an objective test of whether the interference is 'unreasonable' to the extent that persons cannot be expected to put up with it. Licensing authorities and responsible authorities will therefore need to make judgments about what constitutes nuisance and what is needed, in terms of conditions attached to premises licences and CPCs, to prevent it. As regards the impact of licensable activities at particular premises on people living, working and sleeping in the vicinity, excessive noise is probably the matter most likely to give rise to unreasonable interference, although (bright) light pollution, noxious smells and litter may also feature prominently. In relation to noise, authorities will normally seek to control this through conditions controlling its level, in some cases by simple mechanisms like ensuring that doors and windows are kept closed after a particular time in the evening and in other cases by more sophisticated mechanisms like the installation of acoustic curtains or rubber speaker mounts.[16] Bright lighting outside premises that is considered necessary to prevent crime and disorder may itself give rise to light pollution for some neighbours and measures to control light pollution will therefore 'require careful thought' (Guidance, para 2.37). Noxious smells from a takeaway food outlet or a mobile burger bar, and the accumulation of litter, may similarly unreasonably interfere with the reasonable comfort and convenience of life of those living nearby.[17]

For a nuisance to be 'public' there has to be what Lord Bingham in *R v Rimmington, R v Goldstein* referred to (at para 6) as a 'requirement of common injury': 'central to the content of the crime was the suffering of common injury by members of the public by interference with rights enjoyed by them as such'. Not all the public needs to be affected, but a significant section of it does and it is not sufficient if a large number of individual persons are affected:

> To permit a conviction of causing a public nuisance to rest on an injury caused to separate individuals rather than on an injury suffered by the community or a significant section of it as a whole was to contradict the rationale of the offence and pervert its nature . . .[18]

Further, there is a requirement of a mental element for the offence in that the person causing the nuisance 'knew or reasonably should have known' that the acts or omissions would cause 'a sufficiently substantial injury to a significant section of the public' *per* Lord Bingham at [2006] 1 AC 459 (at para 40). Accordingly, it seems that a significant section of the community as a whole will need to be affected for the nuisance to be public and that knowledge or negligence as to the section being so affected is needed for there to be criminal liability.

In the *PYA Quarries* case, vibration and dust from quarrying operations affected householders on two roads in the neighbourhood and it was held that there was sufficient evidence of a public nuisance. Similarly, in *Ruffell*,[19] there was a public nuisance where an acid house party, which was organised in unsuitable premises, was attended by a large number of people, resulting in a road leading to the site being blocked by traffic; local residents being disturbed by noise throughout the night; and litter and excrement being deposited in adjoining woodlands. Less clear is whether it will suffice if only a few people are affected. Paragraph 2.33 of the Guidance, perhaps optimistically, states that it might:

> Public nuisance is . . . not narrowly defined in the 2003 Act and retains its broad common law meaning . . . [and] the prevention of public nuisance could therefore include low-level nuisance perhaps affecting a few people living locally as well as major disturbance affecting the whole community.

Courts have generally been reluctant to recognise a nuisance as public unless the nuisance has been quite widespread in its impact, so, if the expression 'public nuisance' is interpreted in a technical sense and given its normal legal meaning, acting to prevent disturbances affecting only a few persons may not suffice. Where a only few people are affected this might be a private nuisance or a statutory nuisance under s 79(1)(a) of the Environmental Protection Act 1990 ('any premises in such a state as to be prejudicial to health or a nuisance'), for which an abatement notice can be served under s 80, but it is not a public nuisance. However, courts do not always interpret terms in their technical sense if this is not considered to accord with the intention of Parliament and it may be that the expression is given a wider and more flexible meaning, with 'prevention of public nuisance' interpreted to mean 'prevention of nuisance to members of the public'.[20]

## 4.2.10 *Promoting prevention of public nuisance*

4.2.11   If a licensing authority is seeking to promote prevention of public nuisance, it is not necessary to decide whether or not conduct does amount to a public nuisance. An authority, when discharging its functions, is concerned only to promote the objective of *prevention* of public nuisance. There need be no certainty of a public nuisance occurring, although whether an authority can be said to be acting for the prevention of public nuisance will be affected, at least in part, by the likelihood of a public nuisance occurring. Clearly, if there was little chance of its occurrence, it would be difficult to justify actions seeking to promote the objective of preventing a public nuisance, whereas conversely, if one was very likely to occur, actions could easily be justified. Less clear is where the line should be drawn between these two extremes and what degree of likelihood of a public nuisance occurring should be required to justify action to promote this licensing objective. It is submitted that the appropriate threshold should be neither a probability nor a possibility of occurrence, but a real possibility of a public nuisance occurring.

In seeking to promote prevention of public nuisance, it will be important for the authority to determine what conduct on the part of a licence holder might be taken into account. Obviously this might include noise or disturbance (hereafter 'disturbance') emanating from particular licensed premises such as a nightclub or public house or from within the curtilage of the premises. This might include outside areas, which are used by customers, following the smoking ban on smoking in indoor public places introduced by the Health Act 2006. Less clear, however, is the extent or parameters within which disturbance caused outside premises can be considered. According to paras 2.37 and 2.38 of the Guidance, the licensee will not have responsibility for disturbance taking place outside his premises, unless it takes place in the vicinity of the premises, and conditions should not seek to regulate conduct outside this area:

> 2.37 In the context of preventing public nuisance, it is . . . essential that conditions are focused on measures within the direct control of the licence holder. Conditions relating to public nuisance caused by the anti-social behaviour of customers once they are beyond the control of the licence holder, club or premises management cannot be justified and will not serve to promote the licensing objectives.

> 2.38 Beyond the vicinity of the premises, these are matters for personal responsibility of individuals under the law . . .

Under the previous law, the Court of Appeal in *Lidster v Owen* [1983] 1 WLR 516 rejected a contention that only matters taking place internally within the premises could be taken into account when deciding whether to renew the music and dancing licence for the applicant's discotheque premises and held that external considerations could be considered. The court in that case was concerned with whether the word 'regulation' at the beginning of s 51 of the Public Health Acts (Amendment) Act 1890 was 'apt to cover both internal and external considerations' (*per* Waller LJ at 521) and decided that it was. The external consideration in this case was public disorder taking place outside the premises and insofar as the case decided that disorder occurring outside premises could be taken into account it accords with the statement contained in the Guidance. However, as will be seen, the distance away from the premises where the disorder was occurring in that case may well have been greater than that envisaged by the Guidance as sufficing for the licensee to have responsibility for it.

The premises in question in *Lidster* were located in the Stateside Centre, situated in the centre of Bournemouth, adjacent to Glen Fern Road, on which there were two other discotheque premises in close proximity. The justices were of the view that the number of persons leaving the three discotheque premises at 1.00 am nightly was the principal factor creating the public disorder, which occurred in the area of Glen Fern Road and Old Christchurch Road (where there were a large number of other licensed premises with terminal hours of between midnight and 2.00 am). The Chief Constable sought to secure an earlier closing time of midnight (instead of 1.00 am) for the discotheques, which was accepted by the two other discotheques whose licences were renewed with this restriction, but the applicants refused to accept this and the justices accordingly refused to renew the licence. The Court of Appeal held that the justices were entitled to have regard to the character and location of the premises and to refuse renewal of the licence on account of the disorder occurring outside the premises, even though the premises were well managed. Slade LJ stated (at 524):

> the evidence before the justices showed that, throughout 1980, what the justices described as a 'quite unacceptable degree of public disorder' existed in the Glen Fern Road and Old Christchurch Road areas of Bournemouth, and that the principal factor creating this disorder there was the number of persons leaving the applicants' premises at one o'clock in the morning. I have no doubt that the justices were entitled to take these factors into account when considering whether or not to renew the applicants' licence.

4.2.12   It is debatable whether the disorder in this case can be regarded as occurring within the 'vicinity' of the premises, with the behaviour of customers still within the control of the premises management. Waller LJ referred to the evidence showing that there was a 'very considerable amount of violence and crime in the immediate neighbourhood of these discotheques', but it is not clear how far away from the premises this was occurring. According to Slade LJ, the disorder 'existed in the Glen Fern Road and Old Christchurch Road areas', so it seems to have been occurring some distance from the applicants' premises, but his Lordship had 'no doubt' that this could be taken into account.[21] If 'immediate neighbourhood' is equated with 'vicinity', then the statement in the Guidance will represent no more than confirmation of the application of the *Lidster* decision under the 2003 Act; but if 'immediate neighbourhood', in the context of the factual situation in *Lidster*, is a wider area than the 'vicinity' of the premises, as envisaged by the Guidance, the Guidance may be proffering a narrower view of the licensee's responsibilities than that indicated by this case. If this is the position, the question will arise as to whether the view expressed in the Guidance should prevail when an authority is discharging its functions under the 2003 Act, or whether the (arguably broader) view in *Lidster* should continue to have application.

Authorities, when discharging their licensing functions, must promote the licensing objectives, including prevention of public nuisance, and (under s 4(3)(b)) have regard to the Guidance, so they might interpret 'prevention of public nuisance' as encompassing only disturbance within the vicinity of the premises so as to accord with the view expressed in the Guidance. Such an interpretation might not accord with the decision in *Lidster*, although that decision might be distinguished on the ground that it was concerned with interpreting another statutory provision with different wording and with no requirement to promote any licensing objectives. On the other hand, the principle in *Lidster* was generally accepted as having application to later statutes on public entertainment licensing, such as the London Government Act 1963 and the Local Government (Miscellaneous Provisions) Act 1982, where the wording was also different from the statutory provision in *Lidster*. Further, there is nothing to indicate, either in the White Paper or in the Guidance, that any change in the law is envisaged as far as disturbance outside premises is concerned. In the absence of any indication to the contrary in statutory provisions, the normal assumption is that existing principles of law remain unchanged and *Lidster* might therefore continue to apply without modification. It will be appreciated that ascertaining the scope of the *Lidster* principle under the 2003 Act permits no easy answer. If called upon to adjudicate on this matter, the approach of the courts may well be to regard *Lidster* as establishing only that, as a matter of law, external considerations such as disorder outside the premises can be taken into account as a relevant consideration. The view may be taken by the court that it will be a question of fact in all the circumstances whether the disorder, as regards its (geographical) extent, can be related to the prevention of public nuisance. This will leave each case to be determined on its own facts and in accordance with the evidence.

## 4.2.13 Protection of children from harm

### 4.2.14 *Meaning of protection of children from harm*

The expression 'children' is not defined in the Act, but it seems almost certain to mean persons under the age of 18. This accords not only with the position under the general law, but is apparent from references, used elsewhere in the 2003 Act, to 'children'. Thus s 146(1) makes it an offence to sell alcohol to 'an individual aged under 18' (see 11.7.9 below) and the expression 'Sale of alcohol to children' is used in the heading to the section. Similarly, in respect of the mandatory condition for premises licences in s 20 that film exhibitions must require the admission of children to be restricted, s 20(4) provides that for the purposes of the section ' "children" means persons aged under 18' (see 6.4.4 below). However, for the offence in s 145, of allowing unaccompanied children on certain premises, s 145(2)(a) provides that ' "child" means an individual aged under 16' (see 11.7.3 below). As to protection from harm, it is clear that this will extend beyond physical harm, which will be covered by other licensing objectives. The physical safety of children will be protected by the public safety objective, whilst any infliction on children of physical harm may amount to a criminal offence (assault) and will thus be covered by the crime prevention objective. The objective of the protection of children from harm is intended to cover both moral and psychological harm as well as physical harm. Paragraph 2.41 of the Guidance provides:

> The protection of children from harm includes the protection of children from moral, psychological and physical harm, and this would include the protection of children from too early an exposure to strong language and sexual expletives, for example, in the context of film exhibitions, or where adult entertainment is provided.

Whilst 'children' in the context of the objective might include anyone under the age of 18, there may be occasions when protection is required only for younger children. This seems to be recognised in the above statement, with its reference to protection 'from too early an exposure' to strong language and sexual expletives. The implication is that older children (and it cannot seriously be contended to the contrary) do not need such protection. The same may be true in respect of exposure to sexually explicit material in films and plays. Where there is a commercial element involved, as with adult entertainment provided in clubs that feature striptease and lap dancing performances, the view traditionally taken has been that children of all ages need protection. A common condition attached to public entertainment licences authorising lap dancing has been that persons under the age of 18 should not be admitted. If a justification were to be advanced for this, it might be that exposure to the practices of commercial sex might inhibit the emotional development of children and convey a distorted view of sexuality, in which sex is seen as a recreational activity divorced from notions such as love, commitment and mutual respect.[22]

## 4.2.15 *Promoting protection of children from harm*

There is not seen to be a general need to protect children from harm when they are on premises where licensable activities are taking place and only where cogent reasons are evident should their access be restricted. Paragraphs 2.42 and 2.43 of the Guidance provide:

> 2.42 ... in the context of many licensed premises such as pubs, restaurants, café bars and hotels, it should be noted that the Secretary of State recommends that the development of family-friendly environments should not be frustrated by overly restrictive conditions in relation to children

> 2.43 The Secretary of State intends that the admission of children to premises holding a premises licence or club premises certificate should normally be freely allowed without restricting conditions unless the 2003 Act itself imposes such a restriction or there are good reasons to restrict entry or to exclude children completely.

Instances of where there may be good reasons to restrict or exclude entry might include premises:

- where adult entertainment is provided;
- where there have been convictions of the current management for serving alcohol to minors or with a reputation for allowing underage drinking, other than in the context of the exemption in the 2003 Act relating to 16 and 17 year olds consuming beer, wine and cider in the company of adults during a table meal [see s 150(4) and 11.7.25 below];
- where requirements for proof of age cards or other age identification to combat the purchase of alcohol by minors is not the norm;
- with a known association with drug taking or dealing;
- where there is a strong element of gambling on the premises (but not small numbers of cash prize machines); and
- where the supply of alcohol for consumption on the premises is the exclusive or primary purpose of the services provided at the premises (Guidance, para 2.44).

In some cases, such as the first two mentioned above, it may be necessary to exclude children altogether in order to protect them from harm, although in other instances, as where adult entertainment or films with restricted classifications are shown only in part of the premises, it may be sufficient to exclude them from that part at times when such licensable activities are taking place.[23] A further way in which children might be protected is not to exclude them, but to require them to be accompanied by an adult. This has application in respect of the showing of films classified as 12A (although there is no reason for it to be confined to the case of films). For such films, children under the age of 12 can be admitted if accompanied by an adult, in addition to the admission of unaccompanied children over the age of 12.

## 4.2.16 Licensing objectives and planning

There is a recognition that licensing functions under the 2003 Act are only one means of promoting the licensing objectives (Guidance, para 1.20) and that delivery of the licensing objectives should involve working in partnership with other authorities, including the local planning authority (LPA). Whilst licensing and planning are separate systems of regulatory control, similar considerations are likely to arise in licensing cases as in planning applications determined by the local planning authority. This is because, except in respect of the licensing objective of protection of children from harm, there is a clear overlap between the other three licensing objectives and planning, as each of the three is also a land use planning objective. Thus, for instance, the LPA, when considering an application for planning permission, is likely to be concerned with amenity and the public impact of the use of premises, particularly if unsociable hours are involved and use might detrimentally affect local residents, and any planning permission granted may accordingly restrict the opening hours of the premises. Licensing authorities, when considering applications for premises licences, might similarly seek to limit operational hours in order to promote the licensing objectives of prevention of crime and disorder, and prevention of public nuisance. Thus 'planning and licensing regimes involve consideration of different (albeit related) considerations' and each operates independently: 'Licensing committees are not bound by decisions made by a planning committee, and vice versa (Guidance, para 13.65).

Since there is no requirement for planning permission to be obtained before any application is made to the licensing authority under the 2003 Act, it is possible that opening hours might be considered in the first instance either by the LPA or the licensing authority, depending on which application is made first. It might be anticipated that in most cases an application will first be made for planning permission, since para 13.64 of the Guidance states: 'Applications for premises licences for permanent commercial premises should normally be from businesses with planning consent for the property concerned'. If no condition on opening hours was imposed by the LPA, the primary task of regulating opening hours will fall to the licensing authority, as was recognised by the High Court in *R (on the application of Blackwood) v Birmingham Magistrates and Birmingham City Council, Mitchells and Butler Leisure Retail Ltd (Interested Party)* (2006) 170 JP 613 (at paras 58–59):

> 58 ... once planning permission has been granted for licensed premises, an operational matter, such as opening hours, is intended by the Act to be regulated primarily by the licensing authority.

> 59. There are, of course, dangers in laying down any hard-and-fast rule, for the field is complex and there is likely to be a multiplicity of situations. Naturally, I am not saying that the planning authority may not, in appropriate circumstances, impose conditions on granting planning permission for licensed premises that concern operational matters. But there may be many circumstances where the planning authority could properly leave such matters to be regulated by the licensing authority. If the planning authority has not dealt with an operational matter, such as opening hours, the licensing

authority, having regard to the licensing objectives, has the primary task of determining what conditions should be imposed.

In this case, the LPA had not attached any condition on opening hours for a public house in a residential area but had attached a condition C6 requiring car park floodlighting not to be used outside of the hours of 9.00 am and 11.30 pm 'in order to safeguard the amenity of the occupiers of the premises/dwellings in the vicinity'. When an application was made under the 2003 Act to convert the existing justices' licence to a premises licence and to vary the existing hours for the sale of alcohol until 12.00 am, with an extra half-hour for drinking up time, thereby giving, effectively, a closing time of 12.30 am, the authority granted the application subject to conditions which, *inter alia*, limited outside drinking to 11.20 pm and and required the erection of signs asking patrons to be considerate of local residents when leaving the premises. The authority's decision was upheld on appeal in the magistrates' court and, on judicial review in the High Court, it was contended that a licensing authority, and, on appeal, a magistrates' court, must take account of relevant planning matters. This contention was rejected, Deputy Judge Kenneth Parker QC stating (at paras 61–62):

> 61. Looking at the present case, it seems to me that the starting point must be that there was no condition imposed on any relevant grant of planning permission which regulated the hours of opening at the pub. It was for the licensing authority, and, on appeal, for the magistrates, to decide this matter, having regard to the licensing objectives, in particular, the objective in respect of public nuisance. The licensing authority, and, on appeal, the magistrates, had to weigh for themselves objectively the evidence about, in particular, noise late at night at the Covered Wagon.

> 62. For that purpose was it relevant at all that the planning authority had imposed condition C6? Superficially it might seem so, but on closer analysis I am very doubtful of its relevance. Condition C6 . . . reflected a general policy against light pollution in residential areas late at night. For good reason the policy required compelling justification for powerful lighting, such as that emanating from the Covered Wagon's floodlighting, to be allowed at a late hour. Clearly the Covered Wagon could operate until 12.30 in the morning, albeit at some inconvenience to its customers and its staff, even if the floodlighting were turned off at 11.30pm. There was, therefore, no compelling justification for the floodlighting operating after that hour. However, once it is understood how the policies governing, on the one hand, opening hours generally and, on the other, light pollution, operated, there was no real tension between permitting the Covered Wagon to remain open to 12.30 in the morning, but requiring the floodlights to be turned off at 11.30pm.

> Nor, once the policy background is understood, was there any inconsistency between condition C6 and the absence of any relevant representations from the planning authority in relation to the proposed variation of the licence regarding opening hours. The planning authority, in my view, rightly treated the question of opening hours and noise pollution as a matter for the licensing authority. Nor did the planning authority act inconsistently when it later refused the application to vary the planning permission in respect of floodlighting, knowing that Mitchells had a varied licence to remain open until 12.30am. The specific policy restricting light pollution was still applicable, although the opening hours had been extended.

Accordingly, the court held that the magistrates had rightly declined to examine whether the proposed variation required planning permission or to speculate whether, if it did, such permission would be forthcoming, since that was a planning matter falling exclusively within the competence of the LPA. Similarly, the magistrates could not vary the existing planning permission for floodlights under condition C6 and had rightly declined to speculate how the LPA might respond to any hypothetical future application for variation of condition C6.

However, the position may be different if there had been a condition imposed on the planning permission regulating opening hours. Here, the licensing authority may well receive a relevant representation from the LPA as a responsible authority (see 6.4.18 below) drawing attention to this condition and the reasons for its imposition, which might incline the licensing authority to impose a similar restriction in order to promote the licensing objectives. It does not necessary follow that the licensing authority will do so and, in the event that it permits longer opening hours, the position would seem to be that during those longer hours there will be a breach of planning control, although no contravention of the 2003 Act. Accordingly, the earlier closing hours should be observed, with para 13.67 of the Guidance providing:

> when as a condition of planning permission, a terminal hour has been set for the use of premises for commercial purposes . . . [and] these hours are different to the licensing hours, the applicant must observe the earlier closing time. Premises operating in breach of their planning permission would be liable to prosecution under planning law.

In the event that planning permission is not obtained prior to an application being made under the 2003 Act, opening hours will in this instance first be considered by the licensing authority. The LPA, however, as a responsible authority can again make a relevant representation to the effect that, in order to promote the licensing objectives, some restriction in accordance with planning considerations might be needed on opening hours (and might be imposed when planning permission is sought). It will then be a matter for the licensing authority to determine whether or not the application should be granted and, if so, subject to what restrictions (if any) on hours. In reaching a decision on this, it will (presumably) have regard to the need, to accord with planning control, for there to be restrictions on hours.

It can be seen that the interaction between licensing control and planning control is a complex one, consisting of overlapping jurisdictions, in which restrictions on hours might or might not be imposed by licensing authority and/or by the LPA, and any restrictions may or may not be different. This measure of overlap may make the sentiment expressed in para 13.65 of the Guidance, that licensing applications 'should not cut across decisions taken by the local authority planning committee', a difficult one to achieve in practice. There is necessarily a degree of tension here and some degree of inconsistency, where separate jurisdictions employ different criteria, is perhaps inevitable.

## 4.2.17 Competing and additional objectives

According to the Guidance, none of the licensing objectives is to be regarded as having greater importance than the other objectives: 'Each objective is of equal importance.'[24] Whilst this is fine in principle, in practice situations are going to arise where there are competing objectives and action that will promote one licensing objective will impede promotion of another (see 4.1.2 above). In such cases, the competing objectives cannot be accorded equal importance or weight and it will be a question of striking a balance between the competing objectives. This will inevitably involve an assessment of their relative importance and the weight to be given to them in the circumstances of the particular case. Where the balance is a fine one, decisions are likely to be subject to appeal and this may in due course lead to a body of case law affording guidance as to relative weight. Thus, although in terms of importance each objective is equal, some may prove to be more equal than others.[25]

It seems inconceivable that licensing objectives are the only objectives to which a licensing authority must have regard when discharging licensing functions and that there cannot be additional objectives and considerations that can be taken into account. Section 4(1) provides only that a licensing authority 'must carry out its functions under this Act ("licensing functions") with a view to promoting the licensing objectives' and it does not expressly exclude other objectives or considerations. If an authority, when exercising its discretion, is to make a decision on the merits of the case, as it must (and there are frequent references in the Guidance to this, for example, paras 1.15, 10.40 and 13.14), it cannot ignore other objectives and considerations. It must seek to strike a balance between promoting the licensing objectives and promoting the wider social, cultural and economic benefits for the community that are derived from licensable activities taking place. There are several references in the Guidance to strategies and schemes that promote these wider benefits, for example tourism and transport, and these are likely to impact indirectly on the licensing objectives. Where the balance is struck will depend on the extent to which there may be harm to the licensing objectives when weighed against the community benefits. If there is a limited amount of harm to the licensing objectives from some licensable activity, for example some minor annoyance and disturbance is likely to be caused, but there are significant community benefits, for example provision of some facility not previously available, the balance is weighted in favour of authorisation for the activity to go ahead. Notwithstanding the harm, in the context of the application and on the merits, the authority can be said to be promoting the licensing objectives. If, on the other hand, a greater degree of harm was likely and the community benefit was more marginal, the balance may be weighted against authorisation for the activity.

## 4.3   LICENSING STATEMENTS

### 4.3.1   Introduction

Statements of Licensing Policy (SOPs), described in the Act as 'Licensing Statements', are statements of the position or view that the licensing authority wishes to take on particular matters in connection with the discharge of its licensing functions. SOPs, in short, are simply formal documents setting out the policy of the licensing authority on particular matters. Policies have several advantages, ensuring transparency so that individuals know where they stand and can plan their affairs, like cases are dealt with similarly so there is fairness and consistency, and there is promotion of efficient administration. As Lord Clyde observed in *R (on the application of Alconbury Developments Ltd and Others) v Secretary of State for the Environment* [2003] 2 AC 295 (at para 143), 'policies are an essential element in securing the coherent and consistent performance of administrative functions'.

Nevertheless, licensing authorities, like public bodies in general that are exercising discretionary powers, are not entitled to adopt a policy that allows them to dispose of cases before them without any consideration of the merits of the individual applications. To do so would fetter the discretion conferred on the authorities. A general policy is permissible, but due consideration must be given to the merits of the particular case. As Lord Reid stated in the House of Lords in *British Oxygen Co Ltd v Board of Trade* [1971] AC 610 (at 625):

> The general rule is that anyone who has to exercise a statutory discretion must not 'shut his ears to an application' . . . I do not think there is any great difference between a policy and a rule. There may be cases where an officer or authority ought to listen to a substantial argument reasonably presented urging a change of policy. What the authority must not do is to refuse to listen at all. But a Ministry or large authority may have had to deal already with a multitude of similar applications and then they will almost certainly have evolved a policy so precise it could well be called a rule. There can be no objection to that, provided the authority is always willing to listen to anyone with something new to say.

There may, however, be circumstances where this general rule does not apply and where, exceptionally, a policy may lawfully exclude exceptions to the policy adopted if to allow them would be inconsistent with the statutory scheme. As Kenneth Parker QC, sitting as a Deputy High Court judge, observed in *R (on the application of Nicholds and others) v Security Industry Authority* [2007] 1 WLR 2067 (at para 61):

> Mr Cragg's [counsel for the appellant] . . . argument rests upon the premise that the "no fetter" principle applies invariably wherever a discretionary power is conferred, whatever the statutory context. This argument . . . assumes that there is an exception to every case, but . . . it is not, in my view, supported by authority or legal policy. Lord Reid was careful, in the passage cited from the *British Oxygen* case [1971] AC 610 to refer to "the general rule." In most instances where a discretionary power is conferred it would be wrong for the decision-maker to frame a rule in absolute terms because to do so would defeat the statutory purpose. However, it seems to me that there are certain exceptional statutory contexts where a policy may lawfully exclude exceptions to the rule *because to allow exceptions would substantially undermine an important legislative aim which underpins the grant of discretionary power to the authority.* There is, for example, a well-known line of cases concerning "taxi" licensing where licensing rules, which admitted of no exceptions for any "special" circumstances, were held lawful: see, for example, *R v Manchester City Justices, ex p McHugh* [1989] RTR 285 and *R v Wirral MBC ex p The Wirral Licensed Taxi Owners Association* [1983] 3 CMLR 150.

In this case, it was held that the statutory scheme under the Security Industry Act 2001 empowered the Security Industry Authority, when setting out criteria for the grant of licences to work as a door supervisor, to make the commission of certain serious criminal offences an absolute bar to obtaining a licence, which admitted of no exceptions. Instances where a policy does not admit of exceptions are, however, likely to be rare and it is not anticipated that they will arise under the 2003 Act in respect of SOPs drawn up by licensing authorities.

### 4.3.2   Requirement for Statements of Licensing Policy

4.3.3    Section 5 requires each licensing authority to determine, for a three-year period, its policy with regard to the exercise of its licensing functions and the SOP must be published before the beginning of the period. The authority must thereafter determine and publish its policy for each subsequent three-year period. Section 5(1) and (2) provides:

(1) Each licensing authority must in respect of each three year period–

    (a) determine its policy with respect to the exercise of its licensing functions, and

    (b) publish a statement of that policy (a "licensing statement") before the beginning of the period.

(2) In this section "three year period" means–

    (a) the period of three years beginning with such day as the Secretary of State may by order appoint, and

    (b) each subsequent period of three years.

The licensing authority must consult various interested parties before it determines its policy. These include the police, the fire and rescue authority, representatives of licence and certificate holders (premises licences, personal licences and club premises certificates), and representatives of businesses and residents in its area. Section 5(3) provides:

> Before determining its policy for a three year period, a licensing authority must consult–
>
> (a) the chief officer of police for the licensing authority's area,
>
> (b) the fire and rescue authority for that area,
>
> (c) such persons as the licensing authority considers to be representative of holders of premises licences issued by that authority,
>
> (d) such persons as the licensing authority considers to be representative of holders of club premises certificates issued by that authority,
>
> (e) such persons as the licensing authority considers to be representative of holders of personal licences issued by that authority, and
>
> (f) such other persons as the licensing authority considers to be representative of businesses and residents in its area.

It will be for the authority to decide who are representative of the persons described in the above provisions and it is recognised in para 13.7 of the Guidance that 'in some areas, it may be difficult to identify persons or bodies that represent all parts of industry affected by the provisions of the 2003 Act, but licensing authorities must make reasonable efforts to do so'. Persons representative of businesses and residents might include, respectively, the local Chamber of Commerce and residents' associations or tenants' associations. Persons representative of licence holders for night-clubs and public houses might include the local Club Watch or Pub Watch and persons representative of off-licence holders might include the Association of Convenience Stores. Holders of licences for film exhibitions might be represented by the Cinema Exhibitors' Association and holders of theatre licences might be represented by various bodies, for there are several organisations of theatre managers. These include, in the West End, the Society of London Theatres; in regional areas, the Theatrical Management Association; the Independent Theatre Council, for fringe and small-scale theatrical performances; and the National Operatic & Dramatic Association, for amateur dramatics.[26] Holders of club premises certificates might be represented by the Club and Institute Union, although it is less clearly obvious who might represent holders of licences covering late night refreshment services. Personal licence holders may perhaps be represented locally by trade unions, professional bodies or by trade associations.

4.3.4    Paragraph 13.7 of the Guidance states: 'The views of all these persons/bodies listed [in s 5(3)] should be given appropriate weight when the policy is determined.' What will constitute 'appropriate weight' will be a matter for the licensing authority itself to decide. It will not be possible to give equal weight to the views of all these bodies, for there may be competing or different views put forward by them. The licensing authority will then need to decide whether to give greater weight to the views of some consultees than others. Which consultees' views are given greater weight may well depend on the particular licensing objective that is being addressed. With regard to the crime prevention objective, for example, greater weight may be given to the views of the police. Similarly, with regard to the public safety objective, greater weight may be given to the views of the fire and rescue authority. Unless the decision of the licensing authority is irrational or wholly unreasonable in the *Wednesbury* sense (see 3.5.13 above), however, it seems unlikely that the courts would interfere. The views of the consultees are relevant considerations to which the authority must have regard and the weight to be attached to these is a matter for the decision-making body and not the courts.[27]

Whilst the authority is required to consult those mentioned in s 5(3), it is not precluded from consulting other persons or bodies. Paragraph 13.12 of the Guidance, however, pointedly states:

> The Secretary of State has established fee levels to provide full cost recovery of all licensing functions including the preparation and publication of a statement of licensing policy, but this will be based on the statutory requirements. Where licensing authorities exceed these requirements, they will have to absorb those costs themselves.

Others that authorities might want to consult, as mentioned in the Guidance, include Crime and Disorder Reduction Partnerships,[28] British Transport Police, local accident and emergency departments, bodies representing consumers, local police consultive groups or those charged locally with the promotion of tourism.[29] Examples not mentioned might include the area child protection committee and any area Licensing Officers Group or Liaison Committee. Whilst licensing authorities 'should consider very carefully whether a full consultation is appropriate as a limited consultation may not allow all persons sufficient opportunity to comment on and influence local policy' (Guidance, para 13.11), it is nevertheless 'for each licensing authority to decide the full extent of its consultation' (Guidance, para 13.9).

4.3.5    Once an initial policy has been drawn up, each subsequent policy is likely to be a repetition of earlier ones, with modifications in the light of the experience of application of the earlier policy. Authorities must keep their policies under review and provision is made for revisions to policies partway through the three-year period, for consultation with the various interested parties mentioned in s 5(3) in respect of any revisions, and for revisions or a revised licensing statement to be published. Section 5(4)–(6) provides:

(4)  During each three year period, a licensing authority must keep its policy under review and make such revisions to it, at such times, as it considers appropriate.

(5)  Subsection (3) applies in relation to any revision of an authority's policy as it applies in relation to the original determination of that policy.

(6)  Where revisions are made, the licensing authority must publish a statement of the revisions or the revised licensing statement.[30]

The extent to which, at the beginning of a three-year period, or in respect of revisions made partway through such a period, full consultation takes place will depend on the nature of the modifications being made. A full consultation may not be considered necessary in some instances and consultation may be confined to those mentioned in s 5(3), as paras 13.9 and 13.10 of the Guidance indicate:

> 13.9 ... Whilst it is clearly good practice to consult widely and to follow the Consultation Guidance published by the Cabinet Office, this may not always be necessary or appropriate. For instance, where a revision is proposed that merely updates contact details for the licensing authority or responsible authorities a simpler consultation may suffice.

> 13.10 Similarly, where a licensing authority has recently revised its policy within a three year period following a full consultation exercise it may not consider that further changes are necessary when determining the policy for the next three year period. As such, it may decide on a simple consultation with those persons listed in section 5(3) of the 2003 Act.

### 4.3.6   Content of Statements of Licensing Policy

There are some general matters which the Guidance recommends should be incorporated in the SOP. These include statements of the following:

- the licensing objectives (para 13.13);
- licensing is about regulating licensable activities, so conditions will focus on matters within the control of operators, centring on the premises and their vicinity (para 13.16);
- as regards vicinity, the focus is on the direct impact of activities at the premises on members of the public living, working or engaged in normal activity in the area (para 13.17) [but see 6.4.13 below];
- licensing law is not the primary mechanism for controlling nuisance and antisocial behaviour by individuals once they are away from the premises (para 13.18);
- a firm commitment to avoid attaching conditions that duplicate other regulatory regimes as far as possible (para 13.19);
- conditions will be tailored to the specific premises concerned, effectively ruling out standardised conditions, although attention may be drawn to pools of conditions which applicants and others may draw on as appropriate (para 13.20); and
- protocols with the local police and the other enforcing authorities on enforcement issues will be established, to provide for a more efficient deployment of licensing authority staff, police officers[,] environmental health officers, and others who are commonly engaged in enforcing licensing law and inspecting licensed premises, with targeting of agreed problem and high risk premises requiring greater attention and a lighter touch for low risk premises which are well run (paras 13.21 and 13.22).

Although the SOP can contain statements on the above (and other) matters, it cannot prescribe or lay down the contents of an application, which is a matter for the applicant (see 6.3.3 and 6.4 below). If a SOP were to give the misleading impression that an applicant had to meet certain requirements in relation to his application, it would not be in accordance with the scheme in the 2003 Act and would be *ultra vires*. The High Court so held in *R (on the application of The British Beer and Pub Association) v Canterbury City Council* [2006] LGR 596, where Richards J stated (at para 85):

> The licensing authority has no power at all to lay down the contents of an application and has no power to assess an application, or to exercise substantive discretionary powers in relation to it, unless there are relevant representations and the decision-making function under s 18(3) is engaged. If a policy creates a different impression, and in particular if it misleads an applicant into believing that he must meet certain requirements in relation to his application and that he lacks the freedom accorded to him by the Act and regulations, the policy is contrary to the legislative scheme and is unlawful.

The council's SOP was held to be 'over-prescriptive in a number of places, suggesting the existence of requirements that cannot lawfully be imposed on applicants' (para 88) and, whilst a proposed addendum represented 'a substantial improvement' in the policy, 'objectionable passages remain in place, and there is at the very least a marked tension between them and the addendum' (para 89). Careful attention to the wording of the SOP is therefore important to ensure that language is not used which might give a false impression as to what is required.

In addition to the above-mentioned general matters that the Guidance recommends should be included in the SOP, there are more specific matters considered in some detail by the Guidance and they are set out below.

### 4.3.7  Cumulative impact of a concentration of licensed premises

4.3.8    Although not mentioned specifically in the 2003 Act, a concentration of licensed premises in one area may have a potential impact on the promotion of licensing objectives, for example public nuisance and crime and disorder, and 'cumulative impact of licensed premises on the promotion of the licensing objectives is a proper matter for a licensing authority to consider in developing its licensing policy statement' (Guidance, para 13.24). A concentration of licensed premises developed in a number of city (and town) centres following considerable efforts during the 1990s to regenerate central areas, to promote them as '24 hour cities' and to develop the 'night-time economy' of pubs and clubs in 'partnership' with the leisure industry. Planning guidance from the Department of Environment facilitated expansion, with local planning authorities, in consultation with the leisure industry, encouraged 'to develop a clear strategy and policies for uses that support the evening economy of their town centres'.[31] In consequence, the numbers of licensed premises expanded largely unchecked, with concentrations often building up in particular areas.[32] The large number of outlets in relatively confined areas has led to various problems of disorder and nuisance, as para 13.25 of the Guidance makes clear:

> In some areas, where the number, type and density of premises selling alcohol for consumption on the premises are unusual, serious problems of nuisance and disorder may be arising or have begun to arise outside or some distance from licensed premises. For example, concentrations of young drinkers can result in queues at fast food outlets and for public transport. Queuing in turn may be leading to conflict, disorder and anti-social behaviour. While more flexible licensing hours may reduce this impact by allowing a more gradual dispersal of customers from premises, it is possible that the impact on surrounding areas of the behaviour of the customers of all premises taken

together will still be greater in these cases than the impact of customers of individual premises. These conditions are more likely to occur in town and city centres, but may also arise in other urban centres and the suburbs.

Accordingly, in such instances, a licensing authority can include in its SOP a 'special policy' (which might be described as a 'cumulative impact' policy or 'stress' policy or 'saturation' policy), the effect of which is the creation of a rebuttable presumption that applications for new premises licences or CPCs, or applications for variations that are likely to add to the existing cumulative impact, will normally be refused, following relevant representations about cumulative impact on the licensing objectives. This is unless the applicant can demonstrate in his operating schedule that there will be no negative cumulative impact on one or more of the licensing objectives (Guidance, para 13.29).[33] This presumption will operate, however, only if there are relevant representations[34] and, if none are received, the authority must grant the application in terms that are consistent with the operating schedule submitted (Guidance, para 13.30).

Variation applications that are likely to add to the existing cumulative impact can include ones to vary and increase the hours for existing authorised licensable activities and will be covered by a cumulative impact policy provided the variation is directly relevant to the cumulative impact policy. This might be the case, as the High Court held in *R (on the application of JD Wetherspoon plc v Guildford Borough Council* [2006] LLR 312 (*Wetherspoon*), if the variation would create further late hours drinking in a drink-led establishment in an area suffering crime and disorder because of the concentration of licensed premises and late hours drinking in such establishments in the area. In *Wetherspoon* the applicants sought to convert and vary in a number of respects the hours of operation under their existing licence, including opening from 11.00 pm to 2.00 am on every night of the week, for premises which fell within the Bridge Street area of Guildford. This was an area where the total capacity of all licensed premises exceeded 4,000 and for which the licensing authority had included in its SOP a cumulative impact policy for new applications and material variations. The application for variation was refused, the subcommittee hearing the application taking the view that the applicants had not demonstrated that the extended hours would not add to the cumulative impact on crime and disorder in the area. A subsequent appeal to the magistrates' court was abandoned in favour of a judicial review application on the ground that the cumulative impact policy and the presumption against the grant of new licences or material variations could not lawfully be applied to a variation application which merely sought an increase in hours for the existing authorised licensable activities. Such a variation, it was contended, was not a 'material variation' under the SOP. The High Court rejected this contention, stating that there is 'nothing in the guidance that expressly precludes or restricts the applicability of cumulative impact policies to variations which only seek to lengthen licensing hours' (para 66), nor should any limit be implied since this 'would take a common class of applications out of the scope of the special policy and significantly reduce its efficacy' (para 71). The licensing authority's SOP was expressed to include 'material variations' and these 'are capable of including a variation of hours if such variation is directly relevant to the cumulative impact policy' (para 83).

4.3.9    In order to include a special policy, it is not sufficient simply that there is a heavy concentration of licensed premises in the area and there needs to be an evidential basis demonstrating the cumulative impact of the concentration. This might be provided from information collated by Crime and Disorder Reduction Partnerships on antisocial behaviour and crime prevention strategies, from information collected by environmental health officers on complaints relating to noise disturbance, and from information disseminated at local licensing group and forum meetings (Guidance, para 13.26). Additional information might be provided from a postal survey of residents in an area that might be the subject of a cumulative impact policy and from an evening and night-time observational study of low-level nuisance behaviour and crime on busy nights of the week.[35] After considering the available evidence and after consulting various interested parties, the authority then needs to be satisfied that inclusion of a special policy in the SOP is both appropriate and necessary (Guidance, para 13.27). Paragraph 13.28 summarises the steps that need to be taken in order to include a 'special policy':

- identify concern about crime and disorder or public nuisance;
- consider whether there is good evidence that crime and disorder and nuisance are happening and are caused by the customers of licensed premises, or that the risk of cumulative impact is imminent;
- identify the boundaries of the area where problems are arising;
- consult with those specified by section 5(3) of the 2003 Act (see 4.3.3 above) and subject to the outcome of the consultation include and publish details of special policy in licensing policy statement.

Whilst acknowledging that cumulative impact might be considered, the Guidance nevertheless sets parameters for the adoption of the policy and within which it might operate and be applied. First, the policy should normally be adopted only in respect of on-licensed premises and be applied only to premises likely to add to the cumulative effect on licensing objectives. Paragraphs 13.33 and 13.34 of the Guidance provide:

13.33 It would normally not be justifiable to adopt a special policy on the basis of a concentration of shops, stores or supermarkets selling alcohol for consumption off the premises. Special policies will usually address the impact of a concentration of licensed premises selling alcohol for consumption on the premises.

13.34 A special policy should never be absolute. Statements of licensing policy should always allow for the circumstances of each application to be considered properly and for licences and certificates that are unlikely to add to the cumulative impact on the licensing objectives to be granted ... The impact can be expected to be different for premises with different styles and characteristics. For example, while a large nightclub or high capacity public house might add to problems of cumulative impact, a small restaurant or a theatre may not. If the licensing authority decides that an application should be refused, it will still need to show that the grant of the application would undermine the promotion of one of the licensing objectives and that necessary conditions would be ineffective in preventing the problems involved.

Secondly, special policies should never be used as a ground for revoking an existing licence or certificate when relevant representations are received about problems with those premises, nor for rejecting applications to vary except where variation is directly relevant to the special policy, for example where the variation sought is a significant increase in the capacity limits of the premises (Guidance, paras 13.35 and 13.36). Thirdly, special policies cannot justify, and should not include, provisions for a terminal hour in a particular area[36] nor must they impose quotas – based on either the number of premises or the capacity of those premises – that restrict the consideration of any application on its individual merits or which seek to impose limitations on trading hours in particular areas (Guidance, paras 13.37 and 13.38).[37]

Further, even where special policies of refusing licences have been adopted, they 'should be reviewed regularly to assess whether they are needed any longer or need expanding' (Guidance, para 13.31) and the SOP should set out other mechanisms that are available for dealing with problems arising from a concentration of premises, to 'enable the general public to appreciate the breadth of the strategy for addressing these problems' (Guidance, para 13.39). These other mechanisms include:

- planning controls;
- positive measures to create a safe and clean town centre environment in partnership with local businesses, transport operators and other departments of the local authority;
- the provision of CCTV surveillance in town centres, ample taxi ranks, provision of public conveniences open late at night, street cleaning and litter patrols;
- powers of local authorities to designate parts of the local authority area as places where alcohol may not be consumed publicly;
- police enforcement of the general law concerning disorder and antisocial behaviour, including the issuing of fixed penalty notices (see 11.5.9 below);
- prosecution of any personal licence holder or member of staff at such premises who is selling alcohol to people who are drunk;
- confiscation of alcohol from adults and children in designated areas;
- police powers to close down instantly, for up to 24 hours, any licensed premises or temporary event on grounds of disorder, the likelihood of disorder or excessive noise emanating from the premises; and
- power for the police, other responsible authorities or a local resident or business to seek a review of the licence or certificate in question;
- other local initiatives that similarly address these problems.

The Guidance, by focusing on limitations in respect of a special policy, the need for regular review following adoption and by highlighting other mechanisms for resolving problems arising from a concentration of premises, appears to envisage special policies having relatively limited scope.[38] The conclusion seems to be that, whilst such policies are possible, the Guidance does not overly encourage their use. Notwithstanding this, a number of authorities have included a special policy on cumulative impact in their SOPs. The areas where such policies have been adopted have generally been in the larger urban cities and towns, although many authorities whose districts do not include such areas have effectively reserved the right to introduce one by making provision for a special policy in their SOP should the need arise. In some instances where policies have been adopted, they have indicated that all applications within the relevant location will be refused unless they are for 'core' hours set out in the SOP. Where this approach is adopted, this might be applied uniformly to all applications or, less extensively, to applications for new licences or certificates or 'material' variations to existing ones. A 'core' hours approach imposes a significant restriction on the 2003 Act's underlying market-based philosophy that operators should make market-based decisions about how they wish to undertake licensable activities at their premises (see 1.2.4 above) and does not accord with the notion that flexible hours can reduce the impact of large numbers of persons leaving premises at certain times. This is not, however, inconsistent with the recommendation in para 13.40 of the Guidance (see 4.3.10 below) that SOPs should recognise that flexible licensing hours for the sale of alcohol can help to avoid concentrations of customers leaving premises at the same time, since this recommendation for recognition is 'in some circumstances' and presumably these do not include cases where special policies on cumulative impact have been adopted. Further, although the SOP may indicate that all applications outside of 'core' hours will be refused, all applications need to be considered on their merits so there may be a departure from the policy in some instances. Such instances may well arise only rarely, especially if the SOP indicates that the policy is intended to be strict and will not be departed from unless there are genuinely exceptional circumstances.

Where the special policy is intended to be strict, it is likely that one or more of the responsible authorities will make a relevant representation so as to engage the committee's discretion (see 6.4 below), even if the responsible authorities themselves may be able to agree operating terms and conditions with the applicant, which would meet any opposition that they might have to the grant of the application. If the licensing authorty has intended its policy to be strict, it is felt that it should be afforded the opportunity to determine whether or not genuinely exceptional circumstances exist. Where the policy is less strict, however, and terms of operation can be agreed with the applicant, it may be that relevant representations are either not made or, if made, are withdrawn, thereby ensuring that the application is granted and the case does not proceed to a hearing. Whilst cumulative impact policies, on the one hand, can have positive benefits in preventing crime, disorder and nuisance, they do, on the other hand, have a tendency to create a stagnant pool of premises which remain largely unchanged and which are immune from competition from new and innovative premises adopting high standards. Given the increased focus on crime, disorder and nuisance (see 1.4 below), however, it might be anticipated that special policies on cumulative impact are likely to increase rather than decrease as licensing authorities review and determine the contents of their SOP for the next three-year period.

### 4.3.10  Licensing hours

The SOP should contain something about licensing hours, at least in relation to the provision of alcohol. It may also contain something about hours relating to entertainment and late night refreshment, although there is nothing in the Guidance about hours for these activities. As to alcohol, where this is consumed on premises, paras 13.40 and 13.41 of the Guidance provide:

> 13.40  The Government recommends that statements of policy should recognise that, in some circumstances, flexible licensing hours for the sale of alcohol can help to ensure that the concentrations of customers leaving premises simultaneously are avoided. This can help to reduce the friction at late night fast food outlets, taxi ranks and other sources of transport which lead to disorder and disturbance.[39]

> 13.41  The Government also wants to ensure that licensing hours should not inhibit the development of thriving and safe evening and night-time local economies which are important for investment and employment locally and attractive to domestic and international tourists. Providing consumers with greater choice and flexibility is an

important consideration, but should always be balanced carefully against the duty to promote the four licensing objectives and the rights of local residents to peace and quiet.

As to alcohol sold in retail outlets for consumption off the premises, para 13.42 of the Guidance indicates that such outlets should be free to sell alcohol at any time when they are open for shopping, unless there are good reasons for limiting hours (for example, because of persons congregating outside and causing disorder or disturbance):

> Statements of licensing policy should indicate that shops, stores and supermarkets, are free to provide sales of alcohol for consumption off the premises at any times when the retail outlet is open for shopping unless there are good reasons, based on the licensing objectives, for restricting those hours. For example, a limitation may be appropriate following police representations in the case of some shops known to be a focus of disorder and disturbance because youths gather there. Statements of licensing policy should therefore reflect this general approach.

Similarly, restrictions on sales in premises in local communities in the early hours of the morning when children are going to school may be an appropriate limitation to promote the licensing objective of prevention of harm to children.

### 4.3.11 Children

#### 4.3.12 Admission generally

The SOP might contain a statement that children are generally to have access to licensed premises, subject to their exclusion where it is necessary for the prevention of harm to them, although para 13.47 of the Guidance states that it is unlikely any general rules (that is, policies) can be laid down in this respect:

> A statement of licensing policy must not . . . seek to limit the access of children to any premises unless it is necessary for the prevention of physical, moral or psychological harm to them. Licensing policy statements should not attempt to anticipate every issue of concern that could arise in respect of children in relation to individual premises and as such, general rules should be avoided. Consideration of the individual merits of each application remains the best mechanism for judging such matters.

The reference to general rules being avoided seems to relate to rules concerning the prevention of harm rather than to rules generally permitting access for children. This is reinforced by the fact that the Guidance recommends that the SOP should merely 'highlight areas that will give rise to particular concern in respect of children' (para 13.48), which include:

- where entertainment or services of an adult or sexual nature are commonly provided;[40]
- where there have been convictions of members of the current staff at the premises for serving alcohol to minors or with a reputation for underage drinking;
- with a known association with drug taking or dealing;[41]
- where there is a strong element of gambling on the premises (but not, for example, the simple presence of a small number of cash prize gaming machines); and
- where the supply of alcohol for consumption on the premises is the exclusive or primary purpose of the services provided at the premises.

The options for restricting access range from full exclusion of persons under 18 when any licensable activities are taking place (for example, for lap dancing clubs, gaming clubs) to qualified admission for children, which might include:

- limitations on the hours when children may be present;
- limitations excluding the presence of children under certain ages when particular specified activities are taking place;
- limitations on the parts of premises to which children might be given access;
- age limitations (below 18); and
- requirements for accompanying adults (including, for example, a combination of requirements which provide that children under a particular age must be accompanied by an adult).[42]

The implementation of any such restrictions may well follow from representations made by the 'responsible authority' recognised by the licensing authority as being competent to advise it on matters relating to the protection of children from harm (see s 13(4)(f) and 6.4.18 below). Paragraph 13.52 of the Guidance indicates that the SOP should specify which body the authority recognises for these purposes:

> A statement of licensing policy should indicate which body the licensing authority judges to be competent to act as the responsible authority in relation to the protection of children from harm. This may be the local authority social services department, the Area Child Protection Committee, or another competent body. It would be practical and useful for statements of licensing policy to include the correct descriptions of the responsible authorities in any area and appropriate contact details.

### 4.3.13   Admission to film exhibitions

A SOP should make clear that in the case of premises giving film exhibitions the licensing authority will expect licensees to include in their operating schedules arrangements for restricting children from viewing age-restricted films classified according to the recommendations of the British Board of Film Classification or the licensing authority itself. Where a local authority intends to adopt its own system of classification, para 13.53 of the Guidance states that its SOP should indicate where the information regarding such classifications will be published and made available to licensees, clubs and the general public.

## 4.3.14  Integration with other strategies

Licensing is seen as only one means of promoting the delivery of the licensing objectives specified in the 2003 Act and delivery should involve licensing authorities working in partnership with all authorities, including responsible authorities, the licensed trade, local people and businesses, town centre managers, Crime and Disorder Reduction Partnerships,[43] performers and local transport authorities and operators (Guidance, para 1.21).[44] The Government is seeking, through this working in partnership, a more co-ordinated approach to promotion of the licensing objectives and the 'wider Government strategy to tackle crime, disorder and anti-social behaviour and reduce alcohol harm' (Guidance, para 1.23). This will require the integration of licensing with various other strategies that are directed towards promotion of the objectives and reduction of crime, disorder and antisocial behaviour.[45] Accordingly, the Guidance, para 13.55, provides that the SOP 'should provide clear indications of how the licensing authority will secure the proper integration of its licensing policy with local crime prevention, planning, transport, tourism, race equality schemes, and cultural strategies and any other plans introduced for the management of town centres and the night-time economy'. These will include the following:

- an indication that conditions attached to premises licences and club premises certificates will, so far as possible, reflect local crime prevention strategies, for example provision of CCTV cameras in certain premises (para 13.56);

- an undertaking that the impact of licensing on regulated entertainment, and particularly live music and dancing, will be monitored, for example, by considering whether premises that provide live music or culture are represented on licensing stakeholder forums, and ensuring that local cultural officers are regularly consulted about the impact on local culture (para 13.57);[46]

- a description of any protocols agreed between the local police and other licensing enforcement officers and the arrangements made for reporting to local authority transport committees so that those committees may have regard to the need to disperse people from town and city centres swiftly and safely (para 13.61);

- the arrangements for licensing committees to receive, when appropriate, reports on the needs of the local tourist economy and the cultural strategy for the area to ensure that these are reflected in their considerations (para 13.62);

- an indication that licensing committees will be kept appraised of the employment situation in the area and the need for new investment and employment where appropriate (para 13.63);[47] and that planning, building control and licensing regimes will be properly separated to avoid duplication and inefficiency (para 13.64); and

- a reference to legislative requirements to eliminate unlawful discrimination and to promote racial equality (para 13.69).

As part of the integration with and implementation of cultural strategies, the SOP should also recognise that 'proper account should be taken of the need to encourage and promote a broad range of entertainment, particularly live music, dancing and theatre . . . for the wider cultural benefit of communities' (Guidance, para 13.70):

> authorities should be aware of the need to avoid measures which deter live music, dancing and theatre by imposing indirect costs of a disproportionate nature. Performances of live music and dancing are central to the development of cultural diversity and vibrant and exciting communities where artistic freedom of expression is a fundamental right and greatly valued. Traditional music and dancing are parts of the cultural heritage of England and Wales. Music and dancing also help to unite communities and particularly in ethnically diverse communities, new and emerging musical and dance forms can assist the development of a fully integrated society. (Guidance, para 13.71)

Indeed, the Guidance (in para 13.72) goes on to suggest that local authorities should consider establishing a policy of seeking premises licences, in their own name from the licensing authority, for public spaces within the community, for example village greens, market squares, promenades, community halls, local authority owned art centres and similar public areas. It would then not be necessary for performers and entertainers to obtain a licence (or give a temporary event notice) themselves to give a performance in these places, although, as para 13.72 makes clear, they would still require the local authority's permission, as the premises licence holder, for any regulated entertainment that it was proposed should take place in these areas. In order to encourage this, the DCMS has established a Central Register of Local Authority Licensed Public Spaces in England in Wales (see 6.1.3 below). Whilst it is perhaps an attractive solution in principle, there may be practical difficulties with this approach. It will not be easy, for instance, to draw up an operating schedule that can accommodate the diverse activities that may take place and variation applications may have to be made on each occasion when a different type of use of the land or premises is proposed. Further, local authorities may be reluctant to put themselves at risk of incurring criminal liability for the offence, in s 136, of carrying on an unauthorised licensable activity in relation to the activities of the premises user (see 11.2 below).

### 4.3.15 Duplication of regulatory control

Paragraph 13.19 of the Guidance states that the SOP 'should include a firm commitment to avoid duplication with other regulatory regimes so far as possible'. Accordingly, the SOP may indicate that conditions will not be attached covering matters dealt with by other regulatory regimes, for example health and safety at work. These regimes place a range of general duties on employers and operators of venues both in respect of employees and of the general public when on the premises in question:

> Licensing authorities should only impose conditions which are necessary and proportionate for the promotion for the licensing objectives. If other existing law already places certain statutory responsibilities on an employer or operator of premises, it cannot be necessary to impose the same or similar duties. (Guidance, para 10.15)

However, these general duties will not always adequately address specific issues that arise on the premises in connection with, for example, certain types of entertainment and if additional and supplementary measures are necessary to promote the licensing objectives, then conditions will need to be attached (Guidance, para 10.18).

### 4.3.16 Standardised conditions

The Guidance states, in para 13.20, that the SOP 'should make clear that a key concept underscoring the 2003 Act is for conditions to be tailored to the specific premises concerned' and goes on to emphasise that this 'effectively rules out standardised conditions'. The Guidance further provides in para 10.12:

> It is perfectly possible that in certain cases, because the test is one of necessity, where there are other legislative provisions which are relevant and must be observed by the applicant, no additional conditions at all are needed to promote the licensing objectives.

However, certain conditions might be thought necessary in virtually all cases if the licensing objectives are to be promoted, for example a condition that access for emergency vehicles shall be kept clear and free from obstruction (which would promote the public safety objective).[48] The Guidance perhaps goes some way to recognising the need for 'common' conditions, for para 13.20 provides:

> it is acceptable for licensing authorities to draw attention in their statements of policy to pools of conditions from which applicants and others may draw on as appropriate.

### 4.3.17 *Enforcement*

The SOP should say something about enforcement and inspection strategies. Paragraph 13.21 of the Guidance 'strongly recommends' establishing protocols with the local police and other enforcement authorities on enforcement issues, with the emphasis on 'the targeting of agreed problem and high risk premises which require greater attention, while providing a lighter touch in respect of low risk premises which are well run' (para 13.22). The SOP might indicate the approach taken to transgressions of licensing law, for example warning for (minor) first transgression, or prosecution for certain more serious first transgressions.

Inspections are not required at periodic intervals under the Act and their frequency is left to the licensing authority's discretion. The SOP should indicate what policy the licensing authority is adopting on inspections and para 13.22 of the Guidance envisages there being more inspections for 'problem' premises:

> The principle of risk assessment and targeting should prevail and inspections should not be undertaken routinely but when and if they are judged necessary. This should ensure that resources are more effectively concentrated on problem premises.

Notwithstanding the targeting of premises, the view may be taken that annual inspections are required for certain types of premises, for example nightclubs, and, if so, this should be indicated in the SOP.[49] Equally, it may be felt that evidence of inspection of particular matters, such as electrical and lighting installations, should be forwarded to the authority on an annual or other periodic basis and, again, if so, this should be indicated in the SOP.

### 4.3.18 *Administration, exercise and delegation of functions*

The Act provides that licensing functions, which will include the taking of decisions, may be carried out by licensing committees or delegated to subcommittees or, in appropriate (uncontested) cases, to licensing officers (see 2.2.17 above). The Guidance contains recommendations as to delegation in particular cases (see 2.2.19 above) and, in para 13.76, states that the SOP should indicate how the licensing authority intends to approach its various functions. It is envisaged that many of the decisions and functions will be purely administrative in nature and the SOP 'should underline the principle of delegation in the interests of speed, efficiency and cost-effectiveness' (para 13.76). In cases where there are no relevant representations made, para 13.78 states, 'these matters should be dealt with by officers in order to speed matters through the system', although licensing committees 'should receive regular reports on decisions made by officers so that they maintain an overview of the general situation'.

### 4.3.19 *Other matters*

There may be a range of other matters that could be included in the SOP, some of which might relate to matters already considered above, for example, as regards the impact of activities on persons living and working in the vicinity of premises (see 4.3.6 above), adoption of a guide distance for 'vicinity' of 100 metres from the premises. Others might include an indication of whether there are certain types of application that the authority wishes to encourage, both in general and in particular areas, or to discourage, especially if there is likely to be a conflict with the licensing objectives. There may be certain types of conditions that authorities may wish in general to attach to particular types of premises. There may be various procedural matters that authorities may wish to include. There is a wide range of matters that licensing authorities might or might not choose to include in their SOP, and SOPs drawn up by licensing authorities have varied considerably, both in terms of their detail and scope.

## 4.3.20 Challenging Statements of Licensing Policy

4.3.21   The SOP itself, or aspects of it, might be challenged either by judicial review or under the Human Rights Act 1998. Two matters require consideration, the grounds for challenge and the persons having standing or *locus standi* who are able to make a challenge.

The SOP might be challenged by judicial review on the ground that it is unlawful as regards either process or content. The procedure for establishing the SOP may not have been followed because there may have been a failure in the statutory consultation, for example, one of the persons mentioned in s 5(3) whom the authority 'must consult' has not been consulted. If the courts consider this to be a mandatory requirement, the SOP itself may be unlawful. That s 5(3) is worded in mandatory terms does not necessarily mean that the courts will regard it as a mandatory requirement such that failure to comply will invalidate the policy. This will depend on whether, having regard to the consequences of non-compliance, Parliament can fairly be taken to have intended total invalidity (see 6.4.22 below). The SOP might equally be challenged on the ground that its content contains material that is irrelevant, which will be the case, for example, if the material does not relate to the licensing objectives and their promotion. In such a case, only that particular part of the SOP, rather than the SOP itself, is likely to be invalid.

Persons who are able to make a challenge by way of judicial review are persons with a 'sufficient interest'. Section 31(3) Supreme Court Act 1981 provides:

> the court shall not grant leave to make . . . an application unless it considers that the applicant has a sufficient interest in the matter to which the application relates.

Whether there is a sufficient interest depends on whether the applicant's rights, in an individual sense, have been affected in some way by the decision complained of, although whether a person has been affected sufficiently is not easy to determine. As Craig, P, *Administrative Law*, 5th edn, 2003, Oxford: OUP, p 730, points out, whether an applicant has standing will include 'the strength of the applicant's interest, the nature of the statutory power or duty in issue, the subject-matter of the claim and the type of illegality which is being asserted . . . The application of these criteria may, however, be unclear or uncertain'. It seems, however, that an applicant will not be precluded from seeking a judicial review of a SOP by the fact that he has not responded to the statutory consultation undertaken by the licensing authority prior to the formulation of the SOP (see 4.3.3 above). The High Court in *R (on the application of Edwards) v Environment Agency and another* [2004] 2 All ER 21 held that, provided a person was affected by the outcome of a decision, it was irrelevant that he had not participated in consultation prior to a decision (on an application for a permit for the use of tyre chips as a partial substitute for fuels used at a cement plant) being reached. Keith J stated (at para [16]):

> You do not have to be active in a campaign yourself to have an interest in its outcome. If the consultation exercise ends with a decision which affects your interests, you are no less affected by that decision simply because you took no part in the exercise but left it to others to do so. You should not be debarred from subsequently challenging the decision on the ground of inadequate consultation simply because you chose not to participate in the consultation exercise, provided that you are affected by its outcome.

Although this decision was not concerned with a judicial review challenge to a SOP, the principle in the case would seem to have equal application to such a challenge.

4.3.22  The SOP might be challenged under the Human Rights Act 1998 on the ground it contravenes s 6(1), which provides: 'It is unlawful for a public authority to act in a way which is incompatible with a Convention right.' Persons who are able to make a challenge for contravention of s 6(1) of the Human Rights Act 1998 are those who are a 'victim' of the unlawful act.[50] The challenge can be made either by bringing proceedings or by relying on the Convention right(s) concerned in any legal proceedings involving the victim.[51] A challenge might be made, for example, if the content of the SOP, as applied to premises licence or CPC applications, in some way violates Convention rights, for example protection of property under Protocol 1 of Art 1 or freedom of expression under Art 10 (see 3.6 and 3.7 above, respectively). It seems unlikely, however, that any challenge could be made under Art 6(1) since formulation of the policy will not involve the 'determination of civil rights and obligations' (see 3.5.3–3.5.6 above). The High Court has taken this view in respect of development plans in planning in *R (on the application of Aggregate Industries UK Ltd) v English Nature* [2003] Env LR 3, where Forbes J stated (at para [72]):

> the development plan and its policies do not dictate the answer absolutely, because other material considerations (which must also be taken into account by the decision-maker) may point to a different conclusion. Thus the development plan gives important guidance, but it does not of itself provide a decisive answer ... therefore, the development plan and its statements of policy are not, in the ordinary way, directly decisive of the civil rights and obligations in relation to land that falls within its ambit.

The same can be said of a SOP and Art 6(1) therefore seems to be inapplicable.

## 4.4    GUIDANCE

4.4.1    Not only must licensing authorities, by s 4(3)(b), have regard to any Guidance issued by the Secretary of State, but the Secretary of State is obliged, by s 182(1), to issue Guidance to licensing authorities on the discharge of their functions under the Act.[52] The Guidance was drawn up following widespread consultation with interested parties and was first published in July 2004. It is a 'living' document to be updated from time to time in the light of developments and experience and a revised version appeared in June 2006, followed by a more extensively revised version in June 2007. The method of updating, and indeed for issuing of the Guidance, is a matter for the Secretary of State, for s 182(7) provides: 'The Secretary of State must arrange for any guidance issued or revised under this section to be published in such manner as he considers appropriate.' The method adopted has been by publication on the DCMS website.

Nevertheless, there are various constraints on the issuing and revision of the Guidance to ensure that it is properly scrutinised before it has effect. These are set out in s 182(2)–(6), which requires a draft of the Guidance to be laid before and approved by each House of Parliament and for revised versions not to have effect until laid before Parliament. Where a resolution disapproving the Guidance is passed by either House, the Secretary of State must make further revisions as appear to him to be required and lay the further revised version before Parliament before it takes effect. Section 182(2)–(6) provides:

(2) But the Secretary of State may not issue the licensing guidance unless a draft of it has been laid before, and approved by resolution of, each House of Parliament.

(3) The Secretary of State may, from time to time, revise the licensing guidance.

(4) A revised version of the licensing guidance does not come into force until the Secretary of State lays it before Parliament.

(5) Where either House, before the end of the period of 40 days beginning with the day on which a revised version of the licensing guidance is laid before it, by resolution disapproves that version–

(a) the Secretary of State must, under subsection (3), make such further revisions to the licensing guidance as appear to him to be required in the circumstances, and

(b) before the end of the period of 40 days beginning with the date on which the resolution is made, lay a further revised version of the licensing guidance before Parliament.

(6) In reckoning any period of 40 days for the purposes of subsection (5), no account is to be taken of any time during which–

(a) Parliament is dissolved or prorogued, or

(b) both Houses are adjourned for more than four days.

4.4.2    The Guidance is intended to have an extensive remit, as is apparent from the following statements in paras 1.6 and 1.7:

1.6 The Guidance is provided for licensing authorities carrying out their functions. It also provides information for magistrates hearing appeals against licensing decisions and has been made widely available for the benefit of operators of licensed premises, their legal advisers and the general public. It is a key mechanism for promoting best practice, ensuring consistent application of licensing powers across the country and for promoting fairness, equal treatment and proportionality.

1.7 The police remain key enforcers of licensing law. The Guidance has no binding effect on police officers who, within the terms of their force orders and the law, remain operationally independent. However, the Guidance is provided to support and assist police officers in interpreting and implementing the 2003 Act in the promotion of the four licensing objectives.

The Guidance is detailed and not confined to specific areas of the legislation. If not all-encompassing, it certainly covers a wide range of areas and, at the very least, touches on most, if not all, aspects of the legislation. However, the Guidance is different in nature to statutory provisions in the 2003 Act and its accompanying secondary legislation, being primarily concerned with encouraging the spread of best practice and ensuring greater consistency of approach on the part of licensing authorities. Accordingly, it should be not be read in a rigid or legalistic manner, since it has not been strictly drafted in the same way as statutory provisions. As Beatson J observed in *Wetherspoon* [2006] LLR 312 (at paras 58–59):

[58] . . . guidance such as this is not drafted in the tight way in which a statute is drafted. It has similarities to the planning policies and development plans considered by Davis J in *Cranage Parish Council v First Secretary of State* [2004] EWHC 2949 (Admin), [2004] All ER (D) 143 (Dec). At para [49] of the judgment his Lordship stated:

'For one thing, in the planning field of policies and development plans of this kind are commonly drafted by planners for planners and often are very loosely drafted. They are not, putting it broadly, intended to be legally binding documents in the strict sense. For another, the relevant phrases used will often be hardly sensible bearing a strict hard edged interpretive approach and resort will be needed to elements of value judgment . . .'

[59] Similarly, in *R v Rochdale Metropolitan Borough Council ex parte Milne* [2001] Env LR 406, at para 51 Sullivan J stated that 'a legalistic approach to the interpretation of development plan policies is to be avoided'. A similar approach has been taken in contexts other than planning . . . These qualities apply to the licensing guidance in this case . . .

## 4.5   DISCHARGING LICENSING FUNCTIONS: LICENSING OBJECTIVES, THE LICENSING STATEMENT AND THE GUIDANCE

4.5.1   The licensing functions of authorities under the Act are, as the Guidance makes clear, only one means by which the licensing objectives are to be promoted. There is a range of other ways in which it is envisaged that this will be done and the licensing functions of authorities are, in context, only part of the wider picture. Paragraphs 1.20–1.22 provide:

1.20  Licensing functions under the 2003 Act are only one means of promoting delivery of the objectives described. They can make a substantial contribution in respect of the premises affected but cannot be regarded as a panacea for all community problems.

1.21  Licensing authorities should work with all partners to deliver the licensing objectives, including responsible authorities, the licensed trade, local people and businesses, town centre managers, Crime and Disorder Reduction Partnerships,[53] performers and local transport authorities and operators. For example, local businesses and a local authority may develop a Business Improvement District (BID), a partnership arrangement to take forward schemes that are of benefit to the community in that area, subject to the agreement of business rate payers.

1.22  The private sector, local residents and community groups in particular have an equally vital role to play in promoting the licensing objectives in partnership with public bodies. The Secretary of State strongly recommends that licensing authorities form licensing liaison groups and forums that bring together all the interested parties on a regular basis to monitor developments and propose possible solutions to any problems that may arise. The Secretary of State also recommends that licensing authorities should hold well publicised open meetings where local people and businesses can give their views on how well they feel the licensing objectives are being met.

Promotion of the licensing objectives is of paramount importance when a licensing authority is discharging its licensing functions under the Act. Section 4(1) provides that the authority 'must carry out its functions with a view to promoting the licensing objectives'. This is a mandatory requirement.[54] An authority has no discretion to depart from promoting the objectives, except in respect of additional objectives or where there are competing licensing objectives (see 4.2.17 above). If it can be shown that, when carrying out any particular function, an authority is not doing so with a view to promoting any of the licensing objectives, the decision will be unlawful. The four licensing objectives will, to use the words of Lord McIntosh during the Committee Stage of the Bill in the House of Lords, be 'the bedrock on which the activities of licensing authorities will be based' (HL Deb, vol 542, col 629, 17 December 2002).

4.5.2 Drawing up and publishing a 'Licensing Statement', that is a SOP, is one of the licensing functions of an authority and this function must therefore be discharged with a view to promoting the licensing objectives. The SOP sets out the way in which the licensing authority will interpret the four licensing objectives in the context of its own area, over a three-year period. When discharging other functions under the Act, such as determination of applications and the addition of conditions to licences, the authority is required to 'have regard to' the SOP. A requirement to 'have regard to' a particular matter means only that it needs to be considered as a relevant factor in the decision-making process. It may be taken into account and applied or it may be considered and then discounted altogether.

4.5.3 The SOP will set out the authority's general approach to its interpretation of the licensing objectives in its own area and its policy on particular matters. The expectation will be that the policy will be followed in the vast majority of cases, since policies, by definition, set out the general rule to be adopted. In these cases, 'have regard to' will mean 'apply'.[55] However, the SOP can only set out the authority's interpretation of the licensing objectives in its area at a general level. It cannot cater for every eventuality or for the wide variety of circumstances that might exist. Accordingly, there may be cases where the SOP is silent on the matter in question and where the licensing authority may 'have regard to' it, but where it offers no assistance when the matter in question is being determined. The extent to which this is the case will clearly depend on the degree of detail that is contained in the SOP. Nor can it cater for cases where, in an individual instance, application of the policy might work injustice or where the licensing objectives might be met by way of an exception to the policy rather than by application of it. In such circumstances it will not be necessary to apply it in the particular case and the authority will 'have regard to' it, but discount it. These cases of discounting the SOP will, however, be exceptional ones and it will only be possible to depart from it where doing so will promote the licensing objectives. This is because of the mandatory requirement in s 4(1) that an authority must discharge its licensing functions with a view to promoting the licensing objectives. The requirement, in s 4(3)(a), to have regard to the SOP will thus be a 'strong' one. There will be discretion to depart from the SOP, but this will have limited application and cogent reasons will be needed for doing so.

4.5.4 The Guidance is the second matter that an authority must 'have regard to' when discharging its functions. With a similarly expressed statutory requirement, this seems to put it on an equal footing with the SOP and again it will be necessary for the Guidance to be followed unless there are good reasons for departing from it. The Guidance itself provides:

> Section 4 of the 2003 Act provides that in carrying out its functions a licensing authority must have regard to Guidance issued by the Secretary of State under section 182. The requirement is therefore binding on all licensing authorities to that extent.
>
> However, the Guidance cannot anticipate every possible scenario or set of circumstances that may arise and so long as licensing authorities have properly understood the Guidance they may depart from it if they have reason to do so as long as they are able to provide full reasons.
>
> Departure from the Guidance could give rise to an appeal or judicial review, and the reasons given will then be a key consideration for the courts when considering the lawfulness and merits of any decision taken.[56]

That the Guidance is issued by the Secretary of State and there is a statutory requirement to 'have regard to' it does not seem to give the Guidance any enhanced status as a factor to be taken into account in the decision-making process. There is no indication of any such status in the Court of Appeal's judgment in *R (on the application of S (A Child)) v Brent London Borough Council* [2002] EWCA Civ 693, where three schoolchildren sought to challenge the decisions of Local Education Authority Appeal Panels to uphold their exclusion from school on the grounds, *inter alia*, that the Appeals Panels, which are required by s 68 of the School Standards and Framework Act 1998 to have regard to any guidance issued by the Secretary of State, had treated their discretion as being fettered by paragraphs in the Guidance.[57] The challenges were unsuccessful, but the court sought to emphasise the importance of the Appeal Panels not being directed by the Guidance when reaching their decisions. Schiemann LJ stated (at para 15):

> Appeal Panels, and schools too, must keep in mind that guidance is no more than that: it is not direction, and certainly not rules. Any Appeal Panel which, albeit on legal advice, treats the Secretary of State's Guidance as something to be strictly adhered to or simply follows it because it is there will be breaking its statutory remit in at least three ways: it will be failing to exercise its own independent judgment; it will be treating guidance as if it were rules; and it will, in lawyers' terms, be fettering its own discretion. Equally, however, it will be breaking its remit if it neglects the guidance. The task is not an easy one.

The statutory requirement, in s 4(3)(b) of the 2003 Act, to have regard to the Guidance is expressed in similar terms to s 4(3)(a) in respect of the SOP and in principle will apply when a licensing authority is discharging any of its licensing functions. The Guidance, however, seems to be aimed in large measure at ensuring a degree of consistency between SOPs of different authorities. It was described by a Government spokesman in the House of Lords as follows:

> a document produced by the Secretary of State that is designed to secure that no unnecessary conflicts exist between the licensing policies set out by different licensing authorities. It also sets out the kind of issues that licensing authorities must consider when they are producing such a policy.[58]

On this view, the Guidance is focused, in the main, on the particular licensing function of formulation of an SOP and it may be less likely to have application in respect of other licensing functions, in particular, the making of licensing decisions under the Act. Whilst the Guidance may be particularly important when drawing up and revising the SOP, and cogent reasons will need to be given for departing from it when doing so, it may be of less importance thereafter. It may be only of secondary importance once the SOP has been formulated in accordance with the Guidance, for the SOP will then become the guiding factor for the licensing authority in its decision-making (except to the extent that revisions may be needed to the SOP to reflect changes made to the Guidance). Whilst provisions in the SOP may be applied in the vast majority of cases when determining applications made or considering temporary event notices (TENs) given under the Act, provisions in the Guidance (having been considered at the earlier stage of formulation of the SOP) may not have such widespread application. The effect of this may be to promote the SOP ahead of the Guidance in terms of the scope of its application. In the decision-making process, a licensing authority will in all cases be seeking to promote the licensing objectives and, in doing so, is perhaps more likely to 'have regard to' its SOP than to the Guidance. This seems to indicate the following hierarchical structure, as far as decision-making is concerned:

- licensing objectives, which must be promoted in all cases;
- the SOP, the provisions of which (if relevant to the particular case) are to be followed in the vast majority of cases; and
- the Guidance, the provisions of which (if relevant to the particular case) may well require consideration in some instances, but not in others on account of the provisions already having been considered when formulating the SOP.

If this structure is correct, there may be a lack of parity in the requirement in s 4(3) for an authority to 'have regard to' the SOP and the Guidance when discharging its licensing functions. The former may assume a more prominent position than the latter in decision-making and the SOP will justify Lord McIntosh's description of it as 'enormously important' (HL Deb, vol 642, col 630, 17 December 2002). The SOP will not rank ahead of the licensing objectives, but, as the means through which the licensing objectives are to be achieved or delivered at the local level, it could be that it will not be far behind the objectives in terms of importance.

## NOTES

1　This objective is generally referred to throughout the Act as the 'crime prevention objective'. Section 193 provides: ' "crime prevention objective" means the licensing objective mentioned in section 4(2)(a) (prevention of crime and disorder).'

2　An example would be restricting bright lighting (assuming the lighting would unreasonably affect a sufficient number of persons), which would assist in prevention of public nuisance to those living nearby, but might inhibit the prevention of crime and disorder by affording greater opportunities for their commission due to the areas being less well-lit.

3　It was also accepted in *Murray* (at para [13]) that there was no obligation to achieve the objectives: 'the objectives are not absolute requirements in the sense of requiring a local planning authority in each case to *achieve* the result pursued by the objective. That would amount to a requirement to refuse planning permission if there were *any* risk to human health or the environment, which would in turn lead to the refusal of planning permission for any or almost any landfill site'.

4　See also the New Zealand case of *Wainright v Police* [1968] NZLR 101, where it was held that what was disorderly behaviour was a matter of degree depending on the circumstance of the case and where the behaviour took place. Wild CJ stated (at 103) that: 'judgment of the conduct in question is in every case a matter of degree depending upon the relevant time, place, and circumstances . . . Conduct that is acceptable at a football match or boxing may well be disorderly at a musical or dramatic performance. Behaviour that is permissible at a political meeting may deeply offend at a religious gathering.'

5  This matter is further considered at 4.2.10 below in the context of the licensing objective of prevention of public nuisance.

6  See *Severn View Social Club and Institute Ltd v Chepstow (Monmouthshire) Licensing Justices* [1968] 1 WLR 1512, where Lord Parker CJ, referring to guests, stated (at 1514): 'In my judgment, they clearly were not members of the public as such'; and 5.3.8 below.

7  See Arts 8 and 9. For a summary of the 2005 Order, see Guidance, paras 2.20–2.25, and for details, see the Communities and Local Government website, www.communities.gov.uk/ fire. Although the Cinematograph (Safety) Regulations 1955, which contained a significant number of regulations in respect of fire safety provision at cinemas, no longer apply, 'licensing authorities and responsible authorities should recognise the need for steps to be taken to assure public safety at such premises in the absence of the 1995 [sic] Regulations': Guidance, para 2.30.

8  Guidance, para 2.19. There will of course be occasions when a public safety condition could incidentally benefit health, but it should not be the purpose of the condition, as this would be *ultra vires* the 2003 Act. Accordingly, conditions should not be imposed under a premises licence or club premises certificate, which relate to cleanliness or hygiene: Guidance, para 2.19.

9  Paragraph 2.26 goes on to provide:

> However, it would be permissible to require as a condition of a licence or certificate, if necessary, checks on this equipment to be conducted at specified intervals and for evidence of these checks to be retained by the premises licence holder or club provided this does not duplicate or gold-plate a requirement in other legislation. Similarly, it would be permissible for licensing authorities, if they receive relevant representations from responsible authorities or interested parties, to attach conditions which required equipment of particular standards to be maintained on the premises. Responsible authorities – such as health and safety inspectors – should therefore make clear their expectations in this respects [sic] to enable prospective licence holders or clubs to prepare effective operating schedules and club operating schedules.

10  See 7.2.2 below.

11  This is except where the licensing authority and the enforcing authority for the fire safety order are one and the same body, eg in the case of designated sports grounds and stands where local authorities enforce the fire safety order. In such circumstances fire safety conditions should not be set in new licences, but conditions in existing licences will remain in force and be enforceable by the licensing authority (Guidance, para 2.21).

12  There is a general statement in para 2.27 that: 'capacity limits may be necessary in preventing disorder, as overcrowded venues can increase the risks of crowds becoming frustrated and hostile'. This is followed by a reference in para 10.43 in relation to High Volume Vertical Drinking (HVVD) establishments: 'Where necessary and appropriate, conditions can be attached to premises licences for the promotion of the prevention of crime and disorder at such premises (if not volunteered by the venue operator and following representations made on such grounds) which require adherence to . . . a prescribed capacity . . .'

13  A civil action in tort can also be brought by any person who can show that he has suffered special or particular loss or damage over and above the general inconvenience or annoyance suffered by the public at large.

14  [2006] 1 AC 459 (at para 36), *per* Lord Bingham, who described the definition as 'clear, precise, adequately defined and based on a discernible rational principle' and with whose judgment other members of the House agreed. The definition was regarded as sufficiently certain to meet the requirement in Article 7 of the European Convention on Human Rights, which requires that 'No-one shall be held guilty of a criminal offence on account of any act or omission which did not constitute an offence . . . at the time when it was

committed'. Criminal offences which lack sufficient certainty are regarded as contravening this requirement (*SW and CR v UK* (1995) 21 EHRR 363) and a norm cannot be regarded as a law unless it is formulated with sufficient precision to enable the citizen to foresee, if need be with appropriate advice, the consequences which a given course of conduct may entail (*Sunday Times v UK* (1979) 2 EHRR 245, para 49). The definition of public nuisance was regarded by the House in *R v Rimmington* as meeting this requirement.

15 [1957] 2 QB 169, 184.

16 Guidance, para 2.34. The issue of acoustics may well have been dealt with at planning level, although any failure to comply might more easily be enforced through attachment of a licence condition.

17 Guidance, para 2.40 provides:

> The cumulative effects of litter in the vicinity of premises carrying on licensable activities can cause public nuisance. For example, it may be appropriate and necessary for a condition of a licence to require premises serving customers from take-aways, and fast food outlets from 11.00 pm to provide litter bins in the vicinity of the premises in order to prevent the accumulation of litter from its customers. Such conditions may be necessary and appropriate in circumstances where customers late at night may have been consuming alcohol and be inclined to carelessness and anti-social behaviour.

18 [2006] 1 AC 459 (at para 37), *per* Lord Bingham. See also Lord Rodger (at para 48): 'Suppose ... that someone makes a series of obscene telephone calls to people living in a village or neighbourhood. In that situation each call is heard, and is intended to be heard, only by the recipient. Of course, as the calls mount up, more and more residents will be affected and the general peace of the neighbourhood may be disturbed. But each telephone call affects only one individual, not the community in the village or neighbourhood. Therefore, it does not have that quality which is the hallmark of the crime of public nuisance'.

19 (1992) 13 Cr App R (S) 204. See also the Canadian case of *Attorney General for Ontario v Orange Productions Ltd* (1971) 21 DLR (3d) 257, where a pop music festival that generated large-scale noise, traffic problems and apprehension was held to be a public nuisance.

20 Certainly a wide application of the concept of public nuisance seems to have been envisaged; according to a Government Minister, Dr Kim Howells, 'the expression "public nuisance" has been chosen for the Bill as a well known concept that is flexible and capable of application in a huge range of circumstances' (HC Standing Committee D, col 158, 1 April 2003). The views expressed here arguably meet the criteria laid down in *Pepper v Hart* [1993] AC 593 for the admission of statements in Parliament as an aid to legislative interpretation, since there is an element of ambiguity as to whether 'public nuisance' will cover the type of conduct in question; the statement is made by a Government Minister promoting the Bill and the statement seems to be clear.

21 His Lordship, in the quotation mentioned, refers to the justices being 'entitled to take these *factors* into account' (emphasis added) which, in the context of the quotation, must mean the disorder in the areas in question and the disorder being created by the number of persons leaving the applicants' premises.

22 It is naturally more difficult to justify protection of persons over the age of 16 since such persons are likely to have passed the difficult stage of adolescence and can themselves engage in sexual activity under the law.

23 See also the Guidance, which gives the following two examples: 'premises may operate as café bar during the day providing meals for families but also provide entertainment with a sexual content after 8.00 pm' (para 2.45) and 'gambling may take place in part of a leisure centre but not in other parts of those premises' (para 2.46).

24 Paragraph 1.3. This is not easy to reconcile with the fact that on a number of occasions, eg for temporary event notices (TENs) (see 9.5.4 below) and personal licences (see

10.1 below) only the crime prevention objective is relevant and the other licensing objectives are excluded from consideration.

25 Where there are competing objectives, a possible argument might be made that, prima facie, the crime and disorder objective should be regarded as of paramount importance on the basis that it has greater application under the Act than the other objectives.

26 We are grateful to David Adams for supplying us with this information.

27 *Quaere* whether a failure to consult one of the statutory consultees will invalidate the consultation process. If the failure is in respect of a matter that can be regarded as of central significance to the SOP, it is possible that it may do. In *R (on the application of Montpeliers and Trevors Association) v Westminster City Cou*ncil [2006] LGR 304, the High Court held that there had been a failure to consult properly in respect of an experimental traffic order where the council decided to exclude from the consultation process the option of retaining barriers to reduce traffic, and consultation proceeded on alternative courses of action: 'the subsequent process, although a process of consultation, was vitiated by the fact that one of the options [of retaining barriers] – and an option which on any view was of central significance – had already been excluded from further consideration' (*per* Munby J at para 25).

28 CDRPs (or Community Safety Partnerships in Wales) were established by the Crime and Disorder Act 1998 and require responsible authorities to work with other local agencies and organisations to develop and implement strategies to tackle crime and disorder and misuse of drugs in their area. The responsible authorities are the police, local authorities, fire and rescue authorities, police authorities, health authorities in Wales, and primary care trusts in England.

29 Paragraph 13.8, which goes on to state that: 'They may also consider it valuable to consult local performers, performers' unions (such as the Musicians' Union and Equity) and entertainers involved in the cultural life of the local community.'

30 Section 5(7) provides that: 'Regulations may make provision about the determination and revision of policies, and the preparation and publication of licensing statements, under this section.'

31 Department of the Environment, *Planning Policy Guidance Note 6: Town Centres and Retail Development*, June 1996, para. 2.19. For the background to these developments, see Campbell, D, 'Alcohol-Related Disorder and the Nature of the Problem of Social Cost' [2005] *Public Law* 749, 753–754.

32 By the time of the 2003 Act's passage, the Government, whilst keen to stress that the number of licensed premises in an area was essentially a matter for planning control and not licensing law, sought to strengthen planning control to curb further expansion. It announced that the Town and Country Planning (Use Classes) Order 1987, SI 1987/764, would be amended to prevent premises like cinemas and bingo halls turning into night-clubs without planning permission. Article 3(1) of the Order provides: 'where a building or other land is used for a purpose of any class specified in the Schedule, the use of that building or other land shall not be taken to involve development of the land [for which planning permission is required]', but under Art 3(6) certain uses are excluded from the specified classes (and consequently they require planning permission) and nightclubs have been added to these excluded uses by Art 2(1) of the Town and Country Planning (Use Classes) (Amendment) (England) Order 2005, SI 2005/84. Article 2(2) of the 2005 Order has also split the former A3 use class (food and drink) into three separate classes: Class A3 (use as a restaurant or café), Class A4 (use as a public house, wine bar or other drinking establishment) and Class A5 (use as a hot food take-away). This, for instance, prevents a change of use without planning permission from a café to a wine bar, as these are now in different classes (A3 and A4), whereas previously they were in the same class (A3) and the change could be made without planning permission. In addition to these amendments, provision was made in the 2003 Act for planning officers to be included in the list of 'responsible authorities' who might make representations under the 2003 Act – see s 13(4)(d) and 6.4.18 below.

33 For instances of where this was successfully done, see *Bar Sport Ltd v Charnwood Borough Council*, Loughborough Magistrates' Court, 27 April 2006 and *Marc Merran (Moldiva) v Westminster City Council* (2007) 68 *Licensing Review* 16. In the former case, premises with a sports theme, televisions, food as a substantial part of the operation, table service of food and drink, and an older clientele was regarded on appeal as 'the type of premises that is unlikely to add to current problems' in the cumulative impact area. In the latter case, a combination of factors and circumstances (identified at 18) persuaded the Marylebone Magistrates' Court that 'there are genuinely exceptional circumstances that take these [nightclub] premises outside the constraints of the Policy'.

34 Relevant representations on a new application can still be made, even in the absence of a 'special policy', on the grounds that the premises will give rise to a negative cumulative impact on one or more of the licensing objectives: Guidance, para 13.26. Presumably the same is true in respect of a material variation.

35 See Turnham, A and Collins, J, 'Building a better policy evidence base', Licensing Circles, Spring 2007, 32–35 and, for details of such additional information acquired by the London Borough of Richmond, see http://www.erskinecorp.com/case_studies/item/london_borough_of_richmond_twickenham_evening_economy_study/

36 In *Wetherspoon* (see 4.3.8 above) the licensing authority in its cumulative impact policy had not set a fixed closing time for the area in question and did 'not purport to apply its special policy in circumstances in which the Secretary of State's guidance advises that it should not do so' (*per* Beatson J at [2006] LLR 312 at [78]).

37 Quotas should not be used 'because they have no regard to the individual characteristics of the premises concerned. Public houses, nightclubs, restaurants, hotels, theatres, concert halls and cinemas all could sell alcohol, serve food and provide entertainment but with contrasting styles and characteristics. Proper regard should be given to those differences and the differing impact they will have on the promotion of the licensing objectives' (Guidance, para 13.38).

38 Statements elsewhere in the Guidance might lend further support to this view, eg para 13.25 states that: 'In some areas, where the *number, type and density of premises* selling alcohol for consumption on the premises are *unusual, serious problems* of nuisance and disorder may be arising or have begun to arise outside or some distance from licensed premises' (emphasis added).

39 *Quaere* whether the SOP should contain some statement about recognising that flexible hours for certain types of premises, such as community public houses with function rooms, will be needed only on a periodic and irregular basis when particular functions are held. Such premises may require late night drinking only on these occasions, but not on a regular, ongoing basis. This might perhaps be accommodated by specification in a condition of the 'general' hours for opening, with provision for later opening to a specified time on occasions when particular functions take place.

40 Paragraph 13.49 provides: 'it is not possible to give an exhaustive list of what amounts to entertainment or services of an adult or sexual nature . . . However, such entertainment or services, for example, would generally include topless bar staff, striptease, lap-, table- or pole-dancing, performances involving feigned violence or horrific incidents, feigned or actual sexual acts or fetishism, or entertainment involving strong and offensive language.'

41 Under the Anti-Social Behaviour Act 2003, there is a power to close premises where there is the production, supply or use of class A drugs and serious nuisance or disorder, enabling closure in as little as 48 hours should this be necessary: Guidance, para 13.48n.

42 Guidance, para 13.50. The SOP should also make it clear that conditions requiring the admission of children to any premises cannot be attached to licences or certificates. Where no licensing restriction is necessary, admission should be a matter for the discretion of the individual licensee or club or person who has given a TEN (Guidance, para 13.51).

43 See 4.3.4 above.

44 The private sector, local residents and community groups in particular have an equally vital role to play in promoting the licensing objectives in partnership with public bodies: Guidance, para 1.22.

45 These will include the Government's *Alcohol Harm Reduction Strategy for England* (AHRSE), which was published by the Cabinet Office (Prime Minister's Strategy Unit) in March 2004 and which seeks to forge new partnerships with the health and police services, the drinks industry and communities, to combat the range of problems caused by alcohol misuse. The AHRSE puts joint action at the heart of a series of measures that will tackle alcohol-related disorder in town and city centres, improve treatment and support for people with alcohol problems, clamp down on irresponsible promotions by the industry and provide better information to consumers about the dangers of alcohol misuse. An updated version, *Safe, Sensible and Social – next steps for the National Alcohol Strategy*, was published in June 2007, with a focus on ensuring that laws and licensing powers introduced to tackle alcohol-related crime and disorder, protect young people and tackle irresponsibly managed premises are being used widely and effectively, and sharpening the focus on the minority of drinkers who cause or experience the most harm to themselves, their communities and their families. In Wales the Welsh Assembly published *Tackling Substance Misuse in Wales: A Partnership Approach* in September 2000, which is currently being further developed (Guidance, para 1.31).

46 *Quaere* whether this will be promoting the delivery of any licensing objective.

47 Ibid.

48 This is Condition 30 from the *Model National Standard Conditions for Places of Public Entertainment* (2002, London: Entertainment Technology Press). Obviously this will not be applicable in all cases, eg where licensable activities take place on vehicles, but it might in most cases where premises in the form of buildings or other places is concerned.

49 It should be noted that the Guidance does not seek to preclude inspections annually or at any other intervals.

50 The meaning of 'victim' is considered at 3.2.1 above. Passing the 'victim' test, however, only establishes a right of standing, enabling a person to bring the case. It does not mean that the case will succeed. Whether or not it does will depend on legal arguments concerning the interference with the particular convention right in question.

51 Where, in the latter instance, the proceedings are an application for judicial review, the applicant will be taken to have a 'sufficient interest' only if he is a victim: s 7(3) of the Human Rights Act 1998.

52 Section 182(1) provides: 'The Secretary of State must issue guidance ("the licensing guidance") to licensing authorities on the discharge of their functions under this Act.'

53 See 4.3.4 above.

54 Referring to this provision during the Committee Stage of the Bill in the House of Lords, Lord McIntosh, a Government spokesman, stated: 'That means that it has no choice. It is not a weak provision; it is a strong requirement' (HL Deb, vol 642, col 629, 17 December 2002).

55 There would not seem to be much scope here for the application of the principle that, where a relevant factor is to be considered, the weight to be attached to it is a matter for the decision-making body. Traditionally, courts have taken the view that whether a body gives great weight to a particular factor, or regards it as being of marginal significance, is entirely a matter for the body itself, subject only to the decision not being *Wednesbury* unreasonable (see 3.5.13 above). In the case of having regard to a SOP, however, it is more a question of whether the policy was applied or not. It is difficult to see therefore how a little weight might be given to the Statement in its application.

56 Paragraph 1.7. See also HL Deb, vol 642, col 630, 17 December 2002: 'The phrase . . . is quite deliberately "have regard to"; in other words, when we are talking about guidance, which is neither legislation nor an instruction, the words "have regard to" are appropriate because the authority retains an ultimate discretion to depart from the guidance' (Lord McIntosh).

57 The relevant paragraphs, contained in Circular 10/99, provided that, where a pupil was excluded in accordance with clearly stated provisions in the school's discipline policy, 'the appeal panel should not normally direct re-instatement' (para 17) and, where a pupil had been permanently excluded for any of a number of specified reasons (eg serious violence or sexual abuse), the Secretary of State 'would normally regard it as inappropriate to re-instate' (para 18).

58 HL Deb, vol 642, col 630, 17 December 2002 (Lord McIntosh). Promotion of consistency was recognised as a necessary purpose of Guidance in the *Brent* case, but the Court of Appeal did not accept that it was sufficient in itself: 'guidance must not only stay within and promote the statutory purposes but . . . must be Convention-compliant, since [the Secretary of State] . . . is a public authority within s.6 [of the Human Rights Act 1998] . . . Parliament has not authorised the Secretary of State to promote practice which is consistent and wrong' (para 16). Further, a preference was expressed by the court for Guidance to be 'neutrally' expressed: 'One way – perhaps the safest – in which to formulate guidance under s.68 [of the School Standards and Framework Act 1998] is to list the factors to which Appeal Panels ought in general to have regard without indicating any preferred outcome. To do so comes closest to achieving consistency about the right matters without trying to influence individual decisions' (para 19). It might be questioned whether the Guidance issued under the 2003 Act accords, in parts, with this preference – see, in particular, paras 13.18–13.33 on the cumulative impact of premises, considered at 4.3.7–4.3.9 above.

# CHAPTER 5

# LICENSABLE ACTIVITIES: THE SCOPE OF CONTROL

## 5.1   INTRODUCTION

### 5.1.1   Licensable activities and qualifying club activities

5.1.2   Section 1 of the 2003 Act sets out the various licensable activities for which some form of authorisation under the Act, a premises licence, a club premises certificate (CPC) or a temporary event notice (TEN), is required.[1] Licensable activities encompass all three areas covered by the Act, the sale or supply of alcohol (for which a personal licence is needed and, in the case of a premises licence, there needs to be a designated premises supervisor for the premises), the provision of entertainment and the provision of late night refreshment (LNR). Section 1(1) provides:

> For the purposes of this Act the following are licensable activities–
> (a)   the sale by retail of alcohol,
> (b)   the supply of alcohol by or on behalf of a club to, or to the order of, a member of the club,
> (c)   the provision of regulated entertainment, and
> (d)   the provision of late night refreshment.

5.1.3   Some, but not all, of these licensable activities comprise 'qualifying club activities' under the Act, for which a CPC might be obtained. Qualifying club activities extend to the sale or supply of alcohol (although there is no requirement for a personal licence or a designated premises supervisor) and the provision of entertainment, but, as far as LNR is concerned, its provision in qualifying clubs is an 'exempt supply' and no authorisation is needed.[2] Section 1(2) provides:

> For those purposes the following licensable activities are also qualifying club activities–
> (a)   the supply of alcohol by or on behalf of a club to, or to the order of, a member of the club,
> (b)   the sale by retail of alcohol by or on behalf of a club to a guest of a member of the club for consumption on the premises where the sale takes place, and
> (c)   the provision of regulated entertainment where that provision is by or on behalf of a club for members of the club or members of the club and their guests.

Whilst the above licensable activities generally require an authorisation under the Act in order for them to take place, there are various exemptions in ss 173–75, under which, in certain circumstances, activities are excluded from the definition of licensable activities.[3]

### 5.1.4   Authorisation for licensable activities and qualifying club activities

Authorisation for qualifying club activities can only take the form of a CPC, whilst authorisation for licensable activities can take the form of a premises licence or a permitted temporary activity under a TEN. Section 2(1) and (2) provides:

(1) A licensable activity may be carried on–
   (a) under and in accordance with a premises licence (see Part 3), or
   (b) in circumstances where the activity is a permitted temporary activity by virtue of Part 5.
(2) A qualifying club activity may be carried on under and in accordance with a club premises certificate (see Part 4).

Not all clubs will be a 'qualifying club' with a CPC, however, and those that are not will be able to carry out licensable activities under the authorisation of a premises licence or a TEN. Nor, if a club is a qualifying club and has obtained a CPC, does this prevent a premises licence or a TEN being obtained and having effect concurrently in respect of the premises. The legislation makes provision for two or more authorisations in respect of the same premises or in respect of the same person. Section 2(3) and (4) provides:

(3) Nothing in this Act prevents two or more authorisations having effect concurrently in respect of the whole or a part of the same premises or in respect of the same person.
(4) For the purposes of subsection (3) "authorisation" means–
   (a) a premises licence;
   (b) a club premises certificate;
   (c) a temporary event notice.

This enables, for example, a qualifying club that wishes to provide entertainment to members of the public on certain days to hold both a CPC, to cover its normal operation, and a premises licence, to authorise the provision of entertainment, in respect of the same premises (Explanatory Note 31). Equally, a person with a premises licence and a personal licence authorising him to sell alcohol there may wish to sell alcohol under a TEN at some unlicensed premises elsewhere.

### 5.1.5   Licensing authorities

By s 3(1), authorisation for licensable activities and qualifying club activities in the form of premises licences, CPCs and TENs is granted in England by district or county councils, except in London where they are granted by borough councils or the Common Council of the City of London, and in Wales where they are granted by county or county borough councils.[4]

## 5.2   SALE BY RETAIL OR SUPPLY OF ALCOHOL

Section 1(1) specifies two types of licensable activities in relation to alcohol: (a) the sale by retail of alcohol; and (b) the supply of alcohol by or on behalf of a club to or to the order of a member of the club otherwise than by way of sale.

### 5.2.1   Sale by retail of alcohol

5.2.2   'Sale by retail' is defined in s 192, which provides:

(1) For the purposes of this Act "sale by retail", in relation to any alcohol, means a sale of alcohol to any person, other than a sale of alcohol that–

    (a)  is within subsection (2),

    (b)  is made from premises owned by the person making the sale, or occupied by him under a lease to which the provisions of Part 2 of the Landlord and Tenant Act 1954 (c.56) (security of tenure) apply, and

    (c)  if made for consumption off the premises.

(2)  A sale of alcohol is within this subsection if it is–

    (a)  to a trader for the purposes of his trade,

    (b)  to a club, which holds a club premises certificate, for the purposes of that club,

    (c)  to the holder of a personal licence for the purpose of making sales authorised by a premises licence,

    (d)  to the holder of a premises licence for the purpose of making sales authorised by that licence, or

    (e)  to the premises user in relation to a temporary event notice for the purpose of making sales authorised by that notice.

A sale will normally involve proof that money passed in return for the alcohol (see 11.5.8 below) and all sales are included except those specifically excepted by s 192(2). These exceptions are ones where the sale is made to persons who will be buying wholesale and then going on to make a sale by retail to their customers (or in the case of clubs, a supply to their members).

5.2.3    'Alcohol' is defined in s 191 which provides:

(1)  In this Act, "alcohol" means spirits, wine, beer, cider or any other fermented, distilled or spirituous liquor,[5] but does not include–

    (a)  alcohol which is of a strength not exceeding 0.5% at the time of the sale or supply in question,

    (b)  perfume,

    (c)  flavouring essences recognised by the Commissioners of Customs and Excise as not being intended for consumption as or with dutiable alcoholic liquor,

    (d)  the aromatic flavouring essence commonly known as Angostura bitters,

    (e)  alcohol which is, or is included in, a medicinal product or a veterinary medicinal product,

    (f)  denatured alcohol,[6]

    (g)  methyl alcohol,

    (h)  naphtha, or

    (i)  alcohol contained in liqueur confectionery.

(2)  In this section–

"denatured alcohol" has the same meaning as in section 5 of the Finance Act 1995 (c.4);

"dutiable alcoholic liquor" has the same meaning as in the Alcoholic Liquor Duties Act 1979 (c.4);

"liqueur confectionery" means confectionery which–

    (a)  contains alcohol in a proportion not greater than 0.2 litres of alcohol (of a strength not exceeding 57%) per kilogram of the confectionery, and

    (b)  either consists of separate pieces weighing not more than 42g or is designed to be broken into such pieces for the purpose of consumption;

"medicinal product" has the same meaning as in section 130 of the Medicines Act 1968 (c.67);

"strength" is to be construed in accordance with section 2 of the Alcoholic Liquor Duties Act 1979 (c.4); and

"veterinary medicinal product" has the same meaning as in regulation 2 of the Veterinary Medicines Regulations 2006.

Thus 'alcohol' essentially comprises spirits, wine, beer, cider or any other fermented, distilled or spirituous liquor, subject to a number of exceptions of a relatively minor nature.

## 5.2.4  Supply of alcohol by or on behalf of a club or to the order of a member of the club otherwise than by way of sale

5.2.5    It is necessary for the Act to make provision for the supply of alcohol to members of clubs otherwise than by way of sale, as a separate licensable activity from sale by retail. This is because in law, depending on the type of club, a purchase made by a club member may not be regarded in law as a 'sale' but as a 'supply'.[7] There are two types of clubs, 'proprietary clubs' and 'members' clubs'.

Proprietary clubs are clubs run as businesses, where club property (that is, premises, furniture and stores of food and drink) belongs to and is owned by the club proprietor. Where persons are members of such clubs, there is a contractual relationship between them and the proprietor under which they pay a membership subscription in return for which they have a licence (permission) to use the club. The proprietor may run the club himself or may entrust the management of it to a committee (nominated by himself or partly so nominated and partly elected by the members), but in either instance the club is being run as a business. In the case of a proprietary club, whether run by the proprietor or by a committee, there will be a retail sale of alcohol, *not* a supply of alcohol, when a purchase is made by a club member. In law, this is no different from a sale of alcohol in a public house to a member of the public and a premises licence will be needed for making such sales.

5.2.6    Members' clubs are clubs where there is not a club proprietor who owns the property. In a members' club, all of the property belongs to all of the members jointly (usually being vested in trustees for convenience) and this includes the club's stock of alcohol. The members' right to use the club is founded on their joint ownership of club property and not a contractual relationship with the club proprietor. The stock of alcohol is regarded as being owned in equal shares by the club's members and, when a member purchases alcohol from the stock of alcohol, there is a release to him of the proprietary rights of his co-owners. There is not in law a 'sale' of alcohol to the member but a 'supply' to him from the stock of liquor; the making of payment merely ensures that club funds are reimbursed fairly as between one member and another (see 8.1.1 below). The inclusion of the supply of alcohol as a licensable activity in s 1(1) thus reflects the fact that in members' clubs no sale of alcohol takes place.

However, not all members' clubs that supply alcohol will do so as a licensable activity under a premises licence. Members' clubs can supply alcohol without a premises licence if they hold a CPC under Part 4 of the Act. This can be granted if certain qualifications are met, which, broadly speaking, are designed to demonstrate that the club is a bona fide one, run *by* the members *for* the members, and is not simply a 'front' for a particular individual or individuals to make a profit (see 8.2.5–8.2.15 below). Where the qualifications are *not* met for some reason, for example where the club has less than 25 members (s 62(5)), the club cannot obtain a CPC and a premises licence will be needed for the supply of alcohol.

## 5.3    PROVISION OF REGULATED ENTERTAINMENT

### 5.3.1   Introduction

What constitutes regulated entertainment as a licensable activity is covered in Sched 1. Section 1(4) provides:

> Schedule 1 makes provision about what constitutes the provision of regulated entertainment for the purposes of this Act.

What constitutes the 'provision' of regulated entertainment is covered by para 1 of Sched 1, and what constitutes 'regulated entertainment' is covered by paras 2 and 3. 'Provision' is for:

- the public or any section of it; or
- exclusively for members of a qualifying club and their guests; or
- in any other case for consideration and with a view to profit.

'Regulated entertainment' is:

- entertainment of various types (plays, films, indoor sporting events, boxing or wrestling, or music or dancing or entertainment of a similar description, where the entertainment is for an audience);[8] or
- entertainment facilities for certain forms of entertainment (facilities for enabling persons to take part in making music, dancing or entertainment of a similar description).

### 5.3.2   Meaning of 'provision' of regulated entertainment

5.3.3    Paragraph 1(1)–(3) of Sched 1 provides:

(1) For the purposes of this Act the "provision of regulated entertainment" means the provision of–
  (a) entertainment of a description falling within paragraph 2, or
  (b) entertainment facilities falling within paragraph 3, where the conditions in sub-paragraphs (2) and (3) are satisfied.
(2) The first condition is that the entertainment or entertainment facilities are provided–
  (a) to any extent for members of the public or a section of the public,
  (b) exclusively for members of a club which is a qualifying club in relation to the provision of regulated entertainment, or for members of such a club and their guests, or
  (c) in any case not falling within paragraph (a) or (b), for consideration and with a view to profit.
(3) The second condition is that the premises on which the entertainment or entertainment facilities are provided are made available for the purpose, or for purposes which include the purpose, of enabling the entertainment concerned (whether of a description falling within paragraph 2(1) or paragraph 3(2)) to take place.

> To the extent that the provision of entertainment facilities consists of making premises available, the premises are to be regarded for the purposes of this sub-paragraph as premises "on which" entertainment facilities are provided.

5.3.4    It can be seen that 'provision' of regulated entertainment is comprised of two elements. One is making entertainment or entertainment facilities available to certain categories of persons (first condition), each of which is considered below, and the other is making premises available for a purpose that includes enabling the entertainment concerned to take place (second condition). Premises being 'made available' suggests the need for some purposive intent on the part of a person. The mere fact that particular types of entertainment actually take place on premises may not in itself suffice. If entertainment were to take place spontaneously, it could not be said that the premises were made available to those who participated in the spontaneous entertainment. The Guidance, para 3.24, provides:

> The spontaneous performance of music, singing or dancing does not amount to the provision of regulated entertainment and is not a licensable activity. The relevant part of the 2003 Act to consider in this context is paragraph 1(3) of Schedule 1 to the Act. This states that the second condition which must apply before an activity constitutes the provision of regulated entertainment is that the premises (meaning "any place") at which the entertainment is, or entertainment facilities are, provided are made available for the purpose, or purposes which include the purpose, of enabling the entertainment concerned to take place. In the case of genuinely spontaneous music (including singing) and dancing, the place where the entertainment takes place will not have been made available to those taking part for that purpose.

This would seem to be the case whether or not there is an awareness or foresight that such entertainment may take place. Awareness or foresight is not purposive intent and in itself ought not to suffice, although it may be evidence from which such intent can be inferred.

### 5.3.5    Members of the public or a section of the public

5.3.6    The 2003 Act, like its predecessors, does not define 'public' and recourse must be had to case law decided under earlier legislative provisions to ascertain the meaning and scope of the term. There is, however, no single authoritative definition emerging from the decided cases.

For entertainment to be open to members of the public, it needs to be open to the public without discrimination, that is, anyone can obtain entry, whether or not any admission charge is made. In *Allen v Emmerson*, where the High Court had to decide, *inter alia*, whether a licence under a local Act of Parliament was required for fun fair premises, entry to which did not involve the payment of any admission charge, the court was of the opinion that:

> a satisfactory working definition of "public entertainment" was one suggested by Mr Turner [counsel for the appellant] in argument, namely, "a place open to members of the public without discrimination who desire to be entertained and where means of entertainment are provided". Judged by this test, or indeed, by the ordinary use of language, these fun fairs were, in our view, "places of public entertainment", and none the less so because no fee was charged for admission to the premises.[9]

5.3.7    However, it is likely in many cases that there will be an admission charge, in which case the test will be whether the place is open to members of the public on payment for admission. It is the place being open for admission which is important and not whether members of the public are in fact present at the place where the entertainment is being provided. As Lord Parker CJ remarked in *Gardner v Morris* (1961) 59 LGR 187 (at 189):

> the test . . . is not whether one, two, or three or any particular number of members of the public were present, but whether, on the evidence, the proper inference is that the entertainment was open to the public in the sense that any reputable member of the public on paying the necessary admission fee could come into and take part in the entertainment.

Whilst provision of regulated entertainment under para 1(2)(a) may be for members of the public at large, where anyone can obtain entry, it need not be and it will suffice it is for a 'section of the public'. This expression, which is not defined by the Act, seems to envisage entry by anyone falling within a particular category or description, for example anyone over the age of 18 or under the age of 30. However, what comprises a section of the public may not always be easy to ascertain. Persons falling within a particular category or description might be described as a section of the public, although they might equally be described as a private class of persons. As Lord Cross observed in *Dingle v Turner* [1972] AC 601 (at 616):

> The phrase a "section of the public" is in truth a vague phrase which may mean different things to different people . . . No doubt some classes are more naturally describable as sections of the public whilst other classes are more naturally describable as private classes than as sections of the public.

His Lordship went on to give examples of blind persons as more naturally describable as sections of the public and employees in 'some fairly small firm' being more naturally describable as a private class, so the matter seems to be one of degree. The larger the category or descriptions of persons, the more likely it is to be regarded as a section of the public.

### 5.3.8   *Exclusively for members of a qualifying club and their guests*

Where regulated entertainment is provided exclusively for members of a qualifying club[10] and their guests, this will not constitute public entertainment. Here, the entertainment is not open to the public because only members and their bona fide guests are able to obtain admission. The guests will not be considered to be members of the public because they cannot obtain entry in their own right independent of the member introducing them. The Divisional Court, in *Severn View Social Club and Institute Ltd v Chepstow (Monmouthshire) Licensing Justices*,[11] held that it was wrong to take the view that the admission of bona fide guests of members of a club to functions involving music and dancing made those functions public, so that a licence for this entertainment was required. Nevertheless, where regulated entertainment is provided exclusively for members of a qualifying club and their guests, this constitutes a 'provision of regulated entertainment' by virtue of para 1(2)(b) of Sched 1 and this will constitute a licensable activity for which authorisation is required.

However, para 1(2)(b) of Sched 1 applies only in respect of qualifying clubs and does not apply to regulated entertainment provided exclusively for members of other clubs and their guests. Other clubs may well be bona fide members' clubs to which the public are not admitted, but not meet the conditions for a qualifying club, for example because they do not have 25 members. There will not be a 'provision of regulated entertainment' by such a club under either para 1(2)(a) of Sched 1, as regulated entertainment is not provided to any extent for members of the public or a section of the public, or under para 1(2)(b) of Sched 1, as regulated entertainment is not provided exclusively for members of a qualifying club and their guests, although there might be under para 1(2)(c) of Sched 1, which is considered below, if the regulated entertainment is provided for consideration and with a view to profit; but if such clubs operate on a non-profit-making basis, it seems that they fall outside the scope of regulatory control.

### 5.3.9   For consideration and with a view to profit

5.3.10   This applies to the provision of any regulated entertainment not falling within the two preceding paragraphs and will thus include entertainment for persons at private events, although there will only be provision of regulated entertainment if it is 'for consideration and with a view to profit'.

#### 5.3.11   For consideration

5.3.12   Regulated entertainment will be provided for consideration only if a charge is made by those organising or managing the entertainment and is paid by some or all of the persons for whom the entertainment is provided.[12] The charge will most probably be the payment of money, but need not be and anything of value, which is requested and given, will suffice. Paragraph 1(4) and (5) provides:

> (4)  For the purposes of sub-paragraph (2)(c), entertainment is, or entertainment facilities are, to be regarded as provided for consideration only if any charge–
>   (a)  is made by or on behalf of–
>     (i)   any person concerned in the organisation or management of that entertainment, or
>     (ii)  any person concerned in the organisation or management of those facilities who is also concerned in the organisation or management of the entertainment within paragraph 3(2) in which those facilities enable persons to take part, and
>   (b)  is paid by or on behalf of some or all of the persons for whom that entertainment is, or those facilities are, provided.
> (5)  In sub-paragraph (4), "charge" includes any charge for the provision of goods or services.

As far as the making of a charge is concerned, persons concerned in the organisation or management of regulated entertainment will comprise those responsible for putting on, arranging or promoting the entertainment, whilst those concerned in the management will be those who exercise some control over the entertainment and the venue at which it takes place during its performance. The phrase 'concerned in the organisation or management' of an entertainment would not seem to extend beyond such persons (or those acting on their behalf) in this context, given the requirement that a charge is made by them. It is true that the Divisional Court, in *Chichester District Council v Ware* (1992) 157 JP 574, in the context of the offence of providing unlicensed public entertainment under the Local Government (Miscellaneous Provisions) Act 1982, gave a much wider interpretation to this phrase, taking the view that it covered anyone who took part in the running of the entertainment and whose part could be said to contribute significantly to the whole unlicensed entertainment; but, whilst a broader view may be appropriate in the context of liability, it can hardly have application in the present context when the making of a charge is required.

5.3.13   It is not sufficient that a charge is made unless it is made by those concerned in the organisation or management of the entertainment. Thus a person might hire out a room in which regulated entertainment takes place but if he is not involved in the entertainment's organisation or management there will be no provision by him of regulated entertainment. Paragraph 3.18 of the Guidance states:

> a private event for invited guests held in a hired private room with a live band and dancing and no charge for admission intended to make a profit is not a regulated entertainment unless the person who hires out the room (for example, the owner of the house in which the room is situated) is also involved in the organisation or management of the entertainment. An owner may become so involved by, for example, hiring a dancefloor, sound equipment and/or smoke machine along with the room, or by arranging for a DJ or band to play at the event. In this case, the provision by the owner of the room (and any other entertainment facilities they provide) for a charge and with a view to profit will itself be a provision of regulated entertainment. By contrast, if the owner simply hires out the room for an event and is not further involved with the entertainment at the event, they will not be providing a regulated entertainment, and the event would need to be looked at separately from the hire of the room in order to determine whether it was itself an instance of regulated entertainment.[13]

Persons performing or playing the music are not, however, themselves concerned in the organisation or management of the entertainment if their involvement does not extend beyond simply selecting the music to be performed or played, determining how it shall be performed or played, or facilitating its performance or playing, for example by providing facilities such as musical instruments to perform or play the music. Paragraph 1(6) makes the following specific provision to this effect:

> For the purposes of sub-paragraph (4)(a), where the entertainment consists of the performance of live music or the playing of recorded music, a person performing or playing the music is not concerned in the organisation or management of the entertainment by reason only that he does one or more of the following–
> (a)  chooses the music to be performed or played,
> (b)  determines the manner in which he performs or plays it,
> (c)  provides any facilities for the purposes of his performance or playing of the music.

### 5.3.14   *With a view to profit*

Regulated entertainment will be provided with a view to profit if the purpose, or one of the purposes, of it is financial gain and a financial benefit is obtained by some individual or a private (or public) body. There are, however, some instances where a financial gain may be made where a regulated entertainment would not ordinarily be thought of as having been provided 'with a view to profit'. One such case is where a genuine members' club provides regulated entertainment with a view to raising funds to be used for the benefit of its members. Such an activity is not regarded as being undertaken with a view to profit for, as Lord Denning MR stated, in the Court of Appeal in *Tehrani v Rostron* [1971] 3 All ER 790, 793, 'in a members' club, the members ... conduct it for their own benefit, not with a view to profit' (see 8.1.1 below).

Another such case may be where money is raised for charity from a regulated entertainment. It was perhaps because the ordinary meaning of the words 'with a view to profit' would not encompass money raised for charity that the Bill originally included a provision that regulated entertainment was to be regarded as provided with a view to profit where it was with a view to raising money for charity. This was deleted during the course of the legislation's passage and, without such a provision, it might be assumed that such entertainment is not to be so regarded. Nevertheless, according to the Explanatory Notes to the Act, entertainment provided to raise money for charity *is* entertainment provided with a view to profit.[14] If this was the intention, a provision to this effect should have remained in the Act. As this was deleted, this should be taken to indicate that money raised for charity falls *outside* the scope of regulated entertainment. Notwithstanding the statements in the Explanatory Notes (which do not form part of the Act and have not been endorsed by Parliament), it is submitted that 'with a view to profit' should be interpreted so as to exclude money raised for charity through private provision of entertainment. The requirements of 'consideration' and 'profit' seem to be more in keeping with 'commercial' provision rather than 'charitable' provision and ought to be confined to the former instances. Where there is 'charitable' provision and members of the public are admitted, this is a licensable activity, irrespective of the 'profit' issue, but extending it beyond this to encompass private provision seems to take regulatory control too far.

If any charge made is merely to cover costs, it will not be with a view to profit and the entertainment will not be licensable. As the Guidance, para 3.19, states:

> a party organised in a private house by and for friends, (and not open to the public) with music and dancing, and where a charge or contribution is made solely to cover the costs of the entertainment and not with a view to profit would not be an instance of regulated entertainment. In the same vein, any charge made by musicians or other performers or their agents to the organiser of a private event does not of itself make that entertainment licensable unless the guests attending are themselves charged for the entertainment with a view to achieving a profit.

As para 1(2)(c) of Sched 1 to the 2003 Act requires that provision of regulated entertainment is 'with a view' to profit, it would appear to be the intention to make a profit from the activity that is important rather than the fact that a profit might be made. If the intention is merely to cover costs, but the actual costs turn out to be less than anticipated so that a profit is in fact made, this would seem not to make the activity licensable and would not constitute provision of an unlicensed activity if no authorisation had been obtained. This is apparent from the Guidance, which provides: 'The fact that a profit might inadvertently be made would be irrelevant as long as there had not been an intention to make a profit' (para 3.16). Of course, the greater the profit made and the more consistently a profit is made, the harder it may be to rebut any inference that the intention was to make a profit.

### 5.3.15 Exemptions

The provision of regulated entertainment is subject to a number of exemptions set out in Pt 2 of Sched 1 and these are covered below.[15]

## 5.3.16 Meaning of 'regulated entertainment'

Regulated entertainment as defined in Sched 1 includes both entertainment and entertainment facilities. The former is covered by para 2 and the latter by para 3. The categories of entertainment and entertainment facilities are capable of being amended, for para 4 provides that the Secretary of State can modify the descriptions by adding, varying or removing any of them.[16]

## 5.3.17 Entertainment as 'regulated entertainment'

### 5.3.18 Types of entertainment

5.3.19   These are set out in para 2(1), which provides:

The descriptions of entertainment are–
(a)   a performance of a play,
(b)   an exhibition of a film,
(c)   an indoor sporting event,
(d)   a boxing or wrestling entertainment,
(e)   a performance of live music,
(f)   any playing of recorded music,
(g)   a performance of dance,
(h)   entertainment of a similar description to that falling within paragraph (e), (f) or (g),

where the entertainment takes place in the presence of an audience and is provided for the purpose, or for purposes which include the purpose, of entertaining that audience.

The term 'audience' might be more customarily employed for some of these forms of entertainment (for example plays and films) than for others (for example, sporting events and boxing and wrestling), where the term 'spectators' might more normally be used. However, the term 'audience' in sub-para (1) will include a reference to spectators, as para 2(2) makes clear.[17]

It is only where the above activities take place before an audience or spectators that there will be a licensable entertainment. Since the 'provision' of regulated entertainment includes provision not only for the public or a section of it, but also for qualifying club members and guests and in other cases where it is for consideration and with a view to profit, it is clear that the audience or spectators need not comprise or consist of any members of the public. Any audience or spectators privately invited will suffice. Activities which do not, however, involve entertaining an audience or spectators are not licensable under the Act. Paragraph 3.12 of the Guidance provides the following illustrations:

* education – teaching students to perform music or to dance;
* activities which involve participation as acts of worship in a religious context;
* the demonstration of a product – for example, a guitar – in a music shop; or
* the rehearsal of a play or rehearsal of a performance of music to which the public are not admitted.[18]

5.3.20   A licensing authority will thus, first and foremost, need to consider the word 'entertainment' and focus on whether what takes place can be said to constitute an entertainment. It is only when satisfied that activities amount to entertainment that a licensing authority should go on to consider the qualifying conditions, exemptions and other definitions in Sched 1.

Except in the case of indoor sporting events, there is no requirement that the regulated entertainment takes place indoors or that the audience is accommodated indoors. Regulated entertainment is licensable when it takes place on 'premises', which is defined in s 193 to include 'any place', and this is generally understood to include places outdoors (see 6.1.3 below). The fact that entertainment can take place before an audience that is outdoors will obviously include open air music concerts within the definition of 'regulated entertainment', although less clear is whether it will include the activity of busking.

Buskers provide one of the types of entertainment set out in para 2(1), the performance of live music; this takes place in the presence of an 'audience', if passers-by are considered to comprise an audience,[19] and the music is clearly for the purposes of entertaining the 'audience'. If 'any place' (which can include outdoor areas – see 6.1.3 below) in s 193 is given a literal interpretation by the courts, buskers might be included and authorisation in the form of a premises licence or a TEN will be needed.[20] However, this seems unlikely, given that the Court of Appeal in *R v Bow Street Magistrates' Court, ex p McDonald* [1996] 15 LS Gaz R 30 held that a busker who habitually played his guitar at one spot in Leicester Square was not, under para 1(7) of Sched 12 to the London Government Act 1963, providing music at a 'place' and did not require a licence. The court rejected a contention, based on the Oxford Dictionary meaning of 'place', that it encompassed 'any area which is capable of demarcation' and could therefore include any London street. Schiemann LJ stated:

> I do not find the reference to "an area capable of demarcation" helpful. Any area is capable of demarcation . . . the test "is the area capable of demarcation" cannot be a complete test capable of operation in the context of criminal sanctions. Something more must be required.[21]

An alternative, narrower contention that 'place' meant an area regularly used by the busker for his music-making, relying on *Powell v Kempton Park Racecourse Co Ltd* [1899] AC 143[22] and various (unspecified) cases under the Shops Act 1950, was also rejected. Schiemann LJ stated:

> For my part I do not find either that case or the Shops Act cases . . . helpful in the instant exercise. They were dealing with the meaning of the word "place" in different Acts of Parliament. We are dealing with the word "premises" in the 1963 Act, admittedly as further defined in that Act.

> Schedule 12 is concerned with the control of premises to which the public is invited for public dancing or music and any other public entertainment of the like kind. It does not forbid all music-making in public places. That much is common ground. The usual controls concern fire risk, numbers coming and going, hours of music-making, and so on. They envisage a situation in which someone other than the Council has the power to regulate the activities of the public in that place and where it is in the public interest that the Council assume some power of entry and supervision which it would not otherwise have. The Schedule is not designed to deal with situations where what is going on is in a street to which every music-maker or other member of the public has access. One music-maker can replace another at an attractive spot, and the Schedule does not seem to me to envisage situations in which several persons are licensed during one day to operate in one place . . .

What the appellant was doing in the instant case was playing his guitar in a public place to which the public had access and over which the Council, by virtue of its ownership of the land and its many powers as highway and local authority, had innumerable powers. That, in my judgment, is not a situation for which the Schedule was designed or which it should be interpreted to cover.[23]

Since the Court of Appeal adopted a purposive approach in respect of the word 'place' in the London Government Act 1963, if a similar approach is taken under the 2003 Act, as seems likely, busking will not be a licensable activity taking place on 'premises' and no authorisation will be required.

The various types of entertainment set out in para 2(1) are themselves defined in Pt 3 of Sched 1[24] and their meaning is considered immediately below.

### 5.3.21  Performance of a play

Paragraph 14 provides:

(1) A "performance of a play" means a performance of any dramatic piece, whether involving improvisation or not–
   (a) which is given wholly or in part by one or more persons actually present and performing, and
   (b) in which the whole or a major proportion of what is done by the person or persons performing, whether by way of speech, singing or action, involves the playing of a role.
(2) In this paragraph, "performance" includes rehearsal (and "performing" is to be construed accordingly).

Notwithstanding that there is no express provision that 'play' includes a ballet, unlike under the previous law in s 18(1) of the Theatres Act 1968, para 14(1)(a) seems to be wide enough to cover any ballet given. Paragraph 14(2) extends performance of a play to rehearsals, which previously did not fall within the scope of licensing control. However, rehearsals of plays will only constitute regulated entertainment if they take place in the presence of an audience and if one of the purposes for which they are provided is entertaining that audience.[25]

### 5.3.22  Exhibition of a film

Paragraph 15 provides:

An "exhibition of a film" means any exhibition of moving pictures.

An 'exhibition' of moving pictures means the showing of moving pictures to an audience rather than a display of moving objects on a screen. The House of Lords so held, in *British Amusement Catering Trades Association v Westminster City Council* [1989] AC 147, when deciding that a licence was not required under the previous law for an amusement arcade where coin-operated video games were played. Lord Griffiths, with whom other members of the House agreed, stated (at 157):

Mervyn Davies J and the majority of the Court of Appeal accepted the argument that because the screen of a video game displays moving objects there was therefore an exhibition of moving pictures within the meaning of the Act . . . This approach fails in my opinion to take into account the different shades of meaning attached in the English language to the use of the word "exhibition" according to the context in which it is used and, in particular, fails to give sufficient weight to the primary dictionary meaning of "exhibit" – 'especially to show publicly for the purpose of amusement or instruction'.

... reading the Act as a whole and the Regulations made thereunder, I have no doubt that exhibition is used in the sense of a show to an audience and not in the sense of a display of moving objects on the screen of a video game.

This will continue to apply under para 15. It seems implicit in the concept of a film shown to an audience that the audience is there wholly or mainly for the purpose of viewing the show whilst it is taking place. If persons are present for other purposes, and any viewing of moving pictures on a screen is incidental or a secondary activity, then there would not seem to be any 'film exhibition' and the activity would not be licensable. This might be the case with video juke boxes, which have moving images displayed on a screen whilst music is playing, the video presenting a visual representation of the music. It is not uncommon to have video juke boxes in public houses, but their presence there would not appear to involve any film show to an audience as the public are not at the premises for the purpose of viewing a film show. Even if a number of persons were to go to the premises specifically or primarily to watch the video juke box, rather than for a drink, this should make no difference. The test of primary purpose is likely to be objectively determined, by reference to what the reasonable person would regard as the primary purpose for which the premises are used, rather than subjectively by reference to the intent of those going there.

### 5.3.23   *Indoor sporting event*

5.3.24   Paragraph 16(1) provides:

An "indoor sporting event" is a sporting event–
(a) which takes place wholly inside a building, and
(b) at which the spectators present at the event are accommodated wholly inside that building.

Paragraph 16 applies only to indoor sporting events and outdoor sporting events and sports stadia fall outside the scope of licensing control as they are the subject of separate legislation with regard to health and safety and fire safety.[26] Such stadia may, of course, have several bars and restaurants selling alcohol and have a premises licence providing authorisation for this licensable activity, but the sporting events themselves will not be ones for which authorisation under the 2003 Act is required. This will similarly be the case where sporting events are held at major sports grounds with roofs that open and close, such as the Millennium Stadium in Cardiff. These are treated as outdoor premises and sports taking place there are not categorised as 'indoor sports'.[27] Paragraph 16(2) provides:

In this paragraph–

"building" means any roofed structure (other than a structure with a roof which may be opened or closed) and includes a vehicle, vessel or moveable structure.

Where a building has a fixed, rather than a sliding, roof structure, sporting events taking place within it will be indoor sports. No indication is given in the definition as to the nature of the roofed structure or the building itself, unlike under the previous law where reference was made to 'any permanent or temporary building and any tent or inflatable structure'.[28] Nor is any indication given as to the nature of a moveable structure, although the expression seems wide enough to include both structures that can be moved in their completed state and ones that need dismantling before being moved. Temporary buildings, marquees, tents and inflatable structures should all fall within the definition of 'building' in para 16, either as roofed structures or as moveable structures.

5.3.25  The definitions of 'sporting event' and 'sport' are contained in para 16(2), which provides:

> "sporting event" means any contest, exhibition or display of any sport, and "sport" includes–
>
> (a) any game in which physical skill is the predominant factor, and
> (b) any form of physical recreation which is also engaged in for purposes of competition or display.

For activities to constitute a 'sport', one of two characteristics will be needed. One is that physical skill will need to be the main factor, which will be the case for a wide range of activities, such as football, badminton, squash and water polo (to mention but a few examples), which might take place indoors in sports centres and similar premises. If physical skill is not the main factor, as with activities such as chess, dominoes or poker, this will not constitute a 'sporting event' and will not be licensable, even if attended by the public as spectators. The other is where recreational physical activity is undertaken for the purposes of competition or display, as with gymnastics or artistic skating. This will constitute a 'sport' and an indoor sporting event for which authorisation will be required. Whether any activity of dancing similarly undertaken, such as artistic dancing, will be licensable as an indoor sporting event is less clear. Dancing is a form of regulated entertainment and is licensable as such, but when undertaken competitively or for display for an audience it may additionally be an indoor sporting event for which authorisation is also needed. There is no exclusion of dancing from the definition of 'sport', as there was under the previous law.[29] Presumably, this exclusion was deliberate rather than inadvertent and, if this was the case, it would seem that activities, such as artistic dancing, will be licensable as indoor sporting events.

5.3.26  Where sporting events take place indoors and are observed by spectators, but are not primarily taking place for their entertainment, this will not constitute regulated entertainment. The Guidance states:

> Games commonly played in pubs and social and youth clubs like pool, darts, table tennis and billiards may fall within the definition of indoor sports in Schedule 1, but normally they would not be played for the entertainment of spectators but for the private enjoyment of the participants. As such they would not normally constitute the provision of regulated entertainment and the facilities provided (even if a pub provides them with a view to profit) do not fall within the limited list of entertainment facilities in that Schedule . . . It is only when such games take place in the presence of an audience and are provided to, at least in part, entertain that audience, for example, a darts championship competition that the activity would become licensable.[30]

This again illustrates the importance of focusing on whether what is provided constitutes 'entertainment'. If it does, it seems that the activity will be licensable irrespective of whether or not the sporting event is the principal purpose for which the building is being used on that occasion.

### 5.3.27   Boxing or wrestling entertainment

Paragraph 17 provides:

> A "boxing or wrestling entertainment" is any contest, exhibition or display of boxing or wrestling.

Where boxing and wrestling entertainments take place indoors, this will constitute an indoor sporting event under the preceding paragraph, but para 17 makes it a licensable activity wherever such an entertainment takes place. Effectively, therefore, para 17 will apply to boxing and wrestling entertainments held wholly or partially outdoors. Such an entertainment will most obviously include a sporting contest, although para 17 is not so restricted as an entertainment extends to 'any contest, exhibition or display of boxing or wrestling'. Neither 'boxing' nor 'wrestling' is defined and, although 'boxing' is likely to have a clearly understood meaning, 'wrestling' is a term which might be employed to describe more than one type of activity. The expression 'wrestling', as traditionally understood, covers hand-to-hand combat between unarmed contestants, usually in a ring or enclosed area, who try to throw each other around, but the term might be used to describe other activity. This could include, for example, arm wrestling (or Indian wrestling as it is sometimes known), which is where two opponents sit facing each other with usually right hands interlocked and elbows firmly positioned, as on a table surface, and attempt to force each other's arm down. It is less clear whether this constitutes a 'wrestling entertainment'. It is thought not, given that para 17 refers to a 'boxing or wrestling entertainment'. This suggests that 'wrestling', in the context of para 17, is perceived as similar in nature to 'boxing' and this is really only the case where 'wrestling' has its traditionally understood meaning indicated above.

Attempts to extend licensing control beyond boxing and wrestling to include other 'martial arts' sports, such as kick-boxing and karate, in cases where these are provided for the entertainment of an audience, were resisted by the Government during the course of the legislation's passage. This was on the grounds that they were less likely to give rise to public safety concerns. During the committee stage of the Bill in the House of Lords, Lord Davies stated:

> we know that boxing and wrestling and their audiences present a significant issue with regard to public safety ... the relationship between wrestling and its audience is particularly engaging, and its showmanship can engage the audience very directly. But, as has been known for many decades, boxing also engages passions ... but I do not believe that martial arts normally set out to engage the audience in quite the same way as do boxing and wrestling.[31]

### 5.3.28   Performance of live music

Paragraph 18 provides:

> "Music" includes vocal or instrumental music or any combination of the two.

'Music' thus includes both singing and instrumental music, so live music concerts, whether instrumental only or a combination of instrumental and singing, will be regulated entertainment. So also will events involving singing, even without any instrumental accompaniment, as in the case of karaoke, where there is singing to the accompaniment of recorded rather than live music. Here the singing element will constitute 'music' that is being performed live.

The term 'performance', as far as live music is concerned, is not defined, unlike in the case of the performance of a play. Paragraph 14(2) specifically provides that the performance of a play includes a rehearsal (see 5.3.21 above), but there is no provision to this effect for live music. It would seem therefore that a live music concert rehearsal, to which an audience was invited, would not constitute a licensable activity under this provision.

### 5.3.29   Any playing of recorded music

Recorded music is played in many premises, but this will be a licensable activity only where it is done for the entertainment of an audience, as where karaoke is provided. Otherwise it will not be licensable and, further, there are exemptions provided where this is incidental to other activities (see 5.3.36–5.3.37 below). No definition is provided as to what constitutes 'recorded' music. In *Toye v Southwark London Borough Council* (2002) 49 *Licensing Review* 13, the Administrative Court, when considering the meaning of 'reproduction of recorded sound' in s 182 of the Licensing Act 1964, took a broad view of what could constitute 'recorded sound'. Holding that sound could be 'recorded' where it was produced by means of written instructions to a computer or synthesizer, Forbes J stated (at 16): 'the expression recorded sound is capable of wide meaning and application.' It is likely that a similar meaning will be adopted in relation to the 'playing of recorded music' and that music recorded by any means will suffice.

### 5.3.30   Performance of dance

The term 'dancing' is not defined and, if given its ordinary meaning, might, tradition-ally at least, be understood to encompass rhythmical movements of the body with measured steps regulated by a musical tune. The *Shorter Oxford English Dictionary* defines 'dancing' to include 'a rhythmical skipping and stepping, with regular turn-ings and movements, usually to a musical accompaniment'. This emphasis on rhythm as a characteristic of dancing is apparent from earlier case law where the meaning of 'dancing' was considered, as can be seen in the remarks of Cave J in *Fay v Bignell* (1883) Cab & El 112, 113: 'It is not every movement of the legs and feet which con-stitutes dancing. It must be a graceful and rhythmical motion.' However, it is clear that this is no longer a defining characteristic, for, as Roch LJ observed in the Court of Appeal in *Willowcell Ltd v Westminster City Council* (1995) 160 JP 101, 111, 'the concept of dancing has changed fundamentally between Victorian times and the present day'. Consequently, it would seem that the present-day concept of dancing does encompass body movements that may not be rhythmical. Nor would it seem to be necessary that movements are regulated by a musical tune. Indeed, this appeared to be recognised by the Divisional Court in *Sammut v Westminster City Council*, where Smith J stated: 'the word "dancing" must be construed in its modern sense, which includes (as it seems to me that it does nowadays) a wide variety of human move-ments, not necessarily rhythmical and not necessarily related to music.'[32]

A 'performance of dance' will be one where the dancing is provided for the entertainment of an audience. 'Performance' is not defined, however, to include a rehearsal, so a rehearsal of dancing to which an audience has been invited will not constitute a licensable activity.[33] Where the entertainment consists of persons meeting up for the purposes of entertaining themselves by taking part in dancing, as at dance halls and dancing schools, this will not be regulated entertainment under paragraph 2(1)(g), as the entertainment is not provided for an audience. It will, nevertheless, be licensable, since it constitutes the provision of entertainment facilities (see 5.3.32 below).

### 5.3.31   *Entertainment of a similar description to that falling within paragraph (e), (f) or (g)*

This will be entertainment of a like kind to (live or recorded) music or the performance of dance. It might include, for example, a skating performance to music, which could be considered an entertainment of a similar description to music and dancing.[34] Similarly, a striptease performance, a form of erotic entertainment in which performers gradually remove items of clothing or apparel in a slow and seductive manner, if not considered to be dancing itself, might be regarded as entertainment of a similar description to dancing.[35] So also might lap dancing (or table dancing), where performers, in return for a payment of money by a customer seated at a table, take off clothing whilst gyrating their bodies in close proximity to the customer. Such entertainment, if not dancing itself, will certainly be entertainment of a similar description to dancing (and the playing of music if there is musical accompaniment for such a performance, as well there might be).

## 5.3.32  Entertainment facilities as 'regulated entertainment'

The types of entertainment for which the provision of facilities becomes licensable are set out in para 3, which provides:

>   (1)   In this Schedule, "entertainment facilities" means facilities for enabling persons to take part in entertainment of a description falling within subparagraph (2) for the purpose, or for purposes which include the purpose, of being entertained.
>   (2)   The descriptions of entertainment are–
>       (a)   making music,
>       (b)   dancing,
>       (c)   entertainment of a similar description to that falling within paragraph (a) or (b).
>   (3)   This paragraph is subject to Part 3 of this Schedule (interpretation).

This is a more limited list than the forms of entertainment set out in para 2(1), is confined to provision of facilities for music, dancing or entertainment of a similar description, and there is no requirement for an audience or spectators to be present. The 2003 Act for the first time expressly draws a distinction drawn between provision of entertainment and provision of entertainment facilities, although it had long been established under the previous law that a licence for public entertainment was required, not only where the public attended a performance of some person or persons, but also where the public participated in some event or activity that comprised the entertainment, such as taking part in dancing (see *Clarke v Serle* (1793) 1 Esp 25). Both such instances were simply considered to be licensable public entertainment but, as regulated entertainment under the 2003 Act, the instances appear to fall under different provisions. The former instance seems to constitute provision of entertainment under para 2 and the latter provision of entertainment facilities under para 3.

The drawing of an express statutory distinction between provision of entertainment and provision of entertainment facilities may not be without its difficulties. It will be clear in some instances that particular activities involving music and dancing fall only within either para 2 or para 3. Displaying a troupe of dancers, for example, falls only within para 2, as 'a performance of dance' under para 2(1)(g) in the presence of an audience. It does not involve provision of entertainment facilities for dancing under para 3(2)(b), as it does not enable persons to take part in dancing. Similarly, hiring out a music recording studio to musicians falls only within para 3, as entertainment facilities for the musicians to take part in making music under para 3(2)(a). It does not involve provision of entertainment by a performance of live music under para 2(1)(e), as no music is provided for the entertainment of an audience. In other instances, however, particular activities might perhaps fall within both para 2 and para 3. This could be the case where there is provision of an in-house music sound system. On the wording of the relevant provisions, this could be described as 'any playing of recorded music' for the entertainment of an audience under para 2(1)(f) and equally could be described as entertainment facilities for enabling persons to take part in making music under para 3(2)(a), through providing the opportunity for them to sing along to the recording.

Here, difficulties may well arise because it is unclear whether the provisions in para 2 and para 3 are mutually exclusive. The view might be taken that they are mutually exclusive because Parliament, by drawing a distinction between these two categories in Sched 1, intended them to cover different types of provision. However, given that there may be an element of uncertainty as to whether particular activities fall within para 2 or para 3, a rigid approach of regarding the two paragraphs and categories as mutually exclusive might prove unduly restrictive and problematic. Activities would need to fall within one or other category and a determination made as to the category in which an activity was to be placed. A more flexible approach would be to regard them as having a measure of overlap, although this will not necessarily resolve all difficulties. Even if paras 2 and 3 might overlap, a further question may arise which is whether, on a premises licence (or CPC) application form, an indication needs to be given that the licensable activities will include both categories (by ticking the box, in the example of an in-house music sound system, for 'recorded music' *and* for 'making music') or whether it will suffice if an indication is given that the licensable activities will include one or other of these two categories (by ticking *one* of the boxes, but not both).

One view would be that it may suffice if the 'recorded music' box only is ticked, since the category of '*any* playing of recorded music' (emphasis supplied) in para 2(1)(f) is very broadly expressed and might be wide enough to subsume provision of entertainment facilities for making music in para 3(2)(a), in cases where it can be said that there is entertainment for an audience, without the need for provision of entertainment facilities to be additionally specified. An alternative view would be that, if particular activities might fall within the descriptions in both para 2 and para 3, both boxes should be ticked. Neither the Explanatory Notes to the Act nor the Guidance gives a steer on which approach should be adopted here, although the Guidance seems to envisage entertainment facilities as an appropriate category to cover cases where facilities are provided which can entertain an audience, for para 3.11 provides:

> Entertainment facilities include, for example, a karaoke machine provided for the use of and entertainment of customers in a public house.

In the light of this, the prudent course may be to tick both boxes. If this is done, authorisation will be provided, irrespective of whether a broad interpretation is taken of 'any playing of recorded music' in para 2(1)(f) so as to include within this expression the provision of entertainment facilities. Further, if both are specified, even if paras 2 and 3 are regarded as mutually exclusive, then whichever category within which the activity in question is considered to fall, will in any event have authorisation.

Paragraph 3.11 of the Guidance indicates that the facilities must be provided 'for the use of and to entertain customers' and gives the following examples:

- a karaoke machine provided for the use of and entertainment of customers in a public house
- a dance floor provided for use by the public in a nightclub
- musical instruments made available for use by the public to entertain others at licensed premises.

In these instances, there will be other persons present on the premises who may be watching the activities in question, but this would not seem to be necessary to constitute the provision of entertainment facilities. Thus, for example, a person who makes available a music recording studio to enable recording artists to practice or to record music there might be providing 'entertainment facilities'. This could amount to providing facilities for enabling those persons to take part in making music for purposes which include their entertainment.[36]

### 5.3.33 Exemptions

Part 2 of Sched 1 contains a number of exemptions where the provision of regulated entertainment in certain instances does not constitute a licensable activity. One or two exemptions relate only to certain types of regulated entertainment, notably film exhibitions and music, although the majority apply to regulated entertainment generally in the particular circumstances. The exemptions are set out in paras 5–12.

### 5.3.34 *Film exhibitions for demonstration, advertisement or information*

Paragraph 5 provides:

> The provision of entertainment consisting of the exhibition of a film is not to be regarded as the provision of regulated entertainment for the purposes of this Act if its sole or main purpose is to–
> (a) demonstrate any product,
> (b) advertise any goods or services, or
> (c) provide information, education or instruction.

Given the nature of the particular film exhibitions, it may be questioned whether in any event these would constitute the provision of 'entertainment' so as to make their exhibition a licensable activity in the first place. However, perhaps for the avoidance of doubt, an exemption is provided and this applies irrespective of where the exhibition of the film takes place or who attends it. The provision would thus exempt, for example, educational films shown in schools, or special advertisements shown at product display stands in shopping centres (Explanatory Note 302).

If such an exhibition were to take place on premises holding a premises licence, which included authorisation for the exhibition of films, it would seem that conditions relating to the exhibition of films on the premises would not have application in the case of an exhibition falling within para 5. The conditions would have application only where the exhibition of films constituted 'regulated entertainment' and this would not be the case here.[37]

### 5.3.35 *Film exhibitions in museums and art galleries*

Paragraph 6 provides:

> The provision of entertainment consisting of the exhibition of a film is not to be regarded as the provision of regulated entertainment for the purposes of this Act if it consists of or forms part of an exhibit put on show for any purposes of a museum or art gallery.

It is not uncommon for museums and art galleries to include, as part of their attractions, film exhibitions relating to aspects of the contents on display and this will not constitute 'regulated entertainment'. The Act contains no definition of 'museum' or 'art gallery', although, if the terms are given their ordinary and natural meaning, they would seem to encompass institutions or repositories for the collection, exhibition or study of, in the case of museums, objects of artistic, scientific, historic or educational interest and, in the case of art galleries, objects of artistic interest.

### 5.3.36 *Music incidental to certain other activities*

5.3.37 Paragraph 7 provides:

> The provision of entertainment consisting of the performance of live music or the playing of recorded music is not to be regarded as the provision of regulated entertainment for the purposes of this Act to the extent that it is incidental to some other activity which is not itself–
>
> (a) a description of entertainment falling within paragraph 2, or
>
> (b) the provision of entertainment facilities.

The Act contains no definition of 'incidental', so the ordinary dictionary meaning of this term would be likely to apply. The *Shorter Oxford English Dictionary* defines the term to include 'occurring or liable to occur in fortuitous or subordinate conjunction with something else; casual', and whether this is the position will depend on the circumstances of the individual case. As para 3.21 of the Guidance states with regard to the incidental performance of live music and incidental playing of recorded music:

> Whether or not music of this kind is "incidental" to other activities is expected to be judged on a case by case basis and there is no definition in the 2003 Act. It will

ultimately be for the courts to decide whether music is "incidental" in the individual circumstances of any case.

Nevertheless, there may be a number of factors which might point towards music either being incidental or not incidental and para 3.22 of the Guidance states:

> In considering whether or not music is incidental, one factor will be whether or not, against a background of the other activities already taking place, the addition of music will create the potential to undermine the four licensing objectives of the Act. Other factors might include some or all of the following:
>
> - Is the music the main, or one of the main, reasons for people attending the premises?[38]
> - Is the music advertised as the main attraction?[39]
> - Does the volume of the music disrupt or predominate over other activities or could it be described as 'background' music?

Conversely, there may be other factors which would not normally be relevant and these might include the number of musicians (since an orchestra might provide incidental music at a large exhibition), whether the musicians are paid, whether the performance is pre-arranged, and whether a charge is made for admission to the premises (Guidance, para 3.22). Stand-up comedy is not regulated entertainment and musical accompaniment incidental to the main performance would not make it a licensable activity, although as para 3.23 of the Guidance recognises 'there are likely to be some circumstances which occupy a greyer area'.

The 'other activity' to which the music is incidental may be unconnected with any entertainment, as where background music is played in supermarkets, restaurants, hairdressers or lifts, although in other instances the 'other activity' may be some other form of entertainment. This will be the case where there is stand-up comedy, mentioned above, to which there is musical accompaniment, or where music is played at events such as fashion shows or firework displays. Similarly, at fairgrounds there will be entertainment like rides at the fair which have accompanying music and 'a good deal of the musical entertainment may be incidental to the main attractions' (Guidance, para 10.35). Paragraph 10.3 goes on to provide:

> However, in the case of a circus, music and dancing are likely to be main attractions themselves (and would be regulated entertainment) amidst a range of other activities which are not all regulated entertainment.

It might be questioned whether music and dancing are likely to be main attractions themselves in a circus. A circus ordinarily involves a travelling show of horses, riders, acrobats, clowns, performing animals and similar acts and any music, if not dancing, might be regarded as incidental to these activities.

Whilst the 'other activity' to which the music is incidental may be a form of entertainment, the exemption is qualified in that it will not apply if the music is incidental to a form of entertainment falling within para 2 or is incidental to the provision of entertainment facilities within para 3. This means that, where music takes place at entertainment events such as those mentioned above (fashion shows or firework displays), the exemption will apply, for these are not forms of entertainment falling within para 2. However, where music is played, for example, as an accompaniment to a film exhibition or performance of a play, which are forms of entertainment falling within para 2, the exemption will not apply. It seems therefore that cinemas and theatres will need not only authorisation under their premises licences for, respectively, film exhibitions and the performance of plays, but also for any playing of music. Further, music (instrumental or vocal) may feature in films or plays and, since this takes place in the presence of an audience and one of the purposes for which the music is provided is the audience's entertainment, this would seem to make the provision of the music a licensable activity. Again, this will not fall within the exemption and authorisation for it will be needed under the premises licence.[40]

The position will be the same where the music is incidental to an entertainment facility within para 3. An entertainment facility includes the provision of facilities for the making of music for the purpose of being entertained (para 3(2)(a)) and, accordingly, it may be that, where there is the provision of facilities for live music and music that can be described only as incidental takes place, the incidental music will fall outside the exemption. It would not seem in this instance to be 'incidental to some other activity which is not itself . . . the provision of entertainment facilities' within para 7, but in fact to be incidental to the provision of such facilities. If this is correct, it will mean that the exemption will not apply where instruments such as pianos are made available in public houses or similar premises. It is perhaps doubtful that this was intended and it certainly seems to sit uneasily with the statement of Dr Howells during the legislation's passage that a piano played in the background in a restaurant will be incidental music within the exemption (see note 38 below). Perhaps in instances such as pianos in public houses or restaurants, the music should be regarded as incidental to the sale of alcohol or the provision of food rather than incidental to the provision of entertainment facilities by making the piano available for the making of music, in which case it can then be regarded as falling within the exemption.

In the preceding instances, the music takes place at the same time as the other activity in question, but is incidental to it. However, in other instances music may not be taking place simultaneously, but may be for a period of limited duration relative to the length of the other activity in question. Here the music may be regarded as incidental, even though, when performed, it would be the principal part of the performance, because it is incidental to the other activity taken as a whole. There was authority under the previous law indicating that no licence was required in such cases.[41] Whether music would be regarded as 'incidental to some other activity' under para 7 in such circumstances is unclear. The approach of the courts under the previous law may be applied here or, alternatively, the view may be taken that music is a principal part in itself and, notwithstanding that it is of limited duration and incidental when judged by reference to the activity taken as a whole, nevertheless constitutes an independent attraction in itself. The view may be taken that it is one of the main reasons for people attending the premises and it seems implicit from what is said in para 3.22 of the Guidance (see above) that music would not be incidental where this is the case. Ultimately, however, it may be a question of the extent to which music can be regarded as independent from or subsumed within any other activities taking place on the premises and this will inevitably depend on the facts and circumstances of the individual case.

## 5.3.38 *Use of television or radio receivers*

Paragraph 8 provides:

> The provision of any entertainment or entertainment facilities is not to be regarded as the provision of regulated entertainment for the purposes of this Act to the extent that it consists of the simultaneous reception and playing of a programme included in a programme service within the meaning of the Broadcasting Act 1990 (c.42).[42]

This provides an exemption for all regulated entertainment that is broadcast on televisions and radios, irrespective of where the entertainment is provided.

### 5.3.39 *Religious meetings or services and places of worship*

Paragraph 9 provides:

> The provision of any entertainment or entertainment facilities–
>
> (a)  for the purposes of, or for purposes incidental to, a religious meeting or service, or
>
> (b)  at a place of public religious worship,
>
> is not to be regarded as the provision of regulated entertainment for the purposes of this Act.

This exemption applies in respect of any entertainment or entertainment facilities (hereafter 'entertainment'), although it is most likely to have application in respect of music. The exemption in para 9(a), where entertainment is provided as part of any religious meeting or service, will most obviously apply in respect of activities such as the singing of hymns during church services or singing during nativity plays. It might also include wedding ceremonies held in church or in a register office (HL Deb, vol 643, col 350, 12 December 2002), although not, it would seem, civil wedding ceremonies. The exemption applies irrespective of where the entertainment takes place and there is no requirement that it is at a place of worship.

For a place to be one of public religious worship under para 9(b), it will be necessary for the place to be consecrated and it must be available not only to the public for religious worship, but it must be apparent that it is so available (HL Deb, vol 645, col 37, 25 February 2003). Paragraph 9(b) requires only that the entertainment is held at a place of public religious worship and it is not necessary that the entertainment is in any way connected with or forms part of any ceremony of religious worship in such a place. Thus, as Baroness Blackstone stated during the course of the legislation's passage, the exemption 'will include instances in which the entertainment provided is secular' (HL Deb, vol 645, col 32, 25 February 2003). Whilst entertainment held within a church itself will clearly fall within the exemption, the position is less clear if the entertainment is held in some adjacent building such as a church annex. Whether this falls within the exemption will presumably depend on how 'place' is construed. If it means the place in which public worship actually takes place, and the annex is not in fact used for worship, then it would seem that exemption will not apply. If, on the other hand, 'place' is more generally construed and means the whole of the land or property on which worship takes place, then the exemption may apply.

The exemption will extend to church premises being hired out to some outside body to hold such events as well as where these events are held by the church authorities themselves. Further, the exemption in respect of places of public religious worship is all-embracing and extends to all places of public religious worship. Its confinement to places of public religious worship, however, may mean that the exemption is incompatibile with Convention rights under Arts 9, 10 and 14 (see 3.9 above).

## 5.3.40 Garden fêtes and similar events

Paragraph 10 provides:

(1) The provision of any entertainment or entertainment facilities at a garden fête, or at a function or event of a similar character, is not to be regarded as the provision of regulated entertainment for the purposes of this Act.

(2) But sub-paragraph (1) does not apply if the fête, function or event is promoted with a view to applying the whole or part of its proceeds for purposes of private gain.

(3) In sub-paragraph (2) "private gain", in relation to the proceeds of a fête, function or event, is to be construed in accordance with section 19(3) of the Gambling Act 2005.[43]

There is no definition of 'garden fête', although the expression seems to encompass events of an outdoor nature at which there is a range of amusements provided and items of a domestic nature for sale. The exemption also extends to 'a function or event of a similar character' to a garden fête, which might include a bazaar or an event at which a sale of work takes place, although it is less clear whether it will include events such as a sporting or athletic event, an exhibition, and a display, all of which were exempt from the need to obtain a public entertainment licence under the previous law in para 3(3)(a) of Sched 1 to the Local Government (Miscellaneous Provisions) Act 1982. The exemption extends to any entertainment or entertainment facilities (hereafter 'entertainment,) and there is no requirement that the entertainment is incidental to the fête or other event, so the exemption will apply even if it is the primary or predominant feature. However, the exemption will not apply if the event 'is promoted with a view to applying the whole or part of its proceeds for purposes of private gain'. How 'private gain' is interpreted will be important in determining the scope of the exemption.

Events such as garden fêtes are likely to be promoted by some body or society (hereafter 'society'), such as a village hall or church fête committee, or a school parent–teachers association, rather than by an individual, and are normally organised in order to raise funds either for the benefit of the society in question or for some charitable purpose. Whether the exemption has any significant application where funds are raised for the benefit of a society will depend on whether applying the proceeds in whole or in part for the benefit of the society as a whole is or is not interpreted as 'private gain'. In this respect, para 10(3) provides ' "private gain" . . . is to be construed in accordance with section 19(3) of the Gambling Act 2005'. Section 19(3) provides:

The provision of a benefit to one or more individuals is not a provision for the purpose of private gain for the purposes of this Act if made in the course of the activities of a society that is a non-commercial society by virtue of subsection (1)(a) or (b).

A noncommercial society, by virtue of these provisions, is a society established and conducted for charitable purposes (which, by s 19(2), means purposes that are exclusively charitable) or for the purpose of enabling participation in, or of supporting, sport, athletics or a cultural activity. A noncommercial society, by virtue of s 19(1)(c), is also expressed to include a society established and conducted for any other noncommercial purpose other than private gain, although, as can be seen, this is not included within s 19(3). This thus seems to confine funds raised for the benefit of a society only to societies whose purpose is sport, athletics or some cultural activity (although, as indicated above, it is not clear whether sporting or athletic events are 'a function or event of a similar character' to a garden fête). Only in these instances where an individual benefits from raising funds for the society's benefit will the event not be regarded as promoted for private gain and the exemption apply.

This seems to narrow the scope of the exemption from its original formulation in the 2003 Act, under which 'private gain' was to be construed in accordance with s 22 of the Lotteries and Amusements Act 1976. Section 22 provided:

(1) For the purposes of this Act proceeds of any entertainment, lottery or gaming promoted on behalf of a society to which this subsection extends which are applied for any purpose calculated to benefit the society as a whole shall not be held to be applied for purposes of private gain by reason only that their application for that purpose results in benefit to any person as an individual.

(2) Subsection (1) above extends to any society which is established and conducted either–

    (a) wholly for purposes other than purposes of any commercial undertaking; or

    (b) wholly or mainly for the purpose of participation in or support of athletic sports or athletic games.

The exemption seems to be narrower in two ways. First, it was sufficient under s 22(2)(b) if the society was established and conducted 'wholly or mainly' for sport or athletics, whereas under s 19(1)(b) the society has to be established and conducted for '*the* purpose' of sport or athletics (emphasis supplied). This suggests it will no longer suffice if the society is mainly for sport or athletics and that it will need to be exclusively for this purpose. Secondly, it was sufficient under s 22(2)(a) if the society was established and conducted wholly for purposes other than purposes of any commercial undertaking. This might include the other categories mentioned in s 19(1)(a) and (b), which is a society established and conducted for charitable purposes or for the purpose of a cultural activity, but it clearly could extend beyond this. Thus it could include a members' club, since such clubs are run for the benefit of members and not as commercial undertakings (see 8.1.1 below). That funds raised for the benefit of members' clubs might not be construed as private gain under s 22 is apparent from the case of *Avais v Hartford, Shankhouse and District Workingmen's Social Club and Institute Ltd* [1969] 2 AC 1. Here, the House of Lords, considering an earlier legislative enactment of s 22 in s 54 of the Betting, Gaming and Lotteries Act 1963, held that the application of the earnings from a gaming machine for the general purposes of the club so as to benefit its members would, by virtue of s 54, 'not be reckoned as application for purposes of private gain' (*per* Lord Pearson at 9). Members' clubs such as the one in question in this case are essentially established and conducted for social purposes, which seems to take them outside the scope of the exemption now that 'private gain' is construed by reference to s 19(3) of the Gambling Act 2005. Such clubs are not established and conducted exclusively for charitable purposes nor are they for the purpose of sport, athletics or a cultural activity. They might fall within s 19(1)(c) as a society established and conducted for any other non-commercial purpose other than private gain, but the express exclusion of this from s 19(3) suggests a deliberate narrowing of the scope of the exemption.

Whether garden fêtes or similar events organised not by societies but by individuals, for example to raise money for a wheelchair for a local person, are promoted for 'private gain' is less clear. The event cannot be regarded as promoted for private gain (and so within the exemption) if 'private gain' is construed in accordance with s 19(3), since this relates only to events organised by a society. Nevertheless, the view may be taken that s 19(3) is not definitive of the meaning of 'private gain', but applies only where events are organised by societies with a view to their benefit. This would allow for cases falling outside s 19(3) to be regarded as not promoted for private gain in accordance with the ordinary meaning of 'private gain'. Since a fête organised by an individual to raise money for a deserving cause would not ordinarily be thought of as promoted for private gain, it may be that the exemption will apply here. This would seem to be in accordance with the legislative purpose behind the exemption and it is submitted that it should have application in such cases.

### 5.3.41 Morris dancing

Paragraph 11 provides:

> The provision of any entertainment or entertainment facilities is not to be regarded as the provision of regulated entertainment for the purposes of this Act to the extent that it consists of the provision of–
> (a) a performance of morris dancing or any dancing of a similar nature or a performance of unamplified, live music as an integral part of such a performance, or
> (b) facilities for enabling persons to take part in entertainment of a description falling within paragraph (a).

The term 'morris dancing' is not defined in the Act, but its ordinary meaning is well understood, the *Shorter Oxford English Dictionary* defining it as 'traditional dance performed by persons in fancy costume, usually representing characters from the Robin Hood legend'. Although the Government 'would have preferred not to introduce such an amendment', which was incorporated at a late stage in the legislation's passage, believing 'that there would have been few circumstances in which traditional morris dancing would have been licensable under the Bill', the amendment, in the words of Mr Richard Caborn, Minister for Sport, 'does no significant damage to the structure and scheme of the Bill, and if it offers reassurance, there is nothing wrong with that' (HC Deb, vol 408, col 1117, 8 July 2003). Since it appears that there are 14,000 morris men in the country, who take part in 11,000 events annually that could have been licensable, the exemption may prove not to be an insignificant one.[44]

### 5.3.42 Vehicles in motion

Paragraph 12 provides:

> The provision of any entertainment or entertainment facilities–
> (a) on premises consisting of or forming part of a vehicle, and
> (b) at a time when the vehicle is not permanently or temporarily parked,
>
> is not to be regarded as the provision of regulated entertainment for the purposes of this Act.

The purpose of this exemption seems to be to ensure that no licence is required where entertainment, such as music or video shows, is provided for those travelling on coaches or other vehicles. In the case of music, this might fall within the exemption in para 7, as the music is incidental to some other activity (travel), which is not itself entertainment, or the provision of entertainment facilities, but it will also fall within this paragraph. More particularly, video shows would not otherwise be exempt were it not for the provision in this paragraph.

### 5.3.43 *Small premises providing music and dancing*

Section 177 provides an 'exemption' for such premises by restricting the range of conditions that might be imposed with the licensing of these forms of entertainment in such premises. This is not an exemption from licensing – the music and dancing remain licensable activities for which a premises licence or CPC is needed – and it is not therefore considered here, but in Chapter 7, which covers conditions attached to premises licences and CPCs (see 7.5 below).

## 5.4    PROVISION OF LATE NIGHT REFRESHMENT

### 5.4.1   Introduction

What constitutes late night refreshment (LNR) as a licensable activity, and what is excluded for the purposes of the Act, is covered in Sched 2. Section 1(5) provides:

> Schedule 2 makes provision about what constitutes the provision of late night refreshment for those purposes (including provision that certain activities carried on in relation to certain clubs or hotels etc, or certain employees, do not constitute provision of late night refreshment and are, accordingly, not licensable activities).

### 5.4.2   Meaning of 'late night refreshment'

5.4.3    LNR means the supply of hot food or hot drink to the members of the public, or a section of the public, for consumption on or off the premises, between 11.00 pm and 5.00 am. It also includes cases where a person supplies or holds himself out as supplying such refreshment to any person on any premises to which members of the public, or a section of the public, have access. Paragraph 1 of Sched 2 provides:

> (1) For the purposes of this Act, a person "provides late night refreshment" if–
>   (a) at any time between the hours of 11.00 pm and 5.00 am, he supplies hot food or hot drink to members of the public, or a section of the public, on or from any premises, whether for consumption on or off the premises, or
>   (b) at any time between those hours when members of the public, or a section of the public, are admitted to any premises, he supplies, or holds himself out as willing to supply, hot food or hot drink to any persons, or to persons of a particular description, on or from those premises, whether for consumption on or off the premises,
>
> unless the supply is an exempt supply by virtue of paragraph 3, 4 or 5.
> (2) References in this Act to the "provision of late night refreshment" are to be construed in accordance with sub-paragraph (1).

Whilst para 2(1)(a) requires that a person 'supplies' hot food or drink, it is sufficient under para 2(1)(b) if he 'holds himself out as willing to supply' it and no actual supply is required. Further, it will suffice under para 2(1)(b) if there is a supply or a willingness to supply hot food or drink only to private individuals, rather than the public or a section of the public, provided the public or a section of it is admitted to the premises. Canteen facilities provided in premises for use by private individuals working there might thus fall within para 2(1)(b) if the public or a section of it is admitted. Restriction of LNR to supply (or willingness to supply) hot food or hot drink accords with the Government's intention to refocus licensing in this area on the prevention of disorder and unreasonable disturbance to residents in the neighbourhood of premises. As the Home Secretary observed in the Foreword to the White Paper, *Time for Reform: Proposals for the Modernisation of Our Licensing Laws* (2000) Cm 4696, p 6: 'Licensing here is meant to prevent disorder and unreasonable disturbance to residents in the neighbourhood, and needs to be re-focused on these key issues.' The likelihood of disorder and disturbance occurring will be in premises such as night cafés and takeaway food outlets, which provide hot food or drink for consumption on or off the premises and both will fall within the scope of Sched 2. As para 3.33 of the Guidance states:

> The legislation impacts on those premises such as night cafés and take away food outlets where people may gather at any time from 11.00pm and until 5.00am with the possibility of disorder and disturbance.

The same will be true of travelling 'fast food' vehicles such as burger and kebab vans, which will also fall within the scope of Sched 2, since 'premises' in s 193 is defined to include a 'vehicle' (see 6.1.5 below).

5.4.4    With regard to whether food or drink is 'hot', a definition of this term is provided by para 2:

> Food or drink supplied on or from any premises is "hot" for the purposes of this Schedule if the food or drink, or any part of it–
>
> (a) before it is supplied, is heated on the premises or elsewhere for the purpose of enabling it to be consumed at a temperature above the ambient air temperature and, at the time of supply, is above that temperature, or
>
> (b) after it is supplied, may be heated on the premises for the purpose of enabling it to be consumed at a temperature above the ambient air temperature.

The food or drink may thus be supplied already hot or it may be heated on the premises, in either instance for consumption when it is hot, whether on the premises or not. Paragraph 2(a) will typically cover night cafés, takeaways and burger and kebab vans, whilst para 2(b) applies where food or drink, 'after it is supplied, may be heated on the premises' to enable it to be consumed. On its wording, this seems wide enough to encompass premises such as shops, stores and supermarkets that stay open late and provide a microwave facility in which food purchased at the store may be heated. However, if a purposive interpretation is given to para 2 it may be that such provision would not fall within the section. If the purpose is to regulate premises where there is a possibility of disorder and disturbance arising, such a possibility is not likely to arise where shops, stores and supermarkets provide a microwave facility. There would seem to be no substantive difference from these premises selling cold food or drink such as bread, milk or sandwiches and these activities are not licensable as LNR: 'shops, stores and supermarkets selling cold food and cold drink that is immediately consumable from 11.00pm are not licensable as providing late night refreshment' (Guidance, para 3.33). It may be that these premises in any event have a premises licence for other licensable activities such as the sale of alcohol, and the premises licence could include authorisation for LNR, although of course not all such premises will have a premises licence. In sum, it remains uncertain whether there would be provision of 'hot' food where a microwave facility is provided and no indication is given on this matter in the Guidance.

### 5.4.5   Exempt supplies

Certain supplies are exempted from the definition of LNR and are not licensable activities for which authorisation is required. These fall under three categories: where hot food or hot drink is supplied to persons of certain descriptions, where it is supplied in premises already licensed under other legislative provisions, and where it is supplied in certain ways.

### 5.4.6   *Supply to persons of certain descriptions*

The first category concerns: supply to members of certain clubs; supply to persons staying in hotels and similar premises that supply accommodation as their main purpose, such as guest houses, lodging houses, caravan or camping sites; supply to employees of a particular employer (as where refreshment is made available to employees whose shift patterns require them to be present at the workplace between 11.00 pm and 5.00 am); supply to persons in particular trades, professions or vocations; and guests of any of the above. Paragraph 3(1)-(3) provides:

(1) The supply of hot food or hot drink on or from any premises at any time is an exempt supply for the purposes of paragraph 1(1) if, at that time, a person will neither–
  (a) be admitted to the premises, nor
  (b) be supplied with hot food or hot drink on or from the premises, except by virtue of being a person of a description falling within sub-paragraph (2).
(2) The descriptions are that–
  (a) he is a member of a recognised club,
  (b) he is a person staying at a particular hotel, or at particular comparable premises, for the night in question,
  (c) he is an employee of a particular employer,
  (d) he is engaged in a particular trade, he is a member of a particular profession or he follows a particular vocation,
  (e) he is a guest of a person falling within any of paragraphs (a) to (d).
(3) The premises which, for the purposes of sub-paragraph (2)(b), are comparable to a hotel are–
  (a) a guest house, lodging house or hostel,
  (b) a caravan site or camping site, or
  (c) any other premises the main purpose of maintaining which is the provision of facilities for overnight accommodation.

Supply to club members is exempt under para 3(2)(a) in the case of a 'recognised club', which is a genuine members' club and one that meets the general qualifying conditions for obtaining a club premises certificate under Pt 4 of the Act. Section 193 defines a 'recognised club' as 'a club which satisfies conditions 1 to 3 of the general conditions in section 62' (see 8.2.7–8.2.15 below). Where a club is not a recognised club, supply of hot food or hot drink to a club member or his guest will not be exempt. Although this will not be a supply to them as members of the public,[46] such a supply is to be treated as a supply to a member of the public for the purposes of Sched 2, thus making the activity licensable and necessitating authorisation for it. Paragraph 6 provides:

> For the purposes of this Schedule–
> (a) the supply of hot food or hot drink to a person as being a member, or the guest of a member, of a club which is not a recognised club is to be taken to be a supply to a member of the public, and
> (b) the admission of any person to any premises as being such a member or guest is to be taken to be the admission of a member of the public.

In some instances where hot food or hot drink is supplied to persons in accordance with para 3, it may be that the supply does not in any event constitute LNR and no reliance need be placed on the exemption. LNR is a licensable activity only where there is either supply to the public or a section of the public, or supply to other persons where the public or a section of the public are admitted to the premises (see para 1(1) and 5.4.3 above) and this may not be the case, for example where there is supply to an employee (para 3(2)(c)). Where the activity does constitute LNR, however, the exemption will apply and no authorisation will be required.

### 5.4.7  Supply in premises already licensed under other legislative provisions

The second category of exempt supply is where supply takes place in premises that are being used in accordance with a public exhibition licence or a near-beer licence. These licences are required only in London, so this category will have limited application. The former licence is needed for various exhibition centres in the capital,[47] whilst the latter applies to premises consisting to a significant degree of the sale for consumption on the premises of drinks such as non-alcoholic lagers and beers, accompanied by live entertainment and/or companions for customers. Paragraph 4 provides:

> The supply of hot food or hot drink on or from any premises is an exempt supply for the purposes of paragraph 1(1) if it takes place during a period for which–
> (a) the premises may be used for a public exhibition of a kind described in section 21(1) of the Greater London Council (General Powers) Act 1966 (c.xxviii) by virtue of a licence under that section, or
> (b) the premises may be used as near beer premises within the meaning of section 14 of the London Local Authorities Act 1995 (c.x) by virtue of a licence under section 16 of that Act.

Since the exemption applies only where supply takes place during a period for which the premises may be used under licence for public exhibitions or as near-beer premises, supply of LNR outside that period will not be covered by the exemption and will be a licensable activity requiring authorisation.

## 5.4.8   Supply in certain ways

The third category of exempt supply extends to hot food and hot drink supplied in various ways. It includes the provision of hot drinks with an alcoholic content or by vending machines (where the money is inserted by members of the public rather than by the staff at the premises), or hot food or hot drink supplied free of charge, or by a registered charity, or on a moving vehicle. Paragraph 5 provides:

   (1)  The following supplies of hot food or hot drink are exempt supplies for the purposes of paragraph 1(1)–

      (a)  the supply of hot drink which consists of or contains alcohol,

      (b)  the supply of hot drink by means of a vending machine,

      (c)  the supply of hot food or hot drink free of charge,

      (d)  the supply of hot food or hot drink by a registered charity or a person authorised by a registered charity,

      (e)  the supply of hot food or hot drink on a vehicle at a time when the vehicle is not permanently or temporarily parked.

   (2)  Hot drink is supplied by means of a vending machine for the purposes of sub-paragraph (1)(b) only if–

      (a)  the payment for the hot drink is inserted into the machine by a member of the public, and

      (b)  the hot drink is supplied directly by the machine to a member of the public.

   (3)  Hot food or hot drink is not to be regarded as supplied free of charge for the purposes of sub-paragraph (1)(c) if, in order to obtain the hot food or hot drink, a charge must be paid–

      (a)  for admission to any premises, or

      (b)  for some other item.

   (4)  In sub-paragraph (1)(d) "registered charity" means–

      (a)  a charity which is registered under section 3 of the Charities Act 1993 (c.10), or

      (b)  a charity which by virtue of subsection (5) of that section is not required to be so registered.

The supply of hot drink that consists of or contains alcohol is exempt under the 2003 Act as LNR because it is caught by the provisions relating to the sale or supply of alcohol (Guidance, para 3.37). Where hot drinks are supplied by vending machines, the rationale for exclusion seems to be that such machines are commonplace in premises to which the public have access and are widely used, with little likelihood of disorder or disturbance occurring. However, the exemption applies only if the machine is one to which the public have access and it is operated by members of the public without any involvement of the staff (Guidance, para 3.34), which will be the case where members of the public insert payment in the machine. Further, the exemption does not apply to hot food. Thus premises supplying for a charge, hot food by vending machine, will be licensable when the food has been heated for the purposes of supply, even though no staff on the premises may have been involved in the transaction.

    The supply of hot food and hot drink free of charge or by or on behalf of a charity is no doubt exempt because the work of charities is unlikely to be enhanced if, when making provision for those such as the homeless, they are required to obtain a licence. However, where any charge is made for either admission to the premises or for some other item in order to obtain the hot food or hot drink, this will not be regarded as 'free of charge' (Guidance, para 3.38). The rationale for exclusion of supply of hot food and hot drink on a moving vehicle would seem to be similar to that of hot drinks supplied by vending machines – a commonplace occurrence with little likelihood of disorder or disturbance occurring. Accordingly, none of the above-mentioned supplies are licensable activities.

## NOTES

1   Authorisation is required where these licensable activities take place on 'premises', which is widely defined in s 193 to include 'any place' (see 6.1.3 below), and, for the purposes of the Act, 'premises are "used" for a licensable activity if that activity is carried on or from the premises' (s 1(6)).

2   The exemption for LNR is contained in Sched 2, para 3 – see 5.4.6 below.

3   Section 1(7) provides: 'This section is subject to sections 173 to 175 (which exclude activities from the definition of licensable activity in certain circumstances).' The exclusions relate to activities in certain locations, which are not licensable, and incidental noncommercial lotteries in which prizes consist of alcohol – for details, see 6.1.8–6.1.14 below.

4   Section 3(1)(a)–(e). Licensing authorities, in addition, include three other bodies: the Sub-Treasurer of the Inner Temple, the Under-Treasurer of the Middle Temple, and the Council of the Isles of Scilly: s 3(1)(f)–(h). The provision in s 3(1) is set out in full in 1.1.10 above.

5   These terms are more fully defined in s 1 of the Alcoholic Liquor Duties Act 1979. 'Spirits' essentially means spirits of any description, or preparations or liquors made with spirits, which are of a strength exceeding 1.2% (s 1(2)). 'Beer' includes ale, porter, stout and any other description of beer, and any liquor that is made or sold as a description of beer or as a substitute for beer and which is of a strength exceeding 0.5% (s 1(3)). 'Wine' means any liquor of a strength exceeding 1.2% obtained from the alcoholic fermentation of fresh grapes or of the must of fresh grapes, whether or not the liquor is fortified with spirits or flavoured with aromatic extracts (s 1(4)). 'Cider' means cider or perry of a strength exceeding 1.2%, but less than 8.5%, obtained from the fermentation of apple or pear juice (s 1(6)).

6   'Denatured alcohol' is the term used to refer to what is more traditionally described as 'methylated spirits'.

7   A supply to a member of a club is a supply other than by a retail sale. Section 1(3) provides: 'In this Act references to the supply of alcohol by or on behalf of a club to, or to the order of, a member of the club do not include a reference to any supply which is a sale by retail of alcohol.'

8   Public exhibitions and entertainment booking offices, included within Sched 12 to the London Government Act 1963 (which covered public entertainments of various descriptions within London), are not included within 'regulated entertainment' under the 2003 Act, but will continue to be licensed under the 1963 Act. Sched 8, para 31 to the 2003 Act provides:

> Notwithstanding the repeal by this Act of Schedule 12 to the London Government Act 1963 (c.33) (licensing of public entertainment in Greater London), or of any enactment amending that Schedule, that Schedule shall continue to apply in relation to–
>
> (a)   licences granted under section 21 of the Greater London Council (General Powers) Act 1966 (c.xxviii) (licensing of public exhibitions in London), and

(b) licences granted under section 5 of the Greater London Council (General Powers) Act 1978 (c.xiii) (licensing of entertainments booking offices in London), as it applied before that repeal.

For details of these provisions, see Manchester, C, *Entertainment Licensing Law and Practice*, 2nd edn, 1999, London: Butterworths, paras 9.12 and 9.13.

9 [1944] KB 362, 368, *per* Asquith J. The principle that payment for admission is immaterial in deciding whether an entertainment is public or not is a long-established one, supported by authorities decided under the Disorderly Houses Act 1751. In *Archer v Willingrice* (1802) 4 Esp 186, the court held the defendant, a publican, liable for allowing dancing to take place on his premises where an admission fee was paid, not to the defendant himself, but to a person who professed to teach the dancing. Lord Ellenborough stated: 'It is not necessary, in order to subject a party to a penalty given by this Act of Parliament, that he should take money for admission. The taking of money is only evidence that the defendant is the owner of the house where the dancing has been carried on.' Similarly, in *Gregory v Tuffs* (1833) 6 C & P 271, where another publican permitted singing and dancing to take place on his premises, it was held that the defendant was liable even though no payment was made at all. Lord Lyndhurst CB, summing up to the jury, stated (at 272–73): 'it was not essential that the room should be used exclusively for this purpose; nor is it necessary that money should be taken for admission.' (The decision in *Archer*, although cited by counsel, was not referred to by the court in support of this point.)

10 A 'qualifying club', in relation to the provision of regulated entertainment, is one that satisfies the general conditions in s 62 (s 61(3)) – see 8.2.6–8.2.15 below.

11 [1968] 1 WLR 1512. 'In my judgment', Lord Parker CJ stated (at 1514), 'they clearly were not members of the public as such.'

12 If no charge is made, what is provided will fall outside the definition of regulated entertainment. Explanatory Note 299 gives the example of a company or firm providing entertainment for its clients, for which no charge is made, but which is connected with stimulating general goodwill that might be advantageous for the business.

13 A further instance might be someone who owns or manages an historic house or other suitable venue who will not be subject to the licensing regime simply because he hires out the venue to a third party (see HL Deb, vol 645, col 10, 25 February 2003).

14 See Explanatory Notes 298 ('This Schedule defines the provision of regulated entertainment as covering entertainment . . . for which a charge is made, which is provided for profit (which will include to raise money for charity . . .') and 299 ('The definition would cover entertainment staged by a charity for the purposes of fundraising . . .').

15 Paragraph 1(7) provides: 'This paragraph is subject to Part 2 of this Schedule (exemptions)' – see 5.3.33 below.

16 Paragraph 4 provides:

The Secretary of State may by order amend this Schedule for the purpose of modifying–

(a) the descriptions of entertainment specified in paragraph 2, or

(b) the descriptions of entertainment specified in paragraph 3,

and for this purpose "modify" includes adding, varying or removing any description.

17 Paragraph 2(2) provides: 'Any reference in sub-paragraph (1) to an audience includes a reference to spectators.'

18 This illustration should not be confined to rehearsals to which the public are not admitted and should include rehearsals to which *any* audience, even a privately invited one, are not admitted.

19 It is arguable whether passers-by do comprise an 'audience'. Passers-by will obviously comprise an 'audience' if they stop to watch. However, even if they do no more than simply exercise rights of passage, it may be said that entertainment is taking place in the presence of a 'travelling' audience.

20  In London, busking is licensable under Pt V of the London Local Authorities Act 2000, the provisions of which can be adopted if busking is likely to inconvenience passers-by or cause nuisance to occupiers of nearby property.

21  This quotation is taken from a transcript of his Lordship's judgment.

22  The House of Lords in this case was concerned with interpreting the Betting House Act 1853, s 1, which provided that 'No house, office, room or other place shall be opened, kept or used . . . for . . . betting . . .', and decided that the inclosure at Kempton Park could constitute an 'other place' for the purposes of this provision. Reliance was placed in the Bow Street case on the words of Lord James who observed (at 194) that, whilst an open space might constitute 'a place', 'there must be a defined area so marked out that it can be found and recognised as "the place" where the business is carried on'.

23  This quotation is taken from a transcript of his Lordship's judgment.

24  Paragraph 2(3) provides: 'This paragraph is subject to Part 3 of this Schedule (interpretation).'

25  See Guidance, para 3.12: 'The following activities, for example, are not regulated entertainment . . . a rehearsal of a play or a rehearsal of a performance of music to which the public are not admitted'. It would be more correct to say 'to which an audience are not admitted', since whether entertainment is regulated entertainment is dependent on the presence of an audience (which might be privately invited) and not the public. The rationale for including rehearsals is to ensure that events, such as press performances and dress rehearsals, are licensed because 'people attending would expect to be protected as they would for a proper performance' (Lord McIntosh) – see HL Deb, vol 643, col 401, 12 December 2002.

26  This is except in the case of boxing and wrestling matches – see 5.3.27 below.

27  This is to avoid such a stadium being made 'subject to duplicate licensing regimes merely because "indoor sport", when the roof is closed, could cover football or rugby played in the stadium' (Lord Davies) – see HL Deb, vol 643, col 414, 12 December 2002.

28  See para 2(6) of Sched 1 to the Local Government (Miscellaneous Provisions) Act 1982 and para 3A(8) of Sched 12 to the London Government Act 1963.

29  See para 2(6) of Sched 1 to the Local Government (Miscellaneous Provisions) Act 1982 and para 3A(8) of Sched 12 to the London Government Act 1963.

30  Guidance, para 3.15. See also op. cit., Manchester, fn 8, para 2.17, where the darts example was used to illustrate the position under the previous law.

31  HL Deb, vol 643, col 391, 12 December 2002.

32  12 July 1994, unreported. See also *Willowcell Ltd v Westminster City Council* (1995) 160 JP 101, 115, where Roch LJ observed that 'dancing' was 'a word as capable of as wide an interpretation as the infinite range of bodily movements which may be said to constitute the dance'.

33  The position here is the same as for the performance of live music – see 5.3.28 above.

34  Such an activity was considered to be 'public entertainment of a like kind to music and dancing' in *R v Tucker* (1877) 2 QBD 417.

35  See the remarks, *obiter*, of Ward LJ in *Willowcell Ltd v Westminster City Council* (1995) 160 JP 101, 115, that it is 'easy to categorise a striptease as being a form of dancing where the exotic is beginning to shade into the erotic'.

36  There may well be other purposes for which persons are taking part in making music in such cases, such as employment or commercial purposes (if, for example, under contract to make a recording for a record producer); but one of the purposes would arguably be for their entertainment, even if this might not be the primary purpose. Paragraph 3(1) simply requires that the facilities are for persons to take part 'for purposes which include the purpose of being entertained' (see 5.3.32 below) and there is no indication that a purpose which is subsidiary or very much a secondary one will not suffice.

37  The previous law contained an express provision to the effect that the conditions would not apply in such circumstances. Section 5(3)(b) of the Cinemas Act 1985 provided: 'where the exhibition is given in premises in respect of which a licence is in force, no

condition or restriction on or subject to which the licence was granted shall apply to the exhibition.' The position under para 5 should, however, be the same notwithstanding that it contains no equivalent provision.

38  As the Minister for Tourism, Film and Broadcasting, Dr Kim Howells observed during the Committee Stage of the Bill in the House of Commons: 'Incidental live music is music that does not form part of the main attraction for visitors to a premises. Examples might include a piano played in the background in a restaurant, or carol singers in a shopping centre' (HC Standing Committee D, cols 67–68, 1 April 2003).

39  'If the entertainment is advertised and the purpose of the music is to draw in customers and to make a profit for the business, that has a direct bearing on the business and it would be difficult to describe it as incidental . . . There might be a clear attempt by the holder of a licence to draw people into his premises by advertising the music that will be played': HC Standing Committee D, col 69, 1 April 2003 (Dr Kim Howells). See, also, Dr Howells' earlier remarks at cols 67–68: 'if a band in a pub was advertised to draw in customers, or live music was played so loud that it could not possibly be regarded as incidental to another activity, it would be unlikely to benefit from the exemption.'

40  The same may also be true where films and plays contain representations of persons dancing and authorisation for this may be needed under the premises licence.

41  The supporting authority for this point is *Fay v Bignell* (1883) Cab & El 112, where the incidental activity was dancing rather than music (although the principle will equally have application to music). In this case, the defendant only had a licence for music and not dancing. The entertainment in question consisted for the most part of music and singing, but the act of one of the 20 artistes performing comprised dancing, involving changes of national costume with the execution of a national dance. Some of the other artistes also accompanied their songs with slight dancing or rhythmical movements of the feet. The whole entertainment took four to five hours, about half an hour of which was taken up by dancing spread over the whole performance. Cave J directed the jury as follows:

> In this entertainment 20 performers take part, and suppose dancing be a principal part of one performance, still the question remains, is that performance a principal part of the entertainment? Because if the performance is merely subsidiary, and not a principal part of the entertainment, the dancing would still be subsidiary.

The jury found for the defendant and must therefore have regarded the dancing as subsidiary and not requiring a licence. Although not itself a strong precedent, the decision has been subsequently approved by the Court of Appeal in *Willowcell Ltd v Westminster City Council*(1995) 160 JP 101.

42  Section 201 Broadcasting Act 1990 provides:

> (1)  In this Act "programme service" means any of the following services (whether or not it is, or is required to be, licensed . . .), namely–
>
> (aa)  any service which is a programme service within the meaning of the Communications Act 2003;
>
> (c)  any other service which consists in the sending, by means of an electronic communications network (within the meaning of the Communications Act 2003), of sounds or visual images or both either–
>
> > (i)  for the reception at two or more places in the United Kingdom (whether they are so sent for simultaneous reception or at different times in response to requests made by different users of the service); or
> >
> > (ii)  for reception at a place in the United Kingdom for the purpose of being presented there to members of the public or to any group of persons.
>
> (2A)  Subsection (1)(c) does not apply to so much of a service consisting only of sound programmes as–

(a) is a two-way service (within the meaning of section 248(4) of the Communications Act 2003);

(b) satisfies the conditions in section 248(5) of that Act; or

(c) is provided for the purpose only of being received by persons who have qualified as users of the service by reason of being persons who fall within paragraph (a) or (b) of section 248(7) of that Act.

(2B) Subsection (1)(c) does not apply to so much of a service not consisting only of sound programmes as–

(a) is a two-way service (within the meaning of section 232 of the Communications Act 2003);

(b) satisfies the conditions in section 233(5) of that Act; or

(c) is provided for the purpose only of being received by persons who have qualified as users of the service by reason of being persons who fall within paragraph (a) or (b) of section 233(7) of that Act.

43 This reference to s 19(3) replaced a reference to s 22 of the Lotteries and Amusements Act 1976 with effect from 1 September 2007 – see s 356(1) and Sched 16, Pt 2, para 20(1), (3), and s 358, of the Gambling Act 2005, and The Gambling Act 2005 (Commencement No. 6 and Transitional Provisions) Order 2006, SI 2006/3272, art 2(4).

44 See HL Deb, vol 650, col 1055, 3 July 2003, where Lord Redesdale, who disclosed this information on the number of morris dancers, observed: 'Some people have expressed the view that that is quite a scary thought.'

45 As to what constitutes the public or a section of the public, see 5.3.7 above.

46 It is well established that activities taking place in bona fide clubs, which admit only members and their guests, are not public. The guests will not be considered to be members of the public because they cannot obtain entry in their own right, independent of the member introducing them. The Divisional Court, in *Severn View Social Club and Institute Ltd v Chepstow (Monmouthshire) Licensing Justices* [1968] 1 WLR 1512, held that it was wrong to take the view that the admission of bona fide guests of members of a reputable club to functions involving music and dancing made those functions public, so that a licence for this entertainment was required. 'In my judgment', Lord Parker CJ stated (at 1514), 'they clearly were not members of the public as such'.

47 Premises described in Sched 1 to the Greater London Council (General Powers) Act 1966 require an exhibition licence under s 21(1) of that Act. These are: Alexandra Palace, Wood Green, Haringey; Central Hall, Tothill Street, City of Westminster, SW1; Earls Court, Warwick Road, Kensington and Chelsea, SW5; Olympia, Blythe Road and Hammersmith Road, Kensington and Chelsea, SW5; Royal Festival Hall, South Bank, Lambeth, SE1; The Royal Horticultural Halls, Vincent Square, City of Westminster, SW1; and Seymour Hall, Seymour Place, City of Westminster, SW1.

# CHAPTER 6

# PREMISES LICENCES

## 6.1  MEANING AND SCOPE OF PREMISES LICENCES

6.1.1   Premises licences are defined by s 11, which provides:

> In this Act "premises licence" means a licence granted under this Part, in respect of any premises, which authorises the premises to be used for one or more licensable activities.

The term 'premises' is further defined in s 193 to mean 'any place and includes a vehicle, vessel or moveable structure'. This is a broad definition of premises for which a licence, authorising one or more of the licensable activities, can be obtained. This provision, however, needs to be read subject to s 176, which prohibits the sale or supply of alcohol, one of the licensable activities, at certain premises (designated as 'excluded premises'). Further, not all premises providing activities for which a licence is required will need to obtain one, for there are a number of exemptions where activities can be provided without a licence. Each of these matters is considered below.

### 6.1.2  Premises for which a licence can be obtained

### *6.1.3  'Any place'*

The reference to 'any place' makes it clear that a premises licence is not confined in its application to licensable activities that take place within a building and its adjuncts, for an open space may be a 'place'. In *Farndale v Bainbridge*(1898) 42 Sol Jo 192, where the defendant hired a piece of waste land on which entertainment was provided in the form of dancing, music and singing, the Divisional Court held that the piece of ground was a 'place' within the meaning of s 51 of the Public Health Acts Amendment Act 1890 and a public entertainment licence was required for the entertainment. Thus, under the 2003 Act, a premises licence can equally extend to activities that take place outdoors, such as pop concerts and theatre productions or film exhibitions held in the open air.[1] Such activities often take place in public spaces owned by local authorities, such as parks, market squares, promenades and village greens, and para 13.72 of the Guidance encourages local authorities to consider obtaining a premises licence for such areas:

> To ensure that cultural diversity thrives, local authorities should consider establishing a policy of seeking premises licences from the licensing authority for public spaces within the community in their own name . . . Performers and entertainers would then have no need to obtain a licence or give a temporary event notice themselves to enable them to give a performance in these places.

This has been further encouraged by the Department of Culture, Media and Sport (DCMS), establishing a Central Register of Local Authority Licensed Public Spaces in England and Wales, details of which are available on the DCMS website, 'to help event organisers and touring entertainment providers determine whether their event could take place in a particular local authority area without the need for a separate authorisation' (Guidance, para 13.72). Those organising events, however, still require the authority's permission as premises licence holder for any proposed regulated entertainment there and practice seems to vary as to the manner in which permission is given. In some instances, this is done as a matter of contract, under which organisers can use the premises under certain conditions. In other cases, this is done through the premises licence, either through conditions on the licence which specify how events are to be run or with applicants required to submit for approval an operating schedule of what is proposed.

Events held in public spaces for which local authorities have obtained a premises licence may well be ones at which the sale of alcohol takes place, in addition to provision of some form of regulated entertainment. Whilst the holding of events in such places may well have helped to encourage cultural diversity, this also resulted in a potential conflict with Designated Public Places Orders (or 'Alcohol Exclusion Zones' as they are more popularly known) under s 13 of the Criminal Justice and Police Act 2001, under which consumption of alcohol in public places could be controlled where such consumption was likely to lead to nuisance or disorder. The potential conflict arose because s 14 of the 2001 Act, which specified places that are not to be designated public places, was amended by para 123 of Sched 6 to the 2003 Act so that premises in respect of which a premises licence was in force were included. Accordingly, local authority public spaces with premises licences could not be designated public places under the 2001 Act, but this conflict has been resolved by a further amendment to s 14 by s 26 of the Violent Crime Reduction Act 2006. The further amended s 14 now provides that premises with a premises licence authorising the sale of alcohol are not a designated public place (s 14(1)(a)) but, where the premises licence is held by a local authority or held by another person, but the premises are occupied by the authority or managed by or on its behalf, the premises licence will only prevent the premises being a designated public space for the period that the premises are being used for the sale of alcohol and for a period of 30 minutes thereafter (s 14(1A)–(1B)). After the 30 minutes period, the premises effectively revert to being a designated public space under which the consumption of alcohol can be controlled.[2]

In cases where a place constitutes a building, a premises licence will need to be obtained for the building where the licensable activities take place. This is self-evident, except that difficulties may arise where the licensable activity is the sale of alcohol and the contract of sale is made at a different place from that where the alcohol is assigned to the particular purchaser. This will most obviously arise in connection with mail order or internet sales of alcohol. For the purposes of the Act, a sale of alcohol is not to be regarded as having been made where the contract of sale is made (for example, on the internet or at a call centre handling sales), but the sale is treated as being made at the premises from which the alcohol is assigned to the purchaser (for example, the warehouse from which delivery is made).[3] Section 190 provides:

(1)  This section applies where the place where a contract for the sale of alcohol is made is different from the place where the alcohol is appropriated to the contract.

(2)  For the purposes of this Act the sale of alcohol is to be treated as taking place where the alcohol is appropriated to the contract.

The Act makes no provision for a single premises licence to cover more than one site or premises. This is justified on the basis that each premises will give rise to different issues relating to the four licensing objectives, all of which are central to the public interest. Accordingly, businesses such as circuses and fairs must obtain an authorisation for each premises that they use to carry on licensable activities, although the fact that there are local authority public spaces with premises licences may go some way towards ameliorating any difficulties.

### 6.1.4 'Vehicle, vessel or moveable structure'

6.1.5  'Vehicle' is defined in s 193 to mean 'a vehicle intended or adapted for use on roads'. No indication is given that a vehicle needs to be mechanically propelled or capable of self-propulsion, so vehicles that can only be towed, such as caravans and trailers (which are often used by fast-food operators), will be covered. 'Vessel', also defined in s 193, 'includes a ship, boat, raft or other apparatus constructed or adapted for floating on water'. No definition of 'moveable structure' is provided, but the term would seem to encompass structures such as marquees, tents, portakabins and inflatable buildings.

Section 189 makes further provision in respect of vehicles, vessels and moveable structures, primarily in respect of their location when they are not permanently located in one place, for this will be important in determining the relevant licensing authority to which an application will be made.[4] As regards vessels, these will only be regarded as having one location, which is the place where they are usually moored or berthed. Section 189(1) provides:

> This Act applies in relation to a vessel which is not permanently moored or berthed as if it were premises situated in the place where it is usually moored or berthed.

6.1.6    As regards vehicles and moveable structures, they can have more than one location and will be treated as premises located at any place where they are situated. If they are positioned (parked or set) at only one particular place, they are to be treated as situated at that place; but if they are positioned at more than one place, they are to be treated as separate premises for each place. Section 189(2)–(4) provides:

> (2) Where a vehicle which is not permanently situated in the same place is, or is proposed to be, used for one or more licensable activities while parked at a particular place, the vehicle is to be treated for the purposes of this Act as if it were premises situated at that place.
>
> (3) Where a moveable structure which is not permanently situated in the same place is, or is proposed to be, used for one or more licensable activities while set in a particular place, the structure is to be treated for the purposes of this Act as if it were premises situated at that place.
>
> (4) Where subsection (2) applies in relation to the same vehicle, or subsection (3) applies in relation to the same structure, in respect of more than one place, the premises which by virtue of that subsection are situated at each such place are to be treated as separate premises.

This will mean that, for example, travelling 'fast food' vehicles such as burger and kebab vans providing late night refreshment (LNR) in several different locations will need, in respect of each location, a separate premises licence from the licensing authority or licensing authorities if the locations fall within different licensing authority areas.

Where application is made in respect of a vessel, vehicle or moveable structure, it is not possible to obtain a provisional statement, which is a statement indicating the likely prospects of the grant of a premises licence, where premises are 'being or about to be constructed, altered or extended', if the premises are completed as indicated.[5] Such statements are restricted to premises other than buildings, for s 189(5) provides:

> Sections 29 to 31 (which make provision in respect of provisional statements relating to premises licences) do not apply in relation to a vessel, vehicle or structure to which this section applies.

### 6.1.7 Excluded premises

There is a general prohibition, contained in s 176, on the sale or supply of alcohol from certain premises. These premises are service areas on motorways or similar roads and garage forecourts, where a premises licence cannot authorise this particular licensable activity.[6] Although these are the only two premises specified in the section, the Secretary of State may make regulations including or excluding any premises from the scope of the prohibition.[7] Section 176(1)–(3) provides:

(1) No premises licence, club premises certificate or temporary event notice has effect to authorise the sale by retail or supply of alcohol on or from excluded premises.

(2) In this section "excluded premises" means–

    (a) premises situated on land acquired or appropriated by a special road authority, and for the time being used, for the provision of facilities to be used in connection with the use of a special road provided for the use of traffic of class I (with or without other classes);[8] or

    (b) premises used primarily as a garage or which form part of premises which are primarily so used.

(3) The Secretary of State may by order amend the definition of excluded premises in subsection (2) so as to include or exclude premises of such description as may be specified in the order.

Premises are used as a garage for the purposes of s 176 if they are used for selling petrol or diesel or selling or maintaining motor vehicles[9] and need to be primarily so used or to form part of premises that are primarily so used. The question of primary use is particularly likely to arise in cases where premises operate as a filling station and a food or convenience store and, when considering this question, it seems that the matter should be determined by reference to the intensity of use by customers at the premises. In *R v Liverpool Crown Court ex p Goodwin* [2002] LLR 698, 699, Laws J stated: 'The question must be, what is the intensity of use by customers at the premises? So that evidence such as that of customer lists, to take an example, might be highly material.'[10] The court held that there had been an 'erroneous approach' by the Crown Court in regarding 'the appearance of the premises and how it is known in the locality' as material to the question of primary use.[11] Primary use should not therefore be based on an examination of the gross or net turnover or income from non-qualifying products, such as petrol or diesel, and other products, although it seems that a comparison of the 'garage use' net turnover (rather than gross turnover, which includes fuel tax and duties) with the net turnover from the other activities may be taken into account, as well as a consideration of the purposes for which customers visited the site. This was the approach taken by justices in *Green v Inner London*

*Licensing Justices* (1994) 19 *Licensing Review* 13, and no adverse comment was made on this by the High Court.

### 6.1.8  Exemptions

6.1.9    Certain types of premises are exempt and a premises licence is not required for activities, which otherwise would be licensable, when these take place at such premises. The exemptions broadly relate to activities taking place on various forms of transport whilst engaged on journeys, and at certain airports and seaports, royal palaces, premises used by the armed forces, and premises exempt on national security grounds. The specified exemptions are not exhaustive, for they may be extended by regulations made by the Secretary of State. Section 173(1) provides:

> An activity is not a licensable activity if it is carried on–
>
> (a)  aboard an aircraft, hovercraft or railway vehicle engaged on a journey,
>
> (b)  aboard a vessel engaged on an international journey,
>
> (c)  at an approved wharf at a designated port or hoverport,
>
> (d)  at an examination station at a designated airport,
>
> (e)  at a royal palace,
>
> (f)  at premises which, at the time when the activity is carried on, are permanently or temporarily occupied for the purposes of the armed forces of the Crown,
>
> (g)  at premises in respect of which a certificate issued under section 174 (exemption for national security) has effect, or
>
> (h)  at such other place as may be prescribed.

The first two exemptions are necessarily limited by the activity in question, that is the transport journey, but the other exemptions are general in nature and there is no requirement for the licensable activities to have any connection with the use to which the premises are put. Thus, the exemption in s 173(1)(f) for premises occupied by the armed forces, for example, is not confined to licensable activities carried on by the military and extends to all events at the premises.

### 6.1.10  *Transport journeys: s 173(1)(a) and (b)*

The period during which an aircraft, hovercraft, railway vehicle or vessel is engaged on a journey extends beyond the journey time itself to include preparations ahead of departure and continued occupation after arrival, pending disembarking. Section 173(2) provides:

> For the purposes of subsection (1) the period during which an aircraft, hovercraft, railway vehicle or vessel is engaged on a journey includes–
>
> (a)  any period ending with its departure when preparations are being made for the journey, and
>
> (b)  any period after its arrival at its destination when it continues to be occupied by those (or any of those) who made the journey (or any part of it).

### 6.1.11  *Airports and seaports: s 173(1)(c) and (d)*

The exemption relates to particular areas of designated airports and seaports. At an airport, this is the examination station, which is that part of the airport beyond the security check-in (Explanatory Note 265), known colloquially as 'airside', and at a seaport, this is an approved wharf. Both of these areas are ones to which the non-travelling public do not have access and they are subject to stringent byelaws. The purpose of the exemption is to enable the provision of refreshment of all kinds to travellers at all times of the day and night (Guidance, para 5.19). The exemption is restricted to these areas and other parts of designated airports and seaports are subject to the normal licensing controls.

As to designation of ports, all existing ports are to be treated as designated (unless provision to the contrary is made by the Secretary of State by order for any port) and the criterion for designation by the Secretary of State of any future ports is whether there appears to be a substantial amount of international passenger traffic. Section 173(3)–(5) provides:

(3) The Secretary of State may by order designate a port, hoverport or airport for the purposes of subsection (1), if it appears to him to be one at which there is a substantial amount of international passenger traffic.

(4) Any port, airport or hoverport where section 86A or 87 of the Licensing Act 1964 (c.26) is in operation immediately before the commencement of this section is, on and after that commencement, to be treated for the purposes of subsection (1) as if it were designated.

(5) But provision may by order be made for subsection (4) to cease to have effect in relation to any port, airport or hoverport.

## 6.1.12  Royal Palaces: s 173(1)(e)

There are numerous Royal Palaces that are exempt from obtaining a premises licence, including Buckingham Palace and its garden and mews, St James' Palace, Clarence House and Marlborough House Mews, Kensington Palace, Hampton Court Mews and Paddocks, the Tower of London, Windsor Castle, Windsor Castle Mews and the Windsor Home and Great Parks.

## 6.1.13  Premises used by the armed forces or exempt on national security grounds: s 173(1)(f) and (g)

Premises used by the armed forces will include not only those permanently occupied by any of the forces (for example, the British Army's Royal Military Academy at Sandhurst), but also any premises temporarily occupied by the forces.

Premises, to be exempt on national security grounds, require a Minister of the Crown[12] to issue a certificate 'if he considers that it is appropriate to do so for the purposes of safeguarding national security' (s 174(1)). No details are provided in s 174 as to what the certificate should contain, except that 'it may identify the premises in question by means of a general description' (s 174(2)).[13] Section 174(5) states that certificates issued by a minister can subsequently be cancelled by him or any other Minister of the Crown. It is envisaged that the power will be used where the inspection of a particular premises, for the purposes of the licensing regime, will give rise to a security risk (Explanatory Note 266).

### 6.1.14 Incidental noncommerical lottery with alcohol as a prize: s 175

Section 175 provides an exemption in the case of an incidental noncommercial lottery where one or more of the prizes consist of alcohol. An incidental noncommercial lottery is one where the lottery is incidental to a noncommercial event, which will be the case where no sum raised by the organisers of the event (whether by way of fees for entrance or for participation, by way of sponsorship, by way of commission from traders or otherwise) is appropriated for the purpose of private gain and where various conditions set out in Pt 1 of Sched 11 to the Gambling Act 2005 are met.[14] Section 175(1) and (2) provides:

(1) The promotion of a lottery to which this section applies shall not constitute a licensable activity by reason only of one or more of the prizes in the lottery consisting of or including alcohol, provided that the alcohol is in a sealed container.

(2) This section applies to an incidental non-commercial lottery (within the meaning of Part 1 of Schedule 11 to the Gambling Act 2005).

## 6.2  APPLICANTS FOR PREMISES LICENCES

6.2.1    Section 16 lists the categories of persons or bodies who may apply for a premises licence in respect of any premises and, where the applicant is an individual, he must be aged at least 18. Section 16(1) and (2) provides:

(1) The following persons may apply for a premises licence in respect of any premises–
   (a) a person who carries on, or proposes to carry on, a business which involves the use of the premises for the licensable activities to which the application relates,
   (b) any person who makes the application pursuant to–
      (i) any statutory function discharged by that person which relates to those licensable activities, or
      (ii) any function discharged by that person by virtue of Her Majesty's prerogative,
   (c) a recognised club,
   (d) a charity,
   (e) the proprietor of an educational institution,
   (f) a health service body,
   (g) a person who is registered under Part 2 of the Care Standards Act 2000 (c.14) in respect of an independent hospital,
   (h) a chief officer of police of a police force in England and Wales,
   (i) a person of such other description as may be prescribed.
(2) But an individual may not apply for a premises licence unless he is aged 18 or over.

### 6.2.2  Persons carrying on a business

6.2.3    The most common category will be paragraph (a), persons whose business involves the use of the premises for licensable activities. There is no requirement for a person to have any legal or equitable interest in the premises or even any contractual right to use them. This may be so, even if a person is merely proposing to carry on a business at the premises. Persons proposing to carry on a business might include those interested in purchasing or constructing premises with a view to carrying out licensable activities there. As para 8.56 of the Guidance indicates, it is possible to make an application where premises are not constructed provided:

clear plans of the proposed structure exist and the applicant is in a position to complete an operating schedule including details of:

- the activities to take place there;
- the time at which such activities will take place;
- the proposed hours of opening;
- where the applicant wishes the licence to have effect for a limited period, that period;
- the steps to be taken to promote the licensing objectives; and
- where the sale of alcohol is involved, whether supplies are proposed to be for consumption on or off the premises (or both) and the name of the designated premises supervisor the applicant wishes to specify.'

Less clear is whether a person developing a site for use for licensable activities can make an application. It seems unlikely that such a person can be regarded as someone who 'carries on, or proposes to carry on, a business which involves the use of the premises for the licensable activities to which the application relates', since there is not a sufficient nexus between his involvement in the use of premises and the licensable activities. Such a person might, however, apply for a provisional statement (see 6.8.4 below).

Since application can be made by 'a person', this will include both a corporate and unincorporated body as well as an individual[15] and it will be a matter for business operators to decide in which person's name an application is to be made. Para 8.19 of the Guidance provides:

Licensing authorities should not require the nomination of an individual to hold the licence or decide who is the most appropriate person to hold the licence. For example, for most leased public houses, a tenant may run or propose to run the business at the premises in agreement with a pub owning company. Both would be eligible to apply for the appropriate licence and it is for these businesses or individuals to agree contractually amongst themselves who should do so. However, in the case of a managed public house, the pub operating company should apply for the licence as the manager (an employee) would not be entitled to do so. Similarly, with cinema chains, the normal holder of the premises licence would be the company owning the cinema and not the cinema manager (an employee of the main company).

6.2.4     Although para(a) is expressed in the singular ('a person'), it nevertheless seems possible for more than one person to hold a premises licence in respect of the same premises. If, for instance, one person were to use the premises for one licensable activity, showing films, and another for a different licensable activity, the provision of late night refreshment services, each might be entitled to make an application under para(a). If each were to make an application for their particular licensable activity, each would be 'a person who carries on . . . a business which involves the use of the premises for the licensable activities to which the application relates'. This is recognised by para 8.23 of the Guidance, which provides:

There is nothing in the 2003 Act which prevents an application being made for a premises licence at premises for which a premises licence is already held. For example, one individual may hold a premises licence authorising the sale of alcohol and another individual could apply for a premises licence for the same premises or part of those premises which would authorise regulated entertainment. This also ensures that one business could not seek premises licences, for example, for all potential circus sites in England and Wales, and prevent other circuses from using those sites even though they had the permission of the landowner.

Equally, it is possible that, in respect of a single licensable activity, more than one person may carry on a business at the premises, as where premises may be used at weekends by one person as a dance school during the day and by another person as a discotheque during the evening. Again, each might make an application for a premises licence.[16] It is clear from s 2(3) that there can be more than one authorisation, that is, a premises licence, a club premises certificate (CPC) or a temporary event notice (TEN) in respect of the same premises (see 5.1.4 above) and that these may be held by the same person or different people. If this can occur, there is no reason why different persons should not hold one form of authorisation, a premises licence, in respect of different licensable activities or perhaps even the same licensable activities that take place on the premises.

6.2.5    Similarly, it seems possible that there can be an application in the name of more than one person for a single premises licence in respect of some particular licensable activity or activities and the subsequent grant of a licence in joint names. That references in the 2003 Act are in the singular – application is by 'a person' who, if granted a premises licence will be 'the holder' of it – will not necessarily preclude the grant of a licence in joint names, as s 6(c) of the Interpretation Act 1978 provides: 'In any Act, unless the contrary intention appears ... words in the singular include the plural and words in the plural include the singular.' There were similar references in the Licensing Act 1964 and the Local Government (Miscellaneous Provisions) Act 1982 under the previous law; both justices and local authorities granted licences in joint names and there was no suggestion by the courts that this was in any way improper. In *Buchanan v Gresswell* [1995] COD 355, the Divisional Court considered the question of revocation of a justices' licence, which was held jointly by two licensees, without giving any indication that a licence could not be so held.[17] Further, the Guidance envisages that licences might be jointly held, at least in some circumstances. Paragraphs 8.20 and 8.21 provide:

> 8.20 In considering joint applications (which is likely to be a rare occurrence), it must be stressed that under section 16(1)(a) of the 2003 Act each applicant must be carrying on a business which involves the use of the premises for licensable activities at the premises. In the case of public houses, this would be easier for a tenant to demonstrate than for a pub owning company that is not itself carrying on licensable activities.[18] The Secretary of State recommends that where licences are to be held by businesses, it is desirable that this should be a single business to avoid any lack of clarity in terms of accountability.

> 8.21 A public house may be owned or a tenancy held, jointly by a husband and wife or other partnerships of a similar nature, both actively involved in carrying on the licensable activities. In these cases, it is entirely possible for the husband and wife or the partners to apply jointly as applicant for the premises licence, even if they are not formally partners in business terms. This is unlikely to lead to the same issues of clouded accountability that could arise where two separate businesses apply jointly for the licence.

In practice, it is much more likely that licences will be held by a single person, although no doubt there will be instances of licences held in joint names.

## 6.2.6   Other categories

6.2.7    The remaining categories of persons who may apply for a premises licence are ones where the person or body would not traditionally be regarded as carrying on a 'business' in respect of the licensable activities. Section 16(1)(b) covers two groups, the first of which is any person exercising a statutory function (which, by s 16(3) means 'a function conferred by or under any enactment'). This will include local authorities and other state agencies not otherwise included in the list of applicants, such as the Fire Service, Prison Service and Probation Service. The second group is any person exercising a function under Her Majesty's Prerogative, usually referred to as the Royal Prerogative. It is not obvious what this will include. Possibilities might be licensable activities held in Royal Parks (for example, Hyde Park) or to celebrate the grant of honours, awards and privileges (for example, the conferring of city status). Perhaps this provision was intended to ensure inclusion of any ministerial functions that may not be statutory and which might therefore fall outside the first group covered by s 16(1)(b). Section 16(1)(c) includes a recognised club, which is defined in s 193 as one that satisfies the general Conditions 1–3 in s 62. This is, broadly speaking, a club where there is a period of time before a person is admitted to membership or the privileges of membership and which is conducted in good faith (see 8.2.8 below).

6.2.8    As regards applicants falling within s 16(1)(d) to (g), which cover charities, educational institutions and health bodies in the public and private sector, further provision as to meaning is made by s 16(3). 'Charity' has the same meaning as in s 96(1) of the Charities Act 1993, which provides:

> "charity" means any institution, corporate or not, which is established for charitable purposes and is subject to the control of the High Court in the exercise of the court's jurisdiction with respect to charities.

The terms 'educational institution' and the 'proprietor' of such an institution are defined by reference to the Education Act 1996 and the Further and Higher Education Act 1992:

> "educational institution" means–
>
> (a)  a school, or an institution within the further or higher education sector, within the meaning of section 4 of the Education Act 1996 (c.56),[19] or
>
> (b)  a college (including any institution in the nature of a college), school, hall, or other institution of a university, in circumstances where the university receives financial support under section 65 of the Further and Higher Education Act 1992 (c.13);[20]
>
> "proprietor" means–
>
> (a)  in relation to a school within the meaning of section 4 of the Education Act 1996 (c.56), has the same meaning as in section 579(1) of that Act,[21] and
>
> (b)  in relation to an education institution other than such a school, means the governing body of that institution within the meaning of section 90(1) of the Further and Higher Education Act 1992 (c.13).[22]

A health service body will include an NHS Trust, a Primary Care Trust and a Local Health Board. Section 16(3) of the 2003 Act provides:

> "health service body" means–
>
> (a)  an NHS trust established by virtue of section 25 of the National Health Service Act 2006 or section 18 of the National Health Service (Wales) Act 2006,

(b) a Primary Care Trust established by virtue of section 18 of the National Health Service Act 2006, or

(c) a Local Health Board established by virtue of section 11 of the National Health Service (Wales) Act 2006.

As regards the private sector, application can be made by a person who is registered under Part 2 of the Care Standards Act 2000 in respect of an 'independent hospital', which has the same meaning as in s 2(2) of the 2000 Act, which provides: 'A hospital which is not a health service hospital is an independent hospital.'

6.2.9    The remaining specifically identified category, in s 16(1)(h), is police forces in England and Wales, for which the applicant will be the chief officer of police for the force. Finally, there is scope for the Secretary of State to extend the categories of applicant, since s 16(1)(i) makes provision for 'a person of such other description as may be prescribed' to be an applicant.

## 6.3    APPLICATIONS FOR PREMISES LICENCES

### 6.3.1    Form, notices and fees

#### *Form and Notices*

Section 17(1) provides: 'An application for a premises licence must be made to the relevant licensing authority'; and s 12(1) provides: 'For the purposes of this Part the "relevant licensing authority" in relation to any premises is determined in accordance with this section.' The relevant licensing authority will be the authority in whose area the premises are situated, except that where they are situated in the areas of two or more licensing authorities, it will be the authority in whose area the greater (or greatest) part of the premises are situated or, if there is no such authority, the authority nominated by the applicant.[23] Section 12(2)–(4) provides:

(2)  Subject to subsection (3), the relevant licensing authority is the authority in whose area the premises are situated.

(3)  Where the premises are situated in the areas of two or more licensing authorities, the relevant licensing authority is–

(a) the licensing authority in whose area the greater or greatest part of the premises is situated, or

(b) if there is no authority to which paragraph (a) applies, such one of those authorities as is nominated in accordance with subsection (4).

(4)  In a case within subsection (3)(b)–

(a) an applicant for a premises licence must nominate one of the licensing authorities as the relevant licensing authority in relation to the application and any licence granted as a result of it, and

(b) an applicant for a statement under section 29 (provisional statement) in respect of the premises must nominate one of the licensing authorities as the relevant licensing authority in relation to the statement.

With regard to applications for premises licences in respect of vessels, vessels are treated by s 189(1) as if they are premises situated in the place where the vessel is usually moored or berthed (see 6.1.5 above), so the relevant licensing authority will therefore be the licensing authority for the area in which the vessel is usually moored or berthed (Guidance, para 5.11). Applications, are by virtue of s 17(2), subject to regulations[24] made (a) under s 54 in respect of the form, etc, of applications and any notices that need to be given, and (b) under s 55 in respect of fees to accompany applications and notices.[25] The Licensing Act 2003 (Premises Licences and Club Premises Certificates) Regulations 2005, SI 2005/42 (LA 2003 (PL and CPC) Regs 2005) specify the form the application shall take and the information that it must contain.[26]

## Fees

### Generally

Under the Licensing Act 2003 (Fees) Regulations 2005, SI 2005/79 (LA 2003 (Fees) Regs 2005) premises are allocated to specific bands for the purposes of determining the appropriate level of fee to be paid when applying for the grant or variation of a premises licence (or CPC) and the appropriate level of the annual fee that is payable. These bands are based on the 'rateable value' of the premises, which is defined in reg 2(1) as 'the value for the time being in force for the premises entered in the local non-domestic rating list for the purposes of Part III of the Local Government Finance Act 1988' or, in short, what might be described as the 'non-domestic rateable value' (NDRV) of the premises.[27] Premises are allocated to one of five bands, Bands A–E, for each of which an application fee is payable, which ranges from £100 to £635.[28] Provision is made for increased fees in two instances: one is in respect of certain premises in the top two bands, Bands D and E, and the other is in respect of events where 5,000 or more people may attend the premises concerned. Provision is also made for fee exemptions in certain cases. The question of fees has been examined by the Independent Licensing Fees Review Panel under the chairmanship of Sir Les Elton, which reported in January 2007, but at the time of writing no action has been taken by the Government on the Panel's Report.

### Application and annual fees

Regulation 3(1) and Sched 1 set out the rateable values applicable to Bands A–E; regs 4(2)–(3) and Sched 2 the application fee payable; and reg 5 and Sched 5 the annual fee payable.[29] The bands and fees are set out in the table below:

| Band | A | B | C | D | E |
|---|---|---|---|---|---|
| NDRV | £0–£4,300 | £4,301–£33,000 | £33,001–£87,000 | £87,001–£125,000 | £125,001 or over |
| Application fee | £100 | £190 | £315 | £450 | £635 |
| Annual fee | £70 | £180 | £295 | £3,200 | £350 |

In cases where premises do not have an NDRV, because they are not liable to or are exempt from nondomestic rating, a Band A application fee and annual fee are generally payable. This will be the case for domestic premises, public open spaces, for example parks, and vehicles and vessels that lack the degree of permanence required for them to be subject to nondomestic rating. Where, however, premises are in the course of construction they are allocated to Band C. Regulation 2(2) provides: 'Except in a case where a premises is in the course of construction, in which case the premises shall be in Band C, in all other cases, the premises shall be in Band A.'

*Increased fees*

Provision is made for an increased fee for both applications for grant under s 17 and for variation under s 34. Where premises are in Bands D and E and are used 'exclusively or primarily for the carrying on on the premises of the supply of alcohol for consumption on the premises', there is a multiplier of twice the fee for such premises in Band D and three times the fee for such premises in Band E. Regulation 4(2), as substituted by reg 2(2) of the Licensing Act 2003 (Fees) (Amendment) Regulations 2005, SI 2005/357 (LA 2003 (Fees) (Amendment) Regs 2005), provides:

> Subject to paragraphs (4) [which provides for an additional fee where more than 5,000 persons attend] and, in the case of an application under section 34, (6) and (7) [which applied in respect of transition], where the application under section 17 or section 34 relates to a premises in Band D or Band E and the premises is used exclusively or primarily for the carrying on on the premises of the supply of alcohol for consumption on the premises, the amount of the fee shall be–
>
> (a) in the case of premises in Band D, two times the amount of the fee applicable for the Band appearing in column 1 of the table in Schedule 2 specified in column 2 of that table, and
>
> (b) in the case of premises in Band E, three times the amount of the fee applicable for that Band appearing in column 1 of the table in Schedule 2 specified in column 2 of that table.

This regulation makes it clear that the increased fee is payable where premises are used exclusively or primarily for supply of alcohol for consumption there, unlike the provision in reg 4(2) in its original form that referred to a case where the 'application relates to – (a) a premises in Band D or Band E; and (b) the use of the premises exclusively or primarily for the carrying on on the premises of the supply of alcohol for consumption on the premises'.[30] The expression 'application . . . relates to . . . the use of the premises' might have been taken to mean that the increased fee was payable where the *application* related to the use of the premises exclusively or primarily for supply of alcohol for consumption there rather than whether the premises themselves were so used. In other words, exclusive or primary use might have been determined by reference to the licensable activities specified in the premises licence application rather than by reference to the licensable and non-licensable activities taking place at the premises, that is by reference to their overall use. This could have meant that if supply of alcohol was the only licensable activity specified in the premises licence application, as may be the case with casino premises, the increased fee would be payable, irrespective of other activities taking place at the premises. Casino premises themselves are not used exclusively or primarily for the supply of alcohol for consumption there, but the premises licence application would relate exclusively to such supply.

That the original regulation might be so interpreted was clearly not in accordance with the Government's intention, which is for the increased fee to be paid for premises used exclusively or primarily for the supply of alcohol for consumption there. This is apparent from a press release issued by the Department of Culture, Media and Sport on 21 January 2005 (Press Release 005/05 'New Licensing Fees Will

Help Provide Tougher Protections For Local People'), in which it was stated that 'the largest urban pubs would be required to meet a greater share of the cost to licensing authorities ... of running the new licensing regime than previously proposed'. One of the 'key findings' from the consultation into fees following publication of the draft regulations that needed to be addressed was 'that the control of premises selling alcohol would in general give rise to higher costs than other premises ... particularly where these were situated in town and city centres'. The Secretary of State, Tessa Jowell, was quoted as saying:

> In particular, we are asking the largest town and city centre pubs to pay a higher premium. This is only right. They can have the biggest capacities, the highest turnover and often make the greatest profit. They are a major beneficiary of our night time economy. They should put more back into policing it.

Thus the rationale for the increased fee seems to have been that those premises in respect of which the deployment of resources is most likely to be required to promote the licensing objectives (perhaps, in particular, prevention of crime and disorder) should make a greater financial contribution via the fees payable and, generally speaking, this will be the larger establishments, falling within Bands D and E, used exclusively or primarily for supply of alcohol for consumption on the premises.[31] Once it was drawn to the Government's attention that the original reg 4(2) might not have this effect, a new reg 4(2) was substituted by the LA 2003 (Fees) (Amendment) Regs 2005 to ensure that it did.[32]

With regard to determining exclusive or primary use, few premises are used exclusively for the supply of alcohol for consumption there and in most cases it will be necessary to determine primary use. This may not be easy to ascertain in some cases, as is recognised in para 13.45 of the Guidance in respect of the comparable requirement in the offence in s 145 of permitting children under the age of 16 who are not accompanied by an adult to be present on premises being used exclusively or primarily for supply of alcohol for consumption on those premises (see 11.7.4 below). The inherent difficulty is that primary use might be determined by reference to different criteria – these might include turnover, profit, floor space, the general character of the business, the purpose for which customers go to the premises and the intensity of use by customers[33] – and the application of different criteria may produce different results.

The case of a nightclub provides an illustration. The general character of the business may be said to be the provision of music and dancing, suggesting that premises are not used primarily for the supply of alcohol for consumption there and an increased fee is not payable. This might be supported by the fact that under the previous law nightclubs with a special hours certificate (SHC) could supply alcohol beyond the normal permitted hours, only where the alcohol was ancillary to the music and dancing and to the provision of substantial refreshment. Indeed, under s 81 of the Licensing Act 1964 the certificate could be revoked where, on the whole, persons resorting to the premises were there for the purpose of obtaining alcohol rather than for music and dancing and substantial refreshment. Nightclub premises under the 2003 Act need not, however, provide music and dancing as the primary activity, with supply of alcohol as ancillary, and where this is the case application of the above-mentioned factors may produce diverse outcomes. If, for example, regard is had to the purpose for which customers go there and the intensity of use by them, this may indicate that the premises are equally used for the principal purposes of both providing music and dancing, and supplying alcohol. On this basis, they would nevertheless not be used primarily for the supply of alcohol and a higher fee would not be payable. If, on the other hand, regard is had to turnover and profit, much of the turnover and profit is derived from selling alcohol rather than from the music and dancing and any entrance fee for admission. These criteria might suggest that the premises are primarily used for the supply of alcohol and may accordingly be subject to the higher fee.

Given that there are various criteria that can be used, judicial clarification may be needed. However, the courts may well decline to offer any guidance and take the view that there are a number of material considerations that can be taken into account, none of which is decisive, and it is a question of fact in each case which factors are material and what weight should be given to them. This was the approach taken by the courts in respect of the definition of 'sex shop' in para 4(1) of Sched 3 to the Local Government (Miscellaneous Provisions) Act 1982 as a business which consists to a 'significant degree' of the selling, etc, of sex articles. In *Watford Borough Council v Private Alternative Birth Control Information and Education Centres Ltd* [1985] Crim LR 594, Mustill LJ stated:

> The ratio between the sexual and other aspects of the business will always be material. So also will the absolute quantity of sales ... [and] the court will no doubt find it appropriate to consider the character of the remainder of the business. The nature of the display can be a relevant factor, and the nature of the articles themselves will also be material ... It would be wrong to say that in law any single factor is decisive. It is up to the court of trial to decide which considerations are material to the individual case and what weight is to be attached to them.

Before concluding his judgment, Mustill LJ declined an invitation to offer any guidance in the shape of a test to ascertain when the 'significant degree' criterion would be satisfied:

> I appreciate that such guidance would be useful, as much to shopkeepers as to the enforcement and licensing authorities. I believe, however, that no such test could be devised, and if the court were to attempt one it would be placing an illegitimate gloss on a provision which deliberately leaves the question to the broad judgment of those concerned and, in case of need, to the broad judgment of the court.

If the courts adopt the same approach here, it will be left to the broad judgment, initially of the applicant, as to what fee to submit with his application, then of the licensing authority as to whether its judgment accords with that of the applicant, with the matter being resolved either through agreement or ultimately by the courts. It may be that in most cases in practice, if the licensing authority takes a different view from the applicant and considers that the higher fee is payable, applicants are likely to be paid the higher fee requested in order to ensure that their application proceeds rather than resort to a judicial determination of the matter.

*Additional fees*

An additional fee is payable under reg 4(4) where 5,000 or more persons are allowed on the premises at the same time when licensable activities are taking place. However, this is not payable in all cases and, under reg 4(5), does not apply where the premises are 'a structure which is not a vehicle, vessel or moveable structure' and the structure has been constructed or structurally altered for purposes which include enabling licensable activities to take place on the premises where a number of requirements are met. Regulation 4(4)–(5) provides:

> (4) Subject to paragraph (5) and, in the case of an application under section 34, (8), where the maximum number of persons the applicant proposes should, during the times when the licence authorises licensable activities to take place on the premises, be allowed on the premises at the same time is 5,000 or more, an application under paragraph (1) must be accompanied by a fee in addition to any fee determined under paragraphs (2) and (3), the amount of which shall be the fee applicable to the range of number of persons within which falls the maximum number of persons the applicant proposes to be so allowed on the premises in column 1 of the table in Schedule 3 specified in column 2 of that table.
>
> (5) Paragraph (4) does not apply where the premises in respect of which the application has been made–
>
>> (a) is a structure which is not a vehicle, vessel or moveable structure; and
>>
>> (b) has been constructed or structurally altered for the purpose, or for purposes which include the purpose, of enabling–
>>
>>> (i) the premises to be used for the licensable activities the applicant proposes the licence should authorise;
>>>
>>> (ii) the premises to be modified temporarily from time to time, if relevant, for the premises to be used for the licensable activities referred to in the application;
>>>
>>> (iii) at least the number of persons the applicant proposes should, during the times when the licence authorises licensable activities to take place on the premises, be allowed on the premises, to be allowed on the premises at such times; and
>>>
>>> (iv) the premises to be used in a manner which is not inconsistent with the operating schedule accompanying the application.

The reference in reg 4(5)(a) to 'structure', and the exclusion of moveable structures, suggests that no payment of the additional fee is required in respect of structures having some degree of permanence, which for the most part is likely to mean buildings.[34] Thus, the Explanatory Note to the Regulations states: 'the Regulations disapply the requirement to pay the additional fee in respect of premises that are buildings when certain conditions are met (regulation 4(5)).'[35] Less helpfully, the Explanatory Note does not go on to say what those conditions set out in reg 4(5) are.

The conditions are ones that relate in various ways to the structure's construction or structural alteration for the purposes of enabling licensable activities to take place there. The first condition is that the structure has been constructed or altered so that the proposed licensable activities can take place at the premises (reg 4(5)(b)(i)), which suggests it has been purpose-built (or purpose-altered) for those activities, for example an indoor sports arena. The second condition is that the structure has been constructed or altered so as to enable the premises to be temporarily modified on occasions for use for proposed licensable activities (reg 4(5)(b)(ii)), which suggests that the structure has been built (or altered) for other purposes, but might be adapted for occasional use for the proposed licensable activities, for example an exhibition centre such as Earls Court and Olympia, which might be used periodically for musical events.[36] The third condition is that the structure has been constructed or altered so as to allow on the premises at least the number of persons the applicant is proposing to admit at the times when the licence authorises licensable activities to take place (reg 4(5)(b)(iii)), that is, if the applicant is proposing to admit 5,000 persons, the structure must have a capacity of at least 5,000 persons. The fourth condition is that the structure has been constructed or altered so as to enable the premises to be used in a manner that is not inconsistent with the operating schedule (reg 4(5)(b)(iv)). This seems to mean that the premises are fit for the purposes required.

If any of the requirements in reg 4(5) are not met, the additional fee is payable. It may well be that in most cases where the premises comprise a building the requirements will be met and that, in the main, additional fees are likely to be payable in respect of events such as 'outdoor' music concerts held either wholly in the open air or partially in the open air and partially inside moveable structures such as marquees. However, there may be some instances where the additional fee is payable in respect of licensable activities taking place in buildings. Regulation 4(5) provides that 'the premises in respect of which the application has been made – (a) is a structure', which suggests that if the premises *include* a structure, but extend beyond it, as in the case of a music concert held partially in the open air and partially inside a building, an additional fee is payable.

Schedule 3 specifies the additional fees payable, the amount of which is dependent on the number of persons present, as set out in the following table.

ADDITIONAL FEE

| Column 1 | Column 2 |
|---|---|
| Number | Additional fee |
| 5,000 to 9,999 | £1,000 |
| 10,000 to 14,999 | £2,000 |
| 15,000 to 19,999 | £4,000 |
| 20,000 to 29,999 | £8,000 |
| 30,000 to 39,999 | £16,000 |
| 40,000 to 49,999 | £24,000 |
| 50,000 to 59,999 | £32,000 |
| 60,000 to 69,999 | £40,000 |
| 70,000 to 79,999 | £48,000 |
| 80,000 to 89,999 | £56,000 |
| 90,000 and over | £64,000 |

*Fee exemptions*

Where, in respect of certain premises, application is made for a premise licence authorising only the provision of regulated entertainment, there is an exemption in reg 9 from the requirement to pay an application fee. These premises include church halls, chapel halls, village halls, parish and community halls or other premises of a similar nature, as well as schools providing education for pupils up to year 13 or sixth-form colleges (where the regulated entertainment is carried on by and for the purposes of the school or college). Regulation 9(1)–(2) provides:

(1) In respect of an application under section 17, section 34, section 71 or section 84 which relates to the provision of regulated entertainment only, no fee shall be payable and accompany the application or notice if the conditions of this regulation are satisfied in respect of that application or notice.

(2) The conditions referred to in paragraph (1) are–

    (a) in the case of an application by a proprietor[37] of an educational institution in respect of premises that are or form part of an educational institution–

        (i) that the educational institution is a school[38] or a college;[39] and

        (ii) the provision of regulated entertainment on the premises is carried on by the educational institution for and on behalf of the purposes of the educational institution; or

    (b) that the application is in respect of premises that are or form part of a church hall, chapel hall or other similar building or a village hall, parish hall or community hall or other similar building.

Further, under reg 10, there is a similar exemption for such premises in respect of the requirement to pay an annual fee, provided conditions are met at the time an annual fee falls due to be paid. Regulation 10(1)–(2) provides:

(1) The requirement under regulation 5(1) or 7(1), as the case may require, to pay to the relevant licensing authority an annual fee does not apply in a circumstance where on the date the fee shall become due and payable the conditions of this regulation are satisfied.

(2) The conditions referred to in paragraph (1) are that–

    (a) the premises licence or club premises certificate, as the case may require, in respect of the premises to which it relates authorises the provision of regulated entertainment only; and

    (b) either–

        (i) the holder of the premises licence or club premises certificate referred to in paragraph (2)(a) is–

            (aa) the proprietor of an educational institution which is a school or college; and

            (bb) the licence or certificate has effect in respect of premises that are or form part of the educational institution; and

            (cc) the provision of regulated entertainment on the premises is carried on by the educational institution for and on behalf of the purposes of the educational institution; or

        (ii) that the premises licence or club premises certificate has effect in respect of premises that are or form part of a church hall, chapel hall or other similar building or a village hall, parish hall or community hall or other similar building.

### Advertisements

The 2003 Act requires regulations to be made for the advertising of applications, the giving of notice by applicants to responsible authorities and any other persons prescribed by regulations, and the periods within which such notice and any representations by interested parties and responsible authorities must be made.[40] Section 17(5) provides:

    (5) The Secretary of State must by regulations–

(a) require an applicant to advertise the application within the prescribed period–

    (i)  in the prescribed form, and

    (ii)  in a manner which is prescribed and is likely to bring the application to the attention of the interested parties likely to be affected by it,

(b) require an applicant to give notice of the application to each responsible authority, and such other persons as may be prescribed, within the prescribed period,

(c) prescribe the period during which interested parties and responsible authorities may make representations to the relevant licensing authority about the application.

The LA 2003 (PL and CPC) Regs 2005 make provision for the advertising of applications (regs 25–26) and the giving of notice of the application to responsible authorities by giving them a copy of the application and any accompanying documentation on the same day the application is made to the licensing authority (reg 27), and prescribe a period of 28 consecutive days after the application was given to the authority within which representations can be made (reg 22(b)).[41]

## 6.3.2 Accompanying documentation

Applications must be accompanied by various documents as required by s 17(3), which provides:

An application under this section must also be accompanied–

(a) by an operating schedule,

(b) by a plan of the premises to which the application relates, in the prescribed form, and

(c) if the licensable activities to which the application relates ('the relevant licensable activities') include the supply of alcohol,[42] by a form of consent in the prescribed form given by the individual whom the applicant wishes to have specified in the premises licence as the premises supervisor.

## 6.3.3 *Operating schedule: s 17(3)(a)*

The operating schedule has to set out various matters, including the relevant licensable activities to be covered by the licence, the times the premises will be used for these activities and other times the premises will be open to the public, the limited period for which the licence will have effect (if applicable), information concerning the premises supervisor where alcohol is supplied, and the steps proposed to promote the licensing objectives. Section 17(4) provides:

An "operating schedule" is a document which is in the prescribed form,[43] and includes a statement of the following matters–

(a) the relevant licensable activities,

(b) the times during which it is proposed that the relevant licensable activities are to take place,

(c) any other times during which it is proposed that the premises are to be open to the public,

(d) where the applicant wishes the licence to have effect for a limited period, that period,

(e) where the relevant licensable activities include the supply of alcohol, prescribed information in respect of the individual whom the applicant wishes to have specified in the premises licence as the premises supervisor,

(f) where the relevant licensable activities include the supply of alcohol, whether the supplies are proposed to be for consumption on the premises or off the premises, or both,

(g) the steps which it is proposed to take to promote the licensing objectives, and

(h) such other matters as may be prescribed.

The times during which it is proposed that the relevant licensable activities are to take place will not necessarily be identical to the 'opening hours' of the premises, that is the times when premises are open to the public. The times may well be different and, as the operating schedule indicates the times during which it is proposed that the premises are to be open to the public, the licensing authority will know what period of time it is envisaged the premises will be kept open beyond the proposed terminal hour for the licensable activities.[44] This may well be a limited period, and is likely to be so in the case of public houses, but in other instances, as with hotels and premises with letting rooms, the premises may be open to the public all of the time.[45]

There is no specific requirement for inclusion within the operating schedule of any reference to the use of 'Amusement with Prizes' (AWP) machines at the premises, although these are often a feature at premises, in particular those licensed for the sale of alcohol for consumption on the premises. Under s 282 of the Gambling Act 2005 there is an automatic entitlement to have one or two Category C or D gaming machines[46] in premises with an on-premises alcohol licence, provided the person who holds the on-premises alcohol licence has notified the licensing authority of his intention to make gaming machines available and has paid the prescribed fee.[47] Although applicants need not specify AWP machines within their operating schedule, they should nevertheless indicate on the application form whether there are any such machines on the premises. Part 3N of the form requires applicants to 'highlight any . . . matters ancillary to the use of the premises that may give rise to concern in respect of children' and Guidance Note 8 on the form refers to the presence of gaming machines by way of example 'regardless of whether you intend children to have access to the premises'.

The operating schedule will be an important document and will form the basis for the way in which the premises will be operated. As Explanatory Note 59 indicates:

The significance of the operating schedule is that if the application for the premises licence is approved, it will be incorporated into the licence itself and will set out the permitted activities and the limitations on them. As a consequence, it is the applicant who will decide, subject to the determination of applications by the authority, the nature and extent of the activities and the conditions relating to the carrying on of the activities.

Applicants are required by s 17(4)(g) to include a statement of the steps that they propose to take to promote the licensing objectives, although the Explanatory Notes confine themselves to providing a single example, mentioning only the arrangements to be put in place to prevent crime and disorder, such as door security (Note 59). However, it is apparent from the Guidance that applicants should be liaising closely with the licensing authority and the responsible authorities when drawing up their statement. Paragraphs 8.28 and 8.29 of the Guidance provide:

8.28 In preparing an operating schedule, the Secretary of State expects applicants to have had regard to the statement of licensing policy for their area. They should also be aware of the expectations of the licensing authority and the responsible authorities about the steps that are necessary for the promotion of the licensing objectives. Licensing authorities and responsible authorities are therefore expected so far as possible to publish material about the promotion of the licensing objectives and to ensure that applicants can readily access advice about these matters.

8.29 All parties are expected to work together in partnership to ensure that the licensing objectives are promoted collectively. Applicants are not required to seek the views of the key responsible authorities before formally submitting applications, but may find them a useful source of expert advice. Licensing authorities should encourage cooperation in order to minimise the number of disputes which arise. Where there are no disputes, the steps that applicants propose to take to promote the licensing objectives, as set out in the operating schedule, will very often translate directly into conditions that will be attached to premises licences with the minimum of fuss.

The expectations of the licensing authority, material about promotion of the licensing objectives and accessing advice about these are all likely to be contained in the licensing authority's Statement of Licensing Policy (SOP) and, if the applicant has regard to these when drawing up his operating schedule, it is less likely that any opposition to the application will be encountered. As Richards J stated in *R (on the application of The British Beer and Pub Association) v Canterbury City Council* [2006] LGR 596 (at para 82):

An application that takes account of the matters set out in the policy, for example by including what is referred to in the policy or by giving a reasoned justification for not doing so, is less likely to give rise to relevant representations and more likely to be granted without additional conditions, whether under the administrative procedure in the absence of relevant representations or on a decision by the council under s 18(3) in the event of relevant representations.

However, whilst the policy can set out the licensing authority's expectations, it cannot prescribe or dictate the contents of the operating schedule, which remains a matter for the applicant (see 6.4 below). Whilst applicants have the freedom to draw up their own operating schedule, the schedule should be formulated with care and a degree of precision, since loosely worded schedules may lead to similarly worded conditions being attached. This might cause difficulties for premises licences holders and may affect the retail value of the premises upon sale. The desire to incorporate matters into the schedule needs therefore to be balanced against the possible implications of these being translated into conditions that might have an adverse impact in respect of the premises.

### 6.3.4   Plan and premises supervisor consent form: s 17(3)(b)(c)

The requirements and content of the plan of the premises to which the application relates and the prescribed form of consent given by the person who the applicant wishes to be the premises supervisor where alcohol is to be supplied are contained in regs 23 and 24(1), respectively of the LA 2003 (PL and CPC) Regs 2005.[48]

## 6.4     DETERMINATION OF APPLICATIONS FOR PREMISES LICENCES

The Act draws a distinction between cases where no 'relevant representations' are received and where a licence must be issued (mandatory grants) and cases where there are 'relevant representations', in which case the licensing authority has a discretion whether or not to grant a licence (relevant representations and discretion). This is a fundamental distinction and was one of the bases for a judicial review by the British Beer and Pub Association (BBPA) of the Statement of Licensing Policy (SOP) drawn up by Canterbury City Council, which stated: 'All applications will be considered on their merits, as well as against the relevant policy and statutory framework'. It was contended by the BBPA in *R (on the application of The British Beer and Pub Association) v Canterbury City Council* [2006] LGR 596 (at para 24) that this misrepresented the statutory scheme and constituted the correct position only if relevant representations were made. This contention was accepted by the High Court which held (at paras 84–85) that the SOP was unlawful insofar as it gave the impression that the council would exercise substantive discretionary powers in relation to all applications. Richards J stated (at para 85):

> The licensing authority has no power at all to lay down the contents of an application and has no power to assess an application, or to exercise substantive discretionary powers in relation to it, unless there are relevant representations and the decision-making function under s 18(3) is engaged. If a policy creates a different impression, and in particular if it misleads an applicant into believing that he must meet certain requirements in relation to his application and that he lacks the freedom accorded to him by the Act and regulations, the policy is contrary to the legislative scheme and is unlawful.

If, therefore, there are no relevant representations, the operator's market-based decision as to how he will be conducting his licensable activities prevails and the licensing authority's discretion is not engaged here. In such cases, para 13.79 of the Guidance recommends delegation to officers and, where relevant representations are received, delegation to a licensing subcommittee (for recommendations as to delegation, see 2.2.19 above). Each of these cases is considered below.

### 6.4.1   Mandatory grants

The provisions of s 18, which govern the determination of applications, apply where the authority has received an application made in accordance with s 17 and is satisfied that the applicant has complied with the requirements of s 17(5) in relation to publicising and giving notice of the application (s 18(1)). Where this is the case and no relevant representations are received, the authority must grant the licence. Section 18(2) provides:

> Subject to subsection (3) [which applies where relevant representations are received], the authority must grant the licence in accordance with the application subject only to–
>
> (a)  such conditions as are consistent with the operating schedule accompanying the application, and
>
> (b)  any conditions which must under section 19, 20 or 21 be included in the licence.

Paragraph 9.2 of the Guidance envisages that the licensing authority 'must grant the application in the terms sought' and that this 'should be undertaken as a simple administrative process by the licensing authority's officials by whom the proposals contained in the operating schedule to promote the licensing objectives should be translated into clear and understandable conditions.[49] Consistency here means that 'the effect of the condition should be substantially the same as that intended by the terms of the operating schedule' (Guidance, para 10.10). Where applicants are supported by legal representatives or trade associations, they 'can be expected to express steps necessary to promote the licensable objectives in clear and readily translatable terms' but, as the Guidance recognises, other applicants may express the terms of their operating schedules 'less precisely or concisely' and ensuring that conditions are consistent here 'will then be more difficult'.

The extent to which information is included in the applicant's operating schedule will be influenced by the expectations of the licensing authority as set out in its SOP (see 6.3.3 above). Since the applicant will not know at the point in time of submitting the operating schedule along with his application whether or not any relevant representations will be made in respect of it, it is possible that the applicant might be drawn into including in the operating schedule matters that otherwise might not have been included. This was one of the contentions raised by the BBPA in the *Canterbury* case (see 6.4 above), although Richards J (at para 86) thought that these concerns had been 'substantially overstated', as an applicant who failed to take account of the licensing authority's expectations would realise that this could well give rise to relevant representations:

> ... an applicant with freedom to determine for himself the contents of his application will realise that an application that fails to take account of the expectations lawfully expressed in the policy is likely to give rise in practice to relevant representations and thereby to engage the decision-making function of the licensing authority under s 18(3); and the authority, whilst assessing the application on its individual merits, will be guided by the matters set out in the policy in reaching its decision. An applicant who does not tailor his application to the policy therefore faces an uphill struggle.

Further, 'if operating schedules are prepared efficiently, often in consultation with responsible authorities, it is expected that the likelihood of hearings being necessary following relevant representations would be significantly reduced'. As regards conditions that must be imposed under s 18(2)(b), these apply in three circumstances, where alcohol is sold, where films are exhibited and where door supervisors are required.

### 6.4.2 Mandatory conditions where alcohol is sold

Section 19(1) provides: 'Where a premises licence authorises the supply of alcohol, the licence must include the following conditions.' The two conditions, set out in s 19(2) and (3), are as follows:

(2) The first condition is that no supply of alcohol may be made under the premises licence–

    (a) at a time when there is no designated premises supervisor in respect of the premises licence, or

    (b) at a time when the designated premises supervisor does not hold a personal licence or his personal licence is suspended.

(3) The second condition is that supply of alcohol under the premises licence must be made or authorised by a person who holds a personal licence.

The first condition requires a 'designated premises supervisor' (DPS), in relation to the premises licence, who must hold a valid personal licence. A DPS is 'the individual for the time being specified in the licence as the premises supervisor'.[50] Since the term 'individual' is used here and not 'person', only an individual and not a corporate body can be the DPS. Further, reference to 'the individual', who may be the same person who holds the premises licence or a different person,[51] indicates that, at any one time, there can only be one individual as the DPS. This is reinforced by para 4.23 of the Guidance which states: 'Only one designated premises supervisor may be specified in a single premises licence.' This clearly indicates a 'contrary intention' under s 6(c) of the Interpretation Act 1978 that in this instance reference to the singular is not to include the plural and that there can only be one DPS. However, an individual can be a DPS in respect of more than one premises, for para 4.23 goes on to provide:

> a designated premises supervisor may supervise more than one premises as long as they are able to ensure that the four licensing objectives are properly promoted and the premises complies with licensing law and licence conditions.

The function and purpose of the DPS is set out in paras 4.19 and 4.20 of the Guidance, which provide:

> 4.19 In every premises licensed for the supply of alcohol, a personal licence holder must be specified as the 'designated premises supervisor', as defined in the 2003 Act. This will normally be the person who has been given day to day responsibility for running the premises by the premises licence holder.
> 4.20 The Government considers it essential that police officers, fire officers or officers of the licensing authority can identify immediately the designated premises supervisor so that any problems can be dealt with swiftly. For this reason, the name of the designated premises supervisor and contact details must be specified on the premises licence and this must be held at the premises and displayed in summary form.

For a person to be in day-to-day charge and be immediately identifiable by enforcement officers as in a position of authority at premises, that person, at least in the case of premises such as public houses and nightclubs, might generally be expected to be someone who is normally at the premises directing and overseeing the work of others employed there (for example, a manager), although he cannot, of course, be expected to be there at all times.[52]

Not all premises supply alcohol on an everyday basis, however, and some do so only on occasions. Here it is less clear who should be regarded as in 'day to day charge' and who should be selected as the DPS. This might be the case with village halls and community premises, for instance, where a premises licence may be held by the local authority.[53] The local authority in these instances may appoint as its DPS an officer of the council, although the officer, whilst having responsibility for the premises, may be unlikely to be present when supplies of alcohol are taking place there. He may therefore not, in a meaningful sense, be said to be in 'day to day charge' at times when the supply of alcohol is taking place.

However, whoever ought to be the DPS for particular premises will not necessarily be the person who becomes the DPS for the premises. Under s 17(4)(f) applicants for premises licences can specify the individual who they wish to be the DPS and, unless there are relevant representations from the police that 'due to the exceptional circumstances of the case' the appointment of the person named will undermine the crime prevention objective (s 18(9) and see 6.4.23 below), there will be no opportunity for the licensing authority to prevent the individual specified from becoming the DPS. Thus, a premises licence holder (for example, a pub operating company) may seek to specify as a DPS someone in a managerial role within the organisation (for example, an area manager) for a number of its premises, although such a person would not normally be at (any of) the premises and would not be immediately identifiable as in a position of authority at premises. In the absence of any police representation, however, it would seem that the person specified will in fact become the DPS for those premises.

The circumstances in which there will be no DPS in respect of the premises licence are likely to be limited. When an application is made for a premises licence, s 17(3) requires that it must be accompanied by a consent form signed by the individual whom the applicant wishes to be the DPS (if the applicant himself is not to be the DPS) and, if the application with the nominated individual is granted, the individual will thereafter be the DPS unless and until he is replaced.[54] This will be so even if he were to leave the premises or his employment. There may be no DPS on the premises in such a case, but there will still be a DPS in respect of the premises licence. However, s 41 makes provision for an individual to secure his removal as DPS by giving the licensing authority a notice to that effect and there may therefore be a period, once removal has taken effect, but before a new DPS is nominated, when there is no DPS in respect of the premises licence (see 6.9.14 below). This situation apart, it is difficult to envisage circumstances where there will be no DPS, except perhaps where the DPS dies.[55]

The second condition requires that supply of alcohol under the premises licence is made or authorised by a person who holds a personal licence. The DPS himself does not need to make or authorise sales, or be on the premises, provided that sales are made or authorised by a person who holds a personal licence, nor does there need to be any personal licence holder present on the premises when sales are made, provided that a personal licence holder has authorised others, such as bar staff, to make sales.[56] Paragraph 10.49 of the Guidance provides:

> the fact that every supply of alcohol must be made under the authority of a personal licence holder does not mean that only personal licence holders can make such sales or that they must be personally present at every transaction. A personal licence holder may authorise members of staff to make sales of alcohol, but may be absent at times from the premises when a transaction takes place.

In practice, most operating companies have trained a significant number of employees to be personal licence holders, since the personal licence qualification is good training for employees and is relatively inexpensive. There will therefore, at least for town and city centre premises, normally be one or more personal licence holders present at the premises during operating hours.

Where a personal licence holder authorises other persons to make sales, the extent of his responsibility in the event of transgressions of the law by those making the sales under his authority (for example, where underage sales or sales to persons who are drunk take place) remains unclear. Although para 10.49 of the Guidance states that 'the personal licence holder will not be able to escape responsibility for the actions of those he authorises to make such sales' it has been held that a personal licence holder cannot commit the offence in s 146 of underage sales if he does not physically make the sale (see 11.7.9 below).

### 6.4.3    *Authorised sales under the mandatory conditions where alcohol is sold*

The 2003 Act gives no indication as to what constitutes 'authorisation' or what form it should take, although some clarification is provided by the Guidance, which makes it clear that direct supervision by a personal licence holder of each sale is not required and that a number of factors may be taken into account in determining whether authorisation has been given. Paragraphs 10.50 and 10.51 state:

> 10.50 "Authorisation" does not imply direct supervision by a personal licence holder of each sale of alcohol. The question arises as to how sales can be authorised. Ultimately, whether an authorisation has been given is a question of fact that would have to be decided by the courts on the evidence before it in the course of a criminal prosecution.

> 10.51 Nevertheless, it is important that licensing authorities, the police, employers and employees in the alcohol retail industry are given advice which promotes greater clarity and consistency. The Secretary of State considers that the following factors should be relevant in considering whether or not an authorisation has been given:
> - the person(s) authorised to sell alcohol at any particular premises should be clearly identified;
> - the authorisation should have specified the acts which may be carried out by the person being authorised;
> - there should be an overt act of authorisation, for example, a specific written statement given to the individual being authorised; and
> - there should be in place sensible arrangements for the personal licence holder to monitor the activity that they have authorised on a reasonably regular basis.

The overt act of authorisation need not be a written authorisation for there is no requirement in the Act for authorisation to be in writing and 'its absence alone could not give rise to enforcement action' (Guidance, para 10.52). Nevertheless, the Secretary of State 'strongly recommends' that, when authorisation is given to individuals to sell alcohol, personal licence holders give specific written authorisation and para 10.52 of the Guidance states:

> A single written authorisation would be sufficient to cover multiple sales over an unlimited period. This would assist personal licence holders in demonstrating due diligence should issues arise with enforcement authorities; and would protect employees if they themselves are challenged in respect of their authority to sell alcohol.

The form of written authorisation is a matter for the personal licence holder, but the Secretary of State 'recommends that it should satisfy the criteria listed in the paragraph above [para 10.51]' (Guidance, para 10.52).

Once authorisation has been given, it is clear that a personal licence holder does not need to directly supervise sales (Guidance, para 10.50) or be present at the point when sales are made (Guidance, para 10.49 and see 6.4.2 above). He may be present elsewhere on the premises but need not be and may be absent from them. Less clear, however, is the extent to which a personal licence holder may be absent from the premises. Paragraph 10.49 of the Guidance states that a personal licence holder 'may be absent at times from the premises when a transaction takes place'. The period of authorisation referred to here – 'at times' – is obviously short and whether there can be a longer period of authorisation, extending into days or weeks, or possibly months, during which there can be a more prolonged absence from the premises of a personal licence holder, is uncertain. Much will depend on what is considered to be the scope of an 'authorised' sale under s 19(3). One view would be that, since a single authorisation can cover multiple sales over an unlimited period, as indicated in para 10.52 of the Guidance, this authorisation might cover sales made over an extensive period of absence. This might be particularly appropriate in the case of small operators, for whom, if only a short period of absence were permissible, there might be practical difficulties, for example where an off-licence is run by a single individual holding a personal licence, absence for a significant period of time may preclude any sales of alcohol from taking place (perhaps necessitating closure of the premises during that time), unless another personal licence holder can be employed.

An alternative view, however, would be that, if the risks associated with the sale of alcohol are considered so great that a system of personal vetting is needed, sales should in general only be 'authorised' if someone who has been personally vetted – either the DPS or another employee holding a personal licence – is present on the premises to give that authorisation. Whilst this would not require a personal licence holder's presence on the premises at all times and would enable sales to be authorised during brief periods of absence, it would not permit any prolonged absence. This view might be seen as particularly appropriate in the case of larger retail outlets, especially where sale is for consumption on the premises, for example, nightclubs and public houses. It would ensure that, brief periods apart, there is always someone on the premises who has been adjudged suitable to have responsibility for the sale of alcohol. If the position were otherwise for such premises, only a single (absentee) personal licence holder would be needed and all sales of alcohol might be effected from the premises by large numbers of bar staff, none of whom holds a personal licence. The view may be taken that this would not accord with the spirit of the legislation and would conflict with what is necessary to promote the licensing objectives.

It is thus difficult to formulate a legal rule of general application, given that views on the extent to which a personal licence holder may be absent from the premises may well be dependent on the nature of the circumstances and the type of retail outlet. One approach to resolving this difficulty might be to require the giving of authorisation to be consistent with the exercise of proper supervisory control over the sale of alcohol. This would incorporate a degree of flexibility (albeit at the expense of some certainty) into the authorisation test. It would not require the presence on the premises of a personal licence holder at all times except for brief periods, for it would be possible to say that, in the case of a nonspecialist off-licence, such as a convenience store, where the sole personal licence holder is absent for a significant period of time, there is no lack of proper supervisory control in this instance, given the limited number of sales that are likely to take place. Nevertheless, in the case of larger retail outlets selling alcohol for consumption on the premises where there is likely to be a high volume of sales, the view might be taken that proper supervisory control cannot effectively be exercised without the presence (perhaps at all times) of at least one personal licence holder on the premises.

An alternative approach might be to permit the absence, whether prolonged or brief, from the premises of a personal licence holder, irrespective of the type of premises, and to allow sales to take place under his authorisation, unless and until any difficulties arise (for example, disorder, nuisance, sales to children) that might be attributable to no personal licence holder being present. In the event of such difficulties, it might then be open to a licensing authority, on a review of the premises licence, to attach a condition that a personal licence holder be present on the premises at all times when sales of alcohol take place.[57] This is a more individualised approach. It would enable well-run premises, irrespective of their nature and size, to operate without any personal licence holder on the premises, even for significant periods of time. Essentially a reactive approach, presence of a personal licence holder would be required only where experience had shown this was necessary to promote the licensing objectives. Of the two approaches, it is submitted that the first-mentioned one, a proactive approach of aiming to ensure that proper control is exercised over licensed premises, is to be preferred. It remains to be seen whether either (or neither) of these approaches is adopted if and when the matter comes before the courts.

### 6.4.4 *Mandatory condition for film exhibitions*

The mandatory condition for inclusion under s 20 is that, where the licensable activities under the premises licence include the exhibition of films, the admission of children to film exhibitions is to be restricted in accordance with film classification recommendations. These recommendations can be those of the 'film classification body', the British Board of Film Classification (BBFC), or of the licensing authority itself if it operates its own classification system. Section 20 provides:

(1) Where a premises licence authorises the exhibition of films, the licence must include a condition requiring the admission of children to the exhibition of any film to be restricted in accordance with this section.

(2) Where the film classification body is specified in the licence, unless subsection (3)(b) applies, admission of children must be restricted in accordance with any recommendation made by that body.

(3) Where–

 (a) the film classification body is not specified in the licence, or

 (b) the relevant licensing authority has notified the holder of the licence that this subsection applies to the film in question,

admission of children must be restricted in accordance with any recommendation made by that licensing authority.

(4) In this section–

"children" means persons aged under 18; and

"film classification body" means the person or persons designated as the authority under section 4 of the Video Recordings Act 1984 (c.39) (authority to determine suitability of video works for classification).

### 6.4.5 *Mandatory condition for door supervisors*

The condition that must be included under s 21 relates to door supervisors either being licensed under the Private Security Industry Act 2001 (2001 Act) by the Security Industry Authority (SIA) or being exempt from licensing under that Act.[58] Section 21 does not make it mandatory to impose a condition for the employment of door supervisors to act as security personnel but, where such a condition is imposed, makes it mandatory that the individuals employed are licensed or exempt from licensing.[59] Section 21(1) of the 2003 Act provides:

> Where a premises licence includes a condition that at specified times one or more individuals must be at the premises to carry out a security activity, the licence must include a condition that each such individual must
>
> (a) be authorised to carry out that activity by a licence granted under the Private Security Industry Act 2001; or
>
> (b) be entitled to carry out that activity by virtue of section 4 of that Act.

The provision in s 21(1), initially requiring door supervisors to be licensed by the SIA, was amended by s 25 of the Violent Crime Reduction Act 2006 so that door supervisors could be employed where they were exempt from licensing by the SIA, 'to remove an anomaly whereby premises licences could require persons to be licensed by the SIA in circumstances where they were not required to be licensed under the 2001 Act' (Guidance, para 10.59).

The exemption from licensing under s 4 enables persons to engage in licensable conduct where 'suitable alternative arrangements' apply which render it unnecessary for them to be licensed. This includes where certain employees are carrying out conduct in connection with a certified sports grounds in accordance with s 4(6)–(12) of the 2001 Act and where they operate under the SIA's Approved Contractor Scheme under s 4(4) (Guidance, para 10.59). Under the Approved Contractor Scheme, door supervisors can be employed at premises holding a premises licence where they are employed by an Approved Contractor, even though their applications for a licence have not yet been approved.[60] An Approved Contractor can issue a personal Licence Dispensation Notice (LDN) to a door supervisor whose licence application is pending, where certain conditions are met. The personal LDN requires inclusion of the name of the Approved Contractor, contact details and the signature of a representative; the name of the individual operative, contact details and signature; the individual operative's SIA licence application reference number; an expiry date for the personal LDN; and the sectors for which the LDN applies. Even if a personal LDN has been issued, an offence under s 3 of the 2001 Act of engaging in licensable conduct except under and in accordance with a licence is nevertheless committed except in certain circumstances. These are that the person has applied for a licence and the application is pending; the licence applied for is for the activity in which the individual is engaged; the person has not previously been refused a licence for that activity; the employer is an Approved Contractor for the relevant activity in question under the Approved Contractor Scheme; and the SIA has authorised the employer to deploy employees whose licence applications are pending.

For the mandatory condition to be imposed, the individuals must be at the premises 'to carry out a security activity'. Activities that constitute a 'security activity' are set out in Sched 2 to the 2001 Act and include guarding premises against unauthorised access (which covers being wholly or partly responsible for determining the suitability for admission to the premises of persons applying for admission) and against outbreaks of disorder and against damage (see para 2(1) and (2)). This will include persons employed as door supervisors to oversee and control admission to the premises or maintain order in or around the premises. Conditions under s 21 should, as para 10.60 of the Guidance states, 'only relate to an activity to which paragraph 2(1)(a) of Schedule 2 to the 2001 Act applies (certain manned guarding activities) and which is licensable conduct within the meaning of section 3(2) of that Act'. Thus mandatory conditions should not be imposed where other types of activity which are not security-related are carried out by door supervisors. This will include, for example, where door supervisors ensure that doors are kept shut other than when in use for entering or leaving and/or reminding departing customers to leave quietly. It will also include activities related to safety or steward activities to organise, advise and direct members of the public (Guidance, para 10.63). Further, the premises licence has to include a condition that 'at specified times' individuals must be at the premises to carry out a security activity. It seems to be necessary therefore for inclusion not simply of a condition on the licence requiring door supervision at the premises, but for this supervision to be carried out at particular times. In the absence of any specified times, there remains an element of doubt as to whether the mandatory condition can be considered to have effect.

Even where such a condition is imposed, however, this requirement to impose a condition that individuals are licensed or exempt from licensing does not apply in respect of all premises holding a premises licence and exemptions are provided for premises used for certain activities. These include premises with a premises licence authorising plays or films, which means that there will be no mandatory condition for licensing by the SIA for theatres and cinemas. The exemptions also include premises where plays or films are authorised under a TEN, premises being used exclusively by a club with a CPC, premises having a casino premises licence or a bingo premises licence when they are being used wholly or mainly for the purposes for which such a licence is required. Presumably premises providing these facilities are not perceived as giving rise to potential problems of disorder, which might require employment of door supervisors for security activities. Further, the exemption also applies on any occasion prescribed by regulations under the Private Security Industry Act 2001 (although regulations made under the Act, the Private Security Industry (Licences) Regulations 2007, SI 2007/810, have not prescribed any such occasion). Section 21(2) of the 2003 Act provides:

> But nothing in subsection (1) requires such a condition to be imposed–
> (a)  in respect of premises within paragraph 8(3)(a) of Schedule 2 to the Private Security Industry Act 2001 (c.12) (premises with premises licences authorising plays or films), or
> (b)  in respect of premises in relation to–
>   (i)  any occasion mentioned in paragraph 8(3)(b) or (c) of that Schedule (premises being used exclusively by club with club premises certificate, under a temporary event notice authorising plays or films or under a gaming [sic] licence), or
>   (ii)  any occasion within paragraph 8(3)(d) of that Schedule (occasions prescribed by regulations under that Act).[61]

Whilst s 21(2)(a) provides an exemption in respect for premises with a premises licence authorising plays or films, the scope of the exemption is unclear. If the premises licence authorises only one or other of these licensable activities and this is the main licensable activity at the premises, as with a traditional theatre or cinema, this will clearly fall within the exemption. Less clear, however, is the case of premises where this is not the main activity but where it is more secondary or incidental to another licensable activity, for example, video juke boxes in public houses or similar premises where the main activity is the retail sale of alcohol. There is no reference to premises licences authorising only plays or films for the exemption to apply, so it ought to have application even where other licensable activities are authorised under it. The practical effect of application of the exemption where there are other licensable activities may, however, be limited, since it remains open to an authority to impose such a condition even if it may not be mandatory for it to do so. A mandatory condition is also not required in the case of premises used under a TEN, which authorises plays or films and it is similarly unclear here whether this applies where this is secondary or incidental to another licensable activity taking place under the authorisation of the TEN.

### 6.4.6  Prohibited conditions

Apart from the mandatory conditions in ss 19–21, there are two constraints on the power of authorities to impose conditions. First, certain conditions are expressly prohibited and, secondly, authorities can (where there are no relevant representations) only impose such conditions as are consistent with the operating schedule. To the extent that conditions might be inconsistent, therefore, their inclusion is prohibited. Expressly prohibited conditions are covered by s 22, which prevents authorities from imposing conditions as to the nature of plays or the manner of performance where the premises licence authorises the performance of plays. However, this is subject to the proviso that conditions can be imposed where these are considered necessary in the interests of public safety. Section 22 provides:

(1)  In relation to a premises licence which authorises the performance of plays, no condition may be attached to the licence as to the nature of the plays which may be performed, or the manner of performing plays, under the licence.

(2)  But subsection (1) does not prevent a licensing authority imposing, in accordance with section 18(2)(a) or (3)(b), 35(3)(b) or 53(3), any condition which it considers necessary on the grounds of public safety.

6.4.7    The second constraint on the imposition of conditions is that they are consistent with the operating schedule (s 18(2)(a)) and in this respect para 10.10 of the Guidance provides:

Consistency means that the effect of the condition should be substantially the same as that intended by the terms of the operating schedule or club operating schedule. Some applicants for licences or certificates supported by legal representatives or trade associations can be expected to express steps necessary to promote the licensable objectives in clear and readily translatable terms. However, some applicants will express the terms of their operating schedules less precisely or concisely. Ensuring that conditions are consistent with the operating schedule will then be more difficult.

Whether this means that conditions should simply replicate those contained in the operating schedule or whether (and, if so, to what extent) conditions might be imposed that materially differ from those proposed by the applicant is uncertain. The requirement is only for conditions to be 'consistent with' the operating schedule, not for them to be identical to those proposed by the applicant, so at least some measure of variation is permissible. The degree of variation permissible and the extent to which conditions might be materially different from those proposed may depend on how the phrase 'consistent with the operating schedule' is interpreted. The applicant is required in the operating schedule to specify steps to promote the licensing objectives and, if the phrase is interpreted to mean consistent with the steps the applicant proposes to take to promote the licensing objectives, then conditions that are materially different may not be consistent with the operating schedule. If, on the other hand, the phrase is interpreted to mean consistent with the licensing objectives themselves that have application in the particular case (rather than the applicant's proposed steps to promote them because, in the authority's view, the steps proposed do not promote the particular objectives), then materially different conditions that do meet these objectives might be regarded as consistent with the operating schedule. Either interpretation might be possible, but, given that s 17(4)(g) refers to the operating schedule including a statement of steps to promote the objectives and s 18(2) requires conditions to be consistent with the operating schedule, the former view seems to accord more closely with the statutory wording and this generally seems to have been the approach adopted by licensing authorities. Whilst in practice conditions have for the most part been consistent with the operating schedule, in some instances inconsistent conditions were attached in the period immediately following the implementation of the Act. This was no doubt due, at least in part, to the large number of applications then being processed and some were returned for correction and amendment. Not all might have been so returned, however, leaving the possibility of conditions attached to the licence that are inconsistent with the operating schedule. Difficulties may ensue in such instances if the premises are subsequently offered for sale and potential purchasers would be wise to check that the conditions correspond with what is contained in the operating schedule.

Whichever interpretation is adopted, it is clear that authorities can, within the same licence, impose different conditions on different parts of the premises and in relation to different licensable activities. Section 18(10) provides:

In discharging its duty under subsection (2) or (3)(b), a licensing authority may grant a licence under this section subject to different conditions in respect of–

(a) different parts of the premises concerned;

(b) different licensable activities.

### 6.4.8 Relevant representations and discretion

#### 6.4.9 Meaning of 'relevant representations'

If, however, 'relevant representations' have been made, and these might be representations in opposition to or in support of an application (Guidance, para 9.3), s 18(3)(a) provides that the authority must hold a hearing to consider them. Under reg 5 and para 1 of Sched 5 to the LA 2003 (Hearings) Regs 2005, the hearing must be held within a period of 20 working days beginning with the day after the end of the period during which representations may be made as prescribed under section 17(5)(c), which itself, under reg 22(b) of the LA 2003 (PL and CPC) Regs 2005, is 28 consecutive days after the day on which the application is given to the authority. Given the combination of working and consecutive days, the total period of time needs careful thought to avoid error. Under reg 6(4) and para 1 of Sched 2, notice of the hearing must be given to the applicant and persons who made relevant representations no later than 10 working days before the day or the first day on which the hearing is to be held.[63] A hearing need not be held if the authority, the applicant and each person who has made such representations agree that a hearing is unnecessary. This may be the case if the parties have been able, through mediation and compromise, to come to a mutually acceptable solution prior to the hearing of a case and the Guidance, para 9.22, recommends in this respect that applicants 'should be encouraged to contact responsible authorities before formulating their applications so that the mediation process may begin before the statutory time limits come into effect after submission of an application'. It may also be the case in the (perhaps unlikely) event that the only relevant representations received are positively and unqualifiedly in support of the application, instead of being opposed to it. In such cases, the Guidance, para 9.19 recommends that 'the licensing authority should consider whether a hearing is necessary' and 'may wish to notify the interested parties concerned and give them the opportunity to withdraw their representations . . . in sufficient time before the hearing to ensure that parties were not put to unnecessary inconvenience.

Relevant representations will be ones made by an 'interested party' (local residents and businesses) or a 'responsible authority' (statutory bodies) and only such persons are able to make representations. The licensing authority itself is unable to do so. The rationale for this is that only persons with expertise should be entitled to make representations. As Baroness Blackstone explained during the Report Stage of the Bill in the House of Lords:

> Judgment of the merit of an application against the licensing objectives should be left to the experts. The experts on crime and disorder, and the protection of children from harm are the police, and so the police have a voice. The experts on public safety are the health and safety and fire authorities, and so they have a voice too. The experts on public nuisance are the local environmental health authority. It follows that they should have a voice too, and the Bill provides them with one. The experts in what it is like to live and do business in a particular area are local residents and businesses . . .

> What we are not doing, however, is allowing the licensing authority to make representations in its own right. One of the fundamental principles of the Bill is that applications should be granted administratively where the experts have not raised any concerns about them. Where those circumstances apply, there is no reason for the licensing authority as regulatory authority to give a second opinion to those experts, and it would be wrong to give it that opportunity.[64]

The role of the licensing authority is thus envisaged as that of a referee or umpire adjudicating on relevant representations made by 'experts' and the authority is not a 'player' in the licensing process. Its role is more that of a facilitator for communities in making choices where there are competing interests rather than an active participant in the process. Nevertheless, the licensing authority is normally a local authority and might, at least indirectly, have an input into the licensing process through responsible authorities making relevant representations, since the functions of some responsible authorities, for example, planning and environmental health, are carried out by the local authority (see 6.4.18 below).

Any representations made will have to be about the likely effect of the grant of the licence on the promotion of the licensing objectives and, in the case of representations made by an interested party, not be frivolous or vexatious, that is not trifling or futile, or put forward for the purposes of annoyance or oppression. Representations will cease to be relevant if they are withdrawn. Section 18(6) and (7) provides:

(6) For the purposes of this section, "relevant representations" means representations which–

    (a) are about the likely effect of the grant of the premises licence on the promotion of the licensing objectives,

    (b) meet the requirements of subsection (7),

    (c) if they relate to the identity of the person named in the application as the proposed premises supervisor, meet the requirements of subsection (9), and

    (d) are not excluded representations by virtue of section 32 (restriction on making representations following issue of provisional statement).

(7) The requirements are–

    (a) that the representations are made by an interested party or responsible authority within the period prescribed under section 17(5)(c),

    (b) that they have not been withdrawn, and

    (c) in the case of representations made by an interested party (who is not also a responsible authority), that they are not, in the opinion of the relevant licensing authority, frivolous or vexatious.

Only if these criteria are met will a representation be a 'relevant representation' and the Guidance, para 9.11 cautions licensing authorities against taking decisions on whether representations are relevant 'on the basis of any political judgement', whilst recognising that it 'may be difficult for ward councillors receiving complaints from residents within their own wards'.[65]

### 6.4.10 Representations about the likely effect of the grant of the premises licence on the promotion of the licensing objectives: s 18(6)(a)

A first criterion for representations to be 'relevant' is that they are about 'likely effect'. The use of the term 'likely' seems to indicate that the effect has to be more probable than not, but it is not clear whether it is to be judged by reference to the representor (the 'objector') or the representee (the licensing authority). A persuasive argument can be made that it should be judged by reference to the representor. The authority will have the opportunity, when determining the application, to decide what effect the grant will have on the promotion of the licensing objectives, but, if it were able to determine likely effect at this earlier stage, this determination could effectively preclude the holding of a hearing. Representations could be dismissed by the authority as not relevant, since they were not (in its view) concerned with likely effect. The rationale of allowing representations to be made is to improve the quality of decision-making and this would not seem to be met if such an approach could be adopted.

6.4.11 Nevertheless, there needs to be some minimum threshold concerning representations about likely effect to ensure that hearings are not held where trivial complaints are made. This can be achieved if some preliminary investigation is made by the authority. This is not inconsistent with judging likely effect by reference to the representor, which can be done in the vast majority of cases, and a preliminary investigation by the authority to determine relevance may occur only in a relatively small number of cases. As to whether 'likely effect' should be determined subjectively or objectively on such a preliminary investigation, it seems likely that this should be done objectively. This seems to be the test for whether a representation is frivolous or vexatious[66] and the same test should apply when determining relevance and 'likely effect'. If an objective test is applied, it thus will depend on whether a reasonable person in the representor's position would consider the representation to be about the likely effect. The representation will have to be about the likely effect of grant on 'the promotion of the licensing objectives', so a representation will need to relate to the promotion of at least one of the licensing objectives for it to be relevant. The Guidance, para 9.8 provides:

> For example, a representation from a local businessman which argued that his business would be commercially damaged by a new licensed premises would not be relevant. On the other hand, a representation that nuisance caused by the new premises would deter customers from entering the local area and the steps proposed by the applicant to control that nuisance were inadequate would be relevant.

It is sufficient that a representation relates to promotion of at least one licensing objective and there is no need for any supporting record of history of problems at the premises in question to support the representation. Such a record would not be possible for new premises nor is it required for existing ones (Guidance, para 9.8).

### 6.4.12 Representations by an 'interested party' or a 'responsible authority' – persons entitled to submit relevant representations: s 18(6)(b) and (7)(a)

A second criterion for representations to be 'relevant' is that they are made by persons or bodies falling within one of two categories, an 'interested party' or a 'responsible authority'.

### 6.4.13 Interested party

The former category essentially covers residents and businesses in the vicinity of the premises or bodies representing them. Section 13(3) provides:

> "Interested party" means any of the following–
> (a) a person living in the vicinity of the premises,
> (b) a body representing persons who live in that vicinity,
> (c) a person involved in a business in that vicinity,
> (d) a body representing persons involved in such businesses.

The term 'vicinity' was considered by the High Court in *The Queen on the Application of 4 Wins Leisure Ltd v The Licensing Committee of Blackpool Council, Brook Leisure Blackpool Ltd and World Wide Clubs (UK)* [2007] EWHC 2213. Here the applicant sought a judicial review of the licensing authority's decision that it was not a person involved in a business in the vicinity of the application premises, where its premises were 816 metres away, and its representations were not taken into account, although ones made by the third defendant, whose premises were 250 yards away, were considered. Refusing the application, Sullivan J held that the question of 'vicinity' is 'very much a question of fact and degree', is 'highly dependent upon local knowledge' and is 'left for local licensing committees to determine' (para 8). Distance itself is not the deciding factor and recourse is needed to local circumstances. As his Lordship stated (at para 12):

> One is not simply concerned with a mechanical measurement as the crow flies. Regard must be had to local circumstances. Thus, for example, Property A may not be in the vicinity of Property B if, even though it is not very far distant from Property B, the two properties are separated, for example, by a river, by a major road or by a railway.

Conversely, Properties A and B may be quite some distance apart; but given particular geographical considerations they may be said to be in the same vicinity if, for example, there are very strong linkages between them, as there might be (and it would be entirely a matter of fact for the panel to determine) in respect of properties at opposite ends of the promenade in Blackpool.[67]

Whether or not premises are 'in the vicinity' is 'very much a question of judgment on which reasonable people may differ in their views' and accordingly 'any challenge on Wednesbury grounds[68] will be a very difficult road to pursue'. On the facts of the case itself, 'it cannot be said, where two properties are 816 metres apart, as the crow flies, that a committee with local knowledge could not conclude that these two properties were not in the same vicinity' (para 13).

The statutory test is thus essentially the physical or geographical proximity of the premises, in the context of local circumstances, and this applies irrespective of whether interested parties are directly affected by the application premises. Although the Guidance makes reference to individuals being directly affected,[69] Sullivan J stated (at para 16) that 'whilst the question of direct effect may be of assistance in deciding whether or not one premises is in the vicinity of another, it [is] not the statutory test that must be applied'. Accordingly, as his Lordship went on to state (at para 19):

> . . . one might have a business which was wholly unrelated to the proposed application and which indeed would not be affected by it. But, nevertheless, if it was in the vicinity it would be an interested party. Consideration would have to be given to whether or not the representations made by such a business were frivolous or vexatious: see section 18(7)(c), but that does not alter the fact that a business which on the face of it would have no business interests that might be affected can nevertheless be an interested party for the purposes of the 2003 Act. Conversely, one may have a business which has business interests that might indeed be affected, but if that business is not "in the vicinity" then, regardless of the impact on those business interests, it is not an interested party.[70]

Thus provided the proper statutory test is applied and provided the licensing authority's view of 'vicinity' is not wholly unreasonable in the *Wednesbury* sense, its decision should be beyond challenge.

What constitutes the 'vicinity' may or may not be defined with precision. A number of authorities, in their Statements of Licensing Policy, have adopted a guide distance for 'vicinity' of 100 metres from the application premises, which may be varied according to the circumstances. A lesser distance, for instance, might be appropriate where a major road separates a group of residents from the premises or, conversely, a greater distance where premises affect the whole community. It seems unlikely, however, that what constitutes the 'vicinity' will need to be determined with any degree of precision. This is certainly the view that the courts have taken in respect of the meaning of the analogous concept of 'locality' in para 12 of Sched 3 to the Local Government (Miscellaneous Provisions) Act 1982 in relation to sex establishments[71] and there would seem to be no reason why any different approach should be taken here.

6.4.14  In determining whether a person is 'living' in the vicinity of the premises and an interested party within s 13(3)(a), two questions arise. The first is what will constitute 'living' there and the second is the material time(s), in relation to an application, at which a person will need to be 'living' there. As to what constitutes 'living', if a literal interpretation were given to 'living', this would suggest that a person would need to be actually residing in the vicinity to be entitled to make representations, but this would exclude persons ordinarily resident who for some reason happen to be away from where they live at the material time(s). If, however, a purposive interpretation is given to 'living', such persons might be included. The purpose of s 18(3)(a) is to enable representations to be made by those likely to be affected by the application premises and persons ordinarily resident there will be equally affected (once they resume residence) as those who are actually living in the vicinity. They ought therefore to be entitled to make representations and, to ensure that they can, the provision should be given a purposive interpretation. Less clear is whether such an interpretation would include those who have a residential address in the vicinity, but who, for significant periods of the year, might reside elsewhere, for example, students who are away from the parental home at university, persons who work away on weekdays and return at weekends, and persons who have a holiday home in an area. As to the material time(s) at which a person will need to be 'living' in the vicinity, clearly there will be no difficulties where a person is living there at the point in time when representations can be made,[72] when a hearing is held and when the application is determined. Problems may arise, however, where a person is living there at some, but not all, of these points, for example a person living there when representations can be made, although due to move away either immediately before or after the hearing, or a person due to move into property after the period within which representations can be made, but who will be in residence at the time a hearing is held.[73]

6.4.15   Whether a person is 'involved in a business' in the vicinity of the premises and an interested party within s 13(3)(c) will depend on how this is interpreted. It is very widely expressed, to such an extent that, if interpreted literally, it could cover all persons having any involvement with the business, including all employees of the business (whether or not working for the business in the vicinity in question), as well as those involved as directors or partners in running the business. Whether all such persons should be seen as affected by an application for a licence so as to entitle them to make representation is open to doubt. It may be that only those running the business or involved in running it may be considered to be 'involved in a business' for the purposes of s 13(3)(c) – 'involved' may be interpreted to mean involved to a significant or substantial degree rather than involved to any extent. As to what constitutes a 'business' for these purposes, this should not be confined to persons involved in commercial practice, but should include a wide range of other organisations not normally classed as 'businesses', for example, persons involved in education or the professions. As para 8.6 of the Guidance states:

> It is expected that "a person involved in business" will be given its widest possible interpretation, including partnerships, and need not be confined to those engaged in trade and commerce. It is also expected that the expression can be held to embrace the functions of charities, churches and medical practices.

6.4.16   In the case of 'a body representing persons', whether those who live in the vicinity (s 13(3)(b)) or those involved in a business in the vicinity (s 13(3)(d)), this seems clearly designed to enable representations to be made by organisations such as a residents' association or a trade association.[74] Such organisations are likely to have some specific mandate from those that they represent and it is uncertain whether it will encompass only such bodies or whether it will extend to bodies which have no specific mandate but which claim to represent persons living or involved in a business in the vicinity.

Whilst a body representing persons or the persons themselves might make representations as interested parties, a body or persons may nominate others to make representations on their behalf. Paragraph 8.7 of the Guidance provides:

> Any of these individuals or groups may specifically request a representative to make representations on his, her or its behalf. For example, a legal representative, a friend, a Member of Parliament, a Member of the National Assembly for Wales, or a local ward or parish councillor could all act in such a capacity.

Local councillors, in particular, might be instrumental in making representations on behalf of interested parties, with para 8.8 of the Guidance stating:

> Local councillors play an important role in their local communities. They can make representations in writing and at a hearing on behalf of an interested party such as a resident or local business if specifically requested to do so. They can also make representations as an interested party in their own right if they live, or are involved in a business, in the vicinity of the premises in question.

In cases where a local councillor is a member of the licensing committee, decisions in most, if not all, cases are likely to be taken by a licensing subcommittee in accordance with the Guidance's recommendations in para 13.79 (see 2.2.19 above) and the local councillor need not sit on the particular subcommittee hearing an application in respect of premises in his constituency. By not sitting he would not have any involvement in the decision-making process for the application in question. He might thus appear before the subcommittee hearing the application to make representations, whether as an interested party in his personal capacity if he lives in the vicinity of the application premises or in his representative capacity. Councillors in such cases would need, however, to 'consider carefully at a committee meeting whether they had a prejudicial interest in any matter affecting the licence of the premises in question which would require them to withdraw from the meeting when that matter is considered' (Guidance, para 8.10). Where a person has a 'personal interest' in the decision which is also a 'prejudicial interest', he need not, under Arts 12(1)(a) and 12(2) of the Local Authorities (Model Code of Conduct) (England) Order 2007, SI 2007/1159, withdraw from the room or chamber where the meeting considering the business is being held until after he has made the representations (see 2.2.7 above). Further, 'a member with a prejudicial interest in a matter should not seek to influence improperly a decision on the licence in any other way' (Guidance, para 8.10).

6.4.17  For persons to be interested parties, they will need to be in the vicinity of the premises, so it seems that they will need to disclose their name and address to the licensing authority in order for the authority to determine whether they are in the vicinity and therefore meet the criteria to be an 'interested party'. Less clear is whether a person's name and address needs to be disclosed to the applicant. The Act, like most licensing statutes, is silent on this matter. Exceptionally, provision might be made in statute for nondisclosure of a person's name and address without his consent, as in the case of objections to sex establishment licences under para 10(17) of Sched 3 to the Local Government (Miscellaneous Provisions) Act 1982 (LGMPA 1982), but in the absence of any such provision this has generally been regarded as a matter for a licensing authority to determine. Practice on this matter differed under the previous licensing regime for public entertainments under Sched 1 to the LGMPA 1982, with some authorities notifying applicants of objectors' names and addresses as a matter of course but others doing so only if objectors gave their consent.[75] The Divisional Court in *R v Huntingdon DC ex p Cowan* [1984] 1 WLR 501, when considering the duty of an authority to inform an applicant of an objection under Sched 1, appeared to be of the view that disclosure was not required, for Glidewell J stated (at 508) that it was 'not necessary to give him the whole of it, nor to say necessarily who has made it, but to give him the substance of it'. Whilst this may continue to be the position, it is possible that, since the passage of the Human Rights Act 1998, disclosure may be necessary to ensure compliance with the applicant's right to a fair hearing under Art 6(1) of the ECHR (see 3.5 above). In *McMichael v UK* (1995) 20 EHRR 205, a case concerning care proceedings for children, the ECtHR stated (at para 80):

> ... as a matter of general principle the right to a fair – adversarial – trial "means the opportunity to have knowledge of and comment on the observations filed or evidence adduced by the other party" (see the *Ruiz-Mateos v. Spain* judgment of 23 June 1993, Series A no. 262, p. 25, para. 63). In the context of the present case, the lack of disclosure of such vital documents as social reports is capable of affecting the ability of participating parents not only to influence the outcome of the children's hearing in question but also to assess their prospects of making an appeal ...

The Court in this case essentially recognised that, in an adversarial hearing where Art 6(1) civil rights and obligations are at stake, there is a general requirement of full disclosure, without which the parties would be unaware of and unable to comment on the evidence adduced. This principle might be regarded as having application to licensing and disclosure of where persons making representations live. If unaware of this, it might be doubted whether the applicant can comment on whether or not such persons are an 'interested party' living in the vicinity of the premises, being sufficiently close to the premises to be likely to be affected by the licensable activities. It is possible, however, that disclosure of the road or street in which the person making the representations lives, without disclosure of the precise address, might be seen as sufficient to protect the applicant's Art 6(1) rights.

When the Guidance was first published, no reference was made to disclosure of names and addresses of those making representations, but the revised version published in 2007 does contain a section on this matter. Although not explicitly advocating disclosure, it seems to be implicit that this should be the approach adopted in the absence of some exceptional circumstances. Paragraphs 9.15-9.18 provide:

> 9.15 In some exceptional and isolated circumstances interested parties may be reluctant to make representations because of fears of intimidation or violence if their personal details, such as name and address, are divulged to the applicant.
>
> 9.16 Where licensing authorities consider that the interested party has a genuine and well-founded fear of intimidation and may be deterred from making a representation because of this, they may wish to consider alternative approaches.
>
> 9.17 For instance, they could advise interested parties to provide the relevant responsible authority with details of how they consider that the licensing objectives are being undermined so that the responsible authority can make representations if appropriate and justified.

9.18 The licensing authority may also decide to withhold some or all of the interested party's personal details from the applicant, giving only enough details (such as street name or general location within a street) which would allow an applicant to be satisfied that the interested party is within the vicinity of the premises. However, withholding such detail should only be considered where the circumstances justify such action.

Since licensing authorities must have regard to the Guidance under s 4(2)(b) and need a good reason to depart from it, it can be expected that there will generally be disclosure to the applicant of the names and addresses of those making representations.

### 6.4.18 Responsible authority

The other category of persons entitled to make representations is a 'responsible authority' and this comprises various agencies with statutory responsibilities which are specified in s 13(4).[76] The category includes the police and the fire and rescue authority, which have traditionally been consulted on licensing applications, but it is not confined to these two agencies. It does not include the licensing authority itself (see 6.4.9 above), which in most cases will be the local authority, although it can include another licensing authority where part of the premises is situated in that authority's area. Whilst the local authority as licensing authority is not a responsible authority and cannot make representations, representations can nevertheless be made by some sections of the local authority. These include sections dealing with environmental and public health ('the local authority by which statutory functions are exercisable ... in relation to minimising or preventing the risk of pollution to the environment or of harm to human health'[77]), planning ('the local planning authority'), and health and safety where the local enforcement agency for the Health and Safety at Work etc Act 1974 is the local authority (for in certain circumstances it can be the Health and Safety Executive). In some licensing authority areas, it is not uncommon for representations to be made by these sections, in particular by environmental and public health. Other agencies included are a body recognised by the licensing authority as being competent to advise it on matters relating to the protection of children from harm (which is likely to be the area child protection committee);[78] various bodies with responsibilities for waterways where licensable activities take place on a vessel; and any person prescribed by the Secretary of State. Section 13(4) provides that:

"Responsible authority" means any of the following–

(a) the chief officer of police for any police area in which the premises are situated,

(b) the fire and rescue authority for any area in which the premises are situated,

(c) the enforcing authority within the meaning given by section 18 of the Health and Safety at Work etc. Act 1974 (c.37) for any area in which the premises are situated,

(d) the local planning authority within the meaning given by the Town and Country Planning Act 1990 (c.8) for any area in which the premises are situated,

(e) the local authority by which statutory functions are exercisable in any area in which the premises are situated in relation to minimising or preventing the risk of pollution to the environment or of harm to human health,

(f) a body which–

    (i) represents those who, in relation to any such area, are responsible for, or interested in, matters relating to the protection of children from harm, and

      (ii)  is recognised by the licensing authority for that area for the purposes of this section as being competent to advise it on such matters,

  (g)  any licensing authority (other than the relevant licensing authority) in whose area part of the premises is situated,

  (h)  in relation to a vessel–

      (i)  a navigation authority (within the meaning of section 221(1) of the Water Resources Act 1991 (c.57)) having functions in relation to the waters where the vessel is usually moored or berthed or any waters where it is, or is proposed to be, situated at a time when it is used for qualifying club activities,

      (ii)  the Environment Agency,

      (iii) the British Waterways Board, or

      (iv) the Secretary of State,[79]

  (i)  a person prescribed for the purposes of this subsection.

The Secretary of State has, under reg 7 of the LA 2003 (PL and CPC) Regs 2005, prescribed one additional person, the local weights and measures authority for any area in which the premises are situated. This is the trading standards department in the local authority area (see 11.7.12 below). The other responsible authorities mentioned in s 13(4) all have recognised expertise in particular areas that relate to the licensing objectives, but it is not readily apparent where the expertise of trading standards lies in this respect. Perhaps it is in the field of enforcement of certain aspects of the legislation, notably the offence under s 146(1) of selling alcohol to children (see 11.7.11 below).

### 6.4.19 Representations within the prescribed period: s 18(6)(b) and (7)(a)

Section 17(5)(c) provides that regulations may prescribe the period within which relevant representations may be made (see 6.3.1 above) and representations will only be relevant representations if they are made within this period. The definition of 'relevant representations' in s 18(7)(a) contains a requirement that the representations were made by an interested party or responsible authority 'within the period prescribed by section 17(5)(c)' and reg 22(b) of the LA 2003 (PL and CPC) Regs 2005 provides that representations can be made during a period of 28 consecutive days starting on the day after the day on which the application was given to the authority. Whether representations that are relevant (in the sense that they are about the likely effect of the grant of the premises licence on the promotion of the licensing objectives) can be taken into account when they are received outside the 28-day period remains uncertain.

If no other representations are received within the period (or any received are withdrawn), there will be no relevant representations at all and, where this is the case, the authority must under s 18(2) grant the premises licence. It may be that the late representations cannot be taken into account in such a case. However, a failure to do so might be considered to conflict with the authority's duty under s 4(1) to carry out its functions under the Act 'with a view to promoting the licensing objectives'. If the late representations are about the likely effect of the grant of the premises licence on the promotion of the licensing objectives, even if not within the 28-day period, they might be ones that the licensing authority considers it necessary to take into account when reaching a decision on the application in order to promote the licensing objectives. If the authority were to take them into account in relation to attaching conditions consistent with the operating schedule, rather than to refuse a premises licence, this would not be inconsistent with s 18(2). Indeed, it seems open to an authority to hold a hearing to consider the late representations if minded to do so. The authority is obliged under s 18(3)(a) to hold a hearing if there are relevant representations, but is not precluded from doing so where there are none. Paragraph 13.79 of the Guidance recommends delegation to officers where there are no relevant representations (see 2.2.19 above), but an authority can depart from this recommendation if there is good reason to do so and the need to promote the licensing objectives is a good reason.

If relevant representations are received within the 28-day period, the authority must hold a hearing, so there will be an opportunity in such a case for any late representations to be considered. Under the LA 2003 (Hearings) Regs 2005, a 'party to the hearing', which under reg 2 and Sched 2 includes a person making relevant representations (see 2.3.10 above), has various rights, including the right to appear, but these will not apply in respect of a person making late representations. Nevertheless, it may be open to the committee to permit persons other than parties to appear at the hearing (see 2.3.10 above) and this might include persons making late representations. To take late representations into account is not inconsistent with s 18(3)(b), which requires the authority to have regard to relevant representations when determining the steps it considers necessary for the promotion of the licensing objectives. Whilst this requires the authority to have regard to the relevant representations, it does not provide that it can *only* have regard to these, which leaves open the possibility that an authority might have regard to other relevant considerations, such as representations received outside the 28-day period. If regard is had to substance and the primary importance of promotion of the licensing objectives ahead of form and the prescribed period within which representations have to be made, a persuasive case might be made for the authority having a discretion to take into account late representations. Thus the legal position would be that, where relevant representations are made, the authority is obliged to take these into account at the hearing at which the persons making the representations have various rights, but consideration of late representations and any appearance at the hearing by persons making them are at the authority's discretion. This approach would accord with that taken by the House of Lords in *Belfast City Council v Miss Behavin' Ltd* [2007] UKHL 19 (*Miss Behavin'*) in respect of the requirement in para 10(15) of the Local Government (Miscellaneous Provisions) (Northern Ireland) Order 1985 No 1208 (NI 15), that objections to sex establishment licence applications must be made not later than 28 days after the date of the application. The House held that this requirement, which corresponds exactly to the English provision in para 10(15) of Sched 3 to the Local Government (Miscellaneous Provisions) Act 1982, did not preclude the consideration of late objections. The licensing authority was not obliged to take into account late objections, although it had a discretion to do so, whereas it was bound to consider objections received within the 28-day period. Thus Lord Hoffman stated (at para [8]):

> para 10(15) is concerned only with the position of the objector. If he does not comply with the deadline, he cannot complain that the Council did not take his objection into account. But para 10(15) does not prohibit the council from taking all relevant matters into account, whether they have been communicated by objectors or others, early or late, or in any other way. It would be very strange if such a provision, designed to allow the Council to carry on its business in an orderly and expeditious manner, had the effect of requiring it to shut its eyes to facts which it considered relevant to its decision.

Similar sentiments were expressed by Lord Neuberger (at paras [71]–[73]):

[71] It would, in my judgment, be unrealistic and unjust if a council were absolutely precluded from taking into account such objections. If an objection which revealed to a council for the first time certain highly relevant information was received one day late, it would be a little short of absurd if it could not be taken into account. It might reveal, for instance, that a family with a large number of small children had moved into the flat above the subject property, or that the applicant had a string of relevant convictions. In such cases, it would be contrary to the purpose of the 1985 Order, and to the public interest generally, if the council was obliged to ignore the information. Furthermore, it would be the duty of council officers to open and read any letter received; such an officer would be placed in an impossible situation if she or he had read a late letter of objection, with new and important information, but was effectively precluded from communicating this information to council members.

[72] Indeed, unless the 1985 Order provided otherwise in very clear terms, it would seem to me that, if a council received significant relevant information in a late objection, there could be circumstances in which its failure to take that information into account would itself be judicially reviewable. Of course, much would depend on the circumstances of the particular case. It may very well be right to disregard a late objection if it was intentionally last minute, or if it was received so late that taking it into account would lead to unfairness to the applicant (because he would not have had the chance to consider it) or to unacceptable disruption to the council's business . . .

[73] In my view, that is indeed the effect of the provisions of paras 10(15) to (18). Paragraph 10(18) is merely concerned with identifying what a council is obliged to take into account; it says nothing about what the council is entitled to take into account. Accordingly, nothing in para 10(18) would exclude the consideration of late objections. Once one appreciates that that is the effect of para 10(18), the meaning of para 10(15) seems clear. Its effect is that, if an objector wishes to have his objection taken into account as of right under the terms of the Schedule, then he has to ensure that it is sent to the council within the 28 day period. In other words, what those two subparagraphs are concerned with for present purposes is to make it clear that, if an objection is received within 28 days, the council has an obligation to take it into account, and the objector has a right to expect it to be taken into account. Neither sub-paragraph says anything about the parties' respective rights and duties in relation to a late objection. A late objection is therefore governed by general administrative law principles: it is a matter for the council whether to take it into account, and the court will not interfere with its decision in that regard, save on classic administrative law principles, ie unless the decision took into account irrelevant factors or failed to take into account relevant factors or was a decision which no reasonable council could, in all the circumstances, have made.

Although Baroness Hale did not address the matter of late objections in her judgment, Lord Mance expressed specific agreement with the reasons given by both Lords Hoffman and Neuberger on this point[80] and Lord Rodger was in general agreement that the appeal should be allowed for the reasons given by Lord Hoffman. At least one member of the House, however, Lord Neuberger, seemed to recognise that there may be circumstances where late objections should not be considered. His Lordship stated (at para 72):

It may very well be right to disregard a late objection if it was intentionally last minute, or if it was received so late that taking it into account would lead to unfairness to the applicant (because he would not have had the chance to consider it) or to unacceptable disruption to the council's business.

On the facts of the case in question, his Lordship thought that the committee 'could not have reached any conclusion other than that the late objections should be admitted' (para 77) and went on to remark:

> Given that there is no suggestion of the objections being late for lack of good faith, the only reasons for not admitting the late objections would have been prejudice to the Applicant or disruption to the Council's business. Neither suggestion could possibly have been raised in this case, and indeed neither suggestion was raised.

Whether the instances identified are the only ones in which late objections should not be admitted is less clear, not least since no other members of the House made any other observations in this respect. Even if it is implicit in Lord Neuberger's judgment that these are the only instances (and it may be), the observations remain *obiter* since the House did not have to make a decision on this matter.

Whilst the House in this case was hearing an appeal from Northern Ireland, the decision certainly can be regarded as having equal application to the identically worded English provisions on sex shop licensing in Sched 3 to the Local Government (Miscellaneous Provisions) Act 1982 and may well have wider application to other areas of licensing and regulation where late objections or representations are received. The reasons given by the House for consideration of late objections on the sex shop licence application in *Miss Behavin'* (a case which 'must take the prize for the most entertaining name of any that have come before us in recent years', *per* Baroness Hale at para [30]) could well be applied to applications for authorisation for licensable activities under the 2003 Act. Just as it could be said to be contrary to the purpose of the 1985 Order, and to the public interest generally, if the council was obliged to ignore the information (*per* Lord Neuberger at para [71] above), so it could be said to be contrary to promotion of the licensing objectives under the 2003 Act, and the public interest generally, which requires the taking of steps in the overall interests of the local community, if the licensing authority was obliged to ignore late representations. It seems unlikely that the House's decision in *Miss Behavin'* will be regarded as limited in its application to sex establishment licensing and it is submitted that the approach taken in this case should be followed under the 2003 Act.

### 6.4.20 Representations not withdrawn nor frivolous or vexatious: s 18(6)(b) and (7)(b)(c)

6.4.21  To be relevant representations, it is necessary that the representations have not been withdrawn and are not frivolous or vexatious (s 18(7)(b)(c)). As to withdrawal, reg 10 of the LA 2003 (Hearings) Regs 2005 provides that a party who wishes to withdraw any representations can do so by giving notice to the authority no later than 24 hours before the day or the first day on which the hearing is to be held or orally at the hearing (see 2.3.2. above). Representations can be regarded as frivolous if they are trifling or futile or, as para 9.10 of the Guidance puts it, 'essentially categorised by a lack of seriousness'. They can be regarded as vexatious if put forward for the purposes of annoyance or oppression and such representations may well arise because of disputes between rival businesses. Here 'local knowledge will . . . be invaluable in considering such matters' (Guidance, para 9.10). Representations can, however, only be regarded as frivolous or vexatious (frivolous) if made by an interested party and it is presumed (irrebutably) that ones made by a responsible authority are not frivolous.

Representations are frivolous only if they are considered to be so 'in the opinion of the relevant licensing authority' (s 18(7)(c)). For these purposes, the Guidance recommends delegation of this function to officers and the application of an objective test based on what might 'ordinarily be considered' vexatious or frivolous:

> It is for the licensing authority to determine whether any representation by an interested party is frivolous or vexatious on the basis of what might ordinarily be considered to be vexatious or frivolous.[81]

Once a determination is made that representations are frivolous, s 18(8) requires that the authority 'must notify the person who made them of the reasons for the determination'. Such notification will need to be in accordance with s 184 (see 2.5 above) and, under reg 31 of the LA 2003 (PL and CPC) Regs 2005, must be given in writing as soon as is reasonably practicable and in any event before the determination of the application to which the representations relate. If there is a failure to notify or to give reasons, this does not amount to an offence. Although no criminal sanction is provided, this is not to say that the requirement can be ignored and that failure to comply will have no consequences.

6.4.22   Where a statutory duty is imposed and no sanction is provided by the statute for noncompliance, courts can interpret the statute as conferring a civil action for breach of statutory duty. Alternatively, failure by an authority to comply may mean that its conduct is unlawful under s 6 of the Human Rights Act 1998 because the authority is acting in a way which is incompatible with a Convention right.[82] Article 6(1) of the Convention requires that everyone, in the determination of his civil rights and obligations, is entitled to a fair hearing before an independent tribunal. Licensing decisions affecting applicants involve the determination of a civil right and this may also be the case with those making representations, as persons on the 'other side' of the dispute or 'contestation' that is being determined by the licensing authority (see 3.5.4 above). Failure to give applicants reasons for the decision is a violation of Art 6(1) (see 3.5.9 above) and it may be that failure to notify and give interested parties reasons why their representations are considered frivolous and will not be taken into account could similarly be regarded as a violation.[83] Further, there may be a violation in that the requirement for a fair hearing by an 'independent tribunal' is not met. For the purposes of Art 6(1), if the decision-making body is not 'independent' (which is the case with local authorities, as they are part of the executive), it will suffice if there is access to an independent tribunal that has 'full jurisdiction' to hear the complaint that the applicant wishes to bring.[84] This will be the case where there is a right of appeal to a court and this takes the form of a rehearing, but the Act makes no provision for an appeal against a determination that a representation is frivolous. The availability of judicial review and access to the High Court, a ground for challenge mentioned in para 9.10 of the Guidance, may meet the requirement of access to an independent tribunal, but this will depend on whether judicial review proceedings can address the nature of the complaint. This may not necessarily be the case.

An additional consequence of noncompliance with the duty in s 18(8) might be that this could invalidate the licensing decision made in the particular case. Where statute provides a decision-making procedure and there is a failure to comply with some requirement of the procedure when reaching a decision, this may, but not necessarily will, make the decision invalid. Much will depend on the importance of the requirement and traditionally courts have focused on whether the requirement should be regarded as a mandatory one (where failure to comply invalidates the decision) or a directory one (where it does not). However, the usefulness of this distinction has recently been called into question by the House of Lords in *R v Soneji and another* [2005] 4 All ER 321 where Lord Steyn, delivering the leading judgment, stated (at [23]):

> ... the rigid mandatory and directory distinction, and its many artificial refinements, have outlived their usefulness. Instead ... the emphasis ought to be on the consequences of non-compliance, and posing the question whether Parliament can fairly be taken to have intended total invalidity. That is how I would approach what is ultimately a question of statutory construction.

Although the principle in *R v Soneji* was formulated in the context of a criminal case, there is no suggestion from the judgments that its application is confined to such cases and that it has anything other than general application. It should therefore have equal application to noncompliance with requirements under the 2003 Act and it is clear from the decision that the current legal approach is to focus on the consequences of noncompliance with the statutory requirement. If this approach is followed in relation to s 18(8), it is perhaps doubtful whether noncompliance ought to be regarded as invalidating a licensing decision The requirement of notification is not central, or one of crucial importance, in the decision-making process and it seems unlikely that Parliament would have intended total invalidity as a consequence on noncompliance.

### 6.4.23 *Representations relating to the proposed premises supervisor: s 18(6)(c)*

These will be relevant under s 18(6)(c) if they 'relate to the identity of the person named in the application as the proposed premises supervisor', provided the requirements of s 18(9) are met. Section 18(9) provides:

> The requirements of this subsection are that the representations–
>
> (a) were made by the chief officer of police for the police area in which the premises are situated, and
>
> (b) include a statement that, due to the exceptional circumstances of the case, he is satisfied that the designation of the person concerned as the premises supervisor under the premises licence would undermine the crime prevention objective.

Such representations are confined to cases where the licensable activities include the sale or supply of alcohol, since it will only be in such instances that there will be a premises supervisor.

Where the term 'exceptional circumstances' is used in legislation, how unusual circumstances have to be to become 'exceptional' is notoriously difficult to predict. Paragraph 4.27 of the Guidance, however, stresses that they will need to be highly exceptional:

> The portability of personal licences from one premises to another is an important concept within the 2003 Act. The Secretary of State expects that objections by the police on the specification of the designated premises supervisor would arise in only genuinely exceptional circumstances.

An example given is where a personal licence holder has been allowed by the courts to retain his licence, despite convictions for selling alcohol to minors, and transfers into premises which have some degree of notoriety for underage drinking.[85] Less clear is whether exceptional circumstances might include cases where a proposed supervisor does not have any convictions, but where there may be evidence of past criminal activities. For example, a prosecution may have been commenced, but discontinued, an acquittal may have resulted, or a conviction may have been quashed on appeal. Licensing authorities traditionally have regard to such matters in areas of licensing where a 'fit and proper person' test applies, for example, taxi licensing (see 6.12.12 below) and the 'exceptional circumstances' provision in s 18(9)(b) might enable them to continue to do so in appropriate cases. This will, however, be possible only if representations are made by the police in accordance with s 18(9). It is, in addition, unclear whether 'exceptional circumstances' might include instances where, although there is no evidence of past criminal activity, the proposed supervisor may for some reason be thought to be manifestly unsuitable, for example an inexperienced 18-year-old for a large nightclub or a person about to marry a convicted drug dealer.

### 6.4.24  Representations excluded by s 32: s 18(6)(d)

Section 32 contains restrictions on representations that can be made following the issuing of a provisional statement. The restrictions are, broadly, that, unless there has been any material change in circumstances, representations cannot be made following the issuing of a provisional statement and on application for the grant of a premises licence (which is made after the issuing of the statement) if they could have been made at the time the provisional statement was issued.[86] Where these restrictions apply, representations, although they may be relevant in other respects, will not be considered 'relevant representations' by virtue of s 18(6)(d).

## 6.5    GRANT OR REFUSAL OF A PREMISES LICENCE – TAKING STEPS NECESSARY TO PROMOTE THE LICENSING OBJECTIVES

6.5.1    Whether the licence application (which might be for unlicensed premises or equally might be for premises where there is already a premises licence in force) is granted, either as sought by the applicant or in modified form, or whether it is refused will be determined by what the authority considers is necessary to promote the licensing objectives. A hearing must be held to consider relevant representations (unless there is agreement that this is unnecessary) and then, having regard to the representations, the authority must take one of a number of steps that it considers necessary to promote the licensing objectives. Section 18(3) and (4) provide:

(3)  Where relevant representations are made, the authority must–

(a)  hold a hearing to consider them, unless the authority, the applicant and each person who has made such representations agree that a hearing is unnecessary,

(b)  having regard to the representations, take such of the steps mentioned in subsection (4) (if any) as it considers necessary for the promotion of the licensing objectives.

(4)  The steps are–

    (a)  to grant the licence subject to–

        (i)   the conditions mentioned in subsection (2)(a) modified to such extent as the authority considers necessary for the promotion of the licensing objectives, and

        (ii)  any condition which under section 19 or 21 must be included in the licence;

    (b)  to exclude from the scope of the licence any of the licensable activities to which the application relates;

    (c)  to refuse to specify a person in the licence as the premises supervisor;

    (d)  to reject the application.

Section 18(3)(b) requires the authority to 'have regard' to the representations and then take any of the specified steps as necessary to promote the licensing objectives. Most obviously this will include the authority taking into account the particular relevant representations received and taking steps to promote the licensing objectives that are directly linked to particular representations. The particular representations received may well form the focus for the hearing and the Guidance seems to envisage that they should. Paragraph 9.24 provides:

> As a matter of practice, licensing authorities should seek to focus the hearing on the steps needed to promote the particular licensing objective which has given rise to the specific representation and avoid straying into undisputed areas. A responsible authority or interested party . . . may not add further representations to those disclosed to the applicant prior to the hearing, but they may expand on their existing representation.

How far its discretion extends beyond matters detailed in the relevant representations and to what extent it can consider other information which has come to its attention is uncertain. There may be matters other than those specified in a relevant representation that relate to the same licensing objective and come to light after the making of the representation but before the hearing, as where, for example, the police may make a relevant representation in respect of disorder occurring outside the premises and subsequently discover on a visit to the premises that drugs are being sold there. Any representation about the drugs may fall outside the prescribed period for making relevant representations, although this may not necessarily preclude its consideration (see 6.4.19 above), and both the disorder and drugs are about the likely effect of the grant of the licence on the licensing objective of prevention of crime and disorder. Both fall within the police's recognised area of expertise. Further, this would not be an undisputed area that the authority was straying into and the matter could be disclosed to the applicant (if he were not already aware of them) prior to the hearing. Nevertheless, this is information brought to the authority's attention other than through relevant representations and it is uncertain whether the authority's discretion extends to considering this. The same would be the case if the police, in the above example, on visiting the premises, discovered various matters which appeared to compromise public safety. Here the information relates to another licensing objective, public safety, which falls outside the police's recognised area of expertise (although the threat to public safety may in the circumstances be one that is easy to recognise without any particular level of expertise). If representations out of time can be considered by the authority, in accordance with the view expressed earlier (see 6.4.19 above), the authority's discretion should extend to consideration of the matters brought to its attention where, as in the above examples, there is a direct connection with a relevant representation received.

Less clear is the position where information comes to the authority's attention on a matter concerning the licensing objectives where there is no direct connection. Here it is more likely that the authority can be said to be 'straying into undisputed areas', to use the words in para 9.24 of the Guidance. Nevertheless, the wording of s 18(3)(b) may be wide enough to encompass the authority taking into account matters other than those raised in the relevant representations when deciding what is necessary to promote the licensing objectives. Under s 18(3)(a), relevant representations are necessary in order for the holding of a hearing, but the authority is not confined to considering such representations when making its decision on the application. It is simply required to have regard to them. A broad interpretation of s 18(3)(b) would be that, when making a decision on the merits of the case as to the steps necessary to promote the licensing objectives, the authority might consider matters affecting promotion of the licensing objectives generally, whether or not these are contained in any of the relevant representations made and whether or not they have any direct connection with the relevant representations. A narrow interpretation would be that the steps taken can only relate to issues raised by the particular representations received. An intermediate position would be that the steps taken might extend beyond issues raised by the particular representations received but there would need to be some link or direct connection between the steps and the representations. The matter has not yet fallen for judicial determination but comments made, *obiter*, by Richards J in *R (on the application of The British Beer and Pub Association) v Canterbury City Council* [2006] LGR 596 (at para 90) suggest a broad interpretation may be unlikely:

> I think it better to leave open the question of whether the licensing authority's discretion extends beyond the issues raised in the representations and whether it can take account of information received otherwise than through relevant representations received . . . It may well be that the reference [in the authority's Statement of Licensing Policy] to "full discretion" overstates the extent of the council's discretion.

It is submitted that the appropriate level of discretion to confer on the authority would be the intermediate position identified above. This would permit consideration of representations out of time, which it seems authorities might take into account (see 6.4.19 above), or other information received by the authority, in cases where there is some connection with the relevant representations received but not otherwise. This would not be so narrow as to confine the authority to matters raised in the relevant representations, which might be unduly restrictive, nor would it be so wide-ranging as to extend well beyond the relevant representations and be more akin to the largely untrammelled discretion that authorities had under the previous law.

With regard to taking any of the steps mentioned in sub-s (4), it is not necessary that any steps are in fact taken, since s 18(3)(b) refers to the authority taking such of the steps, 'if any', as it considers necessary for the promotion of the licensing objectives. If none of the steps are considered necessary, the authority can grant the licence in the terms sought by the applicant, subject only to such conditions as are consistent with the operating schedule accompanying the application in accordance with s 18(2)(a) (and any mandatory conditions under ss 19–21). The conditions imposed on the grant of the licence in such a case will thus be the same as if no relevant representations had been received and the authority had been obliged to grant the licence.

6.5.2    Apart from rejecting the application and refusing a licence, the authority can grant the licence in accordance with any or all of the three steps mentioned in s 18(4)(a)–(c). First, the licence can be granted subject to conditions consistent with the operating schedule, but modified to such extent as the authority considers necessary for the promotion of the licensing objectives (again, with any mandatory conditions under ss 19–21). As regards conditions being 'modified', s 18(5) provides:

> For the purposes of subsection (4)(a)(i) the conditions mentioned in subsection (2)(a) are modified if any of them is altered or omitted or any new condition is added.

Further, as in the case of a mandatory grant, authorities can, under s 18(10), impose different conditions on different parts of the premises and in relation to different licensable activities (see 6.4.7 above). Given that both the power to modify and the licensing objectives themselves are broadly expressed, this should give authorities a considerable discretion in respect of the imposition of conditions.[87]

Secondly, any of the licensable activities to which the application relates can be excluded from the scope of the licence. An example of where this might occur is given in Explanatory Note 64: 'a licensing authority may remove the performance of amplified music after 11 pm from the scope of the licence applied for by the tenant of a pub in the middle of a quiet residential area.'

6.5.3    Thirdly, the authority can 'refuse to specify a person in the licence as the premises supervisor'. It is not clear from the wording whether this means refuse to specify the person named in the application or refuse to specify a premises supervisor at all, that is anyone (at this stage). Presumably it means the former, although it is perhaps likely to arise only in limited instances. One might be if there have been representations from the police that designation of the person concerned as the premises supervisor would undermine the crime prevention objective. This might be the case if a young, inexperienced person were proposed as the premises supervisor for a large capacity nightclub. Another might be if the person had previously been a premises supervisor for similar premises, but had been removed following a premises licence review for those premises. In general, an authority will not be concerned with the premises supervisor's suitability, since he will need to have a personal licence and his suitability (or lack of it) will have been considered when an application was made for such a licence. If the authority does refuse to specify a person, it is not clear whether it can do so only where the proposed premises supervisor is someone other than the applicant for the premises licence or whether this can also be done if the applicant himself proposes to be the premises supervisor.

Where there is a refusal to specify, the section seems to envisage the licence being granted, but it is not clear how an authority should proceed in such a case. One option would be to grant the licence subject to a condition that the premises must not be open for the supply of alcohol until a satisfactory premises supervisor has been appointed. Another would be to grant the licence and (as an interim measure) specify the applicant as the premises supervisor. This particular step of refusing to specify a premises supervisor is not, in practice, likely to arise very often since police representations about a premises supervisor can be made only in 'exceptional circumstances'.

6.5.4    There is no requirement imposed on the authority to notify the applicant and any person who made relevant representations of its reasons for any decision it makes as to whether or not to take any steps mentioned in s 18(4). However, the authority will be under a duty to give reasons under Art 6(1) of the European Convention on Human Rights, since the right to a fair hearing under this Article extends to the giving of reasons, although reasons will not be required in respect of every point raised (see 3.5.9 above). It will suffice if it is clear to the applicant and any person who made relevant representations what conclusions were reached on the principal issues and why the authority decided the case the way that it did. As Lord Brown stated in *South Bucks District Council v Porter* [2004] 1 WLR 1953, at para 36, when delivering the judgment of the House of Lords as to the adequacy of reasons for a decision for refusal of planning permisssion:

> The reasons for a decision must be intelligible and they must be adequate. They must enable the reader to understand why the matter was decided as it was and what conclusions were reached on the "principal important controversial issues", disclosing how any issue of law or fact was resolved. Reasons can be briefly stated, the degree of particularity required depending entirely on the nature of the issues falling for decision. The reasoning must not give rise to a substantial doubt as to whether the decision-maker erred in law, for example by misunderstanding some relevant policy or some other important matter or by failing to reach a rational decision on relevant grounds. But such adverse inference will not readily be drawn. The reasons need refer only to the main issues in the dispute, not to every material consideration. They should enable disappointed developers to assess their prospects of obtaining some alternative development permission, or, as the case may be, their unsuccessful opponents to understand how the policy or approach underlying the grant of permission may impact upon future such applications. Decision letters must be read in a straight-forward manner, recognising that they are addressed to parties well aware of the issues involved and the arguments advanced. A reasoned challenge will only succeed if the party aggrieved can satisfy the court that he has genuinely been substantially prejudiced by the failure to provide an adequately reasoned decision.

These observations are of general application and were recognised as extending to cases under the 2003 Act by the High Court in *R (on the application of Blackwood) v Birmingham Magistrates and Birmingham City Council, Mitchells and Butler Leisure Retail Ltd (Interested Party)* (2006) 170 JP 613.[88] The court in this case 'also found helpful' its previous decision in *The Queen on the application of Hestview Ltd v Snaresbrook Crown Court* [2001] LLR 214, a betting licensing case, where the court in that case applied the observations of Griffiths LJ in *Eagil Trust v Piggot Brown* [1985] 3 All ER 119, 122 (on which see 12.10.2 below).

## 6.6    NOTIFICATION OF GRANT OR REFUSAL AND ISSUING OF THE PREMISES LICENCE AND SUMMARY

6.6.1    When a premises licence is granted or refused, the licensing authority is required to notify its decision to the applicant, any person who made relevant representations and the chief officer of police. If the licence is granted, the notification must include a statement of the authority's reasons for taking or not taking any of the steps that it did. It must then issue the licence and a summary of it. If refused, notification must be given stating the reasons for doing so. Section 23 provides:

(1)  Where an application is granted under section 18, the relevant licensing authority must forthwith–

    (a)  give a notice to that effect to–

        (i)  the applicant,

        (ii)  any person who made relevant representations in respect of the application, and

        (iii)  the chief officer of police for the police area (or each police area) in which the premises are situated, and

    (b)  issue the applicant with a licence and summary of it.

(2)  Where relevant representations were made in respect of the application, the notice under subsection (1)(a) must state the authority's reasons for its decision as to the steps (if any) to take under section 18(3)(b).

(3)  Where an application is rejected under section 18, the relevant licensing authority must forthwith give a notice to that effect, stating the reasons for the decision, to–

    (a)  the applicant,

    (b)  any person who made relevant representations in respect of the application, and

    (c)  the chief officer of police for the police area (or each police area) in which the premises are situated.

(4)  In this section "relevant representations" has the meaning given in section 18(6).

6.6.2    The authority is required to give notice 'forthwith', the ordinary meaning of which is 'at once, without delay' and, if this meaning is adopted, the authority might be required to give notice as soon as the decision is reached. This seems unrealistic, given that reasons are required and the drafting of reasons will not necessarily be able to take place immediately. The purpose of including the requirement for notice to be given 'forthwith' seems to have been to provide assurance to those in the industry that applications will be dealt with without delay, as can be seen from the following remarks of Baroness Blackstone during the committee stage of the Bill in the House of Lords:

> We sought to reassure the industry that applications for licences will be dealt with promptly and efficiently. The use of the word "forthwith" in Clauses 22 and 35 reflect that aim. It is there to emphasise that there should be no delay in notifying applicants when a matter has been determined. We should not interpret that to mean that, when there is a hearing late in the evening, the licensing authority then has to tell people in the middle of the night. That would be absurd, and I should like to give that reassurance.[89]

In the light of this, a sensible approach would be to interpret 'forthwith' to mean 'forthwith' in practical terms and to equate it with 'as soon as is reasonably practicable'. This approach would in fact accord with that adopted by courts where the term has been used in other legislative provisions. In *Sameen v Abeyewickrema* [1963] AC 597, a case in which a statutory provision required the filing of notice 'forthwith', Lord Dilhorne LC, delivering the judgment of the Privy Council, stated (at 609):

> Their Lordships do not propose to attempt to define "forthwith". The use of that word clearly connotes that the notice must be filed as soon as practicable, but what is practicable must depend on the circumstances of each case.[90]

6.6.3    Notification of the decision to the applicant, those who made relevant representations and the police will be in accordance with s 184(3), under which the authority may give notice by delivery of it to the person in question or by leaving it at his proper address, or by sending it by post to him at that address (see 2.5.4 above). Where granted, the licence and a summary of it will be in a form prescribed in regulations by the Secretary of State. Section 24 makes provision to this effect and sets out the basic requirements as to the information which must be included. Section 24 provides:

(1) A premises licence and the summary of a premises licence must be in the pre-scribed form.

(2) Regulations under subsection (1) must, in particular, provide for the licence to–

    (a) specify the name and address of the holder;

    (b) include a plan of the premises to which the licence relates;

    (c) if the licence has effect for a limited period, specify that period;

    (d) specify the licensable activities for which the premises may be used;

    (e) if the licensable activities include the supply of alcohol, specify the name and address of the individual (if any) who is the premises supervisor in respect of the licence and his address;

    (f) specify the conditions subject to which the licence has effect.

Regulation 33 and Pt A of Sched 12 to the LA 2003 (PL and CPC) Regs 2005 prescribe the form for the premises licence. Under reg 33 the licence must include: (a) an identi-fier for the licensing authority; (b) a number that is unique to the licence; and (c) certain information set out in Pt A of Sched 12. This information includes, but is not confined to, the above-mentioned matters in s 24(2). As regards inclusion of the plan, this is specified in Annex 4 to the Schedule, along with conditions in Annexes 1–3, which strongly suggests that the plan forms part of the licence (see 2.1.10 above). In some instances additional information is required in respect of included matters, for example, the designated premises supervisor's telephone number, personal licence number and the name of the issuing authority as well as his name and address. Matters not specified in s 24(2), but on which information is required include the times at which licensable activities may take place and whether supply of alcohol is for consumption on and off or just on the premises. Regulation 34 requires inclusion of the identifier and premises licence number on the summary of the licence and the information that the summary must contain is set out in Pt B of Sched 12. In large measure, the information replicates that contained in the premises licence, excluding a plan of the premises and licence conditions, and requires reference to whether access to the premises by children is restricted or prohibited. Regulation 34 also requires the summary to be printed on paper of a size equal to or larger than A4.

In the event that the licence or summary is lost, stolen, damaged or destroyed, s 25 enables the licence holder to obtain a copy, in the same form as it existed immediately before it was lost, stolen, damaged or destroyed, on payment of a fee, which under reg 8 and Sched 6 to the LA 2003 (Fees) Regs 2005 is £10.50:

(1) Where a premises licence or summary is lost, stolen, damaged or destroyed, the holder of the licence may apply to the relevant licensing authority for a copy of the licence or summary.

(2) Subsection (1) is subject to regulations under section 55(1) (fee to accompany applications).

(3) Where an application is made in accordance with this section, the relevant licensing authority must issue the holder of the licence with a copy of the licence or summary (certified by the authority to be a true copy) if it is satisfied that–

    (a) the licence or summary has been lost, stolen, damaged or destroyed, and

    (b) where it has been lost or stolen, the holder has reported that loss or theft to the police.

(4) The copy issued under this section must be a copy of the premises licence or summary in the form in which it existed immediately before it was lost, stolen, damaged or destroyed.

(5) This Act applies in relation to a copy issued under this section as it applies in relation to an original licence or summary.

The section does not, however, impose any requirement on the licence holder to return to the licensing authority the licence that is lost or stolen should it come back into his possession, although it might have been expected for such a provision to be included.

## 6.7    DURATION OF PREMISES LICENCE

### 6.7.1   Indefinite duration and exceptions

A premises licence, once granted, will generally remain in force indefinitely. The circumstances in which it will not do so are when it:

- is revoked;
- was granted only for a limited period;
- is suspended;
- lapses due to some incapacity on the part of the licence holder; or
- lapses on surrender.

The first three situations are covered by s 26 and the remaining two by ss 27 and 28, respectively.

    Section 26 provides:

(1) Subject to sections 27 and 28, a premises licence has effect until such time as–

    (a) it is revoked under section 52, or

    (b) if it specifies that it has effect for a limited period, that period expires.

(2) But a premises licence does not have effect during any period when it is suspended under section 52.

Revocation and suspension are covered in 6.12.8–6.12.9 below, and the only other circumstance covered by s 26 is where the licence specifies that it has effect for a limited period and that period expires. Not all applicants will be seeking a 'permanent' premises licence – those wishing to hold pop concerts for larger numbers and/or for longer periods than are permitted by a TEN will need a premises licence (see 6.1.3 above) – and one of the matters that will be included in an applicant's operating schedule will be 'where the applicant wishes the licence to have effect for a limited period, that period' (s 17(4)(d)).

6.7.2    Whilst an applicant may seek a premises licence for a limited period, it is doubtful whether an authority could grant one for such a period if there is no request for this by the applicant in the operating schedule. Although s 26(1)(b) simply refers to a licence specifying that it has effect for a limited period, which on the wording would seem to be wide enough to permit an authority to do so, a narrower interpretation confining this to cases where a limited period was sought would be more in accordance with the intention of Parliament. The legislation is based on the White Paper and it is clear from this that the intention was that premises licences should be of indefinite duration.[91] Nor, in view of the power to impose conditions in s 18, would it seem possible to impose a condition that the licence should have effect in the first instance only for a limited period. If there are no relevant representations, only conditions that are consistent with the operating schedule can be imposed (s 18(2)(a)). If there was no request in the operating schedule for a licence for a limited period, it is hard to see that attaching a condition that it has effect for such a period would be consistent with the operating schedule. If there are relevant representations, conditions can be imposed that are consistent with the operating schedule modified to such extent as the authority considers necessary for the promotion of the licensing objectives. It would, however, be difficult to substantiate a claim that a condition that the licence has effect for a limited period would be necessary for the promotion of the licensing objectives. It is really conditions relating to noise control, prevention of disturbance or access by children, etc that promote the licensing objectives rather than one that the licence is of limited duration.

6.7.3    Lapse of licence due to incapacity on the part of the licence holder covers several situations, including death, mental incapacity, insolvency (of an individual or company), dissolution of a company and, in the case of a club, if it ceases to be a recognised club.[92] Insolvency is widely defined to include voluntary arrangements, bankruptcy, sequestration of an estate, deeds with creditors, appointment of administrators and receivers, and liquidation. Lapse is, however, subject to the possibility of the licence being reinstated under ss 47 or 50 (see 6.11.1 below). Section 27 provides:

(1)  A premises licence lapses if the holder of the licence–
  (a)  dies,
  (b)  becomes a person who lacks capacity (within the meaning of the Mental Capacity Act 2005) to hold the licence,[93]
  (c)  becomes insolvent,
  (d)  is dissolved, or
  (e)  if it is a club, ceases to be a recognised club.
(2)  This section is subject to sections 47 and 50 (which make provision for the reinstatement of the licence in certain circumstances).
(3)  For the purposes of this section, an individual becomes insolvent on–
  (a)  the approval of a voluntary arrangement proposed by him,
  (b)  being adjudged bankrupt or having his estate sequestrated, or
  (c)  entering into a deed of arrangement made for the benefit of his creditors or a trust deed for his creditors.
(4)  For the purposes of this section, a company becomes insolvent on–
  (a)  the approval of a voluntary arrangement proposed by its directors,
  (b)  the appointment of an administrator in respect of the company,

    (c)  the appointment of an administrative receiver in respect of the company, or

    (d)  going into liquidation.

(5)  An expression used in this section and in the Insolvency Act 1986 (c.45) has the same meaning in this section as in that Act.

It is not clear if a licence would lapse in the above circumstances if it were held in joint names with another person (see 6.2.5 above). If a licence does lapse, there is no provision for notification of the holder of any other premises licence in respect of the same premises, although the holder may be notified when a change is made in the licensing register if he has a property interest in the premises and has given notice of that interest to the licensing authority under s 178 (see 2.4.7 above).

6.7.4    A licence will lapse if the licence holder voluntarily surrenders the licence. This is done by a notice of surrender to the licensing authority, accompanied by the return of the licence or a statement of reasons why this cannot be done, for example, because the licence has been lost. Lapse is, however, subject to the possibility of the licence being reinstated under s 50. Section 28 provides:

    (1)  Where the holder of a premises licence wishes to surrender his licence he may give the relevant licensing authority a notice to that effect.

    (2)  The notice must be accompanied by the premises licence or, if that is not practicable, by a statement of the reasons for the failure to provide the licence.

    (3)  Where a notice of surrender is given in accordance with this section, the premises licence lapses on receipt of the notice by the authority.

    (4)  This section is subject to section 50 (which makes provision for the reinstatement in certain circumstances of a licence surrendered under this section).

Perhaps surprisingly, there does not appear to be any requirement for payment of a fee, nor is there any provision for notice of surrender to be given to any other persons, for example, the DPS (if a person other than the premises licence holder), the owner of the premises or the police. This is perhaps unfortunate, given that surrender of a licence may have serious repercussions, such as the DPS being effectively out of a job and the premises owner finding the premises cease to be in use.[94]

## 6.7.5  Updating the premises licence

Once a premises licence has been granted, the holder of the licence is under a duty to notify the licensing authority of any change in either his name or address or that of the DPS (unless the DPS has himself given notice to the authority). The notice given must be accompanied by the appropriate fee (which under reg 8 and Sched 6 to the LA 2003 (Fees) Regs 2005 is £10.50) and the premises licence for the changes to be recorded on it. (A duty to update the licensing document is imposed on the licensing authority by s 56 – see 6.14.1 below.) Section 33(1)–(5) provides:

    (1)  The holder of a premises licence must, as soon as is reasonably practicable, notify the relevant licensing authority of any change in–

        (a)  his name or address, or

        (b)  unless the designated premises supervisor has already notified the authority under subsection (4), the name or address of that supervisor.

    (2)  Subsection (1) is subject to regulations under section 55(1) (fee to accompany application).

(3)  A notice under subsection (1) must also be accompanied by the premises licence (or appropriate part of the licence) or, if that is not practicable, by a statement of the reasons for the failure to produce the licence (or part).

(4)  Where the designated premises supervisor under a premises licence is not the holder of the licence, he may notify the relevant licensing authority under this subsection of any change in his name or address.

(5)  Where the designated premises supervisor gives a notice under subsection (4), he must, as soon as is reasonably practicable, give the holder of the premises licence a copy of that notice.

Failure to comply with the duty without reasonable excuse is a criminal offence, for which the penalty is a level 2 fine on the standard scale. Section 33(6)–(7) provides:

(6)  A person commits an offence if he fails, without reasonable excuse, to comply with this section.

(7)  A person who is guilty of an offence under subsection (6) is liable on summary conviction to a fine not exceeding level 2 on the standard scale.

## 6.8    PROVISIONAL STATEMENTS PRECEDING APPLICATION FOR A PREMISES LICENCE

### 6.8.1   Introduction

6.8.2    Section 29 provides a mechanism whereby a person interested in making a future application for a premises licence can obtain a provisional statement which will give an indication of the prospects of success of the premises licence application. This can be done where premises are about to be or are in the process of being constructed, altered or extended, for s 29(1) provides:

> This section applies to premises which–
> (a)  are being or are about to be constructed for the purpose of being used for one or more licensable activities, or
> (b)  are being or are about to be extended or otherwise altered for that purpose (whether or not they are already being used for that purpose).[95]

Explanatory Note 76 sets out the effect of the section, indicating:

> The effect of the section is to establish a mechanism whereby those engaged in or about to engage in construction or development work at premises to be used for licensable activities can obtain a certain degree of assurance about their potential trading conditions. By obtaining a provisional statement they can receive, at an early stage, a statement describing the likely effect of the intended licensable activities on the licensing objectives and an indication of the prospects of any future application for a premises licence.

A provisional statement does not therefore 'convert' into a premises licence on completion of the construction, alteration or extension and a subsequent premises licence application, with attendant requirements for advertising, will be needed. There will be an opportunity for relevant representations to be made once the premises licence application is submitted, although there are restrictions on the making of relevant representations (imposed by s 32) following the issuing of a provisional statement (see 6.8.9–6.8.12 below).

Provisional statements provide a procedure for leisure industry business operators to obtain an advance indication of the likelihood of obtaining a premises licence, and of the terms and conditions on which this might be granted, in cases where ventures involve a large financial investment, whether for the construction or refurbishment of premises, or for the acquisition of premises (contracts for which are very often conditional on the obtaining of planning permission and any necessary licences). The viability of a venture may well depend on obtaining a licence for alcohol and entertainment and the procedure enables an assessment to be made prior to the incurring of any substantial expenditure.[96] However, in practice the procedure seems not to have been widely used. This may be because of the risk that a premises licence may not subsequently be granted if relevant representations (notwithstanding the restrictions in s 32) are made and because it is not necessary to obtain a provisional statement prior to applying for a premises licence. A premises licence application can be made for partly constructed premises without first obtaining a provisional statement and an application can be made in the first instance for a premises licence even though the premises have not yet been constructed, provided the necessary information required in respect of the application can be supplied. Paragraphs 8.56 and 8.57 of the Guidance provide:

> 8.56 Any person falling within section 16 of the 2003 Act can apply for a premises licence before new premises are constructed, extended or changed. This would be possible where clear plans of the proposed structure exist and the applicant is in a position to complete an operating schedule including details of:
> - the activities to take place there;
> - the time at which such activities will take place;
> - the proposed hours of opening;
> - where the applicant wishes the licence to have effect for a limited period, that period;
> - the steps to be taken to promote the licensing objectives; and
> - where the sale of alcohol is involved, whether supplies are proposed to be for consumption on or off the premises (or both) and the name of the designated premises supervisor the applicant wishes to specify.
>
> 8.54 In such cases, the licensing authority would include in the licence the date upon which it would come into effect. A provisional statement will normally only be required when the information described above is not available.

6.8.3   Premises being or about to be constructed, altered or extended will most obviously apply in respect of buildings, but the meaning of 'premises' extends beyond this to include a vessel, vehicle or moveable structure.[97] Where these types of premises are not permanently located in one place, s 189 makes provision for determining the relevant licensing authority to which an application for a premises licence will be made (see 6.1.6 above) and stipulates, in these cases, that provisional statements will not have application. Section 189(5) provides:

> Sections 29 to 31 (which make provision in respect of provisional statements relating to premises licences) do not apply in relation to a vessel, vehicle or structure to which this section applies.

This provision does not, however, appear to rule out provisional statements in respect of vessels, vehicles or moveable structures in all cases. It states that ss 29–31 on provisional statements do not apply to a vessel, vehicle or structure 'to which this section applies'. Reference to the opening words of s 189(1), (2) and (3) indicate that the section does *not* apply to a vessel that is not permanently moored or berthed or to a vehicle or structure that is not permanently situated in the same place (see 6.1.6 above). Where there *is* a permanent location and a person is interested in making an extension or alteration, it would seem open to him to make an application for a provisional statement prior to making an application for a premises licence.

## 6.8.4  Applicants for a provisional statement

Section 29(2) specifies who may apply for a provisional statement[98] and provides:

> A person may apply to the relevant licensing authority for a provisional statement if–
>
> (a)  he is interested in the premises, and
>
> (b)  where he is an individual, he is aged 18 or over.

As with applicants for a premises licence, 'a person' making application can be either a company or an individual, although in the latter instance there is a requirement that he is aged at least 18 (see 6.2.2–6.2.3 above). The section also requires that the company or individual 'is interested' in the premises, although no guidance is given in the Act, the Explanatory Note (76) to the section or the Guidance as to the nature of the interest that will suffice. Clearly some proprietary interest in the premises, as where a person is the owner or lessee, will suffice, but the section is not restricted in its wording to such interests and should not be interpreted as so restricted. The expression 'interested in the premises' was used in s 6 of the Licensing Act 1964 and its meaning was considered by the High Court in *R v Dudley Crown Court ex p Pask and Moore* (1983) 147 JP 417, which gave it a broad interpretation. Taylor J stated (at 424):

> I see no reason why one should import automatically any requirement of an interest in property, legal or equitable, nor any requirement of any actual contractual right to operate on the premises. In my judgment the phrase is one to be construed in each case by the justices looking broadly at the circumstances of the individual application and what is proposed to be carried out and by whom. Approached in that way, I see no reason why an occupier, who has no interest in the land as such and has no firm contract with the owners, should not be able to make application . . . It may well be that Parliament used the phrase in the broad way that it did to embrace not only those who presently have a legal or equitable interest in the property, but those who are in negotiation and considering acquiring such interest so that they may well be able, without having to make conditional contracts, to make an application and see whether the justices are prepared to grant a licence and so know whether it is commercially viable to proceed with their proposals.

It is likely that the provision in s 29(2)(a) will be similarly interpreted. If it were not, a person interested in acquiring property with a view to carrying out licensable activities there, but who wished to obtain a provisional statement ahead of acquiring any interest in the property would be unable to do so. It ought therefore to include cases where a person has some interest in one or more of the licensable activities to be carrying on at the premises on completion. It might also include those who have some interest in the premises at the time of the application, but who may not have any interest in respect of the licensable activities being carried out there once the premises are completed. This seems to follow from the statement contained in para 8.59 of the Guidance that the applicant 'could be a firm of architects or a construction company or a financier'.

Since it seems that more than one person can hold a premises licence in respect of the same premises if they each were using the premises for a different licensable activity (see 6.2.4 above), it should follow that more than one person can obtain a provisional statement in respect of premises. If each person intended to use the premises for a different licensable activity, each may wish to obtain a provisional statement ahead of incurring any significant expenditure in respect of his particular licensable activity. Where, however, the intention is to use premises with only a single premises licence in respect of some particular licensable activity or activities, it is less clear whether an application for a provisional statement must be made in the name of one person or whether it can be made in joint names. This will depend on whether a (single) premises licence can be held in joint names (see 6.2.5 above). Since it can, then it should be possible to obtain a provisional statement in joint names.

## 6.8.5  Application for a provisional statement

As with a premises licence, application is subject to regulations made (a) under s 54 in respect of the form etc of applications and any notices that need to be given, and (b) under s 55 in respect of fees to accompany applications and notices (s 29(4)). The LA 2003 (PL and CPC) Regs 2005 specify the form the application shall take and the information that it must contain,[99] and under reg 8 and Sched 6 to the LA 2003 (Fees) Regs 2005 the fee payable is £315. Notices can include the publicising of applications and s 30 provides for this to be done in a similar manner to applications for premises licences:

(1)  This section applies where an application is made under section 29.

(2)  The power to make regulations under section 17(5) (advertisement etc of application) applies in relation to an application under section 29 as it applies in relation to an application under section 17.[100]

(3)  Regulations made by virtue of subsection (2) may, in particular, require advertisements to contain a statement in the prescribed form describing the effect of section 32 (restrictions on representations following issue of a provisional statement).[101]

Provision is made in regs 25–26 of the LA 2003 (PL and CPC) Regs 2005 for the advertising of applications (see 2.1.11 above) and, in accordance with s 30(3), reg 26(2)(a) requires the notice posted on the premises and placed in the local newspaper to state that representations are restricted after the issue of a provisional statement. Further, under reg 26(2)(b), the notice may state, where known, the relevant licensable activities which it is proposed will be carried on on or from the premises.

The application must, under s 29(5), be accompanied by a 'schedule of works' and s 29(6) provides:

A schedule of works is a document in the prescribed form which includes–

(a)  a statement made by or on behalf of the applicant including particulars of the premises to which the application relates and of the licensable activities for which the premises are to be used,

(b)  plans of the work being or about to be done at the premises, and

(c)  such other information as may be prescribed.

Regulation 11 and Sched 3 to the LA 2003 (PL and CPC) Regs 2005 prescribe the form for the schedule of works and require the schedule to specify whether the premises are about to be constructed or whether they are being extended or altered, to provide details of the work and attach plans of the work being done or to be done at the premises, to give particulars of the premises to which the application relates, and to indicate the licensable activities for which the premises will be used.[102]

## 6.8.6 Determination of applications for provisional statements

6.8.7    The provisions of s 31, which govern the determination of applications, apply where the authority has received a provisional statement application, that is an application made in accordance with s 29,[103] and is satisfied that the applicant has complied with any requirement imposed on him by virtue of s 30 in relation to publicising and giving notice of the application (s 31(1)). Section 31(2) goes on to provide: 'Where no relevant representations are made, the authority must issue the applicant with a statement to that effect.'[104] However, a statement 'to that effect' will be an indication only that the application has been properly made and advertised, which in itself is of little value to the applicant. What the applicant requires, and what the statement needs to contain, is an indication that the intended licensable activities are likely to have no adverse effect on the licensing objectives and a future premises licence application is likely to be successful. Where there are relevant representations, s 31(3) requires the licensing authority to hold a hearing to consider them (unless the applicant and those making representations agree this is unnecessary). The term 'relevant representations' here has a similar meaning as in respect of premises licences, there is a similar period of 20 working days within which the hearing must be held and 10 working days' notice of the hearing must be given to the applicant and persons who made relevant representations.[105] Section 31(5) and (6), which is defined in broadly similar terms to s 18(6) and (7),[106] provides:

(5)  In this section "relevant representations" means representations–
   (a)  which are about the likely effect on the licensing objectives of the grant of a premises licence in the form described in the provisional statement application, if the work at the premises was satisfactorily completed, and
   (b)  which meet the requirements of subsection (6).
(6)  The requirements are–
   (a)  that the representations are made by an interested party or responsible authority within the period prescribed under section 17(5)(c) by virtue of section 30,[107]
   (b)  that the representations have not been withdrawn, and
   (c)  in the case of representations made by an interested party (who is not also a responsible authority) that they are not, in the opinion of the relevant licensing authority, frivolous or vexatious.[108]

Representations under s 31(5)(a) will be about the likely effect on the licensing objectives if a premises licence is granted in the form described in the provisional statement application 'if the work at the premises was satisfactorily completed'. Work will be satisfactorily completed if it 'substantially complies' with the schedule of works that accompanied the application. Section 29(7) provides:

> For the purposes of this Part, in relation to any premises in respect of which an application for a provisional statement has been made, references to the work being satisfactorily completed are to work at the premises being completed in a manner which substantially complies with the schedule of works accompanying the application.

No indication is provided as to what 'substantially complies' means and this will be a question of fact in the circumstances. The ordinary and natural meaning of 'substantial' in this context suggests 'compliance to a large extent' or 'compliance for the most part', rather than simply 'complying in some measure'.[109] The remaining requirements for representations to be relevant, set out in s 31(6), mirror those in s 18(7) and there is a requirement in s 31(7), comparable to that in s 18(8), for notifying any person whose representations are determined to be frivolous or vexatious of the reasons for that determination (see 6.4.21 above).

6.8.8    If relevant representations are made, the steps which the licensing authority is required to take are set out in s 31(3), which provides:

Where relevant representations are made, the authority must–

(a)  hold a hearing to consider them, unless the authority, the applicant and each person who has made such representations agrees that a hearing is unnecessary,

(b)  determine whether, on the basis of those representations and the provisional statement application, it would consider it necessary to take any steps under section 18(3)(b) if, on the work being satisfactorily completed,[110] it had to decide whether to grant a premises licence in the form described in the provisional statement application, and

(c)  issue the applicant with a statement which

(i)   gives details of that determination and,

(ii)  states the authority's reasons for its decision as to the steps (if any) that it would be necessary to take under section 18(3)(b).

When a hearing is held (or dispensed with if agreed to be unnecessary), the licensing authority must determine whether, if the premises were constructed or altered in the way proposed in the schedule of works and if a premises licence was sought for those premises, it would consider it necessary for the promotion of the licensing objectives to take any of the steps under s 18(3)(b). These steps, set out in s 18(4), are to attach conditions to any licence granted, rule out any of the licensable activities applied for, refuse to accept the person specified as the designated premises supervisor, or reject the application (see 6.5.1 above). Once a determination has been made, the applicant must be issued with a statement under s 31(3)(c)[111] giving details of the steps and the reasons for requiring them.[112] No period of time is specified within which the statement must be issued, but, in cases where no period is specified, reg 28(1) of the LA 2003 (Hearings) Regs 2005 provides that the authority must notify a party of its determination forthwith on making its determination.[113] A copy of the statement must also be given to: (a) each person who made relevant representations; and (b) the chief officer of police for each police area in which the premises are situated (s 31(4)).

## 6.8.9    Restriction on representations following a provisional statement

6.8.10   Where an application is subsequently made for a premises licence for premises in relation to which a provisional statement has been issued, s 32 imposes restrictions on the making of representations in respect of the premises licence application. This is designed to prevent representations being made at the premises licence application stage in respect of matters upon which representations could have been made at the earlier provisional statement application stage. These restrictions will apply where a provisional statement has been issued for premises and there is a subsequent premises licence application in respect of those premises or part of them, or of premises that are substantially the same as those premises or a part of them. Section 32(1) provides:

> This section applies where a provisional statement has been issued in respect of any premises ("the relevant premises") and a person subsequently applies for a premises licence in respect of–
>
> (a)  the relevant premises or a part of them, or
>
> (b)  premises that are substantially the same as the relevant premises or a part of them.

Application therefore can be made for a premises licence for only part of the particular premises for which a provisional statement was issued and the restrictions will still apply. Presumably, this is designed to allow for applicants revising or scaling down their operations between being issued with a provisional statement and making an application for a premises licence and deciding to use only a part of the premises for their licensable activities.

6.8.11   The restrictions will also still apply if the premises licence application is for premises that are 'substantially the same' as the premises in respect of which the provisional statement was issued. The ordinary and natural meaning of these words suggests the premises will have to be 'to a large extent' the same (see 6.8.7 above), although it is not clear whether these have to be the particular premises or whether they might be different premises. The particular premises could be 'substantially the same' if they are completed in a manner which substantially complies with the schedule of works accompanying the provisional statement application. If there is substantial compliance, the work will under s 29(7) be regarded as satisfactorily completed for the purposes of the provisional statement and, although the premises will not be as envisaged in the schedule of works, they may be 'substantially the same'. Equally, it is possible that different premises could be 'substantially the same'. If a number of new units were built in a leisure complex in an area to similar specification, a provisional statement was issued in respect of one unit and an application was made for a premises licence for another unit, the other unit premises could be 'substantially the same' as the unit premises for which the provisional statement was issued.

6.8.12   In order for the s 32 restrictions to apply, the premises licence application has to be in the same form as the application for the provisional statement and the work described in the schedule of works has to have been satisfactorily completed. Section 32(2) provides:

> Where–
>
> (a)  the application for the premises licence is an application for a licence in the same form as the licence described in the application for the provisional statement, and
>
> (b)  the work described in the schedule of works accompanying the application for that statement has been satisfactorily completed,[114]
>
> representations made by a person ("the relevant person") in respect of the application for the premises licence are excluded representations for the purposes of section 18(6)(d) if subsection (3) applies.[115]

It seems likely that an application will not be 'in the same form' if it relates to different licensable activities, although the position is less clear if it relates to the same licensable activities, but with some significant differences. The following example of where representations would *not* be excluded under s 33(1)(a) was given by Lord McIntosh, a Government spokesman, during the committee stage of the Bill in the House of Lords (HL Deb, vol 643, col 317, 16 January 2003):

> A builder may wish to construct a new night club and applies for a provisional state-ment setting out that the club will be open between eight o'clock and two o'clock for six days a week and provide music and dancing. The operator who takes a lease on the club may decide that he wants to stay open until four o'clock on Saturday nights and provide hot food between eleven and one. The builder could not have predicted that, but the information in the premises licence application would be different from that in the provisional statement application. Therefore, further representations could be made by responsible authorities or interested parties.

Here, the application relates both to different activities (hot food instead of just music and dancing) *and* some significant differences as regards the same licensable activities (music and dancing but ending at four o'clock on Saturday nights instead of two o'clock). Whilst, as regards the different activities, the application would not seem to be 'in the same form', whether further representations could be made if the application had only an increase in the hours for music and dancing is uncertain. In one sense it is 'in the same form' (same licensable activity), but in another sense it is not (different hours). It is not easy to predict how this expression, 'in the same form', will be interpreted and ultimately it will be a matter for the courts to decide.

6.8.13   The restrictions on the making of representations are set out in s 32(3), which provides:

> This subsection applies if–
>
> (a) given the information provided in the application for the provisional statement, the relevant person could have made the same, or substantially the same, repre-sentations about that application but failed to do so, without reasonable excuse, and
>
> (b) there has been no material change in circumstances relating either to the relevant premises or to the area in the vicinity of those premises.

The restrictions are, then, that representations cannot be made on the premises licence application in respect of matters upon which representations could have been made when the provisional statement was applied for. The restrictions will not, however, apply in two instances. The first instance is if the person wishing to make those representations has a reasonable excuse for not having made them at the time of the application for the provisional statement. An example given in Explanatory Note 81 is where a person is confined to hospital during the period in which representations could have been made and where arrangements could not have been put in place for representations to be made. This might be the case if the nature of the person's injuries or illness was such that he was unable to make representations, as where a person was unconscious or in a serious, unstable condition. A further example might be if a person had moved into the area in the period between the issuing of the provisional statement and the application for the premises licence.

The second instance where the restrictions will not apply is where there has been a material change in circumstances. As para 8.63 of the Guidance recognises,

> a great deal of time may pass between the issue of a provisional statement and the completion of a premises in accordance with a schedule of works. Genuine and material changes in circumstances may arise during the intervening years.

The material change can be either to the premises or to the area in the vicinity of the premises. A material change relating to the premises might be where they have increased in size through the use of additional storeys or through connection with adjoining property, or where use of an open terrace area is proposed. A material change relating to the area in the vicinity of the premises might include a case where there was a new development of residential properties near to the premises after the issuing of the provisional statement or where there had been a significant increase in the number of licensed premises nearby. The term 'vicinity' here, which is also used in s 13(3), will presumably have the same meaning as under that provision (see 6.4.13 above).

## 6.9    VARIATION OF PREMISES LICENCES

### 6.9.1   Generally

### 6.9.2   *Applications for variation*

Sections 34–36 make provision for variation of premises licences, except as regards a change in the designated premises supervisor, for which there is a separate procedure under s 37. Application is subject to the same fee as for the grant of a premises licence (see 6.3.1 above) and must be accompanied by the premises licence or, if this cannot be provided, a statement of the reasons why this cannot be produced. As with applications for the grant of a licence, provision is made as to the form of applications, advertisement, notification of responsible authorities and the period within which representations can be made (see 2.1.3 above). Section 34 provides:

(1) The holder of a premises licence may apply to the relevant licensing authority for variation of the licence.

(2) Subsection (1) is subject to regulations under–
  (a)  section 54 (form etc of applications etc);
  (b)  section 55 (fees to accompany applications etc).

(3) An application under this section must also be accompanied by the premises licence (or the appropriate part of that licence) or, if that is not practicable, by a statement of the reasons for the failure to provide the licence (or part).

(4) This section does not apply to an application within section 37(1) (application to vary licence to specify individual as premises supervisor).

(5) The power to make regulations under subsection (5) of section 17 (advertisement etc of application) applies in relation to applications under this section as it applies in relation to applications under that section.

Section 34(1), it seems, will encompass all applications to vary the licence in any way, other than to extend its duration (where it is time-limited) or to vary substantially the premises themselves. Such variations are not possible because they are excluded by s 36(6) (see 6.9.5 below). Otherwise, variations might include variation of the licence itself, such as a change in the licensable activities, variation of conditions attached to the licence or variation of the plan of the premises on the basis that this is part of the premises licence (see 2.1.10 above). The LA 2003 (PL and CPC) Regs 2005 specify the form the application shall take and the information that it must contain.[117] They also specify the requirements for advertising, the giving of notices to responsible authorities and for the making of relevant representations within a period of 28 consecutive days after the application was given to the authority.[118]

Variations sought may differ substantially, since some may be little more than minimal or trivial, whilst others may involve significant alterations to the terms of operation of the premises under the premises licence. Section 34, however, which (as indicated) requires advertising, plans and notices to responsible authorities, draws no distinction between the nature of variations sought. Thus, if all applications to vary need to be made under s 34, there will need to be compliance with these requirements in all cases. This might seem unduly onerous for minor variations which may well not have any impact on the licensing objectives. A number of authorities accordingly have, as a matter of practice, adopted an informal minor variation procedure without requiring a s 34 application. This might be justified on the basis that s 34(1) does not impose any obligation on a premises licence holder to apply for a variation, providing only that he 'may' do so, nor does it provide that a variation can be made by a licensing authority only when there is an application under s 34. Other authorites, however, have declined to follow this approach. Perhaps disappointingly, the Guidance provides no steer on how variation applications should be approached, which may reflect the view apparently held by the Government that the 2003 Act requires all variation applications to be dealt with under s 34, that there is no power to deal with minor variations on an informal basis, and that amending legislation is required if there is to be a departure from the s 34 variation procedure in cases which involve only minor variations. Such amending legislation may well be introduced in 2008 to standardise the procedure for minor variations, without any requirement for advertising and for limited giving of notices to responsible authorities.

### 6.9.3   *Determination of applications*

6.9.4    The procedure for determining applications for variation of a licence is set out in s 35. As a prerequisite to determining the application, the application must be made in accordance with s 34 and the authority must be satisfied that the requirements specified under s 34(5) are met (see 6.9.2 above). Section 35(1) provides:

> This section applies where the relevant licensing authority–
> (a)   receives an application, made in accordance with section 34, to vary a premises licence, and
> (b)   is satisfied that the applicant has complied with any requirement imposed on him by virtue of subsection (5) of that section.

It is perhaps doubtful whether a failure to comply with one of the requirements will entitle the authority to refuse to determine the application or invalidate any determination made. If, for instance, a responsible authority had not been notified of the application, but would not have made any relevant representations if it had been, no-one would have been prejudiced or disadvantaged in any way. It surely cannot have been Parliament's intention that the provision in s 35(1)(b) should be interpreted literally so that there cannot be a valid determination of a premises licence variation application under s 35 if there is a failure to comply *to any extent* with *any* requirement imposed on an applicant in respect of the making of an application. The proper construction to be given to s 35(1)(b) should be a purposive one, which requires consideration of whether Parliament can have intended total invalidity from a failure to comply with a statutory requirement. The proper approach here would seem to be to apply the principle in *R v Soneji and another* [2005] 4 All ER 321 (see 6.4.22 above) and focus on the consequences of noncompliance with the statutory requirement. Only if the consequences are sufficiently serious should failure to comply warrant any determination being invalid or entitle the authority to refuse to determine the application. Further, if the application is deficient only in minor respects, it might be expected that the authority would make any necessary amendements, for para 8.25 of the Guidance recommends that 'forms should not be returned if they contain obvious and minor factual errors that can easily be amended'.

The determination procedure is similar to that in respect of grant (see 6.4 above). If no relevant representations are received, the authority must grant the variation and, if there are representations, under reg 5 and para 3 of Sched 1 to the LA 2003 (Hearings) Regs 2005 a hearing must be held within 20 working days to determine what steps should be taken to promote the licensing objectives (unless this is dispensed with by agreement).[119] Notice of the hearing must be given to the applicant and persons who have made relevant representations no later than 10 working days before the day or the first day on which the hearing is to be held.[120] Section 35(2)-(3) provides:

(2)  Subject to subsection (3) and section 36(6),[121] the authority must grant the application.

(3)  Where relevant representations[122] are made, the authority must–

(a)  hold a hearing to consider them, unless the authority, the applicant and each person who has made such representations agree that a hearing is unnecessary, and

(b)  having regard to the representations, take such of the steps mentioned in subsection (4) (if any) as it considers necessary for the promotion of the licensing objectives.

Section 35(3)(b) envisages that no steps may be necessary (and makes provision for this through inclusion of the words 'if any') and, if this is felt to be the case, the variation requested can be granted in the terms sought. If steps are felt to be necessary, the steps that the authority can take include modifying the conditions (either by altering or omitting existing ones or adding new ones) or rejecting the whole or part of the application. Section 35(4) provides:

The steps are–

(a)  to modify the conditions of the licence;

(b)  to reject the whole or part of the application;

and for this purpose the conditions of the licence are modified if any of them is altered or omitted or any new condition is added.

The wording of s 35(4) gives no indication of whether or not these steps are in the alternative, but it seems to be implicit from the reference in s 35(3)(b) to taking 'such of the steps mentioned in subsection (4)' as considered necessary that both steps mentioned might be taken and that they are not alternatives. Thus, an authority might reject an application for an increase in hours whilst at the same time modifying the conditions of the licence, for example, by requiring the use of polycarbonate glasses.

Less clear is whether on a variation application to increase hours an authority might not only refuse to increase the existing hours, but actually reduce them. It is thought this would not be possible for a number of reasons. First, the times at which licensable activities can be carried out are not strictly conditions attached to the licence, but are part of the authorisation granted by the licence. On the format of the premises licence in Sch 12A to the LA 2003 (PL and CPC) Regs 2005, the times are specified in 'Part 1 Premises details' and do not appear in Annexes 1–3, which cover conditions. So, if s 35(4) is construed strictly, it confers the power only to modify conditions, the opening hours are not conditions and therefore existing opening hours cannot be reduced under s 35(4). Secondly, even if s 35(4) is broadly interpreted to include that which is authorised by the licence (whether as conditions or as premises details) and so includes the power to reduce existing opening hours, this can only be done under s 35(3)(b) if there are relevant representations and this is considered necessary to promote the licensing objectives. If existing hours have not given rise to any difficulties, it is hard to see how reducing the hours can be *necessary* to promote the licensing objectives. If relevant representations are received in respect of the application and are to the effect that existing hours should be reduced, it might reasonably be asked why those making representations have not sought a review of the licence, which would be the appropriate course of action to take. If any difficulties were not such as to justify seeking a review, then they should not be considered of sufficient weight to justify a reduction in existing hours on a variation application. Thirdly, where an application is for variation, the relevant issue for the authority to address is what effect the proposed variation, that is the proposed extension in hours, will have on the licensing objectives. If an authority was to reduce existing hours on a variation application, it would not be addressing this issue and might having regard to a consideration that may be relevant on a review application but is irrelevant on a variation application. As such, it may be acting unlawfully and outside the scope of its powers in relation to variations.

6.9.5   When modifying the conditions, the authority can vary the licence so that different conditions apply to different parts of the premises and in respect of different licensable activities. Provision for such variation is made by s 36, which contains supplementary provisions about determinations of applications. Section 36(7) provides:

> In discharging its duty under subsection (2) or (3) of that section [s 35], a licensing authority may vary a premises licence so that it has effect subject to different conditions in respect of–
> (a)  different parts of the premises concerned;
> (b)  different licensable activities.

A variation application in respect of which different conditions are attached to different parts of the premises might typically arise in respect of a variation sought for provision of a shelter for customers following the ban on smoking in indoor public places introduced by the Health Act 2006. Conditions relating to the outdoor area where the shelter is provided might restrict consumption of alcohol there to an earlier time than the time to which sale and consumption of alcohol may take place inside the premises. In addition, a condition may prevent re-entry to the inside areas of the premises by those who have gone into the outside areas (see 7.4.7 below). A variation application might similarly result in conditions being attached only in respect of some licensable actvities, as where there is a noise limiter condition for amplified music, although in other instances the application of conditions might extend to all licensable activities taking place on the premises, for example a condition requiring the exhibition of notices encouraging customers to leave the premises quietly and to respect the rights of people living nearby to a peaceful night.

The power of the authority to modify the conditions of the licence or grant the variation is, however, subject to some limitations. First, it is subject to the provisions of ss 19–21, which provide for the imposition of mandatory conditions relating to the supply of alcohol, the exhibition of films and licensed door supervisors (see 6.4.2–6.4.5 above). Section 35(7) provides:

> Subsections (2) and (3) are subject to sections 19, 20 and 21 (which require certain conditions to be included in premises licences).

Secondly, s 36(6) precludes an authority from varying the licence so as to extend the period of its duration or from making a substantial variation in respect of the premises. It provides:

> A licence may not be varied under section 35 so as–
> (a) to extend the period for which the licence has effect; or
> (b) to vary substantially the premises to which it relates.

Premises licences in most instances will be of an indefinite duration and no question of extending the period will arise, but it is possible for applicants to include in their operating schedule a request for the licence to have effect for a limited period, for example if they wish to hold music concerts only at certain times of the year (see 6.7.1 above). If the licence is granted for a limited duration, s 36(6)(a) precludes any variation that extends the licence's duration and, if an extension is required, it will be necessary for an application for a new premises licence to be made. An application for a new premises licence will similarly be required by virtue of s 36(6)(b) if there is a substantial variation to the premises to which an existing premises licence relates.

### 6.9.6   Notification of decision

The authority must notify its decision to the applicant, the police and any person who made relevant representations. Where the authority decides to grant the variation, persons who made relevant representations must be given reasons for the decision and the notice must specify the time when the variation is to take effect. Section 36(1)-(3) provides:

(1) Where an application (or any part an application) is granted under section 35, the relevant licensing authority must forthwith give a notice to that effect to–

    (a) the applicant,

    (b) any person who made relevant representations[123] in respect of the application, and

    (c) the chief officer of police for the police area (or each police area) in which the premises are situated.

(2) Where relevant representations were made in respect of the application, the notice under subsection (1) must state the authority's reasons for its decision as to the steps (if any) to take under section 35(3)(b).

(3) The notice under subsection (1) must specify the time when the variation in question takes effect.

That time is the time specified in the application or, if that time is before the applicant is given that notice, such later time as the relevant licensing authority specifies in the notice.

Where the authority decides not to grant the variation, similar notification of its decision is required. Section 36(4) provides:

Where an application (or any part an application) is rejected under section 35, the relevant licensing authority must forthwith give a notice to that effect stating its reasons for rejecting the application to–

(a) the applicant,

(b) any person who made relevant representations in respect of the application, and

(c) the chief officer of police for the police area (or each police area) in which the premises are situated.

Whether the variation application is granted or rejected, notification is required 'forthwith', the meaning of which has been considered in 6.6.2 above.

### 6.9.7   Variation of the licence to change the premises supervisor

### *6.9.8   Applications for variation*

6.9.9    Where the premises licence holder wishes to change the DPS, s 37 prescribes a separate procedure. Change may take the form of either naming a person in the licence as DPS, if no person was previously named and the premises licence holder himself was the DPS, or substituting a different person for the person currently named. Application by the premises licence holder, for which a fee of £23 is payable under reg 8 and Sched 6 to the LA 2003 (Fees) Regs 2005, must be accompanied by the premises licence (or, if this cannot be provided, a statement of the reasons why this cannot be produced) and a form of consent by the person who it is proposed will become the DPS. Section 37(1)-(3) provides:

(1) The holder of a premises licence may–

(a) if the licence authorises the supply of alcohol, or

(b) if he has applied under section 34 to vary the licence so that it authorises such supplies,

apply to vary the licence so as to specify the individual named in the application ("the proposed individual") as the premises supervisor.

(2) Subsection (1) is subject to regulations under–

(a) section 54 (form etc of applications etc);

(b) section 55 (fees to accompany applications etc).

(3) An application under this section must also be accompanied by–

(a) a form of consent in the prescribed form given by the proposed individual, and

(b) the premises licence (or appropriate part of that licence) or, if that is not practicable, a statement of the reasons for the failure to provide the licence (or part).

Regulation 13 and Sched 5 to the LA 2003 (PL and CPC) Regs 2005 specify the form the application shall take and the information that it must contain, and reg 24(1) and Pt A of Sched 11 specify the form of consent for the individual who the applicant wishes to have specified in the licence as the premises supervisor. There is no requirement to advertise the application – presumably because changing the premises supervisor is not seen as having any impact on the surrounding area – but notice of the application has to be given to the police and the current DPS (if there is one). Section 37(4) provides:

> The holder of the premises licence must give notice of his application–
>
> (a)  to the chief officer of police for the police area (or each police area) in which the premises are situated, and
>
> (b)  to the designated premises supervisor (if there is one).

Under reg 28(a) of the LA 2003 (PL and CPC) Regs 2005, notice takes the form of the premises licence holder giving the police and (if applicable) the DPS a copy of the application together with any accompanying documents on the same day as he gives the application to the licensing authority. The reason the current DPS needs to be notified is so that he is aware that he will no longer have responsibility as the premises supervisor and the police are to be notified so that they can object if they feel that there are exceptional circumstances whereby the granting of the application to change the DPS would undermine the crime prevention objective.[124] The police can object by giving notice within 14 days and must provide reasons for their decision. Section 37(5) and (6) provides:

> (5)  Where a chief officer of police notified under subsection (4) is satisfied that the exceptional circumstances of the case are such that granting the application would undermine the crime prevention objective, he must give the relevant licensing authority a notice stating the reasons why he is so satisfied.
>
> (6)  The chief officer of police must give that notice within the period of 14 days beginning with the day on which he is notified of the application under subsection (4).

6.9.10  An applicant who seeks a variation can, under s 38(1), include a request that it should have immediate effect. This is a particularly important facility to enable the premises licence holder to continue the supply of alcohol if, for some reason, difficulties arise in relation to the existing DPS. If there is no DPS in respect of the premises, there can be no supply of alcohol under the premises licence, as there is a mandatory condition under s 19(2)(a) that there can be no supplies at a time when there is no DPS in respect of the premises licence (see 6.4.2 above). Section 38(1) provides:

> This section applies where an application made in accordance with section 37, in respect of a premises licence which authorises the supply of alcohol, includes a request that the variation applied for should have immediate effect.

Difficulties may arise in relation to the existing DPS if, for instance, he suddenly becomes indisposed or unable to work (Explanatory Note 87). The incapacity of the existing DPS will not, however, necessarily prevent the continued supply of alcohol since, so long as the existing DPS remains designated as the premises supervisor, any other personal licence holder can authorise the supply of alcohol; but it may prevent the continued supply of alcohol in the cases of small outlets where there are no other personal licence holders apart from the DPS. In such cases, a request for the variation to have immediate effect would be important, since making a change in the DPS under s 37 may take some time, which could have an adverse effect on the operation of premises. Difficulties may also arise if a dispute arises between the DPS and his employer over some matter, for example misappropriation of company money, as a

result of which the DPS may give notice under s 41 to the licensing authority requesting his removal as DPS (see 6.9.14 below). Here, the continued supply of alcohol may
well be at risk because, under s 41(7) and (8), as soon as notice is received by the
licensing authority the individual is to be treated as if he were not the DPS (although
under s 41(4) there is no requirement to notify the premises licence holder for 48
hours). From the point that notice is received there is no DPS in respect of the
premises and accordingly, as indicated above, there can be no supply of alcohol under
the premises licence. If this were to happen in the case of popular premises over a
bank holiday weekend, this could have serious implications, not only for the owner of
the premises in terms of lost custom, but also for the police in terms of potential crime
and disorder if suddenly alcohol, apparently inexplicably, could not be sold at the
premises. Further, making a variation application with immediate effect will be
difficult in such circumstances as these, given that licensing authority premises will
be closed over the weekend period. Although provision is made for electronic communication in reg 21(2) of the LA 2003 (PL and CPC) Regs 2005, the application is not
to be treated as given, under reg 21(3), until the fee has been received by the licensing
authority (see 2.1.5 above).

6.9.11   Where a request is made for variation to have immediate effect, under s 38(2),
the change in DPS has immediate effect as soon as the application is made. The period
for which the variation has immediate effect is determined, under s 37(3), by reference
to the outcome of the application. If the application is granted, it will have immediate
effect until the variation takes effect (s 38(3)(b)(i)). In effect, there will be no change
here – the interim immediate effect will cease to operate at this point (when the
application is granted) and the new DPS will become the premises supervisor for the
premises licence. If the application is rejected, it will have immediate effect only until
the time the rejection is notified to the applicant (s 38(3)(b)(ii)). At this point, the
licence will revert to the form that it took before the application was made. This will
mean that old DPS (if there was one) or the premises licence holder (if there was not
a DPS) will continue to be the premises supervisor. If the application is withdrawn
before it is determined, it will have immediate effect only until the time of the withdrawal (s 38(3)(b)(iii)). From this point, the position will be the same as if the application had been rejected, that is the licence will revert to the form that it took before the
application was made. Section 38(2) and (3) provides:

(2)  By virtue of this section, the premises licence has effect during the application
     period as if it were varied in the manner set out in the application.
(3)  For this purpose "the application period" means the period which–
     (a)  begins when the application is received by the relevant licensing authority,
          and
     (b)  ends–
          (i)   if the application is granted, when the variation takes effect,
          (ii)  if the application is rejected, at the time the rejection is notified to the
                applicant, and
          (iii) if the application is withdrawn before it is determined, at the time of the
                withdrawal.

It seems the variation will have immediate effect, even if the police feel that there
are exceptional circumstances whereby the granting of the application to change the
DPS would undermine the crime prevention objective. Whilst the police can object on

these grounds under s 37(5), they can do so only when notified of the application and any objection will become effective only if upheld by the licensing authority when it determines and rejects the application. This might be regarded as a weakness in the provision, since someone who is completely unsuitable can, albeit for a limited period of time pending determination of the application, become the premises supervisor.

Whether the variation will have immediate effect under s 38(2) if the request for it to do so is not included in the application is uncertain. Section 38(1) refers to 'where an application made in accordance with section 37 . . . includes a request', which suggests that the request has to be included in the application. If this provision is given a literal interpretation, where a request is made at any point subsequent to the application, but before its determination, it would seem that the variation will not have immediate effect by virtue of s 38(2); but there may be circumstances where the premises licence holder might wish it to have immediate effect in this interim period. There may, for instance, be no perceived need for a variation to have immediate effect at the time of the application and no such request may be made, for the existing DPS may not intend to depart until the application is determined; but replacement of the existing DPS may be needed sooner than envisaged, ahead of his intended time of departure, if he suddenly becomes indisposed or unable to work once the application has been made. Such a situation might perhaps be avoided if s 38(1) were given a purposive interpretation. The purpose of the provision is to enable a variation to have immediate effect where circumstances necessitate this and these might just as easily exist when the application is made or when it has been made, but before its determination. A purposive interpretation of 'includes' in s 38(1) might encompass both inclusion at the time of the application and inclusion at any subsequent point ahead of determination. This would avoid the need to make a fresh application with a request for the variation to have immediate effect, as will be necessary if the section is interpreted so as to require the request to be included in the application. However, since either interpretation is possible, perhaps the safest course is for a fresh application to be made.

### 6.9.12 Determination of applications

The procedure here is very similar to that which applies for variations generally.[125] Thus, the application has to be made in accordance with the statutory provisions, in this case s 37; it must be granted if unopposed; if opposed (by the police giving notice that grant would undermine the crime prevention objective), under reg 5 and para 4 of Sched 1 to the LA 2003 (Hearings) Regs 2005 a hearing must be held within 20 working days unless the parties consider this unnecessary; and the application must be refused if the authority is satisfied it is necessary to promote the crime prevention objective. Notice of the hearing must be given to the applicant, the police and the individual proposed as the new premises supervisor, no later than 10 working days before the day or the first day on which the hearing is to be held.[126] Section 39(1)-(3) provides:

(1) This section applies where an application is made, in accordance with section 37, to vary a premises licence so as to specify a new premises supervisor ("the proposed individual").

(2) Subject to subsection (3), the relevant licensing authority must grant the application.

(3) Where a notice is given under section 37(5) (and not withdrawn), the authority must–

    (a) hold a hearing to consider it, unless the authority, the applicant and the chief officer of police who gave the notice agree that a hearing is unnecessary, and

    (b) having regard to the notice, reject the application if it considers it necessary for the promotion of the crime prevention objective to do so.

## 6.9.13 Notification of decision

Whether the application is granted or rejected, notice must be given by the authority to the applicant, the proposed individual who will become the DPS and the chief officer of police for the police area(s) where the premises are situated.[127] Where notice was given by the police to oppose the variation, the notice given by the authority under s 39(4) must state the authority's reasons for granting or rejecting the application and, where the application is granted, the authority's notice must specify the time when the variation takes effect. This will be the time specified in the application or, if the applicant is given notice after that time, such later time as the authority specifies in the notice. Section 39(4)–(6) provides:

(4) Where an application under section 37 is granted or rejected, the relevant licensing authority must give a notice to that effect to–

    (a) the applicant,

    (b) the proposed individual, and

    (c) the chief officer of police for the police area (or each police area) in which the premises are situated.

(5) Where a chief officer of police gave a notice under subsection (5) of that section (and it was not withdrawn), the notice under subsection (4) of this section must state the authority's reasons for granting or rejecting the application.

(6) Where the application is granted, the notice under subsection (4) must specify the time when the variation takes effect.

That time is the time specified in the application or, if that time is before the applicant is given that notice, such later time as the relevant licensing authority specifies in the notice.

Once the applicant has been given notice of the decision under s 39(4), he must forthwith notify the person who was the current DPS when the application was made, provided there was such a person and the applicant himself (as premises licence holder) was not the DPS. Section 40(1) provides:

Where the holder of a premises licence is notified under section 39(4), he must forthwith–

    (a) if his application has been granted, notify the person (if any) who has been replaced as the designated premises supervisor of the variation, and

    (b) if his application has been rejected, give the designated premises supervisor (if any) notice to that effect.

Failure to comply, without reasonable excuse, is a summary offence punishable by a level 3 fine (s 40(2)(3)).

## 6.9.14 Request to be removed as premises supervisor

Section 41 makes provision for an individual to secure his removal as DPS where he no longer wishes to act in this capacity in respect of the premises licence. Section 41(1) provides:

> Where an individual wishes to cease being the designated premises supervisor in respect of a premises licence, he may give the relevant licensing authority a notice to that effect.

The notice, which must be in prescribed form,[128] must be accompanied by the premises licence or appropriate part of it where the premises licence holder is the DPS (or, if he is unable to produce it, a statement of reasons). In cases where the DPS is another individual, that individual must give the premises licence holder a copy of the notice that he has given to the licensing authority (indicating that he no longer wishes to be the DPS) and a notice directing the premises licence holder to send to the licensing authority within 14 days the premises licence or appropriate part of it (or, if unable to do so, a statement of reasons). These must be given to the premises licence holder within 48 hours of the giving of the notice under s 41(1). Section 41(3) and (4) provides:

> (3) Where the individual is the holder of the premises licence, the notice under subsection (1) must also be accompanied by the premises licence (or the appropriate part of the licence) or, if that is not practicable, by a statement of the reasons for the failure to provide the licence (or part).
>
> (4) In any other case, the individual must no later than 48 hours after giving the notice under subsection (1) give the holder of the premises licence–
>
>> (a) a copy of that notice, and
>>
>> (b) a notice directing the holder to send to the relevant licensing authority within 14 days of receiving the notice–
>>
>>> (i) the premises licence (or the appropriate part of the licence), or
>>>
>>> (ii) if that is not practicable, a statement of the reasons for the failure to provide the licence (or part).

When so notified, the authority can then make the appropriate change in the licensing register.[129] Failure to comply with the above requirements, without reasonable excuse, is a summary offence punishable by a level 3 fine (s 41(5)(6)). Where the requirements are complied with, the person requesting removal will cease to be the DPS from the time the notice (under s 41(1)) containing the request is received by the licensing authority or any later time specified in the notice. Section 41(7) and (8) provides:

> (7) Where an individual–
>
>> (a) gives the relevant licensing authority a notice in accordance with this section, and
>>
>> (b) satisfies the requirements of subsection (3) or (4),
>>
>> he is to be treated for the purposes of this Act as if, from the relevant time, he were not the designated premises supervisor.
>
> (8) For this purpose "the relevant time" means–
>
>> (a) the time the notice under subsection (1) is received by the relevant licensing authority, or
>>
>> (b) if later, the time specified in the notice.

The effect of the above provisions seems to be that the individual ceases to be the DPS once the notice indicating he no longer wishes to act in this capacity is received by the authority. If, prior to this time, an application to vary the licence to change the DPS with immediate effect has been made by the premises licence holder, the premises will continue to have a DPS. However, if this is not the case, there may be no DPS in respect of the premises licence, in which case no alcohol can be sold under s 19(2)(a) (see 6.4.2–6.4.3 above) until such time as the premises licence is varied to change the DPS.

## 6.10   TRANSFER OF PREMISES LICENCES

### 6.10.1 Applications

6.10.2 Any person entitled to apply for a premises licence under s 16(1) (see 6.2 above) may apply to the licensing authority for a transfer of a premises licence to him and, where he is an individual, must be aged 18 or over. Section 42(1) and (2) provides:

(1) Subject to this section, any person mentioned in section 16(1) (applicant for premises licence) may apply to the relevant licensing authority for the transfer of a premises licence to him.

(2) Where the applicant is an individual he must be aged 18 or over.

A transfer will only change the identity of the holder of the licence and does not alter the licence in any other way (Guidance, para 8.66). The procedure for applications for transfer of a licence is similar to that in respect of applications for variation (see 6.9.4–6.9.5 above). Thus an application must be in prescribed form,[130] accompanied by the prescribed fee (which under reg 8 and Sched 6 to the LA 2003 (Fees) Regs 2005 is £23), and by the premises licence or, if that is not practicable, a statement of the reasons for failure to provide the licence. Notice of the application must be given to the chief officer of police for the police area(s) in which the premises are situated[131] and, if he is satisfied that the exceptional circumstances of the case are such that the granting of the application would undermine the crime prevention objective, he must give the licensing authority a notice stating the reasons why he is so satisfied.[132] This notice must be given within 14 days beginning with the day on which notification of the application is given.[133] Section 42(3)–(7) provides:

(3) Subsection (1) is subject to regulations under–
    (a) section 54 (form etc of applications etc);
    (b) section 55 (fees to accompany applications etc).

(4) An application under this section must also be accompanied by the premises licence or, if that is not practicable, a statement of the reasons for the failure to provide the licence.

(5) The applicant must give notice of his application to the chief officer of police for the police area (or each police area) in which the premises are situated.

(6) Where a chief officer of police notified under subsection (5) is satisfied that the exceptional circumstances of the case are such that granting the application would undermine the crime prevention objective, he must give the relevant licensing authority a notice stating the reasons why he is so satisfied.

(7) The chief officer of police must give that notice within the period of 14 days beginning with the day on which he is notified of the application under subsection (5).

6.10.3  As in the case of an application to vary the premises licence by changing the DPS (see s 38(1) and 6.9.10 above), an application to transfer the licence can include a request that the transfer has immediate effect. Section 43(1) and (2) provides:

(1) Where–
   (a) an application made in accordance with section 42 includes a request that the transfer have immediate effect, and
   (b) the requirements of this section are met,
   then, by virtue of this section, the premises licence has effect during the application period as if the applicant were the holder of the licence.
(2) For this purpose "the application period" means the period which–
   (a) begins when the application is received by the relevant licensing authority, and
   (b) ends–
      (i) when the licence is transferred following the grant of the application, or
      (ii) if the application is rejected, when the applicant is notified of the rejection, or
      (iii) when the application is withdrawn.

The effect of this provision is to allow licensable activities to be carried on at the premises without interruption, pending the determination of an application to transfer.[134] Where there is a request under s 43(1) for the transfer to have immediate effect and there is a DPS in respect of the premises licence, the applicant must forthwith notify the DPS of the application, except (obviously) in cases where the applicant himself is the DPS. Further, he must notify the DPS if the transfer application is granted. Section 46(1)–(3) provides:

(1) This section applies where–
   (a) an application is made in accordance with section 42 to transfer a premises licence in respect of which there is a designated premises supervisor, and
   (b) the applicant and that supervisor are not the same person.
(2) Where section 43(1) applies in relation to the application, the applicant must forthwith notify the designated premises supervisor of the application.
(3) If the application is granted, the applicant must forthwith notify the designated premises supervisor of the transfer.[135]

6.10.4  In addition, if the applicant requests the transfer to have immediate effect, he must generally obtain the consent of the premises licence holder to the making of the application, although no provision is made for failure to obtain consent to constitute a criminal offence. The procedure for obtaining consent is specified in reg 24(2) and Pt B of Sched 11 to the LA 2003 (PL and CPC) Regs 2005.[136] Consent is, however, not required in two cases: first, if the applicant himself is the holder of the premises licence by virtue of an interim authority under s 47 (see 6.11.1–6.11.11 below) and he is making the application for transfer of the licence into his own name; secondly, if the applicant has taken all reasonable steps to obtain consent and is in a position to use the premises immediately for the licensable activities authorised by the licence. Section 43(3)–(5) provides:

(3) Subject to subsections (4) and (5), an application within subsection (1)(a) may be made only with the consent of the holder of the premises licence.

(4) Where a person is the holder of the premises licence by virtue of an interim authority notice under section 47, such an application may also be made by that person.

(5) The relevant licensing authority must exempt the applicant from the requirement to obtain the holder's consent if the applicant shows to the authority's satisfaction–

    (a) that he has taken all reasonable steps to obtain that consent, and

    (b) that, if the application were one to which subsection (1) applied, he would be in a position to use the premises during the application period for the licensable activity or activities authorised by the premises licence.

The exemption in s 43(5) from obtaining the premises licence holder's consent for a transfer to have immediate effect, which similarly applies in respect of the transfer application itself (see s 44(6) and 6.10.5 below), seems appropriate to cover instances where the applicant for some reason, despite his best efforts, is not in a position to obtain consent. This might be the case, for example, where the premises licence holder lacks capacity to grant consent or cannot be traced. In such cases, although all reasonable steps may be taken to obtain consent, the applicant will be unable to obtain a decision on consent. If he is in a position to use the premises, he might be exempted from the requirement for obtaining consent.

Less clear is whether the exemption might apply where the applicant has sought consent but this has been refused by the premises licence holder. Whilst the provision on its wording seems wide enough to cover such a case, if the view is taken that a request for consent constitutes taking 'all reasonable steps to obtain that consent', it might be doubted whether the exemption should apply here. The underlying Parliamentary intention seems to be to enable an application and a transfer to proceed in circumstances where it is not possible for an applicant to obtain a decision from the premises licence holder on the matter of consent, if he can show that all reasonable steps have been taken by him to try to obtain that consent. It seems unlikely that Parliament would have intended an application and transfer to proceed where the premises licence holder has expressly refused consent, since this might violate his right to protection of his property under Article 1 Protocol 1 of the European Convention on Human Rights (see 3.6 above). There may be an interference with the premises licence holder's economic interests arising from the running of the premises under the premises licence (see *Tre Traktörer Aktiebolag v Sweden* (1991) 13 EHRR 309 and 3.6.2 above) and this interference may not be necessary in accordance with the general interest for advancing the public good, because it does not promote the licensing objectives and/or it imposes a disproportionate burden on him because of the impact it has on his property rights (see 3.6.8 above).

In cases where an authority refuses to exempt an applicant under s 43(5), it must notify the applicant of its reasons for that decision (s 43(6)). In such a case, as Explanatory Note 94 states, the applicant ceases to be treated as the holder of the licence under this section and the licence reverts to the person who held it before the application was made.

## 6.10.5 Determination of applications

The procedure is similar to that which applies for variation of the licence to change the premises supervisor (see 6.9.12 above). Thus the application has to be made in accordance with the statutory provisions, in this case s 42, and it must, in general, be transferred.[137] There are, however, two cases where a transfer is not mandatory. First, where the application has been accompanied by a request that the transfer has immediate effect under s 43, the authority must reject the application unless the premises licence holder consents to the transfer or the applicant is exempted from the need to obtain consent. Section 44(1)–(4) provides:

(1)  This section applies where an application for the transfer of a licence is made in accordance with section 42.

(2)  Subject to subsections (3) and (5), the authority must transfer the licence in accordance with the application.

(3)  The authority must reject the application if none of the conditions in subsection (4) applies.

(4)  The conditions are–

    (a)  that section 43(1) (applications given interim effect) applies to the application,

    (b)  that the holder of the premises licence consents to the transfer, or

    (c)  that the applicant is exempted under subsection (6) from the requirement to obtain the holder's consent to the transfer.

The applicant will be exempt from the need to obtain consent if he has taken reasonable steps to obtain the consent and is in a position to use the premises. Section 44(6) provides:

The relevant licensing authority must exempt the applicant from the requirement to obtain the holder's consent if the applicant shows to the authority's satisfaction–

(a)  that he has taken all reasonable steps to obtain that consent, and

(b)  that, if the application were granted, he would be in a position to use the premises for the licensable activity or activities authorised by the premises licence.[138]

Secondly, if the application has been opposed (by the police giving notice under s 42(6) that grant would undermine the crime prevention objective), a hearing must be held unless the parties consider this unnecessary and the application must be refused if the authority is satisfied it is necessary to promote the crime prevention objective. Section 44(5) provides:

Where a notice is given under section 42(6) (and not withdrawn), and subsection (3) above does not apply, the authority must–

(a)  hold a hearing to consider it, unless the authority, the applicant and the chief officer of police who gave the notice agree that a hearing is unnecessary, and

(b)  having regard to the notice, reject the application if it considers it necessary for the promotion of the crime prevention objective to do so.

The hearing must be held within 20 working days[139] and notice of the hearing must be given to the person applying for transfer, the police and the premises licence holder no later than 10 working days before the day or the first day on which the hearing is to be held.[140]

## 6.10.6 Notification of decision

Whether the application is granted or rejected, notice must be given by the authority to the applicant and to the chief officer of police for the police area(s) in which the premises are situated.[141] Where notice was given by the police under s 42(6) to oppose the transfer, the notice given by the authority under s 45(1) must state the authority's reasons for granting or rejecting the application and, where the application is granted, the authority's notice must specify the time when the transfer takes effect.[142] Section 45(1)–(3) provides:

> (1) Where an application under section 42 is granted or rejected, the relevant licensing authority must give a notice to that effect to–
>     (a) the applicant, and
>     (b) the chief officer of police for the police area (or each police area) in which the premises are situated.
> (2) Where a chief officer of police gave a notice under subsection (6) of that section (and it was not withdrawn) the notice under subsection (1) of this section must state the licensing authority's reasons for granting or rejecting the application.
> (3) Where the application is granted, the notice under subsection (1) must specify the time when the transfer takes effect.

In addition, the authority must give a copy of the notice to the person who was the premises licence holder before the application for transfer was granted or before it was given interim effect (in cases where the application contained a request under s 43 for the transfer to have immediate effect). Section 45(4) provides:

> The relevant licensing authority must also give a copy of the notice given under subsection (1)–
> (a) where the application is granted–
>     (i) to the holder of the licence immediately before the application was granted, or
>     (ii) if the application was one to which section 43(1) applied, to the holder of the licence immediately before the application was made (if any),
> (b) where the application is rejected, to the holder of the premises licence (if any).

Further, in cases where there is a DPS in respect of the premises licence and the application included a request that the transfer has immediate effect, the applicant must forthwith notify the DPS of the transfer if it is granted (see 6.10.3 above).

## 6.11 REINSTATEMENT OF PREMISES LICENCE FOLLOWING LAPSE: INTERIM AUTHORITY NOTICES AND TRANSFER APPLICATIONS HAVING IMMEDIATE EFFECT

### 6.11.1 Introduction

A premises licence, although generally remaining in force indefinitely, can lapse either due to some incapacity on the part of the licence holder or on surrender,[143] but it can be reinstated, within a period of seven days, in one of two ways. One is by the giving of an interim authority notice (IAN) under s 47 and the other is by a transfer application having immediate effect under s 50. The latter might be an appropriate course if there was someone in a position to take over immediately as premises licence holder and to whom the licence could be transferred with immediate effect. Where this is not possible, the former provides an interim authority to carry out the licensable activities until a transfer can be effected at a later date.

## 6.11.2 Reinstatement by interim authority notice

### 6.11.3 *Giving a notice*

6.11.4   A notice can be given where a licence has lapsed due to death, incapacity or insolvency of the premises licence holder and no application has been made for a transfer application to have immediate effect under s 43. Such events may be sudden and unforeseen, leaving little time to make arrangements for transfer, let alone immediate transfer, and the IAN will enable a business to continue in the meantime. As the Guidance, para 8.70 states, the Act:

> provides special arrangements for the continuation of permissions under a premises licence when the holder of a licence dies suddenly or becomes bankrupt or mentally incapable. In the normal course of events, the licence would lapse in such circumstances. However, there may also be some time before, for example, the deceased person's estate can be dealt with or an administrative receiver appointed. This could have a damaging effect on those with interests in the premises, such as an owner, lessor or employees working at the premises in question; and could bring unnecessary disruption to customers' plans. The Act therefore provides for the licence to be capable of being reinstated in a discrete period of time in certain circumstances.

In such circumstances, an IAN may be given to the licensing authority, either by a person with a 'prescribed interest' in the premises or by a person 'connected to' the person who held the premises licence immediately before lapse, within seven days beginning with the day after the licence lapsed.[144] Section 47(1) and (2) provides:

> (1)   This section applies where–
>
>   (a)   a premises licence lapses under section 27 in a case within subsection (1)(a), (b) or (c) of that section (death, incapacity or insolvency of the holder), but
>
>   (b)   no application for transfer of the licence has been made by virtue of section 50 (reinstatement of licence on transfer following death etc).
>
> (2)   A person who–
>
>   (a)   has a prescribed interest in the premises concerned, or
>
>   (b)   is connected to the person who held the premises licence immediately before it lapsed ("the former holder"),
>
> may, during the initial seven day period, give to the relevant licensing authority a notice (an "interim authority notice") in respect of the licence.

6.11.5   Persons with a 'prescribed interest' in the premises are those with a legal interest in the premises as freeholder or leaseholder.[145] Those 'connected to' the former holder of the licence are his personal representative (for death), a person with a power of attorney (for incapacity) or his insolvency practitioner (for insolvency). Section 47(5) provides:

> For the purposes of subsection (2) a person is connected to the former holder of the premises licence if, and only if–
>
> (a)   the former holder has died and that person is his personal representative,

(b) the former holder lacks capacity (within the meaning of the Mental Capacity Act 2005) to hold the licence and that person acts for him under an enduring power of attorney or lasting power of attorney registered under that Act,[146] or

(c) the former holder has become insolvent and that person is his insolvency practitioner.[147]

The initial seven-day period within which notification must be given, which means seven days beginning with the day after the licence lapsed,[148] is not a particularly long period given the traumatic effect that death may have on the personal representative. The personal representative will often be a spouse or other close relative and it would be understandable if, within such a short period, the giving of an IAN were to be overlooked. If it this were to occur, there would be no further opportunity to give an IAN, since s 47(4) provides: 'Only one interim authority notice may be given under subsection (2).' Further, if the licence is not to lapse after the initial seven-day period, a copy of the IAN must be given to the chief officer of police for the police area(s) in which the premises are situated before the end of that period (s 47(7)(a)).[149] Again, it would be understandable if this were to be overlooked.

Once an IAN has been given to the licensing authority, it must issue to the person giving the notice a copy of the licence and summary of the licence in the form in which they existed immediately before the licence lapsed, except for specifying as the premises licence holder the person who gave the IAN. Section 49, which makes supplementary provision for IANs, provides in sub-ss (1) and (2):

(1) On receipt of an interim authority notice, the relevant licensing authority must issue to the person who gave the notice a copy of the licence and a copy of the summary (in each case certified by the authority to be a true copy).

(2) The copies issued under this section must be copies of the premises licence and summary in the form in which they existed immediately before the licence lapsed under section 27, except that they must specify the person who gave the interim authority notice as the person who is the holder.[150]

## 6.11.6 Effect of a notice

6.11.7 The effect of giving an IAN is to reinstate the premises licence in the name of the person giving the notice and thereby allow licensable activities to continue to take place, pending a formal application for transfer (Guidance, para 8.73). Section 47(6) provides:

Where an interim authority notice is given in accordance with this section–

(a) the premises licence is reinstated from the time the notice is received by the relevant licensing authority, and

(b) the person who gave the notice is from that time the holder of the licence.

Whilst the giving of an IAN will reinstate the premises licence, it seems, however, that no licensable activities will be able to take place after the premises licence has lapsed, but before the IAN is given. This is because no premises licence is in existence during this period of time.[151] Where the premises licence is reinstated and a person becomes the holder of it by virtue of this provision, he must, unless he is the DPS under the licence, forthwith notify the DPS (if any) of the IAN (s 49(4)). Failure to comply with this requirement, without reasonable excuse, is a summary offence punishable with a fine not exceeding level 3 on the standard scale (s 49(5)(6)).

6.11.8 Although reinstatement of the premises licence has immediate effect on receipt of the IAN, the licence will lapse again thereafter in two cases; first, as indicated above, if at the end of the initial seven-day period a copy of the notice has not been given to the police;[152] secondly, if an application for transfer with a request under s 43 for the transfer to have immediate effect has not been made at the end of the interim authority period (s 47(7)(b)), which is a period of up to two months from the time when the authority received the IAN.[153] The transfer application can be, but need not be, by the person giving the IAN and, if unsuccessful or withdrawn, will result in the licence lapsing again. Section 47(7)–(9) provides:

> (7) But the premises licence lapses again–
>> (a) at the end of the initial seven day period unless before that time the person who gave the interim authority notice has given a copy of the notice to the chief officer of police for the police area (or each police area) in which the premises are situated;
>> (b) at the end of the interim authority period, unless before that time a relevant transfer application[154] is made to the relevant licensing authority.
> (8) Nothing in this section prevents the person who gave the interim authority notice from making a relevant transfer application.
> (9) If–
>> (a) a relevant transfer application is made during the interim authority period, and
>> (b) that application is rejected or withdrawn,
> the licence lapses again at the time of the rejection or withdrawal.

### 6.11.9 Cancellation of notice following police objections

6.11.10 The police can object within 48 hours of being notified of an IAN, but only if satisfied that exceptional circumstances mean that failure to cancel the IAN would undermine the crime prevention objective (Explanatory Note 100). A notice to this effect must be given to the licensing authority. Section 48(1) and (2) provides:

> (1) This section applies where–
>> (a) an interim authority notice by a person ("the relevant person") is given in accordance with section 47,
>> (b) the chief officer of police for the police area (or each police area) in which the premises are situated is given a copy of the interim authority notice before the end of the initial seven day period (within the meaning of that section), and
>> (c) that chief officer (or any of those chief officers) is satisfied that the exceptional circumstances of the case are such that a failure to cancel the interim authority notice would undermine the crime prevention objective.
> (2) The chief officer of police must no later than 48 hours after he receives the copy of the interim authority notice give the relevant licensing authority a notice stating why he is so satisfied.

The licensing authority must then hold a hearing within five working days[155] to decide whether or not to cancel the IAN, unless the parties agree that this is unnecessary. The need to deal with such matters speedily is emphasised by the Guidance in para 8.72: 'In respect of these matters, it is expected that licensing authorities will be alert to the urgency of the circumstances and the need to consider the objection quickly.' If the authority decides cancellation is necessary for the promotion of the crime prevention objective, it must notify the person who has given the IAN and the police no later than two working days before the day or the first day on which the hearing is to be held,[156] together with the authority's reasons for its decision. Section 48(3)–(5) provides:

(3) Where a notice is given by the chief officer of police (and not withdrawn), the authority must–

    (a) hold a hearing to consider it, unless the authority, the relevant person and the chief officer of police agree that a hearing is unnecessary, and

    (b) having regard to the notice given by the chief officer of police, cancel the interim authority notice if it considers it necessary for the promotion of the crime prevention objective to do so.

(4) An interim authority notice is cancelled under subsection (3)(b) by the licensing authority giving the relevant person a notice stating that it is cancelled and the authority's reasons for its decision.

(5) The licensing authority must give a copy of a notice under subsection (4) to the chief officer of police for the police area (or each police area) in which the premises are situated.

6.11.11 If the IAN is cancelled, the premises licence lapses when the authority gives notice to the person who gave the IAN (although the licence may be reinstated by an appeal against cancellation – see 12.5.5 below). The authority is, however, only able to cancel the IAN up to the time an application for transfer with a request for this to have immediate effect is made. Section 48(6) and (7) provides:

(6) The premises licence lapses if, and when, a notice is given under subsection (4).

    This is subject to paragraph 7(5) of Schedule 5 (reinstatement of premises licence where appeal made against cancellation of interim authority notice).

(7) The relevant licensing authority must not cancel an interim authority notice after a relevant transfer application (within the meaning of section 47) is made in respect of the premises licence.

## 6.11.12    Reinstatement by transfer application

Where a premises licence has either lapsed due to the death, incapacity or insolvency of the premises licence holder (and there is no IAN having effect), or through surrender of the licence, a person entitled to apply for a premises licence can have the licence reinstated by making an application for transfer.[157] The transfer application must include a request under s 43 that the transfer shall have immediate effect and the application must be made not later than seven days after the day that the licence lapsed. Section 50(1)–(4) provides:

(1) This section applies where–

    (a) a premises licence lapses by virtue of section 27 (death, incapacity or insolvency of the holder), but no interim authority notice has effect, or

    (b) a premises licence lapses by virtue of section 28 (surrender).

(2) For the purposes of subsection (1)(a) an interim authority notice ceases to have effect when it is cancelled under section 48 or withdrawn.

(3) Notwithstanding the lapsing of the licence, a person mentioned in section 16(1) (who, in the case of an individual, is aged 18 or over) may apply under section 42 for the transfer of the licence to him provided that the application–

(a)  is made no later than seven days after the day the licence lapsed, and

(b)  is one to which section 43(1)(a) applies.

(4)  Where an application is made in accordance with subsection (3) above, section 43(1)(b) must be disregarded.

The reference in s 50(3)(b) to the application being 'one to which section 43(1)(a) applies' is a reference to the need to include in the transfer application of a request for the transfer to have immediate effect. Normally, for a transfer to have immediate effect under s 43 not only must such a request be included under s 43(1)(a), but also, in accordance with s 43(1)(b), the requirements of s 43 must be met. These requirements include obtaining, or taking reasonable steps to obtain, the consent of the premises licence holder, requirements which are clearly inapplicable in cases where the premises licence has lapsed, not least when this is through death. It is for this reason that s 50(4) provides that s 43(1)(b) must be disregarded for the purposes of s 50.

The premises licence is reinstated once the transfer application is received, but will lapse again if rejected or if the application is withdrawn. Section 50(5) and (6) provides:

(5)  Where such an application is made, the premises licence is reinstated from the time the application is received by the relevant licensing authority.

(6)  But the licence lapses again if, and when–

(a)  the applicant is notified of the rejection of the application, or

(b)  the application is withdrawn.

Finally, not more than one application can be made for transfer so as to effect reinstatement under this section, since s 50(7) provides: 'Only one application for transfer of the premises licence may be made in reliance on this section.'

## 6.12   REVIEW OF PREMISES LICENCES

### 6.12.1 Introduction

According to the Guidance, the proceedings set out in the 2003 Act for reviewing premises licences represent a key protection for the community where problems associated with the licensing objectives are occurring after the grant or variation of a premises licence.[158] Although provision is made for review by interested parties and responsible authorities, it is envisaged that applications for review will be preceded by warnings to premises licence holders of concerns arising and the need for remedial action to be taken, with a review following in the event of a failure to address these concerns:

> It is good practice for authorised persons and responsible authorities to give licence holders early warning of their concerns about problems identified at the premises concerned and of the need for improvement. A failure to respond to such warnings is expected to lead to a decision to request a review.[159]

It is not necessary, in order for a review to be instituted, that any criminal proceedings have been instituted or any conviction obtained in respect of the activity which has given rise to the review. As District Judge Munro stated in *Tesco Express v Birmingham City Council and Chief Constable of West Midlands Police* (2007) 70 *Licensing Review* 34 (at para 16), a case in which the police sought a premises licence review rather than a prosecution for selling alcohol to children under s 146 of the 2003 Act:

> To await the outcome of a prosecution would in my view be counter productive. Indeed I am of the view that Parliament could not have intended that review proceedings would be dependent upon a conviction.

The review provisions have been supplemented by an additional power of summary review introduced by s 21 of the Violent Crime Reduction Act 2006, under which the police can seek an expedited review of premises licences which authorise the sale of alcohol in cases where the premises are associated with serious crime and disorder. This is complemented by a power for the licensing authority to take interim steps in relation to the licence, which can include imposing additional conditions, pending the determination of the review. The general provisions on review are considered in the remainder of this section and the additional power of summary review, with interim steps pending determination, is considered in the following section (see 6.13 below).

## 6.12.2 Application for review

6.12.3 Application is confined to interested parties and responsible authorities. The licensing authority itself cannot institute a review, although the relevant section of the local authority dealing with environmental and public health may (as a responsible authority) do so.[160] Section 53 provides:

> (1) This section applies where a local authority is both–
>    (a) the relevant licensing authority, and
>    (b) a responsible authority,
>    in respect of any premises.
> (2) The authority may, in its capacity as a responsible authority, apply under section 51 for a review of any premises licence in respect of the premises.
> (3) The authority may, in its capacity as licensing authority, determine that application.

Whilst the section makes no reference to the time at which an application can be made, stating only (in s 51(1)) that an interested party or a responsible authority may apply 'where a premises licence has effect', it is clear from the Guidance that an application can be made at any time. Paragraph 11.2 provides:

> At any stage, following the grant of a premises licence, a responsible authority or interested party may ask the licensing authority to review the licence because of a matter arising at the premises in connection with any of the four licensing objectives.[161]

The application is subject to regulations that may make provision for notice to be given to the premises licence holder and each responsible authority, and for advertisement (in this instance, by the authority rather than the applicant) and for the making of representations.[162] Section 51(1)–(3) provides:

> (1) Where a premises licence has effect, an interested party or a responsible authority may apply to the relevant licensing authority for a review of the licence.
> (2) Subsection (1) is subject to regulations under section 54 (form etc. of applications etc.).[163]
> (3) The Secretary of State must by regulations under this section–

(a) require the applicant to give a notice containing details of the application to the holder of the premises licence and each responsible authority within such period as may be prescribed;

(b) require the authority to advertise the application and invite representations about it to be made to the authority by interested parties and responsible authorities;

(c) prescribe the period during which representations may be made by the holder of the premises licence, any responsible authority or any interested party;

(d) require any notice under paragraph (a) or advertisement under paragraph (b) to specify that period.

As regards giving notice to the premises licence holder and each responsible authority, reg 29 of the LA 2003 (PL and CPC) Regs 2005 requires the applicant to give them a copy of the application and any accompanying documents on the same day as he gives the review application to the licensing authority.[164] Regulation 38 requires the authority to advertise the application in two ways. First, the authority must prominently display a notice at, on or near the site of the application premises, where it can conveniently be read from the exterior of the premises, for not less than 28 consecutive days from the day following the giving of the application to the licensing authority. Further, the notice, which must be at least A4 in size, in a pale blue colour, and printed legibly in black ink or typed in black in a font of at least 16-point, must be displayed in a central and conspicuous place at the licensing authority's offices. In addition, where the premises cover more than 50 square metres, a further such notice must be displayed every 50 metres along their external perimeter adjoining any highway. Secondly, the authority must publish a notice (which need not be in the form specified above) on its website where it maintains a website for the purpose of advertisement of applications. Regulation 38 provides:

(1) Subject to the provisions of this regulation and regulation 39, the relevant licensing authority shall advertise an application for the review of a premises licence under section 51(3) or s 53A, of a club premises certificate under section 87(3) or of a premises licence following a closure order under section 167–

    (a) by displaying prominently a notice–

        (i) which is–

            (aa) of a size equal or larger than A4;

            (bb) of a pale blue colour; and

            (cc) printed legibly in black ink or typed in black in a font of a size equal to or larger than 16;

        (ii) at, on or near the site of the premises to which the application relates where it can conveniently be read from the exterior of the premises by the public and in the case of a premises covering an area of more than fifty metres square, one further notice in the same form and subject to the same requirements shall be displayed every 50 metres along the external perimeter of the premises abutting any highway; and

        (iii) at the offices, or the main offices, of the licensing authority in a central and conspicuous place; and

    (b) in a case where the relevant licensing authority maintains a website for the purpose of advertisement of applications given to it, by publication of a notice on that website;

(2) the requirements set out in paragraph (1) shall be fulfilled–

    (a) in the case of a review of a premises licence following a closure order under
        section 167, or of a review of such a licence under section 53A, for a period of
        no less than seven consecutive days starting on the day after the day on which
        the relevant licensing authority received–
        (i) the notice under section 165(4); or
        (ii) the application under section 53A
        (as the case may be); and
    (b) in all other cases, for a period of no less than 28 consecutive days starting on
        the day after the day on which the application was given to the relevant licens-
        ing authority.

The information contained in the premises and website notices must include the
postal address of the premises, the dates within which relevant representations
in writing can be made, the grounds of review, the postal address and any website
address where authority's licensing register is kept and may be inspected, and a
statement of the offence and maximum fine for knowingly or recklessly making
a false statement in connection with an application. Regulation 39 provides:

> Subject to regulation 39A, all notices referred to in regulation 38 shall state–
> (a) the address of the premises about which an application for a review has been
>     made;
> (b) the dates between which interested parties and responsible authorities may make
>     representations to the relevant licensing authority;
> (c) the grounds of the application for review;
> (d) the postal address and, where relevant, the worldwide web address where the
>     register of the relevant licensing is kept and where and when the grounds for
>     the review may be inspected; and
> (e) that it is an offence knowingly or recklessly to make a false statement in connection
>     with an application and the maximum fine for which a person is liable on summary
>     conviction for the offence.

6.12.4 An application for review may be rejected (without a hearing and determination) if the authority is satisfied that the ground of review is not relevant to
the licensing objectives or, if made by an interested party, is frivolous, vexatious or
repetitious. Section 51(4) provides:

> The relevant licensing authority may, at any time, reject any ground for review
> specified in an application under this section if it is satisfied–
> (a) that the ground is not relevant to one or more of the licensing objectives, or
> (b) in the case of an application made by a person other than a responsible authority,
>     that–
>     (i) the ground is frivolous or vexatious, or
>     (ii) the ground is a repetition.

Whether or not a ground is relevant to a licensing objective will depend on how
widely 'relevant' is construed. Clearly grounds which are directly relevant to a
licensing objective will suffice, as where sales of alcohol are made to children, since
such sales are directly related to the licensing objective of protection of children from
harm in respect of the licensable activity of sale of alcohol from the premises. Less
clear is whether grounds which are not directly related will suffice, although the
Guidance seems to envisage that they might, for para 11.22 provides:

> A number of reviews may arise in connection with crime that is not directly connected with licensable activities. For example, reviews may arise because of drugs problems at the premises or money laundering by criminal gangs or the sale of contraband or stolen goods there or the sale of firearms ... In any case, it is for the licensing authority to determine whether the problems associated with the alleged crimes are taking place on the premises and affecting the promotion of the licensing objectives.

Such criminal activity may or may not take place at times when a licensable activity is occurring and may or may not have any connection with it. To the extent that it does, it may be proper for a review to take place but it is submitted that a ground would not be relevant to a licensing objective if it was unconnected with a licensable activity. If, for example, a review was sought for a premises licence authorising the sale of alcohol for consumption on the premises because sales of stolen goods were taking place on the premises, the sales of stolen goods are not relevant to the licensing objective of prevention of crime and disorder. They are relevant to the objective of prevention of crime and disorder, but not the *licensing* objective (emphasis supplied). They are relevant to the objective only in a general sense and are not relevant to the licensing objective because they are unconnected with the licensable activity of sale of alcohol. The statutory powers under the 2003 Act concern licensable activities and authorisation for such activities, and powers of review need to relate to them. Parliament has conferred powers on the licensing authority to regulate licensable activities and it cannot have been intended that review of a premises licence, which may lead to possible loss of the licence, should extend to include matters unconnected with any licensable activity.

For a ground not to be relevant, it would be necessary for it to have no bearing on one or more of the licensing objectives. This may not be easy to establish given that the licensing objectives are expressed in broad terms. However, general concern with crime and disorder in a particular area will not suffice, for the ground for review will need to relate to particular premises. As para 11.6 of the Guidance states:

> a complaint relating to a general (crime and disorder) situation in a town centre should generally not be regarded as a relevant representation unless it can be positively tied or linked by a causal connection to particular premises, which would allow for a proper review of the licence or certificate.

Similarly, it may be that a single complaint about noise from particular premises may not suffice, since, although this is relevant to the licensing objective of prevention of public nuisance in that it demonstrates that there is an element of nuisance, there can be no public nuisance if only one person is affected (see 4.2.9 above). It may be therefore that, if only one representation about noise is received, the application ought not to be determined on the basis that any action taken would not promote the licensing objective of prevention of public nuisance. It may be that the appropriate course here would be for the issuing of a noise abatement notice under the Environmental Protection Act 1990.

Rejection because the ground is frivolous or vexatious is similar to a licensing authority rejecting relevant representations by interested parties for these reasons on an application for grant of a premises licence, which has been considered in 6.4.21–6.4.22 above. Rejection on the ground of repetition is further clarified by s 51(5) which provides:

For this purpose a ground for review is a repetition if–

(a) it is identical or substantially similar to–

    (i) a ground for review specified in an earlier application for review made in respect of the same premises licence and determined under section 52, or

    (ii) representations considered by the relevant licensing authority in accordance with section 18, before it determined the application for the premises licence under that section, or

    (iii) representations which would have been so considered but for the fact that they were excluded representations by virtue of section 32,[165] and

(b) a reasonable interval has not elapsed since that earlier application for review or the grant of the licence (as the case may be).[166]

6.12.5 Neither the legislation nor the Guidance gives any indication when a ground of review is 'substantially similar', but the ordinary and natural meaning of these words suggests 'bearing a strong resemblance' or 'very much of the same kind' rather than simply 'having some similarity'. At the very least, it seems that the ground of review will have to relate not only to the same licensing objective to be substantially similar, but also to the same aspect of the objective (such as public nuisance through noise in a particular area). The onus will be on the licensing authority to show that the ground of review is substantially similar, since the authority has to be satisfied under s 51(4) that the ground is a repetition in order to reject the application for review. Application for review on an identical or substantially similar ground is not automatically ruled out, but only if a reasonable interval has not elapsed since the ground was previously considered. The Guidance indicates that what constitutes a reasonable interval is a matter for the authority to decide, although it then proceeds to indicate that there should normally be an interval of at least 12 months. Having cautioned authorities of the 'need to prevent attempts to review licences merely as a second bite of the cherry following the failure of representations to persuade the licensing authority on earlier occasions', the Guidance states:

> It is for licensing authorities themselves to judge what should be regarded as a reasonable interval in these circumstances. However, the Secretary of State recommends that more than one review originating from an interested party should not be permitted within a period of twelve months on similar grounds save in compelling circumstances or where it arises following a closure order.[167]

If an application for review is rejected, the authority must notify the applicant of its decision. The reason for rejection will be self-evident if it is on the ground that it is repetitious, but reasons must be given if it is rejected on the ground that it is frivolous or vexatious. Section 51(6) provides:

> Where the authority rejects a ground for review under subsection (4)(b), it must notify the applicant of its decision and, if the ground was rejected because it was frivolous or vexatious, the authority must notify him of its reasons for making that decision.

Where an application is rejected because the ground is frivolous, vexatious or a repetition, reg 32 of the LA 2003 (PL and CPC) Regs 2005 requires written notification to be given as soon as is reasonable practicable. An applicant may, of course, seek review on a number of grounds, only some of which may be considered irrelevant, frivolous, vexatious and/or repetitious. In this case, an application may be rejected only to the extent that it is so considered and will need in other respects to be determined. Accordingly, s 51(7) provides:

The application is to be treated as rejected to the extent that any of the grounds for review are rejected under subsection (4).

Accordingly the requirements imposed under subsection (3)(a) and (b) and by section 52 (so far as not already met) apply only to so much (if any) of the application as has not been rejected.

## 6.12.6 Determination of applications

6.12.7   There is a range of powers set out in s 52 that the authority can exercise, when determining applications for review, where it considers them necessary to promote the licensing objectives. Where a review is sought and an application has been made in accordance with the statutory provisions in s 51, under reg 5 and para 7 of Sched 1 to the LA 2003 (Hearings) Regs 2005 the authority must hold a hearing within 20 working days to consider the application and any relevant representations received following advertisement of the application under s 51(3)(b). Notice of the hearing must be given to the premises licence holder, persons who made relevant representations and the person who has made the review application no later than 10 working days before the day or the first day on which the hearing is to be held.[168] Section 52(1) and (2) provides:

(1)   This section applies where–
  (a)   the relevant licensing authority receives an application made in accordance with section 51,
  (b)   the applicant has complied with any requirement imposed on him under subsection (3)(a) or (d) of that section, and
  (c)   the authority has complied with any requirement imposed on it under subsection (3) (b) or (d) of that section.
(2)   Before determining the application, the authority must hold a hearing to consider it and any relevant representations.

It is unclear whether a hearing can be dispensed with if considered unnecessary by the parties and by the licensing authority. Whilst this might be thought of as an unlikely event in the case of a review, it is possible that agreement might be reached by the premises licence holder with interested parties and responsible authorities on their concerns ahead of a review hearing being held. There is no provision contained in s 52 for dispensing with a review hearing, which might indicate that dispensation is not possible, although a general provision is contained in reg 9 of the LA 2003 (Hearings) Regs 2005 for dispensing with a hearing if all parties agree. Regulation 9, headed 'Right to dispense with hearing if all parties agree', enables an authority to dispense with a hearing where it has been given notice by all parties that they consider a hearing unnecesary (reg 9(1)), in which case the authority must forthwith give notice to the parties that the hearing has been dispensed with (reg 9(2)). It is uncertain, however, whether this general provision has effect independently of a specific provision in the 2003 Act, enabling a hearing to be dispensed with where the parties consider this to be unnecessary. Since reg 9(1) provides that the authority can dispense with the hearing 'if all persons *required by the Act* agree that such a hearing is unnecessary' (emphasis supplied), this suggests that there needs to be a requirement in the Act for agreeing that a hearing is unnecessary and that reg 9 does not have effect independently of specific provision in the Act. Accordingly, since there is no specific provision in the Act on reviews, it is thought that reg 9 confers no right to dispense with a review hearing even if all parties agree that it is unnecessary.

At the hearing, relevant representations made by responsible authorities, interested parties and/or by the holder of the premises licence whose licence is being reviewed can be considered. Relevant representations are representations relevant to one or more of the licensing objectives and there is the usual provision for relevant representations not to be considered where they have been withdrawn or when they are regarded as frivolous or vexatious (see 6.4.20–6.4.22 above). Section 52(7) and (8) provides:

> (7)  In this section "relevant representations" means representations which–
>> (a)  are relevant to one or more of the licensing objectives, and
>> (b)  meet the requirements of subsection (8).
> (8)  The requirements are–
>> (a)  that the representations are made–
>>> (i)  by the holder of the premises licence, a responsible authority or an interested party, and
>>> (ii)  within the period prescribed under section 51(3)(c),
>> (b)  that they have not been withdrawn, and
>> (c)  if they are made by an interested party (who is not also a responsible authority), that they are not, in the opinion of the relevant licensing authority, frivolous or vexatious.

The criterion specified for relevant representations in s 52(7)(a) is that the representations 'are relevant to one or more of the licensing objectives'. This differs from that for relevant representations for the grant of a new premises licences or the variation of an existing one, where the requirement is that the representations are 'about the likely effect of the grant . . . on the promotion of the licensing objectives'.[169] This, on the face of it, seems a more stringent standard than being 'relevant' in s 52(7)(a). A representation may be 'relevant' to a licensing objective simply if it has some bearing on it. This would seem to be less onerous than if the representation had to be about the likely effect of the continued operation of the premises on the promotion of the licensing objectives, which would be the equivalent to the criterion adopted for grant or variation.

Further, the requirement in s 52(7)(a) is only that the representations are relevant to one or more of the licensing objectives and not that they are relevant to the particular licensing objective(s) on which the review application is based. Thus, if the police apply for a review based on the licensing objective of prevention of crime and disorder (and only this box is ticked on the application form,) it seems that relevant representations might be made which relate to some other licensing objective. This could include, for example, a representation by the fire authority relating to public safety or a representation by interested parties and/or the environmental health department of the lcoal authority relating to public nuisance by noise. If such representations were to be excluded from the review, they might themselves form the basis for a subsequent review application and could be considered at that review hearing. If there are concurrent concerns relating to other licensing objectives, it makes no sense for relevant representations relating these concerns to be excluded from the review hearing, only for a further review application then to be made in respect of them. The wording of s 52(7)(a) seems to support representations relating to other licensing objectives being relevant representations on a review application, since it provides that representations are relevant representations if they 'are relevant to *one or more* of the licensing objectives' (emphasis supplied). It does not provide that they have to be relevant to the review application and the licensing objective(s) on which the review application is based.

6.12.8  When determining the application, the authority must take one of a number of steps that it considers necessary to promote the licensing objectives. Section 52(3) and (4) provides:

(3)  The authority must, having regard to the application and any relevant representations, take such of the steps mentioned in subsection (4) (if any) as it considers necessary for the promotion of the licensing objectives.

(4)  The steps are–

(a)  to modify the conditions of the licence;

(b)  to exclude a licensable activity from the scope of the licence;

(c)  to remove the designated premises supervisor;

(d)  to suspend the licence for a period not exceeding three months;

(e)  to revoke the licence;

and for this purpose the conditions of the licence are modified if any of them is altered or omitted or any new condition is added.

Once steps are taken and a determination is made, the authority's decision does not, however, have immediate effect. It only takes effect when the period for making an appeal has expired or, if an appeal is lodged, when the appeal is 'disposed of' (which presumably will include either withdrawal or determination of the appeal). Section 52(11) provides:

A determination under this section does not have effect–

(a)  until the end of the period given for appealing against the decision, or

(b)  if the decision is appealed against, until the appeal is disposed of.

It is not necessary that any of the steps mentioned in subsection (4) are taken, since s 52(3) refers to the authority taking such of the steps 'if any' as it considers necessary for the promotion of the licensing objectives. If none of these steps are considered necessary, the authority can decide to take no action. Alternatively, it can decide to take some informal action falling short of the steps specified in sub-s (4), such as issuing a warning or guidance. As para 11.16 of the Guidance states:

The licensing authority may decide that no action is necessary if it finds that the review does not require it to take any steps necessary to promote the licensing objectives. In addition, there is nothing to prevent a licensing authority issuing an informal warning to the licence holder and/or to recommend improvement within a particular period of time. It is expected that licensing authorities will regard such warnings as an important mechanism for ensuring that the licensing objectives are effectively promoted and that warnings should be issued in writing to the holder of the licence.

If the authority decides to modify the conditions of the licence (for example, by reducing the hours of opening or requiring door supervisors at particular times) or to exclude a licensable activity from the scope of the licence (for example, by excluding the playing of live music),[170] it can do so either permanently or for a temporary period of up to three months. Section 52(6) provides:

> Where the authority takes a step mentioned in subsection (4)(a) or (b), it may provide that the modification or exclusion is to have effect only for such period (not exceeding three months) as it may specify.

Suspension, similarly, can be for a period of up to three months, although not for any longer period. Presumably, if an authority feels a three months' suspension period is inadequate to promote the licensing objectives the appropriate course would be to revoke the licence.

In deciding which of these various steps to take, it is expected that licensing authorities should so far as possible seek to establish the cause or causes of the concerns which the representations identify. The remedial action taken should generally be directed at these causes and should always be no more than a necessary and proportionate response, for example the removal and replacement of the designated premises supervisor may be sufficient to remedy a problem where the cause of the identified problem directly relates to poor management decisions made by that individual (Guidance, paras 11.18 and 11.19).

6.12.9  Taking steps to promote the licensing objectives will include steps to prevent the commission of crime, since this is one of the licensing objectives, but the Guidance makes it clear, in para 11.23, that only steps should be taken *in connection with the premises licence* for the promotion of the crime prevention objective:

> Where the licensing authority is conducting a review on the ground that the premises have been used for criminal purposes, its role is solely to determine what steps should be taken in connection with the premises licence for the promotion of the crime prevention objective.

That such activity may take place, notwithstanding the best efforts of the licensee and those working at the premises, does not preclude the authority from taking any necessary steps in the wider interests of the community. As the Guidance goes on to state in the same paragraph:

> It is important to recognise that certain criminal activity or associated problems may be taking place or have taken place despite the best efforts of the licensee and the staff working at the premises and despite full compliance with the conditions attached to the licence. In such circumstances, the licensing authority is still empowered to take any necessary steps to remedy the problems. The licensing authority's duty is to take steps with a view to the promotion of the licensing objectives in the interests of the wider community and not those of the individual holder of the premises licence.

6.12.10 In particular, certain types of criminal activity should be treated particularly seriously and licensing authorities, the police and other law-enforcement agencies should use the review procedures effectively to deter such activities. Revocation of the licence, even in the first instance, should be seriously considered in these cases where the authority determines that the crime prevention objective is being undermined through the premises being used to further crimes (Guidance, paras 11.25 and 11.26). The types of criminal activity in question that should be treated particularly seriously are set out in para 11.25 of the Guidance and these are where there is the use of the licensed premises:

- for the sale and distribution of Class A drugs and the laundering of the proceeds of drugs crime;
- for the use of licensed premises for the sale and distribution of illegal firearms;
- for the evasion of copyright in respect of pirated or unlicensed films and music, which does considerable damage to the industries affected;
- for the purchase and consumption of alcohol by minors, which impacts on the health, educational attainment, employment prospects and propensity for crime of young people;
- for prostitution or the sale of unlawful pornography;
- by organised groups of paedophiles to groom children;
- as the base for the organisation of criminal activity, particularly by gangs;
- for the organisation of racist activity or the promotion of racist attacks;
- for unlawful gaming and gambling; and
- for the sale of smuggled tobacco and alcohol.

6.12.11 The Guidance further provides for review proceedings not to be used as a substitute for criminal proceedings and for authorities to focus on whether problems associated with the alleged criminal activity are taking place on the premises rather than on individual criminal responsibility. Paragraphs 11.22 and 11.23 provide:

> 11.22 A number of reviews may arise in connection with crime that is not directly connected with licensable activities. For example, reviews may arise because of drugs problems at the premises or money laundering by criminal gangs or the sale of contraband or stolen goods there or the sale of firearms. Licensing authorities do not have the power to judge the criminality or otherwise of any issue. This is a matter for the courts of law. The role of the licensing authority when determining such a review is not therefore to establish the guilt or innocence of any individual but to ensure that the crime prevention objective is promoted. Reviews are part of the regulatory process introduced by the 2003 Act and they are not part of criminal law and procedure. Some reviews will arise after the conviction in the criminal courts of certain individuals but not all. In any case, it is for the licensing authority to determine whether the problems associated with the alleged crimes are taking place on the premises and affecting the promotion of the licensing objectives. Where a review follows a conviction, it would also not be for the licensing authority to attempt to go behind any finding of the courts, which should be treated as a matter of undisputed evidence before them.

> 11.23 Where the licensing authority is conducting a review on the ground that the premises have been used for criminal purposes, its role is solely to determine what steps should be taken in connection with the premises licence for the promotion of the crime prevention objective. It is important to recognise that certain criminal activity or associated problems may be taking place or have taken place despite the best efforts of the licensee and the staff working at the premises and despite full compliance with the conditions attached to the licence. In such circumstances, the licensing authority is still empowered to take any necessary steps to remedy the problems. The licensing authority's duty is to take steps with a view to the promotion of the licensing objectives in the interests of the wider community and not those of the individual holder of the premises licence.

6.12.12 Certainly, where review follows a conviction for an offence in respect of activity taking place on the premises, such as drug dealing or the sale of firearms, the authority will be justified in taking steps to promote the prevention of crime objective. Not all reviews, however, will take place after a conviction, but it would seem that if the authority is satisfied, on a balance of probabilities, that some criminal activity is taking place and problems on the premises are associated with that activity, the authority will similarly be justified in taking steps to promote the prevention of crime objective. Less clear is the position where criminal proceedings have been instituted, but there has been no conviction, which will cover cases where there has been an acquittal, a failure by a jury to reach a verdict, a conviction quashed on appeal or discontinuance of a prosecution. In principle, such a case should be no different from one where no criminal proceedings have been instituted. It should, in each case, be a question of whether the authority is satisfied, on a balance of probabilities, that the criminal activity in question is taking place and that it is causing problems on the premises. This is the view that has been traditionally taken in cases of fitness to hold a licence. In civil proceedings, an authority need only be satisfied on a balance of probabilities that criminal conduct took place and the High Court has held, in *R v Crown Court at Maidstone ex p Olson* [1992] COD 496 and *McCool v Rushcliffe Borough Council* [1998] 3 All ER 889, that it is entitled to make such a finding, notwithstanding that criminal proceedings have been unsuccessful.[171] The final sentence of para 11.22 of the Guidance (see above), however, seems to leave it in doubt whether this will continue to be the case as far as reviews under the 2003 Act are concerned. If there is a failure of a criminal prosecution, this sentence in the Guidance might be read as indicating that the authority should not revisit the question of liability for the criminal activity ('not . . . go behind any finding of the courts') and, in accordance with the view of the criminal court, should regard such criminal activity as not having taken place ('should be treated as a matter of undisputed evidence before them').

Alternatively, the sentence might be read in a more restrictive way. The 'finding of the courts' in failed prosecutions is that criminal liability has not been established beyond reasonable doubt and indicating that the authority should 'not . . . go behind' could be read simply as an exhortation not to redetermine the question of criminal liability to a standard beyond reasonable doubt. (This would be consistent and in keeping with the statement in para 11.22 that the role of the authority in a review is 'not . . . to establish the guilt or innocence of any individual'.) On this reading, the failed prosecution 'should be treated as a matter of undisputed evidence before them [the authority]' that criminal liability has not been established beyond reasonable doubt. Treating this as a matter of undisputed evidence would not, however, preclude the authority from examining whether such liability might be established on a balance of probabilities. Given the uncertainty as to the meaning and implications of this sentence in para 11.22, it is submitted that authorities, when having regard to it, should give it a restrictive meaning. The well-established principles in *Olsen* and *McCool* should continue to apply, in the absence of any clear statement to the contrary, and the Guidance cannot be regarded as containing any such clear statement. It may be that too much weight should not be placed on these statements in the Guidance, since, as Beatson J observed in *R on the application of JD Wetherspoon plc v Guildford Borough Council* [2006] LLR 312 (at para 58) 'guidance such as this is not drafted in the tight way in which a statute is drafted' and (at para 58) 'a legalistic approach . . . is to be avoided'.

## 6.12.13   Notification of decision

The authority must notify its decision, with reasons, to the premises licence holder, the applicant, any person who made relevant representations and the police. It must also notify, with reasons, any interested party whose representations were considered to be frivolous or vexatious. Section 52(9) and (10) provides:

> (9)   Where the relevant licensing authority determines that any representations are frivolous or vexatious, it must notify the person who made them of the reasons for that determination.
>
> (10) Where a licensing authority determines an application for review under this section it must notify the determination and its reasons for making it to–
>
> (a)   the holder of the licence,
>
> (b)   the applicant,
>
> (c)   any person who made relevant representations, and
>
> (d)   the chief officer of police for the police area (or each police area) in which the premises are situated.

## 6.13   SUMMARY REVIEW OF PREMISES LICENCES

### 6.13.1 Applications

6.13.2   An application can be made by the police for an expedited or 'fast track' review of a premises licence which authorises the sale of alcohol in cases where a senior police officer of the rank of superintendent or above gives a certificate indicating that in his opinion the premises are associated with serious crime and disorder or both. Such a review, introduced by s 21 of the Violent Crime Reduction Act 2006, can be instituted under s 53A(1) of the 2003 Act, which provides:

> The chief officer of police of a police force for a police area may apply under this section to the relevant licensing authority for a review of the premises licence for any premises wholly or partly in that area if–
>
> (a)   the premises are licensed premises in relation to the sale of alcohol by retail; and
>
> (b)   a senior member[172] of that force has given a certificate that it is his opinion that the premises are associated with serious crime or serious disorder or both;
>
> and that certificate must accompany the application.

The DCMS in October 2007 issued *Expedited/Summary Licence Reviews Guidance* (ESLR Guidance) and this is reproduced in Appendix 13. Paragraph 1.1 of the ESLR Guidance explains how 'to use new provisions in the Licensing Act 2003 . . . which allow a quick process for attaching interim conditions to a licence and a fast track licence review when the police consider that the premises concerned is associated with serious crime or serious disorder (or both)'. No definition is provided of 'serious disorder' and a similar expression, 'serious public disorder', used in s 12 of the Public Order Act 1986 (which provides for conditions to be imposed by the police on public processions where there is reason to believe that they may result in 'serious public disorder'), seems not to have received judicial consideration. Accordingly, as para 2.3 of the ESLR Guidance states, the phrase 'should be understood in its ordinary English sense', there being 'no definitive list of behaviours that constitute serious disorder', and 'the matter is one for judgment by the local police'. The expression 'serious crime' has the same meaning as in s 81(2) and (3) of the Regulation of Investigatory Powers Act 2000. Under s 81(3)(b), an offence constitutes a 'serious crime' if either (a) it is one for which a person who has attained the age of 21 and has no previous convictions could reasonably be expected to be sentenced to imprisonment for a term of three years or more, or (b) the conduct involves the use of violence, results in substantial financial gain or is conduct by a large number of persons in pursuit of a common purpose. Although this might extend to a range of offences, offences at which summary reviews are particularly aimed are those which involve the use of guns and knives (ESLR Guidance, para 1.2). Whilst there may be a causal connection between the retail sale of alcohol at the premises and the premises being associated with serious crime or serious disorder, as where alcohol-related violence occurs at the premises, it does not seem to be necessary on the wording of s 53A(1) that there is any causal connection. Thus premises may be licensed for the retail sale of alcohol and may be associated with serious crime or serious disorder which has no connection, for example, where there is evidence that the premises are used for drug-dealing or for planning large-scale fraud. Here it would seem an application might be made under s 53A(1).

6.13.3   The Licensing Act 2003 (Summary Review of Premises Licences) Regulations 2007, SI 2007/2502 (LA 2003 (SRPL) Regs 2007) prescribe the form in which the application shall be made and the information that it must contain. Provision is made by reg 2(2) and reg 2(7), which respectively amend the LA 2003 (PL and CPC) Regs 2005 by inserting a reg 16A and a Sched 8A into the 2005 Regulations. The application form in Sched 8A (see Appendix 2) is also reproduced in Annex C to the ESLR Guidance (see Appendix 13). The application form must be accompanied by the certificate issued by the senior police officer, which is a formal note that identifies the licensed premises and includes a signed statement by a senior officer that he believes the premises is associated with serious crime, serious disorder or both (ESLR Guidance, para 2.3). This form is not prescribed in the LA 2003 (SRPL) Regs 2007, but a sample form is contained in Annex B to the ESLR Guidance (see Appendix 13). Paragraph 2.4 of the ESLR Guidance goes on to provide that, in deciding whether to sign a certificate, the senior officer will want to consider the following:

- the track record of the licensed premises concerned and whether the police have previously had cause to give advice about serious criminal or disorderly conduct (or the likelihood of such conduct) attributable to activities taking place on the premises, since it is not expected that this power will be used as a first response to a problem;
- the nature of the likely crime and/or disorder and whether the potential incident is sufficiently serious to warrant using this power;
- whether an alternative power should be deployed to address the problem, such as a standard licence review or closure of the premises under s 161, or whether an expedited review could be used in conjunction with modification of licence conditions following the use of a closure power;
- what added value will be brought by use of the expedited process and how any interim steps that the licensing authority might take could effectively address the problem.

It is recommended that the police address these points, in particular why other powers or actions are not felt to be appropriate, and this can be done either in the application for summary review or in the accompanying certificate (ESLR Guidance, para 2.5).

## 6.13.4 Determination of applications

### 6.13.5 Period for determination

Once an application for summary review is made by the police, the authority must determine the application within 28 days, having first considered within 48 hours[173] whether any interim steps are needed pending determination (see 6.13.10 below). Section 53A(2) provides:

> On receipt of such an application, the relevant licensing authority must–
>
> (a) within 48 hours of the time of its receipt, consider under section 53B whether it is necessary to take interim steps pending the determination of a review of the premises licence; and
>
> (b) within 28 days after the day of its receipt, review that licence in accordance with section 53C and reach a determination on that review.

### 6.13.6 Notices, advertising and representations

6.13.7 Where a summary review application is made, the Secretary of State is required to make regulations requiring the licensing authority to give notice of the review to the premises licence holder and responsible authorities; to advertise the review and invite representations from both responsible authorities and interested parties; and to prescribe the periods within which the notice of review must be given, the advertisement must be published, and the representations must be made. Section 53A(3) provides:

> The Secretary of State must by regulations–
>
> (a) require a relevant licensing authority to whom an application for a review under this section has been made to give notice of the review to the holder of the premises licence and to every responsible authority;
>
> (b) prescribe the period after the making of the application within which the notice under paragraph (a) must be given;
>
> (c) require a relevant licensing authority to advertise the review, inviting representations about it to be made to the authority by the responsible authorities and interested parties;
>
> (d) prescribe the period after the making of the application within which the advertisement must be published;
>
> (e) prescribe the period after the publication of the advertisement during which representations may be made by the holder of the premises licence, any responsible authority or any interested party; and
>
> (f) require a notice or advertisement under paragraph (a) or (c) to specify the period prescribed under paragraph (e).

6.13.8 The LA 2003 (SRPL) Regs 2007 make provision for the giving of notice of review to the premises licence holder and each responsible authority. Regulation 2(3) inserts a reg 36A into the LA 2003 (PL and CPC) Regs 2005, under which the licensing authority must give to the premises licence holder and each responsible authority a copy of the application and a copy of the certificate accompanying it, which indicates that in the opinion of the senior police officer the premises are associated with serious crime and disorder or both (see s 53A(1)(b) above). This must be done within 48 hours of receiving the application, with time that is not on a working day disregarded when calculating this period. Regulation 36A provides:

(1) In the case of an application for review of a premises licence under section 53A the relevant licensing authority must, within 48 hours of the time of the receipt of the application, give notice of the review to–

    (a) the holder of the premises licence to which the application relates; and

    (b) each responsible authority.

(2) Notice under paragraph (1) is to be given by giving to the holder and each authority–

    (a) a copy of the application; and

    (b) a copy of the certificate given under section 53A(1)(b) that accompanied the application.

(3) In computing the period of 48 hours mentioned in paragraph (1) time that is not on a working day is to be disregarded.

6.13.9   As regards advertising, provision is made by reg 38 of the LA 2003 (PL and CPC) Regs 2005 (see 6.12.3 above), as amended by reg 2(4) of the LA 2003 (SRPL) Regs 2007, for applications for summary review to be advertised for seven days. This is the same period as for a premises licence review following a closure order, compared to an ordinary review application that must be advertised by the authority for 28 days. Advertisments for review applications must specify information on five matters, in accordance with reg 39 of the LA 2003 (PL and CPC) Regs 2005 (see 6.12.3 above), and this provision, with some modifications set out in reg 39A(1), applies to applications for summary review. The modifications are in respect of the dates between which interested parties and responsible authorities may make representations (reg 39(b)) and the grounds of the review application (reg 39(c)). For summary review applications, the dates for reg 39(b) are the first working day after the day on which the notice was published and the date of the ninth subsequent working day – the period between these two dates is the period within which representations must be made after publication of the advertisement in accordance with s 53A(3)(e) – and the grounds of review for reg 39(c) are to be the opinion of a senior police officer that the premises are associated with serious crime or serious disorder or both. Reg 39A, inserted by reg 2(6) of the LA 2003 (SRPL) Regs 2007, provides:

(1) In the case of a review of a premises licence under section 53A–

    (a) the dates referred to in regulation 39(b) shall be the date of the first working day after the day on which the notice was published, and the date of the ninth subsequent working day;

    (b) the grounds referred to in regulation 39(c) shall be that in the opinion of a senior police officer the premises are associated with serious crime or serious disorder or both.

(2) The period prescribed for the purposes of section 53A(3)(e) of the Act is the period beginning on the first working day after the publication of the notice referred to in regulation 38 and ending on the ninth subsequent working day.

*6.13.10 Interim steps*

6.13.11 As indicated (see 6.13.5 above), before determining the application the authority must decide within 48 hours of receiving the application whether any interim steps are needed pending determination. Deciding whether any interim steps are needed is a decision which must be made by the licensing committee or by a subcommittee, since this is one of the functions that may not be delegated to officers (see s 10(4)(via) and 2.2.17 above). However, there is no requirement for a formal hearing in order to take interim steps and, according to para 3.3 of the ESLR Guidance, this means that 'the relevant sub committee members can communicate by telephone or other remote means in order to reach a decision', although a 'written record should always be produced as soon as possible after a decision is reached'.

The provisions of s 53B apply where the licensing authority considers whether interim steps are needed pending the premises licence review (s 53B(1)). Such consideration may take place without the premises licence holder having been afforded an opportunity to make representations and the steps to be considered are modification of conditions, which can include alteration or omission of existing conditions or addition of new conditions; exclusion of the retail sale of alcohol as a licensable actvitity; removal of the DPS from the licence; and suspension of the licence. Section 53B(2)–(4) provides:

(2) The consideration may take place without the holder of the premises licence having been given an opportunity to make representations to the relevant licensing authority.

(3) The interim steps the relevant licensing authority must consider taking are–
  (a) the modification of the conditions of the premises licence;
  (b) the exclusion of the sale of alcohol by retail from the scope of the licence;
  (c) the removal of the designated premises supervisor from the licence;
  (d) the suspension of the licence.

(4) For the purposes of subsection (3)(a) the conditions of a premises licence are modified if any of them is altered or omitted or any new condition is added.

6.13.12 Whilst s 53B(2) expressly provides that no opportunity needs to be provided for making representations, para 3.2 of the ESLR Guidance states: 'This does not, of course mean that the authority *cannot* afford such an opportunity if it thinks it appropriate and feasible to do so in all the circumstances'. Although an opportunity is later provided for making representations about interim steps (see s 53B(6) and 6.13.14 below), given the possibility that failure to afford an opportunity at the outset may be considered to infringe a premise licence holder's right to a fair hearing under Article 6(1) of the European Convention on Human Rights (see 3.5 above), the prudent course may be to afford an opportunity if at all possible.

Interim steps might include searching for offensive weapons on entry, since summary reviews are particularly aimed at conduct involving the use of guns and knives (see ESLR Guidance, para 1.2 and 6.13.2 above), searching for drugs, or requiring the use of toughened glass (where there is a demonstrable risk that this will help reduce the risk of injury from glassing). They also might include restricting the times at which licensable activities authorised by the licence can take place or having extra door staff on the premises, although as para 3.6 of the ESLR Guidance makes clear the authority 'should consider the practical implications of compliance in relation to the premises' and for door supervisors 'those running the premises may need some time to recruit appropriately qualified and accredited staff'. It is perhaps only in limited instances that the taking of interim steps such as those mentioned above is likely to occur, for Explanatory Note 41 to the Violent Crime Reduction Act 2006 states:

> These are selective measures. It is not the aim to require all licensed premises to undertake these searches [for weapons] or use toughened glass. Rather, the policy aim is to provide a selective tool, to be used proportionately, to limit this condition to those pubs that are at risk either because police intelligence shows there is a risk of knives/guns being carried or because crime and disorder has occurred on the premises.

Further, 'very careful consideration needs to be given to interim steps which would require significant cost or permanent or semi-permanent adjustments to a premises which would be difficult to remove if the outcome of the subsequent full review was to withdraw or modify those steps' (ESLR Guidance, para 3.7). Such instances might include structural changes, additional CCTV or glassware replacement.

6.13.13 If interim steps are taken, the steps have effect immediately, or as soon afterwards as the authority directs, and the authority must immediately notify the premises licence holder and the police, giving reasons for its decision. Section 53B(5) provides:

> Where on its consideration of whether to take interim steps the relevant licensing authority does take one or more such steps–
>
> (a) its decision takes effect immediately or as soon after that as that authority directs; but
>
> (b) it must give immediate notice of its decision and of its reasons for making it to–
>
>     (i) the holder of the premises licence; and
>
>     (ii) the chief officer of police for the police area in which the premises are situated (or for each police area in which they are partly situated).

According to para 3.5 of the ESLR Guidance, there is no requirement that the immediate notice is in writing and this may be given orally initially, with a follow-up version in writing. Paragraph 3.5 provides:

> The Act does not specify that the immediate notice has to be in writing. However, in an individual case the licensing authority may consider that the need for immediate communication at least initially requires a non-written approach, such as a telephone call. This may happen when, for example, the authority decides that the decision should have immediate effect. In such a case, the decision and the reasons for it should be explained clearly and in full to the licence-holder (or someone who is empowered to act for the licence-holder), and the call followed up as soon as possible with a written version of the decision and the reasons (for example by email or fax) which is identical, or not significantly different from the version given by phone.

Whilst an immediate oral communication might as a matter of practice be desirable, it is less clear whether such a communication constitutes a valid 'immediate notice' for the purposes of s 53B(5)(b). It is true that the Act does not specify that the immediate notice has to be in writing, there being no mention of this in s 53B. But summary licence reviews fall within the LA 2003 (PL and CPC) Regs 2005 (see reg 16A and 6.13.2 above) and reg 21 provides: 'An application, a notice or representations shall be given in writing'. Regulation 21 is contained in Part 4 of the LA 2003 (PL and CPC) Regs 2005, which makes general provision under the Regulations, and reg 2 states that ' "notice" means a notice given to a relevant licensing authority under Part 3 or Part 4 of the Act as the case may require and a reference to notices shall be construed accordingly'. An immediate notice under s 53B(5)(b) is a notice given under Part 3 of the 2003 Act and it seems therefore that reg 21 will apply. If this is the case, it seems that a notice must be given in writing if it is to constitute a valid notice.

6.13.14 Where interim steps are taken, if representations are made by the premises licence holder against the taking of such steps, the authority must hold a hearing within 48 hours to consider them. The authority must give advance notice of the hearing to the premises licence holder and to the police, although no indication is given as to what constitutes 'advance notice' for these purposes. Section 53B(6) and (7) provides:

> (6) If the holder of the premises licence makes, and does not withdraw, representations against any interim steps taken by the relevant licensing authority, the authority must, within 48 hours[174] of the time of its receipt of the representations, hold a hearing to consider those representations.
>
> (7) The relevant licensing authority must give advance notice of the hearing to–
>
>  (a) the holder of the premises licence;
>
>  (b) the chief officer of police for the police area in which the premises are situated (or for each police area in which they are partly situated).

No time limit is specified within which the premises licence holder must make representations on interim steps, although in practice the time for making representations 'would at some point be superseded by the full review which would have to be completed within 28 days of the application being received by the licensing authority' (ESLR Guidance, para 4.1).

Given the expedited nature of a hearing on interim steps, not surprisingly many of the provisions of the LA 2003 (Hearings) Regs 2005 are disapplied. They are specifically excluded by reg 3(2), inserted by reg 3(3) of the LA 2003 (SRPL) Regs 2007, with reg 3(2) providing:

> Regulations 4 to 13, 16(a), 18, 20(2)(a) and (4), 22 (from "and shall" to the end), 27, 29 and 34 do not apply to a hearing under section 53B of the Act (interim steps pending review).

The disapplication of reg 6 means that there is no timescale for notifying the premises licence holder of the hearing. Clearly, notification will need to take place before the hearing is held and para 4.2 of ESLR Guidance states that 'it is imperative that the licence holder be given as much notice as is possible in the circumstances to afford him or her the maximum practicable opportunity to attend the hearing'. Further, the disapplication of reg 20(2)(a) means that the licensing authority cannot adjourn the hearing to a later date if the licence holder fails to attend at the specified time, unlike in the case of an ordinary premises licence review under s 52, and, since reg 20(2)(b) is not disapplied, the hearing may be held in his absence.

At the hearing the authority must consider whether interim steps are necessary to promote the licensing objectives and decide whether to withdraw or modify the steps taken. In considering these matters, the authority is required to have regard to the certificate accompanying the police's application for summary review and any representations made by the police and by the premises licence holder. Section 53B(8) and (9) provides:

(8) At the hearing, the relevant licensing authority must–

    (a) consider whether the interim steps are necessary for the promotion of the licensing objectives; and

    (b) determine whether to withdraw or modify the steps taken.

(9) In considering those matters the relevant licensing authority must have regard to–

    (a) the certificate that accompanied the application;

    (b) any representations made by the chief officer of police for the police area in which the premises are situated (or for each police area in which they are partly situated); and

    (c) any representations made by the holder of the premises licence.

The authority's determination in respect of interim steps is not subject to any right of appeal to the magistrates' court (ESLR Guidance, para 4.5), although, as will be seen, appeal can be made against the determination of the summary review application (see 6.3.17 below).

### 6.13.15 Hearing to determine the summary review application

6.13.16 The provisions of s 53C apply where a premises licence review is held following an application made by the police for summary review (s 53C(1)). The authority must hold a hearing to consider the review application and any relevant representations received before reaching a decision on the steps that it considers necessary to promote the licensing objectives. It must also ensure that any interim steps having effect pending determination of the review cease to have effect, except to the extent that they are incorporated in its decision. Section 53C(2) provides:

The relevant licensing authority must–

    (a) hold a hearing to consider the application for the review and any relevant representations;

    (b) take such steps mentioned in subsection (3) (if any) as it considers necessary for the promotion of the licensing objectives; and

    (c) secure that, from the coming into effect of the decision made on the determination of the review, any interim steps having effect pending that determination cease to have effect (except so far as they are comprised in steps taken in accordance with paragraph (b)).

The hearing must, under s 53A(2)(b), be held within 28 days of the date of which the authority received the summary review application (see 6.13.5 above) and the hearing must be held even if the police request withdrawal of the application (ESLR Guidance, para 5.1). As with an ordinary premises licence review, the Act makes no provision for dispensing with a hearing if the parties consider it unnecessary, indicating that dispensation is not possible (see 6.12.7 above). The LA 2003 (Hearings) Regs 2005 have application in full to the summary review hearing, unlike in the case of a hearing to determine the taking of interim steps (see 6.13.14 above), and their application is similar to cases where premises licence reviews take place following closure orders. Thus the authority must give five working days' notice of the hearing (reg 6(3)(a)) and a party wishing to appear must give two working days' notice (reg 8(4)(a)).

6.13.17 The steps which the authority can take are set out in s 53C(3), with the power to modify conditions including alteration or omission of existing conditions as well as the addition of new conditions. Section 53C(3) and (4) provides:

(3) Those steps are–
   (a) the modification of the conditions of the premises licence,
   (b) the exclusion of a licensable activity from the scope of the licence,
   (c) the removal of the designated premises supervisor from the licence,
   (d) the suspension of the licence for a period not exceeding three months, or
   (e) the revocation of the licence.
(4) For the purposes of subsection (3)(a) the conditions of a premises licence are modified if any of them is altered or omitted or any new condition is added.

The power to exclude a licensable activity is generally expressed and is not confined to exclusion of the retail sale of alcohol, although it might be anticipated that, if an authority chooses to exclude a licensable activity, this will be the most likely one to be excluded. Section 53C goes on to make provision, in sub-s (5)–(11), for inclusion of mandatory conditions; for modification or exclusion to be for a specified period not exceeding three months; for the meaning of 'relevant representations'; for notification, with reasons, of those whose representations are considered frivolous or vexatious; for notification, with reasons, of its determination of the application; and for the decision not to have effect until the end of the period for appealing or, where an appeal is made, until the appeal is disposed of. These provisions in s 53C(5)–(11) essentially replicate those in s 52(5)–(11) which apply in the case of a s 51 premises licence review application (see 6.12.7–6.12–8 above).

## 6.14   UPDATING, KEEPING AND PRODUCTION OF PREMISES LICENCE

### 6.14.1 Updating of licence

Where modifications are made to a premises licence, for example where the licence is varied, transferred or amended following a review, the authority must update the licence and, if necessary, issue a new summary of it. Section 56(1) provides:

Where–
(a) the relevant licensing authority, in relation to a premises licence, makes a determination or receives a notice under this Part, or
(b) a premises licence lapses under this Part, or
(c) an appeal against a decision under this Part is disposed of,
   the relevant licensing authority must make the appropriate amendments (if any) to the licence and, if necessary, issue a new summary of the licence.

In order for the authority to make the modifications, it may be necessary for the licence to be returned to the authority and the authority can require the premises licence holder to produce the licence or appropriate part of it within 14 days of being notified of the need to do so. Section 56(2) provides:

Where a licensing authority is not in possession of the licence (or the appropriate part of the licence) it may, for the purposes of discharging its obligations under subsection

(1), require the holder of a premises licence to produce the licence (or the appropriate part) to the authority within 14 days from the date on which he is notified of the requirement.

Failure to comply, without reasonable excuse, with the requirement to produce the licence or part is a summary offence punishable by a fine not exceeding level 2 on the standard scale. Section 56(3) and (4) provides:

(3) A person commits an offence if he fails, without reasonable excuse, to comply with a requirement under subsection (2).

(4) A person guilty of an offence under subsection (3) is liable on summary conviction to a fine not exceeding level 2 on the standard scale.

## 6.14.2 Keeping and production of licence

6.14.3 The premises licence holder is under a duty to keep at the premises and produce the licence or a certified copy of it[175] whenever the premises are being used for licensable activities. The licence or certified copy must be kept in the custody or control of himself or a person working at the premises who he has nominated in writing, and a summary of the licence or certified copy,[176] together with a notice indicating the position held at the premises by the nominated person, must be prominently displayed at the premises. Section 57(1)–(3) provides:

(1) This section applies whenever premises in respect of which a premises licence has effect are being used for one or more licensable activities authorised by the licence.

(2) The holder of the premises licence must secure that the licence or a certified copy of it is kept at the premises in the custody or under the control of–
(a) the holder of the licence, or
(b) a person who works at the premises and whom the holder of the licence has nominated in writing for the purposes of this subsection.

(3) The holder of the premises licence must secure that–
(a) the summary of the licence or a certified copy of that summary, and
(b) a notice specifying the position held at the premises by any person nominated for the purposes of subsection (2), are prominently displayed at the premises.

It might be expected, and clearly would be desirable, for the summary and notice to be prominently displayed in the same place at the premises, although there is no requirement to this effect in s 57(3). It will presumably therefore meet the terms of the section if the summary and notice were to be (prominently) displayed in different parts of the premises.

The information that the summary must contain is set out in Sched 12B to the LA 2003 (PL and CPC) Regs 2005 and includes the postal address of premises or, if there is no postal address, an ordnance survey map reference or description, and telephone number; the dates during which the premises licence has effect, if it is time-limited; the licensable activities authorised by the licence and the times at which those activities may be carried out; the opening hours of the premises; where the licence authorises supplies of alcohol, whether these are on and/or off supplies and the name of the DPS; the name and (registered) address of the premises licence holder; the registered number of the premises licence holder, for example, company number or charity number (where applicable); and whether access to the premises by children is restricted or prohibited.

Failure to comply, without reasonable excuse, with the requirement to display the summary or to keep the licence at the premises is a summary offence punishable by a fine not exceeding level 2 on the standard scale (s 57(4)(8)).

6.14.4 A constable or authorised person may require the person having custody or control of the licence or certified copy to produce it for inspection, the authorised person being required to produce evidence of his authorisation if requested to do so, and a failure to produce the licence or certified copy, without reasonable excuse, is a summary offence punishable by a fine not exceeding level 2 on the standard scale. Section 57(5)–(8) provides:

(5) A constable or an authorised person[177] may require the person who, by virtue of arrangements made for the purpose of subsection (2), is required to have the premises licence (or a certified copy of it) in his custody or under his control to produce the licence (or such a copy) for examination.

(6) An authorised person exercising the power conferred by subsection (5) must, if so requested, produce evidence of his authority to exercise the power.

(7) A person commits an offence if he fails, without reasonable excuse, to produce a premises licence or certified copy of a premises licence in accordance with a requirement under subsection (5).

(8) A person guilty of an offence under this section is liable on summary conviction to a fine not exceeding level 2 on the standard scale.

## 6.15  PREDETERMINATION INSPECTIONS OF PREMISES

6.15.1 Under the previous law, it was common practice for visits to be made to premises to inspect them prior to the grant of a licence to sell intoxicating liquor or provide entertainment and s 59 confers a power on constables and authorised persons (on production of authorisation on request) to enter premises, prior to determination of an application to grant, vary or review a licence, or to issue a provisional statement, to assess the likely effect on the promotion of the licence objectives of the grant. Section 59(1)–(3) provides:

(1) In this section "relevant application" means an application under–
    (a) section 17 (grant of licence),
    (b) section 29 (provisional statement),
    (c) section 34 (variation of licence), or
    (d) section 51 (review of licence).

(2) A constable or an authorised person may, at any reasonable time before the determination of a relevant application, enter the premises to which the application relates to assess–
    (a) in a case within subsection (1)(a), (b) or (c), the likely effect of the grant of the application on the promotion of the licensing objectives, and
    (b) in a case within subsection (1)(d), the effect of the activities authorised by the premises licence on the promotion of those objectives.

(3) An authorised person exercising the power conferred by this section must, if so requested, produce evidence of his authority to exercise the power.

6.15.2  An authorised person for the purposes of this section (and other provisions involving inspection and enforcement) is defined by s 13 to include, in respect of all premises, officers of the licensing authority, fire and rescue authority inspectors, inspectors locally responsible for the enforcement of the Health and Safety at Work etc Act 1974 and environmental health officers. In respect of vessels, they also include an inspector or a surveyor of ships appointed under s 256 of the Merchant Shipping Act 1995. Such persons would normally be officers acting on behalf of the Maritime and Coastguard Agency (Guidance, para 8.4). The Secretary of State may also pre-scribe other authorised persons by means of a statutory instrument. Section 13(2) provides:

"Authorised person" means any of the following–

(a)  an officer of a licensing authority in whose area the premises are situated who is authorised by that authority for the purposes of this Act,

(b)  an inspector appointed by the fire and rescue authority for the area in which the premises are situated,

(c)  an inspector appointed under section 19 of the Health and Safety at Work etc Act 1974 (c.37),

(d)  an officer of a local authority, in whose area the premises are situated, who is authorised by that authority for the purposes of exercising one or more of its statutory functions in relation to minimising or preventing the risk of pollution of the environment or of harm to human health,

(e)  in relation to a vessel, an inspector, or a surveyor of ships, appointed under section 256 of the Merchant Shipping Act 1995 (c.21),

(f)  a person prescribed for the purposes of this subsection.

By virtue of s 59(4), constables and authorised persons may use reasonable force to gain entry, although, for reasons that are not readily apparent, this is restricted to cases involving an application for review and cannot be exercised in cases involving other applications. Section 59(5) makes it an offence for a person to intentionally obstruct an authorised person exercising the power of entry[178] and obstruction of a constable exercising the power will similarly constitute an offence, although falling within the general provision of obstructing a constable in the course of his duties under the Police Act 1996.[179]

## NOTES

1  It seems that it can also extend to partly constructed premises or premises that are to be constructed, without the need for any provisional statement under ss 29–32 to be obtained – see 6.8.2 below.

2  For a detailed consideration of this matter, see Clover, S, 'Violent Reconciliations: Local Authority Licensed Spaces v Designated Public Places Orders' [2007] *Entertainment Law Review* 31–33. The consultation and publicity provisions for designating public places before an order is made, contained in the Local Authorities (Alcohol Consumption in Designated Public Places) Regulations 2007, SI 2007/806, require that the extent and effect of the temporary exclusion of local authority premises with a premises licence whilst alcohol is sold and for 30 minutes thereafter be indicated.

3  Guidance, para 3.6.

4  For the meaning of 'relevant licensing authority', see s 12 and 6.3.1 below.

5  For provisional statements, see 6.8.1–6.8.13 below.

6   The same applies in respect of other authorisations, ie a club premises certificate (CPC) or temporary event notice (TEN): s 176(1).

7   The power to make an order is, however, subject to the 'affirmative resolution procedure', ie a draft of the statutory instrument has to be laid before and approved by a resolution of each House of Parliament: s 197(3)(4).

8   The premises referred to here are, as stated above, service areas on motorways or similar roads, which are provided at intervals and comprise petrol filling stations and refreshment facilities. These are provided by persons holding the land on lease from the special road authority. Section 176(4) provides:

> "special road" and "special road authority" have the same meaning as in the Highways Act 1980 (c.66), except that "special road" includes a trunk road to which (by virtue of paragraph 3 of Schedule 23 to that Act) the provisions of that Act apply as if the road were a special road, (b) "class I" means class I in Schedule 4 to the Highways Act 1980 as varied from time to time by an order under section 17 of that Act, but if that Schedule is amended by such an order so as to add to it a further class of traffic, the order may adapt the reference in subsection (2)(a) to traffic of class I so as to take account of the additional class.

9   Section 176(4)(c) provides:

> Premises are used as a garage if they are used for one or more of the following–
> (i)   the retailing of petrol,
> (ii)  the retailing of derv,
> (iii) the sale of motor vehicles,
> (iv)  the maintenance of motor vehicles.

10  Although the court here was considering the question of 'primary use' under the previous law contained in s 9 of the Licensing Act 1964, this should have equal application to s 176.

11  See also Guidance, para 5.24, which provides: 'The approach endorsed so far by the courts is based on intensity of use by customers to establish primary use. For example, if a garage shop in any rural area is used more intensely by customers purchasing other products than by customers purchasing the products or services listed above [ie petrol, diesel, etc], it may be eligible to seek authority to sell or supply alcohol.'

12  Section 174(7) provides: 'In this section "Minister of the Crown" has the meaning given by the Ministers of the Crown Act 1975'. Section 8 of that Act provides: ' "Minister of the Crown" means the holder of an office in Her Majesty's Government in the United Kingdom, and includes the Treasury, the Board of Trade and the Defence Council.' Further, s 174(6) provides: 'The powers conferred by this section on a Minister of the Crown may be exercised only by a Minister who is a member of the Cabinet or by the Attorney General.'

13  A document purporting to be a certificate 'is to be received in evidence and treated as being a certificate under this section unless the contrary is proved' (s 174(3)) and a document purporting to be certified as a true copy of a ministerial certificate 'is evidence of that certificate' (s 174(4)).

14  These are that the promotors may not deduct from the proceeds more than the sum prescribed by the Secretary of State by regulations in respect of costs incurred in organising the lottery; the lottery must be promoted wholly for a purpose other than that of private gain (which under s 353 is to be construed in accordance with s 19(3), on which see 5.3.40 above); there must be no rollover; and no ticket must be sold or supplied otherwise than on the premises on which the noncommercial event takes place and while that event is taking place.

15  Section 5 of the Interpretation Act 1978 provides that in any Act, 'unless the contrary intention appears', words and expressions listed in Sched 1 to the Act are to be construed according to that Schedule and Sched 1 provides: ' "person" includes a body of persons corporate or unincorporate'.

16 Since the nature of the uses of the premises may differ in such a case, even though the licensable activity is of the same description, different conditions on the premise licence may be appropriate and this might be more easily facilitated if each person held a premises licence in respect of his particular activity.

17 The court held that partial revocation under s 20A of the Licensing Act 1964 was not possible and the justices were wrong to revoke the licence in the name of one licensee, following improper conduct on his part. The licence itself should have been revoked, with an application for transfer into the sole name of the other licensee being made before the revocation took effect.

18 Whilst this may be so, the wording of s 16(1)(a) nevertheless seems wide enough to cover a pub owning company since its business does involve the use of the premises for licensable activities if 'involves' is broadly interpreted.

19 Section 4(1) provides:

> In this Act "school" means an educational institution which is outside the further education sector and the higher education sector and is an institution for providing–
>
> (a) primary education,
>
> (b) secondary education, or
>
> (c) both primary and secondary education,
>
> whether or not the institution also provides part-time education suitable to the requirements of junior pupils or further education.

20 Financial support under s 65 relates to the receipt of funds by the Higher Education Funding Councils established under s 62 of the Act.

21 Section 579(1) provides: ' "proprietor", in relation to a school, means the person or body of persons responsible for the management of the school (so that, in relation to a community, foundation or voluntary or community or foundation special school, it means the governing body).'

22 Section 90(1) provides:

> "governing body", in relation to an institution, means . . .–
>
> (a) in the case of an institution conducted by a further education corporation or a higher education corporation, the corporation,
>
> (b) in the case of a university not falling within paragraph (a) above, the executive governing body which has responsibility for the management and administration of its revenue and property and the conduct of its affairs,
>
> (c) in the case of any other institution not falling within paragraph (a) or (b) above for which there is an instrument of government providing for the constitution of a governing body, the governing body so provided for, and
>
> (d) in any other case, any board of governors of the institution or any persons responsible for the management of the institution, whether or not formally constituted as a governing body or board of governors.

23 Clearly, cases where premises are situated in the areas of two different authorities will be rare, although a notable instance is Earls Court in London, which is in the Royal Borough of Kensington and Chelsea, but which straddles the boundary with the Borough of Hammersmith and Fulham. In such a case, it will be 'important that the licensing authorities concerned maintain close contact' (Guidance, para 8.1). No instance of premises situated in the areas of more than two different authorities is known.

24 These are regulations made by the Secretary of State. Section 193 provides: ' "regulations" means regulations made by the Secretary of State . . .'; and, under s 197, the power of the Secretary of State to make regulations, or any order under the 2003 Act, is exercisable by statutory instrument (s 197(1)). Regulations or orders may include incidental, supplementary, consequential or transitional provision or savings; may make provision generally or only in relation to specified cases; and may make different provision for

different purposes (s 197(2)). Most regulations and orders that can be made under the Act, including those under s 17(2), are subject to the 'negative resolution procedure', ie annulment in pursuance of a resolution of either House of Parliament, although some are subject to the 'affirmative resolution procedure', ie a draft of the statutory instrument has to be laid before and approved by a resolution of each House of Parliament.

25  Regulations may require applications, except applications for review (see 6.12 below), to be accompanied by a fee and may prescribe the amount of the fee; they may also require a premises licence holder to pay an annual fee; and they may prescribe the amount of the annual fee and the time at which any such fee is due. Any annual fee owed to a licensing authority may be recovered as a debt due to the authority. Section 55 provides:

> (1)  Regulations may–
>> (a)  require applications under any provision of this Part (other than section 51) or notices under section 47 to be accompanied by a fee, and
>> (b)  prescribe the amount of the fee.
> (2)  Regulations may also require the holder of a premises licence to pay the relevant licensing authority an annual fee.
> (3)  Regulations under subsection (2) may include provision prescribing–
>> (a)  the amount of the fee, and
>> (b)  the time at which any such fee is due.
> (4)  Any fee which is owed to a licensing authority under subsection (2) may be recovered as a debt due to the authority.

26  See reg 10 and Sched 2; and 2.1.3 above.

27  Where premises form only part of a building that has an NDRV they are treated as having the NDRV for the building. Regulation 3(3) provides: 'For the purposes of this regulation, in a case where the premises forms part only of a hereditament in the local non-domestic rating list for the purposes of Part III of the Local Government Finance Act 1988, the premises shall be treated as having a rateable value equal to the rateable value for the hereditament of which it forms part.' Where the premises comprise two or more buildings they are treated as having the NDRV of the building with the highest rateable value. Regulation 3(4) provides: 'For the purposes of this regulation, in a case where the premises comprises two or more hereditaments in the local non-domestic rating list, the premises shall be treated as having a rateable value equal to the rateable value for the hereditament with the highest rateable value.'

28  NDRVs are subject to periodic revaluations, the last one of which occurred in April 2005, with rateable value based on a property's annual open market rental value as at 1 April 2003. Applicants may therefore find themselves paying a fee for one band when making an application, based on the existing valuation, but an annual fee under a higher band following revaluation.

29  Regulation 5(6) provides that the annual fee is 'due and payable each year on the anniversary of the date of the grant of the premises licence'.

30  It also excluded application of the provisions for increased fees in the case of applications for variation made at the same time as applications for conversion of existing licences into premises licence during the transition period. There had been no such exclusion in the original reg 4(2) and exclusion was achieved by making the regulation subject to paras (6) and (7).

31  Evidence that such premises are more likely to require the deployment of resources to promote the licensing objectives may be found in paras 10.41 and 10.42 of the Guidance, which provides:

> 10.41  Large capacity "vertical drinking" premises, sometimes called High Volume Vertical Drinking establishments (HVVDs), are premises with exceptionally high capacities, used primarily or exclusively for the sale and consumption of alcohol, and have little or no seating for patrons.

10.42 A comprehensive review of the research conducted in the last twenty-five years into alcohol and crime and its relationship to licensed premises, "Alcohol and Crime: Taking Stock" by Ann Deehan, Home Office Crime Reduction Research Series No 3 (1999) can be viewed on www.crimereduction.gov.uk/drugsalcohol8.htm. It shows that the environment within such establishments can have a significant bearing on the likelihood of crime and disorder arising on the premises.

32 It is possible that the original reg 4(2) might have been interpreted in a way that the increased fee was payable only where premises themselves were used exclusively or primarily for the supply of alcohol for consumption there. This would have required a purposive interpretation to be given to the regulation, 'reading in' the word 'is' and reading the reference to 'relates to' in the regulation disjunctively in respect of sub-paras (i) and (ii), so that it read: 'application relates to – (i) premises in Band D or Band E and (ii) use of premises [is] exclusively or primarily for' such supply.

33 Section 176, in essence re-enacting provisions previously contained in s 9 of the Licensing Act 1964, precludes the sale of alcohol at premises used primarily as a garage and under s 9 the courts regarded intensity of use as the determining criterion, although account might be taken of net turnover and the purpose for which customers visited the site – see 6.1.7 above.

34 The additional fee is payable in respect of vehicles or vessels on which 5,000 or more persons are allowed, although these are likely to be few in numbers, since under reg 4(5)(a) exclusion of payment of the fee does not apply in these cases. This is similarly the case with moveable structures.

35 For the use of Explanatory Notes as an aid to interpreting the meaning of a statutory provision, see 9.6.4 below.

36 Although all of the conditions in reg 4(5)(b) need to be met in order for the additional fee not to be payable, reg 4(5)(b)(ii) clearly does not have application in the case of structures purpose-built (or altered) for licensable activities and it can be ignored in such cases. This is apparent from inclusion of the reference to 'if relevant' in reg 4(5)(b)(ii); it will not be relevant for purpose-built structures.

37 For the definition of 'proprietor', see s 16(3) of the 2003 Act and 6.2.8 above.

38 Regulation 2(1) provides: ' "school" means a school within the meaning of section 4 of the Education Act 1996' – see 6.2.8 above.

39 Regulation 2(1) provides: ' "college" means a college or similar institution principally concerned with the provision of full-time education suitable to the requirements of persons over compulsory school age who have not attained the age of 19.'

40 For the meaning of 'interested party' and 'responsible authority', see s 13(3) and (4), and 6.4.13–6.4.18 below.

41 These are covered in detail in 2.1.3–2.1.13 above.

42 Section 14 provides:

'For the purposes of this Part the "supply of alcohol" means–

(a) the sale by retail of alcohol, or

(b) the supply of alcohol by or on behalf of a club to, or to the order of, a member of the club.'

43 See reg 10 and Sched 2 to the LA (PL and CPC) Regs 2005.

44 *Quaere* whether 'open to the public' should indicate only the times proposed for the public to remain on the premises after they have been present at licensable activities or, in addition, any times proposed for the public to be admitted to the premises after licensable activities have ended.

45 Equally, of course, premises may be open to the public prior to the commencement hour for licensable activities, for example, for breakfast or sale of non-alcoholic beverages.

46 Under reg 4 of the Categories of Gaming Machine Regulations 2007, SI 2007/2158 a Category C gaming machine is one where the maximum charge for use is no more than 50 pence and the maximum prize value is no more than £35. Under reg 3, a Category D

gaming machine is defined partly by reference to whether the machine offers money or non-money prizes, or a combination of both. A machine is a Category D gaming machine where a non-money prize is offered, if the maximum charge for use is no more than 30 pence and the maximum prize value is no more than £8 (reg 3(1)); where a money prize is offered, if the maximum charge for use is no more than 10 pence and the maximum prize value is no more than £5 (reg 3(2)); and in any other case, if the maximum charge for use is no more than 10 pence and the maximum prize value is no more than £8, of which no more than £5 can be a money prize (reg 3(3)).

47 The prescribed fee is £50 (under the Gaming Machines in Alcohol Licensed Premises (Notification Fee) (England and Wales) Regulations 2007, SI 2007/1832). Under Art 6 and Sched 4, para 23 of The Gambling Act 2005 (Commencement No. 6 and Transitional Provisions) Order 2006, SI 2006/3272, notification and payment of the prescribed fee are not required where authorisations under s 34 of the Gaming Act 1968 for AWPs are in force before 1 September 2007 or are granted on or after that date. Such authorisations continue in force until 31 August 2010, after which notification and payment are required.

48 See 2.1.8–2.1.10 above for plans and Sched 11, Pt A for consent.

49 Not all proposals contained in the operating schedule are in fact translated into conditions; some are included in the licence itself and do not appear as conditions, eg the times the licence authorises the carrying out of licensable actvities, and the opening hours of the premises – see LA 2003 (PL and CPC) Regs 2005, Sch 12A.

50 Section 15(1) provides: 'In this Act references to the "designated premises supervisor", in relation to a premises licence, are to the individual for the time being specified in that licence as the premises supervisor.'

51 Section 15(2) provides: 'Nothing in this Act prevents an individual who holds a premises licence from also being specified in the licence as the premises supervisor.'

52 The Guidance, para 10.46 provides: 'This does not mean that the condition should require the presence of the designated premises supervisor or any other personal licence holder on the premises at all material times.'

53 See Guidance, para 13.72, which recommends that local authorities 'should consider establishing a policy of seeking premises licences from the licensing authority for public spaces within the community in their own name' and which goes on to mention, by way of example, 'village greens, market squares, promenades, community halls, local authority owned art centres and similar public areas' (see 6.1.3 above).

54 This can be done by an application under s 37 to vary the licence so as to specify the individual named in the application – see 6.9.7–6.9.13 below.

55 However, one of the steps that an authority can take when determining a licence application (where there are relevant representations) is to refuse to specify a person as the premises supervisor (s 18(4)(c)) – see 6.5.1 below and 6.5.3–6.5.4 below – and it may be in such an instance there will also be no DPS.

56 The Guidance, para 10.46 provides: 'This does not mean that the condition should require the presence of the designated premises supervisor or any other personal licence holder on the premises at all material times.'

57 *Quaere* whether an authority might include in its Statement of Licensing Policy a provision that, for (certain types of) premises selling alcohol, its policy will be for a personal licence holder to be present on the premises at all times. Perhaps in the absence of any evidence of difficulties associated with no personal licence holder being present on the premises, such a provision could not be said to meet the requirement of being necessary to promote any of the licensing objectives. If the Statement were to indicate that this would be the policy following a review of the premises licence, however, this requirement might more easily be met.

58 The SIA was established by the Private Security Industry Act 2001 to regulate the private security industry. Although the heading to s 21 refers to 'Mandatory conditions: door supervision', the term 'door supervisor' is not used in the section, which refers to 'a

condition that at specified times one or more individuals must be at the premises to carry out a security activity'. A 'security activity' means an activity to which para 2(1)(a) of Sched 2 to the Private Security Industry Act 2001 applies and which is licensable conduct for the purposes of that Act (see section 3(2) of that Act), ie door supervision by security operatives: s 21(3)(a).

59 The reason for the inclusion of this condition is to ensure that a premises licence holder can be prosecuted where door supervisors supplied by an agency are used. This is not possible under the Private Industry Security Act 2001, which provides only for prosecution of the individual door supervisor or anyone employing him, and door supervisors supplied by an agency are employed by the agency not the holder of the licence.

60 Section 14 of the 2001 Act requires the SIA to establish and maintain a register of approved providers of security industry services, and those organisations that satisfactorily meet the agreed standards may be registered as approved contractors and may advertise themselves as such. For details, see the Private Security Industry Act 2001 (Approved Contractor Scheme) Regulations 2007, SI 2007/808.

61 Paragraph 8 relates to activities of a 'security operative' (ie door supervisor) in relation to licensed premises at times when these are open to the public for the supply of alcohol for consumption on the premises or for the provision of regulated entertainment on the premises and para 8(3) makes provision for occasions on which premises are not to be regarded as 'licensed premises' for the purposes of the paragraph. These occasions include ones where the premises are about to be used or have just been used for the purpose in question, for para 8(5) provides that: 'References in this paragraph to the occasion on which any premises are being used for a particular purpose include references to any time on that occasion when the premises are about to be used for that purpose, or have just been used for that purpose.' This has application under s 21(3)(b) of the 2003 Act, which provides that: 'Paragraph 8(5) of that Schedule (interpretation of references to an occasion) applies as it applies in relation to paragraph 8 of that Schedule.'

62 As the Guidance indicates: 'there is no power for the licensing authority to attach a condition which is merely aspirational: it must be necessary. For example, conditions may not be attached which relate solely to the health of customers rather than their direct physical safety' (para 9.24).

63 As to the giving of notice of hearing, see 2.3.2 above. The applicant must be given the relevant representations with the notice of hearing: reg 7(2) and Sched 3, para 1 of the LA 2003 (Hearings) Regs 2005.

64 HL Deb, vol 645, col 400, 27 February 2003. Various other parties with expert voices have been added to the parties mentioned here, eg the local planning authority, which has particular expertise on the issue of cumulative effect, and a body (likely to be the area child protection committee) recognised by the authority as representing those responsible for or interested in matters relating to the protection of children from harm – see 6.4.18 below.

65 Further, the 'Secretary of State recommends that in borderline cases, the benefit of the doubt should be given to the interested party making the representation. The subsequent hearing would then provide an opportunity for the person or body making the representation to amplify and clarify it. If it then emerged, for example, that the representation should not be supported, the licensing authority could decide not to take any action in respect of the application' (Guidance, para 9.12).

66 The Guidance, para 9.10 provides: 'It is for the licensing authority to determine whether any representation by an interested party is frivolous or vexatious on the basis of what might ordinarily be considered to be vexatious or frivolous'. What might ordinarily be considered to be vexatious or frivolous suggests an objective test.

67 See also the remarks of Lord McIntosh, a Government spokesman, in the House of Lords during the passage of the legislation: ' "Vicinity" . . . will not exclude individuals who live a few streets away from the premises and . . . under certain circumstances, it could be

interpreted to cover a neighbourhood or district if the case warranted that breadth of scope.' (HL Deb, vol 645, col 406, 27 February 2003).

68   This is considered at 3.5.13 above.

69   Paragraph 9.5 provides:'In making their initial decision on the question of vicinity, licensing authorities should consider whether the individual's residence or business is likely to be directly affected by disorder and disturbance occurring or potentially occurring on those premises or immediately outside the premises. In other words, it is the impact of issues relating to the four licensing objectives that is the key consideration'.

70   It was submitted by counsel for the applicant that this 'is an absurd position', to which his Lordship's response was: 'He may well be right, but that is the effect of Parliament's definition of "interested party" in section 13(3)' (para 19).

71   For details, see Manchester, C, *Entertainment Licensing Law and Practice*, 2nd edn, 1999, London: Butterworths, paras 15.33 and 15.34.

72   Under s 17(5)(c) this is a period prescribed by regulations and, under reg 22(b) of the LA 2003 (PL and CPC) Regs 2005, is generally 28 days after the day on which the application is given to the authority – see 6.3.1 above.

73   In the former instance, although such persons would seem to be entitled to make representations, their representations may perhaps not be regarded as relevant representations, either on the ground that they are considered frivolous or vexatious or are considered to have been impliedly withdrawn (since the persons in question will clearly not be affected by the time the premises licence takes effect). In the latter instance, such persons will not literally be living in the vicinity, but might, to all intents and purposes, be regarded as doing so and it might be felt that, on a purposive construction, they should be entitled to make representations, since they undoubtedly will be affected.

74   'A body is included in subsection 3(b) to ensure that residents' associations have a voice without the need to take direct instructions from their members on every single matter' (Baroness Blackstone, HL Deb, vol 645, col 396, 27 February 2003). Residents' and trade associations are mentioned as examples in para 8.5 of the Guidance, along with a parish or town council. *Quaere* whether there is sufficient connection between a parish or town council and those living within its boundaries for it to be 'a body representing persons'.

75   See op. cit., Manchester, fn 71, para 5.10.

76   Section 185 makes provision for the sharing of information by licensing authorities and responsible authorities. Information held by or on behalf of a licensing authority or a responsible authority (including information obtained before the coming into force of s 185) may be supplied to a licensing authority or responsible authority for the purposes of facilitating the exercise of the authority's functions under the Act (s 185(1)(2)). It must not, however, be further disclosed for any other purpose (s 185(3)). A 'responsible authority', for these purposes, means a responsible authority within the meaning of Pt 3 or 4 of the Act (s 185(4)).

77   Section 13(5) provides: 'For the purposes of this section, "statutory function" means a function conferred by or under any enactment.'

78   The Guidance, para 13.52, provides: 'This may be the local authority social services department, the Area Child Protection Committee, or another competent body'.

79   The Guidance, para 8.14, provides: 'The Secretary of State in this case means the Secretary of State for Transport who in practice acts through the Maritime and Coastguard Agency (MCA) . . .' It will therefore effectively be the Maritime and Coastguard Agency that will be making representations and representations made by the MCA on behalf of the Secretary of State should be given particular weight (Guidance, para 5.15). There is no reference to the MCA in the Act since it is an Executive Agency of Government that acts for the Secretary of State for Transport, but which itself has no formal legal existence.

80   See para [40]: 'For the reasons given by Lord Hoffmann and Lord Neuberger, there is nothing in the complaint that the Council should have declined to consider the late representations and objections'.

81  Guidance, para 9.10. The recommendation for delegation is contained in para 13.79 of the
    Guidance – see 2.2.19 above. Although officers cannot determine a premises licence
    application where representations have been received, as delegation to them is excluded
    by s 10(4)(a), determination in the case of frivolous representations is concerned with the
    question of *whether* (relevant) representations have been received and this is *not* excluded
    by s 10(4).
82  This is in effect a breach of the statutory duty in s 6 of the Human Rights Act 1998, as
    distinct from a breach of the statutory duty in s 18(8) of the 2003 Act.
83  This may depend on whether persons making representations are regarded as affected
    to a sufficient degree by the authority's decision and whether they can be classed as a
    'victim' – see 3.2.1 above.
84  On this aspect, see further 3.5.12–3.5.13 above.
85  Paragraph 4.25. The convictions here are for 'relevant offences', which may preclude a
    person from obtaining or retaining a personal licence. These offences are specified in
    Sched 4. Selling alcohol to minors will fall either within para 1 of Sched 4 (an offence
    under the 2003 Act) or 2(b) (an offence under the Licensing Act 1964). For details of
    'relevant offences', see 10.5.6–10.5.12 below. Convictions for offences other than 'relevant
    offences' should not constitute exceptional circumstances. Parliament has made express
    provision in s 120(2) that (provided certain other conditions are met) a person must be
    granted a personal licence if he does not have any convictions for a relevant offence. This,
    by implication, means that he must be granted a licence even if he has convictions for
    other offences. If such convictions could be introduced via s 18(9), this might be regarded
    as countermanding the intention of Parliament as expressed in s 120(2).
86  For details of provisional statements and these restrictions, see 6.8.13 below.
87  An example is given in one of the Explanatory Notes (64) to s 18 – the authority
    may prohibit the admittance of under-18s to premises where adult entertainment is pro-
    vided (which would accord with the licensing objective of protection of children from
    harm).
88  See paras 63–64: 'Mr Pike [counsel for the claimant] correctly submitted that the reasons
    given by a decision-maker must explain at least "the conclusions reached on the principal
    important controversial issues" (see *South Bucks District Council v. Porter* . . .) . . . The
    immediate context . . . was somewhat different but the statements of general principle . . .
    are of course applicable generally . . .'
89  HL Deb, vol 643, cols 302–03, 16 January 2003. Inclusion of the 'forthwith' requirement
    might possibly have the opposite effect to that intended. Authorities might, in con-
    sequence of this requirement, be inclined to delay announcement of a decision. Under
    reg 26(2) of the LA 2003 (Hearings) Regs 2005 authorities must make a determination
    within a period of five working days beginning with the day or the last day on which the
    hearing was held, so they might delay a determination until in a position to provide more
    or less immediate notification.
90  The requirement in this case to file notice of security for the costs of an appeal 'forthwith'
    was held not to require it to be done the same day: 'It is not right to construe "forthwith"
    as meaning "on the same day". If it had been intended that the notice must be filed on the
    same day . . . that could have been expressed [in the statute]' (*per* Lord Dilhorne LC at
    608).
91  See para 46 of Cm 4696, 2000 ('a licence should be issued either for the life of the business
    providing alcohol sales and/or public entertainment at the premises or until such time as
    it is revoked or suspended').
92  For the meaning of 'recognised club', see s 193 and 8.2.3 below.
93  Section 2(1) provides: 'For the purposes of this Act, a person lacks capacity in relation to a
    matter if at the material time he is unable to make a decision for himself in relation to the
    matter because of an impairment of, or a disturbance in the functioning of, the mind or
    brain'.

94  The premises owner may be notified of the surrender of the licence if he has given notice under s 178 to the licensing authority of his property interest in the premises, which will entitle him to be notified of the surrender once this change has been made in the licensing register kept under s 8 – see 2.4.7 above; but persons such as the DPS are unlikely to have any property interest in the premises entitling them to give notice under s 178.

95  Premises might be 'otherwise altered' for the purpose of being used for one or more licensable activities if a previously unlicensed area in the building is to be used for a licensable activity and a provisional statement may be sought in respect of the additional area – see Guidance, para 8.55. Extension or alteration of premises already used for licensable activities under a premises licence might be effected by means of an application to vary the licence, although s 36(6) provides that it is not possible through a variation application to vary substantially the premises to which the licence relates – see 6.9.5 below. If a substantial extension or alteration is sought, application should be made for a provisional statement, followed (on completion of the work) by an application for a (new) premises licence.

96  As para 8.54 of the Guidance recognises, 'investors may be unwilling to commit funds unless they have some assurance that a premises licence covering the desired licensable activities would be granted for the premises when the building work is completed'.

97  See 6.1.4–6.1.6 above.

98  Section 29(3) provides that: 'In this Act "provisional statement" means a statement issued under section 31(2) or (3)(c)' – see 6.8.7–6.8.8 below.

99  See reg 11 and Sched 3.

100  For the provision in s 17(5), see 6.3.1 above.

101  For the restriction imposed by s 32, see 6.8.9–6.8.13 below.

102  The level of detail required is much less than in the case of an operating schedule that must accompany an application for a premises licence (see 6.3.3 above), not least because in many cases the person carrying out the work will not be the same person who will carry out the licensable activities and therefore it is not possible at the stage of an application for a provisional statement to provide such detail – see HL Deb, vol 643, col 316, 16 January 2003.

103  Section 31(8) provides: 'In this section "provisional statement application" means an application made in accordance with section 29.'

104  The statement issued under s 31(2) will be a 'provisional statement': s 29(3) – see 6.8.4 above.

105  Regulation 5 and Sched 1, para 2 and reg 6(1)(4) and Sched 2, para 2 of the LA 2003 (Hearings) Regs 2005. As to the giving of notice of hearing, see 2.3.2 above. Under reg 7(2) and Sched 3, para 2 the applicant must be given the relevant representations with the notice of hearing.

106  See 6.4.9 above. Reference should be made back to commentary on these provisions, which should have equal application in respect of provisional statements.

107  See reg 22(b) of the LA 2003 (PL and CPC) Regs 2005, which provides that representations can be made at any time during a period of 28 consecutive days starting on the day after the day on which the application was given to the authority.

108  For notification of interested parties, see reg 31 of the LA 2003 (PL and CPC) Regs 2005 and 6.4.21 above.

109  The word 'substantial', as Deane J observed in the Australian case of *Tillmans Butcheries Property Ltd v Australasian Meat Industry Employees Union* [1979] 42 FLR 331, 348, 'is not only susceptible of ambiguity: it is a word calculated to conceal a lack of precision'. However, the meaning normally given is large or considerable rather than something above the minimal or trivial: ' "Substantial" . . . is not the same as "not unsubstantial" ie just enough to avoid the *de minimis* principle. One of the primary meanings of the

word is equivalent to considerable, solid or big' (*per* Viscount Simon in *Palser v Grinling* [1948] AC 292, at 316).

110  This will have the meaning ascribed by s 29(7) – see 6.8.7 above.

111  This will be a 'provisional statement': s 29(3) – see 6.8.4 above.

112  The Guidance, para 8.61, states that the licensing authority 'should give full and comprehensive reasons for its decision'.

113  For the meaning of 'forthwith', see 6.6.2 above.

114  This will have the meaning ascribed by s 29(7) – see 6.8.7 above.

115  For sub-s (3), see 6.8.13 below.

116  Variations that seek to extend the time for which the licence has effect or to vary substantially the premises to which it relates are excluded.

117  See reg 12 and Sched 4.

118  See regs 25, 27 and 22(b), respectively, and 2.12, 2.1.6 and 2.17 above.

119  *Quaere* whether if a hearing is dispensed with by agreement, following modifications made to an application, there should be further advertisement under s 34 in the event that modifications have a possible impact on persons who may not have been affected by the application as originally made. This might arise, for instance, if premises had frontages on two streets and the means of exit on the application was in one street but this was changed to exit on the other street. This modification may affect those residing on the other street, although they may not have been affected (or at least not affected to the same extent) by the original application. The Act must envisage modifications being made, as without them there is unlikely to be any agreement to dispense with a hearing, but there does not seem to be any requirement for further advertisement in such cases.

120  Regulation 6(4) and Sched 2, para 3 of the LA 2003 (Hearings) Regs 2005. As to the giving of notice of hearing, see 2.3.2 above. Under reg 7(2) and Sched 3, para 3, the applicant must be given the relevant representations with the notice of hearing.

121  Section 36(6) excludes any variation which seeks to extend the licence's period of duration or to make a substantial variation in respect of the premises – see 6.9.5 below.

122  'Relevant representations', for the purposes of this section, has the same meaning as in s 18(6)(a)(b) and (7) in respect of applications for grant of a premises licence – see 6.4.9 above. Section 35(5) and (6) are expressed in identical terms to these provisions in s 18. If any representations are determined to be frivolous or vexatious, the authority must notify the person who made them of the reasons for the determination: s 36(5). Notification must be given in writing to the person who made the representations as soon as is reasonably practicable and in any event before the determination of the application to which the representations relate: reg 31 of the LA 2003 (PL and CPC) Regs 2005 (see 6.4.21 above).

123  'Relevant representations' has the same meaning as in s 35(5): s 36(8) – see 6.9.4 above.

124  The police have a similar power of objection in respect of the grant of a premises licence and the (initial) designation of the premises supervisor. This matter has been considered at 6.4.23 above and reference should be made back to this section.

125  See 6.9.4–6.9.5 above.

126  Regulation 6(4) and Sched 2, para 4 of the LA 2003 (Hearings) Regs 2005. As to the giving of notice of hearing, see 2.3.2 above. Under reg 7(2) and Sched 3, para 4, the applicant must be given the police notice of objection with the notice of hearing.

127  Notice must be given forthwith on making the determination and the notice must be accompanied by information regarding the right of a party to appeal against the determination of the authority: regs 28–29 of the LA 2003 (Hearings) Regs 2005. For the meaning of 'forthwith', see 6.6.2 above.

128  Section 41(2) provides: 'Subsection (1) is subject to regulations under section 54 (form etc of notices etc).' Regulation 21(1) of the LA 2003 (PL and CPC) Regs 2005 requires only that the notice be in writing, although reg 21(2) makes provision for this requirement to be satisfied by electronic communication where certain criteria are met – see 2.1.5 above.

129 The Guidance, para 13.79, recommends that a request to be removed as the DPS should be delegated to and dealt with by officers – see 2.2.19 above. For details of the licensing register, see 2.4 above.

130 See reg 14 and Sched 6 to the LA 2003 (PL and CPC) Regs 2005.

131 Giving notice requires a copy of the application, together with any attachments, to be given on the same day the application is given to the licensing authority: reg 28(b) of the LA 2003 (PL and CPC) Regs 2005.

132 As in other cases where the police can object on this ground (eg varying the DPS), the Guidance stresses that this should 'only arise in truly exceptional circumstances' (para 8.69).

133 *Quaere* whether an authority has a discretion to take into account any notice given outside the 14-day period. Arguably it has, since the authority must carry out its functions under the Act with a view to promoting the licensing objectives, one of which is the prevention of crime and disorder (s 4(1) and (2)(a)), and it might be seen as failing to discharge this duty if the notice were to be discounted.

134 Explanatory Note 94. See also Guidance, para 8.67: 'Section 43 of the 2003 Act provides a mechanism which allows the transfer to come into immediate effect as soon as the licensing authority receives it, until it is formally determined or withdrawn. This is to ensure that there should be no interruption to normal business at the premises.'

135 For the meaning of 'forthwith', see 6.6.2 above. Failure to comply with the requirement of notification, without reasonable excuse, is a criminal offence punishable on summary conviction with a fine not exceeding level 3 on the standard scale: s 46(4)(5).

136 *Quaere* whether the provisions in s 184 – see 2.5 above – with regard to the giving of notices apply to the giving of consent. These apply 'in relation to any document required or authorised by or under this Act to be given to any person' (s 184(1)). The term 'document' is not defined and, whilst it is clear (from the heading to the section) that it will include the giving of notices, it is less clear whether it will apply to cases where a person gives consent. It could be said that the effect of s 43(3) is to authorise (for it does not require) the giving of consent by the premises licence holder to the applicant for transfer and therefore consent should be given in accordance with s 184.

137 The Guidance, para 8.67 states: 'In the vast majority of cases, it is expected that a transfer will be a very simple administrative process.'

138 Section 44(7) provides: 'Where the relevant licensing authority refuses to exempt an applicant under subsection (6), it must notify the applicant of its reasons for that decision.'

139 Regulation 5 and Sched 1, para 5 of the LA 2003 (Hearings) Regs 2005.

140 Regulation 6(4) and Sched 2, para 5 of the LA 2003 (Hearings) Regs 2005. As to the giving of notice of hearing, see 2.3.2 above. Under reg 7(2) and Sched 3, para 5, the applicant and the holder of the premises licence must be given the police notice of objection with the notice of hearing.

141 Notice must be given forthwith on making the determination and the notice must be accompanied by information regarding the right of a party to appeal against the determination of the authority: regs 28–29 of the LA 2003 (Hearings) Regs 2005. For the meaning of 'forthwith', see 6.6.2 above.

142 Section 45(3) goes on to provide: 'That time is the time specified in the application or, if that time is before the applicant is given that notice, such later time as the relevant licensing authority specifies in the notice.'

143 See 6.7.3–6.7.4 above.

144 The notice must be given within 'the initial seven day period' referred to in s 47(2) and defined in s 47(10) to mean 'the period of seven days beginning with the day after the day the licence lapses'. Section 47(3) provides: 'Subsection (2) is subject to regulations under – (a) section 54 (form etc of notices etc); (b) section 55 (fees to accompany applications etc).' For the form and information to be contained in an IAN, see reg 15

and Sched 7 to the LA 2003 (PL and CPC) Regs 2005. Under reg 8 and Sched 6 to the LA 2003 (Fees) Regs 2005, the fee payable is £23.

145 Regulation 8 of the LA 2003 (PL and CPC) Regs 2005 provides: 'For the purposes of section 47(2)(a) a person has a prescribed interest in the premises concerned if he has a legal interest in the premises as freeholder or leaseholder.'

146 This provision was amended by Sched 6, para 46 of the Mental Capacity Act 2005.

147 Section 47(10) provides: ' "becomes insolvent" is to be construed in accordance with section 27' – see 6.7.3 above – and ' "insolvency practitioner", in relation to a person, means a person acting as an insolvency practitioner in relation to him (within the meaning of section 388 of the Insolvency Act 1986 (c.45))'. Section 388 makes different provision, depending on whether a person is acting as an insolvency practitioner in relation to a company, individual or an insolvent partnership.

148 Section 47(10) provides: ' "initial seven day period", in relation to a licence which lapses as mentioned in subsection (1), means the period of seven days beginning with the day after the day the licence lapses.'

149 A copy of the application, together with any attachments, must be given on the same day the application is given to the licensing authority: reg 28(b) of the LA 2003 (PL and CPC) Regs 2005.

150 Section 49(3) provides: 'This Act applies in relation to a copy issued under this section as it applies in relation to an original licence or summary.'

151 The Guidance, para 8.71, provides:

> The premises licence would lapse until such a notice is given and carrying on licensable activities in that time would be unlawful. Such activity will be an offence as an unauthorised licensable activity under section 136(1)(a) of the 2003 Act, to which there is a "defence of due diligence" provided in section 139. This may be relevant where, for example, the manager of particular premises is wholly unaware for a period of time that the premises licence holder has died.

152 Section 47(7)(a) – see 6.11.5 above. If a copy has been given, the reinstatement of the premises licence continues, although it may thereafter lapse if the licensing authority cancels the IAN following police objections – see 6.11.9–6.11.11 below.

153 Section 47(10) provides:

> "interim authority period" means the period beginning with the day on which the interim authority notice is received by the relevant licensing authority and ending–
>
> (a) two months after that day, or
>
> (b) if earlier, when it is terminated by the person who gave the interim authority notice
>
> notifying the relevant licensing authority to that effect.

154 Section 47(10) provides: ' "relevant transfer application" in relation to the premises licence, is an application under section 42 which is given interim effect by virtue of section 43.'

155 Regulation 5 and Sched 1, para 6 of the LA 2003 (Hearings) Regs 2005.

156 Regulation 6(2)(a), and Sched 2, para 6 of the LA 2003 (Hearings) Regs 2005. As to the giving of notice of hearing, see 2.3.2 above. Under reg 7(2) and Sched 3, para 6, the person giving the IAN must be given the police notice of objection with the notice of hearing.

157 For lapse in the circumstances mentioned, see 6.7.3–6.7.4 above. For persons entitled to apply for a premises licence, see s 16(1) and 6.2 above.

158 Paragraph 11.1. 'The provisions for the review of the premises licence are a powerful means of securing the promotion of the licensing objective[s]. They are reactive provisions which are designed to deal with problems as and when they arise. We need to recognise that exceptional action should be taken when a particular personal licence holder marries up with a certain set of premises and produces a damaging mixture' (Lord McIntosh – see HL Deb, vol 645, col 410, 27 February 2003).

159 Guidance, para 11.8, which also provides: 'It is important to recognise that the promotion of the licensing objectives relies heavily on a partnership between licence holders, authorised persons, interested parties and responsible authorities in pursuit of common aims. It is therefore equally important that reviews are not used to drive a wedge between these groups in a way that would undermine the benefits of co-operation.'

160 The Guidance, para 11.4, provides: 'Licensing authorities may not initiate their own reviews of premises licences. Officers of the local authority who are specified as responsible authorities under the 2003 Act, such as environmental health officers, may however request reviews on any matter which relates to the promotion of one or more of the licensing objectives.'

161 The Guidance, para 11.3, goes on to provide: 'In addition, a review of the licence will normally follow any action by the police to close down the premises for up to 24 hours on grounds of disorder or noise nuisance as a result of a notice of magistrates court's determination sent to the licensing authority.' For such closure, see 11.13 below.

162 No provision, however, is made for the payment by an applicant of a fee for review, presumably so as not to discourage the making of applications.

163 For the form and information to be contained in a premises licence review application, see reg 16 and Sched 8 to the LA 2003 (PL and CPC) Regs 2005.

164 Regulation 29 provides:

> In the case of an application for a review of a premises licence under section 51 or a review of a club premises certificate under section 87, the person making the application shall give notice of his application to each responsible authority and to the holder of the premises licence or the club in whose name the club premises certificate is held and to which the application relates by giving to the authority, the holder or the club a copy of the application for review together with its accompanying documents, if any, on the same day as the day on which the application for review is given to the licensing authority.

165 For excluded representations, see 6.8.12–6.8.13 above.

166 The wording of this provision is similar to that used in s 14(2) of the Freedom of Information Act 2000, which provides: 'Where a public authority has previously complied with a request for information which was made by any person, it is not obliged to comply with a subsequent identical or substantially similar request from that person unless a reasonable interval has elapsed between compliance with the previous request and the making of the current request.' This provision does not appear to have received any judicial consideration.

167 Paragraph 11.12. This recommendation relates only to reviews originating from interested parties and not from responsible authorities.

168 Regulation 6(4), and Sched 2, para 7 of the LA 2003 (Hearings) Regs 2005. As to the giving of notice of hearing, see 2.3.2 above. Under reg 7(2) and Sched 3, para 7, the premises licence holder must be given the relevant representations with the notice of hearing.

169 See s 18(6)(a) and 6.4.11 above, and s 35(5) and 6.9.4 above, respectively.

170 The examples given are mentioned in the Guidance, para 11.17. As regards modifying conditions, this power is subject to ss 19–21, which contain requirements to include certain conditions in premises licences: s 52(5). These are conditions, respectively, relating to the supply of alcohol (requiring a DPS for the premises and for supply to be made or authorised by personal licence holders), for the admission of children to film exhibitions to be restricted in accordance with film classification recommendations and for door supervisors to be licensed by the Security Industry Authority – see 6.4.2–6.4.5 above.

171 In *R v Crown Court at Maidstone ex p Olson* [1992] COD 496, the High Court held that an authority, when refusing to renew a taxi driver's licence, could rely on the evidence of a

female passenger of whom he had been convicted of indecently assaulting, notwith-standing that the conviction had subsequently been quashed by the Court of Appeal as unsafe and unsatisfactory on account of a number of misdirections and non-directions by the trial judge when summing up to the jury. A later High Court, in *McCool v Rushcliffe Borough Council* [1998] 3 All ER 889 (a case with similar facts), applying the *Maidstone* principle, held that hearsay evidence, in this case a newspaper report of the passenger's evidence at the first trial (which was later accepted by the driver as an accurate record following acknowledgment that he had lied to the police and on oath at the trial), might establish unfitness and direct evidence from the victim was not neces-sary. Where, however, criminal proceedings are discontinued and a defendant disputes both liability and admissions made in a police note of the incident, there may be no way of knowing whether the denial was well founded. In this instance hearsay evidence might not establish unfitness and there may be no reasonable cause for the licence to be revoked: *R (Wrexham Borough Council) v Chester Crown Court* [2004] LLR 802 (where the Administrative Court, distinguishing *McCool*, held that that case did not support the proposition that the court should have taken into account the police note and required the defendant to give evidence or offered him the opportunity to do so).

172   Section 53A(4)(a) provides: ' "senior member", in relation to a police force, means a police officer who is a member of that force and of or above the rank of superintendent'.

173   Section 53A(5) provides: 'In computing the period of 48 hours mentioned in subsection (2)(a) time that is not on a working day is to be disregarded'.

174   Section 53B(10) provides: 'In computing the period of 48 hours mentioned in subsection (6) time that is not on a working day is to be disregarded'.

175   Section 58 makes provision about certified copies: s 57(10). A certified copy is a copy certified to be a true copy by the relevant licensing authority, a solicitor or notary, or a person of a prescribed description: s 58(1). Any certified copy produced in accordance with a requirement under s 57(5) (for a person having custody or control of the licence to produce it for examination by a constable or authorised officer) must be a copy of the document in the form in which it exists at the time: s 58(2). A document which purports to be a certified copy is to be taken to be such a copy unless the contrary is shown: s 58(3).

176   The summary is a reference to the summary issued under s 23 – see 6.6.1 above – or, where one or more summaries have been subsequently issued under s 56 following updating of the licence, the most recent summary to have been so issued: s 57(9).

177   For the meaning of 'authorised person', see s 13 and 6.15.2 below.

178   The offence is punishable summarily by a fine not exceeding level 2 on the standard scale: s 59(6).

179   See s 89(2) of the Police Act 1996, which provides: 'Any person who resists or wilfully obstructs a constable in the execution of his duty, or a person assisting a constable in the execution of his duty, shall be guilty of an offence and liable on summary conviction to imprisonment for a term not exceeding one month or to a fine not exceeding level 3 on the standard scale, or to both.'

# CHAPTER 7

# CONDITIONS

## 7.1 INTRODUCTION

Conditions may be attached to a premises licence and to a club premises certificate (CPC), but not to a personal licence or to a temporary event notice (TEN) except where the licensable activities include the supply of alcohol, in which case under s 100(6) a condition must be attached to the TEN that all supplies of alcohol must be made or authorised by the premises user (see 9.2.3 below). When licences and certificates (hereafter 'licences') are granted, there are also some mandatory conditions that must be imposed. For premises licences, these are that no supply of alcohol may be made unless there is a designated premises supervisor (DPS) with a personal licence in respect of the premises licence and unless supply is made or authorised by a personal licence holder; that the admission of children to film exhibitions is to be restricted in accordance with film classification recommendations; and that any condition requiring door supervisors must also require them to be licensed or exempt from licensing by the Security Industry Authority (SIA) (ss 19–21; and see 6.4.2–6.4.5 above). For CPCs that authorise the supply of alcohol for consumption off the premises, there are mandatory conditions that supply must be at a time when the premises are open for supply to club members for consumption on the premises, the alcohol must be supplied in a sealed container and the supply must be made to a member of the club in person.[1] For CPCs that authorise the exhibition of films, there is a mandatory condition that the admission of children to exhibitions is to be restricted in accordance with film classification recommendations (s 74; and see 8.4.2 below).

Conversely, there are some conditions the inclusion of which is prohibited by the 2003 Act. No condition may be attached as to the nature of any plays that may be performed, which applies to both premises licences and CPCs,[2] and, for CPCs, no conditions may be attached preventing the sale by retail of alcohol or the provision of regulated entertainment to any associate member or guest.[3] Apart from the instances of mandatory or prohibited conditions, authorities have a discretion to impose conditions, although this must be exercised in accordance with the general principles set out below. In cases where no representations have been received in respect of an application, an authority can attach such conditions as are consistent with the operating schedule.[4] In other cases, an authority, if it decides to grant a licence or CPC, can attach such conditions as are consistent with the operating schedule with the conditions modified to such extent as it considers necessary for the promotion of the licensing objectives.[5]

## 7.2 GENERAL PRINCIPLES

There are a number of general principles that operate in respect of the imposition of conditions. First and foremost is a requirement that conditions may only be attached where they are necessary for the promotion of one or more of the four licensing objectives. In addition, there is a need to avoid duplication with other statutory provisions, to avoid the imposition of standard conditions, and for conditions to be proportionate.

## 7.2.1  Conditions necessary for promotion of the licensing objectives

The conditions that are necessary for the promotion of the licensing objectives should emerge initially from a risk assessment, which applicants are expected to carry out before making their application for a premises licence or CPC, and the steps they propose to take to promote the licensing objectives will be set out in the operating schedule and translated into conditions (Guidance, para 10.7). In the event that there are no relevant representations received in respect of the application, only conditions consistent with the operating schedule (and any mandatory conditions) will be attached (see 6.4.1 above and 8.4.2 below). This means that the effect of any such condition 'should be substantially the same as that intended by the terms of the operating schedule or club operating schedule' (Guidance, para 10.10). Where relevant representations are received, the authority has a discretion to impose conditions, but only where it has been satisfied at a hearing of the necessity to impose conditions. Paragraph 10.11 of the Guidance states:

> It may then only impose conditions that are necessary to promote one or more of the four licensing objectives. Such conditions must also be expressed in unequivocal and unambiguous terms to avoid legal dispute.

Given the necessity test and the fact that there may be other applicable legislative provisions, the Guidance goes on to state in para 10.12:

> It is perfectly possible that in certain cases, because the test is one of necessity, where there are other legislative provisions which are relevant and must be observed by the applicant, no additional conditions at all are needed to promote the licensing objectives.

Conditions that are necessary for the promotion of the licensing objectives are likely to have application at all times when licensable activities are taking place at the premises in question but less clear is whether they might apply at times when licensable activities are not taking place. In some instances, the conditions will not be necessary to promote the licensing objectives at the times when licensable activities are not taking place. For example, conditions attached to night cafés and takeaway outlets may be necessary to promote the licensing objectives of prevention of crime and disorder and public nuisance when the premises are operating after 11.00 pm, but not when the premises are operating during the daytime period. Here the conditions should not have application. However, in other instances, the conditions may be regarded as necessary to promote the licensing objectives. For example, conditions relating to the quiet dispersal of customers as they leave premises may be necessary to prevent public nuisance to residents in the vicinity of the premises, although licensable activities may no longer be taking place at this time. It is thought that in such instances the conditions should have application.

## 7.2.2  Avoiding duplication with other statutory provisions

Since only conditions that are necessary to achieve the licensing objectives can be attached, it follows that, if the existing law already places certain statutory responsibilities on an employer or operator of premises, it cannot be necessary to impose similar duties or the same duty, by way of conditions, on the holder of a premises licence or CPC. Thus employers and self-employed persons are required by the Management of Health and Safety at Work Regulations 1999, SI 1999/3242, to assess the risks to their workers and any others (for example, members of the public visiting the premises) who may be affected by their business, so as to identify what measures are needed to avoid or control risks. It will not therefore be necessary to include a condition requiring such a risk assessment to be carried out (Guidance, para 10.15). These general duties, however, will not always adequately cover specific issues that arise on the premises in connection with certain entertainments, but it is only in these cases where additional and supplementary measures are required to promote the licensing objectives that proportionate conditions will need to be attached (Guidance, para 10.17).

Similarly, to the extent that public safety is already adequately covered by other provisions, conditions will not be necessary to promote public safety. Thus if a licensing authority receives an application for a premises licence in relation to a vessel not permanently moored or berthed (see 6.1.5 above), it 'should not focus on matters relating to safe navigation or operation of the vessel, the general safety of passengers or emergency provision, all of which are subject to regulations which must be met before the vessel is issued with its Passenger Certificate and Safety Management Certificate' (Guidance, para 5.14).[6]

### 7.2.3   Avoiding standard conditions

The Act envisages that licensing conditions should be tailored to the size, style, characteristics and activities taking place at the premises concerned; this effectively rules out standardised conditions, which would ignore these individual aspects (Guidance, para 10.13). Nevertheless, there are perhaps a number of conditions that might commonly be attached to most, if not all, licences granted and these conditions are likely to continue to be attached. It would be desirable if these were formulated in a consistent manner and, with a view to advancing this objective, Annex D of the Guidance sets out 'pools' of conditions for each of the four licensing objectives, together with a separate part covering the promotion of public safety in theatres, cinemas, concert halls and similar places.[8] When considering conditions in respect of any particular licence granted, an authority can select from the 'pools' the conditions that it feels are necessary to promote the licensing objectives, although para 10.5 of the Guidance is at pains to point out that it is 'important that they should not be applied universally and treated as standard conditions irrespective of circumstances'. The Annexes, however, only in part comprise 'pools' from which formulated conditions can be drawn for immediate inclusion in licences and certificates. In a number of instances, they do no more than indicate the nature of particular conditions that might be attached and it will be necessary for authorities to formulate the conditions themselves. Inevitably, this will lead to differently worded conditions being used and a greater degree of inconsistency, which could have been avoided if conditions with 'model' wording had been included.[9]

### 7.2.4   Proportionality

The principle of proportionality generally means that measures taken need to bear a reasonable and proportionate relationship to their intended objectives and that any disadvantages caused must not be disproportionate to the aims pursued (or, put another way, a sledgehammer should not be used to crack a nut). It is in this sense that the term 'proportionality' is used in the European Convention on Human Rights in respect of measures taken to protect rights or to impose legitimate restrictions or penalties (see 3.4 above). The Guidance applies this concept to conditions to be attached to the licence. Conditions, it seems, need to be proportionate to the financial resources that the holder of the licence can reasonably be expected to devote to promoting the intended objective(s). Paragraph 10.13 provides:

> It is important that conditions are proportionate and properly recognise significant differences between venues. For example, charities, community groups, voluntary groups, churches, schools and hospitals which host smaller events and festivals will not usually be pursuing these events commercially with a view to profit and will inevitably operate within limited resources.

Although the Guidance does not say so expressly, the clear implication is that less onerous conditions should be attached for events organised by bodies such as those mentioned above. The Guidance, in para 10.14, encourages authorities to 'be alive to the indirect costs that can arise because of conditions attached to licences', which 'could be a deterrent to the holding of events that are valuable to the community or for the funding of good and important causes', and goes on to provide, in para 10.14, that authorities:

> should therefore ensure that any conditions they impose are only those which are necessary for the purposes of the licensing objectives, which means that they must not go further than what is needed for that purpose. Public safety concerns (and the concerns identified in the other objectives) should not of course be ignored and in considering a proportionate response to the licensing needs for such events, the physical safety and well-being of attending such events should remain a primary objective.

As regards conditions being necessary only for the purposes of the licensing objectives, this should, of course, be the position in *all* cases and not just ones involving events such as those mentioned. However, views as to what may be necessary may well differ and, if regard is had to the Guidance when an authority is discharging its licensing function of attaching conditions, it seems that a reduced level of conditions might be permissible in some cases.

## 7.3   CONDITIONS REGULATING HOURS

### 7.3.1   Conditions necessary to promote the licensing objectives

7.3.2   The particular licensing objectives that hours for licensable activities may be considered necessary to promote are the objectives of prevention of crime and disorder (crime prevention objective) and/or the prevention of public nuisance. The times to which licensable activities are provided are unlikely to affect the licensing objectives of public safety and the prevention of harm to children. Although conditions regulating hours may be attached to licences where regulated entertainment and late night refreshment services are being provided, the need for such conditions is perhaps most likely to arise in connection with premises supplying alcohol. There is no presumption in favour of extended hours and conditions can restrict hours where this is necessary to promote the licensing objectives. Thus para 10.20 of the Guidance states:

> there is no general presumption in favour of lengthening licensing hours and the four licensing objectives should be paramount considerations at all times. Where there are objections to an application and the committee believes that changing the licensing hours would undermine the licensing objectives, they may reject the application or grant it with appropriate conditions and/or different hours from those requested.

Restrictions on hours for premises providing alcohol for consumption off the premises might be needed in some cases. The example given in the Guidance, para 10.21 is of shops that are known to be a focus for disorder or disturbance because youths gather there. Nuisance and antisocial behaviour by youths, including trying to pressurise shop staff to make unlawful sales of alcohol, might be combated by a restriction on opening hours in such cases. In general, however, conditions regulating hours are not likely to be needed in the vast majority of cases and para 13.42 of the Guidance recommends that Statements of Licensing Policy (SOPs) should indicate that such premises can sell alcohol during the hours in which they are normally open for trading:

> Statements of licensing policy should indicate that shops, stores and supermarkets, are free to provide sales of alcohol for consumption off the premises at any times when the retail outlet is open for shopping unless there are good reasons, based on the licensing objectives, for restricting those hours.

7.3.3    Where alcohol is supplied for consumption on the premises, the Guidance indicates, in paras 13.40 and 13.41, the need for flexibility in closing hours to reduce the concentrations of persons leaving licensed premises at or around the same time(s):

> 13.40  The Government recommends that statements of policy should recognise that, in some circumstances, longer licensing hours for the sale of alcohol can help to ensure that the concentrations of customers leaving premises simultaneously are avoided. This can help to reduce the friction at late night fast food outlets, taxi ranks and other sources of transport which lead to disorder and disturbance.

> 13.41  The Government also wants to ensure that licensing hours should not inhibit the development of thriving and safe evening and night-time local economies which are important for investment and employment locally and attractive to domestic and international tourists. Providing consumers with greater choice and flexibility is an important consideration, but should always be balanced carefully against the duty to promote the four licensing objectives and the rights of local residents to peace and quiet.

Conditions imposing fixed and artificially early closing times, which will undermine this flexibility should therefore be avoided, with paras 1.17 and 1.18 of the Guidance providing:

> 1.17  The Government strongly believes that, prior to the introduction of the Licensing Act 2003, fixed and artificially early closing times (established under the Licensing Act 1964) were one of the key causes of rapid binge drinking prior to closing times; and one

of the causes of disorder and disturbance when large numbers of customers were required to leave the premises simultaneously.

1.18  The aim through the promotion of the licensing objectives should be to reduce the potential for concentrations and achieve a slower dispersal of people from licensed premises through flexible opening times. Arbitrary restrictions that would undermine the principle of flexibility should therefore be avoided.

7.3.4   Notwithstanding the expressed preference in the Guidance for flexible closing hours, it remains only guidance and it is not binding on licensing authorities. If authorities feel that a restriction on hours is necessary to prevent public nuisance or crime and disorder, they are free to impose one. It may perhaps be necessary, however, for flexible closing hours to be adopted in the first instance with a view to resolving difficulties. If authorities, when discharging their licensing function of imposing conditions on licences granted, have regard to the Guidance, as they are required to do by s 4(3)(b), it will be difficult to justify restricting hours without first having recourse to flexible hours to see whether these have any impact on the difficulties. In order for a restriction on hours at which alcohol may be sold to be effective, it may be necessary for premises to close within a relatively short period of time after sales take place. If the premises remain open thereafter for a long period for time, this may well frustrate application of the hours condition and promotion of the licensing objectives. Attaching a condition to the licence or certificate to regulate opening hours may not be necessary, however, since the operating schedule will specify the closing hours for the premises (see s 17(4)(c) and 6.3.3 above, and s 71(5)(c) and 8.3.3 above) and, once the application is determined, these will be specified on the licence or certificate itself.

## 7.3.5   Overriding of conditions on hours by licensing hours orders

The Act makes provision for the general relaxation of opening hours on special occasions by means of a licensing hours order made by the Secretary of State[10] and in these instances hours will be governed by those specified in the order and not by any conditions on hours that are attached to the premises licence or club premises certificate. These orders can be made by the Secretary of State for periods which mark occasions of exceptional international, national, or local significance and the relaxation in hours can be for periods of up to four days. The relaxation can be one having application generally throughout the country, which is likely to be the case for events of national or international significance, or only in particular areas, which will clearly be appropriate where an occasion is one only of exceptional local significance. Not only may orders make provision geographically, but they may also make different provision for different days during a relaxation period and different provision in respect of different licensable activities. Section 172(1)–(3) provides:

(1)  Where the Secretary of State considers that a period ("the celebration period") marks an occasion of exceptional international, national, or local significance, he may make a licensing hours order.

(2)  A licensing hours order is an order which provides that during the specified relaxation period[11] premises licences and club premises certificates have effect (to the extent that it is not already the case) as if specified times were included in the opening hours.[12]

(3)  An order under this section may–

(a) make provision generally or only in relation to premises in one or more specified areas;

(b) make different provision in respect of different days during the specified relaxation period;

(c) make different provision in respect of different licensable activities.

It is not envisaged that orders will be made by the Secretary of State under s 172 in respect of occasions such as bank holidays and days of national importance. Paragraph 8.39 of the Guidance provides:

> It should normally be possible for applicants for premises licences and club premises certificates to anticipate special occasions which occur regularly each year – such as bank holidays and St George's or St Patrick's Day – and to include appropriate opening hours in their operating schedules. Similarly temporary event notices should be sufficient to cover other events which take place at premises that do not have a premises licence or club certificate.

Rather it seems to be envisaged that orders under s 172 will be used in respect of future exceptional events which occur, but which have not been anticipated, for para 8.40 states:

> exceptional events of local, national or international significance may arise which could not have been anticipated when the application was first made. In these circumstances, the Secretary of State may make a licensing hours order to allow premises to open for specified, generally extended, hours on these special occasions. This avoids the need for large numbers of applications to vary premises licences and club certificates. Typical events might include a one-off local festival, a Royal Jubilee, a World Cup or an Olympic Games.

The power in s 172 is not restricted to extending opening hours of premises for the sale of alcohol and the Secretary of State is able to specify times for inclusion in the opening hours of premises for any of the licensable activities or qualifying club activities. It might be expected, however, that extensions in opening hours will most likely have application in respect of those selling or supplying alcohol.

The initiative for the making of an order may come from the Secretary of State, although it seems that any other person may approach the Secretary of State requesting an order. Given the requirement for consultation in s 172(4), if an approach is made, it will need to be made at least six months before the proposed relaxation of opening hours. It is likely, however, that the making of an order, whether in such cases or on the initiative of the Secretary of State, will be rare.[13] The Guidance, in para 8.41, provides:

> Such events should be genuinely exceptional and the Secretary of State will not consider making such an order lightly. Licensing authorities (or any other persons) approaching the Secretary of State about the making of such an order are advised that they should give at least six months notice before the celebration. Before making such an order, the Secretary of State is required to consult such persons as she considers appropriate, and this would generally enable a wide range of bodies to make representations to her for consideration. In addition, such an order will require the approval of both Houses of Parliament. Nine months would be the minimum period in which such a process could be satisfactorily completed.

## 7.4    CONDITIONS PROMOTING THE LICENSING OBJECTIVES

Apart from conditions regulating hours, any other conditions attached will have to be necessary to promote one or more of the licensing objectives. As indicated above, an Annex D of the Guidance sets out, for each licensing objective, 'pools' of conditions from which authorities might select when imposing a condition (see 7.2.3 above).

### 7.4.1    Prevention of crime and disorder

7.4.2    A potentially wide range of conditions might be attached in order to promote this licensing objective. As the Guidance states in para 2.1: 'The steps any licence holder or club might take to prevent crime and disorder are as varied as the premises or clubs where any licensable activities may be carried on.' The pool of conditions will not therefore be able to cover every possible scenario and licensing authorities are advised to 'look to the police as the main source of advice on these matters'.[14]

Whilst conditions seeking to promote this objective might be attached where any licensable activities are provided, they are more likely to be necessary for some licensable activities than others. They are perhaps unlikely to be required where entertainment, such as films and plays, takes place on premises, but they may well be needed for nightclubs and public houses providing late night alcohol and/or entertainment. The provision of close-circuit television (CCTV) cameras is perhaps one of the most obvious conditions that might promote the crime prevention objective in such premises and, properly located inside and outside premises, CCTV may provide a significant deterrent to crime and disorder. Paragraph 2.6 of the Guidance states:

> the presence of close circuit television cameras both inside and immediately outside the premises can actively deter disorder, nuisance and anti-social behaviour and crime generally. Some licensees may wish to have such cameras on their premises for the protection of their own staff and for the prevention of crime directed against the business itself or its customers. But any condition may require a broader approach, and it may be necessary to ensure that the precise location of cameras is set out on plans to enable certain areas are properly covered and to ensure that there is no subsequent dispute over the terms of the condition.

A condition requiring the provision of CCTV is almost universally attached to new premises licences where the premises operate late at night in busy areas, and in the larger bars and nightclubs coverage may well be required of most, and in some cases all, of the licensed area. CCTV can be said to promote the licensing objective of prevention of crime and disorder by acting to some extent as a deterrent, although its main use is perhaps as an aid to identification of perpertrators of criminal activity and verification of what might have happened in the event of conflicting accounts. A condition requiring CCTV may well be coupled with a condition requiring door supervision, which may reduce the potential for crime and disorder by seeking to prevent people who are drunk or underage (if access for children is restricted) from entering the premises.[15] Similarly, a condition requiring that all glasses used on the premises for the sale of alcoholic drinks should be made of plastic or toughened glass or not allowing bottles to pass across a bar may help to prevent violence by denying assailants suitable weapons.[16] Whether such a condition is considered necessary to promote the licensing objective of prevention of crime and disorder may well depend on whether any incidents of crime and disorder involving the use of glasses or bottles as weapons have taken place at the premises. In the absence of any incidents of this nature, it may be difficult to substantiate a case for such a condition being necessary to prevent crime and disorder, since there will be no supporting evidence that might justify the attachment of the condition. In cases where disorder has occurred at premises, with a view to preventing its recurrence if those responsible for causing it move on to other premises, a condition might be attached requiring communication links with local police stations to provide an early warning of potential disorder. Paragraph 2.15 of the Guidance provides:

> Communications between the managers of the premises and the police can also be crucial in preventing crime and disorder. Involvement by operators and managers in voluntary schemes and initiatives may be particularly valuable. Conditions requiring dedicated text or pager links between management teams and local police stations can provide early warning of disorder and also can be used to inform other licence holders that a problem has arisen in the area generally. For example, where a gang of youths is causing problems in one public house and their eviction will only result in them going on elsewhere to cause problems on other premises, there is advantage in communication links between the police and other licensed premises and clubs.

Such a condition may be necessary and effective in some licensing authority areas, although less so in others. Much may depend on the views of the police and these, according to the Guidance, 'should be given considerable weight' (Guidance, para 2.16).

7.4.3   Whilst conditions such as those mentioned above may assist in preventing crime and disorder, maintenance of order on the premises will ultimately come down to the competency of the management team generally and the competency of the DPS, in particular, as the key person with responsibility for day-to-day management of the premises on which alcohol is sold or supplied. The premise on which the Act is based is that anyone who meets the qualifications for a personal licence is in principle a suitable person to run any premises where the sale or supply of alcohol takes place, whether this is a small off-licence or a large nightclub. Not surprisingly, therefore, para 2.13 of the Guidance indicates that 'conditions relating to the management competency of designated premises supervisors should not normally be attached to premises licences'. A DPS may nevertheless prove to be unsuitable and may ultimately be replaced, although this may do little to resolve difficulties in the interim period or prevent them recurring if another DPS is appointed who lacks experience of running the type of premises in question and who also turns out to be unsuitable. There must come a point when continuing difficulties with disorder on premises might justify the attachment of conditions relating to the competence of the DPS. This is recognised by paras 2.13 and 2.14 of the Guidance, which provide:

> 2.13  A condition of this kind could only be justified as necessary in rare circumstances where it could be demonstrated that in the circumstances associated with particular premises, poor management competency could give rise to issues of crime and disorder and public safety.

> 2.14  It will normally be the responsibility of the premises licence holder as an employer, and not the licensing authority, to ensure that the managers appointed at the premises are competent and appropriately trained and licensing authorities must ensure that they do not stray outside their powers and duties under the 2003 Act. This is important to ensure the portability of the personal licence and the offences set out in

the 2003 Act ensure, for example, that the prevention of disorder is in sharp focus for all such managers, licence holders and clubs.

Attaching a condition, where there are continuing difficulties with premises, would not be straying outside licensing authorities' powers and duties and this may well be an appropriate course on a review of the premises licence. The steps that a licensing authority can take when determining an application for review include removal of the DPS and modification of the conditions of the licence (see s 52(4)(c) and (a), respectively, and 6.12.8 above). The premises licence might be permitted to continue in force with removal of an unsuitable DPS and a modification of the conditions so as to include one that the new DPS has some experience of running the type of premises in question.

### 7.4.4  Public safety

7.4.5    The public safety objective is concerned with the physical safety of the people using the relevant premises or place. Conditions should therefore be concerned with this and not public health, which is dealt with in other legislation (Guidance, para 2.19). In most cases, existing legislation will provide adequately for safety of the public or club members and guests (Guidance, Annex D Pt 2), although where this is not the case conditions might be imposed, for example periodic checks on equipment or equipment of particular standards being maintained on the premises.

The Guidance provides:

> Where there is a requirement in other legislation for premises open to the public or for employers to possess certificates attesting to the safety or satisfactory nature of certain equipment or fixtures on the premises, it would be unnecessary for a licensing condition to require possession of such a certificate. However, it would be permissible to require as a condition of a licence or certificate, if necessary, checks on this equipment to be conducted at specified intervals and for evidence of these checks to be retained by the premises licence holder or club provided this does not duplicate or gold-plate a requirement in other legislation. Similarly, it would be permissible for licensing authorities, following the receipt of relevant representations from responsible authorities or interested parties, to attach conditions which required equipment of particular standards to be maintained on the premises. Responsible authorities – such as health and safety inspectors – should therefore make clear their expectations in this respects [sic] to enable prospective licence holders or clubs to prepare effective operating schedules and club operating schedules.[17]

The risk of fire may affect public safety and fires, it seems, are not uncommon in pubs and clubs.[18] Matters relating to fire safety, however, which traditionally might have been included as conditions are now governed by the Regulatory Reform (Fire Safety) Order 2005 and licensing authorities should not seek to impose fire safety conditions where the Order applies (Guidance, para 2–20 and see 4.2.7 above).[19] Excessive numbers of persons may also affect public safety because of the risk of physical injury through crushing. Conditions might therefore be attached restricting numbers on the premises, so that there is a 'safe capacity' limit.[20] The circumstances in which a capacity limit condition may be attached to premises where licensable activities are taking place, and whether this might extend to all or only certain types of licensable activities, is likely to prove a contentious issue and is not a matter addressed by the Guidance.[21]

7.4.6    Public safety may be affected not only by the fabric of the building or any installations in it, but also by the activities of those who are present on the premises. This is likely to have particular application in respect of nightclub premises and the use of drugs by some of those who frequent them. A key element of the strategy described in the 'Safer Clubbing' document produced by the Home Office in conjunction with the London Drug Policy Forum[22] is the use of necessary and appropriate licensing conditions to control the environment at relevant premises.

Public safety will include the safety of all those who are permitted to come on to the premises. This will include persons with disabilities and, with a view to ensuring that operators cannot easily justify their exclusion, authorities 'should avoid well meaning conditions which are intended to provide for the safety of people or performers with disabilities, but which actively deter operators from admitting or employing such people'.[23] An example is given in the Guidance of a condition which states that 'wheelchairs and similar equipment shall not be allowed on the premises except in accordance with the terms of any consent issued by the licensing authority'. Such a condition, states para 10.26, 'can be ambiguous and be used to justify exclusion and may be ultra vires' and conditions should therefore be 'positively worded and assume the presence of people with disabilities on licensed premises'.

### 7.4.7    Prevention of public nuisance

Public nuisance is where conduct endangers the life, health, property, or comfort of the public, or obstructs the public in the exercise or enjoyment of rights common to all Her Majesty's subjects (see 4.2.9 above). A judgment will therefore have to be made by responsible authorities when making relevant representations and by the licensing authority when considering them on what constitutes public nuisance and what is necessary, in terms of conditions attached to specific premises licences and club premises certificates, to prevent it. This will mean focusing on the impact of the licensable activities at the specific premises on people living and working in the vicinity that are disproportionate and unreasonable. The issues will mainly concern noise nuisance, light pollution, noxious smells and litter (Guidance, para 2.32). As regards noise, perhaps the most likely cause of a public nuisance, conditions will normally concern steps necessary to control the levels of noise emanating from premises. Noise often concerns loud music, which usually occurs from mid-evening until either late evening or early morning when residents in adjacent properties may be attempting to go to sleep or are sleeping. Accordingly, conditions to prevent this could focus on these sensitive periods if steps to control the level of noise are considered to be necessary only at particular times of the day rather than at all times. The steps required may vary in terms of sophistication and expenditure required. In some instances, relatively simple preventive requirements, such as ensuring that doors and windows are kept closed after a particular time in the evening, may suffice, whereas in other cases sound-level inhibitors on amplification equipment or sound proofing may be necessary.[24] Conditions relating to noise nuisance, however, may in certain circumstances not be necessary where the provisions of the Environmental Protection Act 1990, the Noise Act 1996 and the Clean Neighbourhoods and Environment

Act 2005 adequately protect those living in the vicinity of the premises in question (Guidance, para 2.35).

Conditions relating to noise can, of course, extend to matters other than music and might include, for example, the conduct of customers in outside areas of the premises who have left the indoor areas where they are unable to smoke following the ban on smoking in indoor public places introduced by the Health Act 2006. The widespread introduction for the benefit of smokers of shelters in outside areas within the curtilage of premises inevitably increases the risk of noise nuisance being occasioned, for example, by conversation or use of mobile phones, to those living within the vicinity of the premises. Conditions which might seek to prevent such nuisance could include restriction of sales of alcohol for consumption only on and inside the premises after a certain time, and a condition imposing a terminal hour for entry inside the premises, including re-entry by those who may have left the premises, albeit for a brief period, in order to smoke in an outside area.

Conditions might also regulate the conduct of customers in the immediate vicinity of the premises, with a view to preventing any disturbance occasioned by customers entering and leaving the premises. A condition might be included requiring the licence holder to display notices near to the exits and in adjacent car parks requesting customers to leave as quietly as possible. The Guidance, para 2.39 provides:

> it would be perfectly reasonable for a licensing authority to impose a condition follow-ing relevant representations from a responsible authority or interested party that requires the licence holder or club to place signs at the exits from the building encouraging patrons to be quiet until they leave the area and to respect the rights of people living near-by to a peaceful night.

Such a condition is focused on the behaviour of customers within the immediate vicinity of the premises, where it is within the direct control of the licence holder, but paras 2.38 and 2.39 of the Guidance provides that conditions should not seek to regulate conduct outside this area:

> 2.38 Conditions relating to public nuisance caused by the anti-social behaviour of customers once they are beyond the control of the licence holder, club or premises management cannot be justified and will not serve to promote the licensing objectives.

> 2.39 Beyond the vicinity of the premises, these are matters for personal responsibility of individuals under the law. An individual who engages in anti-social behaviour is accountable in his own right.[25]

## 7.4.8  Protection of children from harm

### 7.4.9  Conditions restricting or prohibiting entry

Conditions restricting or prohibiting the entry of children to premises where licensable activities are taking place should be attached only where 'the 2003 Act itself imposes such a restriction or there are good reasons to restrict entry or to exclude children completely'.[26] Instances of where there may be such reasons are provided in the Guidance.[27] In some cases, these relate to a particular reputation that the premises may have acquired (for example, for underage drinking or drug taking or dealing) or the nature of other activities taking place on the premises (for example, where there is a strong element of gambling). In other cases, these relate to the nature of the licensable activity itself that is taking place (or one of the licensable activities), as where entertainment of an adult nature is provided.

If activities take place only at certain times, it will only be necessary for conditions to restrict entry at these times. Paragraph 2.45 of the Guidance gives the example of premises operating as a café bar during the day providing meals for families, but also providing entertainment with a sexual content after 8.00 pm. In such a case, conditions need only restrict entry after 8.00 pm. Similarly, gambling may take place in part of a leisure centre, but not in other parts of those premises (Guidance, para 2.46). In this instance, conditions need only restrict entry to those parts of the premises where gambling is taking place. In other circumstances, conditions may require age limitations, adult supervision (for example, that children under a particular age must be accompanied by an adult), and full exclusion of people under 18 from the premises when any licensable activities are taking place (Guidance, para 2.47).

### 7.4.10 Film exhibitions

A condition restricting the admission of children to film exhibitions has for many years been attached to film exhibition (or cinema) licences and, under s 20 and s 74, such a condition must be imposed on premises licences and club premises certificates where these authorise the exhibition of films (see 6.4.4 above and 8.4.2 below, respectively). The condition will include a requirement to adhere to either the age-restriction recommendations of the British Board of Film Classification (BBFC) or to similar classifications imposed by local authorities themselves. Paragraph 2.49 of the Guidance provides that a condition must be included 'requiring the admission of children to films to be restricted in accordance with recommendations given either by a body designated under section 4 of the Video Recordings Act 1984 specified in the licence [the British Board of Film Classification is currently the only body which has been so designated] or by the licensing authority itself'. Most local authorities do include a condition that films should be exhibited in accordance with age classification certificates issued by the Board, a non-statutory body set up originally by the film industry and which, as such, has no statutory powers to regulate the showing of films. The regulatory powers are vested in local authorities through the issuing of licences and for this reason authorities can, and sometimes do, adopt their own classification of films. Paragraph 10.55 of the Guidance, however, discourages authorities from adopting this course:

> The BBFC classifies films in accordance with its published Guidelines which are based on extensive research into public opinion and professional advice. The Secretary of State therefore recommends that licensing authorities should not duplicate this effort by choosing to classify films themselves. The classifications recommended by the Board should be those normally applied unless there are very good local reasons for a licensing authority to adopt this role.

Films would normally be classified by the Board or the local authority in the following way:

- U – Universal. Suitable for all.

- PG – Parental Guidance. Some scenes may be unsuitable for young children.
- 12A – Passed only for viewing by unaccompanied persons aged 12 years or older or younger persons accompanied by an adult.
- 15 – Passed only for viewing by persons aged 15 years and over.
- 18 – Passed only for viewing by persons aged 18 years and over.
- Restricted 18 – Passed only for viewing by persons aged 18 years or over who are members of a properly constituted club or their guests aged 18 or over.

The particular conditions that might be attached in order to give effect to these age classifications will be a matter for the authority to decide, although an example of the type of condition that might be attached would be:

> Where a programme includes a film in the 12A, 15 or 18 category no person appearing to be under the age of 12 (and unaccompanied in that case), 15 or 18 as appropriate shall be admitted to any part of the programme; and the licence holder shall display in a conspicuous position a notice in the following terms–
>
> **PERSONS UNDER THE AGE OF [INSERT APPROPRIATE AGE] CANNOT BE ADMITTED TO ANY PART OF THE PROGRAMME.**

### 7.4.11 *Theatrical performances*

Unlike film exhibitions, there is no classification system for theatrical performances and the admission of children to them is not usually restricted. Admission of children to such performances should normally be left to the discretion of the licence holder and no condition restricting access should be attached. However, theatres present a wide range of entertainment including, for example, variety shows incorporating adult entertainment. A condition restricting the admission of children in such circumstances may be necessary. Entertainments specifically for children may also be presented at theatres and it may be necessary to consider whether a condition should be attached requiring the presence of a sufficient number of adult staff on the premises to ensure the wellbeing of the children during any emergency (Guidance, para 2.50).

## 7.5     RESTRICTIONS ON APPLICATIONS OF CONDITIONS IN SMALL PREMISES PROVIDING MUSIC AND DANCING

### 7.5.1   Introduction

A particularly contentious issue during the course of the legislation's passage was the threat posed to the performance of music in small public houses and similar premises by the need for the entertainment to be licensed. There was apprehension, notably on the part of the Musicians' Union, that those running such premises might be reluctant to allow entertainment to take place if a range of conditions might be imposed with the licensing of the entertainment.[28] Under the previous law there was a limited exemption from the need to obtain a public entertainment licence where recorded music was played or live music was performed by not more than two performers on premises licensed for the sale of alcohol. This exemption, contained in s 182 of the Licensing Act 1964, was removed by the 2003 Act, but amendments restricting the application of conditions on premises licences where there was live music (and dancing) on small premises were incorporated at a late stage as the Bill was nearing the completion of its passage. These amendments represented a compromise measure after an impasse was reached between the House of Lords and the House of Commons over a proposed exemption for small premises, which the former was keen to promote, but the latter was not prepared to accept. The compromise provision, to which the Government acceded with some reluctance as the Parliamentary session was drawing to a close, became s 177 of the Act and took the form of restrictions on the conditions that could be imposed.

### 7.5.2  Restrictions for small premises

Small premises are ones having a premises licence or CPC,[29] where there is a permitted capacity of less than 200 persons[30] and where there is authorisation for 'music entertainment'. The permitted capacity is determined in accordance with any recommendation made by the fire and rescue authority, for s 177(8) provides:

> In this section–
>
> "permitted capacity", in relation to any premises, means–
>
> . . .
>
> (b) the limit on the number of persons who may be on the premises at any one time in accordance with a recommendation made by, or on behalf of, the fire and rescue authority for the area in which the premises are situated (or, if the premises are situated in the area of more than one fire and rescue authority, those authorities) . . .[31]

Where there is no existing permitted capacity, applicants should conduct their own risk assessment as to the appropriate capacity of the premises and send their recommendation to the fire and rescue authority who will consider it and then decide what the 'permitted capacity' of those premises should be (Guidance, para 2.29). Presumably, it will be necessary for operators who wish to take advantage of the provision in s 177 to include a numbers limitation in their operating schedule so that the licensing authority is aware that the restrictions on conditions will apply.

Although s 177 refers to 'music entertainment', this term is defined in s 177(8) so as to include not only the performance of live music, but also the provision of facilities enabling persons to take part in making music and the performance of dance (but not the provision of facilities enabling persons to take part in dancing). The premises are thus ones where the performance of music and/or dancing takes place and/or where music facilities are provided through the making available for use of musical instruments, for example, a piano in a public house for use by customers. 'Music entertainment', in short, might conveniently be described as 'live music and dancing'. Section 177(8) provides:

> In this section–
>
> . . . "music entertainment" means–
>
> (a) entertainment of a description falling within, or of a similar description to that falling within, paragraph 2(1)(e) or (g) of Schedule 1, or
>
> (b) facilities enabling persons to take part in entertainment within paragraph (a) . . .

The restrictions are on the application of conditions relating to 'music entertainment' that will take effect, for, when such activities are taking place, not all conditions on the premises licence or CPC relating to live music and dancing will apply. The conditions contained in the operating schedule will always apply, but not all conditions that have been imposed by the licensing authority ('licensing authority imposed conditions') will be operative. Conditions imposed by the licensing authority will be ones imposed in contested cases, following relevant representations, on the grant or variation of a premises licence or CPC, or on a review of the licence or certificate (whether or not following a closure order made in respect of the premises). They also include the mandatory condition that door supervisors are licensed or exempt from licensing by the SIA, where a condition requiring door supervisors is included in the premises licence or CPC. Section 177(8) provides:

> In this section–
>
> "licensing authority imposed condition" means a condition which is imposed by virtue of section 18(3)(b) (but is not referred to in section 18(2)(a)) or which is imposed by virtue of 35(3)(b), 52(3) or 167(5)(b) or in accordance with section 21 . . .[32]

The restrictions on the application of licensing authority imposed conditions (LAI conditions) relating to live music and dancing are either that only conditions imposed to meet certain of the licensing objectives will have effect or that no conditions at all shall have effect, although in the case of a review the licensing authority can disapply s 177 so that any condition imposed on review can have effect in relation to small premises. Whether only some conditions have effect or no conditions at all have effect depends on the nature of the entertainment and the premises on which it is taking place. Three matters therefore require consideration: first, the cases when only some conditions have effect; secondly, the cases when none have effect; and thirdly, when (on review) any condition might have effect.

### 7.5.3   Some but not all licensing authority imposed conditions having effect

7.5.4    Where a premises licence or CPC authorises the sale of alcohol for consumption on the premises and the provision of live music or dancing, and where the premises are used primarily for the consumption of alcohol on the premises, and where the premises have a capacity limit of up to 200, any conditions relating to the provision of the live music and dancing imposed on the licence by the licensing authority as being necessary for public safety or the prevention of crime and disorder will have effect (in addition to those contained in the operating schedule). Any conditions relating to the provision of the live music and dancing imposed on the licence by the licensing authority as being necessary for the prevention of public nuisance or the protection of children from harm, however, will not apply. Section 177(1) and (2) provides:

> (1)  Subsection (2) applies where–
>       (a)  a premises licence authorises–
>             (i)   the supply of alcohol[33] for consumption on the premises, and
>             (ii)  the provision of music entertainment, and
>       (b)  the premises–
>             (i)   are used primarily for the supply of alcohol for consumption on the premises, and
>             (ii)  have a permitted capacity of not more than 200 persons.

(2) At any time when–

    (a) the premises–

        (i) are open for the purposes of being used for the supply of alcohol for consumption on the premises, and

        (ii) are being used for the provision of music entertainment, and

    (b) subsection (4) does not apply,

any licensing authority imposed condition of the premises licence which relates to the provision of music entertainment does not have effect, in relation to the provision of that entertainment, unless it falls within subsection (5) or (6).[34]

Subsection (5) restricts the application of conditions to those imposed by the licensing authority as being necessary for public safety or the prevention of crime and disorder and provides:

A condition falls within this subsection if the premises licence specifies that the licensing authority which granted the licence considers the imposition of the condition necessary on one or both of the following grounds–

(a) the prevention of crime and disorder,

(b) public safety.

7.5.5 These restrictions, under s 177(1)(b)(i), will apply only where the premises are used 'primarily for the supply of alcohol for consumption on the premises'. The question of 'primary use' has been considered earlier (see 6.1.7 and 6.3.1 above) and the effect of this requirement is that application of these restrictions, in the main, will be confined to public houses and similar premises. The provisions appear not to apply to nightclubs, as the principal uses of such premises seem to be provision of music and dancing, and supply of alcohol, so the premises cannot be said to be primarily used for the consumption of alcohol on the premises. Further, the restrictions will apply, under s 177(2), only where the premises are open for the supply of alcohol and are being used for the provision of live music and dancing, and when 'subsection (4) does not apply'. Subsection (4), as will be seen, covers cases where, during the hours of 8.00 am to midnight, the premises are being used for the provision of live unamplified music, but not for any other description of regulated entertainment (see 7.5.7 below). The restrictions in s 177(5) will therefore apply in all instances falling outside sub-s (4). These will include not only all live amplified music, but also any live unamplified music falling outside the hours of 8.00 am until midnight and any live unamplified music during those hours where any other description of regulated entertainment is also taking place.

## 7.5.6 No licensing authority imposed conditions having effect

Where a premises licence or CPC authorises the provision of live music and dancing and the premises have a capacity limit of 200, then, during the hours of 8.00 am and until midnight, if the premises are being used for the provision of live unamplified music, but no other description of regulated entertainment, any LAI conditions will not apply. The only conditions that will apply will be those contained in the operating schedule. Section 177(3) and (4) provides:

    (3) Subsection (4) applies where–

        (a) a premises licence authorises the provision of music entertainment, and

(b)  the premises have a permitted capacity of not more than 200 persons.

(4)  At any time between the hours of 8 a.m. and midnight when the premises–

   (a)  are being used for the provision of music entertainment which consists of–

      (i)   the performance of unamplified, live music, or

      (ii)  facilities for enabling persons to take part in entertainment within sub-paragraph (i), but

   (b)  are not being used for the provision of any other description of regulated entertainment,

any licensing authority imposed condition of the premises licence which relates to the provision of the music entertainment does not have effect, in relation to the provision of that entertainment, unless it falls within subsection (6).

No LAI conditions apply in these circumstances because of the absence of any reference (in s 177(4)) to conditions falling within sub-s (5) (which provides for the application of conditions imposed by the licensing authority as being necessary for public safety or the prevention of crime and disorder – see 7.5.4 above). The only reference is to a condition that 'falls within subsection (6)', which means that LAI conditions can have application only on a review (see 7.5.7 below). For LAI conditions not to apply, the requirements of s 177(4) will have to be met. There are two requirements. The first is that the premises are being used either for the performance of unamplified live music or there is provision at the premises of facilities for enabling persons to take part in entertainment comprising such a performance (for example, a piano that customers can play). The second is that the premises are not being used for the provision of any other description of regulated entertainment. This will mean that the requirements will not be met at any premises at which other activities (for example, dancing) take place at the same time as the unamplified live music, so consequently nightclubs will fall outside the scope of these provisions.

## 7.5.7   Discretion for any licensing condition having effect on review

Although LAI conditions on a grant or variation apply either only in part or not at all to small premises (as indicated in the two preceding sections), any LAI conditions on review might have application. Such conditions, whether new ones added or existing ones altered, will apply unless the condition includes a statement that s 177 does not apply to the condition. Section 177(6) provides:

A condition falls within this subsection if, on a review of the premises licence–

   (a)  it is altered so as to include a statement that this section does not apply to it, or

   (b)  it is added to the licence and includes such a statement.

The 'default position' therefore is that all LAI conditions on review relating to the provision of the live music and dancing will not have application. They will only have application if the condition specifically disapplies s 177, that is, provides that the restrictions on LAI conditions contained in s 177 do not have effect. Where the condition includes a statement that s 177 does not apply, the altered or added condition will be outside the exemption and will therefore have application.

# NOTES

1  Section 73(2)–(5); and see 8.4.2 below.

2  Sections 22 and 76; and see 6.4.6 above and 8.4.3 below, respectively.

3  Section 75; and see 8.4.3 below. For the meaning of 'associate member' and 'regulated entertainment', see s 67(2) and Sched 1, and 8.2.3 below and 5.3 above, respectively.

4  Sections 18(2)(a) (premises licences) and 72(2)(a) (CPCs); and see 6.4.1 above (and 6.4.7 above) and 8.4.2 below, respectively.

5  Sections 18(4)(a)(i) (premises licences) and 72(4)(a)(i) (CPCs); and see 6.5.1 above and 8.5.1 below, respectively.

6  A vessel carrying more than 12 passengers is a passenger ship and subject to safety regulation by the Maritime and Coastguard Agency (MCA) and if the MCA is satisfied that the vessel complies with merchant shipping standards for a passenger ship, 'the premises should normally be accepted as meeting the public safety objective' (Guidance, para 5.15). A vessel carrying no more than 12 passengers is subject to the Code for the Safety of Small Commercial Vessels (which sets the standards for construction, safety equipment and manning) if it goes to sea and, if it does not, may be regulated or licensed by the competent harbour authority, navigation authority or local authority, with standards for construction, safety equipment and manning set out as best-practice guidance in the non-statutory Inland Waters Small Passenger Boat Code (Guidance, paras 5.16–15.17).

8  See Pt 1 (Prevention of Crime and Disorder), Pt 2 (Public Safety), Pt 3 (Theatres, Cinemas, Concert Halls and Similar Places (Promotion of Public Safety)), Pt 4 (Prevention of Public Nuisance) and Pt 5 (Protection of Children from Harm).

9  Some parts of Annex D, to a greater extent than others, contain conditions suitably formulated for immediate inclusion in licences and certificates, eg there are more in Pt 2 for public safety than in Pt 1 for the prevention of crime and disorder.

10  Section 172(4) provides: 'Before making an order under this section, the Secretary of State must consult such persons as he considers appropriate.' This may perhaps envisage some form of consultation in all cases, since the provision contains no reference to the words 'if any' after 'such persons'. Since any relaxation is most likely to arise in connection with the licensable activities of sale or supply of alcohol, those in the licensed trade would seem to be the most appropriate persons to be consulted.

11  Section 172(5) provides:

> In this section–
>
> ... "relaxation period" means–
>
> (a)  if the celebration period does not exceed four days, that period, or
>
> (b)  any part of that period not exceeding four days; and
>
> "specified", in relation to a licensing hours order, means specified in the order.

12  Section 172(5) provides:

> In this section–
>
> "opening hours" means–
>
> (a)  in relation to a premises licence, the times during which the premises may be used for licensable activities in accordance with the licence, and
>
> (b)  in relation to a club premises certificate, the times during which the premises may be used for qualifying club activities in accordance with the certificate ...

13  The power to make an order is subject to the 'affirmative resolution procedure', a draft of the statutory instrument has to be laid before and approved by a resolution of each House of Parliament: s 197(3)(d) and (4).

14  Guidance, para 2.1. Conditions should not, however, replicate licensing offences that are

set out in the Act, eg by stating that a licence holder shall not permit drunkenness and disorderly behaviour on his premises (Guidance, para 2.5), nor prohibit the public display of indecent matter since such conduct is regulated by the Indecent Displays (Control) Act 1981 (Guidance, para 2.17). The position will be similar in respect of matters covered by other statutory provisions since one of the applicable general principles for the attaching of conditions is avoidance of duplication with other statutory provisions – see 7.2.2 above.

15 Where conditions relating to door supervision are attached to premises licences, s 20 requires that the licence must include a condition that individuals are licensed by the Security Industry Authority or are exempt from licensing – see 6.4.5 above.

16 Guidance, para 2.9. This condition, although primarily focused on the prevention of crime and disorder, will also promote the licensing objective of public safety. It will minimise the damage done to victims when such assaults take place, because there will be no facial injuries resulting from broken glass.

17 Guidance, para 2.26. The way in which this paragraph is worded suggests that there can be conditions for checks on equipment where there is a requirement in other legislation for certificates to be possessed, but no indication is given as to whether there can be if there is no such requirement. There would seem to be no reason why conditions should not be attached in both instances if this is felt to be necessary to promote public safety.

18 A Government spokesman, Lord McIntosh, disclosed during the course of the legislation's passage that 'in 2001 there were over 1,500 fires in pubs and clubs in England and Wales': HL Deb, vol 650, col 1050, 3 Jul 2003.

19 Regarding fire safety at cinemas, the 2003 Act repealed the Cinematograph (Safety) Regulations 1955, SI 1955/1129, which contained a significant number of regulations in respect of fire safety provision at cinemas, and licensing authorities and responsible authorities 'should therefore recognise the need for steps to be taken to assure public safety at such premises in the absence of the 1995 [sic] regulations': Guidance, para 2.30.

20 Capacities attached to premises licences may in certain circumstances be necessary in preventing disorder, as overcrowded venues can increase the risks of crowds becoming frustrated and hostile: Guidance, para 2.27.

21 Paragraph 2.26 provides: ' "Safe capacities" should only be imposed where necessary for the promotion of public safety or the prevention of disorder on the relevant premises.' The types of licensable activities for which a capacity limit condition might be imposed has been considered earlier – see 4.2.7 above.

22 This document, based on the earlier 'Dance Till Dawn Safely' Guide produced in 1996 by the London Drug Policy Forum, has 'proved an extremely useful document for licensing officers, club managers and promoters' (Guidance, Annex E). The aim of reducing the potential for harm through better management of dance venues was affirmed in the 2003 'Updated Drug Strategy', which may be viewed with 'Safer Clubbing' at www.drugs.gov.uk.

23 Guidance, para 10.23. Paragraph 10.24 goes on to provide: 'It is Government policy that facilities for people and performers with disabilities should be provided at places of entertainment. The Secretary of State encourages licence holders and clubs to provide facilities enabling their admission and reminds them of the duties imposed by the Disability Discrimination Act 1995.'

24 Guidance, para 2.34, which goes on to provide: 'Any conditions necessary to promote the prevention of public nuisance should be tailored to the style and characteristics of the specific premises'.

25 The extent to which this view might represent any change from the previous law, set out in *Lidster v Owen* [1983] 1 WLR 516, is considered at 4.2.11–4.2.12 above.

26 Guidance, para 2.43, which goes on to provide: 'Licensing authorities, the police and other authorised persons should focus on the enforcement of those laws.'

27 See para 2.44 and 4.2.15 above. The Guidance, para 2.48, goes on to provide that the Secretary of State 'considers that representations made by the children protection bodies

and the police in respect of individual applications should be given considerable weight when they address necessary issues regarding the admission of children'.

28  A Report by the Live Music Forum, set up in January 2004 under the chairmanship of Feargal Sharkey to monitor the 2003 Act's impact on live music, published in July 2007, found that the Act had had a 'broadly neutral impact on the provision of live music' (para 1.9), although it was 'also true to say that the Licensing Act has not led to the promised increase in live music' ((para 1.10) – see http://www.culture.gov.uk/ Reference_library/Publications/archive_2007/lmf_findings_recommendations.htm

29  Section 177(7) provides: 'This section applies in relation to a club premises certificate as it applies in relation to a premises licence . . .'.

30  Reference to a capacity of 200 persons is contained in s 177(1)(b)(ii) and s 177(3)(b), each of which relates to different types of premises and the provision of different facilities – see 7.5.4 and 7.5.6 below.

31  For some reason (probably an oversight), when this provision was amended by Sched 2, para 50(3) of the Regulatory Reform (Fire Safety) Order 2005, SI 2005/1541, the references in to the 'fire authority' were not amended to 'fire and rescue authority', as has been the case with other references to 'fire authority' in the 2003 Act.

32  Section 177(7) provides:

> This section applies in relation to a club premises certificate as it applies in relation to a premises licence, except that, in the application of this section in relation to such a certificate, the definition of "licensing authority imposed condition" in subsection (8) has effect as if for 'section 18(3)(b)' to the end there were substituted 'section 72(3)(b) (but is not referred to in section 72(2)) or which is imposed by virtue of section 85(3)(b) or 88(3)'.

33  Section 177(8) provides:

> ' "supply of alcohol" means–
> (a)  the sale by retail of alcohol, or
> (b)  the supply of alcohol by or on behalf of a club to, or to the order of, a member of the club.'

34  Subsection (6) makes provision for the licensing authority to disapply s 177 in cases of a review, so that any condition imposed on review can have effect in relation to small premises – see 7.5.7 below.

# CHAPTER 8

# CLUBS AND CLUB PREMISES CERTIFICATES

## 8.1 THE NATURE AND TYPES OF CLUBS

8.1.1 There is no one universal statutory definition or generally understood meaning of the term 'club'. As the *Report of the Departmental Committee on Liquor Licensing* in 1972 observed: 'The word has a range of meanings, and precise definitions tend to be left to legislation dealing either with the criteria which have to be met by clubs for particular purposes or with specific club activities.'[1] Nevertheless, as Lord Denning MR stated in the Court of Appeal *Tehrani v Rostron* [1971] 3 All ER 790, 793: 'The word "club" . . . has a meaning well understood in the law. It denotes a society of persons associated together for the promotion of some common object or objects, such as social intercourse, art, science, literature, politics or sport. In law, it is also well known that a "club" may be one of two kinds: a members' club or a proprietary club.' Clubs invariably have a membership fee and in the case of a members' club the group of persons subscribe to a common fund for the benefit of the members and in the proprietary club they subscribe for the benefit of an individual or body (the proprietor).

In each of these two types of clubs, the nature of the relationship between members and the club differs and this affects the nature of the transaction when members obtain alcohol from the club. In proprietary clubs, members will have a contractual right to use the club by virtue of payment of their subscriptions to the proprietor and there will be a sale by retail of alcohol to members when a purchase is made, in much the same way as alcohol is bought in a public house. But in members' clubs, members will be able to use the club by virtue of property rights because payment of their subscriptions will give them a joint share in the club property, which will include the club's stock of alcohol, and no 'sale' of alcohol to members is regarded as taking place. Rather, there is a 'supply' to members, that is a release to them of their property rights in the alcohol. In *Graff v Evans* (1882) 9 QBD 373, where the matter first seems to have been considered, the Divisional Court held that where the manager of a bona fide club supplied a member with a bottle of whisky and a bottle of beer for consumption off the premises no offence of a 'sale by retail' of intoxicating liquor without a justices' licence was committed. Field J stated (at 378):

> Did Graff, the manager, who supplied the liquors to Foster [the member], effect a sale by retail? I think not. A sale involves the element of a bargain. There was no bargaining here, nor any contract with Graff with respect to the goods. Foster . . . as a member of the club . . . became entitled to have ale and whisky . . . supplied to him as a member at a certain price. There was no contract between two persons, because Foster was a vendor as well as a buyer . . . Foster was as much a co-owner as a vendor. I think it was a transfer of a special property in the goods to Foster, which was not a sale . . .

Courts have routinely followed this approach ever since, although it is regarded as anomalous in respect of the law on the sale of goods.[2] Nevertheless, at least for the purposes of licensing legislation, it is well established that in members' clubs there is a 'supply' of alcohol to members and not a 'sale'. The different nature of the relationship is conveniently summarised in the following passage from the *Report of the Departmental Committee on Liquor Licensing,* Cmnd 5154, 1972, para 1.30:

> Proprietary clubs are clubs in which the premises and stock belong to a proprietor or group of proprietors. If the stock of liquor belongs to the proprietor, a "sale" takes place when a member orders and pays for a drink . . . In the case of "members" clubs, all the property, including the stock of liquor, belongs to the members jointly, and when a member obtains liquor, even on payment, the position is that a "supply" rather than a sale takes place.[3]

8.1.2    Historically, members' clubs, in order to supply alcohol, needed a justices' licence to do so, but provision for registration of clubs was made by the Licensing Act 1902, provided certain conditions were met. This enabled them to supply alcohol under a registration certificate[4] and the conditions for registration, previously set out in s 41 of the Licensing Act 1964, have in large measure been replicated in the 2003 Act for the granting of club premises certificates (CPCs). Under the 2003 Act, members' clubs can obtain a CPC to provide authorisation for their licensable activities and s 1(2) provides that the following licensable activities are also 'qualifying club activities': the supply of alcohol to a member, the sale by retail of alcohol to a guest of a member for consumption on the premises, and the provision of regulated entertainment for a member and guest (see 8.2.2 below). Although members' clubs can obtain a CPC, they are not required to do so. They can, alternatively, obtain a premises licence, which might be appropriate where the requirements for a CPC are not met, or they can obtain a premises licence in addition to a CPC to make provision for licensable activities in circumstances not covered by the CPC.[5]

The provision of CPCs for members' clubs continues the privileged position that such clubs have traditionally enjoyed through registration certificates. The benefits associated with a CPC under the 2003 Act include an exemption from the requirement for any member or employee to hold a personal licence to supply or sell alcohol to members and guests and the absence of any requirement to specify a designated premises supervisor.[6] This reflects the fact that clubs are essentially private premises to which public access is restricted and accordingly they are, in the words of Lord Davies, a Government spokesman in the House of Lords during the report stage of the Bill, 'subject to a different regime with lighter controls' (HL Deb, vol 645, col 482, 27 February 2003). These benefits accrue only if certain conditions are met, so that the club is a 'qualifying club', entitling it to obtain a CPC. Most members' clubs will be a 'qualifying club' and can obtain a CPC, but these conditions are unlikely to be met by proprietary clubs.[7] Proprietary clubs will require a premises licence, for which there will need to be a designated premises supervisor (DPS) holding a personal licence and all supplies of alcohol will need to be made by or under the authority of a personal licence holder.[8]

## 8.2    CLUB PREMISES CERTIFICATES FOR QUALIFYING CLUBS

### 8.2.1   Club premises certificates

8.2.2    A CPC is defined by s 60, which provides:

(1) In this Act "club premises certificate" means a certificate granted under this Part–

   (a) in respect of premises occupied by, and habitually used for the purposes of, a club,[9]

   (b) by the relevant licensing authority,[10] and

   (c) certifying the matters specified in subsection (2).

(2) Those matters are–

   (a) that the premises may be used by the club for one or more qualifying club activities specified in the certificate, and

   (b) that the club is a qualifying club in relation to each of those activities (see section 61).

The CPC will thus certify that the premises may be used for one or more 'qualifying club activities' and these are set out in Part 1 of the Act in s 1(2) as follows:

   (a) the supply of alcohol by or on behalf of a club to, or to the order of, a member of the club,

   (b) the sale by retail of alcohol by or on behalf of a club to a guest of a member of the club for consumption on the premises where the sale takes place, and

   (c) the provision of regulated entertainment where that provision is by or on behalf of a club for members of the club or members of the club and their guests.[11]

The supply of alcohol to members under para (a) can be the only 'qualifying club activity' (if no entertainment is provided) because club rules may provide that there can be no retail sale to guests, that is, drinks can be purchased only by members. However, the sale by retail of alcohol to guests of members clearly cannot be the only 'qualifying club activity'. It can subsist, assuming club rules allow for a sale to guests, as a 'qualifying club activity' only in conjunction with a supply to members. Guests can purchase alcohol only if introduced or admitted to the club by a member and cannot do so in their own right, so if the CPC does not make provision for alcohol to be supplied to members, there can be no provision for it to be sold to guests. Thus para (a) can exist as the sole 'qualifying club activity', but paras (a) and (b) can exist only in conjunction with each other. Paragraph (c) can also be the sole 'qualifying club activity' or equally it can exist either with para (a) or with paras (a) and (b). In many instances, the 'qualifying club activities' are likely to comprise all of the three activities in s 1(2).

8.2.3   With regard to the sale of alcohol to or the provision of entertainment for guests of members, this is not confined to guests of members of the particular club as the Act provides that references to a guest of a member of a club includes references to an 'associate member' of a club and a guest of such a member. Section 67 provides:

(1) Any reference in this Act (other than this section) to a guest includes a reference to–

   (a) an associate member of the club, and

   (b) a guest of an associate member of the club.

(2) For the purposes of this Act a person is an "associate member" of a club if–

   (a) in accordance with the rules of the club, he is admitted to its premises as being a member of another club, and

   (b) that other club is a recognised club (see section 193).

Section 193 provides that a 'recognised club' means 'a club which satisfies conditions 1–3 of the general conditions in section 62'. These general conditions (of which there are five) are ones that need to be met if a club is to be a 'qualifying club', enabling it to obtain a CPC. These are set out in the following section of this chapter and conditions 1–3 relate to admission to club membership, admission to the privileges of member-ship and the club being conducted in good faith (see 8.2.7–8.2.15 below). Associate members of a qualifying club are thus members of other clubs that are either qualify-ing clubs (because they meet all of the general conditions in s 62) or, if not, meet the requirements of the first three conditions as mentioned above.

8.2.4    This provision continues the reciprocal arrangements whereby members of one club can obtain admission to another associated or affiliated club, as where clubs are part of the Club & Institute Union. However, the Act makes no specific provision for sales to be made to 'visitors' on occasions where they attend the club. Such occasions might include when sports teams visit the club, when a golf club permits members of the public to play rounds of golf on payment of a green fee, or when corporate events are held on club premises. They might also include 'visitors' to student union bars that operate as clubs from students holding a National Union of Students card who are at other institutions where the bar is not operated as a club but under a premises licence.[12] It is possible, however, that sales might be made to 'visitors', depending on how the expression 'guest' is interpreted. It might be inter-preted to mean not only a guest of a member of the club, but also a guest of the club itself, in which case 'visitors' might be admitted as a guest of the club. Section 61(2) refers only to the 'supply of alcohol to members or guests' when dealing with whether a club is a qualifying club (see 8.2.6 below) and does not make it explicit that 'guests' have to be guests of members of the club. This appears to leave open the possibility that 'guests' may also include guests of the club, as well as guests of members of the club. Further, s 67(1) states that 'reference in this Act . . . to a guest of a member of a club includes a reference to' an associate member of the club and a guest of an associ-ate member (see 8.2.3 above) and use of the word 'includes' might indicate that this is not comprehensive. Guests might therefore encompass persons other than those to whom reference is made (associated members and their guests) and could include guests of the club.

This seems to be the view held by the Government, as can be seen by the response of Mr Richard Caborn, the Minister for Sport and Tourism, to an oral question in Parliament about whether a non-invited non-qualifying club member turning up unannounced and uninvited and signed in for his green fee to play a round of golf might buy a drink at the bar afterwards. The Minister stated (at HC Deb, vol 423, col 3, 28 June 2004):

> If the hon. Gentleman studies the Act carefully, particularly the provisions dealing with associate members and sees how we have been able to incorporate the definition of "guests" in that, it would allay his fears and those of every golfer'.

No further explanation was given, however, as to how persons who are not members of any other club and who are 'uninvited visitors' are incorporated within the pro-visions dealing with associate members, but the Government's view appears to be that they are and that they can be admitted as 'guests' of the club under s 67(1). That persons might be so admitted is a view reiterated in the 2007 Guidance (although not appearing in the original 2004 version). Paragraph 6.7 provides:

> The 2003 Act does not prevent visitors to a qualifying club being supplied with alcohol as long as they are 'guests' of any member of the club or the club collectively, and nothing in the 2003 Act prevents the admission of such people as guests without prior

notice. For the sake of flexibility, the Act does not define "guest" and whether or not somebody is a genuine guest would in all cases be a question of fact. The term can include a wide variety of people who are invited by the qualifying club or any individual member to use the club facilities. The manner in which they are admitted as 'guests' would be for the club to determine and to consider setting out in their own club rules.

Nevertheless, there are two compelling reasons against the view that 'guests', in s 61(2) and s 67(1), might include guests of the club. First, the 2003 Act provides a definition of the expression 'supply of alcohol to members or guests' that appears in s 61(2). Section 70, which applies for the purposes of Pt 4 of the Act and which makes reference only to a guest of a member of the club, provides:

> In this Part–
>
> . . .
>
> "supply of alcohol to members or guests" means, in the case of any club–
> (a)  the supply of alcohol by or on behalf of the club to, or to the order of, a member of the club, or
> (b)  the sale by retail of alcohol by or on behalf of the club to a guest of a member of the club for consumption on the premises where the sale takes place,
> and related expressions are to be construed accordingly.

Thus, although s 61(2) does not make it explicit that 'guests' have to be guests of members of the club, this is made explicit, in relation to 'guests', by s 70(b). As regards s 67(1), the reference to 'includes' might easily be explained on the basis that the section is giving an extended meaning, beyond its normal meaning, to the expression 'guest of a member of a club'. Thus the expression, in relation to a particular club, covers not only a guest of a member of the club (normal meaning), but also an associate member or his guest (extended meaning). If the provision in s 67(1) is read as giving an extended meaning, the reference to 'includes' will not extend beyond the specific instances mentioned, that is an associate member or his guest, and will not include guests of the club itself. This seems to be the more natural meaning of 'guest of a member of a club' in s 67(1), having regard to the wording, and does not involve 'reading in' to the section any other categories of 'guest'.

Secondly, there was no suggestion under the previous law that 'guests' included guests of the club and that such guests could be supplied with alcohol. The Licensing Act 1964 used the same wording of 'member or guest' (for example, in s 39) and 'guests' was understood to mean only guests of members of the club. Indeed, this is apparent from s 49(1), which enabled intoxicating liquor, where club rules provided for the admission to the premises of 'persons other than members and *their* guests' (emphasis supplied), to be sold to such persons. There is a presumption, when interpreting statutes, that a statutory provision is not intended to make changes in the existing law beyond those expressly stated or arising by necessary implication from the language of the statute. There is an expressly stated change in that s 67(1) extends the meaning of 'guest of a member of a club' to include an associate member or his guest; but extension beyond this to also include a guest of the club does not seem to arise by necessary implication from the language of the 2003 Act.

Whilst the Minister's statement in Parliament might be an extrinsic aid to interpreting the 2003 Act, it may be that only limited weight should be placed on this statement. With regard to the Minister's statement, in the House of Lords, in *Robinson v Secretary of State for Northern Ireland* [2002] UKHL 32, Lord Hoffmann, with whose judgment other members of the House expressed agreement, stated (at para 40):

> it will be very rare indeed for an Act of Parliament to be construed by the courts as meaning something different from what it would be understood to mean by a member of the public who was aware of all the material forming the background to its enactment but who was not privy to what had been said by individual members (including Ministers) during the debates in one or other House of Parliament.

As indicated above, s 67(1) might more naturally be interpreted as providing an extended meaning of the normal meaning of the expression 'guest of a member of a club' and it is in this sense that it might be understood by a member of the public. Whilst greater weight might be placed on the statement in the 2007 Guidance, it is open to doubt whether this is sufficient to rebut the presumption that statutory provisions are not intended to make changes in the existing law beyond those expressly stated or arising by necessary implication. If the statement is to be considered indicative of Parliamentary intent, it might reasonably be asked why this was not included in the Guidance in its original formulation or, indeed, why no mention was made of 'guests of the club' in the White Paper preceding the introduction of the 2003 Act. Notwithstanding this statement, therefore, the better view may be that the provisions in s 67 dealing with associate members do not extend beyond such members and their guests to include guests of the club itself. On this view, persons who are not members of any other qualifying club or are not their guests cannot be supplied with alcohol as 'guests' under the CPC.

If this view represents the correct legal position, some other means of authorisation is needed under which such persons might be admitted to the club. One possibility might be under the authority of a temporary event notice (TEN), which could be suitable for occasions where it is known some time in advance that persons will be visiting the club, for example, where sports teams might be playing at the club, although under s 107(4) there is a limit of 12 TENs per year that can be given in respect of the same premises (see 9.7.1 below). Another possibility might be for visitors to become 'temporary members' of the club. The 2003 Act does not define the expression 'member' of a club and it seems open to clubs to have different categories of 'member'. One might be 'ordinary members', that is persons who are nominated for membership by a current member or who apply for membership and whose nomination or application is accepted in accordance with the rules of the club. Such members would have full voting rights and acquire a joint interest in the property of the club. Another might be 'temporary members', that is, any person attending a private function at the club or any person from a group or organisation visiting the club for a cultural, artistic or sporting event (for example, rugby teams, their officials and spectators). Temporary membership would last for the duration of the function or visit and temporary members would not be entitled to any voting rights or acquire any interest in the property of the club. There seems to be nothing in the 2003 Act to prevent clubs drawing such a distinction between members, since the Act contains no restrictions in respect of membership or voting rights. Certainly the concept of 'temporary members' appears to have been recognised under the previous law, since the High Court in *Coventry City FC v Coventry JJ* (1973) 117 Sol Jo 855 held that temporary members comprising teams and officials from visiting sports clubs could be admitted to the club if their names were on the board at least two days before attendance. This would continue to be the case under the 2003 Act, since under s 61(2) one of the general conditions that a club must satisfy if it is to be a qualifying club entitled to obtain a CPC is that members cannot enjoy the benefits and privileges of club membership until a period of two days has elapsed after they have applied for membership (see 8.2.9 below). Conferment of temporary membership might therefore be suitable for occasions where it is known some time in advance that persons will be visiting the club and only a two-day period is necessary in such cases compared to 10 working days before the event for the issuing of a TEN (see s 100(7) and 9.2.6 below). However, neither means of authorisation enables a visitor to turn up on the day, pay his green fee to play a round of golf and buy a drink at the bar afterwards.

## 8.2.5  Qualifying clubs

8.2.6    Whichever qualifying club activities are specified in the certificate, the club will need to be a 'qualifying club' in relation to each of them. The conditions that need to be met for a club to be a 'qualifying club' are set out in s 61 and they differ according to whether the club is providing entertainment or alcohol for members and guests. General conditions in each instance need to be met, but there are additional conditions that have to be satisfied where alcohol is provided. Section 61 provides:

(1)  This section applies for determining for the purposes of this Part whether a club is a qualifying club in relation to a qualifying club activity.

(2)  A club is a qualifying club in relation to the supply of alcohol to members or guests[13] if it satisfies both–

(a)  the general conditions in section 62, and

(b)  the additional conditions in section 64.

(3)  A club is a qualifying club in relation to the provision of regulated entertainment if it satisfies the general conditions in section 62.

The supply of alcohol to members or guests under a CPC must be for consumption on the premises, although s 73 of the Act also states that a CPC authorising this can additionally authorise supply to members for consumption off the premises. Where this is the case, however, certain conditions must be attached in respect of off-sales (see 8.4.2 below).

## 8.2.7  *General conditions for qualifying clubs*

8.2.8    Section 62(1) provides: 'The general conditions which a club must satisfy if it is to be a qualifying club in relation to a qualifying club activity are the following' and the section then goes on to set out five conditions in sub-ss (2)–(6):

(2)  Condition 1 is that under the rules of the club persons may not–

(a)  be admitted to membership, or

(b)  be admitted, as candidates for membership, to any of the privileges of membership,

without an interval of at least two days between their nomination or application for membership and their admission.

(3)  Condition 2 is that under the rules of the club persons becoming members without prior nomination or application may not be admitted to the privileges of membership without an interval of at least two days between their becoming members and their admission.

(4)  Condition 3 is that the club is established and conducted in good faith as a club (see section 63).

(5)  Condition 4 is that the club has at least 25 members.

(6)  Condition 5 is that alcohol is not supplied, or intended to be supplied, to members on the premises otherwise than by or on behalf of the club.

### 8.2.9    Admission to membership

Conditions 1 and 2 are clearly intended to prevent clubs qualifying for a CPC where club rules permit 'instant membership', with members able to enjoy immediately the benefits and privileges of club membership. A period of two days must elapse between application or nomination for membership and admission to member-ship (Condition 1) and, even if persons can become 'instant members' without prior application or nomination, the same period must elapse before the privileges of membership are made available (Condition 2). The use of the phrase 'two days' leaves it uncertain whether an interval of two whole days is required or whether parts of a day might count towards the two-day period. If parts of a day are to count, there would be an interval of two days if (say) a person applied for membership just before midnight on a Monday and was admitted to membership just after midnight on the following Wednesday. Perhaps it may have been better to use the phrase 'two whole days' or '48 hours' for the avoidance of doubt. However, s 62(2) and (3) replicate the provisions previously contained in s 41(1)(a) and (b) of the Licensing Act 1964 and no difficulties in practice seem to have arisen under the previous legislation from use of the 'two days' terminology.[14]

### 8.2.10   Good faith

8.2.11   Condition 3 requires that the club is established and conducted in good faith as a club and s 63(1) provides that various matters, as specified in s 63(2), may be taken into account in determining the question of good faith. These matters are:

(a)  any arrangements restricting the club's freedom of purchase of alcohol;

(b)  any provision in the rules, or arrangements, under which–

(i)   money or property of the club, or

(ii)  any gain arising from the carrying on of the club,

is or may be applied otherwise than for the benefit of the club as a whole or for charitable, benevolent or political purposes;

(c)  the arrangements for giving members information about the finances of the club;

(d)  the books of account and other records kept to ensure the accuracy of that information;

(e)  the nature of the premises occupied by the club.

If the licensing authority is not satisfied that the club is established and conducted in good faith in accordance with these provisions, it must give notice to the club, with reasons for its decision. Section 63(3) provides:

> If a licensing authority decides for any purpose of this Act that a club does not satisfy condition 3 in subsection (4) of section 62, the authority must give the club notice of the decision and of the reasons for it.[15]

8.2.12   One common situation that might appear to fall within para (a) is a 'brewery tie' arrangement whereby a club agrees, in return for a loan or grant from a brewery, to take all or most of its alcoholic drinks from the brewery. This is certainly, on the face of it, an arrangement restricting the club's freedom of purchase of alcohol, but whether a club with such an arrangement is conducted in good faith seems not to have been judicially determined. Whether such an arrangement is conducted in good faith may depend on the degree of restriction and the extent to which the club remains an independent entity during the course of the 'tie'. If a loan is for some specific purpose (for example, extension of club premises) and repayable within a fixed period, after which the 'tie' arrangement comes to an end, the club is more likely to be regarded as being conducted in good faith. Conversely, it is less likely if a general 'open-ended' payment is made. Even if a 'tie arrangement' (or any other restricting arrangement) points towards a lack of good faith, the 'tie' might be outweighed by the other factors in paras (b)–(e) indicating the presence of good faith.

The requirement, in para (b), that club assets might be applied otherwise than for the benefit of the club or for charitable, benevolent or political purposes, is clearly designed to ensure that assets are not applied for the benefit of others, perhaps in particular a proprietor who might be using the club as a 'front' for his own purposes. It is possible, however, that some common arrangements in genuine members' clubs might be regarded as contravening this provision, for example, where spouses of club stewards are permitted to run the food catering side of the club for their own benefit and profit. On the other hand, this could be seen as assets being used for the benefit of the club, since it amounts to the employment of a professional expertise that the club itself may be unable to supply. Whether there is contravention in any particular instance may, again, be a question of degree and any contravention may similarly be outweighed by factors in the other paragraphs indicating the presence of good faith.

8.2.13   Paragraphs (c) and (d) relate to club finances, which, in view of the joint ownership of club property by members in a genuine members' club (see 8.1.1 above), is a matter of particular interest to the members. This is unlike the case of a proprietary club, where property is owned by the proprietor and there is a much less compelling case for financial accountability to the membership. Information appertaining to club finances and its availability to club members is therefore a significant yardstick by which to measure whether a club is a members' or proprietary club.

Paragraph (e) provides that the nature of the premises occupied by the club may be taken into account when considering the question of good faith. 'Nature' of the premises suggests physical or structural layout and it is hard to see how this might affect whether a club is conducted in good faith, except perhaps the ability of the premises to provide sufficient demarcation between areas used by the public and areas reserved for members. If the premises were such that access to the club could not be controlled or there could be free movement of the public into areas comprising the club, this might indicate that the premises were not being properly run in good faith as a club. Similarly, given that there is no mandatory requirement for guests to be signed in by a member, if 'guests' were able to obtain easy access and purchase alcohol, this might indicate that the club was not being conducted in good faith. As para 6.8 of the Guidance indicates:

There is no mandatory requirement under the 2003 Act for guests to be signed in by a member of the club. However, a point may be reached where a club is providing commercial services to the general public in a way that is contrary to its qualifying club status. It is at this point that the club would no longer be conducted in "good faith" and would no longer meet "general condition 3" for qualifying clubs in section 62 of the 2003 Act.

These instances apart, it would seem to be the use to which the premises are put and the way in which they are conducted as a club that would affect the question of good faith rather than the nature of the premises.[16]

### 8.2.14   Number of members

Condition 4 is that the club has at least 25 members, a requirement that can be traced back to when registration of clubs was first introduced by the Licensing Act 1902 (see s 29(1)(a)) and one that was presumably designed to rule out registration for very small clubs.

### 8.2.15   Supply of alcohol

Condition 5 is that alcohol is not supplied, or intended to be supplied, to members on the premises otherwise than by or on behalf of the club. This means that the bar will need to be run and operated by the club rather than by some third party under, for example, a franchise arrangement whereby a sum of money is paid to the club in return for the right to operate the bar and keep the profits.

## 8.2.16   Additional conditions for qualifying clubs

Section 64 sets out three conditions which must be satisfied for a club to supply alcohol as a qualifying club. Section 64 provides:

(1)   The additional conditions which a club must satisfy if it is to be a qualifying club in relation to the supply of alcohol to members or guests are the following.

(2)   Additional condition 1 is that (so far as not managed by the club in general meeting or otherwise by the general body of members) the purchase of alcohol for the club, and the supply of alcohol by the club, are managed by a committee whose members–

(a)   are members of the club;

(b)   have attained the age of 18 years; and

(c)   are elected by the members of the club.

This subsection is subject to section 65 (which makes special provision for industrial and provident societies, friendly societies etc).

(3)   Additional condition 2 is that no arrangements are, or are intended to be, made for any person to receive at the expense of the club any commission, percentage or similar payment on, or with reference to, purchases of alcohol by the club.

(4)   Additional condition 3 is that no arrangements are, or are intended to be, made for any person directly or indirectly to derive any pecuniary benefit from the supply of alcohol by or on behalf of the club to members or guests, apart from–

(a)   any benefit accruing to the club as a whole; or

(b) any benefit which a person derives indirectly by reason of the supply giving rise or contributing to a general gain from the carrying on of the club.

### 8.2.17   *Management by elected committee*

Additional Condition 1 requires that purchase and supply of alcohol by the club is managed either by the general body of the members in a general meeting or by an elected committee. Where clubs have a significant number of members, and they need at least 25 members in order to satisfy Condition 4 of the general conditions for a qualifying club (see 8.2.14 above), management of the club in a general meeting of members is difficult and it is much more common for management to be undertaken by a committee. It is not necessary that all members of this 'management committee' are elected members, that is, elected by members of the club, but, for a committee to manage the purchase and supply of alcohol, its members must, under s 64(2)(c), be 'elected by the members of the club'. Thus, if the 'management committee' is wholly elected by the members it can manage the purchase and supply of alcohol, but, if not, a separate committee (in all probability a subcommittee of the 'management committee', sometimes called a 'wine committee') will be needed.

### 8.2.18   *Beneficial arrangements*

Additional condition 2 precludes any arrangements for a person receiving, at the expense of the club, a benefit from purchases of alcohol by the club and additional condition 3 precludes any arrangements for a person deriving any pecuniary benefit from the supply of alcohol by the club to members or guests. The aim of these provisions would seem to be, respectively, to prevent possible links between the club management and a particular supplier, and to ensure a proprietor is not obtaining a financial benefit for himself by using a members' club as a 'front'.

## 8.2.19 Special provision for certain societies and institutes

8.2.20   Special provision is made by the 2003 Act, first, for clubs that are registered as Industrial and Provident Societies and Friendly Societies, and secondly, for Miners' Welfare Institutes to obtain CPCs. Such clubs can obtain CPCs, despite the fact that they are differently constituted from most members' clubs, being organisations managed partly be employers and partly by employees or members. As regards the former, which principally cover working men's clubs, the requirement in s 64(2) for the purchase and supply of alcohol to be managed by a committee elected by the members is waived. By virtue of s 65(2) this requirement is taken to be satisfied if purchase and supply is under the control of the members or of a committee appointed by the members. This enables such societies to obtain a CPC where a committee has been appointed, rather than elected, by the members. Section 65 provides:

(1) Subsection (2) applies in relation to any club which is–
   (a) a registered society, within the meaning of the Industrial and Provident Societies Act 1965 (c.12) (see section 74(1) of that Act),
   (b) a registered society, within the meaning of the Friendly Societies Act 1974 (c.46) (see section 111(1) of that Act), or
   (c) a registered friendly society, within the meaning of the Friendly Societies Act 1992 (c.40) (see section 116 of that Act).

(2) Any such club shall be taken for the purposes of this Act to satisfy additional condition 1 in subsection (2) of section 64 if and to the extent that–

    (a) the purchase of alcohol for the club, and

    (b) the supply of alcohol by the club,

are under the control of the members or of a committee appointed by the members.

(3) References in this Act, other than this section, to–

    (a) subsection (2) of section 64, or

    (b) additional condition 1 in that subsection,

are references to it as read with subsection (1) of this section.

(4) Subject to subsection (5), this Act applies in relation to an incorporated friendly society as it applies in relation to a club, and accordingly–

    (a) the premises of the society are to be treated as the premises of a club,

    (b) the members of the society are to be treated as the members of the club, and

    (c) anything done by or on behalf of the society is to be treated as done by or on behalf of the club.

(5) In determining for the purposes of section 55 whether an incorporated friendly society is a qualifying club in relation to a qualifying club activity, the society shall be taken to satisfy the following conditions–

    (a) condition 3 in subsection (4) of section 62,

    (b) condition 5 in subsection (6) of that section,

    (c) the additional conditions in section 64.

(6) In this section "incorporated friendly society" has the same meaning as in the Friendly Societies Act 1992 (see section 116 of that Act).

8.2.21 As regards Miners' Welfare Institutes, these can be treated as clubs by s 66, again without the need for an elected committee. Certain conditions need to be met and these can include an institute being managed by a committee or board consisting of persons appointed or nominated from within the coal industry. When an institute is treated as a club, it can obtain a CPC if it complies with the conditions needed to be a 'qualifying club' and, for these purposes, an institute is taken to satisfy some of the general conditions in s 62 and all of the additional conditions in s 64. Section 66 provides:

(1) Subject to subsection (2), this Act applies to a relevant miners' welfare institute as it applies to a club, and accordingly–

    (a) the premises of the institute are to be treated as the premises of a club,

    (b) the persons enrolled as members of the institute are to be treated as the members of the club, and

    (c) anything done by or on behalf of the trustees or managers in carrying on the institute is to be treated as done by or on behalf of the club.

(2) In determining for the purposes of section 61 whether a relevant miners' welfare institute is a qualifying club in relation to a qualifying club activity, the institute shall be taken to satisfy the following conditions–

    (a) condition 3 in subsection (4) of section 62,

    (b) condition 4 in subsection (5) of that section,

    (c) condition 5 in subsection (6) of that section,

    (d) the additional conditions in section 64.

(3) For the purposes of this section–

(a) "miners' welfare institute" means an association organised for the social well-being and recreation of persons employed in or about coal mines (or of such persons in particular), and

(b) a miners' welfare institute is "relevant" if it satisfies one of the following conditions.

(4) The first condition is that–

(a) the institute is managed by a committee or board, and

(b) at least two thirds of the committee or board consists–

(i) partly of persons appointed or nominated, or appointed or elected from among persons nominated, by one or more licensed operators within the meaning of the Coal Industry Act 1994 (c.21), and

(ii) partly of persons appointed or nominated, or appointed or elected from among persons nominated, by one or more organisations representing persons employed in or about coal mines.

(5) The second condition is that–

(a) the institute is managed by a committee or board, but

(b) the making of–

(i) an appointment or nomination falling within subsection (4)(b)(i), or

(ii) an appointment or nomination falling within subsection (4)(b)(ii),

is not practicable or would not be appropriate, and

(c) at least two thirds of the committee or board consists–

(i) partly of persons employed, or formerly employed, in or about coal mines, and

(ii) partly of persons appointed by the Coal Industry Social Welfare Organisation or a body or person to which the functions of that Organisation have been transferred under section 12(3) of the Miners' Welfare Act 1952 (c.23).

(6) The third condition is that the premises of the institute are held on trusts to which section 2 of the Recreational Charities Act 1958 (c.17) applies.

## 8.3    APPLICATIONS FOR CLUB PREMISES CERTIFICATES

### 8.3.1   Generally

Section 71(1) provides: 'A club may apply for a club premises certificate in respect of any premises which are occupied by, and habitually used for the purposes of, the club.' The reference here to 'any premises' may mean any single premises or any number of premises. If it means the latter, then a club could apply for a CPC for more than one set of premises. This was certainly possible under the previous law.[17] There is nothing to indicate that s 71(1) is intended to change the previous law and its wording is wide enough to encompass this possibility. However, unlike the previous provision, s 71(1) is ambiguous in its wording and it is possible that it may be narrowly construed so that CPCs may apply only in respect of a single premises. A narrow construction may be supported if recourse is had to the Licensing Act 2003 (Premises Licences and Club Premises Certificates) Regulations 2005, SI 2005/42 (LA 2003 (PL and CPC) Regs 2005) as an aid to interpretation. It was recognised by the House of Lords in *British Amusement Catering Trades Association v Westminster City Council* [1988] 1 All E.R. 740 that courts can have regard to statutory provisions in secondary legislation made under primary legislation in order to interpret the meaning of the primary legislation itself[18] and reg 23 of the LA 2003 (PL and CPC) Regs 2005 may indicate that 'premises' in s 71 has only a singular meaning. Regulation 23 prescribes the form of the plan that must accompany the application (see 8.3.3 below) and reg 23(3)(a) requires the plan to show the 'extent of the boundary of *the building* . . . and, if different, the perimeter of *the premises*' (emphasis supplied). The reference here to 'building' in the singular, and (it must be assumed) 'premises' in the singular, may well show that Parliament intended a CPC to have application only to a single premises.

Unlike in the case of premises licences, no provision is made for the issuing of provisional statements in respect of club premises that are being or about to be constructed, altered or extended.[19] Admittedly, it may be less likely to be used than in the case of premises licences, but it is not readily apparent why this procedure should not be available in respect of club premises. In other respects, however, application is very similar to that in respect of premises licences.[20]

### 8.3.2 Form, notices and fees

Applications for CPCs, under s 71(2), are made to the relevant licensing authority[21] and under s 71(3) are subject to regulations made (by the Secretary of State: s 193) (a) under s 91 in respect of the form of applications and any notices that need to be given, and (b) under s 92 in respect of fees to accompany applications and notices. Under s 91, regulations may prescribe the form of the application or notice, the manner in which it is to be made or given and any information and documents that must accompany it. Regulation 18 and Sched 9 to the LA 2003 (PL and CPC) Regs 2005 specify the form the application must take and the information that it must contain and, under reg 17 and Sched 9, on or before making the application, the club must make a declaration as to its qualifying status and provide certain supporting information. Notices in respect of an application can include the publicising of it and in this respect s 71(6) provides:

> Regulations may–
> (a)  require an applicant to advertise the application within the prescribed period–
>   (i)  in the prescribed form, and
>   (ii)  in a manner which is prescribed and is likely to bring the application to the attention of the interested parties likely to be affected by it,
> (b)  require an applicant to give notice of the application to each responsible authority, and such other persons as may be prescribed within the prescribed period,
> (c)  prescribe the period during which interested parties and responsible authorities may make representations to the relevant licensing authority about the application.

This provision is comparable to that in s 17(5) in respect of premises licences and the advertising and notice requirements are set out in regs 25–26 of the LA 2003 (PL and CPC) Regs 2005 (see 2.1.12–2.1.13 above).

Section 92 contains various provisions in respect of the fees payable[22] and under reg 6(1) and Sched 2 to the Licensing Act 2003 (Fees) Regulations 2005, SI 2005/79 (LA 2003 (Fees) Regs 2005) the application fees payable for a CPC application are the same as for a premises licence application, except that such applications do not attract increased (multiplier) fees or additional fees (see 6.3.1 above). Under reg 7(1) this is also the position in respect of payment of an annual fee[23] and under reg 7(2) responsibility to discharge the duty to pay the annual fee is placed on the club secretary.

### 8.3.3 Accompanying documentation

Applications must be accompanied by various documents as required by s 71(4), which provides:

> An application under this section must also be accompanied by–
> (a) a club operating schedule,
> (b) a plan of the premises to which the application relates, in the prescribed form,[24] and
> (c) a copy of the rules of the club.

The club operating schedule has to set out various matters, including the qualifying club activities to be covered by the certificate, the times it will be used for these activities and other times it will be open, whether any supply of alcohol will be for consumption on and off the premises or only on the premises, and the steps proposed to promote the licensing objectives. Section 71(5) provides:

> A "club operating schedule" is a document which is in the prescribed form, and includes a statement of the following matters–
> (a) the qualifying club activities to which the application relates ("the relevant qualifying club activities"),
> (b) the times during which it is proposed that the relevant qualifying club activities are to take place,
> (c) any other times during which it is proposed that the premises are to be open to members and their guests,
> (d) where the relevant qualifying club activities include the supply of alcohol, whether the supplies are proposed to be for consumption on the premises or both on and off the premises,
> (e) the steps which it is proposed to take to promote the licensing objectives, and
> (f) such other matters as may be prescribed.

In terms of requirements, the club operating schedule is broadly comparable to the operating schedule that applicants are required to submit for a premises licence (see 6.3.3 above) and differs in only two respects. One is that there is no requirement for the provision of information in respect of the person who will be specified as the premises supervisor relating to the supply of alcohol since this has no application in the case of clubs and the other is that there is no requirement for inclusion of a statement as to the period the applicant wishes the CPC to have effect, if this is a limited period, since no provision is made in the Act for a CPC to be of limited duration.[25]

## 8.4    DETERMINATION OF APPLICATIONS FOR CLUB PREMISES CERTIFICATES

### 8.4.1   Mandatory grants

8.4.2   The position as regards determination of applications is similar to that in respect of premises licences (see 6.4 above). If the application requirements have been met and no relevant representations received,[26] s 72(2) provides:

> The authority must grant the certificate in accordance with the application, subject only to (a) such conditions as are consistent with the club operating schedule accompanying the application, and (b) any conditions which must under section 73(2) to (5) or 74 be included.

The requirement for conditions to be consistent with the club operating schedule is comparable to the requirement for conditions to be consistent with the operating schedule accompanying a premises licence application, a requirement that has been considered in Chapter 6.[27] Section 73(2)–(5) contains three conditions that must be attached in respect of off-sales of alcohol where a CPC authorises supply of alcohol for consumption off the premises as well as consumption on the premises:[28]

> (2)   A club premises certificate which authorises the supply of alcohol for consumption off the premises must include the following conditions.
>
> (3)   The first condition is that the supply must be made at a time when the premises are open for the purposes of supplying alcohol, in accordance with the club premises certificate, to members of the club for consumption on the premises.
>
> (4)   The second condition is that any alcohol supplied for consumption off the premises must be in a sealed container.
>
> (5)   The third condition is that any supply of alcohol for consumption off the premises must be made to a member of the club in person.

Section 74 requires a mandatory condition, where the qualifying club activities include the exhibition of films, for the admission of children to exhibitions to be restricted in accordance with film classification recommendations. These recommendations can be those of the 'film classification body', the British Board of Film Classification (BBFC), or of the licensing authority itself if it operates its own classification system. Section 74 provides:

> (1)   Where a club premises certificate authorises the exhibition of films, the certificate must include a condition requiring the admission of children to the exhibition of any film to be restricted in accordance with this section.
>
> (2)   Where the film classification body is specified in the certificate, unless subsection (3)(b) applies, admission of children must be restricted in accordance with any recommendation made by that body.
>
> (3)   Where–
>> (a)   the film classification body is not specified in the certificate, or
>> (b)   the relevant licensing authority has notified the club which holds the certificate that this subsection applies to the film in question,
>
> admission of children must be restricted in accordance with any recommendation made by that licensing authority.
>
> (4)   In this section–
> "children" means persons aged under 18; and

"film classification body" means the person or persons designated as the authority under section 4 of the Video Recordings Act 1984 (c.39).

8.4.3     As well as these mandatory conditions, there are certain conditions that an authority is prohibited from attaching. These are set out in ss 75–76. Section 75 prohibits the imposition of conditions preventing the sale by retail of alcohol to or the provision of regulated entertainment for associate members of the club and their guests, where the rules of the club make provision for this.[29] Section 75 provides:

(1)  Where the rules of a club provide for the sale by retail of alcohol on any premises by or on behalf of the club to, or to a guest of, an associate member of the club, no condition may be attached to a club premises certificate in respect of the sale by retail of alcohol on those premises by or on behalf of the club so as to prevent the sale by retail of alcohol to any such associate member or guest.

(2)  Where the rules of a club provide for the provision of any regulated entertainment on any premises by or on behalf of the club to, or to a guest of, an associate member of the club, no condition may be attached to a club premises certificate in respect of the provision of any such regulated entertainment on those premises by or on behalf of the club so as to prevent its provision to any such associate member or guest.

Section 76 applies only where the CPC authorises the performance of plays and prohibits the imposition of conditions as to the nature of plays or the manner of their performance.[30] It provides:

(1)  In relation to a club premises certificate which authorises the performance of plays, no condition may be attached to the certificate as to the nature of the plays which may be performed, or the manner of performing plays, under the certificate.

(2)  But subsection (1) does not prevent a licensing authority imposing, in accordance with section 72(2) or (3)(b), 85(3)(b) or 88(3), any condition which it considers necessary on the grounds of public safety.

### 8.4.4  Relevant representations and discretion

The position as regards determination of applications is again similar to that in respect of premises licences (see 6.4.8 et seq above). Under s 72(3)(a) the authority must hold a hearing to consider them, unless the authority, the applicant and each person who has made such representations agree that a hearing is unnecessary, and under para 8 of Sched 1 to the Licensing Act 2003 (Hearings) Regulations 2005, SI 2005/44 (LA 2003 (Hearings) Regs 2005) the hearing must be held within 20 working days, beginning with the day after the end of the period during which representations may be made as prescribed under s 71(6)(c), which itself, under reg 22(b) of the LA 2003 (PL and CPC) Regs 2005, is 28 consecutive days after the day on which the application is given to the authority. Under reg 6(4) and para 8 of Sched 2, notice of the hearing must be given to the club and persons who made relevant representations no later than 10 working days before the day or the first day on which the hearing is to be held.[31]

### *8.4.5  Meaning of relevant representations*

Relevant representations are defined in s 72(7) and (8) and have the same meaning as for premises licences (see 6.4.9 above):

(7)  For the purposes of this section, "relevant representations" means representations which–

    (a)  are about the likely effect of the grant of the certificate on the promotion of the licensing objectives, and

    (b)  meet the requirements of subsection (8).

(8)  The requirements are–

    (a)  that the representations are made by an interested party or responsible authority in accordance with regulations under section 71(6)(c),

    (b)  that they have not been withdrawn, and

    (c)  in the case of representations made by an interested party (who is not also a responsible authority), that they are not, in the opinion of the relevant licensing authority, frivolous or vexatious.

### 8.4.6   Representations about the likely effect of the grant of the certificate on the promotion of the licensing objectives: s 72(7)(a)

The position is the same as in respect of premises licences (see 6.4.10–6.4.11 above).

### 8.4.7   Persons entitled to submit relevant representations: s 72(7)(b) and (8)(a)

The position is the same as in respect of premises licences, with s 69(3) and (4) making identical provision to s 13(3) and (4) for premises licences (see 6.4.12–6.4.18 above).

### 8.4.8   Representations within the prescribed period: s 72(7)(b), s 72(8)(a) and s 71(6)(c)

Representations by an interested party or responsible authority must be made 'in accordance with regulations under section 71(6)(c)', which provides that regulations may prescribe the period within which relevant representations may be made. The period prescribed by reg 22(b) of the LA 2003 (PL and CPC) Regs 2005 is 28 consecutive days starting on the day after the day on which the application is given to the authority by the applicant. The position in respect of representations received outside the prescribed period is the same as for premises licences (see 6.4.19 above).

### 8.4.9   Representations not withdrawn nor frivolous or vexatious: s 72(7)(b) and (8)(b)(c)

The position is the same as in respect of premises licences (see 6.4.20–6.4.22 above).[32]

## 8.5   GRANT OR REFUSAL OF A CLUB PREMISES CERTIFICATE – TAKING STEPS NECESSARY TO PROMOTE THE LICENSING OBJECTIVES

8.5.1    Except in cases where no relevant representations have been received (in which case the authority must grant the CPC), whether a CPC is granted or refused will be determined by what the authority considers necessary to promote the licensing objectives. A hearing must be held to consider relevant representations (unless there is agreement that this is unnecessary) and then, having regard to the representations, there are a number of steps open to the authority one or more of which it might take depending on what it considers necessary to promote the licensing objectives. Section 72(3) and (4) provides:

> (3)  Where relevant representations are made, the authority must–
>
>> (a)  hold a hearing to consider them, unless the authority, the applicant and each person who has made such representations agree that a hearing is unnecessary, and
>>
>> (b)  having regard to the representations, take such of the steps mentioned in sub-section (4) (if any) as it considers necessary for the promotion of the licensing objectives.[33]
>
> (4)  The steps are–
>
>> (a)  to grant the certificate subject to–
>>
>>> (i)  the conditions mentioned in subsection (2)(a) modified to such extent as the authority considers necessary for the promotion of the licensing objectives, and
>>>
>>> (ii)  any conditions which must under section 73(2) to (5) or 74 be included in the certificate;
>>
>> (b)  to exclude from the scope of the certificate any of the qualifying club activities to which the application relates;
>>
>> (c)  to reject the application.

Section 72(3)(b) only requires the authority to 'have regard' to the representations and the authority might take into account matters other than those raised in the relevant representations when deciding what is necessary to promote the licensing objectives (see 6.5.1 above). It is not necessary that any of the steps mentioned in sub-s (4) be taken since s 72(3)(b) refers to the authority taking such of the steps 'if any' as it considers necessary for the promotion of the licensing objectives. If none of the steps are considered necessary, the authority can grant the CPC in the terms sought by the applicant subject only to such conditions as are consistent with the club operating schedule accompanying the application in accordance with s 72(2)(a). The conditions imposed on the grant of the CPC in such a case will thus be the same as if no relevant representations had been received and the authority had been obliged to grant the CPC.

8.5.2    Apart from rejecting the application and refusing a CPC, the authority can grant the CPC subject to conditions and/or with the exclusion of one or more of the licensable activities for which application has been made in accordance with any or all of the three steps mentioned in s 72(4)(a)–(b). As regards the attachment of conditions, the CPC can be granted subject to conditions consistent with the club operating schedule, but modified to such extent as the authority considers necessary for the promotion of the licensing objectives, again with any mandatory conditions under s 73(2)–(5) or s 74 if applicable (see 8.4.2 above). As regards conditions being 'modified', s 72(6) provides:

> For the purposes of subsection (4)(a)(i) the conditions mentioned in subsection (2)(a) are modified if any of them is altered or omitted or any new condition is added.

Further, as in the case of a mandatory grant, authorities can, under s 72(10), impose different conditions on different parts of the premises and in relation to different licensable activities (see 8.4.2 above).

Where considering the imposition of conditions, it may be that authorities should be more circumspect than in the case of premises licences and take a stricter approach to the imposition of conditions. This seems to follow from paras 6.14 and 6.15 of the Guidance, which provide:

6.14 The Secretary of State wishes to emphasise that non-profit making clubs make an important and traditional contribution to the life of many communities in England and Wales and bring significant benefits. Their activities also take place on premises to which the public do not generally have access and they operate under codes of discipline applying to members and their guests.

6.15 Licensing authorities should bear these matters in mind when considering representations and should not attach conditions to certificates unless they can be demonstrated to be strictly necessary. The indirect costs of conditions will be borne by individual members of the club and cannot be recovered by passing on these costs to the general public.

That conditions should not be imposed unless 'strictly necessary' perhaps suggests a higher threshold than for premises licences, where conditions need only be 'necessary'. It is not easy to see how this will operate in practice, as in each instance the licensing authority must be acting to promote the licensing objectives. Perhaps if the imposition of a condition is considered 'marginal', it might be included on a premises licence, but be excluded in the case of a club.[34]

## 8.6    NOTIFICATION OF GRANT OR REFUSAL AND ISSUING OF THE CLUB PREMISES CERTIFICATE AND SUMMARY

8.6.1    The position in respect of notification is the same as in respect of premises licences (see 6.6 above). Section 77 makes identical provision for CPCs as s 23 does for premises licences and provides:

(1)  Where an application is granted under section 72, the relevant licensing authority must forthwith–
   (a)  give a notice to that effect to–
      (i)   the applicant,
      (ii)  any person who made relevant representations in respect of the application, and
      (iii) the chief officer of police for the police area (or each police area) in which the premises are situated, and
   (b)  issue the club with the club premises certificate and a summary of it.
(2)  Where relevant representations were made in respect of the application, the notice under subsection (1)(a) must specify the authority's reasons for its decision as to the steps (if any) to take under section 72(3)(b).
(3)  Where an application is rejected under section 72, the relevant licensing authority must forthwith give a notice to that effect, stating its reasons for that decision, to–
   (a)  the applicant,
   (b)  any person who made relevant representations in respect of the application, and
   (c)  the chief officer of police for the police area (or each police area) in which the premises are situated.
(4)  In this section "relevant representations" has the meaning given in section 72(6).[35]

8.6.2 Where granted, the CPC and a summary of it will be in a form prescribed in regulations by the Secretary of State. Section 78 makes provision to this effect and sets out the basic requirements that those regulations must include as to the content of the certificate. Section 78 provides:

  (1) A club premises certificate and the summary of such a certificate must be in the prescribed form.

  (2) Regulations under subsection (1) must, in particular, provide for the certificate to–

    (a) specify the name of the club and the address which is to be its relevant registered address, as defined in section 184(7);[36]

    (b) specify the address of the premises to which the certificate relates;

    (c) include a plan of those premises;[37]

    (d) specify the qualifying club activities for which the premises may be used;

    (e) specify the conditions subject to which the certificate has effect.

Regulation 35 and Pt A of Sched 13 to the LA 2003 (PL and CPC) Regs 2005 provide for the certificate to specify, in addition to the above-mentioned matters, the dates in cases where the CPC is time-limited (although s 71(5) in fact makes no provision for inclusion in a club operating schedule of a statement as to the period for which the applicant wishes the CPC to have effect – see 8.3.3 above), the times at which qualifying club activities may take place, the opening hours of the club and whether supply of alcohol is for consumption on and off or just on the premises. Regulation 36 and Pt B of Sched 12 provide for the summary to be printed on paper of a size equal or larger than A4 and to specify all matters mentioned above (except for a plan) and, in addition, to state whether access to the club premises by children is restricted.

8.6.3 In the event that the CPC or summary is lost, stolen, damaged or destroyed, s 79 enables the club to obtain a copy, in the same form as it existed immediately before loss etc, on payment of a fee (which under reg 8 and Sched 6 to the LA 2003 (Fees) Regs 2005 is £10.50):

  (1) Where a club premises certificate or summary is lost, stolen, damaged or destroyed, the club may apply to the relevant licensing authority for a copy of the certificate or summary.

  (2) Subsection (1) is subject to regulations under section 92(1) (power to prescribe fee to accompany application).

  (3) Where an application is made in accordance with this section, the relevant licensing authority must issue the club with a copy of the certificate or summary (certified by the authority to be a true copy) if it is satisfied that–

    (a) the certificate or summary has been lost, stolen, damaged or destroyed, and

    (b) where it has been lost or stolen, the club has reported the loss or theft to the police.

  (4) The copy issued under this section must be a copy of the club premises certificate or summary in the form in which it existed immediately before it was lost, stolen, damaged or destroyed.

  (5) This Act applies in relation to a copy issued under this section as it applies in relation to an original club premises certificate or summary.

The section simply indicates that 'the club' may apply for any copy, without any indication as to who will make the application, but presumably the club will do so through its secretary.

## 8.7    DURATION OF CLUB PREMISES CERTIFICATE

### 8.7.1    Indefinite duration and exceptions

A CPC, once granted, will generally remain in force indefinitely. The circumstances in which it will not do so are when it is withdrawn, lapses on surrender or is suspended. Section 80 provides:

(1)  A club premises certificate has effect until such time as–
   (a)  it is withdrawn under section 88 or 90, or
   (b)  it lapses by virtue of section 81(3) (surrender).
(2)  But a club premises certificate does not have effect during any period when it is suspended under section 88.

In this respect, the CPC is similar to the premises licence, except that a premises licence can cease to remain in force for other reasons in addition to those mentioned above (see 6.7 above). These other reasons – the licence being granted only for a limited period and lapse due to some incapacity on the part of the licence holder – do not have application in the case of CPCs.

### 8.7.2    Withdrawal of club premises certificate

8.7.3    A CPC can be withdrawn[38] in two circumstances. One is where it is withdrawn under s 88 following an application for review (see 8.10.8 below) and the other is where it is withdrawn under s 90 because the club has ceased to meet the qualifying conditions for a CPC. Where the club ceases to be a qualifying club in relation to some qualifying club activity, it is no longer entitled to a CPC and the authority must give the club a notice withdrawing the certificate in relation to that activity.[39] Section 90(1) provides:

Where–
(a)  a club holds a club premises certificate, and
(b)  it appears to the relevant licensing authority that the club does not satisfy the conditions for being a qualifying club in relation to a qualifying club activity to which the certificate relates (see section 61),
the authority must give a notice to the club withdrawing the certificate, so far as relating to that activity.

The authority must give notice if it 'appears' that the club does not satisfy the qualifying conditions. The section does not say that the authority has to be 'satisfied' that the qualifying conditions are not met before notice is given, but it is submitted that notice should not be given unless the authority is so satisfied. Notwithstanding that the wording of the section seems to indicate that the onus on the authority is not a particularly heavy one, the authority should be satisfied on a balance of probabilities before notice is given. This is the normal standard of proof required in civil proceedings and there seems no justification for any lesser standard having application here. Withdrawal of a CPC is a significant interference with property rights which are afforded protection under Art 1 of Protocol 1 of the European Convention on Human Rights (see 3.6 above). It may be that, in the absence of proper proof substantiating withdrawal as necessary because the qualifying conditions are no longer met, the interference is not justified as a control of use of the property in the general interest and is a violation of the right under Art 1 of Protocol 1.

8.7.4    With a view to ascertaining whether or not a club satisfies the qualifying conditions, powers of entry, search and seizure are conferred on a constable (but not an authorised officer). These can be exercised within one month of a justice of the peace issuing a warrant and enable any documents relating to the business of the club to be seized. Section 90(5) and (6) provides:

> (5)  Where a justice of the peace is satisfied, on information on oath, that there are reasonable grounds for believing–
>    (a)  that a club which holds a club premises certificate does not satisfy the conditions for being a qualifying club in relation to a qualifying club activity to which the certificate relates, and
>    (b)  that evidence of that fact is to be obtained at the premises to which the certificate relates,
>    he may issue a warrant authorising a constable to enter the premises, if necessary by force, at any time within one month from the time of the issue of the warrant, and search them.
> (6)  A person who enters premises under the authority of a warrant under subsection (5) may seize and remove any documents relating to the business of the club in question.

Section 90 does not expressly indicate at what point withdrawal takes effect – whether this is from the date of the notice or whether it might be from some later date specified by the authority. However, it may be implicit from s 90(2), which provides for withdrawal to take effect after three months from the date of the notice in cases where the club has fewer members than required,[40] that in other cases withdrawal would be effective from the date of the notice. Section 90(2) seems to be expressed by way of an exception, suggesting that the general rule is withdrawal on notice. As to the exception, it is clearly a pragmatic one, since club membership can obviously fluctuate over time. Membership may dip below the minimum required only for a relatively short period of time before thereafter rising above the minimum. Requiring the notice not to take effect for three months means that there will be no withdrawal if, by the end of the three months, membership has risen to at least the minimum required. It will take effect only if the membership remains below that minimum. Section 90(2) provides:

> Where the only reason that the club does not satisfy the conditions for being a qualifying club in relation to the activity in question is that the club has fewer than the required number of members,[41] the notice withdrawing the certificate must state that the withdrawal–
> (a)  does not take effect until immediately after the end of the period of three months following the date of the notice, and
> (b)  will not take effect if, at the end of that period, the club again has at least the required number of members.

This provision does not prevent an authority from giving a further notice of withdrawal under the section at any time (s 90(4)). If, during the currency of a notice given in accordance with s 90(2), it is discovered that the club does not satisfy another qualifying condition, a further notice might be given and under this withdrawal might have immediate effect. This would effectively supersede the notice given in accordance with s 90(2).

In the event of any dispute, no provision is made for any hearing to take place to determine whether or not the club has ceased to meet the qualifying conditions for a CPC, although a right of appeal to the magistrates' court is provided (see para 14 of Sched 5; and 12.2.21 below).

### 8.7.5    Lapse of CPC on surrender

A CPC will lapse if the club voluntarily surrenders it. Surrender is by way of a notice of surrender to the licensing authority, accompanied by the return of the CPC or a statement of reasons why this cannot be done, for example because the CPC has been lost. As with premises licences, no provision is made for payment of a fee or for notice of surrender to be given to other persons (see 6.7.4 below). Section 81 provides:

(1) Where a club which holds a club premises certificate decides to surrender it, the club may give the relevant licensing authority a notice to that effect.

(2) The notice must be accompanied by the club premises certificate or, if that is not practicable, by a statement of the reasons for the failure to produce the certificate.

(3) Where a notice is given in accordance with this section, the certificate lapses on receipt of the notice by the authority.

Unlike in the case of premises licences, no provision is made for reinstatement of the CPC.[42] Nor is it apparent who may surrender the CPC, for s 81(1) refers only to surrender by 'a club which ... decides to surrender it'. Certainly there could be surrender where there is a formal resolution at a club committee meeting to surrender the CPC and a club officer is mandated to give notice of surrender to the authority, but it is not clear whether anything less than this will suffice.

### 8.7.6    Suspension of club premises certificate

This is covered in 8.10.9 below.

## 8.8    AMENDING THE CLUB PREMISES CERTIFICATE

8.8.1    Once a CPC has been granted, the secretary of the club is under a duty to notify the licensing authority of any change in the name of the club or any alteration made to club rules.[43] The notice given must be accompanied by the appropriate fee (which under reg 8 and Sched 6 to the LA 2003 (Fees) Regs 2005 is £10.50) and the CPC for the changes to be recorded on it. Section 82(1)–(3) provides:

(1) Where a club–

    (a) holds a club premises certificate, or

    (b) has made an application for a club premises certificate which has not been determined by the relevant licensing authority,

the secretary of the club must give the relevant licensing authority notice of any change in the name, or alteration made to the rules, of the club.

(2) Subsection (1) is subject to regulations under section 92(1) (power to prescribe fee to accompany application).

(3) A notice under subsection (1) by a club which holds a club premises certificate must be accompanied by the certificate or, if that is not practicable, by a statement of the reasons for the failure to produce the certificate.

The licensing authority is required under s 82(4) to amend the CPC to record any such change, but the amendment cannot change the premises to which it relates. That such a change cannot be made seems implicit in s 82(1), since notification is confined to changes to the club name or club rules, but s 82(5) nevertheless contains an express provision to this effect. Section 82(4) and (5) provides:

(4) An authority notified under this section of a change in the name, or alteration to the rules, of a club must amend the club premises certificate accordingly.

(5) But nothing in subsection (4) requires or authorises the making of any amendment to a club premises certificate so as to change the premises to which the certificate relates (and no amendment made under that subsection to a club premises certificate has effect so as to change those premises).

8.8.2 Failure by the club secretary to notify the authority of the change within 28 days following the day on which it is made is a criminal offence, for which the maximum penalty is a level 2 fine on the standard scale. Section 82(6)–(7) provides:

(6) If a notice required by this section is not given within the 28 days following the day on which the change of name or alteration to the rules is made, the secretary of the club commits an offence.

(7) A person guilty of an offence under subsection (6) is liable on summary conviction to a fine not exceeding level 2 on the standard scale.

The period of time for notification (28 days) is more precise (and almost certainly longer) than in the case of premises licences, where under s 33(1) notification of changes has to be given 'as soon as is reasonably practicable' (see 6.7.5 above). Whilst perhaps more generous in this respect, s 82 is less so with regard to the offence of failing to notify. Liability seems to be strict, with no provision made for any defence of reasonable excuse. The defence of reasonable excuse is provided in s 33(6) for failure by a premises holder to comply with requirements to notify changes of his name and address and that of the designated premises supervisor, but s 82(6) contains no such provision. It is difficult to see why a reasonable excuse should provide a defence in one case, but not the other, and neither Explanatory Note 143 to s 82 nor the Guidance gives any indication as to why this is the case.

8.8.3 In addition to notifying the licensing authority of any change of name or club rules, the club may notify the authority of any change in the club's relevant registered address. This is the address given in the record for the certificate, which is in the register kept under s 8 by the licensing authority that granted the certificate (see 2.4 below). Notification is mandatory if the club ceases to have authority to use this address and in each case a fee is payable (which under reg 8 and Sched 6 to the LA 2003 (Fees) Regs 2005 is £10.50). Section 83(1)–(3) provides:

(1) A club which holds a club premises certificate may give the relevant licensing authority notice of any change desired to be made in the address which is to be the club's relevant registered address.

(2) If a club which holds a club premises certificate ceases to have any authority to make use of the address which is its relevant registered address, it must as soon as reasonably practicable give to the relevant licensing authority notice of the change to be made in the address which is to be the club's relevant registered address.

(3) Subsections (1) and (2) are subject to regulations under section 92(1) (power to prescribe fee to accompany application).

Although the section does not specify who is responsible for notifying the authority, this will presumably be the club secretary as it is he who will be criminally liable for failure to notify under s 83(2). Section 82(6)–(7) provides:

> (6) If a club fails, without reasonable excuse, to comply with subsection (2) the secretary commits an offence.
>
> (7) A person guilty of an offence under subsection (6) is liable on summary conviction to a fine not exceeding level 2 on the standard scale.

The notice must be accompanied by the CPC (or a statement of reasons why this cannot be produced) for the change to be recorded on it by the authority. Section 83(4)–(5) provides:

> (4) A notice under subsection (1) or (2) must also be accompanied by the club premises certificate or, if that is not practicable, by a statement of the reasons for the failure to produce the certificate.
>
> (5) An authority notified under subsection (1) or (2) of a change to be made in the relevant registered address of a club must amend the club premises certificate accordingly.[44]

## 8.9     VARIATION OF CLUB PREMISES CERTIFICATES

### 8.9.1     Applications for variation

Application for variation might include seeking either a variation of the conditions or a variation of the CPC itself in some way, such as a change in the licensable activities. It might also include variation of the plan of the premises on the basis that this is part of the CPC (see 2.1.10 above). The application is subject to the same fee as for the grant of a CPC (see 8.3.2 above), must be accompanied by the CPC (or, if this cannot be provided, a statement of the reasons why this cannot be produced) and provision is made for advertising applications. Section 84 provides:

> (1) A club which holds a club premises certificate may apply to the relevant licensing authority for variation of the certificate.
>
> (2) Subsection (1) is subject to regulations under–
>
>> (a) section 91 (form etc of applications);
>>
>> (b) section 92 (fees to accompany applications).
>
> (3) An application under this section must also be accompanied by the club premises certificate or, if that is not practicable, by a statement of the reasons for the failure to provide the certificate.
>
> (4) The power to make regulations under subsection (6) of section 71 (advertisement etc of application) applies in relation to applications under this section as it applies in relation to applications under that section.

Regulation 19 and Sched 10 to the LA 2003 (PL and CPC) Regs 2005 specify the form the application shall take and the information that it must contain and regs 25–26 prescribe the advertisement requirements (see 2.1.12–2.1.13 above).

### 8.9.2     Determination of applications

8.9.3     The position here will be the same as in respect of premises licences.[45] Section 85 makes for CPCs identical provision to s 35 for premises licences and provides:

(1) This section applies where the relevant licensing authority–

    (a) receives an application, made in accordance with section 84, to vary a club premises certificate, and

    (b) is satisfied that the applicant has complied with any requirement imposed by virtue of subsection (4) of that section.

(2) Subject to subsection (3) and section 86(4), the authority must grant the application.

(3) Where relevant representations are made, the authority must–

    (a) hold a hearing to consider them, unless the authority, the applicant and each person who has made such representations agree that a hearing is unnecessary, and

    (b) having regard to the representations, take such of the steps mentioned in subsection (4) (if any) as it considers necessary for the promotion of the licensing objectives.

(4) The steps are–

    (a) to modify the conditions of the certificate;

    (b) to reject the whole or part of the application;

and for this purpose the conditions of the certificate are modified if any of them is altered or omitted or any new condition is added.

(5) In this section "relevant representations" means representations which–

    (a) are about the likely effect of the grant of the application on the promotion of the licensing objectives, and

    (b) meet the requirements of subsection (6).

(6) The requirements are–

    (a) that the representations are made by an interested party or responsible authority within the period prescribed under section 71(6)(c) by virtue of section 84(4),

    (b) that they have not been withdrawn, and

    (c) in the case of representations made by an interested party (who is not also a responsible authority), that they are not, in the opinion of the relevant licensing authority, frivolous or vexatious.

(7) Subsections (2) and (3) are subject to sections 73 and 74 (mandatory conditions relating to supply of alcohol for consumption off the premises and to exhibition of films).

8.9.4    There are also similar supplementary provisions in s 86, comparable to those in s 36 for premises licences (see s 36(6) and (7); and 6.9.5 above), which preclude an authority from making a substantial variation in respect of the premises, but enable the authority to vary the CPC so that different conditions apply to different parts of the premises and in respect of different licensable activities. Section 86(6) and (7) provides:

    (6) A club premises certificate may not be varied under section 85 so as to vary substantially the premises to which it relates.

    (7) In discharging its duty under subsection (2) or (3)(b) of that section, a licensing authority may vary a club premises certificate so that it has effect subject to different conditions in respect of–

        (a) different parts of the premises concerned;

        (b) different qualifying club activities.

### 8.9.5   Notification of decision

Supplementary provision on notification, similar to s 36 for premises licences, is made for CPCs by s 86.[46] Thus the authority must notify its decision to the applicant, the police and any person who made relevant representations[47] and, where the authority decides to grant the variation, persons who made relevant representations must be given reasons for the decision and the notice must specify the time when the variation is to take effect. Section 86(1)–(3) provides:

(1) Where an application (or any part of an application) is granted under section 85, the relevant licensing authority must forthwith give a notice to that effect to–

    (a) the applicant,

    (b) any person who made relevant representations[48] in respect of the application, and

    (c) the chief officer of police for the police area (or each police area) in which the premises are situated.

(2) Where relevant representations were made in respect of the application, the notice under subsection (1) must specify the authority's reasons for its decision as to the steps (if any) to take under section 85(3)(b).

(3) The notice under subsection (1) must specify the time when the variation in question takes effect.

That time is the time specified in the application or, if that time is before the applicant is given the notice, such later time as the relevant licensing authority specifies in the notice.

Where the authority decides not to grant the variation, similar notification of its decision is required. This includes giving notice to any person whose representations were determined to be frivolous or vexatious.[49] Section 86(4) and (5) provides:

(4) Where an application (or any part of an application) is rejected under section 85, the relevant licensing authority must forthwith give a notice to that effect stating its reasons for rejecting the application to–

    (a) the applicant,

    (b) any person who made relevant representations, and

    (c) the chief officer of police for the police area (or each police area) in which the premises are situated.

(5) Where the relevant licensing authority determines for the purposes of section 85(6)(c) that any representations are frivolous or vexatious, it must give the person who made them its reasons for that determination.

## 8.10   REVIEW OF CLUB PREMISES CERTIFICATES

### 8.10.1 Application

8.10.2   An application for review can be initiated by an interested party, a responsible authority or a member of the club. As with reviews of premises licences, the licensing authority itself cannot institute a review, although the relevant section of the local authority dealing with environmental health may (as a responsible authority) do so.[50] Applications might be made at any time and regulations must require the applicant to give notice to the club and each responsible authority, and for advertisement (in this instance by the authority rather than the applicant) and for the making of representations within a prescribed period of time. Section 87(1)–(3) provides:

(1) Where a club holds a club premises certificate–

    (a) an interested party,

    (b) a responsible authority, or

    (c) a member of the club,

    may apply to the relevant licensing authority for a review of the certificate.

(2) Subsection (1) is subject to regulations under section 91 (form etc of applications).

(3) The Secretary of State must by regulations under this section–

    (a) require the applicant to give a notice containing details of the application to the club and each responsible authority within such period as may be prescribed;

    (b) require the authority to advertise the application, and invite representations relating to it to be made, to the authority;

    (c) prescribe the period during which representations may be made by the club, any responsible authority and any interested party;

    (d) require any notice under paragraph (a) or advertisement under paragraph (b) to specify that period.

Regulation 20 and Sched 8 to the LA 2003 (PL and CPC) Regs 2005 specify the form the application shall take and the information that it must contain.[51] Under reg 29, the applicant must give a copy of the application, along with any accompanying documents, to the club and each responsible authority on the same day as he gives the review application to the licensing authority. Under regs 38–39, the application for review must be advertised by the licensing authority, as in the case of reviews of premises licences (see 6.12.3 above). Under reg 22(b), representations may be made during a period of 28 consecutive days after the day on which the application is given to the authority.

8.10.3 An application for review may be rejected (without a hearing and determination) if the authority is satisfied that the ground of review is not relevant to the licensing objectives or, if made by an interested party or club member, is frivolous, vexatious or repetitious. Section 87(4) provides:

The relevant licensing authority may, at any time, reject any ground for review specified in an application under this section if it is satisfied–

(a) that the ground is not relevant to one or more of the licensing objectives, or

(b) in the case of an application made by a person other than a responsible authority, that–

    (i) the ground is frivolous or vexatious, or

    (ii) the ground is a repetition.

Rejection because the ground is frivolous or vexatious is similar to a licensing authority rejecting relevant representations for these reasons, which has been considered earlier.[52] Rejection on the ground of repetition has also been considered earlier, in relation to reviews of premises licences, and the position is similar in relation to the review of CPCs.[53] Section 87(5) provides:

For this purpose a ground for review is a repetition if–

(a) it is identical or substantially similar to–

(i)   a ground for review specified in an earlier application for review made in respect of the same club premises certificate and determined under section 88, or

(ii)  representations considered by the relevant licensing authority in accordance with section 72, before it determined the application for the club premises certificate under that section, and

(b)  a reasonable interval has not elapsed since that earlier application or that grant.

The meaning of 'substantially similar' and 'reasonable interval' have been considered in relation to reviews of premises licences (in 6.12.5 above) and presumably will have a similar meaning in relation to the review of CPCs.

Where a ground of review is rejected on the ground that it is frivolous, vexatious or repetitious, reg 32 of the LA 2003 (PL and CPC) Regs 2005 requires that notification in writing is given as soon as reasonably practicable to the person making the application.

8.10.4   If an application for review is rejected, the authority must notify the applicant of its decision.[54] The reason for rejection will be self-evident if it is on the ground that it is repetitious, but reasons must be given if it is rejected on the ground that it is frivolous or vexatious. Section 87(6) provides:

> Where the authority rejects a ground for review under subsection (4)(b), it must notify the applicant of its decision and, if the ground was rejected because it was frivolous or vexatious, the authority must notify him of its reasons for making that decision.

An application may, of course, seek review on a number of grounds, only some of which may be considered irrelevant, frivolous, vexatious and/or repetitious. In this case, an application may be rejected only to the extent that it is so considered and will need in other respects to be determined. Accordingly, s 87(7) provides:

> The application is to be treated as rejected to the extent that any of the grounds for review are rejected under subsection (4).

> Accordingly, the requirements imposed under subsection (3)(a) and (b) and by section 88 (so far as not already met) apply only to so much (if any) of the application as has not been rejected.

## 8.10.5  Determination of applications

8.10.6   The position will be the same as in respect of premises licences (see 6.12.6–6.12.12 above). Where an application for review has been made in accordance with s 87, under para 10 of Sched 1 to the LA 2003 (Hearings) Regs 2005 a hearing must be held within 20 working days to consider it and any relevant representations received following advertisement of the application under s 87(3)(b). Under reg 6(4) and para 10 of Sched 2, notice of the hearing must be given to the club, persons who made relevant representations and the person who has made the review application no later than 10 working days before the day or the first day on which the hearing is to be held.[55] Section 88(1) and (2) provides:

(1)  This section applies where–

(a)  the relevant licensing authority receives an application made in accordance with section 87,

   (b) the applicant has complied with any requirement imposed by virtue of subsection (3)(a) or (d) of that section, and

   (c) the authority has complied with any requirement imposed on it under subsection (3)(b) or (d) of that section.

(2) Before determining the application, the authority must hold a hearing to consider it and any relevant representations.

To constitute 'relevant representations', representations will, by virtue of s 88(7), need to be relevant to one or more of the licensing objectives – see s 4(2) and 4.2 above – and meet the requirements set out in s 88(8). These relate to the persons entitled to make representations making them within the prescribed time period, which under reg 22(b) of the LA 2003 (PL and CPC) Regs 2005 is 28 consecutive days starting on the day after the day on which the application was given to the authority, and there is the usual provision for relevant representations not to be considered where they have been withdrawn or when they are regarded as frivolous or vexatious. Section 88(7) and (8) provides:

(7) In this section "relevant representations" means representations which–

   (a) are relevant to one or more of the licensing objectives, and

   (b) meet the requirements of subsection (8).

(8) The requirements are–

   (a) that the representations are made by the club, a responsible authority or an interested party within the period prescribed under section 87(3)(c),

   (b) that they have not been withdrawn, and

   (c) if they are made by an interested party (who is not also a responsible authority), that they are not, in the opinion of the relevant licensing authority, frivolous or vexatious.

8.10.7 As to the persons entitled to make representations, s 88(7) includes, on the one hand, the club whose CPC is being reviewed and, on other hand, responsible authorities or interested parties. No mention is made, however, of representations by a club member, although a club member is entitled to apply for a review. The ground on which a club member may seek a review may well be relevant to one or more of the licensing objectives. If, for instance, there was a change in the nature of the entertainment provided by the club, which became increasingly of an adult variety, a member might seek a review of the CPC for conditions to be modified in order to protect children from harm (for example, by prohibiting their access to certain areas). It may be that the authority is able to consider representations by a club member, where such representations are relevant to the licensing objectives, but it is less clear whether a club member is *entitled*, as is an interested party and a responsible author-ity, to have his representations considered. The club member's representations will not be 'relevant representations' that the authority is obliged to consider since they will not comply with the requirement in s 88(8)(a) (unless the member, as a person living in the vicinity of the premises, is an interested party). The club member will not therefore be a 'party to the hearing' under the LA 2003 (Hearings) Regs 2005 and will not have the rights afforded to such parties at the hearing, including the right to have his representations considered (see 2.3.5 above). This is unless the view is taken that exclusion of representations by a club member from s 88(8)(a) was not deliberate, but an oversight, in which case the words 'or a club member' might be read into s 88(8)(a) to give effect to the legislature's intention. If this is done, the club member's representations will become 'relevant representations' that the authority is obliged to consider. If this is not done, the authority nevertheless might exercise a discretion to admit the representations in the same way that it might do so for late representations received outside the prescribed period of time of consecutive 28 days (see 6.4.19 above). It remains to be seen whether or not such words will be read into the section.

It may also be that the same words should be read into s 88(8)(c), which makes provision for representations by an interested party to be discounted if the authority considers them to be frivolous or vexatious, but not for the discounting of any such representations made by a club member. Where a ground of review by a person, other than a responsible authority, is considered by the authority to be frivolous or vexatious (or a repetition), the application can be rejected without a hearing under s 87(4)(b)(ii), which means rejection without a hearing can occur where the review was sought by either an interested party or a club member (see 8.10.3 above). If a ground advanced by a club member might be considered frivolous or vexatious and dismissed in advance of a hearing, it would be illogical if representations for consideration at a hearing could not be discounted if they were similarly so regarded. This will be the case, however, unless the words 'or a club member' are also read into s 88(8)(c).

8.10.8  When determining the application, the authority must take one of a number of steps that it considers necessary to promote the licensing objectives (see s 4(2) and 4.2 above). Section 88(3)–(5) provides:

> (3)  The authority must, having regard to the application and any relevant representa-
> tions, take such of the steps mentioned in subsection (4) (if any) as it considers
> necessary for the promotion of the licensing objectives.
>
> (4)  The steps are–
>> (a)  to modify the conditions of the certificate;
>> (b)  to exclude a qualifying club activity from the scope of the certificate;
>> (c)  to suspend the certificate for a period not exceeding three months;
>> (d)  to withdraw the certificate;
>
> and for this purpose the conditions of the certificate are modified if any of them is
> altered or omitted or any new condition is added.
>
> (5)  Subsection (3) is subject to sections 73 and 74 (mandatory conditions relating to
> supply of alcohol for consumption off the premises and to exhibition of films).

Once steps are taken and a determination is made, the authority's decision does not, however, have immediate effect. It takes effect only when the period for making an appeal has expired or, if an appeal is lodged, when the appeal is 'disposed of'(which presumably will include cases of both withdrawal and determination of the appeal). Section 88(11) provides:

> A determination under this section does not have effect–
> (a)  until the end of the period given for appealing against the decision, or
> (b)  if the decision is appealed against, until the appeal is disposed of.

8.10.9  It is not necessary that any of the steps mentioned in sub-s (4) are taken since s 88(3) refers to the authority taking such of the steps 'if any' as it considers necessary for the promotion of the licensing objectives. If none of these steps are considered necessary, the authority can decide to take no action. Alternatively, it may be that some informal action, such as issuing a warning or guidance, can be taken, a step which seems possible for premises licences (see 6.12.8 above), and there is no reason why the position should be any different in relation to CPCs. If the authority decides to modify the conditions of the CPC or to exclude a licensable activity from the scope of the certificate, it seems that it may do so either permanently or for a temporary period up to three months. Section 88(6) provides:

> Where the authority takes a step mentioned in subsection (4)(a) or (b), it may provide that the modification or exclusion is to have effect only for such period (not exceeding three months) as it may specify.

Since the authority 'may' make provision for a temporary exclusion for up to three months under this subsection, but is not obliged to do so since the section is not expressed in mandatory terms, it seems open to an authority to permanently exclude a qualifying club activity. If the exclusion is temporary, however, it must not be for a longer period than three months. Suspension, similarly, can be for a period of up to three months, although not for any longer period. Presumably if an authority feels a three months' suspension period is inadequate to promote the licensing objectives, the appropriate course would be to withdraw the CPC.

When taking steps to promote the licensing objective of preventing the commission of crime, the position will be similar to that in respect of premises licences. The Guidance makes it clear that only steps necessary in connection with the premises licence should be taken for the promotion of the crime prevention objective[56] and for clubs this will mean taking only steps necessary in connection with the CPC.

## 8.10.10 Notification of decision

The authority must notify its decision, with reasons, to the club, the applicant, any person who made relevant representations and the police. It must also notify, with reasons, any interested party whose representations were discounted as frivolous or vexatious.[57] Section 88(9) and (10) provides:

(9) Where the relevant licensing authority determines that any representations are frivolous or vexatious, it must give the person who made them its reasons for that determination.

(10) Where a licensing authority determines an application for review under this section it must notify the determination and its reasons for making it to–

    (a) the club,

    (b) the applicant,

    (c) any person who made relevant representations, and

    (d) the chief officer of police for the police area (or each police area) in which the premises are situated.

# 8.11  UPDATING AND PRODUCTION OF CLUB PREMISES CERTIFICATE

## 8.11.1  Updating of club premises certificate

Where modifications are made to a CPC, for example, where it is varied or amended following a review, the authority must update the CPC and, if necessary, issue a new summary of it. Section 93(1) provides:

> Where–
> (a) the relevant licensing authority, in relation to a club premises certificate, makes a determination or receives a notice under this Part, or
> (b) an appeal against a decision under this Part is disposed of,
> the relevant licensing authority must make the appropriate amendments (if any) to the certificate and, if necessary, issue a new summary of the certificate.

In order for the authority to make the modifications, it may be necessary for the CPC to be returned to the authority and the authority can require the club secretary to produce it or the appropriate part of it within 14 days of being notified of the need to do so. Section 93(2) provides:

> Where a licensing authority is not in possession of the club premises certificate, it may, for the purpose of discharging its obligations under subsection (1), require the secretary of the club to produce the certificate to the authority within 14 days from the date on which the club is notified of the requirement.

Failure to comply, without reasonable excuse, with the requirement to produce the CPC or appropriate part is a summary offence punishable by a fine not exceeding level 2 on the standard scale. Section 93(3) and (4) provides:

> (3) A person commits an offence if he fails, without reasonable excuse, to comply with a requirement under subsection (2).
> (4) A person guilty of an offence under subsection (3) is liable on summary conviction to a fine not exceeding level 2 on the standard scale.

## 8.11.2  Production of club premises certificate

8.11.3  The club secretary is under a duty to keep at the premises and produce the CPC or a certified copy of it[58] whenever the premises are being used for licensable activities. He must ensure: that the CPC or certified copy is kept in the custody or control of himself, any member of the club or any person who works at the premises for the purpose of the club; that the person having custody or control has been nominated by him in writing; and that he has given a notice to the relevant licensing authority identifying that person. The nominated person is responsible for ensuring that a summary of the CPC or certified copy,[59] together with a notice indicating the position held at the premises by the nominated person, must be prominently displayed at the premises. Section 94(1)–(4) provides:

> (1) This section applies whenever premises in respect of which a club premises certificate has effect are being used for one or more qualifying club activities authorised by the certificate.
> (2) The secretary of the club must secure that the certificate, or a certified copy of it, is

kept at the premises in the custody or under the control of a person ("the nominated person") who–

  (a)  falls within subsection (3),

  (b)  has been nominated for the purpose by the secretary in writing, and

  (c)  has been identified to the relevant licensing authority in a notice given by the secretary.

(3)  The persons who fall within this subsection are–

  (a)  the secretary of the club,

  (b)  any member of the club,

  (c)  any person who works at the premises for the purposes of the club.

(4)  The nominated person must secure that–

  (a)  the summary of the certificate or a certified copy of that summary, and

  (b)  a notice specifying the position which he holds at the premises, are prominently displayed at the premises.

8.11.4  Although s 94(2)(b) and (c) require the club secretary to nominate the person in writing and give a notice to the licensing authority, no provision is made in secondary legislation as to the form of nomination or notice. Nor is there any requirement in s 94(4) for the summary and notice to be prominently displayed at the same place in the premises. It might be expected, and clearly would be desirable, if this were the case but it will presumably meet the terms of the section if the summary and notice were to be (prominently) displayed in different parts of the premises. Failure by the club secretary to comply, without reasonable excuse, with the requirement under s 94(2) is a summary offence, as is a failure by the nominated person to comply, without reasonable excuse, with the requirement under s 94(4). In both instances, the offence is punishable by a fine not exceeding level 2 on the standard scale.[60] Section 94(5) and (6) provides:

(5)  The secretary commits an offence if he fails, without reasonable excuse, to comply with subsection (2).

(6)  The nominated person commits an offence if he fails, without reasonable excuse, to comply with subsection (4).

A constable or authorised person may require the nominated person to produce the CPC or certified copy for inspection, the authorised person being required to produce evidence of his authorisation if requested to do so, and a failure to produce the CPC or certified copy, without reasonable excuse, is a summary offence punishable by a fine not exceeding level 2 on the standard scale. Section 94(7)–(10) provides:

(7)  A constable or an authorised person[61] may require the nominated person to produce the club premises certificate (or certified copy) for examination.

(8)  An authorised person exercising the power conferred by subsection (7) must, if so requested, produce evidence of his authority to exercise the power.

(9)  A person commits an offence if he fails, without reasonable excuse, to produce a club premises certificate or certified copy of a club premises certificate in accordance with a requirement under subsection (7).

(10) A person guilty of an offence under this section is liable on summary conviction to a fine not exceeding level 2 on the standard scale.

## 8.12    PREDETERMINATION INSPECTIONS OF PREMISES

8.12.1   Section 96 confers a power on constables and authorised persons (see 8.11.4 above) on production on request of their authorisation, to enter premises, prior to determination of an application to grant, vary or review a CPC. Section 96(1) and (2) provides:

(1)  Subsection (2) applies where–
    (a)  a club applies for a club premises certificate in respect of any premises,
    (b)  a club applies under section 84 for the variation of a club premises certificate held by it, or
    (c)  an application is made under section 87 for review of a club premises certificate.
(2)  On production of his authority–
    (a)  an authorised person, or
    (b)  a constable authorised by the chief officer of police, may enter and inspect the premises.

The section gives no indication of the purpose(s) for which a constable or authorised officer may enter, unlike the comparable provision in s 59(2) relating to premises licences, which specifies that the power of entry is to assess the likely effect on the promotion of the licence objectives of the grant (see 6.15.1 above). Although it seems implicit that entry will be for these purposes, it is not apparent why there is no express provision to this effect, as there is in s 59, and for the avoidance of doubt it might have been better if there had been.

8.12.2   There are more constraints placed on constables and authorised officers in respect of the right to enter and inspect premises with CPCs than with premises licences.[62] First, there is no comparable provision to s 59(4) for premises licences, under which constables and authorised persons may use reasonable force to gain entry in cases of an application for review (see 6.15.2 above). Secondly, whilst for premises licences entry and inspection can take place at any reasonable time before the determination of a relevant application, for clubs, it must be not more than 14 days after (that is, within 14 days of) the making of the application and at least 48 hours' notice must be given. Section 96(3) and (4) provides:

(3)  Any entry and inspection under this section must take place at a reasonable time on a day–
    (a)  which is not more than 14 days after the making of the application in question, and
    (b)  which is specified in the notice required by subsection (4).
(4)  Before an authorised person or constable enters and inspects any premises under this section, at least 48 hours' notice must be given to the club.

It is not indicated to whom notice must be given, but presumably it is to the club secretary. Given the compressed timescale within which entry and inspection must take place, the Act makes provision for a seven-day extension, on application by a responsible authority. However, this can be granted only where, despite taking reasonable steps, it was not possible for the inspection to take place within the time allowed. Section 96(7) and (8) provides:

(7)  The relevant licensing authority may, on the application of a responsible authority, extend by not more than 7 days the time allowed for carrying out an entry and inspection under this section.

(8)  The relevant licensing authority may allow such an extension of time only if it appears to the authority that–

   (a)  reasonable steps had been taken for an authorised person or constable authorised by the applicant to inspect the premises in good time, but

   (b)  it was not possible for the inspection to take place within the time allowed.

8.12.3  It is an offence to obstruct an authorised person exercising the power of entry, an offence punishable summarily by a fine not exceeding level 2 on the standard scale. Section 96(5) and (6) provides:

(5)  Any person obstructing an authorised person in the exercise of the power conferred by this section commits an offence.

(6)  A person guilty of an offence under subsection (5) is liable on summary conviction to a fine not exceeding level 2 on the standard scale.

Unlike in the comparable provision in s 59(5) for premises licences (see 6.15.2 above), there is no reference to a mental element in s 96. Section 59(5) makes it an offence to 'intentionally' obstruct, but this word is absent from s 96(5), suggesting that the offence may be one of strict liability. In the case of a constable who is obstructed, a person commits an offence under the general provision of obstructing a constable in the course of his duties under s 89(2) of the Police Act 1996 only if he 'wilfully' obstructs. It seems illogical if a mental element is required for obstruction of a constable, as it clearly is because of the reference to 'wilfully', but not for obstruction of an authorised officer. Nor is it apparent why an authorised officer needs to be 'intentionally' obstructed when entering and inspecting in the case of premises licence application, but not in the case of a CPC application. It is submitted that s 96(5) should be interpreted so as to require a mental element (by invoking the presumption that statutes creating a criminal offence require a blameworthy state of mind (*mens rea*) on the part of the defendant) and the word 'intentionally' should be read into the section.

8.12.4  Finally, s 97 confers other powers of search on a constable, including the power to use reasonable force if necessary, where he has reason to believe an offence in connection with the supply of controlled drugs has been, is being, or is about to be, committed there or there is likely to be a breach of the peace there:

(1)  Where a club premises certificate has effect in respect of any premises, a constable may enter and search the premises if he has reasonable cause to believe–

   (a)  that an offence under section 4(3)(a), (b) or (c) of the Misuse of Drugs Act 1971 (c.38) (supplying or offering to supply, or being concerned in supplying or making an offer to supply, a controlled drug) has been, is being, or is about to be, committed there, or

   (b)  that there is likely to be a breach of the peace there.

(2)  A constable exercising any power conferred by this section may, if necessary, use reasonable force.

Section 97 confers express authority to enter and search for these purposes without a warrant, although it may be that such a power exists by virtue of s 17(6) of the Police and Criminal Evidence Act 1984. Although s 17(5) of that Act abolishes the common-law power to enter premises without a warrant, s 17(6) provides that this does not affect any power of entry to deal with or prevent a breach of the peace, and the Court of Appeal has held, in *McLeod v Commissioner of Police for the Metropolis* [1994] 4 All ER 553, that this power extends to any type of premises, including private premises. As Neill LJ stated (at 560), 'if the police reasonably believe that a breach of the peace is likely to take place on private premises, they have power to enter those premises to prevent it' and a constable might therefore enter club premises in pursuance of this power, quite apart from the express authority conferred by s 97. Nevertheless, it would be preferable to rely on the express provision in s 97, since there remains an element of doubt as to whether s 17(6) supports the Court of Appeal's conclusion in *McLeod*.[63]

## NOTES

1 Cmnd 5154, 1972, para 16.03. The Report is usually referred to as the Erroll Report after the name of the Committee's chairman, Lord Erroll of Hale.
2 See *Benjamin's Sale of Goods*, 7th edn, 2006, London: Sweet & Maxwell, para 1–121.
3 See also Guidance, para 6.3, which states: 'Where members purchase alcohol, there is no sale (as the member owns part of the alcohol stock) and the money passing across the bar is merely a mechanism to preserve equity between members where one may consume more than another'.
4 Common examples of clubs that operated under a registration certificate included Labour, Conservative and Liberal Clubs; the Royal British Legion and other ex-services clubs; working men's clubs and various sports clubs, such as rugby and cricket clubs.
5 Under s 2(3), there can be two or more authorisations having effect concurrently in respect of the same premises or part thereof – see 5.1.4 above.
6 Guidance, para 6.4. The benefits also include more limited rights of entry for the police and authorised persons, not being subject to police powers of instant closure on grounds of disorder and noise nuisance, and not being subject to orders of the magistrates' court for the closure of all licensed premises in an area when disorder is happening or expected.
7 It is not impossible for a proprietary club to meet the conditions and it depends on the proprietary element. The conditions include whether the club is conducted in good faith (s 63) and this might still be the case even if a person makes a profit out of the general running of the club, although the extent of the gain is clearly relevant in determining whether it is conducted in good faith.
8 See 6.4.2 above
9 This is likely to be a building of some description but, as in the case of a premises licence, a CPC can be obtained in respect of any premises as defined in s 193, ie any place or a vehicle, vessel or moveable structure – see 6.1.2–6.1.6 above.
10 Section 68(1) provides that the 'relevant licensing authority' in relation to any premises 'is determined in accordance with this section'. The relevant licensing authority will be 'the authority in whose area the premises are situated' (s 68(2)), except where the premises are situated in the areas of two or more licensing authorities, in which case it is 'the authority in whose area the greater or greatest part of the premises is situated' (s 68(3)(a)). If there is no such authority, it is the authority nominated by the applicant (s 68(3)(b) and s 68(4)). This provision is more or less identical to the provision in s 12 in respect of premises licences – see 6.3.1 above.
11 Qualifying club activities extend only to the sale or supply of alcohol and the provision of regulated entertainment. The provision of late night refreshment for members and guests is an 'exempt supply' under Sched 2, para 3(2) and no authorisation for this activity is needed – see 5.4.6 above.

12 Practice differs in respect of student union bars. Some operate as a club with a CPC, whereas others operate under a premises licence. Students from another institution that operates under a CPC can obtain admission as guests by virtue of being associate members under s 67 of the 2003 Act, but students from another institution that operates under a premises licence, not being members of any club, are unable to do so.

13 The expression 'supply of alcohol to members and guests' is defined in s 70 – see 8.2.4 above.

14 As a Government spokesman, Lord Davies stated in the House of Lords during the committee stage of the Bill when an amendment to change the period to 48 hours was being considered, 'The two-day requirement has lasted for many years. It is well attested to and it works without difficulty. We have not had substantial representations that it should be changed' (HL Deb, vol 643, col 364, 17 January 2003).

15 The Licensing Act 2003 (Premises Licences and Club Premises Certificates) Regulations 2005, SI 2005/42 (LA 2003 (PL and CPC) Regs 2005), reg 21 provides that a notice must be given in writing, although these Regulations contain no reference to the period of time within which the notice must be given. It may be that notice must be given forthwith, in accordance with the Licensing Act 2003 (Hearings) Regulations 2005, SI 2005/44 (LA 2003 (Hearings) Regs 2005), reg 28, which provides: 'In a case where the Act does not make provision for the period within which the authority must notify a party of its determination, the authority must do so forthwith on making its determination'.

16 The provision in para (e) has existed in licensing legislation since the registration of clubs was first introduced by s 28(2) of the Licensing Act 1902, but the Parliamentary debates to that Act give no indication of how it was envisaged that the nature of the premises might affect good faith. The provision was introduced by the Home Secretary as an amendment to the Bill at the third reading stage, along with a requirement that the supply of alcohol must be under the control of the members. The amendment was introduced without discussion, with the Home Secretary remarking that its object was 'to deal with clubs established simply for the sale of liquor, and for the purpose of profit to those who supplied the liquor' and it was 'directed against what were called bogus clubs' (Parl Debs (Fourth series), vol 110, cols 849 and 850, 4 July 1902).

17 Specific provision was made for a club to be registered for more than one set of premises by s 52 of the Licensing Act 1964, which provided: 'A single registration certificate may relate to any number of premises of the same club . . .' Use of this provision was made, for example, where student union bars operated under a registration certificate and there were bars that were located in several different premises.

18 In this case (on which, see 5.3.22 above), the House of Lords, when deciding that the expression 'exhibition of moving pictures' in s 1(3) of the Cinematograph Act 1909 denoted the showing of moving pictures to an audience rather than a display of moving objects of a (video) screen, had regard to the Cinematograph (Safety) Regulations 1955, SI 1955/1129 made under that Act. Lord Griffiths stated (at 745): '. . . these regulations are inapt to cover amusement arcades and other places where video games are normally located. The regulations only make sense if the 'cinematograph exhibitions' referred to in the regulations are understood in the sense of a show to an audience for example, there are frequent references to the auditorium, of which the definition in the Shorter Oxford English Dictionary is: 'The part of a public building occupied by the audience . . .' The regulations are dealing with the precautions necessary to protect an audience at a film show. Parliament having used the phrase 'cinematograph exhibition' in the sense of a film show in the regulations must in my view have intended to use the phrase in the same sense in the . . . Act in which it adopted the regulations'.

19 For provisional statements for premises licences, see 6.8 above.

20 The Guidance, para 6.11, provides:

> The arrangements for applying for or seeking to vary club premises certificates are extremely similar to those in respect of a premises licence. Licensing authorities should

therefore look to Chapter 8 of this Guidance on the handling of such applications and of hours of opening. In that Chapter most of the references to the premises licence, premises licence holders and application can be read for the purposes of this Chapter and club premises certificates, qualifying clubs and applicants.

21  For the meaning of 'relevant licensing authority', see s 68 and 8.2.2 above.

22  Regulations may require applications to be accompanied by a fee and may prescribe the amount of the fee (s 92(1)). Regulations may also require the holder of a premises licence to pay the relevant licensing authority an annual fee (s 92(2)), may impose liability for the making of the payment of the annual fee on the secretary or such other officers or members of the club as may be prescribed, and may prescribe the amount of the annual fee and the time at which any such fee is due (s 92(3)). Any annual fee owed to a licensing authority may be recovered as a debt due to the authority from any person liable to make the payment (s 92(4)).

23  Under reg 7(3), the annual fee is 'due and payable each year on the anniversary of the date of the grant of the club premises certificate', which is the same as for premises licence applications under reg 5(6).

24  For the form of the plan and the information that it must contain, see 2.1.8–2.1.10 above.

25  Nevertheless, reg 35 and Sched 13, Pt A, which make provision for the form of the CPC, require inclusion of the dates of the CPC where it is time-limited – see 8.6.2 below.

26  For the meaning of 'relevant representations' and the position where these have been received, see 8.4.4–8.4.5 below.

27  See 6.4.7 above. Authorities can similarly, within the same CPC, impose different conditions on different parts of the premises and in relation to different licensable activities: s 72(10).

28  Authorisation of the supply of alcohol to a member of a club is the qualifying club activity under s 1(2)(a) and the CPC must authorise supply for consumption on the premises although it can also authorise supply for consumption off the premises – see s 73(1), which provides: 'A club premises certificate may not authorise the supply of alcohol for consumption off the premises unless it also authorises the supply of alcohol to a member of the club for consumption on those premises.'

29  For associate members and guests, see 8.2.3 above.

30  This is comparable to the provision in s 22 in respect of premises licences – see 6.4.6 above.

31  As to the giving of notice of hearing, see 2.3.2 above. Under reg 7(2) and Sched 3, para 8, the club must be given the relevant representations with the notice of hearing.

32  Where a determination is made that representations are frivolous or vexatious, s 72(9) requires that the authority 'must notify the person who made them of the reasons for the determination'. Under reg 31 of the LA 2003 (PL and CPC) Regs 2005, notification must be in writing as soon as is reasonably practicable and in any event before the determination of the application to which the representations relate.

33  The requirement to take such steps is subject to s 72(5), which provides: 'Subsections (2) and (3)(b) are subject to section 73(1) (certificate may authorise off-supplies only if it authorises on-supplies).'

34  Conditions relating to sex equality should not be included, since 'although equal treatment on the grounds of gender is important to society generally, it is not a licensing objective. Conditions should not therefore be imposed which interfere with the arrangements for granting membership or voting within the club' (Guidance, para 6.16).

35  The reference in the Act to s 72(6) is incorrect. It should read s 72(7).

36  The 'relevant registered address' in s 184(7) (see 2.5.5 below) will be the address given in the record for the certificate that is in the register kept, under s 8, by the licensing authority that granted the certificate (see 2.4 above).

37  As to the plans forming part of the certificate, see 2.1.10 above.

38 It is not obvious why the term 'withdrawn' is used for CPCs, rather than 'revoked', which is used in s 26 for premises licences.

39 The conditions for being a qualifying club are set out in s 61 – see 8.2.6 above.

40 The numbers required are 25: s 62(5) – see 8.2.8 above.

41 Section 90(3) provides: 'The references in subsection (2) to the required number of members are references to the minimum number of members required by condition 4 in section 62(5) (25 at the passing of this Act).'

42 For reinstatement of a premises licence under s 50, see 6.11.12 above.

43 There is no comparable requirement to notify the licensing authority of any change in the name of premises where there is a premises licence in force.

44 Section 83(8) provides: 'In this section "relevant registered address" has the meaning given in section 184(7).' For the provision in s 184(7), see 2.5.5 above.

45 See 6.9.3–6.9.5 above. The provision is comparable to s 34 for variation of premises licences, except that there can be no variation of the designated premises supervisor (under s 37) or the time for having effect, since neither of these is applicable in the case of CPCs. Under reg 5 and Sched 1, para 9 of the LA 2003 (Hearings) Regs 2005 the holding of the hearing under s 85(3)(a) must be within 20 working days and under reg 6(4) and Sched 2, para 9, notice of the hearing must be given to the club and persons who made relevant representations no later than 10 working days before the day or the first day on which the hearing is to be held. As to the giving of notice of hearing, see 2.3.2 above. Under reg 7(2) and Sched 3, para 9, the club must be given the relevant representations with the notice of hearing.

46 These provisions, contained in s 86(6) and (7), are comparable to those in s 34(6) and (7). This is except in respect of the provision in s 36(6), which precludes an authority from varying a premises licence so as to extend the period of its duration, which is inapplicable in the case of CPCs.

47 Notice must be given forthwith on making the determination and the notice must be accompanied by information regarding the right of a party to appeal against the determination of the authority: see regs 28–29 of the LA 2003 (Hearings) Regs 2005 and 2.3.18 above. For the meaning of 'forthwith', see 6.6.2 above.

48 Section 86(8) provides: 'In this section "relevant representations" has the meaning given in section 85(5).'

49 Although there is no provision in the Guidance indicating that licensing authorities may not initiate their own reviews for CPCs, there is for premises licences (see Guidance, para 11.4 and 6.12.3 above) and the position must be the same for CPCs.

50 Section 89 provides that, where a local authority is both the responsible authority and the relevant licensing authority, it may, in its capacity as a responsible authority, apply under s 87 for a review of any premises licence and may, in its capacity as licensing authority, determine that application. This is the same as in the case for premises licences – see s 53 and 6.12.3 above.

51 As in the case of premises licences (see 6.12.3 above), no provision is made for the payment of a fee by an applicant for review.

52 See 8.4.9 above, referring to 6.4.20–6.4.22 above where this matter is considered in detail in relation to the grant of premises licences.

53 See 6.12.4 above. The provision in s 87(5) is comparable to that in s 52(5) for premises licences, except that it does not include representations being identical or substantially similar to those made on an application for a provisional statement since provisional statements have no application in the case of clubs (see 8.3.1 above).

54 Notice must be given forthwith on making the determination and the notice must be accompanied by information regarding the right of a party to appeal against the authority's determination: see regs 28–29 of the LA 2003 (Hearings) Regs 2005 and 2.3.18 above. For the meaning of 'forthwith', see 6.6.2 above.

55 As to the giving of notice of hearing, see 2.3.2 above. Under reg 7(2) and Sched 3, para 10, the club must be given the relevant representations with the notice of hearing.

56 Guidance, para 11.23; and see 6.12.9 above. The further guidance provided in para 11.25, that certain criminal activity should be treated particularly seriously, will also presumably apply – see 6.12.10 above.

57 Where an application for review is rejected because the ground is frivolous, vexatious or a repetition, reg 32 of the LA 2003 (PL and CPC) Regs 2005 requires written notification to be given as soon as reasonably practicable to the person making the application for a review (see 2.3.19 above). For the meaning of 'forthwith', see 6.6.2 above.

58 Section 95 makes provision for certified copies: s 94(12). A certified copy is a copy certified to be a true copy by the relevant licensing authority, a solicitor or notary, or a person of a prescribed description: s 95(1). Any certified copy produced in accordance with a requirement under s 94(7) [for a person having custody or control of the CPC to produce it for examination by a constable or authorised officer] must be a copy of the document in the form in which it exists at the time: s 95(2). A document which purports to be a certified copy is to be taken to be such a copy unless the contrary is shown: s 95(3).

59 The summary is a reference to the summary issued under s 77 – see 8.6.1 above – or, where one or more summaries have been subsequently issued under s 93 following updating of the licence, the most recent summary to have been so issued: s 94(11). As to the certified copy, see previous footnote.

60 Section 94(10) provides: 'A person guilty of an offence under this section is liable on summary conviction to a fine not exceeding level 2 on the standard scale.'

61 'Authorised person' has an identical meaning as in respect to premises licences in Pt 3 of the Act. The definition in s 69(2), for clubs, is the same as in s 13(2) for premises licences, on which see 6.14.2 above.

62 This reflects the fact that clubs' activities 'take place on premises to which the public do not generally have access and they operate under codes of discipline applying to members and their guests' (Guidance, para 9.13).

63 See Feldman, D, 'Interference in the Home and Anticipated Breach of the Peace' (1995) 111 *Law Quarterly Review* 562.

# CHAPTER 9

# TEMPORARY ACTIVITIES: TEMPORARY EVENT NOTICES

## 9.1  INTRODUCTION

9.1.1    Part 5 of the Act provides a system of permitted temporary activities, under which licensable activities can be carried out on a temporary basis (for a period not exceeding 96 hours) without the need for a premises licence or a club premises certificate (CPC). These activities can take place on any premises, which under s 193 means any place, vehicle, vessel or moveable structure (see 6.1.2–6.1.6 above), by the authority of a temporary event notice (TEN) given by an individual, a 'premises user', to the relevant licensing authority.[1] No permission is required from the licensing authority and, in general, only the police may intervene with a view to preventing such an event going ahead or to modify arrangements for it.[2] The TEN is subject to various restrictions (including ones on maximum numbers attending at any one time when licensable activities are taking place, that being less than 500) and limits attaching to the number of events, with different limits applying depending on whether or not the person carrying out the licensable activities holds a personal licence and the frequency of the use of the premises.[3] Where the requirements for obtaining a TEN cannot be met, as where events exceed 96 hours or the maximum numbers are 500 or more, then it will be necessary for a premises licence to be obtained, even if the event is only for a 'one-off' single occasion.

The circumstances in which a personal licence holder may need to obtain a TEN might include where he wishes to carry out one or more licensable activities at premises not covered by a premises licence relating to those activities. Examples provided by para 7.10 of the Guidance include holding an event involving live music, extending the hours when alcohol may be sold for an ad hoc occasion or providing late night refreshment after a quiz night. Individuals who do not hold a personal licence might wish to obtain a TEN to enable them to carry out one or more of the licensable activities at any premises, regardless of whether or not they are covered by a premises licence relating to those activities. This could include running a bar and providing a band at a party to celebrate a 50th wedding anniversary or any similar event (Explanatory Note 164). It could equally include various public events for fund raising, at which licensable activities take place, staged on behalf of charities, and community and voluntary groups,[4] as well as schools, churches and hospitals.

9.1.2    In order for the TEN to have effect, and for the activity to become a permitted temporary activity, there are various conditions that need to be complied with. These include: requirements in respect of the giving of the notice; its acknowledgement by the licensing authority and notification of the police; and the notice not having been withdrawn or being subject to the issuing of a counter-notice, either following a police objection or because the permitted limits have been exceeded. Section 98 provides:

(1)  A licensable activity is a permitted temporary activity by virtue of this Part if–

(a)  it is carried on in accordance with a notice given in accordance with section 100, and

(b)  the following conditions are satisfied.

(2) The first condition is that the requirements of sections 102 (acknowledgement of notice) and 104(1) (notification of police) are met in relation to the notice.

(3) The second condition is that the notice has not been withdrawn under this Part.

(4) The third condition is that no counter notice has been given under this Part in respect of the notice.

If one or more of these conditions is not met, then it would seem that the licensable activity will not be a permitted temporary activity. The rationale for the conditions seems to be that it would be wrong for the event to proceed where these conditions have not been complied with. If a counter-notice has been issued, there will be justifiable reasons why the event should not take place, either that the holding of the event will undermine the crime prevention objective or the requisite number of temporary events has already been held either by the premises user or in respect of the premises. If the TEN has been withdrawn, the premises user will thereby have indicated his intention not to go ahead with the event. If there has been a failure to notify the police under s 104(1), the police will have been denied any opportunity to decide whether to issue a counter-notice on the ground that allowing the event to go ahead will undermine the crime prevention objective. In all these instances it would be wrong for the event to take place, but it is less clear that this is the case where there has been a failure by the licensing authority to acknowledge receipt of the notice in accordance with s 102. If the licensing authority had not been notified of the event, it might be wrong for the event to take place as the authority would have been denied any opportunity to decide whether the requisite number of temporary events had already been held, but s 102 is not concerned with the authority being notified. It is concerned with the authority acknowledging receipt once it has received notice.

9.1.3    Nevertheless, it would seem that, if there is a failure by the authority to acknowledge the notice as required by s 102, the first (part of the first) condition in s 98(2) will not be met. This will mean that the licensable activity will not be a permitted temporary activity and the premises user will be unable to carry it on as such in accordance with the notice. The effect of this appears to be that an authority can prevent a temporary event from taking place as a permitted temporary activity simply by not acknowledging the notice. Obviously this would frustrate the legislative purpose of introducing TENs and it must be assumed that Parliament did not intend this to be the case. However, it is difficult to see how this can be avoided if the provision in s 98(2), that 'the requirements of sections 102 (acknowledgement of notice) . . . are met in relation to the notice', is given its ordinary meaning.

Courts do, of course, depart from the ordinary meaning of words when interpreting statutory provisions and can do so, as Lord Blackburn stated in *River Wear Commissioners v Adamson* (1877) App Cas 743, 764–65, when the ordinary meaning of words will produce 'an inconsistency, or an absurdity or inconvenience so great as to convince the Court that the intention could not have been to use them in their ordinary signification'.[5] His Lordship went on to say (at 765) that in such a case the court will be justified in 'putting on them some other significance, which, though less proper, is one which the Court thinks the words will bear'. The possible frustration of the legislative purpose may be seen as a 'great inconvenience' and it may perhaps be possible to put some significance on the words in s 98(2), other than their ordinary meaning. The requirements of s 102 might be considered to be met, not only where there has been an *actual acknowledgement* of the notice by the authority, but also where an authority is *in a position to acknowledge* receipt by returning to the premises user one notice of the two that it has received. Unless this or some other 'creative' interpretation is given to the provision in s 98(2), the provision has the potential to restrict considerably the scope of TENs under the 2003 Act.

## 9.2    REQUIREMENTS IN RESPECT OF THE GIVING OF THE NOTICE

### 9.2.1    Persons entitled to give notice

Only an individual aged 18 or over who proposes to use premises for one or more of the licensable activities during a period not exceeding 96 hours, designated by the Act as the 'premises user', is entitled to give a TEN. Section 100(1)–(3) provides:

(1)  Where it is proposed to use premises for one or more licensable activities during a period not exceeding 96 hours, an individual may give to the relevant licensing authority notice of that proposal (a "temporary event notice").

(2)  In this Act, the "premises user", in relation to a temporary event notice, is the individual who gave the notice.

(3)  An individual may not give a temporary event notice unless he is aged 18 or over.

In cases where businesses, clubs or organisations wish to use premises for a temporary event, it will be necessary for one individual to be identified as the proposed premises user.

### 9.2.2    Form and content of notice

9.2.3    The TEN must be in a form prescribed in regulations by the Secretary of State and contain various details about the proposed event. These details include: information about the licensable activities and the times at which they will take place; the total length of the event (which must not exceed 96 hours); the maximum numbers (which must be less than 500) that will be allowed on the premises at any one time when licensable activities are taking place; whether any alcohol supplied will be for consumption on or off the premises or both (in all such cases the notice must make it a condition that supplies are made by or under the authority of the premises user); and any other information or matters prescribed. Section 100(4)–(6) provides:

(4)  A temporary event notice must be in the prescribed form and contain–

    (a)  a statement of the matters mentioned in subsection (5),

    (b)  where subsection (6) applies, a statement of the condition mentioned in that subsection, and

    (c)  such other information as may be prescribed.

(5)  Those matters are–

    (a)  the licensable activities to which the proposal mentioned in subsection (1) relates ("the relevant licensable activities"),

    (b)  the period (not exceeding 96 hours) during which it is proposed to use the premises for those activities ("the event period"),

    (c)  the times during the event period when the premises user proposes that those licensable activities shall take place,

(d) the maximum number of persons (being a number less than 500) which the premises user proposes should, during those times, be allowed on the premises at the same time,

(e) where the relevant licensable activities include the supply of alcohol,[6] whether supplies are proposed to be for consumption on the premises or off the premises, or both, and

(f) such other matters as may be prescribed.

(6) Where the relevant licensable activities include the supply of alcohol, the notice must make it a condition of using the premises for such supplies that all such supplies are made by or under the authority of the premises user.

The Secretary of State has prescribed the form of a TEN, and additional information or matters it must contain, in the Licensing Act 2003 (Permitted Temporary Activities) (Notices) Regulations 2005, SI 2005/2918 (LA 2003 (PTA) (Notices) Regs 2005).[7] Regulation 3(1) and Sched 1 provide that the TEN and must state name and address of the relevant licensing authority and its reference number (optional), and must go on to provide: 'I, the proposed premises user, hereby give notice under section 100 of the Licensing Act 2003 of my proposal to carry on a temporary activity at the premises described below'.

Details to be specified in the TEN, contained in Sched 1, include:

- personal and contact details of the premises user;
- the following information concerning the premises:
  - the address or if there is no address a detailed description (including Ordinance Survey references). Since 'premises' means 'any place' (see s 193 and 6.1.3 above), there may be instances where there is no address, as in cases involving public parks, recreation grounds and private land;
  - the area of the premises where it is proposed to carry on licensable activities, if it is intended that only part of the premises is so used. This could include cases such as a single room within a village hall, a plot within a larger area of land, or a discrete area within a marquee (Guidance, para 7.14). As note 3 of Sched 1 to the LA 2003 (PTA) (Notices) Regs 2005 indicates, this is important as any licensable activities conducted outside the area of the premises protected by the authority of the TEN would be unlawful and could lead to prosecution;
  - the nature of the event at which the licensable activities are taking place (for example, a wedding with a pay bar, the supply of beer at a particular farmers' market, a discotheque, the performance of a string quartet, a folk group or a rock band) and the nature of the premises at which it is being provided (for example, a public house, a restaurant, an open field, a village hall or a beer tent), as this assists the police in deciding if any crime prevention issues arise (LA 2003 (PTA) (Notices) Regs 2005, Sched 1, notes 4–5).
- the licensable activities, their dates and times, the maximum numbers of persons intended to be allowed on the premises at any one time when licensable activities are taking place, and where alcohol is supplied whether this is for consumption on or off the premises or both;
- where the premises user is a personal licence holder, information concerning his personal licence;

- whether the event period for the TEN falls within any part of the preceding 24-hour period of any TEN given in respect of the same premises by the premises user or by any associate or business colleagues (see 9.2.9–9.2.10 below);
- numbers of TENs previously given in the same calendar year by the premises user and by any associate or business colleagues.

9.2.4    The 'event period' of not exceeding 96 hours was extended during the course of the legislation's passage from the original specified period of not exceeding 72 hours, the rationale for which seems to have been that it would include a whole bank holiday weekend, a popular time at which festivals and concerts might be held. The 96 hours' period will effectively enable an event to take place on four consecutive days, although s 100(5)(b) does not expressly require the period to be a continuous one. It does not specify a 'continuous' period not exceeding 96 hours, which leaves it open to the possible interpretation of a period of proposed premises use for licensable activities that, in total, does not exceed 96 hours. It is conceivable that an event may not involve a licensable activity on a Sunday, perhaps for religious reasons, but licensable activities may take place on the preceding Friday and Saturday and the following Monday and Tuesday. If the licensable activities can take place for a period not exceeding 96 hours in total, there will be compliance with s 100(5)(b), but, if the period of 96 hours needs to be a continuous one and is the maximum length of time within which licensable activities can take place, there will not. Explanatory Note 168, which may act as an aid to interpretation (see 9.6.4 below), is not conclusive, but suggests a continuous period, stating: 'the total length of the event . . . must not exceed 96 hours.' Similarly, the requirement in s 100(5)(c) for the notice to contain a statement of the times during the event period when the premises user proposes that those licensable activities shall take place is also not conclusive, for it might be used to support either interpretation. It seems more probable that the 96-hour period was intended to be a continuous one, representing the total length of the event, and it is submitted that this is how the section should be interpreted. This would be consistent with the position under the previous law in respect of occasional permissions. Under s 1 of the Licensing (Occasional Permissions) Act 1983, permission authorising the sale of alcohol could be granted 'during a period not exceeding twenty four hours' and this was interpreted by the Divisional Court, in *R v Bromley Licensing Justices ex p Bromley Licensed Victuallers' Association* [1984] 1 All ER 794, to mean a continuous period of 24 hours.

The figure in s 100(5)(d) of (less than) 500 for the maximum number of persons seems to have been a fairly arbitrary one. It appears to have been regarded as a 'reasonable figure', although different views on it were expressed in the consultation period. As a Government spokesman, Lord McIntosh, observed during the committee stage of the Bill in the House of Lords (HL Deb, vol 643, col 385, 17 January 2003):

> . . . we have set a limit of 500 people. In our consultation, some people wanted the limit to be higher; others wanted it to be lower . . . events of more than 500 people – particularly those with significantly more – are of a size close to events that cause disturbance . . . We must find a figure. Five hundred may not be exactly the right one, but the police and others have suggested that it is a reasonable figure.

The figure of less than 500 includes not only the audience, spectators or consumers but also those involved in the licensable activities and present on the premises such as staff, organisers, stewards and performers (LA 2003 (PTA) (Notices) Regs 2005, Sched 1, note 3).

The time period of 96 hours and the maximum permitted number of persons of less than 500 are ones that may be subject to subsequent change, for the Secretary of State has the power by order to alter the period and numbers.[8] Section 100(8) provides:

> The Secretary of State may, by order–
>
> (a) amend subsections (1) and (5)(b) so as to substitute any period for the period for the time being specified there;
>
> (b) amend subsection (5)(d) so as to substitute any number for the number for the time being specified there.

## 9.2.5    Period of notice

9.2.6    The TEN must be given to the authority at least 10 working days before the event. It must be submitted in duplicate – this is to enable the authority to acknowledge receipt of the notice by marking and returning one copy to the premises user – and accompanied by the prescribed fee, which under reg 8 and Sched 6 to the Licensing Act 2003 (Fees) Regulations 2005, SI 2005/79 is £21. Section 100(7) provides:

> The temporary event notice–
>
> (a) must be given to the relevant licensing authority (in duplicate) no later than ten working days before the day on which the event period begins, and
>
> (b) must be accompanied by the prescribed fee.

The period of 10 working days essentially consists of a two-week period, since a 'working day' means Monday to Friday (excluding bank holidays, Christmas Day and Good Friday).[9] For the purposes of calculating this period, para 7.18 of the Guidance provides that 10 working days' notice 'means ten working days exclusive of the day on which the event is to start, and exclusive of the day on which the notice is given'. That the day on which the event occurs is excluded when calculating the period is apparent from the wording of s 100(7)(a), which requires 'ten working days *before* the day on which the event period begins' (emphasis supplied). The section gives no indication of whether the day on which the notice is given is to be regarded as the first day of the 10 working-day period or whether the day after it is given counts as the first day. This will depend on how the expression 'no later than' is interpreted and the DCMS legal view on the matter, reflected in the statement in the Guidance and contained in advice given (on 14 July 2006) to licensing authorities from LACORS, is that the day after counts as the first day:

> In section 100(7)(a) of the 2003 Act, the expression "ten working days before the day on which the event period begins" should be interpreted in accordance with the legal principle that fractions of a day are normally to be disregarded unless the Act expressly says or implies they are to be taken account of.
>
> In addition, the courts have held that it follows from this principle that in the case of a specified time limit the running of which is triggered by an event or action, the whole of the day on which the event or action occurs is disregarded for the purpose of calculating the period. This has been held to be necessary to ensure that time periods specified in legislation do not end up being shorter than Parliament has specified. If a TEN could be given on Friday at 6pm and the Friday still counted as one of the ten

working days, the ten working day period prescribed by Parliament would be closer to nine, and the intention of the Act defeated. (See Bennion, *Statutory Interpretation*, 4th ed. pp 960–962; *Okolo v Secretary of State for the Environment* [1997] 4 All ER 242).

In *Okolo* the Court of Appeal was concerned with the meaning of 'within' a six-week period and, as Schiemann LJ stated at 246, 'the crucial question . . . essentially was when those six weeks ran out'. The case was therefore concerned not only with the meaning of a different expression ('within' rather than 'no later than') but also with when the period ended, not when it commenced, and is thus not directly in point. Further, there appears to be no authority on how the words 'no later than' should be interpreted so there remains an element of doubt as to the legal position. Nevertheless, as a general rule, in cases in which a period is fixed within which a person must act or take the consequences, the day of the act or event from which the period runs is not included.[10] If this general rule is followed, as seems likely, the day after the notice is given will count as the first working day.

Given that the legal position is not settled, licensing authorities are required under s 4(2)(b) of the 2003 Act to have regard to the Guidance and the Guidance provides in para 7.18 that 10 working days' notice is exclusive of the day on which the notice is given, so authorities will need a good reason to depart from this view. This may be the case if notice is given at the beginning of the day, so that almost the whole of that day is available for dealing with the notice. Here it might be said that there is compliance with the substance and spirit of the requirement in s 100(7)(a) of giving notice no later than 10 working days before the event. This may also accord with the Government's intention that TENs should operate with a minimum level of bureacracy, which is reflected in LACORS' advice that events should not be prohibited even if application requirements might not strictly have been met, provided the police are satisfied with the notice given and are not planning to issue a counter-notice:

> The Government's intention is that the TENs regime is utilised to give temporary permission to those operating a licensable activity with minimum bureaucracy. LACORS is of the view that if an authority considers that a Temporary Event Notice has not been properly given then in the first instance the authority should check with the Police they are in receipt of the application, are satisfied with the notice given and whether or not they are planning to issue a counter notice on the grounds of crime and disorder. If no counter notice is intended, and the Police are satisfied with the notice given authorities should not unnecessarily prohibit these events taking place on the grounds of the application not being properly made.

It may be therefore that strict adherence to the 10 working days' notice period, commencing on the day after the notice is given, is not required as a matter of practice in all cases.

A further matter affecting calculation of the 10 working days' notice period is the manner in which notice is 'given' to the authority. What constitutes the giving of notices is prescribed by s 184, which has effect in relation to any document required or authorised by or under the Act to be given to any person.[11] Where notice is given to the licensing authority, the document containing the notice must be given 'by addressing it to the authority and leaving it at or sending it by post' to the principal office of the authority or another office at which the authority is willing to accept documents (s 184(2); and see 2.5.2 above). If it is left at the relevant (principal or other) office of the authority on a particular day, the next working day will constitute the first day of the 10 working days' period: 'posting a copy of the notice addressed to the authority through the letterbox of its principal office before midnight on Friday would count as "giving" the notice to the authority, and Friday would be day zero, Monday day one, etc' (LACORS advice, 30 November 2006). If the notice was posted through the letter box after midnight on Friday, the position is less clear. One view is that the person posting it would not be regarded as 'giving' the notice until the Monday (as Saturday and Sunday are not a 'working day'), in which case the next working day, Tuesday, will constitute the first day of the 10 working days' period. This view is put forward in the LACORS advice: 'If the answer [to when the notice was left at the office] is after midnight on Friday then Monday is day zero'. However, whilst s 100(7)(a) requires 10 working days' notice to be given to the authority, the giving of notices under s 184 is not governed by working days. It is concerned only with when the notice is left at the authority's office and s 184 contains no requirement for this to be on a working day. It seems therefore that a notice left on a Saturday or Sunday is 'given' on that day, in which case Monday is not day zero but day one.

If a notice is sent by post to the authority's office, the normal rules on postal delivery set out in s 7 of the Interpretation Act 1978 will apply and the notice will be regarded as having been given at the time at the time of delivery of the letter in the ordinary course of post.[12] This will be the next day if posted first class, the day after that if posted second class, and, in cases of other methods of postal delivery, whatever day the carrier advertises as the expected or guaranteed day of delivery. The day of delivery under these rules will be day zero and the 10 working day period will begin on the next working day. These rules apply in the absence of any proof to the contrary, for example, of later delivery or non-receipt (proof of which might be by an affidavit from the person who checks the mail).

9.2.7     The 10 working-day period may not give rise to difficulties where a notice is unchallenged – the authority will simply have to acknowledge the notice in such a case within the period – but might do where the police decide to give an objection notice. The police, to whom a copy of the notice must also be given within the same 10 working days' period, have 48 hours within which to object (see 9.5.1 below). If the police do object, the authority must hold a hearing to consider the objection (and then decide whether it is necessary, for the promotion of the crime prevention objective, to give the premises user a counter-notice). This will not leave much time for a hearing to be convened for the matter to be considered by a subcommittee of the authority.[13] Under reg 5 and para 11 of Sched 1 to the Licensing Act 2003 (Hearings) Regulations 2005, SI 2005/44 (LA 2003 (Hearings) Regs 2005), the hearing must be commenced within seven working days beginning with the day after the end of the period within which the police may object, and under reg 26(1)(c) the authority must make its determination at the conclusion of the hearing. Nevertheless, unless the hearing is commenced in the early part of this period, the parties will not be able to exercise any right of appeal in respect of the subcommittee's decision, for Pt 3 of Sched 5, para 16(6), provides: 'no appeal may be brought later than five working days before the day on which the event period specified in the temporary event notice begins.'[14] In short, the timescale is a very compressed one.

The Explanatory Notes to s 100 acknowledge 10 working days to be the minimum specified period[15] and envisage a longer period being given in most cases ('it is antici-pated that in most circumstances greater notice will be given'). The assumption seems to be that, in the spirit of cooperation, a longer period than that required will be given. As the Guidance states in para 7.17:

> licensing authorities should publicise locally their preferences in terms of forward notice and encourage notice givers to provide the earliest possible notice of events likely to take place.

The Guidance goes on to provide in para 7.17:

> Licensing authorities should also consider publicising a preferred maximum time in advance of an event that applications should be made. For example, if an application is made too far in advance of an event, it may be difficult for the police to make a sensible assessment and could lead to objections that could be otherwise avoided.

However, whether a longer period is given is entirely down to the person giving notice. There will be compliance with the requirements of s 100 if 10 working days' notice is given and, whatever the encouragement or exhortations by the licensing authority, there is no power to extend the period.

Although on each occasion at least 10 working days notice must be given, where a person intends holding more than one TEN, there is nothing to prevent simultaneous notification of multiple events at a single time. This is provided that the final event is at least 10 working days away.[16]

### 9.2.8 Minimum period between events by a premises user at the same premises

9.2.9    An additional requirement with which a premises user needs to comply is that a minimum period of 24 hours has elapsed since the last notice was given in respect of the same premises by him or another person with whom he is closely associated. This requirement, in s 101, prevents a premises user from holding numerous consecutive events, not only where notice is given in his own name, but also where it is given in the name of the other person, as a means of avoiding an application for a premises licence (Explanatory Note 171). A TEN that does not comply with the minimum 24-hour period is void (Guidance, para 7.19). Section 101(1) provides:

> A temporary event notice ("notice A") given by an individual ("the relevant premises user") is void if the event period specified in it does not–
>
> (a) end at least 24 hours before the event period specified in any other temporary event notice given by the relevant premises user in respect of the same premises before or at the same time as notice A, or
>
> (b) begin at least 24 hours after the event period specified in any other such notice.

9.2.10    For the purposes of determining whether there is a contravention of s 101, a TEN is treated in certain circumstances as having been given by a premises user where it is given by another individual. This is where it has been given by an individual who is an 'associate' of the premises user, which includes spouses or civil partners, certain other close relatives or their spouses or civil partners, or an agent or employee or their spouse or civil partner, or by an individual who is 'in business' with the premises user. Whilst this goes some way towards preventing consecutive events being staged by an individual premises user, this limitation may not, in practice, prove to be particularly effective for it might easily be circumvented by

TENs given by friends of the individual. Further, a TEN is regarded as given in respect of the same premises if the premises in question includes or forms part of the premises in respect of which a TEN has already been given. Thus two TENs, each given in respect of different parts of premises, will be regarded as given in respect of the same premises. On the other hand, where a premises user gives a TEN and it is withdrawn or a counter-notice is given in respect of it, this is discounted when calculating the minimum period. Section 101(2)–(4) provides:

(2) For the purposes of subsection (1)–

   (a) any temporary event notice in respect of which a counter notice has been given under this Part or which has been withdrawn under section 103 is to be disregarded;

   (b) a temporary event notice given by an individual who is an associate of the relevant premises user is to be treated as a notice given by the relevant premises user;

   (c) a temporary event notice ("notice B") given by an individual who is in business with the relevant premises user is to be treated as a notice given by the relevant premises user if–

      (i) that business relates to one or more licensable activities, and

      (ii) notice A and notice B relate to one or more licensable activities to which the business relates (although not necessarily the same activity or activities);

   (d) two temporary event notices are in respect of the same premises if the whole or any part of the premises in respect of which one of the notices is given includes or forms part of the premises in respect of which the other notice is given.

(3) For the purposes of this section an individual is an associate of another person if he is–

   (a) the spouse or civil partner of that person,

   (b) a child, parent, grandchild, grandparent, brother or sister of that person,

   (c) an agent or employee of that person, or

   (d) the spouse or civil partner of a person within paragraph (b) or (c).

(4) For the purposes of subsection (3) a person living with another as that person's husband or wife is to be treated as that person's spouse.

The scope of an 'associate' is quite wide, covering not only an individual's spouse or civil partner and his close relatives, agents or employees, but also the spouse or civil partner of those persons and anyone with whom those persons are living in a husband-wife relationship. The section gives no indication of when an individual is 'in business' with a premises user, but the wording suggests that both would need to have some sort of proprietary interest in the business (for example, as partners). Simply being employees in the same business would not seem to suffice, although the position may perhaps be different if both were employed in some senior capacity and had some managerial control over the business. It is necessary that each notice relates to one or more licensable activities with which the business is concerned, although they need not necessarily be the same activities, in order for both notices to be treated as given by the premises user. Thus, if the premises user were 'in business' with an individual and the business was a restaurant providing late night refreshment, live music and the sale of alcohol, a TEN given by the premises user for the sale of alcohol at premises will be void if it follows on from a TEN, for either the playing of live music or the provision of late night refreshment, given in respect of the same premises by the individual; but if the TEN given by the individual relates to dancing at the premises, the TEN given by the premises user will not be void. This is because under s 101(2)(c)(ii) both TENs do not relate to one or more licensable activities to which the business relates. Only the TEN given by the premises user for the sale of alcohol does.

## 9.3    ACKNOWLEDGMENT BY THE LICENSING AUTHORITY

9.3.1    The licensing authority must acknowledge the TEN by returning to the premises user one of the duplicate notices received. This must be done within a specified period, which, if the notice was received on a working day, is the end of the following working day and, if received on a non-working day, is the end of the second working day after the day on which it was received. Acknowledgment is not, however, necessary if the authority has already given a counter-notice to the premises user, indicating that the prescribed number of events would be exceeded if the event in respect of which notice has been given were to take place (see 9.7 below). Section 102 provides:

(1)   Where a licensing authority receives a temporary event notice (in duplicate) in accordance with this Part, it must acknowledge receipt of the notice by sending or delivering one notice to the premises user–

   (a)  before the end of the first working day following the day on which it was received, or

   (b)  if the day on which it was received was not a working day, before the end of the second working day following that day.

(2)   The authority must mark on the notice to be returned under subsection (1) an acknowledgement of the receipt in the prescribed form.

(3)   Subsection (1) does not apply where, before the time by which the notice must be returned in accordance with that subsection, a counter notice has been sent or delivered to the premises user under section 107 in relation to the temporary event notice.

Acknowledgment must be in prescribed form, which is the inclusion in section 10 (entitled 'Acknowledgement') of the TEN form, or of a copy of it, of the signature of a person authorised to acknowledge receipt on the authority's behalf (LA 2003 (PTA) (Notices) Regs 2005, reg 4). Acknowledgement can be by electronic copy, since reg 2(d) provides: ' "copy" includes an electronic copy'.

9.3.2    Section 102 requires, if not a more or less instantaneous acknowledgment, then at least a quick response. A notice needs to be sent out by the end of the following working day.[17] It is not clear, however, what the effect of failure to comply with these requirements will be, either as far as the licensing authority or the premises user is concerned. The section provides no sanction against the licensing authority for a failure to comply, although the failure might perhaps prevent the premises user from staging the event as a permitted temporary activity as one of the necessary conditions is that the requirements of this section are met (see s 98(2) and 9.1.2 above). Nor can a failure to comply preclude the giving of a counter-notice by the police, since this follows from the police being given a copy of the TEN and is independent of acknowledgement by the licensing authority. It is difficult therefore to see what effect a failure to comply can have.

Once the authority has acknowledged the TEN by returning to the premises user one of the duplicate notices received, the premises user then has authorisation to stage the temporary event. When the temporary event takes place, however, it must be in accordance with the restrictions imposed by the authorisation and, if these are not adhered to, the event will be unauthorised. Paragraph 7.23 of the Guidance states:

> In the case of an event proceeding under the authority of a temporary event notice, failure to adhere to the requirements of the 2003 Act, such as the limitation of no more than 499 being present at any one time, would mean that the event was unauthorised. In such circumstances, the premises user would be liable to prosecution.

## 9.4 WITHDRAWAL OF THE NOTICE

A premises user can withdraw a TEN at any time up to 24 hours before the event is due to take place by giving a notice to this effect to the licensing authority. Once withdrawn, the notice does not count towards the limit on the number of TENs (see 9.7.1 below) that may be submitted by an individual during a calendar year (Explanatory Note 173). Section 103 provides:

(1) A temporary event notice may be withdrawn by the premises user giving the relevant licensing authority a notice to that effect no later than 24 hours before the beginning of the event period specified in the temporary event notice.

(2) Nothing in section 102 or sections 104 to 107 applies in relation to a notice withdrawn in accordance with this section.

## 9.5 POLICE OBJECTIONS

### 9.5.1 Giving an objection notice

A copy of the TEN must be given to the police at least 10 working days before the beginning of the event period and, if the police are of the view that allowing the event to proceed would undermine the crime prevention objective, they must give an objection notice to the premises user and the licensing authority, giving reasons for their decision. Section 104(1) and (2) provides:

(1) The premises user must give a copy of any temporary event notice to the relevant chief officer of police no later than ten working days before the day on which the event period specified in the notice begins.

(2) Where a chief officer of police who receives a copy notice under subsection (1) is satisfied that allowing the premises to be used in accordance with the notice would undermine the crime prevention objective, he must give a notice stating the reasons why he is so satisfied (an "objection notice")–

    (a) to the relevant licensing authority, and

    (b) to the premises user.

Again, the provisions of s 184 will have application in respect of the giving of notice and, in cases of notice given to a person other than a licensing authority, s 184(3) provides that this can be 'by delivering it to him, or by leaving it at his proper address, or by sending it by post to him at that address' (see 2.5.4 above). The police must give the objection notice no later than 48 hours after receipt of the copy of the notice. There is, however, no requirement to give an objection notice if the police have received a copy of a counter-notice from the licensing authority to the effect that the permitted limits attaching to the number of events have been exceeded. An objection notice, which may lead to the licensing authority giving a counter-notice, would be rather pointless in such a case once a counter-notice had already been given. Section 104(3) and (4) provides:

> (3)  The objection notice must be given no later than 48 hours after the chief officer of police is given a copy of the temporary event notice under subsection (1).
>
> (4)  Subsection (2) does not apply at any time after the relevant chief officer of police has received a copy of a counter notice under section 105 in respect of the temporary event notice.

The period of 48 hours does not give the police long to decide whether or not to make an objection and speedy contact will need to be made with the premises user if any concerns are to be discussed informally. The objection notice has to be given no later than 48 hours after the police are 'given' a copy of the TEN and, as indicated above, this can be done under s 184(3) by posting the copy of the TEN to the police. The period of time surely cannot begin to run from when the copy is put in the post. If it does, it is conceivable (and perhaps likely if second-class post is used) that the 48-hour period will have elapsed before the police actually receive the copy of the TEN. This can be avoided if 'given' (a copy of the TEN) is interpreted in this provision to mean 'received' and the notice provisions in s 184 are regarded as not having application.[18] In the event that the police do not (or are not able to) intervene, they will, however, still be able to rely on their powers of closure (see 11.12–11.14 below) should disorder or noise nuisance disturbance subsequently arise (Guidance, para 7.26).

## 9.5.2  Scope for use

9.5.3    The most important purpose of an objection notice, according to para 7.25 of the Guidance, 'is to give the police the opportunity to consider whether they should object to the event taking place for reasons of preventing crime and disorder'. As to the cases where an objection notice might be given, para 7.26 seems to envisage it being the larger events:

> Such cases might arise because of concerns about the scale, location or timing of the event. However, in most cases, where alcohol is supplied away from licensed premises at a temporary bar under the control of a personal licence holder, (e.g. at weddings or small social, community, charitable or sporting events) this should not give rise to the use of these police powers.

9.5.4    There is likely to be only a single objection notice where these powers are exercised because the premises will be located in only one police area, but there may be two or more objection notices where premises straddle an area or areas. As previously mentioned (see 9.1.1 above), in such a case a TEN needs to be given to each authority and the police in each area are entitled to give an objection notice. Section 104(5) provides:

> In this section "relevant chief officer of police" means–
>
> (a)  where the premises are situated in one police area, the chief officer of police for that area, and

(b)  where the premises are situated in two or more police areas, the chief officer of police for each of those areas.

Objections are confined to those put forward by the police and the only relevant ground is the crime prevention objective. No provision is made for objections by other interested parties, such as residents living in the area (who may be unaware of the events due to the absence of any requirement for advertisement) or 'responsible authorities' such as the fire and rescue authority or the environmental health department of the local authority. Nor is the environmental impact on the area or any safety concern a relevant ground for objection. In some cases where TENs are given, the TENs will be by premises licence holders who wish to use their premises temporarily for events involving licensable activities that may not be covered by their licence, such as the sale of alcohol. The premises will at least be known to the licensing authority and it may be assumed that they will have met certain minimum safety requirements before the licence was granted; but where events are staged by those not holding a premises licence, the premises, and the extent to which they might meet safety requirements, may be unknown to the authority.

An attempt to widen the grounds of objection to include all the licensing objectives (not just the crime prevention objective) and to extend it to interested parties and responsible authorities was resisted by the Government at the committee stage in the House of Lords. Lord McIntosh, a Government spokesman, stated (HL Deb, vol 643, col 390, 17 January 2003):

> Is that what we want for school fêtes, weddings, church fundraisers and discos in the village hall? Why should people be asked to jump through these additional hoops? There is no need to expand the number of bodies needed to scrutinise temporary event notices. There is no reason to widen the grounds. As long as the police are satisfied with the proposals and they meet the appropriate conditions on permitted limits, there should be no additional bureaucracy.[19]

The amendment was resisted on the ground that the crime prevention objective was quite wide[20] and that, in any event, the police have the power to close down for up to 24 hours premises for which a TEN has been given 'where they are a source of noise, nuisance and disorder likely to threaten public safety'.[21]

## 9.6   COUNTER-NOTICE OR MODIFICATION OF NOTICE FOLLOWING POLICE OBJECTION

9.6.1   If the police object, the licensing authority must hold a hearing to determine whether or not it accepts the police objections. Regulation 5 and para 11 of Sched 1 to the LA 2003 (Hearings) Regs 2005 provide that the hearing must be held within seven working days beginning with the day after the end of the period within which the police may give notice under s 104(2). The end of the period within which the police may give notice is, under s 104(3), 48 hours after the premises user has given them a copy of the TEN (see 9.5.1 above). Under reg 6(2)(b), and para 11 of Sched 2, notice of the hearing must be given to the premises user and the police no later than two working days before the day or the first day on which the hearing is to be held. If the objections are accepted, the authority must issue a counter-notice; but at any point between the police receiving a copy of the TEN from the premises user and the licensing authority hearing, the police and premises user may agree to modify the TEN in order that it meets the crime prevention objective. When TENs are modified, the notice of objection by the police is withdrawn and the modified notice then has effect.[22] Counter-notices and modifications are dealt with by ss 105 and 106, respectively and each is considered below.

## 9.6.2 Counter-notice

9.6.3    Unless the authority, the police and the premises user agree that it is unnecessary, the authority must hold a hearing and give the premises user a counter-notice if it considers it necessary for the promotion of the crime prevention objective. Section 105(1) and (2) provides:

> (1) This section applies where an objection notice is given in respect of a temporary event notice.
> (2) The relevant licensing authority must–
>     (a) hold a hearing to consider the objection notice, unless the premises user, the chief officer of police who gave the objection notice and the authority agree that a hearing is unnecessary,[23] and
>     (b) having regard to the objection notice, give the premises user a counter notice under this section if it considers it necessary for the promotion of the crime prevention objective to do so.

Paragraph 7.27 of the Guidance makes it clear that the authority is confined in the hearing to consideration of the crime prevention objective and it cannot uphold an objection notice on other grounds, such as public nuisance. Further, para 7.22 provides that authorities may not attach any terms, limitations or restrictions on the carrying on of licensable activities at temporary events. This suggests an 'all or nothing' approach is needed on the part of the authority.

If the authority decides to give the premises user a counter-notice, this must be accompanied by a notice stating the reasons for its decision, with copies of both notices being given to the police. If a counter-notice is not given, the premises user and the police must be given notice of the decision.[24] There is, however, no requirement imposed on the authority to give reasons to the police as to why their objection has not given rise to a counter-notice. Nevertheless, the authority will be under a duty to give reasons under Art 6(1) of the European Convention on Human Rights since the right to a fair hearing under this Article extends to the giving of reasons (see 3.5.9 above). Section 105(3) provides:

> The relevant licensing authority must–
>     (a) in a case where it decides not to give a counter notice under this section, give the premises user and the relevant chief officer of police notice of the decision, and
>     (b) in any other case–
>         (i) give the premises user the counter notice and a notice stating the reasons for its decision, and
>         (ii) give the relevant chief officer of police a copy of both of those notices.

9.6.4    Section 105 contains no provision as to the form that a counter-notice under the section should take, unlike s 107 (counter-notices where permitted limits are exceeded), sub-s (7) of which provides: 'A counter notice under this section must be in the prescribed form and given to the premises user in the prescribed manner'.[25] Nor does s 105 specify at any point what the effect is of giving a counter-notice, although Explanatory Note 175 provides a clear statement of the intended effect:

> If the authority accepts the police objection it must issue a counter notice to the premises user in which case the event cannot proceed.[26]

Explanatory Notes are to facilitate understanding of the legislation, but do not form part of the Act and have not been endorsed by Parliament, as the Introduction section to all Explanatory Notes makes clear. Recourse might be had to the Explanatory Notes when interpreting an Act's provisions,[27] although it is not necessary to do so here as the absence of any reference in s 105 to the effect of the counter-notice might be explained by the provision in s 98(4). This provides that one of the conditions for a temporary permitted activity to take place is that no counter-notice has been given in respect of the notice. The effect of the counter-notice is therefore to negate one of the conditions necessary for a temporary permitted activity to take place, which will mean that the event cannot proceed.

9.6.5      The authority must have made a decision on whether to give a counter-notice, and give the notices as required by s 105(3), at least 24 hours before the specified event period. Section 105(4) provides:

> A decision must be made under subsection (2)(b), and the requirements of subsection (3) must be met, at least 24 hours before the beginning of the event period specified in the temporary event notice.

As with the effect of giving a counter-notice, s 105 does not specify the effect of failing to comply with this requirement, although again a clear statement of the intended effect is provided by Explanatory Note 175. This states: 'Any decision or counter notice must be issued to the premises user at least 24 hours before the specified event period. A failure to do so will result in the premises user being able to proceed with the event.' Less clear is whether a failure to give to the police a copy of the counter-notice and/or notice stating the reasons for the authority's decision will have the same result. Arguably it should not do so, for if the premises user has been given a counter-notice, he will know that the licensing authority and the police oppose the holding the event and that he should not proceed with it. If he has not himself been given the notice, it is reasonable to assume that his TEN is effective and he is entitled to proceed with staging the event.

     That a counter-notice may be given up to 24 hours before an event is due to begin does not leave much time for a premises user to cancel arrangements that may have been made or to notify those who had planned to perform at, or attend, the event. As in the case of the period for the police to give an objection notice (48 hours), it seems that the period here of 24 hours runs from receipt of the notice (see 9.5.1 above). Since the giving of notice can be complied with under s 184(3) by posting the copy of the counter-notice to the premises user (see 2.5.4 above), the period of time cannot sensibly be regarded as commencing until receipt of the counter-notice.

9.6.6      In cases where premises straddle two or more licensing authority areas, each (or all) of the authorities will need to act jointly, for s 105(5) provides:

> Where the premises are situated in the area of more than one licensing authority, the functions conferred on the relevant licensing authority by this section must be exercised by those authorities jointly.

This means that a joint hearing will need to be held to consider any police objections and decide whether a counter-notice should be issued. This may be complicated by the fact that, if the premises are situated in two (or more) police areas, the police in each area can give an objection notice, which may result in a notice being given by the police in one (or more) area(s), but not in the other(s). If there are competing views by the police as to whether allowing the premises to be used for the event would undermine the crime prevention objective, this may make it more difficult for the authorities to decide whether to give a counter-notice. Whether or not the authorities do decide to give one, there will have to be joint notification given to the premises user and the police in accordance with s 105(3) and compliance with the 24-hour period in s 105(4) (see 9.6.3 and 9.6.4 above). It is not clear whether 'functions . . . exercised . . . jointly' for the purposes of s 105(5) will require each authority to give notification independently or whether notification given by one authority acting on behalf of the other(s) will suffice. It is perhaps as well that this situation is unlikely to arise very often in practice.

### 9.6.7  Modification of TEN

9.6.8    Where the police have given an objection notice, they can, in agreement with the premises user, make alterations to the TEN so that it meets the crime prevention objective and return it to him.[28] This can be done at any stage before a hearing is held to consider the objection notice.[29] Section 106(1) and (2) provides:

(1)  This section applies where a chief officer of police has given an objection notice[30] in respect of a temporary event notice (and the objection notice has not been withdrawn).

(2)  At any time before a hearing is held or dispensed with under section 105(2), the chief officer of police may, with the agreement of the premises user, modify the temporary event notice by making changes to the notice returned to the premises user under section 102.

This is sound in principle, but the method adopted for making the alterations is not. The method ought to be for the police to make alterations to the copy of the TEN that they have received under s 104(1), for this then to be returned to the premises user, and for a copy of the modified TEN to be given to the licensing authority. Instead, s 106(2) requires the police to modify the TEN 'by making changes to the notice returned to the premises user under section 102'. This will be difficult to do for two reasons. First, the notice under s 102 is an acknowledgment of notice sent out *by the authority* on its receipt of the TEN. It will be one of the duplicate TENs sent to the authority, which it is returning to the premises user, duly marked, as an acknowledgement of receipt of his TEN. It is true that the police will have exactly the same document, since a copy will have been sent to them under s 104(1), but the police do not return the TEN under s 102. They are not therefore in any position to make changes to it, except perhaps by communicating the modifications to the licensing authority so that it can make the necessary changes.

A second difficulty is that, in all probability, the TEN will have been returned by the authority to the premises user under s 102 ahead of any modifications that the police might want to make following the objection notice. If the TEN was received on a working day, the authority must under s 102(1) return it by the end of the following working day and, if received on a non-working day, by the end of the second working day after that day (see 9.3 above). By the time of its return, the police may not even have given an objection notice – they have, under s 104(3), until 48 hours after the premises user has given them a copy of the TEN (see 9.5.1 above) – let alone have considered whether the TEN should be modified in agreement with the premises user. It is possible that, if the police give an objection notice more or less immediately, following which there is contact with the premises user and agreement to modify, the authority may not at this point have returned the TEN under s 102; but it is much more likely that the TEN will have been returned before the police decide to make any modifications since, once an objection notice has been given by the police, modifications can be made at any time thereafter up until the time of the hearing.

9.6.9    The solution to these difficulties would seem to be for the police to modify their copy of the TEN and to give a copy of the modified TEN to both the premises user and the licensing authority. Whilst this does not accord with s 106(2) as far as the premises user is concerned (because modifications are not made to the TEN returned to the premises user),[31] that section simply provides that the police 'may' modify the notice that is returned to the premises user under s 102. It does not require the police to make changes to that notice and it should therefore be open to them to adopt the alternative method of modification indicated. It is submitted that this is how the section should be interpreted.

The effect of modifying the TEN is that the notice of objection by the police is withdrawn and the modified TEN has effect. Section 106(3) provides:

> Where a temporary event notice is modified under subsection (2)–
> (a) the objection notice is to be treated for the purposes of this Act as having been withdrawn from the time the temporary event notice is modified, and
> (b) from that time–
>> (i) this Act has effect as if the temporary event notice given under section 100 had been the notice as modified under that subsection, and
>> (ii) to the extent that the conditions of section 98 are satisfied in relation to the unmodified notice they are to be treated as satisfied in relation to the notice as modified under that subsection.

In cases where premises straddle two or more police areas, the TEN can be modified only where the police in each area agree to the modification. Section 106(5) provides:

> Where the premises are situated in more than one police area, the chief officer of police may modify the temporary event notice under this section only with the consent of the chief officer of police for the other police area or each of the other police areas in which the premises are situated.

Presumably the police that modify the TEN will have the responsibility for complying with the requirement in s 106(4) that a copy of the modified TEN is given to the licensing authority.

## 9.7    COUNTER-NOTICE WHERE PERMITTED LIMITS HAVE BEEN EXCEEDED

### 9.7.1    The permitted limits

Section 107, by prescribing limits that apply in respect of the number of TENs that can be held in any one calendar year, contains safeguards to protect the system of temporary permitted activities from being abused. It requires the licensing authority to issue a counter-notice on receipt of a TEN when these limits are exceeded. Different limits apply depending on whether the person giving a TEN holds a personal licence, and there are also limits in respect of the number of temporary events that can be held on the same premises. An individual who does hold a personal licence can give 50 TENs a year, whereas an individual who does not can give only five. Further, no more than 12 TENs can be given for any one premises within the year and these cannot cover a period of more than 15 days. Section 107(1)–(5) provides:

(1)  Where a licensing authority–

    (a)  receives a temporary event notice ("notice A") in respect of any premises ("the relevant premises"), and

    (b)  is satisfied that subsection (2), (3), (4) or (5) applies, the authority must give the premises user ("the relevant premises user") a counter notice under this section.

(2)  This subsection applies if the relevant premises user–

    (a)  holds a personal licence, and

    (b)  has already given at least 50 temporary event notices in respect of event periods wholly or partly within the same year as the event period specified in notice A.

(3)  This subsection applies if the relevant premises user–

    (a)  does not hold a personal licence, and

    (b)  has already given at least five temporary event notices in respect of such event periods.

(4)  This subsection applies if at least 12 temporary event notices have already been given which–

    (a)  are in respect of the same premises as notice A, and

    (b)  specify as the event period a period wholly or partly within the same year as the event period specified in notice A.

(5)  This subsection applies if, in any year in which the event period specified in notice A (or any part of it) falls, more than 15 days are days on which one or more of the following fall–

    (a)  that event period or any part of it,

    (b)  an event period specified in a temporary event notice already given in respect of the same premises as notice A or any part of such a period.

TENs, it seems, might be given by individuals without the knowledge or authority of the person to whom the premises belong, for there is no requirement for a premiser user who wishes to hold a temporary event on another's premises to notify that other that a TEN is being given in respect of the premises. This might be regarded as a signficant weakness, since any TENs given will count towards the permitted annual limit on numbers of 12 and the limit might thus be exhausted or reduced without the knowledge of the premises owner. With regard to the 15-day period over which the 12 events might take place, a day counts as one of the 15 days, under s 107(5)(a), if it is a day on which the 'event period or any part of it' falls. Since s 107(13)(a) provides that ' "day" means a period of 24 hours beginning at midnight', this means that where a 'one day' event takes place and continues after midnight the event will be regarded as taking place on two days. As para 7.7 of the Guidance states:

> In determining whether the maximum total duration of the periods covered by temporary event notices at any individual premises has exceeded 15 days, licensing authorities should be aware that any event beginning before midnight and continuing into the next day would count as two days towards the 15 day limitation.

When it comes to calculating the permitted limits and TENs are given to the same licensing authority, the authority will know how many it has received and will be aware of whether or not the permitted limits have been reached, since each authority must keep a register which will contain a record of each TEN received by it (s 8(1)(b); and see 2.4 above).[32] No difficulties will therefore arise in respect of the permitted limits in s 107(4) and (5) for premises since the TENs will all be given to the same authority, at least where the premises correspond exactly in respect of each TEN given. It will be more problematic, however, to ascertain whether the permitted limits have been reached where this is not the case. Under s 100(1), the premises user may give the licensing authority a TEN where 'it is proposed to use premises for one or more licensable activities' and by s 193 ' "premises" means any place'. When giving a TEN a premises user can specify what constitutes the 'premises' where the licensable activity is to take place. In respect of buildings, this might be the complete building if all of it is being used, but, if only a certain room is being used, it might be only that room.[33] Thus, premises users may give TENs in respect of parts only of buildings. This is clearly envisaged by s 101, which specifies a minimum period of 24 hours between event periods specified by a premises user, for s 101(2)(d) provides:

> two temporary event notices are in respect of the same premises if the whole or any part of the premises in respect of which one of the notices is given includes or forms part of the premises in respect of which the other notice is given,

Further, s 107(13)(a) provides, for the purposes of calculating whether permitted limits have been exceeded so as to require the issuing of a counter-notice:

> a temporary event notice is in respect of the same premises as notice A if it is in respect of the whole or any part of the relevant premises or premises which include the whole or any part of those premises.[34]

That TENs might be issued in respect of parts only of buildings is recognised in para 7.14 of the Guidance, which states:

> A temporary event notice may be given for part of a building such as a single room within a village hall, a plot within a larger area of land, or a discrete area within a marquee as long as it includes a clear description of the area where the licensable activities will take place and the premises user intends to restrict the number of people present in the notified area at any one time to less than 500.

Where this is the case, it will need to be ascertained whether the permitted limit of 12 applies in respect of each room or part of the premises or whether it applies to the premises as a whole. If the expression 'same premises' in s 107(4) is interpreted to mean 'same part of the premises', then, taking the premises as a whole, many TENs may be given in respect of them. Premises with several rooms may, in part, be in more or less constant use for licensable activities under the authority of TENs. If, however, the expression 'same premises' in s 107(4) is interpreted to mean 'part of the same premises', then there will be maximum of 12 TENs for the premises as a whole. Certainly the former interpretation is a much more expansive one than the latter and might facilitate a much greater use of TENs, although whether this would be in accordance with Parliament's intention is less clear.

Difficulties may also arise in respect of the permitted limits in s 105(2) and (3) for individuals. Individuals may give TENs to a number of different authorities, which may make it difficult to ascertain when the permitted limits have been reached. A central register[35] or a central database to which licensing authorities have access might solve the problem, but, in the absence of either, the only course would seem to be to require a person giving a TEN to disclose how many previous TENs he has given. The authorities, however, will obviously be dependent on the honesty of the notice giver when he discloses how many previous TENs he has given.

## 9.7.2 Calculating the permitted limits

9.7.3 The relevant number of events is calculated by reference to a calendar year – s 107(13)(b) provides that, for the purposes of the section, ' "year" means calendar year' – and provision is made in respect of events which straddle two years. Provided an event falls partly within one year, it will count towards the relevant number of events for that year. This is clear from the references to 'wholly or partly' in para (b) of the provisions in s 107(2) and (4) (see 9.7.1 above).[36] Further, it will also count towards the relevant number of events for the following year, for s 107(6) provides:

> If the event period in notice A straddles two years, subsections (2), (3) and (4) apply separately in relation to each of those years.

However, for calculation purposes, any TEN in respect of which the authority has given a counter-notice, either following an objection notice from the police or because the permitted limits are exceeded, is not included. Section 107(9) provides:

> In determining whether subsection (2), (3), (4) or (5) applies, any temporary event notice in respect of which a counter notice has been given under this section or section 105 is to be disregarded.

Where a counter-notice has been given under s 105 following an objection notice from the police, the temporary event will be unable to proceed, and it is right therefore that this should not be included for calculation purposes in the number of events that can take place over the course of the year. An individual may, for example, have given only one TEN and held one temporary event at the beginning of the year when he receives a counter-notice to his second TEN preventing him from holding the proposed event. The second TEN will not count and the individual will be able to give another 49 or four TENs over the remaining part of the year, depending on whether he is or is not a personal licence holder (see 9.7.1 above).

9.7.4 Disregarding, for calculation purposes, a counter-notice given because the permitted limits are exceeded is likely to have application where the permitted limits relate to premises rather than individuals. If an individual has reached his permitted limit and a counter-notice has been given, then any TENs given by him thereafter will obviously result in another counter-notice. There will be no subsequent temporary events that he can hold for which the counter-notice can be disregarded for calculation purposes, as he has already reached his limit. The only exception would seem to be where a counter-notice is given in respect of an event that straddles two years. In this case, for the purposes of calculating the number of events for the second year, the event in question would be disregarded and the individual could give his 50 or five TENs for that year. In the case of premises, however, once the permitted limit of 12 TENS has been reached, a counter-notice must be issued if any further TEN is given in respect of those premises. The individual giving the further TEN may well be below his personal limit and still have a number of TENs left that he can give before the end of the year.[37] When calculating the number left in such a case, the event in respect of which the counter-notice was given will not be taken into account.

A further factor to be taken into account when calculating an individual's permitted limits is whether any TENs have been given by someone who is (closely) associated with or in business with that individual. It will be recalled that, under s 101, the minimum 24-hour period between temporary events held on the same premises applies not only to events held by the premises user, but also to events held by another person who is associated with or in business with that user (see 9.2.8–9.2.10 above). Events given by that other person are treated as events given by the premises user for the purposes of s 101 and the position is similar when calculating the number of permitted events under s 107. Section 107(10) provides:

> In determining for the purposes of subsection (2) or (3) the number of temporary event notices given by the relevant premises user–
> (a) a temporary event notice given by an individual who is an associate of the relevant premises user is to be treated as a notice given by the relevant premises user;
> (b) a temporary event notice ("notice B") given by an individual who is in business with the relevant premises user is to be treated as a notice given by the relevant premises user if–
>    (i) that business relates to one or more licensable activities, and
>    (ii) notice A and notice B relate to one or more licensable activities to which the business relates (but not necessarily the same activity or activities).

For these purposes, 'an associate' has the same meaning as in s 101, that is, a spouse or civil partner, certain other close relatives or their spouses or civil partners, and an agent or employee or their spouse or civil partner.[38]

### 9.7.5 Giving the counter-notice

The counter-notice must be in prescribed form and given to the premises user in the prescribed manner and, as in the case of counter-notices following police objections, must be given at least 24 hours before the event period specified in the TEN. Section 107(7) and (8) provides:

> (7) A counter notice under this section must be in the prescribed form and given to the premises user in the prescribed manner.
> (8) No such counter notice may be given later than 24 hours before the beginning of the event period specified in notice A.

The question of counter-notices being given 24 hours before the specified event period has been considered in relation to counter-notices given under s 105 (see

9.6.2–9.6.6 above) and the position will be the same for counter-notices under s 107 where the permitted limits are exceeded.

The prescribed form for the counter-notice is specified in reg 5 and Sched 2 to the LA 2003 (PTA) (Notices) Regs 2005. The counter-notice must specify the name and address of the licensing authority and its reference number (optional), followed by a prescribed form of words[39] indicating that the authority has received the TEN and is satisfied that, if the event was to go ahead, one of the permitted limits would be exceeded. The counter-notice thereafter sets out in tabular form the different ways in which the permitted limits in s 107(2)–(5) might be exceeded and indicates by an 'X' in the appropriate column in the table which of the limits is contravened. Finally, the person authorised to issue the counter-notice on behalf of the licensing authority is required to append his signature to the notice.

The manner in which the counter-notice can be given is prescribed by reg 6, which provides four alternative methods. First, the counter-notice can be delivered to the relevant premises user in person.[40] Secondly, it can be left at the 'appropriate address', which is either the postal address indicated by the premises user in section 1(8) of the TEN form as the address for correspondence or, if there is no such address, his current postal address indicated in section 1(6). Thirdly, it can be sent to the 'appropriate address' by 'ordinary post', which means ordinary prepaid first-class or second-class post, with or without special arrangements for delivery (reg 2(f)). Fourthly, it can be sent by email to an 'appropriate e-mail address', which means either an email address indicated in section 1(9) of the TEN form as the email address for correspondence or, if no such address has been entered in section 1(8) nor any postal address for correspondence included in section 1(9), an email address entered in contact details in section 1(7) (reg 2(c)).

## 9.8   KEEPING AND PRODUCTION OF NOTICE

9.8.1   The premises user is under a duty to keep at the premises the TEN whenever the premises are being used for licensable activities. The TEN must be kept in the custody or control of himself or a person working at the premises who he has nominated,[41] and a copy of the TEN, together with a notice indicating the position held at the premises by the nominated person, must be prominently displayed at the premises. Section 109(1)–(3) provides:

(1) This section applies whenever premises are being used for one or more licensable activities which are or are purported to be permitted temporary activities by virtue of this Part.

(2) The premises user must either–

    (a) secure that a copy of the temporary event notice is prominently displayed at the premises, or

    (b) meet the requirements of subsection (3).

(3) The requirements of this subsection are that the premises user must–

    (a) secure that the temporary event notice is kept at the premises in–

        (i) his custody, or

        (ii) in the custody of a person who is present and working at the premises and whom he has nominated for the purposes of this section, and

> (b) where the temporary event notice is in the custody of a person so nominated, secure that a notice specifying that fact and the position held at the premises by that person is prominently displayed at the premises.

It might be expected, and clearly would be desirable, for the copy of the TEN and notice to be prominently displayed at the same place in the premises, although neither s 109(2) nor (3) imposes any requirement to this effect. It will presumably therefore meet the terms of the section if the TEN and notice were to be (prominently) displayed in different parts of the premises. Failure to comply, without reasonable excuse, with the requirement to prominently display or to keep the TEN at the premises is a summary offence punishable by a fine not exceeding level 2 on the standard scale (s 109(4)(9)).

9.8.2    A constable or authorised officer may require the person having custody or control of the TEN to produce it for inspection, the authorised person being required to produce evidence of his authorisation if requested to do so, and a failure to produce it, without reasonable excuse, is a summary offence punishable by a fine not exceeding level 2 on the standard scale. Section 109(5)–(9) provides:

> (5)  Where–
>> (a)  the temporary event notice is not displayed as mentioned in subsection (2)(a), and
>> (b)  no notice is displayed as mentioned in subsection (3)(b),
>
>> a constable or authorised officer may require the premises user to produce the temporary event notice for examination.
>
> (6)  Where a notice is displayed as mentioned in subsection (3)(b), a constable or authorised officer may require the person specified in that notice to produce the temporary event notice for examination.
>
> (7)  An authorised officer exercising the power conferred by subsection (5) or (6) must, if so requested, produce evidence of his authority to exercise the power.
>
> (8)  A person commits an offence if he fails, without reasonable excuse, to produce a temporary event notice in accordance with a requirement under subsection (5) or (6).
>
> (9)  A person guilty of an offence under this section is liable on summary conviction to a fine not exceeding level 2 on the standard scale.

The power of inspection is restricted to a constable and 'authorised officer'. An 'authorised officer' will be an officer of the licensing authority and the power of inspection is not open to a wider range of 'authorised persons' as it is in the case of premises licences.[42]

9.8.3    In the event that the acknowledgment of the TEN is lost, stolen, damaged or destroyed, s 110 makes provision for the premises user to obtain a copy of the notice, in the same form as it existed immediately before it was lost, stolen, damaged or destroyed, on payment of a fee. Under reg 8 and Sched 6 to the Licensing Act 2003 (Fees) Regulations 2005, the fee is £10.50 and a copy of the notice can be obtained only if application is made no more than one month after the end of the event period specified in the TEN. Section 110 provides:

> (1)  Where a temporary event notice acknowledged under section 102 is lost, stolen, damaged or destroyed, the premises user may apply to the licensing authority which acknowledged the notice (or, if there is more than one such authority, any of them) for a copy of the notice.

(2) No application may be made under this section more than one month after the end of the event period specified in the notice.

(3) The application must be accompanied by the prescribed fee.

(4) Where a licensing authority receives an application under this section, it must issue the premises user with a copy of the notice (certified by the authority to be a true copy) if it is satisfied that–

    (a) the notice has been lost, stolen, damaged or destroyed, and

    (b) where it has been lost or stolen, the premises user has reported that loss or theft to the police.

(5) The copy issued under this section must be a copy of the notice in the form it existed immediately before it was lost, stolen, damaged or destroyed.

(6) This Act applies in relation to a copy issued under this section as it applies in relation to an original notice.

## 9.9    RIGHT OF ENTRY WHERE NOTICE IS GIVEN

A right of entry, where a TEN is given, to assess its likely effect on the promotion of the crime prevention objective is conferred by s 108. The right is conferred on a constable and 'authorised officer' (on production of authorisation on request) and is broadly comparable to the right conferred on constables and authorised persons by s 59 for premises licences (see 6.14 above). Section 108(1) and (2) provides:

(1) A constable or an authorised officer may, at any reasonable time, enter the premises to which a temporary event notice relates to assess the likely effect of the notice on the promotion of the crime prevention objective.

(2) An authorised officer exercising the power conferred by this section must, if so requested, produce evidence of his authority to exercise the power.

There are, however, a number of differences between the right under this provision and that under s 59. First, the right is confined to constables and authorised officers, whereas for s 59 the right extends to the wider range of authorised persons. Secondly, no provision is made for the use of reasonable force for gaining entry, as it is (in s 59(4)) for premises licences. Thirdly, the right of entry under s 59 is expressly confined to entry 'before the determination of a relevant application', although there is no comparable provision in s 108 of entry having to occur prior to the temporary event taking place. It may, nevertheless, be implicit that entry must be before the event, since the purpose of entry is to assess the likely effect of the TEN on the promotion of the crime prevention objective and likely effect will relate to what might happen before the event rather than once it is taking place.

Section 108(3) provides: 'A person commits an offence if he intentionally obstructs an authorised officer exercising a power conferred by this section.'[43] Obstruction of a constable exercising the power will similarly constitute an offence, although falling within the general provision of obstructing a constable in the course of his duties under the Police Act 1996.[44]

## 9.10   CONCLUSION

The system of temporary permitted activities is one in which authorisation for licensable activities can be obtained simply by the giving of a TEN. The most important aspect of the TENs system, accordingly to para 7.2 of the Guidance, is that

> events do not have to be authorised as such by the licensing authority. Instead the premises user notifies the event to the licensing authority and the police, subject to fulfilling certain conditions.

TENs seek to cover a wide spectrum of activities, ranging from, at one extreme, four-day music concerts attended by up to 499 people, to, at the other extreme, small single-day events such as school fêtes and wedding receptions held in village halls or similar premises. The system regulating these events, described by para 7.5 of the Guidance as 'light touch', is one that applies the same light touch to the former events just as much as to the latter, in essence, adopting a 'one size fits all' approach. Described by Lord McIntosh, a Government spokesman, during the committee stage of the Bill in the House of Lords, as 'a very deregulatory measure', it is one which goes 'as far as we think it is safe and reasonable to go in view of the protection of local people' (HL Deb, vol 643, col 386, 17 January 2003).

## NOTES

1  The 'relevant licensing authority' is defined in s 99, which provides: 'In this Part references to the "relevant licensing authority", in relation to any premises, are references to–

   (a)  the licensing authority in whose area the premises are situated, or

   (b)  where the premises are situated in the areas of two or more licensing authorities, each of those authorities.'

   In the case of premises situated in the areas of two or more licensing authorities, the position differs from that in respect of premises licences and CPCs. A TEN needs to be given to *each* of the authorities, whereas for premises licences and CPCs application is made to one or other of the authorities in accordance with s 12(3) and s 71(3) respectively – see 6.3.1 above and 8.3.2 above. This is because, in the words of Lord McIntosh, a Government spokesman in the House of Lords, a TEN is 'merely a notification . . . [and] it seems to be virtually no burden for it to go to more than one authority at the same time', whereas for premises licences and CPCs 'the requirements . . . are fairly onerous . . . [and] it would be onerous for the applicant to have to go to more than one authority' (HL Deb, vol 643, col 381, 17 January 2003).

2  'The licensing authority may only ever intervene of its own volition if the limits set out in the 2003 Act on the number of temporary event notices that may be given in various circumstances would be exceeded. Otherwise, the licensing authority is only required to issue a timely acknowledgement' (Guidance, para 7.3). For the limits set on the number of events, see 9.7.1 below. Police intervention is on the ground that allowing the event to go ahead will undermine the crime prevention objective – see 9.5 below.

3  Explanatory Note 163. Because of these limitations on numbers, along with limitations on the length of time (96 hours), the maximum aggregate duration of the periods covered by TENs at any individual premises (15 days) and the scale of the event in terms of the maximum number of persons attending at any one time when licensable activities are taking place (less than 500), the system of TENs is 'characterised by an exceptionally light touch bureaucracy': Guidance, para 7.3.

4   Guidance, para 7.8, which acknowledges that premises users such as these 'will not have commercial backgrounds or ready access to legal advice' and authorities 'should therefore ensure that local publicity about the system of temporary permitted activities is clear and understandable and should strive to keep the arrangements manageable and user-friendly for these groups'.

5   This is the so-called 'golden rule' of statutory interpretation.

6   Section 100(9) provides:

> 'In this section "supply of alcohol" means–
> (a) the sale by retail of alcohol, or
> (b) the supply of alcohol by or on behalf of a club to, or to the order of, a member of the club.'

7   See reg 3(1) and Sched 1. Reg (2) goes on to provide: 'A matter appearing in, or required to be stated in the prescribed form in that Schedule (other than a matter mentioned in section 100(5)(a) to (e) of the Act) is a prescribed matter for the purposes of section 100(5) of the Act' and, under reg (3), 'Any other information appearing in, or required to be included in the prescribed form in that Schedule (other than information mentioned in section 100(4)(a) or (b) of the Act) is prescribed information for the purposes of section 100(4) of the Act'.

8   The power to make such regulations is subject to the 'affirmative resolution procedure', ie a draft of the statutory instrument has to be laid before and approved by a resolution of each House of Parliament: s 197(3)(b) and (4).

9   Section 193 provides: ' "working day" means any day other than a Saturday, a Sunday, Christmas Day, Good Friday or a day which is a bank holiday under the Banking and Financial Dealings Act 1971 (c.80) in England and Wales.'

10  See Halsbury's Laws of England (4th edn Reissue), Vol 45(2), *Time*, para 235.

11  Although the section refers to 'documents' and not 'notices', it is apparent from the heading to the section ('Giving of notices etc') that it is intended to cover the latter – see 2.5 above.

12  Section 7 of the Interpretation Act 1978 provides: 'Where an Act authorises or requires any document to be served by post (whether the expression "serve" or the expression "give" or "send" or any other expression is used) then, unless the contrary intention appears, the service is deemed to be effected by properly addressing, prepaying and posting a letter containing the document and, unless the contrary is proved, to have been effected at the time at which the letter would be delivered in the ordinary course of post.'

13  The Guidance, para 13.79, recommends that such cases are heard by a subcommittee – see 2.2.19 above. A hearing need not be held if the parties agree that this is unnecessary: s 105(2)(a).

14  Under para 16(2), the premises user can appeal if the authority issues a counter-notice and under para 16(3) the police can appeal if the authority refuses to do so – see 12.2.22 below.

15  Explanatory Note 169. The Guidance contains a similar acknowledgement in para 7.17: 'ten working days is the minimum possible notice that may be given.'

16  Para 7.16. The Guidance goes on to give the example of an individual personal licence holder wishing to exhibit and sell beer at a series of country shows who may wish to give several notices simultaneously: 'However, this would only be possible where the events are to take place in the same licensing authority (and police area) and the premises to be used at the show would be occupied by no more than 499 people at any one time.'

17  The first working day is treated, to all intents and purposes, as the day of receipt, when s 102(1)(b) applies.

18  This is on the basis that s 184 prescribes only the methods of giving notice and not additionally the time from which the notice is considered to have effect – see 9.2.6 above. Even if this is the case, it is still possible in some instances that the police may have less than 48 hours' notice, eg if a copy of the TEN were delivered over a weekend to a police station that was unmanned at weekends.

19  The first question posed clearly invites and anticipates a response in the negative. However, if the question were rephrased as, 'Is that what we want for four day music festivals attended by nearly five hundred people held on premises of which the local authority has no knowledge', the response may well be different.

20  'Anyone who is concerned about the restriction to prevention of crime should bear in mind that that is a wide definition. If there were any suggestion that there was a threat to children from underage drinking or grooming by paedophiles, that would be covered by prevention of crime. The police could intervene on those grounds. That is wide enough' (Lord McIntosh at HL Deb, vol 643, col 391, 17 January 2003).

21  See ibid. cols 385–86. This power exists by virtue of the provision in s 161 – see 11.13 below.

22  Explanatory Note 176. Where the objection notice is withdrawn following modification, or for any other reason, the authority is not required to hold a hearing and consider whether to issue a counter-notice. Nor is it required to do so if it has given the premises user a counter-notice to the effect that the permitted limits attaching to the number of events have been exceeded.

>  Section 105(6) provides: 'This section does not apply–
>
>  (a)  if the objection notice has been withdrawn (whether by virtue of section 106 or otherwise), or
>
>  (b)  if the premises user has been given a counter notice under section 107.'

23  'In this section "objection notice" and "relevant chief officer of police" have the same meaning as in section 104': s 105(7).

24  Notice must be given forthwith on making the determination and the notice must be accompanied by information regarding the right of a party to appeal against the determination of the authority: regs 28–29 of the LA 2003 (Hearings) Regs 2005. For the meaning of 'forthwith', see 6.6.2 above.

25  For the prescribed form, see reg 5 and Sched 2 to the LA 2003 (PTA) (Notice) Regs 2005, and 9.7.5 below.

26  The Guidance mentions intended effect only obliquely, with a reference in para 7.3 to the police being able to 'intervene to prevent such an event taking place'.

27  In *Westminster City Council v National Asylum Support Service* [2002] UKHL 38, para 5, Lord Steyn stated, *obiter*: 'Insofar as the Explanatory Notes cast light on the objective setting or contextual scene of the statute, and the mischief at which it is aimed, such materials are . . . admissible aids to construction . . ., although his Lordship went on to say at para 6: 'What is impermissible is to treat the wishes and desires of the Government about the scope of the statutory language as reflecting the will of Parliament. The aims of the Government in respect of the meaning of clauses as revealed in Explanatory Notes cannot be attributed to Parliament. The object is to see what is the intention expressed by the words enacted.' Although no other members of the House of Lords in the case made reference to the use of Explanatory Notes, the House has since acknowledged, in *R v Montila* [2005] 1 All ER 113, para 35, that it 'has become common practice for their Lordships to ask to be shown the explanatory notes when issues are raised about the meaning of words used in an enactment'.

28  This is provided the licensing authority has not given the premises user a counter-notice under s 107 to the effect that the permitted limits attaching to the number of events have been exceeded. Section 106(6) provides: 'This section does not apply if a counter notice has been given under section 107.'

29  Guidance, para 7.29, provides: 'The police may withdraw their objection notice at any stage if the proposed premises user agrees to modify his proposal to meet their concerns. For example, if the premises user agrees to modify the period during which alcohol may be sold. The licensing authority will then be sent or delivered a copy of the modified notice by the police as proof of their agreement . . .'

30  'Objection notice' has the same meaning as in s 104(2): s 106(7) – see 9.5.1 above.

31  There is compliance with s 106 as far as giving a copy of the modified TEN to the licensing authority is concerned, for the police are required to do this under s 106(4). Section 106(4) provides: 'A copy of the temporary event notice as modified under subsection (2) must be sent or delivered by the chief officer of police to the relevant licensing authority before a hearing is held or dispensed with under section 105(2).'

32  With regard to the information recorded, para 7.24 of the Guidance provides: 'Licensing authorities should be aware that there is no requirement to record all the personal information given on a temporary event notice, and should avoid recording certain details, such as national insurance numbers, which may give rise to identity fraud'.

33  See 9.2.3 above. The position may be similar in respect of open spaces, such as parks, where only part of the area may be used.

34  Where the permitted limits have been reached, they are then exceeded when a licensing authority receives a further TEN (designated 'notice A') in respect of the premises in question.

35  Section 8(6) makes provision for the Secretary of State to arrange for any duties imposed in respect of the keeping of a register under s 8 to be discharged by means of one or more central registers – see 2.4.6 above.

36  Although these words are not used in s 107(3)(b), they are incorporated by reference back to s 107(2)(b) through the words 'such event periods'.

37  This could be so whether or not the individual is a personal licence holder. It is more likely where he is, since a personal licence holder can give 50 TENs a year, but an individual who is not a licence holder may have given none (or only some) of the five TENs that constitutes the limit for the premises.

38  Section 107(13)(d) provides: 'subsections (3) and (4) of section 101 (meaning of "associate") apply as they apply for the purposes of that section.' As to what might constitute being 'in business', see 9.2.10 above.

39  The prescribed form of words are: 'On [insert date] the licensing authority received from you, [insert name], a temporary event notice ("the notice") in respect of proposed temporary licensable activities due to take place on [insert date] at [insert address or description of premises]. The licensing authority is satisfied that if the activities were to take place, one of the permitted limits set out in section 107(2), (3), (4) and (5) of the Licensing Act 2003 ("the Act") would be exceeded'.

40  'Relevant premises user' has the same meaning as in s 107(1): reg 2(g).

41  There is no requirement that such nomination be in writing, as there is in the case of premises licences (see s 57(2)(b) and 6.13.3 above).

42  Section 109(10) provides: 'In this section "authorised officer" has the meaning given in section 108(5)'; and s 108(5) provides: 'In this section "authorised officer" means–

(a)  an officer of the licensing authority in whose area the premises are situated, or

(b)  if the premises are situated in the area of more than one licensing authority, an officer of any of those authorities, authorised for the purposes of this Act.'

The exclusion of the power of inspection for other persons, such as environmental health officers or fire authority officers, reflects the fact that such persons are not able to object or make representations as they are in the case of premises licences.

43  Section 108(4) provides: 'A person guilty of an offence under this section is liable on summary conviction to a fine not exceeding level 2 on the standard scale.'

44  See s 89(2) of the Police Act 1996, which provides: 'Any person who resists or wilfully obstructs a constable in the execution of his duty, or a person assisting a constable in the execution of his duty, shall be guilty of an offence and liable on summary conviction to imprisonment for a term not exceeding one month or to a fine not exceeding level 3 on the standard scale, or to both.'

# CHAPTER 10

# PERSONAL LICENCES

## 10.1    INTRODUCTION

Part 6 of the Act establishes a regime for the supply of alcohol to be regulated by the granting of personal licences to individuals. The personal licence relates only to the sale of alcohol, not to the provision of regulated entertainment or late night refreshment services, because, according to para 4.2 of the Guidance

> sale and supply of alcohol, because of its impact on the wider community and on crime and anti-social behaviour, carries with it greater responsibility than the provision of regulated entertainment and late night refreshment. This is why individuals who may be engaged in making and authorising the sale and supply of alcohol require a personal licence.[1]

Further, a personal licence is required only in respect of sale or supply of alcohol under a premises licence and not where alcohol is supplied under a club premises certificate (CPC) or a temporary event notice (TEN). This presumably reflects the view that sale and supply of alcohol in the latter instances are not perceived to have the same social impact on the community as sale and supply in premises (such as public houses and nighclubs) that operate under a premises licence. Absence of a personal licence for clubs where there is a CPC should not give rise to difficulties given that members' clubs, in the main, are well run and relatively unproblematic. A premises user giving a TEN may in fact have a personal licence, although it is not necessary that he has and where no personal licence is held, difficulties may be more likely to arise. Premises users may give TENs for events at which alcohol will be supplied and may turn out to be totally unsuitable persons to supply alcohol. Whilst the police may be able to prevent this occurring in some instances (if they can give an objection notice and this is upheld by the licensing authority), they may not be able to do so in others. In these instances, it will be left to the police to deal with any difficulties that arise through their powers of closure under the 2003 Act (see 11.12 below).

Applicants for a personal licence are required to possess an accredited qualification and a personal licence is issued for 10 years in the first instance. There is a statutory presumption in favour of renewal for further periods of 10 years if the licence holder has not been subject to penalties under licensing law. A personal licence may be sought by any individual whether or not they have current employment or business interests associated with the use of the licence.[2] It is not linked to particular premises and the licensing of individuals, separately from the licensing of premises, permits the movement of licence holders from one set of premises to another. However, a personal licence holder may become associated directly with particular premises covered by a premises licence by being made the 'designated premises supervisor' (DPS) for those premises. The DPS is a personal licence holder who is the nominated individual responsible for the day-to-day running of the licensed premises (see 6.4.2 above). There may be other individuals at the licensed premises holding a personal licence apart from the DPS, although it will not be necessary for all staff to hold personal licences. However, under s 19(3), all supplies of alcohol under a premises licence must be made by or under the authority of a personal licence holder (see 6.4.2–6.4.3 above). A personal licence does not, however, authorise its holder to supply alcohol anywhere, but only from premises having a premises licence (Explanatory Note 184), although a personal licence holder may supply alcohol elsewhere under the authority of a TEN (see 9.1.1 above).

## 10.2   MEANING OF PERSONAL LICENCE

A personal licence is a licence granted by a licensing authority to an individual, permitting him to sell alcohol by retail or to supply alcohol by or on behalf of a club to club members. In the latter instance, this will relate to supply of alcohol in clubs holding a premises licence since no personal licence is needed where alcohol is supplied in clubs holding a club premises certificate (see 8.1.2 above). Section 111 provides:

> (1)  In this Act "personal licence" means a licence which–
>> (a)  is granted by a licensing authority to an individual, and
>> (b)  authorises that individual to supply alcohol, or authorise the supply of alcohol, in accordance with a premises licence.
> (2)  In subsection (1)(b) the reference to an individual supplying alcohol is to him–
>> (a)  selling by retail alcohol, or
>> (b)  supplying alcohol by or on behalf of a club to, or to the order of, a member of the club.

## 10.3   APPLICANTS FOR PERSONAL LICENCES

Application can be made only by an individual and not by a company or corporate body. Section 117(1) provides:

> An individual may apply–
> (a)  for the grant of a personal licence, or
> (b)  for the renewal of a personal licence held by him.

An application can also be made by an individual only if he does not already hold a personal licence or does not have an outstanding application for a personal licence awaiting determination. An individual is permitted to hold only one personal licence and, once an application has been made for a licence, no further application can be made until the initial application has been determined or withdrawn. Further, any licence granted is void if it transpires that the individual already holds a personal licence. Section 118 provides:

> (1)  An individual who makes an application for the grant of a personal licence under section 117 ("the initial application") may not make another such application until the initial application has been determined by the licensing authority to which it was made or has been withdrawn.
> (2)  A personal licence is void if, at the time it is granted, the individual to whom it is granted already holds a personal licence.

## 10.4 APPLICATIONS FOR PERSONAL LICENCES

### 10.4.1 The relevant licensing authority

Application for the grant of a personal licence must normally be made to the authority for the area in which the applicant is ordinarily resident, although, if for some reason a person is not ordinarily resident in an authority's area, for example, a person has no fixed abode or is ordinarily resident abroad, application can be made to any licensing authority. Section 117(2) provides:

> An application for the grant of a personal licence–
>
> (a) must, if the applicant is ordinarily resident in the area of a licensing authority, be made to that authority, and
>
> (b) may, in any other case, be made to any licensing authority.

As to when a person will be 'ordinarily resident' in an area, the meaning of this phrase has been considered by the House of Lords in the context of s 1(1) of the Education Act 1962, under which local authorities were under a duty to bestow awards for designated courses to students who were 'ordinarily resident' within their areas. In *Shah v Barnet London Borough Council* [1983] 1 All ER 226, 235, Lord Scarman stated:

> Unless . . . it can be shown that the statutory framework or the legal context in which the words are used requires a different meaning, I unhesitatingly subscribe to the view that 'ordinarily resident' refers to a man's abode in a particular place or country which he has adopted voluntarily and for settled purposes as part of the regular order of his life for the time being, whether of short or long duration.

There would seem to be no reason to give the phrase any different meaning in s 117(2).

The authority granting the personal licence then becomes the 'relevant licensing authority' as far as the personal licence holder is concerned.[3] It will thereafter continue to have responsibility for the licence and application will need to be made to it for renewal of the licence at 10-year periods.[4] Section 117(3) provides: 'An application for the renewal of a personal licence must be made to the relevant licensing authority.'

Once the licence is granted, the licensing authority that issued it remains the relevant licensing authority for it, even though the individual may move out of the area or take employment elsewhere. The personal licence itself will give details of the issuing licensing authority. The holder of the licence is required by the Act to notify the licensing authority of all changes of name or address. These changes will be recorded by the licensing authority. The holder is also required to notify the licensing authority of any convictions for 'relevant offences' (see 10.5.6–10.5.12 below) and the courts are similarly required to inform the licensing authority of such convictions, whether or not they have ordered the suspension or forfeiture of the licence. These measures ensure that a single record will be held of the holder's history in terms of licensing matters.[5] In order to make these records available to licensing authorities, the Government, supported by licensing authorities, aims to develop a central database which will, among other things, include details of all personal licence holders (Guidance, para 4.17).

## 10.4.2 Form, notices and accompanying documentation

Application is subject to regulations made under s 133 in respect of the form, etc of applications and fees to accompany applications and notices. Section 133(1) and (2) provides:

(1)  In relation to any application under section 117 or notice[6] under this Part, regulations may prescribe–

    (a)  its form,

    (b)  the manner in which it is to be made or given, and

    (c)  the information and documents that must accompany it.

(2)  Regulations may also–

    (a)  require applications under section 117 or 126 or notices under section 127 to be accompanied by a fee,[7] and

    (b)  prescribe the amount of the fee.

Regulation 6(1) and Sched 1 to the Licensing Act 2003 (Personal Licences) Regulations 2005, SI 2005/41 (LA 2003 (Personal Licences) Regs 2005) prescribe the form of the application for the grant of a licence and the information that it shall contain.[8] Under reg 7(1), the documents that must accompany an application are two photographs of the applicant (one of which must be endorsed), a certificate or search results on criminal convictions obtained within the last month and a declaration in respect of criminal convictions for relevant or foreign offences (see 10.5.4–10.5.13 below). Regulation 7(1) provides:

(a)  two photographs of the applicant, which shall be–

    (i)  taken against a light background so that the applicant's features are distinguishable and contrast against the background,

    (ii)  45 millimetres by 35 millimetres,

    (iii)  full face uncovered and without sunglasses and, unless the applicant wears a head covering due to his religious beliefs, without a head covering,

    (iv)  on photographic paper, and

    (v)  one of which is endorsed with a statement verifying the likeness of the photograph to the applicant by a solicitor, notary, a person of standing in the community or any individual with a professional qualification; and

(b)  either–

    (i)  a criminal conviction certificate issued under section 112 of the Police Act 1997,

    (ii)  a criminal record certificate issued under section 113A of the Police Act 1997 or

    (iii)  the results of a subject access search under the Data Protection Act 1998 of the Police National Computer by the National Identification Service, and

    in any case such certificate or search results shall be issued no earlier than one calendar month before the giving of the application to the relevant licensing authority, and

(c)  a declaration by the applicant, in the form set out in Schedule 3, that either he has not been convicted of a relevant offence or a foreign offence or that he has been convicted of a relevant offence or a foreign offence accompanied by details of the nature and date of the conviction and any sentence imposed on him in respect of it.

As regards persons entitled to endorse the photograph, a 'person of standing in the community' under reg 2 'includes a bank or building society official, a police officer, a civil servant or a minister of religion'. It seems unlikely that any bank or building society employee will suffice for these purposes since such persons might be employed in a very junior capacity and would not be equated with a 'person of standing in the community'. Clearly it will include persons such as managers or assistant managers of branches, although it is less clear how far this might extend below this level of employee. Similarly, it seems unlikely that any person employed as a civil servant will satisfy this test and at least some degree of seniority might be expected. Police officers, unless perhaps at probationary level, and ministers of religion, however, might ordinarily be expected to meet the criteria. As regards an individual with a 'professional qualification', this will obviously include persons working in areas regulated by professional bodies, for example, doctors, accountants, teachers, barristers and solicitors, although it is uncertain whether it will extend beyond such professions.[9]

As regards certificates and search results on criminal convictions, one of three documents to accompany the application will suffice. First, a criminal conviction certificate,[10] which shows all convictions held at national level, which are not 'spent' under the Rehabilitation of Offenders Act 1974 (see 10.5.14 below), but not 'spent' convictions or cautions, can be obtained from the Criminal Records Bureau by anyone on payment of the required fee. Secondly, a criminal record certificate, which can be either a standard criminal record certificate or an enhanced criminal record certificate, can be obtained from the Criminal Records Bureau, although only by a 'registered person' in accordance with s 120 of the Police Act 1997 as these certificates also include details of 'spent' convictions and cautions. Local authorities will be registered persons under the Act as they discharge functions where such details may need to be disclosed. The standard certificate includes details of 'spent' convictions and any cautions held at national level and is available in respect of posts or for purposes that are exceptions to the Rehabilitation of Offenders Act 1974. The enhanced certificate is issued for work that involves regularly caring for, training, supervising or being in sole charge of persons under the age of 18 or vulnerable adults. In addition to the information contained in the standard certificate, it includes information from local police records, including relevant non-conviction information. Thirdly, under s 7 of the Data Protection Act 1998 data subjects have a right of access to any personal data held by a data controller. Information in respect of criminal convictions is personal data and the police are a 'data controller' in respect of information that they hold on individuals ('data subjects'). This information can be obtained from the police, on request, by means of a data access search. Any one of these three documents can accompany the personal licence application.

For renewals, the form of the application and the information that the application shall contain are prescribed by reg 6(2) and Sched 2. The accompanying documentation required by reg 6(2) is the same as that set out in reg 7 above. As the applicant already has a licence, no copy of his licensing qualification is needed, although the application needs to be accompanied by the personal licence or a statement of reasons if this cannot be produced. Section 117(4) provides:

> Where the application is for renewal of a personal licence, the application must be accompanied by the personal licence or, if that is not practicable, by a statement of the reasons for the failure to provide the licence.

The applicant is also required, under para 3 of Sched 2, to confirm that he does not hold any other personal licences other than the one submitted for renewal, since under s 118 only one personal licence can be held (see 10.3 above). In addition, in the case of a renewal application, it is also necessary for the application to be lodged within a two-month period beginning three months before the licence's expiry. Section 117(6) provides:

> An application for renewal may be made only during the period of two months beginning three months before the time the licence would expire in accordance with section 115(1) if no application for renewal were made.[11]

Under the Licensing Act 2003 (Fees) Regulations 2005, SI 2005/79 (LA 2003 (Fees) Regs 2005), the application fee for the grant and renewal of a personal licence is £37.

## 10.5   DETERMINATION OF APPLICATIONS FOR PERSONAL LICENCES

The Act draws a distinction between cases where certain qualifications criteria are met and where a licence must be issued (mandatory grants) and cases where these criteria are not met. Where they are not met, in some cases the licensing authority must reject the application and refuse to grant a licence (mandatory refusals). In other cases where the criteria are not met, the licensing authority must notify the police who can then decide whether to object. If there is no objection, the authority must grant the licence and, if there is objection, the authority must hold a hearing to decide whether or not to grant a licence (discretionary grants). Where no police objection is received, para 13.79 of the Guidance recommends delegation to officers and, where representations are received, delegation to a licensing subcommittee (see 2.2.19 above). Each of these cases is considered below.

### 10.5.1 Mandatory grants

#### 10.5.2 *The criteria*

The provisions of s 120, which govern the determination of applications, apply where the authority has received an application made in accordance with s 117 (s 120(1)) and, where this is the case, the authority must grant the licence if the following criteria set out in s 120(2) are satisfied:

> The authority must grant the licence if it appears to it that–
> (a)  the applicant is aged 18 or over,
> (b)  he possesses a licensing qualification or is a person of a prescribed description,
> (c)  no personal licence held by him has been forfeited in the period of five years ending with the day the application was made, and
> (d)  he has not been convicted of any relevant offence or any foreign offence.

Provided the criteria are met, it seems that the authority must grant the licence, irrespective of whether other considerations may preclude an applicant from exercising any control over the premises.[12]

### 10.5.3 Age, qualification and absence of forfeiture

As regards the age of the applicant, it is necessary only that he is aged 18 or over at the time of the determination of his application and he need not be this age at the time the application is made. This is in contrast to the position of premises licence applications, where an applicant is precluded by s 16(2) from applying for a premises licence unless he is aged 18 or over (see 6.2.1 above). It is not obvious why the position should be different here, but it would appear to be since there is no comparable provision to s 16(2) in Part 6 of the Act as regards personal licences.

As regards licensing qualifications, s 120(8) provides:

In this section "licensing qualification" means–

(a) a qualification–

    (i) accredited at the time of its award, and

    (ii) awarded by a body accredited at that time,

(b) a qualification awarded before the coming into force of this section which the Secretary of State certifies is to be treated for the purposes of this section as if it were a qualification within paragraph (a), or

(c) a qualification obtained in Scotland or Northern Ireland or in an EEA State (other than the United Kingdom) which is equivalent to a qualification within paragraph (a) or (b).[13]

Under s 120(9), a qualification is 'accredited' if it is accredited by the Secretary of State and on 7 February 2005 the Secretary of State accredited the first two personal licence qualifications, the British Institute of Innkeeping Associated Board (BIIAB) Level 2 National Certificate for Personal Licence Holders (QCA Accreditation Number: 100/4866/2) and the Global Online Assessment for Learning (GOAL) Level 2 Certificate for Personal Licence Holders (QCA Accreditation Number: 100/4865/0). To these has been added a third qualification, the Graded Qualifications Alliance (GQAL) Level 2 Certificate for Personal Licence Holders (QCA Accreditation Number: 100/5040/1).[14] Persons not possessing a recognised licensing qualification may nevertheless satisfy the requirement in s 120(2)(b) if they are a 'person of a prescribed description'. Under reg 4 of the LA 2003 (Personal Licences) Regs 2005, the Secretary of State has prescribed one category of persons who may obtain a personal licence without a licensing qualification and these are persons who are a member of the company of the Master, Wardens, Freemen and Commonality of Mistery of the Vintners of the City of London.[15] Such persons can obtain a personal licence, provided the other requirements are met, without the need for a licensing qualification as the Vintners 'adopt very high standards for admission to their Company, membership of which is a significant honour . . . [and] the Secretary of State is satisfied that it would be fair and equitable to regard admission to the Company as the equivalent of obtaining a licensing qualification' (*Consultation on Draft Regulations and Order to be Made under the Licensing Act 2003*, para 3.9).

As regards absence of forfeiture, it is necessary for the applicant not to have forfeited any personal licence held within the preceding five-year period. Forfeiture of a personal licence may occur where the licence holder is convicted of a 'relevant offence' by a court in England or Wales and the court orders the licence to be forfeited.[16]

### 10.5.4 *Absence of convictions for any relevant offence or any foreign offence*

10.5.5   Not all convictions will preclude a mandatory grant, but only ones for a 'relevant offence' or 'foreign offence'. Further, some convictions for such offences are to be disregarded and do not count as a 'conviction' for the purposes of premises licences under Pt 6 of the Act. These are where the conviction for a relevant offence or foreign offence has become 'spent' for the purposes of the Rehabilitation of Offenders Act 1974. The three matters requiring consideration, therefore, are the meaning of 'relevant offence', the meaning of 'foreign offence' and when convictions for these offences become 'spent'. These are considered below.

#### 10.5.6   *Relevant offence*

Section 113(1) provides: 'In this Part "relevant offence" means an offence listed in Schedule 4.' This list may be amended from time to time, for s 113(2) provides: 'The Secretary of State may by order amend that list so as to add, modify or omit any entry'. The offences listed in the Schedule are, for the most part, set out in chronological order by reference to the statutory provisions in which they appear, although they broadly fall into the following categories:

- offences involving licensing, alcohol (including drugs) or gambling;
- offences involving firearms;
- offences involving fraudulent or dishonest conduct;
- offences involving sexual conduct; and
- offences involving violence.

The relevant offences are mentioned below under these categories, with a reference in parentheses, after the statutory provision(s), to the relevant paragraph(s) in Sched 4 in which the offences appear.

#### 10.5.7   *Offences involving licensing or alcohol (including drugs)*

The following offences are included:

- Offences under the Licensing Act 2003 (para 1);
- Offences under previous licensing legislation governing the areas of alcohol, entertainment and late night refreshment. The relevant legislative provisions are:
  - for alcohol, the Licensing Act 1964 and the Licensing (Occasional Permissions) Act 1983 (para 2(b) and (g)),
  - for entertainment, Sched 12 to the London Government Act 1963, the Private Places of Entertainment (Licensing) Act 1967, s 13 of the Theatres Act 1968, s 6 of or Sched 1 to the Local Government (Miscellaneous Provisions) Act 1982 and the Cinemas Act 1985 (para 2(a), (c), (d), (f) and (h)),
  - for late night refreshment, the Late Night Refreshment Houses Act 1969 and the London Local Authorities Act 1990 (para 2(e) and (i)).
- An offence under s 3 of the Private Security Industry Act 2001 of engaging in certain activities relating to security without a licence (para 20);

- An offence under s 7(2) of the Gaming Act 1968 of allowing a child to take part in gaming on premises licensed for the sale of alcohol (para 6);
- An offence under section 46 of the Gambling Act 2005 if the child or young person was invited, caused or permitted to gamble on premises in respect of which a premises licence under this Act had effect (para 21) (added by para 20(4) of Sched Pt 2 to the Gambling Act 2005);
- Offences under the Road Traffic Act 1988 that involve alcohol or drugs and motor vehicles, which are:
  - causing death by careless driving while under the influence of drink or drugs (s 3A),
  - driving, attempting to drive or being in charge of a vehicle when under the influence of drink or drugs (s 4), and
  - driving, attempting to drive or being in charge of a vehicle with alcohol concentration above the prescribed limit (s 5) (para 14).
- Offences under the Misuse of Drugs Act 1971, which are:
  - production of a controlled drug (s 4(2)),
  - supply of a controlled drug (s 4(3)),
  - possession of a controlled drug with intent to supply (s 5(3)), and
  - permitting [various drug-related] activities to take place on premises (s 8) (para 7).

### 10.5.8   Offences involving firearms

The following offences are included:

- Offences under the Firearms Act 1968 (para 3);
- Offences under the Firearms (Amendment) Act 1988 (para 12);
- Offences under the Firearms (Amendment) Act 1997 (para 17).

### 10.5.9   Offences involving fraudulent or dishonest conduct

The following offences are included:

- An offence under s 1 of the Trade Descriptions Act 1968 of applying a false trade description of goods, or supplying or offering to supply goods to which a false trade description is applied, in circumstances where the goods in question are or include alcohol (para 4);
- Most offences under the Theft Act 1968:
  - theft (s 1),
  - robbery (s 8),
  - burglary (s 9),
  - aggravated burglary (s 10),
  - removal of articles from places open to the public (s 11),
  - aggravated vehicle-taking (s 12A),[17]
  - abstracting of electricity (s 13),
  - obtaining property by deception (s 15),

- obtaining a money transfer by deception (s 15A),
- obtaining pecuniary advantage by deception (s 16),
- false accounting (s 17),
- false statements by company directors, etc (s 19),
- suppression, etc of documents (s 20),
- blackmail (s 21),
- handling stolen goods (s 22),
- dishonestly retaining a wrongful credit (s 24A), and
- going equipped for stealing, etc (s 25) (para 5(a)–(q)).[18]
- Deception offences under the Theft Act 1978:
  - obtaining services by deception (s 1), and
  - evasion of liability by deception (s 2) (para 8(a) and (b)).[19]
- Offences under the Fraud Act 2006:
  - fraud (s 1),
  - possession of articles for use in frauds (s 6),
  - making or supplying articles for use in frauds (s 7),
  - participating in fraudulent business carried on by sole trader (s 9),
  - obtaining services dishonestly (s 11) (para 22).[20]
- Offences under the Customs and Excise Management Act 1979:
  - fraudulent evasion of duty (s 170), and
  - taking preparatory steps for evasion of duty (s 170B) (para 9(a) and (b)).[21]
- Offences under the Tobacco Products Duty Act 1979:
  - possession and sale of unmarked tobacco (s 8G), and
  - use of premises for sale of unmarked tobacco (s 8H) (para 9(a) and (b)).[22]
- Offences under the Forgery and Counterfeiting Act 1981 (other than an offence under ss 18 or 19) (para 11);[23]
- Offences under the Copyright, Designs and Patents Act 1988:
  - public exhibition in the course of business of an article infringing copyright (s 107(1)(d)(iii)),
  - infringment of copyright by public performance of a work (s 107(3)),
  - broadcast, etc of recording of a performance made without sufficient consent (s 198(2)),
  - fraudulent reception of transmission (s 297(1)), and
  - supply, etc, of unauthorised decoder (s 297A(1)) (para 13).
- Offences under the Food Safety Act 1990, in circumstances where the food in question is or includes alcohol:
  - selling food or drink not of the nature, substance or quality demanded (s 14), and
  - falsely describing or presenting food or drink (s 15) (para 15).
- An offence under s 92(1) or (2) of the Trade Marks Act 1994 of unauthorised use of trademark, etc in relation to goods, in circumstances where the goods in question are or include alcohol (para 16).

## 10.5.10 Offences involving sexual conduct

A sexual offence, being an offence:

- listed in Pt 2 of Sched 15 to the Criminal Justice Act 2003, other than the offence mentioned in para 95 (an offence under s 4 of the Sexual Offences Act 1967 (procuring others to commit homosexual acts));
- an offence under s 8 of the Sexual Offences Act 1956 (intercourse with a defective); and
- an offence under s 18 of the Sexual Offences Act 1956 (fraudulent abduction of an heiress) (para 18).[24]

## 10.5.11 Offences involving violence

A violent offence, being any offence that leads, or is intended or likely to lead, to a person's death or to physical injury to a person, including an offence that is required to be charged as arson (whether or not it would otherwise fall within this definition) (para 19).[25]

## 10.5.12 Secondary party and inchoate liability for relevant offences

A general criminal law principle is that no distinction is drawn between principals and secondary parties for prosecution purposes and under s 8 of the Accessories and Abettors Act 1861 and s 44 of the Magistrates Courts Act 1980 secondary parties are liable to be tried and convicted as principal offenders. Conviction for a relevant offence should therefore include those whose participation has been as a principal offender, that is, those whose conduct is the most immediate cause of the commission of the offence, and also those who may have participated as secondary parties by providing encouragement or assistance. Nevertheless, for sexual offences, express provision is made by para 153(a) of Sched 15 to the Criminal Justice Act 2003 for secondary party liability. Paragraph 153(a) provides that 'aiding, abetting, counselling, procuring'[26] the commission of any specified sexual offence is itself an offence under the schedule, although it is thought that there would be liability in such cases under the general criminal law, even in the absence of this express statutory provision.

Section 153(a)–(c) also makes express provision for inchoate liability in respect of any specified sexual offence, that is, for incitement, conspiracy or attempt to commit such an offence. This means that a conviction incurred, for instance, for attempted rape is a conviction for a relevant offence. Apart from in the case of sexual offences, no express provision is made for inchoate offences to be relevant offences. Since the conviction in such cases is for incitement, conspiracy or attempt to commit the offence in question, and not for the substantive offence itself, inchoate offences will not be included as relevant offences in the absence of express provision (as for sexual offences) or unless they can be considered to fall within the definition of a relevant offence itself. This might be the case for a violent offence. Since the defintion of 'violent offence' includes 'any offence . . . intended . . . to lead to a person's death or to physical injury to a person' (see 10.5.11 above), this might include offences of incitement, conspiracy and attempt to commit murder, grievous bodily harm or actual bodily harm, since intention to bring death or harm is of the essence of these offences.

With regard to other relevant offences, however, it seems that convictions for incitement, conspiracy and attempt to commit the offences in question will not be relevant offences for the purposes of s 113(1). There are possible exceptions in the Theft Act 1968 for robbery under s 8, which involves the threat or use of force immediately before or at the time of stealing; for burglary under s 9, which can take the form of entering premises as a trespasser with intent to commit grievous bodily harm; and for aggravated burglary under s 10, which can take the form of commission of burglary where a person has with him a weapon of offence. These offences might perhaps fall within the definition of 'violent offence' in Sched 4, para 19 of the Licensing Act 2003 (see 10.5.11 above).

### 10.5.13 'Foreign offence'

Section 113(3) provides: 'In this Part "foreign offence" means an offence (other than a relevant offence) under the law of any place outside England and Wales.' The effect of this provision seems to be that, if relevant offences are excluded,[27] the requirements for the mandatory grant of a licence will not be met where an applicant has a conviction for any foreign offence. This is because, if the words '(other than a relevant offence)' are excluded, all that this leaves in s 113(3) is 'an offence . . . under the law of any place outside England and Wales', without any other limiting or qualifying words. This is not to say, however, that an applicant with a conviction for any foreign offence will not obtain a personal licence, but only that this will preclude a mandatory grant. Where there is a conviction, it will mean, as will be seen, that the authority must give notice to the police under s 120(4) so the police have an opportunity to object (see 10.5.17 below).[28]

It is doubtful whether convictions for all foreign offences will be drawn to the attention of the local authority and police since the Guidance envisages only offences equivalent to relevant offences being disclosed. Paragraph 4.6 states that all applicants are 'required to make a clear statement as to whether or not they have been convicted outside England and Wales of a relevant offence or an *equivalent* foreign offence' (emphasis added). If only these offences are disclosed, then only these offences will prevent a mandatory grant. It may be, of course, that applicants disclose convictions that are not equivalent to relevant offences. This will still have the effect of preventing a mandatory grant and will require a notice to be given to the police, although the police will not be in a position to object on the basis of such convictions. This is because, in deciding whether to make an objection in the case of a conviction for a foreign offence, the police can only do so under s 120(5)(b) where the foreign offence is one 'which the chief officer of police considers to be comparable to a relevant offence' (see 10.5.19 below).

### 10.5.14 Spent convictions

Section 114 provides:

> For the purposes of this Part a conviction for a relevant offence or a foreign offence must be disregarded if it is spent for the purposes of the Rehabilitation of Offenders Act 1974 (c.53).

For certain 'less serious' offences, a conviction is to be treated as 'spent' under s 1 of the Rehabilitation of Offenders Act 1974, and a person is to be treated as a 'rehabilitated person', once the required period of time under the Act (the 'rehabilita-tion period') has elapsed.[29] The requirement in s 114 that a conviction must be dis-regarded 'if it is spent for the purposes of the Rehabilitation of Offenders Act 1974' might mean simply that, in accordance with s 1, the rehabilitation period has passed. One view would be that it does have this meaning and, if this is the case, *all* spent convictions must *in all circumstances* be disregarded and can never be taken into account. However, an alternative view would be that this provision in s 114 should be read and interpreted in the wider context of the 1974 Act as a whole. Where a conviction is to be treated as spent, s 4(1) of the 1974 Act goes on to make provision for the effect of rehabilitation, which is that the conviction must be disregarded. It pro-vides that the person convicted is to be treated in law as if he had neither committed nor been tried for the offence(s) in question and that no evidence as to the conviction shall be admissible in proceedings before a judicial authority. This is, however, subject to the provision in s 7(3) that, in any proceedings before a judicial authority, the authority can admit or require evidence as to a person's spent conviction if satisfied that justice cannot otherwise be done. The 1974 Act does not therefore require spent convictions to be disregarded in *all* circumstances.

10.5.15 If the reference in s 114 to 'spent for the purposes of the Rehabilitation of Offenders Act 1974' means spent for the purposes of the Act taken as a whole, the section might be seen as representing no more than a declaratory statement of the law as regards spent convictions under the 1974 Act. On this view, s 7(3) might still have application and spent convictions need not be disregarded in absolutely all circumstances. A local authority, when reaching a decision on a licensing application, is a 'judicial authority' for the purposes of s 7(3),[30] and it might therefore admit evidence of spent convictions if satisfied that justice cannot otherwise be done. In short, on the first view, the power to admit spent convictions under s 7(3) would be impliedly excluded by s 114, but, on the second view, it will continue to have applica-tion notwithstanding s 114. Either view might be supported on the wording of s 114.

Neither the Explanatory Notes to the Act nor the Guidance provides any real indication of whether or not s 7(3) is to have application, for neither makes any mention of the section. The Explanatory Notes do state that convictions must be disregarded 'when spent' under the 1974 Act,[31] which might perhaps be seen as supporting the view that spent convictions are to be disregarded in all circumstances; but this is not conclusive and a persuasive argument might be made against this view. Under the previous law, licensing authorities were able to take into account spent convictions under s 7(3) and can continue to do so in other areas where licensing control is exercised. To exclude the application of s 7(3) under the 2003 Act would therefore not only be a major change in the law, but also a departure from the well-established legal position operating in other areas. It might be said that, in the absence of clear words, a change of such fundamental importance should not be made. After all, the section does not say, as it might have done, that spent convictions must be disregarded in all circumstances or that the provision in s 7(3) of the 1974 Act does not have application for the purposes of Pt 6 of the 2003 Act. Had it done so, the position would have been clear, but it is not and there is at the very least an element of doubt as to whether s 7(3) is impliedly excluded by s 114.

10.5.16 It remains to be seen what view will be taken of the provision in s 114(1). Of the two views, disregarding spent convictions in all circumstances perhaps accords more closely with the ordinary and natural meaning of the section, but a tentative view is offered that, as a matter of policy, the best course would be to regard s 7(3) as still having application. The courts have made it clear that s 7(3) does not confer a discretion on authorities to admit spent convictions, and the circumstances in which they can be taken into account are tightly circumscribed by the requirement that justice cannot be done otherwise than by admitting the conviction. This can be seen from the remarks of Sedley J in a liquor licensing case, *R v Hastings Magistrates' Court ex p McSpirit* (1994) 162 JP 44 (at 48):

> In my judgment the purpose of section 7(3) is not to confer a dispensing power by way of discretion by adjudicating bodies but to ensure that spent convictions stay spent, unless in the classes of case where it is permissible to do so the party applying to put the spent conviction in can satisfy the judicial authority concerned that there is no other way of doing justice.

Similar remarks were made by his Lordship in *Adamson v Waveney District Council* (1997) 161 JP 787, 793, where justices had dismissed an appeal against the local authority's refusal to grant a hackney carriage licence following reception from the police of a list of the applicant's spent convictions:

> the justices . . . were . . . wrongly advised . . . that they had a discretion to admit spent convictions. It is misleading so to describe the power conferred by s 7(3). Section 7(3) creates a specific and limited exception to an otherwise overriding statutory exclusion of evidence of spent convictions. It is an exception that has to be applied with regard both to the letter of s 7(3) and to the overriding purpose of the Act itself. It is a matter of judgment, not discretion.

Given the limited extent to which spent convictions can be admitted under s 7(3), but the crucial importance that they may have in a relatively small number of cases, it is submitted that the preferable course would be to interpret s 114 so as not to impliedly exclude the application of s 7(3). To do so would not go against the general tenor of the 2003 Act, which is to reduce the level of discretion, for s 7(3) is not concerned with discretion. The provision is concerned with preventing injustice in the circumstances of an individual case and this may not be possible if there is a hard and fast rule, rigidly applied, that spent convictions must be disregarded in all circumstances.

## 10.5.17   Mandatory refusals

Where an applicant fails to meet any of the criteria in s 120(2)(a)–(c) as to age, licensing qualification and absence of forfeiture of a personal licence within the preceding five years (see 10.5.2 above), then the authority must refuse the licence. Section 120(3) provides:

> The authority must reject the application if it appears to it that the applicant fails to meet the condition in paragraph (a), (b) or (c) of subsection (2).

Mandatory refusal does not apply if an applicant fails to meet the criteria in s 120(2)(d), that being that he has not been convicted of any relevant offence or any foreign offence. If the above three criteria are met, but this one is not, then the authority must give the police a notice to this effect. Section 120(4) provides:

> If it appears to the authority that the applicant meets the conditions in paragraphs (a), (b) and (c) of that subsection but fails to meet the condition in paragraph (d) of that

subsection, the authority must give the chief officer of police for its area a notice to that effect.

This will then give the police an opportunity to object to the application on the ground that to grant it might undermine the crime prevention objective.

## 10.5.18 Discretionary grants

10.5.19 The licensing authority has a discretion whether or not to grant the personal licence only if an objection is received from the police. Once the police have received a notice from the authority that the applicant has a conviction for a relevant offence or foreign offence, they have 14 days within which to give the authority an objection notice. If a foreign offence is involved, it has to be one that the police consider is comparable to a relevant offence. The police can object only if they are satisfied that granting the licence would undermine the crime prevention objective and reasons why this would be the case must be given. Section 120(5) provides:

> Where, having regard to–
>
> (a) any conviction of the applicant for a relevant offence, and
>
> (b) any conviction of his for a foreign offence which the chief officer of police considers to be comparable to a relevant offence,
>
> the chief officer of police is satisfied that granting the licence would undermine the crime prevention objective, he must, within the period of 14 days beginning with the day he received the notice under subsection (4), give the authority notice stating the reasons why he is so satisfied ("an objection notice").

10.5.20 If there is no objection within the 14-day period, or if any objection is withdrawn, the licence must be granted. Section 120(6) provides:

> Where no objection notice is given within that period (or the notice is withdrawn), the authority must grant the application.

On the wording of the section it would appear that if an objection notice is received outside the period, the authority must nevertheless grant the licence, irrespective of the merits of the objection. However, to do so might conflict with the authority's duty under s 4(1) to carry out its functions under the Act with a view to promoting the licensing objectives, one of which under s 4(2)(a) is the prevention of crime and disorder (see 4.1.1 above). If the authority shares the police's view that granting the licence will undermine the crime prevention objective, but grants the application because the objection is given outside the required period, it will not be complying with its duty in s 4(1). Conversely, if it does not grant the licence in order to comply with its duty under s 4(1), it will be failing to comply with the requirement in s 120(6). Both s 4(1) and s 120(6) are expressed in mandatory terms and there cannot be compliance with both. Priority will have to be accorded to one and the other will need to be read subject to it. One view would be that, as s 4(1) is only a general provision, whereas s 120(6) is dealing with a specific matter, the specific should be accorded priority. This would be in keeping with general principles of statutory construction, with s 4(1) having application insofar as the Act permits it to do so. A contrary view would be that promotion of the licensing objectives is of overriding importance and other provisions in the Act should be read subject to it. In this instance, it is submitted that the latter view is to be preferred. The requirement in s 120(6), unlike s 4(1), is one of form rather than substance and the provision in s 120(6) should be read subject to s 4(1). If the objection is late, but the authority considers it has substance, it should hold a hearing, in the same way as if the objection is within the required period, to decide whether or not to grant the licence.[32]

10.5.21 Where an objection notice is received from the police (either within or outside the required period, if the view advocated above is correct), the authority must, under reg 5 and para 12 of Sched 1 to the Licensing Act 2003 (Hearings) Regulations 2005, SI 2005/44 (LA 2003 (Hearings) Regs 2005), hold a hearing within 20 working days to consider the application (unless the parties consider it unnecessary). Under reg 6(4), and para 12 of Sched 2, notice of the hearing must be given to the applicant and the police no later than 10 working days before the day or the first day on which the hearing is to be held.[33] Then, having regard to the objection notice, the authority must reject the application if it considers it necessary to promote the crime prevention objective and or otherwise grant it. Section 120(7) provides:

> In any other case, the authority–
> (a) must hold a hearing to consider the objection notice, unless the applicant, the chief officer of police and the authority agree that it is unnecessary, and
> (b) having regard to the notice, must–
>   (i) reject the application if it considers it necessary for the promotion of the crime prevention objective to do so, and
>   (ii) grant the application in any other case.

There is no provision in the Act or any indication in Explanatory Notes 197–200 to s 120 or in the Guidance that the giving of objection notices, or the rejection of applications having regard to them, should be confined to exceptional circumstances.[34] Indeed, once an objection notice is given, the position is quite the reverse and the expectation is that the licensing committee *will* reject the application. Paragraph 4.9 of the Guidance states: 'The Secretary of State recommends that, where the police have issued an objection notice, the licensing authority should normally refuse the application unless there are exceptional and compelling circumstances which justify granting it'.[35]

## 10.6  DETERMINATION OF RENEWAL APPLICATIONS FOR PERSONAL LICENCES

10.6.1  The provisions of s 121, which govern the determination of renewal applications, apply where the authority has received an application made in accordance with s 117 (s 121(1)). These provisions relate only to cases where it appears to the authority that the applicant has been convicted of a relevant offence or foreign offence in the period since the licence was granted or last renewed. It seems implicit from the section, although there is no express provision to this effect, that in the absence of convictions the authority must grant the renewal application.[36] Where it appears there are convictions, the authority must give notice to the police, who, if satisfied that renewal of the licence would undermine the crime prevention objective, must give an objection notice to the authority within 14 days, stating their reasons. Section 121(2) and (3) provides:

(2) If it appears to the authority that the applicant has been convicted of any relevant offence or foreign offence since the relevant time,[37] the relevant licensing authority must give notice to that effect to the chief officer of police for its area.

(3) Where, having regard to–

(a) any conviction of the applicant for a relevant offence, and

(b) any conviction of his for a foreign offence which the chief officer of police considers to be comparable to a relevant offence,

the chief officer of police is satisfied that renewing the licence would undermine the crime prevention objective, he must, within the period of 14 days beginning with the day he received the notice under subsection (2), give the authority a notice stating the reasons why he is so satisfied ("an objection notice").

10.6.2 In deciding whether to give an objection notice, the police are not confined to considering convictions incurred in the period since the licence was granted or last renewed. Any convictions incurred either before or after this period can also be taken into account.[38] Section 121(4) provides:

For the purposes of subsection (3)(a) and (b) it is irrelevant whether the conviction occurred before or after the relevant time.

If the police decide not to give an objection notice, the authority must renew the licence and, if a notice is given, a hearing must, under reg 5 and para 13 of Sched 1 to the LA 2003 (Hearings) Regs 2005, be held within 20 working days (unless the parties agree this is unnecessary) to determine the application. Under reg 6(4), and para 13 of Sched 2, notice of the hearing must be given to the applicant and the police no later than 10 working days before the day or the first day on which the hearing is to be held.[39] When considering the application, the authority must reject it if it considers it necessary for the promotion of the crime prevention objective and, if not necessary for that objective, grant it. Section 121(5) and (6) provides:

(5) Where no objection notice is given within that period (or any such notice is withdrawn), the authority must grant the application.

(6) In any other case, the authority–

(a) must hold a hearing to consider the objection notice unless the applicant, the chief officer of police and the authority agree that it is unnecessary, and

(b) having regard to the notice, must–

(i) reject the application if it considers it necessary for the promotion of the crime prevention objective to do so, and

(ii) grant the application in any other case.

Where a renewal application has been made, the existing licence will remain in effect, even if its expiry date has passed, until the application has been determined or withdrawn. Section 119 provides:

(1) Where–

(a) an application for renewal is made in accordance with section 117, and

(b) the application has not been determined before the time the licence would, in the absence of this section, expire,

then, by virtue of this section, the licence continues to have effect for the period beginning with that time and ending with the determination or withdrawal of the application.

(2)  Subsection (1) is subject to section 115(3) and (4) (revocation, forfeiture and suspension) and section 116 (surrender).

## 10.7   NOTIFICATION OF GRANT OR REFUSAL AND ISSUING OF THE PERSONAL LICENCE

10.7.1   When an application for the grant or renewal of a personal licence is determined, the licensing authority is required to notify its decision to the applicant and the police.[40] If the licence is granted and the police objected, the notification must include a statement of the authority's reasons for granting the licence. Similarly, if the licence is refused, notification must be given stating the reasons for rejection of the application. Section 122 provides:

(1)  Where a licensing authority grants an application–
   (a)  it must give the applicant and the chief officer of police for its area a notice to that effect, and
   (b)  if the chief officer of police gave an objection notice (which was not withdrawn), the notice under paragraph (a) must contain a statement of the licensing authority's reasons for granting the application.
(2)  A licensing authority which rejects an application must give the applicant and the chief officer of police for its area a notice to that effect containing a statement of the authority's reasons for rejecting the application.
(3)  In this section–
   "application" means an application for the grant or renewal of a personal licence; and
   "objection notice" has the meaning given in section 120 or 121, as the case may be.

On the wording of s 122(1)(a), the giving of notice to the police seems to be required in all cases, even in ones where the requirements for a mandatory grant under s 120(2) are satisfied, although in such a case the police are involved (through notification of convictions and the opportunity to object) in the application process.

10.7.2   Where granted, the licence must be issued forthwith,[41] specify the holder's name and address and the issuing licensing authority, and be in a form prescribed by regulations. Section 125 provides:

(1)  Where a licensing authority grants a personal licence, it must forthwith issue the applicant with the licence.
(2)  The licence must–
   (a)  specify the holder's name and address, and
   (b)  identify the licensing authority which granted it.
(3)  It must also contain a record of each relevant offence and each foreign offence of which the holder has been convicted, the date of each conviction and the sentence imposed in respect of it.
(4)  Subject to subsections (2) and (3), the licence must be in the prescribed form.

Regulation 5(1) of the LA 2003 (Personal Licences) Regs 2005 prescribes the form of the personal licence and requires it to be a physical document in two separate parts. The first part, which must be in durable form and of a size no larger than 70mm × 100mm, requires inclusion of the matters referred to in s 125(2), a photograph of the holder, a number allocated by the licensing authority and unique to the licence, an identifier for the licensing authority granting the licence and the date of the expiry of the licence. The second part requires inclusion of the matters referred to in s 125(3) of the Act and the matters referred to in the first part, except for the photograph of the holder. Regulation 5(1) provides:

> A personal licence shall be in the form of a physical document in two separate parts and shall contain–
>
> (a)  in the first part, the matters referred to in section 125(2) of the Act, a photograph of the holder, a number allocated by the licensing authority that is unique to the licence, an identifier for the licensing authority granting the licence and the date of the expiry of the licence and this part shall be produced in durable form and shall be of a size no larger than 70mm × 100mm, and
>
> (b)  in the second part, the matters referred to in section 125(3) of the Act and the matters referred to in (a) except that the photograph of the holder shall be omitted.

In the event that the licence is lost, stolen, damaged or destroyed, s 126 enables the licence holder to obtain a copy, in the same form as it existed immediately before it was lost, stolen, damaged or destroyed, on payment of a fee (which under reg 8 and Sched 6 to the LA 2003 (Fees) Regs 2005 is £10.50):

(1)  Where a personal licence is lost, stolen, damaged or destroyed, the holder of the licence may apply to the relevant licensing authority for a copy of the licence.

(2)  Subsection (1) is subject to regulations under section 133(2) (power to prescribe fee to accompany application).

(3)  Where the relevant licensing authority receives an application under this section, it must issue the licence holder with a copy of the licence (certified by the authority to be a true copy) if it is satisfied that–

   (a)  the licence has been lost, stolen, damaged or destroyed, and

   (b)  where it has been lost or stolen, the holder of the licence has reported the loss or theft to the police.

(4)  The copy issued under this section must be a copy of the licence in the form in which it existed immediately before it was lost, stolen, damaged or destroyed.

(5)  This Act applies in relation to a copy issued under this section as it applies in relation to an original licence.

The section does not, however, place any requirement on the licence holder to return to the licensing authority the licence that is lost or stolen should it come back into his possession, although it might have been expected that such a provision would have been included.

## 10.8  CONVICTIONS INCURRED DURING THE APPLICATION PERIOD

10.8.1  Sections 123 and 124 make provision where convictions for a relevant offence or a foreign offence are incurred during the application period, that is, the period beginning when the application is made and ending when it is determined or withdrawn. The former section requires an applicant to disclose such convictions to the authority and the latter makes provision for revocation of the licence by the authority. Section 123 provides that an applicant convicted of a relevant offence or foreign offence during the application period must notify the authority as soon as is reasonably practicable and a failure to do so is a summary offence punishable by a fine not exceeding level 4 on the standard scale:

(1) Where an applicant for the grant or renewal of a personal licence is convicted of a relevant offence or a foreign offence during the application period, he must as soon as reasonably practicable notify the conviction to the authority to which the application is made.

(2) A person commits an offence if he fails, without reasonable excuse, to comply with subsection (1).

(3) A person guilty of an offence under this section is liable on summary conviction to a fine not exceeding level 4 on the standard scale.

(4) In this section "the application period" means the period that–

    (a) begins when the application for grant or renewal is made, and

    (b) ends when the application is determined or withdrawn.

10.8.2 Where the authority becomes aware of such a conviction, whether through disclosure by the applicant under s 123(1) or notification by a court under s 131 or by the licence holder under s 132 (see 10.9.12 below), s 124 requires the police to be notified to give them an opportunity to object on the ground that continuation of the licence would undermine the crime prevention objective. The police have 14 days within which to object and, if they do, the authority must, under reg 5 and para 14 of Sched 1 to the LA 2003 (Hearings) Regs 2005, hold a hearing within 20 working days to determine whether or not to revoke the licence. This is unless the parties agree this is unnecessary. Under reg 6(4) and para 14 of Sched 2, notice of the hearing must be given to the licence holder and the police no later than 10 working days before the day or the first day on which the hearing is to be held.[42] If the authority considers it necessary for the promotion of the crime prevention objective to revoke the licence, it must do so. Section 124(1)–(4) provides:

(1) This section applies where, after a licensing authority has granted or renewed a personal licence, it becomes aware (whether by virtue of section 123(1), 131 or 132 or otherwise) that the holder of a personal licence ("the offender") was convicted during the application period[43] of any relevant offence or foreign offence.

(2) The licensing authority must give a notice to that effect to the chief officer of police for its area.

(3) Where, having regard to–

    (a) any conviction of the applicant for a relevant offence, and

    (b) any conviction of his for a foreign offence which the chief officer of police considers to be comparable to a relevant offence,

which occurred before the end of the application period, the chief officer of police is satisfied that continuation of the licence would undermine the crime prevention objective, he must, within the period of 14 days beginning with the day he received the notice under subsection (2), give the authority a notice stating the reasons why he is so satisfied ("an objection notice").

(4) Where an objection notice is given within that period (and not withdrawn), the authority–

    (a) must hold a hearing to consider the objection notice, unless the holder of the licence, the chief officer of police and the authority agree it is unnecessary, and

(b)  having regard to the notice, must revoke the licence if it considers it necessary for the promotion of the crime prevention objective to do so.

10.8.3  Once a decision is reached, the authority must notify the offender and the police of its decision and its reasons.[44] The decision does not, however, have effect whilst an appeal can be made or is outstanding, so, even if revoked, the licence will be deemed to remain in force pending appeal. Section 124(5) and (6) provides:

(5)  Where the authority revokes or decides not to revoke a licence under subsection (4) it must notify the offender and the chief officer of police of the decision and its reasons for making it.

(6)  A decision under this section does not have effect–

(a)  until the end of the period given for appealing against the decision, or

(b)  if the decision is appealed against, until the appeal is disposed of.

## 10.9  CONVICTIONS DURING THE CURRENCY OF THE LICENCE

### 10.9.1 Introduction

Where a personal licence holder is charged with a relevant offence, he must under s 128 notify the court that he is the holder of a personal licence. This is to enable the court to decide, in the event of a conviction, whether to exercise its powers under s 129 to order forfeiture or suspension of the licence. If an order is made it may have immediate effect, although the court has power under s 130 to suspend its operation pending an appeal. The court must under s 131 also notify the licensing authority of the conviction and the Guidance in para 4.30 provides that, on receipt of such a notification, the authority should contact the holder and request his licence so that the necessary action can be taken.[45] On receipt of the licence, the details of the conviction should be recorded in the authority's records and endorsed on the licence, as should any period of suspension if so ordered. The licence should then be returned to the holder. If the licence is declared forfeit, it should be retained by the licensing authority.

Although the authority will become aware of convictions for relevant offences when notified by the court, this will only occur if the court is aware of the existence of the personal licence. There may be cases where the court is not so aware and, to ensure that the authority knows of the convictions, s 132 imposes a duty on the licence holder to notify the authority of them. The duty under s 132 also extends to notifying the authority of convictions for any foreign offence for which the personal licence holder is convicted, since unless these are disclosed, the authority is unlikely to become aware of their existence.

### 10.9.2 Notifying the court that a personal licence is held

10.9.3  A personal licence holder charged with a relevant offence must, by the time of his first court appearance, produce his licence or, if unable to do so, give reasons to the court and notify the court of the relevant licensing authority that issued the licence. Section 128(1) provides:

Where the holder of a personal licence is charged with a relevant offence, he must, no later than the time he makes his first appearance in a magistrates' court in connection with that offence–

(a) produce to the court the personal licence, or

(b) if that is not practicable, notify the court of the existence of the personal licence and the identity of the relevant licensing authority and of the reasons why he cannot produce the licence.

Section 128(2) and (3) make similar provision where a person is granted a personal licence in the period between his first court appearance and the conclusion of his trial or, if an appeal is made, the disposal of the appeal. In such circumstances, the person must comply when he next appears in court. Section 128(2) and (3) provides:

(2) Subsection (3) applies where a person charged with a relevant offence is granted a personal licence–

(a) after his first appearance in a magistrates' court in connection with that offence, but

(b) before–

(i) his conviction, and sentencing for the offence, or his acquittal, or,

(ii) where an appeal is brought against his conviction, sentence or acquittal, the disposal of that appeal.

(3) At his next appearance in court in connection with that offence, that person must–

(a) produce to the court the personal licence, or

(b) if that is not practicable, notify the court of the existence of the personal licence and the identity of the relevant licensing authority and of the reasons why he cannot produce the licence.

10.9.4 If, after having first produced the licence (or after having explained why he cannot), the licence is surrendered, revoked or renewed, or there is a licence renewal application (made or withdrawn), in the interim period up to the conclusion of the trial, the personal licence holder is under a duty to notify the court at his next court appearance. Section 128(4) and (5) provides:

(4) Where–

(a) a person charged with a relevant offence has produced his licence to, or notified, a court under subsection (1) or (3), and

(b) before he is convicted of and sentenced for, or acquitted of, that offence, a notifiable event occurs in respect of the licence,

he must, at his next appearance in court in connection with that offence, notify the court of that event.

(5) For this purpose a "notifiable event" in relation to a personal licence means any of the following–

(a) the making or withdrawal of an application for renewal of the licence;

(b) the surrender of the licence under section 116;

(c) the renewal of the licence under section 121;

(d) the revocation of the licence under section 124.

Failure to comply with the duty without reasonable excuse is a criminal offence, for which the penalty is a level 2 fine on the standard scale. Section 128(6) and (7) provides:

(6) A person commits an offence if he fails, without reasonable excuse, to comply with this section.

(7) A person guilty of an offence under subsection (6) is liable on summary conviction to a fine not exceeding level 2 on the standard scale.

A reasonable excuse for not producing the licence might arise in cases where it was not practicable for the licence holder to produce the licence and he notified the court of its existence (under s 128(1)(b)) by a letter sent by post, but the letter was not delivered to the court.

### 10.9.5 Forfeiture or suspension of the licence on conviction for relevant offence

10.9.6 Where a personal licence holder is convicted of a relevant offence, the court has power under s 129 to make an order for forfeiture of the licence or suspension for a period of up to six months. Section 129(1) and (2) provides:

(1) This section applies where the holder of a personal licence is convicted of a relevant offence by or before a court in England and Wales.

(2) The court may–

   (a) order the forfeiture of the licence, or

   (b) order its suspension for a period not exceeding six months.

Presumably if the court feels a six months' suspension period is inadequate the appropriate course would be to order forfeiture of the licence.

The court, when deciding whether to make an order, is not confined to considering the relevant offence for which the licence holder was convicted, but can take into account any previous conviction for a relevant offence.[46] If an order is made, it will have immediate effect, unless the court suspends the order pending an appeal against it, in which case the licence will continue in force. Section 129(3)–(5) provides:

(3) In determining whether to make an order under subsection (2), the court may take account of any previous conviction of the holder for a relevant offence.

(4) Where a court makes an order under this section it may suspend the order pending an appeal against it.

(5) Subject to subsection (4) and section 130, an order under this section takes effect immediately after it is made.

10.9.7 Orders made under s 129 can be suspended by the court where the licence holder appeals against his conviction or sentence to the Crown Court (if the case was heard in the magistrates' court) or if there is a subsequent appeal, or application for leave to appeal, to the Court of Appeal and/or the House of Lords. In the case of appeals to the Crown Court and the Court of Appeal, it is these courts, that is the court to which the appeal is made, which have the power to suspend the order. In the case of appeals to the House of Lords, it is the court from which the appeal is made that has the power, that is the High Court (in cases where there can be an appeal direct to the House of Lords)[47] or Court of Appeal. Section 130(1)–(4) provides:

(1) This section applies where–

   (a) a person ("the offender") is convicted of a relevant offence, and

(b)  an order is made under section 129 in respect of that conviction ("the section 129 order").

(2)  In this section any reference to the offender's sentence includes a reference to the section 129 order and to any other order made on his conviction and, accordingly, any reference to an appeal against his sentence includes a reference to an appeal against any order forming part of his sentence.

(3)  Where the offender–

(a)  appeals to the Crown Court, or

(b)  appeals or applies for leave to appeal to the Court of Appeal,

against his conviction or his sentence, the Crown Court or, as the case may be, the Court of Appeal may suspend the section 129 order.

(4)  Where the offender appeals or applies for leave to appeal to the House of Lords–

(a)  under section 1 of the Administration of Justice Act 1960 (c.65) from any decision of the High Court which is material to his conviction or sentence, or

(b)  under section 33 of the Criminal Appeal Act 1968 (c.19) from any decision of the Court of Appeal which is material to his conviction or sentence,

the High Court or, as the case may require, the Court of Appeal may suspend the section 129 order.

10.9.8  Suspension is not confined to appeals against conviction or sentence, but also extends to appeals by case stated to the High Court and applications to the High Court for a quashing order.[48] In both cases, it is the High Court that has the power to suspend the order. Section 130(5) and (6) provides:

(5)  Where the offender makes an application in respect of the decision of the court in question under section 111 of the Magistrates' Courts Act 1980 (c.43) (statement of case by magistrates' court) or section 28 of the Supreme Court Act 1981 (c.54) (statement of case by Crown Court) the High Court may suspend the section 129 order.

(6)  Where the offender–

(a)  applies to the High Court for a quashing order to remove into the High Court any proceedings of a magistrates' court or of the Crown Court, being proceedings in or in consequence of which he was convicted or his sentence was passed, or

(b)  applies to the High Court for permission to make such an application,

the High Court may suspend the section 129 order.

If the court decides to suspend the order, it can do so on such terms as it thinks fit and must notify the licensing authority of the suspension. Suspension of the order will allow the licence holder to continue trading during the period of suspension either by reinstating the licence where the order is for its forfeiture or permitting it to remain in force where the order is for its suspension. Section 130(7)–(9) provides:

(7)  Any power of a court under this section to suspend the section 129 order is a power to do so on such terms as the court thinks fit.

(8)  Where, by virtue of this section, a court suspends the section 129 order it must send notice of the suspension to the relevant licensing authority.

(9)  Where the section 129 order is an order for forfeiture of the licence, an order under this section to suspend that order has effect to reinstate the licence for the period of the suspension.

## 10.9.9 Court's duty to notify licensing authority of convictions

10.9.10 Where a personal licence holder is convicted of a relevant offence and the court is aware that he holds a personal licence, it must notify the licensing authority, through the appropriate court officer, of the person's name and address, the nature and date of the conviction and details of any sentence passed. The court must also send a copy of the notice to the person himself. Section 131(1) and (2) provides:

> (1) This section applies where a person who holds a personal licence ("the relevant person") is convicted, by or before a court in England and Wales, of a relevant offence in a case where–
>
>   (a) the relevant person has given notice under section 128 (notification of personal licence), or
>
>   (b) the court is, for any other reason, aware of the existence of that personal licence.
>
> (2) The appropriate officer[49] of the court must (as soon as reasonably practicable)–
>
>   (a) send to the relevant licensing authority a notice specifying–
>
>     (i) the name and address of the relevant person,
>
>     (ii) the nature and date of the conviction, and
>
>     (iii) any sentence passed in respect of it, including any order made under section 129, and
>
>   (b) send a copy of the notice to the relevant person.

On receiving notification, the licensing authority should request that the licence holder return the licence so that details of the conviction can be recorded and endorsed on the licence (Guidance, para 4.30).

10.9.11 In cases where there is an appeal and the conviction is quashed or the sentence altered, the appeal court must notify the licensing authority of the outcome and also send a copy of the notice to the person himself. Similar action must be taken by the Court of Appeal in cases where it takes action in relation to a sentence it regards as unduly lenient on references to it under s 36 of the Criminal Justice Act 1988. Section 131(3) and (4) provides:

> (3) Where, on an appeal against the relevant person's conviction for the relevant offence or against the sentence imposed on him for that offence, his conviction is quashed or a new sentence is substituted for that sentence, the court which determines the appeal must (as soon as reasonably practicable) arrange–
>
>   (a) for notice of the quashing of the conviction or the substituting of the sentence to be sent to the relevant licensing authority, and
>
>   (b) for a copy of the notice to be sent to the relevant person.
>
> (4) Where the case is referred to the Court of Appeal under section 36 of the Criminal Justice Act 1988 (c.33) (review of lenient sentence), the court must cause–
>
>   (a) notice of any action it takes under subsection (1) of that section to be sent to the relevant licensing authority, and
>
>   (b) a copy of the notice to be sent to the relevant person.

## 10.9.12    Licence holder's duty to notify licensing authority of convictions

The licence holder will be aware of convictions notified by the court to the licensing authority under s 131 as he will have received a copy of the notice containing details of convictions sent by the court to the authority, but in other cases the onus is upon the licence holder, under s 132, to notify the licensing authority. This will be the case with convictions for relevant offences where the court was not aware of the existence of the licence and convictions for foreign offences of which the licensing authority will otherwise be unaware. The licence holder must, as soon as reasonably practicable after the conviction, give to the authority a notice containing details of the conviction, any sentence imposed and the outcome of any appeal. He must also return with the notice his personal licence or give reasons why it is not practicable to do so. Section 132(1)–(3) provides:

> (1) Subsection (2) applies where the holder of a personal licence–
>   (a) is convicted of a relevant offence, in a case where section 131(1) does not apply, or
>   (b) is convicted of a foreign offence.
> (2) The holder must–
>   (a) as soon as reasonably practicable after the conviction, give the relevant licensing authority a notice containing details of the nature and date of the conviction, and any sentence imposed on him in respect of it, and
>   (b) as soon as reasonably practicable after the determination of any appeal against the conviction or sentence, or of any reference under section 36 of the Criminal Justice Act 1988 (c.33) in respect of the case, give the relevant licensing authority a notice containing details of the determination.
> (3) A notice under subsection (2) must be accompanied by the personal licence or, if that is not practicable, a statement of the reasons for the failure to provide the licence.

Failure to comply, without reasonable excuse, is a summary offence punishable by a level 2 fine. Section 132(4) and (5) provides:

> (4) A person commits an offence if he fails, without reasonable excuse, to comply with this section.
> (5) A person guilty of an offence under subsection (4) is liable on summary conviction to a fine not exceeding level 2 on the standard scale.

Where a licence holder complies with the duty to notify the licensing authority, there seem to be limited sanctions available to the authority even where the relevant offence or foreign offence is a particularly serious one, for example, rape or grievous bodily harm. The licensing authority can request return of the licence for details of the conviction to be recorded and endorsed on the licence, but has no power to revoke or suspend the licence. Only a court, following conviction for a relevant offence, can make an order for revocation or suspension under s 129 (see 10.9.5–10.9.8 above). The licensing authority can, when the licence is due for renewal, notify the police of the licence holder's conviction(s) for a relevant offence and/or foreign offence and, if an objection notice is given by the police on the ground that renewing the licence would undermine the crime prevention objective, the authority can refuse to renew the licence if it considers it necessary to promote the crime prevention objective (see 10.6 above). However, as personal licences require renewal only after a 10-year period (see 10.10.1 below), renewal of the licence may be some years away, by which time it is possible that the conviction(s) might in any event have become spent and may not be able to be taken into account (see 10.5.14–10.5.16 above). It is possible that a prosecution might be brought against the licence holder, under s 132, for failing to notify the court that he holds a personal licence (see 10.9.2–10.9.4 above) and, if a conviction is secured, the court might then order forfeiture or suspension of the licence.[50] This is nevertheless dependent on securing a conviction, something which might not occur if the licence holder had a reasonable excuse for the court not being aware that he held a personal licence, for example, if he had notified the court by post and the letter had not been delivered (see 10.9.4 above). It seems surprising that no power of revocation or suspension is conferred on the licensing authority in cases where it is notified by the licence holder of convictions under s 132. Given that a licensing authority can revoke or suspend a premises licences and a CPC following a review of the licence or certificate, there seems no obvious reason why it should not be able to revoke or suspend a personal licence and it is difficult to resist the conclusion that the absence of such a power is the result of an oversight.

## 10.10  DURATION OF PERSONAL LICENCE

### 10.10.1  Ten-year duration

A personal licence, once granted, will generally remain in force for 10 years (although it also will continue in force pending renewal or disposal of an appeal) and is renewable at intervals of 10 years. The circumstances in which it will not do so are when it is surrendered, revoked, suspended or forfeited. Section 115 provides:

(1) A personal licence–
   (a) has effect for an initial period of ten years beginning with the date on which it is granted, and
   (b) may be renewed in accordance with this Part for further periods of ten years at a time.
(2) Subsection (1) is subject to subsections (3) and (4) and to–
   (a) section 116 (surrender),
   (b) section 119 (continuation of licence pending renewal), and
   (c) paragraph 17 of Schedule 5 (continuation of licence pending disposal of appeal).
(3) A personal licence ceases to have effect when it is revoked under section 124 or forfeited under section 129.
(4) And a personal licence does not have effect during any period when it is suspended under section 129.
(5) Subsections (3) and (4) are subject to any court order under sections 129(4) or 130.

### 10.10.2  Exceptions: surrender, revocation, suspension and forfeiture

Provision for surrender of a personal licence is made by s 116, which provides:

(1) Where the holder of a personal licence wishes to surrender his licence he may give the relevant licensing authority a notice to that effect.

(2) The notice must be accompanied by the personal licence or, if that is not practicable, by a statement of the reasons for the failure to provide the licence.

(3) Where a notice of surrender is given in accordance with this section, the personal licence lapses on receipt of the notice by the authority.

No provision is made for notification of anyone other than the licensing authority, although surrender of a personal licence may have serious repercussions for other persons, notably the premises licence holder, for example, if a DPS were to surrender his personal licence without the knowledge of the premises licence holder and sales of alcohol were to continue, there would be a breach of the mandatory condition attached to the premises licence that no supply of alcohol can be made at a time when the DPS does not hold a personal licence.[51] Nevertheless, it is open to the premises licence holder, under s 178, as a person with a 'property interest' in the premises, to give notice of his interest to the licensing authority as a result of which he will be notified if a 'change relating to the premises' is made in the licensing register (see 2.4.7–2.4.9 above). Since the post of DPS is linked to particular premises for which there is a premises licence, surrender by the DPS of his licence could be regarded as a 'change relating to the premises'. The premises licence holder will, however, be notified only if he has, under s 178, given notice (which is renewable annually) to the licensing authority of his interest and the notice still has effect. Further, notification may occur at some point after the surrender of the licence has taken effect. Under s 116(3), the personal licence lapses on receipt by the authority of the notice of surrender, but, until a change recording surrender is made to the register (and this may not be done immediately), there is no obligation on the authority under s 178 to notify the premises licence holder.

Revocation of the licence might occur where the authority becomes aware of convictions incurred by the licence holder during the application period and considers that, following a police objection, revocation is necessary for the promotion of the crime prevention objective (see s 124(4)(b) and 10.8.2 above). It seems that revocation by the authority is confined to these circumstances.

Suspension or forfeiture of a licence can be ordered only by a court where a personal licence holder is convicted of a relevant offence (see 10.9.5–10.9.8 above). There is no power available to the authority to suspend the licence or require its forfeiture.

## 10.11 UPDATING AND PRODUCTION OF PERSONAL LICENCE

### 10.11.1 Updating of licence

10.11.2 Once a licence has been granted, the holder of the licence is under a duty to notify the licensing authority of any change in his name or address. The notice given must be accompanied by the appropriate fee, which under under reg 8 and Sched 6 to the LA 2003 (Fees) Regs 2005 is £10.50, and the licence for the changes to be recorded on it. (A duty to update the licensing document is imposed on the licensing authority by s 134 – see 10.11.3 below.) Section 127(1)–(3) provides:

(1) The holder of a personal licence must, as soon as reasonably practicable, notify the relevant licensing authority of any change in his name or address as stated in the personal licence.

(2) Subsection (1) is subject to regulations under section 133(2) (power to prescribe fee to accompany notice).

(3) A notice under subsection (1) must also be accompanied by the personal licence or, if that is not practicable, by a statement of the reasons for the failure to provide the licence.

Failure to comply with the duty without reasonable excuse is a criminal offence, for which the penalty is a level 2 fine on the standard scale. Section 127(4) and (5) provides:

(4) A person commits an offence if he fails, without reasonable excuse, to comply with this section.

(5) A person guilty of an offence under subsection (4) is liable on summary conviction to a fine not exceeding level 2 on the standard scale.

10.11.3 The licensing authority itself is under a duty to update the licence where it renews or revokes it; where it is notified by a licence applicant that he has been convicted of a relevant offence or foreign offence, or that he has changed his name or address; where it is notified by a court that the licence holder has been convicted of a relevant offence; and where it is notified by the licence holder himself that he has been so convicted. It must similarly update the licence following the disposal of any appeal that has been made in respect of a personal licence. Section 134(1) provides:

Where–

(a) the relevant licensing authority makes a determination under section 121 or 124(4),

(b) it receives a notice under section 123(1), 127, 131 or 132, or

(c) an appeal against a decision under this Part is disposed of,

in relation to a personal licence, the authority must make the appropriate amendments (if any) to the licence.

If, on conviction of the licence holder for a relevant offence, the court makes an order under s 129 for the forfeiture or suspension of the licence, the licensing authority must make an endorsement on the licence indicating the terms of the forfeiture or suspension. This endorsement must, however, be cancelled in the event of an appeal leading to the quashing of the forfeiture or suspension order. Section 134(2) and (3) provides:

(2) Where, under section 131, notice is given of the making of an order under section 129, the relevant licensing authority must make an endorsement on the licence stating the terms of the order.

(3) Where, under section 131, notice is given of the quashing of such an order, any endorsement previously made under subsection (2) in respect of it must be cancelled.

In order to update the licence, the licensing authority can require the licence holder to produce it to the authority within 14 days of being notified and failure on the part of the licence holder to do so, without reasonable excuse, is a summary offence punishable with a fine not exceeding level 2 on the standard scale. Section 134(4)–(6) provides:

(4) Where a licensing authority is not in possession of a personal licence, it may, for the purposes of discharging its obligations under this section, require the holder of the licence to produce it to the authority within 14 days beginning with the day on which he is notified of the requirement.

(5) A person commits an offence if he fails, without reasonable excuse, to comply with a requirement under subsection (4).

(6) A person guilty of an offence under subsection (5) is liable on summary conviction to a fine not exceeding level 2 on the standard scale.

Notification to the personal licence holder to produce the licence will be in accordance with the provision in s 184(3). Thus, notice can be given to him by delivering it to him or by leaving it at his proper address, or by sending it by post to him at that address (see 2.5.4 above), although if notice is given by the last mentioned method, the licence holder will in fact have less than 14 days within which to produce the licence. As the requirement in s 134(4) is for the licence holder to 'produce' the licence to the authority where it is not in the authority's possession, the requirement would not seem to be met until the authority has actually acquired possession of it. If the licence were to be sent by the post to the licensing authority, but not arrive, the licence holder has arguably failed to 'produce' it to the authority as required by s 134(4), although he may, under s 134(5), have a reasonable excuse for failing to comply with this requirement.

## 10.11.4  Production of licence

Where a personal licence holder is on premises making or authorising the supply of alcohol under a premises licence or TEN, a constable or authorised officer (on production on request of authorisation) can require him to produce the licence for examination. Section 135(1)–(3) provides:

(1) This section applies where the holder of a personal licence is on premises to make or authorise the supply of alcohol, and such supplies–

  (a) are authorised by a premises licence in respect of those premises, or

  (b) are a permitted temporary activity on the premises by virtue of a temporary event notice given under Part 5 in respect of which he is the premises user.

(2) Any constable or authorised officer[52] may require the holder of the personal licence to produce that licence for examination.

(3) An authorised officer exercising the power conferred by subsection (2) must, if so requested, produce evidence of his authority to exercise the power.

A failure to produce the licence, without reasonable excuse, is a summary offence punishable by a fine not exceeding level 2 on the standard scale. Section 135(4) and (5) provides:

(4) A person who fails, without reasonable excuse, to comply with a requirement under subsection (2) is guilty of an offence.

(5) A person guilty of an offence under subsection (4) is liable on summary conviction to a fine not exceeding level 2 on the standard scale.

## NOTES

1  Not every person selling or supplying alcohol needs to hold a personal licence, but every sale or supply of alcohol must be at least authorised by such a licence holder (Guidance, para 4.2).

2  Guidance, para 4.4.

3 Section 112 provides: 'For the purposes of this Part the "relevant licensing authority", in relation to a personal licence, is the licensing authority which granted the licence.'

4 The personal licence has effect for an initial period of 10 years and is thereafter renewable for further periods of 10 years – see s 115(1) and, for determination of renewal applications, 10.6 below.

5 Guidance, para 4.15. The requirements for notification of change of name and address are contained in s 127, and for convictions in ss 123 and 131–32 – see 10.11.2 below, and 10.8 and 10.9 below, respectively. The Guidance goes on to provide: 'Licensing authorities should maintain easily accessible records and a service which can advise the police in any area and other licensing authorities promptly of any details they require about the holder of the personal licence in relation to their licensing functions' (para 4.16).

6 Notices relate to various matters such as notifying the licensing authority of changes of name and address or convictions incurred – see 10.11.2 below, and 10.8 and 10.9 below, respectively.

7 Applications under s 126 are ones for a replacement licence where the original has been lost, stolen, damaged or destroyed and notices under s 127 concern changes of name and address – see 10.7.2 and 10.11.2 below, respectively.

8 The information required includes personal details, licensing qualification (if applicable), and previous and outstanding personal licence applications, along with that required by reg 7(1) – see below.

9 *Quaere* whether it will include the first-mentioned author of this work and persons who have obtained a Certificate of Higher Education in Licensing Law from the Universities of Birmingham, Warwick or Westminster, each of which is recognised by the Institute of Licensing as entitling persons to membership of the Institute.

10 This is often referred to as 'basic disclosure'.

11 If the licence expires before the application for renewal has been determined by the licensing authority, the licence continues to have effect until a decision is made – see s 119 and 10.6.2 below.

12 This might be the case, eg where an applicant suffers from physical or mental incapacity, such as paralysis or brain damage.

13 Section 120(9) provides: ' "EEA State" means a state which is a contracting party to the Agreement on the European Economic Area signed at Oporto on 2nd May 1992, as adjusted by the Protocol signed at Brussels on 17th March 1993.'

14 See http://www.culture.gov.uk/what_we_do/Alcohol_entertainment/licensing_act_2003_explained/offences.htm

15 Two other categories were also prescribed, a person operating under a licence granted by the University of Cambridge and a person operating premises under a licence granted by the Board of the Green Cloth (which licensed inns that were formerly within the private grounds of Buckingham Palace), but such persons were able to obtain a personal licence without a licensing qualification only during the transitional period up until 24 November 2005.

16 A court can order forfeiture under s 129 – see 10.9.6 below. As to what constitutes a 'relevant offence', see 10.5.6–10.5.12 below.

17 This applies only in circumstances where s 12A(2)(b) applies and the accident caused the death of any person: para 5(f).

18 There are only a few offences under the Act that are not included, such as taking a conveyance without authority (s 12), theft or robbery of mail outside the jurisdiction (s 14), and advertising rewards for the return of goods lost or stolen with no questions asked, etc (s 23).

19 The only offence under the Act which is not included is making off without payment (s 3).

20 This paragraph was inserted by Sched 1, para 34 of the Fraud Act 2006 and was originally numbered para 21, although this was a paragraph number already used for the offence in

s 46 of the Gambling Act 2005 (see above). It was subsequently renumbered as para 22 by The Licensing Act 2003 (Amendment of Schedule 4) Order 2007, SI 2007/2075.

21 For the offence of fraudulent evasion of duty under s 170, s 170(1)(a) is to be disregarded: para 9(a). Under s 170(1)(a), it is an offence if any person, with intent to defraud, knowingly acquires possession of various goods, including ones that are chargeable with a duty that has not been paid. This means that fraudulent evasion, as a relevant offence, is confined to the offence in s 170(1)(b) of knowingly being concerned in carrying, removing, depositing, harbouring, keeping or concealing or in any manner dealing with any such goods, with intent to defraud.

22 These fall broadly under fraudulent or dishonest conduct since unmarked tobacco consists of tobacco products not carrying a fiscal mark indicating that excise duty has been paid on them.

23 The offences under ss 18 and 19 relate respectively to reproduction of British currency notes and making imitation British coins.

24 A new para 18 was inserted by Art 2 of the LA2003 (Personal licence: relevant offences) (Amendment) Order 2005, SI 2005/2366, following changes introduced by the Sexual Offences Act 2003 and the Criminal Justice Act 2003. There is a wide range of sexual offences listed in Pt 2 of Sched 15 to the Criminal Justice Act 2003 and para 153 expressly includes secondary party liability and inchoate liability (which covers incitement, attempts and conspiracy) for these offences. The offences can be accessed at: http://www.opsi.gov.uk/acts/acts2003/30044-bi.htm_sch15pt2.

25 This provision, inserted into Sched 4 by Art 2 of the LA2003 (Personal licence: relevant offences) (Amendment) Order 2005, SI 2005/2366, replicates the definition previously contained in s 161(3) of the Powers of Criminal Courts (Sentencing) Act 2000. This is a wide definition that might include even common assault. A threatening act sufficient to raise in the mind of the person threatened a fear of immediate violence could be an offence that is likely to lead to physical injury to a person. Although a matter of interpretation for a court as to whether common assault falls within this definition, it appears that the Government's view is that it should be included – see Poppleston Allen, *Licensed Trade E-News*, 8 February 2005 and Annex C to the Secretary of State's Guidance, June 2007 (see Appendix 11).

26 These are the terms traditionally used to describe secondary participation.

27 The effect of the words in parentheses in s 113(3) is to exclude them and exclusion is not surprising. It is most unlikely that any such offences, as defined in Sched 4, will be offences under the law elsewhere, since the 'extent' sections in the applicable legislation will in all probability confine application to England and Wales. It is possible that in some cases application may extend to Scotland or Northern Ireland, in which case in these instances the 'relevant offence' will be an offence in either of these jurisdictions. This will enable account to be taken of it as a 'relevant offence', but it will not be a 'foreign offence' under s 113(3), because of the excluding words in parentheses.

28 It is not obvious why a conviction for any foreign offence should preclude a mandatory grant of a personal licence, whereas only a conviction for certain offences in England and Wales ('relevant offences') will do so. Perhaps it is felt that the licensing authority may not be in a position to determine whether a foreign offence is comparable to a relevant offence and that this matter is best left to the police to decide. The police will be able to do this when a notice is given and they have the opportunity to object.

29 The length of the rehabilitation period is specified in s 5 of the Act and depends on the sentence imposed. Length ranges from six months, in the case of an absolute discharge, to 10 years, in the case of a sentence of imprisonment for more than six months, but not more than 30 months. In cases where a sentence exceeds 30 months' imprisonment, the conviction cannot become spent. The 1974 Act applies both to convictions for offences in England and Wales and to convictions for 'foreign offences' since s 1(4) provides that 'references to a conviction . . . include references (a) to a conviction by or before a court outside Great Britain . . .'.

30  In *Adamson v Waveney District Council* (1997) 161 JP 787, 789, it was stated by the High Court that 'it is common ground in this case that the initial consideration by the local authority of an application under s 59 of the [Local Government (Miscellaneous Provisions)] Act of 1976 for a hackney carriage driver's licence is a proceeding before a judicial authority within this provision' (*per* Sedley J). The position will clearly be the same in respect of other licensing functions exercised by local authorities.

31  Explanatory Note 192. On the question of the use of Explanatory Notes as an aid to interpreting statutory provisions, see 9.6.4 above.

32  This seems to be the position where there are late representations in respect of premises licence applications, following the House of Lords' decision in *Belfast City Council v Miss Behavin' Ltd* [2007] UKHL 19 – see 6.4.19 above – and the position should be the same here.

33  As to the giving of notice of hearing, see 2.3.2 above. Under reg 7(2) and Sched 3, para 11, the applicant must be given the police notice of objection with the notice of hearing.

34  This can be contrasted with the position in respect of police objections to designated premises supervisors for premises licences – see 6.4.23 above.

35  An example of such circumstances might be where an applicant is able to demonstrate that, because the offence in question took place so long ago and there is no longer any propensity to reoffend, any risk to the community is so diminished that it would be right to grant the application: Guidance, para 4.9. A further example might be if a conviction were shortly to become spent and the authority would grant the licence once it had become so.

36  Explanatory Note 201 states: 'The licensing authority must renew a personal licence except where the applicant has been convicted of one or more relevant offences since the original grant of the licence or its last renewal.' An obligation to renew the licence seems implicit from s 121(5), which provides that the authority must grant the application if there is no objection from the police. A fortiori, the application must be granted if there are no convictions.

37  Section 121(7) provides:

> 'In this section "the relevant time" means–
>
> (a)  if the personal licence has not been renewed since it was granted, the time it was granted, and
>
> (b)  if it has been renewed, the last time it was renewed.'

38  These might include, for example, convictions of which the authority was unaware at the time of the earlier grant or renewal and that have only since come to light.

39  As to the giving of notice of hearing, see 2.3.2 above. Under reg 7(2) and Sched 3, para 12, the applicant must be given the police notice of objection with the notice of hearing.

40  Notice must be given forthwith on making the determination and the notice must be accompanied by information regarding the right of a party to appeal against the determination of the authority: regs 28–29 LA 2003 (Hearings) Regs 2005. For the meaning of 'forthwith', see 6.6.2 above.

41  For the meaning of 'forthwith', see 6.6.2 above.

42  As to the giving of notice of hearing, see 2.3.2 above. Under reg 7(2) and Sched, para 13, the licence holder must be given the police notice of objection with the notice of hearing.

43  Section 124(7) contains a provision comparable to s 123(4) (see 10.8.1 above), and provides: 'In this section "application period", in relation to the grant or renewal of a personal licence, means the period that–

> (a)  begins when the application for the grant or renewal is made, and
>
> (b)  ends at the time of the grant or renewal.'

44  Notice must be given forthwith on making the determination and the notice must be accompanied by information regarding the right of a party to appeal against the

determination of the authority: regs 28–29 of the LA 2003 (Hearings) Regs 2005. For the meaning of 'forthwith', see 6.6.2 above.

45   On request, the holder must then produce his licence to the authority within 14 days. The Guidance goes on to provide: 'It is expected that the chief officer of police for the area in which the holder resides would be advised if they do not respond promptly' (para 4.30). It does not, however, give any indication of what action should be taken by the police should the holder not respond.

46   *Quaere* whether spent convictions might be taken into account under s 7(3) of the Rehabilitation of Offenders Act 1974 – see 10.5.14–10.5.16 above.

47   This is a so-called 'leapfrog' appeal direct to the House of Lords from the High Court, where a point of law of general public importance is involved and leave to appeal is given either by the High Court or the House of Lords. The relevant part of the High Court from which such an appeal can be made is the Administrative Court, to which an appeal may have been made by way of case stated from the court before which the personal licence holder was convicted of a relevant offence. The 'leapfrog' appeal is in practice rarely used.

48   For such appeals, see 12.11 and 12.12 below.

49   Section 131(5) provides:

> For the purposes of subsection (2) "the appropriate officer" is–
>
> (a) in the case of a magistrates' court, the clerk of the court, and
>
> (b) in the case of the Crown Court, the appropriate officer;
>
> and section 141 of the Magistrates' Courts Act 1980 (c.43) (meaning of "clerk of a magistrates' court") applies in relation to this subsection as it applies in relation to that section.

50   *Quaere* whether forfeiture or suspension of the licence for conviction for this offence might be seen as a disproportionate sentence. Arguably it might be, as the offence is summary only and under s 128(7) subject only to a level 2 fine – see 10.9.5 above. However, the consequence of not notifying the court may be that forfeiture or suspension could not be imposed for a conviction for a much more serious offence for which this would have been a proportionate sentence. On the basis of this causal link, it may be said that the sentence is not disproportionate.

51   See s 19(2)(b) and 6.4.2 above. In such circumstances, the premises licence holder may well have a defence of 'due diligence', under s 139, to a charge of carrying on an unauthorised licensable activity – see 11.2.11 below.

52   Section 135(6) provides: 'In this section "authorised officer" means an officer of a licensing authority authorised by the authority for the purposes of this Act.'

# CHAPTER 11

# ENFORCEMENT

## 11.1    INTRODUCTION

11.1.1    Parts 7–9 of the 2003 Act contain provisions for the enforcement of licensing control. These include the creation in Pt 7 of a number of offences, powers of closure in respect of licensed premises contained in Pt 8, and rights of entry to investigate licensable activities and the commission of offences in Pt 9.

Part 7 contains some offences for which the conduct element (*actus reus*) alone will suffice for criminal liability, although a 'due diligence' defence may be provided, whereas other offences require a mental element (*mens rea*), normally knowledge, to be proved by the prosecution. The three main categories of offences are unauthorised licensable activities, drunkenness and disorderly conduct, and children and alcohol, with additional categories of smuggled goods, vehicles and trains, and false statements in relation to licensing. There are numerous other offences in the Act directed at failure to comply with procedural requirements and these are dealt with at the points in the book at which these requirements are considered. However, a comprehensive list of all offences is contained in Appendix 10. This appendix covers the relevant statutory provision, a description of the offence, persons who may be liable for the offence, any applicable defence and the maximum penalty for the offence.

11.1.2    The offence in s 136, of carrying out or attempting to carry out unauthorised licensable activities or knowingly allowing such activities to be carried on, is the one that will have primary application and 'is central to the enforcement of the licensing regime introduced by the Act' (Explanatory Note 219). This is supplemented by ss 137–38, which create offences of exposing alcohol for unauthorised sale or keeping alcohol on the premises for unauthorised sale. The effect of these provisions is that an offence is committed where no sale or attempted sale of alcohol takes place, which would be necessary for the offence under s 136 to have been committed. A defence of due diligence to these offences (with the exception of allowing unauthorised licensable activities to be carried on, for which the defence is inapplicable since the prosecution must prove knowledge) is provided by s 139.

A number of other offences, most of which are alcohol-related, are also contained in Pt 7. These include: offences dealing with drunkenness and disorderly conduct (ss 140–43); the keeping of smuggled goods (s 144);[1] the involvement of children with alcohol (ss 145–55); the sale of alcohol on moving vehicles and on trains (ss 156–57); and the making of false statements in connection with licensing applications and notices (s 158). There are also some general provisions relating to offences in Pt 9 which cover the institution of proceedings for offences (s 186), offences by bodies corporate (s 187), and jurisdiction and procedure in respect of offences (s 188).

11.1.3    Part 8 contains provisions for the closure of licensed premises either by the police or (in some instances) by trading standards officers. The police can make an order for the closure of all licensed premises in an area experiencing disorder for a period not exceeding 24 hours (s 160). Closure orders, again for a period not exceeding 24 hours, may also be made by the police in respect of identified premises where there is, or is likely imminently to be, disorder on, or in, the vicinity of the premises and closure is necessary for public safety, or where a public nuisance is created by noise and closure is necessary to prevent the nuisance (s 161). Provisions are included for extension (s 162) and cancellation (s 163) of closure orders, for their consideration by magistrates' courts (ss 164–66), for review of a premises licence following a closure order (ss 167–68), and for enforcement of closure orders (s 169). Closure orders can be made only by the police, but similar powers of closure are available to local authorities under ss 40–41 of the Anti-Social Behaviour Act 2003 in respect of 'noisy premises'.[2] Closure notices, on the other hand, can be given by either the police or trading standards officers where there are persistent sales of alcohol to children (s 169A). Such orders propose closure of the premises for the sale of alcohol for a period not exceeding 48 hours and can, but need not, be accepted by the premises licence holder(s) as an alternative to criminal proceedings (s 169B). An exemption from liability for damages in respect of closure of licensed premises is provided both for the police and for trading standards officers (s 170).

11.1.4 Part 9 of the 2003 Act contains powers of entry and inspection for police officers and authorised persons. Under s 179, they can enter to investigate licensable activities taking place on premises and an offence is committed by any person who intentionally obstructs a person exercising this power. Under s 180, a police officer may enter and search premises if he has reason to believe an offence under the Act has been, is being, or is about to be, committed.

## OFFENCES

## 11.2  UNAUTHORISED LICENSABLE ACTIVITIES

11.2.1  Section 136(1) provides:

> A person commits an offence if–
>
> (a)  he carries on or attempts to carry on a licensable activity on or from any premises otherwise than under and in accordance with an authorisation, or
>
> (b)  he knowingly allows a licensable activity to be so carried on.

This offence is wide-ranging in scope and applies in respect of all premises lacking 'an authorisation', that is, authorisation under a premises licence, a club premises certificate (CPC) or temporary event notice (TEN).[3] It will thus encompass premises that have no authorisation at all for licensable activities to take place, premises that have authorisation, but not for the particular licensable activity in question, and premises where, although there is authorisation for the licensable activity in question, either a breach of conditions occurs[4] or there is some failure to comply with matters specified in the licence[5]. The offences, however, are subject to qualification by s 136(2), which provides:

> Where the licensable activity in question is the provision of regulated entertainment, a person does not commit an offence under this section if his only involvement in the provision of the entertainment is that he–
>
> (a)  performs in a play,
>
> (b)  participates as a sportsman in an indoor sporting event,
>
> (c)  boxes or wrestles in a boxing or wrestling entertainment,

(d) performs live music,

(e) plays recorded music,

(f) performs dance, or

(g) does something coming within paragraph 2(1)(h) of Schedule 1 (entertainment similar to music, dance, etc).[6]

This provision precludes application of the offence in s 136(1) to those who are performers or participants in regulated entertainment. A person undertaking any of the above-mentioned activities will not be a person who 'carries on or attempts to carry on' a licensable activity without authorisation for the purposes of this section if his only involvement is as a performer.[7] The exclusion of such persons from the scope of the offence followed a Report of the Joint Committee on Human Rights (JCHR), which raised doubts about whether criminalisation of the actions of performers who participated in the entertainment could be justified in terms of the right to freedom of expression under Art 10 of the European Convention on Human Rights. The JCHR concluded that inclusion of performers within the offence would give rise to 'a significant risk of disproportionality, and hence incompatibility under Article 10'[8] and the provision in s 136(2) was duly incorporated on the third reading of the Bill in the House of Lords.

There are two categories of persons who might commit the offence in s 136(1), for which the penalty is prescribed by s 136(4):

> A person guilty of an offence under this section is liable on summary conviction to imprisonment for a term not exceeding six months or to a fine not exceeding £20,000, or to both.

One category is those who carry on or attempt to carry on an unauthorised licensable activity and the other category is those who allow such an activity to be so carried on.

## 11.2.2 Carrying on or attempting to carry on an unauthorised licensable activity

### 11.2.3 Carrying on

1.2.4 This category will most obviously include those who have some organisational or managerial involvement in the licensable activity. This will be in accordance with the ordinary dictionary meaning of 'carry on', which includes (in reference to a business) to 'manage'.[9] In the case of premises lacking any authorisation for a licensable activity, this could be the person running the premises. Alternatively, in the case of entertainment, it could be those responsible for putting on, arranging, promoting or managing the entertainment and, in the case of late night refreshment (LNR), those providing the refreshment. In the case of premises for which there is an authorisation, but not for the particular licensable activity in question, this could be (where the authorisation is a premises licence) the premises licence holder or (where the authorisation is a CPC) the club secretary or the club committee or (where the authorisation is a TEN) the premises user.

11.2.5 How far liability extends beyond such persons will depend on how 'carries on' is interpreted. If a broad interpretation is given, this might include those who take part in the licensable activity in a way that contributes significantly to the activity, apart of course from participation as a performer since this activity is specifically excluded by s 136(2) (see 11.2.1 above). Such an interpretation would accord with the approach taken by the courts under the previous law in respect of the offence of being concerned in the organisation or management of unlicensed public entertainment under para 12(1) of Sched 1 to the Local Government (Miscellaneous Provisions) Act 1982. The Divisional Court, in *Chichester District Council v Ware* (1992) 157 JP 574, held that this offence was wide enough to include anyone who took part in the running of the entertainment and whose part could be said to contribute significantly to the whole unlicensed entertainment. In the *Chichester* case, an unlicensed public musical entertainment in the nature of an 'acid house' party[10] was held in a barn near Chichester and prosecutions were instituted against four defendants who either played a part in taking equipment to the barn or who made use of the equipment in the course of the entertainment. One defendant, Byrne, hired the audio equipment and two electric generators; a second defendant, Simpkins, drove a van transporting Byrne and this equipment at least part of the way to the barn; a third defendant, Sylvester, hired the record turntable and lighting equipment used; and a fourth defendant, Ware (who according to the evidence was the only one present at the party), although he had not been engaged to act as a disc jockey, did so at the start of the party as no other disc jockey had arrived. The defendants denied taking part in organising the party, alleging that they had 'independently either come across, or been approached by that chimerical go-between, so frequently figuring in criminal courts, a man in a pub' (*per* Beldam LJ at 575). The justices, before whom the defendants appeared, took the view that the conduct of the defendants was not proximate enough to constitute being concerned in the organisation of unlicensed public entertainment and acquitted the defendants.

There was an appeal by case stated to the Divisional Court, which took a broad view of the nature and degree of participation required to bring an act within the description of acts 'concerned in the organisation . . . of that entertainment' and held that the justices were not correct in deciding that the defendants' conduct was not proximate enough. Beldam LJ stated (at 581):

> Looking at the subsection [sic] broadly, a distinction is first of all drawn between those who are concerned in the organisation and management of the entertainment and those who are in a position to permit an entertainment to be held at some place. Those two categories cover all those who take part in the provision of such unlicensed musical entertainment except those who simply attend for the purpose of being entertained.

This remark might have equal application to s 136(1), which similarly draws a distinction between carrying on or attempting to carry on (hereafter 'carrying on') a licensable activity and allowing such an activity to be carried on. If these two categories are looked at broadly, they might cover all who take part (to a significant extent)[11] in a licensable activity, except those who attend the premises to purchase alcohol, to be entertained or to purchase LNR.

11.2.6  No reference is made in s 136(1)(a) to any mental element for the offence of carrying on a licensable activity. Absence of any reference is often indicative of strict liability, particularly where provision is made for a defence of due diligence, as it is for this offence (see s 139 and 11.2.10 below), although sometimes courts 'read in' a mental element for the offence. This is because there is a presumption that statutes creating criminal offences require a blameworthy state of mind (*mens rea*) on the part of a defendant. It is uncertain whether it would be consistent for a court to 'read in' a requirement of knowledge for an offence for which there is a due diligence defence. In principle, it may be consistent since it seems that the presumption of *mens rea* applies to all criminal offences. This was the view taken by the Court of Appeal in *R v Muhamad* [2003] QB 1031 where Dyson LJ stated (at para [15]):

> The question, whether the presumption of law that mens rea is required applies, and, if so, whether it has been displaced, can be approached in two ways. One approach is to ask whether the act is truly criminal, on the basis that, if it is not, then the presumption does not apply at all. The other approach is to recognise that any offence in respect of which a person may be punished in a criminal court is prima facie sufficiently "criminal" for the presumption to apply. But the more serious the offence, the greater the weight to be attached to the presumption, and conversely, the less serious the offence, the less weight to be attached. It is . . . this latter approach which, according to our domestic law, must be applied.

If this is the case, the presumption of *mens rea* will apply to offences for which a due diligence defence is provided, the same as for any other offence, and will need to be displaced in accordance with the criteria set out by the Privy Council in *Gammon (Hong Kong) Ltd. v Attorney General of Hong Kong* [1985] AC 1.[12] It would therefore seem open to the defence to run alternative contentions that knowledge (or some other form of *mens rea*) is needed for the offence or, if not, then the due diligence defence applies. Whether the former contention would ever be likely to succeed where, as here, the statute provides a due diligence defence is open to question. The implicit assumption by courts seems to have been that provision of a due diligence defence where there is no specified mental element *ipso facto* makes the offence one of strict liability and it may well be that, notwithstanding the view expressed above by the Court of Appeal in *R v Muhamad*, that this continues to be the case.[13]

The view that a mental element may not be required for the offence in s 136(1)(a) might be reinforced by the fact that, whilst there is no reference to any mental element in this provision, there is an express reference to knowledge in s 136(1)(b) for the offence of allowing a licensable activity to be carried on. The position is comparable here to that under the previous law for the offence of providing unlicensed public entertainment and in the *Chichester* case the Divisional Court held that that offence was one of strict liability, taking the view that the wording of the offence was the decisive factor:[14]

> In subparagraph (1) of para 12 [of Schedule 1 to the Local Government (Miscellaneous Provisions) Act 1982] the clear distinction is drawn between persons who are concerned in the organisation and management of the unlicensed entertainment and other persons who, knowing or having reasonable cause to suspect that such an entertainment would be so provided, permit a place to be used for the provision of entertainment.

> It seems to me impossible to infer that the draftsman of that provision intended it to be a requirement of the offence under s [sic] 12(1)(a) that it would have to be proved that the person concerned in the organisation and management of the entertainment knew or had reasonable cause to suspect that the entertainment would be provided at the place referred to.

> Thus, in the drafting of the section [sic] there was a clear distinction drawn between the two subparagraphs and my interpretation that no particular mental requirement is necessary for an offence to be proved under para 12(1)(a) is reinforced by the provision

in sub para (3), that it is to be a defence to a person charged with an offence under the paragraph to prove that he took all reasonable precautions and exercised all due diligence to avoid the commission of the offence, words which strongly suggest that the offence is one of strict liability though I accept, of course, that they are not determinative.[15]

In the light of the above, it is likely that s 136(1)(a) will be similarly interpreted, notwithstanding that under s 136(4), a relatively high maximum penalty of six months' imprisonment and a fine not exceeding £20,000 might be imposed for the offence.[16] Imposing strict liability under s 136(1)(a) would accord not only with the previous law relating to the provision of unlicensed public entertainment, but also with the previous law relating to the sale of intoxicating liquor without a licence,[17] and there is nothing to indicate that Parliament intended there to be any change in this position.

### 11.2.7 Attempting to carry on

11.2.8   The offence under s 136(1)(a) extends to cases where a person is 'attempting to carry on' an unauthorised licensable activity. In general, statutory provisions creating criminal offences do not include references to attempts since liability for attempts is imposed by s 1(1) of the Criminal Attempts Act 1981. However, liability under s 1(1) arises only in respect of attempts to commit indictable offences (those which can or, in some cases, must be tried before a jury). Section 1(4) provides (subject to some exceptions): 'This section applies to any offence which, if it were completed, would be triable in England and Wales as an indictable offence . . .'. The Act does not therefore apply to summary-only offences (those that are triable only before magistrates)[18] and, since the offence in s 136(1) is summary only, it is for this reason that reference is made in the section to attempting to carry on an unauthorised licensable activity.

The principles governing liability for attempting summary-only offences, in cases where there is a special statutory provision creating an offence of attempting to commit another offence, are nevertheless the same as those that apply to attempts under s 1(1) of the 1981 Act. Section 3 of the 1981 Act contains provisions to this effect and s 3(4), essentially replicating s 1(1), provides:

> A person is guilty of an attempt under a special statutory provision if, with intent to commit the relevant full offence, he does an act which is more than merely preparatory to the commission of that offence.

11.2.9   The conduct element required for the offence is whether an act has been done which is 'more than merely preparatory' to the commission of an offence and, where there is evidence to support such a finding, the Act, in s 4(3), explicitly provides that this 'is a question of fact'. Although the courts have provided some guidance, much will depend on the circumstances of the particular case.[19] The mental element required is intent to commit the offence, which means 'a decision to bring about, in so far as it lies within the accused's power, the commission of the offence which it is alleged the accused intended to commit, no matter whether the accused desired that consequence of his act or not'.[20] Although it seems that the full offence itself under s 136(1)(a) is one of strict liability, nevertheless it will still probably be necessary for intent to be proved on a charge of attempt.[21]

## 11.2.10   Defence of due diligence

11.2.11 A defence of due diligence is provided for the offence in s 136(1)(a). Section 139 provides:

> (1)   In proceedings against a person for an offence to which subsection (2) applies, it is a defence that–
>
> > (a)   his act was due to a mistake, or to reliance on information given to him, or to an act or omission by another person, or to some other cause beyond his control, and
> >
> > (b)   he took all reasonable precautions and exercised all due diligence to avoid committing the offence.
>
> (2)   This subsection applies to an offence under–
>
> > (a)   section 136(1)(a) (carrying on unauthorised licensable activity),
> >
> > (b)   section 137 (exposing alcohol for unauthorised sale), or
> >
> > (c)   section 138 (keeping alcohol on premises for unauthorised sale).

In some instances where a due diligence defence is provided, all that seems to be required is that the defendant exercised all due diligence to avoid committing the offence. This is the case for the offences of allowing an unaccompanied child under 16 on premises on which his or her presence is prohibited (see s 145(8) and 11.7.6 below), of selling alcohol to children (see s 146(6) and 11.7.10 below) and selling liqueur chocolates to a person under 16 (see s 148(5) and 11.7.16 below). For the offence in s 136(1)(a), and for the offences in ss 137–138, however, due diligence is only one component of the defence and additional elements must be established. Section 139(1) also requires that all reasonable precautions were taken and that the act in question has to be attributable to one of the four causes mentioned in s 139(1)(a). The element of reasonable precautions essentially involves the setting up of a proper and efficient system for the avoidance of offences, whilst due diligence involves the taking of effective checks to ensure that the system is properly operating and working as intended.[22] If the offence occurred despite these facts, the defence is made out.[23]

A further limitation on the application of the defence is that there needs to be some 'external' cause beyond the defendant's control to which commission of the offence can be attributed. The reference to 'some other cause beyond his control' seems to indicate that the previously mentioned causes (mistake etc) are to be understood in the sense of having application only if the cause is one beyond the defendant's control. This suggests that it is not sufficient if there is a mistake if the defendant had been capable of doing something to rectify it, nor if there is reliance on information given to him if the defendant might have verified the information for himself, nor if there is an omission by another person if the defendant had been in a position to prevent the omission.[24] On the other hand, any cause beyond the defendant's control will meet the requirement in the defence and this might include, for example, where the manager of particular premises is wholly unaware of the death of the premises licence holder, which under s 27(1)(a) causes the premises licence to lapse (see 6.7.3 above) and which will make the provision of licensable activities unauthorised under s 136.[25] It might also include the malfunctioning of a till machine programmed to make the cashier aware whenever a customer presents an item for sale that is age-controlled.[26] The use of such a till machine has been judicially recognised as being of considerable importance in respect of the due diligence defence – in

*Davies v Carmarthenshire County Council* [2005] LLR 276 at para 11 (*Davies*), a case concerning underage sales of alcohol under s 169(1) of the Licensing Act 1964, Maurice Kay LJ stated: 'For my part, I place particular importance on the way in which the till worked in relation to each transaction' – and it is clear from *Bibby-Cheshire v Golden Wonder Ltd* [1972] 1 WLR 1487 that malfunctioning of a machine can be a cause beyond the control of those using the machine. In this case a packeting machine of the best kind available, which in the ordinary course of functioning was expected to produce the correct weight into packets, produced underweight packets of the product and the cause of the deficiency was held to be 'some other cause beyond his [the product manufacturers'] control' within the meaning of s 26(1)(a) of the Weights and Measures Act 1963.

Unless the cause is beyond the defendant's control, even if the defendant had in the circumstances taken reasonable precautions and exercised due diligence to prevent the offence, the defence will not be made out. This more restrictive form of the due diligence defence has not previously applied to licensing offences, although it does feature in other regulatory offences schemes, notably trade descriptions, fair trading and consumer credit.[27] The reasons for its importation into the 2003 Act are unclear, with no indication provided in the Parliamentary debates during the course of the Act's passage, the Explanatory Notes to the Act or the Secretary of State's Guidance. Given that the causes beyond the defendant's control are broadly expressed and may be broadly interpreted,[28] it may be that this additional requirement will have little practical effect in restricting successful pleas of the defence. It remains to be seen whether the courts will in due course provide further clarification of the scope of this more restrictive formulation of the due diligence defence.

11.2.12 Whether or not due diligence can be established in any particular case will be a question of fact in all the circumstances.[29] Where there is clear evidence that there is an adequately implemented and supervised system to deal with sales of alcohol to persons under the age of 18, the defence will be made out and it will be wrong for a court to come to the view that it is not. The High Court in *Davies* held that a magistrates' court had erred in rejecting a defence of due diligence by a supermarket manageress (a joint licensee) who was charged with selling intoxicating liquor to a person under the age of 18 contrary to s 169 of the Licensing Act 1964, following a sale made by a sales assistant at the supermarket, where a number of undisputed matters that were material and of considerable importance to the defence had been made out. These included the sales assistant having been provided with written material aimed at preventing underage sales, a prominent display throughout the store of the supermarket's policy of requesting age identification from anyone who looked under the age of 21 before alcohol would be sold, the use of tills that required a sales assistant to be satisfied as to a person's age before a sale of alcohol could be effected and a completed record by the sales assistant logging previous occasions when sales had been refused. Allowing the appeal by case stated, the High Court held that all this material showed that the defendant had taken adequate steps to train and supervise the sales assistant and the magistrates' court had erred in holding that the defendant had not established the defence.

Where some steps have been taken but not others, it will be for the court to decide on balance whether due diligence has been established. Thus in *Cambridgeshire City Council v Kama* (2007) 171 JP 196, where a licensee of a small corner shop was charged with the offence under s 169A of the Licensing Act 1964 when a 15-year-old girl was sold intoxicating liquor by an employee in the licensee's absence, the defence of due diligence was found to be made out by the magistrates' court on the basis that the licensee had:

- taken up references for the employee (who had been there about five weeks), which indicated he was a good employee, with previous experience in the licensed trade and full knowledge of the licensing laws;
- closely supervised him at the start of his employment and had not permitted him to serve in the shop until he was satisfied that he had been fully trained and inducted; and
- included a reference to the fact that it was illegal to sell alcohol to a child in the employee's contract, the terms of which had been orally explained to the employee and there was a section in the contract indicating that the employee had read and accepted its terms.

Dismissing the appeal by case stated, the High Court held that the magistates' court was entitled to find that due diligence had been exercised, notwithstanding that there was:

- no system involving a refusals book or a log;
- no evidence of formal training courses having been given nor any written training records; and
- no till prompt system, either electronic or manual, which would remind staff and thus ensure that persons purchasing such items were aged over 18.

The magistrates' court had found due diligence notwithstanding the absence of any such arrangements because 'a small corner shop could not reasonably be expected to have in place all of the systems that, for example. a supermarket would have in place'. This was regarded by the High Court as a 'highly significant finding' because it indicated that the magistrates' court was 'plainly having regard to the question of whether matters such as the absence of a refusals book were indicative in this case of a failure to take all due diligence' (*per* Treacy J at para [14]). In upholding the magistrates' court's decision, albeit with 'some hesitation', since the decision was 'not one that every court would necessarily have come to' (at para [15]), the High Court distinguished the earlier decision in *Davies*:

> . . . in that case the court was not identifying steps which must be taken in order to satisfy due diligence, it was enumerating matters which the Justices had in that case failed to take into account in considering the defence in that particular case. Moreover, the Davies case is concerned with a multi-branch supermarket style retailer whereas this case involves a small corner shop.

It thus seems that less may be expected of a small corner shop than larger premises such as multibranch supermarkets, although the High Court was keen to emphasize (at para [15]) that its decision was not to be seen as sanctioning the absence of arrangements such as refusals books for corner shops:

> This decision is not to be taken as one which gives a licence to small corner shops, for example, not to have a refusals book. There may well be other circumstances and other cases where a court could legitimately find that the keeping of such a record is a step which should be taken. It occurs to me, for example, that if there had been evidence

before the court of advice or warning by a Trading Standards Officer of the desirability of keeping such a book, the case might well have been different. Or if indeed there had been evidence that the keeping of such a record in corner shops in Cambridge was common practice, again the Justices might have taken a different view of the case.

Where a person is relying on the defence, it may not be necessary for him to have personally taken reasonable precautions and exercised all due diligence to avoid the commission of the offence. The Divisional Court so held in *Russell v DPP* (1996) 161 JP 185, where, the defendant, a trainee branch manager acting as relief manager for the licensee in off-licensed premises, sold intoxicating liquor to a person under the age of 18 contrary to s 169(1) of the Licensing Act 1964 after false documentary proof of age had been given by the purchaser to the company's area manager, who was working alongside the defendant in the premises. The Divisional Court held that the 'due diligence' defence in s 169(4A) did not require that the defendant personally had exercised all due diligence to avoid the commission of the offence. McCowan LJ stated (at 188–89):

> the Crown Court went wrong in approaching the matter on the basis that the appellant had to show that he had exercised an independent judgment in the matter. That was not required by the Act. He was operating a good system put in place by his employers and he was at the time under the immediate control of a superior and very much more experienced employee of the company. There was no finding that CR [the purchaser] was obviously [under] 18 and there is a specific finding that there was nothing on the face of the card to indicate that it was a forgery. I think it entirely reasonable that the appellant should accept Mr Manthorpe's [the area manager's] assessment of CR and his document. Indeed, to expect the appellant to contradict Mr Manthorpe's assessment would, in my judgment, be a wholly excessive and unrealistic expectation.

This principle should have similar application to the defence of due diligence under s 139.

11.2.13 No reference is made in s 139 to the burden of proof in respect of the defence, which means that ultimately it will be a matter for the courts to determine whether the legal burden of proof will be on the defendant to prove the defence on the balance of probabilities or whether the defendant will merely have an evidential burden, with the legal burden of disproving the defence resting on the prosecution. This issue, linked with the presumption of innocence in Art 6(2) of the European Convention on Human Rights, has been considered elsewhere and the view has been advanced that the legal burden of proof will be on the defendant (see 3.5.17–3.5.23 above). A similar view was expressed in para 14.14 of the 2004 Guidance, which stated: 'The burden of satisfying the court that this defence has been met falls on the individual raising it.'[30] Although this statement does not appear in the 2007 Guidance, it might be seen as indicative of Parliamentary intent and be admissible as an aid to interpreting the Act. Although courts are not required to have regard to the Guidance when interpreting the provisions of the Act – the requirement to do so applies only to licensing authorities under s 4(3)(b) when carrying out their licensing functions under the Act – courts can have regard to intrinsic material within a statute, such as other sections in the Act or the Act's long title, as well as a range of extrinsic material including parliamentary and pre-parliamentary publications like Government White Papers and Reports of Royal Commissions.[31] There would seem to be no reason why they might not therefore have regard to Guidance issued pursuant to a statutory provision in an Act as an extrinsic aid to the Act's interpretation. If recourse is had to para 14.14

of the 2004 Guidance, this suggests that s 139, correctly interpreted, imposes the legal burden of proof on the defendant.

### 11.2.14 Knowingly allowing a licensable activity to be carried on without authorisation

### *11.2.15 Knowingly*

11.2.16 Inclusion of a reference to 'knowingly' in an offence makes the mental element clear only where there is a single component in the conduct element for the offence. Where there is more than one component, the reference to 'knowingly' might be construed as having application conjunctively to some or all components, or disjunctively, applying only to the first-mentioned component. The question of which of these constructions should be adopted arises here since the conduct element concerns not only the licensable activity being carried on, but also it being carried on without authorisation. It is clear that knowledge is needed as to first-mentioned component, allowing a licensable activity to be carried on, but less clear whether knowledge is needed as to the carrying on being without authorisation.

As a matter of general principle, where a reference to 'knowingly' is included in the definition of an offence, this should be considered to have application conjunctively to all the elements of the offence. This was the view taken by Robert Goff LJ when the case of *Westminster City Council v Croyalgrange Ltd* [1985] 1 All ER 740 (*Croyalgrange*) was heard in the Divisional Court. His Lordship stated (at 744):

> Prima facie, as a matter of ordinary construction, when the word 'knowingly' is so introduced in a provision of this kind, it required [sic] knowledge by the accused of each of the facts constituting the actus reus of the offence.

The Divisional Court's decision in this case was affirmed by the House of Lords (at [1986] 1 WLR 674) although the House, when reaching its decision, did not adopt or make any reference to this statement. Nevertheless, it is submitted that Robert Goff LJ's view represents the correct approach and, indeed, might be regarded simply as an alternative way of stating the well-known presumption that *mens rea* is required for criminal offences, the presumption being that it is required in respect of all elements of the offence. The 'ordinary construction' principle, that knowledge applies to all elements of the offence is, however, only the prima facie construction to be adopted. Whilst this construction might ultimately prevail and become the conclusive construction, it can be displaced if the court is of the view that, to accord with Parliament's intention, the knowledge requirement needs to be applied selectively to the elements of the offence. Whether or not it is to be displaced in a given statutory provision, and under what criteria, is far from easy to determine.[32]

Certainly the view might be taken that Parliament cannot have intended the knowledge requirement to be applied selectively if the language of the offence is not reasonably capable of supporting both a disjunctive (selective) interpretation as well as a conjunctive one. If knowledge cannot be regarded as having any meaningful application if confined to one component only, this should be conclusive in favour of application of the ordinary construction principle. Such an approach is consistent with the House of Lords' decision in *Croyalgrange*, where the defendants sublet premises for use as a sex establishment and were prosecuted for knowingly permitting the use of the premises without a licence. No licence was obtained by the person operating the establishment, although the defendants contended that they had no knowledge a licence had not been obtained and honestly believed an application had been made. The council argued that knowledge was needed only as to the use of the premises, but this argument was rejected by the House of Lords. Lord Bridge stated (at 681–82):

> it seems to me that the word 'knowingly' in paragraph 20(1)(a) [of Sched 3 to the Local Government (Miscellaneous Provisions) Act 1982] cannot sensibly have been introduced merely to apply to the use which the defendant is making, or causing or permitting another to make, of premises as a sex establishment. I can conceive of no circumstances in which a person could be said to be using premises, still less of causing or permitting them to be used, 'to a significant degree for the exhibition' of pornographic films or 'for a business which consists to a significant degree' of the sale of pornographic material if that person were ignorant of the nature of the offending use. If the argument for the council is right, the word 'knowingly' is tautologous.
>
> ... If the argument for the council were accepted, it would lead to the conclusion that paragraph 20(1)(a) had in effect created an offence of strict liability. The offence would consist in the unlawful use of premises as a sex establishment and even an honest belief in facts which, if true, would make the use lawful would afford no defence. It is trite law that the legislature's intention to create an offence of strict liability must be signified by clear language. To find such an intention in paragraph 20(1)(a) is obviously impossible. The only meaning of which the language is reasonably capable makes knowledge that the use of premises as a sex establishment is in contravention of the prohibition imposed by paragraph 6 a necessary ingredient of the offence.

A similar view might be taken in respect of the offence in s 136(1)(b), where the knowledge requirement is unlikely to have any meaningful application if confined to the element of allowing the licensable activity to be carried on. This is certainly so in cases where there has been active facilitation and some positive conduct on the defendant's part. Whilst it may have meaningful application in cases of 'allowing' where a person has omitted to exercise any control to prevent an activity in cases where he has the power to do so, since here the defendant needs knowledge as to the activity occurring on particular occasions or at particular periods (see 11.2.19 below), this will only be a meaningful application in the restricted instance of omissions and should not justify a departure from the ordinary construction principle. The language of s 136(1)(b), for the most part, does not seem to be reasonably capable of supporting a disjunctive interpretation of the knowledge requirement and so the requirement of knowledge should extend to both allowing the licensable activity to be carried on and to this being without authorisation.

This might be reinforced by taking the view that the ordinary construction principle should not easily be displaced in cases where, as here, there is express inclusion of 'knowingly' in the offence. Whilst courts commonly 'read in' a requirement of *mens rea* (knowledge) where there is an absence of any reference to a mental element in a statutory offence, in accordance with the criteria set out by Lord Scarman in the Privy Council case of *Gammon (Hong Kong) Ltd v Attorney General of Hong Kong* [1985] AC 1,[33] this is more akin to 'reading out' such a requirement by confining 'knowingly' to only one component of the offence. No instance of such an approach being taken by a court is known in respect of a licensing offence,[34] again indicating that knowledge should be required as to both elements of the offence.

11.2.17 As to the meaning of 'knowingly', knowledge is equated with positive belief that a circumstance (in this case that a licensable activity is carried on without authorisation) exists, although it is not necessary for a person to think that the circumstance exists with ascertainable certainty. He need only accept or assume it exists or entertain no serious doubts that this is the case. However, a belief or knowledge that a circumstance *may* exist and indifference to it, which is more akin to the concept of recklessness, will not suffice where knowledge is required.[34] Nevertheless, where there is an awareness that the circumstance might well exist and a person deliberately refrains from further investigation, shutting his eyes to an obvious means of knowledge, knowledge may be readily inferred and attributed to him under the doctrine of 'wilful blindness'. As Lord Bridge observed in *Croyalgrange* (at 684):

> It is always open to a tribunal of fact, when knowledge on the part of a defendant is required to be proved, to base a finding of knowledge on evidence that the defendant had deliberately shut his eyes to the obvious or refrained from enquiry because he suspected the truth but did not want to have his suspicion confirmed.[35]

It is a person's deliberate shutting of his eyes to the obvious and refraining from enquiry that is of the essence of wilful blindness. This is not the same as indifference and the fact that the person *ought* to have known had proper enquiries been made. As Devlin J stated, in *Taylor's Central Garages (Exeter) Ltd v Roper* [1951] 2 TLR 284 (at 289):

> There is a vast distinction between a state of mind which consists of deliberately refraining from making inquiries, the result of which the person does not care to have, and a state of mind which is merely neglecting to make such inquiries as a reasonable and prudent person would make.

In practice, however, it may not always be easy to distinguish between cases of wilful blindness, which constitutes knowledge, and cases of indifference or neglecting to make enquiries, which does not, since there is a fine dividing line between them and the concepts do tend to shade into each other.

### 11.2.18 Allows

11.2.19 It may be that a person 'allows' a licensable activity to be carried on at premises not only where he has done something positive to facilitate the activity, but also where he has omitted to exercise any control to prevent it in cases where he has the power to do so. This was the view taken by the Divisional Court, in *Barking and Dagenham London Borough Council v Bass Taverns* [1993] COD 453, in respect of the offence under para 10(1)(b)(i) of Sched 12 to the London Government Act 1963, under which it was an offence if a person 'allowed' a place to be used in the Greater London area for the provision of unlicensed public entertainment. Glidewell LJ stated:

> . . . provided that the person who knows, or has reasonable cause to suspect, that there will be unlicensed dancing at the premises has means in his power to prevent that dancing taking place, and does not use those means, then it can be said that he allowed the premises to be used for the purposes of that entertainment. He does not need to do something active. Of course, if he does do something such as actively encouraging or advertising the dancing, then there could be no difficulty about construing that as "allowing".

11.2.20 His Lordship went on to state that knowledge or reasonable cause to suspect that there will be unlicensed entertainment needed to relate to the particular occasion(s) on which, or the particular periods at which, unlicensed entertainment took place, before it could be said that a person 'allowed' the entertainment by failing to exercise a power to prevent it. A general suspicion that unlicensed entertainment might take place, coupled with an actual occurrence of unlicensed entertainment, would not suffice:

> Mr Pittaway, for the London Borough Council, submits that once it has been established, as it was here, that Bass had reasonable cause to suspect that the unlicensed dancing would be provided or would take place, then if Bass failed to take steps which were open to them to prevent such dancing, they allowed it . . .

> Mr Beckett, for Bass argues, on the other hand, that while "allowing" can include failing to take steps which are open to the particular party, nevertheless it must, in its context, mean doing or failing to do something related to the particular occasion when dancing took place.

> Here, the Justices decided that Bass had reasonable cause to suspect that music and dancing would be provided in the public house because they had received two letters of 1987 and January 1989 – particularly the letter of January 1989, which referred to a specific occasion when there had been unlicensed dancing. But that finding, Mr Beckett submits, can only have been that they had such a suspicion in a general sense. It cannot have been intended to be a finding that there would be a suspicion that there would be dancing on that particular day, or perhaps even in that particular week. In order to allow dancing to take place Bass, or their employees on their behalf, must have had some reason to suspect that dancing was going to take place at or about the time when it did. There must be some connection between that reasonable suspicion and what actually happened on 6 March 1992. There was none here . . .

> I agree with Mr Beckett's submission that there had to be some connection between the suspicion and the actual event that took place so as to provide a nexus from which it can be said that they allowed to happen that which they suspected might happen . . .

The interpretation of 'allowed' in this case would seem to have application under s 136(1)(b), not only to allowing entertainment to be carried on, but also other licensable activities, namely the sale and supply of alcohol and the provision of late LNR.

## 11.3   EXPOSING ALCOHOL FOR UNAUTHORISED SALE

11.3.1  Section 137(1) provides:

> A person commits an offence if, on any premises, he exposes for sale by retail any alcohol in circumstances where the sale by retail of that alcohol on those premises would be an unauthorised licensable activity.

The conduct element of the offence is exposure for retail sale of alcohol where such sale would be an unauthorised licensable activity. This will cover cases where there is no sale or attempted sale, and therefore no offence under s 136(1), but where alcohol is nevertheless exposed for unauthorised sale. In view of the fact that s 138(1) creates an offence of keeping alcohol on premises for unauthorised sale, it seems likely that the element of 'exposes' in s 137(1) will mean 'exposes to view' so that those visiting the premises can actually see the alcohol on sale, rather than 'makes available' for sale so that those visiting are aware alcohol is on sale even if it might not be visibly on display. This latter situation would seem to be covered by s 138(1) and ought therefore to fall outside the scope of the offence in s 137(1).

The offence will not be confined to cases where there is no authorisation at all for the sale by retail of alcohol, for s 137(2) provides:

> For that purpose a licensable activity is unauthorised unless it is under and in accordance with an authorisation.

Thus, where there is authorisation for the sale by retail of alcohol, but not in the particular circumstances, for example because there is a breach of condition relating to hours, the licensable activity will be unauthorised because it is not under and in accordance with an authorisation. Exposing alcohol for sale outside authorised hours will therefore constitute an offence under s 137(1).

11.3.2   No mention is made of any mental element for the offence and, with provision of a defence of due diligence by s 139 (see 11.2.11–11.2.13 above), it is likely that one will not be required (see 11.2.6 above).

The same maximum penalty as for the offence in s 136(1) is prescribed by s 137(3), which provides:

> A person guilty of an offence under this section is liable on summary conviction to imprisonment for a term not exceeding six months or to a fine not exceeding £20,000, or to both.

Where a person is convicted of this offence, the court may order the confiscation of the alcohol exposed for sale and its containers, which may then be either destroyed or otherwise dealt with as the court sees fit. Section 137(4) provides:

> The court by which a person is convicted of an offence under this section may order the alcohol in question, and any container for it, to be forfeited and either destroyed or dealt with in such other manner as the court may order.

## 11.4   KEEPING ALCOHOL ON PREMISES FOR UNAUTHORISED SALE

11.4.1   Section 138(1) provides:

> A person commits an offence if he has in his possession or under his control alcohol which he intends to sell by retail or supply[36] in circumstances where that activity would be an unauthorised licensable activity.

This section makes it an offence to keep alcohol with the intention of selling it by retail or supplying it by or on behalf of a club or to the order of a member of the club where that sale or supply is an unauthorised licensable activity. The conduct element is having possession or control of the alcohol where sale would be an unauthorised licensable activity and it is not necessary that a person has ownership of the alcohol or any other proprietary right in it. 'Possession' is an established legal concept that normally requires a mental element, an intention to possess or an awareness of having possession,[37] and some degree of dominion over the property, which will vary according to the circumstances. Often a person with 'possession' of property will have 'control' of it, although, since either will suffice under the section, it is not necessary to distinguish between the two.[38] Although the heading to the section refers to keeping alcohol on premises for unauthorised sale, the section itself refers only to a person having alcohol in his possession or under his control and makes no mention of the alcohol itself being on premises. The wording of the section therefore seems wide enough to encompass cases where a person has possession or control of alcohol other than on premises, for example, on his person or whilst travelling in a vehicle. It is possible, however, that a court might interpret the section so as to exclude this, having recourse to the heading as an indication that Parliament's intention was to confine liability to cases where alcohol was kept on premises. The use of headings (which have replaced sidenotes following a change in practice in 2001 by the Parliamentary Counsel Office) as an aid to interpretation has been approved by the House of Lords in *R v Montila* [2005] 1 All ER 113 where it was stated (at para 34):

> The question then is whether headings and sidenotes, although unamendable, can be considered in construing a provision in an Act of Parliament. Account must, of course, be taken of the fact that these components were included in the Bill not for debate but for ease of reference. This indicates that less weight can be attached to them than to the parts of the Act that are open for consideration and debate in Parliament. But ... [t]hey provide the context for an examination of those parts of the Bill that are open for debate. Subject, of course, to the fact that they are unamendable, they ought to be open to consideration as part of the enactment when it reaches the statute book.[39]

If the mischief at which the offence is aimed is the keeping of the alcohol for unauthorised sale, as the heading seems to indicate, where it is kept is of no real significance and it may be better if a broad interpretation is given to the section to include keeping alcohol whether on or off premises.

11.4.2   Although a mental element is needed for possession and there needs to be an intention to sell by retail or supply, it may be sufficient if the sale or supply is in circumstances where that activity would be an unauthorised licensable activity, whether or not the person keeping the alcohol is aware of this. No reference is made to any mental element, such as knowledge or reasonable cause to suspect that the sale or supply would be an unauthorised licensable activity. This, coupled with the provision of a due diligence defence for this offence by s 139(2)(c) (see 11.2.11 above), strongly suggests that awareness for this element of the offence (the licensable activity being unauthorised) is not needed and that liability in this respect is strict (see 11.2.6 above).

As with the preceding offence, liability will not be confined to cases where there is no authorisation at all for the sale by retail or supply of alcohol, for s 138(2) provides:

> For that purpose a licensable activity is unauthorised unless it is under and in accordance with an authorisation.

Thus a club with a CPC that keeps alcohol, intending to sell it by retail to persons who are not members and guests, will commit an offence under the section since the sale will be otherwise than in accordance with its CPC.

11.4.3   The offence of keeping alcohol for unauthorised sale attracts a much lower maximum penalty, a level 2 fine, than the preceding offences of selling or attempting to sell alcohol (s 136) or exposing it for sale (s 137), although a similar power of the court to order confiscation of the alcohol and its containers applies in respect of this offence. Section 138(4) and (5) provides:

(4) A person guilty of an offence under this section is liable on summary conviction to a fine not exceeding level 2 on the standard scale.

(5) The court by which a person is convicted of an offence under this section may order the alcohol in question, and any container for it, to be forfeited and either destroyed or dealt with in such other manner as the court may order.

## 11.5 OFFENCES INVOLVING DRUNKENNESS AND DISORDERLY CONDUCT

11.5.1 Sections 140–43 contain various offences involving drunkenness or disorderly conduct on premises that have authorisation for licensable activities to take place. These premises, designated as 'relevant premises' in Pt 7 of the Act, are premises for which there is in force a premises licence ('licensed premises') or CPC, or which may be used for a permitted temporary activity following the giving of a TEN.[40] Persons who may be liable for the offences of allowing disorderly conduct on relevant premises under s 140 and selling or attempting to sell[41] alcohol to a person who is drunk on relevant premises under s 141 include:

- any person who works at the premises in a capacity, whether paid or unpaid, which authorises him to prevent the conduct;[42]
- the premises licence holder and the designated premises supervisor (DPS) (if any);
- any member or officer of a club holding a club premises certificate who at the time the conduct takes place is present on the premises in a capacity that enables him to prevent it;[43]
- the premises user in relation to a TEN.

Persons obtaining alcohol for a person who is drunk commit an offence under s 142 and persons who are drunk and disorderly and fail to leave relevant premises following a request to do so commit an offence under s 143.

### 11.5.2 Allowing disorderly conduct on relevant premises

11.5.3 Section 140 provides:

(1) A person to whom subsection (2) applies commits an offence if he knowingly allows disorderly conduct on relevant premises.

(2) This subsection applies–
(a) to any person who works at the premises in a capacity, whether paid or unpaid, which authorises him to prevent the conduct,
(b) in the case of licensed premises, to–
(i) the holder of a premises licence in respect of the premises, and
(ii) the designated premises supervisor (if any) under such a licence,
(c) in the case of premises in respect of which a club premises certificate has effect, to any member or officer of the club which holds the certificate who at the time the conduct takes place is present on the premises in a capacity which enables him to prevent it, and

(d)  in the case of premises which may be used for a permitted temporary activity by virtue of Part 5, to the premises user in relation to the temporary event notice in question.

(3)  A person guilty of an offence under this section is liable on summary conviction to a fine not exceeding level 3 on the standard scale.

This offence will apply to premises where any licensable activities are taking place. It is, however, likely to have particular application where alcohol is sold and may be regarded as of crucial importance for the safety of persons on the premises.

11.5.4  The conduct element of the offence requires that a person who commits it 'allows disorderly conduct' to take place on relevant premises. The term 'allow' includes not only doing something positive to facilitate the conduct, but also failing to exercise any control to prevent it in cases where there is the power to do so (see 11.2.19 above). In this context, it is much more likely that 'allow' will involve the latter than the former. As to what constitutes 'disorderly conduct', no definition is provided in the Act, but 'disorder', in the context of licensing, seems to involve conduct that seriously offends against values generally recognised by society as being of a character likely to cause annoyance to others who are present, although not having reached the stage of criminal conduct calculated to provoke a breach of the peace (see 4.2.3 above). The offence requires only the allowing of disorderly conduct 'on relevant premises', which are those having authorisation for licensable activities. It does not specify that the disorderly conduct should occur at the same time as or as a result of licensable activities taking place under the authorisation, only that such conduct occurs on premises with an authorisation. On a literal interpretation of the section, a person who may commit the offence may do so if such conduct were to occur at any time and for reasons unconnected with the provision of licensable activities. The position is less clear if a purposive interpretation is adopted. One view may be that the purpose of the legislation is the regulation of licensable activities and disorderly conduct therefore needs to be related to such activities if it is to fall within the scope of the statutory offence. Another view, however, may be that the legislative purpose is to ensure that premises in respect of which there is an authorisation for licensable activities are properly run in all circumstances. If they are not properly run when non-licensable activities are occurring there is equally a risk that they will not be properly run when licensable activities are taking place and allowing disorderly conduct on the premises at any time ought therefore to fall within the offence. It is submitted that the offence should be given a broad interpretation to include disorderly conduct even if unconnected with licensable activities. The s 140 offence re-enacted in part the offence in s 172 of the Licensing Act 1964, where conduct did not need to occur when alcohol was being sold,[44] and there is no indication that Parliament intended the position to be different for the s 140 offence.

11.5.5  The mental element required for the offence is knowledge (see 11.2.15–11.2.17 above) on the part of the person who may commit it. Prima facie the requirement of knowledge should apply to all elements of the offence, that is, that the conduct is taking place, that it is disorderly, and that it is on relevant premises. It may be that this construction should become the conclusive one here, as with the offence under s 136(1)(b) (see 11.2.16 above), since the knowledge requirement is unlikely to have any meaningful application if it is confined simply to the first-mentioned element (conduct taking place). If knowledge is needed that the conduct is disorderly, this might, however, be readily be inferred. If conduct being disorderly is seen as a question of law, it is easy to infer knowledge since everyone is presumed to know the law. If it is seen as a question of fact, a finding that the conduct in the circumstances of the case is disorderly may give rise to an (irresistible) inference of knowledge that it is disorderly. The requirement of knowledge as to the conduct being disorderly may therefore be one that is easily satisfied.

Liability for this offence is not dependent on a person being present on the premises at the time the disorderly conduct takes place, except in the case of a club member or officer where a CPC has effect in relation to the premises. In many cases the person alleged to have committed the offence may well have been present and personally aware of the occurrence of the disorderly conduct, although in some instances this will not be so, for example, in the case of premises licences, the DPS may be absent for a period of time from the premises or the premises licence holder may not be in day-to-day control of the premises. In such cases, the question will arise whether personal knowledge will be needed or whether knowledge might be imputed to establish liability. It would seem that the principle of delegated authority, whereby knowledge can be imputed where there has been a delegation of authority, will have application, as it did under the Licensing Act 1964. For knowledge to be imputed under the delegation principle, it seems that there must be a complete and not partial transfer of authority and responsibilities to another person. Thus, in *Vane v Yiannopoullos* [1965] AC 486, the House of Lords held that knowledge could not be imputed to the licensee of a restaurant where a sale of alcohol was made by a waitress without his knowledge to persons not taking meals contrary to the terms of the licence, for he had merely given her authority to sell alcohol and there had not been a delegation of authority to manage the business. Although in this case some doubts were cast on the validity of the delegation principle, it has been endorsed by the Court of Appeal in *R v Winson* [1969] 1 QB 371[45] and applied in subsequent cases. It seems, however, that the delegation principle may apply only where 'the delegator's offence is precisely the offence actually committed by the person to whom he delegated the responsibility', *per* Mitchell J in *Southwark LBC v Allied Domecq Leisure Ltd* [1999] EHLR 231.

## 11.5.6 Selling or attempting to sell alcohol to a person who is drunk

11.5.7 Section 141 provides:

(1) A person to whom subsection (2) applies commits an offence if, on relevant premises, he knowingly–
    (a) sells or attempts to sell alcohol to a person who is drunk, or
    (b) allows alcohol to be sold to such a person.

(2) This subsection applies–
    (a) to any person who works at the premises in a capacity, whether paid or unpaid, which gives him authority to sell the alcohol concerned,
    (b) in the case of licensed premises, to–
        (i) the holder of a premises licence in respect of the premises, and
        (ii) the designated premises supervisor (if any) under such a licence,
    (c) in the case of premises in respect of which a club premises certificate has effect, to any member or officer of the club which holds the certificate who at the time the sale (or attempted sale) takes place is present on the premises in a capacity which enables him to prevent it, and

(d) in the case of premises which may be used for a permitted temporary activity by virtue of Part 5, to the premises user in relation to the temporary event notice in question.

(3) This section applies in relation to the supply of alcohol by or on behalf of a club to or to the order of a member of the club as it applies in relation to the sale of alcohol.

(4) A person guilty of an offence under this section is liable on summary conviction to a fine not exceeding level 3 on the standard scale.

The section creates two offences, one in s 141(1)(a) of selling or attempting to sell alcohol to a person who is drunk and another in s 141(1)(b) of allowing alcohol to be sold to such a person.[46] These offences will extend to premises in respect of which there is in force a premises licence (s 141(2)(b)), a club premises certificate (s 141(2)(c) and s 141(3)) or a TEN (s 141(2)(d). Whether in such cases, for an offence to be committed, the licensable activities under the premises licence, TEN or CPC will need to include a sale by retail or supply of alcohol or whether it will suffice if there is an unauthorised sale or supply is less clear. It is perhaps implicit from the categories of persons mentioned in s 141(2), who might commit the offence that authorisation for the sale or supply of alcohol will be needed – s 141(2)(a) refers to a person working at the premises in a capacity which 'gives him authority to sell the alcohol concerned', whilst s 141(2)(b)(ii) refers to the 'designated premises supervisor' (DPS) and there will only be such a person if alcohol can be sold under a premises licence. However, the wording of the section is wide enough to encompass an unauthorised sale or supply of alcohol from premises whose licensable activities do not include alcohol and the mischief aimed at by the offence is preventing a person who is drunk from consuming more alcohol. It may be, therefore, that the offence can be committed where consumption occurs on premises where the licensable activities do not include the sale by retail or supply of alcohol either at all or in the particular circumstances, although in such cases there is in any event likely to be an offence of carrying on or attempting to carry an unauthorised licensable activity under s 136(1) (see 11.2.1 above).

11.5.8   The conduct element of the offence in s 141(1)(a) requires that a person who may commit it 'sells or attempts to sell' alcohol to a person who is 'drunk'. A sale will normally involve proof that money passed in return for the alcohol, so if a bona fide gift of alcohol is made to a person who is drunk, this would seem to fall outside the offence.[47] Less clear is the case where there is a transaction in the nature of a sale, as where a person who is drunk is given alcohol in exchange for some valuable consideration. Under the Licensing Act 1964, a sale might be regarded as having taken place in such circumstances, for there was a provision in s 196(1) whereby evidence that a transaction in the nature of a sale took place was to be evidence of a sale without proof that money passed. There is, however, no equivalent provision in the 2003 Act. It seems, therefore, that unless 'sale' is to be construed to include an exchange for valuable consideration other than money, no offence may be committed. No reference is made in the section to a retail sale of alcohol, so it must be assumed that any sale, whether retail or otherwise, falls within the offence.[48] In cases of an 'attempt to sell', the requirements set out in the Criminal Attempts Act 1981 will have application in determining whether an attempt has taken place (see 11.2.8–11.2.9 above). The term 'allow' for the offence in s 141(1)(b) includes not only doing something positive to facilitate the activity, but also failing to exercise any control to prevent it in cases where there is the power to do so (see 11.2.19 above).

As to whether a person is 'drunk', no definition is provided in the Act and the word should therefore be given its ordinary and natural meaning. Such a meaning was considered by the Divisional Court in *Neale v RJME (A Minor)* (1985) 80 Cr App R 20 in respect of the offence under s 12 of the Licensing Act 1872 of disorderly behaviour in a public place whilst drunk, where Robert Goff LJ stated (at 23):

> the natural and ordinary meaning of the word, as found in the statute, appears to me to coincide with the primary dictionary meaning. The primary meaning set out in the Shorter Oxford Dictionary (1933) is as follows: "That has drunk intoxicating liquor to an extent which affects steady self-control." . . . In my judgment, that is indeed the natural and ordinary meaning of the word "drunk" in ordinary common speech in 1984.

There seems no reason why the ordinary and natural meaning should not apply in respect of the offences in s 141 or why any different meaning should be given to the word 'drunk' at the present time from that given by the court in this case.

It is clear from the wording of s 141(1) that the person selling or attempting to sell must be on relevant premises when the sale or attempted sale to the person who is drunk takes place, but it is less clear whether the person who is drunk needs to be on the relevant premises at the time or whether there needs to be consumption (or intended consumption) by him of the alcohol on the premises. The reference to being 'on relevant premises' in s 141(1) might be read as having application only to the person selling or attempting to sell or as having application both to that person and the person who is drunk. If read in the former sense, the section might encompass a case where there is a sale or attempted sale from public house premises through an off-sales window to a person outside the premises who is drunk and who seeks to purchase alcohol for consumption off the premises. If read in the latter sense, such a case would fall outside the offence. As the mischief at which the offence is aimed is preventing a person who is drunk from consuming more alcohol, whether or not that person is on the premises is of no real significance and it may be better if a broad interpretation is given to the section to require only the person making the sale or attempted sale to be on the premises.

The mental element required for each of the offences is knowledge (see 11.2.15–11.2.17 above) on the part of the person who may commit it and for s 141(1)(a) this might be interpreted to mean knowledge that a sale or attempted sale is being made to a person who is in fact drunk or knowledge as to both elements, that is, the sale or attempted sale and the person being drunk. The position is similar for s 141(1)(b) in respect of allowing the sale and the person being drunk. Neither of the previous offences that these offences replaced, ss 172(3) and 172(3A) of the Licensing Act 1964,[49] included any reference to 'knowledge' nor was any provision made for a 'due diligence' defence in respect of them, so liability was strict. By including a mental element of knowledge for the offences in s 141, it seems unlikely that Parliament intended it simply to relate to the element of sale, where it serves little meaningful purpose, and it is submitted that knowledge should be required as to both sale and as to the person being drunk. This would accord with the 'ordinary construction' principle set out in *Croyalgrange* (see 11.2.16 above). Proof of knowledge should not present an insuperable burden for the prosecution where there is compelling evidence in the form of unsteady gait or slurred speech (shurely shome mishtake . . .) on the part of that person intending to purchase. In cases where the charge is one of allowing alcohol to be sold to a person who is drunk, knowledge may be imputed where there has been a delegation of authority (see 11.5.5 above).

11.5.9  The offences are ones for which a penalty notice for disorder (PND) carrying an £80 fixed penalty can be given under s 2 of the Criminal Justice and Police Act 2001 in cases where a constable has reason to believe that a person has committed the offence. PNDs were introduced in 2001, specifically to tackle low-level antisocial behaviour for certain offences that were of a more serious nature than that for which Fixed Penalty Notices of £50 could be given and to reduce police bureaucracy in dealing with these types of crimes. The offences for which a PND might be issued encompass various offences under the Licensing Act 2003, including the offence in s 141, as a result of the Licensing Act 2003 (Consequential Amendments) Order 2005, SI 2005/3048, which replaced previous references to offences under the Licensing Act 1964.[50]

Under s 2(4) of the 2001 Act a PND offers a person the opportunity, by paying the fixed penalty, to discharge any liability to be convicted of the offence to which the PND relates. If the person declines the opportunity and asks to be tried for the alleged offence, a PND cannot be issued and proceedings may be brought against the person (s 4(2)). But if the opportunity is accepted and a PND is issued, no proceedings may be brought within 21 days and, if the penalty is paid within that period, no proceedings may be brought thereafter for the offence (s 5). If there has been no request to be tried for the offence and the fixed penalty is not paid within the 21-day period, a sum equal to one and a half times the amount of the penalty may be registered under s 8 for enforcement against that person as a fine (s 4(5)). Where a PND is accepted, however, this does not count as getting a conviction for the offence nor does payment of the fixed penalty constitute an admission of guilt (Explanatory Note 8 to the 2001 Act).

## 11.5.10   Obtaining alcohol for a person who is drunk

11.5.11 Section 142 provides:

   (1)  A person commits an offence if, on relevant premises, he knowingly obtains or attempts to obtain alcohol for consumption on those premises by a person who is drunk.

   (2)  A person guilty of an offence under this section is liable on summary conviction to a fine not exceeding level 3 on the standard scale.

Liability for this offence is confined to cases where alcohol is obtained for consumption on the premises, for which there will need to be in force a premises licence, CPC or TEN (otherwise they will not be 'relevant premises' – see 11.5.1 above), although it would not seem to be necessary for the licensable activities to include the sale by retail or supply of alcohol on the premises. If only regulated entertainment and/or the provision of LNR can be provided, but a person obtains or attempts to obtain alcohol for consumption on the premises by a person who is drunk, the offence would seem to be made out. As with s 141, the mischief aimed at by the offence is preventing a person who is drunk from consuming more alcohol and it may be that the offence should not be restricted to cases where consumption occurs on premises where the licensable activities include the sale by retail or supply of alcohol. It is, however, necessary that the obtaining or attempted obtaining is for consumption on the premises and no offence is committed if the obtaining or attempted obtaining is for consumption off the premises.[51]

11.5.12 The conduct element of the offence requires that a person 'obtains or attempts to obtain' alcohol. 'Obtain' seems wide enough to cover not only cases where a person purchases alcohol for someone who is drunk, but also instances where a person acquires alcohol either for valuable consideration other than money or without payment, as where a free drink is given. No reference is made in the section to obtaining alcohol by a retail sale so it must be assumed that any obtaining of alcohol, through whatever means, falls within the offence. In cases of an 'attempt to sell', the requirements set out in the Criminal Attempts Act 1981 will have application in determining whether an attempt has taken place (see 11.2.8–11.2.9 above). The mental element required for the offence is knowledge (see 11.2.15–11.2.17 above), which should be knowledge both as to the element of obtaining or attempted obtaining and as to the person being drunk.[52] This would accord with the 'ordinary construction' principle set out in *Croyalgrange* (see 11.2.16 above).

### 11.5.13   Failure to leave relevant premises

11.5.14 Section 143 provides:

(1) A person who is drunk or disorderly commits an offence if, without reasonable excuse–
  (a) he fails to leave relevant premises when requested to do so by a constable or by a person to whom subsection (2) applies, or
  (b) he enters or attempts to enter relevant premises after a constable or a person to whom subsection (2) applies has requested him not to enter.

(2) This subsection applies–
  (a) to any person who works at the premises in a capacity, whether paid or unpaid, which authorises him to make such a request,
  (b) in the case of licensed premises, to–
    (i)  the holder of a premises licence in respect of the premises, or
    (ii) the designated premises supervisor (if any) under such a licence,
  (c) in the case of premises in respect of which a club premises certificate has effect, to any member or officer of the club which holds the certificate who is present on the premises in a capacity which enables him to make such a request, and
  (d) in the case of premises which may be used for a permitted temporary activity by virtue of Part 5, to the premises user in relation to the temporary event notice in question.

(3) A person guilty of an offence under subsection (1) is liable on summary conviction to a fine not exceeding level 1 on the standard scale.

(4) On being requested to do so by a person to whom subsection (2) applies, a constable must–
  (a) help to expel from relevant premises a person who is drunk or disorderly,
  (b) help to prevent such a person from entering relevant premises.

11.5.15 The conduct element of the offence requires that a person be drunk or disorderly and either fails to leave the relevant premises (see 11.5.1 above) on request or enters or attempts to enter following a request not to do so.[53] A request may be made by a constable or any of the persons who may themselves be liable either for selling or attempting to sell alcohol to a person who is drunk on relevant premises or for allowing disorderly conduct to take place on the premises. Any such persons may, under s 143(4), require a constable to provide assistance in removing a person who has been requested to leave or in preventing a person entering who has been requested not to enter. No provision is made, however, for the constable to use such force as may be required for this purpose nor is a constable authorised to arrest an offender.

11.5.16 No reference is made to any mental element, although it may perhaps be implicit that the person appreciates that a request has been made for him to leave or not to enter. In any event, a defence of reasonable excuse is provided, which might apply, for example, if a person is ill, disabled or injured, and so unable to leave the premises. The legal burden of proof for this defence will probably be on the defence on a balance of probabilities (see 11.2.13 above).

## 11.6   SMUGGLED GOODS

11.6.1  Section 144 provides:

(1) A person to whom subsection (2) applies commits an offence if he knowingly keeps or allows to be kept, on any relevant premises, any goods which have been imported without payment of duty or which have otherwise been unlawfully imported.

(2) This subsection applies–

(a) to any person who works at the premises in a capacity, whether paid or unpaid, which gives him authority to prevent the keeping of the goods on the premises,

(b) in the case of licensed premises, to–

(i) the holder of a premises licence in respect of the premises, and

(ii) the designated premises supervisor (if any) under such a licence,

(c) in the case of premises in respect of which a club premises certificate has effect, to any member or officer of the club which holds the certificate who is present on the premises at any time when the goods are kept on the premises in a capacity which enables him to prevent them being so kept, and

(d) in the case of premises which may be used for a permitted temporary activity by virtue of Part 5, to the premises user in relation to the temporary event notice in question.

(3) A person guilty of an offence under this section is liable on summary conviction to a fine not exceeding level 3 on the standard scale.

(4) The court by which a person is convicted of an offence under this section may order the goods in question, and any container for them, to be forfeited and either destroyed or dealt with in such other manner as the court may order.

This offence is aimed primarily at the sale in relevant premises (see 11.5.1 above) of cigarettes and alcohol smuggled in from abroad, as is apparent from para 14.22 of the 2004 Guidance:

The sale of contraband cigarettes and alcohol is a matter of considerable concern to the Government. In addition, some of the goods sold have not been manufactured by responsible manufacturers but are fake products smuggled from Eastern European countries and China on behalf of organised criminal gangs and could therefore contain dangerous ingredients.[54]

11.6.2   The conduct element of the offence, however, extends considerably beyond the sale of these goods. First, it is not necessary for any sale to take place or even that the goods are kept for sale. It is only necessary that the goods are kept or allowed to be kept on the premises by any of the persons specified in s 144(2),[55] so mere possession will suffice. Secondly, the offence applies not only to 'any goods which have been imported without payment of duty', which will include but are not limited to contraband cigarettes and alcohol, but also to 'any goods . . . which have otherwise been unlawfully imported'. This might include any goods in respect of which there is an import prohibition, such as obscene material, drugs, or counterfeit currency. Allowing any of these goods to be kept on the premises, even if not commercially imported and only in small quantities and for personal use, will suffice for the commission of the offence.

11.6.3   The mental element required for the offence is knowledge (see 11.2.15–11.2.17 above) on the part of the person who keeps the goods or allows them to be kept on the premises. As with the offence in s 136(1)(b), there is more than one component to which the element of knowledge might apply – knowledge might be confined to the first-mentioned element of keeping or it might also be required in respect of the element of the goods having being imported unlawfully – and under the 'ordinary construction' principle in *Croyalgrange* prima facie knowledge is required for each component (see 11.2.16 above). This construction may become the conclusive one if knowledge cannot be regarded as having any meaningful application if it is confined to the first-mentioned component only, but this does not seem to be the case here. A person may be aware that he is keeping goods but equally may well not be aware that he is doing so if, for example, they are brought onto the premises by a third party without his authority or they remain on the premises when he has expected them to be removed. Knowledge might therefore have a meaningful application if confined to the requirement of keeping. Notwithstanding this, the construction should become the conclusive one unless there is a good reason for departure from the 'ordinary construction' principle that knowledge is needed for each component.

One reason might be that, where a person 'keeps' goods, this seems not to be substantively different from where he has goods 'in his possession or under his control', as is required for the offence in s 138,[56] and 'possession' cases require only knowledge of having control of the goods and not knowledge as to their nature or identity (see 11.4.1 above). On this basis, knowledge might similarly be required only as to the goods being kept on the premises and not that they have been unlawfully imported, although against this it might be said that s 138, unlike s 144, contains no reference to 'knowingly'. A further reason might be that knowledge of unlawful importation might be difficult for the prosecution to prove. The difficulty for the prosecution in establishing knowledge, whilst it may be advanced as a justification for dispensing with the need for the prosecution to prove *mens rea*, does not generally seem to have found much favour with the courts in relation to licensing offences. When the Court of Appeal, for example, in *R v Edwards* [1975] QB 27 (which was subsequently approved by the House of Lords in *R v Hunt* [1987] AC 352), decided that for the offence of selling intoxicating liquor without a licence under s 160 of the Licensing Act 1964 the burden of proof (exceptionally) was on the defendant to prove that he had a licence, it expressly declined to base its decision on the difficulty of the prosecution proving knowledge. Referring to the exception's application to the general rule of the burden being on the prosecution, Lawton LJ stated (at 40):

> In our judgment its application does not depend on either the fact, or the presumption, that the defendant has peculiar knowledge enabling him to prove the positive of any negative averment. As Wigmore pointed out in his great treatise on evidence this concept of peculiar knowledge furnishes no working rule. If it did, defendants would have to prove lack of intent.[57]

Similarly, the House of Lords in *Croyalgrange* (see 11.2.16 above), rejected difficulty of proof of knowledge that sex establishment premises were unlicensed as a basis for confining the knowledge requirement to use of premises as a sex establishment. Lord Bridge stated (at [1986] 1 WLR 674 at 682–83):

> The main thrust of the argument for the council was . . . [that] it will put an impossible burden on the controlling authorities . . . if they are required to prove against those who use, or permit the use of, premises as sex establishments that they knew that the use was unlicensed . . . [but] if the problem of controlling sex establishments is so acute as to require the creation of an offence of strict liability, it is, of course, for Parliament, not for your Lordships, exercising the judicial function of the House, to take that step.

There seems therefore to be a strong judicial preference for not displacing the 'ordinary construction' principle in licensing cases where there is an express reference to 'knowingly' in a statutory provision, which suggests that the knowledge requirement in s 144 should have application to both the elements of keeping and unlawful importation. With regard to the requirement of knowledge that goods have been unlawfully imported, it should not be necessary to prove that the defendant knows the particular nature of the goods. It should suffice if he knows that the goods were ones the importation of which was prohibited. This seems to follow from decisions on unlawful importation of drugs such as *R v Hussain* [1969] 2 QB 567 and *R v Shivpuri* [1987] AC 1.[58] That this is how s 144 should be interpreted might be reinforced by the fact that, if knowledge is needed only as to keeping, a person who buys some goods in good faith, acting impeccably with no reason to suppose that the goods have been unlawfully imported, will be liable for the offence, as no 'due diligence' defence is provided by the section.[59]

Where a person is convicted of this offence, the court may, under s 144(4), order the confiscation of the goods and any container for them, which may then be either destroyed or otherwise dealt with as the court sees fit.

## 11.7    CHILDREN AND ALCOHOL

11.7.1   Sections 145–55 contain a range of offences involving children and alcohol, which broadly fall into four categories:

- unaccompanied children prohibited from certain premises;
- sales of alcohol to children;

- acquisition of alcohol by or for children; and
- sales to others involving children.

'Children', for these purposes, are generally persons under the age of 18 (see 4.2.14 above), although the prohibition on unaccompanied children relates to children under 16 and in some instances alcohol may be consumed by children who are aged 16 or 17.

In addition, a power is conferred on the police, by s 155, to confiscate from persons under the age of 18 alcohol in sealed containers, which complements the existing right to require surrender of alcohol where it is in open containers (see 11.7.36 below).[60]

## 11.7.2 Unaccompanied children prohibited from certain premises

11.7.3  Section 145 makes it an offence to allow children under 16 to be on certain categories of 'relevant premises' (see 11.5.1 above) if they are not accompanied by an adult when those premises are open for the supply of alcohol for consumption there. The elements of the offence differ according to the category of premises and there are two categories. One is premises used exclusively or primarily for the supply of alcohol for consumption on the premises (hereafter 'exclusive or primary use'). This includes not only premises used on a permanent basis for such supplies, under either a premises licence or CPC, but also premises open for the supply of alcohol for consumption on the premises under a TEN which, at the time the TEN has effect, are used exclusively or primarily for such supplies. The other is premises that are open for the supply for alcohol for consumption there, although not used exclusively or primarily for such supplies.

For the former category, it is an offence to allow an unaccompanied child under 16 on the premises at any time when the premises are open for the supply of alcohol, whereas for the latter category it is offence to do so only at a time between midnight and 5.00 am when the premises are open for the supply for alcohol. Persons who can commit the offence are those who are in a position to request that a child under 16 who is unaccompanied by an adult leaves the premises. These are any person working there in a capacity which authorises him to request the child leaves, a premises licence holder or DPS, a member or officer of a club holding a CPC who is present in a capacity that authorises him to request the child leaves and, in the case of a TEN, the premises user. Section 145(1)–(4) provides:

(1)  A person to whom subsection (3) applies commits an offence if–

    (a)  knowing that relevant premises are within subsection (4), he allows an unaccompanied child to be on the premises at a time when they are open for the purposes of being used for the supply of alcohol[61] for consumption there, or

    (b)  he allows an unaccompanied child to be on relevant premises at a time between the hours of midnight and 5 am when the premises are open for the purposes of being used for the supply of alcohol for consumption there.

(2)  For the purposes of this section–

    (a)  "child" means an individual aged under 16,

    (b)  a child is unaccompanied if he is not in the company of an individual aged 18 or over.

(3)  This subsection applies–

   (a)  to any person who works at the premises in a capacity, whether paid or unpaid, which authorises him to request the unaccompanied child to leave the premises,

   (b)  in the case of licensed premises, to–

      (i)   the holder of a premises licence in respect of the premises, and

      (ii)  the designated premises supervisor (if any) under such a licence,

   (c)  in the case of premises in respect of which a club premises certificate has effect, to any member or officer of the club which holds the certificate who is present on the premises in a capacity which enables him to make such a request, and

   (d)  in the case of premises which may be used for a permitted temporary activity by virtue of Part 5, to the premises user in relation to the temporary event notice in question.

(4)  Relevant premises are within this subsection if–

   (a)  they are exclusively or primarily used for the supply of alcohol for consumption on the premises, or

   (b)  they are open for the purposes of being used for the supply of alcohol for consumption on the premises by virtue of Part 5 (permitted temporary activities) and, at the time the temporary event notice in question has effect, they are exclusively or primarily used for such supplies.

11.7.4  Whether there is exclusive or primary use will be a question of fact in the circumstances of the particular case and this will presumably be determined by reference to use of the premises as a whole. (Exclusive or primary use additionally arises in connection with the fee payable for premises licence applications and reference should also be made to 6.3.1 above.) Public houses or (drinking) clubs will most obviously be premises so used, but, given that many provide a measure of refreshment and/or entertainment, it may not always be easy to establish whether alcohol is the primary use. Whilst this will be a question of degree, the Guidance, in para 13.45, cautions against adoption of any particular formula or method of calculation:

> It is not intended that the definition "exclusively or primarily" in relation to the consumption of alcohol should be applied in a particular way by reference to turnover, floorspace or any similar measure. The expression should be given its ordinary and natural meaning in the context of the particular circumstances. It will normally be quite clear that the business being operated at the premises is predominantly the sale and consumption of alcohol. Mixed businesses may be harder to pigeon hole and it would be sensible for both operators and enforcement agencies to consult where necessary about their respective interpretations of the activities taking place on the premises before any moves are taken which might lead to prosecution.

The effect of the above provisions is that, where there is exclusive or primary use, it will be an offence to allow unaccompanied children under 16 to be on the premises at any time. Whilst this may effectively bar unaccompanied children under 16 from such premises, this does not mean that children between 16 and 18 are necessarily permitted to have access to such premises, if accompanied, or to any other licensed premises. The Guidance, para 13.46, states:

> The fact that the . . . offence may effectively bar children under 16 unaccompanied by an adult from premises where the consumption of alcohol is the exclusive or primary activity does not mean that the 2003 Act automatically permits unaccompanied

children under the age of 18 to have free access to other premises or to the same premises even if they are accompanied or to premises where the consumption of alcohol is not involved. Subject only to the provisions of the 2003 Act and any licence or certificate conditions, admission will always be at the discretion of those managing the premises. The 2003 Act includes on the one hand, no presumption of giving children access or on the other hand, no presumption of preventing their access to licensed premises. Each application and the circumstances obtaining at each premises must be considered on its own merits.

However, allowing unaccompanied children to be on premises where there is no exclusive or primary use will be an offence only where they are there between the hours of midnight and 5.00 am. As the Guidance, para 13.44 states:

> Between 5am and midnight the offence would not necessarily apply to many restaurants, hotels, cinemas and even many pubs where the main business activity is the consumption of both food and drink.

Equally, between these hours the offence would not necessarily apply to many night-clubs; but whilst the offence may not apply, this 'does not mean that children should automatically be admitted to such premises'.[62]

11.7.5 The conduct element of the offence requires that the premises are 'relevant premises' within s 145(4), that is, they fall into one of the two categories specified, that they are open for the purposes of being used for the supply of alcohol, and that the person who allows (see 11.2.18–11.2.20 above) an unaccompanied child under 16 to be on the premises (at any time or between midnight and 5.00 am as applicable) is in a position to request the child to leave. No mental element is specified in s 145(1), except in relation to the requirement of the premises being exclusively or primarily used for the supply of alcohol for consumption on the premises, for which knowledge (see 11.2.15–11.2.17 above) is required. If the premises are found as a matter of fact to be so used it is likely that knowledge will be readily inferred since a number of persons who might commit the offence (for example, a premises licence holder, a DPS, a premises user under a TEN) will clearly be aware of the use of the premises. It is perhaps only in respect of persons working at the premises (in a capacity that authorises them to request the unaccompanied child to leave) that knowledge might be more difficult to establish.

No reference being made to any mental element and provision of the defences in s 145(6) and (8) (see 11.7.6 below) strongly suggests that liability is strict (see 11.2.6 above). It will thus not be necessary for the prosecution to establish that a person is aware that the premises are open for the purposes of being used for the supply of alcohol, that the child is under 16 and is unaccompanied, and that the child is on the premises.

The offence is summary only and punishable by a level 3 fine on the standard scale. Section 145(9) provides:

> A person guilty of an offence under this section is liable on summary conviction to a fine not exceeding level 3 on the standard scale.

However, no offence is committed where the unaccompanied child is merely passing through the premises, where this is the only convenient route, for s 145(5) provides:

> No offence is committed under this section if the unaccompanied child is on the premises solely for the purpose of passing to or from some other place to or from which there is no other convenient means of access or egress.

It is unclear on whom the burden of proof will lie in this respect. Section 145(5) is not expressed to be by way of defence, so it may be that the burden will be on the prosecution to show beyond reasonable doubt that the requirements of this subsection are not met. On the other hand, the Court of Appeal in *R v Edwards* [1975] QB 27 (see 11.6.3 above) held that, in cases where the true construction of a statute is that it prohibits the doing of an act subject to provisos or exceptions, the prosecution are not required to prove that the proviso or exception does not have application. The legal burden is on the defence in such cases to prove on a balance of probabilities the existence of the proviso or exception. This may well be the case here, since s 145(5) seems to provide a proviso or exception to the general prohibition on unaccompanied children being on the premises.

11.7.6   Section 145(6) and (8) each provides a defence, the former where there is a 'reasonable belief' that the child was over 16 or that the person accompanying him was an adult and the latter where there has been 'due diligence' to avoid the commission of the offence. Section 145(6)–(8) provides:

> (6) Where a person is charged with an offence under this section by reason of his own conduct it is a defence that–
>
>   (a) he believed that the unaccompanied child was aged 16 or over or that an individual accompanying him was aged 18 or over, and
>
>   (b) either–
>
>     (i) he had taken all reasonable steps to establish the individual's age, or
>
>     (ii) nobody could reasonably have suspected from the individual's appearance that he was aged under 16 or, as the case may be, under 18.
>
> (7) For the purposes of subsection (6), a person is treated as having taken all reasonable steps to establish an individual's age if–
>
>   (a) he asked the individual for evidence of his age, and
>
>   (b) the evidence would have convinced a reasonable person.
>
> (8) Where a person ("the accused") is charged with an offence under this section by reason of the act or default of some other person, it is a defence that the accused exercised all due diligence to avoid committing it.

The requirements for the defence of 'reasonable belief' are comparable to those for the defence in s 146(4) for the offence in s 146 of selling alcohol to children (see 11.7.10 below), but the due diligence defence in s 145(8) differs from that for that provided by s 139 for the offences in ss 136–38 (see 11.2.10–11.2.13 above). It is less restrictive in its formulation, requiring only that the offence occurs by reason of the act or default of another and that all due diligence has been exercised. There is no requirement of taking reasonable precautions or the act in question being attributable to specified causes. The absence of a reasonable precautions element may reflect the fact that, as the defence in s 145(8) is available only where a person is charged by reason of the act or default of another, the person might not be in a position to have taken reasonable precautions by setting up a proper prevention system for avoiding commission of the offence.[63] Notwithstanding the absence of any specified reasonable precautions element, it remains possible that the defence in s 145(8) may be interpreted as requiring both a proper prevention system and a proper checking system in the same way as if a reference to reasonable precautions had also been expressly included in its formulation. No further explanation for the different formulations of the due diligence defence is provided in either the Explanatory Notes or the Guidance and it remains to be seen whether in practice they will differ significantly in terms of their scope and application.

### 11.7.7  Sales of alcohol to children

### *11.7.8  Sale of alcohol to children*

11.7.9   The main offence involving sales of alcohol to children is contained in s 146(1), which provides:

> A person commits an offence if he sells alcohol to an individual aged under 18.

An offence will also be committed where there is a supply of alcohol to children on premises where supplies of alcohol are authorised by a CPC, for s 146(2) and (3) provides:

> (2)  A club commits an offence if alcohol is supplied by it or on its behalf–
>> (a)  to, or to the order of, a member of the club who is aged under 18, or
>> (b)  on the order of a member of the club, to an individual who is aged under 18.
> (3)  A person commits an offence if he supplies alcohol on behalf of a club–
>> (a)  to, or to the order of, a member of the club who is aged under 18, or
>> (b)  to the order of a member of the club, to an individual who is aged under 18.

The conduct element of these offences requires that a sale or supply of alcohol is made to an individual who is under the age of 18, so liability arises only where there is a sale or supply and not where there is an attempted sale or supply.[64] It is clear that the offence can be committed either personally, by reason of a person's own conduct, or through the act or default of another person, not least since s 146(4) and (6) expressly so provides when making provision for a defence in each instance (see 11.7.10 below).

*Section 146(1)*

The offence in s 146(1) applies to sales that take place anywhere and by any person. It might therefore apply not only where a retail sale of alcohol takes place as a licensable activity, but also in cases where it does not, as where an exemption is provided (see s 173 and 6.1.8–6.1.14 above). Nevertheless, proceedings are likely to be initiated, in the main, where sales or supply take place where there is an authorisation under the 2003 Act. The offence requires that a person 'sells' alcohol to an individual aged under 18 and this will most obviously include the person who is the owner of the alcohol, since it is the owner who is in a position to make a contractual sale of the alcohol to the purchaser. Where the sale of alcohol is authorised under a premises licence, the person owning the alcohol in most cases is likely to be the premises licence holder (and where sale is authorised under a TEN, it is likely to be premises user). The premises licence holder may be an individual or a corporate or unincorporated body such as a company or a partnership, since both individuals and bodies fall within the various categories of persons who can make an application for a premises licence (see s 16 and 6.2 above). Section 146(1) refers to a 'person' committing the offence and it is well established that this expression can include both individuals as well as corporate and unincorporated bodies (see 6.2.3 above), so premises licence holders might be liable irrespective of their status.[65]

Whilst it has not been definitely established that premises licence holders can be liable for the offence in s 146(1), successful prosecutions have been brought in Magistrates' Courts against corporate premises licence holders and these provide some persuasive supporting authority. Thus, in *Carmarthenshire County Council v Co-operative Group (CWS) Ltd, Tesco Stores Ltd and Others* (2007) 70 *Licensing Review* 32 (*Carmarthenshire*), District Judge Watkins stated (at para 9):

> The sale of alcohol for the purposes of s146(1) Licensing Act 2003 can be made by the owner of the alcohol where that person is the premises licence holder and employs the designated premises supervisor and/or the personal licence holder by whom and under whose authority the alcohol was sold.

Similarly, in *Tesco Express v Birmingham City Council and Chief Constable of West Midlands Police* (2007) 70 *Licensing Review* 34, District Judge Munro, in holding that Tesco Express as premises licence holder could be prosecuted under s 146, stated (at para 16):

> In coming to my decision I have had regard to the *Guidance* issued under the Licensing Act 2003, *Patersons*, and s187 of the Licensing Act.[66] My view is that the Appellant could have been prosecuted under this section. The Respondents say that s147A[67] has been specifically created to deal with this type of offending by corporate bodies. I take the view that s146 and s147A are distinct sections and therefore distinct offences.

Premises licence holders who are individuals equally might be liable where they are owners of the alcohol. They might personally 'sell' the alcohol and be liable by reason of their own conduct or the sale may be made by another person, such as a personal licence holder, in which case they might be liable by reason of the act or default of that person. Not all premises licence holders, however, will be owners of the alcohol since there may be cases where, for example, premises licences are held by pub-operating companies in respect of premises that are run by tenants. It will be tenants who have ownership of the alcohol and who make sales of it, not the premises licence holder. Accordingly, the premises licence holder will not 'sell' alcohol as the owner and be liable under the section. This view is reflected in Guidance issued by LACORS in August 2007 which, having stated (at para 4.3) that 'having regard to section 187 and the wording of section 146 of the Licensing Act 2003, a corporate body that sells alcohol may commit an offence of selling alcohol to a person under the age of 18', goes on to provide: ' a pub-owning company, using tenants, that has no title to the stock, and does not "sell" cannot, therefore commit an offence under section 146'. However, there would seem to be no reason why the tenant should not be liable in such a case. It is likely that the tenant will be the DPS for the premises, and as such will hold a personal licence (since this is a requirement for a person to be the DPS), although the position should be the same if he is neither the DPS nor a personal licence holder. The basis of his liability is that he 'sells' as owner, so it should not matter whether he is the DPS or a personal licence holder as he is not making the sale in this capacity.

A narrow construction of s 146(1) might confine liability for the offence to the owner of the alchol, although it is likely that a broader construction will be given to the section. Courts have traditionally regarded liability for regulatory offences where a person 'sells' as extending to those who, although not the owner of the goods, physically make the sale transaction itself. Thus, in *Hotchin v Hindmarsh* [1891] 2 QB 181, the High Court held that an employee of a dairy company who made a sale of adulterated milk to a purchaser was liable as a person who 'sells' an article of food that was not of the nature, substance and quality demanded by the purchaser, contrary to s 6 of the Sale of Food and Drugs Act 1875. The court rejected an argument (at 184) that there 'can be no sale by a person who does not render himself liable on the contract of sale' (which would have confined liability to the owner), with Lord Coleridge CJ stating (at 186–187) that 'a person who takes the article in his hand, and performs the physical act of transferring the adulterated thing to the purchaser, is a person who sells within this section'. The person who physically transacts the sale might be any one of a number of persons. It could conceivably be a premises licence holder who is not the owner of the alcohol, although this would perhaps be unlikely. More likely is that it would be the DPS or a personal licence holder, or a person authorised to make the sale by one or other of these persons.

Whilst the owner of the alcohol and the person physically selling it might be liable for the offence under s 146(1), it is less clear whether other persons, by reason of the position that they may hold in respect of the premises, may have responsibility for sales attributed to them and be liable. Authorisation for sales of alcohol taking place at particular premises is vested in the premises licence holder for the premises, although it is uncertain whether the premises licence holder can be liable (through the act of default of the person who makes the sale) if he neither owns the alcohol nor physically transacts the sale. More certain is the position of the DPS, for it was held in *Carmarthenshire* (at para 9) that a DPS 'cannot be liable under section 146(1) Licensing Act 2003 merely because of the position he holds'. The court stated (at para 8):

> The Act does not stiputate the duties and responsibilities of the designated premises supervisor. Under s15 he is required to be specified in that role in the premises licence. In sections 140, 141, 143 and 144 the DPS is identified as a prospective defendant. Section 146 is silent about the activity of the DPS under that section.

That the DPS may not be liable by virtue of his position is reinforced by having regard to the main purpose and function of the DPS. The DPS is 'the key person who will usually be charged with day to day management of the premises by the premises licence holder' (Guidance, para 2.13) and is the one specified individual, readily identifiable to enforcement authorities, as the person who is in day-to-day charge of the premises. This purpose is not advanced by making the DPS responsible for the offence in s 146(1).

As regards the position of personal licence holders who do not physically transact sales themselves but authorise others to do so (which could include the DPS since, as a personal licence holder, he may authorise others to make sales), the court in *Carmarthenshire* (at para 9) was of the view that there would be no liability on the part of the personal licence holder: 'A personal licence holder cannot commit an offence under s146 if he does not physically make the sale'. Little is provided in the way of explanation, however, as to why a personal licence holder who has authorised another to make a sale may not be liable. In the absence of any persuasive reasoning, an alternative view in favour of liability might be advanced. The view may be taken that a personal licence holder 'sells' alcohol in such circumstances by reason of the act or default of the person who he has authorised to physically make the sale, in much the same way as the owner of alcohol 'sells' by reason of the act or default of the person who physically makes the sale on his behalf. Parliament has entrusted responsibility for alcohol sales under premises licences to personal licence holders and its intention may have been that, although they can authorise others to make sales, they should retain responsibility for those sales. This would be consistent with para 10.53 of the Guidance, which states that 'whilst the designated premises supervisor or a personal licence holder may authorise other individuals to sell alcohol in their absence, they are responsible for any sales that may be made'. If personal licence holders were not liable where they authorised others to make sales, however inadequate their instructions might be to those persons, and were liable only where they personally effected sales, this might be regarded as frustrating the purpose of requiring the authority of a personal licence to underpin sales of alcohol in licensed premises. Against this, it may be said that imposing liability on personal licence holder may prove to be problematic. As one commentator has observed:

> Imposing liability on personal licence holders would be fraught with practical difficulties. Many premises have more than one personal licence holder, all of whom will have authorised members of staff to make sales. Which one would be liable for any particular offence? Would it be all of them? Perhaps the ones on duty? What if one of them was on leave? Could he still be liable?[68]

In the light of the possible practical difficulties and the ruling in *Carmarthenshire*, it is possible that, if and when the matter comes before a higher court, personal licence holders may be held not to commit the offence under s 146 when they authorise others to commit sales. However, it may be premature at this stage to regard the matter as settled.

*Section 146(2) and (3)*

Whilst the offence in s 146(1) has application to premises with a premises licence or where permitted temporary events take place, the offences in s 146(2) and (3) apply to premises with a CPC. For the offence of supply of alcohol to children where there is a CPC, s 146(2) refers to an offence being committed by a 'club', which suggests that it will be the club that will commit the offence and be charged with it rather than any official who might represent the club, such as the club secretary. A club incurring liability for the offence in s 146(2) might do so as a corporate body (if the club is run as a company limited by guarantee) or as an unincorporated association (if club property is held by trustees for the benefit of members), in accordance with the provision in s 187, which makes general provision for offences by corporate bodies and unincorporated associations (see 11.11.2 below). Where alcohol is supplied by a person on behalf of the club under s 146(3), this will include supplies by club employees and members who are present in a capacity enabling them to prevent the supply such as committee members.

11.7.10 No mention is made of any mental element for the offences in s 146 and, where there is provision of a defence such as due diligence or, as here, 'reasonable belief' that the person is aged 18 or over, it is likely that one will not be required (see 11.2.6 above). Thus alcohol does not have to be knowingly sold or supplied to a person who is aged under 18 and it is sufficient that the person is in fact under that age, although a defendant may rely on the defence of 'reasonable belief' set out in s 146(4), which provides:

Where a person is charged with an offence under this section by reason of his own conduct it is a defence that–

(a) he believed that the individual was aged 18 or over, and

(b) either–

    (i) he had taken all reasonable steps to establish the individual's age, or

    (ii) nobody could reasonably have suspected from the individual's appearance that he was aged under 18.

This applies where the person has been charged with the offence 'by reason of his own conduct', which suggests this will apply where the person charged has personally made the sale or supply. For the defence to succeed, in all cases it will be necessary for there to be an honest belief that the person was aged 18 or over. This alone may suffice if nobody could reasonably have suspected that the person was aged under 18, as may be the case if the purchaser who was under 18 looked exceptionally old for his age. In such a case, it would not occur to anyone to ask for any proof of age and the defence could succeed without any proof being requested. Whether a person looked exceptionally old will depend on 'the individual's appearance', which would seem to be wide enough to include both physical characteristics and the manner of dress. Looking exceptionally old in itself will not suffice for the defence unless the person charged honestly believes the person to be aged 18 or over. If there is a suspicion that the person may be under 18, perhaps because others with whom the person is associating are known to be under that age, the defence will not be made out.

Where the purchaser does not look exceptionally old, it will be necessary for 'all reasonable steps' to be taken to establish the individual's age and s 146(5) makes provision for when a person is deemed to have taken all reasonable steps:

For the purposes of subsection (4), a person is treated as having taken all reasonable steps to establish an individual's age if–

(a) he asked the individual for evidence of his age, and

(b) the evidence would have convinced a reasonable person.

The threshold in respect of the evidence, that it would have 'convinced' a reasonable person, is a high one and seems almost akin to a reasonable person being satisfied 'beyond reasonable doubt'. This may be met where there is production of a nationally-recognised Proof of Age Standards Scheme (PASS)[69] card or a birth certificate coupled with some photographic identification of the person whose name appears on the certificate. Less clear, however, is a case where evidence takes the form of a photographic card where the cardholder is very likely to be over the age of 18, but may not necessarily be (for example, a National Union of Students card). Clearly, if the evidence of age was such that no reasonable person would have been convinced by it, as where the proof of age was either an obvious forgery or clearly belonged to another person, the defence will fail.

Whilst a person may be treated as having taken all reasonable steps if he has complied with s 146(5), this ought not to be the only way that a person can establish that he has taken all reasonable steps to establish the individual's age. If, for instance, a regular customer, well known to the manager of a public house, was to assure the manager that the person accompanying him was over the age of 18 and the manager, believing him to be over 18, was to sell alcohol to him, this might in the circumstances constitute taking all reasonable steps. Section 146(5) does not provide that a person may be treated as having taken all reasonable steps *only* if he asked the individual for evidence of his age and the evidence would have convinced a reasonable person. Whilst this may be conclusive evidence, other evidence of having taken all reasonable steps should suffice for the purposes of s 146(4)(b)(i).

A further defence is provided in circumstances where the sale or supply was not made personally by the person charged with the offence, but by someone else. Here it is a defence where the person charged exercised all due diligence to avoid committing the offence. Section 146(6) provides:

> Where a person ("the accused") is charged with an offence under this section by reason of the act or default of some other person it is a defence that the accused exercised all due diligence to avoid committing it.

For this defence, and for the defence of 'reasonable belief' in s 146(4), the legal burden of proof will probably be on the defence on a balance of probabilities (see 11.2.13 above). Defences are provided in both instances where a 'person' is charged with an offence under the section and need not be confined to cases where an individual commits an offence. They should also extend to cases where a club does so under s 146(2), since the term 'person' in law can include a corporate entity or unincorporated body and provision is made in s 187 for offences by corporate bodies, partnerships and unincorporated associations (see 11.11.2 below).

11.7.11 The maximum penalty for the offences of selling alcohol to children, under s 146(1), or supplying alcohol to children on premises where supplies of alcohol are authorised by a club premises certificate, under s 146(2)(3), is a level 5 fine. Section 146(7) provides:

> A person guilty of an offence under this section is liable on summary conviction to a fine not exceeding level 5 on the standard scale.

Responsibility for enforcement for this offence rests with local trading standards departments so far as sales from premises to which the public have access are concerned and test purchases, including ones by children,[70] can be made to ensure compliance with the provisions of s 146. Section 154 provides:

(1) It is the duty of every local weights and measures authority[71] in England and Wales to enforce within its area the provisions of sections 146 and 147, so far as they apply to sales of alcohol made on or from premises to which the public have access.

(2) A weights and measures inspector[72] may make, or authorise any person to make on his behalf, such purchases of goods as appear expedient for the purpose of determining whether those provisions are being complied with.

This enforcement duty is confined to sales of alcohol made on or from premises 'to which the public have access' and thus does not extend to members' clubs, as these are private premises which are not open to the public.

The offences in s 146(1) and s 146(3) are ones for which a PND carrying an £80 fixed penalty can be given under s 2 of the Criminal Justice and Police Act 2001 in cases where a constable has reason to believe that a person has committed the offence (see 11.5.9 above).

## 11.7.12  *Allowing the sale of alcohol to children*

Section 147 provides:

(1) A person to whom subsection (2) applies commits an offence if he knowingly allows the sale of alcohol on relevant premises to an individual aged under 18.

(2) This subsection applies to a person who works at the premises in a capacity, whether paid or unpaid, which authorises him to prevent the sale.

(3) A person to whom subsection (4) applies commits an offence if he knowingly allows alcohol to be supplied on relevant premises by or on behalf of a club–

   (a) to or to the order of a member of the club who is aged under 18, or

   (b) to the order of a member of the club, to an individual who is aged under 18.

(4) This subsection applies to–

   (a) a person who works on the premises in a capacity, whether paid or unpaid, which authorises him to prevent the supply, and

   (b) any member or officer of the club who at the time of the supply is present on the relevant premises in a capacity which enables him to prevent it.

(5) A person guilty of an offence under this section is liable on summary conviction to a fine not exceeding level 5 on the standard scale.

Section 147 creates two offences – one in s 147(1) and the other in s 147(3). The conduct element of these offences are allowing sale of alcohol to an individual under the age of 18 (s 147(1)) and allowing supply of alcohol to a club member under that age or to a club member for an individual under that age (s 147(3)), where sale or supply is on 'relevant premises' (see 11.5.1 above). The term 'allow' includes not only doing something positive to facilitate the conduct, but also failing to exercise any control to prevent it in cases where there is the power to do so (see 11.2.19 above). No reference is made in the section to a retail sale of alcohol so it seems that in principle any sale, whether retail or otherwise, might fall within the offence. However, the instances in which a sale other than by retail might occur (on which, see s 192 and 5.2.2 above) are unlikely to have application in the case of sales to children, so the offence will, to all intents and purposes, be confined to cases of retail sale. The only persons who can commit the offence are those who work at the premises in a capacity that gives them the authority to prevent the sale or supply and, additionally in the case of a supply on club premises, an officer or member of the club who is present at the time of the supply in a capacity that gives him authority to prevent that supply.

The mental element required for the offence is knowledge (see 11.2.15–11.2.17 above) and, if the 'ordinary construction' principle set out in *Croyalgrange* (see 11.2.16 above) is applied, this will mean that prima facie knowledge is required as to all elements. Accordingly, knowledge will be needed as to allowing the sale to a person and as to the person being under the age of 18. It may be that this construction should become the conclusive one here, as with the offence under s 136(1)(b) (see 11.2.16 above), since the knowledge requirement is unlikely to have any meaningful application if it is confined simply to the first-mentioned element (allowing the sale). Requiring knowledge as to all elements would also be consistent with the scheme of offences in the 2003 Act as a whole. Where there is a sale to a person under the age of 18, s 146 provides a defence of 'reasonable belief' as to the person's age where the sale is made personally and a defence of due diligence based on the act or default of another person where it is not (see 11.7.10 above), but no defence of 'reasonable belief' or 'due diligence' is provided by s 147. If knowledge were to be required only in respect of allowing the sale, there will be liability even if there is no reason to suspect that the person to whom the sale is made might be under the age of 18. This would make the offence stricter in this respect than s 146. If, on the other hand, knowledge were to be required, both as to allowing the sale and as to the person being under the age of 18, the offence would be more difficult to prove than that in s 146 since the prosecution would need to prove knowledge as to age. It would not seem to be consistent with the inclusion of a requirement of knowledge for this offence, but not for s 146, if this offence were to be stricter than s 146 in relation to the age of the person (which is the essence of both offences). Knowledge ought therefore to be required as to the person being under the age of 18 as well as in respect of allowing the sale.[73]

As with the offence in s 146, responsibility for enforcement rests with local trading standards departments (see 11.7.11 above).

### 11.7.13  Persistently Selling alcohol to children

11.7.14 Section 23(1) of the Violent Crime Redecution Act 2006 inserted a new offence into the Licensing Act 2003 of persistently selling alcohol to children. The offence, contained in s 147A, carries a maximum penalty of £10,000 (s 147A(8)), which is double the maximum penalty for the offences of selling alcohol to children under s 146.[74] This offence was introduced because it was felt that the penalties for selling alcohol to children may be insufficient in themselves to curb the level of unlawful sales taking place and that a power was needed for the police and trading standards officers to close premises for up to 48 hours where there was evidence of persistent unlawful sales. Such a power, linked to the offence in s 147A, is provided by ss 169A and 169B (see 11.15 below). Guidance on the offence in s 147A, along with the power of closure, has been issued by the DCMS to police and trading standards officers and is contained in *Interpreting and implementing sections 23 and 24 of the Violent Crime Reduction Act 2006 – Persistently selling to children*[75] (hereafter 'Police and TS Guidance').

The conduct offence of the offence in s 147A requires that, on three or more separate occasions over a three-month period, a person unlawfully sells alcohol to a person under the age of 18 from the same premises where there is in force a premises licence or TEN. Section 147A(1) provides:

(1) A person is guilty of an offence if–
   (a) on 3 or more different occasions within a period of 3 consecutive months alcohol is unlawfully sold on the same premises to an individual aged under 18;
   (b) at the time of each sale the premises were either licensed premises or premises authorised to be used for a permitted temporary activity by virtue of Part 5; and
   (c) that person was a responsible person in relation to the premises at each such time.

The offence is confined to sales from premises where there is in force a premises licence or TEN and does not apply where sales are made under a CPC. However, clubs that operate under a premises licence rather than a CPC will fall within the scope of the offence. In cases where clubs have both a CPC and a premises licence, it seems that an unlawful sale will need to take place under the premises licence authorisation and not the CPC authorisation, in order for it to count as one of the three sales. Although s 147A(1)(b) simply requires that at the time of each sale the premises were licensed premises (or authorised under a TEN), it seems implicit in this provision that the premises need to be operating under the premises licence (or TEN) at the time of the sale, as well as having such an authorisation.

The persons who can commit this offence (a 'responsible person') are the person or one of the persons who, in the case of a premises licence, holds the premises licence or, in the case of a TEN, is the premises user who gave the TEN. Section 147A(4) provides:

(4) A person is, in relation to premises and a time, a responsible person for the purposes of subsection (1) if, at that time, he is–
(a) the person or one of the persons holding a premises licence in respect of the premises; or
(b) the person or one of the persons who is the premises user in respect of a temporary event notice by reference to which the premises are authorised to be used for a permitted temporary activity by virtue of Part 5.

It is not necessary that such persons themselves personally make the sale or are in any way a party to it, for it is sufficient that alcohol is 'unlawfully sold' on the premises to a child. Indeed, where premises licences are held in the name of businesses or organisations, which for instance is a widespread practice with public house operating companies, sales will not be made personally by them. Section 147A does not define 'unlawfully sold' or identify the particular offence or offences in question, but it would seem that the offence will certainly include sale of alcohol to children under s 146 and might also include allowing the sale of alcohol to children under s 147 (see 11.7.7 and 11.7.12 above). For the purposes of the s 147A offence, the individual to whom the alcohol is sold need not be the same person on each of the occasions in question, for s 147A(5) provides: 'The individual to whom the sales mentioned in subsection (1) are made may, but need not, be the same in each case'.

No mental element is specified for the offence for the premises licence holder or premises user to be liable, and, where there is provision of a defence such as due diligence or, as here, 'reasonable belief' that the person is aged 18 or over, it is likely that one will not be required (see 11.2.6 above). Section 147A(1)(a) requires only that alcohol 'is unlawfully sold' and this will be so under s 147A(2) and (3) if the person making the sale believed the individual to be under the age of 18 or did not have reasonable grounds for believing him to be 18 or over. A person has reasonable grounds for so believing only if he asked the individual for evidence of his age and either the evidence produced would have convinced a reasonable person or no person could reasonably have suspected that the person was under the age of 18. Section 147A(2) and (3) provides:

(2) For the purposes of this section alcohol sold to an individual aged under 18 is unlawfully sold to him if–
(a) the person making the sale believed the individual to be aged under 18; or
(b) that person did not have reasonable grounds for believing the individual to be aged 18 or over.
(3) For the purposes of subsection (2) a person has reasonable grounds for believing an individual to be aged 18 or over only if—

(a)  he asked the individual for evidence of his age and that individual produced evidence that would have convinced a reasonable person; or

(b)  nobody could reasonably have suspected from the individual's appearance that he was aged under 18.

It is unclear on whom the burden of proof will lie in respect of belief of age. If s 147A(2) had been expressed to be by way of a defence to the s 147A(1) offence, as is the case with the comparable provision in s 146(4) for the offence of sale of alcohol to children (see 11.7.10 above), it is likely the burden of proof would be on the defence. This would similarly be the case if it was prohibiting the doing of an act subject to a proviso or exception (see 11.7.5 above). However, s 147A(2) is not expressed to be by way of defence nor does it seem to be making any proviso or exception. Accordingly, the burden of proving absence of belief or absence of reasonable grounds for belief may be on the prosecution, in which case this provision incorporates a mental element into the offence for liability. Since reasonable grounds can exist only in either of the two instances mentioned in s 147A(3), the prosecution will need to prove that neither of these instances has application. How this burden might be discharged will depend on what form the proof of unlawful sale takes (see 11.7.15 below).

11.7.15 The question of unlawful sale for the purposes of the offence is determined solely by reference to the person making the sale and whether that person believed the individual to be aged under 18 or lacked any reasonable grounds for believing him to be aged 18 or over. Whilst s 146(4) makes similar provision, there is, in addition, no unlawful sale under s 146 where a person is charged with the offence by reason of the act or default of another person, provided it can be shown that the accused exercised all due diligence to avoid committing the offence. Section 146(6) provides a defence in such a case (see 11.7.10 above). There is, however, no equivalent provision in s 147A, which means that the 'responsible persons' who may commit the s 147A offence – the premises licence holder(s) or the premises user who gave the TEN (see s 147A(4) and 11.7.14 above) – will be liable, in cases where they themselves have not made the sale, without any opportunity to raise a due diligence defence. Perhaps it was felt that a due diligence defence could not have application in light of the nature of the offence in s 147A. The view might have been taken that, if the offence requires unlawful sales to have taken place on three separate occasions within a period of three consecutive months, as it does, this is inconsistent with any possible finding of due diligence.

As regards proof of unlawful sale, this might take the form of a conviction, caution or the issuing of a PND requiring payment of a fixed penalty for the offence in s 146. Section 147A(7) provides:

In determining whether an offence under this section has been committed, the following shall be admissible as evidence that there has been an unlawful sale of alcohol to an individual aged under 18 on any premises on any occasion–

(a)  the conviction of a person for an offence under section 146 in respect of a sale to that individual on those premises on that occasion;

(b)  the giving to a person of a caution (within the meaning of Part 5 of the Police Act 1997) in respect of such an offence; or

(c)  the payment by a person of a fixed penalty under Part 1 of the Criminal Justice and Police Act 2001 in respect of such a sale.

Section 147A(7) makes specific reference to the forms of evidence that are admissible for an unlawful sale. These are a conviction, caution or PND for the offence in s 146, but less clear is whether other forms of evidence might suffice, for example, evidence from an enforcement campaign or undercover operation where no subsequent action has been taken other than the giving of a warning. Similarly it is unclear whether a conviction or caution for the offence of allowing alcohol to be sold under s 147 may be admissible. That the forms specified may be admissible as evidence does not necessarily preclude the admission of other forms of evidence and it is possible that the section may be interpreted to extend beyond the specified forms. Such an interpretation may be supported if recourse is had to Police and TS Guidance (see 11.7.14 above) as an aid to interpretation and this is seen as indicative of Parliamentary intent, for para 22 provides:

> This is not an exclusive list. Other relevant evidence would be admissible. The purpose of this sub-section is to make it clear that although, for example, the payment of a fixed penalty under Part 1 of the 2001 Act discharges further criminal liability for the seller on a specific occasion, the fact of the acceptance of a fixed penalty could be evidence relating to commission of an offence under section 147A for the holder of the premises licence.

Unlawful sale is dependent on the person making the sale believing the individual to be aged under 18 or lacking any reasonable grounds for believing him to be aged 18 or over (see 11.7.14 above) and where there has been a conviction for a s 146 offence the issue of belief or reasonable grounds will have been examined at trial. In such a case, the fact of conviction should be sufficient for the prosecution to discharge the burden of proof on it of proving absence of belief or reasonable grounds. For a caution, there will have been no examination of the issue of belief or reasonable grounds, but a caution is given only where there is sufficient evidence for prosecution and where the person cautioned acknowledges that he is guilty for the offence. In accepting the caution, there is therefore an acknowledgment of absence of belief or reasonable grounds and the fact of caution should again be sufficient for the prosecution to discharge the burden of proof on it of proving these elements. However, the position seems to be different for a PND, which does not appear to involve an acknowledgment of guilt. Although there is no provision to this effect in ss 1–11 of the Criminal Justice and Police Act 2001 which make provision for PNDs, Explanatory Note 8 to the Act provides:

> A penalty notice is notice of the opportunity to discharge any liability to conviction of the offence by payment of a fixed penalty. There is thus no criminal conviction or admission of guilt associated with payment of the penalty, though the alleged offender has the right to opt for trial by a court, and risk conviction, if he so chooses.

If the PND carries no admission of guilt, the fact that a PND has been issued will not be sufficient for the prosecution to discharge the burden of proving absence of belief or reasonable grounds. Whilst the PND is admissible as evidence of an unlawful sale, further evidence will be required if the prosecution is to show that the person making the sale believed the individual was under 18 or had no reasonable grounds for believing he was 18 or over.

Where a prosecution has been instituted under s 146 and a conviction incurred, the premises licence holder will almost certainly be aware of the conviction, but may not be where a caution or PND has been given. There is no requirement for a premises licence holder to be notified of this and the person receiving the caution or PND may choose not to disclose this. It is possible therefore that the premises licence holder may not know of the existence of previous unlawful sales that might count towards the total of three in a three-month period and that might lead to liability being incurred for the s 147A offence.

Whatever form the unlawful sale takes, the same sale may be counted only once for the purpose of enabling the same person to be convicted of the offence under s 147A(1). A person convicted, cautioned or given a PND for a s 146 offence in (say) January, February, March and April may be convicted of only one offence under s 147A(1). This can be based on offences on three occasions in the period of the three consecutive months of January, February and March, or February, March and April. He cannot, however, be convicted of more than one offence under s 147A(1) since the s 146 offence in February cannot (under s 147A(6)(a)) be counted in respect of different s 147A(1) offences (that is, it cannot be counted twice). Similarly, the same sale cannot be counted both for the purposes of an offence under s147A(1) and an offence under either s 146 or s 147. So if a person, after making two unlawful sales of alcohol, makes a third unlawful sale within a period of three consecutive months, he cannot be convicted of an offence under s 147A(1). The same (third) sale cannot, under s 147A(6)(b), be counted for the purposes of a s 146 or s 147 offence (as applicable) and at the same time be counted for the purposes of a s 147A(1) offence. Again, essentially, it cannot be counted twice. Section 147A(6) provides:

> The same sale may not be counted in respect of different offences for the purpose–
>
> (a)  of enabling the same person to be convicted of more than one offence under this section; or
>
> (b)  of enabling the same person to be convicted of both an offence under this section and an offence under section 146 or 147.

For the purposes of calculating whether or not alcohol has been unlawfully sold at the same premises on three occasions within a period of three consecutive months, it is not necessary that on each occasion the premises are operating under the same form of authorisation, that is, a premises licence or TEN. Alcohol may be unlawfully sold to a child on two occasions when the premises are operating under a premises licence and an unlawful sale may take place on a third occasion when a TEN has been issued for the same premises so that sales of alcohol can be made outside the hours authorised by the premises licence. As to whether unlawful sales are within a period of three consecutive months, no definition of 'month' is provided in the section. However, s 5 of and Sched 1 to the Interpretation Act 1978 provides that ' "month" means calendar month', which suggests that s 147A(1)(a) should be interpreted to mean three consective calendar months (for example, January, February and March) and that the three occasions will need to fall within three such calendar months for the offence to be made out. This will not be the case if there are three occasions within a three-month period, but the months in which they occur are not consecutive (for example, a first occasion at the end of January, a second at the beginning of February and a third at the beginning of April). Although these fall within a three-month period, they do not fall within a period of three consecutive months. Further, under s 147A(4), a sale of alcohol does not count for the purposes of s 147A if it took place before the section came into force.

Where a premises licence holder is convicted of this offence, the court may make an order suspending the retail sale of alcohol on the premises for a period not exceeding three months. If any sales were to take place following suspension, this would constitute the offence carrying on an unauthorised licensable activity under s 136(1) and may involve exposing alcohol for unathorised sale under s 137 (see 11.2 and 11.3 above). Only one order of suspension can be made, however, notwithstanding that more than one person may, as premises licence holder, be convicted of this offence (see s 147A(4)(b) and 11.7.14 above). Section 147B(1) and (2) provides:

(1) Where the holder of a premises licence is convicted of an offence under section 147A in respect of sales on the premises to which the licence relates, the court may order that so much of the licence as authorises the sale by retail of alcohol on those premises is suspended for a period not exceeding three months.

(2) Where more than one person is liable for an offence under section 147A relating to the same sales, no more than one order under subsection (1) may be made in relation to the premises in question in respect of convictions by reference to those sales.

Such an order comes into force at a time specified by the court, which may suspend it coming into effect pending an appeal. The powers available to the court to suspend the licence are similar to those available to the court where it orders forfeiture or suspension of a personal licence where the licence holder is convicted of a relevant offence (see ss 129–130 and 10.9.5–10.9.8 above). Section 147B(3)–(5) provides:

(3) Subject to subsections (4) and (5), an order under subsection (1) comes into force at the time specified by the court that makes it.

(4) Where a magistrates' court makes an order under subsection (1), it may suspend its coming into force pending an appeal.

(5) Section 130 (powers of appellate court to suspend section 129 order) applies (with the omission of subsection (9)) where an order under subsection (1) is made on conviction of an offence under section 147A as it applies where an order under section 129 is made on conviction of a relevant offence in Part 6.

Where a person is convicted of the offence under s 147A, or indeed whilst proceedings for the offence are pending, it is open to the police to seek a review of the premises licence under s 51 (see 6.12.3 below).

### 11.7.16 Sale of liqueur confectionery to children under 16

It is an offence for a person to sell liqueur confectionery to a child under the age of 16, or for a club or a person on behalf of a club to supply it to such a child. Section 148(1) and (2) provides:

(1) A person commits an offence if he–
    (a) sells liqueur confectionery to an individual aged under 16, or
    (b) he supplies such confectionery, on behalf of a club–
        (i) to or to the order of a member of the club who is aged under 16, or
        (ii) to the order of a member of the club, to an individual who is aged under 16.

(2) A club commits an offence if liqueur confectionery is supplied by it or on its behalf–
    (a) to or to the order of a member of the club who is aged under 16, or
    (b) to the order of a member of the club, to an individual who is aged under 16.

Section 148 creates two offences, one which can be committed by any person (s 148(1)) and the other which can be committed by a club (s 148(2)). The conduct element of these offences is sale of liqueur confectionery by a person to an individual under the age of 16 (s 148(1)(a)) or supply of liqueur confectionery by a person (s 148(1)(b)) or by a club (s 148(2)) to a club member under that age or to a club member for an individual under that age. The meaning of 'liqueur confectionery' is set out in s 191(2),[76] which provides:

"liqueur confectionery" means confectionery which–

(a)   contains alcohol in a proportion not greater than 0.2 litres of alcohol (of a strength not exceeding 57%) per kilogram of the confectionery, and

(b)   either consists of separate pieces weighing not more than 42g or is designed to be broken into such pieces for the purpose of consumption.

No offence is committed if liqueur confectionery is sold or supplied to persons aged 16 and 17, although the exemption which permits such persons to buy alcohol in the form of liqueur confectionery does not extend to any other foodstuffs that contain alcohol exceeding the prescribed limits.

No mental element is specified for the offence, but defences of 'reasonable belief' and 'due diligence' are provided, which strongly suggest that liability is strict (see 11.2.6 above). Thus liqueur confectionery does not have to be knowingly sold or supplied to a person who is aged under 16 and it is sufficient that the person is in fact under that age. The defences of 'reasonable belief' and 'due diligence' are set out in s 148(3)–(5), which provides:

(3)   Where a person is charged with an offence under this section by reason of his own conduct it is a defence that–

(a)   he believed that the individual was aged 16 or over, and

(b)   either–

(i)   he had taken all reasonable steps to establish the individual's age, or

(ii)   nobody could reasonably have suspected from the individual's appearance that he was aged under 16.

(4)   For the purposes of subsection (3), a person is treated as having taken all reasonable steps to establish an individual's age if–

(a)   he asked the individual for evidence of his age, and

(b)   the evidence would have convinced a reasonable person.

(5)   Where a person ("the accused") is charged with an offence under this section by reason of the act or default of some other person, it is a defence that the accused exercised all due diligence to avoid committing it.

These defences are similar to those applying to the offence, under s 146, of selling or supplying alcohol to children under 18 (see 11.7.10 above).

The maximum penalty for the offence of selling or supplying liqueur confectionery to a person under the age of 16 is a level 2 fine. Section 148(6) provides:

A person guilty of an offence under this section is liable on summary conviction to a fine not exceeding level 2 on the standard scale.

### 11.7.17 Acquisition of alcohol by or for children

### *11.7.18 Purchase of alcohol by or on behalf of children*

11.7.19  Section 149(1) makes it an offence for a child under 18 to purchase or attempt to purchase alcohol, or, if he is a member of a club, for him to have or attempt to have alcohol supplied to him by the club.[77] Section 149(1) provides:

> An individual aged under 18 commits an offence if–
>
> (a)  he buys or attempts to buy alcohol, or
>
> (b)  where he is a member of a club –
>
>   (i)   alcohol is supplied to him or to his order by or on behalf of the club, as a result of some act or default of his, or
>
>   (ii)  he attempts to have alcohol supplied to him or to his order by or on behalf of the club.

The conduct element under s 149(1)(a) is a purchase or attempted purchase of alcohol by an individual under 18, which may take place anywhere and need not be on licensed premises. Under s 149(1)(b), it is the supply or attempted supply where he is a member of a club and it seems this will need to be in circumstances where the individual actively caused the supply, for s 149(1)(b)(i) requires the supply to be 'as a result of some act or default of his'. This does not appear to be necessary, however, in the case of an attempt to have alcohol supplied, for there is no equivalent provision in s 149(1)(b)(ii).

The offence will not be committed if the child buys or attempts to buy alcohol as part of a test purchasing operation carried out by a police constable or trading standards officer to establish whether licensees and staff working in licensed premises are complying with the prohibition on underage sales.[78] Although test purchasing operations are only likely to be carried out in licensed premises, no offence will be committed wherever a child buys or attempts to buy alcohol as part of such an operation, for the provision in s 149(2) is not limited in its application. Section 149(2) provides:

> But subsection (1) does not apply where the individual buys or attempts to buy the alcohol at the request of–
>
> (a)  a constable, or
>
> (b)  a weights and measures inspector,[79]
>
> who is acting in the course of his duty.

As with the provision in s 145(5), the burden of proof here may be on the defence (see 11.7.5 above).

No mental element is specified for the offence, although a mental element may be necessary. This is likely to be the case for an attempt, since attempt requires an intention to commit the offence (see 11.2.9 above). An individual will therefore need an intention to purchase alcohol to be liable, so if he does not know that what he is buying is alcohol (for example, he thinks it is a non-alcoholic drink), he would seem not to have the required intention. If this is the case for an attempted purchase, it would be odd if the position were different where a purchase was made. It seems unlikely that Parliament would have intended there to be a mental element for an attempted purchase but not for an actual purchase. Accordingly, it is submitted that an individual must intend to purchase alcohol and will commit no offence if he is intending to purchase a non-alcholic drink but in fact purchases an alcoholic one.

11.7.20 Section 149(3) makes it an offence for a person to purchase or attempt to purchase alcohol for a child or, if he is a member of a club, for him to have or attempt to have alcohol supplied to him by the club. Section 149(3) provides:

> A person commits an offence if–
> (a) he buys or attempts to buy alcohol on behalf of an individual aged under 18, or
> (b) where he is a member of a club, on behalf of an individual aged under 18 he–
>   (i) makes arrangements whereby alcohol is supplied to him or to his order by or on behalf of the club, or
>   (ii) attempts to make such arrangements.

The conduct element for the offence is a purchase or attempted purchase of alcohol by a person for an individual under 18, which may take place anywhere and need not be on licensed premises, or the supply or attempted supply by a member of a club for such an individual. The general offence provided by this subsection might be an appropriate charge where a child gives money to an adult to buy alcohol in an off-licence for consumption by the child, or where a club member has alcohol supplied to a child or attempts to do so.

No mental element is specified for the offence, but, as with s 149(1), it may be that a person must intend to purchase or secure the supply of alcohol for the individual concerned (see 11.7.19 above). With regard to the child's age, provision of a defence by s 149(6), if there is no reason to suspect that he was under the age of 18, strongly suggests that liability in this respect is strict (see 11.2.6 above). Section 149(6) provides:

> Where a person is charged with an offence under subsection (3) or (4) it is a defence that he had no reason to suspect that the individual was aged under 18.

11.7.21 Section 149(4) creates a more specific offence than s 149(3) to cover cases of purchase or attempted purchase, or supply or attempted supply, for a child where the alcohol is for consumption on the premises and s 149(5) makes provision for this offence not to have application in certain circumstances. Section 149(4) and (5) provides:

> (4) A person ("the relevant person") commits an offence if–
>   (a) he buys or attempts to buy alcohol for consumption on relevant premises by an individual aged under 18, or
>   (b) where he is a member of a club–
>     (i) by some act or default of his, alcohol is supplied to him, or to his order, by or on behalf of the club for consumption on relevant premises by an individual aged under 18, or
>     (ii) he attempts to have alcohol so supplied for such consumption.
> (5) But subsection (4) does not apply where–
>   (a) the relevant person is aged 18 or over,
>   (b) the individual is aged 16 or 17,
>   (c) the alcohol is beer, wine or cider,

(d) its purchase or supply is for consumption at a table meal on relevant premises, and

(e) the individual is accompanied at the meal by an individual aged 18 or over.

The conduct element for the offence is a purchase or attempted purchase of alcohol on relevant premises (see 11.5.1 above) by a person for an individual under 18 and this offence might be an appropriate charge where a father buys a drink for his son under 18 in a public house, or where a club member or officer has alcohol supplied to a child (in circumstances where by act or default he actively caused the supply) or attempted to do so. The position in respect of the mental element for the offence is the same as for s 149(3) (see 11.7.20 above).

This offence, however, is not committed where a person aged 18 or over buys beer, wine or cider for a 16- or 17-year-old to consume with a table meal on relevant premises (see 11.5.1 above) when accompanied by an adult (s 149(5)). As with the provision in s 145(5), the burden of proof here may be on the defence to establish that the requirements of this provision are met (see 11.7.5 above). It is not necessary that the person who purchases the alcohol accompanies the 16- or 17-year-old at the meal and it will suffice if the 16- or 17-year-old is accompanied by any adult, for s 149(5)(e) requires only that there is accompaniment at the meal 'by an individual aged 18 or over'.[80] The purchase or supply must be for consumption 'at' a table meal, which appears to confine the exemption from liability to cases where the alcohol is consumed during the course of the meal and to exclude cases where it is consumed as an aperitif to a meal. The meal must be a 'table meal', which is defined by s 159:

> "table meal" means a meal eaten by a person seated at a table, or at a counter or other structure which serves the purpose of a table and is not used for the service of refreshments for consumption by persons not seated at a table or structure serving the purpose of a table.

Under this definition table meals are 'sit down' meals, where meals are eaten in traditional fashion with persons seated at tables or, in keeping with present-day practices, they may be eaten at a counter or similar structure. Counters where refreshments might be consumed by persons who are not seated, as where persons may be standing at a counter eating sandwiches, will not qualify (in accordance with the latter part of the definition in s 159) as a counter at which a table meal may be served. The counter needs to be one that is *not* used for such purposes, that is, it needs to be a counter for 'sit down' meals.

A 'table meal' will need to be a meal in the ordinary sense of the word, and something more than a snack, for alcohol to be served to a 16- or 17-year-old as an accompaniment. Rather surprisingly, what constitutes a 'meal' or 'table meal' has not generated much in the way of case law guidance and the only two authorities seem to be *Solomon v Green* (1955) 119 JP 289 and *Timmins v Millman* (1965) 109 Sol Jo 31. In *Solomon*, the High Court refused to interfere with a finding by justices that sandwiches and sausages on sticks constituted a 'meal', although Lord Goddard CJ stated (at 290) that the justices, who had themselves described the case as 'borderline', 'might easily have come to the conclusion that it was on the other side of the line'. In *Timmins*, where justices decided that a substantial sandwich accompanied by beetroot and pickles, eaten at a table, might be a 'table meal', the High Court, in a case decided on other grounds, gave no indication that the justices were wrong to take this view.

11.7.22 The two offences in s 149(3) and (4) are regarded as more serious than the offence in s 149(1), where a person under 18 seeks himself to obtain alcohol, and they carry a level 5 fine, as compared to a level 3 fine for the offence in s 149(1). Section 149(7) provides:

> A person guilty of an offence under this section is liable on summary conviction–
> (a) in the case of an offence under subsection (1), to a fine not exceeding level 3 on the standard scale, and
> (b) in the case of an offence under subsection (3) or (4), to a fine not exceeding level 5 on the standard scale.

The offences in s 149 are ones for which a PND carrying an £80 fixed penalty can be given under s 2 of the Criminal Justice and Police Act 2001 in cases where a constable has reason to believe that a person has committed the offence (see 11.5.9 above).

### 11.7.23    Consumption of alcohol by children

11.7.24 Section 150(1) provides:

> An individual aged under 18 commits an offence if he knowingly consumes alcohol on relevant premises.

The conduct element requires consumption of alcohol on relevant premises (see 11.5.1 above) and the offence might be committed not only where there is consumption in premises such as public houses that operate under a premises licence and are open to the public, but also where consumption takes place in clubs operating under a CPC or on premises where events (which may well be private occasions) are taking place under the authority of a TEN. The mental element required for the offence is knowledge (see 11.2.15–11.2.17 above), so no offence is committed where consumption is inadvertent, as in the case of a child whose drink was 'spiked' (Guidance, para 12.16) or where a child thought he was drinking a non-alcoholic drink, but was not in fact doing so.

Section 150(2) makes it an offence for a person knowingly to allow the consumption of alcohol by a child on relevant premises. By s 150(3), those who can commit this offence are any person who works at the premises in a capacity that gives him the authority to prevent the consumption and, in the case of a club, any officer or member of a club who is present at the time of the consumption in a capacity that allows him to prevent the supply of alcohol. Section 150(2) and (3) provides:

> (2) A person to whom subsection (3) applies commits an offence if he knowingly allows the consumption of alcohol on relevant premises by an individual aged under 18.
> (3) This subsection applies–
>     (a) to a person who works at the premises in a capacity, whether paid or unpaid, which authorises him to prevent the consumption, and
>     (b) where the alcohol was supplied by a club to or to the order of a member of the club, to any member or officer of the club who is present at the premises at the time of the consumption in a capacity which enables him to prevent it.

The conduct element requires allowing a child to consume alcohol on relevant premises and 'allow' includes not only doing something positive to facilitate the conduct, but also failing to exercise any control to prevent it in cases where there is the power to do so (see 11.2.19 above). The mental element required for the offence is knowledge (see 11.2.15–11.2.17 above), and, if the 'ordinary construction' principle set out in *Croyalgrange* (see 11.2.16 above) is applied, this will mean that prima facie knowledge is required as to all elements. Accordingly, knowledge will be needed as to allowing consumption and as to the person being under the age of 18. It may be that this construction should become the conclusive one here, as with the offence under s 136(1)(b) (see 11.2.16 above), since the knowledge requirement is unlikely to have any meaningful application if it is confined simply to the first-mentioned element (allowing consumption). The view has been expressed in respect of the offence, in s 147, of allowing sale to a person under the age of 18 that knowledge should be required as to age (see 11.7.12 above) and it would be illogical if the position were different here. Neither this section nor s 147 provides a defence of 'reasonable belief' or 'due diligence' and it is submitted that knowledge that the person is under the age of 18 ought to be required in both instances.

11.7.25 No offence under s 150(1) or (2) is committed, however, where a person aged 16 or 17 consumes beer, wine or cider for consumption with a table meal on relevant premises when accompanied by an adult. Section 150(4) contains a similar exemption to s 149(5), by which no offence is committed (see 11.7.21 above) and provides:

> Subsections (1) and (2) do not apply where–
> (a) the individual is aged 16 or 17,
> (b) the alcohol is beer, wine or cider,
> (c) its consumption is at a table meal on relevant premises, and
> (d) the individual is accompanied at the meal by an individual aged 18 or over.

As with the provision in s 145(5), the burden of proof here may be on the defence (see 11.7.5 above). A maximum sentence for the offence comparable to that for purchase of alcohol under s 149 (see 11.7.22 above) is provided by s 150(5):

> A person guilty of an offence under this section is liable on summary conviction–
> (a) in the case of an offence under subsection (1), to a fine not exceeding level 3 on the standard scale, and
> (b) in the case of an offence under subsection (2), to a fine not exceeding level 5 on the standard scale.

The offences in s 150 are ones for which a PND carrying an £80 fixed penalty can be given under s 2 of the Criminal Justice and Police Act 2001 in cases where a constable has reason to believe that a person has committed the offence (see 11.5.9 above).

### 11.7.26 *Delivering alcohol to children*

11.7.27 Section 151(1) provides:

> A person who works on relevant premises in any capacity, whether paid or unpaid, commits an offence if he knowingly delivers to an individual aged under 18–
> (a) alcohol sold on the premises, or
> (b) alcohol supplied on the premises by or on behalf of a club to or to the order of a member of the club.

The conduct element requires a delivery to a child of alcohol sold on premises or supplied on club premises to the order of a member and will cover, for example, circumstances where a child takes delivery of a consignment of alcohol ordered by an adult by telephone. This is provided that none of the exemptions apply (see 11.7.28 below).

Section 151(2) makes it an offence for a person working on relevant premises (see 11.5.1 above), and in a position that gives him authority to prevent it (s 151(3)), knowingly to allow another person to deliver alcohol to children. This offence will cover, for example, a person who authorises a delivery of the sort mentioned above in the knowledge that the recipient will be a child. Section 151(2) and (3) provides:

(2)  A person to whom subsection (3) applies commits an offence if he knowingly allows anybody else to deliver to an individual aged under 18 alcohol sold on relevant premises.

(3)  This subsection applies to a person who works on the premises in a capacity, whether paid or unpaid, which authorises him to prevent the delivery of the alcohol.

Section 151(4) makes it an offence for a person working in a club, and in a position that gives him authority to prevent it, knowingly to allow another person to deliver to children alcohol supplied on the club premises for members. Persons who are in a position to prevent this are anyone working on the premises in a capacity that gives him authority to prevent it (for example, the club steward) and any member or officer present in a capacity that enables him to prevent the supply. Section 151(4) and (5) provides:

(4)  A person to whom subsection (5) applies commits an offence if he knowingly allows anybody else to deliver to an individual aged under 18 alcohol supplied on relevant premises by or on behalf of a club to or to the order of a member of the club.

(5)  This subsection applies–

    (a)  to a person who works on the premises in a capacity, whether paid or unpaid, which authorises him to prevent the supply, and

    (b)  to any member or officer of the club who at the time of the supply in question is present on the premises in a capacity which enables him to prevent the supply.

The conduct element for the offences in s 151(2) and(4) requires allowing a person to deliver to a child alcohol sold, or alcohol supplied by a club to a club member, on relevant premises (see 11.5.1 above) and 'allow' includes not only doing something positive to facilitate the conduct, but also failing to exercise any control to prevent it in cases where there is the power to do so (see 11.2.19 above).

The mental element required for the offences in s 151(1), (2) and (4) is knowledge (see 11.2.15–11.2.17 above) and, if the 'ordinary construction' principle set out in *Croyalgrange* (see 11.2.16 above) is applied, this will mean that prima facie knowledge is required as to all elements. Accordingly, knowledge will be needed as to the making or allowing of delivery and as to the person to whom delivery is made being under the age of 18. It may be that this construction should become the conclusive one here, as with the offence under s 136(1)(b) (see 11.2.16 above), since the knowledge requirement is unlikely to have any meaningful application if it is confined simply to the first-mentioned element (making or allowing delivery). No defence of 'reasonable belief' or 'due diligence' is provided and it is submitted that knowledge ought to be required both as to making or allowing delivery and as to the person being under the age of 18.[81]

11.7.28 There are, however, a number of exemptions where no offence under s 151(1), (2) and (4) is committed. These include where alcohol is delivered to the home or place of work of the purchaser or person who is supplied (for example, where a child answers the door and signs for the delivery of his father's order at his house), where the job of the child who took delivery of the alcohol involves delivery of alcohol (for example, where a 16-year-old office worker is sent to collect a delivery for his employer), and where the alcohol is sold or supplied for consumption on the relevant premises. This last-mentioned exemption would appear to include cases where alcohol is delivered to premises, such as public houses, and delivery is taken there by a child. Section 151(6) provides:

> Subsections (1), (2) and (4) do not apply where–
> (a) the alcohol is delivered at a place where the buyer or, as the case may be, person supplied lives or works, or
> (b) the individual aged under 18 works on the relevant premises in a capacity, whether paid or unpaid, which involves the delivery of alcohol, or
> (c) the alcohol is sold or supplied for consumption on the relevant premises.

As with the provision in s 145(5), the burden of proof in respect of these exemptions may be on the defence (see 11.7.5 above).

All of the offences under this section are punishable by a maximum level 5 fine. Section 151(7) provides:

> A person guilty of an offence under this section is liable on summary conviction to a fine not exceeding level 5 on the standard scale.

The offences in s 151(1) and (2) are ones for which a PND carrying an £80 fixed penalty can be given under s 2 of the Criminal Justice and Police Act 2001 in cases where a constable has reason to believe that a person has committed the offence (see 11.5.9 above).

## 11.7.29 *Sending a child to obtain alcohol*

11.7.30 Section 152(1) provides:

> A person commits an offence if he knowingly sends an individual aged under 18 to obtain–
> (a) alcohol sold or to be sold on relevant premises for consumption off the premises, or
> (b) alcohol supplied or to be supplied by or on behalf of a club to or to the order of a member of the club for such consumption.

The conduct element requires sending a child to obtain alcohol sold on relevant premises (see 11.5.1 above), or supplied by a club to a club member, for consumption off the premises and the offence will cover, for example, circumstances where a parent sends his child to an off-licence to collect some alcohol that had been bought over the telephone. It will similarly apply where a member of a club sends his child to the club to fetch some alcohol. Where a child is sent to obtain alcohol, the alcohol will normally be obtained from the relevant premises in question, but need not be, for s 152(2) provides:

For the purposes of this section, it is immaterial whether the individual aged under 18 is sent to obtain the alcohol from the relevant premises or from other premises from which it is delivered in pursuance of the sale or supply.

The mental element required is knowledge (see 11.2.15–11.2.17 above) and, if the 'ordinary construction' principle set out in *Croyalgrange* (see 11.2.16 above) is applied, this will mean that prima facie knowledge is required as to all elements. Accordingly, knowledge will be needed as to the sending and as to the individual being under the age of 18. It may be that this construction should become the conclusive one here, as with the offence under s 136(1)(b) (see 11.2.16 above), since the knowledge requirement is unlikely to have any meaningful application if it is confined simply to the first-mentioned element (sending). A person who sends an individual to obtain alcohol and does not know that that individual is a child would not therefore commit the offence.

11.7.31 Nor will the offence be committed where the child works at the premises in question and his job involves taking deliveries of alcohol or if the child is sent by a police or trading standards officer as part of a test purchase operation to check compliance of the retailer or club with the prohibition on underage sales.[82] Section 152(3) and (4) provides:

(3) Subsection (1) does not apply where the individual aged under 18 works on the relevant premises in a capacity, whether paid or unpaid, which involves the delivery of alcohol.

(4) Subsection (1) also does not apply where the individual aged under 18 is sent by–

(a) a constable, or

(b) a weights and measures inspector,[83]

who is acting in the course of his duty.

As with the provision in s 145(5), the burden of proof here may be on the defence (see 11.7.5 above). This offence is punishable by a maximum level 5 fine. Section 152(5) provides:

A person guilty of an offence under this section is liable on summary conviction to a fine not exceeding level 5 on the standard scale.

## 11.7.32   Sales involving children

### 11.7.33   *Prohibition of unsupervised sales by children*

11.7.34 Section 153 makes it an offence for a 'responsible person' on relevant premises (see 11.5.1 above) knowingly to allow an individual under the age of 18 to sell or, in the case of a club, to supply alcohol unless the sale or supply has been specifically approved by him or another responsible person. Section 153(1) provides:

A responsible person commits an offence if on any relevant premises he knowingly allows an individual aged under 18 to make on the premises–

(a) any sale of alcohol, or

(b) any supply of alcohol by or on behalf of a club to or to the order of a member of the club,

unless the sale or supply has been specifically approved by that or another responsible person.

The persons who can commit this offence (a 'responsible person') are, in the case of a premises licence, the premises licence holder, the DPS or someone aged over 18 authorised by them; in the case of a club, any member or officer of the club who is present on the premises in a capacity that enables him to prevent the supply; or in a case where the premises are used for a permitted temporary activity under a TEN, the premises user or a person over 18 authorised by him. Section 153(4) provides:

> In this section "responsible person" means–
>
> (a) in relation to licensed premises–
>
>   (i)   the holder of the premises licence in respect of the premises,
>
>   (ii)  the designated premises supervisor (if any) under such a licence, or
>
>   (iii) any individual aged 18 or over who is authorised for the purposes of this section by such a holder or supervisor,
>
> (b) in relation to premises in respect of which there is in force a club premises certificate, any member or officer of the club present on the premises in a capacity which enables him to prevent the supply in question, and
>
> (c) in relation to premises which may be used for a permitted temporary activity by virtue of Part 5–
>
>   (i)   the premises user, or
>
>   (ii)  any individual aged 18 or over who is authorised for the purposes of this section by the premises user.

The conduct element requires allowing (see 11.2.18–11.2.20 above) a child to make a sale of alcohol on relevant premises (see 11.5.1 above), or a supply of alcohol by a club to a club member, unless this has been specifically approved by a responsible person. Since s 153(1) refers to 'the' sale or supply being specifically approved by a responsible person, it seems that each such sale or supply will need to be specifically approved if an offence is not to be committed. However, since specific approval can be by a responsible person other than the one charged, it seems that the term 'allow' might include cases where the person charged fails to exercise any control to prevent the sale or supply in cases where there is the power to do so. This would accord with the normal meaning of 'allow' as including cases of omission as well as doing something positive to facilitate the conduct (see 11.2.19 above). Provided the sale or supply is specifically approved, it seems that no offence will be committed, irrespective of the age of the individual making the sale or supply. Section 153(1) simply refers to 'an individual aged under 18' and there is no proscribed minimum age for the individual as far as making the sale or supply is concerned.[84]

The mental element required for the offence is knowledge (see 11.2.15–11.2.17 above) and, if the 'ordinary construction' principle set out in *Croyalgrange* (see 11.2.16 above) is applied, this will mean that prima facie knowledge is required as to all elements. Accordingly, knowledge will be needed as to allowing an individual to make the sale or supply and as to the individual being under the age of 18. It may be that this construction should become the conclusive one here, as with the offence under s 136(1)(b) (see 11.2.16 above), since the knowledge requirement is unlikely to have any meaningful application if it is confined simply to the first-mentioned element (allowing an individual to make the sale or supply).

11.7.35 No offence is committed where the alcohol is sold for consumption with a table meal in a part of the premises used only for this purpose. Section 153(2) provides:

492 Alcohol and Entertainment Licensing Law

But subsection (1) does not apply where–

(a) the alcohol is sold or supplied for consumption with a table meal,

(b) it is sold or supplied in premises which are being used for the service of table meals (or in a part of any premises which is being so used), and

(c) the premises are (or the part is) not used for the sale or supply of alcohol otherwise than to persons having table meals there and for consumption by such a person as an ancillary to his meal.

As with the provision in s 145(5), the burden of proof here may be on the defence (see 11.7.5 above). The effect of this exception is that, for example, a child working as a waiter or waitress in a restaurant is able to serve alcohol lawfully in the restaurant. So also can a child working as a waiter or waitress in premises such as public houses that serve table meals, provided this is in a part of the premises being used only for the service of such meals. If table meals can be taken anywhere in the premises at tables that can be used by persons who are only drinking, this would seem to fall outside the exception. In this instance, the premises *would* be used for the sale or supply of alcohol otherwise than to persons having table meals and s 153(2)(c) requires that they are *not* so used. Further, the alcohol will have to be sold or supplied to the persons taking table meals for consumption by them as an 'ancillary' to their meal. To be ancillary, it will have to be subservient or subordinate to the meal (*per* Glidewell, J in *Young v O'Connell* [2001] LLR 158, 163), but this does mean that it will have to be supplied at the same time as the meal and consumed with it. Drinks taken as an aperitif before the meal and brandy or liqueurs taken after it will be consumed as an ancillary to the meal and, if these are served by a child, no offence will be committed under s 153(1).

Where an offence is committed under s 153(1), it is punishable by a maximum level 1 fine. Section 153(3) provides:

A person guilty of an offence under this section is liable on summary conviction to a fine not exceeding level 1 on the standard scale.

## 11.7.36 Confiscation of alcohol in sealed containers

Section 155 amends the Criminal Justice and Police Act 2001 and the Confiscation of Alcohol (Young Persons) Act 1997 so that the police have the power to confiscate alcohol in sealed containers from anyone under 18 in any public place and from anyone in an area which has been designated by the local authority for the purposes of curbing antisocial behaviour. It provides:

(1) In section 1 of the Confiscation of Alcohol (Young Persons) Act 1997 (c.33) (right to require surrender of alcohol)–

(a) in subsection (1), omit "(other than a sealed container)",

(b) after that subsection insert–

"(1A) But a constable may not under subsection (1) require a person to surrender any sealed container unless the constable reasonably believes that the person is, or has been, consuming, or intends to consume, alcohol in any relevant place.", and

(c) in subsection (6), after "subsection (1)" insert "and (1A)".

(2) In section 12(2)(b) of the Criminal Justice and Police Act 2001 (c.16) (right to require surrender of alcohol), omit the words "(other than a sealed container)".

The 1997 Act was introduced to permit the confiscation of alcohol from the possession of young persons under the age of 18 in public places and other places to which they have unlawfully gained access. There is no requirement that possession of the alcohol is associated with nuisance to other persons or disorderly conduct, although the power of confiscation was introduced for these reasons. Under s 1(1) a constable can require such a person to surrender anything in his possession which is, or which the constable reasonably believes to be, alcohol. Failure without reasonable excuse to comply is an offence under s 1(4), the maximum penalty for which is a fine not exceeding level 2 on the standard scale, and under s 1(5), a constable may arrest without warrant anyone who fails to comply. This power of confiscation was extended by s 12 of the Criminal Justice and Police Act 2001, which enabled local authorities, with a view to reducing the incidence of nuisance and disorder arising from alcohol consumption in public places, to designate areas where it was an offence to consume alcohol after being requested by a constable not to do so. These powers remain unchanged by the 2003 Act, except for their extension, by s 155, to confiscation where the alcohol is contained in sealed containers.

## 11.8   SALE OF ALCOHOL ON MOVING VEHICLES

11.8.1   Section 156(1) provides:

> A person commits an offence under this section if he sells by retail alcohol on or from a vehicle at a time when the vehicle is not permanently or temporarily parked.

The conduct element requires a retail sale of alcohol on or from a vehicle when permanently or temporarily parked and the offence does not extend to an attempted sale nor does it prohibit consumption on vehicles. It does not therefore amount to a ban on the consumption of alcohol on coach trips or similar excursions. A 'vehicle' is defined by s 193 as 'a vehicle intended or adapted for use on roads' and most obviously this will include vehicles, such as coaches, minibuses and stretch limousines, from which sales of alcohol might be made whilst on the move. There is no requirement under s 193 that a vehicle needs to be mechanically propelled or capable of self-propulsion, so it should also be an offence when alcohol is sold from a caravan or trailer whilst being towed by another vehicle. An offence is committed, however, only if a vehicle is moving and not if it is parked. This is because there can be authorisation for the sale of alcohol under a premises licence, CPC or TEN in respect of a vehicle when it is parked at a particular place, as vehicles fall within the definition in s 193 of 'premises' (see 6.1.2–6.1.6 above).

11.8.2   No mental element is specified for this offence, but a 'due diligence' defence is available under s 156(3), which strongly suggests that liability is strict (see 11.2.6 above). Section 156(3) provides:

> In proceedings against a person for an offence under this section, it is a defence that–
>
> (a) his act was due to a mistake, or to reliance on information given to him, or to an act or omission by another person, or to some other cause beyond his control, and
>
> (b) he took all reasonable precautions and exercised all due diligence to avoid committing the offence.

This defence is comparable to that in s 139, which has application to offences in ss 136–38 (see 11.2.10–11.2.13 above). Such a defence might arise, for example, if a person mistakenly believes the beverages he is serving are non-alcoholic (Explanatory

Note 245). The maximum penalty for failure to comply carries both a term of imprisonment and a high fine. Section 156(2) provides:

> A person guilty of an offence under this section is liable on summary conviction to imprisonment for a term not exceeding three months or to a fine not exceeding £20,000, or to both.

## 11.9   POWER TO PROHIBIT SALE OF ALCOHOL ON TRAINS

11.9.1   The sale of alcohol on trains is not automatically an offence, but will become so if a magistrates' court, on application by a police officer of at least the rank of inspector, exercises its power to make an order prohibiting its sale in order to prevent disorder. Section 157(1)–(3) provides:

> (1) A magistrates' court acting for the local justice area may make an order prohibiting the sale of alcohol, during such period as may be specified,[85] on any railway vehicle–[86]
>   (a) at such station[87] or stations as may be specified, being stations in that area, or
>   (b) travelling between such stations as may be specified, at least one of which is in that area.
> (2) A magistrates' court may make an order under this section only on the application of a senior police officer.[88]
> (3) A magistrates' court may not make such an order unless it is satisfied that the order is necessary to prevent disorder.

Once an order is made, the police officer who applied for the order, or any other police officer of at least the rank of inspector who has been designated by the chief officer of police for this purpose, must forthwith serve a copy of the order on any train operator concerned. Section 157(4) provides:

> Where an order is made under this section, the responsible senior police officer[89] must, forthwith, serve a copy of the order on the train operator[90] (or each train operator) affected by the order.

The requirement to serve notice 'forthwith', a common requirement under the 2003 Act, might sensibly be interpreted as 'as soon as reasonably practicable' rather than 'immediately' (see 6.6.2 above).

11.9.2   A person who fails to comply with an order commits an offence if he knowingly sells, attempts to sell or allows the sale of alcohol in contravention of the order. Section 157(5) provides:

> A person commits an offence if he knowingly–
> (a) sells or attempts to sell alcohol in contravention of an order under this section, or
> (b) allows the sale of alcohol in contravention of such an order.

The conduct element requires the making or allowing of a sale or attempted sale[91] of alcohol on a train where an order has been made prohibiting sale. No reference is made in the section to a retail sale of alcohol, so it must be assumed that any sale, whether retail or otherwise, falls within the offence. The term 'allow' includes not only doing something positive to facilitate the conduct, but also failing to exercise any control to prevent it in cases where there is the power to do so (see 11.2.19 above).

The mental element required for the offence is knowledge (see 11.2.15–11.2.17 above) and, if the 'ordinary construction' principle set out in *Croyalgrange* (see 11.2.16 above) is applied, this will mean that prima facie knowledge is required as to all elements. Accordingly, knowledge will be needed as to sale, attempted sale or allowing sale and as to the existence of a prohibition order. It may be that this construction should become the conclusive one here, as with the offence under s 136(1)(b) (see 11.2.16 above), since the knowledge requirement is unlikely to have any meaningful application if it is confined simply to the first-mentioned element (sale, attempted sale or allowing sale).

The maximum penalty for the offence includes a term of imprisonment and a high fine. Section 157(6) provides:

A person guilty of an offence under this section is liable on summary conviction to imprisonment for a term not exceeding three months or to a fine not exceeding £20,000, or to both.

## 11.10 FALSE STATEMENTS RELATING TO APPLICATIONS

11.10.1 Section 158(1) provides:

A person commits an offence if he knowingly or recklessly makes a false statement in or in connection with–
(a) an application for the grant, variation, transfer or review of a premises licence or club premises certificate,
(b) an application for a provisional statement,
(c) a temporary event notice, an interim authority notice or any other notice under this Act, or
(d) an application for the grant or renewal of a personal licence;
(e) a notice within section 178(1) (notice by freeholder etc conferring right to be notified of changes to licensing register).

The conduct element will be the making of a false statement in connection with an application or notice. The statement will need to be false in fact and it will not suffice if a person believes a statement to be false if it in fact turns out to be true. There might, however, be an attempt to make a false statement in such a case, as held in *R v Deller* (1952) 36 Cr App R 184, a case of obtaining by false pretences under the Larceny Act 1916. Making a false statement will generally mean making an express representation on some matter that is factually incorrect rather than a failure to disclose information or an omission to remedy a mistake or misunderstanding. However, there are circumstances where the law imposes a duty to speak and where a failure or omission will constitute the making of a false statement. A duty will arise if a statement is true when made, but due to a change of circumstances, it later, to the knowledge of the person making it, becomes false. Here there is a duty on the person to disclose the change of circumstances.[92] A duty might also arise if, in the circumstances, a person is under a duty to disclose the information.[93]

11.10.2 For the purposes of the offence, a person makes a false statement not only where he makes this himself in some document, but also where he uses some other document that contains a false statement. In this latter instance, he is to be treated as having made a false statement by s 158(2), which provides:

> For the purposes of subsection (1) a person is to be treated as making a false statement if he produces, furnishes, signs or otherwise makes use of a document that contains a false statement.

The mental element is 'knowingly or recklessly' making a false statement. The meaning of 'knowledge' has been considered in 11.2.15–11.2.17 above. The meaning of 'reckless', reaffirmed by the House of Lords in *R v G* [2004] 1 Cr App R 21, is an awareness on the part of the defendant of the risk of something occurring and a willingness to run the risk. It does not include cases where the defendant has not given any thought to the possibility of there being any such risk, but where the risk would have been obvious to the reasonable person.[94] In the context of s 158(1), a defendant will be reckless if he is aware of the risk that a statement he makes may be false, but goes ahead anyway.

A person who commits the offence under s 158(1) is liable to a maximum sentence of a level 5 fine. Section 158(3) provides:

> A person guilty of an offence under this section is liable on summary conviction to a fine not exceeding level 5 on the standard scale.

## 11.11  GENERAL PROVISIONS RELATING TO OFFENCES

Sections 186–88 contain provisions having general application in respect of the above offences. Section 186 makes provision for the institution of proceedings for offences, s 187 for offences by bodies corporate and s 188 for jurisdiction and procedure in respect of offences.

### 11.11.1　Institution of proceedings

Either the licensing authority (except for the offence of persistently selling alcohol to children under s 147A) or the Director of Public Prosecutions (DPP) can institute proceedings for offences under the Act and in certain circumstances, involving offences of selling or allowing the sale of alcohol under ss 146–147A (see 11.7.7–11.7.15 above), a trading standards department of the local authority can do so. The reason that the licensing authority is precluded from instituting proceedings for the offence under s 147A is because it may be required to consider an application for a review of the premises licences on grounds relating to the commission of such offences and it should not have predetermined any related matters.[95] Section 186(1) and (2) provides:

> (1)  In this section "offence" means an offence under this Act.
> (2)  Proceedings for an offence may be instituted–
>> (a)  by a licensing authority except in the case of an offence under s 147A,
>> (b)  by the Director of Public Prosecutions, or
>> (c)  in the case of an offence under section 146 or 147 or 147A (sale of alcohol to children), by a local weights and measures authority (within the meaning of section 69 of the Weights and Measures Act 1985 (c.72)).[96]

In determining whether to institute proceedings, Crown Prosecutors exercising the functions of the DPP will be governed by the Code for Crown Prosecutors and licensing authorities will need to have regard to their own prosecution policy (which is likely to follow the general principles set out in the Code for Crown Prosecutors). A failure to act in accordance with this policy may result in proceedings being stayed by the court on the grounds that to proceed would be oppressive. The Court of Appeal so held in *R v Adaway* (2004) 168 JP 645, a case involving a prosecution for offences under the Trade Descriptions Act 1968, where Rose LJ stated (at 652):

> We cannot emphasize too strongly that before criminal proceedings are instituted by a local authority, acting in relation to the strict liability offences created by the Trade Descriptions Act, they must consider with care the terms of their own prosecuting policy. If they fail to do so, or if they reach a conclusion which is wholly unsupported, as the conclusion to prosecute in this case was, by material establishing the criteria for prosecution, it is unlikely that the courts will be sympathetic, in the face of the other demands upon their time at Crown Court and appellate level, to attempts to justify such prosecutions.

These remarks are likely to have equal application to offences under the 2003 Act, several of which, as seen earlier, are ones of strict liability.

All of the offences under the Act are summary only and normally prosecutions for such offences need to be commenced within six months from the commission of the offence. However, perhaps in recognition of the increased responsibilities that licensing authorities have under the Act, this limitation period is extended to 12 months by s 186(3), which provides:

> In relation to any offence, section 127(1) of the Magistrates' Courts Act 1980 (information to be laid within six months of offence) is to have effect as if for the reference to six months there were substituted a reference to 12 months.

## 11.11.2  Offences by bodies corporate

Where an offence is committed a corporate body, for example, a limited company, provision is made for there to be additional liability on the part of persons in a senior management capacity within the company where it can be shown that the offence has been committed with their consent or connivance or through neglect that can be attributed to them. This additional liability extends to a director, member of the management committee, chief executive, manager, secretary or similar officer (including persons purporting to act in such a capacity), or person controlling the corporate body, and, where the body is managed by its members, a member of the body. Section 187(1)–(3) provides:

> (1) If an offence[97] committed by a body corporate is shown–
>
>     (a) to have been committed with the consent or connivance[98] of an officer, or
>
>     (b) to be attributable to any neglect on his part, the officer as well as the body corporate is guilty of the offence and liable to be proceeded against and punished accordingly.
>
> (2) If the affairs of a body corporate are managed by its members, subsection (1) applies in relation to the acts and defaults of a member in connection with his functions of management as if he were a director of the body.
>
> (3) In subsection (1) "officer", in relation to a body corporate, means–
>
>     (a) a director, member of the committee of management, chief executive, manager, secretary or other similar officer of the body, or a person purporting to act in any such capacity, or
>
>     (b) an individual who is a controller of the body.

A similar provision is made for additional liability of partners where an offence is committed by a partnership and, in the case of unincorporated associations, for additional liability of an officer of the association or member of its governing body. Section 187(4)–(6) provides:

> (4) If an offence[99] committed by a partnership is shown–
>> (a) to have been committed with the consent or connivance of a partner, or
>> (b) to be attributable to any neglect on his part, the partner as well as the partnership is guilty of the offence and liable to be proceeded against and punished accordingly.
> (5) In subsection (4) "partner" includes a person purporting to act as a partner.
> (6) If an offence[100] committed by an unincorporated association (other than a partnership) is shown–
>> (a) to have been committed with the consent or connivance of an officer of the association or a member of its governing body, or
>> (b) to be attributable to any neglect on the part of such an officer or member, that officer or member as well as the association is guilty of the offence and liable to be proceeded against and punished accordingly.

The Secretary of State has a power to make regulations under s 187(7) for the application of any of the above provisions with such modifications as he considers appropriate. Section 187(7) provides:

> Regulations may provide for the application of any provision of this section, with such modifications as the Secretary of State considers appropriate, to a body corporate or unincorporated association formed or recognised under the law of a territory outside the United Kingdom.

### 11.11.3   Jurisdiction and procedure in respect of offences

Although headed 'jurisdiction and procedure in respect of offences', s 188 relates only in part to this and is concerned as much, if not more so, with matters pertaining to unincorporated associations. It makes provision for any fine imposed following conviction for an offence under the 2003 Act to be paid out of an unincorporated association's funds and for any proceedings brought against such associations to be brought in the name of the association (not in the name of any of its members). Section 188(1) and (2) provides:

> (1) A fine imposed on an unincorporated association on its conviction for an offence[101] is to be paid out of the funds of the association.
> (2) Proceedings for an offence alleged to have been committed by an unincorporated association must be brought in the name of the association (and not in that of any of its members).

The section also makes provision for certain legal procedures and rules relating to the service of documents that apply to bodies corporate to have application to unincorporated associations. Section 188(3) and (4) provides:

> (3) Rules of court relating to the service of documents are to have effect as if the association were a body corporate.
> (4) In proceedings for an offence brought against an unincorporated association, section 33 of the Criminal Justice Act 1925 (c.86) and Schedule 3 to the Magistrates' Courts Act 1980 (c.43) (procedure) apply as they do in relation to a body corporate.

Finally, general provision is made in respect of jurisdiction, as far as the institution of proceedings for an offence is concerned, that is, the geographical area(s) in which proceedings can be taken. In the case of an unincorporated association or a body corporate, proceedings may be instituted at any place at which it has a place of business and, for individuals, at any place where they are for the time being. Section 188(5) and (6) provides:

(5) Proceedings for an offence may be taken–

    (a) against a body corporate or unincorporated association at any place at which it has a place of business;

    (b) against an individual at any place where he is for the time being.

(6) Subsection (5) does not affect any jurisdiction exercisable apart from this section.

## CLOSURE OF PREMISES

## 11.12 INTRODUCTION TO CLOSURE OF PREMISES

Two separate powers of closure of premises were originally provided in Pt 8 of the 2003 Act when it was passed: first, a power of closure under a magistrates' court order, on application by the police, under s 160, under which all premises with authorisation for licensable activities in an identified area can be closed for a period of up to 24 hours where they are situated at or near a place where disorder is occurring or anticipated; and, secondly, a police power of closure, under s 161, of individual premises for a similar period where closure is necessary in the interests of public safety because disorder is occurring or is imminent, or where a nuisance is being caused by noise from the premises. The arrangements for closing premises, contained in s 160, are likely to be used by the police, with the sanction of the courts, where contingency planning is possible, although the powers may be used in a geographical area that is experiencing or expected to experience disorder in emergency too. The arrangements for closing down individual licensed premises, contained in ss 161–70, are likely to be used only where unanticipated events arise and emergency action proves necessary and, in order to give effect to these arrangements, police officers can use such force as is necessary to secure closure of the premises.[102] These powers are important, not only as regards their actual use, but also their potential use. That the powers may be invoked should have a significant deterrent value in curbing disorder and public nuisance through noise, as well as enabling disorder and noise nuisance to be brought to an end when they occur.

A third power of closure has been added under s 169A, which is a police power of closure of individual premises in cases of persistently selling alcohol to children contrary to s 147A of the 2003 Act. The introduction of this third power of closure by s 24 of the Violent Crime Reduction Act 2006 followed Alcohol Misuse Enforcement Campaigns in the summer of 2004 and during the Christmas/New Year period of 2004/2005, which found high levels of offences of selling alcohol to children in premises targeted by test purchasing operations.[103] Guidance to police officers in the exercise of these closure powers under the 2003 Act has been issued by the DCMS. Intially, this was contained within the 2004 Guidance issued under s 182 of the Act, but separate guidance, *Police Powers to Close Premises under the Licensing Act 2003* (hereafter 'Police Guidance'), was issued in June 2007 (see Appendix 12).

A fourth power of closure is contained in s 19 of the Criminal Justice and Police Act 2001, under which the police and the local authority can close premises that are being, or within the last 24 hours have been, used for the unauthorised sale of alcohol for consumption on, or in the vicinity of, the premises.

Each of these four powers of closure is considered in turn below.

## 11.13 CLOSURE OF PREMISES IN A GEOGRAPHICAL AREA: MAGISTRATES' CLOSURE ORDERS

11.13.1 Under s 160, a senior police officer of the rank of superintendent or above may ask a magistrates' court to make an order requiring all premises holding premises licences, or subject to a TEN, which are situated at or near the place of the disorder or anticipated disorder, to be closed for a period of up to 24 hours. The magistrates' court may make the order only if it is satisfied that the order is necessary to prevent disorder. Section 160(1)–(3) provides:

(1) Where there is or is expected to be disorder in any local justice area, a magistrates' court acting for the area may make an order requiring all premises–

    (a) which are situated at or near the place of the disorder or expected disorder, and

    (b) in respect of which a premises licence or a temporary event notice has effect, to be closed for a period, not exceeding 24 hours, specified in the order.

(2) A magistrates' court may make an order under this section only on the application of a police officer who is of the rank of superintendent or above.

(3) A magistrates' court may not make such an order unless it is satisfied that it is necessary to prevent disorder.

The use of this power in emergency situations will be where there is disorder, but its more frequent use will be anticipatory, where there is 'expected to be disorder'. An expectation of disorder suggests that disorder must be more likely to occur than not, rather than its occurrence being merely a possibility, and some evidence should be required to substantiate this. As para 11 of the Police Guidance states:

> These orders should normally be sought where the police anticipate public order problems (very often fuelled by the ready availability of alcohol) as a result of intelligence or publicly available information.

11.13.2 Evidence to substantiate an expectation of disorder from a particular event might take the form of disorder having previously occurred when that event took place in the area. It might be anticipated from this that disorder might recur if and when that event was to take place again. Football matches between teams where there has been a history of public order problems and disorder between rival fans is an obvious example. Disorder might be expected to occur, if it has previously done so at this particular fixture. The mere fact that it had previously occurred may not, however, in itself be sufficient and it may be that some intelligence indicating a likely recurrence on this occasion will be required to justify an order requiring closure of premises in such circumstances. Even if there has been no earlier occurrence of disorder, which will be the case if events have not previously taken place, intelligence that disorder is likely may justify the making of an order. This might arise, for instance, if a political demonstration was to be held and there was evidence that it was likely to be hijacked by extreme and violent groups (an example given, along with football matches, in para 12 of the Police Guidance).

The premises that can be required to close do not include clubs with a CPC, since such premises are not open to members of the public and are unlikely to be the focus of or have any effect on the disorder. Closure is confined to premises with a premises licence or where a TEN has effect and will extend only to those 'situated at or near the place of disorder'. Whether the expression 'near', as used here, has any different meaning from 'vicinity', which is used in respect of closure orders under s 161 as well as elsewhere in the Act,[104] is unclear. Since the normal meaning of 'vicinity' is the state of being near in space,[105] it may well be that there is no significance in the different expression used here. Perhaps the explanation is that the power in s 160 replaced that in s 188 of the Licensing Act 1964; the expression 'near' was used in s 188 and has simply been repeated in the 2003 Act. What constitutes being near in space to the disorder will depend on how wide the disorder is seen as extending and will be a question of fact for the court to determine. Whether the area needs to be defined with a degree of precision is less clear. With regard to persons being entitled to make relevant representations as interested parties living within the 'vicinity' of application premises, the view has been expressed that what constitutes the 'vicinity' will not need to be determined with any degree of precision (see 6.4.13 above). However, in the context of closing all premises with authorisation for licensable activities (except clubs with a CPC) in an area, it may be that the area will need to be more accurately prescribed, either by reference to a radius distance from the place of disorder (or anticipated disorder) or by reference to roads or other identifying features which surround the area.

11.13.3 The court will, under s 160(3), need to be 'satisfied that it [the order] is necessary to prevent disorder' before it can grant the order and 'the burden of proof will fall on the police to satisfy the court that their intelligence or evidence is sufficient to demonstrate that such action is necessary' (Police Guidance, para 13). As to when intelligence or evidence is sufficient, since the proceedings for a closure order are civil in nature, it might be expected that the normal standard of proof in civil proceedings will apply, that is, the court will need to be satisfied on a balance of probabilities that the closure order is necessary to prevent disorder. However, courts have not always required proof to this standard where there is a statutory requirement for magistrates to be satisfied on a particular matter. In *R (on the application of McCann) v Manchester Crown Court* [2003] AC 787, the House of Lords held, in respect of the requirement under s 1(1)(b) of the Crime and Disorder Act 1998 of satisfying magistrates that an Anti-Social Behaviour Order (ASBO) is necessary to protect persons from further antisocial behaviour by a specific person, once it had established beyond reasonable doubt under s 1(1)(a) that that person has acted in an antisocial manner, did not involve a standard proof on a balance of probabilities, but simply an exercise of judgment or evaluation. Whilst this approach may be justified in the case of an ASBO in respect of the s 1(1)(b) requirement, however, it is submitted that it cannot be for a closure order because of the wide-ranging impact that exercise of the power under s 160 will have, that is, closure for a period up to 24 hours of all premises with a premises licences or TEN, which are situated near the place of the disorder or anticipated disorder. The impact of an ASBO is much more limited. *McCann* ought not to be followed in respect of a closure order, but distinguished on the ground that the nature of the order is substantially different, and the burden of proof on the police should be to satisfy the court on a balance of probabilities that the closure order is necessary to prevent disorder.

Having to be satisfied that the order is necessary to 'prevent' disorder imposes a high standard of proof for the grant of an order and, if the court is satisfied only that closure may help to minimise disorder rather than prevent it, the statutory criterion in s 160(3) would not seem to be made out. Even if the court is satisfied that an order is necessary to prevent disorder, it seems to be a matter for the court's discretion whether or not to grant an order. Section 160(3) does not require the court to grant an order when it is satisfied this is necessary to prevent disorder; it merely provides that the court may not make an order unless it is so satisfied. When deciding whether to exercise its discretion to make an order, the court will need to balance the degree to which disorder might be expected to take place against the impact on the community of closure of premises in the area. The greater the degree of disorder expected and the more tightly circumscribed the area affected, the more the balance will be tipped in favour of the closure of premises. Conversely, only a limited degree of anticipated disorder, which might be spread over a wide area, will make it harder to justify the closure of a large number of premises. The seeking of a closure order under s 160 is seen as a last resort and para 13 of the Police Guidance encourages voluntary closure where possible:

> Where serious disorder is anticipated, many holders of premises licences and premises users who have given temporary event notices will want to co-operate with the police, not least for the protection of their premises and customers. So far as possible, and where time is available, police officers should initially seek voluntary agreement to closure in an area for a particular period of time. The courts should therefore only be involved where other alternatives are not available.

11.13.4 Once a closure order is made, it is an offence for the premises licence holder, a DPS, the premises user (in the case of a TEN) and any manager of the premises in question – a 'manager' being a person who has authority to close the premises[106] – to knowingly keep open or allow the premises to be kept open during the period of the order. Section 160(4) and (5) provides:

> (4) Where an order is made under this section, a person to whom subsection (5) applies commits an offence if he knowingly keeps any premises to which the order relates open, or allows any such premises to be kept open, during the period of the order.
>
> (5) This subsection applies–
>> (a) to any manager of the premises,
>> (b) in the case of licensed premises, to–
>>> (i) the holder of a premises licence in respect of the premises, and
>>> (ii) the designated premises supervisor (if any) under such a licence, and
>> (c) in the case of premises in respect of which a temporary event notice has effect, to the premises user in relation to that notice.

11.13.5 The conduct element required for the offence is keeping premises that are subject to a closure order, open, or allowing such premises to be kept open. The term 'allow' includes not only doing something positive to facilitate the conduct, but also failing to exercise any control to prevent it in cases where there is the power to do so (see 11.2.19 above). Subject to various exceptions, premises are kept 'open' for the purposes of this offence if a person enters the premises and either obtains food, drink or anything usually sold, or remains there whilst they are used for the provision of regulated entertainment. Exceptions relate both to those who enter and to the particular use of the premises. Premises are not 'open' if the only persons who enter are those who might commit the offence, those who usually live at the premises and (in both instances) a member of their family. Nor are premises 'open' if they are used for non-licensable activities falling outside the event period under a TEN (where no premises licence is in force in respect of the premises); if they are used for a qualifying club activity under a CPC;[107] or if the obtaining of the food or drink does not amount to the licensable activity of provision of LNR services because, under para 3 of Sched 2, it is an 'exempt supply' made to a member of a recognised club (see 5.4.6 above). Section 171(2)–(5) provides:

(2) Relevant premises are open if a person who is not within subsection (4) enters the premises and–

    (a) he buys or is otherwise supplied with food, drink or anything usually sold on the premises, or

    (b) while he is on the premises, they are used for the provision of regulated entertainment.

(3) But in determining whether relevant premises are open the following are to be disregarded–

    (a) where no premises licence has effect in respect of the premises, any use of the premises for activities (other than licensable activities) which do not take place during an event period specified in a temporary event notice having effect in respect of the premises,

    (b) any use of the premises for a qualifying club activity under and in accordance with a club premises certificate, and

    (c) any supply exempted under paragraph 3 of Schedule 2 (certain supplies of hot food and drink by clubs, hotels etc not a licensable activity) in circumstances where a person will neither be admitted to the premises, nor be supplied as mentioned in sub-paragraph (1)(b) of that paragraph, except by virtue of being a member of a recognised club or a guest of such a member.

(4) A person is within this subsection if he is–

    (a) an appropriate person in relation to the premises,

    (b) a person who usually lives at the premises, or

    (c) a member of the family of a person within paragraph (a) or (b).

(5) The following expressions have the meanings given–

"appropriate person", in relation to any relevant premises, means–

    (a) any person who holds a premises licence in respect of the premises,

    (b) any designated premises supervisor under such a licence,

    (c) the premises user in relation to any temporary event notice which has effect in respect of the premises, or

    (d) a manager of the premises.

The mental element required for the offence is knowledge (see 11.2.15–11.2.17 above), and, if the 'ordinary construction' principle set out in *Croyalgrange* (see 11.2.16 above) is applied, this will mean that prima facie knowledge is required as to all elements. Accordingly, knowledge will be needed as to the keeping open of the premises, or as to allowing them to be kept open, and as to them being subject to a closure order. It may be that this construction should become the conclusive one here, as with the offence under s 136(1)(b) (see 11.2.16 above), since the knowledge requirement is unlikely to have any meaningful application if it is confined simply to the first-mentioned element (keeping open the premises or allowing them to be kept open). Although there is no requirement for the police to notify persons affected by the order, it might be anticipated that persons will be notified as soon as possible (and they may, in any event, be 'on notice' of an order if there has been voluntary closure of the premises – see 11.13.3 above). This should facilitate proof of the requirement of knowledge of the closure order. The maximum penalty for the offence is a level 3 fine and a constable may use necessary force to close any premises covered by such an order. Section 160(6) and (7) provides:

(6)  A person guilty of an offence under subsection (4) is liable on summary conviction to a fine not exceeding level 3 on the standard scale.

(7)  A constable may use such force as may be necessary for the purpose of closing premises ordered to be closed under this section.

No provision is made for cancellation of a magistrates' closure order under s 160, unlike for police closure orders under s 161 (see 11.14.13–11.14.15 above), so presumably the order will continue to have effect notwithstanding that the basis for it being made no longer has application, that is, continued closure is no longer necessary to prevent disorder.

## 11.14  CLOSURE OF IDENTIFIED PREMISES FOR PUBLIC SAFETY OR PREVENTION OF NOISE NUISANCE: POLICE CLOSURE ORDERS

### 11.14.1  Making a closure order

11.14.2 The circumstances in which disorder might be expected, and where the power in s 160 can have application, will be relatively few and disorder will more commonly arise in circumstances that cannot readily be anticipated. Section 161 makes provision for this by enabling a senior police officer of the rank of inspector or above to make an order closing individual premises covered by premises licences or a TEN for up to 24 hours where disorder is taking place or is imminent and closure is necessary in the interests of public safety. Such an order can also be made where a nuisance is being caused by noise emanating from the premises. Section 161(1) and (2) provides:

(1)  A senior police officer[108] may make a closure order in relation to any relevant premises[109] if he reasonably believes that–

(a)  there is, or is likely imminently to be, disorder on, or in the vicinity of and related to, the premises and their closure is necessary in the interests of public safety, or

(b)  a public nuisance is being caused by noise coming from the premises and the closure of the premises is necessary to prevent that nuisance.

(2)  A closure order is an order under this section requiring relevant premises to be closed for a period not exceeding 24 hours beginning with the coming into force of the order.[110]

An officer's reasonable belief, under s 161(1)(a), will need to relate to three matters. First, he will need a reasonable belief that disorder is actually occurring, either on the premises or in the vicinity (see 6.4.13 above), or is likely to be imminent. If he reasonably believes it is likely to occur at some point in the future, then the power in s 160 should be used. This might be the case if, for example, intelligence was received on a Thursday about a football match to be played on a Saturday. Here, there is sufficient time to obtain a magistrates' court order under s 160, but, in cases where there is not, then disorder ought to be regarded as 'imminent' for the purposes of s 161. Otherwise, there may be a 'lacuna', where neither the power under s 160 nor s 161 can be used. Secondly, an officer will need a reasonable belief that the disorder or imminent disorder 'relates to' the premises, that is, causally linked with the premises. If disorder is occurring or is imminent in the vicinity, but the officer does not reasonably believe it to be connected with the premises, a closure order should not be made. Thirdly, he will need a reasonable belief that closure is necessary in the interests of public safety, which will mean a reasonable belief that 'closure of the licensed premises should actively diminish the probability that disorder will take place in the immediate future' (Police Guidance, para 26).

11.14.3 An officer's reasonable belief, under s 161(1)(b), will need to relate to four matters. First, he will need a reasonable belief that a public nuisance is being caused. Secondly, he will need a reasonable belief that it is being caused by noise. A reasonable belief that such a nuisance may be imminent will not, it seems, justify the exercise of the power since there will not be a reasonable belief that a nuisance is 'being caused' if a nuisance by noise is not actually occurring. In this instance, it appears necessary for the officer to wait until the noise (most probably music) has commenced. Thirdly, he will need a reasonable belief that a public nuisance by noise is coming from the premises. The premises might extend beyond a building and could include areas such as a beer garden, courtyard or street terrace (Police Guidance, para 28). However, it will not suffice if an officer reasonably believes the noise is coming from the vicinity of the premises rather than the premises themselves: 'Noise nuisance arising solely from people in the street outside the perimeter of the licensed premises would not be sufficient to justify the use of these powers' (ibid.). Fourthly, he will need a reasonable belief that closure of the premises is necessary to prevent the noise nuisance and 'the senior police officer should normally have cause to believe that particular individuals in the vicinity are being annoyed by the noise from the licensed premises' (Police Guidance, para 29).

11.14.4 An officer's decision whether to make a closure order will in large measure be determined by the nature of the activities taking place, but s 161(3) requires the officer to have regard to the conduct of those involved in running the premises who may be in a position to close them. It provides:

> In determining whether to make a closure order in respect of any premises, the senior police officer must have regard, in particular, to the conduct of each appropriate person in relation to the disorder or disturbance.[111]

Thus, if the licence holder, manager or DPS (or premises user in the case of a TEN) has 'acted incompetently, inadequately or has actually provoked or caused the problems', the officer may take that into account when deciding whether to make a closure order (Police Guidance, para 15). Conversely, if such persons 'have called the police in promptly and acted sensibly to try to prevent disorder or noise nuisance', such good conduct may also be taken into account (ibid.). The effect of s 161(3) is that, at the very least, the conduct of those involved will be a relevant consideration to be taken into account in reaching a decision and, where there is an element of blameworthiness, this will be more likely to result in an order being made. It may perhaps, at best, be seen as an important relevant consideration, given that the section directs the officer to have regard 'in particular' to the conduct of those involved, but it will be no more than a relevant consideration. If there is disorder or excessive noise, a closure order might be made irrespective of how good the conduct of those involved might have been. The power of closure is, first and foremost, designed to protect the public, whether or not any person involved in running the premises is at fault. Even where everything possible has been done to prevent the disorder or noise nuisance, a senior police officer may on occasions still believe that closure is necessary to safeguard the public or to prevent the public nuisance (Police Guidance, para 17).

11.14.5 If a decision is taken to make a closure order, the period of closure will need to be determined before the order is given. By s 161(2), the duration of the order cannot exceed 24 hours. This does not necessarily mean that the length of the closure should automatically be set for 24 hours on every occasion. The period should be that which the senior police officer estimates would be needed to end the threat to public safety from disorder or the prevention of public nuisance by noise. According to para 36 of the Police Guidance, 'closure orders could last between 30 minutes and 24 hours depending on the circumstances of each case' and para 37 goes on to provide:

> If, for example, a closure is made at 9pm on a Monday evening because of disorder caused by gangs fighting in a public house, closure might only be appropriate for up to the time when the premises licence requires the premises to close, perhaps midnight. This could be because the senior police officer reasonably believes that there is a threat of gang members (those not arrested) returning to the premises before closing time but after the police have left. However, if the threat is not expected to have subsided by closing time, it may be appropriate to impose a closure for a period extending into the following day.

There may in practice be a reluctance on the part of the police to make a closure order for a short period of time and it may be more likely in such cases that the police will seek voluntary closure of the premises. This should in any event be the approach adopted in the first instance, for para 18 of the Police Guidance provides that the police should 'whenever possible, seek the voluntary co-operation of licensees, managers and others in resolving incidents of disorder, potential disorder and noise nuisance rather than move directly to a decision to use a closure order'. Paragraph 20 goes on to provide that the police should 'wherever possible, give them an opportunity to close the premises voluntarily, on police advice, until the following day' and a 'closure order will normally only have to be made if police advice is disputed or rejected and it becomes necessary to take action to impose closure'.

## 11.14.6   Giving a closure order

11.14.7 If a decision is taken to make a closure order, there is no prescribed form that this must be taken, but there is certain information that must be contained in it. Section 161(4) provides:

> A closure order must–
> (a)  specify the premises to which it relates,
> (b)  specify the period for which the premises are to be closed,

(c)  specify the grounds on which it is made, and

(d)  state the effect of sections 162 to 168.

Annex I to the Guidance provides a Specimen Closure Order made under s 161. The Notes to the Order state the effect of ss 162–168, as required by s 161(4)(d). The Order contains a section headed 'Premises to be closed', in which the premises to which the order relates is to be specified and all that would seem to be required is identification of the premises by their address (and perhaps trading name). A section headed 'Period of closure (until – time and date)' requires insertion of the time and date until which the premises should remain closed, the Order itself indicating the date and time when it is made, which is the period from when closure runs. A section headed 'Reason (ground) for closure' meets the requirement in s 161(4)(c), to specify the grounds on which it is made, although it is uncertain what degree of detail is to be given here. More than simple identification of the relevant statutory provision, that is, s 161(1)(a) or (b), should be required (since the Notes to the Order, although referring to disorder and nuisance, do not make reference to these provisions). At the very least an indication should be given in the Order as to whether the ground relied on is disorder (or its likelihood) or nuisance by noise. Whether reasons need also to be given in this section is unclear, since the section heading 'Reason (grounds) for Closure' is ambiguous. It might mean reason(s) that substantiate the ground on which reliance is placed or it might mean simply the ground itself.

The Act contains no provision as to the effect of a closure order in the event of a failure to comply with any of these requirements in s 161(4). It might reasonably be assumed that relatively minor inaccuracies or deficiencies will not invalidate the notice, but that any major ones might do so.

11.14.8 Where a senior police officer decides to make a closure order under s 161, notice of the order, providing the above details, may be given by that officer personally or, where the decision is made remotely, by any constable. The senior police officer does not have to be present at the premises to authorise service of an order (otherwise, particularly in rural areas, an unreasonable period may pass during which public safety might be at risk). He may make his decision on the basis of information supplied to him by other police officers, although the decision remains his and he remains accountable for that decision (Police Guidance, para 39). It will be important in such cases that the information passed to the relevant senior officer is 'comprehensive and contemporaneously recorded', so that the senior officer 'can be clear about the reasons for closure'. Senior police officers should, however, as a matter of good practice, 'attempt to attend wherever possible in order to make a full and personal assessment of the situation' (Police Guidance, para 40). 'Giving' the notice, in this context, is the delivery of the notice to an 'appropriate person' (see s 171(5) and 11.13.5 above), who is essentially a person in a position to close the premises. Such persons will be the holder of the premises licence, the DPS, the manager of the relevant premises or the premises user. Delivery will normally be by personal service and if there is a refusal to accept the notice of a closure order, the notice might be left in the sight of the relevant person on whom it is being served, with an oral indication of its contents. In such cases, the refusal to accept might be drawn to the attention of the relevant magistrates' court at the hearing that will follow (Police Guidance, para 41).

Once the notice is given, it will at that point take effect. Section 161(5) provides:

A closure order in respect of any relevant premises comes into force at the time a constable gives notice of it to an appropriate person who is connected with any of the activities to which the disorder or nuisance relates.

The Act does not require the licence holder or the police to clear the premises of customers following the service of a closure order. It is assumed that customers will leave the premises, given that licensable activities cannot take place during the period of closure. However, the licence holder or manager of the premises commits no offence arising from the mere presence of customers who might remain. Similarly, customers themselves commit no offence if they are not asked to leave the premises and choose to stay.[112] Different means might be employed, however, when it comes to customers leaving the premises. Thus there might be a phased emptying of the premises so as to disperse disorderly gangs or 'it might be in the interests of public safety to keep law-abiding citizens inside for a temporary period while troublemakers outside are dispersed by the police' (Police Guidance, para 32). Dispersal of trouble-makers might lead to such persons seeking out other licensed premises and 'it is good practice to ensure that other licensed premises nearby are warned of the action being taken and of licence holders' and others' obligations not to allow disorderly conduct on their premises' (Police Guidance, para 34).

### 11.14.9   Extension of a closure order

11.14.10 Once a closure order comes into force, the senior police officer must, under s 164(1), as soon as reasonably practicable, apply to the magistrates' court for it to consider the order (see 11.14.16–11.14.19 above). However, there will clearly be some circumstances where the officer may reasonably believe that it will not be possible to make an application before the closure period ends and s 162 accordingly makes provision for extension of the closure period for up to a further 24 hours. Such an extension might be made by the officer (before the closure period ends), provided he also reasonably believes closure is (still) necessary on grounds of disorder or public nuisance by noise. Section 162(1) and (2) provides:

(1)   Where, before the end of the period for which relevant premises are to be closed under a closure order or any extension of it ("the closure period"), the responsible senior police officer reasonably believes that–

    (a)   a relevant magistrates' court will not have determined whether to exercise its powers under section 165(2) in respect of the closure order, and any extension of it, by the end of the closure period, and

    (b)   the conditions for an extension are satisfied,

    he may extend the closure period for a further period not exceeding 24 hours beginning with the end of the previous closure period.

(2)   The conditions for an extension are that–

    (a)   in the case of an order made by virtue of section 161(1)(a), closure is necessary in the interests of public safety because of disorder or likely disorder on, or in the vicinity of and related to, the premises,

    (b)   in the case of an order made by virtue of section 161(1)(b), closure is necessary to ensure that no public nuisance is, or is likely to be, caused by noise coming from the premises.[113]

It seems from the wording of the section that there may be more than one extension period. Section 162(1) indicates that the officer 'may extend the closure period' and the 'closure period' is designated as the period when the 'relevant premises are to be closed under a closure order or any extension of it'.

11.14.11 For the extension to come into force, notice must be given before the end of the closure period and the extension will take effect when the notice is given. Section 162(3) and (4) provides:

> (3) An extension in relation to any relevant premises comes into force when a constable gives notice of it to an appropriate person connected with any of the activities to which the disorder or nuisance relates or is expected to relate.
>
> (4) But the extension does not come into force unless the notice is given before the end of the previous closure period.

## 11.14.12   Failure to comply with a closure order or extension

Where a closure order or extension is in force, a person who permits the premises to remain open (see 11.13.5 above) without reasonable excuse in contravention of the order or extension commits an offence punishable both by imprisonment and a fine. Section 161(6) and (7) provides:

> (6) A person commits an offence if, without reasonable excuse, he permits relevant premises to be open in contravention of a closure order or any extension of it.
>
> (7) A person guilty of an offence under subsection (6) is liable on summary conviction to imprisonment for a term not exceeding three months or to a fine not exceeding £20,000, or to both.

The commission of this offence is not confined to an 'appropriate person', under s 171(5) a person who has power to close the premises (see 11.14.8 above), for s 161(6) makes reference only to 'a person'. In principle, therefore, it would seem that any person, including perhaps a barman, might commit the offence. However, if a person 'permits' premises to remain open, it might be implicit that he must have it within his authority to enable them to remain open, either doing something positive to facilitate this or failing to exercise any control to prevent them from remaining open. In this respect, 'permit' has a similar meaning to 'allow' (see 11.2.19 above) and it may be that a barman does not have it within his authority to enable the premises to remain open. No mental element is specified for the offence but a defence of 'reasonable excuse' is provided, which strongly suggests that liability is strict (see 11.2.6 above).

## 11.14.13   Cancellation of a closure order or extension

11.14.14 Once a closure order or extension has come into force, it can be cancelled at any time thereafter by the senior police officer, at his discretion, up to the time when it is considered by the magistrates' court. Further, it must be cancelled by him if he no longer reasonably believes that it is necessary in the interests of public safety because of disorder or likely disorder or to ensure that no public nuisance is or is likely to be caused by noise coming from the premises. Section 163(1) and (2) provides:

> (1) The responsible senior police officer may cancel a closure order and any extension of it at any time–
>
> (a) after the making of the order, but
>
> (b) before a relevant magistrates' court has determined whether to exercise its powers under section 165(2) in respect of the order and any extension of it.

(2) The responsible senior police officer must cancel a closure order and any extension of it if he does not reasonably believe that–

    (a) in the case of an order made by virtue of section 161(1)(a), closure is necessary in the interests of public safety because of disorder or likely disorder on, or in the vicinity of and related to, the premises,

    (b) in the case of an order made by virtue of section 161(1)(b), closure is necessary to ensure that no public nuisance is, or is likely to be, caused by noise coming from the premises.

If a closure order or extension is cancelled, notice of the cancellation must be given to an 'appropriate person' (which under s 171(5) is the premises licence holder, the DPS, premises user or the manager of the premises) connected with any of the activities related to the disorder or nuisance (see 11.14.8 above). Section 163(3) provides:

> Where a closure order and any extension of it are cancelled under this section, the responsible senior police officer must give notice of the cancellation to an appropriate person connected with any of the activities related to the disorder (or anticipated disorder) or nuisance in respect of which the closure order was made.

11.14.15 The section does not provide that the person to whom notice of cancellation is given must be the same person as was given the closure order. Whilst this may well be the case in most instances, it does not seem necessary according to this provision, which simply requires that notice is given to 'an appropriate person' who is connected with any of the activities in question. Since this will normally be by personal service (see 11.14.8 above), it might be expected that notice of cancellation will similarly be given. However, it need not be and notice to a person might be given by any of the means specified in s 184(3), which are delivering it to him, leaving it at his proper address, or sending it by post to him at that address (see 2.5.4 above). Although the section provides that the senior police officer must give the notice of cancellation, presumably this need not be done by him personally and may be done by a constable on his behalf. Notice of a closure order can be given by a constable, where a decision to make an order is made remotely by the senior police officer, and it would be odd if the position were different for notice of cancellation. Although there is no specific provision authorising notice of cancellation to be given by a constable – there is, under s 161(5), in the case of notice of a closure order (see 11.14.8 above) – the giving of such notice should be permissible in accordance with the ordinary principles of the law of agency.

### 11.14.16    Consideration of a closure order or extension by a magistrates' court

11.14.17 Whilst the giving of a closure order enables the instant closure of premises, it is necessary for the senior police officer to make an application as soon as reasonably practicable to the magistrates' court for the court to consider the order. He must also notify the licensing authority of the order and the court application if the order concerns licensed premises, that is, premises in respect of which there is in force a premises licence (s 193). This is to enable a review of the premises licence to take place (see 11.14.20–11.14.24 below). Section 164(1) and (2) provides:

(1) The responsible senior police officer must, as soon as reasonably practicable after a closure order comes into force in respect of any relevant premises, apply to a relevant magistrates' court for it to consider the order and any extension of it.

(2) Where an application is made under this section in respect of licensed premises, the responsible senior officer must also notify the relevant licensing authority–

    (a) that a closure order has come into force,

    (b) of the contents of the order and of any extension of it, and

    (c) of the application under subsection (1).

The magistrates' court must consider the application as soon as reasonably practicable and decide whether to exercise any of its powers, which include revoking the order (or extension) or ordering the premises to remain closed until the licensing authority has conducted a review of the order under s 167.[114] If closure is ordered until review, complete closure may not be necessary. Exceptions can be specified in the order, under which the premises can remain open, and the premises can also remain open if specified conditions are satisfied. Section 165(1) and (2) provides:

(1) A relevant magistrates' court must as soon as reasonably practicable after receiving an application under section 164(1)–

    (a) hold a hearing to consider whether it is appropriate to exercise any of the court's powers under subsection (2) in relation to the closure order or any extension of it, and

    (b) determine whether to exercise any of those powers.

(2) The relevant magistrates' court may–

    (a) revoke the closure order and any extension of it;

    (b) order the premises to remain or to be closed until such time as the relevant licensing authority has made a determination in respect of the order for the purposes of section 167;

    (c) order the premises to remain or to be closed until that time subject to such exceptions as may be specified in the order;

    (d) order the premises to remain or to be closed until that time unless such conditions as may be specified in the order are satisfied.

Exceptions specified in the closure order, which could allow for premises to remain open, might include opening during daytime hours rather than evenings or opening on some, but not all, evenings. Exceptions specified to remain open where conditions are satisfied might include the DPS or a certain number of personal licence holders being present on the premises, certain persons, for example, football supporters, not being admitted to the premises, or recorded or amplified music not being played without certain soundproofing precautions being taken.

11.14.18 The criteria that the court must apply, in deciding whether to revoke or extend the closure order, will include whether closure is necessary either in the interests of public safety because of disorder (or likely disorder) or to ensure that no public nuisance is (or is likely to be) caused by noise coming from the premises.[115] Section 165(3) provides:

In determining whether the premises will be, or will remain, closed the relevant magistrates' court must, in particular, consider whether–

    (a) in the case of an order made by virtue of section 161(1)(a), closure is necessary in the interests of public safety because of disorder or likely disorder on the premises, or in the vicinity of and related to, the premises;

    (b) in the case of an order made by virtue of section 161(1)(b), closure is necessary to ensure that no public nuisance is, or is likely to be, caused by noise coming from the premises.

The criteria specified in the section seem not to be the only ones to which the court can have regard. The section provides that the court must consider the matters specified 'in particular', which suggests that there may be other considerations that the court might also take into account. These might include the impact of closure of the premises on the premises licence holder (for example, financial hardship and possible loss of livelihood) and perhaps also the impact on other persons working there (for example possible loss of employment) and on the community generally (for example, possible loss of a facility at which licensable activities are provided). Certainly the impact of closure on the premises licence holder ought to be considered as closure will be an interference with his property under Art 1 of Protocol 1 of the European Convention on Human Rights. In determining whether this is justified, a fair balance will need to be struck between the general interest in closure to advance the public good (the purpose of the interference, in this case closure in accordance with the grounds mentioned above in s 165(3)) and the burden on the individual of the interference and whether the measures taken are proportionate to the aims to be achieved, that is, the impact on property rights (see 3.6.8 above). If an excessive burden is imposed on the premises licence holder and/or the measures taken are disproportionate, there might be a violation of Art 1 of Protocol 1. This might be the case if the premises are ordered to remain closed completely until review, if public safety might be assured or public nuisance by noise prevented by closure subject to exceptions under which the premises might remain open for periods of time (see 11.14.17 above). In determining whether to revoke or extend the closure order, the court therefore must consider whether closure is necessary in the interests of public safety or to prevent public nuisance by noise, as it is required to do by s 165(3), but cannot confine its consideration to these matters.

If the court decides to exercise its powers to revoke or extend the closure order, it must notify the licensing authority of its decision if the order concerns licensed premises. Section 165(4) provides:

> In the case of licensed premises, the relevant magistrates' court must notify the relevant licensing authority of any determination it makes under subsection (1)(b).

11.14.19 Where a court has extended the closure order, a person who permits the premises to remain open (see 11.13.5 above) in contravention of the order without reasonable excuse commits an offence punishable both by imprisonment and a fine. Section 165(7) and (8) provides:

(7) A person commits an offence if, without reasonable excuse, he permits relevant premises to be open in contravention of an order under subsection (2)(b), (c) or (d).

(8) A person guilty of an offence under subsection (7) is liable on summary conviction to imprisonment for a term not exceeding three months or to a fine not exceeding £20,000, or to both.

The requirements in respect of this offence are the same as those for the offence in s 161(6) (see 11.14.12 above). There is a right of appeal to the Crown Court against the magistrates' court order, which must be exercised within 21 days of the court's decision. Section 166 provides:

(1) Any person aggrieved by a decision of a magistrates' court under section 165 may appeal to the Crown Court against the decision.

(2) An appeal under subsection (1) must be commenced by notice of appeal given by the appellant to the designated officer for the magistrates' court within the period of 21 days beginning with the day the decision appealed against was made.

The right of appeal is available to 'any person aggrieved'. If the order is revoked by the magistrates' court, this will include the senior police officer who made the closure order, although it ought not to include the licensing authority, which will be notified of the magistrates' court's determination under s 165(4) to enable it to hold a review of the premises licence under s 167. This is because, even if the order is revoked, the licensing authority is still able to hold the review. It would not therefore seem to be 'aggrieved' by the decision to revoke and so should have no right of appeal under s 166(1). If the closure order is extended, then any 'appropriate person' would seem to be entitled to appeal.[116]

## 11.14.20   Review of premises licence following closure order

11.14.21 Where a closure order has been made in respect of licensed premises and the licensing authority receives notification of the magistrates' court's determination under s 165(4), it must review the premises licence and reach a decision on the action to be taken (if any) within 28 days of the notice. Section 167(1)–(3) provides:

(1) This section applies where–
    (a) a closure order has come into force in relation to premises in respect of which a premises licence has effect, and
    (b) the relevant licensing authority has received a notice under section 165(4) (notice of magistrates' court's determination), in relation to the order and any extension of it.
(2) The relevant licensing authority must review the premises licence.
(3) The authority must reach a determination on the review no later than 28 days after the day on which it receives the notice mentioned in subsection (1)(b).

Provision is made for regulations to require notice to be given to the premises licence holder and each responsible authority, for advertisement of the review by the authority and for the making of representations by responsible authorities and interested parties.[117] Section 167(4), which contains a comparable provision to that in s 51(3) for review of a premises licence under s 51 (see 6.12.3 above), provides:

The Secretary of State must by regulations–
(a) require the relevant licensing authority to give, to the holder of the premises licence and each responsible authority, notice of–
    (i) the review,
    (ii) the closure order and any extension of it, and
    (iii) any order made in relation to it under section 165(2);
(b) require the authority to advertise the review and invite representations about it to be made to the authority by responsible authorities and interested parties;
(c) prescribe the period during which representations may be made by the holder of the premises licence, any responsible authority or any interested party;
(d) require any notice under paragraph (a) or advertisement under paragraph (b) to specify that period.

Regulation 37 of the Licensing Act 2003 (Premises Licences and Club Premises Certificates) Regulations 2005, SI 2005/42 requires the authority to give notice in writing to the premises licence holder and each responsible authority of the matters specified in s 167(4)(a), and of the dates between which interested parties and responsible authorities may make representations. This must be done within one working day beginning on the day following the authority being notified (under s 165(4)) of the magistrates' court's decision to exercise its powers in relation to closure. Under reg 22(a), the period of time within which representations may be made is seven working days, beginning on the day following the authority's notification under s 165(4). Under regs 38–39, the licensing authority must advertise a review of a premises licence following a closure order in the same way as an application for a review of a premises licence under s 51 or a CPC under s 87 (see 6.12.3 above).

11.14.22 Relevant representations, which need to be relevant to one or more of the licensing objectives, will include those made by responsible authorities and interested parties, as well as those made by the holder of the premises licence whose licence is being reviewed. There is the usual provision for relevant representations not to be considered where they have been withdrawn or when they are regarded as frivolous or vexatious.[118] Section 167(9) and (10) provides:

> (9)  In this section "relevant representations" means representations which–
>> (a)  are relevant to one or more of the licensing objectives, and
>> (b)  meet the requirements of subsection (10).
>
> (10) The requirements are–
>> (a)  that the representations are made by the holder of the premises licence, a responsible authority or an interested party within the period prescribed under subsection (4)(c),
>> (b)  that they have not been withdrawn, and
>> (c)  if they are made by an interested party (who is not also a responsible authority), that they are not, in the opinion of the relevant licensing authority, frivolous or vexatious.

Under reg 5 and para 15 of Sched 1 to the Licensing Act 2003 (Hearings) Regulations 2005, SI 2005/44 (LA 2003 (Hearings) Regs 2005), the licensing authority must hold a hearing to review the premises licence within 10 working days, beginning with the day after the day the relevant licensing authority is notified by the magistrates' court under s 165(4) of its determination (see 11.14.18 above). Under reg 6(3)(a) and para 15 of Sched 2, notice of the hearing must be given to the premises licence holder and persons who made relevant representations no later than five working days before the day or the first day on which the hearing is to be held (see 2.3.2 above).[119] The authority must take such steps, if any, that it considers necessary to further the licensing objectives, which are the same ones open to it when reviewing a licence under s 52 where no closure order has been made (see s 52(4) and 6.12.8 above). The steps include revocation of the licence, modification of licence conditions, exclusion of certain licensable activities, suspension of the licence for up to three months or the removal of the DPS. For example, where the licensing authority determines that the lack of experience or expertise of the DPS has contributed to the level of disorder that has given rise to a closure order, it may specify that the individual concerned should be removed from that position. Similarly, it may determine that imposing a condition on the licence to the effect that additional security staff should be employed would reduce disorder (Explanatory Note 259). Section 167(5) and (6) provides:

>   (5)  The relevant licensing authority must–
>     (a)  hold a hearing to consider–
>       (i)   the closure order and any extension of it,
>       (ii)  any order under section 165(2), and
>       (iii) any relevant representations, and
>     (b)  take such of the steps mentioned in subsection (6) (if any) as it considers necessary for the promotion of the licensing objectives.
>   (6)  Those steps are–
>     (a)  to modify the conditions of the premises licence,
>     (b)  to exclude a licensable activity from the scope of the licence,
>     (c)  to remove the designated premises supervisor from the licence,
>     (d)  to suspend the licence for a period not exceeding three months, or
>     (e)  to revoke the licence;
>   and for this purpose the conditions of a premises licence are modified if any of them is altered or omitted or any new condition is added.[120]

11.14.23 If the authority decides to modify the conditions of the licence or to exclude a licensable activity from the scope of the licence, it can do so either permanently or for a temporary period up to three months. Section 167(8) provides:

> Where the authority takes a step within subsection (6)(a) or (b), it may provide that the modification or exclusion is to have effect only for a specified period (not exceeding three months).

Once the authority has conducted the review and made its determination, notification must be given (see 2.5 above) to the premises licence holder, anyone who made relevant representations and the chief officer of police, giving reasons for its decision. Section 167(12) provides:

> Where a licensing authority determines a review under this section it must notify the determination and its reasons for making it to–
> (a)  the holder of the licence,
> (b)  any person who made relevant representations, and
> (c)  the chief officer of police for the police area (or each police area) in which the premises are situated.

The authority's determination takes effect in accordance with the provisions in s 168.[121] In some cases the determination will not have effect pending appeal, that is, during the appeal period (21 days) or, if an appeal is made, until the appeal is disposed of, whereas in other cases it will have an effect, as it takes effect once the premises licence holder is notified of the decision. In general, the authority's decision will not have effect pending appeal. Section 168(1) and (2) provides:

>   (1)  Subject to this section, a decision under section 167 does not have effect until the relevant time.
>   (2)  In this section "the relevant time", in relation to any decision, means–
>     (a)  the end of the period given for appealing against the decision, or
>     (b)  if the decision is appealed against, the time the appeal is disposed of.

However, in cases where the magistrates' court, when considering the closure order, made an order under s 165 requiring the premises to remain closed pending a review of the premises licence, the determination of the review will generally take effect when the premises licence holder is notified of the decision. It will thus have effect pending appeal. This is unless either the magistrates' court to which the appeal is made decides to suspend the decision pending the appeal, which it has power to do under para 18(3) of Sched 5 (see 12.5.7 below), or the licensing authority itself decides to do so in accordance with its power under s 168(5). In cases where premises have remained closed and the licensing authority decides to revoke the premises licence, the authority's decision will not have effect pending appeal. Section 168(3)–(5) provides:

(3) Subsections (4) and (5) apply where–

   (a) the relevant licensing authority decides on a review under section 164 to take one or more of the steps mentioned in subsection (6)(a) to (d) of that section, and

   (b) the premises to which the licence relates have been closed, by virtue of an order under section 165(2)(b), (c) or (d), until that decision was made.

(4) The decision by the relevant licensing authority to take any of the steps mentioned in section 167(6)(a) to (d) takes effect when it is notified to the holder of the licence under section 167(12).

   This is subject to subsection (5) and paragraph 18(3) of Schedule 5 (power of magistrates' court to suspend decision pending appeal).

(5) The relevant licensing authority may, on such terms as it thinks fit, suspend the operation of that decision (in whole or in part) until the relevant time.

11.14.24 Where the licensing authority decides to revoke the premises licence, provision is made for premises to remain closed during any appeal against the licensing authority's decision, although the premises licence itself remains in force. The magistrates' court, although not, it appears, the licensing authority,[122] may, however, modify the closure order pending appeal and modification might include suspending the effect of the order during the appeal. Section 168(6) and (7) provides:

(6) Subsection (7) applies where–

   (a) the relevant licensing authority decides on a review under section 170 to revoke the premises licence, and

   (b) the premises to which the licence relates have been closed, by virtue of an order under section 165(2)(b), (c) or (d), until that decision was made.

(7) The premises must remain closed (but the licence otherwise in force) until the relevant time.

   This is subject to paragraph 18(4) of Schedule 5 (power of magistrates' court to modify closure order pending appeal).

Where premises remain closed pending appeal following revocation of the premises licence, a person who permits the premises to remain open (see 11.13.5 above) in contravention of the order and without reasonable excuse commits an offence punishable both by imprisonment and a fine.[123] Section 168(8) and (9) provides:

(8) A person commits an offence if, without reasonable excuse, he allows premises to be open in contravention of subsection (7).

(9) A person guilty of an offence under subsection (8) is liable on summary conviction to imprisonment for a term not exceeding three months or to a fine not exceeding £20,000, or to both.

The requirements in respect of this offence are the same as those for the offence in s 161(6) (see 11.14.12 above), except for the reference to 'allows', rather than 'permits', although the use of these different terms should not indicate any substantive difference.

## 11.15 CLOSURE OF IDENTIFIED PREMISES FOR PERSISTENTLY SELLING ALCOHOL: POLICE CLOSURE NOTICES

### 11.15.1 Making a closure notice

Section 169A makes provision for a closure notice to be given either by a police officer of the rank of superintendent or above or a trading standards officer[124] in respect of premises where there is evidence that a person who is the premises licence holder has committed the offence of persistently selling alcohol under s 147A. Guidance for police and trading standards officers on the power of closure, along with the offence in s 147A, has been issued by the DCMS and is contained in *Interpreting and implementing sections 23 and 24 of the Violent Crime Reduction Act 2006 – Persistently selling to children* (hereafter 'Police and TS Guidance'). There is no requirement for the premises licence holder to have been convicted of the s 147A offence for a closure notice to be given and it is sufficient if there is evidence that the offence has been committed and the person serving the notice considers the evidence to be such that there would be a realistic prospect of conviction. Section 169A(1) provides:

> A relevant officer[125] may give a notice under this section (a 'closure notice') applying to any premises if–
> (a) there is evidence that a person ('the offender') has committed an offence under section 147A in relation to those premises;
> (b) the relevant officer considers that the evidence is such that, if the offender were prosecuted for the offence, there would be a realistic prospect of his being convicted; and
> (c) the offender is still, at the time when the notice is given, the holder of a premises licence in respect of those premises, or one of the holders of such a licence.

The concept of a 'realistic prospect' of conviction is one that appears in other legislation, for example, in s 65 of the Crime and Disorder Act 1998, under which a constable can issue a reprimand or warning to a young offender, although the meaning and scope of the concept seems not yet to have been judicially considered.

The closure notice can propose a prohibition of alcohol sales on the premises for a period of up to 48 hours, which can be offered as an alternative to incurring criminal liability for the s 147A offence. If the proposed prohibition in the closure notice is accepted, this operates to discharge any criminal liability in respect of the offence. Section 169A (2) provides:

> (2) A closure notice is a notice which–
> (a) proposes a prohibition for a period not exceeding 48 hours on sales of alcohol on the premises in question; and
> (b) offers the opportunity to discharge all criminal liability in respect of the alleged offence by the acceptance of the prohibition proposed by the notice.

Whilst acceptance will preclude sales of alcohol, it will not in fact be necessary to close the premises, as the designation 'closure notice' perhaps implies. The premises need only be closed for the sale of alcohol. In other respects the premises can continue to operate and provision of any other licensable activities, that is regulated entertainment or late night refreshment, can continue.

## 11.15.2    Giving a closure notice

11.15.3 The closure notice must be in the form prescribed by the Secretary of State in regulations and must provide various details, including specification of the premises to which applies; provision of reasonable information and particulars of the alleged offence; specification of the length of the prohibition period proposed for alcohol sales, which must not be more than 48 hours, and, if the prohibition is accepted, when that period would commence, which must not be less than 14 days after the date the closure notice is served; explanation of the effect of the proposed prohibition and the consequences of noncompliance; explanation of the right of any person holding the premises licence to be tried for the offence if the proposed prohibition is not accepted; and explanation of how the right to be tried or acceptance of the proposed prohibition is to be accepted. Section 169A(3) and (4) provides:

(3) A closure notice must–

    (a) be in the form prescribed by regulations made by the Secretary of State;

    (b) specify the premises to which it applies;

    (c) give such particulars of the circumstances believed to constitute the alleged offence (including the sales to which it relates) as are necessary to provide reasonable information about it;

    (d) specify the length of the period during which it is proposed that sales of alcohol should be prohibited on those premises;

    (e) specify when that period would begin if the prohibition is accepted;

    (f) explain what would be the effect of the proposed prohibition and the consequences under this Act (including the maximum penalties) of a sale of alcohol on the premises during the period for which it is in force;

    (g) explain the right of every person who, at the time of the alleged offence, held or was one of the holders of a premises licence in respect of those premises to be tried for that offence; and

    (h) explain how that right may be exercised and how (where it is not exercised) the proposed prohibition may be accepted.

(4) The period specified for the purposes of subsection (3)(d) must be not more than 48 hours; and the time specified as the time from which that period would begin must be not less than 14 days after the date of the service of the closure notice in accordance with subsection (6).

11.15.4 Provision is made by s 169A(5) as to how the proposed prohibition is to be accepted or the right to be tried for the offence is to be exercised. As to acceptance of the prohibition, the closure notice is required to identify the police officer or trading standards officer to whom notice of acceptance is to be given, within 14 days of service of the closure notice, and set out particulars of where and how notice of acceptance is to be given. As to exercise of the right to be tried for the offence, this is to be taken as having been exercised unless every person who is a holder of the premises licence accepts the proposed prohibition. Section 169A(5) provides:

The provision included in the notice by virtue of subsection (3)(h) must–

(a)  provide a means of identifying a police officer or trading standards officer to whom notice exercising the option to accept the prohibition may be given;

(b)  set out particulars of where and how that notice may be given to that police officer or trading standards officer;

(c)  require that notice to be given within 14 days after the date of the service of the closure notice; and

(d)  explain that the right to be tried for the alleged offence will be taken to have been exercised unless every person who, at the time of the notice, holds or is one of the holders of the premises licence for the premises in question accepts the proposed prohibition.

11.15.5 The method of service of the closure order is not governed by the normal rules of service of notices contained in s 184 of the 2003 Act (see 2.5 above). The closure notice must be served on the premises, with a police officer or trading standards officer personally handing in the notice at the premises, at a time when licensable activities are taking place there, to a person who appears to have control or responsibility for the premises. Whilst the giving of a notice can be only by a police officer of the rank of superintendent or above (see s 169A(11) and 11.5.1 above), service of the notice can be by a constable and this can include a person, for example, a community support officer, exercising the powers of a constable by virtue of a designation under s 38 of the Police Reform Act 2002.[126] Similarly, a trading standards officer has to be at inspector level (s 169A(11)), that is, appointed under s 72(1) of the Weights and Measures Act 1985, to be able to give a closure notice, although the notice can be physically served at the premises by any authorised trading standards enforcement officer (Police and TS Guidance, para 62). Further, a copy of the closure notice must be sent to the holder of the premises licence at whatever address for him is currently on the premises licence. Section 169A(6)–(8) provides:

(6)  Section 184 (giving of notices) does not apply to a closure notice; but such a notice must be served on the premises to which it applies.

(7)  A closure notice may be served on the premises to which it applies–

(a)  only by being handed by a constable or trading standards officer to a person on the premises who appears to the constable or trading standards officer to have control of or responsibility for the premises (whether on his own or with others); and

(b)  only at a time when it appears to that constable or trading standards officer that licensable activities are being carried on there.

(8)  A copy of every closure notice given under this section must be sent to the holder of the premises licence for the premises to which it applies at whatever address for that person is for the time being set out in the licence.

11.15.6 The requirement to hand over the notice is simply at a time when licensable activities are taking place, which may well be when alcohol sales are being made, but need not be. Other licensable activities may be taking place outside of the hours at which alcohol is being sold and service of the notice at such a time will meet the requirement in s 169A(7)(b). The person to whom the closure notice is handed, who will be a person appearing to have control or responsibility for the premises, is likely to be either the premises licence holder himself or the DPS (if a different person from the premises licence holder), if either is present on the premises. If not, the closure notice may be handed to another manager or a more junior member of staff if the premises have been left in the charge of such a person. In the event that the closure notice is handed to the premises licence holder, it would still seem necessary, in order to comply with s 169A(8), for a copy of the notice to be sent to him at the address set out in the premises licence, even if that is the same address as the premises at which the closure notice had been handed to him. Whilst there is an element of duplication here, s 169A(8) is expressed in mandatory terms and appears to require service in all cases. However, a failure to comply with s 169(8) will not invalidate or otherwise affect the closure notice, for s 169B(8) provides: 'The operation of this section is not affected by any contravention of section 169A(8)'.

In the event that the closure notice is handed to a person other than the premises licence holder, there is no express requirement for that person to pass it on to the premises licence holder. It should be apparent to the person receiving it that it needs passing on, since the notice will be addressed to the premises licence holder and his name and address will appear on the notice.[127] Further, the officer handing over the notice may well instruct the recipient to pass it on to the premises licence holder. Nevertheless, the notice contains no requirement for it to be passed on, providing only:

> If you have been handed this notice and are not the premises licence holder, you may wish to inform the premises licence holder the [sic] this notice has been served.

Whilst the premises licence holder may well have a copy of the notice sent to him under s 169A(8), even if the notice is not passed on to him by the person to whom it is handed at the premises, a failure to send the copy will not, as indicated above, invalidate or otherwise affect the closure notice by virtue of the provision in s 169B(8). It is possible therefore that the premises licence holder may be unaware of the service of the closure notice and, accordingly, not realise that the opportunity is available to discharge all criminal liability in respect of the alleged offence by the acceptance of the prohibition on alcohol sales proposed by the notice. Essentially, this is seen as the retailer's responsibility. As para 67 of the Police and TS Guidance states:

> It is for the retailer to ensure adequate arrangements and processes are in place for information about unlawful sales and results of test purchase operations to be passed to the most appropriate person(s) in the organisation.

Nevertheless, the Police and TS Guidance goes on to state that, as a matter of good practice, instances of unlawful sales should be drawn to the retailer's attention:

> 67. . . . it may be in the best interest of the licensing objectives, and particularly those of children, for enforcers to draw the attention of the premises licence holder, or the store or area manager, to instances where unlawful sales of alcohol have been detected.

> 69. There will be a few cases where local enforcement agencies will decide it is not appropriate to notify the retailer of the result of a test purchase operation at the earliest opportunity. This might include where the operation is part of an on going criminal investigation or where a retailer is relying on police/trading standards information on non-compliance rather than putting their own monitoring of staff performance in place.

> 70. Such cases should be rare and the Home Office and ACPO agree that the default position is that police/trading standards officers should share information of passes and failures with premises as soon as practicable.

Paragraph 70 concludes by observing pointedly that 'administrative convenience should not be the deciding factor'.

11.15.7 A closure notice must be given not more than three months after the last alleged offence under s 147A, no more than one closure notice can be given in respect of offences relating to the same sales, and no notice can be given in respect of an offence for which a prosecution has already been brought. Section 169A(9) and (10) provides:

> (9)  A closure notice must not be given more than 3 months after the time of the last of the sales to which the alleged offence relates.
>
> (10)  No more that one closure notice may be given in respect of offences relating to the same sales; nor may such a notice be given in respect of an offence in respect of which a prosecution has already been brought.

There is no requirement that the closure notice is given, and the closure of the premises takes effect, as soon as is reasonably practicable after the alleged offence and the closure notice can be given at any time within three months of the last unlawful sales taking place. Section 169A thus contains no element of 'urgency' in respect of the giving of the closure notice, which would seem to confer on the police a discretion to select whatever period of up to 48 hours that they choose for the premises to be closed, which might include times at which the premises are likely to be busy, such as Bank Holidays or the Christmas/New Year periods. However, para 47 of the Police and TS Guidance indicates that the closure notice should be given as soon as possible:

> If there is a problem of persistent sales of alcohol to children, the notice should normally be given as soon as possible after the third relevant unlawful sale is detected. The purpose of the new provisions is to protect children from harm and delays in resolving such problems should be avoided wherever possible.

## 11.15.8    Effect of a closure notice

Where a closure notice is given, s 169B makes provision as to its effect (s 169B(1)). The giving of a notice precludes the bringing of any proceedings either for the alleged offence of persistently selling alcohol to children under s 147A, or for the offences of selling alcohol to children under s 146 or knowingly allowing the sale of alcohol to children under s 147 to which the alleged offence relates, at any time before the proposed prohibition on sale takes effect. Section 169B(2) provides:

> No proceedings may be brought for the alleged offence or any related offence[128] at any time before the time when the prohibition proposed by the notice would take effect.

If, prior to the proposed prohibition on sale taking effect, the person holding the premises licence, or all persons holding it if there is more than one, accept the proposed prohibition, the prohibition will take effect at the time specified in the notice. This will preclude the bringing of any proceedings subsequently for the above-mentioned offences and will also preclude the use of the premises for the retail sale of alcohol for the specified period of closure (but not for any other licensable activities authorised by the premises licence). Section 169B(3) and (4) provides:

> (3)  If before that time every person who, at the time of the notice, holds or is one of the holders of the premises licence for the premises in question accepts the proposed prohibition in the manner specified in the notice
>
> (a)  that prohibition takes effect at the time so specified in relation to the premises in question; and

(b)  no proceedings may subsequently be brought against any such person for the alleged offence or any related offence.

(4)  If the prohibition contained in a closure notice takes effect in accordance with subsection (3)(a) in relation to any premises, so much of the premises licence for those premises as authorises the sale by retail of alcohol on those premises is suspended for the period specified in the closure notice.

However, acceptance of the proposed prohibition does not preclude any application for a review of the premises licence from being progressed (Police and TS Guidance, para 52).

## 11.16  CLOSURE OF IDENTIFIED PREMISES FOR UNAUTHORISED SALE OF ALCOHOL: CLOSURE NOTICES AND CLOSURE ORDERS

### 11.16.1  Making a closure notice

A power to close premises, contained in s 19 of the Criminal Justice and Police Act 2001, is available to the police and to the local authority where premises are being, or within the last 24 hours have been, used for the unauthorised sale of alcohol for consumption on, or in the vicinity of, the premises. Section 19(1) and (2) provides:

(1)  Where a constable is satisfied that any premises are being, or within the last 24 hours have been, used for the unauthorised sale of alcohol for consumption on, or in the vicinity of, the premises, he may serve under subsection (3) a notice in respect of the premises.

(2)  Where a local authority is satisfied that any premises in the area of the authority are being, or within the last 24 hours have been, used for the unauthorised sale of alcohol for consumption on, or in the vicinity of, the premises, the authority may serve under subsection (3) a notice in respect of the premises.

This power was introduced primarily to enable the closure of unlicensed bars by operators who had no licence and who tended to move from one location to another to avoid local enforcement action being taken against them. That the purpose of the provision was the closure of unlicensed premises is apparent from the heading to the section, 'Closure of unlicensed premises', and from its original wording, 'unlicensed sale of intoxicating liquor'. The original wording has now been amended by paras 119 and 126(a) of Sched 6 to the 2003 Act and 'unlicensed sale of intoxicating liquor' has been replaced by 'unauthorised sale of alcohol'. As to what constitutes an 'unauthorised sale', para 128 amends s 28 of the 2001 Act (which is concerned with interpretation of provisions relating to closure) by providing that 'unauthorised sale' means any supply of alcohol that is a licensable activity under the 2003 Act and 'is made otherwise than under and in accordance with an authorisation (within the meaning of section 136 of that Act)'. Whilst this will include an unlicensed sale, it is not restricted to such sales for a sale 'otherwise than . . . in accordance with an authorisation' includes a sale in breach of licence conditions (see 11.2.1 above).

The effect of the amendments to s 19 seems to be a considerable extension in the scope of the closure power by enabling it to be invoked in cases of failure to comply with conditions, for example, noncompliance with CCTV requirements as to coverage or as to the period footage should be kept. Although Sched 6 to the 2003 Act deals with 'Minor and consequential amendments', this amendment is certainly not a minor one, even if it is a consequential one as a result of inclusion in s 136 of offences of both supply of alcohol without authorisation and in breach of (conditions attached to) an authorisation.[129] It might be questioned whether it is appropriate for a change of this magnitude to be effected through its inclusion in a schedule dealing with 'Minor and consequential amendments', which by its very nature is unlikely to attract much attention and will effectively preclude any Parliamentary debate on the matter. Notwithstanding this, it is probably the case that the words 'in accordance with an authorisation' in the amended s 28 of the 2001 Act leave no room for ambiguity, since they cannot really mean anything other than noncompliance with a condition. If the power of closure was confined to unlicensed sales (which is covered by the expression 'otherwise than under . . . an authorisation'), this would effectively mean that the words 'in accordance with' have no meaning at all. Whilst courts occasionally do regard words in statutes as surplusage and as having no meaning,[130] they do not do so very often and usually only where there is a compelling reason. Effecting a major change via a 'Minor and consequential amendments' schedule is unlikely to be seen as a compelling reason for not giving the words 'in accordance with' the meaning that they can clearly bear, that is, breach of conditions.

## 11.16.2 Giving a closure notice

11.16.3 There are three categories of persons on whom a closure notice must be served. First, a closure notice must be served on the person having control or responsibility for the activities carried on at the premises. Section 19(3) provides:

> A notice under subsection (1) or (2) ("a closure notice") shall be served by the constable or local authority concerned on a person having control of, or responsibility for, the activities carried on at the premises.

This includes anyone who aims to profit from the activities, manages them or employs another to do so, or is involved in their conduct. Section 19 (10) provides:

> For the purposes of subsections (3) and (5) a person having control of, or responsibility for, the activities carried on at the premises includes a person who—
> (a) derives or seeks to derive profit from the carrying on of the activities;
> (b) manages the activities;
> (c) employs any person to manage the activities; or
> (d) is involved in the conduct of the activities.

Having 'control or responsibility' is widely defined here and, for unlicensed sales, might extend to anyone taking an operational part in the sales. For breach of conditions, this might be, in the case of a premises licence, the licence holder and/or the DPS (and perhaps a personal licence holder, who may be 'involved in the conduct of the activities') and, in the case of a CPC, the club, club secretary and/or a club committee member.

Secondly, a closure notice must be served on any person occupying part of the premises if the police or local authority reasonably believe that person's access would be impeded if the premises were closed. Section 19(4) provides:

A closure notice shall also be served by the constable or local authority concerned on any person occupying another part of any building or other structure of which the premises form part if the constable or (as the case may be) the local authority concerned reasonably believes, at the time of serving notice under subsection (3), that the person's access to the other part of the building or other structure would be impeded if an order under section 21 providing for the closure of the premises were made.

Thirdly, a closure notice must be served on any other person having control or responsibility for the activities carried on at the premises (other than the person on whom the notice is served under s 19(3)) and any person who has an interest in the premises. Section 19(5) provides:

A closure notice may also be served by a constable or the local authority concerned on—

(a)  any other person having control of, or responsibility for, the activities carried on at the premises;

(b)  any person who has an interest in the premises.

11.16.4 No method of service is specified. As service is not under the 2003 Act, the provisions on the giving of notices in s 184 (see 2.5 above) do not apply and giving the closure notice will be in accordance with the normal rules of service.

The notice must specify the alleged use of the premises and grounds for being satisfied that there has been an unauthorised sale of alcohol for consumption on or in the vicinity of the premises, the effect of the notice and specify the steps to ensure the alleged use ends or does not recur. Section 19(6) provides:

A closure notice shall—

(a)  specify the alleged use of the premises and the grounds on which the constable or (as the case may be) the local authority concerned is satisfied as mentioned in subsection (1) or (as the case may be) subsection (2);

(b)  state the effect of section 20; and

(c)  specify the steps which may be taken to ensure that the alleged use of the premises ceases or (as the case may be) does not recur.

## 11.16.5   Effect of a closure notice

### 11.16.6   *Application for a closure order*

Where a closure notice is given, application can be made, between seven days and six months, to a magistrate (by complaint) for a closure order. Section 20(1) and (2) provides:

(1)  Where a closure notice has been served under section 19(3), a constable or (as the case may be) the local authority concerned may make a complaint to a justice of the peace for an order under section 21 (a "closure order").

(2)  A complaint under subsection (1) shall be made not less than seven days, and not more than six months, after the service of the closure notice under section 19(3).

This is provided the police or local authority are satisfied that use of the premises for unauthorised sale of alcohol for consumption there or in the vicinity has not ceased and there is a reasonable likelihood that the premises will be so used in future. Section 19(3) provides:

No complaint shall be made under subsection (1) if the constable or (as the case may be) the local authority is satisfied that–

(a) the use of the premises for the unauthorised sale of alcohol for consumption on, or in the vicinity of, the premises has ceased; and

(b) there is no reasonable likelihood that the premises will be so used in the future.

Where an application for a closure order is made, the magistrate may issue a summons requiring any person having control of, or responsibility for, the activities carried on at the premises on whom a closure notice was served to attend at a specified place, on a specified date and time, to answer the complaint. Section 20(4)–(6) provides:

(4) Where a complaint has been made to a justice of the peace under subsection (1), the justice may issue a summons to answer to the complaint.

(5) The summons shall be directed to–

(a) the person on whom the closure notice was served under section 19(3); and

(b) any other person on whom the closure notice was served under section 19(5)(a).

(6) Where a summons is served in accordance with subsections (4) and (5), a notice stating the date, time and place at which the complaint will be heard shall be served on all persons on whom the closure notice was served under section 19(4) and (5)(b).

The procedure on a complaint for a closure order is generally governed by the Magistrates' Courts Act 1980, which for the most part has application here. Section 20(7) provides:

The procedure on a complaint for a closure order shall (except as otherwise provided) be in accordance with the Magistrates' Courts Act 1980 (c. 43).

### 11.16.7   Cancellation of a closure notice

Although a closure order might be sought by the police or local authority, it is open to them to cancel the closure notice without proceeding with an application for a closure order. This is done by serving a notice of cancellation, which will presumably occur if unauthorised sale of alcohol for consumption on the premises, or in the vicinity, is no longer taking place nor is there any reasonable likelihood of this recurring. Section 19(7) provides:

A closure notice served by a constable or local authority may be cancelled by a notice of cancellation served by a constable or (as the case may be) the local authority concerned.

The notice of cancellation must be served on all persons on whom the closure notice was served, although cancellation is effective as soon as notice is served on any one of those persons. Section 19(8) and (9) provides:

(8) Any such notice of cancellation shall have effect as soon as it is served by a constable or (as the case may be) the authority concerned on at least one person on whom the closure notice was served.

(9) The constable or (as the case may be) the local authority concerned shall also serve the notice of cancellation on any other person on whom the closure notice was served.

## 11.16.8  *Making a closure order*

Where an application is made for a closure order, the magistrates' court hearing the complaint, provided it is satisfied the closure notice was properly served and the premises continue to be used for unauthorised sale of alcohol for consumption there or in the vicinity, can make such order as it considers appropriate. Section 21(1) provides:

> (1) On hearing a complaint made under section 20(1), the court may make such order as it considers appropriate if it is satisfied that–
>
>    (a) the closure notice was served under section 19(3); and
>
>    (b) the premises continue to be used for the unauthorised sale of alcohol for consumption on, or in the vicinity of, the premises or there is a reasonable likelihood that the premises will be so used in the future.

The requirement to be satisfied as to proper service of the notice relates only to the person served under s 19(3) as having control or responsibility for the activities carried on at the premises. There are other persons on whom the notice must be served (see 11.16.3 above), but it seems that a failure for them to be served with the notice will not preclude the magistrates' court from hearing the complaint.

Whilst s 21(1) confers a broad discretion on the court, s 21(2) and (3) goes on to provide instances of what action the court might take, which include immediate closure of the premises, immediate discontinuance of the sale of alcohol for consumption there or in the vicinity, payment of a sum into court, and imposition of conditions on admission to the premises or access to other parts of them. Section 21(2) and (3) provides:

> (2) An order under this section may, in particular, require–
>
>    (a) the premises in respect of which the closure notice was served to be closed immediately to the public and to remain closed until a constable or (as the case may be) the local authority concerned makes a certificate under section 22(1);
>
>    (b) the use of the premises for the unauthorised sale of alcohol for consumption on, or in the vicinity of, the premises to be discontinued immediately;
>
>    (c) any defendant to pay into court such sum as the court determines and that the sum will not be released by the court to that person until the other requirements of the order are met.[131]
>
> (3) An order of the kind mentioned in subsection (2)(a) may, in particular, include such conditions as the court considers appropriate relating to–
>
>    (a) the admission of persons onto the premises;
>
>    (b) the access by persons to another part of any building or other structure of which the premises form part.

Once the order is made, the complainant, that is, the police or local authority, must as soon as practicable, affix a copy of the notice in a conspicuous position on the premises. Section 21(4) provides:

> The complainant shall, as soon as practicable after the making of an order under this section, give notice of the order by fixing a copy of it in a conspicuous position on the premises in respect of which it was made.

## 11.16.9   Termination of a closure order

11.16.10  Where a closure order has been made, the police or local authority can make a certificate indicating that they are satisfied there is no longer any need for the order, whereupon the order ceases to have effect and any sum paid into court under the order under s 21(2)(c) (see 11.16.8 above) is released. Section 22(1)–(3) provides:

(1) Where a closure order has been made, a constable or (as the case may be) the local authority concerned may make a certificate to the effect that the constable or (as the case may be) the authority is satisfied that the need for the order has ceased.[132]

(2) Where such a certificate has been made, the closure order shall cease to have effect.

(3) Where a closure order containing provision of the kind mentioned in section 21(2)(c) ceases to have effect by virtue of the making of a certificate under subsection (1), any sum paid into court by a defendant under the order shall be released by the court.

The order ceases to have effect on the making of the certificate and not when a copy of the certificate is served on those against whom the closure order was made, as is required under s 22(5)(a), which may be some time later (as service is required only as soon as practicable after the making of the certificate). A copy of the certificate must also be served on anyone who requests a copy and a copy fixed in a conspicuous position on the premises. Section 22(5) and (6) provides:

(5) The constable or (as the case may be) the local authority concerned shall, as soon as practicable after the making of a certificate under subsection (1)–

(a) serve a copy of it on the person against whom the closure order has been made and the designated officer for the court which made the order; and

(b) fix a copy of it in a conspicuous position on the premises in respect of which the order was made.

(6) The constable or (as the case may be) the local authority concerned shall also serve a copy of the certificate on any person who requests such a copy.

11.16.11  An alternative way in which a closure order may be terminated is by application to a magistrate by way of complaint by a person on whom the order was served for its discharge and in such cases the court can make an order for discharge if satisfied that the need for the closure order has ceased. Section 23(1) and (2) provides:

(1) Where a closure order has been made–

(a) any person on whom the closure notice concerned was served under section 19; or

(b) any person who has an interest in the premises in respect of which the closure order was made but on whom no closure notice was served,

may make a complaint to a justice of the peace . . . for an order that the closure order be discharged.

(2) The court may not make an order under subsection (1) unless it is satisfied that the need for the closure order has ceased.

Where such an application is made, the magistrate may issue a summons requiring the police or local authority to attend at a specified place, on a specified date and time, to answer the complaint. Section 23(3) and (4) provides:

(3) Where a complaint has been made to a justice of the peace under subsection (1), the justice may issue a summons directed to such constable as he considers

appropriate or (as the case may be) the local authority concerned requiring that person to appear before the magistrates' court to answer to the complaint.

(4) Where a summons is served in accordance with subsection (3), a notice stating the date, time and place at which the complaint will be heard shall be served on all persons on whom the closure notice concerned was served under section 19 (other than the complainant).[133]

### 11.16.12    *Appeal against a closure order or its termination*

Since closure orders are not orders under the 2003 Act, the appeal provisions in the 2003 Act do not have application and s 24 of the 2001 Act provides rights of appeal to the Crown Court against a closure order and against a decision as to whether it should be terminated through discharge under s 23. Section 24(1) provides:

> An appeal against a closure order, an order under section 23(1) or a decision not to make an order under section 23(1) may be brought to the Crown Court at any time before the end of the period of 21 days beginning with the day on which the order or (as the case may be) the decision was made.

Section 24(2) goes on to specify the persons able to bring an appeal against a closure order, which are anyone on whom a closure notice was served and anyone with an interest in the premises on whom no notice was served:

> An appeal under this section against a closure order may be brought by–
>
> (a) any person on whom the closure notice concerned was served under section 19; or
>
> (b) any person who has an interest in the premises in respect of which the closure order was made but on whom no closure notice was so served.

If only such persons are able to appeal, as seems to be the case, this appears to rule out appeal by the police or licensing authority where a magistrate declines to issue a summons under s 20 requiring the attendance of persons on whom a closure notice was served (see 11.16.6 above) or where the magistrates' court declines to make a closure order under s 22 following attendance to answer the complaint (see 11.16.8 above).

As is common in cases where there is a right of appeal to the Crown Court, the court can 'make such order as it considers appropriate' and provision to this effect is made by s 24(3).

## 11.17  IMMUNITY FROM DAMAGES

Section 170 confers an immunity from liability for damages in certain types of cases concerning closure orders or closure notices. Immunity covers, in the case of closure orders, both the police officer exercising the power and the chief officer of police. Similarly, in the case of closure notices, immunity covers both the police officer or trading standards officer exercising the power and the chief officer of police or the trading standards department.[134] Section 170(1) and (2) provides:

> (1) Neither a constable nor a trading standards officer is liable for relevant damages in respect of any act or omission of his in the performance or purported performance of his functions in relation to a closure order or any extension of it or of his functions in relation to a closure notice.

(2) Neither a chief officer of police nor a local weights and measures authority is liable for relevant damages in respect of any act or omission of a person in the performance or purported performance, while under the direction or control of such a chief officer or local weights and measures authority–

   (a) of a function of that person in relation to a closure order, or any extension of it; or

   (b) of a function in relation to a closure notice.

Section 170, which provides immunity only in accordance with the terms of the section and does not affect any other exemption from liability for damges that might exist,[135] identifies three cases in which immunity might exist. The types of cases in question, identified by reference to the term 'relevant damages' in the section, are proceedings for judicial review and for the torts of negligence or misfeasance in public office. Section 170(5) provides:

> In this section, "relevant damages" means damages awarded in proceedings for judicial review, the tort of negligence or misfeasance in public office.

Whilst this confers immunity in these cases, it seems to leave open the possibility of action on other legal grounds, for example, the torts of trespass to land and (perhaps) conversion.

There are, however, qualifications to the immunity, in that it does not apply if the power of closure has been exercised in bad faith or if the conduct involves acting incompatibly with Convention rights contrary to s 6 of the Human Rights Act 1998. Section 170(3) provides:

> But neither subsection (1) nor (2) applies–
>
> (a) if the act or omission is shown to have been in bad faith, or
>
> (b) so as to prevent an award of damages in respect of an act or omission on the grounds that the act or omission was unlawful as a result of section 6(1) of the Human Rights Act 1998 (c.42) (incompatibility of act or omission with Convention rights).

The meaning of 'bad faith', when used in statutory provisions, varies according to the context and it may or may not be equated with dishonesty. It might be subjectively or objectively determined, but, whatever standard is adopted in this context, even if it is a relatively low one on the scale of 'bad faith', it is likely to be a difficult hurdle to surmount.

The act or omission being unlawful as a result of s 6(1) of the Human Rights Act 1998 is likely to be easier to prove. This requires proof that a public authority, which under s 6(3)(b) will include the police, has acted in a way that is incompatible with a Convention right. The Convention right in question is likely to be Art 1 of Protocol 1 (see 3.6 above). In determining whether there is a breach of Art 1 of Protocol 1 (and, in turn, whether the public authority is acting unlawfully under s 6(1) of the Human Rights Act 1998), the 'fair balance' test applies, that is, the need for controlling the use of property in the general interest for advancing the public good (the purpose of the interference) will have to be balanced against the burden on the individual of the interference and whether the measures taken are proportionate to the aims to be achieved (impact on property rights). Clearly, the State has a need to control the use of licensed premises to prevent nuisance and disorder, but the public good is advanced by closing licensed premises only in extreme cases where disorder threatens public safety or excessive noise causes disturbance, since other mechanisms are available to deal with general disorder and noise. Where closure of premises occurs, the burden on the individual is particularly severe and the 'fair balance' test is likely to require that the power be exercised only sparingly and where there is compelling prima facie evidence of a likelihood of disorder and a necessity to protect public safety.

## 11.18　ALCOHOL DISORDER ZONES AND PAYMENT OF CHARGES FOR PREMISES

### 11.18.1　Introduction

11.18.2 Under Chapter 2 of Pt 1 of the Violent Crime Reduction Act 2006, local authorities can, with the consent of the police, make an order designating a locality as an 'alcohol disorder zone' (ADZ) if there are problems with alcohol-related nuisance and disorder there. The purpose of ADZs is set out in Explanatory Notes 37 and 38 to the Act:

> 37. Alcohol disorder zones are designed to tackle the problem of alcohol-related crime and disorder in town and city centres by focussing intervention activity on the public space around licensed premises and/or the management of individual premises.

> 38. Alcohol disorder zones will sit alongside other measures to change individuals' behaviour, enforce the provisions of the Licensing Act 2003 and secure the collective responsibility of licensed premises to help build a robust local infrastructure to manage the night time economy. They are intended to be an intervention of the last resort.

ADZs enable local authorities to impose monthly charges on holders of premises licences allowing the retail sale of alcohol and on holders of CPCs allowing supply of alcohol to members and guests whose premises fall within the ADZ. Where designation is proposed, an 'action plan', drawn up by the local authority and the police, will require steps to be taken over a period of eight weeks by licensed premises and clubs to address the problems that have arisen. Charges at a nationally set rate can be imposed by the local authority if the steps are not implemented, 'reflecting the cost of a typical basket of initiatives which could be used by local authorities and other public authorities to tackle the problem' (Explanatory Note 4). Further, payments can also be required under the action plan, for example, to fund additional service provision such as extra late-night transport and any designation is subject to a three-monthly review of its appropriateness.

11.18.3 Whilst ADZs are part of a range of measures aimed at enforcing the provisions of the 2003 Act, they are not seen as appropriate unless there is a general problem in the area, as is apparent from statements made by Government Ministers during the course of the legislation's passage:

> If there are one or two rogue premises in an area, we should not necessarily reach for an alcohol disorder zone as our first tool. (Ms Hazel Blears, HC Deb, Standing Committee B, col 129, 20 October 2005)

> Where evidence reveals a few clearly identifiable problem premises, local authorities and the police should not reach for an ADZ; the Licensing Act should be used. Alcohol disorder zones become an option where this and other interventions have been tried

and there is still a more general problem. ADZs cannot and will not become a routine intervention. (Lord Bassam, HLDeb, vol 685, col 557, 16 October 2006)

In order to ensure that ADZs do not become routinely used, his Lordship gave a commitment to 'review their operation two years following their implementation', with an indication that the review will be 'undertaken earlier, if necessary—for example, if we find that their use escalates out of control, which we will take action to rectify'. Nor are ADZs envisaged as having anything other than a limited duration; as Ms Blears stated:

> I do not envisage alcohol disorder zones as long-term solutions. That would be a matter of accommodating our current problems. The policy intention is to prevent them, and to reduce the mayhem that goes on in town and city centres. (HC Deb, Standing Committee B, col 136, 20 October 2005)

It remains to be seen to what extent use will be made of ADZs and how their use is envisaged in the statutory Guidance that the Secretary of State is required to issue under s 19 about the manner in which powers and duties in relation to ADZs are exercised. There will need to be good reasons for departing from this Guidance since local authorities, the police and police authorities are under a duty to have regard to it when exercising these powers and discharging these duties (s 19(4)).

### 11.18.4  The imposition of monthly charges

### *11.18.5  Making of payments*

11.18.6 Section 15(1) enables the Secretary of State to make provision by regulations[136] for local authorities to impose monthly charges on holders of premises licences that authorise the retail sale of alcohol and clubs holding CPCs that authorise supply of alcohol to members and guests where the premises are in an ADZ. A monthly payment is required where a premises licence or CPC is held for either the whole or part only of the month in question. Section 15(1) provides:

> The Secretary of State may, by regulations, make provision for the imposition by a local authority of charges to be paid to the authority for each month by–
> (a) persons who for the whole or a part of that month held premises licences authorising the use of premises in alcohol disorder zones in the authority's area for the sale of alcohol by retail; and
> (b) clubs which for the whole or a part of that month were authorised by virtue of club premises certificates to use premises in such zones for the supply of alcohol to members or guests.

No indication is given as to the purposes for which the charges might be imposed, although, if the charges are to fall within the scope of the statutory power, it would seem that they will need in some way to relate to alcohol disorder. Provision is made, however, for the Secretary of State to specify or determine in regulations purposes for which revenue from the charges might be used, although there is no requirement for the Secretary of State to do so. Section 15(2) provides:

> The Secretary of State may by regulations make provision requiring a local authority that impose charges by reference to an alcohol disorder zone to use sums received by them in respect of those charges for the purposes specified in or determined under the regulations.

The Government's reluctance to commit itself in the legislation to detail on the matter seems to have been due to a desire to retain local flexibility so that 'local authorities and the police can determine their priorities and exercise discretion' (HC Deb, Standing Committee B, col 118, 20 October 2005). Nevertheless, some indication as to purposes can be obtained from statements made by Government Ministers during the course of the legislation's passage. It seems that purposes will include extra enforcement measures over and above what is normally required – this might include targeted policing activity, trading standards operations, joint agency visits and noise abatement enforcement – and directed particularly at problem premises:

> We are clear that income from alcohol disorder zones should not be used simply to subsidise existing activity. The charge is a special one and should be used to fund extra enforcement, particularly on the premises that cause the most problems, because that is how the community will get a real benefit from the measures. If the money were used simply to subsidise existing activity, local authorities and the police might have a perverse incentive to keep a zone in place because of the extra income generated from it. (HC Deb, Standing Committee B, col 118, 20 October 2005)

Purposes might also include a need to provide extra late-night transport (as indicated in the Explanatory Notes to the Act) or more public conveniences:

> An example that comes to mind is Westminster city council, which has provided a huge number of extra toilets on the streets. That has made a great difference to disorder on the streets and is exactly the sort of thing that we envisage for alcohol disorder zones. (HC Deb, Standing Committee B, col 118, 20 October 2005)

11.18.7 The rates set for the charges must be such that, after meeting costs, there are funds available, at a level considered by the Secretary of State to be appropriate, for use for any of the purposes specified in or determined under the regulations; and the different rates may be fixed for different descriptions of local authority, different descriptions of ADZs and different descriptions of premises. Section 15(3) and(4) provides:

(3) The rates of charges fixed under this section must be such as the Secretary of State considers appropriate for securing that the funds that he considers appropriate are available (after the costs[137] of the scheme have been met from the charges) to be used for any purposes specified or determined under subsection (2).

(4) Regulations under this section fixing the rates of charges may fix different rates for different descriptions of local authority, different descriptions of alcohol disorder zones and different descriptions of premises and may do so either–

    (a) by setting out the different rates in the regulations; or

    (b) by specifying the methods of computing the different rates in the regulations.

As to the level of charges, the Government's intention, as Lord Bassam stated during the Report Stage of the Bill in the House of Lords, is to set them 'at a meaningful level that is sufficient to recoup local agencies' costs in mounting effective enforcement interventions based on what is required to reduce crime and disorder locally'. The charges, he went on to say, 'must be realistic', whilst recognising that they must not set 'at a level that forces people to stop trading' (HLDeb, vol 685, col 561, 16 October 2006).

As to different rates, it is clearly envisaged that there will be differentials for different descriptions of premises, quite apart from any discounts and exemptions that might apply (see 11.18.9 below). The different rates will reflect the level of risk presented by particular types of premises, in the light of the way that they operate:

> In relation to charging premises, we recognise that not all premises should pay the same. We propose a national charging framework that will be structured and calibrated so that account will be taken of the risk that individual premises pose. This will be linked to the level of service that they receive and the amount that they pay. For example, a small pub on the corner closing at 11 pm will pay much less than a large bar closing at 3 am ... constructing the charge in this way will allow us to gear both the charge and the service received to reflect the different nature of licensed premises. There will not be a flat-rate charge for all. (HLDeb, vol 685, col 557, 16 October 2006)

His Lordship went on to say that there will be a charging formula that 'takes account of a premises' size, hours of opening and management practice' and the 'clear aim is to have charges that are proportionate, reflecting the level of risk proposed [sic] by licensed premises and the level of enforcement activity required' (HLDeb, vol 685, col 561, 16 October 2006). Similarly, there may be different rates for a different local authority areas, with large urban centres likely to have a higher rate than rural areas with a single small market town, and for different types of ADZs, which might depend on the number of premises within the ADZ's boundaries (Explanatory Note 134).

11.18.8 The charging formula, with its differential rates, will, however, have application in respect of *all* premises in the locality of the ADZ, even those that fall partly in the locality,[138] except to the extent that discounts or exemptions apply (see 11.18.9 below). The Government resisted amendents seeking to exclude payment for responsibly run premises that did not contribute in any way to the disorder taking place. Payment for all premises, regarded by those promoting the amendments as unfair and unjust, has proved to be particularly contentious. But the Government, taking the view that establishing a clear link with particular premises causing problems would be 'unworkable' (see HL Deb, vol 685, col 557, 16 October 2006), firmly committed itself to the collective responsibility approach that it had advocated during the Committee Stage of the Bill in the House of Commons (at HC Deb, Standing Committee B, cols 125–126, 20 October 2005):

> ... the intention of the policy is to try to get licensed premises in an area where there is serious disorder due to the misuse of alcohol to take some collective responsibility for that, and to come together to agree an action plan with a local authority before an alcohol disorder zone is ever designated. If they agree a plan, and they get together to ensure that behaviour in their neighbourhood is conducted responsibly, there will be no need to designate an alcohol disorder zone.

> The policy intention is that off-licences, on-licences, pubs and clubs ... in an area where people's behaviour is out of control as a result of consuming alcohol, will come together and say, "We have a responsibility to do something about this", they will agree with the local authority about the action that needs to be taken, implement it, and make a difference, so that there is no longer a problem, and we do not need an alcohol disorder zone.

> ... As far as we can, we shall ensure that the premises that cause the greatest problem, pose the highest risk and need the most intensive and targeted enforcement, pay the highest costs. However, we are not in the business of letting people simply say, "It wasn't me. It wasn't in my pub that someone had the four alcopops that two hours later

led them to fight in the bus queue or conduct a serious assault against somebody on the way home."

## 11.18.9   Discounts and exemptions

11.18.10 Provision is made for the making of regulations to authorise or require local authorities to grant discounts from the monthly charges and, in limited instances, for exemptions from the requirement to pay the charge. There is a requirement for the regulations to provide exemptions, but only where two criteria are met. These are that the principal use of the premises does not include the sale or supply of alcohol and the availability of alcohol there is not the main reason, or one of the main reasons, why individuals enter or remain on those premises. Thus the premises must pass a dual test of principal use and what might be described as a 'patronage test' to qualify for an exemption. Discounts or exemptions can be subject to compliance with conditions, either as set out in the regualtions or specified by local authorities in accordance with provisions in the regulations, and conditions can include the seeking of approval from specified persons. Section 15(5)–(7) provides:

> (5)  Regulations under this section fixing such rates–
>
>   (a)  may authorise or require a local authority to grant discounts from the charges; and
>
>   (b)  must provide for exemptions from the charges for the purpose mentioned subsection (6).
>
> (6)  The only exemptions from charges for which regulations under this section may provide are exemptions for the purpose of securing that charges are not imposed in relation to premises where–
>
>   (a)  the principal use to which the premises are put does not consist in or include the sale or supply of alcohol; and
>
>   (b)  the availability of alcohol on those premises is not the main reason, or one of the main reasons, why individuals enter or remain on those premises (whether generally or at particular times of the day or on particular days of the week, or both).[139]
>
> (7)  Regulations providing for a discount or exemption from charges may make a discount or exemption subject to compliance with conditions which–
>
>   (a)  are set out in the regulations; or
>
>   (b)  are specified by the local authority in accordance with provision made under the regulations;
>
> and those conditions may include conditions requiring approvals to be given in respect of premises by such persons, and in accordance with such scheme, as may be provided for in the regulations.

11.18.11 The principal use test is similar to the primary use test, which has application in other areas under the 2003 Act, namely, the prohibition on supplying alcohol where premises are used primarily as a garage (see 6.1.7 above) and payment of increased premises licence fees where premises are used exclusively or primarily for supply of alcohol for consumption on the premises (see 6.3.1 above). The principal use test, as formulated in s 15(6)(a), however, seems to be broader than the primary use test employed in these instances. The primary use test envisages a main, dominant purpose for which the premises are used, but the s 15 principal use test can either 'consist in or *include*' sale or supply (hereafter 'supply') of alcohol (emphasis supplied). Where it consists in supply, as in the case of public houses, supply will be the main, dominant purpose for which the premises are used and will be the primary use. Where it includes supply, however, supply may be one of the principal uses, although not the only one, and supply here may not be the primary use. This may be the case with nightclubs, where the principal uses may be regarded as provision of music and dancing, and supply of alcohol. Here, the principal use might be said to include supply and this will mean that the s 15(6)(a) requirement, of principal use not including supply, is not met. The position of nightclubs and the principal use test was in fact raised during the course of the legislation's passage (at HC Deb, Standing Committee B, cols 121–12, 20 October 2005):

> Is the principal activity in such places drinking or not? Do people go to dance so that drinking is incidental, or is it the other way around? Those are rather difficult questions, on which it would be helpful to have an authoritative answer from the Minister.

No authoritative answer, or indeed any answer at all, was, however, forthcoming from the Minister when responding on principal use in the course of dealing with a range of points raised (see col 130). If what is said above is correct, however, it seems the principal use test in s 15(6)(a) is not met. In the case of other premises that supply alcohol, the position is clearer and it is evident that the principal use does not consist in or include supply of alcohol. Thus for restaurants the principal use consists in the provision of food, for hotels it is overnight accommodation, for cinemas and theatres it is entertainment, for gyms it is physical exercise facilities and for supermarkets and convenience stores it is the sale of foodstuffs. Here, the provision of alcohol is secondary and the principal use test for the exemption will be satisfied.

11.18.12 The patronage test requires that the availability of alcohol is not the main reason, or one of the main reasons, why individuals enter or remain on the premises. Even if (contrary to what is said above) principal use of nightclubs is regarded as consisting in provision of dancing and not including supply of alcohol, nightclubs may not meet the patronage test. To meet this test, the availability of alcohol on the premises must not be one of the main reasons why individuals enter or remain on those premises and the view may be taken that it *is* one of the main reasons. It may not be *the* main reason, if dancing is regarded as the principal use, but it may be one of the main reasons, along with dancing, why persons enter and remain there. On this basis, nightclubs will not be exempt from payment of the monthly charge.

Although s 15 provides that there can be exemptions only where both the principal use and patronage tests are satisfied, there may in practice be further exemptions if the Government proceeds with its stated intention, expressed during the course of the legislation's passage, that in some circumstances there may be discounts of 100%. The Government's intention is that, where premises have closed before any crime or disorder arises, a 100% discount, which will effectively be the same as an exemption, should be given: 'Outlets that close before ADZ enforcement activity commences will receive a 100 per cent discount' (Lord, Bassam, HL Deb, vol 685, col 558, 16 October 2006). If a local authority is to designate an area as an ADZ, it seems it will have to establish a time for ADZ services to commence, which will need to be evidence-based in relation to when crime and disorder occurred. Premises closing before that time will receive no direct benefit from any ADZ services and will not be required to pay for services delivered after they have closed.

### 11.18.13   *Enforcement, appeals and nonpayment*

The regulations may make provision for payment, collection and enforcement of charges; for determinations about liability, applicable charge rates or compliance with discount or exemption conditions; and appeals against decisions made. They may also make provision for interest to be charged on overdue payments and for suspension of premises licences and CPCs for nonpayment of charges. Section 15(8) and (9) provides:

> (8) The Secretary of State may by regulations make provision about–
>> (a) the payment, collection and enforcement of charges imposed in accordance with regulations under this section;
>> (b) the determination of questions about liability for such charges, about the rate of charge applicable in relation to a particular set of premises or about compliance with the conditions of any exemption or discount; and
>> (c) appeals against decisions determining such questions.
>
> (9) Such regulations may include provision–
>> (a) for interest to be charged at such rate and in such manner as may be specified in or determined under the regulations on charges that are overdue; and
>> (b) for the suspension of premises licences and club premises certificates for non payment of a charge.

Whilst the regulations may make provision for appeals against decisions on charges, no provision is made in the regulations or in the Act itself for appeals against the designation of a locality as an ADZ.

## 11.18.14   Designation of alcohol disorder zones

### 11.18.15   *Criteria for designation*

11.18.16 There are four requirements that need to be met for designation of a locality as an ADZ. They are that, first, there has, in or near the locality, been nuisance or annoyance to members of the public, or a section of it, or disorder; secondly, this is associated with consumption of alcohol either taking place in the locality or supplied at premises that are in the locality; thirdly, there is a likely repetition of such associated nuisance, annoyance or disorder; and fourthly, an eight-week period has elapsed between publication of an action plan to take steps to render designation unnecessary without such steps having been implemented. Section 16(1) and (8) provides:

> (1) A local authority may by order designate a locality in their area as an alcohol disorder zone if they are satisfied–
>> (a) that there has been nuisance or annoyance to members of the public, or a section of the public, or disorder, in or near that locality;
>> (b) that the nuisance, annoyance or disorder is associated with the consumption of alcohol in that locality or with the consumption of alcohol supplied at premises in that locality;
>> (c) that there is likely to be a repetition of nuisance, annoyance or disorder that is so associated; and
>> (d) that subsection (8) allows the making of the order.
>
> (8) A local authority may only make an order designating a locality as an alcohol disorder zone if–

(a)  the period of 8 weeks beginning with the day after the publication of the action plan has expired without such steps for implementing the action plan having been taken as, in that authority's opinion, make the designation of the locality unnecessary; or

(b)  the local authority are satisfied (whether before or after the end of that period) that the plan will not be implemented, that the steps required by the plan are no longer being taken or that effect is no longer being given to arrangements made in accordance with the plan.

11.18.17 To satisfy the first requirement, the nuisance, annoyance or disorder (here-after 'NAD') need not occur in the locality and it is sufficient if it occurs 'near' the locality. This would ordinarily be the case if it is in the vicinity of the locality. The locality itself may be quite a small area, since s 20(1) provides that references to 'locality' include a part of a locality and the Government has stated that 'the zone will be tightly drawn around the premises concerned' (HL Deb, vol 685, col 563, 16 October 2006). This suggests a rather narrowly defined area for the locality and the surrounding area, which is 'near' the locality is likely to be correspondingly small.

There does not seem to be any need for the NAD to occur on more than one occasion, although it seems that the Guidance will emphasize the need for some degree of persistence or repetition and will 'specifically refer to full use of the Licensing Act 2003 before designating an alcohol disorder zone' (ibid., col 563). In practice, given that ADZs are 'an intervention of last resort', isolated occurrences are most unlikely to result in designation. If conduct amounts to no more than 'annoyance', which presumably is something short of what is required for a nuisance, then, in order to take action under the 2003 Act, this will need to be justified on the basis that this is necessary to promote the licensing objective of prevention of public nuisance. The mere existence of annoyance, coupled with a likely repetition, will not in itself suffice, although it appears that it will for designation of an ADZ (assuming the other requirements are met). This seems difficult to justify.

For the second requirement, it is necessary only that the NAD is 'associated with' consumption of alcohol, which indicates the need for the NAD to be alcohol-related, but without any requirement for a causal link between the two. The consumption of alcohol with which the NAD is associated can be consumption either within or out-side the ADZ. Where it is consumption outside, the consumption has to be of alcohol supplied at premises in the ADZ. Where it is consumption inside, the alcohol need not have been supplied at premises in the ADZ. Indeed, it seems on the wording that an area could be designated as an ADZ where alcohol-related NAD has occurred in the locality, even though none of the alcohol consumed there has been supplied by any of the premises within the ADZ.

On the third requirement of a likely repetition of associated NAD, the authority will need to be of the view that repetition is more probable than not. That there may have been a number of similar previous occurences of NAD may well substantiate the view that further occurrences are likely and satisfy this requirement.

The final requirement of the elapsing of an eight-week period since publication of an action plan is to give the action plan every opportunity of success to avoid having to designate the locality as an ADZ. It is only after this period, if there are no signs that the plan is going to be implemented, that designation can take place.

11.18.18 If the four requirements are met, the local authority must, before proceeding to designate an ADZ, publicise its proposal to do so. This must be done by publishing a notice setting out the proposal and inviting persons interested to make representations within 28 days about the proposal, and what the action plan, which is to be drawn up, might include. Section 16(2) and (3) provides:

> (2) Before designating a locality as an alcohol disorder zone, a local authority must publish a notice–
>  (a) setting out their proposal to designate the locality; and
>  (b) inviting persons interested to make representations about the proposal, and about what might be included in the action plan under subsection (4).
>
> (3) That notice must require the representations to be made before the end of the period of 28 days beginning with the day after publication of the notice.

No indication is given as to what form the notice should take, what detail it should contain about the proposal, or how or where the notice should be published, although it might be expected that these matters will be addressed in the regulations. Representations can be made by 'persons interested', an expression that is not defined in the Act. It is possible that the regulations may prescribe who are 'persons interested' for these purposes or, if not, some indication may be given in the ADZ Guidance issued under s 19 (see 11.18.28 below). However, the intention may be to leave the expression undefined in order to enable representations to be received from a broad range of persons.

Similarly, no indication is given as to what the content of the representations might relate to. Representations that relate to the criteria for designation under a 15(1) or to what the local authority is proposing clearly seem to be relevant, as perhaps might representations that relate more generally in some way to the licensing objectives, but how far representations extending beyond this should be considered is less clear. It may be that these matters will be dealt with either in the regulations or in the s 19 ADZ Guidance.

### 11.18.19  Preparation of the action plan

11.18.20 Once the 28-day period for making representations has passed, the local authority and police must, as soon as reasonably practicable, prepare an 'action plan' indicating the steps to be taken to avoid the need for designation of an ADZ, publish the plan in whatever way they think is suitable for drawing it to the attention of those likely to be interested, and send a copy of it to all those holding either a premises licence authorising the retail sale of alcohol or a CPC authorising the supply of alcohol to members or guests. Given that representations have been invited, it seems implicit that the local authority and police will have regard to them when preparing the action plan and indicating what steps should be taken, although there is no express requirement for them to do so. Section 16(4) provides:

> As soon as reasonably practicable after the end of the period for making representations about a proposal by a local authority to designate a locality, the local authority and the local chief officer of police must–
>  (a) prepare a document ("the action plan") setting out the steps the taking of which would, in their opinion, make the designation of the locality unnecessary;

(b) publish the action plan in such manner as they consider appropriate for bringing it to the attention of persons likely to be interested in it; and

(c) send a copy of the plan to every person who holds–

(i) a premises licence authorising the use of premises in the locality for the sale of alcohol by retail; or

(ii) a club premises certificate by virtue of which authorisation is given to the use of premises in the locality for the supply of alcohol to members or guests.

The requirement in s 16(4) (a) seems to assume that the local authority and police will be able to achieve a consensus on what steps should be taken, which may or may not prove to be the case. Presumably in the absence of agreement the proposal for designation will not proceed but, assuming agreement is reached, the action plan will set out details of the proposed action by the local authority and the police. Examples of what might be included were alluded to during the course of the legislation's passage, with the Government Minister Hazel Blears stating (at HC Deb, Standing Committee B, cols 153–54, 20 October 2005) that steps to be taken might cover:

> . . . additional high-visibility policing, and the application of the industry principles and standards . . . code of practice . . . which covers "no ID no sale", irresponsible promotions and a dispersal policy.

> . . . coffee bars being open at 3, 4 or 5 o'clock in the morning [so] [p]eople waiting for their parents to collect them or waiting for an all-night bus can have a cup of coffee and perhaps sober up a little before dad arrives; they are in a better state to be taken home . . .

> Toughened drinking glasses will help solve the problem of people cutting each other's faces with broken glasses . . . Another big flash-point for violence can be people trying to jump the taxi queue at 2 am, so having fairly large, burly and sober people [as taxi marshalls] can make a big difference.

> There will be extra enforcement work, with frequent visits to premises, and trading standards will run test purchasing operations with under-age youngsters being sent in. Environmental health visits can help deal with excessive noise, which is another big problem. CCTV can be installed outside licensed premises, and cleaning the streets directly outside licensed premises in the zone, perhaps where people have had unfortunate incidents and left appalling messes on the pavements, could also be charged for.

Further, the proposed action will vary between different areas, as Explanatory Note 143 recognises:

> As an example, the proposed alcohol disorder zone may be in an area where there is a need to raise operating standards in pubs and clubs within the zone. In this case, the action plan might contain, for example, a requirement for pubs and clubs to display information about their proof of age policy. In a different scenario, the proposed alcohol disorder zone might be in an area where the pubs and clubs are quite well run, but there is a public space problem – for example, there is a lack of late-night transport, and the taxi rank is poorly lit and the scene of a lot of trouble. Here the action plan might require premises to fund extra transport provision, and provide door staff for an extra hour after closing time to monitor the taxi rank.

Section 16(4)(b) leaves it to the local authority and police to decide how best to bring the action plan to the attention of persons likely to be interested in it and s 16(4)(c) requires them to send a copy of the action plan to every person holding either a premises licence authorising the retail sale of alcohol or a CPC authorising the supply of alcohol to members or guests. Explanatory Note 143 states that the plan must be 'sent to those who would be liable to pay the charge if the area was to be designated', but the section, on its wording, does not so restrict the sending of the plan. It is expressed in wider terms and essentially requires a copy to be sent to *all* premises authorising sale or supply. This will include not only those liable to pay the monthly charge, but also those exempt from making payment of it under s 15(6) because the principal use of the premises does not consist in or include the sale or supply of alcohol and the availability of alcohol is not the main reason, or one of the main reasons, why individuals enter or remain there (see 11.18.10 above).

11.18.21 The action plan can include steps for establishing and maintaining a scheme for making payments to the local authority and, if such a scheme is set up, the Secretary of State can make regulations requiring the local authority to use the sums received for any purposes specified or determined in the regulations, as is the case with sums received from monthly charges (see 11.18.6 above). The plan must also indicate what proposed action will be taken by the local authority and the police if the plan is implemented. Section 16(5)–(7) provides:

> (5) The steps set out in the action plan may include the establishment and mainten-ance of a scheme for the making of payments to the local authority.
> (6) The action plan must also contain proposals by–
>> (a) the local authority in whose area the locality to which the proposed designa-tion relates is situated, and
>> (b) the local chief officer of police,
>> about what action they will take in relation to that locality if the plan is imple-mented.
> (7) The power of the Secretary of State to make regulations under subsection (2) of section 15 shall be exercisable in relation to sums received by a local authority in accordance with a scheme established under an action plan as it is exercisable in relation to sums received by a local authority in respect of charges imposed by virtue of regulations under that section.

Whilst s 16(5) makes it clear that an action plan can make provision for a payments scheme, no mention is made of the premises that might contribute payments. Given that ADZs are concerned with premises authorising sale or supply of alcohol, it seems evident that payment should be required only from such premises and requiring payment from any other premises would be *ultra vires* as falling outside the scope of the statutory power. But it is less clear whether payment might be required from all premises in the proposed ADZ area which authorise sale or supply of alcohol. The monthly charge payable under s 15 where an area is designated as an ADZ is not payable by all such premises because there is an exemption under s 15(6) from pay-ment for some premises (see 11.18.10 above). However, this exemption is expressed to apply only to 'charges', with which s 15 is concerned, whereas the action plan under s 16(5) enables the making of 'payments'. It seems likely therefore, on the wording of the relevant provisions, that premises may be required to contribute payments under an action plan, although they might be exempt from the monthly charge if the area is designated as an ADZ. This might or might not accord with the legislative intent on a purposive construction of the provisions. On the one hand, the view may be taken that there is no inconsistency here. The action plan might be felt to have a greater chance of success in preventing designation of an ADZ with payments from a wider spread of premises, but, if the plan fails and designation goes ahead, charges should then be more restricted (as they will be under s 15(6)). On the other hand, the action plan is an integral part of the designation process and if premises are excluded from collective responsibility in one part of the process (by exemption from the monthly charge) it might be felt that they should similarly be excluded in another part (by not making payments under the action plan). Whilst a purposive construction is equivocal, a literal interpretation points to payments under the scheme being able to include all premises in the proposed ADZ area which authorise sale or supply of alcohol.

However, since the action plan has to be prepared by the local authority and the police and they will establish the payments scheme (if they decide to have one), it may be that they can choose to adopt a scheme that does not seek to secure payments from all such premises, but excludes those that would be exempt from a charge in the event of the area being designated as an ADZ. The extent to which premises are required to make payments under an action plan may thus be a matter for the local authority and the police to determine. It is possible that the premises from which payments should be required may be addressed in the Secretary of State's s 19 ADZ Guidance, although it seems unlikely that any provision in this respect can be included in regulations made by the Secretary of State under s 16(7). This is because the power to make regulations under s 16(7) relates only to the purposes for which sums received are used and, as such, does not extend to determining whether or not sums should or should not be received from particular premises. However, it is possible that such provision might be included in regulations made under s 17(6), which enable the Secretary of State to supplement the provisions in ss 16–17 by prescribing additional procedures to be followed in relation to the making or revocation of orders for the designation of a locality as an ADZ (see 11.18.23 below). Since the action plan is part of the procedure for making ADZ orders and the plan can include provision for the making of payments, the regulations might prescribe the premises from which those payments should be required.

## *11.18.22 Designation procedure for ADZs*

11.18.23 Section 17 sets out the designation procedure, which is by an order identifying the ADZ locality either by name or by description of its boundaries. Provision is made for revocation of the order, which can take place at any time, and for its variation. Section 17(1)–(3) provides:

(1) An order designating an alcohol disorder zone must identify the locality being designated either by name or, if appropriate, by describing its boundaries.

(2) A local authority who have designated a locality as an alcohol disorder zone may by order revoke the designation.

(3) If a local authority consider that the locality designated by an alcohol disorder zone should be varied, they may–

    (a) make a proposal for the purposes of section 16 for a replacement order designating a locality that includes the whole or part of the locality already designated; and

    (b) in any designation order made to give effect to that proposal, revoke the previous designation with effect from the coming into force of the replacement order.

The power to make a variation is seen as important, because there may well be unforeseen displacement of activity and, if an ADZ is designated in one place, problems might emerge elsewhere. Accordingly, local authorities have the flexibility to vary the ADZ. In the case of variation, s 17(3)(a) requires the local authority to 'make a proposal for the purposes of section 16 for a replacement order', but there is some uncertainty as to what is required in order to do this. At its lowest, this may require no more than a simple proposal for varying the original order in some specified way. However, more than this may be required because s 16(2)(a) refers to the local authority publishing a notice 'setting out their proposal to designate the locality' and s 16(6) refers to the action plan containing proposals about what action will be taken if the plan is implemented. It may therefore be necessary for the local authority to publish a notice setting out the variation proposal, invite representations within 28 days, and for the local authority and the police to prepare and publish an action plan based on the variation. A purposive interpretation would support this view, for the Government Minister Hazel Blears stated (at HC Deb, Standing Committee B, col 157, 20 October 2005): 'That means that it must make a proposal in accordance with the original procedure in clause 13 [which became s 16], so premises to which it would be extended would have exactly the same opportunity as others to make their representations and be included in the plan'. If the proposal for variation is to be in accordance with the original procedure, it would seem to follow that copies of the plan should also be sent to premises having a premises licence authorising sale of alcohol or a CPC authorising supply under s 16(4)(c) (see 11.18.20 above).

Additional procedures for making or revoking ADZs (though not, it seems, for varying them) can be prescribed by the Secretary of State in regulations and these must include publicising the making and effect of orders designating localities as ADZs. Section 17(6) and (7) provides:

(6)  The Secretary of State may make regulations which, for the purpose of supplementing the provisions of section 16 and this section, prescribe additional procedures to be followed in relation to the making or revocation of orders for the designation of a locality as an alcohol disorder zone.

(7)  Those regulations must include, in particular, provision requiring local authorities to publicise the making and effect of orders designating localities as alcohol disorder zones.

11.18.24  As ADZs are not envisaged as having long-term effect, provision is made for review by the local authority and the police at intervals of three months and on each review they must consider whether revocation or variation would be appropriate. Section 17(4) and (5) provides:

(4)  The local authority who have designated a locality as an alcohol disorder zone and the local chief officer of police must–

(a)  as soon as reasonably practicable after the end of three months from the coming into force of the designation, and

(b)  as soon as reasonably practicable after the end of each subsequent period of three months,

together carry out a review of the need for the designation.

(5)  On each such review the local authority and local chief officer of police must consider whether it would be appropriate for any of the powers in subsections (2) and (3) to be exercised.

The purpose of a three-month review is, as the Government Minister Hazel Blears indicated (at HC Deb, Standing Committee B, col 158, 20 October 2005), 'to ensure a constant focus on the area, rather than allowing the designation to run and run' It remains to be seen how long ADZs will remain in existence and a duration of one year seems to be envisaged as exceptional, with the Minister stating that 'possibly only a handful of alcohol disorder zones will still be in existence 12 months on'.

## 11.18.25 Functions of the police

### 11.18.26 *Police applications for ADZs*

The impetus for designation of an ADZ may come from either the police or the local authority. If it comes from the police and the police apply to the local authority for a designation, the local authority must consider whether a proposal should be made. If the authority decides against making a proposal, it must give notice of its decision and its reasons to the police and send a copy of the notice to both the Secretary of State and the police authority for the area where the ADZ is proposed. Section 18(1) and (2) provides:

(1) It is the duty of a local authority to consider whether to make a proposal for the designation of a locality as an alcohol disorder zone if the local chief officer of police applies to them to do so.

(2) If on such an application the local authority decide not to make a proposal, they must–
   (a) give notice of their decision (setting out their reasons) to the local chief officer of police; and
   (b) send a copy of that notice to the Secretary of State and to the police authority for the police area in which the locality to which the proposal relates is situated.

### 11.18.27 *Consultees on local authority proposals for ADZs*

If the impetus for designation of an ADZ comes from the local authority, without any application from the police, the authority must consult the police before publishing notice of their designation proposal. If the action plan prepared is not implemented and the authority wishes to proceed to designate the locality as an ADZ, it must obtain the consent of the police. In the event that consent is not forthcoming, the police must give notice of their decision and reasons to the Secretary of State and to the police authority. The police's consent must similarly be obtained if the local authority intends to revoke the designation under s 17(2), although there is no provision for giving notice of this decision and the reasons for it. Section 18(3)–(5) provides:

(3) A local authority which–
   (a) are proposing to designate a locality as an alcohol disorder zone, and
   (b) are not doing so on an application from the local chief officer of police,
   must consult that chief officer before publishing notice of their proposal.

(4) The consent of the local chief officer of police is required for the making of–
   (a) an order designating a locality as an alcohol disorder zone; or
   (b) the making of an order under section 17(2).

(5) Where the local chief officer of police does not give a consent required by sub-section (4)(a), he must give notice of his decision (setting out his reasons) to the Secretary of State and to the police authority for his police area.

## 11.18.28    Guidance about designation of alcohol disorder zones

### 11.18.29    Issuing of ADZ Guidance

The Secretary of State is required to issue Guidance about the designation of ADZs and the manner in which local authorities, police authorities and the police exercise and perform their powers and duties in relation to ADZs. The ADZ Guidance, which may be revised from time to time, must make provision as to what alternative steps should be considered before a proposal to designate an ADZ is made. Section 19(1) and (2) provides:

(1) The Secretary of State–
- (a) must issue such guidance as he considers appropriate about the manner in which local authorities, police authorities and chief officers of police are to exercise and perform their powers and duties by virtue of this Chapter; and
- (b) may from time to time revise that guidance.
(2) The guidance must include guidance about what alternative steps should be considered before a proposal is made for the designation of a locality as an alcohol disorder zone.

Local authorities, police authorities and the police are all under a duty to have regard to the s 19 ADZ Guidance when exercising their powers and duties, for s 19(4) provides: 'It shall be the duty of every local authority, police authority and chief officer of police, in exercising their powers and duties by virtue of this Chapter, to have regard to the guidance for the time being in force under this section'.

### 11.18.30    Consultation on the ADZ Guidance

As with the Secretary of State's Guidance under s 182 of the 2003 Act, provision is made for widespread consultation prior to the issuing or revising of the s 19 ADZ Guidance. Consultation extends to representatives of local authorities, the police, police authorities, premises licences holders and CPC holders, in addition to such other persons as the Secretary of State thinks fit. Section 19(3) provides:

Before issuing or revising any guidance under this section, the Secretary of State must consult–

(a) persons he considers represent the interests of local authorities;
(b) persons he considers represent the interests of chief officers of police;
(c) persons he considers represent the interests of police authorities;
(d) persons he considers represent the interests of holders of premises licences;
(e) persons he considers represent the interests of holders of club premises certificates; and
(f) such other persons as he thinks fit.

## RIGHTS OF ENTRY

## 11.19 RIGHTS OF ENTRY TO INVESTIGATE LICENSABLE ACTIVITIES

11.19.1 Section 179 provides that police officers and authorised persons (on production of authority) may enter premises where there is reason to believe that premises are being, or are about to be, used for a licensable activity without authorisation, and may use reasonable force to gain entry. Section 179(1)–(3) provides:

(1) Where a constable or an authorised person[140] has reason to believe that any premises are being, or are about to be, used for a licensable activity, he may enter the premises with a view to seeing whether the activity is being, or is to be, carried on under and in accordance with an authorisation.

(2) An authorised person exercising the power conferred by this section must, if so requested, produce evidence of his authority to exercise the power.

(3) A person exercising the power conferred by this section may, if necessary, use reasonable force.

The section expressly confers a right of entry (for which no warrant is needed), but not a power of search. In the case of a constable entering, there will in any event be a power of search under s 180 where the constable has reason to believe that an offence under the Act has been, is being or is about to be committed (see 11.20 below). However, this power in s 180 is confined to constables and does not extend to authorised persons. Although s 179 does not expressly confer a power of search, this may be implicit in that the right of entry is 'with a view to seeing whether the activity ... is carried on under ... an authorisation'. Any search of the premises might be with a view to seeing whether this is the case and so would fall within the scope of the section.

11.19.2 Whether activities are carried out under 'authorisation' will mean whether they are carried out under a premises licence, a club premises certificate or a TEN. Section 179(6) provides:

In this section–

"authorisation" means–

(a) a premises licence,

(b) a club premises certificate, or

(c) a temporary event notice in respect of which the conditions of section 98(2) to (4) are satisfied.

This right of entry does not, however, apply in respect of premises for which there is only a CPC in force. Exclusion of the right in such a case reflects the fact that clubs operating under a CPC are private premises to which public access is restricted. However, if there is, additionally, authorisation under either a premises licence or a TEN, the right will apply. Section 179(7) provides:

Nothing in this section applies in relation to premises in respect of which there is a club premises certificate but no other authorisation.

It seems that the right will apply in *all* cases, provided there is another authorisation in existence, including occasions on which the premises are being operated as a club in accordance with a CPC, and it will not be confined to cases where the premises are being used under another authorisation. Carrying on licensable activities otherwise than in accordance with an authorisation includes, under s 179(6)(b), an authorisation under a CPC, so it is clearly envisaged that there can be entry to see whether there is compliance with such an authorisation. The effect of s 179(7) is to exclude the right of entry only where premises are used exclusively as a club under a CPC.

11.19.3 Section 179(1) confers a power of entry to premises to see whether a licensable activity 'is being, or is to be, carried on under and in accordance with an authorisation'. The wording here is comparable to the offence in s 136, which applies both in respect of premises where a licensable activity is carried on without authorisation and premises where there is authorisation, but where a breach of conditions occurs (see 11.2.1 above). However, it may be doubted whether the power in s 179(1) extends to entering premises where there is no authorisation for a licensable activity, in cases where there is reason to believe that premises are being, or are about to be, used for a licensable activity. Although s 179(1) is wide enough on its wording to permit entry in such a case, this may not accord with Parliament's intention if s 179 is read in conjunction with s 180, which provides a right of entry for constables (only) to investigate offences (see 11.20 below). This right under s 180 applies where a constable has reasonable grounds for believing an offence under the 2003 Act has been, or is about to be, committed. Section 180 extends to premises of any kind and the right to enter can obviously include cases where premises lack any authorisation for a licensable activity.

If the power of entry under s 179 also extends to premises lacking authorisation, a constable would simply need to believe that the premises are being used for a licensable activity in order to enter – he need not have any reasonable grounds for believing an offence has been, or is about to be, committed. If this were the case, this would seem to render s 180 largely redundant – the constable could always enter under the power in s 179 and no recourse to s 180 would be needed. It must be assumed that Parliament did not intend this and this result can be avoided if the power of entry under s 179 is confined in its application to premises having an authorisation. There is perhaps some support for the view that Parliament envisaged s 179 as applying to premises having an authorisation, for the Explanatory Note to s 179 states: 'This section provides for police officers or other authorised persons to enter premises to ensure that any licensable activities are being carried on under the appropriate authorisations'. It may be implicit from this statement that the premises have an authorisation in the first place and entry by police officers or other authorised persons is to ensure that there is compliance with this.

11.19.4 It is an offence to intentionally obstruct an authorised person exercising a right of entry under s 179, an offence punishable summarily by a fine not exceeding level 3 on the standard scale. Section 179(4) and (5) provides:

    (4)  A person commits an offence if he intentionally obstructs an authorised person exercising a power conferred by this section.

    (5)  A person guilty of an offence under subsection (4) is liable on summary conviction to a fine not exceeding level 3 on the standard scale.

In the case of a constable who is obstructed, a person commits an offence under the general provision of wilfully obstructing a constable in the course of his duties under s 89(2) of the Police Act 1996, so no provision is made by the 2003 Act in this respect.

## 11.20 RIGHT OF ENTRY TO INVESTIGATE OFFENCES

Section 180 confers on police officers a right to enter and search premises, and to use reasonable force if necessary, where they have reason to believe an offence under the Act has been, is being or is about to be committed. Section 180(1) and (2) provides:

(1) A constable may enter and search any premises in respect of which he has reason to believe that an offence under this Act has been, is being or is about to be committed.

(2) A constable exercising a power conferred by this section may, if necessary, use reasonable force.

As under s 179, intentionally preventing a constable from exercising these powers will amount to the offence of wilfully obstructing a constable in the course of his duties under s 89(2) of the Police Act 1996.

## NOTES

1 This is not restricted to alcohol, but could include any goods on which duty has not been paid, such as cigarettes, or which have been unlawfully imported (see 11.6 below).
2 Under s 40 a closure order may be made by the chief executive officer of a local authority (who may, under s 41(2), authorise an environmental health officer to exercise the power) for premises where a premises licence or temporary event notice (TEN) has effect in respect of them and where there is a reasonable belief that a public nuisance is being caused by noise coming from the premises, and closure of the premises is necessary to prevent that nuisance.
3 Section 136(5) provides:

'In this Part "authorisation" means–

(a) a premises licence,

(b) a club premises certificate, or

(c) a temporary event notice in respect of which the conditions of section 98(2) to (4) are satisfied.'

4 It seems likely that there will be only one offence committed irrespective of the number of conditions breached. This was the view taken by the Divisional Court, in *Mendip District Council v Glastonbury Festivals Ltd* (1993) 91 LGR 447, in respect of the offence, under Sched 1, para 12(2) of the Local Government (Miscellaneous Provisions) Act 1982, of providing public entertainment 'otherwise than in accordance with the terms, conditions or restrictions on or subject to which the licence is held'.
5 Some matters are specified in the licence itself and do not appear as conditions, eg the times the licence authorises the carrying out of licensable activities, and the opening hours of the premises – see LA2003 (PL and CPC) Regs 2005, Sch 12A. *Quaere* whether there will be a lack of authorisation for licensable activities under s 136(1) if there is a failure to comply with the opening hours of the premises in cases where these hours extend beyond the hours at which licensable actvities take place.
6 Section 136(3) provides: 'Subsection (2) is to be construed in accordance with Part 3 of Schedule 1', Pt 3 being concerned with interpretation of the terms used to describe the various types of regulated entertainment – see 5.3.21–5.3.32 above.
7 However, if the individual also organised or helped to organise the event, an offence may be committed, notwithstanding the fact that the individual was also a performer, although this is subject to the defence of due diligence – see 11.2.10 below.

8 JCHR, Fourth Report of 2002–03, *Scrutiny of Bills: Further Progress Report*, HL Paper 50, HC 397, para 19 – see 3.4.6 above.

9 See, eg *Chambers English Dictionary, Collins English Dictionary* and *Shorter Oxford English Dictionary*; and also *Brown v London and Northern Western Rly Co* (1863) 32 LJQB 318, 321, *per* Blackburn J: 'Business can only be said to be carried on where it is managed.'

10 The term 'acid house' is commonly supposed to derive from the colloquial name for the drug LSD, the use of which may be associated with parties of the kind in question, but this may not be the correct explanation. According to Tony Colston-Hayter, Chairman of the Association of Dance Party Promotions:

> the name "Acid House" comes from the streets of Chicago, where "acid" means to steal: Chicago House music is made up of "samples" taken from recordings and thus, in a sense, stolen: hence Acid House. Only the tabloids and the ill-informed maintain that it derives from LSD. Nobody else uses the term "Acid House party". The police use the self-explanatory "pay party"; we prefer "warehouse party" or "rave". ('Why Should Having Fun Be Against the Law?', *Independent*, 3 March 1990.)

11 Beldam LJ, qualifying the above statement, went on to remark (at 582): 'it may be that there will arise a case in which it can be said that a part played is so minor and so small that it should not be regarded as being concerned in the organisation or management of the entertainment.'

12 These criteria are set out in the judgment of Lord Scarman (at 14): '. . . (1) there is a presumption of law that mens rea is required before a person can be held guilty of a criminal offence; (2) the presumption is particularly strong where the offence is 'truly criminal' in character; (3) the presumption applies to statutory offences, and can be displaced only if this is clearly or by necessary implication the effect of the statute; (4) the only situation in which the presumption can be displaced is where the statute is concerned with an issue of social concern, and public safety is such an issue; (5) even where a statute is concerned with such an issue, the presumption of mens rea stands unless it can also be shown that the creation of strict liability will be effective to promote the objects of the statute by encouraging greater vigilance to prevent the commission of the prohibited act.'

13 On this area generally, see Manchester, C, 'Knowledge, Due Diligence and Strict Liability in Regulatory Offences' [2006] *Criminal Law Review* 213 (an article focused on offences under the 2003 Act).

14 Other factors to which the court had regard were:

(a) the offence regulates specific activities involving potential danger to public safety and not the general conduct of citizens in the course of their everyday life, so placing it in the category of offences for which strict liability might be imposed, according to Lord Diplock in *Sweet v Parsley* [1970] AC 132, 162;

(b) the presumption of mens rea is not particularly strong since the offence is not, in the words of Lord Scarman in *Gammon (Hong Kong) Ltd v Attorney General of Hong Kong* [1985] AC 1, 14, 'truly criminal' in character; and

(c) the presumption of mens rea could be displaced, in accordance with the criteria set out by Lord Scarman in the *Gammon (Hong Kong)* case, as the statute is concerned with matters of social policy and the offence was created to promote the enforcement of the provisions of Sched 1 to the 1982 Act for ensuring safety and welfare.

15 (1992) 157 JP 574, 581. A subsequent Divisional Court, in *Marshall v South Oxfordshire District Council* (12 June 1996, unreported), declined an invitation to regard as incorrect the ruling in *Chichester* that the offence was one of strict liability. Henry LJ stated:

> We are asked to say that *Chichester District Council v Ware* is wrong. Although that decision is not technically binding on us, it is a decision of a court of equivalent

jurisdiction, another constitution of the court in which we sit, and in those circumstances we should follow it unless we are clearly of the opinion that it is wrong. I, on the material before me, am not satisfied that that decision is clearly wrong. It seems to me that it should be followed . . .

16  A similar sentence was available for the offence of providing unlicensed music and dancing and licensed music and dancing where there was a breach of condition relating to the numbers of persons present, following the passing of the Entertainments (Increased Penalties) Act 1990. Although this Act was not in force at the time of the *Chichester* case, it was at the time of the decision in *Marshall*.

17  See *French v Hoggett* [1968] 1 WLR 94 (steward of working men's club served a plain-clothes policeman, who he honestly believed was a club member and to whom he was not therefore making a sale, held liable for making a sale to the policeman of intoxicating liquor without a justices' licence contrary to s 160 of the Licensing Act 1964).

18  The rationale for this is that attempts are less serious than the perpetration of substantive offences and do not merit criminalisation where the substantive crime is of a relatively minor nature, which tends to be the case with summary-only offences. There are, however, a number of specific statutory offences of attempting to commit particular summary-only offences.

19  See, eg *R v Gullefer* [1990] 3 All ER 882, where the Court of Appeal stated (*per* Lord Lane CJ at 885) that attempt 'begins when the merely preparatory acts come to an end and the defendant embarks upon the crime proper'. As Allen, M (*Textbook of Criminal Law*, 9th edn, 2007, Oxford: OUP, pp 297 and 300) observes: 'The inclusion of the word 'merely' . . . suggests a grey area of ill-defined proportions between acts which are purely preparatory and the last act of commission . . . [and] while . . . a distinction may be drawn between acts which fall within the 'preparation phase' of the intended crime from those which fall within the 'commission phase', it is clear that courts have difficulty in identifying where the line between the two is to be drawn.'

20  *R v Mohan* [1976] QB 1, 3 (*per* James LJ), a pre-Act case, but subsequently stated by the Court of Appeal, in *R v Pearman* (1985) 80 Cr App R 259, to remain an authoritative guide to interpretation of 'intent' under the Act.

21  This seems to be generally accepted by commentators, although there is no authority directly on the point.

22  See, eg *Tesco Supermarkets Ltd. v Nattrass* [1972] AC 153, 191.

23  As to what might constitute relevant considerations in determining whether there have been reasonable precautions and due diligence, see Fidler, 'The Due Diligence Defence' (1998) 148 *New Law Journal* 328 and 379.

24  The word 'omission' rather than 'default' may have been used to avoid an undue narrowing of the defence. In *Tesco Supermarkets Ltd v Nattrass* [1972] AC 153 at 196, Lord Diplock stated, in relation to s 24(1)(a) of the Trades Description Act 1968, that 'use of the word "default" instead of the neutral expression "omission" connotes a failure to act which constitutes a breach of a legal duty to act'

25  See Guidance, para 8.71. Under s 47 an interim authority notice can be given within seven days of the lapse that reinstates the licence – see 6.11.1 above.

26  Tills so programmed beep to alert the cashier and a readily visible message appears on the till screen enquiring if the customer is 18 and indicating what is the latest acceptable birth date. Before the transaction can be effected by the till operator a command button indicating 'Yes' or 'No' in answer to the question about the age of the customer has to be pressed.

27  See s 24 of the Trade Descriptions Act 1968, s 25 of the Fair Trading Act 1973 and s 168 of the Consumer Credit Act 1974.

28  See, eg *Coventry City Council v Lazarus* (1996) 160 JP 188, *per* Potts J: 'The word "information" in s 168(1)(a) [of the Consumer Credit Act 1974] is unqualified. Section 168(1) provides a defence to a penal statute. 'The expression "information supplied" must be

strictly construed. If there is doubt as to its meaning the respondent should be given the benefit of that doubt'. His Lordship held that advice given from the Area Manager and Legal Department of a Trade Association in respect of credit advertisements was 'information supplied' within s 168(1) and 'forms an exception to the general principle that ignorance of the law is no excuse'.

29  See *RC Hammett Ltd v Crabb* (1931) 47 TLR 623, 625, a case decided under the Sale of Food (Weights & Measures) Act 1926. ('It is a question of fact in every case whether what the principal has done constitutes due diligence on his part to enforce the execution of the Act', *per* Avory J.) As to measures that might be taken to substantiate a due diligence defence, see Light, R, 'Criminal liability for under-age sales of alcohol' (2006) 64 *Licensing Review* 11, 12–13.

30  It seems clear that the burden of proof means the legal burden, although not referred to expressly as such.

31  See Manchester, C, and Salter, D, *Exploring the Law: The Dynamics of Precedent and Statutory Interpretation*, 3rd edn, 2006, London: Sweet & Maxwell, pp 52–60.

32  For an interpretative framework for considering and determining the scope of the knowledge requirement in such cases, see Manchester, C, 'Knowledge, Due Diligence and Strict Liability in Regulatory Offences' [2006] *Criminal Law Review* 213.

33  The criteria set out in this case (at 14) are:

> (1) there is a presumption of law that mens rea is required before a person can be held guilty of a criminal offence; (2) the presumption is particularly strong where the offence is 'truly criminal' in character; (3) the presumption applies to statutory offences, and can be displaced only if this is clearly or by necessary implication the effect of the statute; (4) the only situation in which the presumption can be displaced is where the statute is concerned with an issue of social concern, and public safety is such an issue; (5) even where a statute is concerned with such an issue, the presumption of mens rea stands unless it can also be shown that the creation of strict liability will be effective to promote the objects of the statute by encouraging greater vigilance to prevent the commission of the prohibited act.

34  A reference to 'knowingly' has been read as not having application in respect of an exception contained within a statutory licensing offence in *Brooks v Mason* [1902] 2 KB 743, but the exception was not considered to be a component part of the definition of that offence.

34  For some offences, recklessness may suffice for liability, eg the offence of knowingly or recklessly making false statements when making licence applications or giving notices under s 158 (see 11.10 below), but it does not suffice for this offence.

35  See also the remarks of Lord Brightman at 684 that knowledge might readily be inferred where the defendant chooses not to give evidence of his absence of knowledge and there are no circumstances that sufficiently suggest an absence of knowledge. ('But although such knowledge is an ingredient of the offence under paragraph 20(1)(a), and although the onus of establishing all the ingredients of the offence must lie on the prosecution, this does not impose on the prosecution an undue burden: if (1) all the other ingredients of the offence are proved, (2) the defendant (or the responsible officer of a corporate defendant) chooses not to give evidence of his absence of knowledge, and (3) there are no circumstances which sufficiently suggest absence of knowledge, the court may properly infer without direct evidence that the defendant did indeed possess the requisite knowledge.')

36  Section 138(3) provides:

> 'In subsection (1) the reference to the supply of alcohol is a reference to the supply of alcohol by or on behalf of a club to, or to the order of, a member of the club.'

37  A person who is not aware that he has possession of an item, as where the item is slipped into his bag or pocket without his knowledge, is not in 'possession' of it, although if a

person is aware that a container or receptacle has come under his control, he will (be deemed to) be in 'possession' of it, even if mistaken about its contents, unless the contents are of a wholly different nature than was believed. These principles, derived from the (confusing) House of Lords' case of *Warner v Metropolitan Police Commissioner* [1969] 2 AC 256, which involved possession of dangerous drugs, were subsequently restated by the Court of Appeal in *R v McNamara* (1988) 87 Cr App R 246. If these principles are applied, it may be that a person who has possession of containers, intending to sell or supply the contents mistakenly believing them not to be alcohol, will commit the offence if in the circumstances the sale of the alcohol would be an unauthorised licensable activity.

38 There may be cases where a person who has possession does not have control, eg an employer will legally retain possession of property given to an employee to deliver to a third party, but will not have control of it whilst the employee has it during delivery.

39 The House went on to state (at paras 35–36): '[35] . . . It has become common practice for their Lordships to ask to be shown the explanatory notes when issues are raised about the meaning of words used in an enactment. [36] The headings and sidenotes are as much part of the contextual scene as these materials, and there is no logical reason why they should be treated differently.'

40 Section 159 provides:

> ' "relevant premises" means–
>
> (a)  licensed premises, or
>
> (b)  premises in respect of which there is in force a club premises certificate, or
>
> (c)  premises which may be used for a permitted temporary activity by virtue of Part 5.'
>
> Section 193 provides that: ' "Licensed premises" means premises in respect of which a premises licence has effect.'

41 On attempts, see 11.2.8–11.2.9 above.

42 This would seem to encompass persons who work at the premises in some type of managerial capacity, although it might extend beyond this to include persons such as door supervisors employed at premises and, where alcohol is served, personal licence holders.

43 This might include the club steward and (perhaps) bar staff, as well as officers such as the club secretary and club members who have been elected to the club committee. It is difficult to conceive of circumstances where persons, such as the club secretary and committee members would be on the premises other than in a capacity that enables them to prevent the disorderly conduct and it may be that such persons could be liable for the offence whenever they are on the premises.

44 See, eg *Lawson v Edminson* [1908] 2 KB 952, where a licensee who, after closing hours on his licensed premises, supplied guests with drink at his own expense was held to have been rightly convicted of permitting drunkenness on the premises when the guests were found to be drunk.

45 Lord Parker CJ stated (at 385–86), that when introducing the legislation:

> Parliament must be taken . . . to know that the doctrine of delegation had been applied in a number of licensing cases, and that the principle of those cases was that a man cannot get out of the responsibilities and duties attached to the licence by absenting himself. The position of course is quite different if he remains in control. It would be only right he should not be liable if a servant behind his back did something which contravened the terms of the licence. If, however, he wholly absents himself leaving somebody else in control, he cannot claim that what has happened has happened without his knowledge if the delegate has knowingly carried on in contravention of the licence.

46 On attempts, see 11.2.8–11.2.9 above.

47 *Petherick v Sargent* (1862) 26 JP 135. However, if the person making the gift made it not to

the person who was drunk, but to another person who obtained it for the person who was drunk, he might aid and abet an offence by the person who obtained it, under s 142, of obtaining alcohol for a person who is drunk – see 11.5.10–11.5.12 below.

48 For the meaning of 'sale by retail' and sales falling outside the defintion, see s 192 and 5.2.2 above.

49 Section 172(3) made it an offence for the holder of a justices' licence to sell intoxicating liquor to a drunken person and s 172A(3) made it an offence for any person to do so who worked in the licensed premises in a capacity, whether paid or unpaid, which gave him authority to sell the intoxicating liquor concerned.

50 The other offences are those contained in ss 146(1) and (3), 149, 150 and 151.

51 *Quaere* whether any offence is committed if the person obtaining alcohol does so with a view to the drunk consuming it on the premises, but the drunk leaves and consumes it off the premises.

52 The reasoning here is the same as in respect of s 141, namely, that if knowledge simply relates to the first-mentioned element (obtaining), it serves little meaningful purpose (see 11.5.9 above).

53 As to the requirement of 'disorderly' see 11.5.4 above, for 'drunk' see 11.5.9 above and for 'attempts' see 11.2.8–11.2.9 above.

54 This statement does not appear in the 2007 Guidance, which, unlike the 2004 Guidance, does not contain a section on Offences.

55 These persons are the same persons who might be liable for the offences of allowing disorderly conduct on relevant premises under s 140 and selling or attempting to sell alcohol to a person who is drunk on relevant premises under s 141 – see s 140(2) and s 141(2), and 11.5.3 and 11.5.7 above, respectively.

56 That the heading to each section refers to 'keeping' is indicative of the fact that there is no substantive difference.

57 For the reference to Wigmore, see *A Treatise on the System of Evidence in Trials at Common Law* (1905), vol 4, p 3525.

58 In *R v Hussein*, approved in *R v Shivpuri*, Lord Widgery CJ stated (at 571–572):

> It seems perfectly clear that the word "knowingly" in section 304(b) [of the Customs and Excise Act 1952) is concerned with knowing that a fraudulent evasion of a prohibition in respect of goods is taking place. If, therefore, the accused knows that what is on foot is the evasion of a prohibition against importation and he knowingly takes part in that operation, it is sufficient to justify his conviction, even if he does not know precisely what kind of goods are being imported. It is, of course, essential that he should know that the goods which are being imported are goods subject to a prohibition. It is essential he should know that the operation with which he is concerning himself is an operation designed to evade that prohibition and evade it fraudulently. But it is not necessary that he should know the precise category of the goods the importation of which has been prohibited.

59 The authors are conscious that the view expressed here sits uneasily with the statement in the first edition of this work that "the balance might be tipped marginally in favour of knowledge being required only as to keeping". We can say only that we have revised our views on this matter and, to adopt the words of Bramwell B in *Andrews v Styrap* (1872) 26 LT 704, 706, the matter does not appear to us now as it appears to have appeared to us then.

60 Section 155 amends s 1 of the Confiscation of Alcohol (Young Persons) Act 1997, which uses the term 'young persons', rather than the term 'children', which is used in the 2003 Act, although in both instances this means (for the most part) persons under 18.

61 Section 145(10) provides:

> In this section "supply of alcohol" means–
> (a) the sale by retail of alcohol, or

(b)  the supply of alcohol by or on behalf of a club to, or to the order of, a member of the club.

62  Guidance, para 13.44. As to whether children should or should not be admitted to any particular premises, para 13.47 provides: 'A statement of licensing policy must not . . . seek to limit the access of children to any premises unless it is necessary for the prevention of physical, moral or psychological harm to them.'

63  Under the previous law, the defence in respect of selling alcohol to a person under 18, contained in s 169A(3) of the Licensing Act 1964, was similarly worded and perhaps the defence in s 145(8), and similar defences in ss 146(6) and 148(5) (see 11.7.10 and 11.7.16 below), were all modelled on this.

64  Cf. the offences of sale or supply of alcohol to, and obtaining alcohol for, a person who is drunk under ss 141–42 – see 11.5.6–11.5.12 above. As the offences in s 146 are summary only (see s 146(7) and 11.7.11 below), there will be no liability for attempt under the Criminal Attempts Act 1981 as this Act does not apply to summary only offences – see s 1(4) and 11.2.8–11.2.9 above.

65  Section 146(1) is, however, perhaps unhappily worded, since it makes reference to a person committing an offence if 'he' sells alcohol and 'he' is an expression which would normally be used in respect of individuals and not companies. A more appropriate wording for the offence might have been: 'A person who sells alcohol to an individual aged under 18 commits an offence'.

66  Section 187 makes provision for liability of corporate bodies, partnerships and unincorporated assocations for offences under the 2003 Act (see 11.11.2 below).

67  Under s 147A a premises licence holder can be charged with the offence of persistently selling alcohol to children where underage sales have occurred at the premises on three or more separate occasions over a three-month period (see s 147A(4)(a) and 11.7.13 below).

68  Hollis, D, 'Liability for offences under the 2003 Act' (2007) 70 *Licensing Review* 9, 11–12.

69  PASS is a national proof of age accreditation scheme endorsed by the Government, which sets minimum standards for proof of age cards. Cards incorporate the holder's date of birth, full name, a passport standard photograph, an image of the holder's signature and a PASS hologram, which is a hallmark indicating that the card issuer has passed a stringent and rigorous audit process carried out by trading standards officers and that the card may be relied upon.

70  Provision is made for test purchases by children in s 149(2) – see 11.7.19 below.

71  This is the technical term used for a trading standards department.

72  Section 159 provides: ' "weights and measures inspector" means an inspector of weights and measures appointed under section 72(1) of the Weights and Measures Act 1985 (c.72).'

73  This would accord with the previous law, contained in s 169B(1) of the Licensing Act 1964, where the wording was comparable to s 147, and in *Goodwin v Baldwin* (1975) 139 JP 147 (at which time the offence in s 169B was contained in s 169) it was held that proof of actual knowledge as to age or deliberate avoidance of attention to obvious means of acquiring knowledge was necessary. May J stated (at 149):

> In my judgment, in s 169 of the Licensing Act, 1964, as indeed in other statutes creating offences, the use of the word "knowingly" requires proof against the person charged before he is rightly convicted that he had actual knowledge of the facts creating the offence or that he wilfully turned away and deliberately avoided paying attention to an obvious means of knowledge from which, had he paid attention, he would have acquired the appropriate degree of knowledge.

If actual knowledge (or wilful blindness) is needed 'of the facts creating the offence', one such fact is whether the person is under the age of 18 and this decision supports the need for knowledge as to age being a requirement of the offence.

74  The £10,000 maximum fine may be increased, for s 147A(9) provides: 'The Secretary of State may by order amend subsection (8) to increase the maximum fine for the time being specified in that subsection'.

75  See      www.culture.gov.uk/what_we_do/Alcohol_entertainment/licensing_act_2003_ explained/offences

76  Section 148(7) provides: 'In this section "liqueur confectionery" has the meaning given in section 191(2)'.

77  In cases of an attempt, this and other offences in s 150 are summary only (s 150(7)) and the requirements for liability are set out in s 3(4) of the Criminal Attempts Act 1981 – see 11.2.8 above.

78  It is expected that enforcement officers will have regard to the LACORS and Trading Standards Institute Code of Best Practice on test purchasing operations, which includes advice on the protection of children engaged in such operations.

79  Section 159 provides: ' "weights and measures inspector" means an inspector of weights and measures appointed under section 72(1) of the Weights and Measures Act 1985 (c.72).' This is the technical term used for a trading standards officer.

80  Whether the adult accompanying the 16- or 17-year-old himself needs to be taking a meal is less clear. It will depend on whether 'accompanied' in s 149(5)(e) is interpreted to mean simply 'present with' at the meal or 'present with and partaking'. The view taken may depend on what is seen as being the purpose of having an accompanying adult. If it is to exercise proper restraint in a supervisory capacity, it may not matter whether or not the adult is also partaking of a meal. If it is to enable alcohol (other than spirits) to be consumed by 16- or 17-year-olds when having a meal with family or (adult) friends, it may be that the adult will need to be partaking of a meal.

81  The reasoning here is the same as in respect of s 147 – see 11.7.12 above.

82  No offences of delivering alcohol to children, under s 151, or of children purchasing alcohol, under s 149, will be committed in these circumstances – see s 151(6)(b) and s 149(2), and 11.7.28 above and 11.7.19 above, respectively.

83  Section 159 provides: ' "weights and measures inspector" means an inspector of weights and measures appointed under section 72(1) of the Weights and Measures Act 1985 (c.72).' This is the technical term used for a trading standards officer.

84  For an instance of where a 12-year-old, the son of the person running a pub, was serving alcohol in accordance with this provision, see *Daily Mail*, 29 November 2006.

85  Section 159(7) provides: ' "specified" means specified in the order under this section.'

86  Section 159(7) provides: ' "railway vehicle" has the meaning given by section 83 of the Railways Act 1993 (c.43).' Section 83 provides: ' "railway vehicle" includes anything which, whether or not it is constructed or adapted to carry any person or load, is constructed or adapted to run on flanged wheels over or along track.'

87  Section 159(7) provides: ' "station" has the meaning given by section 83 of the Railways Act 1993.' Section 83 provides: ' "station" means any land or other property which consists of premises used as, or for the purposes of, or otherwise in connection with, a railway passenger station or railway passenger terminal (including any approaches, forecourt, cycle store or car park), whether or not the land or other property is, or the premises are, also used for other purposes.'

88  Section 159(7) provides: ' "senior police officer" means a police officer of, or above, the rank of inspector.'

89  Section 159(7) provides: ' "responsible senior police officer", in relation to an order under this section, means the senior police officer who applied for the order or, if the chief officer of police of the force in question has designated another senior police officer for the purpose, that other officer.'

90  Section 159(7) provides: ' "train operator" means a person authorised by a licence under section 8 of that Act to operate railway assets (within the meaning of section 6 of that

Act).' Railway assets under s 6(2) comprise any train, network, station or light maintenance depot.

91  For 'attempt' see 11.2.18–11.2.20 above.

92  *R v Rai* [2000] Crim LR 192. (An application was made for a council grant to install a
downstairs bathroom in the defendant's house for use by his elderly mother. His mother
died two days after approval of the grant, the council was not informed and the bathroom was installed. Held that the failure to inform the council was capable of constituting
a deception (representing something to be true which is false) and the defendant was
liable for obtaining (building) services by deception under s 1 of the Theft Act 1978).
Although s 1 has been repealed by the Fraud Act 2006, the position remains the same,
for the general offence of fraud in s 1 of the 2006 Act can be committed where there is a
failure to disclose information that a person is under a legal duty to disclose, provided
there is an intention to make a gain for himself or another, or an intention to cause loss to
another or to expose another to a risk of loss – see s 3 of the 2006 Act.

93  *R v Firth* (1989) 91 Cr App R 217. (A hospital consultant was convicted of obtaining by
deception an exemption from liability to make payment under s 2(1)(c) of the Theft Act
1978 for private patients he had treated, when he failed to inform the hospital that they
were private patients, knowing that they would be treated as NHS patients without
charge.)

94  Such cases of 'objective' recklessness, considered to fall within the meaning of the word
'reckless' in s 1 of the Criminal Damage Act 1971 in an earlier House of Lords' case, *R v
Caldwell* [1982] AC 341, were held in *R v G* to have been based on a misinterpretation of
that term.

95  See Guidance issued by the DCMS to police and trading standards officers, *Interpreting
and implementing sections 23 and 24 of the Violent Crime Reduction Act 2006 – Persistently
selling to children*, para 31.

96  This is the technical term used for a trading standards department of the local authority.

97  Section 187(8) provides: 'In this section "offence" means an offence under this Act.'

98  The meaning of 'connivance' seems not to have been judicially considered, but connivance is likely to cover the case where it cannot be established that a person has
given actual consent to the commission of the offence, but has tacitly acquiesced in its
commission by failing to take steps to prevent or discourage it.

99  Section 187(8) provides: 'In this section "offence" means an offence under this Act.'

100  Section 187(8) provides: 'In this section "offence" means an offence under this Act.'

101  Section 188(7) provides: 'In this section "offence" means an offence under this Act.'

102  Section 169 provides: 'A constable may use such force as may be necessary for the
purposes of closing premises in compliance with a closure order.' Under s 171(5),
' "closure order" has the meaning given in section 161(2)'.

103  The first campaign found that offences were committed in almost 50 per cent of cases
and the second in 32 per cent of cases (Explanatory Note 48).

104  See 11.14.2 below and, for other instances where the term is used, see s 13(3), s 32(3),
s 69(3), s 161(1), s 162(2), s 163(2) and s 165(3).

105  See *Adler v George* [1964] 1 All ER 628, 629, *per* Lord Parker CJ. In *The Queen on the
Application of 4 Wins Leisure Ltd v The Licensing Committee of Blackpool Council, Brook
Leisure Blackpool Ltd and World Wide Clubs (UK)* [2007] EWHC 2213, the meaning of
'vicinity' in s 13(3) of the 2003 Act was considered to be physical or geographical
proximity of the premises, in the context of local circumstances (see 6.4.13 above).

106  Section 171(5) provides: 'A "manager", in relation to any premises, means a person who
works at the premises in a capacity, whether paid or unpaid, which authorises him
to close them.' It is not relevant whether or not the individual has the expression
"manager" in their job title or description: Police Guidance, para 38.

107  For the meaning of 'qualifying club activity', see s 1(2) and 8.2.2 above.

108  Section 161(8) provides: 'In this section – . . . "senior police officer" means a police officer
of, or above, the rank of inspector.'

109   Section 161(8) provides:

> In this section –
>
> "relevant premises" means premises in respect of which one or more of the following have effect–
>
> (a)   a premises licence,
>
> (b)   a temporary event notice.

110   The order will come into force when notice of the order is given to 'an appropriate person', who is a person who is in a position to close the premises – see 11.14.8 below.

111   An 'appropriate person' is a person who is in a position to close the premises – see the definition in s 171(5) and 11.14.8 below.

112   Police Guidance, para 31. However, if an individual who is drunk or disorderly is asked to leave and refuses to do so, this is an offence under s 143 (see 11.5.13–11.5.16 above).

113   The condition for securing an extension in the case of public nuisance by noise seems to be wider than in the case of making an order. For an extension, it will suffice, under s 162(2)(b), that such a nuisance is *likely to be* caused by noise coming from the premises, but, for the making of an order, s 161(1)(b) requires that a nuisance *is* being caused by noise coming from the premises – see 11.14.3 above.

114   For reviews under s 167, see 11.14.20–11.14.24 below. These powers cannot be exercised if a premises licence is no longer in force in respect of the premises, in which case the premises cease to be 'relevant premises' (as defined by s 171(5) and s 161(8)). Section 165(5) provides: 'Subsection (2) does not apply if, before the relevant magistrates' court discharges its functions under that subsection, the premises cease to be relevant premises.' If the powers have been exercised and an order made, the order will cease to have effect if the premises thereafter cease to be 'relevant premises'. Section 165(6) provides: 'Any order made under subsection (2) ceases to have effect if the premises cease to be relevant premises.' The powers can be exercised by a single justice and it is necessary for evidence to be given on oath in the proceedings. Section 165(9) and (10) provides:

> (9)   The powers conferred on a magistrates' court by this section are to be exercised in the place required by the Magistrates' Courts Act 1980 (c.43) for the hearing of a complaint and may be exercised by a single justice.
>
> (10)  Evidence given for the purposes of proceedings under this section must be given on oath.

115   These are the same criteria as must be considered by the senior police officer when he is deciding whether to make an extension of a closure order – see s 162(2) and 11.14.10 above.

116   For the definition of 'appropriate person' – a person who is in a position to (open or) close the premises – see s 171(5) and 11.14.8 above.

117   Section 167(14) provides: 'In this section "interested party" and "responsible authority" have the same meaning as in Part 3.' See s 13(3) and (4) and 6.4.13–6.4.18 above.

118   Section 167(11) provides: 'Where the relevant licensing authority determines that any representations are frivolous or vexatious, it must notify the person who made them of the reasons for that determination.' Frivolous or vexatious representations are considered at 6.4.20–6.4.22 above and notification procedures at 2.5 above.

119   Under reg 7(2) and Sched 3, para 14, the premises licence holder must be given the relevant representations with the notice of hearing.

120   The power to modify conditions is subject to ss 19–21, which require the inclusion of mandatory conditions in respect of the supply of alcohol, the exhibition of films and the licensing of door supervisors – see 6.4.2–6.4.5 above. Section 167(7) provides: 'Subsection (5)(b) is subject to sections 19, 20 and 21 (requirement to include certain conditions in premises licences).'

121   Section 167(13) provides: 'Section 168 makes provision about when the determination takes effect.'

122  Section 168(5), which gives the licensing authority power to suspend, relates to 'that decision', which must mean the decision mentioned in s 168(3)(a), to take one or more of the steps mentioned in subsection (6)(a) to (d) of s 164. These steps do not include revocation, which is the step mentioned in s 167(6)(e) – see 11.14.22 above.

123  A constable may use force to prevent the premises remaining open, for s 169 provides: 'A constable may use such force as may be necessary for the purposes of closing premises in compliance with a closure order.'

124  Section 171(5) provides: ' "trading standards officer", in relation to any premises to which a premises licence relates, means a person authorised by a local weights and measures authority to act in the area where those premises are situated in relation to proposed prohibitions contained in closure notices'. The section goes on to provide: ' "local weights and measures authority" has the meaning given by section 69 of the Weights and Measures Act 1985'.

125  Section 169A(11) provides:

>  In this section 'relevant officer' means–
>
>  (a)  a police officer of the rank of superintendent or above; or
>
>  (b)  an inspector of weights and measures appointed under section 72(1) of the Weights and Measures Act 1985.

126  Sched 4, para 5A of the Police Reform Act 2002 provides:

>  Where a designation applies this paragraph to any person, that person shall have–
>
>  (a)  within the relevant police area, and
>
>  (b)  if it appears to him as mentioned in subsection (7) of section 169A of the Licensing Act 2003 (closure notices served on licensed premises persistently serving children),
>
>  the capacity of a constable under that subsection to be the person by whose delivery of a closure notice that notice is served.

127  See the prescribed form of closure notice in the Licensing Act 2003 (Persistent Selling of Alcohol to Children) (Prescribed Form of Closure Notice) Regulations 2007, SI 2007/1183, which is set out in Appendix 8.

128  Section 169B(5) provides: 'In this section "related offence", in relation to the alleged offence, means an offence under section 146 or 147 in respect of any of the sales to which the alleged offence relates.'

129  *Quaere* whether 'Minor and consequential' means that amendments must be both minor and consequential or whether it is sufficient that they are either minor or consequential. The former would seem to be the more natural meaning, although according to the DCMS the expression 'includes either minor amendments to other statutes or amendments which are consequential on Parliament's approval of the Act as a whole' (letter from Andrew Cunningham to Jeremy Allen). If this is the case, it might reasonably be asked why the expression 'Minor or consequential' is not used.

130  For an example, see *R v R* [1992] 1 AC 599 (the word 'unlawful' in s 1 of the Sexual Offences (Amendment) Act 1976 was 'mere surplusage', per Lord Keith at 623).

131  Such sum must be paid to a designated officer for the court. Section 21(5) provides: 'A sum which has been ordered to be paid into court under this section shall be paid to the designated officer for the court'.

132  When a closure order is made, it may make provision for dealing with any consequences that might arise from cancellation. Section 22(4) provides: 'Subject to this, a closure order may include such provision as the court considers appropriate for dealing with any consequences which would arise if the order were to cease to have effect by virtue of the making of a certificate under subsection (1)'.

133 The procedure on a complaint is generally governed by the Magistrates' Courts Act 1980 and s 23(5) makes identical provision to s 20(7) for application for a closure order (see 11.16.6 above).

134 The immunity will also extend to any person exercising the powers of a constable by virtue of a designation under s 38 of the Police Reform Act 2002 (see 11.5.5 above) as well as to the police authority, for s 170(4A) provides: 'In this section references to a constable include references to a person exercising the powers of a constable by virtue of a designation under section 38 of the Police Reform Act 2002 (community support officers etc.); and, in relation to such a person, the first reference in subsection (2) to a chief officer of police has effect as a reference to a police authority'.

135 Section 172(4) provides: 'This section does not affect any other exemption from liability for damages (whether at common law or otherwise).'

136 These regulations, and any other regulations that the Secretary of State can make in respect of ADZs, are made by statutory instrument. Section 20(4) provides: 'The powers of the Secretary of State to make regulations under this Chapter shall be exercisable by statutory instrument'. These powers include making provision for different cases, for exemptions and exceptions, and for incidental, supplemental, consequential and transitional matters. Section 20(5) provides: 'Those powers all include power- (a) to make different provision for different cases; (b) to make provision subject to such exemptions and exceptions as the Secretary of State thinks fit; and (c) to make such incidental, supplemental, consequential and transitional provision as he thinks fit'. A draft of the regulations must be laid before Parliament and approved by a resolution of each House. Section 20(6) provides: 'The Secretary of State must not make regulations containing (with or without other provision) any provision that he is authorised to make by this Chapter unless a draft of the regulations has been laid before Parliament and approved by a resolution of each House'.

137 Costs, for these purposes, include the administration and enforcement costs in connection with the monthly charges. Section 15(10) provides: 'In subsection (3) the reference, in relation to any charges, to the costs of the scheme is a reference to the costs of the arrangements made for or in connection with the imposition, collection and recovery of those charges'.

138 Section 20(3) provides: 'References in this Chapter to premises being in a locality (however described) include references to their being partly in that locality'.

139 Although the Secretary of State has a general power under s 20(5)(b) to make provision for exemptions and exceptions in regulations (see 11.18.6 above), this power cannot be used to make any other provision for exemptions in this respect. Section 20(7) provides: 'Subsection (5)(b) is subject to the restriction on exemptions contained in section 15(6)'.

140 Section 181(6) provides: ' "authorised person" means an authorised person within the meaning of Part 3 or 4 or an authorised officer within the meaning of section 108(5).' For the meaning of 'authorised person' in Pts 3 (premises licences) and 4 (clubs), see 6.15.2 above and 8.11.4 above, respectively, and, for 'authorised officer' under s 108(5), see 9.8.2 above.

# CHAPTER 12

# APPEALS

## APPEALS UNDER THE 2003 ACT[1]

### 12.1 INTRODUCTION

Section 181 and Sched 5 provide for a right of appeal to the magistrates' court against decisions of licensing authorities and the court has a number of options when determining an appeal. These include dismissing the appeal, making any decision that the licensing authority itself could have made in substitution for the decision reached by the authority, or remitting the case to the authority with a direction as to how it should be dealt with. The court may also make an order for the award of costs. Section 181 provides:

> (1) Schedule 5 (which makes provision for appeals against decisions of licensing authorities) has effect.
>
> (2) On an appeal in accordance with that Schedule against a decision of a licensing authority, a magistrates' court may–
>
> (a) dismiss the appeal,
>
> (b) substitute for the decision appealed against any other decision which could have been made by the licensing authority, or
>
> (c) remit the case to the licensing authority to dispose of it in accordance with the direction of the court,
>
> and may make such order as to costs as it thinks fit.

The power of the court to substitute a decision is broadly expressed. It will clearly include cases where the court reaches a more favourable decision than dismissing the appeal, for example, granting a variation in hours until 11.30 pm on appeal against a refusal to vary the hours from 11.00 pm until 12.00 am. However, there is nothing to indicate that the provision in para (b) is so confined and that it might not extend to cases where the court reaches the same decision as the licensing authority but on less favourable terms, for example, upholding the licensing authority's decision to refuse a variation in hours from 11.00 pm until 12.00 am, but additionally imposing a condition confining consumption of alcohol within the curtilage of the premises. Here the court is not simply dismissing the appeal under para (a), but substituting a similar (but not identical) decision to that which the authority could have made. It seems unlikely that a court would want to constrain the options available to an appeal court by adopting a narrow interpretation of the wording of para (b) and confining it to cases where the appeal court makes decisions more favourable than dismissing the appeal. The expression in para (b) is wide enough, on a literal interpretation, to include appeal court decisions that are both more favourable and less favourable. A purposive construction might support this too, since it is difficult to see why Parliament might have intended the provision to be restrictively interpreted. Further, a broad interpretation would accord with the nature of an appeal hearing as a re-hearing of the case, with evidence of events occurring between the licensing authority's decision and the appeal hearing being admissible (see 12.7 below). Such evidence might justify a less favourable outcome than simply dismissing the appeal and this would not be possible if the power to substitute a decision under para (b) was confined only to more favourable decisions than dismissal of the appeal.

Appeal under the 2003 Act is, in all instances, to the magistrates' court, with the exception of closure orders made by the police under s 161 and upheld by the magistrates' court, in which case appeal under s 166 is to the Crown Court (see 11.14.19 above). Rights of appeal are set out in Sched 5, which is divided into three parts. Part 1 covers premises licences, Pt 2 covers club premises certificates (CPCs) and Pt 3 covers other appeals, that is, temporary event notices (TENs), personal licences and closure orders.[2] No secondary legislation governing appeals has been introduced and the section on appeals in the Guidance is relatively short (see paras 12.1–12.11). Much has been left to the Magistrates' Association, the Justices' Clerks' Society and LACORS (Local Authority Co-ordinators of Regulatory Services, a part of the Local Government Association), to develop procedure within a broad statutory framework and to provide guidance to licensing authorities and those entitled to appeal. LACORS has issued some Guidance on licensing appeals, *Appeals Process – Licensing Act 2003*, which was first published in August 2005 and a revised version was issued in March 2007.

## 12.2  PARTIES ENTITLED TO APPEAL

12.2.1  Rights of appeal extend to any party involved in the decision – licence applicants/licence holders[3] and responsible authorities and interested parties who have made 'relevant representations' (see 6.4.9 above). No right of appeal is, however, available where a representation does not meet the criteria to constitute a 'relevant representation'. This is the case, for instance, where a representation is made outside the prescribed 28-day period or by an interested party and is judged to be frivolous or vexatious (see 6.4.19–6.4.20 above).

### 12.2.2  Premises licence appeals

Appeals may be made in the following circumstances:

- where premises licence applications are rejected;
- where there is a grant, variation, transfer or review of a premises licence;
- where an interim authority notice seeking reinstatement of the licence following lapse is given; and
- where a provisional statement is issued (following which an application may be made for the grant of a premise licence).

### 12.2.3  *Where premises licence applications are rejected*

Applications that are rejected may be for the grant of a licence, for its variation (including variation by specifying an individual as the designated premises supervisor (DPS)), or for its transfer. Where any of these are rejected, the applicant has a right of appeal. Paragraph 1 provides:

Where a licensing authority–
(a)  rejects an application for a premises licence under section 18,

(b) rejects (in whole or in part) an application to vary a premises licence under section 35,

(c) rejects an application to vary a premises licence to specify an individual as the premises supervisor under section 39, or

(d) rejects an application to transfer a premises licence under section 44,

the applicant may appeal against the decision.

### 12.2.4 Where there is a grant, variation, transfer or review of a premises licence

#### 12.2.5 Grant

12.2.6 Rights of appeal where a premises licence is granted are governed by para 2, sub-para (1) of which provides: 'This paragraph applies where a licensing authority grants a premises licence under section 18.' Rights of appeal are available both to the holder of the licence and persons who made relevant representations.

The holder can appeal against any conditions imposed on the licence (except, of course, mandatory conditions), the exclusion of any licensable activity or the refusal to specify an individual as the DPS. Paragraph 2(2) provides:

The holder of the licence may appeal against any decision–
(a) to impose conditions on the licence under subsection (2)(a) or (3)(b) of that section, or
(b) to take any step mentioned in subsection (4)(b) or (c) of that section (exclusion of licensable activity or refusal to specify person as premises supervisor).

12.2.7 Those who made relevant representations – responsible authorities or interested parties – may appeal against the grant of the licence, or against the conditions subject to which it was granted (contending that different or additional ones should have been imposed). They may also appeal on the ground that the licensing authority should have excluded one or more of the licensable activities to which the application related or should have refused to specify the person in the licence as the DPS. Paragraph 2(3) provides:

Where a person who made relevant representations[4] in relation to the application desires to contend–
(a) that the licence ought not to have been granted, or
(b) that, on granting the licence, the licensing authority ought to have imposed different or additional conditions, or to have taken a step mentioned in subsection (4)(b) or (c) of that section,

he may appeal against the decision.

Where a licence has been granted, it seems that the holder of the licence will be able to operate the premises in accordance with the licensing authority's decision pending determination of the appeal, for there is no provision that the decision is not to have effect until such time as the appeal is disposed of.

#### 12.2.8 Variation

12.2.9 Applications for variation differ according to whether they are for the variation of conditions or of the licence itself in some way (such as a change in the licensable activities) or whether they are for variation by changing the DPS. Different procedures apply to these two types of variation and separate provisions are contained in paras 4 and 5 for appeals in each case where variation is granted.[5]

Rights of appeal for the former type of variation application are governed by para 4, sub-para (1) of which provides: 'This paragraph applies where an application to vary a premises licence is granted (in whole or in part) under section 35.' Rights of appeal are available both to the applicant and persons who made relevant representations. The applicant can appeal against any decision to modify the conditions. Paragraph 4(2) provides:

> The applicant may appeal against any decision to modify the conditions of the licence under subsection (4)(a) of that section.

Those who made relevant representations may appeal against the variation granted (for example, a change in the licensable activities) or against the modification of any conditions. Paragraph 4(3) provides:

> Where a person who made relevant representations[6] in relation to the application desires to contend–
>
> (a) that any variation made ought not to have been made, or
>
> (b) that, when varying the licence, the licensing authority ought not to have modified the conditions of the licence, or ought to have modified them in a different way, under subsection (4)(a) of that section,
>
> he may appeal against the decision.

12.2.10 Rights of appeal for a variation by changing the DPS are governed by para 5, sub-para (1) of which provides:

> This paragraph applies where an application to vary a premises licence is granted under section 39(2) in a case where a chief officer of police gave a notice under section 37(5) (which was not withdrawn).

If the application is granted, the premises licence holder will not be in any way be 'aggrieved' and thus needs no right of appeal available to him. Since the chief officer of police is the only person entitled to object and will be the only person 'aggrieved' by the grant, the right to appeal is confined to him. Paragraph 5(2) provides: 'The chief officer of police may appeal against the decision to grant the application.'

### 12.2.11 Transfer

Applications to transfer the premises licence must, in general, be granted and can be opposed only by the police giving notice that grant would undermine the crime prevention objective (see 6.10.5 above). Accordingly, rights of appeal where a transfer application is granted are confined to cases where the police have opposed the transfer, but the licensing authority has granted it. Paragraph 6 provides:

> (1) This paragraph applies where an application to transfer a premises licence is granted under section 44 in a case where a chief officer of police gave a notice under section 42(6) (which was not withdrawn).
>
> (2) The chief officer of police may appeal against the decision to grant the application.

*12.2.12 Review and summary review*

Rights of appeal where there has been a review of a premises licence are governed by para 8, sub-para (1) of which provides: 'This paragraph applies where an application for a review of a premises licence is decided under section 52.' Rights of appeal are available to the applicant for the review, the premises licence holder and persons who made relevant representations. Paragraph 8(2) provides:

An appeal may be made against that decision by–
(a)  the applicant for the review,
(b)  the holder of the premises licence, or
(c)  any other person who made relevant representations[7] in relation to the application.

No right of appeal, however, is available to the person owning the freehold of the premises that are subject to a premises licence review where that person is not the premises licence holder. Although such a person might be a 'person aggrieved' and entitled to appeal under s 166 where a closure order is made in respect of the premises (see 12.2.29 below), para 8(2) makes no provision for appeal by such a person.

The right to seek a summary review of a premises licence was introduced by s 21 of the Violent Crime Reduction Act 2006 (see 6.13 above) and rights of appeal where there has been a summary review are governed by para 8A, sub-para (1) of which provides: 'This paragraph applies where a review of a premises licence is decided under section 53A(2)(b) (review of premises licence following review notice)'. Rights of appeal are available to the police, the premises licence holder and persons who made relevant representations. Paragraph 8A(2) provides:

An appeal may be made against that decision by–
(a)  the chief officer of police for the police area (or each police area) in which the premises are situated,
(b)  the holder of the premises licence, or
(c)  any other person who made relevant representations[8] in relation to the application for review.

As in the case of a review, no right of appeal is available to the person owning the freehold of the premises that are subject to a summary review where that person is not the premises licence holder.

## 12.2.13  *Where an interim authority notice seeking reinstatement of the licence following lapse is given*

A premises licence, although generally remaining in force indefinitely, can lapse either due to some incapacity on the part of the licence holder or on surrender, but can be reinstated by the giving of an interim authority notice (IAN) under s 47 (see 6.11.4–6.11.8 above). The police (to whom a copy of the IAN is given) can, however, object if satisfied that exceptional circumstances mean that failure to cancel the IAN would undermine the crime prevention objective. The IAN may or may not be cancelled by the licensing authority and para 7 provides for rights of appeal by the person giving the notice (where it is cancelled) and by the police (where their objection is not upheld). Paragraph 7(1)–(3) provides:

(1) This paragraph applies where–
  (a) an interim authority notice is given in accordance with section 47, and
  (b) a chief officer of police gives a notice under section 48(2) (which is not withdrawn).
(2) Where the relevant licensing authority decides to cancel the interim authority notice under subsection (3) of section 48, the person who gave the interim authority notice may appeal against that decision.
(3) Where the relevant licensing authority decides not to cancel the notice under that subsection, the chief officer of police may appeal against that decision.

### 12.2.14   *Where a provisional statement is issued*

Rights of appeal where a provisional statement has been issued are governed by para 3, sub-para (1) of which provides: 'This paragraph applies where a provisional statement is issued under subsection (3)(c) of section 31.' Rights of appeal are available both to the applicant and persons who made relevant representations. Paragraph 3(2) provides:

An appeal against the decision may be made by–
(a) the applicant, or
(b) any person who made relevant representations[9] in relation to the application.

### 12.2.15   Club premises certificate appeals

The appeal provisions in Pt 2 for CPCs follow a similar format to those in Pt 1 for premises licences and appeals may be made in the following circumstances:

• where CPC applications are rejected; or
• where there is a grant, variation, review or withdrawal of a CPC.

### 12.2.16   *Where CPC applications are rejected*

Applications that are rejected may be for the grant of a CPC or for its variation and the club that made the application has a right of appeal in these cases. Paragraph 10 provides:

Where a licensing authority–
(a) rejects an application for a club premises certificate under section 72, or
(b) rejects (in whole or in part) an application to vary a club premises certificate under section 85,

the club that made the application may appeal against the decision.

### 12.2.17   *Where there is a grant, variation, review or withdrawal of a CPC*

#### 12.2.18   *Grant*

Rights of appeal where a CPC is granted are governed by para 11, sub-para (1) of which provides: 'This paragraph applies where a licensing authority grants a club premises certificate under section 72.' Rights of appeal are available both to the club holding the CPC and persons who made relevant representations.

The club can appeal against any conditions imposed on the CPC or any exclusion of a qualifying club activity. Paragraph 11(2) provides:

> The club holding the certificate may appeal against any decision–
>
> (a) to impose conditions on the certificate under subsection (2) or (3)(b) of that section, or
>
> (b) to take any step mentioned in subsection (4)(b) of that section (exclusion of qualifying club activity).

Those who made relevant representations may appeal against the grant of the CPC, or against the conditions subject to which it was granted (contending that different or additional ones should have been imposed), or on the ground that the licensing authority should have excluded one or more of the qualifying club activities to which the application related. Paragraph 11(3) provides:

> Where a person who made relevant representations[10] in relation to the application desires to contend–
>
> (a) that the certificate ought not to have been granted, or
>
> (b) that, on granting the certificate, the licensing authority ought to have imposed different or additional conditions, or to have taken a step mentioned in subsection (4)(b) of that section,
>
> he may appeal against the decision.

## 12.2.19 Variation

Rights of appeal where an application is made for variation of a CPC are governed by para 12, sub-para (1) of which provides: 'This paragraph applies where an application to vary a club premises certificate is granted (in whole or in part) under section 85.' Rights of appeal are available both to the club holding the CPC and persons who made relevant representations. The club can appeal against any decision to modify the conditions. Paragraph 12(2) provides:

> The club may appeal against any decision to modify the conditions of the certificate under subsection (3)(b) of that section.

Those who made relevant representations may appeal against the variation granted (for example, a change in the qualifying club activities) or against the modification of any conditions. Paragraph 12(3) provides:

> Where a person who made relevant representations[11] in relation to the application desires to contend–
>
> (a) that any variation ought not to have been made, or
>
> (b) that, when varying the certificate, the licensing authority ought not to have modified the conditions of the certificate, or ought to have modified them in a different way, under subsection (3)(b) of that section,
>
> he may appeal against the decision.

## 12.2.20 Review

Rights of appeal where there has been a review of a CPC are governed by para 13, sub-para (1) of which provides: 'This paragraph applies where an application for a review of a club premises certificate is decided under section 88.' Rights of appeal are available to the applicant for the review, the club holding the CPC and persons who made relevant representations. Paragraph 13(2) provides:

> An appeal may be made against that decision by–
> (a) the applicant for the review,
> (b) the club that holds or held the club premises certificate, or
> (c) any other person who made relevant representations[12] in relation to the application.

### 12.2.21 Withdrawal

A CPC can be withdrawn following an application for review, in which case the club can appeal against the decision under para 13(2)(b), but it can also be withdrawn by the licensing authority under s 90 because the club has ceased to meet the qualifying conditions for a CPC (see 8.7.3 above). In this latter instance, the club can appeal against the decision to withdraw the CPC under para 14, which provides:

> Where the relevant licensing authority gives notice withdrawing a club premises certificate under section 90, the club which holds or held the certificate may appeal against the decision to withdraw it.

## 12.2.22 Temporary event notice appeals

TEN appeals, which will arise only where there has been a police objection (see 9.1.1 above), are governed by para 16, sub-para (1) of which provides:

> This paragraph applies where–
> (a) a temporary event notice is given under section 98, and
> (b) a chief officer of police gives an objection notice in accordance with section 104(2).[13]

Rights of appeal are available both to the premises user who gave the TEN and to the police. The premises user can appeal where the licensing authority has given a counter-notice and the police can appeal where their objection has not been upheld and no counter-notice has been given. Paragraph 16(2) and (3) provides:

> (2) Where the relevant licensing authority[14] gives a counter notice under section 105(3), the premises user may appeal against that decision.
> (3) Where that authority decides not to give such a counter notice, the chief officer of police may appeal against that decision.

## 12.2.23 Personal licence appeals

Appeals may be made in the following circumstances:

- where applications for the grant or renewal of a personal licence are rejected;
- where there is a grant or renewal of a personal licence following police objections;
- where there is a revocation of a personal licence following police objections on convictions coming to light after grant or renewal; and
- where there is a decision not to revoke a personal licence following police objections on convictions coming to light after grant or renewal.

## 12.2.24 Where personal licence applications are rejected

In this case, the applicant has a right of appeal under para 17(1), which provides:

Where a licensing authority–

(a) rejects an application for the grant of a personal licence under section 120, or

(b) rejects an application for the renewal of a personal licence under section 121,

the applicant may appeal against that decision.

## 12.2.25 Where there is a grant or renewal of a personal licence following police objections

Police objections to grant or renewal, made respectively under s 120(5) or s 121(6), will be on the ground that grant or renewal will undermine the crime prevention objective (see 10.5.19 and 10.6.2 respectively). If these objections are not upheld, the police have a right of appeal under para 17(2) and (3), which provides:

(2) Where a licensing authority grants an application for a personal licence under section 120(7), the chief officer of police who gave the objection notice (within the meaning of section 120(5)) may appeal against that decision.

(3) Where a licensing authority grants an application for the renewal of a personal licence under section 121(6), the chief officer of police who gave the objection notice (within the meaning of section 121(3)) may appeal against that decision.

## 12.2.26 Where there is a revocation of a personal licence following police objections on convictions coming to light after grant or renewal

A licensing authority has the power to revoke a personal licence under s 124(4) in such circumstances where there have been police objections on the ground that continuation of the licence would undermine the crime prevention objective (see 10.8.2 above). Where the licence is revoked, the licence holder has a right of appeal under para 17(4), which provides:

Where a licensing authority revokes a personal licence under section 124(4), the holder of the licence may appeal against that decision.

## 12.2.27 Where there is a decision not to revoke a personal licence following police objections on convictions coming to light after grant or renewal

Where, in the circumstances outlined in the preceding paragraph, the licensing authority decides not to revoke the licence, the police have a right of appeal under para 17(5), which provides:

Where in a case to which section 124 (convictions coming to light after grant or renewal) applies–

(a) the chief officer of police for the licensing authority's area gives a notice under subsection (3) of that section (and does not later withdraw it), and

(b) the licensing authority decides not to revoke the licence,

the chief officer of police may appeal against the decision.

## 12.2.28   Closure order appeals

### *12.2.29   Consideration of closure order by magistrates' court*

Rights of appeal to the Crown Court are available by any person aggrieved when a closure order has been upheld or revoked by a magistrates' court (see s 166 and 11.14.19 above). This will most obviously include the licence holder, but a 'person aggrieved' might extend beyond this to include other persons. In *Garrett v Middlesex JJ* (1884) 12 QBD 620 it was held that a mortgagee of licensed premises was a 'person aggrieved' in respect of a refusal to renew a justices' licence for the sale of intoxicating liquor and in *Cooke v Cooper* [1912] 2 KB 248 a similar decision was reached in respect of a premises owner. On the basis of these decisions, a mortgagee and premises owner might similarly be a 'person aggrieved' in cases where a closure order is made.

### *12.2.30   Review of premises licence following closure order*

12.2.31 Rights of appeal (to the magistrates' court) where there has been a review of a premises licence under s 167 following a closure order are governed by para 18, sub-para (1) of which provides:

> This paragraph applies where, on a review of a premises licence under section 167, the relevant licensing authority[15] decides under subsection (5)(b) of that section–
>
> (a)  to take any of the steps mentioned in subsection (6) of that section, in relation to a premises licence for those premises, or
>
> (b)  not to take any such step.

The steps, which are mentioned in sub-s (6) are: (a) to modify the conditions of the premises licence; (b) to exclude a licensable activity from the scope of the licence; (c) to remove the designated premises supervisor from the licence; (d) to suspend the licence for a period not exceeding three months; or (e) to revoke the licence.

12.2.32 Rights of appeal are available to the premises licence holder and persons who made relevant representations. Paragraph 18(2) provides:

> An appeal may be made against that decision by–
>
> (a)  the holder of the premises licence, or
>
> (b)  any other person who made relevant representations[16] in relation to the review.

## 12.3   RESPONDENTS TO AN APPEAL

12.3.1  The licensing authority will always be a respondent to the appeal, but in cases where a favourable decision has been made for an applicant against the representations of a responsible authority or an interested party, or the objections of the police, the holder of the premises licence or CPC or the person who gave an interim authority notice will also be a respondent (and the person who made the relevant representation or the chief officer of police will be the appellant).[17] Similarly, in the case of a personal licence where a favourable decision has been made against a police objection – this will be where, despite the police objection, a personal licence has been granted, renewed or not revoked on convictions coming to light after grant or renewal – the personal licence applicant or holder will also be a respondent.[18] Again, in the case of a

TEN, where a favourable decision has been made against a police objection (which will be where the authority decides not to issue a counter-notice), the premises user will also be a respondent.[19] In all of these cases, the person making the application for authorisation will be a respondent, along with the licensing authority, and will be a participant in the appeal process. He will thus be able to challenge any evidence put forward by the appellants opposing the application (responsible authorities or interested parties who have made relevant representations or the police who have made an objection).

12.3.2 However, in cases where the person making the application is unsuccessful and he appeals, Sched 5 makes provision only for the licensing authority to be a respondent to the appeal. There are no provisions in Sched 5 enabling those opposing the application to be respondents and this, it seems, was not an oversight but a deliberate policy choice. The policy intention has been set out in correspondence between Andrew Cunningham, Head of Licensing Policy at the DCMS, and Mark Du Val, of LACORS who raised the matter of behalf of local government lawyers.[20] Mr Cunningham's response, dated 25 October 2005, was:

> With regard to appeals, applicants/licence holders are different to those who have made representations for two connected reasons. Firstly, the livelihood of the individuals owning the business and their employees would always be at risk in any appeal. Secondly, and more importantly, the appeal is their last chance. If the outcome of the appeal is a rejected licence application or a revoked licence that would be the end of the road under the terms of the Licensing Act 2003. The appeal to the magistrates' court is a final appeal. In the case of interested parties or responsible authorities, the review procedures offer them the chance to come back on issues if they are proved right and problems in connection with the four licensing objectives emerge. There is no such second chance to re-visit the issue for an applicant.

> Any interested party or responsible authority that is satisfied with a decision can, of course, reasonably expect the licensing authority to seek to uphold its own decision. If the licensing authority wishes to present evidence supporting its decision, it may, with the court's leave, call interested parties or responsible authorities to give evidence. This will be for the licensing authority to decide (and the court to approve) in each case. However, the record of the hearing will itself constitute evidence recording what interested parties or responsible authorities said in writing and at the hearing.

The view that those making relevant representations were not entitled to be respondents was subsequently reiterated in DCMS's *Guidance for Interested Parties: Appealing Licensing Decisions* issued in November 2005: 'If applicants appeal licensing authority's decisions, responsible authorities, such as the police, and interested parties, such as local residents, that made representations about the application, will not, in the terms of the Licensing Act be "responding parties" at appeal hearings'. Whilst this might have brought it to the attention of some parties, notably those interested in appealing, it might have been helpful if this policy justification had been made more widely known, for example by including it in the Guidance issued under s 182.

Whether those making relevant representations were entitled to be respondents was in fact considered by the Horseferry Road Magistrates' Court in *Lucas v Westminster City Council* on 11 November 2005, at or around the time that the above-mentioned DCMS *Guidance* was issued. The court in this case was asked to rule whether three interested parties who had made relevant representations were entitled to be respondents (and it is understood that the court was at the time of reaching its decision was aware of the policy justification). Both the council and the appellant (who was appealing against a refusal to extend opening hours at the Candy Bar in Soho) contended that the interested parties could not appear as they were not mentioned in Sched 5 and could not be joined as of right, with leave, or at all.[21] Referring to this contention, District Judge Purdy remarked:

> The statute being silent on the issue must mean either by accident or design, the only construction I am permitted to make is that there is no provision and thus no entitlement. For the Appellant there was the submission that schedule 5 paragraph 9 lists exhaustively who may be respondents. There was a degree of Pilate like hand wringing in submitting that perhaps this omission was an error but if so too bad. Westminster City Council goes further submitting there is no accidental omission. Parliament, mindful of a more lengthy hearing before the court, wanted to restrict the parties.

The council's contention found little favour with the district judge[22] who ruled that para 9 of Sched 5 provides no more than a positive duty to be a respondent on certain parties and cannot be construed to exclude as respondents previous interested parties:

> . . . the regime of the Licensing Act 2003 must be construed as intending a wider range of parties beyond public undertakings and actual applicants to be heard . . .Schedule 5 can quite properly be construed and must be, to imply without question that an 'interested party' before the sub-committee can, as of right, be a respondent. Such a party need not respond and may withdraw from further participation or actively become involved. Once making clear a desire to be a respondent then that is on equal terms with the local authority . . .[23]

Thus those opposing an application, according to *Lucas*, have an implied right to appear as respondents and their participation is not dependent on whether the licensing authority, as respondent, chooses to rely on their evidence. This means that the licensing authority will have to consider not only the terms on which it might wish to proceed with the appeal (whether by way of contesting, withdrawing or settling it), but also how those opposing the application might wish to proceed. The parties may not necessarily see their interests as co-terminus, so some negotiation may be required to arrive at a strategy for pursuing the appeal (or not, as the case may be).

12.3.3  Whilst *Lucas* represents a considered decision on this point at magistrates' court level, a contrary view, against the right to appear as respondents, might be advanced. The view might equally be taken that, had Sched 5 intended interested parties or responsible authorities to have the right to appear as a respondent, express provision to this effect would have been made for this. The position might be compared to that under the Licensing Act 1964, s 21 of which permitted an appeal by a 'person aggrieved' and s 22(3) of which made express provision for such a person to be a respondent, in addition to the licensing justices, where there was a refusal to grant a justices' licence. The absence of any such provision in the 2003 Act might thus be taken to indicate that Parliament did not intend any right of appeal as a respondent and that no right to appear should accordingly be implied.

If this view is followed, those opposing the application will be denied any right to participate in the appeal process. Whether they can participate will be dependent on whether the licensing authority, as the only respondent to the appeal, chooses to rely on their evidence. If, for instance, on an appeal against the refusal to grant a premises licence where relevant representations had been made by residents about the risk of public nuisance and by the police about the risk to crime and disorder, the licensing authority sought to adduce evidence only on the former issue at the appeal hearing, the police would be unable to be heard. Further, the public nuisance issue might be resolved following discussions between the applicant, the licensing authority and the residents, and the appeal withdrawn. The police may not have been a party to these discussions, but, since they are not a respondent to the appeal, it is open to the licensing authority to settle the appeal without regard to their objections and without them having an opportunity to present their case on appeal. It is arguable that in such cases there would be a violation of the right of the police to a fair hearing under Art 6(1) of the European Convention on Human Rights on the ground that there is no right to be heard by an 'independent' tribunal (see 3.5.12–3.5.13 above). Whilst the right will exist in cases where the application has been successful – those opposing the application are entitled to appeal and do have the right to be heard in this instance – there appears to be no such right where the application has been unsuccessful.[24]

12.3.4   In the absence of any authoritative decision – *Lucas*, as a magistrates' court decision, carries little weight as a judicial precedent and it has been followed in some areas, but not in others[25] – the legal position remains uncertain. It is thought, however, that the view more closely according with Parliamentary intent, applying ordinary principles of statutory construction, is that there should be no right to appear. It has to be conceded, however, that if the human rights point has substance, the position may be different as the 2003 Act has to be 'read and given effect in a way which is compatible with . . . Convention rights', where it is possible to do so, under s 3(1) of the Human Rights Act 1998 (see 3.2.1 above). One way in which this might be done is for Sched 5 to the 2003 Act to be read as implying a right to appear as a respondent in a magistrates' court appeal so as to be compatible with Art 6. Given that the competing arguments seem finely balanced on the issue of the right to appear, there is a pressing need for some judicial clarification of the position.

## 12.4   COMMENCING AN APPEAL

12.4.1   Appeal is commenced by the appellant giving to the magistrates' court a notice of appeal. Perhaps surprisingly, although there are prescribed forms in secondary legislation governing many aspects of the scheme under the 2003 Act (for example, making applications for licences and certificates), there is no set form or procedure for giving notice of appeal. Whilst some courts have created an 'appeals form', others have not and it is left to appellants to contact the relevant court to check how to make an appeal (see *Guidance for Interested Parties: Appealing Licensing Decisions*, DCMS, November 2005, p 2), although LACORS' *Appeals Process – Licensing Act 2003*, March 2007 does contain a suggested draft version in Annex D. An appeal is commenced in all cases by the appellant giving a notice of appeal for to the 'designated officer' for the magistrates' court within 'a period of 21 days beginning with the day on which the appellant was notified by the licensing authority of the decision to be appealed against'.[26]

12.4.2   Unless the Act makes provision for the period within which the authority must notify a party of its decision, under reg 28 of the Licensing Act 2003 (Hearings)

Regulations 2005, this must be done by the authority 'forthwith on making its determination'. The meaning of 'forthwith' seems to be as soon as reasonably practicable (see 6.6.2 above) and under reg 34(1) this notice 'must be given in writing', although reg 34(2) goes on to provide that this requirement is satisfied where the text of the notice is transmitted by electronic means, provided certain requirements are met (see 2.1.5 above). The 21-day period will thus run from the date the written notice is given or, in the case of electronic transmission, when the text is received. Section 184 makes provision for the giving of notices under the Act, so the 21-day period should begin with the day on which notice of decision is given in accordance with that section. Where under s 184 notice is given to a person other than the licensing authority (which will be the case where it is given to the designated officer of a magistrates' court), sub-s (3) provides that notice may be given 'by delivering it to him, or by leaving it at his proper address, or by sending it by post to him at that address' (see 2.5.4 above).

No indication is given, however, as to what might constitute good service in accordance with the chosen method. The Civil Procedure Rules 1998 make provision for the deemed day of service for particular methods of service (for example, second day after posting for a document sent by first-class post), but these Rules do not apply to magistrates' courts.[27] Magistrates' courts are governed by the Criminal Procedure Rules 2005, but these contain no comparable provision.[28] The position in respect of giving notice by posting may, however, be governed by s 7 of the Interpretation Act 1978, which provides that, where an Act authorises or requires any document to be served by post, service is deemed, unless the contrary is proved, to 'have been effected at the time at which the letter would be delivered in the ordinary course of post.' This may be the same time as set out in r 6.7 of the Civil Procedure Rules 1998 for deemed service for first-class post, that is, second day after posting.[29] This would accord with the view taken by the Justices' Clerks' Society, which has recommended first-class post or recorded delivery for posting of the notice and has advised allowing two days from date of posting in determining the date when the 21-day period begins to run.[30]

12.4.3  A person entitled to appeal may, however, have been aware of the licensing decision prior to being notified under s 184, since the decision may have been announced at the end of the oral hearing to determine it. This may well be prior to written notification being given, for, where a hearing is held, the authority has in general five working days within which to make its determination.[31] Although in practice it is unlikely to delay a decision beyond the end of the hearing, even a determination made at the end of the hearing may not result in written notice under the 2003 Act being given immediately, since reasons need to be given for the decision and it may take some time for them to be properly formulated. Since there may be a difference in point of time at which an oral and a written notification is given, it is important to determine whether the 21-day appeal period begins to run from oral or written notification, especially as no provision is made for granting any extension of time. The provisions in Sched 5 simply make reference to the 21-day period beginning on the day that the appellant was 'notified by the licensing authority of the decision to be appealed against' and it is not clear from the wording whether this means being given written notice of the determination or being informed orally of the decision at the end of a hearing.

12.4.4 Whether an oral announcement of a committee's decision constitutes being 'notified' of the decision, with the 21-day period running from this date rather than the later date of written notification, is a matter that has been considered at magistrates' court level in an appeal against the refusal to grant a sex establishment licence. In *Quietlynn Ltd v Oldham Borough Council*,[32] magistrates took the view that a notice of appeal dated 5 March 1984, which was within 21 days of the date of written notification on 14 February 1984 of refusal to grant a licence, but more than 21 days from the date of the oral hearing on 9 February 1984, was out of time. Following the dismissal of the appeal, the appellants asked the justices to state a case for the High Court and this was done, but the case stated was not lodged in the required time and did not proceed.[33] Notwithstanding the approach taken in this case, the position under the 2003 Act may well be different. Schedule 3 to the Local Government (Miscellaneous Provisions) Act 1982 for sex establishment licensing contains no specific provision for the giving of notices, simply providing, in para 27, for appeal within 21 days of 'the date on which the person in question is notified of the refusal of his application, the imposition of the term, condition or restriction by which he is aggrieved or the revocation of his licence, as the case may be'. There is nothing to which reference can be made when determining what constitutes being 'notified'. There is, however, in the 2003 Act, with the specific provision in s 184 (see 2.5 above). References, in paragraphs in Sched 5, to the 21-day appeal period beginning with the day on which the appellant was 'notified' of the decision can be related to the giving of notices under s 184. If being 'notified' of the decision means being given notice in accordance with s 184, the 21-day period runs from the date of written notification in accordance with that section. However, to be on the safe side, it may be prudent to ensure that notice of appeal is given within 21 days of any notification given at an oral hearing.

## 12.5 INTERIM EFFECT OF APPEALS

12.5.1 Whether a licensing authority's decision under the 2003 Act takes immediate effect or is suspended pending the determination of an appeal depends on the nature of the decision and whether it is affecting existing rights to trade. If authorisation for a licensable activity already exists and the decision is seeking to modify or remove existing trading rights, provision is made for suspension until after the appeal, with suspension either taking place automatically or at the discretion of the licensing authority or magistrates' court to which the appeal is made.

### 12.5.2 Automatic suspension of the licensing authority's decision

A licensing authority's decision following a review of a premises licence or a CPC, or a summary review of a premises licence in serious cases of crime and disorder, does not have effect until the end of the 21-day period within which an appeal can be made or, if the decision is appealed against, until the appeal is disposed of. Section 52(11) makes provision to this effect for premises licences (see 6.12.8 above), s 88(11) for CPCs (see 8.10.8 above) and s 53C(11) for summary reviews (see 6.13.17 above). Similarly, under s 124(6), where there is a decision by the licensing authority either to revoke or not revoke a personal licence following police objections on convictions coming to light after its grant or renewal, the decision is automatically suspended pending the determination of an appeal (see 10.8.3 above).

### 12.5.3 Discretionary suspension of the licensing authority's decision

#### 12.5.4 *Refusal to renew a personal licence*

Where there is a refusal to renew a personal licence and the licence holder gives notice of appeal, either the licensing authority or the magistrates' court to which appeal is made has the power to order the personal licence to remain in force if it would cease to have effect before the appeal or, if it has already ceased to have effect, to reinstate it. Schedule 5, para 17(9) and (10) provides:

> (9) Sub-paragraph (10) applies where the holder of a personal licence gives notice of appeal against a decision of a licensing authority to refuse to renew it.
>
> (10) The relevant licensing authority, or the magistrates' court to which the appeal has been made, may, on such conditions as it thinks fit–
>
> > (a) order that the licence is to continue in force until the relevant time,[34] if it would otherwise cease to have effect before that time, or
> >
> > (b) where the licence has already ceased to have effect, order its reinstatement until the relevant time.

#### 12.5.5 *Cancellation of an interim authority notice*

Where an appeal is made against a licensing authority's decision to cancel an IAN (see 6.11.10 above) following a police objection under s 48(3), cancellation of which will cause the premises licence in respect of which the notice was given to lapse, the magistrates' court has a discretion to reinstate the premises licence pending determination of the appeal. By its very nature an IAN is only of temporary effect and its purpose is to enable a business to continue when a premises licence holder dies suddenly or becomes incapacitated in some way. This purpose would be frustrated if an IAN could not be reinstated until an appeal was heard. Accordingly, the court has a discretion to order reinstatement of the IAN and, where it does so, the premises licence will be reinstated from that time. Schedule 5, para 7(4) and (5) provides:

> (4) Where an appeal is brought under sub-paragraph (2) [by the person who gave the interim authority notice in respect of the licensing authority's decision to cancel it], the court to which it is brought may, on such terms as it thinks fit, order the reinstatement of the interim authority notice pending—
>
> > (a) the disposal of the appeal, or
> >
> > (b) the expiry of the interim authority period,[35]
> >
> > whichever first occurs.
>
> (5) Where the court makes an order under sub-paragraph (4), the premises licence is reinstated from the time the order is made, and section 47 has effect in a case where the appeal is dismissed or abandoned before the end of the interim authority period as if—
>
> > (a) the reference in subsection (7)(b) to the end of the interim authority period were a reference to the time when the appeal is dismissed or abandoned, and
> >
> > (b) the reference in subsection (9)(a) to the interim authority period were a reference to that period disregarding the part of it which falls after that time.

## 12.5.6 *Review of premises licence following closure order*

12.5.7   When making a decision on review on which steps it should take (see 12.2.31 above), the licensing authority (except in the case of revocation) may or may not have ordered suspension of the operation of that decision under s 168(5) until the end of the period for making an appeal or, if an appeal is made, until it is disposed of.[36] Where an appeal is made against a decision to take any of these steps (except revocation), the magistrates' court itself may suspend the operation of that decision, if the licensing authority has not so suspended it, or it may cancel any order made by the licensing authority or make an order in substitution for any order made by the licensing authority. Schedule 5, para 18(3) provides:

> Where an appeal is made under this paragraph against a decision to take any of the steps mentioned in section 167(6)(a) to (d) (modification of licence conditions etc), the magistrates' court may in a case within section 168(3) (premises closed when decision taken)–
>
> (a)  if the relevant licensing authority has not made an order under section 168(5) (order suspending operation of decision in whole or part), make any order under section 168(5) that could have been made by the relevant licensing authority, or
>
> (b)  if the authority has made such an order, cancel it or substitute for it any order which could have been made by the authority under section 168(5).

12.5.8   In cases where the licensing authority has made a decision to revoke the premises licence, s 168(7) requires that the premises must remain closed until the end of the period for making an appeal or, if an appeal is made, until it is disposed of. The licensing authority has no power under s 168(5) to order suspension of the operation of that decision (see 11.14.24 above). However, where an appeal is made, the magistrates' court may make an order that s 168(7) is not to have application so that the premises are not to remain closed pending appeal. Paragraph 18(4) provides:

> Where an appeal is made under this paragraph in a case within section 168(6) (premises closed when decision to revoke made to remain closed pending appeal), the magistrates court may, on such conditions as it thinks fit, order that section 168(7) (premises to remain closed pending appeal) is not to apply to the premises.

Apart from the above-mentioned instances, the 2003 Act makes no other references to suspension of decisions of a licensing authority pending the determination of an appeal, so it must be assumed that all other decisions have immediate effect. In some instances, this might not give rise to any hardship or additional expense, but in other instances it might do so. If a variation in hours is sought and is simply refused, continuing to operate with the existing hours pending the hearing of an appeal is not in itself particularly onerous nor is any expense likely to be incurred in the interim period. However, the position may be different in the event that refusal to vary is accompanied, as it seems it can be (see 6.9.4 above), by the imposition of conditions. If, for example, a condition was imposed requiring the use of polycarbonate glasses, the replacement of existing breakable glasses would, for those operating large premises, represent a significant expenditure which might, in the event of a successful appeal, prove to be unnecessary if such a condition was not imposed by the magistrates' court. Suspension of the effect of such a condition pending appeal might be thought to be desirable in such cases but there appears to be no provision in the Act under which this might be done. Failure to comply with the condition pending appeal would constitute an offence under s 136(1) (see 11.2.1 above), although the sensible and pragmatic solution in such instances would seem to be for the licensing authority to refrain from taking any enforcement action until determination of the appeal.

## 12.6   PRE-HEARING PROCEDURE

12.6.1   The procedure on appeal against the licensing authority's decision is governed by Pt 7 of the Criminal Procedure Rules 2005, SI 2005/384, which makes provision for commencing proceedings in magistrates' courts. Rule 7.1, previously contained in r 4(1) of the Magistrates' Courts Rules 1981, SI 1981/552, provides: 'An information may be laid or complaint made by the prosecutor or complainant in person or by his counsel or solicitor or other person authorised in that behalf'. The making of a complaint is the standard form for appeals against local authority decisions and r 34 of the Magistrates' Courts Rules 1981 ensures that a uniform system operates for appeals irrespective of the particular enactment under which the appeal is brought. It provides:

> Where under any enactment an appeal lies to a magistrates' court against the decision or order of a local authority or other authority, or other body or person, the appeal shall be by way of complaint for an order.

For appeals under the 2003 Act, an 'initial appeal hearing' at the magistrates' court will normally be held at least 28 days after the 21-day period for making appeals for the court to decide whether it wishes to hear the appeal or remit the case back to the licensing authority. The court has power to take either course. When an appeal is made the court may, under s 181(2) of the 2003 Act, dismiss the appeal, substitute for the decision appealed against any other decision that could have been made by the licensing authority, or remit the case to the licensing authority to dispose of it in accordance with the direction of the court (see 12.1 above). If the parties are disposed towards the case being remitted, it is clearly desirable that this matter is considered and a decision reached prior to the evidence being received at a full hearing of the case. Cases in which the court might wish to remit the case back to the licensing authority might include where conditions duplicating other statutory requirements have been attached[37] (which can be removed by the licensing authority on remission back) or where it appears that the particular subcommittee hearing the application has rigidly applied the authority's Statement of Licensing Policy (SOP) without considering the merits of the application (in which case the application can be re-heard by a differently constituted subcommittee).[38] If the case in not remitted, it will normally be adjourned for a separate hearing date.

12.6.2   The initial appeal hearing may well encompass a pre-trial review to consider matters affecting the length of the hearing, including any disputed legal issues for which skeleton arguments may be required, whether any legal authorities are likely to be relied upon by the parties, any evidence that can be agreed, exchange of documents, and numbers of witnesses to be called.[39] No statutory provision is made for either initial hearings or pre-trial reviews, which seem to have developed as a matter of local practice in the light of the likely numbers of appeals under the 2003 Act. Similarly, local practice appears to determine whether the relevant matters are considered by a bench of magistrates and the justices' clerk sitting together or by the justices' clerk presiding alone. Although the Justices' Clerks Rules 2005, SI 2005/545 make provision for certain matters authorised to be dealt with by a single magistrate to be dealt with by a court clerk and these include the making of a complaint (r 2 and Sched, para 1), pre-trial reviews and initial hearings are not specifically included within the Rules. The Rules are not regarded as having application to them and there can accordingly be no delegation to a court clerk. When considering matters at a pre-trial review, it may be that the parties can come to a mutually acceptable agreement on what action should be taken (for example, modification of the conditions in the applicant's operating schedule). Where this occurs, the case need not proceed to a hearing and effect can be given to the agreement by a consent order made by the court without the need for evidence to be called. In *R v Kings Lynn Magistrates' Court ex p M* [1988] 2 FLR 393 the Divisional Court held that, where a man admitted paternity in affiliation proceedings and consented to an order requiring him to pay maintenance as the putative father of the child, the justices were entitled to make the order without the need for further evidence and this principle should have equal application to an agreement reached on a licensing application at a pre-trial review.[40]

12.6.3 Not all courts have an initial hearing and pre-trial review and cases may simply be set down for a full hearing once notice of appeal has been given. When and if the case does proceed to a full hearing, this is before a bench of magistrates sitting as a court. The bench is likely to consist of three magistrates, although in some instances there may be only two, for a magistrates' court can sit with only two members (or, alternatively, a district judge may sit alone). Most benches have established Appeals Panels to hear cases; these consist of magistrates who have received training on the provisions of the 2003 Act and include some members who have had previous experience of sitting as licensing justices. Creation of Appeals Panels was recommended at an early stage by the Magistrates' Association and the Justices' Clerks Society and a supporting letter (dated 28 July 2004) was sent out by the chairman of the Association's Licensing Committee to all bench chairman and all Appeals Panel chairmen, in which it was stated:

> The Association remains fully committed to the creation of Appeals Panels and would ask all chairmen to support their creation. Panels will ensure that a limited number of magistrates are trained in this new area of law and can then apply the specialist knowledge they will require of Local Authority procedure and policy, whilst also having regard to the National Guidance document. We are aware that many benches have already accepted this advice.
>
> As we approach the October bench meetings, this is an ideal opportunity to ensure that the matter is properly aired on your bench with the bench being asked to decide on the creation of the panel, and then move to elect that panel if that is deemed appropriate. Current views are that no more than 50% of existing Licensing Committee members should serve due to possible conflict of interests in the transitional period.

It is thought that about 80% of benches in the country have established Appeals Panels. Those not doing so, in the main, tend to be benches in the larger city areas. The likely reason for this seems to be the high volume of anticipated work, with such benches not wishing to place any fetter on their discretion to list magistrates to sit on licensing appeals.

12.6.4 In the period before the appeal is heard, attempts may be made to reach a compromise in respect of the particular application, thereby obviating the need for the case to be heard. This might result from a review of the evidence available to the parties. The licensing authority, as respondent to the appeal, may or may not wish to accede to the proposed compromise. Much may depend on the period of time before the appeal is due to be heard, on the views of interested parties and responsible authorities who made relevant representations in respect of the application made to the licensing authority, and on whether the proposal seeks to extend the original application. If the proposed compromise is made just before the appeal hearing is to commence, it may not be open to the licensing authority's legal representative to accept the compromise. The representative may have been instructed by the licensing authority not to accept any compromise, on the basis that decision-making is a matter for the licensing committee or subcommittee, although it is possible that delegated authority may have been given to accept within certain confines. If the proposed compromise is well ahead of the appeal hearing, there will be the opportunity for the proposal to be referred back to the licensing committee or subcommittee for its future consideration and to consult interested parties and responsible authorities. This will be of particular importance if the proposal seeks in some way to extend the original application and LACORS Guidance on licensing appeals recommends that in such cases the proposal should be refused pending the appeal, with consideration given only to offers limiting the original application in some way, for example, by offering to reduce the operating hours, premises capacity or to accept additional conditions (*Appeals Process – Licensing Act 2003*, March 2007, p 9).

Interested parties and responsible authorities who are consulted in respect of a proposed compromise will clearly be aware of the pending appeal, but otherwise may not be so aware. They are not necessarily parties to the appeal and there is no requirement for them to be notified of the appeal, although clearly they will be informed by the licensing authority if it wishes to call them as witnesses. Otherwise, it seems to be a matter of practice for the licensing authority to decide whether or not it wishes to inform them and LACORS, in its Guidance on licensing appeals, 'believes that it is up to the individual licensing authority to decide' (*Appeals Process – Licensing Act 2003*, March 2007, p 12).

## 12.7  NATURE OF THE APPEAL HEARING

12.7.1  Neither s 181 of nor Sched 5 to the 2003 Act gives any indication as to the nature of the appeal hearing. The previous legislative provisions similarly gave no indication, but the appeal was regarded as taking the form of a re-hearing of the case, based on the Court of Appeal's decision in *Sagnata Investments Ltd v Norwich Corporation* [1971] 2 QB 614. This was a case concerning appeal to Quarter Sessions[41] against a refusal to grant a permit for amusement with prizes machines. The court had to decide whether the appeal at quarter sessions before the recorder was to be treated as a new hearing to be determined on evidence *de novo*, with the court having a complete and unfettered discretion and without being influenced by the local authority's decision, or whether the hearing was to be treated as an 'appeal proper', in which the local authority's decision was to be regarded as of considerable weight and was not to be reversed unless its decision was shown to be wrong. A majority of the court adopted an 'intermediate' position of regarding the appeal as a re-hearing, in which the court could substitute its decision for that of the local authority, but with a requirement for due regard to be paid to the local authority's decision.

Edmund Davies LJ, delivering the leading judgment of the majority, stated (at 636–637):

> I hold that the proceedings before this recorder were by way of a complete rehearing. But, contrary to what has been contended, this conclusion does not involve that the views earlier formed by the local authority have to be entirely disregarded by quarter sessions . . . *Stepney Borough Council v. Joffe* [1949] 1 K.B. 599 establishes what I regard as the proper approach, for, having made the point that there was in that case an unrestricted appeal, Lord Goddard C.J. continued, at pp. 602, 603:
>
> > "That does not mean to say that the court of appeal, in this case the metropolitan magistrate, ought not to pay great attention to the fact that the duly constituted and elected local authority have come to an opinion on the matter, and ought not lightly, of course, to reverse their opinion. It is constantly said (although I am not sure that it is always sufficiently remembered) that the function of a court of appeal is to exercise its powers when it is satisfied that the judgment below is wrong, not merely because it is not satisfied that the judgment was right."

Similar sentiments were expressed by Phillimore LJ (at 639–640), although without reliance on the decision in *Joffe*:

> The position seems to me to be so well established that it is not susceptible of legal subtlety. The hearing of an appeal at quarter sessions is a rehearing. It cannot be less so if the decision from which the appeal is brought is an administrative decision by the committee of a local authority which heard no evidence, before which no one took an oath, or was cross-examined . . .
>
> I think that the recorder [in the appeal] must hear evidence – all the more so because none was called before the committee. I think he must give effect to that evidence and reach what he regards as a just conclusion. Of course, he will bear in mind the views expressed by the local authority and will be slow to disagree . . .[42]

No supporting reasons were advanced for this view by Phillimore LJ, but Edmund Davies LJ based his view on the fact that, since there was no formal record of proceedings before the local authority, it was impractical for an appeal to be anything other than by way of a re-hearing. His Lordship (at 633–634) placed reliance on observations of Lord Goddard CJ in *Drover v Rugman* [1951] 1 KB 380 when dealing with a case stated by quarter sessions on an appeal from the juvenile court:

> . . . Lord Goddard C.J. said, at p.382: "When a case goes to quarter sessions it is reheard; the person seeking an order proves his case over again. That only means that quarter sessions are taking the place, as it may be expressed, of petty sessions; but the proceedings are none the less an appeal." This, he explained, was due to the fact that there was no formal record of proceedings before justices, an observation equally true of proceedings before the licensing committee of this local authority . . .
>
> For my part, I cannot see how it is practicable in cases such as the present for an appeal to quarter sessions to be other than by way of a complete rehearing. Having no record before him of what transpired before the local authority, how could the recorder otherwise begin to judge the cogency of the written reasons placed before him?

12.7.2 The decision in *Sagnata* subsequently seems to have been regarded as having application to licensing decisions generally and to appeals before courts other than quarter sessions (which were in fact abolished and replaced by the Crown Court in 1971 shortly after the *Sagnata* case). Certainly the Crown Court was considered to have succeeded to the administrative jurisdiction of quarter sessions and it was recognised that appeals before the Crown Court could take the form of a rehearing. This is apparent from *Kavanagh v Chief Constable of Devon and Cornwall* [1974] QB 624 where the Court of Appeal decided that hearsay evidence might be admitted in a Crown Court appeal against a decision by the chief constable under the Firearms Act 1968 to refuse to grant the applicant a shot gun certificate and to register him as a firearms dealer on the ground that the proceedings were neither criminal nor civil ones to which the normal rules of evidence applied, but were administrative in nature. Cusack J stated (at 629):

> It is quite true it [appeal] lies to the Crown Court, but it is the successor of quarter sessions, and certainly quarter sessions had many administrative functions . . . It [the Crown Court] clearly has to consider the matter from the beginning afresh . . . [and] apply its own discretion in exactly the same way as, in the first instance, the chief constable would have to apply his discretion.

Appeals to the magistrates' court against decisions of local authorities were similarly considered to take the form of a re-hearing. Thus Glidewell J in the Divisional Court in *R v Huntingdon District Council ex p Cowan*, when referring to the provision in Sched 1, para 17(4) of the Local Government (Miscellaneous Provisions) Act 1982 that 'On an appeal to the magistrates' court or the Crown Court, under this paragraph the court may make such order as it thinks fit', took it to be self-evident that a public entertainment licensing appeal was a re-hearing. His Lordship stated (at 504):

> It follows from the latter part of that provision that the appeal is by way of rehearing and the powers of the magistrates' court to inquire into relevant matters and of the Crown Court on appeal from them are not in any way trammelled.

Similarly, in *Westminster City Council v Zestfair Ltd* (1989) 153 JP 613, where the Divisional Court held that the magistrates' court hearing an appeal against refusal to register premises as a night café had been wrong to refuse to admit evidence of a council officer about nuisance complaints on the basis that it was inadmissible as hearsay evidence, it was 'common ground that the [magistrates'] court should re-hear the application on the merits and not simply decide whether the council was wrong in law' (*per* Pill J at 615).

12.7.3  In none of these cases was the nature of the appeal hearing in issue and no reference was made in the judgments to *Sagnata*. However, in *Rushmoor Borough Council v Richards* (1996) 160 LG Rev 460, the Divisional Court, considering an appeal by a local authority against a magistrates' court's variation of the hours of a night-club's public entertainment licence, held that the magistrates' court should have admitted new evidence that the club was being badly run in the period between the date of the licensing authority's decision and the date of the appeal hearing. Tuckey J, placing reliance on *Sagnata* and the other decisions mentioned above (except *Huntingdon*, to which no reference was made), stated:

> These cases support the view that I form from looking at the legislation, that appeals under this legislation are by way of a rehearing de novo and that Magistrates are not restricted to hearing evidence about events before the authority's decision under appeal'[43]

Thus, since fresh evidence might be admitted, new witnesses might be called to give evidence in the appeal hearing, even though they might not have been called to give evidence at the hearing before the licensing authority.

12.7.4 In the light of the above it might be thought that there should be little doubt that an appeal under the 2003 Act is a *de novo* re-hearing of the case. But doubts persist primarily because para 12.6 of the Guidance states that the court on appeal may 'review the merits of the decision on the facts and consider points of law or address both'. This reference to 'review the merits' suggests more an examination of the licensing authority's decision, perhaps (if applicable) with reception of any new evidence between the decision and the appeal hearing, rather than a complete re-hearing of the case. The Guidance may be no more than an aid to interpretation of legislative intent if a court were required to ascertain the nature of an appeal hearing, but the statement in the Guidance may be sufficient to influence the view taken by magistrates' courts when hearing licensing appeals under the 2003 Act and arguments might be advanced for not following the approach in *Sagnata*. These might include the fact that a broad, largely unfettered discretion was to be exercised by the licensing authority in that case (and in *Rushmoor*, the only other case where the nature of the appeal hearing was in issue), whereas under the 2003 Act there is a more restricted discretion which must be exercised in accordance with specified licensing objectives. Further, in the leading judgment of the majority in *Sagnata* (Edmund Davies LJ), the rationale advanced for deciding that the appeal was a re-hearing was that there was no formal record of proceedings before the licensing authority which made it impractical for the hearing to take any other form.[44] But it is now recognised that there is a general duty on decision-makers to give reasons for their decisions (see 12.10.2 below), unlike at the time of *Sagnata*, and under reg 30 of the LA 2003 (Hearings) Regs 2005, authorities are required to keep a record of the hearing in a permanent and intelligible form which they must keep for a period of six years or until the disposal of any appeal (see 2.3.18 above). It is possible therefore that the decision in *Sagnata* might be distinguished if the largely unfettered nature of the statutory discretion in that case and/or the absence of any formal record of proceedings are considered to be material facts in the decision.

Notwithstanding this, it seems to be generally accepted that *Sagnata* continues to have application and that appeal takes the form of a re-hearing. Indeed, in *R (on the application of Blackwood) v Birmingham Magistrates and Birmingham City Council, Mitchells and Butler Leisure Retail Ltd (Interested Party)* (2006) 170 JP 613 the High Court stated (at para 18):

> It is common ground in these proceedings that the appeal to a magistrates' court is a rehearing of the decision (see *Sagnata Investments Ltd v. Norwich Corporation* [1971] 2 QB 614).

It is submitted that this is the correct approach for two reasons. First, in the absence of any indication that the position under the previous law is to be changed, it should continue to apply. Secondly, provision of a re-hearing would more easily ensure compliance with the requirement in Art 6(1) of the European Convention on Human Rights of the right to a fair hearing by an independent tribunal.[45]

## 12.8 PROCEDURE AT THE APPEAL HEARING

12.8.1 Appeal procedure is governed by Pt 7 of the Criminal Procedure Rules 2005 (CPR 2005), SI 2005/384, which makes provision for commencing proceedings in magistrates' courts, and appeals against the decision of a local authority are by way of complaint for an order (see 12.6.1 above). In such cases, the order of speeches and the calling of evidence appear to be governed by r 37.1 of the CPR 2005, which regulates the order of evidence and speeches in summary trials. Rule 37.1, although referring only to the 'summary trial of an information' and making no mention of the making of a complaint, essentially seems to replicate the provisions previously contained in rr 13 and 14 of the Magistrates' Courts Rules 1981, which applied, respectively, to the summary trial of an information and the hearing of a complaint. In the absence of any specific provision in the CPR 2005 regulating the order of evidence and speeches in complaint hearings, it is thought that this provision in r 37.1 has application.[46] Rule 37(1), as applied to complaint hearings, requires the complainant, that is, the person making the appeal to present his case first, although the court may, with the consent of the parties, invite the licensing authority as respondent to proceed first. There are significant advantages in doing so in that the court is better able to comprehend the authority's decision and reasoning for it if the authority presents its evidence at the outset. This is preferable to the court hearing evidence why the authority made the wrong decision before it hears information about what that decision is.[47]

12.8.2 The degree of information provided by the licensing authority of its decision may well vary, although it has not been uncommon for decision notices to go no further than setting out the decision taken and the particular licensing objective(s) on which reliance was placed. In such cases, it will be necessary for an outline of the history of the case to be given.[48] It is likely that this will be given by a licensing officer of the authority, although under s 223 of the Local Government Act 1972, any member or officer of a local authority may be authorised by the authority to appear on its behalf and this might include the Chair of the licensing committee or relevant sub-committee. Whilst the Chair may be able to give reasons why the particular decision was reached, reasons should be apparent from the committee or subcommittee's determination notice and from the minutes of the hearing. Although the Chair may appear on behalf of the authority, licensing officers usually prepare a witness statement explaining the administrative history of the application, what happened at the subcommittee hearing, who appeared as parties at the hearing and exhibiting all of the relevant documents (the application, the representations received, the report prepared for the subcommittee, the notice of decision and, if applicable, the licence or certificate granted). This evidence will very probably be agreed and simply read. Although it may be more efficient for written evidence to be provided, if the court agrees this is acceptable, the court is not obliged to accept written evidence and can insist that oral evidence is given.

12.8.3 Each party may call evidence in support of its case, which can include evidence given by witnesses and, with the court's agreement, written evidence. Parties are generally free to call witnesses on appeals, unlike in hearings before the licensing authority where the LA 2003 (Hearings) Regs 2005 impose constraints on witnesses appearing and their examination (see 2.3.10 above). But these Regulations and restrictions do not apply to licensing appeals. Thus parties to the appeal are generally able, at least as a matter of practice, to call any witnesses in support of their application without the need to obtain any permission and witnesses called might include persons refused permission by the authority to appear at the hearing. The appeal proceedings, unlike hearings before the licensing authority, remain essentially adversarial in nature with the opportunity for cross-examination by the parties.

12.8.4   At appeal hearings, evidence will be admitted on the same basis as it was when the case was heard by the licensing authority. Although the licence appeal hearing is administrative and in the nature of a civil proceeding, the court will not be bound by the rules of evidence applicable in civil proceedings and can take into account all matters that were before the licensing authority. Thus, any evidence that is logically probative and goes to prove a relevant issue can be admitted. As Diplock LJ stated in *R v Deputy Industrial Injuries Comr ex p Moore* [1965] 1 QB 456 (at 488):

> "evidence" is not restricted to evidence which would be admissible in a court of law . . . The requirement that a person exercising quasi-judicial functions must base his decision on evidence means no more than it must be based upon material which tends logically to show the existence or non-existence of facts relevant to the issue to be determined, or to show the likelihood or unlikelihood of the occurrence of some future event the occurrence of which would be relevant. It means he must not spin a coin or consult an astrologer, but he may take into account any material which, as a matter of reason, has some probative value in the sense mentioned above. If it is capable of having any probative value, the weight to be attached to it is a matter for the person to whom Parliament has entrusted the responsibility of deciding the issue. The supervisory jurisdiction of the High Court does not entitle it to usurp this responsibility and to substitute its own view for his.

Since evidence is not restricted to that admissible before a court, hearsay evidence can be received, even in those instances where such evidence continues to be inadmissible in civil proceedings after the Civil Evidence Act 1995.[49] The right to admit hearsay evidence in licensing appeals in the magistrates' court was recognised by the Divisional Court in *Westminster City Council v Zestfair Ltd* (1989) 153 JP 613, following the Court of Appeal's ruling in *Kavanagh v Chief Constable of Devon and Cornwall* [1974] QB 624 (affirming [1973] 3 All ER 657) that hearsay evidence was admissible in a Crown Court licensing appeal. In the *Westminster* case, it was held that the magistrates' court, when hearing an appeal under s 49(10) of the Greater London Council (General Powers) Act 1968 against the local authority's refusal to register premises for use as a night café, was wrong to decline to receive any hearsay evidence. The court rejected an argument that by s 53(2) of the Magistrates' Courts Act 1980, under which the court, after hearing the evidence and the parties, has to make the order for which the complaint was made or dismiss the complaint, only evidence that was admissible in normal judicial proceedings could be considered. The court considered itself bound by the decision in *Kavanagh* and did not think that that case was (*per* Pill J at 618) 'distinguishable on the grounds that the present appeal was to the magistrates' court whereas the appeal in *Kavanagh* was to the Crown Court'. This ruling ought to continue to have application under the 2003 Act.

12.8.5   In addition, local knowledge might be taken into account when reaching decisions. It had long been established, prior to the 2003 Act, that local knowledge might be considered. There was Court of Appeal authority in support of this in relation to justices' licences for the sale or supply of alcohol, *R v Howard ex p Farnham Licensing Justices* [1902] 2 KB 363, and this principle was regarded as having application to local authority decisions on licensing in the field of entertainment and other areas. In *Howard*, the justices' attention had been drawn to the excessive number of licensed premises in the area, so an investigation was undertaken by a number of members of the licensing committee and a report compiled. Justices subsequently objected to all renewals and required all licensees to attend the general annual licensing meeting. Evidence was heard in each case and the justices thereafter refused renewal of nine licences. The Court of Appeal held that the justices were entitled to object themselves and could take into account local knowledge acquired from the report in considering whether to renew. Collins MR stated (at 376):

> justices, in dealing with licences, are not a judicial body; they are deliberately appointed because from their circumstances they are likely to have local knowledge; and it cannot have been the intention of the Legislature that they should divest themselves of all such knowledge in dealing with questions of licences.

Whether justices might act solely on local knowledge on an issue was less clear. The Court of Appeal declined to express a view on the matter, Cozens Hardy LJ stating (at 382) that it 'is not necessary to consider whether the justices can act solely upon their own local knowledge – for example, as to the number of public houses compared with the population . . .'. The principle that local knowledge can be taken into account when decisions are being reached, whether by the licensing authority when hearing the case in the first instance or by the magistrates' court in a rehearing on appeal, ought to continue to have application under the 2003 Act, although it will be important to ensure that this is consistent with the right to a fair hearing under Art 6(1) of the European Convention on Human Rights (see 3.5 above).

12.8.6   As well as taking into account all matters and evidence before the licensing authority, the court can receive new evidence, including evidence of events occurring between the date of the licensing authority's decision and the date of the appeal hearing. In *Rushmoor Borough Council v Richards* (1996) 160 LG Rev 460, the Divisional Court held that magistrates, hearing an appeal against a refusal to vary the terms of a public entertainment licence, were wrong to exclude evidence relating to how a nightclub had been run in the interim period between refusal and the appeal hearing. Tucker J stated:

> Magistrates are not restricted to hearing evidence about events before the authority's decision under appeal. They are able and, indeed, must consider all the relevant evidence that is put before them whether it relates to events before or after the decision under appeal.[50]

Any new evidence will clearly need to relate to promotion of the licensing objectives in order for it to be relevant under the 2003 Act. However, it is less clear whether any such relevant evidence might be admitted, or whether new evidence is restricted either to matters contained in any of the relevant representations received by the authority or to grounds specified in the notice of appeal. Evidence may be restricted to grounds specified in the notice of appeal if the approach under the previous law is followed. When renewing justices' licences, it had long been established that the grounds set out in the notice of objection were the only ones on which justices could adjudicate. In *R v Walley* [1916] Brewing Trade Review Law Reports 44, notice of objection to renewal of a justices' licence was served on the licensee on the grounds that the premises had been ill-conducted and that the licensee was not a fit and proper person to hold the licence. The justices decided not to refuse renewal on either of these grounds but to refer the matter to the compensation authority on the ground of redundancy.[51] The Divisional Court held that the justices had no power to refer and were confined to considering the grounds specified in the notice, which related only to nonrenewal without compensation. If a similar approach is taken in respect of appeals under the 2003 Act, this would permit new information relating to the grounds specified in the notice of appeal to be introduced on appeal, but would preclude new grounds of objection being raised. Since the appeal by its very nature is in respect of matters raised before the licensing authority, it seems right that the parties should be confined to those matters. Insofar as new grounds of objection might need to be raised other than those brought to the attention of the licensing authority at the initial hearing, the 2003 Act provides a mechanism for doing so through the right of interested parties and responsible authorities to seek a review of the licence or certificate.[52] Where new evidence is admitted, the magistrates' court might either reach a different decision from the licensing authority or reach the same decision, but for different reasons, in accordance with this evidence.

## 12.9   DISCHARGING THE LICENSING FUNCTION

A licensing authority, when discharging licensing functions under the 2003 Act, is under a duty to promote the licensing objectives and to have regard both to its Statement of Licensing Policy and the Secretary of State's Guidance issued under s 182 (see s 4(1)–(3) and 4.1.1 above). Although no similar duty is expressly imposed on a magistrates' court on appeal, it seems clear that the appeal court should proceed in a similar manner.

### 12.9.1 Promoting the licensing objectives

The licensing objectives and their promotion, which are of paramount importance, determine the scope of the statutory power that is to be exercised and must therefore be adhered to by the court. When the licensing authority is discharging licensing functions, it must, where relevant representations are made, have regard to them and take such steps (if any) as are specified in the Act as it considers necessary for the promotion of the licensing objectives (see 6.5.1 above). The court when determining the appeal will be under a similar obligation.

### 12.9.2 Having regard to the Statement of Licensing Policy and the Guidance

12.9.3  Although the licensing authority is required, under s 4(3), to have regard to the authority's Statement of Licensing Policy (SOP) and the Secretary of State's Guidance in reaching its decision (see 4.1.1 above), there is no express statutory requirement on the magistrates' court to do so. Nevertheless, it is clearly envisaged that the magistrates' court will have regard to these, for para 12.7 of the Guidance provides: 'In hearing an appeal against any decision made by a licensing authority, the magistrates' court concerned will have regard to that licensing authority's statement of licensing policy and this Guidance'. Like the licensing authority, however, the court is entitled to depart from them if it considered this was justified in the individual circumstances of the case.[53] Paragraph 12.7 of the Guidance goes on to provide:

> . . . the court would be entitled to depart from either the statement of licensing policy or this Guidance if it considered it was justified to do so because of the individual circumstances of any case.

> In other words, while the appellate court will normally consider the matter as if it was "standing in the shoes" of the licensing authority, it would be entitled to find that the licensing authority should have departed from its own policy or the Guidance because the particular circumstances would have justified such a decision.

The importance of the appeal court considering the matter as if it were 'standing in the shoes' of the licensing authority is to ensure consistency and fairness, which might be undermined if on appeal the SOP were not regarded as having general application. This was emphasized under the previous law in *R (on the application of Westminster City Council) v Middlesex Crown Court and Chorion plc* [2002] LLR 538 (*Chorion*), where Scott Baker J stated, *obiter*, (at para 21) that the Crown Court, when hearing an appeal against the grant of a public entertainment licence under Schedule 12 to the London Government Act 1963, 'must accept the policy and apply it as if it was standing in the shoes of the council considering the application'.

12.9.4 Doubts may, of course, arise as to the legality of some aspect of the SOP (or, indeed, the Guidance) on an appeal and, perhaps surprisingly, the Guidance envisages the magistrates' court determining legality and not applying any part of the SOP which is *ultra vires* the 2003 Act and has a direct bearing on the case before it. Paragraph 12.8 provides:

> ... the appellate court is entitled to disregard any part of a licensing policy statement or this Guidance that it holds to be ultra vires the 2003 Act and therefore unlawful. The normal course for challenging a statement of licensing policy or this Guidance should be by way of judicial review, but where it is submitted to an appellate court that a statement of policy is itself ultra vires the 2003 Act and this has a direct bearing on the case before it, it would be inappropriate for the court, on accepting such a submission, to compound the original error by relying on that part of the statement of licensing policy affected.

Whilst it would be inappropriate to do so, it would also seem inappropriate for the magistrates' court to determine the question of legality of a SOP, given the potentially complex legal arguments that may be involved. As Webster J recognised in *Quietlynn Ltd v Plymouth City Council* [1987] 2 All ER 1040 (at 1046), the 'law relating to judicial review has become increasingly more sophisticated in the past few decades'; there is 'now a complex body of law' affecting the validity of decisions and 'justices are not to be expected to assume the functions of the Divisional Court'. Surely the appropriate course would be for the magistrates' court to adjourn proceedings pending determination by the High Court, on a judicial review application, of the legality of the relevant part of the SOP. This was regarded as the correct way to proceed by the High Court in *Quietlynn*, a sex establishment licensing case, when a challenge was made in the magistrates' court to the validity of a local authority licensing decision. Webster J stated (at 1046):

> If a bona fide challenge to the validity of the decision in question is raised before them, then the proceedings should be adjourned to enable an application for judicial review to be made and determined ... except in the case of a decision which is invalid on its face, every decision of the licensing authority ... is to be presumed to have been validly made and to continue in force unless and until it has been struck down by the High Court; and neither the justices nor a Crown Court have power to investigate and decide on its validity.

Similar sentiments were expressed by Scott Baker J in *Chorion* where his Lordship stated (at para 21):

Neither the magistrates' court nor the Crown Court is the right place to challenge the policy. The remedy, if it is alleged that a policy has been unlawfully established, is an application to the Administrative Court for judicial review.

The views expressed in these cases, it is submitted, have application to decisions under the 2003 Act, including matters such as the validity of a SOP on which such decisions are based, and should be regarded as binding on magistrates' courts. It seems doubtful that statements contained in the Guidance are indicative of any intention on the part of Parliament to change the established legal position, set out in *Quietlynn* and *Chorion*, that *ultra vires* and validity are matters for the High Court in judicial review proceedings.[54]

## 12.10 REASONS, COSTS AND NOTIFICATION OF DECISION

### 12.10.1 Reasons

12.10.2 Having reached a decision on the appeal, the magistrates' court is under a duty to give reasons in accordance with what is now regarded as the 'general obligation of judicial and administrative decision-makers to explain, however succinctly, why they are deciding as they are' (*per* Sedley LJ in *R (on the application of Tofik) v Immigration Appeal Tribunal* [2003] ECWA Civ 1138, para 17). The degree of particularity required in reasons will inevitably depend on the circumstances of the case and not every point raised will need to be addressed, provided it is clear why the matter was decided as it was and what conclusions were reached on the principal issues. As Griffiths LJ observed in the Court of Appeal in *Eagil Trust Co Ltd v Piggott-Brown and Another* [1985] 3 All ER 119 (at 122):

> ... the judge should set out his reasons, but the particularity with which he is required to set them out must depend on the circumstances of the case before him and the nature of the decision he is giving ... They need not be elaborate. I cannot stress too strongly that there is no duty on a judge, in giving his reasons, to deal with every argument presented by counsel in support of his case. It is sufficient if what he says shows the parties and, if need be, the Court of Appeal the basis on which he has acted, and if it be that the judge has not dealt with some particular argument but it can be seen that there are grounds on which he would have been entitled to reject it, this court should assume that he acted on those grounds unless the appellant can point to convincing reasons leading to a contrary conclusion.[55]

These observations were regarded by the Court of Appeal in *English v Emery Reimbold & Strick Ltd* [2002] 1 WLR 2409 as applying 'to judgments of all descriptions' (*per* Lord Phillips MR at para 18) and so should have equal application to decisions made by magistrates' courts on appeals under the 2003 Act.[56] In some instances it may be that brief, even minimal, reasons suffice, as perhaps where the court accepts the evidence of one witness in preference to that of another. In other cases, more depth might be required, which may be the case where the court's decision involves a departure from the authority's SOP or the Secretary of State's Guidance (or, equally, where the court declines to make a departure when requested to do so).

12.10.3 In the event that reasons are felt to be inadequate, it is open to the person aggrieved to seek a judicial review of the court's decision, although it may be that in the first instance a more appropriate course would be to proceed with a request for more detailed reasons. This procedure has recently been encouraged by the Court of Appeal in respect of judgments given by trial judges. In *English v Emery Reimbold & Strick Ltd* [2002] 1 WLR 2409 the Court of Appeal regarded it as desirable, in an effort to avoid appellate proceedings, for an appeal court faced with an application for permission to appeal to remit the case to the trial judge with an invitation to provide additional reasons or reasons for making a specific finding. Lord Phillips MR stated (at para 25):

> If an application for permission to appeal on the ground of lack of reasons is made to the appellate court and it appears to the appellate court that the application is well founded, it should consider adjourning the application and remitting the case to the trial judge with an invitation to provide additional reasons for his decision or, where appropriate, his reasons for making a specific finding or findings.[57]

It remains to be seen whether the Administrative Court will regard this as an appropriate procedure when considering applications for judicial review from decisions of magistrates' courts made on appeals under the 2003 Act.

## 12.10.4   Costs

12.10.5 Under s 181(2), the magistrates' court 'may make such order as to costs as it thinks fit', although no further guidance is provided either by the 2003 Act or the Secretary of State's Guidance. This provision is, strictly speaking, unnecessary, as a magistrates' court in a case where the appeal is by way of complaint for an order, which it is for appeals under the 2003 Act (see 12.8.1 above), has 'a power in its discretion to make such order as to costs . . . as it thinks just and reasonable' under s 64(1) of the Magistrates' Courts Act 1980. It has been recognised by the High Court in *Crawley Borough Council v Attenborough* [2006] EWHC 127 (at para 8), that there is 'no practical distinction' between the terms of these two provisions. The principles to be applied on a licensing appeal in respect of the award of costs under s 64(1) were considered by the High Court in *City of Bradford Metropolitan District Council v Booth* [2001] LLR 151 (*Bradford*). Here, the complainant successfully challenged in the magistrates' court the council's decision to refuse renewal of his licence to operate private hire vehicles and was awarded costs, the magistrates' court deciding that it was 'just and reasonable' to apply the normal civil law principle that costs 'follow the event', that is, they are paid by the losing party. The council was of the view that this was an erroneous approach and a case was stated for the opinion of the High Court as to whether the normal civil law principle should be applied. The correct principle, the council contended (at para 10), was

> . . . that a local authority ought not to be ordered to pay costs unless it has acted unreasonably, improperly or dishonestly . . . it would be gravely detrimental to the protection of the public if local authorities were to be deterred from making whatever decisions they thought were right by the fear that if those decisions were challenged, and if the challenge were successful, they would be mulcted in costs.

The High Court held that the principle that 'costs follow the event' did not apply against local authorities making decisions on licensing functions that they were required to perform and Lord Bingham CJ stated (at para 25) that 'the proper approach to questions of this kind can for convenience be summarized in three propositions':

1. Section 64(1) confers a discretion upon a magistrates' court to make such order as to costs as it thinks just and reasonable. That provision applies both to quantum of costs (if any) to be paid, but also as to the party (if any) which should pay them.

2. What the court will think is just and reasonable will depend on the relevant facts and circumstances of the case before the court. The court may think it just and reasonable that costs should follow the event but need not think so in all cases covered by the subsection.

3. Where a complainant has successfully challenged before justices an administrative decision made by a police or regulatory authority acting honestly, reasonably, properly and on grounds that reasonably appeared to be sound, in exercise of its public duty, the court should consider, in addition to any other relevant fact or circumstances, both (i) the financial prejudice to the particular complainant in the particular circumstances if an order for costs is not made in his favour; and (ii) the need to encourage public authorities to make and stand by honest, reasonable and apparently sound administrative decisions made in the public interest without fear of exposure to undue financial prejudice if the decision is successfully challenged.

Although formulated in the context of a taxi licensing decision and relating to an award of costs under s 64(1), it is clear from the reference to administrative decisions 'by a police or regulatory authority' that these principles are intended to have general application to licensing appeal decisions. That they will apply under the 2003 Act has been explicitly recognised by a later High Court in *R (on the Application of Cambridge City Council) v Alex Nestling Ltd* [2006] LLR 397 (*Nestling*), where Toulson J stated (at para 11):

> Local authorities have many licensing functions. It is clear that Lord Bingham's guidance did not depend on considerations specific to the licensing of vehicles, but is equally applicable in comparable cases where there is a statutory appeal from a decision of the local authority and the court has a broad discretion as to costs.

12.10.6 With regard to the application of these principles, under the third proposition formulated by the court, it seems to be a prerequisite that, for an award of costs not to be made against an authority, it must have acted honestly, reasonably, properly and on grounds that reasonably appeared to be sound. That the authority has acted reasonably and in good faith in the discharge of its public function was regarded by the court in *Nestling* (at para 11) as 'plainly a most important factor' and a failure in any of the respects mentioned in the third proposition should in all probability result in costs being awarded against the authority.[58] Further, it may be that attempts by applicants to resolve matters ahead of a hearing and the fact that the applicant is a publicly funded corporation may be relevant considerations in a decision on whether to award costs against an authority. In *Uttlesford District Council v English Heritage* [2007] EWHC 816 (Admin), an appeal was made against the imposition of conditions on a premises licence for a mansion house (Audley End House in Saffron Walden) that any amplified sound from the licensed premises shall not be 'clearly audible' at the boundary of any noise-sensitive premises and that, when regulated entertainment was taking place, regular assessments of noise levels should be made and steps taken to reduce levels 'where it is likely to cause a disturbance to local residents'. An expert report from sound engineers, obtained by English Heritage prior to the appeal, equated a noise level of between 50 and 55 decibels with the perception of 'clearly audible' at the nearest residential locations and, on appeal, the magistrates' court duly varied the condition to require a level not exceeding 52 decibels over any 15-minute period at a distance of one metre from any residential premises. It was held that the term 'clearly audible' was not sufficiently precise; it was not a scientific measurement and left too much open to interpretation. The condition requiring regular assessments was similarly varied so that the noise did not exceed a 52-decibels level. The court, in awarding costs against the licensing authority, had regard to the fact that the licensing authority had an opportunity to resolve the matter before the appeal hearing,[59] and that English Heritage, as a publicly funded organisation, had interests that needed to be balanced with those of the licensing authority. On appeal by case stated to the Administrative Court, it was held that it was just and reasonable for costs to be awarded to English Heritage (although the quantum of costs was regarded as excessive and was reduced – see 12.10.8 below) and the court, in a short judgment, gave no indication that the magistrates' court had acted in any way improperly in having regard to the considerations which it took into account.

Where these criteria are met, essentially a balance then needs to be struck between the impact on the complainant if no costs are awarded and the impact on the authority if they are. A number of factors might be taken into account in striking this balance. These could include:

- the quantum of costs that might be awarded and the complainant's ability to absorb them (which may be easier for a large, national operator than for a small, sole trader);
- the extent to which the authority may be discouraged through an award of costs against it from properly discharging its licensing functions, which may depend on the quantum of costs, the authority's ability to absorb them, and the importance the authority attaches to the outcome of the particular case in question.

It seems, however, that the appeal court cannot take into account decisions reached by the licensing authority in respect of other premises in the vicinity of the application premises when reaching a decision on costs. In *Nestling* the magistrates' court had stated that one factor in its decision as regards costs[60] 'was the fact that the licensing authority had seen fit to grant more generous hours of trading to two other premises in the same street', but the High Court stated (at para 16) that criticism of this approach by counsel for the licensing authority was 'well founded'. 'The only possible relevance of that matter', stated Toulson J (at para 15), 'could be if it led them to think that the local authority had been applying double standards and acted unreasonably', a finding would have been 'wholly inconsistent' with the magistrates' court's decision that the local authority had acted reasonably and conscientiously.

12.10.7 Less clear is whether the principles set out in the *Bradford* case are confined to decisions made by a licensing authority under the 2003 Act or whether they might also apply if responsible authorities and interested parties are respondents to an appeal. If it is accepted that they can be respondents to an appeal, such authorities and parties are equally at risk of costs being awarded against them if a complaint by an applicant is upheld. The position of responsible authorities may perhaps be considered analogous to administrative decision-makers, in that both are public authorities acting under a statutory duty to discharge their responsibilities. Although responsible authorities are not under any express statutory duty to make representations, there is a statutory requirement under reg 27 of the LA 2003 (PL and CPC) Regs 2005 for them to be notified of applications (see 2.1.6 above), with a view to them making representations. There might therefore be an implied obligation on the part of responsible authorities to make representations if they consider that granting an application might have an adverse effect on the promotion of the licensing objectives. Not to do so might be seen as a dereliction of public duty by a public authority and, if this is the case, their position may be comparable with administrative decision-makers. It may thus be in the public interest for responsible authorities to make and stand by their representations without fear of exposure to undue financial prejudice if their representations are discounted. The position of interested parties is less obviously analogous in this respect. Although they are entitled to make representations, there is no statutory requirement for them to be individually notified[61] and no exercise by them of any public duty, as there may be with responsible authorities. However, a broader view of the public interest might be that, since allowing representations improves the quality of decision-making, anyone making representations should not be discouraged from standing by them through fear of an award of costs and that they would not be so discouraged if the *Bradford* principles had application. Further, one of the key and aims purposes of the 2003 Act, according to the Secretary of State in her Foreword to the 2004 Guidance, was 'the necessary protection of local residents, whose lives can be blighted by disturbance and anti-social behaviour associated with the behaviour of some people visiting places of entertainment'. These key aims and purposes were stated to be 'of vital importance and should be principal aims for all involved in licensing work' and it might therefore be felt that costs ought not to be awarded against interested parties who are unsuccessful, but meet the *Bradford* criteria. Certainly the Magistrates' Association and the Justices' Clerks' Society have advised that awarding costs for a licensing appeal should be an exception and not a rule, and any resident with reasonable grounds for appeal should not be penalised (see DCMS, *Guidance for Interested Parties: Appealing Licensing Decisions*, November 2005, p 4). Whether the courts will be inclined to extend the *Bradford* principles to those making representations where these have been made honestly, reasonably, properly and on grounds that reasonably appeared to be sound, or whether they will confine them to decisions so made by licensing authorities, remains to be seen.

12.10.8 There appears to be little or no guidance as to quantum of costs in respect of orders made in magistrates' court and the leading work on costs, *Cook on Costs*, makes no reference to costs in magistrates' courts. Where costs are awarded to the applicant or a person making relevant representations, the appropriate figure would appear to be the level of remuneration under the contract between the person and his legal representative, although it seems that this has not always been the criterion employed. Some courts have apparently applied legal aid rates to the work undertaken, but these seem inappropriate since they apply only to criminal work and licensing appeals are civil or administrative in nature.

The level of remuneration, however, may not necessarily extend to all aspects of work under the contract. Whilst it may include work involving preparation for and attendance at the hearing, it may not extend to other work such as that in relation to an expert report. In *Uttlesford District Council v English Heritage* [2007] EWHC 816 (Admin) (see 12.10.6 above), the magistrates' court in a licensing appeal had ordered the licensing authority to pay English Heritage's costs of £14,300, which included solicitors' costs and the costs of an expert report on noise, but the Administrative Court stated that 'the quantum was excessive . . . given that the hours claimed by the solicitor extended not only to preparation and attendance at the hearing, but also in relation to the expert report' and it duly reduced costs to £4,750 plus VAT.

Where costs are awarded to the licensing authority, they will be calculated on the basis of time spent by licensing officers in preparing the case, any expenses (for example, lost earnings or travel expenses) paid to witnesses appearing at the hearing, and work undertaken by the legal services department at its normally applicable rates. In cases where an interested party or responsible authority appears with the licensing authority as a co-respondent, in principle it would seem that each should be entitled to costs, although there may be some apportionment in the event that the position of the co-respondents is not very far apart.

12.10.9 As to whether courts should give reasons for their decisions on costs, the general rule traditionally has been that there is no obligation to do so. As Griffiths LJ stated in *Eagil Trust Co Ltd v Pigott-Brown* [1985] 3 All ER 119 (at 122):

> A professional judge should, as a rule, give reasons for his decision. I say "as a general rule" because in the field of discretion there are well-established exceptions. The most obvious and frequently used is the exercise of the judge's discretion on costs. As a general rule the judge gives no reasons for the way in which he is exercising his discretion on costs, although if he were to make an unusual award of costs, it is clearly desirable that he should give his reasons for doing so.

This ruling, applied by the High Court in *R v Stafford Crown Court ex parte Wilf Gilbert (Staffs) Ltd* [2001] LLR 138 (*Stafford*) in a judicial review of a betting licensing decision, recognises that reasons need only be given exceptionally, although some doubt as to the continued application of this position has been expressed by the High Court in *Crawley Borough Council v Attenborough* [2006] EWHC 1278. In this case Scott Baker LJ stated (at para 10) that it 'seems to me very doubtful whether that decision [*Stafford*] has survived the new Criminal Procedure Rules [2005] which have loosened the opportunity to appeal on costs decisions'. Whilst a greater freedom to appeal in respect of costs decisions might indicate a possible relaxation in the general rule that reasons are not required, it seems that in any event 'there is no obligation on justices in cases of this kind to go in detail into the reasons for their decision, and it is sufficient that they have made it clear that they appreciated the principle under which they were operating' (*per* Scott Baker LJ at para 11). The court in *Attenborough* (at para 15) was of the view that the magistrates' court 'had all material matters in mind and it was within the ambit of their discretion to make the order that they did entitling Mr and Mrs Attenborough to have the costs of the appeal' and accordingly declined to interfere with the award of costs, making the general observation (at para 11) that it was 'highly undesirable that the courts should do anything to encourage satellite litigation on questions such as costs'. It is only where it is evident that a magistrates' court has not properly appreciated and applied the principles established in *Bradford* that a decision on costs will be set aside by the High Court, as it was in *Nestling*. Here the magistrates' court referred to being advised of the usual rule in civil cases that 'costs follow the event', which it appeared to regard as at least capable of carrying some weight, and there was no indication that it had been advised that *Bradford* had established that such a rule had no part to play in licensing cases. It was apparent that the usual rule had permeated the magistrates' court's thinking, for costs were awarded against the licensing authority following the court's reaching of a different conclusion from the authority, although the court had found that the authority had 'carried out its statutory duties in a conscientious and proper manner'. If the authority had so acted, costs should not have been awarded against it in accordance with *Bradford* and, as, Toulson J stated (at para 16), 'I do not see, on the facts as found, how the magistrates could properly have awarded costs against the local authority in these circumstances'.

### 12.10.10   Notification of decision

Once the court has made its decision, it must notify the licensing authority and the other party or parties to the appeal of its decision and the reasons for it. No provision is contained in the 2003 Act or in secondary legislation as to notification, although courts will usually provide notification within three working days of the appeal hearing (see LACORS, *Appeals Process – Licensing Act 2003*, March 2007, p 15). Once notified, it is envisaged that the decision will be implemented by the licensing authority without delay. The Guidance, para 12.10, provides:

> As soon as the decision of the magistrates' courts has been promulgated, licensing authorities should not delay its implementation. Any attempt to delay such implementation will only bring the appeal system into disrepute. Standing orders should therefore be in place that on receipt of the decision, necessary action should be taken forthwith unless ordered by the magistrates' court or a higher court to suspend such action (for example, as a result of an on-going judicial review).

The necessary action may involve the licensing authority issuing a licence or certificate where there is a successful appeal by a licence applicant or withdrawing a licence or certificate where there is a successful appeal by a responsible authority or interested party. In each instance, this is a matter for the licensing authority to undertake and not the magistrates' court.

## APPEALS TO THE HIGH COURT

## 12.11   APPEALS TO THE HIGH COURT BY CASE STATED FROM THE MAGISTRATES' COURT

12.11.1 Under s 111(1) of the Magistrates' Courts Act 1980 (MCA 1980), any person who is a party to any proceedings before a magistrates' court, or (although not a party) who is 'aggrieved' by the court's order, may appeal to the High Court on the ground that the proceedings were wrong in law or in excess of jurisdiction. This right exists, provided there is no right of appeal to the High Court itself against the decision and provided the decision is not expressed by statute to be final, neither of which is the case for appeals under the 2003 Act. Thus licence applicants and holders, licensing authorities and persons who made relevant representations, as parties to the proceedings, will have a right of appeal under this provision. So also will any person 'aggrieved', which will be anyone whose legal rights are adversely affected by the decision, for example, a person with a legal or equitable interest in the licensed premises.

12.11.2 Before stating a case, the magistrates must finish dealing with the case before them. In *Streames v Copping* [1985] QB 920, the Divisional Court held that, on a proper construction of s 111(1) of the MCA 1980, magistrates had no power to state a case thereunder until they had reached a final determination of the matter before them and, further, the High Court had no jurisdiction to consider and determine a case stated by magistrates in excess of their powers. The magistrates were accordingly held to have acted wrongly in acceding to a request to state a case, following rejection of a defence submission that an information against the defendant for selling an unroadworthy vehicle was bad for duplicity. The case should have proceeded to final determination before a case was stated. The requirement to proceed to final determination will not apply, however, where the magistrates have declined to exercise jurisdiction to hear a case.

12.11.3 Under s 111(2) of the MCA 1980, applications for a case stated need to be made within 21 days of the date of the magistrates' court's decision. If magistrates think an application is frivolous, they can refuse to state a case,[62] although they can be required to do so by the High Court issuing an order of *mandamus* (Mandatory Order) in judicial review proceedings.[63] A person exercising the right of appeal by case stated under s 111 of the MCA 1980 must comply with the requirements set out in r 64.1 of the Criminal Procedure Rules 2005. The application must be made in writing, be signed by or on behalf of the applicant and identify the question(s) of law or jurisdiction on which the opinion of the High Court is sought.[64] Where one of the questions is whether there was evidence on which the magistrates' court could come to its decision, the particular finding of fact that it is claimed cannot be supported by the evidence must, under r 64.1(2) of the Criminal Procedure Rules 2005, be specified in the application. Within 21 days of receiving the application, a court officer must, under r 64.2(1), send a draft case to the applicant or his legal representative, with a copy to the respondent and his legal representative.[65] This is unless the justices refuse to state a case under section 111(5) of the MCA 1980, although under r 64.2(3) the court officer must so act if the justices are subsequently required to state a case by a Mandatory Order of the High Court under section 111(6). Under r 64.2(2), the applicant and respondent have 21 days in which to make representations as to the contents of the case, which must be in writing, signed and sent to the magistrates' court officer. Under r 64.3(1), the magistrates then have a further 21 days in which to make any adjustments to the stated case, after considering representations received, and to state and sign the case.[66] The stated case must, under r 64.3(3), forthwith be sent to the applicant or his legal representative.[67] The stated case should contain a statement of the facts found by the court and should not contain a statement of the evidence, unless it is contended that there was no evidence to support a particular finding of fact (r 64.6(1)–(3)).

12.11.4 The powers of the High Court in respect of a stated case are contained in s 28A(3) of the Supreme Court Act 1981. The High Court can determine the question(s) of law and either reverse, affirm or amend the determination appealed against, or remit the case to the magistrates with a direction to take certain action or with an expression of the opinion of the High Court. It may make such other order in relation to the matter (including as to costs) as it thinks fit. These powers can be exercised not only to correct errors of law, such as an incorrect interpretation of a statutory provision, but also to correct any decision which is unsupported by the evidence.[68] The High Court's decision under this section is final, subject to a right of appeal to the House of Lords in criminal cases under the Administration of Justice Act 1960 (s 28A(4)). Where the decision is not in respect of any criminal cause or matter, as is likely to be the case where licensing functions are being exercised, no further appeal is possible. The Court of Appeal, in *Westminster City Council v Horseferry Road Justices*

[2004] 1 WLR 195, stated that the provisions of s 18(1) and s 28A(4) of the Supreme Court Act 1981 precluded any further appeal in respect of a case stated and held the court did not have jurisdiction to hear it.[69]

## 12.12  APPEALS TO THE HIGH COURT BY WAY OF APPLICATION FOR JUDICIAL REVIEW

12.12.1 Section 31 of the Supreme Court Act 1981 embodies the inherent jurisdiction of the High Court to control inferior courts and tribunals and an application can be made, with leave of the High Court, for judicial review of a decision of the magistrates' court or other tribunal (which will include the licensing committee and subcommittees under the 2003 Act). Under s 31(3), leave will be granted only if the High Court considers that the applicant has a 'sufficient interest' in the matter to which the application relates (see 4.3.21 above). If leave is granted, the High Court may grant relief in the form of a Quashing Order (formerly *certiorari*), a Prohibiting Order (formerly prohibition), a Mandatory Order (formerly *mandamus*), or it may award a declaration or damages.

The granting of a Quashing Order will be appropriate to quash a decision where there is some element of unlawfulness concerning the process by which the decision was reached. This might arise in a number of ways. First, there may be an error of law on the face of the record. This may be the case, for example, where a TEN is given once the maximum number of notices that can be given in the calendar year has been exceeded (for these numbers, see 9.7.1 above). Secondly, a decision may be made that is invalid through lack of power. This may arise, for instance, under the 2003 Act where a licensing authority grants a personal licence to an applicant who already holds a personal licence, for under s 113 an individual is permitted to hold only one personal licence (see 10.3 above). Thirdly, there may be the power to make the decision, but there is something about the way in which it is exercised, in the circumstances of the individual case, which constitutes an abuse of that power, that is, the decision in some way is procedurally defective and has not been reached in the correct manner. This might include exercise of the power for an improper purpose (for example a purpose not falling within promotion of the licensing objectives), taking into account an irrelevant consideration or failing to have regard to a relevant consideration (for example, the SOP or the Secretary of State's Guidance) or reaching a decision which no reasonable court or tribunal could have reached.[70]

12.12.2 That there may be an abuse of power does not, however, necessarily mean that the licensing decision itself will be quashed. If, for instance, a condition is attached to a licence that does not promote the licensing objectives, the condition may be invalid, but this may not invalidate the decision itself to grant the licence. Whether or not it does will depend on whether the licence, with the condition deleted from it, is fundamentally different from the licence with the condition incorporated. If it is not, the condition may be severed and the licensing decision upheld, but if severance would alter the essential character or substance of that which remained, the entire licence will be invalid. Thus, in *R v North Hertfordshire District Council ex p Cobbold* [1985] 3 All ER 486, the respondent local authority granted to the applicant a public entertainment licence to hold two open-air musical entertainments on private land, subject to a condition that the concert promoters would reimburse both the local authority and the county council for all reasonable expenses incurred in the provision of additional public services required in connection with the concerts. Expenses incurred by the county council related to policing, but the promoters and the police authority were unable to agree on the appropriate level of police manning (and consequently on the amount of reimbursement). The applicant duly sought an order of *certiorari* to quash the condition. The respondent accepted that the condition was invalid, on the basis that, as a local authority, although they were concerned with safety under the legislation, they were not concerned with questions of payment for policing and how that payment was to be secured. However, it was contended that the failure of the condition vitiated the entire licence and this contention was upheld by the Divisional Court. Mann J stated (at 492):

> a licence with this provision removed would then be a licence totally silent on policing. I regard policing as fundamental. To remove the requirement as to policing would alter the character of the document. It follows that this clause, failing as it does, brings down with it the whole of the licence.

12.12.3 Whilst a Quashing Order will be the appropriate remedy to quash a decision in instances such as those mentioned above where there has been some element of unlawfulness concerning the way in which the decision was reached, a Prohibiting Order can be sought on the same grounds as a Quashing Order to prevent some future unlawful action being taken. Whereas a Quashing Order quashes past unlawful conduct, a Prohibiting Order is concerned with prevention of any future or continued unlawful conduct by the decision-making body. There is, in addition, a Mandatory Order, which compels a court or tribunal to carry out the proper performance of its functions. This is often sought in addition to a Quashing Order, although it need not be and may be the only order sought, such as where a licensing authority wrongly declines to hear and determine a licence application because the premises in respect of which the application is made are mistakenly considered to fall outside its jurisdictional boundaries.

12.12.4 The High Court may, however, decline to grant relief on an application for judicial review if an alternative remedy is available that is more effective and convenient as regards the applicant and in the public interest. This was made clear by Glidewell J, in *R v Huntingdon District Council ex p Cowan* [1984] 1 WLR 501, where his Lordship stated (at 507):

> where there is an alternative remedy available but judicial review is sought, then in my judgment the court should always ask itself whether the remedy that is sought in the court, or the alternative remedy which is available to the applicant by way of appeal, is the most effective and convenient, in other words, which of them will prove to be the most effective and convenient in all the circumstances, not merely for the applicant, but in the public interest. In exercising discretion whether or not to grant relief, that is a major factor to be taken into account.

Accordingly, the High Court may refuse to grant relief if it considers that an appeal by case stated would have been more appropriate. This may well be the case if the facts are particularly complicated. As McNeill J stated, in *R v Crown Court at Ipswich ex p Baldwin* (1990) 72 Cr App Rep 131, 134, 'in a case such as this which bristles with factual difficulties the only convenient and proper way to get it before the Divisional Court is by case stated and not by way of application for judicial review'.

12.12.5 Relief may also be refused if the applicant has not exercised other rights of appeal open to him. In *R v Hammersmith and Fulham London Borough Council ex p Earls Court Ltd, The Times*, 15 July 1993, the High Court, whilst holding that a condition imposed on a public entertainment licence that did not enable the applicants to know with a reasonable degree of certainty what must be done to comply with it was unreasonable and invalid, declined to grant relief on the ground that the applicants had a right of appeal to a magistrates' court (and thereafter to the Crown Court), which they should have exercised before making any application for judicial review. Similarly, in *R v Peterborough Magistrates' Court ex p Dowler* [1996] 2 Cr App Rep 561, the High Court refused an application for judicial review of a defendant's conviction before magistrates for driving without due care and attention, where there was pro-cedural unfairness because of a failure to disclose to him a potentially helpful witness statement, on the ground that there was a right of appeal to the Crown Court and a complete rehearing of the case could take place there.[71]

However, the fact that such a right of appeal may exist will not necessarily preclude an application for judicial review. A later High Court, in *R v Hereford Magis-trates' Court ex p Rowlands* [1998] QB 110, held that an applicant was entitled to challenge a conviction in the magistrates' court by way of judicial review, notwith-standing the existence of a right of appeal to the Crown Court. Lord Bingham CJ, without referring to the *Earl's Court* case, stated (at 125):

> While we do not doubt that *Dowler* was correctly decided, it should not in our view be treated as authority that a party complaining of procedural unfairness or bias in the magistrates' court should be denied leave to move for judicial review and left to what-ever rights he may have in the Crown Court. So to hold would be to emasculate the long-established supervisory jurisdiction of this court over magistrates' courts, which has over the years proved an invaluable guarantee of the integrity of proceedings in those courts . . .

> Two notes of caution should however be sounded. First, leave to move should not be granted unless the applicant advances an apparently plausible complaint which, if made good, might arguably be held to vitiate the proceedings in the magistrates' court . . . Secondly, the decision whether or not to grant relief by way of judicial review is always, in the end, a discretionary one . . . We do not, however, consider that the existence of a right of appeal to the Crown Court, particularly if unexercised, should ordinarily weigh against the grant of leave to move for judicial review, or the grant of substantive relief, in a proper case.

Although these decisions concern the existence of a right of appeal to the Crown Court, they have equal application to cases where, as under the 2003 Act, the right of appeal is to the magistrates' court. Whether the case is a 'proper one' for judicial review will depend on whether or not the matter can be suitably addressed in a magistrates' court appeal hearing. As the High Court stated in *R v Leeds City Council ex p Hendry* [1994] 6 Admin LR 443, it is a question of whether 'the real issue to be determined can sensibly be determined' by the alternative procedure and, as the same court observed in *R v London Borough of Newham ex p R* [1995] ELR 156 (at 163), whether 'the alternative statutory remedy will resolve the question at issue fully and directly'.

The decision whether to grant relief on an application for judicial review in the end is always a discretionary one for the court, although the conflicting judicial approaches make it hard to predict how that discretion might be exercised in cases where other rights of appeal open to an applicant have not been exercised. As a general rule, the preferable course would seem to be to exercise, in the first instance, the right of appeal to the magistrates' court under the 2003 Act. It has been accepted, *obiter*, by the High Court in *R (JD Wetherspoon Plc) v Guildford Borough Council* [2006] LLR 312 that, in respect of the 2003 Act, 'licensing applications are primarily a matter to be dealt with at local level first by local licensing authorities and then by local magistrates' courts' (*per* Beatson J, at para 91). However, it was recognised that, where the issue raised is 'one on which there is a need for uniformity in the understanding of licensing authorities', judicial review may be an appropriate approach at the expense of a magistrates' court appeal.[72]

12.12.6 Appeal to the High Court, either by case stated or for judicial review of the magistrates' court decision, are courses of action open to an aggrieved party who feels that any complaint has not been properly addressed on a re-hearing of the case in the magistrates' court. The former is the more appropriate course where it is alleged that the magistrates' court has incorrectly interpreted the law or that there is an inadequate factual basis to support its findings, although in appeals by case stated the High Court is a final appeal court and no further appeal is thereafter possible (see 12.11.4 above). The latter is the more appropriate course where it is alleged that the magistrates' court has acted in some way improperly in reaching its decision, (see 12.12.1 above) and in judicial review appeals the High Court is not the final appeal court. Further appeals can be made to the Court of Appeal, with leave of that court, and thereafter to the House of Lords, with leave of either the Court of Appeal or the House of Lords.

## NOTES

1   See Manchester, C, 'Licensing Act 2003 Appeals' (2006) 25 *Civil Justice Quarterly* 380–403.
2   Premises licences are covered by Sched 5, paras 1–9, CPCs by paras 10–15, TENs by para 16, personal licences by para 17 and closure orders by para 18. All references to paras hereafter are to paragraphs in Sched 5, unless otherwise stated.
3   This will apply in respect of both a premises licence and (where the licensable activities include the supply of alcohol) a personal licence. It will also encompass an applicant for or holder of a CPC and a premises user who has given a TEN.
4   Paragraph 2(4) provides: 'In sub-paragraph (3) "relevant representations" has the meaning given in section 18(6).' For s 18(6), see 6.4.9 above.
5   Paragraph 3, which makes provision for appeals in respect of the issuing of provisional statements, is considered below – see 12.2.14 below.
6   Paragraph 4(4) provides: 'In sub-paragraph (3) "relevant representations" has the meaning given in section 35(5).' For s 35(5), see 6.9.4 above.
7   Paragraph 8(3) provides: 'In sub-paragraph (2) "relevant representations" has the meaning given in section 52(7).' For s 52(7), see 6.12.7 above.
8   Paragraph 8A(3) provides: 'In sub-paragraph (2) "relevant representations" has the meaning given in section 53C(7).' For s 53C(7), see 6.13.17 above.
9   Paragraph 3(3) provides: 'In sub-paragraph (2) "relevant representations" has the meaning given in subsection (5) of that section.' For s 31(5), see 6.8.7 above.
10   Paragraph 11(4) provides: 'In sub-paragraph (3) "relevant representations" has the meaning given in section 72(7).' For s 72(7), see 8.4.5 above.
11   Paragraph 12(4) provides: 'In sub-paragraph (3) "relevant representations" has the meaning given in section 85(5).' For s 85(5), see 8.9.3 above.

12 Paragraph 13(3) provides: 'In sub-paragraph (2) "relevant representations" has the meaning given in section 88(7).' For s 88(7), see 8.10.6 above.

13 Paragraph 16(8) provides: 'In this paragraph – "objection notice" has the same meaning as in section 104'. For s 104, see 9.5.1 above.

14 Paragraph 16(8) provides: 'In this paragraph – . . . "relevant licensing authority" has the meaning given in section 99.' For s 99, see 9.1.1 above.

15 Paragraph 18(7) provides: 'In this paragraph – . . . "relevant licensing authority" has the same meaning as in Part 3 of this Act.' The 'relevant licensing authority' for the purposes of Pt 3 is defined in s 12 – see 6.3.1 above.

16 Paragraph 18(7) provides: 'In this paragraph – . . . "relevant representations" has the meaning given in section 167(9).' For s 167(9), see 11.14.22 above.

17 Guidance, para 12.4. For premises licences, the cases where the licence holder will be a respondent are identified in para 9(3), which provides: 'On an appeal under paragraph 2(3), 3(2)(b), 4(3), 5(2), 6(2) or 8(2)(a) or (c), the holder of the premises licence is to be the respondent in addition to the licensing authority.' For club premises certificates, the cases where the certificate holder will be a respondent are identified in para 15(3), which provides: 'On an appeal under paragraph 11(3), 12(3) or 13(2)(a) or (c), the club that holds or held the club premises certificate is to be the respondent in addition to the licensing authority.' For interim authority notices, the only case where the person giving the notice will be a respondent is where there is an appeal by the police under para 7(3). Paragraph 9(4) provides: 'On an appeal under paragraph 7(3), the person who gave the interim authority notice is to be the respondent in addition to the licensing authority.'

18 Paragraph 17(8) provides: 'On an appeal under sub-paragraph (2), (3) or (5), the holder of the personal licence is to be the respondent in addition to the licensing authority.'

19 Paragraph 16(7) provides: 'On an appeal under sub-paragraph (3), the premises user is to be the respondent in addition to the licensing authority.'

20 Letter from Mark Du Val to Andrew Cunningham, September 23, 2005: 'Colleagues are keen to understand the Government's policy intention behind the decision to make the applicant a corespondent where those who make representations appeal but not to make the latter co-respondents if the situation is the other way round i.e. the applicant appeals.'

21 See (2006) 65 *Licensing Review* 44. The interested parties—a resident, the Dean Street Residents' Association and the Soho Society—would not accept the council's offer to appear as witnesses: 'In short, politely but clearly, they expressed in argument a distrust of Westminster City Council to advance issues they feel are relevant and if so advanced to do so in a manner they feel is most effective. They wish to be heard as parties and nothing less.'

22 'I expressed surprise during argument that the workload and listing/hearing considerations of these courts would trouble Parliament. No authority from the Explanatory Notes, Hansard or elsewhere has been produced in support of the submission . . . [which] I reject . . . as being, with all due respect, plainly wrong.'

23 The court did not find it necessary to rule on two further contentions. These were that the court should exercise its discretion under s 52 of the Magistrates' Courts Act 1980 to permit, in fairness, the interested parties to be joined as respondents and that the court should, under s 3(1) of the Human Rights Act 1998, construe Sched 5 to include interested parties so that the schedule is compatible with the Convention right in Art 6(1) to a fair hearing (see 3.5 above). For a consideration of these issues, see Hollis, D, 'Who are parties to an appeal?' (2006) 66 *Licensing Review* 16, 17–18.

24 Whilst the view might be taken that there is no 'civil right' meriting protection under Art 6, because there is no general right for residents (or responsible authorities) to have *locus standi* in all court proceedings that affect decisions being made in their area (see Hollis, D, 'Who are parties to an appeal?' (2006) 66 *Licensing Review* 16, 18), it is thought that a 'civil

right' is created in the specific instance of decisions under the 2003 Act because of express provisions enabling relevant representations to be made by interested parties and responsible authorities. If these provisions do give rise to a 'civil right', the question of whether there is a right to be heard by an 'independent' tribunal then arises.

25 Eg Redhill Magistrates Court declined to follow *Lucas* when hearing an appeal by Woldingham Golf Club and residents were not permitted to appear in their own right – see Clover, S, 'Licensing: rejection of "Candy Bar" decision – postcode lottery' (2006) 17 *Entertainment Law Review* 48.

26 Guidance, para 12.3; and see paras 9(2) (premises licences), 15(2) (CPCs), 16(5) (TENs), 17(7) (personal licences) and 18(5) (closure orders), as amended by Courts Act 2003 (Consequential Provisions) Order 2005, SI 2005/886, Art 1 and Sched, para 93, each of which provides: 'An appeal under this Part must be commenced by notice of appeal given by the appellant to the designated officer for the magistrates' court within the period of 21 days beginning with the day on which the appellant was notified by the licensing authority of the decision appealed against.' In the case of TENs, however, this is subject to para 16(6), which provides: 'But no appeal may be brought later than five working days before the day on which the event period specified in the temporary event notice begins.' Where an appeal is made out of time, there is no provision for granting an extension of time.

27 The provisions on deemed service are contained in r 6.7, but application of the Rules is governed by r 2.1, which refers only to proceedings in county courts, the High Court and Civil Division of the Court of Appeal.

28 Pt 4 of the Rules covers service of documents but extends only to service of summonses or other documents by a justice of the peace (r 4.1), proof of service in magistrates' courts (r 4.2) and service of documents in Crown Court proceedings (r 4.3).

29 Service by Royal Mail 'Special Delivery', which guarantees following day delivery, is regarded as equivalent to first-class post: *Petford v Saw* [2002] 11 CL 53.

30 See Pink, M, 'Appeals: Procedure before the Magistrates' (2005) 62 *Licensing Review* 5.

31 See LA 2003 (Hearings) Regs 2005, reg 26 (2), and 2.3.18 above. For exceptions, where determination must be made at the conclusion of the hearing, see reg 26(1).

32 (1984) unreported, 6 July, Oldham Magistrates' Court. It is understood that this view has been followed by magistrates' courts in other local authority areas.

33 The appellants were thereafter prosecuted for operating a sex establishment without a licence and sought unsuccessfully, both in the magistrates' court and on appeal in the Crown Court, to raise by way of defence the alleged invalidity of the licence refusal decision. The appellants thereafter appealed by case stated to the Divisional Court, which heard simultaneously appeals by Quietlynn involving Plymouth and Portsmouth City Councils, where the Crown Court's decision was upheld: *Quietlynn Ltd v Plymouth City Council* [1988] QB 114 (approved by the House of Lords in *Boddington v British Transport Police* [1998] 2 All ER 203). The question of whether the time for notice of appeal against a licence refusal decision ran from the date of the oral hearing or from the written notification was not, however, considered.

34 Paragraph 17(11) provides:

> In sub-paragraph (10) "the relevant time" means–
>
> (a) the time the appeal is dismissed or abandoned, or
>
> (b) where the appeal is allowed, the time the licence is renewed.

35 The interim authority period is the period within which a transfer application must be made if the licence is not to lapse again following the giving of an IAN. Under s 47(10), the period is two months from the date the IAN was received by the licensing authority (unless the period is terminated earlier by the person giving the IAN). This period applies here, for para 7(6) provides: 'In this paragraph "interim authority period" has the same meaning as in section 47.'

36  See 11.14.23 above.
37  Only conditions that are necessary to achieve the licensing objectives can be attached, so it follows that, if the existing law already places certain statutory responsibilities on an employer or operator of premises, it cannot be necessary to impose similar duties or the same duty by way of conditions (see 7.2.2 above).
38  It is thought that remission cannot be conditional, ie on terms that, if the licensing authority does not comply with the direction to it to dispose of the case, the matter can be referred back to and reconsidered by the court. Remission would seem to conclude the appeal proceedings so that the court's interest in the matter would then be closed. Where a case has been remitted, a further appeal against any decision subsequently made by the authority might be made, since there is a further determination by the licensing authority, which may well be different from that initially made, and an appeal can lie against this determination.
39  Alternatively, a pre-trial review may be held on a separate date before the actual hearing of the appeal or may be conducted by correspondence without the parties attending court.
40  The agreement may require approval of the local authority's licensing committee (or subcommittee) before the consent order is made. If the committee agrees the proposed course of action, officers can reach a nonbinding agreement with the appellant on the agreed terms and the court can then be asked to exercise its discretion to make an order on those terms.
41  Quarter sessions were general sessions of the peace, held quarterly before the whole body of justices in counties or before recorders in boroughs, and they were abolished by the Courts Act 1971, which created the Crown Court to replace quarter sessions and assizes.
42  Lord Denning MR dissented, considering (at 628) that the recorder had misdirected himself in law in taking the view that he must approach the matter afresh with a complete and unfettered discretion: 'I do not think this is correct . . . Seeing that Parliament has entrusted the discretion to the local authority, it must intend then that their views should carry great weight . . . [and] should not be pushed on one side by the courts as worth nothing'.
43  This quotation does not appear in the report and is taken from a transcript of his Lordship's judgment.
44  See 12.7.1 above, where his Lordship placed reliance on earlier observations of Lord Goddard CJ in *Drover v Rugman* [1951] 1 KB 380, 382.
45  Determination by the licensing authority does not satisfy this requirement, as the licensing authority, being part of the executive, is not an 'independent' tribunal for these purposes, but the requirement is satisfied if there is a right of appeal to a body (such as the magistrates' court in this instance) that is independent. The possibility of appeal to the High Court by way of judicial review may satisfy this requirement, depending on whether the complaint is one that can be addressed in judicial review proceedings, but the requirement is more easily met if there is a right of appeal to court which has 'full jurisdiction' to re-hear the case – see 3.5.12–3.5.13 above.
46  Rule 37.1 provides:

    (1)  On the summary trial of an information, where the accused does not plead guilty, the prosecutor shall call the evidence for the prosecution, and before doing so may address the court.
    (2)  At the conclusion of the evidence for the prosecution, the accused may address the court, whether or not he afterwards calls evidence.
    (3)  At the conclusion of the evidence, if any, for the defence, the prosecutor may call evidence to rebut that evidence.
    (4)  At the conclusion of the evidence for the defence and the evidence, if any, in rebuttal, the accused may address the court if he has not already done so.

(5) Either party may, with the leave of the court, address the court a second time, but where the court grants leave to one party it shall not refuse leave to the other.

(6) Where both parties address the court twice the prosecutor shall address the court for the second time before the accused does so.

47 Where there is a second respondent (eg a licence applicant in cases where an appeal is made by an interested party or responsible authority), such respondent may follow the licensing authority, with the appellant presenting his evidence at the end. Alternatively, the appellant may follow first, with the second respondent giving evidence last. Either option is open to the court, although it may be more logically for the former course to be adopted.

48 The position here seems analogous to a court not having sufficient information from the record of a court decision to properly consider the case before it. In *R v Knightsbridge Crown Court ex p Aspinall Curzon Ltd* [1982] *The Times* 16 December, where the Divisional Court was considering a judicial review application in respect of a gaming licence appeal decision of the Crown Court, Woolf J stated:

> In many cases, and indeed in the majority of cases, the reasoned judgment of the court will be all that it is necessary to have regard to, but where, as in this case, you have extremely short reasons, it is not possible in these sort of proceedings, which were taking place before the Crown Court, to see what the issues are just by looking at the decision of the learned Judge. At least in order to find what were the issues, in my view, it must be possible to look at an affidavit of the sort relied upon by Mr. Mathew [outlining a history of the case] albeit that it did not technically form part of the record.

49 Although s 1 of the 1995 Act abolishes the rule making hearsay evidence inadmissible in civil proceedings, this applies only in respect of hearsay as defined in the Act. The definition, in s 1(2), provides that 'hearsay' means 'a statement made otherwise than by a person while giving oral evidence in the proceedings which is tendered as evidence of the matters stated'. This may exclude hearsay which does not consist of statements made, but which comprises conduct about which a person gives evidence, eg as in *R v Kearley* [1992] 2 AC 228, where police evidence of calls by telephone and calls at the door of a person's flat inquiring about the purchase of drugs was tendered as evidence of that person being a supplier of drugs. Such evidence was held, by the House of Lords, to be inadmissible hearsay in that case and, as it would fall outside s 1(2), it would continue to be inadmissible after the 1995 Act.

50 This quotation does not appear in the report and is taken from a transcript of his Lordship's judgment.

51 The Licensing Act 1904 made provision for a reduction in the number of licensed premises, with a view to reducing levels of drunkenness, where premises were considered surplus to the needs of the neighbourhood and for the payment of compensation to licence holders on grounds of redundancy. Justices could refer cases to the compensation authority for their area, which consisted of local magistrates and councillors, and the authority could recommend to justices that renewal of licences be refused. A licensee whose licence was refused in this way was compensated by a sum equal to the difference between the value of their premises with a licence and without one. The compensation scheme, the money for which was raised by a levy on the licensees whose licences were renewed, was abolished by the Licensing (Alcohol and Educational Research) Act 1981.

52 See ss 51–53 for premises licences (and 6.12 above) and ss 87–89 for CPCs (and 8.10 above).

53 The application of the SOP may be in issue in the appeal, with one of the parties seeking to rely upon it and another seeking to justify a departure from it. Where a person is seeking to establish an exception to the policy, the burden of proof rests on that person – see *R v Crown Court at Sheffield, ex p Consterdine* (1998) 34 *Licensing Review* 19,

23 ('. . . it is for the party seeking to persuade the committee to depart from its policy to show that that can be done without imperilling it or the reasons which underlie it', *per* Turner J).

54 This is reinforced by the fact that, whilst the High Court has power to quash a policy found to be unlawful or uphold it where no substantial injustice has been caused by refusing to grant relief, no similar powers are available to magistrates' courts. The magistrates' court would be confined to considering the policy in the context of the case before it, leaving it uncertain whether the policy would continue to govern future cases, whether decisions made in reliance on the policy would continue to be valid, and what the position would be if different magistrates' courts were to come to different decisions as to the validity of the policy.

55 This continues to be the case after the Human Rights Act 1998, since the European Court of Human Rights in *Hiro Balani v Spain* (1994) 19 EHRR 565, para 27 has stated: 'Article 6(1) [of the European Convention on Human Rights] obliges the courts to give reasons for their judgments, but cannot be understood as requiring a detailed answer to every argument. The extent to which this duty to give reasons applies may vary according to the nature of the decision' – see 3.5.9 above.

56 The observations have been regarded as having application to licensing decisions of the Crown Court – see, eg *The Queen on the application of Hestview Ltd v Snaresbrook Crown Court* [2001] LLR 214, paras 55 and 76 (betting licensing). See also 6.5.4 above in respect of reasons given by licensing authorities.

57 See, also, Arden LJ in *Re T (Contact)* [2003] FLR 532, para 41: 'It would be unsatisfactory to use an omission by a judge to deal with a point in a judgment as grounds for an application for appeal if the matter has not been brought to the judge's attention when there was a ready opportunity to do so'.

58 See, eg *Powell v City and County of Swansea* [2004] LLR 145, where the High Court held that magistrates had erred in concluding that a decision made by the local authority was on grounds that appeared to be reasonably sound, when the local authority had conceded that it had wrongly applied its policy of taxis needing to be wheelchair-compliant to the appellant's application, which should have been treated as a renewal to which the policy did not apply rather than a new application to which the policy did apply. Costs were accordingly awarded against the council.

59 It is not clear whether these were attempts to resolve the matter ahead of the hearing before the licensing authority or ahead of the appeal hearing (or both). The case for awarding costs where attempts are made before the appeal hearing is stronger, since costs are being awarded in respect of the appeal and the applicant's conduct relates directly to the appeal. Where attempts are made only ahead of the hearing before the licensing authority, the applicant's conduct is less clearly connected to the appeal and the view may be taken that it is not sufficiently causally connected.

60 The court's decision was to order the licensing authority to pay £2,000 towards the applicant's costs, which represented half the costs incurred in the appeal, reflecting the fact that the appeal against the licensing authority's decision had not been successful in its entirety (the appeal was successful in that the court extended opening hours from 11.00 pm until midnight on Fridays and Saturdays, but unsuccessful in that a condition was attached that the garden be closed at 11.00 pm).

61 The requirement is for an applicant to advertise his application 'in a manner which is prescribed and likely to bring it to the attention of the interested parties likely to be affected by it' (see s 17(5)(a)(ii)) and 6.3.1 above for grants of premises licences and s 71(6)(a)(ii) and 8.3.2 above for grants of CPCs). Again, these provisions have application to variations – see respectively s 34(5) and s 84(4). Some licensing authorities have, however, as a matter of practice contacted individually interested parties living in the vicinity of the application premises to draw to their attention the application.

62 Section 111(5) of the Magistrates' Courts Act 1980.

63 Section 111(6) of the Magistrates' Courts Act 1980. The order is now called a Mandatory Order, although the reference to *mandamus* in s 111(6) remains.

64 Criminal Procedure Rules 2005, r 64.1(1). Any such application must be sent to a court officer for the magistrates' court whose decision is questioned: r 64.1(3).

65 Within 21 days after receipt of the draft case under r 64.2(1), each party may make representations thereon. Any such representations shall be in writing and signed by or on behalf of the party making them and shall be sent to the magistrates' court officer: r 64.2(2). In the event that a magistrates' court officer is unable to send to the applicant a draft case under r 64.2(1) within the 21-day period, he shall do so as soon as practicable thereafter and the provisions of that rule apply accordingly; but in that event a court officer must attach to the draft case, and to the final case when it is sent to the applicant or his legal representative under r 64.3(3), a statement of the delay and the reasons for it: r 64.4(1). An applicant or respondent can make a request, with reasons, both of which must be in writing, for an extension of time within which to make representations under r 64.2(2) and the period can be extended by the court officer: r 64.4(2).

66 A case may be stated on behalf of the justices whose decision is questioned by any two or more of them and may, if the justices so direct, be signed on their behalf by the justices' clerk: r 64.3(2). In the event that the justices cannot state a case within 21 days, they must do so as soon as practicable thereafter and the court officer must attach to the final case, when it is sent to the applicant or his legal representative under rule 64.3(3), a statement of the delay and the reasons for it: r 64.4(3).

67 If an extension of time has been granted by the court officer under r 64.4(2) of the period within which representations can be made on the draft case, he must attach a statement of the extension of time and the reasons for it: r 64.4(2).

68 *Bracegirdle v Oxley* [1947] 1 All ER 126 ('In the opinion of the court, it is impossible to say that a reasonably-minded bench of justices, having facts . . . before them, could come to a decision that no offence [of driving a vehicle at a speed dangerous to the public] had been committed', per Lord Goddard CJ at 129).

69 Section 18(1)(c) provides that no appeal should lie to the Court of Appeal 'from any order, judgment or decision of the High Court or any other court or tribunal which by virtue of any provision (however expressed) of this or any other Act is final', and s 28A(4) provides that a decision of the High Court on an appeal by way of case stated under s 111 of the Magistrates' Courts Act 1980, which is not in respect of any criminal cause or matter, is final. The appeal by case stated in the case in question was not in respect of a criminal cause or matter, being concerned with whether a special hours certificate could be granted to the holder of a justices' on-licence for part of premises for which no music and dancing licence had been granted.

70 Such a decision is usually termed '*Wednesbury* unreasonable', following the principles laid down in *Associated Provincial Picture Houses Ltd v Wednesbury Corporation* [1948] 1 KB 223 – see 3.5.13 above.

71 The court regarded the judicial review application in this case as having been made with the ulterior object of procuring such delay as would lead to the dropping of the prosecution, which may well have influenced its decision to refuse the application.

72 The court thought this to be so in the case in question, as it concerned the scope of 'cumulative impact' policies (see 4.3.7–4.3.9 above) in the light of the Secretary of State's Guidance. It accordingly held that a deliberate decision to abandon a magistrates' court appeal in favour of judicial review was not, in this instance, an abuse of process and, had the claimant succeeded, the court indicated that it would not have denied a remedy on the basis that there was an alternative avenue of appeal.

# APPENDIX CONTENTS

# APPENDIX 1: LICENSING ACT 2003

## Licensing Act 2003
## 2003 Chapter 17
## CONTENTS

## PART 5

### PERMITTED TEMPORARY ACTIVITIES

#### *Introductory*

#### *Temporary event notices*

#### *Police objections*

#### *Limits on temporary event notices*

#### *Rights of entry, production of notice, etc*

## PART 8

### CLOSURE OF PREMISES

# Licensing Act 2003
## 2003 Chapter 17

An Act to make provision about the regulation of the sale and supply of alcohol, the provision of entertainment and the provision of late night refreshment, about offences relating to alcohol and for connected purposes.                                             [10th July 2003]

BE IT ENACTED by the Queen's most Excellent Majesty, by and with the advice and consent of the Lords Spiritual and Temporal, and Commons, in this present Parliament assembled, and by the authority of the same, as follows:–

## PART 1

### LICENSABLE ACTIVITIES

**1      Licensable activities and qualifying club activities**

(1)    For the purposes of this Act the following are licensable activities–

    (a)    the sale by retail of alcohol,

    (b)    the supply of alcohol by or on behalf of a club to, or to the order of, a member of the club,

    (c)    the provision of regulated entertainment, and

    (d)    the provision of late night refreshment.

(2)    For those purposes the following licensable activities are also qualifying club activities–

    (a)    the supply of alcohol by or on behalf of a club to, or to the order of, a member of the club,

    (b)    the sale by retail of alcohol by or on behalf of a club to a guest of a member of the club for consumption on the premises where the sale takes place, and

    (c)    the provision of regulated entertainment where that provision is by or on behalf of a club for members of the club or members of the club and their guests.

(3)    In this Act references to the supply of alcohol by or on behalf of a club to, or to the order of, a member of the club do not include a reference to any supply which is a sale by retail of alcohol.

(4)    Schedule 1 makes provision about what constitutes the provision of regulated entertainment for the purposes of this Act.

(5)    Schedule 2 makes provision about what constitutes the provision of late night refreshment for those purposes (including provision that certain activities carried on in relation to certain clubs or hotels etc, or certain employees, do not constitute provision of late night refreshment and are, accordingly, not licensable activities).

(6)    For the purposes of this Act premises are "used" for a licensable activity if that activity is carried on or from the premises.

(7)    This section is subject to sections 173 to 175 (which exclude activities from the definition of licensable activity in certain circumstances).

**2      Authorisation for licensable activities and qualifying club activities**

(1)    A licensable activity may be carried on–

    (a)    under and in accordance with a premises licence (see Part 3), or

    (b)    in circumstances where the activity is a permitted temporary activity by virtue of Part 5.

(2)    A qualifying club activity may be carried on under and in accordance with a club premises certificate (see Part 4).

(3)    Nothing in this Act prevents two or more authorisations having effect concurrently in respect of the whole or a part of the same premises or in respect of the same person.

(4)    For the purposes of subsection (3) "authorisation" means–

    (a)    a premises licence;

    (b)    a club premises certificate;

    (c)    a temporary event notice.

PART 2

LICENSING AUTHORITIES

*The authorities*

**3      Licensing authorities**

(1)      In this Act "licensing authority" means–

    (a)   the council of a district in England,

    (b)   the council of a county in England in which there are no district councils,

    (c)   the council of a county or county borough in Wales,

    (d)   the council of a London borough,

    (e)   the Common Council of the City of London,

    (f)   the Sub-Treasurer of the Inner Temple,

    (g)   the Under-Treasurer of the Middle Temple, or

    (h)   the Council of the Isles of Scilly.

(2)      For the purposes of this Act, a licensing authority's area is the area for which the authority acts.

*Functions of licensing authorities etc*

**4      General duties of licensing authorities**

(1)      A licensing authority must carry out its functions under this Act ("licensing functions") with a view to promoting the licensing objectives.

(2)      The licensing objectives are–

    (a)   the prevention of crime and disorder;

    (b)   public safety;

    (c)   the prevention of public nuisance; and

    (d)   the protection of children from harm.

(3)      In carrying out its licensing functions, a licensing authority must also have regard to–

    (a)   its licensing statement published under section 5, and

    (b)   any guidance issued by the Secretary of State under section 182

**5      Statement of licensing policy**

(1)      Each licensing authority must in respect of each three year period–

    (a)   determine its policy with respect to the exercise of its licensing functions, and

    (b)   publish a statement of that policy (a "licensing statement") before the beginning of the period.

(2)      In this section "three year period" means–

    (a)   the period of three years beginning with such day as the Secretary of State may by order appoint, and

    (b)   each subsequent period of three years.

(3)      Before determining its policy for a three year period, a licensing authority must consult–

    (a)   the chief officer of police for the licensing authority's area,

    (b)   the fire and rescue authority for that area,

    (c)   such persons as the licensing authority considers to be representative of holders of premises licences issued by that authority,

    (d)   such persons as the licensing authority considers to be representative of holders of club premises certificates issued by that authority,

    (e)   such persons as the licensing authority considers to be representative of holders of personal licences issued by that authority, and

    (f)   such other persons as the licensing authority considers to be representative of businesses and residents in its area.

(4)      During each three year period, a licensing authority must keep its policy under review and make such revisions to it, at such times, as it considers appropriate.

(5)    Subsection (3) applies in relation to any revision of an authority's policy as it applies in relation to the original determination of that policy.

(6)    Where revisions are made, the licensing authority must publish a statement of the revisions or the revised licensing statement.

(7)    Regulations may make provision about the determination and revision of policies, and the preparation and publication of licensing statements, under this section.

**6    Licensing committees**

(1)    Each licensing authority must establish a licensing committee consisting of at least ten, but not more than fifteen, members of the authority.

(2)    This section does not apply in relation to the Sub-Treasurer of the Inner Temple or the Under-Treasurer of the Middle Temple.

**7    Exercise and delegation of functions**

(1)    All matters relating to the discharge by a licensing authority of its licensing functions are, by virtue of this subsection, referred to its licensing committee and, accordingly, that committee must discharge those functions on behalf of the authority.

(2)    Subsection (1) does not apply to–

(a)    any function conferred on the licensing authority by section 5 (statement of licensing policy), or

(b)    any function discharged under subsection (5)(a) below by a committee (other than a licensing committee), or any matter relating to the discharge of any such function.

(3)    A licensing authority may arrange for the discharge by its licensing committee of any function of the authority which–

(a)    relates to a matter referred to that committee by virtue of subsection (1), but

(b)    is not a licensing function.

(4)    Where the licensing authority does not make arrangements under subsection (3) in respect of any such function, it must (unless the matter is urgent) consider a report of its licensing committee with respect to the matter before discharging the function.

(5)    Where a matter relates to a licensing function of a licensing authority and to a function of the authority which is not a licensing function ("the other function"), the authority may–

(a)    refer the matter to another of its committees and arrange for the discharge of the licensing function by that committee, or

(b)    refer the matter to its licensing committee (to the extent it is not already so referred under subsection (1)) and arrange for the discharge of the other function by the licensing committee.

(6)    In a case where an authority exercises its power under subsection (5)(a), the committee to which the matter is referred must (unless the matter is urgent) consider a report of the authority's licensing committee with respect to the matter before discharging the function concerned.

(7)    Before exercising its power under subsection (5)(b), an authority must consult its licensing committee.

(8)    In a case where an authority exercises its power under subsection (5)(b), its licensing committee must (unless the matter is urgent) consider any report of any of the authority's other committees with respect to the matter before discharging the function concerned.

(9)    Where a licensing committee is unable to discharge any function delegated to it in accordance with this section because of the number of its members who are unable to take part in the consideration or discussion of any matter or vote on any question with respect to it, the committee must refer the matter back to the licensing authority and the authority must discharge that function.

(10)    This section does not apply in relation to the Sub-Treasurer of the Inner Temple or the Under-Treasurer of the Middle Temple.

**8          Requirement to keep a register**

(1)    Each licensing authority must keep a register containing–

    (a)    a record of each premises licence, club premises certificate and personal licence issued by it,

    (b)    a record of each temporary event notice received by it,

    (c)    the matters mentioned in Schedule 3, and

    (d)    such other information as may be prescribed.

(2)    Regulations may require a register kept under this section to be in a prescribed form and kept in a prescribed manner.

(3)    Each licensing authority must provide facilities for making the information contained in the entries in its register available for inspection (in a legible form) by any person during office hours and without payment.

(4)    If requested to do so by any person, a licensing authority must supply him with a copy of the information contained in any entry in its register in legible form.

(5)    A licensing authority may charge such reasonable fee as it may determine in respect of any copy supplied under subsection (4).

(6)    The Secretary of State may arrange for the duties conferred on licensing authorities by this section to be discharged by means of one or more central registers kept by a person appointed pursuant to the arrangements.

(7)    The Secretary of State may require licensing authorities to participate in and contribute towards the cost of any arrangements made under subsection (6).

*Licensing committees*

**9          Proceedings of licensing committee**

(1)    A licensing committee may establish one or more subcommittees consisting of three members of the committee.

(2)    Regulations may make provision about–

    (a)    the proceedings of licensing committees and their subcommittees (including provision about the validity of proceedings and the quorum for meetings),

    (b)    public access to the meetings of those committees and subcommittees,

    (c)    the publicity to be given to those meetings,

    (d)    the agendas and records to be produced in respect of those meetings, and

    (e)    public access to such agendas and records and other information about those meetings.

(3)    Subject to any such regulations, each licensing committee may regulate its own procedure and that of its sub-committees.

**10         Sub-delegation of functions by licensing committee etc**

(1)    A licensing committee may arrange for the discharge of any functions exercisable by it–

    (a)    by a sub-committee established by it, or

    (b)    subject to subsection (4), by an officer of the licensing authority.

(2)    Where arrangements are made under subsection (1)(a), then, subject to subsections (4) and (5), the sub-committee may in turn arrange for the discharge of the function concerned by an officer of the licensing authority.

(3)    Arrangements under subsection (1) or (2) may provide for more than one sub-committee or officer to discharge the same function concurrently.

(4)    Arrangements may not be made under subsection (1) or (2) for the discharge by an officer of–

    (a)    any function under–

        (i)    section 18(3) (determination of application for premises licence where representations have been made),

        (ii)   section 31(3) (determination of application for provisional statement where representations have been made),

(iii) section 35(3) (determination of application for variation of premises licence where representations have been made),

(iv) section 39(3) (determination of application to vary designated premises supervisor following police objection),

(v) section 44(5) (determination of application for transfer of premises licence following police objection),

(vi) section 48(3) (consideration of police objection made to interim authority notice),

(via) section 53A(2)(a) or 53B (determination of interim steps pending summary review),

(vii) section 72(3) (determination of application for club premises certificate where representations have been made),

(viii) section 85(3)(determination of application to vary club premises certificate where representations have been made),

(ix) section 105(2) (decision to give counter notice following police objection to temporary event notice),

(x) section 120(7) (determination of application for grant of personal licence following police objection),

(xi) section 121(6) (determination of application for renewal of personal licence following police objection), or

(xii) section 124(4) (revocation of licence where convictions come to light after grant etc),

(b) any function under section 52(2) or (3) (determination of application for review of premises licence) in a case where relevant representations (within the meaning of section 52(7)) have been made,

(ba) any function under section 53C (review following review notice), in a case where relevant representations within the meaning of section 53C(7) have been made,

(c) any function under section 88(2) or (3) (determination of application for review of club premises certificate) in a case where relevant representations (within the meaning of section 88(7)) have been made, or

(d) any function under section 167(5) (review following closure order), in a case where relevant representations (within the meaning of section 167(9)) have been made.

(5) The power exercisable under subsection (2) by a subcommittee established by a licensing committee is also subject to any direction given by that committee to the sub-committee.

PART 3

PREMISES LICENCES

*Introductory*

**11  Premises licence**

In this Act "premises licence" means a licence granted under this Part, in respect of any premises, which authorises the premises to be used for one or more licensable activities.

**12  The relevant licensing authority**

(1) For the purposes of this Part the "relevant licensing authority" in relation to any premises is determined in accordance with this section.

(2) Subject to subsection (3), the relevant licensing authority is the authority in whose area the premises are situated.

(3) Where the premises are situated in the areas of two or more licensing authorities, the relevant licensing authority is–

(a) the licensing authority in whose area the greater or greatest part of the premises is situated, or

(b) if there is no authority to which paragraph (a) applies, such one of those authorities as is nominated in accordance with subsection (4).

(4)    In a case within subsection (3)(b)–

   (a)   an applicant for a premises licence must nominate one of the licensing authorities as the relevant licensing authority in relation to the application and any licence granted as a result of it, and

   (b)   an applicant for a statement under section 29 (provisional statement) in respect of the premises must nominate one of the licensing authorities as the relevant licensing authority in relation to the statement.

**13     Authorised persons, interested parties and responsible authorities**

(1)    In this Part in relation to any premises each of the following expressions has the meaning given to it by this section–

"authorised person",

"interested party",

"responsible authority".

(2)    "Authorised person" means any of the following–

   (a)   an officer of a licensing authority in whose area the premises are situated who is authorised by that authority for the purposes of this Act,

   (b)   an inspector appointed by the fire and rescue authority for the area in which the premises are situated,

   (c)   an inspector appointed under section 19 of the Health and Safety at Work etc. Act 1974 (c.37),

   (d)   an officer of a local authority, in whose area the premises are situated, who is authorised by that authority for the purposes of exercising one or more of its statutory functions in relation to minimising or preventing the risk of pollution of the environment or of harm to human health,

   (e)   in relation to a vessel, an inspector, or a surveyor of ships, appointed under section 256 of the Merchant Shipping Act 1995 (c.21),

   (f)   a person prescribed for the purposes of this subsection.

(3)    "Interested party" means any of the following–

   (a)   a person living in the vicinity of the premises,

   (b)   a body representing persons who live in that vicinity,

   (c)   a person involved in a business in that vicinity,

   (d)   a body representing persons involved in such businesses.

(4)    "Responsible authority" means any of the following–

   (a)   the chief officer of police for any police area in which the premises are situated,

   (b)   the fire authority and rescue authority for any area in which the premises are situated,

   (c)   the enforcing authority within the meaning given by section 18 of the Health and Safety at Work etc. Act 1974 for any area in which the premises are situated,

   (d)   the local planning authority within the meaning given by the Town and Country Planning Act 1990 (c.8) for any area in which the premises are situated,

   (e)   the local authority by which statutory functions are exercisable in any area in which the premises are situated in relation to minimising or preventing the risk of pollution of the environment or of harm to human health,

   (f)   a body which–

      (i)   represents those who, in relation to any such area, are responsible for, or interested in, matters relating to the protection of children from harm, and

      (ii)  is recognised by the licensing authority for that area for the purposes of this section as being competent to advise it on such matters,

   (g)   any licensing authority (other than the relevant licensing authority) in whose area part of the premises is situated,

   (h)   in relation to a vessel–

App 1

    (i)    a navigation authority (within the meaning of section 221(1) of the Water Resources Act 1991 (c.57) having functions in relation to the waters where the vessel is usually moored or berthed or any waters where it is, or is proposed to be, navigated at a time when it is used for licensable activities,

    (ii)   the Environment Agency,

    (iii)  the British Waterways Board, or

    (iv)  the Secretary of State,

  (i)    a person prescribed for the purposes of this subsection.

(5)    For the purposes of this section, "statutory function" means a function conferred by or under any enactment.

**14**    **Meaning of "supply of alcohol"**

For the purposes of this Part the "supply of alcohol" means–

  (a)    the sale by retail of alcohol, or

  (b)    the supply of alcohol by or on behalf of a club to, or to the order of, a member of the club.

**15**    **Meaning of "designated premises supervisor"**

(1)    In this Act references to the "designated premises supervisor", in relation to a premises licence, are to the individual for the time being specified in that licence as the premises supervisor.

(2)    Nothing in this Act prevents an individual who holds a premises licence from also being specified in the licence as the premises supervisor.

*Grant of premises licence*

**16**    **Applicant for premises licence**

(1)    The following persons may apply for a premises licence–

  (a)    a person who carries on, or proposes to carry on, a business which involves the use of the premises for the licensable activities to which the application relates,

  (b)    a person who makes the application pursuant to–

    (i)    any statutory function discharged by that person which relates to those licensable activities, or

    (ii)   any function discharged by that person by virtue of Her Majesty's prerogative,

  (c)    a recognised club,

  (d)    a charity,

  (e)    the proprietor of an educational institution,

  (f)    a health service body,

  (g)    a person who is registered under Part 2 of the Care Standards Act 2000 (c.14) in respect of an independent hospital,

  (h)    the chief officer of police of a police force in England and Wales,

  (i)    a person of such other description as may be prescribed.

(2)    But an individual may not apply for a premises licence unless he is aged 18 or over.

(3)    In this section–

"charity" has the same meaning as in section 96(1) of the Charities Act 1993 (c.10);

"educational institution" means–

  (a)    a school, or an institution within the further or higher education sector, within the meaning of section 4 of the Education Act 1996 (c.56), or

  (b)    a college (including any institution in the nature of a college), school, hall or other institution of a university, in circumstances where the university receives financial support under section 65 of the Further and Higher Education Act 1992 (c.13);

"health service body" means–

  (a)    an NHS trust established by virtue of section 25 of the National Health Service Act 2006 or section 18 of the National Health Service (Wales) Act 2006,

(b)   a Primary Care Trust established by virtue of section 18 of the National Health Service Act 2006, or

(c)   a Local Health Board established by virtue of section 11 of the National Health Service (Wales) Act 2006;

"independent hospital" has the same meaning as in section 2 (2) of the Care Standards Act 2000 (c.14);

"proprietor"–

(a)   in relation to a school within the meaning of section 4 of the Education Act 1996, has the same meaning as in section 579(1) of that Act, and

(b)   in relation to an educational institution other than such a school, means the governing body of that institution within the meaning of section 90(1) of the Further and Higher Education Act 1992; and

"statutory function" means a function conferred by or under any enactment.

**17     Application for premises licence**

(1)   An application for a premises licence must be made to the relevant licensing authority.

(2)   Subsection (1) is subject to regulations under–

(a)   section 54 (form etc. of applications etc.);

(b)   section 55 (fees to accompany applications etc.).

(3)   An application under this section must also be accompanied–

(a)   by an operating schedule,

(b)   by a plan of the premises to which the application relates, in the prescribed form, and

(c)   if the licensable activities to which the application relates ("the relevant licensable activities") include the supply of alcohol, by a form of consent in the prescribed form given by the individual whom the applicant wishes to have specified in the premises licence as the premises supervisor.

(4)   An "operating schedule" is a document which is in the prescribed form and includes a statement of the following matters–

(a)   the relevant licensable activities,

(b)   the times during which it is proposed that the relevant licensable activities are to take place,

(c)   any other times during which it is proposed that the premises are to be open to the public,

(d)   where the applicant wishes the licence to have effect for a limited period, that period,

(e)   where the relevant licensable activities include the supply of alcohol, prescribed information in respect of the individual whom the applicant wishes to have specified in the premises licence as the premises supervisor,

(f)   where the relevant licensable activities include the supply of alcohol, whether the supplies are proposed to be for consumption on the premises or off the premises, or both,

(g)   the steps which it is proposed to take to promote the licensing objectives,

(h)   such other matters as may be prescribed.

(5)   The Secretary of State must by regulations–

(a)   require an applicant to advertise his application within the prescribed period–

(i)   in the prescribed form, and

(ii)   in a manner which is prescribed and is likely to bring the application to the attention of the interested parties likely to be affected by it;

(b)   require an applicant to give notice of his application to each responsible authority, and such other persons as may be prescribed, within the prescribed period;

(c)   prescribe the period during which interested parties and responsible authorities may make representations to the relevant licensing authority about the application.

**18      Determination of application for premises licence**

(1)    This section applies where the relevant licensing authority–

    (a)    receives an application for a premises licence made in accordance with section 17, and

    (b)    is satisfied that the applicant has complied with any requirement imposed on him under subsection (5) of that section.

(2)    Subject to subsection (3), the authority must grant the licence in accordance with the application subject only to–

    (a)    such conditions as are consistent with the operating schedule accompanying the application, and

    (b)    any conditions which must under sections 19, 20 or 21 be included in the licence.

(3)    Where relevant representations are made, the authority must–

    (a)    hold a hearing to consider them, unless the authority, the applicant and each person who has made such representations agree that a hearing is unnecessary, and

    (b)    having regard to the representations, take such of the steps mentioned in sub-section (4) (if any) as it considers necessary for the promotion of the licensing objectives.

(4)    The steps are–

    (a)    to grant the licence subject to–

        (i)    the conditions mentioned in subsection (2)(a) modified to such extent as the authority considers necessary for the promotion of the licensing objectives, and

        (ii)    any condition which must under section 19, 20 or 21 be included in the licence;

    (b)    to exclude from the scope of the licence any of the licensable activities to which the application relates;

    (c)    to refuse to specify a person in the licence as the premises supervisor;

    (d)    to reject the application.

(5)    For the purposes of subsection (4)(a)(i) the conditions mentioned in subsection (2)(a) are modified if any of them is altered or omitted or any new condition is added.

(6)    For the purposes of this section, "relevant representations" means representations which–

    (a)    are about the likely effect of the grant of the premises licence on the promotion of the licensing objectives,

    (b)    meet the requirements of subsection (7),

    (c)    if they relate to the identity of the person named in the application as the proposed premises supervisor, meet the requirements of subsection (9), and

    (d)    are not excluded representations by virtue of section 32 (restriction on making representations following issue of provisional statement).

(7)    The requirements of this subsection are–

    (a)    that the representations were made by an interested party or responsible authority within the period prescribed under section 17(5)(c),

    (b)    that they have not been withdrawn, and

    (c)    in the case of representations made by an interested party (who is not also a responsible authority), that they are not, in the opinion of the relevant licensing authority, frivolous or vexatious.

(8)    Where the authority determines for the purposes of subsection (7)(c) that any repre-sentations are frivolous or vexatious, it must notify the person who made them of the reasons for its determination.

(9)    The requirements of this subsection are that the representations–

    (a)    were made by a chief officer of police for a police area in which the premises are situated, and

    (b)   include a statement that, due to the exceptional circumstances of the case, he is satisfied that the designation of the person concerned as the premises supervisor under the premises licence would undermine the crime prevention objective.

(10)  In discharging its duty under subsection (2) or (3)(b), a licensing authority may grant a licence under this section subject to different conditions in respect of–

    (a)   different parts of the premises concerned;

    (b)   different licensable activities.

**19     Mandatory conditions where licence authorises supply of alcohol**

(1)   Where a premises licence authorises the supply of alcohol, the licence must include the following conditions.

(2)   The first condition is that no supply of alcohol may be made under the premises licence–

    (a)   at a time when there is no designated premises supervisor in respect of the premises licence, or

    (b)   at a time when the designated premises supervisor does not hold a personal licence or his personal licence is suspended.

(3)   The second condition is that every supply of alcohol under the premises licence must be made or authorised by a person who holds a personal licence.

**20     Mandatory condition: exhibition of films**

(1)   Where a premises licence authorises the exhibition of films, the licence must include a condition requiring the admission of children to the exhibition of any film to be restricted in accordance with this section.

(2)   Where the film classification body is specified in the licence, unless subsection (3)(b) applies, admission of children must be restricted in accordance with any recommendation made by that body.

(3)   Where–

    (a)   the film classification body is not specified in the licence, or

    (b)   the relevant licensing authority has notified the holder of the licence that this subsection applies to the film in question,

admission of children must be restricted in accordance with any recommendation made by that licensing authority.

(4)   In this section–

"children" means persons aged under 18; and

"film classification body" means the person or persons designated as the authority under section 4 of the Video Recordings Act 1984 (c.39) (authority to determine suitability of video works for classification).

**21     Mandatory condition: door supervision**

(1)   Where a premises licence includes a condition that at specified times one or more individuals must be at the premises to carry out a security activity, the licence must include a condition that each such individual must

    (a)   be authorised to carry out that activity by a licence granted under the Private Security Industry Act 2001; or

    (b)   be entitled to carry out that activity by virtue of section 4 of that Act.

(2)   But nothing in subsection (1) requires such a condition to be imposed–

    (a)   in respect of premises within paragraph 8(3)(a) of Schedule 2 to the Private Security Industry Act 2001 (c.12) (premises with premises licences authorising plays or films), or

    (b)   in respect of premises in relation to–

        (i)   any occasion mentioned in paragraph 8(3)(b) or (c) of that Schedule (premises being used exclusively by club with club premises certificate, under a temporary event notice authorising plays or films or under a gaming licence), or

        (ii)  any occasion within paragraph 8(3)(d) of that Schedule (occasions prescribed by regulations under that Act).

App 1

(3) For the purposes of this section–
  (a) "security activity" means an activity to which paragraph 2 (1)(a) of that Schedule applies and which is licensable conduct for the purposes of that Act (see section 3(2) of that Act) and
  (b) paragraph 8(5) of that Schedule (interpretation of references to an occasion) applies as it applies in relation to paragraph 8 of that Schedule.

## 22 Prohibited conditions: plays

(1) In relation to a premises licence which authorises the performance of plays, no condition may be attached to the licence as to the nature of the plays which may be performed, or the manner of performing plays, under the licence.

(2) But subsection (1) does not prevent a licensing authority imposing, in accordance with section 18(2)(a) or (3)(b), 35(3)(b) or 52(3), any condition which it considers necessary on the grounds of public safety.

## 23 Grant or rejection of application

(1) Where an application is granted under section 18, the relevant licensing authority must forthwith–
  (a) give a notice to that effect to–
    (i) the applicant,
    (ii) any person who made relevant representations in respect of the application, and
    (iii) the chief officer of police for the police area (or each police area) in which the premises are situated, and
  (b) issue the applicant with the licence and a summary of it.

(2) Where relevant representations were made in respect of the application, the notice under subsection (1)(a) must state the authority's reasons for its decision as to the steps (if any) to take under section 18(3)(b).

(3) Where an application is rejected under section 18, the relevant licensing authority must forthwith give a notice to that effect, stating its reasons for the decision, to–
  (a) the applicant,
  (b) any person who made relevant representations in respect of the application, and
  (c) the chief officer of police for the police area (or each police area) in which the premises are situated.

(4) In this section "relevant representations" has the meaning given in section 18(6).

## 24 Form of licence and summary

(1) A premises licence and the summary of a premises licence must be in the prescribed form.

(2) Regulations under subsection (1) must, in particular, provide for the licence to–
  (a) specify the name and address of the holder;
  (b) include a plan of the premises to which the licence relates;
  (c) if the licence has effect for a limited period, specify that period;
  (d) specify the licensable activities for which the premises may be used;
  (e) if the licensable activities include the supply of alcohol, specify the name and address of the individual (if any) who is the premises supervisor in respect of the licence;
  (f) specify the conditions subject to which the licence has effect.

## 25 Theft, loss, etc. of premises licence or summary

(1) Where a premises licence or summary is lost, stolen, damaged or destroyed, the holder of the licence may apply to the relevant licensing authority for a copy of the licence or summary.

(2) Subsection (1) is subject to regulations under section 55(1) (fee to accompany applications).

(3)    Where an application is made in accordance with this section, the relevant licensing authority must issue the holder of the licence with a copy of the licence or summary (certified by the authority to be a true copy) if it is satisfied that–

     (a)    the licence or summary has been lost, stolen, damaged or destroyed, and

     (b)    where it has been lost or stolen, the holder has reported that loss or theft to the police.

(4)    The copy issued under this section must be a copy of the premises licence or summary in the form in which it existed immediately before it was lost, stolen, damaged or destroyed.

(5)    This Act applies in relation to a copy issued under this section as it applies in relation to an original licence or summary.

*Duration of licence*

**26      Period of validity of premises licence**

(1)    Subject to sections 27 and 28, a premises licence has effect until such time as–

     (a)    it is revoked under section 52, or

     (b)    if it specifies that it has effect for a limited period, that period expires.

(2)    But a premises licence does not have effect during any period when it is suspended under section 52.

**27      Death, incapacity, insolvency etc. of licence holder**

(1)    A premises licence lapses if the holder of the licence–

     (a)    dies,

     (b)    becomes a person who lacks capacity (within the meaning of the Mental Capacity Act 2005) to hold the licence,

     (c)    becomes insolvent,

     (d)    is dissolved, or

     (e)    if it is a club, ceases to be a recognised club.

(2)    This section is subject to sections 47 and 50 (which make provision for the reinstatement of the licence in certain circumstances).

(3)    For the purposes of this section, an individual becomes insolvent on–

     (a)    the approval of a voluntary arrangement proposed by him,

     (b)    being adjudged bankrupt or having his estate sequestrated, or

     (c)    entering into a deed of arrangement made for the benefit of his creditors or a trust deed for his creditors.

(4)    For the purposes of this section, a company becomes insolvent on–

     (a)    the approval of a voluntary arrangement proposed by its directors,

     (b)    the appointment of an administrator in respect of the company,

     (c)    the appointment of an administrative receiver in respect of the company, or

     (d)    going into liquidation.

(5)    An expression used in this section and in the Insolvency Act 1986 (c.45) has the same meaning in this section as in that Act.

**28      Surrender of premises licence**

(1)    Where the holder of a premises licence wishes to surrender his licence he may give the relevant licensing authority a notice to that effect.

(2)    The notice must be accompanied by the premises licence or, if that is not practicable, by a statement of the reasons for the failure to provide the licence.

(3)    Where a notice of surrender is given in accordance with this section, the premises licence lapses on receipt of the notice by the authority.

(4)    This section is subject to section 50 (which makes provision for the reinstatement in certain circumstances of a licence surrendered under this section).

*Provisional statement*

**29    Application for a provisional statement where premises being built, etc.**

(1)    This section applies to premises which–

(a)    are being or are about to be constructed for the purpose of being used for one or more licensable activities, or

(b)    are being or are about to be extended or otherwise altered for that purpose (whether or not they are already being used for that purpose).

(2)    A person may apply to the relevant licensing authority for a provisional statement if–

(a)    he is interested in the premises, and

(b)    where he is an individual, he is aged 18 or over.

(3)    In this Act "provisional statement" means a statement issued under section 31(2) or (3)(c).

(4)    Subsection (2) is subject to regulations under–

(a)    section 54 (form etc. of applications etc.);

(b)    section 55 (fees to accompany applications etc.).

(5)    An application under this section must also be accompanied by a schedule of works.

(6)    A schedule of works is a document in the prescribed form which includes–

(a)    a statement made by or on behalf of the applicant including particulars of the premises to which the application relates and of the licensable activities for which the premises are to be used,

(b)    plans of the work being or about to be done at the premises, and

(c)    such other information as may be prescribed.

(7)    For the purposes of this Part, in relation to any premises in respect of which an application for a provisional statement has been made, references to the work being satisfactorily completed are to work at the premises being completed in a manner which substantially complies with the schedule of works accompanying the application.

**30    Advertisement of application for provisional statement**

(1)    This section applies where an application is made under section 29.

(2)    The duty to make regulations imposed on the Secretary of State by section 17(5) (advertisement etc. of application) applies in relation to an application under section 29 as it applies in relation to an application under section 17.

(3)    Regulations made under section 17(5)(a) by virtue of subsection (2) may, in particular, require advertisements to contain a statement in the prescribed form describing the effect of section 32 (restriction on representations following issue of a provisional statement).

**31    Determination of application for provisional statement**

(1)    This section applies where the relevant licensing authority–

(a)    receives a provisional statement application, and

(b)    is satisfied that the applicant has complied with any requirement imposed on him by virtue of section 30.

(2)    Where no relevant representations are made, the authority must issue the applicant with a statement to that effect.

(3)    Where relevant representations are made, the authority must–

(a)    hold a hearing to consider them, unless the authority, the applicant and each person who has made such representations agree that a hearing is unnecessary,

(b)    determine whether, on the basis of those representations and the provisional statement application, it would consider it necessary to take any steps under section 18(3)(b) if, on the work being satisfactorily completed, it had to decide whether to grant a premises licence in the form described in the provisional statement application, and

(c)    issue the applicant with a statement which–

(i)    gives details of that determination, and

(ii)   states the authority's reasons for its decision as to the steps (if any) that it would be necessary to take under section 18(3)(b).

(4)   The licensing authority must give a copy of the provisional statement to–

(a)   each person who made relevant representations, and

(b)   the chief officer of police for each police area in which the premises are situated.

(5)   In this section "relevant representations" means representations–

(a)   which are about the likely effect on the licensing objectives of the grant of a premises licence in the form described in the provisional statement application, if the work at the premises was satisfactorily completed, and

(b)   which meet the requirements of subsection (6).

(6)   The requirements are–

(a)   that the representations are made by an interested party or responsible authority within the period prescribed under section 17(5)(c) by virtue of section 30,

(b)   that the representations have not been withdrawn, and

(c)   in the case of representations made by an interested party (who is not also a responsible authority), that they are not, in the opinion of the relevant licensing authority, frivolous or vexatious.

(7)   Where the authority determines for the purposes of subsection (6)(c) that any representations are frivolous or vexatious, it must notify the person who made them of the reasons for its determination.

(8)   In this section "provisional statement application" means an application made in accordance with section 29.

**32      Restriction on representations following provisional statement**

(1)   This section applies where a provisional statement has been issued in respect of any premises ("the relevant premises") and a person subsequently applies for a premises licence in respect of–

(a)   the relevant premises or a part of them, or

(b)   premises that are substantially the same as the relevant premises or a part of them.

(2)   Where–

(a)   the application for the premises licence is an application for a licence in the same form as the licence described in the application for the provisional statement, and

(b)   the work described in the schedule of works accompanying the application for that statement has been satisfactorily completed,

representations made by a person ("the relevant person") in respect of the application for the premises licence are excluded representations for the purposes of section 18(6)(d) if subsection (3) applies.

(3)   This subsection applies if–

(a)   given the information provided in the application for the provisional statement, the relevant person could have made the same, or substantially the same, representations about that application but failed to do so, without reasonable excuse, and

(b)   there has been no material change in circumstances relating either to the relevant premises or to the area in the vicinity of those premises since the provisional statement was made.

*Duty to notify certain changes*

**33      Notification of change of name or address**

(1)   The holder of a premises licence must, as soon as is reasonably practicable, notify the relevant licensing authority of any change in–

(a)   his name or address,

(b)   unless the designated premises supervisor has already notified the authority under subsection (4), the name or address of that supervisor.

(2)   Subsection (1) is subject to regulations under section 55(1) (fee to accompany application).

(3)   A notice under subsection (1) must also be accompanied by the premises licence (or the appropriate part of the licence) or, if that is not practicable, by a statement of the reasons for the failure to produce the licence (or part).

(4)   Where the designated premises supervisor under a premises licence is not the holder of the licence, he may notify the relevant licensing authority under this subsection of any change in his name or address.

(5)   Where the designated premises supervisor gives a notice under subsection (4), he must, as soon as is reasonably practicable, give the holder of the premises licence a copy of that notice.

(6)   A person commits an offence if he fails, without reasonable excuse, to comply with this section.

(7)   A person guilty of an offence under subsection (6) is liable on summary conviction to a fine not exceeding level 2 on the standard scale.

*Variation of licences*

**34    Application to vary premises licence**

(1)   The holder of a premises licence may apply to the relevant licensing authority for variation of the licence.

(2)   Subsection (1) is subject to regulations under–

   (a)   section 54 (form etc. of applications etc.);

   (b)   section 55 (fees to accompany applications etc.).

(3)   An application under this section must also be accompanied by the premises licence (or the appropriate part of that licence) or, if that is not practicable, by a statement of the reasons for the failure to provide the licence (or part).

(4)   This section does not apply to an application within section 37 (1) (application to vary licence to specify individual as premises supervisor).

(5)   The duty to make regulations imposed on the Secretary of State by subsection (5) of section 17 (advertisement etc. of application) applies in relation to applications under this section as it applies in relation to applications under that section.

**35    Determination of application under section 34**

(1)   This section applies where the relevant licensing authority–

   (a)   receives an application, made in accordance with section 34, to vary a premises licence, and

   (b)   is satisfied that the applicant has complied with any requirement imposed on him by virtue of subsection (5) of that section.

(2)   Subject to subsection (3) and section 36(6), the authority must grant the application.

(3)   Where relevant representations are made, the authority must–

   (a)   hold a hearing to consider them, unless the authority, the applicant and each person who has made such representations agree that a hearing is unnecessary, and

   (b)   having regard to the representations, take such of the steps mentioned in sub-section (4) (if any) as it considers necessary for the promotion of the licensing objectives.

(4)   The steps are–

   (a)   to modify the conditions of the licence;

   (b)   to reject the whole or part of the application; and for this purpose the conditions of the licence are modified if any of them is altered or omitted or any new condition is added.

(5)   In this section "relevant representations" means representations which–

   (a)   are about the likely effect of the grant of the application on the promotion of the licensing objectives, and

   (b)   meet the requirements of subsection (6).

(6) The requirements are–

    (a) that the representations are made by an interested party or responsible authority within the period prescribed under section 17(5)(c) by virtue of section 34(5),

    (b) that they have not been withdrawn, and

    (c) in the case of representations made by an interested party (who is not also a responsible authority), that they are not, in the opinion of the relevant licensing authority, frivolous or vexatious.

(7) Subsections (2) and (3) are subject to sections 19, 20 and 21 (which require certain conditions to be included in premises licences).

**36    Supplementary provision about determinations under section 35**

(1) Where an application (or any part of an application) is granted under section 35, the relevant licensing authority must forthwith give a notice to that effect to–

    (a) the applicant,

    (b) any person who made relevant representations in respect of the application, and

    (c) the chief officer of police for the police area (or each police area) in which the premises are situated.

(2) Where relevant representations were made in respect of the application, the notice under subsection (1) must state the authority's reasons for its decision as to the steps (if any) to take under section 35(3)(b).

(3) The notice under subsection (1) must specify the time when the variation in question takes effect.

That time is the time specified in the application or, if that time is before the applicant is given that notice, such later time as the relevant licensing authority specifies in the notice.

(4) Where an application (or any part of an application) is rejected under section 35, the relevant licensing authority must forthwith give a notice to that effect stating its reasons for rejecting the application to–

    (a) the applicant,

    (b) any person who made relevant representations in respect of the application, and

    (c) the chief officer of police for the police area (or each police area) in which the premises are situated.

(5) Where the relevant licensing authority determines for the purposes of section 35(6)(c) that any representations are frivolous or vexatious, it must notify the person who made them of the reasons for that determination.

(6) A licence may not be varied under section 35 so as–

    (a) to extend the period for which the licence has effect, or

    (b) to vary substantially the premises to which it relates.

(7) In discharging its duty under subsection (2) or (3)(b) of that section, a licensing authority may vary a premises licence so that it has effect subject to different conditions in respect of–

    (a) different parts of the premises concerned;

    (b) different licensable activities.

(8) In this section "relevant representations" has the meaning given in section 35(5).

**37    Application to vary licence to specify individual as premises supervisor**

(1) The holder of a premises licence may–

    (a) if the licence authorises the supply of alcohol, or

    (b) if he has applied under section 34 to vary the licence so that it authorises such supplies, apply to vary the licence so as to specify the individual named in the application ("the proposed individual") as the premises supervisor.

(2) Subsection (1) is subject to regulations under–

    (a) section 54 (form etc. of applications etc.);

    (b) section 55 (fees to accompany applications etc.).

(3)    An application under this section must also be accompanied by–
　　(a)    a form of consent in the prescribed form given by the proposed individual, and
　　(b)    the premises licence (or the appropriate part of that licence) or, if that is not practicable, a statement of the reasons for the failure to provide the licence (or part).
(4)    The holder of the premises licence must give notice of his application–
　　(a)    to the chief officer of police for the police area (or each police area) in which the premises are situated, and
　　(b)    to the designated premises supervisor (if there is one), and that notice must state whether the application is one to which section 38 applies.
(5)    Where a chief officer of police notified under subsection (4) is satisfied that the exceptional circumstances of the case are such that granting the application would undermine the crime prevention objective, he must give the relevant licensing authority a notice stating the reasons why he is so satisfied.
(6)    The chief officer of police must give that notice within the period of 14 days beginning with the day on which he is notified of the application under subsection (4).

38    **Circumstances in which section 37 application given interim effect**
(1)    This section applies where an application made in accordance with section 37, in respect of a premises licence which authorises the supply of alcohol, includes a request that the variation applied for should have immediate effect.
(2)    By virtue of this section, the premises licence has effect during the application period as if it were varied in the manner set out in the application.
(3)    For this purpose "the application period" means the period which–
　　(a)    begins when the application is received by the relevant licensing authority, and
　　(b)    ends–
　　　　(i)    if the application is granted, when the variation takes effect,
　　　　(ii)    if the application is rejected, at the time the rejection is notified to the applicant, or
　　　　(iii)    if the application is withdrawn before it is determined, at the time of the withdrawal.

39    **Determination of section 37 application**
(1)    This section applies where an application is made, in accordance with section 37, to vary a premises licence so as to specify a new premises supervisor ("the proposed individual").
(2)    Subject to subsection (3), the relevant licensing authority must grant the application.
(3)    Where a notice is given under section 37(5) (and not withdrawn), the authority must–
　　(a)    hold a hearing to consider it, unless the authority, the applicant and the chief officer of police who gave the notice agree that a hearing is unnecessary, and
　　(b)    having regard to the notice, reject the application if it considers it necessary for the promotion of the crime prevention objective to do so.
(4)    Where an application under section 37 is granted or rejected, the relevant licensing authority must give a notice to that effect to–
　　(a)    the applicant,
　　(b)    the proposed individual, and
　　(c)    the chief officer of police for the police area (or each police area) in which the premises are situated.
(5)    Where a chief officer of police gave a notice under subsection (5) of that section (and it was not withdrawn), the notice under subsection (4) of this section must state the authority's reasons for granting or rejecting the application.
(6)    Where the application is granted, the notice under subsection (4) must specify the time when the variation takes effect.
　　That time is the time specified in the application or, if that time is before the applicant is given that notice, such later time as the relevant licensing authority specifies in the notice.

**40     Duty of applicant following determination under section 39**

(1)    Where the holder of a premises licence is notified under section 39(4), he must forth-with–

    (a)    if his application has been granted, notify the person (if any) who has been replaced as the designated premises supervisor of the variation, and

    (b)    if his application has been rejected, give the designated premises supervisor (if any) notice to that effect.

(2)    A person commits an offence if he fails, without reasonable excuse, to comply with subsection (1).

(3)    A person guilty of an offence under subsection (2) is liable on summary conviction to a fine not exceeding level 3 on the standard scale.

**41     Request to be removed as designated premises supervisor**

(1)    Where an individual wishes to cease being the designated premises supervisor in respect of a premises licence, he may give the relevant licensing authority a notice to that effect.

(2)    Subsection (1) is subject to regulations under section 54 (form etc. of notices etc.).

(3)    Where the individual is the holder of the premises licence, the notice under subsection (1) must also be accompanied by the premises licence (or the appropriate part of the licence) or, if that is not practicable, by a statement of the reasons for the failure to provide the licence (or part).

(4)    In any other case, the individual must no later than 48 hours after giving the notice under subsection (1) give the holder of the premises licence–

    (a)    a copy of that notice, and

    (b)    a notice directing the holder to send to the relevant licensing authority within 14 days of receiving the notice–

        (i)     the premises licence (or the appropriate part of the licence), or

        (ii)    if that is not practicable, a statement of the reasons for the failure to provide the licence (or part).

(5)    A person commits an offence if he fails, without reasonable excuse, to comply with a direction given to him under subsection (4) (b).

(6)    A person guilty of an offence under subsection (5) is liable on summary conviction to a fine not exceeding level 3 on the standard scale.

(7)    Where an individual–

    (a)    gives the relevant licensing authority a notice in accordance with this section, and

    (b)    satisfies the requirements of subsection (3) or (4),

he is to be treated for the purposes of this Act as if, from the relevant time, he were not the designated premises supervisor.

(8)    For this purpose "the relevant time" means–

    (a)    the time the notice under subsection (1) is received by the relevant licensing authority, or

    (b)    if later, the time specified in the notice.

*Transfer of premises licence*

**42     Application for transfer of premises licence**

(1)    Subject to this section, any person mentioned in section 16(1) (applicant for premises licence) may apply to the relevant licensing authority for the transfer of a premises licence to him.

(2)    Where the applicant is an individual he must be aged 18 or over.

(3)    Subsection (1) is subject to regulations under–

    (a)    section 54 (form etc. of applications etc.);

    (b)    section 55 (fees to accompany applications etc.).

(4)    An application under this section must also be accompanied by the premises licence or, if that is not practicable, a statement of the reasons for the failure to provide the licence.

(5) The applicant must give notice of his application to the chief officer of police for the police area (or each police area) in which the premises are situated.

(6) Where a chief officer of police notified under subsection (5) is satisfied that the exceptional circumstances of the case are such that granting the application would undermine the crime prevention objective, he must give the relevant licensing authority a notice stating the reasons why he is so satisfied.

(7) The chief officer of police must give that notice within the period of 14 days beginning with the day on which he is notified of the application under subsection (5).

**43 Circumstances in which transfer application given interim effect**

(1) Where–

    (a) an application made in accordance with section 42 includes a request that the transfer have immediate effect, and

    (b) the requirements of this section are met, then, by virtue of this section, the premises licence has effect during the application period as if the applicant were the holder of the licence.

(2) For this purpose "the application period" means the period which–

    (a) begins when the application is received by the relevant licensing authority, and

    (b) ends–

        (i) when the licence is transferred following the grant of the application, or

        (ii) if the application is rejected, when the applicant is notified of the rejection, or

        (iii) when the application is withdrawn.

(3) Subject to subsections (4) and (5), an application within subsection (1)(a) may be made only with the consent of the holder of the premises licence.

(4) Where a person is the holder of the premises licence by virtue of an interim authority notice under section 47, such an application may also be made by that person.

(5) The relevant licensing authority must exempt the applicant from the requirement to obtain the holder's consent if the applicant shows to the authority's satisfaction–

    (a) that he has taken all reasonable steps to obtain that consent, and

    (b) that, if the application were one to which subsection (1) applied, he would be in a position to use the premises during the application period for the licensable activity or activities authorised by the premises licence.

(6) Where the relevant licensing authority refuses to exempt an applicant under subsection (5), it must notify the applicant of its reasons for that decision.

**44 Determination of transfer application**

(1) This section applies where an application for the transfer of a licence is made in accordance with section 42.

(2) Subject to subsections (3) and (5), the authority must transfer the licence in accordance with the application.

(3) The authority must reject the application if none of the conditions in subsection (4) applies.

(4) The conditions are–

    (a) that section 43(1) (applications given interim effect) applies to the application,

    (b) that the holder of the premises licence consents to the transfer,

    (c) that the applicant is exempted under subsection (6) from the requirement to obtain the holder's consent to the transfer.

(5) Where a notice is given under section 42(6) (and not withdrawn), and subsection (3) above does not apply, the authority must–

    (a) hold a hearing to consider it, unless the authority, the applicant and the chief officer of police who gave the notice agree that a hearing is unnecessary, and

    (b) having regard to the notice, reject the application if it considers it necessary for the promotion of the crime prevention objective to do so.

(6) The relevant licensing authority must exempt the applicant from the requirement to obtain the holder's consent if the applicant shows to the authority's satisfaction–

    (a) that he has taken all reasonable steps to obtain that consent, and

    (b) that, if the application were granted, he would be in a position to use the premises for the licensable activity or activities authorised by the premises licence.

(7) Where the relevant licensing authority refuses to exempt an applicant under subsection (6), it must notify the applicant of its reasons for that decision.

**45     Notification of determination under section 44**

(1) Where an application under section 42 is granted or rejected, the relevant licensing authority must give a notice to that effect to–

    (a) the applicant, and

    (b) the chief officer of police for the police area (or each police area) in which the premises are situated.

(2) Where a chief officer of police gave a notice under subsection (6) of that section (and it was not withdrawn), the notice under subsection (1) of this section must state the licensing authority's reasons for granting or rejecting the application.

(3) Where the application is granted, the notice under subsection (1) must specify the time when the transfer takes effect.

That time is the time specified in the application or, if that time is before the applicant is given that notice, such later time as the relevant licensing authority specifies in the notice.

(4) The relevant licensing authority must also give a copy of the notice given under subsection (1)–

    (a) where the application is granted–

        (i) to the holder of the licence immediately before the application was granted, or

        (ii) if the application was one to which section 43(1) applied, to the holder of the licence immediately before the application was made (if any),

    (b) where the application is rejected, to the holder of the premises licence (if any).

**46     Duty to notify designated premises supervisor of transfer**

(1) This section applies where–

    (a) an application is made in accordance with section 42 to transfer a premises licence in respect of which there is a designated premises supervisor, and

    (b) the applicant and that supervisor are not the same person.

(2) Where section 43(1) applies in relation to the application, the applicant must forthwith notify the designated premises supervisor of the application.

(3) If the application is granted, the applicant must forthwith notify the designated premises supervisor of the transfer.

(4) A person commits an offence if he fails, without reasonable excuse, to comply with this section.

(5) A person guilty of an offence under subsection (4) is liable on summary conviction to a fine not exceeding level 3 on the standard scale.

*Interim authority notices*

**47     Interim authority notice following death etc. of licence holder**

(1) This section applies where–

    (a) a premises licence lapses under section 27 in a case within subsection (1)(a), (b) or (c) of that section (death, incapacity or insolvency of the holder), but

    (b) no application for transfer of the licence has been made by virtue of section 50 (reinstatement of licence on transfer following death etc.).

(2) A person who–

    (a) has a prescribed interest in the premises concerned, or

    (b)   is connected to the person who held the premises licence immediately before it lapsed ("the former holder"),

may, during the initial seven day period, give to the relevant licensing authority a notice (an "interim authority notice") in respect of the licence.

(3)    Subsection (2) is subject to regulations under–

    (a)   section 54 (form etc. of notices etc.);

    (b)   section 55 (fees to accompany applications etc.).

(4)    Only one interim authority notice may be given under subsection (2).

(5)    For the purposes of subsection (2) a person is connected to the former holder of the premises licence if, and only if–

    (a)   the former holder has died and that person is his personal representative,

    (b)   the former holder lacks capacity (within the meaning of the Mental Capacity Act 2005) to hold the licence and that person acts for him under an enduring power of attorney or lasting power of attorney registered under that Act, or

    (c)   the former holder has become insolvent and that person is his insolvency practitioner.

(6)    Where an interim authority notice is given in accordance with this section–

    (a)   the premises licence is reinstated from the time the notice is received by the relevant licensing authority, and

    (b)   the person who gave the notice is from that time the holder of the licence.

(7)    But the premises licence lapses again–

    (a)   at the end of the initial seven day period unless before that time the person who gave the interim authority notice has given a copy of the notice to the chief officer of police for the police area (or each police area) in which the premises are situated;

    (b)   at the end of the interim authority period, unless before that time a relevant transfer application is made to the relevant licensing authority.

(8)    Nothing in this section prevents the person who gave the interim authority notice from making a relevant transfer application.

(9)    If–

    (a)   a relevant transfer application is made during the interim authority period, and

    (b)   that application is rejected or withdrawn,

the licence lapses again at the time of the rejection or withdrawal.

(10)    In this section–

"becomes insolvent" is to be construed in accordance with section 27;

"initial seven day period" in relation to a licence which lapses as mentioned in subsection (1), means the period of seven days beginning with the day after the day the licence lapses;

"insolvency practitioner", in relation to a person, means a person acting as an insolvency practitioner in relation to him (within the meaning of section 388 of the Insolvency Act 1986 (c.45));

"interim authority period" means the period beginning with the day on which the interim authority notice is received by the relevant licensing authority and ending–

    (a)   two months after that day, or

    (b)   if earlier, when it is terminated by the person who gave the interim authority notice notifying the relevant licensing authority to that effect;

"relevant transfer application" in relation to the premises licence, is an application under section 42 which is given interim effect by virtue of section 43.

**48**    **Cancellation of interim authority notice following police objections**

(1)    This section applies where–

    (a)   an interim authority notice by a person ("the relevant person") is given in accordance with section 47,

(b)   the chief officer of police for the police area (or each police area) in which the premises are situated is given a copy of the interim authority notice before the end of the initial seven day period (within the meaning of that section), and

(c)   that chief officer (or any of those chief officers) is satisfied that the exceptional circumstances of the case are such that a failure to cancel the interim authority notice would undermine the crime prevention objective.

(2)   The chief officer of police must no later than 48 hours after he receives the copy of the interim authority notice give the relevant licensing authority a notice stating why he is so satisfied.

(3)   Where a notice is given by the chief officer of police (and not withdrawn), the authority must–

(a)   hold a hearing to consider it, unless the authority, the relevant person and the chief officer of police agree that a hearing is unnecessary, and

(b)   having regard to the notice given by the chief officer of police, cancel the interim authority notice if it considers it necessary for the promotion of the crime prevention objective to do so.

(4)   An interim authority notice is cancelled under subsection (3)(b) by the licensing authority giving the relevant person a notice stating that it is cancelled and the authority's reasons for its decision.

(5)   The licensing authority must give a copy of a notice under subsection (4) to the chief officer of police for the police area (or each police area) in which the premises are situated.

(6)   The premises licence lapses if, and when, a notice is given under subsection (4). This is subject to paragraph 7(5) of Schedule 5 (reinstatement of premises licence where appeal made against cancellation of interim authority notice).

(7)   The relevant licensing authority must not cancel an interim authority notice after a relevant transfer application (within the meaning of section 47) is made in respect of the premises licence.

**49    Supplementary provision about interim authority notices**

(1)   On receipt of an interim authority notice, the relevant licensing authority must issue to the person who gave the notice a copy of the licence and a copy of the summary (in each case certified by the authority to be a true copy).

(2)   The copies issued under this section must be copies of the premises licence and summary in the form in which they existed immediately before the licence lapsed under section 27, except that they must specify the person who gave the interim authority notice as the person who is the holder.

(3)   This Act applies in relation to a copy issued under this section as it applies in relation to an original licence or summary.

(4)   Where a person becomes the holder of a premises licence by virtue of section 47, he must (unless he is the designated premises supervisor under the licence) forthwith notify the supervisor (if any) of the interim authority notice.

(5)   A person commits an offence if he fails, without reasonable excuse, to comply with subsection (4).

(6)   A person guilty of an offence under subsection (5) is liable on summary conviction to a fine not exceeding level 3 on the standard scale.

*Transfer following death etc of licence holder*

**50    Reinstatement of licence on transfer following death etc of holder**

(1)   This section applies where–

(a)   a premises licence lapses by virtue of section 27 (death, incapacity or insolvency etc. of the holder), but no interim authority notice has effect, or

(b)   a premises licence lapses by virtue of section 28 (surrender).

(2)   For the purposes of subsection (1)(a) an interim authority notice ceases to have effect when it is cancelled under section 48 or withdrawn.

(3) Notwithstanding the lapsing of the licence, a person mentioned in section 16(1) (who, in the case of an individual, is aged 18 or over) may apply under section 42 for the transfer of the licence to him provided that the application–

(a) is made no later than seven days after the day the licence lapsed, and

(b) is one to which section 43(1)(a) applies.

(4) Where an application is made in accordance with subsection (3), section 43(1)(b) must be disregarded.

(5) Where such an application is made, the premises licence is reinstated from the time the application is received by the relevant licensing authority.

(6) But the licence lapses again if, and when–

(a) the applicant is notified of the rejection of the application, or

(b) the application is withdrawn.

(7) Only one application for transfer of the premises licence may be made in reliance on this section.

*Review of licences*

**51 Application for review of premises licence**

(1) Where a premises licence has effect, an interested party or a responsible authority may apply to the relevant licensing authority for a review of the licence.

(2) Subsection (1) is subject to regulations under section 54 (form etc. of applications etc.).

(3) The Secretary of State must by regulations under this section–

(a) require the applicant to give a notice containing details of the application to the holder of the premises licence and each responsible authority within such period as may be prescribed;

(b) require the authority to advertise the application and invite representations about it to be made to the authority by interested parties and responsible authorities;

(c) prescribe the period during which representations may be made by the holder of the premises licence, any responsible authority or any interested party;

(d) require any notice under paragraph (a) or advertisement under paragraph (b) to specify that period.

(4) The relevant licensing authority may, at any time, reject any ground for review specified in an application under this section if it is satisfied–

(a) that the ground is not relevant to one or more of the licensing objectives, or

(b) in the case of an application made by a person other than a responsible authority, that–

(i) the ground is frivolous or vexatious, or

(ii) the ground is a repetition.

(5) For this purpose a ground for review is a repetition if–

(a) it is identical or substantially similar to–

(i) a ground for review specified in an earlier application for review made in respect of the same premises licence and determined under section 52, or

(ii) representations considered by the relevant licensing authority in accordance with section 18, before it determined the application for the premises licence under that section, or

(iii) representations which would have been so considered but for the fact that they were excluded representations by virtue of section 32, and

(b) a reasonable interval has not elapsed since that earlier application for review or the grant of the licence (as the case may be).

(6) Where the authority rejects a ground for review under subsection (4)(b), it must notify the applicant of its decision and, if the ground was rejected because it was frivolous or vexatious, the authority must notify him of its reasons for making that decision.

(7) The application is to be treated as rejected to the extent that any of the grounds for review are rejected under subsection (4).

Accordingly the requirements imposed under subsection (3)(a) and (b) and by section 52 (so far as not already met) apply only to so much (if any) of the application as has not been rejected.

**52   Determination of application for review**

(1)   This section applies where–

    (a)   the relevant licensing authority receives an application made in accordance with section 51,

    (b)   the applicant has complied with any requirement imposed on him under subsection (3)(a) or (d) of that section, and

    (c)   the authority has complied with any requirement imposed on it under subsection (3)(b) or (d) of that section.

(2)   Before determining the application, the authority must hold a hearing to consider it and any relevant representations.

(3)   The authority must, having regard to the application and any relevant representations, take such of the steps mentioned in subsection (4) (if any) as it considers necessary for the promotion of the licensing objectives.

(4)   The steps are–

    (a)   to modify the conditions of the licence;

    (b)   to exclude a licensable activity from the scope of the licence;

    (c)   to remove the designated premises supervisor;

    (d)   to suspend the licence for a period not exceeding three months;

    (e)   to revoke the licence;

and for this purpose the conditions of the licence are modified if any of them is altered or omitted or any new condition is added.

(5)   Subsection (3) is subject to sections 19, 20 and 21 (requirement to include certain conditions in premises licences).

(6)   Where the authority takes a step mentioned in subsection (4)(a) or (b), it may provide that the modification or exclusion is to have effect for only such period (not exceeding three months) as it may specify.

(7)   In this section "relevant representations" means representations which–

    (a)   are relevant to one or more of the licensing objectives, and

    (b)   meet the requirements of subsection (8).

(8)   The requirements are–

    (a)   that the representations are made–

        (i)   by the holder of the premises licence, a responsible authority or an interested party, and

        (ii)   within the period prescribed under section 51(3)(c),

    (b)   that they have not been withdrawn, and

    (c)   if they are made by an interested party (who is not also a responsible authority), that they are not, in the opinion of the relevant licensing authority, frivolous or vexatious.

(9)   Where the relevant licensing authority determines that any representations are frivolous or vexatious, it must notify the person who made them of the reasons for that determination.

(10)   Where a licensing authority determines an application for review under this section it must notify the determination and its reasons for making it to–

    (a)   the holder of the licence,

    (b)   the applicant,

    (c)   any person who made relevant representations, and

    (d)   the chief officer of police for the police area (or each police area) in which the premises are situated.

(11)   A determination under this section does not have effect–

    (a)   until the end of the period given for appealing against the decision, or

    (b)   if the decision is appealed against, until the appeal is disposed of.

**53    Supplementary provision about review**

  (1)   This section applies where a local authority is both–

    (a)   the relevant licensing authority, and

    (b)   a responsible authority,

    in respect of any premises.

  (2)   The authority may, in its capacity as a responsible authority, apply under section 51 for a review of any premises licence in respect of the premises.

  (3)   The authority may, in its capacity as licensing authority, determine that application.

*Summary reviews in serious cases of crime or disorder*

**53A   Summary reviews on application of senior police officer**

  (1)   The chief officer of police of a police force for a police area may apply under this section to the relevant licensing authority for a review of the premises licence for any premises wholly or partly in that area if–

    (a)   the premises are licensed premises in relation to the sale of alcohol by retail; and

    (b)   a senior member of that force has given a certificate that it is his opinion that the premises are associated with serious crime or serious disorder or both;

    and that certificate must accompany the application.

  (2)   On receipt of such an application, the relevant licensing authority must–

    (a)   within 48 hours of the time of its receipt, consider under section 53B whether it is necessary to take interim steps pending the determination of a review of the premises licence; and

    (b)   within 28 days after the day of its receipt, review that licence in accordance with section 53C and reach a determination on that review.

  (3)   The Secretary of State must by regulations–

    (a)   require a relevant licensing authority to whom an application for a review under this section has been made to give notice of the review to the holder of the premises licence and to every responsible authority;

    (b)   prescribe the period after the making of the application within which the notice under paragraph (a) must be given;

    (c)   require a relevant licensing authority to advertise the review, inviting representations about it to be made to the authority by the responsible authorities and interested parties;

    (d)   prescribe the period after the making of the application within which the advertisement must be published;

    (e)   prescribe the period after the publication of the advertisement during which representations may be made by the holder of the premises licence, any responsible authority or any interested party; and

    (f)   require a notice or advertisement under paragraph (a) or (c) to specify the period prescribed under paragraph (e).

  (4)   In this section–

    'senior member', in relation to a police force, means a police officer who is a member of that force and of or above the rank of superintendent; and

    'serious crime' has the same meaning as in the Regulation of Investigatory Powers Act 2000 (c. 23) (see section 81(2) and (3) of that Act).

  (5)   In computing the period of 48 hours mentioned in subsection (2)(a) time that is not on a working day is to be disregarded.

**53B   Interim steps pending review**

  (1)   This section applies to the consideration by a relevant licensing authority on an application under section 53A whether it is necessary to take interim steps pending the determination of the review applied for.

(2) The consideration may take place without the holder of the premises licence having been given an opportunity to make representations to the relevant licensing authority.

(3) The interim steps the relevant licensing authority must consider taking are–

    (a)   the modification of the conditions of the premises licence;

    (b)   the exclusion of the sale of alcohol by retail from the scope of the licence;

    (c)   the removal of the designated premises supervisor from the licence;

    (d)   the suspension of the licence.

(4) For the purposes of subsection (3)(a) the conditions of a premises licence are modified if any of them is altered or omitted or any new condition is added.

(5) Where on its consideration of whether to take interim steps the relevant licensing authority does take one or more such steps–

    (a)   its decision takes effect immediately or as soon after that as that authority directs; but

    (b)   it must give immediate notice of its decision and of its reasons for making it to–

        (i)   the holder of the premises licence; and

        (ii)   the chief officer of police for the police area in which the premises are situated (or for each police area in which they are partly situated).

(6) If the holder of the premises licence makes, and does not withdraw, representations against any interim steps taken by the relevant licensing authority, the authority must, within 48 hours of the time of its receipt of the representations, hold a hearing to consider those representations.

(7) The relevant licensing authority must give advance notice of the hearing to–

    (a)   the holder of the premises licence;

    (b)   the chief officer of police for the police area in which the premises are situated (or for each police area in which they are partly situated).

(8) At the hearing, the relevant licensing authority must–

    (a)   consider whether the interim steps are necessary for the promotion of the licensing objectives; and

    (b)   determine whether to withdraw or modify the steps taken.

(9) In considering those matters the relevant licensing authority must have regard to–

    (a)   the certificate that accompanied the application;

    (b)   any representations made by the chief officer of police for the police area in which the premises are situated (or for each police area in which they are partly situated); and

    (c)   any representations made by the holder of the premises licence.

(10) In computing the period of 48 hours mentioned in subsection (6) time that is not on a working day is to be disregarded.

**53C    Review of premises licence following review notice**

(1) This section applies to a review of a premises licence which a relevant licensing authority has to conduct on an application under section 53A.

(2) The relevant licensing authority must–

    (a)   hold a hearing to consider the application for the review and any relevant representations;

    (b)   take such steps mentioned in subsection (3) (if any) as it considers necessary for the promotion of the licensing objectives; and

    (c)   secure that, from the coming into effect of the decision made on the determination of the review, any interim steps having effect pending that determination cease to have effect (except so far as they are comprised in steps taken in accordance with paragraph (b)).

(3) Those steps are–

    (a)   the modification of the conditions of the premises licence,

    (b)   the exclusion of a licensable activity from the scope of the licence,

(c) the removal of the designated premises supervisor from the licence,

(d) the suspension of the licence for a period not exceeding three months, or

(e) the revocation of the licence.

(4) For the purposes of subsection (3)(a) the conditions of a premises licence are modified if any of them is altered or omitted or any new condition is added.

(5) Subsection (2)(b) is subject to sections 19, 20 and 21 (requirement to include certain conditions in premises licences).

(6) Where the authority takes a step within subsection (3)(a) or (b), it may provide that the modification or exclusion is to have effect only for a specified period (not exceeding three months).

(7) In this section 'relevant representations' means representations which–

(a) are relevant to one or more of the licensing objectives, and

(b) meet the requirements of subsection (8).

(8) The requirements are–

(a) that the representations are made by the holder of the premises licence, a responsible authority or an interested party within the period prescribed under subsection 53A(3)(e),

(b) that they have not been withdrawn, and

(c) if they are made by an interested party (who is not also a responsible authority), that they are not, in the opinion of the relevant licensing authority, frivolous or vexatious.

(9) Where the relevant licensing authority determines that any representations are frivolous or vexatious, it must notify the person who made them of the reasons for that determination.

(10) Where a relevant licensing authority determines a review under this section it must notify the determination and its reasons for making it to–

(a) the holder of the premises licence,

(b) any person who made relevant representations, and

(c) the chief officer of police for the police area in which the premises are situated (or for each police area in which they are partly situated).

(11) A decision under this section does not have effect until–

(a) the end of the period given for appealing against the decision, or

(b) if the decision is appealed against, the time the appeal is disposed of."

*General provision*

**54      Form etc of applications and notices under Part 3**

In relation to any application or notice under this Part, regulations may prescribe–

(a) its form;

(b) the manner in which it is to be made or given;

(c) information and documents that must accompany it.

**55      Fees**

(1) Regulations may–

(a) require applications under any provision of this Part (other than section 51) or notices under section 47 to be accompanied by a fee, and

(b) prescribe the amount of the fee.

(2) Regulations may also require the holder of a premises licence to pay the relevant licensing authority an annual fee.

(3) Regulations under subsection (2) may include provision prescribing–

(a) the amount of the fee, and

(b) the time at which any such fee is due.

(4) Any fee which is owed to a licensing authority under subsection (2) may be recovered as a debt due to the authority.

*Production of licence, rights of entry, etc*

**56    Licensing authority's duty to update licence document**

(1)    Where–

(a)    the relevant licensing authority, in relation to a premises licence, makes a determination or receives a notice under this Part,

(b)    a premises licence lapses under this Part, or

(c)    an appeal against a decision under this Part is disposed of,

the relevant licensing authority must make the appropriate amendments (if any) to the licence and, if necessary, issue a new summary of the licence.

(2)    Where a licensing authority is not in possession of the licence (or the appropriate part of the licence) it may, for the purposes of discharging its obligations under subsection (1), require the holder of a premises licence to produce the licence (or the appropriate part) to the authority within 14 days from the date on which he is notified of the requirement.

(3)    A person commits an offence if he fails, without reasonable excuse, to comply with a requirement under subsection (2).

(4)    A person guilty of an offence under subsection (3) is liable on summary conviction to a fine not exceeding level 2 on the standard scale.

**57    Duty to keep and produce licence**

(1)    This section applies whenever premises in respect of which a premises licence has effect are being used for one or more licensable activities authorised by the licence.

(2)    The holder of the premises licence must secure that the licence or a certified copy of it is kept at the premises in the custody or under the control of–

(a)    the holder of the licence, or

(b)    a person who works at the premises and whom the holder of the licence has nominated in writing for the purposes of this subsection.

(3)    The holder of the premises licence must secure that–

(a)    the summary of the licence or a certified copy of that summary, and

(b)    a notice specifying the position held at the premises by any person nominated for the purposes of subsection (2),

are prominently displayed at the premises.

(4)    The holder of a premises licence commits an offence if he fails, without reasonable excuse, to comply with subsection (2) or (3).

(5)    A constable or an authorised person may require the person who, by virtue of arrangements made for the purposes of subsection (2), is required to have the premises licence (or a certified copy of it) in his custody or under his control to produce the licence (or such a copy) for examination.

(6)    An authorised person exercising the power conferred by subsection (5) must, if so requested, produce evidence of his authority to exercise the power.

(7)    A person commits an offence if he fails, without reasonable excuse, to produce a premises licence or certified copy of a premises licence in accordance with a requirement under subsection (5).

(8)    A person guilty of an offence under this section is liable on summary conviction to a fine not exceeding level 2 on the standard scale.

(9)    In subsection (3) the reference to the summary of the licence is a reference to the summary issued under section 23 or, where one or more summaries have subsequently been issued under section 56, the most recent summary to have been so issued.

(10)    Section 58 makes provision about certified copies of documents for the purposes of this section.

**58    Provision supplementary to section 57**

(1)    Any reference in section 57 to a certified copy of any document is a reference to a copy of that document which is certified to be a true copy by–

(a)   the relevant licensing authority,

(b)   a solicitor or notary, or

a person of a prescribed description.

(2)   Any certified copy produced in accordance with a requirement under section 57(5) must be a copy of the document in the form in which it exists at the time.

(3)   A document which purports to be a certified copy of a document is to be taken to be such a copy, and to comply with the requirements of subsection (2), unless the contrary is shown.

**59    Inspection of premises before grant of licence etc**

(1)   In this section "relevant application" means an application under–

(a)   section 17 (grant of licence),

(b)   section 29 (provisional statement),

(c)   section 34 (variation of licence), or

(d)   section 51 (review of licence).

(2)   A constable or an authorised person may, at any reasonable time before the determination of a relevant application, enter the premises to which the application relates to assess–

(a)   in a case within subsection (1)(a), (b) or (c), the likely effect of the grant of the application on the promotion of the licensing objectives, and

(b)   in a case within subsection (1)(d), the effect of the activities authorised by the premises licence on the promotion of those objectives.

(3)   An authorised person exercising the power conferred by this section must, if so requested, produce evidence of his authority to exercise the power.

(4)   A constable or an authorised person exercising the power conferred by this section in relation to an application within subsection (1)(d) may, if necessary, use reasonable force.

(5)   A person commits an offence if he intentionally obstructs an authorised person exercising a power conferred by this section.

(6)   A person guilty of an offence under this section is liable on summary conviction to a fine not exceeding level 2 on the standard scale.

## PART 4

### CLUBS

*Introductory*

**60    Club premises certificate**

(1)   In this Act "club premises certificate" means a certificate granted under this Part–

(a)   in respect of premises occupied by, and habitually used for the purposes of, a club,

(b)   by the relevant licensing authority, and

(c)   certifying the matters specified in subsection (2).

(2)   Those matters are–

(a)   that the premises may be used by the club for one or more qualifying club activities specified in the certificate, and

(b)   that the club is a qualifying club in relation to each of those activities (see section 61).

*Qualifying clubs*

**61    Qualifying clubs**

(1)   This section applies for determining for the purposes of this Part whether a club is a qualifying club in relation to a qualifying club activity.

(2)   A club is a qualifying club in relation to the supply of alcohol to members or guests if it satisfies both–

        (a)   the general conditions in section 62, and

        (b)   the additional conditions in section 64.

(3)     A club is a qualifying club in relation to the provision of regulated entertainment if it satisfies the general conditions in section 62.

## 62      The general conditions

(1)     The general conditions which a club must satisfy if it is to be a qualifying club in relation to a qualifying club activity are the following.

(2)     Condition 1 is that under the rules of the club persons may not–

        (a)   be admitted to membership, or

        (b)   be admitted, as candidates for membership, to any of the privileges of membership,

     without an interval of at least two days between their nomination or application for membership and their admission.

(3)     Condition 2 is that under the rules of the club persons becoming members without prior nomination or application may not be admitted to the privileges of membership without an interval of at least two days between their becoming members and their admission.

(4)     Condition 3 is that the club is established and conducted in good faith as a club (see section 63).

(5)     Condition 4 is that the club has at least 25 members.

(6)     Condition 5 is that alcohol is not supplied, or intended to be supplied, to members on the premises otherwise than by or on behalf of the club.

## 63      Determining whether a club is established and conducted in good faith

(1)     In determining for the purposes of condition 3 in subsection (4) of section 62 whether a club is established and conducted in good faith as a club, the matters to be taken into account are those specified in subsection (2).

(2)     Those matters are–

        (a)   any arrangements restricting the club's freedom of purchase of alcohol;

        (b)   any provision in the rules, or arrangements, under which–

            (i)    money or property of the club, or

            (ii)   any gain arising from the carrying on of the club, is or may be applied otherwise than for the benefit of the club as a whole or for charitable, benevolent or political purposes;

        (c)   the arrangements for giving members information about the finances of the club;

        (d)   the books of account and other records kept to ensure the accuracy of that information;

        (e)   the nature of the premises occupied by the club.

(3)     If a licensing authority decides for any purpose of this Act that a club does not satisfy condition 3 in subsection (4) of section 62, the authority must give the club notice of the decision and of the reasons for it.

## 64      The additional conditions for the supply of alcohol

(1)     The additional conditions which a club must satisfy if it is to be a qualifying club in relation to the supply of alcohol to members or guests are the following.

(2)     Additional condition 1 is that (so far as not managed by the club in general meeting or otherwise by the general body of members) the purchase of alcohol for the club, and the supply of alcohol by the club, are managed by a committee whose members–

        (a)   are members of the club;

        (b)   have attained the age of 18 years; and

        (c)   are elected by the members of the club.

     This subsection is subject to section 65 (which makes special provision for industrial and provident societies, friendly societies etc).

(3)    Additional condition 2 is that no arrangements are, or are intended to be, made for any person to receive at the expense of the club any commission, percentage or similar payment on, or with reference to, purchases of alcohol by the club.

(4)    Additional condition 3 is that no arrangements are, or are intended to be, made for any person directly or indirectly to derive any pecuniary benefit from the supply of alcohol by or on behalf of the club to members or guests, apart from–

    (a)    any benefit accruing to the club as a whole, or

    (b)    any benefit which a person derives indirectly by reason of the supply giving rise or contributing to a general gain from the carrying on of the club.

**65    Industrial and provident societies, friendly societies etc**

(1)    Subsection (2) applies in relation to any club which is–

    (a)    a registered society, within the meaning of the Industrial and Provident Societies Act 1965 (c.12) (see section 74(1) of that Act),

    (b)    a registered society, within the meaning of the Friendly Societies Act 1974 (c.46) (see section 111(1) of that Act), or

    (c)    a registered friendly society, within the meaning of the Friendly Societies Act 1992 (c.40) (see section 116 of that Act).

(2)    Any such club is to be taken for the purposes of this Act to satisfy additional condition 1 in subsection (2) of section 64 if and to the extent that–

    (a)    the purchase of alcohol for the club, and

    (b)    the supply of alcohol by the club, are under the control of the members or of a committee appointed by the members.

(3)    References in this Act, other than this section, to–

    (a)    subsection (2) of section 64, or

    (b)    additional condition 1 in that subsection, are references to it as read with subsection (1) of this section.

(4)    Subject to subsection (5), this Act applies in relation to an incorporated friendly society as it applies in relation to a club, and accordingly–

    (a)    the premises of the society are to be treated as the premises of a club,

    (b)    the members of the society are to be treated as the members of the club, and

    (c)    anything done by or on behalf of the society is to be treated as done by or on behalf of the club.

(5)    In determining for the purposes of section 61 whether an incorporated friendly society is a qualifying club in relation to a qualifying club activity, the society is to be taken to satisfy the following conditions–

    (a)    condition 3 in subsection (4) of section 62,

    (b)    condition 5 in subsection (6) of that section,

    (c)    the additional conditions in section 64.

(6)    In this section "incorporated friendly society" has the same meaning as in the Friendly Societies Act 1992 (see section 116 of that Act).

**66    Miners' welfare institutes**

(1)    Subject to subsection (2), this Act applies to a relevant miners' welfare institute as it applies to a club, and accordingly–

    (a)    the premises of the institute are to be treated as the premises of a club,

    (b)    the persons enrolled as members of the institute are to be treated as the members of the club, and

    (c)    anything done by or on behalf of the trustees or managers in carrying on the institute is to be treated as done by or on behalf of the club.

(2)    In determining for the purposes of section 61 whether a relevant miners' welfare institute is a qualifying club in relation to a qualifying club activity, the institute is to be taken to satisfy the following conditions–

    (a)    condition 3 in subsection (4) of section 62,

      (b)    condition 4 in subsection (5) of that section,

      (c)    condition 5 in subsection (6) of that section,

      (d)    the additional conditions in section 64.

(3)    For the purposes of this section–

      (a)    "miners' welfare institute" means an association organised for the social well-being and recreation of persons employed in or about coal mines (or of such persons in particular), and

      (b)    a miners' welfare institute is "relevant" if it satisfies one of the following conditions.

(4)    The first condition is that–

      (a)    the institute is managed by a committee or board, and

      (b)    at least two thirds of the committee or board consists–

            (i)    partly of persons appointed or nominated, or appointed or elected from among persons nominated, by one or more licensed operators within the meaning of the Coal Industry Act 1994 (c.21), and

            (ii)   partly of persons appointed or nominated, or appointed or elected from among persons nominated, by one or more organisations representing persons employed in or about coal mines.

(5)    The second condition is that–

      (a)    the institute is managed by a committee or board, but

      (b)    the making of–

            (i)    an appointment or nomination falling within subsection (4)(b)(i), or

            (ii)   an appointment or nomination falling within subsection (4)(b)(ii), is not practicable or would not be appropriate, and

      (c)    at least two thirds of the committee or board consists–

            (i)    partly of persons employed, or formerly employed, in or about coal mines, and

            (ii)   partly of persons appointed by the Coal Industry Social Welfare Organisation or a body or person to which the functions of that Organisation have been transferred under section 12(3) of the Miners' Welfare Act 1952 (c.23).

(6)    The third condition is that the premises of the institute are held on trusts to which section 2 of the Recreational Charities Act 1958 (c.17) applies.

*Interpretation*

**67    Associate members and their guests**

(1)    Any reference in this Act (other than this section) to a guest of a member of a club includes a reference to–

      (a)    an associate member of the club, and

      (b)    a guest of an associate member of the club.

(2)    For the purposes of this Act a person is an "associate member" of a club if–

      (a)    in accordance with the rules of the club, he is admitted to its premises as being a member of another club, and

      (b)    that other club is a recognised club (see section 193).

**68    The relevant licensing authority**

(1)    For the purposes of this Part the "relevant licensing authority" in relation to any premises is determined in accordance with this section.

(2)    Subject to subsection (3), the relevant licensing authority is the authority in whose area the premises are situated.

(3)    Where the premises are situated in the areas of two or more licensing authorities, the relevant licensing authority is–

      (a)    the licensing authority in whose area the greater or greatest part of the premises is situated, or

(b)    if there is no authority to which paragraph (a) applies, such one of those authorities as is nominated in accordance with subsection (4).

(4)    In a case within subsection (3)(b), an applicant for a club premises certificate must nominate one of the licensing authorities as the relevant licensing authority in relation to the application and any certificate granted as a result of it.

**69    Authorised persons, interested parties and responsible authorities**

(1)    In this Part in relation to any premises each of the following expressions has the meaning given to it by this section–

"authorised person",

"interested party",

"responsible authority".

(2)    "Authorised person" means any of the following–

(a)    an officer of a licensing authority in whose area the premises are situated who is authorised by that authority for the purposes of this Act,

(b)    an inspector appointed by the fire and rescue authority for the area in which the premises are situated,

(c)    an inspector appointed under section 19 of the Health and Safety at Work etc. Act 1974 (c.37),

(d)    an officer of a local authority, in whose area the premises are situated, who is authorised by that authority for the purposes of exercising one or more of its statutory functions in relation to minimising or preventing the risk of pollution of the environment or of harm to human health,

(e)    in relation to a vessel, an inspector, or a surveyor of ships, appointed under section 256 of the Merchant Shipping Act 1995 (c.21),

(f)    a person prescribed for the purposes of this subsection.

(3)    "Interested party" means any of the following–

(a)    a person living in the vicinity of the premises,

(b)    a body representing persons who live in that vicinity,

(c)    a person involved in a business in that vicinity,

(d)    a body representing persons involved in such businesses.

(4)    "Responsible authority" means any of the following–

(a)    the chief officer of police for any police area in which the premises are situated,

(b)    the fire and rescue authority for any area in which the premises are situated,

(c)    the enforcing authority within the meaning given by section 18 of the Health and Safety at Work etc. Act 1974 (c.37) for any area in which the premises are situated,

(d)    the local planning authority within the meaning given by the Town and Country Planning Act 1990 (c.8) for any area in which the premises are situated,

(e)    the local authority by which statutory functions are exercisable in any area in which the premises are situated in relation to minimising or preventing the risk of pollution of the environment or of harm to human health,

(f)    a body which–

(i)    represents those who, in relation to any such area, are responsible for, or interested in, matters relating to the protection of children from harm, and

(ii)    is recognised by the licensing authority for that area for the purposes of this section as being competent to advise it on such matters,

(g)    any licensing authority (other than the relevant licensing authority) in whose area part of the premises is situated,

(h)    in relation to a vessel–

(i)    a navigation authority (within the meaning of section 221(1) of the Water Resources Act 1991 (c.57)) having functions in relation to the waters where the vessel is usually moored or berthed or any waters where it is, or is proposed to be, navigated at a time when it is used for qualifying club activities,

        (ii)   the Environment Agency,

        (iii)  the British Waterways Board, or

        (iv)  the Secretary of State,

    (i)    a person prescribed for the purposes of this subsection.

(5)    For the purposes of this section, "statutory function" means a function conferred by or under any enactment.

## 70    Other definitions relating to clubs

In this Part–

> "secretary", in relation to a club, includes any person (whether or not an officer of the club) performing the duties of a secretary;
>
> "supply of alcohol to members or guests" means, in the case of any club,–
>
> (a)   the supply of alcohol by or on behalf of the club to, or to the order of, a member of the club, or
>
> (b)   the sale by retail of alcohol by or on behalf of the club to a guest of a member of the club for consumption on the premises where the sale takes place,
>
> and related expressions are to be construed accordingly.

*Grant of club premises certificate*

## 71    Application for club premises certificate

(1)    A club may apply for a club premises certificate in respect of any premises which are occupied by, and habitually used for the purposes of, the club.

(2)    Any application for a club premises certificate must be made to the relevant licensing authority.

(3)    Subsection (2) is subject to regulations under–

    (a)   section 91 (form etc of applications and notices under this Part);

    (b)   section 92 (fees to accompany applications and notices).

(4)    An application under this section must also be accompanied by–

    (a)   a club operating schedule,

    (b)   a plan of the premises to which the application relates, in the prescribed form, and

    (c)   a copy of the rules of the club.

(5)    A "club operating schedule" is a document which is in the prescribed form, and includes a statement of the following matters–

    (a)   the qualifying club activities to which the application relates ("the relevant qualifying club activities"),

    (b)   the times during which it is proposed that the relevant qualifying club activities are to take place,

    (c)   any other times during which it is proposed that the premises are to be open to members and their guests,

    (d)   where the relevant qualifying club activities include the supply of alcohol, whether the supplies are proposed to be for consumption on the premises or both on and off the premises,

    (e)   the steps which it is proposed to take to promote the licensing objectives, and

    (f)   such other matters as may be prescribed.

(6)    The Secretary of State must by regulations–

    (a)   require an applicant to advertise the application within the prescribed period–

        (i)   in the prescribed form, and

        (ii)  in a manner which is prescribed and is likely to bring the application to the attention of the interested parties likely to be affected by it;

    (b)   require an applicant to give notice of the application to each responsible authority, and such other persons as may be prescribed within the prescribed period;

    (c)   prescribe the period during which interested parties and responsible authorities may make representations to the relevant licensing authority about the application.

**72    Determination of application for club premises certificate**

(1)    This section applies where the relevant licensing authority–

    (a)    receives an application for a club premises certificate made in accordance with section 71, and

    (b)    is satisfied that the applicant has complied with any requirement imposed on the applicant under subsection (6) of that section.

(2)    Subject to subsection (3), the authority must grant the certificate in accordance with the application subject only to–

    (a)    such conditions as are consistent with the club operating schedule accompanying the application, and

    (b)    any conditions which must under section 73(2) to (5) or 74 be included in the certificate.

(3)    Where relevant representations are made, the authority must–

    (a)    hold a hearing to consider them, unless the authority, the applicant and each person who has made such representations agree that a hearing is unnecessary, and

    (b)    having regard to the representations, take such of the steps mentioned in subsection (4) (if any) as it considers necessary for the promotion of the licensing objectives.

(4)    The steps are–

    (a)    to grant the certificate subject to–

        (i)    the conditions mentioned in subsection (2)(a) modified to such extent as the authority considers necessary for the promotion of the licensing objectives, and

        (ii)    any conditions which must under section 73(2) to (5) or 74 be included in the certificate;

    (b)    to exclude from the scope of the certificate any of the qualifying club activities to which the application relates;

    (c)    to reject the application.

(5)    Subsections (2) and (3)(b) are subject to section 73(1) (certificate may authorise off-supplies only if it authorises on supplies).

(6)    For the purposes of subsection (4)(a)(4)(a) the conditions mentioned in subsection (2)(a) are modified if any of them is altered or omitted or any new condition is added.

(7)    For the purposes of this section, "relevant representations" means representations which–

    (a)    are about the likely effect of the grant of the certificate on the promotion of the licensing objectives, and

    (b)    meet the requirements of subsection (8).

(8)    The requirements are–

    (a)    that the representations were made by an interested party or responsible authority within the period prescribed under section 71(6)(c),

    (b)    that they have not been withdrawn, and

    (c)    in the case of representations made by an interested party (who is not also a responsible authority), that they are not, in the opinion of the relevant licensing authority, frivolous or vexatious.

(9)    Where the authority determines for the purposes of subsection (8)(c) that any representations are frivolous or vexatious, it must notify the person who made them of the reasons for its determination.

(10)    In discharging its duty under subsection (2) or (3)(b) a licensing authority may grant a club premises certificate subject to different conditions in respect of–

    (a)    different parts of the premises concerned;

    (b)    different qualifying club activities.

**73**      **Certificate authorising supply of alcohol for consumption off the premises**

(1)      A club premises certificate may not authorise the supply of alcohol for consumption off the premises unless it also authorises the supply of alcohol to a member of the club for consumption on those premises.

(2)      A club premises certificate which authorises the supply of alcohol for consumption off the premises must include the following conditions.

(3)      The first condition is that the supply must be made at a time when the premises are open for the purposes of supplying alcohol, in accordance with the club premises certificate, to members of the club for consumption on the premises.

(4)      The second condition is that any alcohol supplied for consumption off the premises must be in a sealed container.

(5)      The third condition is that any supply of alcohol for consumption off the premises must be made to a member of the club in person.

**74**      **Mandatory condition: exhibition of films**

(1)      Where a club premises certificate authorises the exhibition of films, the certificate must include a condition requiring the admission of children to the exhibition of any film to be restricted in accordance with this section.

(2)      Where the film classification body is specified in the certificate, unless subsection (3)(b) applies, admission of children must be restricted in accordance with any recommendation made by that body.

(3)      Where–

     (a)      the film classification body is not specified in the certificate, or

     (b)      the relevant licensing authority has notified the club which holds the certificate that this subsection applies to the film in question,

     admission of children must be restricted in accordance with any recommendation made by that licensing authority.

(4)      In this section–

     "children" means persons aged under 18; and

     "film classification body" means the person or persons designated as the authority under section 4 of the Video Recordings Act 1984 (c.39) (authority to determine suitability of video works for classification).

**75**      **Prohibited conditions: associate members and their guests**

(1)      Where the rules of a club provide for the sale by retail of alcohol on any premises by or on behalf of the club to, or to a guest of, an associate member of the club, no condition may be attached to a club premises certificate in respect of the sale by retail of alcohol on those premises by or on behalf of the club so as to prevent the sale by retail of alcohol to any such associate member or guest.

(2)      Where the rules of a club provide for the provision of any regulated entertainment on any premises by or on behalf of the club to, or to a guest of, an associate member of the club, no condition may be attached to a club premises certificate in respect of the provision of any such regulated entertainment on those premises by or on behalf of the club so as to prevent its provision to any such associate member or guest.

**76**      **Prohibited conditions: plays**

(1)      In relation to a club premises certificate which authorises the performance of plays, no condition may be attached to the certificate as to the nature of the plays which may be performed, or the manner of performing plays, under the certificate.

(2)      But subsection (1) does not prevent a licensing authority imposing, in accordance with section 72(2) or (3)(b), 85(3)(b) or 88, any condition which it considers necessary on the grounds of public safety.

**77**      **Grant or rejection of application for club premises certificate**

(1)      Where an application is granted under section 72, the relevant licensing authority must forthwith–

     (a)      give a notice to that effect to–

      (i)    the applicant,

      (ii)   any person who made relevant representations in respect of the application, and

      (iii)  the chief officer of police for the police area (or each police area) in which the premises are situated, and

   (b)  issue the club with the club premises certificate and a summary of it.

(2)   Where relevant representations were made in respect of the application, the notice under subsection (1)(a) must specify the authority's reasons for its decision as to the steps (if any) to take under section 72(3)(b).

(3)   Where an application is rejected under section 72, the relevant licensing authority must forthwith give a notice to that effect, stating its reasons for that decision, to–

   (a)  the applicant,

   (b)  any person who made relevant representations in respect of the application, and

   (c)  the chief officer of police for the police area (or each police area) in which the premises are situated.

(4)   In this section "relevant representations" has the meaning given in section 72(6).

**78   Form of certificate and summary**

(1)   A club premises certificate and the summary of such a certificate must be in the prescribed form.

(2)   Regulations under subsection (1) must, in particular, provide for the certificate to–

   (a)  specify the name of the club and the address which is to be its relevant registered address, as defined in section 184(7);

   (b)  specify the address of the premises to which the certificate relates;

   (c)  include a plan of those premises;

   (d)  specify the qualifying club activities for which the premises may be used;

   (e)  specify the conditions subject to which the certificate has effect.

**79   Theft, loss, etc of certificate or summary**

(1)   Where a club premises certificate or summary is lost, stolen, damaged or destroyed, the club may apply to the relevant licensing authority for a copy of the certificate or summary.

(2)   Subsection (1) is subject to regulations under section 92(1) (power to prescribe fee to accompany application).

(3)   Where an application is made in accordance with this section, the relevant licensing authority must issue the club with a copy of the certificate or summary (certified by the authority to be a true copy) if it is satisfied that–

   (a)  the certificate or summary has been lost, stolen, damaged or destroyed, and

   (b)  where it has been lost or stolen, the club has reported the loss or theft to the police.

(4)   The copy issued under this section must be a copy of the club premises certificate or summary in the form in which it existed immediately before it was lost, stolen, damaged or destroyed.

(5)   This Act applies in relation to a copy issued under this section as it applies in relation to an original club premises certificate or summary.

*Duration of certificate*

**80   Period of validity of club premises certificate**

(1)   A club premises certificate has effect until such time as–

   (a)  it is withdrawn under section 88 or 90, or

   (b)  it lapses by virtue of section 81(3) (surrender).

(2)   But a club premises certificate does not have effect during any period when it is suspended under section 88.

**81    Surrender of club premises certificate**

(1)    Where a club which holds a club premises certificate decides to surrender it, the club may give the relevant licensing authority a notice to that effect.

(2)    The notice must be accompanied by the club premises certificate or, if that is not practicable, by a statement of the reasons for the failure to produce the certificate.

(3)    Where a notice is given in accordance with this section, the certificate lapses on receipt of the notice by the authority.

*Duty to notify certain changes*

**82    Notification of change of name or alteration of rules of club**

(1)    Where a club–

     (a)    holds a club premises certificate, or

     (b)    has made an application for a club premises certificate which has not been determined by the relevant licensing authority,

the secretary of the club must give the relevant licensing authority notice of any change in the name, or alteration made to the rules, of the club.

(2)    Subsection (1) is subject to regulations under section 92(1) (power to prescribe fee to accompany application).

(3)    A notice under subsection (1) by a club which holds a club premises certificate must be accompanied by the certificate or, if that is not practicable, by a statement of the reasons for the failure to produce the certificate.

(4)    An authority notified under this section of a change in the name, or alteration to the rules, of a club must amend the club premises certificate accordingly.

(5)    But nothing in subsection (4) requires or authorises the making of any amendment to a club premises certificate so as to change the premises to which the certificate relates (and no amendment made under that subsection to a club premises certificate has effect so as to change those premises).

(6)    If a notice required by this section is not given within the 28 days following the day on which the change of name or alteration to the rules is made, the secretary of the club commits an offence.

(7)    A person guilty of an offence under subsection (6) is liable on summary conviction to a fine not exceeding level 2 on the standard scale.

**83    Change of relevant registered address of club**

(1)    A club which holds a club premises certificate may give the relevant licensing authority notice of any change desired to be made in the address which is to be the club's relevant registered address.

(2)    If a club which holds a club premises certificate ceases to have any authority to make use of the address which is its relevant registered address, it must as soon as reasonably practicable give to the relevant licensing authority notice of the change to be made in the address which is to be the club's relevant registered address.

(3)    Subsections (1) and (2) are subject to regulations under section 92(1) (power to prescribe fee to accompany application).

(4)    A notice under subsection (1) or (2) must also be accompanied by the club premises certificate or, if that is not practicable, by a statement of the reasons for the failure to produce the certificate.

(5)    An authority notified under subsection (1) or (2) of a change to be made in the relevant registered address of a club must amend the club premises certificate accordingly.

(6)    If a club fails, without reasonable excuse, to comply with subsection (2) the secretary commits an offence.

(7)    A person guilty of an offence under subsection (6) is liable on summary conviction to a fine not exceeding level 2 on the standard scale.

(8)    In this section "relevant registered address" has the meaning given in section 184(7).

*Variation of certificates*

**84  Application to vary club premises certificate**

(1)  A club which holds a club premises certificate may apply to the relevant licensing authority for variation of the certificate.

(2)  Subsection (1) is subject to regulations under–

(a)  section 91 (form etc of applications);

(b)  section 92 (fees to accompany applications).

(3)  An application under this section must also be accompanied by the club premises certificate or, if that is not practicable, by a statement of the reasons for the failure to provide the certificate.

(4)  The duty to make regulations imposed on the Secretary of State by subsection (6) of section 71 (advertisement etc of application) applies in relation to applications under this section as it applies in relation to applications under that section.

**85  Determination of application under section 84**

(1)  This section applies where the relevant licensing authority–

(a)  receives an application, made in accordance with section 84, to vary a club premises certificate, and

(b)  is satisfied that the applicant has complied with any requirement imposed by virtue of subsection (4) of that section.

(2)  Subject to subsection (3) and section 86(6), the authority must grant the application.

(3)  Where relevant representations are made, the authority must–

(a)  hold a hearing to consider them, unless the authority, the applicant and each person who has made such representations agree that a hearing is unnecessary, and

(b)  having regard to the representations, take such of the steps mentioned in subsection (4) (if any) as it considers necessary for the promotion of the licensing objectives.

(4)  The steps are–

(a)  to modify the conditions of the certificate;

(b)  to reject the whole or part of the application;

and for this purpose the conditions of the certificate are modified if any of them is altered or omitted or any new condition is added.

(5)  In this section "relevant representations" means representations which–

(a)  are about the likely effect of the grant of the application on the promotion of the licensing objectives, and

(b)  meet the requirements of subsection (6).

(6)  The requirements are–

(a)  that the representations are made by an interested party or responsible authority within the period prescribed under section 71(6)(c) by virtue of section 84(4),

(b)  that they have not been withdrawn, and

(c)  in the case of representations made by an interested party (who is not also a responsible authority), that they are not, in the opinion of the relevant licensing authority, frivolous or vexatious.

(7)  Subsections (2) and (3) are subject to sections 73 and 74 (mandatory conditions relating to supply of alcohol for consumption off the premises and to exhibition of films).

**86  Supplementary provision about applications under section 84**

(1)  Where an application (or any part of an application) is granted under section 85, the relevant licensing authority must forthwith give a notice to that effect to–

(a)  the applicant,

(b)  any person who made relevant representations in respect of the application, and

(c)  the chief officer of police for the police area (or each police area) in which the premises are situated.

(2)  Where relevant representations were made in respect of the application, the notice under subsection (1) must specify the authority's reasons for its decision as to the steps (if any) to take under section 85(3)(b).

(3)  The notice under subsection (1) must specify the time when the variation in question takes effect.

That time is the time specified in the application or, if that time is before the applicant is given the notice, such later time as the relevant licensing authority specifies in the notice.

(4)  Where an application (or any part of an application) is rejected under section 85, the relevant licensing authority must forthwith give a notice to that effect stating its reasons for rejecting the application to–

(a)  the applicant,

(b)  any person who made relevant representations, and

(c)  the chief officer of police for the police area (or each police area) in which the premises are situated.

(5)  Where the relevant licensing authority determines for the purposes of section 85(6)(c) that any representations are frivolous or vexatious, it must give the person who made them its reasons for that determination.

(6)  A club premises certificate may not be varied under section 85 so as to vary substantially the premises to which it relates.

(7)  In discharging its duty under subsection (2) or (3)(b) of that section, a licensing authority may vary a club premises certificate so that it has effect subject to different conditions in respect of–

(a)  different parts of the premises concerned;

(b)  different qualifying club activities.

(8)  In this section "relevant representations" has the meaning given in section 85(5).

*Review of certificates*

**87    Application for review of club premises certificate**

(1)  Where a club holds a club premises certificate–

(a)  an interested party,

(b)  a responsible authority, or

(c)  a member of the club,

may apply to the relevant licensing authority for a review of the certificate.

(2)  Subsection (1) is subject to regulations under section 91 (form etc of applications).

(3)  The Secretary of State must by regulations under this section–

(a)  require the applicant to give a notice containing details of the application to the club and each responsible authority within such period as may be prescribed;

(b)  require the authority to advertise the application and invite representations relating to it to be made to the authority;

(c)  prescribe the period during which representations may be made by the club, any responsible authority and any interested party;

(d)  require any notice under paragraph (a) or advertisement under paragraph (b) to specify that period.

(4)  The relevant licensing authority may, at any time, reject any ground for review specified in an application under this section if it is satisfied–

(a)  that the ground is not relevant to one or more of the licensing objectives, or

(b)  in the case of an application made by a person other than a responsible authority, that–

(i)  the ground is frivolous or vexatious, or

(ii)  the ground is a repetition.

(5)  For this purpose a ground for review is a repetition if–

(a)  it is identical or substantially similar to–

      (i)    a ground for review specified in an earlier application for review made in respect of the same club premises certificate and determined under section 88, or

      (ii)   representations considered by the relevant licensing authority in accordance with section 72, before it determined the application for the club premises certificate under that section, and

   (b)   a reasonable interval has not elapsed since that earlier application or that grant.

(6)   Where the authority rejects a ground for review under subsection (4)(b), it must notify the applicant of its decision and, if the ground was rejected because it was frivolous or vexatious, the authority must notify him of its reasons for making that decision.

(7)   The application is to be treated as rejected to the extent that any of the grounds for review are rejected under subsection (4).

Accordingly, the requirements imposed under subsection (3)(a) and (b) and by section 88 (so far as not already met) apply only to so much (if any) of the application as has not been rejected.

**88    Determination of application for review**

(1)   This section applies where–

   (a)   the relevant licensing authority receives an application made in accordance with section 87,

   (b)   the applicant has complied with any requirement imposed by virtue of subsection (3)(a) or (d) of that section, and

   (c)   the authority has complied with any requirement imposed on it under subsection (3)(b) or (d) of that section.

(2)   Before determining the application, the authority must hold a hearing to consider it and any relevant representations.

(3)   The authority must, having regard to the application and any relevant representations, take such of the steps mentioned in subsection (4) (if any) as it considers necessary for the promotion of the licensing objectives.

(4)   The steps are–

   (a)   to modify the conditions of the certificate;

   (b)   to exclude a qualifying club activity from the scope of the certificate;

   (c)   to suspend the certificate for a period not exceeding three months;

   (d)   to withdraw the certificate;

and for this purpose the conditions of the certificate are modified if any of them is altered or omitted or any new condition is added.

(5)   Subsection (3) is subject to sections 73 and 74 (mandatory conditions relating to supply of alcohol for consumption off the premises and to exhibition of films).

(6)   Where the authority takes a step within subsection (4)(a) or (b), it may provide that the modification or exclusion is to have effect for only such period (not exceeding three months) as it may specify.

(7)   In this section "relevant representations" means representations which–

   (a)   are relevant to one or more of the licensing objectives, and

   (b)   meet the requirements of subsection (8).

(8)   The requirements are–

   (a)   that the representations are made by the club, a responsible authority or an interested party within the period prescribed under section 87(3)(c),

   (b)   that they have not been withdrawn, and

   (c)   if they are made by an interested party (who is not also a responsible authority), that they are not, in the opinion of the relevant licensing authority, frivolous or vexatious.

(9)   Where the relevant licensing authority determines that any representations are frivolous or vexatious, it must give the person who made them its reasons for that determination.

(10)   Where a licensing authority determines an application for review under this section it must notify the determination and its reasons for making it to–

     (a)   the club,

     (b)   the applicant,

     (c)   any person who made relevant representations, and

     (d)   the chief officer of police for the police area (or each police area) in which the premises are situated.

(11)   A determination under this section does not have effect–

     (a)   until the end of the period given for appealing against the decision, or

     (b)   if the decision is appealed against, until the appeal is disposed of.

## 89   Supplementary provision about review

(1)   This section applies where a local authority is both–

     (a)   the relevant licensing authority, and

     (b)   a responsible authority,

in respect of any premises.

(2)   The authority may, in its capacity as responsible authority, apply under section 87 for a review of any club premises certificate in respect of the premises.

(3)   The authority may in its capacity as licensing authority determine that application.

*Withdrawal of certificates*

## 90   Club ceasing to be a qualifying club

(1)   Where–

     (a)   a club holds a club premises certificate, and

     (b)   it appears to the relevant licensing authority that the club does not satisfy the conditions for being a qualifying club in relation to a qualifying club activity to which the certificate relates (see section 61),

the authority must give a notice to the club withdrawing the certificate, so far as relating to that activity.

(2)   Where the only reason that the club does not satisfy the conditions for being a qualifying club in relation to the activity in question is that the club has fewer than the required number of members, the notice withdrawing the certificate must state that the withdrawal–

     (a)   does not take effect until immediately after the end of the period of three months following the date of the notice, and

     (b)   will not take effect if, at the end of that period, the club again has at least the required number of members.

(3)   The references in subsection (2) to the required number of members are references to the minimum number of members required by condition 4 in section 62(5) (25 at the passing of this Act).

(4)   Nothing in subsection (2) prevents the giving of a further notice of withdrawal under this section at any time.

(5)   Where a justice of the peace is satisfied, on information on oath, that there are reasonable grounds for believing–

     (a)   that a club which holds a club premises certificate does not satisfy the conditions for being a qualifying club in relation to a qualifying club activity to which the certificate relates, and

     (b)   that evidence of that fact is to be obtained at the premises to which the certificate relates,

he may issue a warrant authorising a constable to enter the premises, if necessary by force, at any time within one month from the time of the issue of the warrant, and search them.

(6)   A person who enters premises under the authority of a warrant under subsection (5) may seize and remove any documents relating to the business of the club in question.

*General provision*

**91      Form etc of applications and notices under Part 4**

In relation to any application or notice under this Part, regulations may prescribe–

    (a)   its form;

    (b)   the manner in which it is to be made or given;

    (c)   information and documents that must accompany it.

**92      Fees**

  (1)   Regulations may–

    (a)   require applications under any provision of this Part (other than section 87) to be accompanied by a fee, and

    (b)   prescribe the amount of the fee.

  (2)   Regulations may also require the payment of an annual fee to the relevant licensing authority by or on behalf of a club which holds a club premises certificate.

  (3)   Regulations under subsection (2) may include provision–

    (a)   imposing liability for the making of the payment on the secretary or such other officers or members of the club as may be prescribed,

    (b)   prescribing the amount of any such fee, and

    (c)   prescribing the time at which any such fee is due.

  (4)   Any fee which is owed to a licensing authority under subsection (2) may be recovered as a debt due to the authority from any person liable to make the payment by virtue of subsection (3)(a).

*Production of certificate, rights of entry, etc*

**93      Licensing authority's duty to update club premises certificate**

  (1)   Where–

    (a)   the relevant licensing authority, in relation to a club premises certificate, makes a determination or receives a notice under this Part, or

    (b)   an appeal against a decision under this Part is disposed of,

the relevant licensing authority must make the appropriate amendments (if any) to the certificate and, if necessary, issue a new summary of the certificate.

  (2)   Where a licensing authority is not in possession of the club premises certificate, it may, for the purpose of discharging its obligations under subsection (1), require the secretary of the club to produce the certificate to the authority within 14 days from the date on which the club is notified of the requirement.

  (3)   A person commits an offence if he fails, without reasonable excuse, to comply with a requirement under subsection (2).

  (4)   A person guilty of an offence under subsection (3) is liable on summary conviction to a fine not exceeding level 2 on the standard scale.

**94      Duty to keep and produce certificate**

  (1)   This section applies whenever premises in respect of which a club premises certificate has effect are being used for one or more qualifying club activities authorised by the certificate.

  (2)   The secretary of the club must secure that the certificate, or a certified copy of it, is kept at the premises in the custody or under the control of a person (the "nominated person") who–

    (a)   falls within subsection (3),

    (b)   has been nominated for the purpose by the secretary in writing, and

    (c)   has been identified to the relevant licensing authority in a notice given by the secretary.

  (3)   The persons who fall within this subsection are–

    (a)   the secretary of the club,

    (b)   any member of the club,

(c)    any person who works at the premises for the purposes of the club.

(4)    The nominated person must secure that–

(a)    the summary of the certificate or a certified copy of that summary, and

(b)    a notice specifying the position which he holds at the premises,

are prominently displayed at the premises.

(5)    The secretary commits an offence if he fails, without reasonable excuse, to comply with subsection (2).

(6)    The nominated person commits an offence if he fails, without reasonable excuse, to comply with subsection (4).

(7)    A constable or an authorised person may require the nominated person to produce the club premises certificate (or certified copy) for examination.

(8)    An authorised person exercising the power conferred by subsection (7) must, if so requested, produce evidence of his authority to exercise the power.

(9)    A person commits an offence if he fails, without reasonable excuse, to produce a club premises certificate or certified copy of a club premises certificate in accordance with a requirement under subsection (7).

(10)   A person guilty of an offence under this section is liable on summary conviction to a fine not exceeding level 2 on the standard scale.

(11)   In subsection (4) the reference to the summary of the certificate is a reference to the summary issued under section 77 or, where one or more summaries have subsequently been issued under section 93, the most recent summary to be so issued.

(12)   Section 95 makes provision about certified copies of club premises certificates and of summaries of club premises certificates for the purposes of this section.

**95    Provision supplementary to section 94**

(1)    Any reference in section 94 to a certified copy of a document is a reference to a copy of the document which is certified to be a true copy by–

(a)    the relevant licensing authority,

(b)    a solicitor or notary, or

(c)    a person of a prescribed description.

(2)    Any certified copy produced in accordance with a requirement under subsection 94(7) must be a copy of the document in the form in which it exists at the time.

(3)    A document which purports to be a certified copy of a document is to be taken to be such a copy, and to comply with the requirements of subsection (2), unless the contrary is shown.

**96    Inspection of premises before grant of certificate etc**

(1)    Subsection (2) applies where–

(a)    a club applies for a club premises certificate in respect of any premises,

(b)    a club applies under section 84 for the variation of a club premises certificate held by it, or

(c)    an application is made under section 87 for review of a club premises certificate.

(2)    On production of his authority–

(a)    an authorised person, or

(b)    a constable authorised by the chief officer of police, may enter and inspect the premises.

(3)    Any entry and inspection under this section must take place at a reasonable time on a day–

(a)    which is not more than 14 days after the making of the application in question, and

(b)    which is specified in the notice required by subsection (4).

(4)    Before an authorised person or constable enters and inspects any premises under this section, at least 48 hours' notice must be given to the club.

(5)    Any person obstructing an authorised person in the exercise of the power conferred by this section commits an offence.

(6)    A person guilty of an offence under subsection (5) is liable on summary conviction to a fine not exceeding level 2 on the standard scale.

(7)    The relevant licensing authority may, on the application of a responsible authority, extend by not more than 7 days the time allowed for carrying out an entry and inspection under this section.

(8)    The relevant licensing authority may allow such an extension of time only if it appears to the authority that–

    (a)    reasonable steps had been taken for an authorised person or constable authorised by the applicant to inspect the premises in good time, but

    (b)    it was not possible for the inspection to take place within the time allowed.

**97    Other powers of entry and search**

(1)    Where a club premises certificate has effect in respect of any premises, a constable may enter and search the premises if he has reasonable cause to believe–

    (a)    that an offence under section 4(3)(a), (b) or (c) of the Misuse of Drugs Act 1971 (c.38) (supplying or offering to supply, or being concerned in supplying or making an offer to supply, a controlled drug) has been, is being, or is about to be, committed there, or

    (b)    that there is likely to be a breach of the peace there.

(2)    A constable exercising any power conferred by this section may, if necessary, use reasonable force.

## PART 5

### PERMITTED TEMPORARY ACTIVITIES

*Introductory*

**98    Meaning of "permitted temporary activity"**

(1)    A licensable activity is a permitted temporary activity by virtue of this Part if–

    (a)    it is carried on in accordance with a notice given in accordance with section 100, and

    (b)    the following conditions are satisfied.

(2)    The first condition is that the requirements of sections 102 (acknowledgement of notice) and 104(1) (notification of police) are met in relation to the notice.

(3)    The second condition is that the notice has not been withdrawn under this Part.

(4)    The third condition is that no counter notice has been given under this Part in respect of the notice.

**99    The relevant licensing authority**

In this Part references to the "relevant licensing authority", in relation to any premises, are references to–

    (a)    the licensing authority in whose area the premises are situated, or

    (b)    where the premises are situated in the areas of two or more licensing authorities, each of those authorities.

*Temporary event notices*

**100    Temporary event notice**

(1)    Where it is proposed to use premises for one or more licensable activities during a period not exceeding 96 hours, an individual may give to the relevant licensing authority notice of that proposal (a "temporary event notice").

(2)    In this Act, the "premises user", in relation to a temporary event notice, is the individual who gave the notice.

(3)    An individual may not give a temporary event notice unless he is aged 18 or over.

(4)    A temporary event notice must be in the prescribed form and contain–

    (a)    a statement of the matters mentioned in subsection (5),

(b) where subsection (6) applies, a statement of the condition mentioned in that sub-section, and

(c) such other information as may be prescribed.

(5) Those matters are–

(a) the licensable activities to which the proposal mentioned in subsection (1) relates ("the relevant licensable activities"),

(b) the period (not exceeding 96 hours) during which it is proposed to use the premises for those activities ("the event period"),

(c) the times during the event period when the premises user proposes that those licensable activities shall take place,

(d) the maximum number of persons (being a number less than 500) which the premises user proposes should, during those times, be allowed on the premises at the same time,

(e) where the relevant licensable activities include the supply of alcohol, whether supplies are proposed to be for consumption on the premises or off the premises, or both, and

(f) such other matters as may be prescribed.

(6) Where the relevant licensable activities include the supply of alcohol, the notice must make it a condition of using the premises for such supplies that all such supplies are made by or under the authority of the premises user.

(7) The temporary event notice–

(a) must be given to the relevant licensing authority (in duplicate) no later than ten working days before the day on which the event period begins, and

(b) must be accompanied by the prescribed fee.

(8) The Secretary of State may, by order–

(a) amend subsections (1) and (5)(b) so as to substitute any period for the period for the time being specified there;

(b) amend subsection (5)(d) so as to substitute any number for the number for the time being specified there.

(9) In this section "supply of alcohol" means–

(a) the sale by retail of alcohol, or

(b) the supply of alcohol by or on behalf of a club to, or to the order of, a member of the club.

**101    Minimum of 24 hours between event periods**

(1) A temporary event notice ("notice A") given by an individual ("the relevant premises user") is void if the event period specified in it does not–

(a) end at least 24 hours before the event period specified in any other temporary event notice given by the relevant premises user in respect of the same premises before or at the same time as notice A, or

(b) begin at least 24 hours after the event period specified in any other such notice.

(2) For the purposes of subsection (1)–

(a) any temporary event notice in respect of which a counter notice has been given under this Part or which has been withdrawn under section 103 is to be dis-regarded;

(b) a temporary event notice given by an individual who is an associate of the relevant premises user is to be treated as a notice given by the relevant premises user;

(c) a temporary event notice ("notice B") given by an individual who is in business with the relevant premises user is to be treated as a notice given by the relevant premises user if–

(i) that business relates to one or more licensable activities, and

(ii) notice A and notice B relate to one or more licensable activities to which the business relates (although not necessarily the same activity or activities);

(d) two temporary event notices are in respect of the same premises if the whole or any part of the premises in respect of which one of the notices is given includes or forms part of the premises in respect of which the other notice is given.

(3) For the purposes of this section an individual is an associate of another person if that individual is–

    (a) the spouse or civil partner of that person,

    (b) a child, parent, grandchild, grandparent, brother or sister of that person,

    (c) an agent or employee of that person, or

    (d) the spouse or civil partner of a person within paragraph (b) or (c).

(4) For the purposes of subsection (3) a person living with another as that person's husband or wife is to be treated as that person's spouse.

## 102 Acknowledgement of notice

(1) Where a licensing authority receives a temporary event notice (in duplicate) in accordance with this Part, it must acknowledge receipt of the notice by sending or delivering one notice to the premises user–

    (a) before the end of the first working day following the day on which it was received, or

    (b) if the day on which it was received was not a working day, before the end of the second working day following that day.

(2) The authority must mark on the notice to be returned under subsection (1) an acknowledgement of the receipt in the prescribed form.

(3) Subsection (1) does not apply where, before the time by which the notice must be returned in accordance with that subsection, a counter notice has been sent or delivered to the premises user under section 107 in relation to the temporary event notice.

## 103 Withdrawal of notice

(1) A temporary event notice may be withdrawn by the premises user giving the relevant licensing authority a notice to that effect no later than 24 hours before the beginning of the event period specified in the temporary event notice.

(2) Nothing in section 102 or sections 104 to 107 applies in relation to a notice withdrawn in accordance with this section.

*Police objections*

## 104 Objection to notice by the police

(1) The premises user must give a copy of any temporary event notice to the relevant chief officer of police no later than ten working days before the day on which the event period specified in the notice begins.

(2) Where a chief officer of police who receives a copy notice under subsection (1) is satisfied that allowing the premises to be used in accordance with the notice would undermine the crime prevention objective, he must give a notice stating the reasons why he is so satisfied (an "objection notice")–

    (a) to the relevant licensing authority, and

    (b) to the premises user.

(3) The objection notice must be given no later than 48 hours after the chief officer of police is given a copy of the temporary event notice under subsection (1).

(4) Subsection (2) does not apply at any time after the relevant chief officer of police has received a copy of a counter notice under section 107 in respect of the temporary event notice.

(5) In this section "relevant chief officer of police" means–

    (a) where the premises are situated in one police area, the chief officer of police for that area, and

    (b) where the premises are situated in two or more police areas, the chief officer of police for each of those areas.

**105    Counter notice following police objection**

(1) This section applies where an objection notice is given in respect of a temporary event notice.

(2) The relevant licensing authority must–
   (a) hold a hearing to consider the objection notice, unless the premises user, the chief officer of police who gave the objection notice and the authority agree that a hearing is unnecessary, and
   (b) having regard to the objection notice, give the premises user a counter notice under this section if it considers it necessary for the promotion of the crime prevention objective to do so.

(3) The relevant licensing authority must–
   (a) in a case where it decides not to give a counter notice under this section, give the premises user and the relevant chief officer of police notice of the decision, and
   (b) in any other case–
      (i) give the premises user the counter notice and a notice stating the reasons for its decision, and
      (ii) give the relevant chief officer of police a copy of both of those notices.

(4) A decision must be made under subsection (2)(b), and the requirements of subsection (3) must be met, at least 24 hours before the beginning of the event period specified in the temporary event notice.

(5) Where the premises are situated in the area of more than one licensing authority, the functions conferred on the relevant licensing authority by this section must be exercised by those authorities jointly.

(6) This section does not apply–
   (a) if the objection notice has been withdrawn (whether by virtue of section 106 or otherwise), or
   (b) if the premises user has been given a counter notice under section 107.

(7) In this section "objection notice" and "relevant chief officer of police" have the same meaning as in section 104.

**106    Modification of notice following police objection**

(1) This section applies where a chief officer of police has given an objection notice in respect of a temporary event notice (and the objection notice has not been withdrawn).

(2) At any time before a hearing is held or dispensed with under section 105(2), the chief officer of police may, with the agreement of the premises user, modify the temporary event notice by making changes to the notice returned to the premises user under section 102.

(3) Where a temporary event notice is modified under subsection (2)–
   (a) the objection notice is to be treated for the purposes of this Act as having been withdrawn from the time the temporary event notice is modified, and
   (b) from that time–
      (i) this Act has effect as if the temporary event notice given under section 100 had been the notice as modified under that subsection, and
      (ii) to the extent that the conditions of section 98 are satisfied in relation to the unmodified notice they are to be treated as satisfied in relation to the notice as modified under that subsection.

(4) A copy of the temporary event notice as modified under subsection (2) must be sent or delivered by the chief officer of police to the relevant licensing authority before a hearing is held or dispensed with under section 105(2).

(5) Where the premises are situated in more than one police area, the chief officer of police may modify the temporary event notice under this section only with the consent of the chief officer of police for the other police area or each of the other police areas in which the premises are situated.

(6) This section does not apply if a counter notice has been given under section 107.

(7) In this section "objection notice" has the same meaning as in section 104(2).

*Limits on temporary event notices*

**107    Counter notice where permitted limits exceeded**

(1) Where a licensing authority–

    (a)    receives a temporary event notice ("notice A") in respect of any premises ("the relevant premises"), and

    (b)    is satisfied that subsection (2), (3), (4) or (5) applies,

    the authority must give the premises user ("the relevant premises user") a counter notice under this section.

(2) This subsection applies if the relevant premises user–

    (a)    holds a personal licence, and

    (b)    has already given at least 50 temporary event notices in respect of event periods wholly or partly within the same year as the event period specified in notice A.

(3) This subsection applies if the relevant premises user–

    (a)    does not hold a personal licence, and

    (b)    has already given at least five temporary event notices in respect of such event periods.

(4) This subsection applies if at least 12 temporary event notices have already been given which–

    (a)    are in respect of the same premises as notice A, and

    (b)    specify as the event period a period wholly or partly within the same year as the event period specified in notice A.

(5) This subsection applies if, in any year in which the event period specified in notice A (or any part of it) falls, more than 15 days are days on which one or more of the following fall–

    (a)    that event period or any part of it,

    (b)    an event period specified in a temporary event notice already given in respect of the same premises as notice A or any part of such a period.

(6) If the event period in notice A straddles two years, subsections (2), (3) and (4) apply separately in relation to each of those years.

(7) A counter notice under this section must be in the prescribed form and given to the premises user in the prescribed manner.

(8) No such counter notice may be given later than 24 hours before the beginning of the event period specified in notice A.

(9) In determining whether subsection (2), (3), (4) or (5) applies, any temporary event notice in respect of which a counter notice has been given under this section or section 105 is to be disregarded.

(10) In determining for the purposes of subsection (2) or (3) the number of temporary event notices given by the relevant premises user–

    (a)    a temporary event notice given by an individual who is an associate of the relevant premises user is to be treated as a notice given by the relevant premises user;

    (b)    a temporary event notice ("notice B") given by an individual who is in business with the relevant premises user is to be treated as a notice given by the relevant premises user if–

        (i)    that business relates to one or more licensable activities, and

        (ii)    notice A and notice B relate to one or more licensable activities to which the business relates (but not necessarily the same activity or activities).

(11) Where a licensing authority gives a counter notice under this section it must, forthwith, send a copy of that notice to the chief officer of police for the police area (or each of the police areas) in which the relevant premises are situated.

(12) The Secretary of State may, by order, amend subsection (2)(b), (3)(b), (4) or (5) so as to substitute any number for the number for the time being specified there.

(13) For the purposes of this section–

    (a) a temporary event notice is in respect of the same premises as notice A if it is in respect of the whole or any part of the relevant premises or premises which include the whole or any part of those premises,

    (b) "year" means calendar year,

    (c) "day" means a period of 24 hours beginning at midnight, and

    (d) subsections (3) and (4) of section 101 (meaning of "associate") apply as they apply for the purposes of that section.

*Rights of entry, production of notice, etc*

**108    Right of entry where temporary event notice given**

(1) A constable or an authorised officer may, at any reasonable time, enter the premises to which a temporary event notice relates to assess the likely effect of the notice on the promotion of the crime prevention objective.

(2) An authorised officer exercising the power conferred by this section must, if so requested, produce evidence of his authority to exercise the power.

(3) A person commits an offence if he intentionally obstructs an authorised officer exercising a power conferred by this section.

(4) A person guilty of an offence under this section is liable on summary conviction to a fine not exceeding level 2 on the standard scale.

(5) In this section "authorised officer" means–

    (a) an officer of the licensing authority in whose area the premises are situated, or

    (b) if the premises are situated in the area of more than one licensing authority, an officer of any of those authorities,

authorised for the purposes of this Act.

**109    Duty to keep and produce temporary event notice**

(1) This section applies whenever premises are being used for one or more licensable activities which are or are purported to be permitted temporary activities by virtue of this Part.

(2) The premises user must either–

    (a) secure that a copy of the temporary event notice is prominently displayed at the premises, or

    (b) meet the requirements of subsection (3).

(3) The requirements of this subsection are that the premises user must–

    (a) secure that the temporary event notice is kept at the premises in–

        (i) his custody, or

        (ii) in the custody of a person who is present and working at the premises and whom he has nominated for the purposes of this section, and

    (b) where the temporary event notice is in the custody of a person so nominated, secure that a notice specifying that fact and the position held at the premises by that person is prominently displayed at the premises.

(4) The premises user commits an offence if he fails, without reasonable excuse, to comply with subsection (2).

(5) Where–

    (a) the temporary event notice is not displayed as mentioned in subsection (2)(a), and

    (b) no notice is displayed as mentioned in subsection (3)(b),

a constable or authorised officer may require the premises user to produce the temporary event notice for examination.

(6) Where a notice is displayed as mentioned in subsection (3)(b), a constable or authorised officer may require the person specified in that notice to produce the temporary event notice for examination.

(7) An authorised officer exercising the power conferred by subsection (5) or (6) must, if so requested, produce evidence of his authority to exercise the power.

(8) A person commits an offence if he fails, without reasonable excuse, to produce a temporary event notice in accordance with a requirement under subsection (5) or (6).

(9) A person guilty of an offence under this section is liable on summary conviction to a fine not exceeding level 2 on the standard scale.

(10) In this section "authorised officer" has the meaning given in section 108(5).

*Miscellaneous*

**110    Theft, loss, etc of temporary event notice**

(1) Where a temporary event notice acknowledged under section 102 is lost, stolen, damaged or destroyed, the premises user may apply to the licensing authority which acknowledged the notice (or, if there is more than one such authority, any of them) for a copy of the notice.

(2) No application may be made under this section more than one month after the end of the event period specified in the notice.

(3) The application must be accompanied by the prescribed fee.

(4) Where a licensing authority receives an application under this section, it must issue the premises user with a copy of the notice (certified by the authority to be a true copy) if it is satisfied that–

   (a)   the notice has been lost, stolen, damaged or destroyed, and

   (b)   where it has been lost or stolen, the premises user has reported that loss or theft to the police.

(5) The copy issued under this section must be a copy of the notice in the form it existed immediately before it was lost, stolen, damaged or destroyed.

(6) This Act applies in relation to a copy issued under this section as it applies in relation to an original notice.

PART 6

PERSONAL LICENCES

*Introductory*

**111    Personal licence**

(1) In this Act "personal licence" means a licence which–

   (a)   is granted by a licensing authority to an individual, and

   (b)   authorises that individual to supply alcohol, or authorise the supply of alcohol, in accordance with a premises licence.

(2) In subsection (1)(b) the reference to an individual supplying alcohol is to him–

   (a)   selling alcohol by retail, or

   (b)   supplying alcohol by or on behalf of a club to, or to the order of, a member of the club.

**112    The relevant licensing authority**

For the purposes of this Part the "relevant licensing authority", in relation to a personal licence, is the licensing authority which granted the licence.

**113    Meaning of "relevant offence" and "foreign offence"**

(1) In this Part "relevant offence" means an offence listed in Schedule 4.

(2) The Secretary of State may by order amend that list so as to add, modify or omit any entry.

(3) In this Part "foreign offence" means an offence (other than a relevant offence) under the law of any place outside England and Wales.

**114    Spent convictions**

For the purposes of this Part a conviction for a relevant offence or a foreign offence must be disregarded if it is spent for the purposes of the Rehabilitation of Offenders Act 1974 (c.53).

**115    Period of validity of personal licence**

   (1)  A personal licence–

       (a)  has effect for an initial period of ten years beginning with the date on which it is granted, and

       (b)  may be renewed in accordance with this Part for further periods of ten years at a time.

   (2)  Subsection (1) is subject to subsections (3) and (4) and to–

       (a)  section 116 (surrender),

       (b)  section 119 (continuation of licence pending renewal), and (c) paragraph 17 of Schedule 5 (continuation of licence pending disposal of appeal).

   (3)  A personal licence ceases to have effect when it is revoked under section 124 or forfeited under section 129.

   (4)  And a personal licence does not have effect during any period when it is suspended under section 129.

   (5)  Subsections (3) and (4) are subject to any court order under sections 129(4) or 130.

**116    Surrender of personal licence**

   (1)  Where the holder of a personal licence wishes to surrender his licence he may give the relevant licensing authority a notice to that effect.

   (2)  The notice must be accompanied by the personal licence or, if that is not practicable, by a statement of the reasons for the failure to provide the licence.

   (3)  Where a notice of surrender is given in accordance with this section, the personal licence lapses on receipt of the notice by the authority.

*Grant and renewal of licences*

**117    Application for grant or renewal of personal licence**

   (1)  An individual may apply–

       (a)  for the grant of a personal licence, or

       (b)  for the renewal of a personal licence held by him.

   (2)  An application for the grant of a personal licence–

       (a)  must, if the applicant is ordinarily resident in the area of a licensing authority, be made to that authority, and

       (b)  may, in any other case, be made to any licensing authority.

   (3)  An application for the renewal of a personal licence must be made to the relevant licensing authority.

   (4)  Where the application is for renewal of a personal licence, the application must be accompanied by the personal licence or, if that is not practicable, by a statement of the reasons for the failure to provide the licence.

   (5)  Subsection (1) is subject to regulations under section 133 (form etc of applications and notices under this Part).

   (6)  An application for renewal may be made only during the period of two months beginning three months before the time the licence would expire in accordance with section 115(1) if no application for renewal were made.

**118    Individual permitted to hold only one personal licence**

   (1)  An individual who makes an application for the grant of a personal licence under section 117 ("the initial application") may not make another such application until the initial application has been determined by the licensing authority to which it was made or has been withdrawn.

   (2)  A personal licence is void if, at the time it is granted, the individual to whom it is granted already holds a personal licence.

**119    Licence continued pending renewal**

   (1)  Where–

       (a)  an application for renewal is made in accordance with section 117, and

(b)   the application has not been determined before the time the licence would, in the absence of this section, expire,

then, by virtue of this section, the licence continues to have effect for the period beginning with that time and ending with the determination or withdrawal of the application.

(2)   Subsection (1) is subject to section 115(3) and (4) (revocation, forfeiture and suspension) and section 116 (surrender).

**120   Determination of application for grant**

(1)   This section applies where an application for the grant of a personal licence is made to a licensing authority in accordance with section 117.

(2)   The authority must grant the licence if it appears to it that–

(a)   the applicant is aged 18 or over,

(b)   he possesses a licensing qualification or is a person of a prescribed description,

(c)   no personal licence held by him has been forfeited in the period of five years ending with the day the application was made, and

(d)   he has not been convicted of any relevant offence or any foreign offence.

(3)   The authority must reject the application if it appears to it that the applicant fails to meet the condition in paragraph (a), (b) or (c) of subsection (2).

(4)   If it appears to the authority that the applicant meets the conditions in paragraphs (a), (b) and (c) of that subsection but fails to meet the condition in paragraph (d) of that subsection, the authority must give the chief officer of police for its area a notice to that effect.

(5)   Where, having regard to–

(a)   any conviction of the applicant for a relevant offence, and

(b)   any conviction of his for a foreign offence which the chief officer of police considers to be comparable to a relevant offence,

the chief officer of police is satisfied that granting the licence would undermine the crime prevention objective, he must, within the period of 14 days beginning with the day he received the notice under subsection (4), give the authority a notice stating the reasons why he is so satisfied (an "objection notice").

(6)   Where no objection notice is given within that period (or the notice is withdrawn), the authority must grant the application.

(7)   In any other case, the authority–

(a)   must hold a hearing to consider the objection notice, unless the applicant, the chief officer of police and the authority agree that it is unnecessary, and

(b)   having regard to the notice, must–

(i)   reject the application if it considers it necessary for the promotion of the crime prevention objective to do so, and

(ii)   grant the application in any other case.

(8)   In this section "licensing qualification" means–

(a)   a qualification–

(i)   accredited at the time of its award, and

(ii)   awarded by a body accredited at that time,

(b)   a qualification awarded before the coming into force of this section which the Secretary of State certifies is to be treated for the purposes of this section as if it were a qualification within paragraph (a), or

(c)   a qualification obtained in Scotland or Northern Ireland or in an EEA State (other than the United Kingdom) which is equivalent to a qualification within paragraph (a) or (b).

(9)   For this purpose–

"accredited" means accredited by the Secretary of State; and

"EEA State" means a state which is a contracting party to the Agreement on the

European Economic Area signed at Oporto on 2nd May 1992, as adjusted by the Protocol signed at Brussels on 17th March 1993.

**121    Determination of application for renewal**

(1)   This section applies where an application for the renewal of a personal licence is made to the relevant licensing authority in accordance with section 117.

(2)   If it appears to the authority that the applicant has been convicted of any relevant offence or foreign offence since the relevant time, the relevant licensing authority must give notice to that effect to the chief officer of police for its area.

(3)   Where, having regard to–

   (a)   any conviction of the applicant for a relevant offence, and

   (b)   any conviction of his for a foreign offence which the chief officer of police considers to be comparable to a relevant offence,

   the chief officer of police is satisfied that renewing the licence would undermine the crime prevention objective, he must, within the period of 14 days beginning with the day he received the notice under subsection (2), give the authority a notice stating the reasons why he is so satisfied (an "objection notice").

(4)   For the purposes of subsection (3)(a) and (b) it is irrelevant whether the conviction occurred before or after the relevant time.

(5)   Where no objection notice is given within that period (or any such notice is withdrawn), the authority must grant the application.

(6)   In any other case, the authority–

   (a)   must hold a hearing to consider the objection notice unless the applicant, the chief officer of police and the authority agree that it is unnecessary, and

   (b)   having regard to the notice, must–

      (i)    reject the application if it considers it necessary for the promotion of the crime prevention objective to do so, and

      (ii)   grant the application in any other case.

(7)   In this section "the relevant time" means–

   (a)   if the personal licence has not been renewed since it was granted, the time it was granted, and

   (b)   if it has been renewed, the last time it was renewed.

**122    Notification of determinations**

(1)   Where a licensing authority grants an application–

   (a)   it must give the applicant and the chief officer of police for its area a notice to that effect, and

   (b)   if the chief officer of police gave an objection notice (which was not withdrawn), the notice under paragraph (a) must contain a statement of the licensing authority's reasons for granting the application.

(2)   A licensing authority which rejects an application must give the applicant and the chief officer of police for its area a notice to that effect containing a statement of the authority's reasons for rejecting the application.

(3)   In this section–

   "application" means an application for the grant or renewal of a personal licence; and

   "objection notice" has the meaning given in section 120 or 121, as the case may be.

**123    Duty to notify licensing authority of convictions during application period**

(1)   Where an applicant for the grant or renewal of a personal licence is convicted of a relevant offence or a foreign offence during the application period, he must as soon as reasonably practicable notify the conviction to the authority to which the application is made.

(2)   A person commits an offence if he fails, without reasonable excuse, to comply with subsection (1).

(3)   A person guilty of an offence under this section is liable on summary conviction to a fine not exceeding level 4 on the standard scale.

(4)   In this section "the application period" means the period that–

(a)   begins when the application for grant or renewal is made, and

(b)   ends when the application is determined or withdrawn.

**124   Convictions coming to light after grant or renewal**

(1)   This section applies where, after a licensing authority has granted or renewed a personal licence, it becomes aware (whether by virtue of section 123(1), 131 or 132 or otherwise) that the holder of a personal licence ("the offender") was convicted during the application period of any relevant offence or foreign offence.

(2)   The licensing authority must give a notice to that effect to the chief officer of police for its area.

(3)   Where, having regard to–

(a)   any conviction of the applicant for a relevant offence, and

(b)   any conviction of his for a foreign offence which the chief officer of police considers to be comparable to a relevant offence,

which occurred before the end of the application period, the chief officer of police is satisfied that continuation of the licence would undermine the crime prevention objective, he must, within the period of 14 days beginning with the day he received the notice under subsection (2), give the authority a notice stating the reasons why he is so satisfied (an "objection notice").

(4)   Where an objection notice is given within that period (and not withdrawn), the authority–

(a)   must hold a hearing to consider the objection notice, unless the holder of the licence, the chief officer of police and the authority agree it is unnecessary, and

(b)   having regard to the notice, must revoke the licence if it considers it necessary for the promotion of the crime prevention objective to do so.

(5)   Where the authority revokes or decides not to revoke a licence under subsection (4) it must notify the offender and the chief officer of police of the decision and its reasons for making it.

(6)   A decision under this section does not have effect–

(a)   until the end of the period given for appealing against the decision, or

(b)   if the decision is appealed against, until the appeal is disposed of.

(7)   In this section "application period", in relation to the grant or renewal of a personal licence, means the period that–

(a)   begins when the application for the grant or renewal is made, and

(b)   ends at the time of the grant or renewal.

**125   Form of personal licence**

(1)   Where a licensing authority grants a personal licence, it must forthwith issue the applicant with the licence.

(2)   The licence must–

(a)   specify the holder's name and address, and

(b)   identify the licensing authority which granted it.

(3)   It must also contain a record of each relevant offence and each foreign offence of which the holder has been convicted, the date of each conviction and the sentence imposed in respect of it.

(4)   Subject to subsections (2) and (3), the licence must be in the prescribed form.

**126   Theft, loss, etc of personal licence**

(1)   Where a personal licence is lost, stolen, damaged or destroyed, the holder of the licence may apply to the relevant licensing authority for a copy of the licence.

(2)   Subsection (1) is subject to regulations under section 133(2) (power to prescribe fee to accompany application).

(3)  Where the relevant licensing authority receives an application under this section, it must issue the licence holder with a copy of the licence (certified by the authority to be a true copy) if it is satisfied that–

(a)  the licence has been lost, stolen, damaged or destroyed, and

(b)  where it has been lost or stolen, the holder of the licence has reported the loss or theft to the police.

(4)  The copy issued under this section must be a copy of the licence in the form in which it existed immediately before it was lost, stolen, damaged or destroyed.

(5)  This Act applies in relation to a copy issued under this section as it applies in relation to an original licence.

*Duty to notify certain changes*

**127    Duty to notify change of name or address**

(1)  The holder of a personal licence must, as soon as reasonably practicable, notify the relevant licensing authority of any change in his name or address as stated in the personal licence.

(2)  Subsection (1) is subject to regulations under section 133(2) (power to prescribe fee to accompany notice).

(3)  A notice under subsection (1) must also be accompanied by the personal licence or, if that is not practicable, by a statement of the reasons for the failure to provide the licence.

(4)  A person commits an offence if he fails, without reasonable excuse, to comply with this section.

(5)  A person guilty of an offence under subsection (4) is liable on summary conviction to a fine not exceeding level 2 on the standard scale.

*Conviction of licence holder for relevant offence*

**128    Duty to notify court of personal licence**

(1)  Where the holder of a personal licence is charged with a relevant offence, he must, no later than the time he makes his first appearance in a magistrates' court in connection with that offence–

(a)  produce to the court the personal licence, or

(b)  if that is not practicable, notify the court of the existence of the personal licence and the identity of the relevant licensing authority and of the reasons why he cannot produce the licence.

(2)  Subsection (3) applies where a person charged with a relevant offence is granted a personal licence–

(a)  after his first appearance in a magistrates' court in connection with that offence, but

(b)  before–

(i)  his conviction, and sentencing for the offence, or his acquittal, or,

(ii)  where an appeal is brought against his conviction, sentence or acquittal, the disposal of that appeal.

(3)  At his next appearance in court in connection with that offence, that person must–

(a)  produce to the court the personal licence, or

(b)  if that is not practicable, notify the court of the existence of the personal licence and the identity of the relevant licensing authority and of the reasons why he cannot produce the licence.

(4)  Where–

(a)  a person charged with a relevant offence has produced his licence to, or notified, a court under subsection (1) or (3), and

(b)  before he is convicted of and sentenced for, or acquitted of, that offence, a notifiable event occurs in respect of the licence,

he must, at his next appearance in court in connection with that offence, notify the court of that event.

(5) For this purpose a "notifiable event" in relation to a personal licence means any of the following–

    (a) the making or withdrawal of an application for renewal of the licence;

    (b) the surrender of the licence under section 116;

    (c) the renewal of the licence under section 121;

    (d) the revocation of the licence under section 124.

(6) A person commits an offence if he fails, without reasonable excuse, to comply with this section.

(7) A person guilty of an offence under subsection (6) is liable on summary conviction to a fine not exceeding level 2 on the standard scale.

**129    Forfeiture or suspension of licence on conviction for relevant offence**

(1) This section applies where the holder of a personal licence is convicted of a relevant offence by or before a court in England and Wales.

(2) The court may–

    (a) order the forfeiture of the licence, or

    (b) order its suspension for a period not exceeding six months.

(3) In determining whether to make an order under subsection (2), the court may take account of any previous conviction of the holder for a relevant offence.

(4) Where a court makes an order under this section it may suspend the order pending an appeal against it.

(5) Subject to subsection (4) and section 130, an order under this section takes effect immediately after it is made.

**130    Powers of appellate court to suspend order under section 129**

(1) This section applies where–

    (a) a person ("the offender") is convicted of a relevant offence, and

    (b) an order is made under section 129 in respect of that conviction ("the section 129 order").

(2) In this section any reference to the offender's sentence includes a reference to the section 129 order and to any other order made on his conviction and, accordingly, any reference to an appeal against his sentence includes a reference to an appeal against any order forming part of his sentence.

(3) Where the offender–

    (a) appeals to the Crown Court, or

    (b) appeals or applies for leave to appeal to the Court of Appeal,

    against his conviction or his sentence, the Crown Court or, as the case may be, the Court of Appeal may suspend the section 129 order.

(4) Where the offender appeals or applies for leave to appeal to the House of Lords–

    (a) under section 1 of the Administration of Justice Act 1960 (c.65) from any decision of the High Court which is material to his conviction or sentence, or

    (b) under section 33 of the Criminal Appeal Act 1968 (c.19) from any decision of the Court of Appeal which is material to his conviction or sentence,

    the High Court or, as the case may require, the Court of Appeal may suspend the section 129 order.

(5) Where the offender makes an application in respect of the decision of the court in question under section 111 of the Magistrates' Courts Act 1980 (c.43) (statement of case by magistrates' court) or section 28 of the Supreme Court Act 1981 (c.54) (statement of case by Crown Court) the High Court may suspend the section 129 order.

(6) Where the offender–

    (a) applies to the High Court for a quashing order to remove into the High Court any proceedings of a magistrates' court or of the Crown Court, being proceedings in or in consequence of which he was convicted or his sentence was passed, or

    (b) applies to the High Court for permission to make such an application,

    the High Court may suspend the section 129 order.

(7) Any power of a court under this section to suspend the section 129 order is a power to do so on such terms as the court thinks fit.

(8) Where, by virtue of this section, a court suspends the section 129 order it must send notice of the suspension to the relevant licensing authority.

(9) Where the section 129 order is an order for forfeiture of the licence, an order under this section to suspend that order has effect to reinstate the licence for the period of the suspension.

## 131    Court's duty to notify licensing authority of convictions

(1) This section applies where a person who holds a personal licence ("the relevant person") is convicted, by or before a court in England and Wales, of a relevant offence in a case where–

   (a) the relevant person has given notice under section 128 (notification of personal licence), or

   (b) the court is, for any other reason, aware of the existence of that personal licence.

(2) The appropriate officer of the court must (as soon as reasonably practicable)–

   (a) send to the relevant licensing authority a notice specifying–

      (i) the name and address of the relevant person,

      (ii) the nature and date of the conviction, and

      (iii) any sentence passed in respect of it, including any order made under section 129, and

   (b) send a copy of the notice to the relevant person.

(3) Where, on an appeal against the relevant person's conviction for the relevant offence or against the sentence imposed on him for that offence, his conviction is quashed or a new sentence is substituted for that sentence, the court which determines the appeal must (as soon as reasonably practicable) arrange–

   (a) for notice of the quashing of the conviction or the substituting of the sentence to be sent to the relevant licensing authority, and

   (b) for a copy of the notice to be sent to the relevant person.

(4) Where the case is referred to the Court of Appeal under section 36 of the Criminal Justice Act 1988 (c.33) (review of lenient sentence), the court must cause–

   (a) notice of any action it takes under subsection (1) of that section to be sent to the relevant licensing authority, and

   (b) a copy of the notice to be sent to the relevant person.

(5) For the purposes of subsection (2) "the appropriate officer" is–

   (a) in the case of a magistrates' court, the clerk of the court, and

   (b) in the case of the Crown Court, the appropriate officer;

and section 141 of the Magistrates' Courts Act 1980 (c.43) (meaning of "clerk of a magistrates' court") applies in relation to this subsection as it applies in relation to that section.

## 132    Licence holder's duty to notify licensing authority of convictions

(1) Subsection (2) applies where the holder of a personal licence–

   (a) is convicted of a relevant offence, in a case where section 131(1) does not apply, or

   (b) is convicted of a foreign offence.

(2) The holder must–

   (a) as soon as reasonably practicable after the conviction, give the relevant licensing authority a notice containing details of the nature and date of the conviction, and any sentence imposed on him in respect of it, and

   (b) as soon as reasonably practicable after the determination of any appeal against the conviction or sentence, or of any reference under section 36 of the Criminal Justice Act 1988 (c.33) in respect of the case, give the relevant licensing authority a notice containing details of the determination.

(3) A notice under subsection (2) must be accompanied by the personal licence or, if that is not practicable, a statement of the reasons for the failure to provide the licence.

(4) A person commits an offence if he fails, without reasonable excuse, to comply with this section.

(5) A person guilty of an offence under subsection (4) is liable on summary conviction to a fine not exceeding level 2 on the standard scale.

*General provision*

**133 Form etc of applications and notices under Part 6**

(1) In relation to any application under section 117 or notice under this Part, regulations may prescribe–

   (a) its form,

   (b) the manner in which it is to be made or given, and

   (c) the information and documents that must accompany it.

(2) Regulations may also–

   (a) require applications under section 117 or 126 or notices under section 127 to be accompanied by a fee, and

   (b) prescribe the amount of the fee.

**134 Licensing authority's duty to update licence document**

(1) Where–

   (a) the relevant licensing authority makes a determination under section 121 or 124(4),

   (b) it receives a notice under sections 123(1), 127, 131 or 132, or

   (c) an appeal against a decision under this Part is disposed of,

in relation to a personal licence, the authority must make the appropriate amendments (if any) to the licence.

(2) Where, under section 131, notice is given of the making of an order under section 129, the relevant licensing authority must make an endorsement on the licence stating the terms of the order.

(3) Where, under section 131, notice is given of the quashing of such an order, any endorsement previously made under subsection (2) in respect of it must be cancelled.

(4) Where a licensing authority is not in possession of a personal licence, it may, for the purposes of discharging its obligations under this section, require the holder of the licence to produce it to the authority within 14 days beginning with the day on which he is notified of the requirement.

(5) A person commits an offence if he fails, without reasonable excuse, to comply with a requirement under subsection (4).

(6) A person guilty of an offence under subsection (5) is liable on summary conviction to a fine not exceeding level 2 on the standard scale.

*Production of licence*

**135 Licence holder's duty to produce licence**

(1) This section applies where the holder of a personal licence is on premises to make or authorise the supply of alcohol, and such supplies–

   (a) are authorised by a premises licence in respect of those premises, or

   (b) are a permitted temporary activity on the premises by virtue of a temporary event notice given under Part 5 in respect of which he is the premises user.

(2) Any constable or authorised officer may require the holder of the personal licence to produce that licence for examination.

(3) An authorised officer exercising the power conferred by subsection (2) must, if so requested, produce evidence of his authority to exercise the power.

(4) A person who fails, without reasonable excuse, to comply with a requirement under subsection (2) is guilty of an offence.

(5) A person guilty of an offence under subsection (4) is liable on summary conviction to a fine not exceeding level 2 on the standard scale.

(6) In this section "authorised officer" means an officer of a licensing authority authorised by the authority for the purposes of this Act.

PART 7

OFFENCES

*Unauthorised licensable activities*

**136    Unauthorised licensable activities**

(1) A person commits an offence if–

    (a) he carries on or attempts to carry on a licensable activity on or from any premises otherwise than under and in accordance with an authorisation, or

    (b) he knowingly allows a licensable activity to be so carried on.

(2) Where the licensable activity in question is the provision of regulated entertainment, a person does not commit an offence under this section if his only involvement in the provision of the entertainment is that he–

    (a) performs in a play,

    (b) participates as a sportsman in an indoor sporting event,

    (c) boxes or wrestles in a boxing or wrestling entertainment,

    (d) performs live music,

    (e) plays recorded music,

    (f) performs dance, or

    (g) does something coming within paragraph 2(1)(h) of Schedule 1 (entertainment similar to music, dance, etc).

(3) Subsection (2) is to be construed in accordance with Part 3 of Schedule 1.

(4) A person guilty of an offence under this section is liable on summary conviction to imprisonment for a term not exceeding six months or to a fine not exceeding £20,000, or to both.

(5) In this Part "authorisation" means–

    (a) a premises licence,

    (b) a club premises certificate, or

    (c) a temporary event notice in respect of which the conditions of section 98(2) to (4) are satisfied.

**137    Exposing alcohol for unauthorised sale**

(1) A person commits an offence if, on any premises, he exposes for sale by retail any alcohol in circumstances where the sale by retail of that alcohol on those premises would be an unauthorised licensable activity.

(2) For that purpose a licensable activity is unauthorised unless it is under and in accordance with an authorisation.

(3) A person guilty of an offence under this section is liable on summary conviction to imprisonment for a term not exceeding six months or to a fine not exceeding £20,000, or to both.

(4) The court by which a person is convicted of an offence under this section may order the alcohol in question, and any container for it, to be forfeited and either destroyed or dealt with in such other manner as the court may order.

**138    Keeping alcohol on premises for unauthorised sale etc**

(1) A person commits an offence if he has in his possession or under his control alcohol which he intends to sell by retail or supply in circumstances where that activity would be an unauthorised licensable activity.

(2) For that purpose a licensable activity is unauthorised unless it is under and in accordance with an authorisation.

(3) In subsection (1) the reference to the supply of alcohol is a reference to the supply of alcohol by or on behalf of a club to, or to the order of, a member of the club.

(4)    A person guilty of an offence under this section is liable on summary conviction to a fine not exceeding level 2 on the standard scale.

(5)    The court by which a person is convicted of an offence under this section may order the alcohol in question, and any container for it, to be forfeited and either destroyed or dealt with in such other manner as the court may order.

**139    Defence of due diligence**

(1)    In proceedings against a person for an offence to which subsection (2) applies, it is a defence that–

    (a)    his act was due to a mistake, or to reliance on information given to him, or to an act or omission by another person, or to some other cause beyond his control, and

    (b)    he took all reasonable precautions and exercised all due diligence to avoid committing the offence.

(2)    This subsection applies to an offence under–

    (a)    section 136(1)(a) (carrying on unauthorised licensable activity),

    (b)    section 137 (exposing alcohol for unauthorised sale), or

    (c)    section 138 (keeping alcohol on premises for unauthorised sale).

*Drunkenness and disorderly conduct*

**140    Allowing disorderly conduct on licensed premises etc**

(1)    A person to whom subsection (2) applies commits an offence if he knowingly allows disorderly conduct on relevant premises.

(2)    This subsection applies–

    (a)    to any person who works at the premises in a capacity, whether paid or unpaid, which authorises him to prevent the conduct,

    (b)    in the case of licensed premises, to–

        (i)    the holder of a premises licence in respect of the premises, and

        (ii)    the designated premises supervisor (if any) under such a licence,

    (c)    in the case of premises in respect of which a club premises certificate has effect, to any member or officer of the club which holds the certificate who at the time the conduct takes place is present on the premises in a capacity which enables him to prevent it, and

    (d)    in the case of premises which may be used for a permitted temporary activity by virtue of Part 5, to the premises user in relation to the temporary event notice in question.

(3)    A person guilty of an offence under this section is liable on summary conviction to a fine not exceeding level 3 on the standard scale.

**141    Sale of alcohol to a person who is drunk**

(1)    A person to whom subsection (2) applies commits an offence if, on relevant premises, he knowingly–

    (a)    sells or attempts to sell alcohol to a person who is drunk, or

    (b)    allows alcohol to be sold to such a person.

(2)    This subsection applies–

    (a)    to any person who works at the premises in a capacity, whether paid or unpaid, which gives him authority to sell the alcohol concerned,

    (b)    in the case of licensed premises, to–

        (i)    the holder of a premises licence in respect of the premises, and

        (ii)    the designated premises supervisor (if any) under such a licence,

    (c)    in the case of premises in respect of which a club premises certificate has effect, to any member or officer of the club which holds the certificate who at the time the sale (or attempted sale) takes place is present on the premises in a capacity which enables him to prevent it, and

    (d)   in the case of premises which may be used for a permitted temporary activity by virtue of Part 5, to the premises user in relation to the temporary event notice in question.

  (3)  This section applies in relation to the supply of alcohol by or on behalf of a club to or to the order of a member of the club as it applies in relation to the sale of alcohol.

  (4)  A person guilty of an offence under this section is liable on summary conviction to a fine not exceeding level 3 on the standard scale.

**142     Obtaining alcohol for a person who is drunk**

  (1)  A person commits an offence if, on relevant premises, he knowingly obtains or attempts to obtain alcohol for consumption on those premises by a person who is drunk.

  (2)  A person guilty of an offence under this section is liable on summary conviction to a fine not exceeding level 3 on the standard scale.

**143     Failure to leave licensed premises etc**

  (1)  A person who is drunk or disorderly commits an offence if, without reasonable excuse–

    (a)   he fails to leave relevant premises when requested to do so by a constable or by a person to whom subsection (2) applies, or

    (b)   he enters or attempts to enter relevant premises after a constable or a person to whom subsection (2) applies has requested him not to enter.

  (2)  This subsection applies–

    (a)   to any person who works at the premises in a capacity, whether paid or unpaid, which authorises him to make such a request,

    (b)   in the case of licensed premises, to–

       (i)   the holder of a premises licence in respect of the premises, or

      (ii)   the designated premises supervisor (if any) under such a licence,

    (c)   in the case of premises in respect of which a club premises certificate has effect, to any member or officer of the club which holds the certificate who is present on the premises in a capacity which enables him to make such a request, and

    (d)   in the case of premises which may be used for a permitted temporary activity by virtue of Part 5, to the premises user in relation to the temporary event notice in question.

  (3)  A person guilty of an offence under subsection (1) is liable on summary conviction to a fine not exceeding level 1 on the standard scale.

  (4)  On being requested to do so by a person to whom subsection (2) applies, a constable must–

    (a)   help to expel from relevant premises a person who is drunk or disorderly;

    (b)   help to prevent such a person from entering relevant premises.

*Smuggled goods*

**144     Keeping of smuggled goods**

  (1)  A person to whom subsection (2) applies commits an offence if he knowingly keeps or allows to be kept, on any relevant premises, any goods which have been imported without payment of duty or which have otherwise been unlawfully imported.

  (2)  This subsection applies–

    (a)   to any person who works at the premises in a capacity, whether paid or unpaid, which gives him authority to prevent the keeping of the goods on the premises,

    (b)   in the case of licensed premises, to–

       (i)   the holder of a premises licence in respect of the premises, and

      (ii)   the designated premises supervisor (if any) under such a licence,

    (c)   in the case of premises in respect of which a club premises certificate has effect, to any member or officer of the club which holds the certificate who is present on the premises at any time when the goods are kept on the premises in a capacity which enables him to prevent them being so kept, and

(d)   in the case of premises which may be used for a permitted temporary activity by virtue of Part 5, to the premises user in relation to the temporary event notice in question.

(3)   A person guilty of an offence under this section is liable on summary conviction to a fine not exceeding level 3 on the standard scale.

(4)   The court by which a person is convicted of an offence under this section may order the goods in question, and any container for them, to be forfeited and either destroyed or dealt with in such other manner as the court may order.

*Children and alcohol*

**145      Unaccompanied children prohibited from certain premises**

(1)   A person to whom subsection (3) applies commits an offence if–

(a)   knowing that relevant premises are within subsection (4), he allows an unaccompanied child to be on the premises at a time when they are open for the purposes of being used for the supply of alcohol for consumption there, or

(b)   he allows an unaccompanied child to be on relevant premises at a time between the hours of midnight and 5 a.m. when the premises are open for the purposes of being used for the supply of alcohol for consumption there.

(2)   For the purposes of this section–

(a)   "child" means an individual aged under 16,

(b)   a child is unaccompanied if he is not in the company of an individual aged 18 or over.

(3)   This subsection applies–

(a)   to any person who works at the premises in a capacity, whether paid or unpaid, which authorises him to request the unaccompanied child to leave the premises,

(b)   in the case of licensed premises, to–

(i)    the holder of a premises licence in respect of the premises, and

(ii)   the designated premises supervisor (if any) under such a licence,

(c)   in the case of premises in respect of which a club premises certificate has effect, to any member or officer of the club which holds the certificate who is present on the premises in a capacity which enables him to make such a request, and

(d)   in the case of premises which may be used for a permitted temporary activity by virtue of Part 5, to the premises user in relation to the temporary event notice in question.

(4)   Relevant premises are within this subsection if–

(a)   they are exclusively or primarily used for the supply of alcohol for consumption on the premises, or

(b)   they are open for the purposes of being used for the supply of alcohol for consumption on the premises by virtue of Part 5 (permitted temporary activities) and, at the time the temporary event notice in question has effect, they are exclusively or primarily used for such supplies.

(5)   No offence is committed under this section if the unaccompanied child is on the premises solely for the purpose of passing to or from some other place to or from which there is no other convenient means of access or egress.

(6)   Where a person is charged with an offence under this section by reason of his own conduct it is a defence that–

(a)   he believed that the unaccompanied child was aged 16 or over or that an individual accompanying him was aged 18 or over, and

(b)   either–

(i)    he had taken all reasonable steps to establish the individual's age, or

(ii)   nobody could reasonably have suspected from the individual's appearance that he was aged under 16 or, as the case may be, under 18.

(7)   For the purposes of subsection (6), a person is treated as having taken all reasonable steps to establish an individual's age if–

    (a)   he asked the individual for evidence of his age, and

    (b)   the evidence would have convinced a reasonable person.

(8)   Where a person ("the accused") is charged with an offence under this section by reason of the act or default of some other person, it is a defence that the accused exercised all due diligence to avoid committing it.

(9)   A person guilty of an offence under this section is liable on summary conviction to a fine not exceeding level 3 on the standard scale.

(10) In this section "supply of alcohol" means–

    (a)   the sale by retail of alcohol, or

    (b)   the supply of alcohol by or on behalf of a club to, or to the order of, a member of the club.

## 146   Sale of alcohol to children

(1)   A person commits an offence if he sells alcohol to an individual aged under 18.

(2)   A club commits an offence if alcohol is supplied by it or on its behalf–

    (a)   to, or to the order of, a member of the club who is aged under 18, or

    (b)   to the order of a member of the club, to an individual who is aged under 18.

(3)   A person commits an offence if he supplies alcohol on behalf of a club–

    (a)   to, or to the order of, a member of the club who is aged under 18, or

    (b)   to the order of a member of the club, to an individual who is aged under 18.

(4)   Where a person is charged with an offence under this section by reason of his own conduct it is a defence that–

    (a)   he believed that the individual was aged 18 or over, and

    (b)   either–

        (i)   he had taken all reasonable steps to establish the individual's age, or

        (ii)  nobody could reasonably have suspected from the individual's appearance that he was aged under 18.

(5)   For the purposes of subsection (4), a person is treated as having taken all reasonable steps to establish an individual's age if–

    (a)   he asked the individual for evidence of his age, and

    (b)   the evidence would have convinced a reasonable person.

(6)   Where a person ("the accused") is charged with an offence under this section by reason of the act or default of some other person, it is a defence that the accused exercised all due diligence to avoid committing it.

(7)   A person guilty of an offence under this section is liable on summary conviction to a fine not exceeding level 5 on the standard scale.

## 147   Allowing the sale of alcohol to children

(1)   A person to whom subsection (2) applies commits an offence if he knowingly allows the sale of alcohol on relevant premises to an individual aged under 18.

(2)   This subsection applies to a person who works at the premises in a capacity, whether paid or unpaid, which authorises him to prevent the sale.

(3)   A person to whom subsection (4) applies commits an offence if he knowingly allows alcohol to be supplied on relevant premises by or on behalf of a club–

    (a)   to or to the order of a member of the club who is aged under 18, or

    (b)   to the order of a member of the club, to an individual who is aged under 18.

(4)   This subsection applies to–

    (a)   a person who works on the premises in a capacity, whether paid or unpaid, which authorises him to prevent the supply, and

    (b)   any member or officer of the club who at the time of the supply is present on the relevant premises in a capacity which enables him to prevent it.

(5)   A person guilty of an offence under this section is liable on summary conviction to a fine not exceeding level 5 on the standard scale.

**147A    Persistently selling alcohol to children**

(1) A person is guilty of an offence if–

    (a)   on 3 or more different occasions within a period of 3 consecutive months alcohol is unlawfully sold on the same premises to an individual aged under 18;

    (b)   at the time of each sale the premises were either licensed premises or premises authorised to be used for a permitted temporary activity by virtue of Part 5; and

    (c)   that person was a responsible person in relation to the premises at each such time.

(2) For the purposes of this section alcohol sold to an individual aged under 18 is unlawfully sold to him if–

    (a)   the person making the sale believed the individual to be aged under 18; or

    (b)   that person did not have reasonable grounds for believing the individual to be aged 18 or over.

(3) For the purposes of subsection (2) a person has reasonable grounds for believing an individual to be aged 18 or over only if–

    (a)   he asked the individual for evidence of his age and that individual produced evidence that would have convinced a reasonable person; or

    (b)   nobody could reasonably have suspected from the individual's appearance that he was aged under 18.

(4) A person is, in relation to premises and a time, a responsible person for the purposes of subsection (1) if, at that time, he is–

    (a)   the person or one of the persons holding a premises licence in respect of the premises; or

    (b)   the person or one of the persons who is the premises user in respect of a temporary event notice by reference to which the premises are authorised to be used for a permitted temporary activity by virtue of Part 5.

(5) The individual to whom the sales mentioned in subsection (1) are made may, but need not be, the same in each case.

(6) The same sale may not be counted in respect of different offences for the purpose–

    (a)   of enabling the same person to be convicted of more than one offence under this section; or

    (b)   of enabling the same person to be convicted of both an offence under this section and an offence under section 146 or 147.

(7) In determining whether an offence under this section has been committed, the following shall be admissible as evidence that there has been an unlawful sale of alcohol to an individual aged under 18 on any premises on any occasion–

    (a)   the conviction of a person for an offence under section 146 in respect of a sale to that individual on those premises on that occasion;

    (b)   the giving to a person of a caution (within the meaning of Part 5 of the Police Act 1997) in respect of such an offence; or

    (c)   the payment by a person of a fixed penalty under Part 1 of the Criminal Justice and Police Act 2001 in respect of such a sale.

(8) A person guilty of an offence under this section shall be liable, on summary conviction, to a fine not exceeding £10,000.

(9) The Secretary of State may by order amend subsection (8) to increase the maximum fine for the time being specified in that subsection.

**147B    Order suspending a licence in respect of offence under section 147A**

(1) Where the holder of a premises licence is convicted of an offence under section 147A in respect of sales on the premises to which the licence relates, the court may order that so much of the licence as authorises the sale by retail of alcohol on those premises is suspended for a period not exceeding three months.

(2) Where more than one person is liable for an offence under section 147A relating to the same sales, no more than one order under subsection (1) may be made in relation to the premises in question in respect of convictions by reference to those sales.

(3) Subject to subsections (4) and (5), an order under subsection (1) comes into force at the time specified by the court that makes it.

(4) Where a magistrates' court makes an order under subsection (1), it may suspend its coming into force pending an appeal.

(5) Section 130 (powers of appellate court to suspend section 129 order) applies (with the omission of subsection (9)) where an order under subsection (1) is made on conviction of an offence under section 147A as it applies where an order under section 129 is made on conviction of a relevant offence in Part 6.

**148    Sale of liqueur confectionery to children under 16**

(1) A person commits an offence if he–
     (a) sells liqueur confectionery to an individual aged under 16, or
     (b) supplies such confectionery, on behalf of a club–
         (i) to or to the order of a member of the club who is aged under 16, or
         (ii) to the order of a member of the club, to an individual who is aged under 16.

(2) A club commits an offence if liqueur confectionery is supplied by it or on its behalf–
     (a) to or to the order of a member of the club who is aged under 16, or
     (b) to the order of a member of the club, to an individual who is aged under 16.

(3) Where a person is charged with an offence under this section by reason of his own conduct it is a defence that–
     (a) he believed that the individual was aged 16 or over, and
     (b) either–
         (i) he had taken all reasonable steps to establish the individual's age, or
         (ii) nobody could reasonably have suspected from the individual's appearance that he was aged under 16.

(4) For the purposes of subsection (3), a person is treated as having taken all reasonable steps to establish an individual's age if–
     (a) he asked the individual for evidence of his age, and
     (b) the evidence would have convinced a reasonable person.

(5) Where a person ("the accused") is charged with an offence under this section by reason of the act or default of some other person, it is a defence that the accused exercised all due diligence to avoid committing it.

(6) A person guilty of an offence under this section is liable on summary conviction to a fine not exceeding level 2 on the standard scale.

(7) In this section "liqueur confectionery" has the meaning given in section 191(2).

**149    Purchase of alcohol by or on behalf of children**

(1) An individual aged under 18 commits an offence if–
     (a) he buys or attempts to buy alcohol, or
     (b) where he is a member of a club–
         (i) alcohol is supplied to him or to his order by or on behalf of the club, as a result of some act or default of his, or
         (ii) he attempts to have alcohol supplied to him or to his order by or on behalf of the club.

(2) But subsection (1) does not apply where the individual buys or attempts to buy the alcohol at the request of–
     (a) a constable, or
     (b) a weights and measures inspector,
who is acting in the course of his duty.

(3) A person commits an offence if–
     (a) he buys or attempts to buy alcohol on behalf of an individual aged under 18, or
     (b) where he is a member of a club, on behalf of an individual aged under 18 he–

       (i)    makes arrangements whereby alcohol is supplied to him or to his order by or on behalf of the club, or

       (ii)   attempts to make such arrangements.

(4)  A person ("the relevant person") commits an offence if–

    (a)   he buys or attempts to buy alcohol for consumption on relevant premises by an individual aged under 18, or

    (b)   where he is a member of a club–

       (i)    by some act or default of his, alcohol is supplied to him, or to his order, by or on behalf of the club for consumption on relevant premises by an individual aged under 18, or

       (ii)   he attempts to have alcohol so supplied for such consumption.

(5)  But subsection (4) does not apply where–

    (a)   the relevant person is aged 18 or over,

    (b)   the individual is aged 16 or 17,

    (c)   the alcohol is beer, wine or cider,

    (d)   its purchase or supply is for consumption at a table meal on relevant premises, and

    (e)   the individual is accompanied at the meal by an individual aged 18 or over.

(6)  Where a person is charged with an offence under subsection (3) or (4) it is a defence that he had no reason to suspect that the individual was aged under 18.

(7)  A person guilty of an offence under this section is liable on summary conviction–

    (a)   in the case of an offence under subsection (1), to a fine not exceeding level 3 on the standard scale, and

    (b)   in the case of an offence under subsection (3) or (4), to a fine not exceeding level 5 on the standard scale.

**150    Consumption of alcohol by children**

(1)  An individual aged under 18 commits an offence if he knowingly consumes alcohol on relevant premises.

(2)  A person to whom subsection (3) applies commits an offence if he knowingly allows the consumption of alcohol on relevant premises by an individual aged under 18.

(3)  This subsection applies–

    (a)   to a person who works at the premises in a capacity, whether paid or unpaid, which authorises him to prevent the consumption, and

    (b)   where the alcohol was supplied by a club to or to the order of a member of the club, to any member or officer of the club who is present at the premises at the time of the consumption in a capacity which enables him to prevent it.

(4)  Subsections (1) and (2) do not apply where–

    (a)   the individual is aged 16 or 17,

    (b)   the alcohol is beer, wine or cider,

    (c)   its consumption is at a table meal on relevant premises, and

    (d)   the individual is accompanied at the meal by an individual aged 18 or over.

(5)  A person guilty of an offence under this section is liable on summary conviction–

    (a)   in the case of an offence under subsection (1), to a fine not exceeding level 3 on the standard scale, and

    (b)   in the case of an offence under subsection (2), to a fine not exceeding level 5 on the standard scale.

**151    Delivering alcohol to children**

(1)  A person who works on relevant premises in any capacity, whether paid or unpaid, commits an offence if he knowingly delivers to an individual aged under 18–

    (a)   alcohol sold on the premises, or

    (b)   alcohol supplied on the premises by or on behalf of a club to or to the order of a member of the club.

(2) A person to whom subsection (3) applies commits an offence if he knowingly allows anybody else to deliver to an individual aged under 18 alcohol sold on relevant premises.

(3) This subsection applies to a person who works on the premises in a capacity, whether paid or unpaid, which authorises him to prevent the delivery of the alcohol.

(4) A person to whom subsection (5) applies commits an offence if he knowingly allows anybody else to deliver to an individual aged under 18 alcohol supplied on relevant premises by or on behalf of a club to or to the order of a member of the club.

(5) This subsection applies–

    (a) to a person who works on the premises in a capacity, whether paid or unpaid, which authorises him to prevent the supply, and

    (b) to any member or officer of the club who at the time of the supply in question is present on the premises in a capacity which enables him to prevent the supply.

(6) Subsections (1), (2) and (4) do not apply where–

    (a) the alcohol is delivered at a place where the buyer or, as the case may be, person supplied lives or works, or

    (b) the individual aged under 18 works on the relevant premises in a capacity, whether paid or unpaid, which involves the delivery of alcohol, or

    (c) the alcohol is sold or supplied for consumption on the relevant premises.

(7) A person guilty of an offence under this section is liable on summary conviction to a fine not exceeding level 5 on the standard scale.

**152  Sending a child to obtain alcohol**

(1) A person commits an offence if he knowingly sends an individual aged under 18 to obtain–

    (a) alcohol sold or to be sold on relevant premises for consumption off the premises, or

    (b) alcohol supplied or to be supplied by or on behalf of a club to or to the order of a member of the club for such consumption.

(2) For the purposes of this section, it is immaterial whether the individual aged under 18 is sent to obtain the alcohol from the relevant premises or from other premises from which it is delivered in pursuance of the sale or supply.

(3) Subsection (1) does not apply where the individual aged under 18 works on the relevant premises in a capacity, whether paid or unpaid, which involves the delivery of alcohol.

(4) Subsection (1) also does not apply where the individual aged under 18 is sent by–

    (a) a constable, or

    (b) weights and measures inspector,

who is acting in the course of his duty.

(5) A person guilty of an offence under this section is liable on summary conviction to a fine not exceeding level 5 on the standard scale.

**153  Prohibition of unsupervised sales by children**

(1) A responsible person commits an offence if on any relevant premises he knowingly allows an individual aged under 18 to make on the premises–

    (a) any sale of alcohol, or

    (b) any supply of alcohol by or on behalf of a club to or to the order of a member of the club,

unless the sale or supply has been specifically approved by that or another responsible person.

(2) But subsection (1) does not apply where–

    (a) the alcohol is sold or supplied for consumption with a table meal,

    (b) it is sold or supplied in premises which are being used for the service of table meals (or in a part of any premises which is being so used), and

    (c) the premises are (or the part is) not used for the sale or supply of alcohol otherwise than to persons having table meals there and for consumption by such a person as an ancillary to his meal.

(3)  A person guilty of an offence under this section is liable on summary conviction to a fine not exceeding level 1 on the standard scale.

(4)  In this section "responsible person" means–

   (a)  in relation to licensed premises–

      (i)   the holder of a premises licence in respect of the premises,

      (ii)  the designated premises supervisor (if any) under such a licence, or

      (iii) any individual aged 18 or over who is authorised for the purposes of this section by such a holder or supervisor,

   (b)  in relation to premises in respect of which there is in force a club premises certificate, any member or officer of the club present on the premises in a capacity which enables him to prevent the supply in question, and

   (c)  in relation to premises which may be used for a permitted temporary activity by virtue of Part 5–

      (i)   the premises user, or

      (ii)  any individual aged 18 or over who is authorised for the purposes of this section by the premises user.

**154   Enforcement role for weights and measures authorities**

(1)  It is the duty of every local weights and measures authority in England and Wales to enforce within its area the provisions of sections 146 and 147, so far as they apply to sales of alcohol made on or from premises to which the public have access.

(2)  A weights and measures inspector may make, or authorise any person to make on his behalf, such purchases of goods as appear expedient for the purpose of determining whether those provisions are being complied with.

*Confiscation of alcohol*

**155   Confiscation of sealed containers of alcohol**

(1)  In section 1 of the Confiscation of Alcohol (Young Persons) Act 1997 (c.33) (right to require surrender of alcohol)–

   (a)  in subsection (1), omit "(other than a sealed container)",

   (b)  after that subsection insert–

      "(1A)  But a constable may not under subsection (1) require a person to surrender any sealed container unless the constable reasonably believes that the person is, or has been, consuming, or intends to consume, alcohol in any relevant place."
      , and

   (c)  in subsection (6), after "subsection (1)" insert "and (1A)".

(2)  In section 12(2)(b) of the Criminal Justice and Police Act 2001 (c.16) (right to require surrender of alcohol), omit "(other than a sealed container)".

*Vehicles and trains*

**156   Prohibition on sale of alcohol on moving vehicles**

(1)  A person commits an offence under this section if he sells by retail alcohol on or from a vehicle at a time when the vehicle is not permanently or temporarily parked.

(2)  A person guilty of an offence under this section is liable on summary conviction to imprisonment for a term not exceeding three months or to a fine not exceeding £20,000, or to both.

(3)  In proceedings against a person for an offence under this section, it is a defence that–

   (a)  his act was due to a mistake, or to reliance on information given to him, or to an act or omission by another person, or to some other cause beyond his control, and

   (b)  he took all reasonable precautions and exercised all due diligence to avoid committing the offence.

**157   Power to prohibit sale of alcohol on trains**

(1)  A magistrates' court acting for the local justice area may make an order prohibiting the sale of alcohol, during such period as may be specified, on any railway vehicle–

(a)   at such station or stations as may be specified, being stations in that area, or

(b)   travelling between such stations as may be specified, at least one of which is in that area.

(2)   A magistrates' court may make an order under this section only on the application of a senior police officer.

(3)   A magistrates' court may not make such an order unless it is satisfied that the order is necessary to prevent disorder.

(4)   Where an order is made under this section, the responsible senior police officer must, forthwith, serve a copy of the order on the train operator (or each train operator) affected by the order.

(5)   A person commits an offence if he knowingly–

(a)   sells or attempts to sell alcohol in contravention of an order under this section, or

(b)   allows the sale of alcohol in contravention of such an order.

(6)   A person guilty of an offence under this section is liable on summary conviction to imprisonment for a term not exceeding three months or to a fine not exceeding £20,000, or to both.

(7)   In this section–

"railway vehicle" has the meaning given by section 83 of the Railways Act 1993;

"responsible senior police officer", in relation to an order under this section, means the senior police officer who applied for the order or, if the chief officer of police of the force in question has designated another senior police officer for the purpose, that other officer;

"senior police officer" means a police officer of, or above, the rank of inspector;

"specified" means specified in the order under this section;

"station" has the meaning given by section 83 of the Railways Act 1993 (c.43); and

"train operator" means a person authorised by a licence under section 8 of that Act to operate railway assets (within the meaning of section 6 of that Act).

*False statement relating to licensing etc*

**158   False statements made for the purposes of this Act**

(1)   A person commits an offence if he knowingly or recklessly makes a false statement in or in connection with–

(a)   an application for the grant, variation, transfer or review of a premises licence or club premises certificate,

(b)   an application for a provisional statement,

(c)   a temporary event notice, an interim authority notice or any other notice under this Act,

(d)   an application for the grant or renewal of a personal licence, or

(e)   a notice within section 178(1) (notice by freeholder etc conferring right to be notified of changes to licensing register).

(2)   For the purposes of subsection (1) a person is to be treated as making a false statement if he produces, furnishes, signs or otherwise makes use of a document that contains a false statement.

(3)   A person guilty of an offence under this section is liable on summary conviction to a fine not exceeding level 5 on the standard scale.

*Interpretation*

**159   Interpretation of Part 7**

In this Part–

"authorisation" has the meaning given in section 136(5);

"relevant premises" means–

(a)   licensed premises, or

(b)   premises in respect of which there is in force a club premises certificate, or

(c)   premises which may be used for a permitted temporary activity by virtue of Part 5;

"table meal" means a meal eaten by a person seated at a table, or at a counter or other structure which serves the purpose of a table and is not used for the service of refreshments for consumption by persons not seated at a table or structure serving the purpose of a table; and

"weights and measures inspector" means an inspector of weights and measures appointed under section 72(1) of the Weights and Measures Act 1985 (c.72).

## PART 8

### CLOSURE OF PREMISES

*Closure of premises in an identified area*

**160    Orders to close premises in area experiencing disorder**

(1)   Where there is or is expected to be disorder in any local justice area, a magistrates' court acting for the area may make an order requiring all premises–

(a)   which are situated at or near the place of the disorder or expected disorder, and

(b)   in respect of which a premises licence or a temporary event notice has effect,

to be closed for a period, not exceeding 24 hours, specified in the order.

(2)   A magistrates' court may make an order under this section only on the application of a police officer who is of the rank of superintendent or above.

(3)   A magistrates' court may not make such an order unless it is satisfied that it is necessary to prevent disorder.

(4)   Where an order is made under this section, a person to whom subsection (5) applies commits an offence if he knowingly keeps any premises to which the order relates open, or allows any such premises to be kept open, during the period of the order.

(5)   This subsection applies–

(a)   to any manager of the premises,

(b)   in the case of licensed premises, to–

(i)    the holder of a premises licence in respect of the premises, and

(ii)   the designated premises supervisor (if any) under such a licence, and

(c)   in the case of premises in respect of which a temporary event notice has effect, to the premises user in relation to that notice.

(6)   A person guilty of an offence under subsection (4) is liable on summary conviction to a fine not exceeding level 3 on the standard scale.

(7)   A constable may use such force as may be necessary for the purpose of closing premises ordered to be closed under this section.

*Closure of identified premises*

**161    Closure orders for identified premises**

(1)   A senior police officer may make a closure order in relation to any relevant premises if he reasonably believes that–

(a)   there is, or is likely imminently to be, disorder on, or in the vicinity of and related to, the premises and their closure is necessary in the interests of public safety, or

(b)   a public nuisance is being caused by noise coming from the premises and the closure of the premises is necessary to prevent that nuisance.

(2)   A closure order is an order under this section requiring relevant premises to be closed for a period not exceeding 24 hours beginning with the coming into force of the order.

(3)   In determining whether to make a closure order in respect of any premises, the senior police officer must have regard, in particular, to the conduct of each appropriate person in relation to the disorder or nuisance.

(4) A closure order must–

    (a) specify the premises to which it relates,

    (b) specify the period for which the premises are to be closed,

    (c) specify the grounds on which it is made, and

    (d) state the effect of sections 162 to 168.

(5) A closure order in respect of any relevant premises comes into force at the time a constable gives notice of it to an appropriate person who is connected with any of the activities to which the disorder or nuisance relates.

(6) A person commits an offence if, without reasonable excuse, he permits relevant premises to be open in contravention of a closure order or any extension of it.

(7) A person guilty of an offence under subsection (6) is liable on summary conviction to imprisonment for a term not exceeding three months or to a fine not exceeding £20,000, or to both.

(8) In this section–

"relevant premises" means premises in respect of which one or more of the following have effect–

    (a) a premises licence,

    (b) a temporary event notice; and

"senior police officer" means a police officer of, or above, the rank of inspector.

**162    Extension of closure order**

(1) Where, before the end of the period for which relevant premises are to be closed under a closure order or any extension of it (the "closure period"), the responsible senior police officer reasonably believes that–

    (a) a relevant magistrates' court will not have determined whether to exercise its powers under section 165(2) in respect of the closure order, and any extension of it, by the end of the closure period, and

    (b) the conditions for an extension are satisfied,

he may extend the closure period for a further period not exceeding 24 hours beginning with the end of the previous closure period.

(2) The conditions for an extension are that–

    (a) in the case of an order made by virtue of section 161(1)(a), closure is necessary in the interests of public safety because of disorder or likely disorder on, or in the vicinity of and related to, the premises,

    (b) in the case of an order made by virtue of section 161(1)(b), closure is necessary to ensure that no public nuisance is, or is likely to be, caused by noise coming from the premises.

(3) An extension in relation to any relevant premises comes into force when a constable gives notice of it to an appropriate person connected with any of the activities to which the disorder or nuisance relates or is expected to relate.

(4) But the extension does not come into force unless the notice is given before the end of the previous closure period.

**163    Cancellation of closure order**

(1) The responsible senior police officer may cancel a closure order and any extension of it at any time–

    (a) after the making of the order, but

    (b) before a relevant magistrates' court has determined whether to exercise its powers under section 165(2) in respect of the order and any extension of it.

(2) The responsible senior police officer must cancel a closure order and any extension of it if he does not reasonably believe that–

    (a) in the case of an order made by virtue of section 161(1)(a), closure is necessary in the interests of public safety because of disorder or likely disorder on, or in the vicinity of and related to, the premises,

(b)  in the case of an order made by virtue of section 161(1)(b), closure is necessary to ensure that no public nuisance is, or is likely to be, caused by noise coming from the premises.

(3)  Where a closure order and any extension of it are cancelled under this section, the responsible senior police officer must give notice of the cancellation to an appropriate person connected with any of the activities related to the disorder (or anticipated disorder) or nuisance in respect of which the closure order was made.

**164    Application to magistrates' court by police**

(1)  The responsible senior police officer must, as soon as reasonably practicable after a closure order comes into force in respect of any relevant premises, apply to a relevant magistrates court for it to consider the order and any extension of it.

(2)  Where an application is made under this section in respect of licensed premises, the responsible senior officer must also notify the relevant licensing authority–

(a)  that a closure order has come into force,

(b)  of the contents of the order and of any extension of it, and

(c)  of the application under subsection (1).

**165    Consideration of closure order by magistrates' court**

(1)  A relevant magistrates' court must as soon as reasonably practicable after receiving an application under section 164(1)–

(a)  hold a hearing to consider whether it is appropriate to exercise any of the court's powers under subsection (2) in relation to the closure order or any extension of it, and

(b)  determine whether to exercise any of those powers.

(2)  The relevant magistrates' court may–

(a)  revoke the closure order and any extension of it;

(b)  order the premises to remain, or to be, closed until such time as the relevant licensing authority has made a determination in respect of the order for the purposes of section 167;

(c)  order the premises to remain or to be closed until that time subject to such exceptions as may be specified in the order;

(d)  order the premises to remain or to be closed until that time unless such conditions as may be specified in the order are satisfied.

(3)  In determining whether the premises will be, or will remain, closed the relevant magistrates' court must, in particular, consider whether–

(a)  in the case of an order made by virtue of section 161(1)(a), closure is necessary in the interests of public safety because of disorder or likely disorder on the premises, or in the vicinity of and related to, the premises;

(b)  in the case of an order made by virtue of section 161(1)(b), closure is necessary to ensure that no public nuisance is, or is likely to be, caused by noise coming from the premises.

(4)  In the case of licensed premises, the relevant magistrates' court must notify the relevant licensing authority of any determination it makes under subsection (1)(b).

(5)  Subsection (2) does not apply if, before the relevant magistrates' court discharges its functions under that subsection, the premises cease to be relevant premises.

(6)  Any order made under subsection (2) ceases to have effect if the premises cease to be relevant premises.

(7)  A person commits an offence if, without reasonable excuse, he permits relevant premises to be open in contravention of an order under subsection (2)(b), (c) or (d).

(8)  A person guilty of an offence under subsection (7) is liable on summary conviction to imprisonment for a term not exceeding three months or to a fine not exceeding £20,000, or to both.

(9)  The powers conferred on a magistrates' court by this section are to be exercised in the place required by the Magistrates' Courts Act 1980 (c.43) for the hearing of a complaint and may be exercised by a single justice.

(10) Evidence given for the purposes of proceedings under this section must be given on oath.

**166    Appeal from decision of magistrates' court**

(1)  Any person aggrieved by a decision of a magistrates' court under section 165 may appeal to the Crown Court against the decision.

(2)  An appeal under subsection (1) must be commenced by notice of appeal given by the appellant to the designated officer for the magistrates' court within the period of 21 days beginning with the day the decision appealed against was made.

**167    Review of premises licence following closure order**

(1)  This section applies where–

    (a)  a closure order has come into force in relation to premises in respect of which a premises licence has effect, and

    (b)  the relevant licensing authority has received a notice under section 165(4) (notice of magistrates' court's determination), in relation to the order and any extension of it.

(2)  The relevant licensing authority must review the premises licence.

(3)  The authority must reach a determination on the review no later than 28 days after the day on which it receives the notice mentioned in subsection (1)(b).

(4)  The Secretary of State must by regulations–

    (a)  require the relevant licensing authority to give, to the holder of the premises licence and each responsible authority, notice of–

        (i)   the review,

        (ii)  the closure order and any extension of it, and

        (iii) any order made in relation to it under section 165(2);

    (b)  require the authority to advertise the review and invite representations about it to be made to the authority by responsible authorities and interested parties;

    (c)  prescribe the period during which representations may be made by the holder of the premises licence, any responsible authority or any interested party;

    (d)  require any notice under paragraph (a) or advertisement under paragraph (b) to specify that period.

(5)  The relevant licensing authority must–

    (a)  hold a hearing to consider–

        (i)   the closure order and any extension of it,

        (ii)  any order under section 165(2), and

        (iii) any relevant representations, and

    (b)  take such of the steps mentioned in subsection (6) (if any) as it considers necessary for the promotion of the licensing objectives.

(6)  Those steps are–

    (a)  to modify the conditions of the premises licence,

    (b)  to exclude a licensable activity from the scope of the licence,

    (c)  to remove the designated premises supervisor from the licence,

    (d)  to suspend the licence for a period not exceeding three months, or

    (e)  to revoke the licence;

and for this purpose the conditions of a premises licence are modified if any of them is altered or omitted or any new condition is added.

(7)  Subsection (5)(b) is subject to sections 19, 20 and 21 (requirement to include certain conditions in premises licences).

(8)  Where the authority takes a step within subsection (6)(a) or (b), it may provide that the modification or exclusion is to have effect only for a specified period (not exceeding three months).

(9)  In this section "relevant representations" means representations which–

(a)  are relevant to one or more of the licensing objectives, and

(b)  meet the requirements of subsection (10).

(10)  The requirements are–

   (a)  that the representations are made by the holder of the premises licence, a responsible authority or an interested party within the period prescribed under subsection (4)(c),

   (b)  that they have not been withdrawn, and

   (c)  if they are made by an interested party (who is not also a responsible authority), that they are not, in the opinion of the relevant licensing authority, frivolous or vexatious.

(11)  Where the relevant licensing authority determines that any representations are frivolous or vexatious, it must notify the person who made them of the reasons for that determination.

(12)  Where a licensing authority determines a review under this section it must notify the determination and its reasons for making it to–

   (a)  the holder of the licence,

   (b)  any person who made relevant representations, and

   (c)  the chief officer of police for the police area (or each police area) in which the premises are situated.

(13)  Section 168 makes provision about when the determination takes effect.

(14)  In this section "interested party" and "responsible authority" have the same meaning as in Part 3.

**168  Provision about decisions under section 167**

(1)  Subject to this section, a decision under section 167 does not have effect until the relevant time.

(2)  In this section "the relevant time", in relation to any decision, means–

   (a)  the end of the period given for appealing against the decision, or

   (b)  if the decision is appealed against, the time the appeal is disposed of.

(3)  Subsections (4) and (5) apply where–

   (a)  the relevant licensing authority decides on a review under section 167 to take one or more of the steps mentioned in subsection (6)(a) to (d) of that section, and

   (b)  the premises to which the licence relates have been closed, by virtue of an order under section 165(2)(b), (c) or (d), until that decision was made.

(4)  The decision by the relevant licensing authority to take any of the steps mentioned in section 167(6)(a) to (d) takes effect when it is notified to the holder of the licence under section 167(12).

This is subject to subsection (5) and paragraph 18(3) of Schedule 5 (power of magistrates' court to suspend decision pending appeal).

(5)  The relevant licensing authority may, on such terms as it thinks fit, suspend the operation of that decision (in whole or in part) until the relevant time.

(6)  Subsection (7) applies where–

   (a)  the relevant licensing authority decides on a review under section 167 to revoke the premises licence, and

   (b)  the premises to which the licence relates have been closed, by virtue of an order under section 165(2)(b), (c) or (d), until that decision was made.

(7)  The premises must remain closed (but the licence otherwise in force) until the relevant time.

This is subject to paragraph 18(4) of Schedule 5 (power of magistrates' court to modify closure order pending appeal).

(8)  A person commits an offence if, without reasonable excuse, he allows premises to be open in contravention of subsection (7).

(9)   A person guilty of an offence under subsection (8) is liable on summary conviction to imprisonment for a term not exceeding three months or to a fine not exceeding £20,000, or to both.

**169    Enforcement of closure order**

A constable may use such force as may be necessary for the purposes of closing premises in compliance with a closure order.

*Closure notices*

**169A    Closure notices for persistently selling alcohol to children**

(1)   A relevant officer may give a notice under this section (a 'closure notice') applying to any premises if–

(a)   there is evidence that a person ('the offender') has committed an offence under section 147A in relation to those premises;

(b)   the relevant officer considers that the evidence is such that, if the offender were prosecuted for the offence, there would be a realistic prospect of his being convicted; and

(c)   the offender is still, at the time when the notice is given, the holder of a premises licence in respect of those premises, or one of the holders of such a licence.

(2)   A closure notice is a notice which–

(a)   proposes a prohibition for a period not exceeding 48 hours on sales of alcohol on the premises in question; and

(b)   offers the opportunity to discharge all criminal liability in respect of the alleged offence by the acceptance of the prohibition proposed by the notice.

(3)   A closure notice must–

(a)   be in the form prescribed by regulations made by the Secretary of State;

(b)   specify the premises to which it applies;

(c)   give such particulars of the circumstances believed to constitute the alleged offence (including the sales to which it relates) as are necessary to provide reasonable information about it;

(d)   specify the length of the period during which it is proposed that sales of alcohol should be prohibited on those premises;

(e)   specify when that period would begin if the prohibition is accepted;

(f)   explain what would be the effect of the proposed prohibition and the consequences under this Act (including the maximum penalties) of a sale of alcohol on the premises during the period for which it is in force;

(g)   explain the right of every person who, at the time of the alleged offence, held or was one of the holders of a premises licence in respect of those premises to be tried for that offence; and

(h)   explain how that right may be exercised and how (where it is not exercised) the proposed prohibition may be accepted.

(4)   The period specified for the purposes of subsection (3)(d) must be not more than 48 hours; and the time specified as the time from which that period would begin must be not less than 14 days after the date of the service of the closure notice in accordance with subsection (6).

(5)   The provision included in the notice by virtue of subsection (3)(h) must–

(a)   provide a means of identifying a police officer or trading standards officer to whom notice exercising the option to accept the prohibition may be given;

(b)   set out particulars of where and how that notice may be given to that police officer or trading standards officer;

(c)   require that notice to be given within 14 days after the date of the service of the closure notice; and

(d)   explain that the right to be tried for the alleged offence will be taken to have been exercised unless every person who, at the time of the notice, holds or is one of the holders of the premises licence for the premises in question accepts the proposed prohibition.

(6) Section 184 (giving of notices) does not apply to a closure notice; but such a notice must be served on the premises to which it applies.

(7) A closure notice may be served on the premises to which it applies–

    (a) only by being handed by a constable or trading standards officer to a person on the premises who appears to the constable or trading standards officer to have control of or responsibility for the premises (whether on his own or with others); and

    (b) only at a time when it appears to that constable or trading standards officer that licensable activities are being carried on there.

(8) A copy of every closure notice given under this section must be sent to the holder of the premises licence for the premises to which it applies at whatever address for that person is for the time being set out in the licence.

(9) A closure notice must not be given more than 3 months after the time of the last of the sales to which the alleged offence relates.

(10) No more that one closure notice may be given in respect of offences relating to the same sales; nor may such a notice be given in respect of an offence in respect of which a prosecution has already been brought.

(11) In this section 'relevant officer' means–

    (a) a police officer of the rank of superintendent or above; or

    (b) an inspector of weights and measures appointed under section 72(1) of the Weights and Measures Act 1985.

**169B    Effect of closure notices**

(1) This section applies where a closure notice is given under section 169A in respect of an alleged offence under section 147A.

(2) No proceedings may be brought for the alleged offence or any related offence at any time before the time when the prohibition proposed by the notice would take effect.

(3) If before that time every person who, at the time of the notice, holds or is one of the holders of the premises licence for the premises in question accepts the proposed prohibition in the manner specified in the notice–

    (a) that prohibition takes effect at the time so specified in relation to the premises in question; and

    (b) no proceedings may subsequently be brought against any such person for the alleged offence or any related offence.

(4) If the prohibition contained in a closure notice takes effect in accordance with sub-section (3)(a) in relation to any premises, so much of the premises licence for those premises as authorises the sale by retail of alcohol on those premises is suspended for the period specified in the closure notice.

(5) In this section 'related offence', in relation to the alleged offence, means an offence under section 146 or 147 in respect of any of the sales to which the alleged offence relates.

(6) The operation of this section is not affected by any contravention of section 169A(8).

**170    Exemption of police from liability for damages**

(1) Neither a constable nor a trading standards officer is liable for relevant damages in respect of any act or omission of his in the performance or purported performance of his functions in relation to a closure order or any extension of it or of his functions in relation to a closure notice.

(2) Neither a chief officer of police nor a local weights and measures authority is liable for relevant damages in respect of any act or omission of a person in the performance or purported performance, while under the direction or control of such a chief officer or local weights and measures authority–

    (a) of a function of that person in relation to a closure order, or any extension of it; or

    (b) of a function in relation to a closure notice.

(3) But neither subsection (1) nor (2) applies–

(a) if the act or omission is shown to have been in bad faith, or

(b) so as to prevent an award of damages in respect of an act or omission on the grounds that the act or omission was unlawful as a result of section 6(1) of the Human Rights Act 1998 (c.42) (incompatibility of act or omission with Convention rights).

(4) This section does not affect any other exemption from liability for damages (whether at common law or otherwise).

(4A) In this section references to a constable include references to a person exercising the powers of a constable by virtue of a designation under section 38 of the Police Reform Act 2002 (community support officers etc.); and, in relation to such a person, the first reference in subsection (2) to a chief officer of police has effect as a reference to a police authority.

(5) In this section, "relevant damages" means damages awarded in proceedings for judicial review, the tort of negligence or misfeasance in public office.

*Interpretation*

**171 Interpretation of Part 8**

(1) This section has effect for the purposes of this Part.

(2) Relevant premises are open if a person who is not within subsection (4) enters the premises and–

(a) he buys or is otherwise supplied with food, drink or anything usually sold on the premises, or

(b) while he is on the premises, they are used for the provision of regulated entertainment.

(3) But in determining whether relevant premises are open the following are to be disregarded–

(a) where no premises licence has effect in respect of the premises, any use of the premises for activities (other than licensable activities) which do not take place during an event period specified in a temporary event notice having effect in respect of the premises,

(b) any use of the premises for a qualifying club activity under and in accordance with a club premises certificate, and

(c) any supply exempted under paragraph 3 of Schedule 2 (certain supplies of hot food and drink by clubs, hotels etc not a licensable activity) in circumstances where a person will neither be admitted to the premises, nor be supplied as mentioned in sub-paragraph (1)(b) of that paragraph, except by virtue of being a member of a recognised club or a guest of such a member.

(4) A person is within this subsection if he is–

(a) an appropriate person in relation to the premises,

(b) a person who usually lives at the premises, or

(c) a member of the family of a person within paragraph (a) or (b).

(5) The following expressions have the meanings given–

"appropriate person", in relation to any relevant premises, means–

(a) any person who holds a premises licence in respect of the premises,

(b) any designated premises supervisor under such a licence,

(c) the premises user in relation to any temporary event notice which has effect in respect of the premises, or

(d) a manager of the premises;

"closure notice" has the meaning given in section 169A;

"closure order" has the meaning given in section 161(2);

"extension", in relation to a closure order, means an extension of the order under section 162;

"local weights and measures authority" has the meaning given by section 69 of the Weights and Measures Act 1985;

"manager", in relation to any premises, means a person who works at the premises in a capacity, whether paid or unpaid, which authorises him to close them;

"relevant licensing authority", in relation to any licensed premises, has the same meaning as in Part 3;

"relevant magistrates' court", in relation to any relevant premises, means a magistrates' court acting for the local justice area in which the premises are situated;

"relevant premises" has the meaning given in section 161(8);

"responsible senior police officer", in relation to a closure order, means–

(a)   the senior police officer who made the order, or

(b)   if another senior police officer is designated for the purpose by the chief officer of police for the police area in which the premises are situated, that other officer;

"senior police officer" has the meaning given in section 161(8);

"trading standards officer", in relation to any premises to which a premises licence relates, means a person authorised by a local weights and measures authority to act in the area where those premises are situated in relation to proposed prohibitions contained in closure notices.

(6)   A temporary event notice has effect from the time it is given in accordance with Part 5 until–

(a)   the time it is withdrawn,

(b)   the time a counter notice is given under that Part, or

(c)   the expiry of the event period specified in the temporary event notice,

whichever first occurs.

## PART 9

### MISCELLANEOUS AND SUPPLEMENTARY

#### *Special occasions*

**172   Relaxation of opening hours for special occasions**

(1)   Where the Secretary of State considers that a period ("the celebration period") marks an occasion of exceptional international, national, or local significance, he may make a licensing hours order.

(2)   A licensing hours order is an order which provides that during the specified relaxation period premises licences and club premises certificates have effect (to the extent that it is not already the case) as if specified times were included in the opening hours.

(3)   An order under this section may–

(a)   make provision generally or only in relation to premises in one or more specified areas;

(b)   make different provision in respect of different days during the specified relaxation period;

(c)   make different provision in respect of different licensable activities.

(4)   Before making an order under this section, the Secretary of State must consult such persons as he considers appropriate.

(5)   In this section–

"opening hours" means–

(a)   in relation to a premises licence, the times during which the premises may be used for licensable activities in accordance with the licence, and

(b)   in relation to a club premises certificate, the times during which the premises may be used for qualifying club activities in accordance with the certificate;

"relaxation period" means–

(a)   if the celebration period does not exceed four days, that period, or

(b)    any part of that period not exceeding four days; and

"specified", in relation to a licensing hours order, means specified in the order.

*Exemptions etc*

**173**    **Activities in certain locations not licensable**

(1)    An activity is not a licensable activity if it is carried on–

     (a)    aboard an aircraft, hovercraft or railway vehicle engaged on a journey,

     (b)    aboard a vessel engaged on an international journey,

     (c)    at an approved wharf at a designated port or hoverport,

     (d)    at an examination station at a designated airport,

     (e)    at a royal palace,

     (f)    at premises which, at the time when the activity is carried on, are permanently or temporarily occupied for the purposes of the armed forces of the Crown,

     (g)    at premises in respect of which a certificate issued under section 174 (exemption for national security) has effect, or

     (h)    at such other place as may be prescribed.

(2)    For the purposes of subsection (1) the period during which an aircraft, hovercraft, railway vehicle or vessel is engaged on a journey includes–

     (a)    any period ending with its departure when preparations are being made for the journey, and

     (b)    any period after its arrival at its destination when it continues to be occupied by those (or any of those) who made the journey (or any part of it).

(3)    The Secretary of State may by order designate a port, hoverport or airport for the purposes of subsection (1), if it appears to him to be one at which there is a substantial amount of international passenger traffic.

(4)    Any port, airport or hoverport where section 86A or 87 of the Licensing Act 1964 (c.26) is in operation immediately before the commencement of this section is, on and after that commencement, to be treated for the purposes of subsection (1) as if it were designated.

(5)    But provision may by order be made for subsection (4) to cease to have effect in relation to any port, airport or hoverport.

(6)    For the purposes of this section–

"approved wharf" has the meaning given by section 20A of the Customs and Excise Management Act 1979 (c.2);

"designated" means designated by an order under subsection (3);

"examination station" has the meaning given by section 22A of that Act;

"international journey" means–

     (a)    a journey from a place in the United Kingdom to an immediate destination outside the United Kingdom, or

     (b)    a journey from a place outside the United Kingdom to an immediate destination in the United Kingdom; and

"railway vehicle" has the meaning given by section 83 of the Railways Act 1993 (c.43).

**174**    **Certifying of premises on grounds of national security**

(1)    A Minister of the Crown may issue a certificate under this section in respect of any premises, if he considers that it is appropriate to do so for the purposes of safeguarding national security.

(2)    A certificate under this section may identify the premises in question by means of a general description.

(3)    A document purporting to be a certificate under this section is to be received in evidence and treated as being a certificate under this section unless the contrary is proved.

(4)    A document which purports to be certified by or on behalf of a Minister of the Crown as a true copy of a certificate given by a Minister of the Crown under this section is evidence of that certificate.

(5)   A Minister of the Crown may cancel a certificate issued by him, or any other Minister of the Crown, under this section.

(6)   The powers conferred by this section on a Minister of the Crown may be exercised only by a Minister who is a member of the Cabinet or by the Attorney General.

(7)   In this section "Minister of the Crown" has the meaning given by the Ministers of the Crown Act 1975 (c.26).

**175    Exemption for incidental non-commercial lottery**

(1)   The promotion of a lottery to which this section applies shall not constitute a licensable activity by reason only of one or more of the prizes in the lottery consisting of or including alcohol, provided that the alcohol is in a sealed container.

(2)   This section applies to an incidental non-commercial lottery (within the meaning of Part 1 of Schedule 11 to the Gambling Act 2005).

*Service areas and garages etc*

**176    Prohibition of alcohol sales at service areas, garages etc**

(1)   No premises licence, club premises certificate or temporary event notice has effect to authorise the sale by retail or supply of alcohol on or from excluded premises.

(2)   In this section "excluded premises" means–

    (a)   premises situated on land acquired or appropriated by a special road authority, and for the time being used, for the provision of facilities to be used in connection with the use of a special road provided for the use of traffic of class I (with or without other classes); or

    (b)   premises used primarily as a garage or which form part of premises which are primarily so used.

(3)   The Secretary of State may by order amend the definition of excluded premises in subsection (2) so as to include or exclude premises of such description as may be specified in the order.

(4)   For the purposes of this section–

    (a)   "special road" and "special road authority" have the same meaning as in the Highways Act 1980 (c.66), except that "special road" includes a trunk road to which (by virtue of paragraph 3 of Schedule 23 to that Act) the provisions of that Act apply as if the road were a special road,

    (b)   "class I" means class I in Schedule 4 to the Highways Act 1980 as varied from time to time by an order under section 17 of that Act, but if that Schedule is amended by such an order so as to add to it a further class of traffic, the order may adapt the reference in subsection (2)(a) to traffic of class I so as to take account of the additional class, and

    (c)   premises are used as a garage if they are used for one or more of the following–

        (i)    the retailing of petrol,

        (ii)   the retailing of derv,

        (iii)  the sale of motor vehicles,

        (iv)   the maintenance of motor vehicles.

*Small premises*

**177    Dancing and live music in certain small premises**

(1)   Subsection (2) applies where–

    (a)   a premises licence authorises–

        (i)    the supply of alcohol for consumption on the premises, and

        (ii)   the provision of music entertainment, and

    (b)   the premises–

        (i)    are used primarily for the supply of alcohol for consumption on the premises, and

        (ii)   have a permitted capacity of not more than 200 persons.

(2)  At any time when–
   (a)  the premises–
      (i)  are open for the purposes of being used for the supply of alcohol for consumption on the premises, and
      (ii)  are being used for the provision of music entertainment, and
   (b)  subsection (4) does not apply,
   any licensing authority imposed condition of the premises licence which relates to the provision of music entertainment does not have effect, in relation to the provision of that entertainment, unless it falls within subsection (5) or (6).

(3)  Subsection (4) applies where–
   (a)  a premises licence authorises the provision of music entertainment, and
   (b)  the premises have a permitted capacity of not more than 200 persons.

(4)  At any time between the hours of 8 a.m. and midnight when the premises–
   (a)  are being used for the provision of music entertainment which consists of–
      (i)  the performance of unamplified, live music, or
      (ii)  facilities for enabling persons to take part in entertainment within sub-paragraph (i), but
   (b)  are not being used for the provision of any other description of regulated entertainment,
   any licensing authority imposed condition of the premises licence which relates to the provision of the music entertainment does not have effect, in relation to the provision of that entertainment, unless it falls within subsection (6).

(5)  A condition falls within this subsection if the premises licence specifies that the licensing authority which granted the licence considers the imposition of the condition necessary on one or both of the following grounds–
   (a)  the prevention of crime and disorder,
   (b)  public safety.

(6)  A condition falls within this subsection if, on a review of the premises licence–
   (a)  it is altered so as to include a statement that this section does not apply to it, or
   (b)  it is added to the licence and includes such a statement.

(7)  This section applies in relation to a club premises certificate as it applies in relation to a premises licence except that, in the application of this section in relation to such a certificate, the definition of "licensing authority imposed condition" in subsection (8) has effect as if for "section 18(3)(b)" to the end there were substituted "section 72(3)(b) (but is not referred to in section 72(2)) or which is imposed by virtue of section 85(3)(b) or 88(3)".

(8)  In this section–
   "licensing authority imposed condition" means a condition which is imposed by virtue of section 18(3)(b) (but is not referred to in section 18(2)(a)) or which is imposed by virtue of 35(3)(b), 52(3) or 167(5)(b) or in accordance with section 21;
   "music entertainment" means–
   (a)  entertainment of a description falling within, or of a similar description to that falling within, paragraph 2(1)(e) or (g) of Schedule 1, or
   (b)  facilities enabling persons to take part in entertainment within paragraph (a);
   "permitted capacity", in relation to any premises, means–
      . . .
   (b)  the limit on the number of persons who may be on the premises at any one time in accordance with a recommendation made by, or on behalf of, the fire and rescue authority for the area in which the premises are situated (or, if the premises are situated in the area of more than one fire and rescue authority, those authorities); and
   "supply of alcohol" means–
   (a)  the sale by retail of alcohol, or

(b)    the supply of alcohol by or on behalf of a club to, or to the order of, a member of the club.

*Rights of freeholders etc*

**178    Right of freeholder etc to be notified of licensing matters**

(1)    This section applies where–

(a)    a person with a property interest in any premises situated in the area of a licensing authority gives notice of his interest to that authority, and

(b)    the notice is in the prescribed form and accompanied by the prescribed fee.

(2)    The notice has effect for a period of 12 months beginning with the day it is received by the licensing authority.

(3)    If a change relating to the premises to which the notice relates is made to the register at a time when the notice has effect, the licensing authority must forthwith notify the person who gave the notice–

(a)    of the application, notice or other matter to which the change relates, and

(b)    of his right under section 8 to request a copy of the information contained in any entry in the register.

(4)    For the purposes of this section a person has a property interest in premises if–

(a)    he has a legal interest in the premises as freeholder or leaseholder,

(b)    he is a legal mortgagee (within the meaning of the Law of Property Act 1925 (c.20)) in respect of the premises,

(c)    he is in occupation of the premises, or

(d)    he has a prescribed interest in the premises.

(5)    In this section–

(a)    a reference to premises situated in the area of a licensing authority includes a reference to premises partly so situated, and

(b)    "register" means the register kept under section 8 by the licensing authority mentioned in subsection (1)(a).

*Rights of entry*

**179    Rights of entry to investigate licensable activities**

(1)    Where a constable or an authorised person has reason to believe that any premises are being, or are about to be, used for a licensable activity, he may enter the premises with a view to seeing whether the activity is being, or is to be, carried on under and in accordance with an authorisation.

(2)    An authorised person exercising the power conferred by this section must, if so requested, produce evidence of his authority to exercise the power.

(3)    A person exercising the power conferred by this section may, if necessary, use reasonable force.

(4)    A person commits an offence if he intentionally obstructs an authorised person exercising a power conferred by this section.

(5)    A person guilty of an offence under subsection (4) is liable on summary conviction to a fine not exceeding level 3 on the standard scale.

(6)    In this section–

"authorisation" means–

(a)    a premises licence,

(b)    a club premises certificate, or

(c)    a temporary event notice in respect of which the conditions of section 98(2) to (4) are satisfied; and

"authorised person" means an authorised person within the meaning of Part 3 or 4 or an authorised officer within the meaning of section 108(5).

(7)    Nothing in this section applies in relation to premises in respect of which there is a club premises certificate but no other authorisation.

**180    Right of entry to investigate offences**

(1)    A constable may enter and search any premises in respect of which he has reason to believe that an offence under this Act has been, is being or is about to be committed.

(2)    A constable exercising a power conferred by this section may, if necessary, use reasonable force.

*Appeals*

**181    Appeals against decisions of licensing authorities**

(1)    Schedule 5 (which makes provision for appeals against decisions of licensing authorities) has effect.

(2)    On an appeal in accordance with that Schedule against a decision of a licensing authority, a magistrates' court may–

(a)    dismiss the appeal,

(b)    substitute for the decision appealed against any other decision which could have been made by the licensing authority, or

(c)    remit the case to the licensing authority to dispose of it in accordance with the direction of the court,

and may make such order as to costs as it thinks fit.

*Guidance, hearings etc*

**182    Guidance**

(1)    The Secretary of State must issue guidance ("the licensing guidance") to licensing authorities on the discharge of their functions under this Act.

(2)    But the Secretary of State may not issue the licensing guidance unless a draft of it has been laid before, and approved by resolution of, each House of Parliament.

(3)    The Secretary of State may, from time to time, revise the licensing guidance.

(4)    A revised version of the licensing guidance does not come into force until the Secretary of State lays it before Parliament.

(5)    Where either House, before the end of the period of 40 days beginning with the day on which a revised version of the licensing guidance is laid before it, by resolution disapproves that version–

(a)    the Secretary of State must, under subsection (3), make such further revisions to the licensing guidance as appear to him to be required in the circumstances, and

(b)    before the end of the period of 40 days beginning with the date on which the resolution is made, lay a further revised version of the licensing guidance before Parliament.

(6)    In reckoning any period of 40 days for the purposes of subsection (5), no account is to be taken of any time during which–

(a)    Parliament is dissolved or prorogued, or

(b)    both Houses are adjourned for more than four days.

(7)    The Secretary of State must arrange for any guidance issued or revised under this section to be published in such manner as he considers appropriate.

**183    Hearings**

(1)    Regulations may prescribe the procedure to be followed in relation to a hearing held by a licensing authority under this Act and, in particular, may–

(a)    require a licensing authority to give notice of hearings to such persons as may be prescribed;

(b)    make provision for expedited procedures in urgent cases;

(c)    make provision about the rules of evidence which are to apply to hearings;

(d)    make provision about the legal representation at hearings of the parties to it;

(e)    prescribe the period within which an application, in relation to which a hearing has been held, must be determined or any other step in the procedure must be taken.

(2) But a licensing authority may not make any order as to the costs incurred by a party in connection with a hearing under this Act.

**184 Giving of notices, etc**

(1) This section has effect in relation to any document required or authorised by or under this Act to be given to any person ("relevant document").

(2) Where that person is a licensing authority, the relevant document must be given by addressing it to the authority and leaving it at or sending it by post to–

(a) the principal office of the authority, or

(b) any other office of the authority specified by it as one at which it will accept documents of the same description as that document.

(3) In any other case the relevant document may be given to the person in question by delivering it to him, or by leaving it at his proper address, or by sending it by post to him at that address.

(4) A relevant document may–

(a) in the case of a body corporate (other than a licensing authority), be given to the secretary or clerk of that body;

(b) in the case of a partnership, be given to a partner or a person having the control or management of the partnership business;

(c) in the case of an unincorporated association (other than a partnership), be given to an officer of the association.

(5) For the purposes of this section and section 7 of the Interpretation Act 1978 (c.30) (service of documents by post) in its application to this section, the proper address of any person to whom a relevant document is to be given is his last known address, except that–

(a) in the case of a body corporate or its secretary or clerk, it is the address of the registered office of that body or its principal office in the United Kingdom,

(b) in the case of a partnership, a partner or a person having control or management of the partnership business, it is that of the principal office of the partnership in the United Kingdom, and

(c) in the case of an unincorporated association (other than a partnership) or any officer of the association, it is that of its principal office in the United Kingdom.

(6) But if a relevant document is given to a person in his capacity as the holder of a premises licence, club premises certificate or personal licence, or as the designated premises supervisor under a premises licence, his relevant registered address is also to be treated, for the purposes of this section and section 7 of the Interpretation Act 1978 (c.30), as his proper address.

(7) In subsection (6) "relevant registered address", in relation to such a person, means the address given for that person in the record for the licence or certificate (as the case may be) which is contained in the register kept under section 8 by the licensing authority which granted the licence or certificate.

(8) The following provisions of the Local Government Act 1972 (c.70) do not apply in relation to the service of a relevant document–

(a) section 231 (service of notices on local authorities etc),

(b) section 233 (service of notices by local authorities).

**185 Provision of information**

(1) This section applies to information which is held by or on behalf of a licensing authority or a responsible authority (including information obtained by or on behalf of the authority before the coming into force of this section).

(2) Information to which this section applies may be supplied–

(a) to a licensing authority, or

(b) to a responsible authority,

for the purposes of facilitating the exercise of the authority's functions under this Act.

(3)  Information obtained by virtue of this section must not be further disclosed except to a licensing authority or responsible authority for the purposes mentioned in subsection (2).

(4)  In this section "responsible authority" means a responsible authority within the meaning of Part 3 or 4.

*General provisions about offences*

**186  Proceedings for offences**

(1)  In this section "offence" means an offence under this Act.

(2)  Proceedings for an offence may be instituted–

   (a)  by a licensing authority except in the case of an offence under s 147A,

   (b)  by the Director of Public Prosecutions, or

   (c)  in the case of an offence under section 146 or 147 or 147A (sale of alcohol to children), by a local weights and measures authority (within the meaning of section 69 of the Weights and Measures Act 1985 (c.72)).

(3)  In relation to any offence, section 127(1) of the Magistrates' Courts Act 1980 (information to be laid within six months of offence) is to have effect as if for the reference to six months there were substituted a reference to 12 months.

**187  Offences by bodies corporate etc**

(1)  If an offence committed by a body corporate is shown–

   (a)  to have been committed with the consent or connivance of an officer, or

   (b)  to be attributable to any neglect on his part,

   the officer as well as the body corporate is guilty of the offence and liable to be proceeded against and punished accordingly.

(2)  If the affairs of a body corporate are managed by its members, subsection (1) applies in relation to the acts and defaults of a member in connection with his functions of management as if he were a director of the body.

(3)  In subsection (1) "officer", in relation to a body corporate, means–

   (a)  a director, member of the committee of management, chief executive, manager, secretary or other similar officer of the body, or a person purporting to act in any such capacity, or

   (b)  an individual who is a controller of the body.

(4)  If an offence committed by a partnership is shown–

   (a)  to have been committed with the consent or connivance of a partner, or

   (b)  to be attributable to any neglect on his part,

   the partner as well as the partnership is guilty of the offence and liable to be proceeded against and punished accordingly.

(5)  In subsection (4) "partner" includes a person purporting to act as a partner.

(6)  If an offence committed by an unincorporated association (other than a partnership) is shown–

   (a)  to have been committed with the consent or connivance of an officer of the association or a member of its governing body, or

   (b)  to be attributable to any neglect on the part of such an officer or member,

   that officer or member as well as the association is guilty of the offence and liable to be proceeded against and punished accordingly.

(7)  Regulations may provide for the application of any provision of this section, with such modifications as the Secretary of State considers appropriate, to a body corporate or unincorporated association formed or recognised under the law of a territory outside the United Kingdom.

(8)  In this section "offence" means an offence under this Act.

**188  Jurisdiction and procedure in respect of offences**

(1)  A fine imposed on an unincorporated association on its conviction for an offence is to be paid out of the funds of the association.

App 1

(2) Proceedings for an offence alleged to have been committed by an unincorporated association must be brought in the name of the association (and not in that of any of its members).

(3) Rules of court relating to the service of documents are to have effect as if the association were a body corporate.

(4) In proceedings for an offence brought against an unincorporated association, section 33 of the Criminal Justice Act 1925 (c. 86) and Schedule 3 to the Magistrates' Courts Act 1980 (c.43) (procedure) apply as they do in relation to a body corporate.

(5) Proceedings for an offence may be taken–

  (a) against a body corporate or unincorporated association at any place at which it has a place of business;

  (b) against an individual at any place where he is for the time being.

(6) Subsection (5) does not affect any jurisdiction exercisable apart from this section.

(7) In this section "offence" means an offence under this Act.

*Vessels, vehicles and moveable structures*

**189    Vessels, vehicles and moveable structures**

(1) This Act applies in relation to a vessel which is not permanently moored or berthed as if it were premises situated in the place where it is usually moored or berthed.

(2) Where a vehicle which is not permanently situated in the same place is, or is proposed to be, used for one or more licensable activities while parked at a particular place, the vehicle is to be treated for the purposes of this Act as if it were premises situated at that place.

(3) Where a moveable structure which is not permanently situated in the same place is, or is proposed to be, used for one or more licensable activities while set in a particular place, the structure is to be treated for the purposes of this Act as if it were premises situated at that place.

(4) Where subsection (2) applies in relation to the same vehicle, or subsection (3) applies in relation to the same structure, in respect of more than one place, the premises which by virtue of that subsection are situated at each such place are to be treated as separate premises.

(5) Sections 29 to 31 (which make provision in respect of provisional statements relating to premises licences) do not apply in relation to a vessel, vehicle or structure to which this section applies.

*Interpretation*

**190    Location of sales**

(1) This section applies where the place where a contract for the sale of alcohol is made is different from the place where the alcohol is appropriated to the contract.

(2) For the purposes of this Act the sale of alcohol is to be treated as taking place where the alcohol is appropriated to the contract.

**191    Meaning of "alcohol"**

(1) In this Act, "alcohol" means spirits, wine, beer, cider or any other fermented, distilled or spirituous liquor, but does not include–

  (a) alcohol which is of a strength not exceeding 0.5%; at the time of the sale or supply in question,

  (b) perfume,

  (c) flavouring essences recognised by the Commissioners of Customs and Excise as not being intended for consumption as or with dutiable alcoholic liquor,

  (d) the aromatic flavouring essence commonly known as Angostura bitters,

  (e) alcohol which is, or is included in, a medicinal product or a veterinary medicinal product,

  (f) denatured alcohol,

  (g) methyl alcohol,

    (h)   naphtha, or

    (i)   alcohol contained in liqueur confectionery.

(2)  In this section–

"denatured alcohol" has the same meaning as in section 5 of the Finance Act 1995 (c.4);

"dutiable alcoholic liquor" has the same meaning as in the Alcoholic Liquor Duties Act 1979 (c.4);

"liqueur confectionery" means confectionery which–

    (a)   contains alcohol in a proportion not greater than 0.2 litres of alcohol (of a strength not exceeding 57%) per kilogram of the confectionery, and

    (b)   either consists of separate pieces weighing not more than 42g or is designed to be broken into such pieces for the purpose of consumption;

"medicinal product" has the same meaning as in section 130 of the Medicines Act 1968 (c.67);

"strength" is to be construed in accordance with section 2 of the Alcoholic Liquor Duties Act 1979; and

"veterinary medicinal product" has the same meaning as in regulation 2 of the Veterinary Medicines Regulations 2006.

**192    Meaning of "sale by retail"**

(1)  For the purposes of this Act "sale by retail", in relation to any alcohol, means a sale of alcohol to any person, other than a sale of alcohol that–

    (a)   is within subsection (2),

    (b)   is made from premises owned by the person making the sale, or occupied by him under a lease to which the provisions of Part 2 of the Landlord and Tenant Act 1954 (c.56) (security of tenure) apply, and

    (c)   is made for consumption off the premises.

(2)  A sale of alcohol is within this subsection if it is–

    (a)   to a trader for the purposes of his trade,

    (b)   to a club, which holds a club premises certificate, for the purposes of that club,

    (c)   to the holder of a personal licence for the purpose of making sales authorised by a premises licence,

    (d)   to the holder of a premises licence for the purpose of making sales authorised by that licence, or

    (e)   to the premises user in relation to a temporary event notice for the purpose of making sales authorised by that notice.

**193    Other definitions**

In this Act–

"beer" has the same meaning as in the Alcoholic Liquor Duties Act 1979 (c.4);

"cider" has the same meaning as in that Act;

"crime prevention objective" means the licensing objective mentioned in section 4(2)(a) (prevention of crime and disorder);

"licensed premises" means premises in respect of which a premises licence has effect;

"licensing functions" is to be construed in accordance with section 4(1);

"order", except so far as the contrary intention appears, means an order made by the Secretary of State;

"premises" means any place and includes a vehicle, vessel or moveable structure;

"prescribed" means prescribed by regulations;

"recognised club" means a club which satisfies conditions 1 to 3 of the general conditions in section 62;

"regulations" means regulations made by the Secretary of State;

"vehicle" means a vehicle intended or adapted for use on roads;

"vessel" includes a ship, boat, raft or other apparatus constructed or adapted for floating on water;

"wine" means–

(a) "wine" within the meaning of the Alcoholic Liquor Duties Act 1979, and

(b) "made-wine" within the meaning of that Act;

"working day" means any day other than a Saturday, a Sunday, Christmas Day, Good Friday or a day which is a bank holiday under the Banking and Financial Dealings Act 1971 (c.80) in England and Wales.

**194      Index of defined expressions**

In this Act the following expressions are defined or otherwise explained by the provisions indicated–

| *Expression* | *Interpretation provision* |
|---|---|
| Alcohol | section 191 |
| associate member | section 67(2) |
| authorised person, in Part 3 | section 13 |
| authorised person, in Part 4 | section 69 |
| beer | section 193 |
| cider | section 193 |
| club premises certificate | section 60 |
| conviction, in Part 6 | section 114 |
| crime prevention objective | section 193 |
| designated premises supervisor | section 15 |
| foreign offence, in Part 6 | section 113 |
| given, in relation to a notice, etc | section 184 |
| guest | section 67(1) |
| interested party, in Part 3 | section 13 |
| interested party, in Part 4 | section 69 |
| interim authority notice | section 47 |
| late night refreshment | Schedule 2 |
| licensable activity | section 1(1) |
| licensed premises | section 193 |
| licensing authority | section 3(1) |
| licensing authority's area | section 3(2) |
| licensing functions | sections 4(1) and 193 |
| licensing objectives | section 4(2) |
| order | section 193 |
| permitted temporary activity | section 98 |
| personal licence | section 111(1) |
| premises | section 193 |
| premises licence | section 11 |
| premises user, in relation to a temporary event notice | section 100(2) |
| prescribed | section 193 |
| provisional statement | section 29(3) |
| qualifying club | section 61 |
| qualifying club activity | section 1(2) |
| recognised club | section 193 |
| regulated entertainment | Schedule 1 |
| regulations | section 193 |
| relevant licensing authority, in Part 3 | section 12 |
| relevant licensing authority, in Part 4 | section 68 |

| | |
|---|---|
| relevant licensing authority, in Part 5 | section 99 |
| relevant licensing authority, in Part 6 | section 112 |
| relevant offence, in Part 6 | section 113 |
| responsible authority, in Part 3 | section 13 |
| responsible authority, in Part 4 | section 69 |
| sale by retail, in relation to alcohol | section 192 |
| secretary, in Part 4 | section 70 |
| supply of alcohol, in Part 3 | section 14 |
| supply of alcohol to members or guests, in relation to a club, in Part 4 | section 70 |
| temporary event notice | section 100(1) |
| vehicle | section 193 |
| vessel | section 193 |
| wine | section 193 |
| working day | section 193 |

*Supplementary and general*

**195    Crown application**

(1)   This Act binds the Crown and has effect in relation to land in which there is–

(a)   an interest belonging to Her Majesty in right of the Crown,

(b)   an interest belonging to a government department, or

(c)   an interest held in trust for Her Majesty for the purposes of such a department.

(2)   This Act also applies to–

(a)   land which is vested in, but not occupied by, Her Majesty in right of the Duchy of Lancaster, and

(b)   land which is vested in, but not occupied by, the possessor for the time being of the Duchy of Cornwall.

(3)   No contravention by the Crown of any provision made by or under this Act makes the Crown criminally liable; but the High Court may declare unlawful any act or omission of the Crown which constitutes such a contravention.

(4)   Provision made by or under this Act applies to persons in the public service of the Crown as it applies to other persons.

(5)   But nothing in this Act affects Her Majesty in Her private capacity.

**196    Removal of privileges and exemptions**

No privilege or exemption mentioned in section 199(a) or (b) of the Licensing Act 1964 (c.26) (University of Cambridge and the Vintners of the City of London) operates to exempt any person from the requirements of this Act.

**197    Regulations and orders**

(1)   Any power of the Secretary of State to make regulations or an order under this Act is exercisable by statutory instrument.

(2)   Regulations or an order under this Act–

(a)   may include incidental, supplementary, consequential or transitional provision or savings;

(b)   may make provision generally or only in relation to specified cases;

(c)   may make different provision for different purposes.

(3)   A statutory instrument containing regulations or an order under this Act, other than one containing–

(a)   an order under section 5(2) (order appointing start of first period for which statement of licensing policy to be prepared),

(b)   an order under section 100(8)(alteration of maximum temporary event period),

(c)   an order under section 107(12) (alteration of limit on number of temporary event notices), (ca) an order under section 147A(9) (increase of maximum fine for offence of persistently selling alcohol to children) to which subsection (4A) applies;

(d) an order under section 172 (relaxation of opening hours for special occasions),

(e) an order under section 176(3) (order amending definition of "excluded premises" where alcohol sales are prohibited),

(f) an order under section 201 (commencement), or

(g) an order under paragraph 4 of Schedule 1 (power to amend meaning of regulated entertainment),

is subject to annulment in pursuance of a resolution of either House of Parliament.

(4) A statutory instrument containing an order within subsection (3)(b), (c), (ca), (d), (e) or (g) is not to be made unless a draft of the instrument containing the order has been laid before and approved by a resolution of each House of Parliament.

(4A) This subsection applies to an order under section 147A(9) if it appears to the Secretary of State that the power to make the order is being exercised for purposes that are not confined to the increase of the maximum fine to take account of changes in the value of money.

(5) If a draft of an order within subsection (3)(d) would, apart from this subsection, be treated for the purposes of the Standing Orders of either House of Parliament as a hybrid instrument, it is to proceed in that House as if it were not such an instrument.

## 198 Minor and consequential amendments

(1) Schedule 6 (which makes minor and consequential amendments) has effect.

(2) The Secretary of State may, in consequence of any provision of this Act or of any instrument made under it, by order make such amendments (including repeals or revocations) as appear to him to be appropriate in–

(a) any Act passed, or

(b) any subordinate legislation (within the meaning of the Interpretation Act 1978 (c.30) made,

before that provision comes into force.

## 199 Repeals

The enactments mentioned in Schedule 7 (which include provisions that are spent) are repealed to the extent specified.

## 200 Transitional provision etc

Schedule 8 (which makes transitional and transitory provision and savings) has effect.

## 201 Short title, commencement and extent

(1) This Act may be cited as the Licensing Act 2003.

(2) The preceding provisions (and the Schedules) come into force in accordance with provision made by order.

(3) Subject to subsections (4) and (5), this Act extends to England and Wales only.

(4) Section 155(1) also extends to Northern Ireland.

(5) An amendment or repeal contained in Schedule 6 or 7 has the same extent as the enactment to which it relates.

# SCHEDULES

## SCHEDULE 1

Section 1

### PROVISION OF REGULATED ENTERTAINMENT

#### PART 1

##### GENERAL DEFINITIONS

*The provision of regulated entertainment*

1    (1)    For the purposes of this Act the "provision of regulated entertainment" means the provision of–

   (a)    entertainment of a description falling within paragraph 2, or

   (b)    entertainment facilities falling within paragraph 3,

   where the conditions in sub-paragraphs (2) and (3) are satisfied.

   (2)    The first condition is that the entertainment is, or entertainment facilities are, provided–

   (a)    to any extent for members of the public or a section of the public,

   (b)    exclusively for members of a club which is a qualifying club in relation to the provision of regulated entertainment, or for members of such a club and their guests, or

   (c)    in any case not falling within paragraph (a) or (b), for consideration and with a view to profit.

   (3)    The second condition is that the premises on which the entertainment is, or entertainment facilities are, provided are made available for the purpose, or for purposes which include the purpose, of enabling the entertainment concerned (whether of a description falling within paragraph 2(1) or paragraph 3(2)) to take place.

   To the extent that the provision of entertainment facilities consists of making premises available, the premises are to be regarded for the purposes of this sub-paragraph as premises "on which" entertainment facilities are provided.

   (4)    For the purposes of sub-paragraph (2)(c), entertainment is, or entertainment facilities are, to be regarded as provided for consideration only if any charge–

   (a)    is made by or on behalf of–

      (i)    any person concerned in the organisation or management of that entertainment, or

      (ii)    any person concerned in the organisation or management of those facilities who is also concerned in the organisation or management of the entertainment within paragraph 3(2) in which those facilities enable persons to take part, and

   (b)    is paid by or on behalf of some or all of the persons for whom that entertainment is, or those facilities are, provided.

   (5)    In sub-paragraph (4), "charge" includes any charge for the provision of goods or services.

   (6)    For the purposes of sub-paragraph (4)(a), where the entertainment consists of the performance of live music or the playing of recorded music, a person performing or playing the music is not concerned in the organisation or management of the entertainment by reason only that he does one or more of the following–

   (a)    chooses the music to be performed or played,

   (b)    determines the manner in which he performs or plays it,

   (c)    provides any facilities for the purposes of his performance or playing of the music.

   (7)    This paragraph is subject to Part 2 of this Schedule (exemptions).

*Entertainment*

2 (1) The descriptions of entertainment are–

    (a)   a performance of a play,

    (b)   an exhibition of a film,

    (c)   an indoor sporting event,

    (d)   a boxing or wrestling entertainment,

    (e)   a performance of live music,

    (f)   any playing of recorded music,

    (g)   a performance of dance,

    (h)   entertainment of a similar description to that falling within paragraph (e), (f) or (g),

where the entertainment takes place in the presence of an audience and is provided for the purpose, or for purposes which include the purpose, of entertaining that audience.

  (2) Any reference in sub-paragraph (1) to an audience includes a reference to spectators.

  (3) This paragraph is subject to Part 3 of this Schedule (interpretation).

*Entertainment facilities*

3 (1) In this Schedule, "entertainment facilities" means facilities for enabling persons to take part in entertainment of a description falling within sub-paragraph (2) for the purpose, or for purposes which include the purpose, of being entertained.

  (2) The descriptions of entertainment are–

    (a)   making music,

    (b)   dancing,

    (c)   entertainment of a similar description to that falling within paragraph (a) or (b).

  (3) This paragraph is subject to Part 3 of this Schedule (interpretation).

*Power to amend Schedule*

4 The Secretary of State may by order amend this Schedule for the purpose of modifying–

    (a)   the descriptions of entertainment specified in paragraph 2, or

    (b)   the descriptions of entertainment specified in paragraph 3,

and for this purpose "modify" includes adding, varying or removing any description.

## PART 2

### EXEMPTIONS

*Film exhibitions for the purposes of advertisement, information, education, etc*

5 The provision of entertainment consisting of the exhibition of a film is not to be regarded as the provision of regulated entertainment for the purposes of this Act if its sole or main purpose is to–

    (a)   demonstrate any product,

    (b)   advertise any goods or services, or

    (c)   provide information, education or instruction.

*Film exhibitions: museums and art galleries*

6 The provision of entertainment consisting of the exhibition of a film is not to be regarded as the provision of regulated entertainment for the purposes of this Act if it consists of or forms part of an exhibit put on show for any purposes of a museum or art gallery.

*Music incidental to certain other activities*

7 The provision of entertainment consisting of the performance of live music or the playing of recorded music is not to be regarded as the provision of regulated entertainment

for the purposes of this Act to the extent that it is incidental to some other activity which is not itself–

(a)   a description of entertainment falling within paragraph 2, or

(b)   the provision of entertainment facilities.

*Use of television or radio receivers*

8      The provision of any entertainment or entertainment facilities is not to be regarded as the provision of regulated entertainment for the purposes of this Act to the extent that it consists of the simultaneous reception and playing of a programme included in a programme service within the meaning of the Broadcasting Act 1990 (c. 42).

*Religious services, places of worship etc*

9      The provision of any entertainment or entertainment facilities–

(a)   for the purposes of, or for purposes incidental to, a religious meeting or service, or

(b)   at a place of public religious worship,

is not to be regarded as the provision of regulated entertainment for the purposes of this Act.

*Garden fêtes, etc*

10    (1)   The provision of any entertainment or entertainment facilities at a garden fête, or at a function or event of a similar character, is not to be regarded as the provision of regulated entertainment for the purposes of this Act.

(2)   But sub-paragraph (1) does not apply if the fête, function or event is promoted with a view to applying the whole or part of its proceeds for purposes of private gain.

(3)   In sub-paragraph (2) "private gain", in relation to the proceeds of a fête, function or event, is to be construed in accordance with section 19(3) of the Gambling Act 2005.

*Morris dancing etc*

11    The provision of any entertainment or entertainment facilities is not to be regarded as the provision of regulated entertainment for the purposes of this Act to the extent that it consists of the provision of–

(a)   a performance of morris dancing or any dancing of a similar nature or a performance of unamplified, live music as an integral part of such a performance, or

(b)   facilities for enabling persons to take part in entertainment of a description falling within paragraph (a).

*Vehicles in motion*

12    The provision of any entertainment or entertainment facilities–

(a)   on premises consisting of or forming part of a vehicle, and

(b)   at a time when the vehicle is not permanently or temporarily parked, is not to be regarded as the provision of regulated entertainment for the purposes of this Act.

### PART 3

### INTERPRETATION

*General*

13    This Part has effect for the purposes of this Schedule.

*Plays*

14    (1)   A "performance of a play" means a performance of any dramatic piece, whether involving improvisation or not,–

(a)   which is given wholly or in part by one or more persons actually present and performing, and

(b)   in which the whole or a major proportion of what is done by the person

or persons performing, whether by way of speech, singing or action, involves the playing of a role.

(2)   In this paragraph, "performance" includes rehearsal (and "performing" is to be construed accordingly).

*Film exhibitions*

15    An "exhibition of a film" means any exhibition of moving pictures.

*Indoor sporting events*

16    (1)    An "indoor sporting event" is a sporting event–

      (a)    which takes place wholly inside a building, and

      (b)    at which the spectators present at the event are accommodated wholly inside that building.

    (2)    In this paragraph–

"building" means any roofed structure (other than a structure with a roof which may be opened or closed) and includes a vehicle, vessel or moveable structure,

"sporting event" means any contest, exhibition or display of any sport, and

"sport" includes–

      (a)    any game in which physical skill is the predominant factor, and

      (b)    any form of physical recreation which is also engaged in for purposes of competition or display.

*Boxing or wrestling entertainments*

17    A "boxing or wrestling entertainment" is any contest, exhibition or display of boxing or wrestling.

*Music*

18    "Music" includes vocal or instrumental music or any combination of the two.

### SCHEDULE 2

Section 1

PROVISION OF LATE NIGHT REFRESHMENT

*The provision of late night refreshment*

1    (1)    For the purposes of this Act, a person "provides late night refreshment" if–

      (a)    at any time between the hours of 11.00 p.m. and 5.00 a.m., he supplies hot food or hot drink to members of the public, or a section of the public, on or from any premises, whether for consumption on or off the premises, or

      (b)    at any time between those hours when members of the public, or a section of the public, are admitted to any premises, he supplies, or holds himself out as willing to supply, hot food or hot drink to any persons, or to persons of a particular description, on or from those premises, whether for consumption on or off the premises,

unless the supply is an exempt supply by virtue of paragraphs 3, 4 or 5.

    (2)    References in this Act to the "provision of late night refreshment" are to be construed in accordance with sub-paragraph (1).

    (3)    This paragraph is subject to the following provisions of this Schedule.

*Hot food or hot drink*

2    Food or drink supplied on or from any premises is "hot" for the purposes of this Schedule if the food or drink, or any part of it–

      (a)    before it is supplied, is heated on the premises or elsewhere for the purpose of enabling it to be consumed at a temperature above the ambient air temperature and, at the time of supply, is above that temperature, or

      (b)    after it is supplied, may be heated on the premises for the purpose of enabling it to be consumed at a temperature above the ambient air temperature.

*Exempt supplies: clubs, hotels etc and employees*

3    (1)    The supply of hot food or hot drink on or from any premises at any time is an exempt supply for the purposes of paragraph 1(1) if, at that time, a person will neither–

      (a)    be admitted to the premises, nor

(b)   be supplied with hot food or hot drink on or from the premises, except by virtue of being a person of a description falling within sub-paragraph (2).

(2)   The descriptions are that–

(a)   he is a member of a recognised club,

(b)   he is a person staying at a particular hotel, or at particular comparable premises, for the night in question,

(c)   he is an employee of a particular employer,

(d)   he is engaged in a particular trade, he is a member of a particular profession or he follows a particular vocation,

(e)   he is a guest of a person falling within any of paragraphs (a) to (d).

(3)   The premises which, for the purposes of sub-paragraph (2)(b), are comparable to a hotel are–

(a)   a guest house, lodging house or hostel,

(b)   a caravan site or camping site, or

(c)   any other premises the main purpose of maintaining which is the provision of facilities for overnight accommodation.

*Exempt supplies: premises licensed under certain other Acts*

4     The supply of hot food or hot drink on or from any premises is an exempt supply for the purposes of paragraph 1(1) if it takes place during a period for which–

(a)   the premises may be used for a public exhibition of a kind described in section 21(1) of the Greater London Council (General Powers) Act 1966 (c. xxviii) by virtue of a licence under that section, or

(b)   the premises may be used as near beer premises within the meaning of section 14 of the London Local Authorities Act 1995 (c. x) by virtue of a licence under section 16 of that Act.

*Miscellaneous exempt supplies*

5     (1)   The following supplies of hot food or hot drink are exempt supplies for the purposes of paragraph 1(1)–

(a)   the supply of hot drink which consists of or contains alcohol,

(b)   the supply of hot drink by means of a vending machine,

(c)   the supply of hot food or hot drink free of charge,

(d)   the supply of hot food or hot drink by a registered charity or a person authorised by a registered charity,

(e)   the supply of hot food or hot drink on a vehicle at a time when the vehicle is not permanently or temporarily parked.

(2)   Hot drink is supplied by means of a vending machine for the purposes of sub-paragraph (1)(b) only if–

(a)   the payment for the hot drink is inserted into the machine by a member of the public, and

(b)   the hot drink is supplied directly by the machine to a member of the public.

(3)   Hot food or hot drink is not to be regarded as supplied free of charge for the purposes of sub-paragraph (1)(c) if, in order to obtain the hot food or hot drink, a charge must be paid–

(a)   for admission to any premises, or

(b)   for some other item.

(4)   In sub-paragraph (1)(d) "registered charity" means–

(a)   a charity which is registered under section 3 of the Charities Act 1993 (c. 10), or

(b)   a charity which by virtue of subsection (5) of that section is not required to be so registered.

*Clubs which are not recognised clubs: members and guests*

6     For the purposes of this Schedule–

(a)    the supply of hot food or hot drink to a person as being a member, or the guest of a member, of a club which is not a recognised club is to be taken to be a supply to a member of the public, and

(b)    the admission of any person to any premises as being such a member or guest is to be taken to be the admission of a member of the public.

## SCHEDULE 3

Section 8

### MATTERS TO BE ENTERED IN LICENSING REGISTER

The licensing register kept by a licensing authority under section 8 must contain a record of the following matters–

(a)    any application made to the licensing authority under section 17 (grant of premises licence),

(b)    any application made to it under section 25 (theft etc of premises licence or summary),

(c)    any notice given to it under section 28 (surrender of premises licence),

(d)    any application made to it under section 29 (provisional notice in respect of premises),

(e)    any notice given to it under section 33 (change of name, etc of holder of premises licence),

(f)    any application made to it under section 34 (variation of premises licence),

(g)    any application made to it under section 37 (variation of licence to specify individual as premises supervisor),

(h)    any notice given to it under section 41 (request from designated premises supervisor for removal from premises licence),

(i)    any application made to it under section 42 (transfer of premises licence),

(j)    any notice given to it under section 47 (interim authority notice),

(k)    any application made to it under section 51 (review of premises licence),

(l)    any application made to it under section 71 (application for club premises certificate),

(m)    any application made to it under section 79 (theft, loss, etc. of certificate or summary),

(n)    any notice given to it under section 81 (surrender of club premises certificate),

(o)    any notice given to it under section 82 or 83 (notification of change of name etc),

(p)    any application made to it under section 84 (application to vary club premises certificate),

(q)    any application made to it under section 87 (application for review of club premises certificate),

(r)    any notice given to it under section 103 (withdrawal of temporary event notice),

(s)    any counter notice given by it under section 105 (counter notice following police objection to temporary event notice),

(t)    any copy of a temporary event notice give to it under section 106 (notice given following the making of modifications to a temporary event notice with police consent),

(u)    any application made to it under section 110 (theft etc. of temporary event notice),

(v)    any notice given to it under section 116 (surrender of personal licence),

(w)    any application made to it under section 117 (grant or renewal of personal licence),

(x)    any application made to it under section 126 (theft, loss or destruction of personal licence),

(y)    any notice given to it under section 127 (change of name, etc. of personal licence holder),

(z)    any notice given to it under section 165(4) (magistrates' court to notify any determination made after closure order),

(zi)    any application under paragraph 2 of Schedule 8 (application for conversion of old licences into premises licence),

(zii)    any application under paragraph 14 of that Schedule (application for conversion of club certificate into club premises certificate).

## SCHEDULE 4

Section 113

PERSONAL LICENCE: RELEVANT OFFENCES

1    An offence under this Act.

2    An offence under any of the following enactments–

(a)    Schedule 12 to the London Government Act 1963 (c. 33) (public entertainment licensing);

(b)    the Licensing Act 1964 (c. 26);

(c)    the Private Places of Entertainment (Licensing) Act 1967 (c. 19);

(d)    section 13 of the Theatres Act 1968 (c. 54);

(e)    the Late Night Refreshment Houses Act 1969 (c. 53);

(f)    section 6 of, or Schedule 1 to, the Local Government (Miscellaneous Provisions) Act 1982 (c. 30);

(g)    the Licensing (Occasional Permissions) Act 1983 (c. 24);

(h)    the Cinemas Act 1985 (c. 13);

(i)    the London Local Authorities Act 1990 (c. vii).

3    An offence under the Firearms Act 1968 (c. 27).

4    An offence under section 1 of the Trade Descriptions Act 1968 (c. 29) (false trade description of goods) in circumstances where the goods in question are or include alcohol.

5    An offence under any of the following provisions of the Theft Act 1968 (c. 60)–

(a)    section 1 (theft);

(b)    section 8 (robbery);

(c)    section 9 (burglary);

(d)    section 10 (aggravated burglary);

(e)    section 11 (removal of articles from places open to the public);

(f)    section 12A (aggravated vehicle-taking), in circumstances where subsection (2)(b) of that section applies and the accident caused the death of any person;

(g)    section 13 (abstracting of electricity);

(h)    section 15 (obtaining property by deception);

(i)    section 15A (obtaining a money transfer by deception);

(j)    section 16 (obtaining pecuniary advantage by deception);

(k)    section 17 (false accounting);

(l)    section 19 (false statements by company directors etc);

(m)    section 20 (suppression, etc of documents);

(n)    section 21 (blackmail);

(o)    section 22 (handling stolen goods);

(p)    section 24A (dishonestly retaining a wrongful credit);

(q)    section 25 (going equipped for stealing etc).

6    An offence under section 7(2) of the Gaming Act 1968 (c. 65) (allowing child to take part in gaming on premises licensed for the sale of alcohol).

7    An offence under any of the following provisions of the Misuse of Drugs Act 1971 (c. 38)–

(a)    section 4(2) (production of a controlled drug);

(b)    section 4(3) (supply of a controlled drug);

(c)    section 5(3) (possession of a controlled drug with intent to supply);

(d)    section 8 (permitting activities to take place on premises).

8    An offence under either of the following provisions of the Theft Act 1978 (c. 31)–

(a)    section 1 (obtaining services by deception);

(b)    section 2 (evasion of liability by deception).

App 1

9    An offence under either of the following provisions of the Customs and Excise Management Act 1979 (c. 2)–
     (a)    section 170 (disregarding subsection (1)(a)) (fraudulent evasion of duty etc.);
     (b)    section 170B (taking preparatory steps for evasion of duty).

10   An offence under either of the following provisions of the Tobacco Products Duty Act 1979 (c. 7)–
     (a)    section 8G (possession and sale of unmarked tobacco);
     (b)    section 8H (use of premises for sale of unmarked tobacco).

11   An offence under the Forgery and Counterfeiting Act 1981 (c. 45) (other than an offence under section 18 or 19 of that Act).

12   An offence under the Firearms (Amendment) Act 1988 (c. 45).

13   An offence under any of the following provisions of the Copyright, Designs and Patents Act 1988 (c. 48)–
     (a)    section 107(1)(d)(iii) (public exhibition in the course of a business of article infringing copyright);
     (b)    section 107(3) (infringement of copyright by public performance of work etc);
     (c)    section 198(2) (broadcast etc of recording of performance made without sufficient consent);
     (d)    section 297(1) (fraudulent reception of transmission);
     (e)    section 297A(1) (supply etc of unauthorised decoder).

14   An offence under any of the following provisions of the Road Traffic Act 1988 (c. 52)–
     (a)    section 3A (causing death by careless driving while under the influence of drink or drugs);
     (b)    section 4 (driving etc a vehicle when under the influence of drink or drugs);
     (c)    section 5 (driving etc a vehicle with alcohol concentration above prescribed limit).

15   An offence under either of the following provisions of the Food Safety Act 1990 (c. 16) in circumstances where the food in question is or includes alcohol–
     (a)    section 14 (selling food or drink not of the nature, substance or quality demanded);
     (b)    section 15 (falsely describing or presenting food or drink).

16   An offence under section 92(1) or (2) of the Trade Marks Act 1994 (c. 26) (unauthorised use of trade mark, etc in relation to goods) in circumstances where the goods in question are or include alcohol.

17   An offence under the Firearms (Amendment) Act 1997 (c. 5).

18   A sexual offence, being an offence listed in Pt 2 of Sched 15 to the Criminal Justice Act 2003, other than the offence mentioned in para 95 (an offence under section 4 of the Sexual Offences Act 1967 (procuring others to commit homosexual acts)); an offence under section 8 of the Sexual Offences Act 1956 (intercourse with a defective); and an offence under section 18 of the Sexual Offences Act 1956 (fraudulent abduction of an heiress).

19   A violent offence, being any offence which leads, or is intended or likely to lead, to a person's death or to physical injury to a person, including an offence which is required to be charged as arson (whether or not it would otherwise fall within this definition).

20   An offence under section 3 of the Private Security Industry Act 2001 (c. 12) (engaging in certain activities relating to security without a licence).

21   An offence under section 46 of the Gambling Act 2005 if the child or young person was invited, caused or permitted to gamble on premises in respect of which a premises licence under this Act had effect.

22   An offence under the Fraud Act 2006.

## SCHEDULE 5

Section 181

### APPEALS

### PART 1

### PREMISES LICENCES

*Rejection of applications relating to premises licences*

1      Where a licensing authority–

    (a)   rejects an application for a premises licence under section 18,

    (b)   rejects (in whole or in part) an application to vary a premises licence under section 35,

    (c)   rejects an application to vary a premises licence to specify an individual as the premises supervisor under section 39, or

    (d)   rejects an application to transfer a premises licence under section 44, the applicant may appeal against the decision.

*Decision to grant premises licence or impose conditions etc*

2      (1)   This paragraph applies where a licensing authority grants a premises licence under section 18.

    (2)   The holder of the licence may appeal against any decision–

        (a)   to impose conditions on the licence under subsection (2)(a) or (3)(b) of that section, or

        (b)   to take any step mentioned in subsection (4)(b) or (c) of that section (exclusion of licensable activity or refusal to specify person as premises supervisor).

    (3)   Where a person who made relevant representations in relation to the application desires to contend–

        (a)   that the licence ought not to have been granted, or

        (b)   that, on granting the licence, the licensing authority ought to have imposed different or additional conditions, or to have taken a step mentioned in subsection (4)(b) or (c) of that section,

    he may appeal against the decision.

    (4)   In sub-paragraph (3) "relevant representations" has the meaning given in section 18(6).

*Issue of provisional statement*

3      (1)   This paragraph applies where a provisional statement is issued under subsection (3)(c) of section 31.

    (2)   An appeal against the decision may be made by–

        (a)   the applicant, or

        (b)   any person who made relevant representations in relation to the application.

    (3)   In sub-paragraph (2) "relevant representations" has the meaning given in subsection (5) of that section.

*Variation of licence under section 35*

4      (1)   This paragraph applies where an application to vary a premises licence is granted (in whole or in part) under section 35.

    (2)   The applicant may appeal against any decision to modify the conditions of the licence under subsection (4)(a) of that section.

    (3)   Where a person who made relevant representations in relation to the application desires to contend–

        (a)   that any variation made ought not to have been made, or

        (b)   that, when varying the licence, the licensing authority ought not to have modified the conditions of the licence, or ought to have modified them in a different way, under subsection (4)(a) of that section,

    he may appeal against the decision.

(4) In sub-paragraph (3) "relevant representations" has the meaning given in section 35(5).

*Variation of licence to specify individual as premises supervisor*

5 (1) This paragraph applies where an application to vary a premises licence is granted under section 39(2) in a case where a chief officer of police gave a notice under section 37(5) (which was not withdrawn).

(2) The chief officer of police may appeal against the decision to grant the application.

*Transfer of licence*

6 (1) This paragraph applies where an application to transfer a premises licence is granted under section 44 in a case where a chief officer of police gave a notice under section 42(6) (which was not withdrawn).

(2) The chief officer of police may appeal against the decision to grant the application.

*Interim authority notice*

7 (1) This paragraph applies where–

(a) an interim authority notice is given in accordance with section 47, and

(b) a chief officer of police gives a notice under section 48(2) (which is not withdrawn).

(2) Where the relevant licensing authority decides to cancel the interim authority notice under subsection (3) of section 48, the person who gave the interim authority notice may appeal against that decision.

(3) Where the relevant licensing authority decides not to cancel the notice under that subsection, the chief officer of police may appeal against that decision.

(4) Where an appeal is brought under sub-paragraph (2), the court to which it is brought may, on such terms as it thinks fit, order the reinstatement of the interim authority notice pending–

(a) the disposal of the appeal, or

(b) the expiry of the interim authority period,

whichever first occurs.

(5) Where the court makes an order under sub-paragraph (4), the premises licence is reinstated from the time the order is made, and section 47 has effect in a case where the appeal is dismissed or abandoned before the end of the interim authority period as if–

(a) the reference in subsection (7)(b) to the end of the interim authority period were a reference to the time when the appeal is dismissed or abandoned, and

(b) the reference in subsection (9)(a) to the interim authority period were a reference to that period disregarding the part of it which falls after that time.

(6) In this paragraph "interim authority period" has the same meaning as in section 47.

*Review of premises licence*

8 (1) This paragraph applies where an application for a review of a premises licence is decided under section 52.

(2) An appeal may be made against that decision by–

(a) the applicant for the review,

(b) the holder of the premises licence, or

(c) any other person who made relevant representations in relation to the application.

(3) In sub-paragraph (2) "relevant representations" has the meaning given in section 52(7).

*Summary review of premises licence*

8A (1) This paragraph applies where a review of a premises licence is decided under section 53A(2)(b) (review of premises licence following review notice).

(2) An appeal may be made against that decision by–

      (a)  the chief officer of police for the police area (or each police area) in which the premises are situated,

      (b)  the holder of the premises licence, or

      (c)  any other person who made relevant representations in relation to the application for the review.

    (3)  In sub-paragraph (2) 'relevant representations' has the meaning given in section 53C(7).

*General provision about appeals under this Part*

9    (1)  An appeal under this Part must be made to a magistrates' court.

    (2)  An appeal under this Part must be commenced by notice of appeal given by the appellant to the designated officer for the magistrates' court within the period of 21 days beginning with the day on which the appellant was notified by the licensing authority of the decision appealed against.

    (3)  On an appeal under paragraphs 2(3), 3(2)(b), 4(3), 5(2), 6(2) or 8(2)(a) or (c), the holder of the premises licence is to be the respondent in addition to the licensing authority.

    (4)  On an appeal under paragraph 7(3), the person who gave the interim authority notice is to be the respondent in addition to the licensing authority.

PART 2

CLUB PREMISES CERTIFICATES

*Rejection of applications relating to club premises certificates*

10    Where a licensing authority–

      (a)  rejects an application for a club premises certificate under section 72, or

      (b)  rejects (in whole or in part) an application to vary a club premises certificate under section 85,

    the club that made the application may appeal against the decision.

*Decision to grant club premises certificate or impose conditions etc*

11    (1)  This paragraph applies where a licensing authority grants a club premises certificate under section 72.

    (2)  The club holding the certificate may appeal against any decision–

      (a)  to impose conditions on the certificate under subsection (2) or (3)(b) of that section, or

      (b)  to take any step mentioned in subsection (4)(b) of that section (exclusion of qualifying club activity).

    (3)  Where a person who made relevant representations in relation to the application desires to contend–

      (a)  that the certificate ought not to have been granted, or

      (b)  that, on granting the certificate, the licensing authority ought to have imposed different or additional conditions, or to have taken a step mentioned in subsection (4)(b) of that section,

    he may appeal against the decision.

    (4)  In sub-paragraph (3) "relevant representations" has the meaning given in section 72(7).

*Variation of club premises certificate*

12    (1)  This paragraph applies where an application to vary a club premises certificate is granted (in whole or in part) under section 85.

    (2)  The club may appeal against any decision to modify the conditions of the certificate under subsection (3)(b) of that section.

    (3)  Where a person who made relevant representations in relation to the application desires to contend–

      (a)  that any variation ought not to have been made, or

(b)  that, when varying the certificate, the licensing authority ought not to have modified the conditions of the certificate, or ought to have modified them in a different way, under subsection (3)(b) of that section,

he may appeal against the decision.

(4)  In sub-paragraph (3) "relevant representations" has the meaning given in section 85(5).

*Review of club premises certificate*

13  (1)  This paragraph applies where an application for a review of a club premises certificate is decided under section 88.

(2)  An appeal may be made against that decision by–

(a)  the applicant for the review,

(b)  the club that holds or held the club premises certificate, or

(c)  any other person who made relevant representations in relation to the application.

(3)  In sub-paragraph (2) "relevant representations" has the meaning given in section 88(7).

*Withdrawal of club premises certificate*

14  Where the relevant licensing authority gives notice withdrawing a club premises certificate under section 90, the club which holds or held the certificate may appeal against the decision to withdraw it.

*General provision about appeals under this Part*

15  (1)  An appeal under this Part must be made to a magistrates' court.

(2)  An appeal under this Part must be commenced by notice of appeal given by the appellant to the designated officer for the magistrates' court within the period of 21 days beginning with the day on which the appellant was notified by the licensing authority of the decision appealed against.

(3)  On an appeal under paragraph 11(3), 12(3) or 13(2)(a) or (c), the club that holds or held the club premises certificate is to be the respondent in addition to the licensing authority.

PART 3

OTHER APPEALS

*Temporary event notices*

16  (1)  This paragraph applies where–

(a)  a temporary event notice is given under section 100, and

(b)  a chief officer of police gives an objection notice in accordance with section 104(2).

(2)  Where the relevant licensing authority gives a counter notice under section 105(3), the premises user may appeal against that decision.

(3)  Where that authority decides not to give such a counter notice, the chief officer of police may appeal against that decision.

(4)  An appeal under this paragraph must be made to a magistrates' court.

(5)  An appeal under this paragraph must be commenced by notice of appeal given by the appellant to the designated officer for the magistrates' court within the period of 21 days beginning with the day on which the appellant was notified by the licensing authority of the decision appealed against.

(6)  But no appeal may be brought later than five working days before the day on which the event period specified in the temporary event notice begins.

(7)  On an appeal under sub-paragraph (3), the premises user is to be the respondent in addition to the licensing authority.

(8)  In this paragraph–

"objection notice" has the same meaning as in section 104; and

"relevant licensing authority" has the meaning given in section 99.

*Personal licences*

17  (1)  Where a licensing authority–

(a)  rejects an application for the grant of a personal licence under section 120, or

(b)  rejects an application for the renewal of a personal licence under section 121,

the applicant may appeal against that decision.

(2)  Where a licensing authority grants an application for a personal licence under section 120(7), the chief officer of police who gave the objection notice (within the meaning of section 120(5)) may appeal against that decision.

(3)  Where a licensing authority grants an application for the renewal of a personal licence under section 121(6), the chief officer of police who gave the objection notice (within the meaning of section 121(3)) may appeal against that decision.

(4)  Where a licensing authority revokes a personal licence under section 124(4), the holder of the licence may appeal against that decision.

(5)  Where in a case to which section 124 (convictions coming to light after grant or renewal) applies–

(a)  the chief officer of police for the licensing authority's area gives a notice under subsection (3) of that section (and does not later withdraw it), and

(b)  the licensing authority decides not to revoke the licence, the chief officer of police may appeal against the decision.

(6)  An appeal under this paragraph must be made to a magistrates' court.

(7)  An appeal under this paragraph must be commenced by notice of appeal given by the appellant to the designated officer for the magistrates' court within the period of 21 days beginning with the day on which the appellant was notified by the licensing authority of the decision appealed against.

(8)  On an appeal under sub-paragraph (2), (3) or (5), the holder of the personal licence is to be the respondent in addition to the licensing authority.

(9)  Sub-paragraph (10) applies where the holder of a personal licence gives notice of appeal against a decision of a licensing authority to refuse to renew it.

(10)  The relevant licensing authority, or the magistrates' court to which the appeal has been made, may, on such conditions as it thinks fit–

(a)  order that the licence is to continue in force until the relevant time, if it would otherwise cease to have effect before that time, or

(b)  where the licence has already ceased to have effect, order its reinstatement until the relevant time.

(11)  In sub-paragraph (10) "the relevant time" means–

(a)  the time the appeal is dismissed or abandoned, or

(b)  where the appeal is allowed, the time the licence is renewed.

*Closure orders*

18  (1)  This paragraph applies where, on a review of a premises licence under section 167, the relevant licensing authority decides under subsection (5)(b) of that section–

(a)  to take any of the steps mentioned in subsection (6) of that section, in relation to a premises licence for those premises, or

(b)  not to take any such step.

(2)  An appeal may be made against that decision by–

(a)  the holder of the premises licence, or

(b)  any other person who made relevant representations in relation to the review.

(3)  Where an appeal is made under this paragraph against a decision to take any of the steps mentioned in section 167(6)(a) to (d) (modification of licence conditions etc), the magistrates' court may in a case within section 168(3) (premises closed when decision taken)–

(a)  if the relevant licensing authority has not made an order under section 168(5) (order suspending operation of decision in whole or part), make any order under section 168(5) that could have been made by the relevant licensing authority, or

(b)   if the authority has made such an order, cancel it or substitute for it any order which could have been made by the authority under section 168(5).

(4)   Where an appeal is made under this paragraph in a case within section 168(6) (premises closed when decision to revoke made to remain closed pending appeal), the magistrates court may, on such conditions as it thinks fit, order that section 168(7) (premises to remain closed pending appeal) is not to apply to the premises.

(5)   An appeal under this paragraph must be commenced by notice of appeal given by the appellant to the designated officer for the magistrates' court within the period of 21 days beginning with the day on which the appellant was notified by the relevant licensing authority of the decision appealed against.

(6)   On an appeal under this paragraph by a person other than the holder of the premises licence, that holder is to be the respondent in addition to the licensing authority that made the decision.

(7)   In this paragraph–

"relevant licensing authority" has the same meaning as in Part 3 of this Act; and

"relevant representations" has the meaning given in section 167(9).

## SCHEDULE 6

Section 198

### MINOR AND CONSEQUENTIAL AMENDMENTS

*Universities (Wine Licences) Act 1743 (c. 40)*

1     The Universities (Wine Licences) Act 1743 ceases to have effect.

*Disorderly Houses Act 1751 (c. 36)*

2     The Disorderly Houses Act 1751 does not apply in relation to relevant premises within the meaning of section 159 of the Licensing Act 2003.

*Sunday Observance Act 1780 (c. 49)*

3     The Sunday Observance Act 1780 ceases to have effect.

*Town Police Clauses Act 1847 (c. 89)*

4     Section 35 of the Town Police Clauses Act 1847 (harbouring thieves or prostitutes at a public venue) ceases to have effect.

*Cambridge Award Act 1856 (c. xvii)*

5     The following provisions of the Cambridge Award Act 1856 cease to have effect–

(a)   section 9 (revocation of alehouse licence by justice of the peace following complaint by Vice Chancellor of the University), and

(b)   section 11 (power to grant wine licence, etc to remain vested in the Chancellor, Masters and Scholars of the University).

*Inebriates Act 1898 (c. 60)*

6     In the First Schedule to the Inebriates Act 1898 (offences by reference to which section 6 of the Licensing Act 1902 operates)–

(a)   omit the entry relating to section 18 of the Licensing Act 1872 and the entry relating to section 41 of the Refreshment Houses Act 1860, and

(b)   after the entries relating to the Merchant Shipping Act 1894 insert–

| "Failing to leave licensed premises, etc. when asked to do so. Entering, or attempting to enter, licensed premises, etc when asked not to do so. | Licensing Act 2003, s 143." |

*Licensing Act 1902 (c. 28)*

7     The Licensing Act 1902 is amended as follows.

8   (1)   Section 6 (prohibition of sale of alcohol to person declared by the court to be a habitual drunkard) is amended as follows.

    (2)   For subsection (2) substitute–

"(2) Subsections (2A) to (2C) apply where a court, in pursuance of this Act, orders notice of a conviction to be sent to a police authority.

(2A) The court shall inform the convicted person that the notice is to be sent to a police authority.

(2B) The convicted person commits an offence if, within the three year period, he buys or obtains, or attempts to buy or obtain, alcohol on relevant premises.

(2C) A person to whom subsection (2D) applies commits an offence if, within the three year period, he knowingly–

     (a)   sells, supplies or distributes alcohol on relevant premises, or

     (b)   allows the sale, supply or distribution of alcohol on relevant premises,

to, or for consumption by, the convicted person.

(2D) This subsection applies–

     (a)   to any person who works at the premises in a capacity, whether paid or unpaid, which gives him authority to sell, supply or distribute the alcohol concerned,

     (b)   in the case of licensed premises, to–

        (i)   the holder of a premises licence which authorises the sale or supply of alcohol, and

        (ii)   the designated premises supervisor (if any) under such a licence,

     (c)   in the case of premises in respect of which a club premises certificate authorising the sale or supply of alcohol has effect, to any member or officer of the club which holds the certificate who at the time the sale, supply or distribution takes place is present on the premises in a capacity which enables him to prevent it, and

     (d)   in the case of premises which may be used for a permitted temporary activity by virtue of Part 5 of the Licensing Act 2003, the premises user in respect of a temporary event notice authorising the sale or supply of alcohol.

(2E) A person guilty of an offence under this section is liable on summary conviction–

     (a)   in the case of an offence under subsection (2B), to a fine not exceeding level 1 on the standard scale, and

     (b)   in the case of an offence under subsection (2C), to a fine not exceeding level 2 on the standard scale."

    (3)   In subsection (3), for "licensed persons, and secretaries of clubs registered under Part III of this Act," substitute "persons to whom subsection (4) applies".

    (4)   After that subsection insert–

"(4) This subsection applies to–

     (a)   the holder of a premises licence which authorises the sale or supply of alcohol,

     (b)   the designated premises supervisor (if any) under such a licence,

     (c)   the holder of a club premises certificate authorising the sale or supply of alcohol, and

     (d)   the premises user in relation to a temporary event notice authorising the sale or supply or alcohol.

    (5)   In this section–

"alcohol", "club premises certificate", "designated premises supervisor", "licensed premises", "permitted temporary activity", "premises licence", "premises user" and "temporary event notice" have the same meaning as in the Licensing Act 2003,

"relevant premises" means premises which are relevant premises within the meaning of section 159 of that Act and on which alcohol may be lawfully sold or supplied, and "the three year period", in relation to the convicted person, means the period of three years beginning with the day of the conviction."

9    After section 8 (meaning of "public place") insert–

**"8A Interpretation of "licensed premises"**

For those purposes, "licensed premises" includes–

(a)    any licensed premises within the meaning of section 193 of the Licensing Act 2003, and

(b)    any premises which may be used for a permitted temporary activity by virtue of Part 5 of that Act."

*Celluloid and Cinematograph Film Act 1922 (c. 35)*

10    At the end of section 2 of the Celluloid and Cinematograph Film Act 1922 (premises to which the Act does not apply), add "or which may, by virtue of an authorisation (within the meaning of section 136 of the Licensing Act 2003), be used for an exhibition of a film (within the meaning of paragraph 15 of Schedule 1 to that Act)".

*Sunday Entertainments Act 1932 (c. 51)*

11    The Sunday Entertainments Act 1932 ceases to have effect.

*Children and Young Persons Act 1933 (c. 12)*

12    The Children and Young Persons Act 1933 is amended as follows.

13    In section 5 (giving alcohol to a child under five) for "intoxicating liquor" substitute "alcohol (within the meaning given by section 191 of the Licensing Act 2003, but disregarding subsection (1)(f) to (i) of that section)".

14    In section 12 (failing to provide for safety of children at entertainments)–

(a)    in subsection (3) omit the words from ", and also" to the end,

(b)    in subsection (5), for paragraph (a) substitute–

"(a)    in the case of a building in respect of which a premises licence authorising the provision of regulated entertainment has effect, be the duty of the relevant licensing authority;", and

(c)    after that subsection, insert–

"(5A)  For the purposes of this section–

(a)    "premises licence" and "the provision of regulated entertainment" have the meaning given by the Licensing Act 2003, and

(b)    "the relevant licensing authority", in relation to a building in respect of which a premises licence has effect, means the relevant licensing authority in relation to that building under section 12 of that Act."

15    In section 107 (interpretation), omit the definition of "intoxicating liquor".

*Public Health Act 1936 (c. 49)*

16    In section 226 of the Public Health Act 1936 (power of local authority to close swimming bath and use it instead for other purposes)–

(a)    for subsection (3) substitute–

"(3)    Nothing in this section shall authorise the use of a swimming bath or bathing place for the provision of regulated entertainment (within the meaning of the Licensing Act 2003), unless that activity is carried on under and in accordance with an authorisation (within the meaning given in section 136 of that Act).", and

(b)    omit subsection (4).

*London Building Acts (Amendment) Act 1939 (c. xcvii)*

17    In each of the following provisions of the London Building Acts (Amendment) Act 1939, for "the premises are so licensed" substitute "the premises are premises which, by virtue of a premises licence under the Licensing Act 2003, may be used for the supply of alcohol (within the meaning of section 14 of that Act) for consumption on the premises"–

(a)    section 11(9)(b) (exemption of licensed premises from provision as to naming of buildings),

(b)   paragraph (A) of the proviso to section 13 (offences as to numbering or naming of buildings).

*Civic Restaurants Act 1947 (c. 22)*

18    In section 1(4) of the Civic Restaurants Act 1947 (civic restaurant authority to be subject to law relating to sale of alcohol), for "the enactments relating to the sale of intoxicating liquor" substitute "the Licensing Act 2003 and any other enactment relating to the sale of intoxicating liquor".

*London County Council (General Powers) Act 1947 (c. xlvi)*

19    In section 6(1)(b) of the London County Council (General Powers) Act 1947 (saving in connection with the provision of entertainment for enactments relating to the sale of alcohol), for "any enactment relating to the sale of intoxicating liquor" substitute "the Licensing Act 2003 and any other enactment relating to the sale of intoxicating liquor".

*National Parks and Access to the Countryside Act 1949 (c. 97)*

20    In each of the following provisions of the National Parks and Countryside Act 1949, for "intoxicating liquor" substitute "alcohol (within the meaning of the Licensing Act 2003)"–

(a)   section 12(1)(a) (provision of facilities in National Park),

(b)   section 54(2) (provision of facilities along long-distance routes).

*Reserve and Auxiliary Forces (Protection of Civil Interests) Act 1951 (c. 65)*

21    The Reserve and Auxiliary Forces (Protection of Civil Interests) Act 1951 is amended as follows.

22    In section 14(2)(a) (protection against insecurity of tenure of place of residence), after "premises" insert "in England and Wales which, by virtue of a premises licence under the Licensing Act 2003, may be used for the supply of alcohol (within the meaning of section 14 of that Act) on the premises or in Scotland which are".

23    In section 18(3)(a) (protection against insecurity of tenure in connection with employ-ment), after "premises" insert "in England and Wales which, by virtue of a premises licence under the Licensing Act 2003, may be used for the supply of alcohol (within the meaning of section 14 of that Act) on the premises for consumption on the premises or in Scotland which are".

24    In section 27(1) (renewal of tenancy expiring during period of service), in the second paragraph (c), for the words "licensed for the sale of intoxicating liquor for consump-tion on the premises" substitute "which, by virtue of a premises licence under the Licensing Act 2003, may be used for the supply of alcohol (within the meaning of section 14 of that Act) for consumption on the premises".

*Hypnotism Act 1952 (c. 46)*

25    The Hypnotism Act 1952 is amended as follows.

26    (1)   Section 1 (inclusion in an entertainment licence of conditions in relation to demonstrations of hypnotism) is amended as follows.

(2)   In subsection (1)–

(a)   after "any area" insert "in Scotland", and

(b)   for "places kept or ordinarily used for public dancing, singing, music or other public entertainment of the like kind" substitute "theatres or other places of public amusement or public entertainment".

(3)   Omit subsection (2).

27    In section 2 (requirement for authorisation for demonstration of hypnotism)–

(a)   in subsection (1), for the words from "in relation" to the end substitute ", unless–

(a)   the controlling authority have authorised that exhibition, demonstration or performance under this section, or

(b)   the place is in Scotland and a licence mentioned in section 1 of this Act is in force in relation to it.",

(b)   in subsection (1A) for the words from "either at premises" to the end substitute "at premises in Scotland in respect of which a licence under that Act is in force",

(c)  after subsection (3) insert–

"(3A) A function conferred by this section on a licensing authority is, for the purposes of section 7 of the Licensing Act 2003 (exercise and delegation by licensing authority of licensing functions), to be treated as a licensing function within the meaning of that Act.", and

(d)  for subsection (4) substitute–

"(4) In this section–

"controlling authority" means–

(a)  in relation to a place in England and Wales, the licensing authority in whose area the place, or the greater or greatest part of it, is situated, and

(b)  in relation to a place in Scotland, the authority having power to grant licences of the kind mentioned in section 1 in that area, and "licensing authority" has the meaning given by the Licensing Act 2003."

*Obscene Publications Act 1959 (c. 66)*

28  (1)  Section 2 of the Obscene Publications Act 1959 (prohibition of publication of obscene matter) is amended as follows.

(2)  In subsections (3A) and (4A), for "a film exhibition" in each place it occurs, substitute "an exhibition of a film".

(3)  For subsection (7) substitute–

"(7) In this section, "exhibition of a film" has the meaning given in paragraph 15 of Schedule 1 to the Licensing Act 2003."

. . .

*Children and Young Persons Act 1963 (c. 37)*

32  For section 37(2)(b) of the Children and Young Persons Act 1963 (restriction on performance by child in licensed premises) substitute–

"(b)  any performance in premises–

(i)  which, by virtue of an authorisation (within the meaning of section 136 of the Licensing Act 2003), may be used for the supply of alcohol (within the meaning of section 14 of that Act), or

(ii)  which are licensed premises (within the meaning of the Licensing (Scotland) Act 1976) or in respect of which a club is registered under that Act;".

*Offices, Shops and Railway Premises Act 1963 (c. 41)*

33  In section 90 of the Offices, Shops and Railway Premises Act 1963 (interpretation), omit the definition of "place of public entertainment".

*Greater London Council (General Powers) Act 1966 (c. xxviii)*

34  The Greater London Council (General Powers) Act 1966 is amended as follows.

35  In section 21(1) (licensing of public exhibitions, etc.)–

(a)  for "intoxicating liquor" substitute "alcohol (within the meaning of the Licensing Act 2003)", and

(b)  for "a film exhibition within the meaning of the Cinemas Act 1985" substitute "an exhibition of a film (within the meaning of paragraph 15 of Schedule 1 to the Licensing Act 2003)".

36  In section 22 (application to old buildings of provisions for protection against fire in the London Building Acts (Amendment) Act 1939)–

(a)  in subsection (1), for the words from "being in either case" to "for that purpose" substitute "which may lawfully be used for the provision of regulated entertainment (within the meaning of the Licensing Act 2003) only by virtue of an authorisation under that Act", and

(b)  in subsection (2), for the words from "where" to "that licence" substitute "where a building, or part of a building, is being used for the provision of regulated entertainment by virtue of a premises licence (under the Licensing Act 2003) granted by a borough council, the Common Council, the Sub-Treasurer of the Inner Temple or the Under-Treasurer of the Middle Temple".

*Finance Act 1967 (c. 54)*

37  In section 5 of the Finance Act 1967 (no requirement for excise licence)–
   (a)  in subsection (1), omit paragraph (c), and
   (b)  in subsection (3), omit "which is registered within the meaning of the Licensing Act 1964 or".

*Criminal Appeal Act 1968 (c. 19)*

38  The Criminal Appeal Act 1968 is amended as follows.

39  In section 10 (appeal against sentence to Crown Court), at the end of subsection (3)(c) add–
   "(viii) an order under section 129 of the Licensing Act 2003 (forfeiture or suspension of personal licence); or".

40  In section 31 (powers of Court of Appeal under Part 1 exercisable by single judge), after subsection (2B) insert–
   "(2C) The power of the Court of Appeal, under section 130 of the Licensing Act 2003, to suspend an order under section 129 of that Act may be exercised by a single judge in the same manner as it may be exercised by the Court."

41  In section 44 (powers of Court of Appeal under Part 2 exercisable by single judge), after subsection (2) insert–
   "(3) The power of the Court of Appeal, under section 130 of the Licensing Act 2003, to suspend an order under section 129 of that Act may be exercised by a single judge, but where the judge refuses an application to exercise that power the applicant shall be entitled to have the application determined by the Court of Appeal."

42  In section 50 (meaning of "sentence"), at the end of subsection (1) insert
   "; and
   (i) an order under section 129(2) of the Licensing Act 2003 (forfeiture or suspension of personal licence)."

*Theatres Act 1968 (c. 54)*

43  The Theatres Act 1968 is amended as follows.

44  The following provisions cease to have effect in England and Wales–
   (a)  section 1(2) (local authority may not impose conditions on nature of plays),
   (b)  sections 12 to 14 (licensing of premises for public performance of plays),
   (c)  Schedule 1 (provision about licences to perform plays).

45  In section 15 (warrant to enter theatre where offence suspected)–
   (a)  in subsection (1)–
       (i)  paragraph (b) and the word "or" immediately preceding it, and
       (ii)  the words "or, in a case falling within paragraph (b) above, any police officer or authorised officer of the licensing authority",
       cease to have effect in England and Wales,
   (b)  subsections (2) to (5) cease to have effect in England and Wales, and
   (c)  subsection (6) is omitted.

46  Section 17 (existing letters patent) ceases to have effect.

47  In section 18(1) (interpretation), in the definition of "licensing authority", omit paragraphs (a), (b) and (bb).

. . .

*City of London (Various Powers) Act 1968 (c. xxxvii)*

53  For section 5(3) of the City of London (Various Powers) Act 1968 (entitlement of Corporation of London to apply for and hold licence to sell alcohol in arrangements for catering facilities) substitute–
   "(3) The Corporation of London or any person appointed by them in that behalf may, subject to section 16 of the Licensing Act 2003, for the purposes of this section apply for and hold a premises licence under that Act for the sale by retail of alcohol within the meaning of that Act."

*Finance Act 1970 (c. 24)*

54    In section 6(2)(b) of the Finance Act 1970 (Angostura bitters)–

(a)    omit ", the Licensing Act 1964", and

(b)    for "either of those Acts" substitute "that Act".

*Sunday Theatre Act 1972 (c. 26)*

55    The Sunday Theatre Act 1972 ceases to have effect.

*Local Government Act 1972 (c. 70)*

56    The Local Government Act 1972 is amended as follows.

57    In section 78(1) (supplementary provision relating to changes in local government areas), omit the definition of "public body".

58    In section 101 (arrangements for discharge of functions by local authorities), after subsection (14) insert–

"(15)  Nothing in this section applies in relation to any function under the Licensing Act 2003 of a licensing authority (within the meaning of that Act)."

59    In section 145(4) (provision of entertainment), for "intoxicating liquor" substitute "alcohol".

60    Section 204 (licensed premises) ceases to have effect.

61    (1)    Schedule 12 (meetings and proceedings of local authorities) is amended as follows.

(2)    In the following provisions, for "premises licensed for the sale of intoxicating liquor" substitute "premises which at the time of such a meeting may, by virtue of a premises licence or temporary event notice under the Licensing Act 2003, be used for the supply of alcohol (within the meaning of section 14 of that Act)"–

(a)    paragraph 10(1) (location of parish council meetings),

(b)    paragraph 26(1) (location of community council meetings).

(3)    In the following provisions, for "premises licensed for the sale of intoxicating liquor" substitute "premises which at the time of the meeting may, by virtue of a premises licence or temporary event notice under the Licensing Act 2003, be used for the supply of alcohol (within the meaning of section 14 of that Act)"–

(a)    paragraph 14(5) (location of parish meetings),

(b)    paragraph 32(2) (location of community meetings).

. . .

*Rent Act 1977 (c. 42)*

67    In section 11 of the Rent Act 1977 (tenancy of licensed premises not to be protected or statutory tenancy), for "premises licensed for the sale of intoxicating liquors" substitute "premises which, by virtue of a premises licence under the Licensing Act 2003, may be used for the supply of alcohol (within the meaning of section 14 of that Act)".

*Greater London Council (General Powers) Act 1978 (c. xiii)*

68    The Greater London Council (General Powers) Act 1978 is amended as follows.

69    Section 3 (human posing to be treated as entertainment) ceases to have effect.

70    In section 5(4)(a) (definition of "booking office")–

(a)    omit sub-paragraph (ii) and the word "or" immediately preceding it, and

(b)    for "sub-paragraphs (i) and (ii)" substitute "sub-paragraph (i)".

*Alcoholic Liquor Duties Act 1979 (c. 4)*

71    The Alcoholic Liquor Duties Act 1979 is amended as follows.

72    In section 4 (interpretation)–

(a)    in the definition of "justices' licence" and "justices' on-licence", omit paragraph (a), and

(b)    in the definition of "registered club", omit "which is for the time being registered within the meaning of the Licensing Act 1964 or".

. . .

*Licensed Premises (Exclusion of Certain Persons) Act 1980 (c. 32)*

74      In section 4(1) of the Licensed Premises (Exclusion of Certain Persons) Act 1980 (interpretation), in the definition of "licensed premises" for the words "a justices' on-licence (within the meaning of section 1 of the Licensing Act 1964)" substitute "a premises licence under the Licensing Act 2003 authorising the supply of alcohol (within the meaning of section 14 of that Act) for consumption on the premises".

*Magistrates' Courts Act 1980 (c. 43)*

75      In Part 3 of Schedule 6 to the Magistrates' Courts Act 1980 (matters to which provision relating to fees taken by clerks to justices does not apply), paragraphs 3 and 5 are omitted.

*Local Government, Planning and Land Act 1980 (c. 65)*

76      The Local Government, Planning and Land Act 1980 is amended as follows.

77      Sections 131 and 132 (licensing in new towns) cease to have effect.

78      In section 133 (miscellaneous provision about new towns), in subsection (1), omit the following definitions–

     (a)    "development corporation",

     (b)    "the 1964 Act".

79      In section 146 (disposal of land by urban development corporation)–

     (a)    in subsection (3), for "intoxicating liquor" substitute "alcohol", and

     (b)    in subsection (6), for " "intoxicating liquor" has the meaning assigned by section 201 of the Licensing Act 1964" substitute " "alcohol" has the meaning given by section 191 of the Licensing Act 2003".

*Indecent Displays (Control) Act 1981 (c. 42)*

80      In section 1(4) of the Indecent Displays (Control) Act 1981 (exemptions from offence of displaying indecent matter)–

     (a)    for paragraph (d) substitute–

         "(d) included in a performance of a play (within the meaning of paragraph 14(1) of Schedule 1 to the Licensing Act 2003) in England and Wales or of a play (within the meaning of the Theatres Act 1968) in Scotland;", and

     (b)    in paragraph (e) for "included in a film exhibition as defined in the Cinemas Act 1985" substitute "included in an exhibition of a film, within the meaning of paragraph 15 of Schedule 1 to the Licensing Act 2003, in England and Wales, or a film exhibition, as defined in the Cinemas Act 1985, in Scotland".

*New Towns Act 1981 (c. 64)*

81      In section 18 of the New Towns Act 1981 (disposal by development corporation of land to occupiers of it before acquisition by corporation), in subsection (3) for the words "intoxicating liquor ("intoxicating liquor" having the meaning given in section 201(1) of the Licensing Act 1964)" substitute "alcohol (within the meaning of section 191 of the Licensing Act 2003)".

*Local Government (Miscellaneous Provisions) Act 1982 (c. 30)*

82      The Local Government (Miscellaneous Provisions) Act 1982 is amended as follows.

83      The following provisions cease to have effect–

     (a)    section 1 (licensing of public entertainment outside Greater London),

     (b)    sections 4 to 6 (controls on take-away food shops),

     (c)    Schedule 1 (licensing of public entertainment outside Greater London).

84      In section 10(11) (requirement that apparatus to be installed should be provided with cut-off switch disapplied in relation to cinemas) for the words "premises in respect of which a licence under section 1 of the Cinemas Act 1985 is for the time being in force" substitute "premises in respect of which a premises licence under the Licensing Act 2003 has effect authorising the use of the premises for an exhibition of a film, within the meaning of paragraph 15 of Schedule 1 to that Act".

85      (1)    Schedule 3 (control of sex establishments) is amended as follows.

(2) In paragraph 3(2) (premises not to be treated as a sex cinema merely because the exhibition of a film there must be authorised by a licence, etc.)–

    (a) for paragraph (a) substitute–

        "(a) if they may be used for an exhibition of a film (within the meaning of paragraph 15 of Schedule 1 to the Licensing Act 2003) by virtue of an authorisation (within the meaning of section 136 of that Act), of their use in accordance with that authorisation", and

    (b) in paragraph (b), for "that Act" substitute "the Cinemas Act 1985".

(3) In paragraph 3A (exemption for theatres and cinemas from provisions about sex encounter establishments) for paragraphs (i) and (ii) of the proviso substitute–

    "(i) for the time being, being used for the provision of regulated entertainment (within the meaning of the Licensing Act 2003), in circumstances where that use is authorised under that Act; or

    (ii) for the time being, being used for the purposes of late night refreshment (within the meaning of that Act), in circumstances where that use is so authorised; or".

*Representation of the People Act 1983 (c. 2)*

86 The Representation of the People Act 1983 is amended as follows.

87 In section 185 (interpretation of Part relating to legal proceedings), for the definition of "Licensing Acts" substitute–

    " "Licensing Acts" means the Licensing (Scotland) Act 1976 and the Licensing (Northern Ireland) Order 1996 (as that Act or Order may from time to time have effect);"

88 In Schedule 7 (transitional and saving provision), omit paragraph 4.

*Video Recordings Act 1984 (c. 39)*

89 In section 3(7) of the Video Recordings Act 1984 (exempted supply of video recording)–

    (a) before paragraph (a) insert–

        "(za) premises in England and Wales which, by virtue of an authorisation within the meaning of section 136 of the Licensing Act 2003, may be used for the exhibition of a film within the meaning of paragraph 15 of Schedule 1 to that Act,", and

    (b) in paragraphs (a) and (c) after "premises", and in paragraph (b) after the first "premises", insert "in Scotland".

*Building Act 1984 (c. 55)*

90 The Building Act 1984 is amended as follows.

91 In section 24(4) (provision of exits in buildings) for paragraph (c) substitute–

    "(c) premises in respect of which a club premises certificate has effect under the Licensing Act 2003,".

92 In section 74(2) (exemption for certain premises from requirement for local authority's consent for cellars and rooms below subsoil water level), omit paragraph (a) and the word "or" immediately following it.

. . .

*Greater London Council (General Powers) Act 1984 (c. xxvii)*

94 In section 15(1) of the Greater London Council (General Powers) Act 1984 (exceptions to power of Council to refuse to register sleeping accommodation), at the end insert "; or

    (v) a building–

        (a) in respect of which there is in force immediately before the appointed day a premises licence under the Licensing Act 2003 authorising the supply of alcohol (within the meaning of section 14 of that Act) for consumption on the premises, and

        (b) the use of which for a specified purpose would not contravene the Town and Country Planning Act 1990."

*Cinemas Act 1985 (c. 13)*

95      The Cinemas Act 1985 ceases to have effect in England and Wales.

*Sporting Events (Control of Alcohol etc) Act 1985 (c. 57)*

96      The Sporting Events (Control of Alcohol etc) Act 1985 is amended as follows.

97      In the following provisions, for "intoxicating liquor" substitute "alcohol"–

     (a)    section 1(2) and (3) (alcohol on coaches and trains),

     (b)    section 1A(2) and (3) (alcohol on certain other vehicles),

     (c)    section 2(1) (alcohol at sports grounds).

98      Omit section 2(1A) (application to private rooms of offence of having alcohol at designated sporting event).

99      The following provisions cease to have effect–

     (a)    sections 3 and 4 (order about licensing hours in sports grounds),

     (b)    section 5 (appeal against such an order),

     (c)    section 5A (restricted periods in relation to possession of alcohol in private rooms at sports grounds),

     (d)    section 5B (occasional licences at sports grounds),

     (e)    section 5C (supply of alcohol by clubs at sports grounds),

     (f)    section 5D (non-retail sales of alcohol during sporting event),

     (g)    section 6 (closure of bar during sporting event),

     (h)    the Schedule (procedure for obtaining order about licensing hours in sports grounds).

100     In section 8 (offences)–

     (a)    in paragraph (b), for ", 2A(1), 3(10), 5B(2), 5C(3), 5D(2) or 6(2)" substitute "or 2A(1)", and

     (b)    omit paragraphs (d) and (e).

101     In section 9 (interpretation)–

     (a)    omit subsection (5), and

     (b)    for subsection (7) substitute–

        "(7) An expression used in this Act and in the Licensing Act 2003 has the same meaning in this Act as in that Act."

*Housing Act 1985 (c. 68)*

102     The Housing Act 1985 is amended as follows.

103     In section 11 (provision of board facilities by local housing authority)–

     (a)    for subsection (3) substitute–

        "(3) Where a premises licence under Part 3 of the Licensing Act 2003 authorises the sale by retail of alcohol in connection with the provision of facilities of the kind mentioned in subsection (1)(a), then, notwithstanding the terms of that licence, it does not have effect so as to authorise the sale by retail of alcohol for consumption otherwise than with a meal.",

     (b)    in subsection (4) after "the sale of intoxicating liquor" insert "or the sale by retail of alcohol", and

     (c)    after that subsection insert–

        "(5) An expression used in this section and in the Licensing Act 2003 has the same meaning in this section as in that Act."

104     In Schedule 1 (tenancies which are not secure tenancies), in paragraph 9, for "premises licensed for the sale of intoxicating liquor" substitute "premises which, by virtue of a premises licence under the Licensing Act 2003, may be used for the supply of alcohol (within the meaning of section 14 of that Act)".

*Sex Discrimination Act 1986 (c. 59)*

105     Section 5 of the Sex Discrimination Act 1986 (discrimination required by public entertainment licence) ceases to have effect.

*Fire Safety and Safety of Places of Sport Act 1987 (c. 27)*

106    After section 33(2) of the Fire Safety and Safety of Places of Sport Act 1987 (requirements of safety certificate to take precedence over conflicting conditions imposed in licence, etc.) insert–

"(2A) For the purposes of subsection (2)–

> (a)    "the licensing of premises" includes the granting of a premises licence or club premises certificate under the Licensing Act 2003, and
>
> (b)    "licence" is to be construed accordingly."

*Norfolk and Suffolk Broads Act 1988 (c. 4)*

107    In paragraph 40(1) of Schedule 3 to the Norfolk and Suffolk Broads Act 1988 (provision of facilities by Broads Authority), in paragraph (b) for "intoxicating liquor" substitute "alcohol (within the meaning of the Licensing Act 2003)".

*Housing Act 1988 (c. 50)*

108    In Schedule 1 to the Housing Act 1988 (tenancies which cannot be assured tenancies), in paragraph 5, for "premises licensed for the sale of intoxicating liquors" substitute "premises which, by virtue of a premises licence under the Licensing Act 2003, may be used for the supply of alcohol (within the meaning of section 14 of that Act)".

*Town and Country Planning Act 1990 (c. 8)*

109    Section 334 of the Town and Country Planning Act 1990 (licensing planning areas) ceases to have effect.

*Sunday Trading Act 1994 (c. 20)*

110    (1)    Schedule 1 to the Sunday Trading Act 1994 (restrictions on Sunday opening of large shops) is amended as follows.

        (2)    In paragraph 1–

> (a)    for the definition of "intoxicating liquor" substitute–" "alcohol" has the same meaning as in the Licensing Act 2003,", and
>
> (b)    in paragraph (a) of the definition of "sale of goods", for "intoxicating liquor" substitute "alcohol".

        (3)    In paragraph 3(1)(b) for "intoxicating liquor" substitute "alcohol".

*Criminal Justice and Public Order Act 1994 (c. 33)*

111    In section 63 of the Criminal Justice and Public Order Act 1994 (power to remove persons attending raves, etc), for subsection (9)(a) substitute–

"(a)    in England and Wales, to a gathering in relation to a licensable activity within section 1(1)(c) of the Licensing Act 2003 (provision of certain forms of entertainment) carried on under and in accordance with an authorisation within the meaning of section 136 of that Act;".

*Deregulation and Contracting Out Act 1994 (c. 40)*

112    Section 21 of the Deregulation and Contracting Out Act 1994 (Sunday Observance Act 1780 not to apply to sporting events) ceases to have effect.

*London Local Authorities Act 1995 (c.x)*

113    In section 14 of the London Local Authorities Act 1995 (interpretation of Part relating to near beer premises), in the definition of "near beer premises"–

> (a)    for "intoxicating liquor is provided exemption or saving from the provisions of the Act of 1964 by virtue of section 199 of that Act" substitute "alcohol is not a licensable activity under or by virtue of section 173 of the Licensing Act 2003",
>
> (b)    for paragraph (A) substitute–
>
> > "(A) a premises licence under Part 3 of that Act which authorises the supply of alcohol (within the meaning of section 14 of that Act) for consumption on the premises;",
>
> (c)    in paragraph (B)–
>
> > (i)    omit "Schedule 12 to the London Government Act 1963," and "or the Private Places of Entertainment (Licensing) Act 1967", and

        (ii)   at the end insert "or a premises licence granted under Part 3 of the Licensing Act 2003 which authorises the provision of any form of regulated entertainment (within the meaning of Schedule 1 to that Act)",

(d)   omit paragraphs (C) to (E),

(e)   for paragraphs (f) and (G) substitute–

"(f)   a temporary event notice under the Licensing Act 2003, by virtue of which the premises may be used for the supply of alcohol (within the meaning of section 14 of that Act);",

(f)   for the words from "during the hours" to "licence:" substitute "during the hours permitted by such licence or notice:", and

(g)   for "such licence; and" substitute "such licence or notice; and".

*Employment Rights Act 1996 (c. 18)*

114    In section 232(7) of the Employment Rights Act 1996 (definition of "catering business")–

    (a)   in paragraph (a) for "intoxicating liquor" substitute "alcohol", and

    (b)   for " "intoxicating liquor" has the same meaning as in the Licensing Act 1964" substitute " "alcohol" has the same meaning as in the Licensing Act 2003".

*Confiscation of Alcohol (Young Persons) Act 1997 (c. 33)*

115    (1)   Section 1 of the Confiscation of Alcohol (Young Persons) Act 1997 (confiscation of alcohol) is amended as follows.

    (2)   In subsection (1)–

       (a)   for "intoxicating liquor", in each place it occurs, substitute "alcohol",

       (b)   in paragraph (b) for "liquor" substitute "alcohol", and

       (c)   for "such liquor" substitute "alcohol".

    (3)   For subsection (7) substitute–

    "(7)   In this section–

       "alcohol"–

       (a)   in relation to England and Wales, has the same meaning as in the Licensing Act 2003;

       (b)   in relation to Northern Ireland, has the same meaning as "intoxicating liquor" in the Licensing (Northern Ireland) Order 1996; and

       "licensed premises"–

       (a)   which may by virtue of Part 3 or Part 5 of the Licensing Act 2003 (premises licence; permitted temporary activity) be used for the supply of alcohol within the meaning of section 14 of that Act;

       (b)   in relation to Northern Ireland, has the same meaning as in the Licensing (Northern Ireland) Order 1996."

. . .

*London Local Authorities Act 2000 (c. vii)*

117    In section 32 of the London Local Authorities Act 2000 (interpretation of provisions about the licensing of buskers), in the definition of "busking", for paragraph (b) substitute–

"(b)   under and in accordance with a premises licence under Part 3 of the Licensing Act 2003, or a temporary event notice having effect under Part 5 of that Act, which authorises the provision of regulated entertainment (within paragraph 2(1)(e) to (h) or 3(2) of Schedule 1 to that Act (music and dancing));".

*Private Security Industry Act 2001 (c. 12)*

118    (1)   Paragraph 8 of Schedule 2 to the Private Security Industry Act 2001 (door supervisors etc for licensed premises) is amended as follows.

    (2)   In sub-paragraph (2), for paragraphs (a) to (d) substitute–

    "(a)   any premises in respect of which a premises licence or temporary event notice has effect under the Licensing Act 2003 to authorise the supply of alcohol (within the meaning of section 14 of that Act) for consumption on the premises;

     (b)   any premises in respect of which a premises licence or temporary event notice has effect under that Act to authorise the provision of regulated entertainment;".

  (3)  For sub-paragraph (3) substitute–

     "(3)  For the purposes of this paragraph, premises are not licensed premises–

        (a)  if there is in force in respect of the premises a premises licence which authorises regulated entertainment within paragraph 2(1)(a) or (b) of Schedule 1 to the Licensing Act 2003 (plays and films);

        (b)  in relation to any occasion on which the premises are being used–

           (i)   exclusively for the purposes of a club which holds a club premises certificate in respect of the premises, or

           (ii)  for regulated entertainment of the kind mentioned in paragraph (a), in circumstances where that use is a permitted temporary activity by virtue of Part 5 of that Act;

        (c)  in relation to any occasion on which a licence is in force in respect of the premises under the Gaming Act 1968 (c. 65) and the premises are being used wholly or mainly for the purposes of gaming to which Part 2 of that Act applies; or

        (d)  in relation to any such other occasion as may be prescribed for the purposes of this sub-paragraph."

  (4)  After sub-paragraph (5) insert–

     "(6)  Sub-paragraphs (2)(a) and (b) and (3)(a) and (b) are to be construed in accordance with the Licensing Act 2003."

*Criminal Justice and Police Act 2001 (c. 16)*

119     The Criminal Justice and Police Act 2001 is amended as follows.

120     In section 1(1) (offences leading to penalties on the spot), at the end of the Table insert–

"Section 149(4) of the Licensing Act 2003     Buying or attempting to buy alcohol for consumption on licensed premises, etc. by child"

121     In section 12 (alcohol consumption in designated public place)–

     (a)  in subsections (1) and (2), for "intoxicating liquor", in each place it occurs, substitute "alcohol", and

     (b)  in subsection (2) for "such liquor" substitute "alcohol".

122     In section 13 (designated public places), in subsection (2) for "intoxicating liquor" substitute "alcohol".

123     (1)  Section 14 (places which are not designated public places) is amended as follows.

     (2)  In subsection (1)–

        (a)  for paragraphs (a) to (d) substitute–

          "(a)  premises in respect of which a premises licence or club premises certificate, within the meaning of the Licensing Act 2003, has effect;

          (b)  a place within the curtilage of premises within paragraph (a);

          (c)  premises which by virtue of Part 5 of the Licensing Act 2003 may for the time being be used for the supply of alcohol or which, by virtue of that Part, could have been so used within the last 20 minutes;", and

        (b)  in paragraph (e), for "intoxicating liquor" substitute "alcohol".

     (3)  Omit subsection (2).

124     In section 15(1)(a) (byelaw prohibiting consumption of alcohol), for "intoxicating liquor" substitute "alcohol".

125     In section 16(1) (interpretation of sections 12 to 15)–

     (a)  before the definition of "designated public place" insert–

        " 'alcohol' has the same meaning as in the Licensing Act 2003;",

     (b)  omit the definition of "intoxicating liquor", and the word "and" immediately following it, and

    (c)    after the definition of "public place" insert"; and

           "supply of alcohol" has the meaning given by section 14 of the Licensing Act 2003".

126    In each of the following provisions, for "unlicensed sale of intoxicating liquor" substitute "unauthorised sale of alcohol"–

    (a)    section 19(1) and (2) (service of closure notice by constable or local authority),

    (b)    section 20(3)(a) (no application for closure order where unauthorised sale of alcohol has ceased),

    (c)    section 21(1)(b) and (2)(b) (closure order),

    (d)    section 27(6) (fixing notice on premises where personal service cannot be effected).

127    In section 28 (interpretation of provisions relating to closure of unlicensed premises)–

    (a)    before the definition of "closure notice" insert–

           " 'alcohol' has the same meaning as in the Licensing Act 2003;",

    (b)    omit the definition of "intoxicating liquor", and

    (c)    for the definition of "unlicensed sale" substitute–

           " 'unauthorised sale', in relation to any alcohol, means any supply of the alcohol (within the meaning of section 14 of the Licensing Act 2003) which–

           (a)    is a licensable activity within the meaning of that Act, but

           (b)    is made otherwise than under and in accordance with an authorisation (within the meaning of section 136 of that Act)."

128    In Schedule 1 (powers of seizure)–

    (a)    at the end of Part 1 insert–

           *"Licensing Act 2003*

           74.    The power of seizure conferred by section 90 of the Licensing Act 2003 (seizure of documents relating to club).", and

    (b)    at the end of Part 3 insert–

           *"Licensing Act 2003*

           110. The power of seizure conferred by section 90 of the Licensing Act 2003 (seizure of documents relating to club)."

## SCHEDULE 7

Section 199

REPEALS

| Short title and chapter | Extent of repeal |
| --- | --- |
| Universities (Wine Licences) Act 1743 (c. 40) | The whole Act. |
| Sunday Observance Act 1780 (21 Geo. 3 c. 49) | The whole Act. |
| Metropolitan Police Act 1839 (c. 47) | Section 41. |
| Town Police Clauses Act 1847 (c. 89) | Section 35. |
| Cambridge Award Act 1856 (c. xvii) | Sections 9 and 11. |
| Inebriates Act 1898 (c. 60) | In the First Schedule– the entry relating to section 18 of the Licensing Act 1872, and the entry relating to section 41 of the Refreshment Houses Act 1860. |

| Short title and chapter | Extent of repeal |
|---|---|
| Sunday Entertainments Act 1932 (c. 51) | The whole Act. |
| Children and Young Persons Act 1933 (c. 12) | In section 12(3), the words from, "and also" to the end. In section 107, the definition of "intoxicating liquor". |
| Public Health Act 1936 (c. 49) | Section 226(4). |
| Common Informers Act 1951 (c. 39) | In the Schedule– the entry relating to section 11 of the Universities (Wine Licences) Act 1743, and the entry relating to the Sunday Observance Act 1780. |
| Hypnotism Act 1952 (c. 46) | Section 1(2). |
| London Government Act 1963 (c. 33) | Section 52(3). Schedule 12. |
| Offices, Shops and Railway Premises Act 1963 (c. 41) | In section 90, the definition of "place of public entertainment". |
| Licensing Act 1964 (c. 26) | The whole Act. |
| Administration of Justice Act 1964 (c. 42) | In Schedule 3, paragraph 31. |
| Refreshment Houses Act 1964 (c. 88) | The whole Act. |
| Private Places of Entertainment (Licensing) Act 1967 (c. 19) | The whole Act. |
| Licensing (Amendment) Act 1967 (c. 51) | The whole Act. |
| Finance Act 1967 (c. 54) | In section 5– in subsection (1), the words"; and accordingly as from that date– "and paragraphs (c) and (e), and in subsection (3), the words "which is registered within the meaning of the Licensing Act 1964 or" Section 45(4). Schedule 7. |
| Theatres Act 1968 (c. 54) | Section 15(6). Section 17. In section 18(1), in the definition of "licensing authority", paragraphs (a), (b) and (bb). In Schedule 2– the entries relating to the Licensing Act 1964, and the entry relating to the Private Places of Entertainment (Licensing) Act 1967. |
| Gaming Act 1968 (c. 65) | In Schedule 9– paragraph 11(5), paragraph 14, and paragraph 24. In Schedule 11, in Part 3, the entries relating to the Licensing Act 1964. |

| Short title and chapter | Extent of repeal |
|---|---|
| Greater London Council (General Powers) Act 1968 (c.xxxix) | Sections 47 to 55. |
| Late Night Refreshment Houses Act 1969 (c. 53) | The whole Act. |
| Finance Act 1970 (c. 24) | In section 6(2)(b), the words ", the Licensing Act 1964". |
| Courts Act 1971 (c. 23) | In Schedule 6, paragraphs 7 and 13.<br>In Schedule 8, paragraph 42.<br>In Schedule 9, in Part 1, the entries relating to–<br>    the London Government Act 1963,<br>    the Licensing Act 1964,<br>    the Private Places of Entertainment (Licensing) Act 1967,<br>    the Theatres Act 1968, and<br>    the Late Night Refreshment Houses Act 1969. |
| Sunday Theatre Act 1972 (c. 26) | The whole Act. |
| Local Government Act 1972 (c. 70) | In section 78(1), the definition of "public body".<br>Section 204.<br>In Schedule 25, paragraphs 1 to 9. |
| Local Government Act 1974 (c. 7) | In Schedule 6, paragraph 24. |
| Licensing (Amendment) Act 1976 (c. 18) | The whole Act. |
| Lotteries and Amusements Act 1976 (c.32) | In Schedule 3–<br>in paragraph 1(2), the definition of "the proper officer of the authority", and<br>paragraphs 8(4) and 11. |
| Licensing (Scotland) Act 1976 (c. 66) | In Schedule 7, paragraphs 9(a), (b), (d) and (f), 10, 11 and 12. |
| Greater London Council (General Powers) Act 1976 (c. xxvi) | Sections 5 to 8. |
| Licensing (Amendment) Act 1977 (c. 26) | The whole Act. |
| Greater London Council (General Powers) Act 1978 (c.xiii) | Sections 3 and 4.<br>Section 5(4)(a)(ii) and the word "or" immediately preceding it. |
| Customs and Excise Management Act 1979 (c. 2) | In Schedule 4, in paragraph 12, in the Table, the entry relating to the Licensing Act 1964. |
| Alcoholic Liquor Duties Act 1979 (c. 4) | In section 4–<br>    in the definition of "justices' licence" and "justices' on-licence", paragraph (a), and<br>    in the definition of "registered club", the words "which is for the time being registered within the meaning of the Licensing Act 1964 or".<br>In section 71(5)–<br>    the words "England and Wales or", and paragraph (c).<br>In Schedule 3, paragraph 5. |

| Short title and chapter | Extent of repeal |
|---|---|
| Greater London Council (General Powers) Act 1979 (c. xxiii) | Section 3 |
| Licensing (Amendment) Act 1980 (c. 40) | The whole Act. |
| Magistrates' Courts Act 1980 (c. 43) | In Schedule 6, in Part 3, paragraphs 3 and 5. In Schedule 7, paragraphs 45 to 48 and 50. |
| Local Government, Planning and Land Act 1980 (c.65) | Sections 131 and 132. In section 133(1), the definitions of "development corporation" and "the 1964 Act". |
| Highways Act 1980 (c. 66) | In Schedule 24, paragraph 12. |
| Finance Act 1981 (c. 35) | In Schedule 8, paragraphs 24 and 25. |
| Licensing (Amendment) Act 1981 (c. 40) | The whole Act. |
| Supreme Court Act 1981 (c. 54) | In section 28(2)(b), the words "the Licensing Act 1964,". |
| New Towns Act 1981 (c. 64) | In Schedule 2, paragraph 2. In Schedule 12, paragraphs 1 and 29(a)(i). |
| Local Government (Miscellaneous Provisions) Act 1982 (c.30) | Section 1. Sections 4 to 7. Schedule 1. In Schedule 2, paragraphs 1 to 6. |
| Greater London Council (General Powers) Act 1982 (c. i) | Section 7. |
| Representation of the People Act 1983 (c. 2) | In Schedule 7, paragraph 4. In Schedule 8, paragraphs 7 to 10. |
| Licensing (Occasional Permissions) Act 1983 (c. 24) | The whole Act. |
| Building Act 1984 (c. 55) | In section 74(2), paragraph (a) and the word "or" immediately following it. |
| Greater London Council (General Powers) Act 1984 (c.xxvii) | Section 4(1) and (3). Sections 19 to 22. |
| Cinemas Act 1985 (c. 13) | Section 3(1A). Section 9. Sections 17 and 18. In section 19(3), paragraph (a) and the word "or" immediately following it. In Schedule 2, paragraphs 2, 3, 6, 7, 8, 14, 15 and 16(a) and the word "and" immediately following it. |
| Licensing (Amendment) Act 1985 (c. 40) | The whole Act. |
| Local Government Act 1985 (c. 51) | In Schedule 8– paragraph 1(1), in paragraph 1(3), the words following paragraph (c), and paragraphs 2 to 5. |

| Short title and chapter | Extent of repeal |
|---|---|
| Sporting Events (Control of Alcohol etc.) Act 1985 (c. 57) | Section 2(1A).<br>Sections 3 to 6.<br>Section 8(d) and (e).<br>Section 9(5).<br>The Schedule. |
| Insolvency Act 1985 (c. 65) | In Schedule 8, paragraph 12. |
| Insolvency Act 1986 (c. 45) | In Schedule 14, the entries relating to the Licensing Act 1964. |
| Sex Discrimination Act 1986 (c. 59) | Section 5. |
| Public Order Act 1986 (c. 64) | In Schedule 1, paragraphs 4, 5, 7(5) and 8. |
| Greater London Council (General Powers) Act 1986 (c. iv) | Section 3. |
| Fire Safety and Safety of Places of Sport Act 1987 (c. 27) | Sections 42, 43, 45 and 46.<br>Schedule 3.<br>In Schedule 5–<br>    in paragraph 1, the definition of "the 1963 Act" and the definition of "the 1982 Act" and the word "and" immediately preceding it, and paragraphs 8 to 10. |
| Licensing Act 1988 (c. 17) | The whole Act. |
| Licensing (Retail Sales) Act 1988 (c. 25) | The whole Act. |
| Licensing (Amendment) Act 1989 (c. 20) | The whole Act. |
| Employment Act 1989 (c. 38) | In Schedule 6, paragraph 30. |
| Town and Country Planning Act 1990 (c. 8) | Section 334. |
| Entertainments (Increased Penalties) Act 1990 (c. 20) | Section 1. |
| Licensing (Low Alcohol Drinks) Act 1990 (c. 21) | Section 1. |
| Broadcasting Act 1990 (c. 42) | In Schedule 20, paragraphs 7 and 8. |
| London Local Authorities Act 1990 (c. vii) | Sections 4 to 17, 19 and 20. |
| London Local Authorities (No. 2) Act 1990 (c. xxx) | Section 6. |
| Finance Act 1991 (c. 31) | In Schedule 2, in paragraph 1, the words, "the Licensing Act 1964". |
| London Local Authorities Act 1991 (c. xiii) | Sections 18 to 21. |
| Sporting Events (Control of Alcohol etc.) (Amendment) Act 1992 (c.57) | The whole Act. |
| Charities Act 1993 (c.10) | In Schedule 6, paragraph 27. |

| Short title and chapter | Extent of repeal |
|---|---|
| Local Government (Wales) Act 1994 (c. 19) | In Schedule 2, paragraph 2.<br>In Schedule 15, paragraph 41.<br>In Schedule 16, paragraphs 22, 29, 32, 36, 69 and 73. |
| Coal Industry Act 1994 (c. 21) | In Schedule 9, paragraph 8. |
| Criminal Justice and Public Order Act 1994 (c. 33) | In section 63–<br>in subsection (10), the definitions of "entertainment licence" and "local authority", and subsection (11). |
| Deregulation and Contracting Out Act 1994 (c. 40) | Section 18(1).<br>Section 19.<br>Section 21.<br>Schedule 7.<br>In Schedule 11, paragraph 1. |
| London Local Authorities Act 1994 (c. xii) | Section 5. |
| Licensing (Sunday Hours) Act 1995 (c. 33) | The whole Act. |
| London Local Authorities Act 1995 (c. x) | In section 14–<br>in paragraph (B), the words "Schedule 12 to the London Government Act 1963," and "or the Private Places of Entertainment (Licensing) Act 1967", and paragraphs (C) to (E).<br>Section 28.<br>Sections 45 and 46. |
| London Local Authorities Act 1996 (c. ix) | Sections 20 to 23. |
| Justices of the Peace Act 1997 (c. 25) | In Schedule 4, in paragraph 17(3), the words, "other than any duties as secretary to a licensing planning committee under Part VII of the Licensing Act 1964". |
| Confiscation of Alcohol (Young Persons) Act 1997 (c. 33) | In section 1(1), the words "(other than a sealed container)". |
| Public Entertainments Licences (Drug Misuse) Act 1997 (c. 49) | The whole Act. |
| Access to Justice Act 1999 (c. 22) | In Schedule 10, paragraphs 23 to 29 and 31.<br>In Schedule 11, paragraph 17.<br>In Schedule 13, paragraphs 36 to 56, 61, 62, 87, 124 and 132. |
| Greater London Authority Act 1999 (c. 29) | In Schedule 29, paragraphs 6, 67, 70 and 71. |
| Licensing (Young Persons) Act 2000 (c. 30) | The whole Act. |
| Freedom of Information Act 2000 (c. 36) | In Schedule 1, paragraph 17. |
| London Local Authorities Act 2000 (c. vii) | Sections 22 to 26.<br>Schedule 1. |

| Short title and chapter | Extent of repeal |
|---|---|
| Criminal Justice and Police Act 2001 (c. 16) | In section 1(1), in the Table, the entry relating to section 169C(3) of the Licensing Act 1964. In section 12(2)(b), the words "(other than a sealed container)". Section 14(2). In section 16(1), the definition of "intoxicating liquor" and the word "and" immediately following it. Sections 17 and 18. In section 28, the definition of "intoxicating liquor". Sections 30 to 32. In Schedule 1, paragraphs 7 and 90. |

## SCHEDULE 8

Section 200

TRANSITIONAL PROVISION ETC

PART 1

PREMISES LICENCES

*Introductory*

1    (1)    In this Part–

"canteen licence" has the same meaning as in section 148 of the 1964 Act (licences for seamen's canteens);

"children's certificate" has the same meaning as in section 168A of that Act;

"existing licence" means–

(a)    a justices' licence,

(b)    a canteen licence,

(c)    a licence under Schedule 12 to the London Government Act 1963 (c. 33) (licensing of public entertainment in Greater London),

(d)    a licence under the Private Places of Entertainment (Licensing) Act 1967 (c. 19),

(e)    a licence under the Theatres Act 1968 (c. 54),

(f)    a licence under the Late Night Refreshment Houses Act 1969 (c. 53),

(g)    a licence under Schedule 1 to the Local Government (Miscellaneous Provisions) Act 1982 (c. 30) (licensing of public entertainments outside Greater London),

(h)    a licence under section 1 of the Cinemas Act 1985 (c. 13), or

(i)    a licence under Part 2 of the London Local Authorities Act 1990 (c.vii) (night cafe licensing);

"existing licensable activities", under an existing licence, are–

(a)    the licensable activities authorised by the licence, and

(b)    any other licensable activities which may be carried on, at the premises in respect of which the licence has effect, by virtue of the existence of the licence (see sub-paragraph (2));

"first appointed day" means such day as may be specified as the first appointed day for the purposes of this Part;

"new licence" has the meaning given in paragraph 5(1);

"relevant existing licence", in relation to an application under paragraph 2, means an existing licence to which the application relates;

"relevant licensing authority" has the same meaning as in Part 3 of this Act (premises licences);

"second appointed day" means such day as may be specified as the second appointed day for the purposes of this Part; and

"supply of alcohol" means–

(a)   sale by retail of alcohol, or

(b)   supply of alcohol by or on behalf of a club to, or to the order of, a member of the club.

(2)   In determining, for the purposes of paragraph (b) of the definition of "existing licensable activities", the other licensable activities which may be carried on by virtue of a licence–

(a)   section 182 of the 1964 Act (relaxation of law relating to music and dancing licences) is to be disregarded so far as it relates to public entertainment by way of music and singing provided by not more than two performers, and

(b)   in the case of an existing licence granted under the Theatres Act 1968 (c. 54), the reference in that paragraph to the licence is to be read as including a reference to any notice in force under section 199(c) of the 1964 Act (notice of intention to sell alcohol by retail at licensed theatre premises) in relation to that licence.

(3)   In the application of section 12 (relevant licensing authority in Part 3 of this Act) for the purposes of this Part, the reference in subsection (4)(a) of that section to an applicant for a premises licence is to be read as a reference to an applicant under paragraph 2 for the grant of a licence under paragraph 4.

*Application for conversion of existing licence*

2   (1)   This paragraph applies where, in respect of any premises, one or more existing licences have effect on the first appointed day.

(2)   A person may, within the period of six months beginning with the first appointed day, apply to the relevant licensing authority for the grant of a licence under paragraph 4 to succeed one or more of those existing licences.

(3)   But an application may be made under this paragraph in respect of an existing licence only if–

(a)   it is held by the applicant, or

(b)   the holder of the licence consents to the application being made.

(4)   An application under this paragraph must specify–

(a)   the existing licensable activities under the relevant existing licence or, if there is more than one, the relevant existing licences,

(b)   if any relevant existing licence authorises the supply of alcohol, specified information about the person whom the applicant wishes to be the premises supervisor under the licence granted under paragraph 4, and

(c)   such other information as may be specified.

(5)   The application must also be in the specified form and accompanied by–

(a)   the relevant documents, and

(b)   the specified fee.

(6)   The relevant documents are–

(a)   the relevant existing licence or, if there is more than one, each of them (or a certified copy of the licence or licences in question),

(b)   a plan in the specified form of the premises to which the relevant existing licence or licences relate,

(c)   if any relevant existing licence authorises the supply of alcohol, any children's certificate in force in respect of the premises (or a certified copy of any such certificate),

- (d) a form of consent in the specified form, given by the individual (if any) named in the application in accordance with sub-paragraph (4)(b),
- (e) a form of consent in the specified form, given by any person who is required to consent to the application under sub-paragraph (3), and
- (f) such other documents as may be specified.

(7) In this paragraph any reference to a certified copy of a document is a reference to a copy of that document certified to be a true copy–

- (a) in the case of a justices' licence, children's certificate or canteen licence, by the chief executive of the licensing justices for the licensing district in which the premises are situated,
- (b) in any other case, by the chief executive of the local authority which issued the licence,
- (c) by a solicitor or notary, or
- (d) by a person of a specified description.

(8) A document which purports to be a certified copy of an existing licence or children's certificate is to be taken to be such a copy unless the contrary is shown.

*Police consultation*

3 (1) Where a person makes an application under paragraph 2, he must give a copy of the application (and any documents which accompanied it) to the chief officer of police for the police area (or each police area) in which the premises are situated no later than 48 hours after the application is made.

(2) Where–

- (a) an appeal is pending against a decision to revoke, or to reject an application for the renewal of, the relevant existing licence or, if there is more than one such licence, a relevant existing licence, and
- (b) a chief officer of police who has received a copy of the application under sub-paragraph (1) is satisfied that converting that existing licence in accordance with this Part would undermine the crime prevention objective,

he must give the relevant licensing authority and the applicant a notice to that effect.

(3) Where a chief officer of police who has received a copy of an application under sub-paragraph (1) is satisfied that, because of a material change in circumstances since the relevant time, converting the relevant existing licence or, if there is more than one such licence, a relevant existing licence in accordance with this Part would undermine the crime prevention objective, he must give the relevant licensing authority and the applicant a notice to that effect.

(4) For this purpose "relevant time" means the time when the relevant existing licence was granted or, if it has been renewed, the last time it was renewed.

(5) The chief officer of police may not give a notice under subparagraph (2) or (3) after the end of the period of 28 days beginning with the day on which he received a copy of the application under sub-paragraph (1).

*Determination of application*

4 (1) This paragraph applies where an application is made in accordance with paragraph 2 and the applicant complies with paragraph 3(1).

(2) Subject to sub-paragraphs (3) and (5), the relevant licensing authority must grant the application.

(3) Where a notice is given under paragraph 3(2) or (3) in respect of an existing licence (and not withdrawn), the authority must–

- (a) hold a hearing to consider it, unless the authority, the applicant and the chief officer of police who gave the notice agree that a hearing is unnecessary, and
- (b) having regard to the notice–
  - (i) in a case where the application relates only to that licence, reject the application, and

        (ii)   in any other case, reject the application to the extent that it relates to that licence,

if it considers it necessary for the promotion of the crime prevention objective to do so.

(4)    If the relevant licensing authority fails to determine the application within the period of two months beginning with the day on which it received it, then, subject to sub-paragraph (5), the application is to be treated as granted by the authority under this paragraph.

(5)    An application must not be granted (and is not to be treated as granted under sub-paragraph (4))–

    (a)   if the relevant existing licence has or, if there is more than one, all the relevant existing licences have ceased to be held by the applicant before the relevant time, or

    (b)   where there is more than one relevant existing licence (but paragraph (a) does not apply), to the extent that the application relates to an existing licence which has ceased to be held by the applicant before the relevant time.

(6)    For the purposes of sub-paragraph (5)–

    (a)   where, for the purposes of paragraph 2(3)(b) a person has consented to an application being made in respect of a relevant existing licence, sub-paragraph (5)(a) and (b) applies in relation to that licence as if the reference to the applicant were a reference to–

        (i)   that person, or

        (ii)   any other person to whom the existing licence has been transferred and who has given his consent for the purposes of this paragraph, and

    (b)   "the relevant time" is the time of the determination of the application or, in a case within sub-paragraph (4), the end of the period mentioned in that sub-paragraph.

(7)    Section 10 applies as if the relevant licensing authority's functions under sub-paragraph (3) were included in the list of functions in subsection (4) of that section (functions which cannot be delegated to an officer of the licensing authority).

*Notification of determination and issue of new licence*

5    (1)    Where an application is granted (in whole or in part) under paragraph 4, the relevant licensing authority must forthwith–

    (a)   give the applicant a notice to that effect, and

    (b)   issue the applicant with–

        (i)   a licence in respect of the premises (a "new licence") in accordance with paragraph 6, and

        (ii)   a summary of the new licence.

(2)    Where an application is rejected (in whole or in part) under paragraph 4, the relevant licensing authority must forthwith give the applicant a notice to that effect stating the authority's reasons for its decision to reject the application.

(3)    The relevant licensing authority must give a copy of any notice it gives under sub-paragraph (1) or (2) to the chief officer of police for the police area (or each police area) in which the premises to which the notice relates are situated.

*The new licence*

6    (1)    This paragraph applies where a new licence is granted under paragraph 4 in respect of one or more existing licences.

(2)    Where an application under paragraph 2 is granted in part only, any relevant existing licence in respect of which the application was rejected is to be disregarded for the purposes of the following provisions of this paragraph.

(3)    The new licence is to be treated as if it were a premises licence (see section 11), and sections 19, 20 and 21 (mandatory conditions for premises licences) apply in relation to it accordingly.

(4)    The new licence takes effect on the second appointed day.

(5)   The new licence must authorise the premises in question to be used for the existing licensable activities under the relevant existing licence or, if there is more than one relevant existing licence, the relevant existing licences.

(6)   Subject to sections 19, 20 and 21 and the remaining provisions of this paragraph, the new licence must be granted subject to such conditions as reproduce the effect of–

    (a)   the conditions subject to which the relevant existing licence has effect at the time the application is granted, or

    (b)   if there is more than one relevant existing licence, all the conditions subject to which those licences have effect at that time.

(7)   Where the new licence authorises the supply of alcohol, the new licence must designate the person named in the application under paragraph 2(4)(b) as the premises supervisor.

(8)   The new licence must also be granted subject to conditions which reproduce the effect of any restriction imposed on the use of the premises for the existing licensable activities under the relevant existing licence or licences by any enactment specified for the purposes of this Part.

(9)   In determining those restrictions, the relevant licensing authority must have regard to any children's certificate which accompanied (or a certified copy of which accompanied) the application and which remains in force.

(10)   Nothing in sub-paragraph (6) or (8) requires the new licence to be granted for a limited period.

(11)   But, where the application under paragraph 2 includes a request for the new licence to have effect for a limited period, the new licence is to be granted subject to that condition.

*Variation of new licence*

7   (1)   A person who makes an application under paragraph 2 may (notwithstanding that no licence has yet been granted in consequence of that application) at the same time apply–

    (a)   under section 37 for any licence so granted to be varied so as to specify the individual named in the application as the premises supervisor, or

    (b)   under section 34 for any other variation of any such licence,

and for the purposes of an application within paragraph (a) or (b) the applicant is to be treated as the holder of that licence.

(2)   In relation to an application within sub-paragraph (1)(a) or (b), the relevant licensing authority may discharge its functions under section 35 or 39 only if, and when, the application under paragraph 2 has been granted.

(3)   Where an application within sub-paragraph (1)(a) or (b) is not determined by the relevant licensing authority within the period of two months beginning with the day the application was received by the authority, it is to be treated as having been rejected by the authority under section 35 or 39 (as the case may be) at the end of that period.

*Existing licence revoked after grant of new licence*

8   (1)   This paragraph applies where the relevant licensing authority grants a new licence under this Part in respect of one or more existing licences.

(2)   If sub-paragraph (4) applies to the existing licence (or each of the existing licences) which the new licence succeeds, the new licence lapses.

(3)   If–

    (a)   where the new licence relates to more than one relevant existing licence, sub-paragraph (4) applies to one or more, but not all, of those licences, or

    (b)   sub-paragraph (4) applies to a children's certificate in respect of the premises,

the licensing authority must amend the new licence so as to remove from it any provision which would not have been included in it but for the existence of any existing licence or certificate to which subparagraph (4) applies.

(4)   This sub-paragraph applies to an existing licence or children's certificate if–

(a)   it is revoked before the second appointed day, or

(b)   where an appeal against a decision to revoke it is pending immediately before that day, the appeal is dismissed or abandoned.

(5)   Any amendment under sub-paragraph (3) takes effect when it is notified to the holder of the new licence by the relevant licensing authority.

(6)   The relevant licensing authority must give a copy of any notice under sub-paragraph (5) to the chief officer of police for the police area (or each police area) in which the premises to which the new licence relates are situated.

*Appeals*

9    (1)   Where an application under paragraph 2 is rejected (in whole or in part) by the relevant licensing authority, the applicant may appeal against that decision.

(2)   Where a licensing authority grants such an application (in whole or in part), any chief officer of police who gave a notice in relation to it under paragraph 3(2) or (3) (that was not withdrawn) may appeal against that decision.

(3)   Where a licence is amended under paragraph 8, the holder of the licence may appeal against that decision.

(4)   Section 181 and paragraph 9(1) and (2) of Schedule 5 (general provision about appeals against decisions under Part 3 of this Act) apply in relation to appeals under this paragraph as they apply in relation to appeals under Part 1 of that Schedule.

(5)   Paragraph 9(3) of that Schedule applies in relation to an appeal under sub-paragraph (2).

*False statements*

10    (1)   A person commits an offence if he knowingly or recklessly makes a false statement in or in connection with an application under paragraph 2.

(2)   For the purposes of sub-paragraph (1) a person is to be treated as making a false statement if he produces, furnishes, signs or otherwise makes use of a document that contains a false statement.

(3)   A person guilty of an offence under this section is liable on summary conviction to a fine not exceeding level 5 on the standard scale.

*Opening hours*

11    (1)   This paragraph applies where–

(a)   within such period (of not less than six months) as may be specified, the holder of a justices' licence for any premises applies, in accordance with Part 3 of this Act, for the grant of a premises licence in respect of those premises, and

(b)   the licence, if granted in the form applied for, would authorise the sale by retail of alcohol.

(2)   In determining the application for the premises licence under section 18, the relevant licensing authority may not, by virtue of subsection (3)(b) of that section, grant the licence subject to conditions which prevent the sale of alcohol on the premises during the permitted hours.

(3)   But sub-paragraph (2) does not apply where–

(a)   there has been a material change in circumstances since the relevant time, and

(b)   the relevant representations made in respect of the application include representations made by the chief officer of police for the police area (or any police area) in which the premises are situated advocating that, for the purposes of promoting the crime prevention objective, the premises licence ought to authorise the sale of alcohol during more restricted hours than the permitted hours.

(4)   In this paragraph–

"permitted hours" means the permitted hours during which the holder of the justices' licence is permitted to sell alcohol on the premises under Part 3 of the 1964 Act;

"relevant representations" has the meaning given in section 18(6); and

"relevant time" means the time when the justices' licence was granted or, if it has been renewed, the last time it was renewed.

*Provisional licences*

12    (1)    Where–

(a)    during such period as may be specified the relevant licensing authority receives an application in accordance with Part 3 of this Act for the grant of a premises licence in respect of any premises ("the relevant premises"),

(b)    under section 6 of the 1964 Act, a provisional grant of a justices' licence has been made for–

(i)    the relevant premises or a part of them, or

(ii)    premises that are substantially the same as the relevant premises or a part of them, and

(c)    the conditions of sub-paragraph (2) are satisfied,

the licensing authority must have regard to the provisional grant of the justices' licence when determining the application for the grant of the premises licence.

(2)    The conditions are–

(a)    that the provisional grant of the justices' licence has not been declared final, and

(b)    that the premises to which the provisional grant relates have been completed in a manner which substantially complies with the plans deposited under the 1964 Act or, as the case may be, with those plans with modifications consented to under section 6(3) of that Act.

## Part 2

### Club premises certificates

*Introductory*

13    (1)    In this Part–

"existing club certificate" means a certificate held by a club under Part 2 of the 1964 Act for any premises;

"existing qualifying club activities" means the qualifying club activities authorised by the relevant existing club certificate in respect of those premises;

"first appointed day" means such day as may be specified as the first appointed day for the purposes of this Part;

"relevant existing club certificate", in relation to an application under paragraph 14, means the existing club certificate to which the application relates;

"relevant licensing authority" has the same meaning as in Part 4 of this Act (club premises certificates); and

"second appointed day" means such day as may be specified as the second appointed day for the purposes of this Part.

(2)    In the application of section 68 (relevant licensing authority in Part 4 of this Act) for the purposes of this Part, the reference in subsection (4) of that section to an applicant for a club premises certificate is to be read as a reference to an applicant under paragraph 14 for the grant of a certificate under paragraph 16.

*Application for conversion of existing club certificate*

14    (1)    This paragraph applies where, in respect of any premises, a club holds an existing club certificate on the first appointed day.

(2)    The club may, within the period of six months beginning with the first appointed day, apply to the relevant licensing authority for the grant of a certificate under paragraph 16 to succeed the existing club certificate so far as it relates to those premises.

(3) An application under this Part must specify the existing qualifying club activities and such other information as may be specified.

(4) The application must also be in the specified form and accompanied by–

    (a) the relevant documents, and

    (b) the specified fee.

(5) The relevant documents are–

    (a) the relevant existing club certificate (or a certified copy of it),

    (b) a plan in the specified form of the premises to which that certificate relates, and

    (c) such other documents as may be specified.

(6) In this paragraph any reference to a certified copy of a document is a reference to a copy of that document certified to be a true copy–

    (a) by the chief executive of the licensing justices for the licensing district in which the premises are situated,

    (b) by a solicitor or notary, or

    (c) by a person of a specified description.

(7) A document which purports to be a certified copy of an existing club certificate is to be taken to be such a copy unless the contrary is shown.

*Police consultation*

15 (1) Where a person makes an application under paragraph 14, he must give a copy of the application (and any documents which accompany it) to the chief officer of police for the police area (or each police area) in which the premises are situated no later than 48 hours after the application is made.

(2) Where–

    (a) an appeal is pending against a decision to revoke, or to reject an application for the renewal of, the relevant existing club certificate, and

    (b) a chief officer of police who has received a copy of the application under sub-paragraph (1) is satisfied that converting that existing club certificate in accordance with this Part would undermine the crime prevention objective,

he must give the relevant licensing authority and the applicant a notice to that effect.

(3) Where a chief officer of police who has received a copy of the application under sub-paragraph (1) is satisfied that, because of a material change in circumstances since the relevant time, converting the relevant existing club certificate in accordance with this Part would undermine the crime prevention objective, he must give the relevant licensing authority and the applicant a notice to that effect.

(4) For this purpose "the relevant time" means the time when the relevant existing club certificate was granted or, if it has been renewed, the last time it was renewed.

(5) The chief officer of police may not give a notice under subparagraph (2) or (3) after the end of the period of 28 days beginning with the day on which he received a copy of the application under sub-paragraph (1).

*Determination of application*

16 (1) This paragraph applies where an application is made in accordance with paragraph 14 and the applicant complies with paragraph 15(1).

(2) Subject to sub-paragraphs (3) and (5), the licensing authority must grant the application.

(3) Where a notice is given under paragraph 15(2) or (3) (and not withdrawn), the authority must–

    (a) hold a hearing to consider it, unless the authority, the applicant and the chief officer of police who gave the notice agree that a hearing is unnecessary, and

    (b) having regard to the notice, reject the application if it considers it necessary for the promotion of the crime prevention objective to do so.

(4) If the relevant licensing authority fails to determine the application within the period of two months beginning with the day on which it received it, then, subject to sub-paragraph (5), the application is to be treated as granted by the authority under this paragraph.

(5) An application must not be granted (and is not to be treated as granted under sub-paragraph (4)) if the existing club certificate has ceased to have effect at–

  (a) the time of the determination of the application, or

  (b) in a case within sub-paragraph (4), the end of the period mentioned in that sub-paragraph.

(6) Section 10 applies as if the relevant licensing authority's functions under sub-paragraph (3) were included in the list of functions in subsection (4) of that section (functions which cannot be delegated to an officer of the licensing authority).

*Notification of determination and issue of new certificate*

17    (1) Where an application is granted under paragraph 16, the relevant licensing authority must forthwith–

  (a) give the applicant a notice to that effect, and

  (b) issue the applicant with–

    (i) a certificate in respect of the premises ("the new certificate") in accordance with paragraph 18, and

    (ii) a summary of the new certificate.

(2) Where an application is rejected under paragraph 16, the relevant licensing authority must forthwith give the applicant a notice to that effect containing a statement of the authority's reasons for its decision to reject the application.

(3) The relevant licensing authority must give a copy of any notice it gives under sub-paragraph (1) or (2) to the chief officer of police for the police area (or each police area) in which the premises to which the notice relates are situated.

*The new certificate*

18    (1) The new certificate is to be treated as if it were a club premises certificate (see section 60), and sections 73, 74 and 75 apply in relation to it accordingly.

(2) The new certificate takes effect on the second appointed day.

(3) The new certificate must authorise the premises to be used for the existing qualifying club activities.

(4) Subject to sections 73, 74 and 75, the new certificate must be granted subject to such conditions as reproduce the effect of the conditions subject to which the relevant existing club certificate has effect at the time the application is granted.

(5) The new certificate must also be granted subject to conditions which reproduce the effect of any restriction imposed on the use of the premises for the existing qualifying club activities by any enactment specified for the purposes of this Part.

(6) Nothing in sub-paragraph (4) or (5) requires the new certificate to be granted for a limited period.

*Variation of new certificate*

19    (1) A person who makes an application under paragraph 14 may (notwithstanding that no certificate has yet been granted in consequence of that application) at the same time apply under section 84 for a variation of the certificate, and, for the purposes of such an application, the applicant is to be treated as the holder of that certificate.

(2) In relation to an application within sub-paragraph (1), the relevant licensing authority may discharge its functions under section 85 only if, and when, the application under this Part has been granted.

(3) Where an application within sub-paragraph (1) is not determined by the relevant licensing authority within the period of two months beginning with the day the application was received by the authority, it is to be treated as having been rejected by the authority under section 85 at the end of that period.

App 1

*Existing club certificate revoked after grant of new certificate*

20 Where the relevant licensing authority grants a new certificate under this Part, that certificate lapses if and when–

    (a) the existing club certificate is revoked before the second appointed day, or

    (b) where an appeal against a decision to revoke it is pending immediately before that day, the appeal is dismissed or abandoned.

*Appeals*

21 (1) Where an application under paragraph 14 is rejected by the relevant licensing authority, the applicant may appeal against that decision.

    (2) Where a licensing authority grants such an application, any chief officer of police who gave a notice under paragraph 15(2) or (3) (that was not withdrawn) may appeal against that decision.

    (3) Section 181 and paragraph 15(1) and (2) of Schedule 5 (general provision about appeals against decisions under Part 4 of this Act) apply in relation to appeals under this paragraph as they apply in relation to appeals under Part 2 of that Schedule.

    (4) Paragraph 15(3) of that Schedule applies in relation to an appeal under sub-paragraph (2).

*False statements*

22 (1) A person commits an offence if he knowingly or recklessly makes a false statement in or in connection with an application under paragraph 14.

    (2) For the purposes of sub-paragraph (1) a person is to be treated as making a false statement if he produces, furnishes, signs or otherwise makes use of a document that contains a false statement.

    (3) A person guilty of an offence under this section is liable on summary conviction to a fine not exceeding level 5 on the standard scale.

PART 3

PERSONAL LICENCES

*Introductory*

23 (1) Paragraphs 24 to 27 apply where–

    (a) during the transitional period, the holder of a justices' licence applies to the relevant licensing authority for the grant of a personal licence under section 117,

    (b) the application is accompanied by the documents mentioned in sub-paragraph (3), and

    (c) the applicant gives a copy of the application to the chief officer of police for the relevant licensing authority's area within 48 hours from the time the application is made.

    (2) In this paragraph "transitional period" means such period (of not less than six months) as may be specified for the purposes of this Part.

    (3) The documents are–

    (a) the justices' licence (or a certified copy of that licence),

    (b) a photograph of the applicant in the specified form which is endorsed, by a person of a specified description, with a statement verifying the likeness of the photograph to the applicant, and

    (c) where the applicant has been convicted of any relevant offence or foreign offence on or after the relevant date, a statement giving details of the offence.

    (4) In this paragraph any reference to a certified copy of a justices' licence is to a copy of that licence certified to be a true copy–

    (a) by the designated officer for the licensing justices for the licensing district concerned,

    (b)  by a solicitor or notary, or

    (c)  by a person of a specified description.

(5)  A document which purports to be a certified copy of a justices' licence is to be taken to be such a copy, unless the contrary is shown.

*Section 120 disapplied*

24    Section 120 (determination of application for grant) does not apply in relation to the application.

*Police objections*

25    (1)  Sub-paragraph (2) applies where–

    (a)  the applicant has been convicted of any relevant offences or foreign offences on or after the relevant date, and

    (b)  having regard to–

        (i)  any conviction of the applicant for a relevant offence, and

        (ii)  any conviction of his for a foreign offence which the chief officer of police considers to be comparable to a relevant offence,

      whether occurring before or after the relevant date, the chief officer of police is satisfied that the exceptional circumstances of the case are such that granting the application would undermine the crime prevention objective.

    (2)  The chief officer of police must give a notice stating the reasons why he is so satisfied (an "objection notice")–

    (a)  to the relevant licensing authority, and

    (b)  to the applicant.

    (3)  The objection notice must be given no later than 28 days after the day on which the chief officer of police receives a copy of the application in accordance with paragraph 23(1)(c).

    (4)  For the purposes of this paragraph–

    (a)  "relevant offence" and "foreign offence" have the meaning given in section 113, and

    (b)  section 114 (spent convictions) applies for the purposes of this paragraph as it applies for the purposes of section 120.

*Determination of application*

26    (1)  The relevant licensing authority must grant the application if–

    (a)  it is satisfied that the applicant holds a justices' licence, and

    (b)  no objection notice has been given within the period mentioned in paragraph 25(3) or any notice so given has been withdrawn.

    (2)  Where the authority is not satisfied that the applicant holds a justices' licence, it must reject the application.

    (3)  Where the authority is so satisfied, but sub-paragraph (1)(b) does not apply, it–

    (a)  must hold a hearing to consider the objection notice, and

    (b)  having regard to the notice, must–

        (i)  reject the application if it considers it necessary for the promotion of the crime prevention objective to do so, and

        (ii)  grant the application in any other case.

    (4)  If the authority fails to determine the application within the period of three months beginning with the day on which it receives it, then, the application is to be treated as granted by the authority under this paragraph.

    (5)  Section 10 applies as if the relevant licensing authority's functions under sub-paragraph (3) were included in the list of functions in subsection (4) of that section (functions which cannot be delegated to an officer of the licensing authority).

    (6)  In the application of section 122 (notification of determinations) to a determination under this paragraph, the references to an objection notice are to be read as references to an objection notice within the meaning of paragraph 25(2).

*Appeals*

27 (1) Where a licensing authority rejects an application under paragraph 26, the applicant may appeal against that decision.

   (2) Where a licensing authority grants an application for a personal licence under paragraph 26(3), the chief officer of police who gave the objection notice may appeal against that decision.

   (3) Section 181 and paragraph 17(6) and (7) of Schedule 5 (general provision about appeals relating to personal licences) apply in relation to appeals under this paragraph as they apply in relation to appeals under paragraph 17 of that Schedule.

   (4) Paragraph 17(8) of that Schedule applies in relation to an appeal under sub-paragraph (2) above.

*Interpretation of Part 3*

28 For the purposes of this Part–

   "relevant date", in relation to the holder of a justices' licence, means–

   (a) the date when the licence was granted, or

   (b) where it has been renewed, the last date when it was renewed, or

   (c) where it has been transferred to the holder and has not been renewed since the transfer, the date when it was transferred; and

   "relevant licensing authority", in relation to an application for a personal licence under section 117, means the authority to which the application is made in accordance with that section.

## PART 4

### MISCELLANEOUS AND GENERAL

*Consultation on licensing policy*

29 Until such time as section 59 of the 1964 Act (prohibition of sale, etc of alcohol except during permitted hours and in accordance with justices' licence etc) ceases to have effect in accordance with this Act, section 5(3) of this Act (licensing authority's duty to consult before determining licensing policy) has effect as if for paragraphs (c) to (e) there were substituted–

   "(c) such persons as the licensing authority considers to be representative of holders of existing licences (within the meaning of Part 1 of Schedule 8) in respect of premises situated in the authority's area,

   (d) such persons as the licensing authority considers to be representative of clubs registered (within the meaning of the Licensing Act 1964 (c. 26)) in respect of any premises situated in the authority's area,".

*Meaning of "methylated spirits" (transitory provision)*

30 Until such time as an order is made under subsection (6) of section 5 of the Finance Act 1995 (c. 4) (denatured alcohol) bringing that section into force, section 191 of this Act (meaning of "alcohol") has effect as if–

   (a) for subsection (1)(f) there were substituted–

   "(f) methylated spirits,", and

   (b) in subsection (2), the definition of "denatured alcohol" were omitted and at the appropriate place there were inserted–

   ""methylated spirits" has the same meaning as in the Alcoholic Liquor Duties Act 1979 (c. 4);".

*Savings*

31 Notwithstanding the repeal by this Act of Schedule 12 to the London Government Act 1963 (c. 33) (licensing of public entertainment in Greater London), or of any enactment amending that Schedule, that Schedule shall continue to apply in relation to–

   (a) licences granted under section 21 of the Greater London Council (General Powers) Act 1966 (c. xxviii) (licensing of public exhibitions in London), and

(b)   licences granted under section 5 of the Greater London Council (General Powers) Act 1978 (c. xiii) (licensing of entertainments booking offices in London), as it applied before that repeal.

32    (1)   In Schedule 3 to the Local Government (Miscellaneous Provisions) Act 1982 (c. 30) (control of sex establishments), paragraph (ii) of the proviso to paragraph 3A (as substituted by paragraph 85(3) of Schedule 6 to this Act) does not apply in relation to a borough of a participating council (within the meaning of section 2 of the London Local Authorities Act 1990 (c. vii)) which has appointed a day under section 3 of that Act for the coming into force of section 18 of that Act (repeal of paragraph (ii) of the proviso to paragraph 3A of Schedule 3 to that Act).

      (2)   On or after the coming into force of paragraph 85(3) of Schedule 6 to this Act, the reference in section 18 of that Act to paragraph (ii) of the proviso to paragraph 3A of Schedule 3 to that Act is to be read as a reference to that paragraph as substituted by paragraph 85(3) of Schedule 6 to this Act.

33    Notwithstanding that by virtue of this Act the Cinemas Act 1985 (c.13) ceases to have effect in England and Wales, section 6 of that Act (other than subsection (3)), and sections 5, 20 and 21 of that Act so far as relating to that section, shall continue to have effect there for the purposes of–

(a)   paragraph 3(2)(b) of Schedule 3 to the Local Government (Miscellaneous Provisions) Act 1982 (definition of "sex cinema"), and

(b)   section 3(6)(b) of the Video Recordings Act 1984 (c. 39) (exempted supplies).

*Interpretation*

34    In this Schedule–

           "justices' licence" means a justices' licence under Part 1 of the 1964 Act;

           "specified" means specified by order; and

           "the 1964 Act" means the Licensing Act 1964 (c. 26).

# APPENDIX 2: THE LICENSING ACT 2003 (PREMISES LICENCES AND CLUB PREMISES CERTIFICATES) REGULATIONS 2005

## 2005 No. 42

## LICENCES AND LICENSING

The Licensing Act 2003 (Premises licences and club premises certificates) Regulations 2005

| | |
|---|---|
| *Made* | *12th January 2005* |
| *Laid before Parliament* | *13th January 2005* |
| *Coming into force* | *7th February 2005* |

The Secretary of State, in exercise of the powers conferred upon her by sections 13(4)(i), 17(3)(b), 17(4)(h), 17(5)(a)(i), 17(5)(a)(ii), 17(5)(b), 17(5)(c), 24(1), 29(6), 30(2), 34(5), 37(3)(a), 47(2)(a), 51(3), 54, 69(4), 71(4)(b), 71(5), 71(6), 78(1), 84(4), 87(3), 91, 167(4), 178(1)(b), 178(4)(a) and 197 of the Licensing Act 2003[1], hereby makes the following Regulations:

### Citation and commencement

**1.** These Regulations may be cited as the Licensing Act 2003 (Premises licences and club premises certificates) Regulations 2005 and shall come into force on 7th February 2005.

### Interpretation

**2.**—(1) In these Regulations, unless the context requires otherwise—

"the Act" means the Licensing Act 2003;

"alternative scale plan" means a plan in a scale other than the standard scale;

"application" means an application made to a relevant licensing authority under Part 3 or Part 4 of the Act as the case may require and a reference to applications shall be construed accordingly;

"club" means a qualifying club within the meaning of section 61 of the Act;

"fire and other safety equipment" includes fire extinguishers, fire doors, fire alarms, marine safety equipment, marine evacuation equipment and other similar equipment;

"legible in all material respects" means that the information contained in the application, notice or representations is available to the recipient to no lesser extent than it would be if given by means of a document in written form;

"notice" means a notice given to a relevant licensing authority under Part 3 or Part 4 of the Act as the case may require and a reference to notices shall be construed accordingly;

"prescribed fee" in relation to an application or notice, shall be the fee for such application or notice calculated in accordance with regulations made by the Secretary of State under Part 3 and Part 4 of the Act or in accordance with an order made by the Secretary of State under Schedule 8 to the Act;

"relevant licensing authority" shall be construed in accordance with section 12, 68 or 171 of, or paragraph 1 or 13 of Schedule 8 to, the Act, as the case requires;

"representations" means representations made to a relevant licensing authority under Part 3, Part 4 or Part 8 of the Act as the case may require made by an interested party or a responsible authority in relation to an application or a review;

"review" means a review under Part 3, 4 or 8 of the Act as the case may require and a reference to reviews shall be construed accordingly;

---

"second appointed day" in relation to a premises licence, means the day as specified as such for the purposes of Part 1 of Schedule 8 to the Act and, in relation to a club premises certificate means the day as specified as such for the purposes of Part 2 of Schedule 8 to the Act; and

"standard scale" means that 1 millimetre represents 100 millimetres.

(2) For the purposes of these Regulations a reference to—

    (a) a paragraph in a regulation or in a Schedule, a Schedule or a Part is a reference to the paragraph in that regulation or that Schedule, the Schedule or the Part in these Regulations; and

    (b) a section should be construed as a reference to the section of the Act.

## PART 1

### INTRODUCTORY

**Scope of Regulations**

3. These Regulations apply to applications, notices, representations and reviews.

4. A person applying for a premises licence, a provisional statement, a variation of a premises licence, a review of a premises licence or a transfer of a premises licence or giving an interim authority notice shall comply with the appropriate provisions of Parts 2 and 4.

5. A club applying for a club premises certificate or a variation of a club premises certificate or a person applying for a review of a club premises certificate shall comply with the appropriate provisions of Parts 3 and 4.

6. The relevant licensing authority in relation to an application, notice, representations or a review shall comply with the appropriate provisions of Parts 4 and 5.

**Responsible authorities**

7. For the purposes of sections 13(4) and 69(4), the local weights and measures authority (within the meaning of section 69 of the Weights and Measures Act 1985[2]) for any area in which the premises is situated is a responsible authority.

**Person giving interim authority notice**

8. For the purposes of section 47(2)(a), a person has a prescribed interest in the premises concerned if he has a legal interest in the premises as freeholder or leaseholder.

**Rights of freeholder etc. to be notified of licensing matters**

9. In a case of a person giving a notice of his property interest in any premises under section 178, that notice shall be in the form and shall contain the information set out in Schedule 1 and shall be accompanied by the prescribed fee.

## PART 2

### PREMISES LICENCES

**Premises licences**

10. An application for a premises licence under section 17 shall be in the form and shall contain the information set out in Schedule 2 and shall be accompanied by the prescribed fee.

**Provisional statements**

11. An application for a provisional statement under section 29 shall be in the form and shall contain the information set out in Schedule 3 and shall be accompanied by the prescribed fee.

---

2  1985 c.72

### Variation of premises licences

**12.** An application to vary a premises licence under section 34 shall be in the form and shall contain the information set out in Schedule 4 and shall be accompanied by the prescribed fee (provided that in a case where the application to vary is made at the same time as an application under paragraph 2 of Schedule 8 to the Act, the application shall be in the form and shall contain the information set out in Part B of Schedule 1 to the Licensing Act 2003 (Transitional provisions) Order 2005[3]).

### Variation of premises licences to specify premises supervisor

**13.** An application to vary a premises licence so as to specify the individual named in the application as the premises supervisor under section 37 shall be in the form and shall contain the information set out in Schedule 5 and shall be accompanied by the prescribed fee (provided that in a case where the application is made at the same time as an application under paragraph 2 of Schedule 8 to the Act, the application shall be in the form and shall contain the information set out in Part B of Schedule 1 to the Licensing Act 2003 (Transitional provisions) Order 2005).

### Transfer of premises licences

**14.** An application to transfer a premises licence under section 42 shall be in the form and shall contain the information set out in Schedule 6 and shall be accompanied by the prescribed fee.

### Interim authority notices

**15.** An interim authority notice given under section 47 shall be in the form and shall contain the information set out in Schedule 7 and shall be accompanied by the prescribed fee.

### Review of premises licences

**16.** An application for a review of a premises licence under section 51 shall be in the form and shall contain the information set out in Schedule 8.

### 16A. Summary review of premises licences: serious crime and disorder

An application for a review of a premises licence under section 53A shall be in the form and shall contain the information set out in Schedule 8A.

PART 3

CLUB PREMISES CERTIFICATES

### Qualifying club

**17.** A club applying for a club premises certificate under section 71 on or before making such an application shall make a declaration to the relevant licensing authority in the form and containing the information set out in Part A of Schedule 9.

### Club premises certificates

**18.** An application for a club premises certificate under section 71 shall be in the form and shall contain the information set out in Part B of Schedule 9 and shall be accompanied by the prescribed fee.

### Variation of club premises certificates

**19.** An application to vary a club premises certificate under section 84 shall be in the form and shall contain the information set out in Schedule 10 and shall be accompanied by the prescribed fee (provided that in a case where the application to vary is made at the same time as an application under paragraph 14 of Schedule 8 to the Act, the application shall be in the form and shall contain the information set out in Part B of Schedule 4 to the Licensing Act 2003 (Transitional provisions) Order 2005).

### Review of club premises certificates

**20.** An application to review a club premises certificate under section 87 shall be in the form and shall contain the information set out in Schedule 8.

PART 4

GENERAL

### Applications, notices and representations

**21.**—(1) An application, a notice or representations shall be given in writing.

(2) Notwithstanding the requirement in paragraph (1) and subject to paragraph (3), that requirement shall be satisfied in a case where—

    (a)   the text of the application, notice or representations—

        (i)    is transmitted by electronic means;

        (ii)   is capable of being accessed by the recipient;

        (iii)  is legible in all material respects; and

        (iv)  is capable of being read and reproduced in written form and used for subsequent reference;

    (b)   the person to whom the application or notice is to be given or the representations are to be made has agreed in advance that an application or a notice may be given or representations may be made by electronic means; and

    (c)   forthwith on sending the text of the application, notice or representations by electronic means, the application, notice or representations is given or made, as applicable, to the recipient in writing.

(3) Where the text of the application, notice or representations is or are transmitted by electronic means, the giving of the application or notice or the making of the representation shall be effected at the time the requirements of paragraph 2(a) are satisfied, provided that where any application or notice is required to be accompanied by a fee, plan or other document or information that application or notice shall not be treated as given until the fee, plan or other document or information has been received by the relevant licensing authority.

### Representations

**22.**—An interested party or a responsible authority making representations to a relevant licensing authority, may make those representations—

    (a)   in the case of a review of a premises licence following a closure order, at any time up to and including seven days starting on the day after the day on which the authority received the notice under section 165(4) in relation to the closure order and any extension to it;

    (b)   in any other case, at any time during a period of 28 consecutive days starting on the day after the day on which the application to which it relates was given to the authority by the applicant.

### Plans

**23.**—(1) An application for a premises licence under section 17, or a club premises certificate under section 71, shall be accompanied by a plan of the premises to which the application relates and which shall comply with the following paragraphs of this regulation.

(2) Unless the relevant licensing authority has previously agreed in writing with the applicant following a request by the applicant that an alternative scale plan is acceptable to it, in

which case the plan shall be drawn in that alternative scale, the plan shall be drawn in standard scale.

(3)   The plan shall show—

(a)   the extent of the boundary of the building, if relevant, and any external and internal walls of the building and, if different, the perimeter of the premises;

(b)   the location of points of access to and egress from the premises;

(c)   if different from sub-paragraph (3)(b), the location of escape routes from the premises;

(d)   in a case where the premises is to be used for more than one licensable activity, the area within the premises used for each activity;

(e)   fixed structures (including furniture) or similar objects temporarily in a fixed location (but not furniture) which may impact on the ability of individuals on the premises to use exits or escape routes without impediment;

(f)   in a case where the premises includes a stage or raised area, the location and height of each stage or area relative to the floor;

(g)   in a case where the premises includes any steps, stairs, elevators or lifts, the location of the steps, stairs, elevators or lifts;

(h)   in the case where the premises includes any room or rooms containing public conveniences, the location of the room or rooms;

(i)   the location and type of any fire safety and any other safety equipment including, if applicable, marine safety equipment; and

(j)   the location of a kitchen, if any, on the premises.

(4)   The plan may include a legend through which the matters mentioned or referred to in paragraph (3) are sufficiently illustrated by the use of symbols on the plan.

## Consents

**24.**—(1) In the case of an application under section 17 which relates to the supply of alcohol or section 37, the consent of the individual who the applicant wishes to have specified in the licence as the premises supervisor under section 17(3)(c) or 37(3)(a) in the premises licence shall be in the form set out in Part A of Schedule 11.

(2)   In the case of an application to transfer a premises licence under section 42 or 43, the consent of the holder of the premises licence under section 43(4) or 44(4) shall be in the form set out in Part B of Schedule 11.

## Advertisement of applications

**25.** In the case of an application for a premises licence under section 17, for a provisional statement under section 29, to vary a premises licence under section 34, for a club premises certificate under section 71 or to vary a club premises certificate under section 84, the person making the application shall advertise the application, in both cases containing the appropriate information set out in regulation 26—

(a)   for a period of no less than 28 consecutive days starting on the day after the day on which the application was given to the relevant licensing authority, by displaying a notice,

(i)   which is—

(aa) of a size equal or larger than A4,

(bb) of a pale blue colour,

(cc)  printed legibly in black ink or typed in black in a font of a size equal to or larger than 16;

(ii)   in all cases, prominently at or on the premises to which the application relates where it can be conveniently read from the exterior of the premises and in the case of a premises covering an area of more than fifty metres square, a further notice in the same form and subject to the same requirements every fifty metres along the external perimeter of the premises abutting any highway; and

(b)   by publishing a notice—

(i)   in a local newspaper or, if there is none, in a local newsletter, circular or similar document, circulating in the vicinity of the premises;

(ii)   on at least one occasion during the period of ten working days starting on the day after the day on which the application was given to the relevant licensing authority.

26.—(1) In the case of an application for a premises licence or a club premises certificate, the notices referred to in regulation 25 shall contain a statement of the relevant licensable activities or relevant qualifying club activities as the case may require which it is proposed will be carried on on or from the premises.

(2)   In the case of an application for a provisional statement, the notices referred to in regulation 25—

(a)   shall state that representations are restricted after the issue of a provisional statement; and

(b)   where known, may state the relevant licensable activities which it is proposed will be carried on on or from the premises.

(3)   In the case of an application to vary a premises licence or a club premises certificate, the notices referred to in regulation 25 shall briefly describe the proposed variation.

(4)   In all cases, the notices referred to in regulation 25 shall state—

(a)   the name of the applicant or club;

(b)   the postal address of the premises or club premises, if any, or if there is no postal address for the premises a description of those premises sufficient to enable the location and extent of the premises or club premises to be identified;

(c)   the postal address and, where applicable, the worldwide web address where the register of the relevant licensing authority is kept and where and when the record of the application may be inspected;

(d)   the date by which an interested party or responsible authority may make representations to the relevant licensing authority;

(e)   that representations shall be made in writing; and

(f)   that it is an offence knowingly or recklessly to make a false statement in connection with an application and the maximum fine for which a person is liable on summary conviction for the offence.

## Notice to responsible authority

27. In the case of an application for a premises licence under section 17, a provisional statement under section 29, a variation of a premises licence under section 34, a review under section 51, a club premises certificate under section 71, a review under section 87 or a variation of a club premises certificate under section 84, the person making the application shall give notice of his application to each responsible authority by giving to each authority a copy of the application together with its accompanying documents, if any, on the same day as the day on which the application is given to the relevant licensing authority.

## Notice to chief officer of police etc.

28. In the case of—

(a)   an application to vary a premises licence under section 37 (to specify an individual as premises supervisor), the person making the application shall give to—

(i)   the chief officer of police, and

(ii)   the designated premises supervisor, if any,

a copy of the application together with its accompanying documents, if any, on the same day as the day on which the application is given to the relevant licensing authority;

(b)   an application for the transfer of a premises licence under section 42 or the giving of an interim authority notice under section 47, the person making the application or giving the notice shall give to the chief officer of police a copy of the application or interim authority notice together with its accompanying documents, if any, on the same day as the day on which the application or notice is given to the relevant licensing authority.

### Notification of review

**29.** In the case of an application for a review of a premises licence under section 51 or a review of a club premises certificate under section 87, the person making the application shall give notice of his application to each responsible authority and to the holder of the premises licence or the club in whose name the club premises certificate is held and to which the application relates by giving to the authority, the holder or the club a copy of the application for review together with its accompanying documents, if any, on the same day as the day on which the application for review is given to the licensing authority.

### PART 5

### LICENSING AUTHORITIES – MISCELLANEOUS

### Validity of premises licences and club premises certificates

**30.** A relevant licensing authority may not grant a premises licence or club premises certificate to have effect before the second appointed day.

### Frivolous, vexatious or repetitious representations

**31.** Where the relevant licensing authority notifies the person who made the representations that the representations are frivolous, vexatious or a repetition as the case requires, that notification shall be given in writing to the person who made the representations and as soon as is reasonably practicable and in any event before the determination of the application to which the representations relate.

### Notification that any ground for review is frivolous, vexatious or a repetition

**32.** Where the relevant licensing authority rejects a ground for a review under section 51(4)(b) or section 87(4)(b) it shall give notification in writing as soon as is reasonably practicable to the person making the application for a review.

### Form of premises licence and summary

**33.** A premises licence shall—
(a)   include an identifier for the relevant licensing authority;
(b)   include a number that is unique to the licence; and
(c)   be in the form and shall contain the information set out in Part A of Schedule 12.
**34.** A summary of a premises licence shall—
(a)   include the identifier for the relevant licensing authority;
(b)   include the licence number referred to in regulation 33; and
(c)   be in the form and shall contain the information set out in Part B of Schedule 12, printed on paper of a size equal to or larger than A4.

### Form of club premises certificate and summary

**35.** A club premises certificate shall—
(a)   include an identifier for the relevant licensing authority;
(b)   include a number that is unique to the certificate; and
(c)   be in the form and shall contain the information set out in Part A of Schedule 13.
**36.** A summary of a club premises certificate summary shall—
(a)   include the identifier for the relevant licensing authority;
(b)   include the certificate number referred to in regulation 35; and

(c)   be in the form and shall contain the information set out in Part B of Schedule 13, printed on paper of a size equal to or larger than A4.

## Summary review of premises licences: serious crime and disorder

**36A.**—(1) In the case of an application for review of a premises licence under section 53A the relevant licensing authority must, within 48 hours of the time of the receipt of the application, give notice of the review to—

(a)   the holder of the premises licence to which the application relates; and

(b)   each responsible authority.

(2) Notice under paragraph (1) is to be given by giving to the holder and each authority—

(a)   a copy of the application; and

(b)   a copy of the certificate given under section 53A(1)(b) that accompanied the application.

(3)   In computing the period of 48 hours mentioned in paragraph (1) time that is not on a working day is to be disregarded.

## Review of premises licence following closure order

**37.** In the case of a review of a premises licence under section 167 (review of premises licence following a closure order), within the period of one working day starting on the day after the day on which the relevant licensing authority received the notice under section 165(4) from the magistrates' court, the relevant licensing authority shall give to the holder of the premises licence and each responsible authority notice in writing of—

(a)   the review;

(b)   the dates between which interested parties and responsible authorities may make representations relating to the review to the relevant licensing authority;

(c)   the closure order and any extension of it; and

(d)   any order made in relation to it under section 165(2).

## Advertisement of review by licensing authority

**38.**—(1) Subject to the provisions of this regulation and regulation 39, the relevant licensing authority shall advertise an application for the review of a premises licence under section 51(3) or 53A, of a club premises certificate under section 87(3) or of a premises licence following a closure order under section 167—

(a)   by displaying prominently a notice—

(i)   which is—

(aa) of a size equal or larger than A4;

(bb) of a pale blue colour; and

(cc)  printed legibly in black ink or typed in black in a font of a size equal to or larger than 16;

(ii)   at, on or near the site of the premises to which the application relates where it can conveniently be read from the exterior of the premises by the public and in the case of a premises covering an area of more than fifty metres square, one further notice in the same form and subject to the same requirements shall be displayed every 50 metres along the external perimeter of the premises abutting any highway; and

(iii)   at the offices, or the main offices, of the licensing authority in a central and conspicuous place; and

(b)   in a case where the relevant licensing authority maintains a website for the purpose of advertisement of applications given to it, by publication of a notice on that website;

(2)   the requirements set out in paragraph (1) shall be fulfilled—

    (a)   in the case of a review of a premises licence following a closure order under section 167, or of a review of such a licence under section 53A, for a period of no less than seven consecutive days starting on the day after the day on which the relevant licensing authority received—

        (i)    the notice under section 165(4); or

        (ii)   the application under section 53A

        (as the case may be); and

    (b)   in all other cases, for a period of no less than 28 consecutive days starting on the day after the day on which the application was given to the relevant licensing authority.

**39.** Subject to regulation 39A, all notices referred to in regulation 38 shall state—

(a)   the address of the premises about which an application for a review has been made,

(b)   the dates between which interested parties and responsible authorities may make representations to the relevant licensing authority,

(c)   the grounds of the application for review,

(d)   the postal address and, where relevant, the worldwide web address where the register of the relevant licensing authority is kept and where and when the grounds for the review may be inspected; and

(e)   that it is an offence knowingly or recklessly to make a false statement in connection with an application and the maximum fine for which a person is liable on summary conviction for the offence.

**39A.**—(1) In the case of a review of a premises licence under section 53A—

(a)   the dates referred to in regulation 39(b) shall be the date of the first working day after the day on which the notice was published, and the date of the ninth subsequent working day;

(b)   the grounds referred to in regulation 39(c) shall be that in the opinion of a senior police officer the premises are associated with serious crime or serious disorder or both.

(2)   The period prescribed for the purposes of section 53A(3)(e) of the Act is the period beginning on the first working day after the publication of the notice referred to in regulation 38 and ending on the ninth subsequent working day.

## Provision of forms, notices and applications

**40.** The relevant licensing authority—

(a)   must provide on request the forms listed in the Schedules printed on paper; or

(b)   in a case where the relevant licensing authority maintains a website, it may provide electronic copies of the forms listed in the Schedules on such a website.

## Validity of forms, notices and application

**41.** A relevant licensing authority shall not reject any application or notice by reason only of the fact that it is given on a form provided otherwise than from the relevant licensing authority but which complies with the requirements of these Regulations.

## Acknowledgement of notification of an interest

**42.** The relevant licensing authority shall as soon as reasonably practicable on receipt of a notification to it under section 178 acknowledge its receipt by returning a copy of the notification to the notifier duly endorsed.

*Richard Caborn*
Minister of State
Date 12th January 2005                                   Department for Culture, Media and Sport

## EXPLANATORY NOTE

*(This note is not part of the Regulations)*

The Licensing Act 2003 (c.17) (the Act) provides for the licensing of premises for the sale by retail of alcohol, the supply of alcohol by or on behalf of a club to, or to the order of a member of the club, the provision of regulated entertainment and the provision of late night refreshment. These Regulations set out the detailed requirements relating to applications, notices and representations given or made under Parts 3 and 4 of the Act and reviews made under those Parts and Part 8 of the Act.

In particular, these Regulations, provide that weights and measures authorities are responsible authorities (regulation 7). Also, that persons with a prescribed interest in a premises include those with a legal interest as freeholder or leaseholder (regulation 8) and Schedule 1 sets out the form of the notice to be given by a person to notify a relevant licensing authority or his, her or its interest in a licensed premises (regulation 9).

Regulations 10 to 16 and Schedules 2 to 8 set out the form of applications and notices for the grant of a premises licence, the issue of a provisional statement, an application for variation of a premises licence, an application to vary a premises licence to specify the premises supervisor, an application to transfer a premises licence, the giving of an interim authority notice and an application for the review of a premises licence.

Regulations 17 to 20 and Schedules 9 and 10 set out the form of applications and declarations given by qualifying clubs. These include the form of the club declaration in which a club shows that it is a qualifying club, an application for a club premises certificate, and an application to vary a club premises certificate. Schedule 8 also sets out the form for an application to review a club premises certificate.

The Regulations provide that applications, notices and representations must be given or made in writing but includes a discretion for this requirement to be fulfilled by electronic means (regulation 21).

Regulation 22 sets out the time limits during which representations must be made. Regulation 23 sets out the detailed requirements for plans of premises and club premises to be submitted with applications.

Regulation 24 and Schedule 11 set out the form of consents to be given by the premises supervisor of a premises and the holder of the premises licence in certain circumstances.

Regulations 25, 26, 38 and 39 set out the requirements for the advertisement of applications and reviews by applicants and by relevant licensing authorities.

Regulation 27 requires that persons or clubs applying for a premises licence, club premises certificate, provisional statement, variation of a premises licence or club premises certificate, review of a premises licence or club premises certificate give notice of the application by giving each responsible authority a copy of the application together with its accompanying documents on the same day as the day on which that application is given to the relevant licensing authority. Further, regulations 28 and 29 set out the requirements for giving of notices to the chief officer of police, the premises supervisor, the responsible authorities, the holder of the premises licence and the club holding the club premises certificate in a number of circumstances where this is required by the Act.

Regulations 33 to 36 provide for the form of a premises licence and club premises certificate and regulation 30 states that they may not be granted to have effect until the second appointed day.

Regulations 31 and 32 provide that the notification from a licensing authority that any representations or a ground for review is frivolous, vexatious or repetitious must be given in writing and as soon as reasonably practicable.

Regulation 37 sets out the requirements for the notice given by the relevant licensing authority to the holder of the premises licence and responsible authorities in respect of the review of a premises licence following a closure order under Part 8 of the Act.

Regulations 40 and 41 provide that the relevant licensing authority must provide the forms listed in the Schedules to these Regulations on request and that a licensing authority cannot reject any application or notice by reason only that it is given on a form provided from another source other than that relevant licensing authority. Finally, regulation 42 requires the relevant licensing authority to acknowledge a notice received by it under section 178 of the Act.

A Regulatory Impact Assessment in relation to these Regulations has been placed in the libraries of both Houses of Parliament and copies may be obtained from the Alcohol and Entertainment Licensing Branch of the Department of Culture, Media and Sport, 3rd Floor, 2-4 Cockspur Street, London SW1Y 5DH or view on the Department's website, www.culture.gov.uk.

# APPENDIX 3: THE LICENSING ACT 2003 (PERSONAL LICENCES) REGULATIONS 2005

## 2005 No.41

## LICENCES AND LICENSING

### The Licensing Act 2003 (Personal licences) Regulations 2005

| | |
|---|---|
| Made- - - - - - - - - - - - - - - - - - - - - - - - - - - - - - - -12th January 2005 | |
| Laid before Parliament- - - - - - - - - - - - - - - - - - 13th January 2005 | |
| Coming into force- - - - - - - - - - - - - - - - - - - - - -7th February 2005 | |

The Secretary of State, in exercise of the powers conferred upon her by sections 125(4) and 133(1) of the Licensing Act 2003[1], hereby makes the following Regulations:

### Citation and commencement

**1.** These Regulations may be cited as the Licensing Act 2003 (Personal licences) Regulations 2005 and shall come into force on 7th February 2005.

### Interpretation

**2.**—In these Regulations—

"the Act" means the Licensing Act 2003;

"legible in all material respects" means that the information contained in the application is available to the recipient to no lesser extent than it would be if it were given by means of a document in written form;

"person of standing in the community" includes a bank or building society official, a police officer, a civil servant or a minister of religion; and

"prescribed fee" in relation to an application, shall be the fee for such application calculated in accordance with the regulations made by the Secretary of State under Part 6 of the Act.

### Scope

**3.** These Regulations apply to applications made under and in relation to Part 6 (personal licences) of the Act.

### Person to whom a personal licence may be granted who does not possess a licensing qualification

**4.**—The following persons are prescribed for the purposes of section 120(2)(b) of the Act–

(a) a member of the company of the Master, Wardens, Freemen and Commonalty of the Mistery of the Vintners of the City of London;

(b) a person operating under a licence granted by the University of Cambridge; or

(c) a person operating premises under a licence granted by the Board of the Green Cloth.

### Form of personal licence

**5.** A personal licence shall be in the form of a physical document in two separate parts and shall contain—

(a) in the first part, the matters referred to in section 125(2) of the Act, a photograph of the holder, a number allocated by the licensing authority that is unique to the licence, an

---

1   2003 c. 17

identifier for the licensing authority granting the licence and the date of the expiry of the licence and this part shall be produced in durable form and shall be of a size no larger than 70mm × 100mm, and

(b)    in the second part, the matters referred to in section 125(3) of the Act and the matters referred to in (a) except that the photograph of the holder shall be omitted.

### Application for grant or renewal of a personal licence

6.—(1) Except in the case of an application for the grant of a personal licence by the holder of a justices' licence during the period commencing on 7th February 2005 and ending on 6th August 2005, in which case the provisions of regulation 8 shall apply, an application for the grant of a personal licence made under section 117 of the Act (application for grant or renewal of a personal licence) shall be in the form and shall contain the information set out in Schedule 1 to these Regulations and shall be accompanied by the prescribed fee.

(2)    An application for the renewal of a personal licence made under section 117 of the Act (application for grant or renewal of a personal licence) shall be in the form and shall contain the information set out in Schedule 2 to these Regulations and shall be accompanied by the prescribed fee.

7.—(1) An application made under regulation 6(1) or 6(2) shall be accompanied by the following documents–

(a)    two photographs of the applicant, which shall be–
   (i)    taken against a light background so that the applicant's features are distinguishable and contrast against the background,
   (ii)   45 millimetres by 35 millimetres,
   (iii)  full face uncovered and without sunglasses and, unless the applicant wears a head covering due to his religious beliefs, without a head covering,
   (iv)   on photographic paper, and
   (v)    one of which is endorsed with a statement verifying the likeness of the photograph to the applicant by a solicitor, notary, a person of standing in the community or any individual with a professional qualification; and

(b)    either—
   (i)    a criminal conviction certificate issued under section 112 of the Police Act 1997[2],
   (ii)   a criminal record certificate issued under section 113A of the Police Act 1997 or
   (iii)  the results of a subject access search under the Data Protection Act 1998[3] of the Police National Computer by the National Identification Service, and

   in any case such certificate or search results shall be issued no earlier than one calendar month before the giving of the application to the relevant licensing authority, and

(c)    a declaration by the applicant, in the form set out in Schedule 3, that either he has not been convicted of a relevant offence or a foreign offence or that he has been convicted of a relevant offence or a foreign offence accompanied by details of the nature and date of the conviction and any sentence imposed on him in respect of it.

(2)    Except in the case of a person prescribed under regulation 4, an application under regulation 6(1) shall be accompanied by the licensing qualification of the applicant.

8.—(1) An application for the grant of a personal licence made under section 117 of the Act by a holder of a justices' licence during the period commencing on 7th February 2005 and ending on 6th August 2005 shall be in the form and contain the information set out in Schedule 3, insofar as the provisions are relevant to the application, and Schedule 4 and shall comply with the remaining provisions of this regulation.

---

2   1997 c. 50
3   1998 c. 29

(2) The application shall be accompanied by—

    (a) the prescribed fee;

    (b) in addition to the documents mentioned in paragraph 23(3) of Schedule 8 to the Act, by a second photograph of the applicant in identical form to the requirements in respect of a photograph of the applicant set out in article 10 of the Licensing Act (Transitional provisions) Order 2005[4] except that the second photograph does not need to be endorsed with a statement verifying the likeness of the photograph to the applicant.

**9.**—(1) An application shall be given in writing.

(2) Notwithstanding the requirement in paragraph (1) and subject to paragraph (3), that requirement shall be satisfied in a case where—

    (a) The text of the application—

        (i) is transmitted by electronic means;

        (ii) is capable of being accessed by the recipient;

        (iii) is legible in all material respects; and

        (iv) is capable of being read and reproduced in legible written form and used for subsequent reference;

    (b) the person to whom the application is to be given has agreed in advance that an application may be given to them by those means; and

    (c) forthwith on sending the text of the application by electronic means, the application is given to the recipient in writing.

(3) Where the text of the application is transmitted by electronic means, the giving of the application shall be effected at the time the requirements of paragraph 2(a) are satisfied, provided that where any application is required to be accompanied by a fee, or any document that application shall not be treated as given until the fee or document has been received by the relevant licensing authority.

**Provision of forms**

**10.** The relevant licensing authority—

(a) must provide on request the forms listed in the Schedules printed on paper; or

(b) in a case where the relevant licensing authority maintains a website, it may provide electronic copies of the forms listed in the Schedules on such a website.

**Validity of forms**

**11.** A licensing authority shall not reject any application by reason only of the fact that it is given on a form provided otherwise than from the relevant licensing authority but which complies with the requirements of these Regulations.

*Richard Caborn*
Minister of State
Date 12th January 2005          Department for Culture, Media and Sport

## EXPLANATORY NOTE

*(This note is not part of the Regulations)*

These Regulations make provision for the detailed requirements to be fulfilled by applicants for personal licences under Part 6 of the Licensing Act 2003 (c.17) ("the Act").

In addition the Regulations prescribe those persons to whom a licence may be granted who do not possess a licensing qualification (regulation 4). The form of the personal licence is prescribed in regulation 5.

The Regulations prescribe the application form to be used by the applicant, the information to be supplied and the documents to accompany the application for an application for the grant or renewal of a personal licence (regulations 6 and 7 and Schedules 1 to 3). In respect of an application for a personal licence made by the holder of a justices' licence during the period commencing on 7th February 2005 and ending on 6th August 2005 regulation 8 and Schedules 3 and 4 prescribe the application form to be used by the applicant, the information to be supplied and the documents to accompany the application. In the case of such applications reference should also be made to the Licensing Act 2003 (Transitional provisions) Order 2005 S.I. 2005/40.

The Regulations require the relevant licensing authority to provide the application forms for applicants on request and provides a discretion to provide these on its website.

A Regulatory Impact Assessment in relation to these Regulations has been placed in the libraries of both Houses of Parliament and copies may be obtained from the Alcohol and Entertainment Licensing Branch of the Department of Culture, Media and Sport, 3rd Floor, 2–4 Cockspur Street, London SW1Y 5DH or viewed on the Department's website, www.culture.gov.uk.

# APPENDIX 4: THE LICENSING ACT 2003 (HEARINGS) REGULATIONS 2005

## 2005 No. 44

## LICENCES AND LICENSING

### The Licensing Act 2003 (Hearings) Regulations 2005)

| | |
|---|---|
| *Made-* | *12th January 2005* |
| *Laid before Parliament-* | *13th January 2005* |
| *Coming into force-* | *7th February 2005* |

The Secretary of State, in exercise of the powers conferred upon her by sections 9(2) and 183(1) of the Licensing Act 2003(**a**)[1], hereby makes the following Regulations:

### Citation and commencement

**1.** These Regulations may be cited as the Licensing Act 2003 (Hearings) Regulations 2005 and shall come into force on 7<sup>th</sup> February 2005.

### Interpretation

**2.**—(1) In these Regulations—

"the Act" means the Licensing Act 2003;

"authority" means, in relation to a hearing, the relevant licensing authority which has the duty under the Act to hold the hearing which expression includes the licensing committee or licensing sub-committee discharging the function of holding the hearing;

"determination" is to be interpreted in accordance with Schedule 4;

"hearing" means the hearing referred to in column 1 of the table in Schedule 1 as the case may require;

"legible in all material respects" means that the information contained in the notice is available to the recipient to no lesser extent than it would be if given by means of a document in written form;

"notice of hearing" means the notice given under regulation 6(1);

"party to the hearing" means a person to whom the notice of hearing is to be given in accordance with regulation 6(1) and "party" and "parties" shall be construed accordingly.

(2) In these Regulations, a reference to the application, representations or notice made by a party means the application, representations or notice referred to in relation to that party in column 2 of the table in Schedule 2.

(3) In these Regulations, a reference to a section, or a paragraph of a Schedule is a reference to the section of, or the paragraph of the Schedule to, the Act.

(4) For the purposes of regulation 19(b), a notice given by a chief officer of police does not include an application made, or a certificate given under, section 53A(1) of the Act.

### Scope

**3.**—(1) These Regulations make provision for the procedure to be followed in relation to hearings held under the Act by an authority.

(2) Regulations 4 to 13, 16(a), 18, 20(2)(a) and (4), 22 (from "and shall" to the end), 27, 29 and 34 do not apply to a hearing under section 53B of the Act (interim steps pending review).

---

1  2003, c.17.

**Period of time within which hearing to be held**

**4.** The authority shall arrange for the date on which and time and place at which a hearing is to be held in accordance with regulation 5 and shall give a notice of hearing in accordance with regulations 6 and 7.

**5.** Hearings to be held under the provisions listed in column 1 of the table in Schedule 1 must be commenced within the period of time specified in column 2 of the table and in a case where the hearing is to be held on more than one day, the hearing must be arranged to take place on consecutive working days.

**Notice of hearing**

**6.**—(1) In the case of hearings under the provisions listed in column 1 of the table in Schedule 2, the authority shall give to the persons listed in column 2 of the table a notice stating the date on which and time and place at which the hearing is to be held (the "notice of hearing") in accordance with the following provisions of this regulation.

(2) In the case of a hearing under—

    (a) section 48(3)(a) (cancellation of interim authority notice following police objection), or

    (b) section 105(2)(a) (counter notice following police objection to temporary event notice),

the authority shall give the notice of hearing no later than two working days before the day or the first day on which the hearing is to be held.

(3) In the case of a hearing under—

    (a) section 167(5)(a) (review of premises licence following closure order) or section 53C (review of premises licence following review notice),

    (b) paragraph 4(3)(a) of Schedule 8 (determination of application for conversion of existing licence),

    (c) paragraph 16(3)(a) of Schedule 8 (determination of application for conversion of existing club certificate), or

    (d) paragraph 26(3)(a) of Schedule 8 (determination of application by holder of justices' licence for grant of personal licence),

the authority shall give the notice of hearing no later than five working days before the day or the first day on which the hearing is to be held.

(4) In any other case, the authority shall give notice of hearing no later than ten working days before the day of the first day on which the hearing is to be held.

**Information to accompany notice of hearing**

**7.**—(1) The notice of hearing shall be accompanied by information regarding the following—

    (a) the rights of a party provided for in regulations 15 and 16;

    (b) the consequences if a party does not attend or is not represented at the hearing;

    (c) the procedure to be followed at the hearing;

    (d) any particular points on which the authority considers that it will want clarification at the hearing from a party.

(2) In relation to hearings under the provisions listed in column 1 of the table in Schedule 3, the notice of hearing given to the persons listed in column 2 of the table shall also be accompanied by the documents listed in column 3 of the table.

**Action following receipt of notice of hearing**

**8.**—(1) A party shall give to the authority within the period of time provided for in the following provisions of this regulation a notice stating—

    (a) whether he intends to attend or be represented at the hearing;

    (b) whether he considers a hearing to be unnecessary.

(2) In a case where a party wishes any other person (other than the person he intends to represent him at the hearing) to appear at the hearing, the notice referred to in paragraph (1)

shall contain a request for permission for such other person to appear at the hearing accompanied by details of the name of that person and a brief description of the point or points on which that person may be able to assist the authority in relation to the application, representations or notice of the party making the request.

(3)   In the case of a hearing under—

(a)   section 48(3)(a) (cancellation of interim authority notice following police objection), or

(b)   section 105(2)(a) (counter notice following police objection to temporary event notice),

the party shall give the notice no later than one working day before the day or the first day on which the hearing is to be held.

(4)   In the case of a hearing under—

(a)   section 167(5)(a) (review of premises licence following closure order) or section 53C (review of premises licence following review notice),

(b)   paragraph 4(3)(a) of Schedule 8 (determination of application for conversion of existing licence),

(c)   paragraph 16(3)(a) of Schedule 8 (determination of application for conversion of existing club certificate), or

(d)   paragraph 26(3)(a) of Schedule 8 (determination of application by holder of justices' licence for grant of personal licence),

the party shall give the notice no later than two working days before the day or the first day on which the hearing is to be held.

(5)   In any other case, the party shall give the notice no later than five working days before the day or the first day on which the hearing is to be held.

### Right to dispense with hearing if all parties agree

**9.**—(1) An authority may dispense with holding a hearing if all persons required by the Act to agree that such a hearing is unnecessary, other than the authority itself, have done so by giving notice to the authority that they consider a hearing to be unnecessary.

(2)   Where all the persons required by the Act to agree that a hearing is unnecessary have done so in accordance with paragraph (1), the authority, if it agrees that a hearing is unnecessary, must forthwith give notice to the parties that the hearing has been dispensed with.

### Withdrawal of representations

**10.** A party who wishes to withdraw any representations they have made may do so—

(a)   by giving notice to the authority no later than 24 hours before the day or the first day on which the hearing is to be held; or

(b)   orally at the hearing.

### Power to extend time etc.

**11.**—(1) Subject to regulation 13, an authority may extend a time limit provided for in these Regulations for a specified period where it considers this to be necessary in the public interest.

(2)   Where the authority has extended a time limit it must forthwith give a notice to the parties stating the period of the extension and the reasons for it.

**12.**—(1) Subject to regulation 13, an authority may—

(a)   adjourn a hearing to a specified date, or

(b)   arrange for a hearing to be held on specified additional dates,

where it considers this to be necessary for its consideration of any representations or notice made by a party.

(2)   Where an authority has adjourned a hearing to a specified date it must forthwith notify the parties of the date, time and place to which the hearing has been adjourned.

(3)   Where an authority has arranged for a hearing to be held on a specified additional date it must forthwith notify the parties of the additional date on which and time and place at which the hearing is to be held.

**13.** An authority may not exercise its powers under regulations 11 and 12 in such a way that the effect will be that—

(a)   an application will be treated as granted or rejected under paragraph 4(4), 7(3), 16(4), 19(3) or 26(4) of Schedule 8 (transitional provision etc.); or

(b)   it would fail to reach a determination on the review under section 167 (review of premises licence following closure order) within the period specified in subsection (3) of that section;

(c)   it would fail to reach a determination on a review under section 53A (summary reviews on application of senior police officer) within the period specified in subsection (2)(b) of that section."

### Hearing to be public

**14.**—(1) Subject to paragraph (2), the hearing shall take place in public.

(2)   The licensing authority may exclude the public from all or part of a hearing where it considers that the public interest in so doing outweighs the public interest in the hearing, or that part of the hearing, taking place in public.

(3)   For the purposes of paragraph (2), a party and any person assisting or representing a party may be treated as a member of the public.

### Right of attendance, assistance and representation

**15.** Subject to regulations 14(2) and 25, a party may attend the hearing and may be assisted or represented by any person whether or not that person is legally qualified.

### Representations and supporting information

**16.** At the hearing a party shall be entitled to—

(a)   in response to a point upon which the authority has given notice to a party that it will want clarification under regulation 7(1)(d), give further information in support of their application, representations or notice (as applicable),

(b)   if given permission by the authority, question any other party; and

(c)   address the authority.

**17.** Members of the authority may ask any question of any party or other person appearing at the hearing.

**18.** In considering any representations or notice made by a party the authority may take into account documentary or other information produced by a party in support of their application, representations or notice (as applicable) either before the hearing or, with the consent of all the other parties, at the hearing.

**19.** The authority shall disregard any information given by a party or any person to whom permission to appear at the hearing is given by the authority which is not relevant to—

(a)   their application, representations or notice (as applicable) or in the case of another person, the application representations or notice of the party requesting their appearance, and

(b)   the promotion of the licensing objectives or, in relation to a hearing to consider a notice given by a chief officer of police, the crime prevention objective.

### Failure of parties to attend the hearing

**20.**—(1) If a party has informed the authority that he does not intend to attend or be represented at a hearing, the hearing may proceed in his absence.

(2)   If a party who has not so indicated fails to attend or be represented at a hearing the authority may—

(a) where it considers it to be necessary in the public interest, adjourn the hearing to a specified date, or

(b) hold the hearing in the party's absence.

(3) Where the authority holds the hearing in the absence of a party, the authority shall consider at the hearing the application, representations or notice made by that party.

(4) Where the authority adjourns the hearing to a specified date it must forthwith notify the parties of the date, time and place to which the hearing has been adjourned.

### Procedure at hearing

**21.** Subject to the provisions of these Regulations, the authority shall determine the procedure to be followed at the hearing.

**22.** At the beginning of the hearing, the authority shall explain to the parties the procedure which it proposes to follow at the hearing and shall consider any request made by a party under regulation 8(2) for permission for another person to appear at the hearing, such permission shall not be unreasonably withheld.

**23.** A hearing shall take the form of a discussion led by the authority and cross-examination shall not be permitted unless the authority considers that cross-examination is required for it to consider the representations, application or notice as the case may require.

**24.** The authority must allow the parties an equal maximum period of time in which to exercise their rights provided for in regulation 16.

**25.** The authority may require any person attending the hearing who in their opinion is behaving in a disruptive manner to leave the hearing and may—

(a) refuse to permit that person to return, or

(b) permit him to return only on such conditions as the authority may specify,

but such a person may, before the end of the hearing, submit to the authority in writing any information which they would have been entitled to give orally had they not been required to leave.

### Determination of applications

**26.**—(1) In the case of a hearing under—

(a) section 35 or 39 which is in respect of an application made at the same time as an application for conversion of an existing licence under paragraph 2 of Schedule 8 (determination of application under section 34 or 37),

(aa) section 53B (interim steps pending review),

(ab) section 53C (review of premises licence following review notice),

(b) section 85 which is in respect of an application made at the same time as an application for conversion of an existing club certificate under paragraph 14 of Schedule 8 (determination of application under section 85),

(c) section 105(2)(a) (counter notice following police objection to temporary event notice),

(d) section 167(5)(a) (review of premises licence following closure order),

(e) paragraph 4(3)(a) of Schedule 8 (determination of application for conversion of existing licence),

(f) paragraph 16(3)(a) of Schedule 8 (determination of application for conversion of existing club certificate), or

(g) paragraph 26(3)(a) of Schedule 8 (determination of application by holder of a justices' licence for grant of personal licence),

the authority must make its determination at the conclusion of the hearing.

(2) In any other case the authority must make its determination within the period of five working days beginning with the day or the last day on which the hearing was held.

**27.** Where a hearing has been dispensed with in accordance with regulation 9, the authority must make its determination within the period of ten working days beginning with the day the authority gives notice to the parties under regulation 9(2).

**Notification of determination**

**28.**—(1) In a case where the Act does not make provision for the period within which the authority must notify a party of its determination, the authority must do so forthwith on making its determination.

(2) In a case where—

(a) the Act provides for a chief officer of police to be notified of the determination of an authority, and

(b) that chief officer of police has not been a party to the hearing,

the authority shall notify that chief officer of police of its determination, forthwith on making its determination.

**29.** Where the authority notifies a party of its determination, the notice given (or, in the case of a hearing under section 31(3)(a) (determination of application for provisional statement), the statement issued) to the party must be accompanied by information regarding the right of a party to appeal against the determination of the authority.

**Record of proceedings**

**30.** The authority shall provide for a record to be taken of the hearing in a permanent and intelligible form and kept for six years from the date of the determination or, where an appeal is brought against the determination of the authority, the disposal of the appeal.

**Irregularities**

**31.** Any irregularity resulting from any failure to comply with any provision of these Regulations before the authority has made a determination shall not of itself render the proceedings void.

**32.** In any case of such an irregularity, the authority shall, if it considers that any person may have been prejudiced as a result of the irregularity, take such steps as it thinks fit to cure the irregularity before reaching its determination.

**33.** Clerical mistakes in any document recording a determination of the authority or errors arising in such document from an accidental slip or omission may be corrected by the authority.

**Notices**

**34.**—(1) Any notices required to be given by these Regulations must be given in writing.

(2) Notwithstanding the requirement in paragraph (1) and subject to paragraph (3), that requirement shall be satisfied in a case where –

(a) the text of the notice—

(i) is transmitted by electronic means;

(ii) is capable of being accessed by the recipient;

(iii) is legible in all material respects; and

(iv) is capable of being reproduced in written form and used for subsequent reference;

(b) the person to whom the notice is to be given has agreed in advance that such a notice may be given to them by electronic means; and

(c) forthwith on sending the text of the notice by electronic means, the notice is given to the recipient in writing.

(3) Where the text of the notice is transmitted by electronic means, the giving of the notice shall be effected at the time the requirements of paragraph (2)(a) are satisfied.

*Richard Caborn*
Minister of State
Department for Culture, Media and Sport

Date 12th January 2005

SCHEDULE 1

regulation 5

|  | Column 1 | Column 2 |
|---|---|---|
|  | **Provision under which hearing is held.** | **Period of time within which hearing must be commenced.** |
| 1. | Section 18(3)(a) (determination of application for premises licence). | 20 working days beginning with the day after the end of the period during which representations may be made as prescribed under section 17(5)(c). |
| 2. | Section 31(3)(a) (determination of application for a provisional statement). | 20 working days beginning with the day after the end of the period during which representations may be made as prescribed under section 17(5)(c) by virtue of section 30. |
| 3. | Section 35(3)(a) (determination of application to vary premises licence). | 20 working days beginning with the day after the end of the period during which representations may be made as prescribed under section 17(5)(c) by virtue of section 34(5). |
| 4. | Section 39(3)(a) (determination of application to vary premises licence to specify individual as premises supervisor). | 20 working days beginning with the day after the end of the period within which a chief officer of police may give notice under section 37(5). |
| 5. | Section 44(5)(a) (determination of application for transfer of premises licence). | 20 working days beginning with the day after the end of the period within which a chief officer of police may give notice under section 42(6). |
| 6. | Section 48(3)(a) (cancellation of interim authority notice following police objection). | 5 working days beginning with the day after the end of the period within which a chief officer of police may give notice under section 48(2). |
| 7. | Section 52(2) (determination of application for review of premises licence). | 20 working days beginning with the day after the end of the period during which representations may be made as prescribed under section 51(3)(c). |
| 8. | Section 72(3)(a) (determination of application for club premises certificate). | 20 working days beginning with the day after the end of the period during which representations may be made as prescribed under section 71(6)(c). |
| 9. | Section 85(3) (determination of application to vary club premises certificate). | 20 working days beginning with the day after the end of the period during which representations may be made as prescribed under section 71(6)(c) by virtue of section 84(4). |
| 10. | Section 88(2) (determination of application for review of club premises certificate). | 20 working days beginning with the day after the end of the period during which representations may be made as prescribed under section 87(3)(c). |
| 11. | Section 105(2)(a) (counter notice following police objection to temporary event notice). | 7 working days beginning with the day after the end of the period within which a chief officer of police may give a notice under section 104(2). |
| 12. | Section 120(7)(a) (determination of application for grant of personal licence). | 20 working days beginning with the day after the end of the period within which the chief officer of police may give a notice under section 120(5). |
| 13. | Section 121(6)(a) (determination of application for the renewal of personal licence). | 20 working days beginning with the day after the end of the period within which the chief officer of police may give a notice under section 121(3). |

| 14. | Section 124(4)(a) (convictions coming to light after grant or renewal of personal licence). | 20 working days beginning with the day after the end of the period within which the chief officer of police may give a notice under section 124(3). |
| 15. | Section 167(5)(a) (review of premises licence following closure order). | 10 working days beginning with the day after the day the relevant licensing authority receives the notice given under section 165(4). |
| 16. | Paragraph 4(3)(a) of Schedule 8 (determination of application for conversion of existing licence). | 10 working days beginning with the day after the end of the period within which a chief officer of police may give a notice under paragraph 3(2) or (3) of Schedule 8. |
| 17. | Paragraph 16(3)(a) of Schedule 8 (determination of application for conversion of existing club certificate). | 10 working days beginning with the day after the end of the period within which a chief officer of police may give a notice under paragraph 15(2) or (3) of Schedule 8. |
| 18. | Paragraph 26(3)(a) of Schedule 8 (determination of application by holder of a justices' licence for grant of personal licence). | 10 working days beginning with the day after the end of the period within which the chief officer of police may give a notice under paragraph 25(2) of Schedule 8. |

SCHEDULE 2

regulation 6

| | Column 1 | Column 2 |
| --- | --- | --- |
| | **Provision under which hearing is held.** | **Persons to whom notice of hearing is to be given.** |
| 1. | Section 18(3)(a) (determination of application for premises licence). | (1) The person who has made the application under section 17(1); (2) persons who have made relevant representations as defined in section 18(6). |
| 2. | Section 31(3)(a) (determination of application for provisional statement). | (1) The person who has made the application under section 29(2); (2) persons who have made relevant representations as defined in section 31(5). |
| 3. | Section 35(3)(a) (determination of application to vary premises licence). | (1) The holder of the premises licence who has made the application under section 34(1); (2) persons who have made relevant representations as defined in section 35(5). |
| 4. | Section 39(3)(a) (determination of application to vary premises licence to specify individual as premises supervisor). | (1) The holder of the premises licence who has made the application under section 37(1); (2) each chief officer of police who has given notice under section 37(5); (3) the proposed individual as referred to in section 37(1). |

| 5. | Section 44(5)(a) (determination of application for transfer of premises licence). | (1) The person who has made the application under section 42(1);<br>(2) each chief officer of police who has given notice under section 42(6);<br>(3) the holder of the premises licence in respect of which the application has been made or, if the application is one to which section 43(1) applies, the holder of that licence immediately before the application was made. |
| --- | --- | --- |
| 6. | Section 48(3)(a) (cancellation of interim authority notice following police objection). | (1) The person who has given notice under section 47(2);<br>(2) each chief officer of police who has given notice under section 48(2). |
| 7. | Section 52(2) (determination of application for review of premises licence). | (1) The holder of the premises licence in respect of which the application has been made;<br>(2) persons who have made relevant representations as defined in section 52(7);<br>(3) the person who has made the application under section 51(1). |
| 7A | Section 53C (review of premises licence following review notice) | The holder of the premises licence in respect of which the application has been made;<br>persons who have made relevant representations as defined in section 53C(7); and<br>the chief officer of police who made the application under section 53A(1). |
| 8. | Section 72(3)(a) (determination of application for club premises certificate). | (1) The club which has made the application under section 71(1);<br>(2) persons who have made relevant representations as defined in section 72(7). |
| 9. | Section 85(3)(a) (determination of application to vary club premises certificate). | (1) The club which has made the application under section 84(1);<br>(2) persons who have made relevant representations as defined in section 85(5). |
| 10. | Section 88(2) (determination of application for review of club premises certificate). | (1) The club which holds the club premises certificate in respect of which the application has been made;<br>(2) persons who have made relevant representations as defined in section 88(7);<br>(3) the person who has made the application under section 87(1). |
| 11. | Section 105(2)(a) (counter notice following police objection to temporary event notice). | (1) The premises user;<br>(2) each chief officer of police who has given notice under section 104(2). |
| 12. | Section 120(7)(a) (determination of application for grant of personal licence). | (1) The person who has made the application under section 117(1);<br>(2) the chief officer of police who has given notice under section 120(5). |
| 13. | Section 121(6)(a) (determination of application for renewal of personal licence). | (1) The person who has made the application under section 117(1);<br>(2) the chief officer of police who has given notice under section 121(3). |

App 4

| | | |
|---|---|---|
| 14. | Section 124(4)(a) (convictions coming to light after grant or renewal of personal licence). | (1) The holder of the licence in respect of which the notice has been given; (2) the chief officer of police who has given notice under section 124(3). |
| 15. | Section 167(5)(a) (review of premises licence following closure order). | (1) The holder of the premises licence in respect of which the review has been made; (2) persons who have made relevant representations as defined in section 167(9). |
| 16. | Paragraph 4(3)(a) of Schedule 8 (determination of application for conversion of existing licence). | (1) The person who has made the application under paragraph 2(2) of Schedule 8; (2) each chief officer of police who has given notice under paragraph 3(2) or (3) of Schedule 8. |
| 17. | Paragraph 16(3)(a) of Schedule 8 (determination of application for conversion of existing club certificate). | (1) The club which has made the application under paragraph 14(2) of Schedule 8; (2) each chief officer of police who has given notice under paragraph 15(2) or (3) of Schedule 8. |
| 18. | Paragraph 26(3)(a) of Schedule 8 (determination of application by holder of a justices' licence for grant of personal licence). | (1) The person who has made the application under section 117 to which paragraph 23(1) of Schedule 8 applies; (2) the chief officer of police who has given notice under paragraph 25(2) of Schedule 8. |

SCHEDULE 3

regulation 7

| | Column 1 | Column 2 | Column 3 |
|---|---|---|---|
| | **Provision under which hearing is held.** | **Person to whom notice of hearing is given.** | **Documents to accompany notice of hearing.** |
| 1. | Section 18(3)(a) (determination of application for premises licence). | The person who has made the application under section 17(1). | The relevant representations as defined in section 18(6) which have been made. |
| 2. | Section 31(3)(a) (determination of application for provisional statement). | The person who has made the application under section 29(2). | The relevant representations as defined in section 31(5) which have been made. |
| 3. | Section 35(3)(a) (determination of application to vary premises licence). | The holder of the premises licence who has made the application under section 34(1). | The relevant representations as defined in section 35(5) which have been made. |
| 4. | Section 39(3)(a) (determination of application to vary premises licence to specify individual as premises supervisor). | (1) The holder of the premises licence who has made the application under section 37(1); (2) the proposed individual as referred to in section 37(1). | The notices which have been given under section 37(6). |

| | | | |
|---|---|---|---|
| 5. | Section 44(5)(a) (determination of application for transfer of premises licence). | (1) The person who has made the application under section 42(1); (2) the holder of the premises licence in respect of which the application has been made or, if the application is one to which section 43(1) applies, the holder of that licence immediately before the application was made. | The notices which have been given under section 42(6). |
| 6. | Section 48(3)(a) (cancellation of interim authority notice following police objection). | The person who has given notice under section 47(2). | The notices which have been given under section 48(2). |
| 7. | Section 52(2) (determination of application for review of premises licence). | The holder of the premises licence in respect of which the application has been made. | The relevant representations as defined in section 52(7) which have been made. |
| 7A. | Section 53C (review of premises licence following review notice) | The holder of the premises licence in respect of which the application has been made. | The relevant representations as defined in section 53C(7) which have been made. |
| 8. | Section 72(3)(a) (determination of application for club premises certificate). | The club which has made the application under section 71(1). | The relevant representations as defined in section 72(7) which have been made. |
| 9. | Section 85(3)(a) (determination of application to vary club premises certificate). | The club which has made the application under section 84(1). | The relevant representations as defined in section 85(5) which have been made. |
| 10. | Section 88(2) (determination of application for review of club premises certificate). | The club which holds the club premises certificate in respect of which the application has been made. | The relevant representations as defined in section 88(7) which have been made. |
| 11. | Section 120(7)(a) (determination of application for grant of personal licence). | The person who has made the application under section 117(1). | The notice which has been given under section 120(5) |
| 12. | Section 121(6)(a) (determination of application for renewal of personal licence). | The person who has made the application under section 117(1). | The notice which has been given under section 121(3). |
| 13. | Section 124(4)(a) (convictions coming to light after grant or renewal of personal licence). | The holder of the licence in respect of which the notice has been given. | The notice which has been given under section 124(3). |
| 14. | Section 167(5)(a) (review of premises licence following closure order). | The holder of the premises licence in respect of which the review has been made. | The relevant representations as defined in section 167(9) which have been made. |

App 4

SCHEDULE 4

regulation 2

### Meaning of "determination"

The determination of the authority is the outcome of its consideration, as applicable, of—

1.  the relevant representations as defined in section 18(6), in accordance with section 18,

2.  the relevant representations as defined in section 31(5), in accordance with section 31,

3.  the relevant representations as defined in section 35(5), in accordance with section 35,

4.  a notice given under section 37(5), in accordance with section 39,

5.  a notice given under section 42(6), in accordance with section 44,

6.  a notice given under section 48(2), in accordance with section 48,

7.  an application made in accordance with section 51 and any relevant representations as defined in section 52(7), in accordance with section 52,

8.  the relevant representations as defined in section 72(7), in accordance with section 72,

9.  the relevant representations as defined in section 85(5), in accordance with section 85,

10. an application made in accordance with section 87 and any relevant representations as defined in section 88(7), in accordance with section 88,

11. a notice given under section 104(2), in accordance with section 105,

12. a notice given under section 120(5), in accordance with section 120,

13. a notice given under section 121(3), in accordance with section 121,

14. a notice given under section 124(3), in accordance with section 124,

15. the matters referred to in section 167(5)(a), in accordance with section 167,

16. the notice given under paragraph 3(2) or (3) of Schedule 8, in accordance with its paragraph 4,

17. the notice given under paragraph 15(2) or (3) of Schedule 8, in accordance with its paragraph 16, or

18. the notice given under paragraph 25(2) of Schedule 8, in accordance with its paragraph 26.


### EXPLANATORY NOTE

*(This note is not part of the Regulations)*

These Regulations make provision for the holding of hearings required to be held by licensing authorities under the Licensing Act 2003 (c.17) ("the Act").

In particular, the Regulations provide for the timing of hearings and the notification requirements to parties to a hearing of the date, time and place of a hearing and information to accompany that notification (regulations 4 to 7 and Schedules 1, 2 and 3). In addition, provision is made for a party to a hearing to provide information to the licensing authority about attendance at a hearing, representations, the seeking of permission for another person to attend to assist the authority and whether the party believes a hearing to be necessary (regulation 8).

The Regulations provide for a range of procedural issues to govern the way in which preparations are made for a hearing, for the procedures to be followed, the rights of parties at a hearing, and various administrative matters, for example, the keeping of a record of the hearing and the manner of giving notices (regulations 9 to 33). The Regulations also make provision for the timing of the licensing authority's determination following a hearing (Schedule 4).

Insofar as these Regulations do not make provision for procedures for and at hearings, section 9 of the Act provides that the authority can determine its own procedure.

A Regulatory Impact Assessment in relation to these Regulations has been placed in the libraries of both Houses of Parliament and copies may be obtained from the Alcohol and Entertainment Licensing Branch of the Department for Culture, Media and Sport, 3<sup>rd</sup> Floor, 2–4 Cockspur Street, London SW1Y 5DH or viewed on the Department's website, www.culture.gov.uk.

# APPENDIX 5: THE LICENSING ACT 2003 (LICENSING AUTHORITY'S REGISTER) (OTHER INFORMATION) REGULATIONS 2005

## 2005 No. 43

### LICENCES AND LICENSING

The Licensing Act 2003 (Licensing authority's register)
(other information) Regulations 2005

| | |
|---|---|
| *Made-* | *12th January 2005* |
| *Laid before Parliament-* | *13th January 2005* |
| *Coming into force-* | *7th February 2005* |

The Secretary of State, in exercise of the powers conferred upon her by section 8(1)(d) of the Licensing Act 2003, hereby makes the following Regulations:

### Citation, commencement and interpretation

**1.**—(1) These Regulations may be cited as the Licensing Act (Licensing authority's register) (other information) Regulations 2005 and shall come into force on 7th February 2005.

(2) In these Regulations, "the Act" means the Licensing Act 2003.

### Other information to be contained in the register

**2.**—(1) For the purposes of subsection (1)(d) of section 8 of the Act, in addition to the records referred to in sections 8(1)(a) and (b) of and the matters mentioned in Schedule 3 to the Act, the register kept by each licensing authority shall contain a record of the information set out in this regulation.

(2) In the case of an application under the following provisions of the Act–

  (a) section 17 (application for premises licence), the accompanying operating schedule (provided that the name and address of the premises supervisor, if any, shall be removed from the schedule before it is recorded) and plan of the premises to which the application relates;

  (b) section 29 (application for a provisional statement where premises being built, etc.), the accompanying schedule of works and plans of the work being or about to be done at the premises;

  (c) section 34 (application to vary premises licence), the accompanying revised operating schedule (provided that the name and address of the premises supervisor, if any, shall be removed from the schedule before it is recorded), if any;

  (d) section 71 (application for club premises certificate), the accompanying club operating schedule and plan of the premises to which the application relates; and

  (e) section 84 (application to vary club premises certificate), the accompanying revised club operating schedule, if any.

(3) In the case of an application for review under section 51 (application for review of premises licence) and 87 (application for review of club premises certificate) of the Act or a review under section 167 (review of premises licence following closure order) of the Act, the ground or grounds for the review.

(3A) In the case of an application for review of a premises licence under section 53A of the Act (summary reviews on application of senior police officer) the fact that the application has been made, and that it has been made on the basis of the opinion of a senior police officer that the premises are associated with serious crime or serious disorder or both.

(4) In the case of an application under paragraph 2 (application for conversion of existing licence) or 14 (application for conversion of existing club certificate) of Schedule 8 to the Act, the existing licensable activities or existing qualifying club activities, as the case may require, and

the accompanying plan of the premises to which the existing licence or licences or existing club certificate relates.

*Richard Caborn*
Minister of State
Date 12th January 2005                Department for Culture, Media and Sport

## EXPLANATORY NOTE

*(This note is not part of the Regulations)*

These Regulations prescribe the further information each licensing authority is required to record in the register it is required to keep under section 8 of the Licensing Act 2003 (c.17) (the Act). In addition to the records identified in section 8(1) of and Schedule 3 to the Act, each licensing authority must record in its register operating schedules and club operating schedules, or revisions of these, and plans of premises which accompany applications for premises licences or club premises certificates, or variations of these and Schedules of works and plans of the work being or about to be done which accompany applications for provisional statements (regulation 2(2)). Further, each licensing authority must record in its register the ground or grounds for reviews set out in applications for a review of a premises licence or club premises certificate and the determination of the magistrates' court on its consideration of a closure order (regulation 2(3)). Finally, a record must be kept of the existing licensable activities and existing qualifying club activities and plans of the premises which accompany applications (for conversion of existing licences and existing club certificates (regulation 2(4)).

A Regulatory Impact Assessment in relation to these Regulations has been placed in the libraries of both Houses of Parliament and copies may be obtained from the Alcohol and Entertainment Licensing Branch of the Department for Culture, Media and Sport, 3rd Floor, 2–4 Cockspur Street, London SW1Y 5DH or viewed on the Department's website, www.culture.gov.uk.

# APPENDIX 6: THE LICENSING ACT 2003 (FEES) REGULATIONS 2005

## 2005 No. 79

## LICENCES AND LICENSING

## The Licensing Act 2003 (Fees) Regulations 2005

| | |
|---|---|
| Made- - - - - - - - - - - - - - - - - - - - - - - - - - - - - - | 20th January 2005 |
| Laid before Parliament- - - - - - - - - - - - - - - - - - | 20th January 2005 |
| Coming into force- - - - - - - - - - - - - - - - - - - - - | 7th February 2005 |

The Secretary of State, in exercise of the powers conferred upon her by sections 55, 92, 100(7)(b), 110(3), 133(2) and 178(1)(b) of the Licensing Act 20039a)[1], hereby makes the following Regulations:

### PART 1

### GENERAL

**Citation and commencement**

**1.** These Regulations may be cited as the Licensing Act 2003 (Fees) Regulations 2005 and shall come into force on 23rd February 2005.

**Interpretation**

**2.**—(1) In these Regulations—

"the Act" means the Licensing Act 2003;

"college" means a college or similar institution principally concerned with the provision of full-time education suitable to the requirements of persons over compulsory school age who have not attained the age of 19;

"rateable value" as regards a premises, is the value for the time being in force for the premises entered in the local non-domestic rating list for the purposes of Part III of the Local Government Finance Act 1988[2]; and

"school" means a school within the meaning of section 4 of the Education Act 1996[3]

(2) For the purposes of these Regulations, a reference to—

(a) a paragraph in a regulation or Schedule, a Schedule or a Part is a reference to the paragraph in that regulation or Schedule, the Schedule or the Part in these Regulations; and

(b) a section shall be construed as a reference to the section in the Act.

**Bands for premises**

**3.**—(1) In a case where a premises has a rateable value specified in column 1 of the table in Schedule 1, the premises shall be in the band specified for that rateable value in column 2 of that table.

(2) Except in a case where a premises is in the course of construction, in which case the premises shall be in Band C, in all other cases, the premises shall be in Band A.

(3) For the purposes of this regulation, in a case where the premises forms part only of a hereditament in the local non-domestic rating list for the purposes of Part III of the Local

---

1   2003 c.17. See section 193 for the definitions of "prescribed" and "regulations".
2   1998 c.41
3   1996 c.56

Government Finance Act 1988, the premises shall be treated as having a rateable value equal to the rateable value for the hereditament of which it forms part.

(4) For the purposes of this regulation, in a case where the premises comprises two or more hereditaments in the local non-domestic rating list, the premises shall be treated as having a rateable value equal to the rateable value for the hereditament with the highest rateable value.

## PART 2

### PREMISES LICENCES

**Fee to accompany application for grant or variation of premises licence**

**4.**—(1) Subject to regulation 9, in respect of an application under section 17 (application for premises licence) or section 34 (application to vary premises licence), the fee to accompany the application shall be determined in accordance with the following provisions of this regulation.

(2) Subject to paragraphs (4) and, in the case of an application under section 34, (6) and (7), where the application under section 17 or section 34 relates to a premises in Band D or Band E and the premises is used exclusively or primarily for the carrying on on the premises of the supply of alcohol for consumption on the premises, the amount of the fee shall be—

    (a) in the case of premises in Band D, two times the amount of the fee applicable for the Band appearing in column 1 of the table in Schedule 2 specified in column 2 of that table, and

    (b) in the case of premises in Band E, three times the amount of the fee applicable for that Band appearing in column 1 of the table in Schedule 2 specified in column 2 of that table.

(3) Subject to paragraphs (4) and, in the case of an application under section 34, (6) and (7), in all other cases, the fee to accompany the application shall be the fee applicable to the band appearing in column 1 of the table in Schedule 2 for the premises to which the application relates, determined in accordance with regulation 3, specified in column 2 of that table.

(4) Subject to paragraph (5) and, in the case of an application under section 34, (8), where the maximum number of persons the applicant proposes should, during the times when the licence authorises licensable activities to take place on the premises, be allowed on the premises at the same time is 5,000 or more, an application under paragraph (1) must be accompanied by a fee in addition to any fee determined under paragraphs (2) or (3), the amount of which shall be the fee applicable to the range of number of persons within which falls the maximum number of persons the applicant proposes to be so allowed on the premises in column 1 of the table in Schedule 3 specified in column 2 of that table.

(5) Paragraph (4) does not apply where the premises in respect of which the application has been made—

    (a) is a structure which is not a vehicle, vessel or moveable structure; and

    (b) has been constructed or structurally altered for the purpose, or for purposes which include the purpose, of enabling—

        (i) the premises to be used for the licensable activities the applicant proposes the licence should authorise,

        (ii) the premises to be modified temporarily from time to time, if relevant, for the premises to be used for the licensable activities referred to in the application;

        (iii) at least the number of persons the applicant proposes should, during the times when the licence authorises licensable activities to take place on the premises, be allowed on the premises, to be allowed on the premises at such times, and

        (iv) the premises to be used in a manner which is not inconsistent with the operating schedule accompanying the application.

(6) In respect of an application under section 34 made at the same time as an application under paragraph 2 of Schedule 8 to the Act and which relates in any way or to any extent to the supply of alcohol for consumption on the premises to which the application relates,

the fee to accompany the application under section 34 shall be the fee applicable to the band appearing in column 1 of the table in Schedule 4 for the premises to which the application relates, determined in accordance with regulation 3, specified in column 2 of that table.

(7) In respect of an application under section 34 made at the same time as an application under paragraph 2 of Schedule 8 to the Act and which does not relate in any way or to any extent to the supply of alcohol for consumption on the premises to which the application relates, the requirement under paragraph (1) for a fee determined in accordance with paragraphs (2) or (3) of this regulation, as applicable, to accompany the application under section 34 does not apply.

(8) Subject to paragraph (9), in respect of an application under section 34 made at the same time as an application under paragraph 2 of Schedule 8 to the Act, the requirement under paragraph (4) for a fee in addition to any fee determined under paragraphs (2) or (3) to accompany the application under section 34 does not apply.

(9) Paragraph (8) does not apply where the application to vary under section 34 is made in respect of a licence which at the time of the application does not authorise licensable activities to take place on the premises when the maximum number of people allowed on the premises at the same time is 5,000 or more and the application seeks a variation of the licence to authorise licensable activities to take place on the premises when the maximum number of persons allowed on the premises at the same time is 5,000 or more.

**Annual fee for premises licence**

5.—(1) Subject to regulation 10, the holder of a premises licence shall pay to the relevant licensing authority an annual fee, the amount of which shall be determined in accordance with the following provisions of this regulation.

(2) In the case of premises in Band D or Band E that are relevant premises, the amount of the annual fee shall be—

(a) in the case of premises in Band D, two times the amount of the fee applicable for that Band appearing in column 1 of the table in Part 1 of Schedule 5 specified in column 2 of that table; and

(b) in the case of premises in Band E, three times the amount of the fee applicable for that Band appearing in column 1 of the table in Part 1 of Schedule 5 specified in column 2 of that table.

(3) In all other cases, the amount of the fee shall be the fee applicable to the band appearing in column 1 of the table in Part 1 of Schedule 5 for the premises, determined in accordance with regulation 3, specified in column 2 of that table.

(4) Subject to paragraph (5), in the case of a premises licence authorising licensable activities to take place where the number of persons the holder of the licence may allow on the premises at the same time is 5,000 or more, the holder of the licence shall pay to the said authority an additional annual fee, the amount of which shall be the fee applicable to the range of number of persons within which falls the maximum number of persons the applicant so allows on the premises in column 1 of the table in Part 2 of Schedule 5 specified in column 2 of that table.

(5) Paragraph (4) does not apply where the premises in respect of which the premises licence has effect—

(a) is a structure which is not a vehicle, vessel or moveable structure; and

(b) has been constructed or structurally altered for the purpose, or for purposes which include the purpose, of enabling—

(i) the premises to be used for the licensable activities authorised by the licence,

(ii) the premises to be modified temporarily from time to time, if relevant, for the premises to be used for the licensable activities;

(iii) at least the number of persons the applicant proposes should, during the times when the licence authorises licensable activities to take place on the premises, be allowed on the premises, to be allowed on the premises at such times, and

(iv) the premises to be used in a manner which is not inconsistent with the licence.

(6)   The fee determined under paragraphs (2), (3) or (4) shall become due and payable each year on the anniversary of the date of the grant of the premises licence.

(7)   In this regulation "relevant premises" are premises which are exclusively or primarily used for the supply of alcohol for consumption on the premises.

## PART 3

### CLUB PREMISES CERTIFICATES

**Fee to accompany application for grant or variation of club premises certificate**

**6.**—(1) Subject to regulation 9, in respect of an application under section 71 (application for club premises certificate) or, subject to paragraph (2), section 84 (application to vary club premises certificate), the fee to accompany the application shall be the fee applicable to the band appearing in column 1 of the table in Schedule 2 for the premises to which the application relates, determined in accordance with regulation 3, specified in column 2 of that table.

(2)   In respect of an application under section 84 made at the same time as an application under paragraph 14 of Schedule 8 to the Act, the requirement under paragraph (1) for a fee to accompany the application under section 84 does not apply.

**Annual fee for club premises certificate**

**7.**—(1) Subject to regulation 10, the club holding a club premises certificate shall pay to the relevant licensing authority an annual fee, the amount of which shall be the fee applicable to the band appearing in column 1 of the table in Part 1 of Schedule 5 for the premises, determined in accordance with regulation 3, specified in column 2 of that table.

(2)   It shall be the responsibility of the secretary of a club holding a club premises certificate to discharge the duty imposed on the club in paragraph (1).

(3)   The fee determined under paragraph (1) shall become due and payable each year on the anniversary of the date of the grant of the club premises certificate.

## PART 4

### PERMITTED TEMPORARY ACTIVITIES, PERSONAL LICENCES ETC

**Fees for other applications and notices**

**8.** In the case of an application or a notice listed in column 1 of the table in Schedule 6, a person making that application or giving that notice shall accompany it with a fee, the amount of which is specified in column 2 of that table.

## PART 5

### MISCELLANEOUS EXEMPTIONS

**9.**—(1) In respect of an application under section 17, section 34, section 71 or section 84 which relates to the provision of regulated entertainment only, no fee shall be payable and accompany the application or notice if the conditions of this regulation are satisfied in respect of that application or notice.

(2)   The conditions referred to in paragraph (1) are –

   (a)   in the case of an application by a proprietor[4] of an educational institution in respect of premises that are or form part of an educational institution—

      (i)    that the educational institution is a school or a college; and

      (ii)   the provision of regulated entertainment on the premises is carried on by the educational institution for and on behalf of the purposes of the educational institution; or

   (b)   that the application is in respect of premises that are or form part of a church hall, chapel hall or other similar building or a village hall, parish hall or community hall or other similar building.

---

4   See section 16(3) of 2003 c.17 for the definition of "proprietor".

**10.**—(1) The requirement under regulation 5(1) or 7(1), as the case may require, to pay to the relevant licensing authority an annual fee does not apply in a circumstance where on the date the fee shall become due and payable the conditions of this regulation are satisfied.

(2) The conditions referred to in paragraph (1) are that—

    (a) the premises licence or club premises certificate, as the case may require, in respect of the premises to which it relates authorises the provision of regulated entertainment only; and

    (b) either—

        (i) the holder of the premises licence or club premises certificate referred to in paragraph (2)(a) is—

    (aa) the proprietor of an educational institution which is a school or college; and

    (bb) the licence or certificate has effect in respect of premises that are or form part of the educational institution; and

    (cc) the provision of regulated entertainment on the premises is carried on by the educational institution for and on behalf of the purposes of the educational institution; or

        (ii) that the premises licence or club premises certificate has effect in respect of premises that are or form part of a church hall, chapel hall or other similar building or a village hall, parish hall or community hall or other similar building.

*Andrew McIntosh*
Minister of State
Department for Culture, Media and Sport

Date 20th January 2005

SCHEDULE 1          regulation 3

RATEABLE VALUES AND BANDS

| *Column 1* | *Column 2* |
|---|---|
| *RATEABLE VALUE* | *BAND* |
| No rateable value to £4,300 | A |
| £4,300 to £33,000 | B |
| £33,001 to £87,000 | C |
| £87,001 to £125,000 | D |
| £125,001 and above | E |

SCHEDULE 2          regulation 4(2), (3) and 6(1)

PREMISES LICENCES AND CLUB PREMISES CERTIFICATES

| *Column 1* | *Column 2* |
|---|---|
| *BAND* | *FEE* |
| A | £100 |
| B | £190 |
| C | £315 |
| D | £450 |
| E | £635 |

SCHEDULE 3                                              regulation 4(4)

ADDITIONAL FEE

| Column 1 | Column 2 |
|---|---|
| *Number* | *Additional fee* |
| 5,000 to 9,999 | £1,000 |
| 10,000 to 14,999 | £2,000 |
| 15,000 to 19,999 | £4,000 |
| 20,000 to 29,999 | £8,000 |
| 30,000 to 39,999 | £16,000 |
| 40,000 to 49,999 | £24,000 |
| 50,000 to 59,999 | £32,000 |
| 60,000 to 69,999 | £40,000 |
| 70,000 to 79,999 | £48,000 |
| 80,000 to 89,999 | £56,000 |
| 90,000 and over | £64,000 |

SCHEDULE 4                                              regulation 4(b)

VARIATION FEE IN TRANSITION

| Column 1 | Column 2 |
|---|---|
| *BAND* | *FEE* |
| A | £20 |
| B | £60 |
| C | £80 |
| D | £100 |
| E | £120 |

SCHEDULE 5                                              regulation 5, 7

ANNUAL FEE

PART 1

| Column 1 | Column 2 |
|---|---|
| *BAND* | *FEE* |
| A | £70 |
| B | £180 |
| C | £295 |
| D | £320 |
| E | £350 |

PART 2

| Column 1 | Column 2 |
|---|---|
| Number | Additional fee |
| 5,000 to 9,999 | £500 |
| 10,000 to 14,999 | £1,000 |
| 15,000 to £19,999 | £2,000 |
| 20,000 to £29,999 | £4,000 |
| 30,000 to £39,999 | £8,000 |
| 40,000 to £49,999 | £12,000 |
| 50,000 to £59,999 | £16,000 |
| 60,000 to £69,999 | £20,000 |
| 70,000 to £79,999 | £24,000 |
| 80,000 to £89,999 | £28,000 |
| 90,000 and over | £32,000 |

SCHEDULE 6                                    regulation 8

PERMITTED TEMPORARY ACTIVITIES, PERSONAL LICENCES AND MISCELLANEOUS

| Column 1<br>Application or notice | Column 2<br>Fee |
|---|---|
| section 25 (theft, loss, etc. of premises licence or summary) | £10.50 |
| section 29 (application for a provisional statement where premises being built, etc.) | £315.00 |
| section 33 (notification of change of name or address) | £10.50 |
| section 37 (application to vary licence to specify individual as premises supervisor) | £23 |
| section 42 (application for transfer of premises licence) | £23 |
| section 47 (interim authority notice following death etc. of licence holder) | £23 |
| section 79 (theft, loss etc. of certificate or summary) | £10.50 |
| section 82 (notification of change of name or alteration of rules of club) | £10.50 |
| section 83(1) or (2) (change of relevant registered address of club) | £10.50 |
| section 100 (temporary event notice) | £21 |
| section 110 (theft, loss etc. of temporary event notice) | £10.50 |
| section 117 (application for a grant or renewal of personal licence) | £37 |
| section 126 (theft, loss etc. of personal licence) | £10.50 |
| section 127 (duty to notify change of name or address) | £10.50 |
| section 178 (right of freeholder etc. to be notified of licensing matters) | £21 |

App 6

## EXPLANATORY NOTE

*(This note is not part of the Regulations)*

These Regulations provide for the determination of the fees to accompany the making of applications and the giving of notices under the Licensing Act 2003 (c.17) (the Act) and the payment of those fees. Further, they make provision for the payment of annual fees in respect of premises licences and club premises certificates granted under the Act.

In particular, these Regulations provide for the manner in which premises are allocated to specific bands for the purposes of determining the appropriate level of fee to be paid when applying for a premises licence or club premises certificate and for variations of the licences and certificates by reference mainly to the non-domestic value of the premises (regulation 3 and Schedule 1).

The Regulations make provision for the fee levels in respect of applications for premises licences and identify circumstances in which a particular application in respect of premises in the higher bands attract a multiplier in respect of the fee and when an additional fee needs to be paid in respect of events where 5,000 or more people may attend the premises concerned (regulation 4 and Schedules 2 and 3). However, the Regulations disapply the requirement to pay the additional fee in respect of premises that are buildings when certain conditions are met (regulation 4(5)). In respect of an application to vary which is made at the same time as an application to convert existing licences to new premises licences under paragraph 2 of Schedule 8 to the Act, the Regulations provide for a reduced fee to be paid for the application to vary (regulation 4(6) and Schedule 4).

Provision is made for the payment of an annual fee and the timing of that payment in respect of premises licences and provides for multipliers to be applied to the fee in relation to premises in higher bands and for the payment of an additional fee where the premises accommodate 5,000 or more people at the same time (regulation 5 and Schedule 5). The requirement to pay an additional annual fee is disappplied in relation to premises that comprise a building if certain conditions are met (regulation 5(5)).

Similar provision is made in respect of applications for club premises certificates and variations of these, except that such applications do not attract multiplier fees or additional fees (regulation 6 and Schedule 2). Also, provision is made for the payment of an annual fee in respect of club premises certificates and the timing of that payment. A duty is placed on the secretary of a club to pay the fee on behalf of the club (regulation 7 and Schedule 5).

A number of fixed fees in relation to other applications made or notices given under the Act are provided for, for example in respect of the giving of a temporary event notice under Part 5 of the Act (regulation 8 and Schedule 6).

Exemption from the payment of an application fee is provided in respect of applications relating only to regulated entertainment made in respect of certain premises where conditions are met, these being schools and colleges where the school or college premises are used for the entertainment by the school or college on behalf of the school or college or the use of church halls, village halls and the like for the provision of entertainment (regulation 9). A similar exemption is provided from the requirement to pay an annual fee in these circumstances provided conditions are met at the time an annual fee falls due to be paid (regulation 10).

Fees to be paid in respect of applications under paragraphs 2 or 14 of Schedule 8 to the Act are provided in the Licensing Act 2003 (Transitional conversions fees) Order 2005 (S.I. 2005/80).

A Regulatory Impact Assessment in relation to these Regulations has been placed in the libraries of both Houses of Parliament and copies may be obtained from Alcohol and Entertainment Licensing Branch of the Department for Culture, Media and Sport, 3rd Floor, 2–4 Cockspur Street, London, SW1Y 5DH or viewed on the Department's website, www.culture.gov.uk.

# APPENDIX 7: THE LICENSING ACT 2003 (PERMITTED TEMPORARY ACTIVITIES) (NOTICES) REGULATIONS 2005

## 2005 No. 2918

## LICENCES AND LICENSING

### The Licensing Act 2003 (Permitted Temporary Activities) (Notices) Regulations 2005

Made- - - - - - - - - - - - - - - - - - - - - - - - - - - - -19th October 2005
Laid before Parliament- - - - - - - - - - - - - - - - - - 20th October 2005
Coming into force- - - - - - - - - - - - - - - - - - - -10th November 2005

The Secretary of State makes the following Regulations in exercise of the powers conferred by sections 100(4) and (5), 102(2) and 107(7) of the Licensing Act 2003:[1]

### Citation and commencement

**1.** These Regulations may be cited as the Licensing Act 2003 (Permitted Temporary Activities) (Notices) Regulations 2005 and come into force on 10th November 2005.

### Interpretation

**2.** In these Regulations—

(a) "the Act" means the Licensing Act 2003;

(b) "appropriate address" in relation to a counter notice means—

    (i) the postal address indicated in section 1(8) of the temporary event notice in respect of which the counter notice is given, or

    (ii) if there is no such address the postal address indicated in section 1(6) of the notice;

(c) "appropriate e-mail address" in relation to a counter notice means—

    (i) an e-mail address indicated in section 1(9) of the temporary event notice in respect of which the counter notice is given, or

    (ii) if sections 1(8) and 1(9) of the notice have not been completed, an e-mail address indicated in section 1(7) of the notice;

(d) "copy" includes an electronic copy;

(e) "counter notice" means a counter notice under section 107 of the Act;

(f) "ordinary post" means ordinary prepaid first-class or second-class post (with or without special arrangements for delivery);

(g) "relevant premises user" has the same meaning as in section 107(1) of the Act;

(h) "signature" includes an electronic signature within the meaning of section 7 of the Electronic Communications Act 2000;[2]

(i) "temporary event notice" has the same meaning as in section 100(1) of the Act.

### Form of temporary event notice

**3.**—(1) The prescribed form for a temporary event notice is set out in Schedule 1.

(2) A matter appearing in, or required to be stated in the prescribed form in that Schedule (other than a matter mentioned in section 100(5)(a) to (e) of the Act) is a prescribed matter for the purposes of section 100(5) of the Act.

---

1   2003 c. 17. See the definitions of "prescribed" and "regulations" in section 193 of the Act.
2   2000 c. 7.

(3) Any other information appearing in, or required to be included in the prescribed form in that Schedule (other than information mentioned in section 100(4)(a) or (b) of the Act) is prescribed information for the purposes of section 100(4) of the Act.

### Form of acknowledgement of receipt of temporary event notice

**4.** The prescribed form for an acknowledgement of the receipt by a licensing authority of a temporary event notice is the signature of a person authorised to acknowledge such receipt on the authority's behalf appearing in section 10 (entitled "Acknowledgement") of the notice, or of a copy of the notice.

### Form of counter notice

**5.** The prescribed form for a counter notice is set out in Schedule 2.

### Manner of giving counter notice

**6.** A counter notice is given in the prescribed manner if it is—

(a) delivered to the relevant premises user in person;

(b) left at the appropriate address;

(c) sent to that address by ordinary post; or

(d) sent by e-mail to an appropriate e-mail address.

*Richard Caborn*
Minister of State
Department for Culture, Media and Sport

19th October 2005

SCHEDULE 1                           regulation 3

PRESCRIBED FORM OF TEMPORARY EVENT NOTICE

The Prescribed form for a temporary event notice is as follows:

[Insert name and address of relevant licensing authority and its reference number (optional)]

Temporary Event Notice

Information on the Licensing Act 2003 is available on the website of the Department for Culture, Media and Sport (http://www.culture.gov.uk/alcohol_and_entertainment/default.htm) or from your local licensing authority.

Before completing this notice please read the guidance notes at the end of the notice. If you are completing this notice by hand please write legibly in block capitals. In all cases ensure that your answers are inside the boxes and written or typed in black ink. Use additional sheets if necessary.

You should keep a copy of the completed notice for your records. You must send two copies of this notice to the licensing authority and an additional copy must be sent to the chief officer of police for the area in which the premises are situated. The licensing authority will endorse one of the two copies and return it to you as an acknowledgement of receipt.

**I, the proposed premises user, hereby give notice under section 100 of the Licensing Act 2003 of my proposal to carry on a temporary activity at the premises described below.**

| **1. The personal details of premises user (Please read note 1)** | | | |
|---|---|---|---|
| **1.** YOUR NAME | | | |
| Title<br>Surname<br>Forenames | **(delete as appropriate) Mr Mrs Miss Ms Other (please state)** | | |
| **2.** PREVIOUS NAMES (Please enter details of any previous names or maiden names, if applicable. Please continue on a separate sheet if necessary) | | | |
| Title<br>Surname<br>Forenames | **(delete as appropriate) Mr Mrs Miss Ms Other (please state)** | | |
| **3.** Your date of birth | Day | Mth | Yr |
| **4.** Your place of birth | | | |
| **5.** National Insurance Number | | | |
| **6.** YOUR CURRENT ADDRESS (We will use this address to correspond with you unless you complete the separate correspondence box below) | | | |
| **Post town** | **Post code** | | |
| **7.** OTHER CONTACT DETAILS | | | |
| TELEPHONE NUMBERS<br>Daytime | | | |
| Evening (optional) | | | |
| Mobile (optional) | | | |
| FAX NUMBER (optional) | | | |
| E-Mail Address (optional) | | | |
| **8.** ALTERNATIVE ADDRESS FOR CORRESPONDENCE (If you complete the details below, we will use this address to correspond with you) | | | |
| **Post town** | **Post code** | | |

| **9.** ALTERNATIVE CONTACT DETAILS (IF APPLICABLE) | |
|---|---|
| TELEPHONE NUMBERS<br>Daytime | |
| Evening (optional) | |
| Mobile (optional) | |
| FAX NUMBER (optional) | |
| E-Mail Address (optional) | |

App 7

**2. The premises**

**Please give the address of the premises where you intend to carry on the licensable activities or if it has no address give a detailed description (including the Ordnance Survey references)**
(Please read note 2)

<br><br><br><br>

**If you intend to use only part of the premises at this address or intend to restrict the area to which this notice applies, please give a description and details below.** (Please read note 3)

<br><br><br>

**Please describe the nature of the premises below.** (Please read note 4)

<br><br>

**Please describe the nature of the event below.** (Please read note 5)

<br><br><br>

**3. The licensable activities**

**Please state the licensable activities that you intend to carry on at the premises (please mark an "X" next to the licensable activities you intend to carry on).** (Please read note 6)

| | |
|---|---|
| The sale by retail of alcohol | |
| The supply of alcohol by or on behalf of a club to, or to the order of, a member of the club | |
| The provision of regulated entertainment | |
| The provision of late night refreshment | |

**Please state the dates on which you intend to use these presmises for licensable activities.** (Please read note 7)

<br><br><br>

| Please state the times during the event period that you propose to carry on licensable activities (please give times in 24 hour clock). (Please read note 8) | |
|---|---|
| Please state the maximum number of people at any one time that you intend to allow to be present at the premises during the times when you intend to carry on licensable activities, including any staff, organisers or performers. (Please read note 9) | |

| If the licensable activities will include the supply of alcohol, please state whether the supplies will be for consumption on or off the premises, or both (please mark an "X" next to the appropriate box). (Please read note 10) | On the premises only | |
| | Off the premises only | |
| | Both | |

| 4. Personal licence holders (Please read note 11) | | |
|---|---|---|
| Do you currently hold a valid personal licence? (Please mark an "X" in the box that applies to you) | Yes | No |
| If "Yes" please provide the details of your personal licence below. | | |

| Issuing licensing authority | |
|---|---|
| Licence number | |
| Date of issue | |
| Date of expiry | |
| Any further relevant details | |

App 7

| 5. Previous temporary event notices you have given (Please read note 12) | | |
|---|---|---|
| Have you previously given a temporary event notice in respect of any premises for events falling in the same calendar year as the event for which you are now giving this temporary event notice? (Please mark an "X" in the box that applies to you) | Yes | No |
| If answering yes, please state the number of temporary event notices you have given for events in that same calendar year | | |
| Have you already given a temporary event notice for the same premises in which the event period:<br>a) ends 24 hours or less before; or<br>b) begins 24 hours or less after<br>the event period proposed in this notice?<br>(Please mark an "X" in the box that applies to you) | Yes | No |

| 6 Associates and business colleagues (Please read note 13) | | |
|---|---|---|
| Has any associate of yours given a temporary event notice for an event in the same calendar year as the event for which you are now giving a temporary event notice? (Please mark an "X" in the box that applies to you) | Yes | No |
| If answering yes, please state the total number of temporary event notices your associate(s) have given for events in the same calendar year | | |
| Has any associate of yours already given a temporary event notice for the same premises in which the event period: a) ends 24 hours or less before; or b) begins 24 hours or less after the event period proposed in this notice? (Please mark an "X" in the box that applies to you) | Yes | No |
| Has any person with whom you are in business carrying on licensable activities given a temporary event notice for an event in the same calendar year as the event for which you are now giving a temporary event notice? (Please mark an "X" in the box that applies to you) | Yes | No |
| If answering yes, please state the total number of temporary event notices your business colleague(s) have given for events in the same calendar year. | | |
| Has any person with whom you are in business carrying on licensable activities already given a temporary event notice for the same premises in which the event period: a) ends 24 hours or less before; or b) begins 24 hours or less after the event period proposed in this notice? (Please mark an "X" in the box that applies to you) | Yes | No |

| 7. Checklist (Please read note 14) | |
|---|---|
| I shall (Please mark the appropriate boxes with an "X") | |
| Send two copies of this notice to the licensing authority for the area in which the premises are located | |
| Send a copy of this notice to the chief officer of police for the area in which the premises are located | |
| If the premises are situated in one or more licensing authority areas, send two copies of this notice to each additional licensing authority | |
| If the premises are situated in one or more police areas, send a copy of this notice to each additional chief officer of police | |
| Make or enclose payment of the fee for the application | |
| Sign the declaration in Section 9 below | |

| 8. Condition (Please read note 15) |
|---|
| It is a condition of this temporary event notice that where the relevant licensable activities described in Section 3 above include the supply of alcohol that all such supplies are made by or under the authority of the premises user. |

**9. Declarations** (Please read note 16)

The information contained in this form is correct to the best of my knowledge and belief.

I understand that it is an offence:
(i)  to knowingly or recklessly make a false statement in connection with this temporary event notice and that a person is liable on conviction for such an offence to a fine up to level 5 on the standard scale; and
(ii)  to permit an unauthorised licensable activity to be carried on at any place and that a person is liable on conviction for any such offence to a fine not exceeding £20,000, or to imprisonment for a term not exceeding six months, or to both.

| SIGNATURE | | DATE | |
|---|---|---|---|
| Name of Person signing | | | |

**10. Acknowledgement** (Please read note 17)

I acknowledge receipt of this temporary event notice.

| SIGNATURE | | DATE | |
|---|---|---|---|
| | On behalf of the Licensing Authority | | |
| Name of Officer Signing | | | |

App 7

## NOTES

*General*

In general, only the police may intervene on crime prevention grounds to prevent the occurrence of an event at which permitted temporary activities are to take place or to agree a modification of the arrangements for such an event. However, the licensing authority may intervene of its own volition by issuing a counter notice if the first, second and fourth of the limits set out below would be exceeded. If any of the limits below are breached or if a counter notice has been issued, any licensable activities taking place would be unauthorised and the premises user would be liable to prosecution. The limitations apply to:

— the number of times a person (the "premises user") may give a temporary event notice (50 times per year for a personal licence holder and 5 times per year for other people);
— the number of times a temporary event notice may be given in respect of any particular premises (12 times in a calendar year);
— the length of time a temporary event may last for these purposes (96 hours);
— the maximum aggregate duration of the periods covered by temporary event notices at any individual premises (15 days per calendar year); and
— the scale of the event in terms of the maximum number of people attending at any one time (a maximum of 499).

For the purposes of determining the overall limits of 50 temporary event notices per personal licence holder (in a calendar year) and of 5 for a non-personal licence holder (in a calendar year), temporary event notices given by an associate or a person who is in business with a premises user (and that business involves carrying on licensable activities) count towards those totals. Note 13 below explains the definition of an "associate".

When permitted temporary activities take place, a premises user must ensure that either:

— a copy of the temporary event notice endorsed as acknowledged by the licensing authority is prominently displayed at the premises; or that

— the temporary event notice endorsed as acknowledged by the licensing authority is kept at the premises either in his own custody or in the custody of a person present and working at the premises and whom he has nominated for that purpose.

Where the temporary event notice is in the custody of a nominated person, a notice specifying that fact and the position held by that person must be displayed prominently at the premises.

Where neither the temporary event notice nor a notice specifying the nominated person are displayed, a constable or an authorised person (for example, a licensing officer, fire officer or environmental health officer) may require the premises user to produce the temporary event notice for examination. Similarly, where the nominated person has the temporary event notice in his custody, a constable or authorised person may require that person to produce it for examination. Failure to produce the temporary event notice without reasonable excuse would be an offence.

It should also be noted that the following, among other things, are offences under the Licensing Act 2003:

— the sale or supply of alcohol to children under 18 years of age (maximum fine on conviction is a fine up to level 5 on the standard scale, currently £5,000);

— allowing the sale of alcohol to children under 18 (maximum fine on conviction is a fine up to level 5 on the standard scale, currently £5,000);

— knowingly allowing the consumption of alcohol on the premises by a person aged under 18 (maximum fine on conviction is a fine up to level 5 on the standard scale, currently £5,000);

— allowing disorderly behaviour on the premises (maximum fine on conviction is a fine up to level 3 on the standard scale, currently £1,000);

— the sale of alcohol to a person who is drunk (maximum fine on conviction is a fine up to level 3 on the standard scale, currently £1,000);

— obtaining alcohol for a person who is drunk (maximum fine on conviction is a fine up to level 3 on the standard scale, currently £1,000);

— knowingly allowing a person aged under 18 to make any sale or supply of alcohol unless the sale or supply has been specifically approved by the premises user or any individual aged 18 or over who has been authorised for this purpose by the premises user (maximum fine on conviction is a fine up to level 1 on the standard scale, currently £200); and

— knowingly keeping or allowing to be kept on the premises any smuggled goods which have been imported without payment of duty or which have otherwise been unlawfully imported (maximum fine on conviction is a fine up to level 3 on the standard scale, currently £1,000).

In addition, where the premises are to be used primarily or exclusively for the sale or supply of alcohol for consumption on the premises, it is an offence to allow children under 16 to be present when the premises are open for that purpose unless they are accompanied by an adult. In the case of any premises at which sales or supplies of alcohol are taking place at all, it is an offence for a child under 16 to be present there between the hours of midnight and 5am unless accompanied by an adult. In both instances, the penalty on conviction is a fine not exceeding level 3 on the standard scale, currently £1,000.

**Note 1**

A temporary event notice may only be given by an individual and not, for example, by an organisation or club or business. The individual giving the notice is the proposed "premises user". Within businesses, clubs or organisations one individual will therefore need to be identified as the proposed premises user.

If you include an e-mail address in section 1(7) or 1(9) the licensing authority may use the address to send any counter notice it is required to give under section 107 of the Licensing Act 2003.

## Note 2

For the purposes of the Licensing Act 2003, "premises" means any place. Premises will therefore not always be a building with a formal address and postcode. Premises can include, for example, public parks, recreation grounds and private land.

## Note 3

A temporary event notice can be given for part of a building, such as a single room or a plot within a larger area of land. You should provide a clear description of the area in which you propose to carry on licensable activities. This is important as any licensable activities conducted outside the area of the premises protected by the authority of this temporary event notice would be unlawful and could lead to prosecution.

In addition, when holding the proposed event, the premises user would need to be able to restrict the number of people on the premises at any one time when licensable activities are taking place to less than 500.

If more than 499 are on the premises when licensable activities are being carried on, the licensable activities would be unlawful and the premises user would be liable to prosecution. The maximum figure of 499 includes, for example, staff, organisers, stewards and performers.

## Note 4

A description of the nature of the premises assists the chief officer of police in deciding if any crime prevention issues are likely to arise. You should state clearly that the premises to be used are, for example, a public house, a restaurant, an open field, a village hall or a beer tent.

## Note 5

A description of the nature of the event similarly assists the chief officer of police in making his decision whether or not to make an objection. You should state clearly that the event taking place at the premises would be, for example, a wedding with a pay bar, the supply of beer at a particular farmers' market, a discotheque, the performance of a string quartet, a folk group or a rock band.

## Note 6

The licensable activities are:

— the sale by retail of alcohol;
— the supply of alcohol by or on behalf of a club to, or to the order of, a member of a club;
— the provision of regulated entertainment; and
— the provision of late night refreshment.

Please refer to Schedules 1 and 2 to the Licensing Act 2003 for fuller details of the definitions and exemptions relating to regulated entertainment and late night refreshment.

Regulated entertainment, subject to specified conditions and exemptions, includes:

(a) a performance of a play;
(b) an exhibition of a film;
(c) an indoor sporting event;
(d) a boxing or wrestling entertainment;
(e) a performance of live music;
(f) any playing of recorded music;
(g) a performance of dance;
(h) entertainment of a similar description to that falling within (e), (f) or (g).

Regulated entertainment also includes the provision of "entertainment facilities" for:

(a) making music;

(b)   dancing; and

(c)   entertainment of a similar description to that falling within (a) or (b).

If you are uncertain whether or not the activities that you propose are licensable, you should contact your licensing authority for further advice.

## Note 7

The maximum period for using premises for licensable activities under the authority of a temporary event notice is 96 hours (four days).

## Note 8

You should state here the times during the event period, for example 48 hours, when you intend to carry on licensable activities. For example, you may not intend to carry on licensable activities throughout the entire 48 hour event period, and may intend to sell alcohol between 8.00 hrs and 23.00 hrs on each of the two days.

## Note 9

No more than 499 may be on the premises for a temporary event at any one time when licensable activities are being carried on. If you intend to have more than 499 attending the event, you should obtain a premises licence for the event. Your licensing authority should be able to advise you. The maximum figure of 499 does not just include the audience, spectators or consumers and includes, for example, staff, organisers, stewards and performers who will be present on the premises.

## Note 10

If you indicate that alcohol will be supplied only for consumption on the premises, you would be required to ensure that no person leaves the premises with alcohol supplied there. If such a supply takes place, the premises user may be liable to prosecution for carrying on an unauthorised licensable activity. Similarly, if the premises user gives notice that only supplies of alcohol for consumption off the premises will take place, he/she must ensure that alcohol supplied is not consumed on the premises. The premises user is free to give notice that he/she intends to carry on both types of supplies. For this purpose the supply of alcohol includes both of the first two licensable activities listed in note 6 above.

## Note 11

The holder of a valid personal licence issued under the Licensing Act 2003 may give up to 50 temporary event notices in any calendar year subject to the other limitations in the 2003 Act. A proposed premises user who holds such a licence should give the details requested.

## Note 12

As stated under Note 11 the holder of a valid personal licence holder issued under the Licensing Act 2003 may give up to 50 temporary event notices in any calendar year. An individual who does not hold a valid personal licence may only give 5 temporary event notices in England and Wales within a calendar year. A calendar year is the period between 1 January to 31 December, inclusive, in any year.

If an event straddles two calendar years, it will count against the limits on temporary event notices (12 for each premises, 15 days for each premises, 50 per personal licence holder and 5 for non-holders) for each year, however, only one notice needs to be given.

For the purposes of determining the overall limits of 50 temporary event notices per personal licence holder (in a calendar year) and of 5 for a non-personal licence holder (in a calendar year), temporary event notices given by an associate or a person who is in business with a premises user (and that business involves carrying on licensable activities) count towards those totals. Note 13 below sets out the definition of an "associate".

If a temporary event notice has been given for the same premises, by the same premises user, and would have effect within 24 hours before the start of the event period under the current proposal or within 24 hours after the end of that period, the temporary event notice given would be void and any licensable activities carried on under it would therefore be unlicensed.

For the purposes of determining whether or not the required gap of 24 hours is upheld, temporary event notices given by an associate or a person who is in business with a premises user (and that business involves carrying on licensable activities) count as if they had been given by the premises user himself. Note 13 below sets out the definition of an "associate".

## Note 13

An "associate" of the proposed premises user is:

   (a)   the spouse of that person;

   (b)   a child, parent, grandchild, grandparent, brother or sister of that person;

   (c)   an agent or employee of that person; or

   (d)   the spouse of a person within (b) or (c).

For these purposes, a person living with another as that person's husband or wife is to be treated as that person's spouse.

These provisions will be subject to amendment by the Civil Partnerships Act. These amendments are due to take effect from 5th December 2005.

## Note 14

It is a requirement that you send two copies of this notice to the licensing authority at least ten working days before the commencement of the proposed licensable activities. The authority will endorse one of the two copies and return it to you as an acknowledgement. This will be important proof that you gave the notice and when you gave it for the purposes of the Act. Some premises may be situated in two licensing authority areas, for example, where a building or field straddles the local authority boundary. Where this is the case, two copies must be sent to each of the licensing authorities identified, together with the appropriate fee in each case. In such circumstances, you need to receive acknowledgements from all the relevant licensing authorities.

One copy must be sent to the chief officer of police for the area in which the premises is situated at least ten working days before the commencement of the proposed licensable activities. Where the premises are situated in two police areas, a further copy will need to be sent to the second police force.

## Note 15

Under the Licensing Act 2003, all temporary event notices are given subject to a mandatory condition requiring that where the licensable activities involve the supply of alcohol, all such supplies must be made by or under the authority of the named premises user. If there is a breach of this condition, the premises user and the individual making the supply in question would be liable to prosecution. For this purpose the supply of alcohol includes both of the first two licensable activities listed in note 6 above.

## Note 16

It is an offence knowingly or recklessly to make a false statement in, or in connection with, a temporary event notice. (A person is to be treated as making a false statement if he produces, furnishes, signs or otherwise makes use of a document that contains a false statement). To do so could result in prosecution and a fine not exceeding level 5 on the standard scale.

## Note 17

You should not complete section 10 of the notice, which is for use by the licensing authority. They will complete this section and return one of the copies that you have sent to them as an acknowledgement of the notice you have given.

App 7

**SCHEDULE 2**             regulation 5

PRESCRIBED FORM OF COUNTER NOTICE

The prescribed form for a counter notice is as follows:

[Insert name and address of relevant licensing authority and its reference number (optional)]

Counter Notice—Permitted Temporary Activities

On [*insert date*] the licensing authority received from you, [*insert name*], a temporary event notice ("the notice") in respect of proposed temporary licensable activities due to take place on [*insert date*] at [*insert address or description of premises*]. The licensing authority is satisfied that if the activities were to take place, one of the permitted limits set out in section 107(2), (3), (4) and (5) of the Licensing Act 2003 ("the Act") would be exceeded.

The limit (and subsection) which applies is indicated by an "X" in the following table.

| Relevant limit (and subsection of the Licensing Act 2003) | Insert "X" as applicable |
|---|---|
| You are a personal licence holder and you have already given at least 50 temporary event notices in respect of event periods wholly or partly within the same calendar year as the event period specified in the notice. (See section 107(2) of the Act) | |
| You are not a personal licence holder and you have already given at least 5 temporary event notices in respect of event periods wholly or partly within the same calendar year as the event period specified in the notice. (See section 107(3) of the Act) | |
| At least 12 temporary event notices have already been given which are in respect of the premises indicated in the notice and which specify as the event period a period wholly or partly within the same calendar year as the event specified in the notice. (See section 107(4) of the Act) | |
| In the calendar year in which the event period specified in the notice (or any part of it) falls, more than 15 days are days on which one or both of the following fall– <br> a) that event period or any part of it, <br> b) an event period specified in a temporary event notice already given in respect of the same premises as the notice, or any part of such period. (See section 107(5) of the Act) | |

A copy of this counter notice will be sent to the chief officer of police for the area in which the premises specified in the temporary event notice you gave is situated.

The Licensing Act 2003 does not make provision for you to appeal against this counter notice.

Under section 136 of the Licensing Act 2003 a person commits an offence if he carries on a licensable activity on or from any premises otherwise than under and in accordance with an authorisation; or if he knowingly allows a licensable activity to be so carried on. A person convicted of such an offence is liable to imprisonment for a term not exceeding six months or to a fine not exceeding £20,000, or to both.

| SIGNATURE | On behalf of the Licensing Authority | DATE | |
|---|---|---|---|
| **Name of Officer Signing** | | | |

### EXPLANATORY NOTE

*(This note is not part of the Regulations)*

These Regulations prescribe the forms to be used for temporary event notices given by premises users under section 100 of the Licensing Act 2003 (c. 17), and the prescribed matters and information to be contained in such notices. They also prescribe the form for the acknowledgement of the receipt by a licensing authority of a temporary event notice.

In addition the Regulations prescribe the form to be used for counter notices given by licensing authorities under section 107 of the 2003 Act, and the manner in which a counter notice must be given to the premises user.

App 7

# APPENDIX 8: THE LICENSING ACT 2003 (PERSISTENT SELLING OF ALCOHOL TO CHILDREN) (PRESCRIBED FORM OF CLOSURE NOTICE) REGULATIONS 2007

## 2007 No. 1183
## CRIMINAL LAW, ENGLAND AND WALES
## LICENCES AND LICENSING

The Licensing Act 2003 (Persistent Selling of Alcohol to Children) (Prescribed Form of Closure Notice) Regulations 2007

*Made* - - - - - - - - - - - - - - - - - - - - - - - - - - - - - - *11th April 2007*
*Laid before Parliament* - - - - - - - - - - - - - - - - - - - - *12th April 2007*
*Coming into force* - - - - - - - - - - - - - - - - - - - - - - - *3rd May 2007*

The Secretary of State makes the following Regulations in exercise of the power conferred by section 169A(3)(a) of the Licensing Act 2003:[1]

### Citation and commencement

**1.** These Regulations may be cited as the Licensing Act 2003 (Persistent Selling of Alcohol to Children) (Prescribed Form of Closure Notice) Regulations 2007 and come into force on 3rd May 2007.

### Prescribed form

**2.** A closure notice given pursuant to section 169A of the Licensing Act 2003 (Closure notices for persistently selling alcohol to children) is to be in the form set out in the Schedule.

*Shaun Woodward*
Parliamentary Under Secretary of State
Department for Culture, Media and Sport

11th April 2007

SCHEDULE 1        regulation 2

## CLOSURE NOTICE FOR PERSISTENTLY SELLING ALCOHOL TO CHILDREN

### Section 169A(2) of the Licensing Act 2003

**This notice offers a period of closure as an alternative to criminal prosecution for an offence of repeatedly selling alcohol to underage persons. It is addressed to the person(s) (which may include a company etc) who hold the relevant premises licence for the premises concerned. A copy of this closure notice will be sent to the holder of the premises licence at the address for that person set out in the licence.**

**The premise licence holder(s) should read parts 10, 11, 12 and 13 of this notice with particular care as they contain information concerning their rights. If you have been handed this notice and are not the premises licence holder, you may wish to inform the premises licence holder(s) the [sic] this notice has been served.**

---

1    2003 c. 17. Section 169A was inserted by section 24(1) of the Violent Crime Reduction Act 2006 (c. 38).

| 1. Name and rank of the police officer (must hold the rank of superintendent or above)/ name of the inspector of weights and measures *[delete as appropriate]* giving this closure notice |
|---|
|  |

| 2. Name of the police, community support or trading standards officer [delete as appropriate] serving this closure notice. *(A closure notice may be served by being handed to a person on the premises who appears to have control of or responsibility for the premises and who need not be the premises licence holder).* |
|---|
|  |

| 3. Date on which closure notice is given | D | D | M | M | Y | Y | Y | Y |
|---|---|---|---|---|---|---|---|---|

| Details of premises and premises licence holder(s) | |
|---|---|
| 4. Address of premises in respect of which this notice is being given |  |
| 5. Premises Licence Reference number and issuing licensing authority |  |
| 6. Name of premises licence holder(s) |  |
| 7. Address of premises licence holder(s). *(This is the address to which a copy of this closure notice will be sent)* |  |

8. Particulars of alleged offence under section 147A of the Licensing Act 2003, including:

- particulars of unlawful sales made to persons under 18:
- dates of the sales; and
- the individuals making the sales (so far as known).

(Note: you can be liable for the offence if you were a premises licence holder at the time each unlawful sale took place on the premises)

| First unlawful sale: |  |
|---|---|
| Second unlawful sale: |  |
| Third unlawful sale: |  |

**9. Proposed period (maximum 48 hours) during which sales of alcohol by retail are to be prohibited (commencing not less than 14 days after this closure notice was served):**

| From | Time: | To | Time: |
|------|-------|-----|-------|
|      | Date: |     | Date: |

**10. Effect of accepting of the proposed prohibition (closure)**

If you decide to accept the proposed closure (on how to do this, see part 12 below), all sales by retail of alcohol at the premises during the period specified in part 9 of this notice will be unauthorised. An unauthorised sale is a criminal offence (see section 136 of the Licensing Act 2003). A person guilty of an offence under that section is liable on summary conviction to imprisonment for a term not exceeding six months or to a fine not exceeding £20,000, or to both.

**11.Right to elect to go to trial**

You do not have to accept the proposed closure. As an alternative, you may elect to be tried in a court of law for the offence described in part 8 above. That right may be exercised by informing the officer named in part 14 in writing or by e-mail.

**12. How to accept the proposed prohibition**

In order to accept the proposed closure, _all_ premises licence holder(s) should notify the officer named in part 14 of their decision in writing or by e-mail **within 14 days** of this notice being served. Failure to notify the officer named in part 14 of acceptance of the prohibition within 14 days will be taken as a decision to elect for trial for the alleged offence described in part 8.

**13. Effect of a failure by one or more of the premises licence holders to accept the proposed prohibition**

The right to be tried for the alleged offence described in part 8 of this closure notice will be taken to have been exercised unless every person who was a holder of the premises licence at the time this notice was given accepts the proposed prohibition.

**14. Name of the police officer or trading standards officer to whom notice exercising the option to accept the prohibition should be given, or election to go to trial must be sent, within 14 days**

The address of the officer in part 14

E-mail address and telephone number of the officer in part 14

## EXPLANATORY NOTE

*(This note is not part of the Regulations)*

These Regulations prescribe the form of a closure notice given under section 169A of the Licensing Act 2003 ("the 2003 Act").

A closure notice offers an alternative to prosecution under section 147A of the 2003 Act for persistently selling alcohol to children. That offence may be committed by the holder of a premises licence (a form of authorisation for alcohol sales under the 2003 Act) if on 3 or more occasions within 3 consecutive months alcohol is sold unlawfully to an individual aged under 18 on the premises to which the licence relates.

If he considers on the evidence that there is a realistic prospect of conviction of the licence holder for such an offence, a police officer (of the rank of superintendent or above), or an inspector of weights and measures may give a closure notice under s169A proposing that the premises concerned be "closed" (that is, alcohol sales be prohibited) for a period of up to 48 hours beginning not less than 14 days after the date the closure notice is served.

If the closure notice is accepted by the premises licence holder (or if there is more than one, all of them), the prohibition on alcohol sales proposed in it takes effect, and no proceedings may subsequently be brought against the holder or holders for the alleged s 147A offence or any related offence (see section 169B(3) and (5) of the 2003 Act). If the closure notice is not accepted by all relevant licence holders they may be liable for prosecution for the s 147A offence in the usual way.

Sections 147A and 169A and 169B were inserted into the 2003 Act by the Violent Crime Reduction Act 2006 (c. 38).

# APPENDIX 9

# TABLE OF FEES

## PREMISES LICENCES AND CPC FEES

Applications for grant and for variation (other than changes of name and address etc or changes of designated premises supervisor)

| Band | A | B | C | D* | E** |
|---|---|---|---|---|---|
| NDRV | £0–£4,300 | £4,301–£33,000 | £33,001–£87,000 | £87,001–£125,000 | £125,001 or over |
| Fee | £100 | £190 | £315 | £450 | £635 |
| Annual charge | £70 | £180 | £295 | £320 | £350 |

\* A multiplier of twice the fee and annual charge applies where use of the premises is exclusively or primarily for the carrying on on the premises of the supply of alcohol for consumption on the premises

\** A multiplier of three times the fee and annual charge applies where use of the premises is exclusively or primarily for the carrying on on the premises of the supply of alcohol for consumption on the premises

(Premises with no NDRV = Band A; premises under construction = Band C)

## Additional fees for exceptionally large events of a temporary nature requiring premises licences

| Number of persons present | Additional Fee | Annual Fee |
|---|---|---|
| 5,000–9,999 | £1,000 | £500 |
| 10,000–14,999 | £2,000 | £1,000 |
| 15,000–19,999 | £4,000 | £2,000 |
| 20,000–29,999 | £8,000 | £4,000 |
| 30,000–39,999 | £16,000 | £8,000 |
| 40,000–49,999 | £24,000 | £12,000 |
| 50,000–59,999 | £32,000 | £16,000 |
| 60,000–69,999 | £40,000 | £20,000 |
| 70,000–79,999 | £48,000 | £24,000 |
| 80,000–89,999 | £56,000 | £28,000 |
| 90,000 and over | £64,000 | £32,000 |

**Notification of change of name or address of premises licence holder or club** £10.50

**Application to vary to specify individual as designated premises supervisor** £23

**Notification of change of address of designated premises supervisor** £10.50

| | |
|---|---|
| Notification of alteration of club rules | £10.50 |
| Application to transfer premises licence | £23 |
| Interim authority notice | £23 |
| Application for copy or summary | £10.50 |
| Application for making of a provisional statement | £315 |
| Application for conversion and conversion/variation during transitional period | £105 |

## PERSONAL LICENCES FEES

| | |
|---|---|
| Application for grant | £37 |
| Application for conversion during transitional period | £37 |
| Application for copy | £10.50 |
| Notification of change of name or address | £10.50 |

## TEMPORARY EVENT NOTICES FEES

| | |
|---|---|
| Notification of a temporary event | £21 |
| Application for copy | £10.50 |

## OTHER FEES

| | |
|---|---|
| Supply of copy of information contained in licensing register (fee determined by licensing authority based on costs) | £Variable |
| Notification of an interest in any premises | £21 |

# APPENDIX 10: TABLE OF OFFENCES

| SECTION | OFFENCE | OFFENDER | DEFENCE(S) | PENALTY LEVEL 1–5 FINES Level 1 – £250 Level 2 – £500 Level 3 – £1,000 Level 4 – £2,500 Level 5 – £5,000 PENALTY NOTICE FOR DISORDER (PND) – £80 |
|---|---|---|---|---|
| **Premises Licence Holders** | | | | |
| 33(6) | Failure to notify licensing authority of change in name or address | Premises licence holder | Reasonable excuse | Level 2 fine |
| 40(2) | Failure to notify existing designated premises supervisor that premises licence has been varied to replace them with another or that such application has been rejected | Premises licence holder | Reasonable excuse | Level 3 fine |
| 41(5) | Failure to provide premises licence (or statement of reasons for failure to do so) to licensing authority within 14 days of direction from the designated premises supervisor who has given notice of intention to cease | Premises licence holder | Reasonable excuse | Level 3 fine |
| 46(4) | Failure to notify designated premises supervisor of application for transfer with interim effect (applicant and premises supervisor not the same person) | Applicant for transfer of premises licence | Reasonable excuse | Level 3 fine |
| 49(5) | Failure to notify designated premises supervisor of interim authority notice | Interim authority holder | Reasonable excuse | Level 3 fine |
| 56(3) | Failure to produce premises licence at the request of the licensing authority so that it may be amended | Premises licence holder | Reasonable excuse | Level 2 fine |

| SECTION | OFFENCE | OFFENDER | DEFENCE(S) | PENALTY LEVEL 1–5 FINES Level 1 – £250 Level 2 – £500 Level 3 – £1,000 Level 4 – £2,500 Level 5 – £5,000 PENALTY NOTICE FOR DISORDER (PND) – £80 |
|---|---|---|---|---|
| 57(4) | Failure to keep premises licence or certified copy at the premises | Premises licence holder | Reasonable excuse | Level 2 fine |
| 57(4) | Failure to display summary of premises licence or certified copy and notice specifying any nominated person | Premises licence holder | Reasonable excuse | Level 2 fine |
| 57(7) | Failure to produce premises licence or certified copy to authorised person for examination | Premises licence holder or nominated person | Reasonable excuse | Level 2 fine |
| 59(5) | Intentional obstruction of authorised person exercising power of inspection prior to grant, variation or review of premises licence or issuing or provisional statement | Any person | Lack of intent | Level 2 fine |
| Qualifying Clubs | | | | |
| 82(6) | Failure to notify licensing authority of change of name or alteration of rules of the club | Secretary | None | Level 2 fine |
| 83(6) | Failure to notify licensing authority of change of registered address of club | Secretary | Reasonable excuse | Level 2 fine |
| 93(3) | Failure to produce club premises certificate (CPC) to licensing authority within 14 days of request | Secretary | Reasonable excuse | Level 2 fine |

| SECTION | OFFENCE | OFFENDER | DEFENCE(S) | PENALTY LEVEL 1–5 FINES Level 1 – £250 Level 2 – £500 Level 3 – £1,000 Level 4 – £2,500 Level 5 – £5,000 PENALTY NOTICE FOR DISORDER (PND) – £80 |
|---|---|---|---|---|
| 94(5) | Failure to keep CPC or certified copy at the premises | Secretary | Reasonable excuse | Level 2 fine |
| 94(6) | Failure to display at premises the summary of the CPC or certified copy, together with a notice stating the position held by the nominated person | Nominated person | Reasonable excuse | Level 2 fine |
| 94(9) | Failure to produce CPC to constable or authorised person for examination | Nominated person | Reasonable excuse | Level 2 fine |
| 96(5) | Failure to permit entry to authorised person for purposes of inspection prior to grant, variation or review of CPC | Any person | None | Level 2 fine |
| **Permitted Temporary Activities** | | | | |
| 108(3) | Intentional obstruction of authorised officer inspecting temporary event premises to assess likely effect of temporary event notice (TEN) upon promotion of crime prevention objective | Any person | Lack of intent | Level 2 fine |
| 109(4) | Failure to display TEN, or keep it in the custody of the premises user (who is at the premises) or nominated person (for whom a notice of nomination must also be on display at the premises) | Premises user | Reasonable excuse | Level 2 fine |

**App 10**

| SECTION | OFFENCE | OFFENDER | DEFENCE(S) | PENALTY<br>LEVEL 1–5 FINES<br>Level 1 – £250<br>Level 2 – £500<br>Level 3 – £1,000<br>Level 4 – £2,500<br>Level 5 – £5,000<br>PENALTY NOTICE<br>FOR DISORDER<br>(PND) – £80 |
|---|---|---|---|---|
| 109(8) | Failure to produce TEN to authorised officer | Premises user or nominated person | Reasonable excuse | Level 2 fine |
| **Personal Licences** | | | | |
| 123(2) | Failure to notify licensing authority of relevant offence or foreign offence during grant or renewal | Applicant | Reasonable excuse | Level 4 fine |
| 127(5) | Failure to notify licensing authority of change of name or address of personal licence holder | Personal licence holder | Reasonable excuse | Level 2 fine |
| 128(6) | Failure to notify court of personal licence when being dealt with for relevant offence | Personal licence holder | Reasonable excuse | Level 2 fine |
| 132(4) | Failure to notify licensing authority of conviction for relevant or foreign offence | Personal licence holder | Reasonable excuse | Level 2 fine |
| 134(5) | Failure to produce personal licence within 14 days to licensing authority to be updated | Personal licence holder | Reasonable excuse | Level 2 fine |
| 135(4) | Failure to produce personal licence to authorised person or a constable | Personal licence holder | Reasonable excuse | Level 2 fine |
| **General Offences** | | | | |
| 136(1) | Knowingly allowing or carrying on unauthorised licensable activities | Any person (exceptions: s 134(2)) | Due diligence (s 139) | 6 months' imprisonment and/or £20,000 fine |

| SECTION | OFFENCE | OFFENDER | DEFENCE(S) | PENALTY LEVEL 1–5 FINES Level 1 – £250 Level 2 – £500 Level 3 – £1,000 Level 4 – £2,500 Level 5 – £5,000 PENALTY NOTICE FOR DISORDER (PND) – £80 |
|---|---|---|---|---|
| 137(1) | Unauthorised exposure for sale of alcohol | Any person | Due diligence (s 139) | 6 months' imprisonment and/or £20,000 fine |
| 138(1) | Unauthorised possession of alcohol with intent to sell or supply | Any person | Due diligence (s 139) | Level 2 fine |
| 140(1) | Knowingly allowing disorderly conduct on premises with premises licence, CPC or TEN | Any person authorised to prevent | Lack of knowledge | Level 3 fine |
| 141(1) | Knowingly selling, attempting to sell or allowing sale, or supplying, attempting to supply or allowing supply, of alcohol to person who is drunk | Any person authorised to prevent | Lack of knowledge | Level 3 fine or PND £80 |
| 142(1) | Knowingly obtaining or attempting to obtain alcohol for consumption by person who is drunk | Any person | Lack of knowledge | Level 3 fine or PND £80 |
| 143(1) | Failure to leave premises with premises licence, CPC or TEN, or attempting to enter premises, by a person who is drunk or disorderly, following request by person in authority | Any person | Reasonable excuse | Level 1 fine |
| 144(1) | Knowingly keeping unlawfully imported goods on relevant premises | Any person authorised to prevent | Lack of knowledge | Level 3 fine |

App 10

| SECTION | OFFENCE | OFFENDER | DEFENCE(S) | PENALTY LEVEL 1–5 FINES Level 1 – £250 Level 2 – £500 Level 3 – £1,000 Level 4 – £2,500 Level 5 – £5,000 PENALTY NOTICE FOR DISORDER (PND) – £80 |
|---|---|---|---|---|
| 156(3) | Selling alcohol on or from moving vehicles | Any person | Due diligence | 3 months' imprisonment and/or £20,000 fine |
| 157(5) | Knowingly selling, attempting to sell or allowing sale of alcohol on trains contrary to prohibition order | Any person | Lack of knowledge | 3 months' imprisonment and/or £20,000 fine |
| 158(1) | Knowingly or recklessly making false statement in connection with licensing application | Any person | Lack of knowledge or recklessness | Level 5 fine |
| 179(4) | Intentional obstruction of entry of authorised person to investigate unauthorised use of premises for licensable activity | Any person | Lack of intent | Level 3 fine |
| **Underage Offences** | | | | |
| 145(1) | Knowingly allowing unaccompanied child under 16 on premises when open and used for sale or supply of alcohol | Any person authorised to prevent | 1. Lack of knowledge 2. Child using premises for passage | Level 3 fine |

| SECTION | OFFENCE | OFFENDER | DEFENCE(S) | PENALTY LEVEL 1–5 FINES Level 1 – £250 Level 2 – £500 Level 3 – £1,000 Level 4 – £2,500 Level 5 – £5,000 PENALTY NOTICE FOR DISORDER (PND) – £80 |
|---|---|---|---|---|
| 146(1)(2) (3) | Selling alcohol to person under 18 or supplying alcohol to club member or guest under 18 | Any person or club | 1. Reasonable belief aged 18 + reasonable steps or no reasonable suspicion 2. Due diligence | Level 5 fine or PND £80 (s 146(1) and (3)) |
| 147(1)(3) | Knowingly allowing sale of alcohol to person under 18 or knowingly allowing supply of alcohol to club member or guest under 18 | Any person authorised to prevent | Lack of knowledge | Level 5 fine |
| 147A(1) | Unlawful sale of alcohol on 3 or more different occasions on same premises within period of 3 consecutive months | Premises licence holder or premises user under a TEN | Reasonable belief aged 18 + reasonable steps or no reasonable suspicion | £10,000 fine |
| 148(1)(2) | Sale or supply of liqueur confectionary to person under 16 | Any person or a club | 1. Reasonable belief aged 16 + reasonable steps or no reasonable suspicion 2. Due diligence | Level 2 fine |

App 10

| SECTION | OFFENCE | OFFENDER | DEFENCE(S) | PENALTY LEVEL 1–5 FINES Level 1 – £250 Level 2 – £500 Level 3 – £1,000 Level 4 – £2,500 Level 5 – £5,000 PENALTY NOTICE FOR DISORDER (PND) – £80 |
|---|---|---|---|---|
| 149(1)(3) (4) | Purchase or supply of alcohol by or on behalf of person under 18, or attempt to do so | Person under 18 or person purchasing on his behalf | 1. Beer, wine or cider for 16–17 year old for consumption at table meal in accompaniment of person 18 or over. 2. No reason to suspect person was under 18. 3. Purchase at request of constable or weights and measures inspector | Level 3 fine (person under 18) Level 5 fine (person on behalf of under 18) or PND £80 |
| 150(1) | Knowingly consuming alcohol on premises with premises licence, CPC or TEN when under 18 | Person under 18 | Lack of knowledge | Level 3 fine or PND £80 |
| 150(2) | Knowingly allowing consumption of alcohol by person under 18 on premises with premises licence, CPC or TEN | Person working at premises, member or officer of club who could have prevented | Lack of knowledge | Level 5 fine or PND £80 |

| SECTION | OFFENCE | OFFENDER | DEFENCE(S) | PENALTY LEVEL 1–5 FINES Level 1 – £250 Level 2 – £500 Level 3 – £1,000 Level 4 – £2,500 Level 5 – £5,000 PENALTY NOTICE FOR DISORDER (PND) – £80 |
|---|---|---|---|---|
| 151(1)(2) (4) | Delivering or allowing delivery to person under 18 | Person working at premises, member or officer of club who could have prevented | 1. Lack of knowledge 2. Place where buyer lives or works 3. Person under 18 works on premises in capacity which involves delivery of alcohol 4. Alcohol sold or supplied for consumption on premises | Level 5 fine or PND £80 (s 151(1) and (2)) |
| 152(1) | Sending person under 18 to obtain alcohol for consumption off the premises | Any person | 1. Lack of knowledge 2. Purchase at request of constable or weights and measures inspector 3. Person under 18 works on premises in capacity which involves delivery of alcohol | Level 5 fine |

App 10

| SECTION | OFFENCE | OFFENDER | DEFENCE(S) | PENALTY LEVEL 1–5 FINES Level 1 – £250 Level 2 – £500 Level 3 – £1,000 Level 4 – £2,500 Level 5 – £5,000 PENALTY NOTICE FOR DISORDER (PND) – £80 |
|---|---|---|---|---|
| 153(1) | Knowingly allowing person under 18 to sell or supply alcohol without approval on premises with premises licence, CPC or TEN | Premises licence holder, designated premises supervisor, or person over 18 authorised by either | 1. Lack of knowledge 2. Sale for consumption with table meal in area used for meals | Level 1 fine |
| **Closure Order Offences** | | | | |
| 160(4) | Knowingly keeping premises open or allowing premises to be kept open in breach of closure order in identified area | Any manager, premises licence holder, designated premises supervisor or premises user for temporary event | Lack of knowledge | Level 3 fine |
| 161(6) | Permitting identified premises to be kept open in breach of closure order | Any person | Reasonable excuse | 3 months' imprisonment and/or £20,000 fine |
| 165(7) | Permitting premises to be kept open in breach of magistrates' court closure order | Any person | Reasonable excuse | 3 months' imprisonment and/or £20,000 fine |
| 168(8) | Allowing premises to be kept open in breach of closure order pending appeal against revocation of premises licence | Any person | Reasonable excuse | 3 months' imprisonment and/or £20,000 fine |

# APPENDIX 11: SECRETARY OF STATE'S GUIDANCE ISSUED UNDER SECTION 182 OF THE LICENSING ACT 2003

Issued by **The Secretary of State for Culture, Media and Sport**, 28 June 2007

This document represents the Guidance and is issued by the Secretary of State for Culture, Media and Sport. The Guidance has been published on the DCMS website and on UK Online. Any local authority or other organisation is free to publish the Guidance on its own website or provide an appropriate link to either of these websites.

The Guidance has been prepared in consultation with other Government Departments, executive agencies and an Advisory Group comprising stakeholder representatives.

It will be kept under constant review in consultation with key stakeholder groups and will be amended or supplemented as necessary at any time.

# Contents

App 11

# Foreword

By the Secretary of State for Culture, Media and Sport

When this Guidance was first published in July 2004, we were on the brink of the introduction of a wholly new and exciting approach to licensing. The purpose of the regime was about to be given much needed clarity by four statutory objectives becoming paramount when any relevant matters were considered. The objectives are:

- the prevention of crime and disorder;
- public safety;
- the prevention of public nuisance; and
- the protection of children from harm.

Thanks to the exceptional efforts of many officers and councillors in local authorities, the Licensing Act 2003 came into force on 24 November 2005 and it immediately began to give local people a bigger voice in licensing decisions and to help local authorities' broader efforts to create safer and more civilised evening and night-time economies.

It also began to add impetus to our aims of providing a better system of regulation for business, greater choice for consumers and where possible, help for areas in need of economic regeneration.

We were criticised by some for our conviction that these major changes would have a positive impact on and support our wider strategy for tackling crime and disorder, under-age drinking, public nuisance and anti-social behaviour.

We now have a clearer picture of how the Act is working in practice and I am greatly encouraged by the very positive feedback we are receiving from licensing authorities, local residents, the police and the licensed trade.

There is evidence that licensees have made good progress towards taking seriously their responsibilities under the Act and are actively working with the police and each other to eliminate sales of alcohol to underage drinkers and to combat alcohol related crime and disorder.

There is widespread evidence of good and effective partnership working. In many areas, local authorities have set up licensing forums that bring together residents, licensees, responsible authorities such as the police and others to discuss and try to resolve licensing issues. Enforcement has also benefited from this partnership approach with improved targeting of problem premises and better co-ordination and cooperation to clamp down on the irresponsible minority of retailers. The new closure and review powers are working.

Local people are starting to show a much greater understanding of their rights to make objections and seek reviews and are becoming more aware of and engaged in the licensing process. Representations from residents have resulted in new conditions being placed on thousands of licences and often this has been achieved through mediation without the need to go to a formal hearing.

We will continue to monitor and evaluate the impact of the 2003 Act on the prevention of crime and disorder and the other licensing objectives. The Licensing Act in isolation cannot provide a remedy to many of the ills of society associated with alcohol misuse. It must be part of a broader strategy to achieve better management of the night-time economy and a better balance between the rights and responsibilities of everyone living and working in each community.

We realise too that we are at the beginning of a long road towards the cultural change that must eventually underpin the modernisation of the law.

While this revised version of the Guidance is my advice to licensing authorities, it is the product of partnership between central Government and a wide range of stakeholders including, local authorities, the police, industry, the voluntary sector, the club movement, musicians and other performers, representatives of the community and a wider public consultation. I am grateful to all those who have participated and look forward to further work together to promote the four licensing objectives.

I am confident that this revised version of the Guidance will encourage the spread of best practice and help to ensure even greater consistency of approach across licensing authorities.

We will, of course, continue to monitor the impact of the Act on the licensing objectives and if necessary, consider the introduction of further legislation with the consent of Parliament to strengthen or alter any provisions.

*Tessa Jowell*

**Tessa Jowell MP Secretary of State for Culture, Media and Sport**

# 1. Introduction

## THE LICENSING ACT 2003

1.1 The 2003 Act, the associated explanatory notes and any statutory instruments made under its provisions may be viewed on the OPSI website www.opsi.gov.uk. All statutory instruments may also be viewed on the DCMS website www.culture.gov.uk. The main statutory instruments are:

- The Licensing Act 2003 (Transitional provisions) Order 2005
- The Licensing Act 2003 (Personal licences) Regulations 2005
- The Licensing Act 2003 (Premises licences and club premises certificates) Regulations 2005
- The Licensing Act 2003 (Licensing authority's register) (other information) Regulations 2005
- The Licensing Act 2003 (Hearings) Regulations 2005
- The Licensing Act 2003 (Hearings) (Amendment) Regulations 2005
- The Licensing Act 2003 (Permitted Temporary Activities) (Notices) Regulations 2005
- The Licensing Act 2003 (Transitional conversions fees) Order 2005
- The Licensing Act 2003 (Fees) (Amendment) Regulations 2005

## LICENSING OBJECTIVES AND AIMS

1.2 The legislation provides a clear focus on the promotion of four statutory objectives which must be addressed when licensing functions are undertaken:

**The licensing objectives**

- The prevention of crime and disorder.
- Public safety.
- The prevention of public nuisance.
- The protection of children from harm.

1.3 Each objective is of equal importance. It is important to note that there are no other licensing objectives, so that these four objectives are paramount considerations at all times.

1.4 But the legislation also supports a number of other key aims and purposes. These are vitally important and should be principal aims for everyone involved in licensing work. They include:

- the necessary protection of local residents, whose lives can be blighted by disturbance and anti-social behaviour associated with the behaviour of some people visiting licensed premises of entertainment;
- the introduction of better and more proportionate regulation to give business greater freedom and flexibility to meet customers' expectations;
- greater choice for consumers, including tourists, about where, when and how they spend their leisure time;
- the encouragement of more family friendly premises where younger children can be free to go with the family;
- the further development within communities of our rich culture of live music, dancing and theatre, both in rural areas and in our towns and cities; and
- the regeneration of areas that need the increased investment and employment opportunities that a thriving and safe night-time economy can bring.

## THE GUIDANCE

1.5 Section 182 of the Licensing Act 2003 ("the 2003 Act") provides that the Secretary of State must issue and, from time to time, may revise

App 11

guidance to licensing authorities on the discharge of their functions under the 2003 Act.

## Purpose

1.6    The Guidance is provided for licensing authorities carrying out their functions. It also provides information for magistrates hearing appeals against licensing decisions and has been made widely available for the benefit of operators of licensed premises, their legal advisers and the general public. It is a key mechanism for promoting best practice, ensuring consistent application of licensing powers across the country and for promoting fairness, equal treatment and proportionality.

1.7    The police remain key enforcers of licensing law. The Guidance has no binding effect on police officers who, within the terms of their force orders and the law, remain operationally independent. However, the Guidance is provided to support and assist police officers in interpreting and implementing the 2003 Act in the promotion of the four licensing objectives.

## Legal status

**Section 4 of the 2003 Act provides that in carrying out its functions a licensing authority must 'have regard to' guidance issued by the Secretary of State under section 182. The requirement is therefore binding on all licensing authorities to that extent.**

**However, the guidance cannot anticipate every possible scenario or set of circumstances that may arise and as long as licensing authorities have properly understood the Guidance they may depart from it if they have reason to do so as long as they are able to provide full reasons.**

**Departure from the Guidance could give rise to an appeal or judicial review, and the reasons given will then be a key consideration for the courts when considering the lawfulness and merits of any decision taken.**

1.8    Nothing in this Guidance should be taken as indicating that any requirement of licensing law or any other law may be overridden (including the obligations placed on

the authorities under human rights legislation). The Guidance does not in any way replace the statutory provisions of the 2003 Act or add to its scope and licensing authorities should note that interpretation of the Act is a matter for the courts. Licensing authorities and others using the Guidance must take their own professional and legal advice about its implementation.

## LICENSING POLICIES

1.9    Section 5 of the Act requires a licensing authority to prepare and publish a statement of its licensing policy every three years. The policy must be published before the authority carries out any licensing function in relation to applications made under the Act.

1.10    However, making a statement is a licensing function and as such the authority must have regard to the Secretary of State's Guidance when making and publishing its policy. A licensing authority may depart from its own policy if the individual circumstances of any case merit such a decision in the interests of the promotion of the licensing objectives. But once again, it is important that they should be able to give full reasons for departing from their published statement of licensing policy. Where revisions to this Guidance are issued by the Secretary of State, there may be a period of time when the local policy statement is inconsistent with the Guidance, for example, during any consultation by the licensing authority. In these circumstances, the licensing authority should have regard, and give appropriate weight, to the Guidance and its own licensing policy statement.

## LICENSABLE ACTIVITIES

1.11    For the purposes of the Act, the following are licensable activities:

## Licensable activities

- The sale by retail of alcohol.
- The supply of alcohol by or on behalf of a club to, or to the order of, a member of the club.

- The provision of regulated entertainment.
- The provision of late night refreshment.

1.12    Further explanation of these terms is provided in Chapter 3.

## AUTHORISATIONS

1.13    The Act provides for four different types of authorisation, as follows:

### Authorisations

- Personal licences – to sell or supply alcohol and/or authorise the sale/supply.
- Premises Licences – to use a premises for licensable activities.
- Club Premises Certificates – to allow a qualifying club to engage in qualifying club activities as set out in Section 1 of the Act.
- Temporary Event Notices – to carry out licensable activities at a temporary event.

## GENERAL PRINCIPLES

1.14    If an application for a premises licence or club premises certificate has been made lawfully and there have been no representations from responsible authorities or interested parties, the licensing authority must grant the application, subject only to conditions that are consistent with the operating schedule and relevant mandatory conditions.

### Each application on its own merits

1.15    Each application must be considered on its own merits and any conditions attached to licences and certificates must be tailored to the individual style and characteristics of the premises and events concerned. This is essential to avoid the imposition of disproportionate and overly burdensome conditions on premises where there is no need for such conditions. Standardised conditions should be avoided and indeed, may be unlawful where they cannot be shown to be necessary for the promotion of the licensing objectives in any individual case.

### Avoiding duplication of other legal requirements

1.16    The licensing authority should only impose conditions on a premises licence or club premises certificate which are necessary and proportionate for the promotion of the licensing objectives. If other existing law already places certain statutory responsibilities on an employer or operator of premises, it cannot be necessary to impose the same or similar duties on the premises licence holder or club. It is only where additional and supplementary measures are necessary to promote the licensing objectives that necessary, proportionate conditions will need to be attached to a licence.

### Hours of opening

1.17    The Government strongly believes that, prior to the introduction of the Licensing Act 2003, fixed and artificially early closing times (established under the Licensing Act 1964) were one of the key causes of rapid binge drinking prior to closing times; and one of the causes of disorder and disturbance when large numbers of customers were required to leave the premises simultaneously.

1.18    The aim through the promotion of the licensing objectives should be to reduce the potential for concentrations and achieve a slower dispersal of people from licensed premises through flexible opening times. Arbitrary restrictions that would undermine the principle of flexibility should therefore be avoided.

1.19    The four licensing objectives should be paramount considerations at all times and licensing authorities should always consider the individual merits of a case.

### Partnership working

1.20    Licensing functions under the Act are only one means of promoting the delivery of the objectives described. They can make a substantial contribution in relation to licensed premises, but are not the panacea for all community problems.

1.21    Licensing authorities should work with all partners to deliver the licensing objectives, including responsible authorities, the licensed trade, local people and businesses, town centre managers, Crime and Disorder Reduction Partnerships,

App 11

performers and local transport authorities and operators. For example, local businesses and a local authority may develop a Business Improvement District (BID), a partnership arrangement to take forward schemes that are of benefit to the community in that area, subject to the agreement of business rate payers.

1.22    The private sector, local residents and community groups in particular have an equally vital role to play in promoting the licensing objectives in partnership with public bodies. The Secretary of State strongly recommends that licensing authorities form licensing liaison groups and forums that bring together all the interested parties on a regular basis to monitor developments and propose possible solutions to any problems that may arise. The Secretary of State also recommends that licensing authorities should hold well publicised open meetings where local people and businesses can give their views on how well they feel the licensing objectives are being met.

## RELATED LEGISLATION AND STRATEGIES

1.23    The Licensing Act is part of a wider Government strategy to tackle crime, disorder and anti-social behaviour and reduce alcohol harm. Licensing authorities should develop effective strategies with the police, and the other enforcement agencies as appropriate, for the management of the night-time economy. Central to this would be the enforcement of the law relating to the sales of alcohol to drunk and underage people and drunkenness or disorder on, or in the immediate vicinity of licensed premises. Targeted enforcement of this kind, in line with the recommendations in the 'Hampton' report[1] should have a positive impact on the immediate vicinity of the licensed premises concerned.

1.24    Local authorities are also empowered under section 13 of the Criminal Justice and Police Act 2001 to make 'designated public place orders' (DPPOs) to control the consumption of alcohol in a public place outside of licensed premises.

1.25    In addition there is nothing to prevent the police, licensing authorities and the hospitality industry reaching agreement about best practice in areas where problems are likely to arise.

1.26    Licensing law is not the primary mechanism for the general control of individuals once they are away from a licensed premises and therefore beyond the direct control of individual licensees or certificate holders. However, licensees and certificate holders should take reasonable steps to prevent the occurrence of crime and disorder and public nuisance immediately outside their premises, for example on the pavement, in a beer garden, or (once the smoking ban comes into force) in a smoking shelter, where and to the extent that these matters are within their control.

1.27    In addition, when considering a new premises licence or following reviews that have identified problems with a particular premises, licensing authorities may consider imposing conditions as appropriate, such as preventing customers from taking open containers outside the premises or installing CCTV. However, any conditions imposed must not be aspirational and must be within the control of the licensee. For example, a condition may require a premises to adopt a particular dispersal policy, but a licensee cannot force customers to abide by it.

### Crime and Disorder Act 1998

1.28    All local authorities must fulfil their obligations under section 17 of the Crime and Disorder Act 1998 when carrying out their functions as licensing authorities under the 2003 Act.

---

1   'Reducing administrative burdens: effective inspection and enforcement' by Philip Hampton. March 2003

1.29    Section 17 is aimed at giving the vital work of crime and disorder reduction a focus across the wide range of local services and putting it at the heart of local decision-making. It places a duty on certain key authorities, including local authorities and police and fire and rescue authorities to do all they reasonably can to prevent crime and disorder in their area.

1.30    The Government believes that licensing authorities should, as a matter of good practice, involve Crime and Disorder Reduction Partnerships (CDRPs) in decision-making in order to ensure that statements of licensing policy include effective strategies that take full account of crime and disorder implications.

## Alcohol Harm Reduction Strategy

1.31    Licensing authorities should familiarise themselves with the relevant government's alcohol harm reduction strategy. In England this is *Safe. Sensible. Social. The next steps in the National Alcohol Strategy* published in June 2007 and in Wales the Welsh Assembly published *Tackling Substance Misuse in Wales: A Partnership Approach* in September 2000, which is currently being further developed. Licensing authorities should ensure that their licensing policies complement the relevant strategy, and subsequent measures, where these may help to promote one or more of the licensing objectives.

## The Anti-Social Behaviour Act 2003

1.32    Licensing authorities need to be aware of new powers that will be available to local authorities under sections 40 and 41 of the Anti Social Behaviour Act 2003. The Act provides that if the noise from any licensed premises is causing a public nuisance, an authorised environmental health officer would have the power to issue a closure order effective for up to 24 hours. Under this provision, it is for the Chief Executive of the local authority to delegate their power to environmental health officers within their authority. If after receiving a

closure order the premises remain open, the person responsible may upon summary conviction receive a fine of up to £20,000 or imprisonment for a term not exceeding three months, or both. This complements the police powers under Part 8 of the 2003 Act to close licensed premises for temporary periods.

## Violent Crime Reduction Act 2006

1.33    The Violent Crime Reduction Act 2006 received Royal Assent on 8 November 2006. The Act introduces new measures to ensure that police and local communities have the powers they need to tackle guns, knives and alcohol-related violence. Relevant measures include:

– (from 3 May 2007) an amendment to the Licensing Act to introduce a new offence of persistently selling alcohol to children. The offence will be committed if, on three or more different occasions in a period of three consecutive months, alcohol is unlawfully sold to a minor on the same premises – new powers for local authorities and the police to designate Alcohol Disorder Zones (ADZs) as a last resort to tackle alcohol related crime and disorder. The designation of an area as an ADZ will empower local authorities to charge licensees for additional enforcement activity affecting all licensed premises within the zone. The earliest date for commencement of ADZs is 1 October 2007. On commencement, relevant guidance and regulations will be placed on the Home Office website (www.homeoffice.gov.uk).

– an amendment to the Licensing Act which will enable licensing authorities, on the application of a senior police officer in cases of serious crime and disorder, to attach interim conditions to licences pending a full review. The earliest date for commencement of these powers is 1 October 2007.

## LACORS Practical Guide to Test Purchasing

1.34    Licensing authorities should also familiarise themselves with the LACORS Practical Guide to Test

Purchasing insofar as it relates to the test purchasing of alcohol by trading standards officers. LACORS continues to fulfil an important co-ordinating role in advising and informing licensing authorities about the requirements of the 2003 Act. LACORS' website may be viewed at www.lacors.gov.uk.

1.35    Details of other relevant industry initiatives can be found at Annex E.

## The Health Act 2006 – workplace smoking ban

1.36    The ban on smoking in all enclosed workplaces and public spaces will come into force on 1 July 2007. The ban will include smoking in pubs, restaurants and members' clubs where bar or other staff are employed. In this context 'enclosed' will mean anywhere with more than 50% of wall and ceiling space infilled.

## The Clean Neighbourhoods and Environment Act 2005

1.37    This provides local authorities with an additional power to issue a fixed penalty notice to any licensed premises emitting noise that exceeds the permitted level between the hours of 11pm and 7am.

# 2. The licensing objectives

## CRIME AND DISORDER

2.1     The steps any licence holder or club might take to prevent crime and disorder are as varied as the premises or clubs where licensable activities may be carried on. Licensing authorities should therefore look to the police as the main source of advice on these matters. They should also seek to involve the local CDRP, as recommended in paragraph 1.21 of this Guidance.

2.2     The Government's expectation is that the police will have a key role in undertaking the following tasks:

- developing a constructive working relationship with licensing authority licensing officers and bodies such as the local authority social services department, the Area Child Protection Committee or another competent body;

- developing a constructive working relationship with designated premises supervisors and other managers of premises, including premises providing late night refreshment;

- advising, where necessary, on the development of a venue drug policy;

- developing a constructive working relationship with the Security Industry Authority including joint visits and enforcement action where appropriate;

- agreeing the protocols for actions taken by door supervisors in relation to illegal drugs or violent behaviour, particularly when police officers should be called immediately;

- advising on and approving search procedures and the storage procedures for confiscated drugs;

- gathering and sharing intelligence on drug dealing and use with partner organisations and local venues;

- advising on the installation and monitoring of security devices such as CCTV;

- advising on the provision of safe and accessible transport home in consultation with community safety colleagues, local transport authorities and transport operators;

- working with venue owners and managers to resolve drug-related problems and problems of disorder, drunkenness and antisocial behaviour; and

- advising on the protection of employees on licensed premises who may be targets for attacks and reprisals.

2.3     The Security Industry Authority also plays an important role in preventing crime and disorder by ensuring that door supervisors are properly licensed and, in partnership with police and other agencies, that security companies are not being used as fronts for serious and organised criminal activity and that door supervisors are properly licensed. This may include making specific enquiries or visiting premises through intelligence led operations in conjunction with the police, local authorities and other partner agencies. In the exercise of their functions licensing authorities should seek to co-operate with the SIA as far as possible and consider adding relevant conditions to licences where necessary and appropriate.

2.4     The essential purpose of the licence or certificate in this context is to regulate behaviour on premises and access to them where this relates to licensable activities and the licensing objectives. Conditions attached to licences cannot seek to manage the behaviour of customers once they are beyond the direct management of the licence holder and their staff or agents, but can directly impact on

App 11

the behaviour of customers on, or in the immediate vicinity of, the premises as they seek to enter or leave.

2.5     Licence conditions should not replicate licensing offences that are set out in the 2003 Act. For example, a condition that states that a licence holder shall not permit drunkenness and disorderly behaviour on his premises would be superfluous because this is already a criminal offence. A condition that states that a licence holder shall not permit the sale of controlled drugs on the premises would be similarly superfluous.

2.6     Conditions are best targeted on deterrence and preventing crime and disorder. For example, where there is good reason to suppose that disorder may take place, the presence of closed-circuit television cameras both inside and immediately outside the premises can actively deter disorder, nuisance and anti-social behaviour and crime generally. Some licensees may wish to have cameras on their premises for the protection of their own staff and for the prevention of crime directed against the business itself or its customers. But any condition may require a broader approach, and it may be necessary to ensure that the precise location of cameras is set out on plans to ensure that certain areas are properly covered and there is no subsequent dispute over the terms of the condition.

2.7     Similarly, the provision of requirements for door supervision may be necessary to ensure that people who are drunk or drug dealers or carrying firearms do not enter the premises, reducing the potential for crime and disorder, and that the police are kept informed.

2.8     Text and radio pagers allow premises licence holders, designated premises supervisors and managers of premises and clubs to communicate instantly with the local police and facilitate a rapid response to any disorder which may be endangering the customers and staff on the premises. The Secretary of State recommends that text or radio pagers should be considered appropriate necessary conditions for public houses, bars and nightclubs operating in city and town centre leisure areas with a high density of licensed premises.

2.9     Some conditions primarily focused on the prevention of crime and disorder will also promote other licensing objectives. For example, a condition requiring that all glasses used on the premises for the sale of alcoholic drinks should be made of plastic or toughened glass or not allowing bottles to pass across a bar may be necessary to prevent violence by denying assailants suitable weapons, but may also benefit public safety by minimising the injury done to victims when such assaults take place (for example, facial injuries resulting from broken glass).

2.10    A condition must also be capable of being met. For example, while beer glasses may be available in toughened glass, wine glasses may not. Licensing authorities should carefully consider conditions of this kind to ensure that they are not only necessary but both practical and achievable.

2.11    Similarly, although most commonly made a condition of a licence on public safety grounds, licensing authorities should also consider conditions which set capacity limits for licensed premises or clubs where it may be necessary to prevent overcrowding likely to lead to disorder and violence. If such a condition is considered necessary, the licensing authority should consider whether door supervisors are needed to control numbers.

2.12    In the context of crime and disorder and public safety, the preservation of order on premises may give rise to genuine concerns about the competency of the management team charged with the maintenance of order. This may occur, for example, on premises where there are very large numbers of people and alcohol is supplied for consumption, or in premises where there are public order problems.

2.13  The designated premises supervisor is the key person who will usually be charged with day to day management of the premises by the premises licence holder, including the prevention of disorder. However, conditions relating to the management competency of designated premises supervisors should not normally be attached to premises licences. A condition of this kind could only be justified as necessary in rare circumstances where it could be demonstrated that in the circumstances associated with particular premises, poor management competency could give rise to issues of crime and disorder and public safety.

2.14  It will normally be the responsibility of the premises licence holder as an employer, and not the licensing authority, to ensure that the managers appointed at the premises are competent and appropriately trained and licensing authorities must ensure that they do not stray outside their powers and duties under the 2003 Act. This is important to ensure the portability of the personal licence and the offences set out in the 2003 Act ensure, for example, that the prevention of disorder is in sharp focus for all such managers, licence holders and clubs.

2.15  Communications between the managers of the premises and the police can also be crucial in preventing crime and disorder. Involvement by operators and managers in voluntary schemes and initiatives may be particularly valuable. Conditions requiring dedicated text or pager links between management teams and local police stations can provide early warning of disorder and also can be used to inform other licence holders that a problem has arisen in the area generally. For example, where a gang of youths is causing problems in one public house and their eviction will only result in them going on elsewhere to cause problems on other premises, there is advantage in communication links between the police and other licensed premises and clubs.

2.16  However, while this may be necessary and effective in certain parts of licensing authority areas, it may be less effective or even unnecessary in others. Police views on such matters should be given considerable weight and licensing authorities must remember that only necessary conditions, which are within the control of the licence holder or club, may be imposed.

2.17  The Indecent Displays Act 1981 prohibits the public display of indecent matter, subject to certain exceptions. It should not therefore be necessary for any conditions to be attached to licences or certificates concerning such displays in or outside the premises involved. For example, the display of advertising material on or immediately outside such premises is regulated by this legislation. Similarly, while conditions relating to public safety in respect of dancing may be necessary in certain circumstances, the laws governing indecency and obscenity are adequate to control adult entertainment involving striptease and lap-dancing which goes beyond what is lawful. Accordingly, conditions relating to the content of such entertainment which have no relevance to crime and disorder, public safety, public nuisance or the protection of children from harm could not be justified. In this context, however, it should be noted that it is in order for conditions relating to the exclusion of minors or the safety of performers to be included in premises licence or club premises certificate conditions where necessary. The Local Government (Miscellaneous Provisions) Act 1982 insofar as its adoptive provisions relate to sex establishments – sex shops, sex cinemas and in London sex encounter establishments – also remains in force.

2.18  Guidance to the police on powers to close premises (formerly Chapter 11 of this Guidance) can now be found on the DCMS website at www.culture.gov.uk.

App 11

## PUBLIC SAFETY

2.19    Licensing authorities and responsible authorities should note that the public safety objective is concerned with the physical safety of the people using the relevant premises and not with public health, which is dealt with in other legislation. There will of course be occasions when a public safety condition could incidentally benefit health, but it should not be the purpose of the condition as this would be ultra vires the 2003 Act. Accordingly, conditions should not be imposed on a premises licence or club premises certificate which relate to cleanliness or hygiene.

2.20    From 1 October 2006 the Regulatory Reform (Fire Safety) Order 2005 ('the Fire Safety Order') replaced previous fire safety legislation. As such any fire certificate issued under the Fire Precautions Act 1971 will have ceased to have effect. Licensing authorities should note that under article 43 of the Fire Safety Order any conditions imposed by the licensing authority that relate to any requirements or prohibitions that are or could be imposed by the Order automatically cease to have effect, without the need to vary the licence. This means that licensing authorities should not seek to impose fire safety conditions where the Order applies.

2.21    The exception to this will be in cases where the licensing authority and the enforcing authority for the fire safety order are one and the same body. For example, designated sports-grounds and stands where local authorities enforce the fire safety order. In such circumstances fire safety conditions should not be set in new licences, but conditions in existing licences will remain in force and be enforceable by the licensing authority.

2.22    The Fire Safety Order applies in England and Wales. It covers 'general fire precautions' and other fire safety duties which are needed to protect 'relevant persons' in case of fire in and around 'most premises'. The Order requires fire precautions to be put in place 'where necessary' and to the extent that it is reasonable and practicable in the circumstances of the case.

2.23    Responsibility for complying with the Order rests with the 'responsible person', which may be the employer, or any other person or people who may have control of the premises. Each responsible person must carry out a fire risk assessment which must focus on the safety in case of fire for all 'relevant persons'. The fire risk assessment is intended to identify risks that can be removed or reduced and to decide the nature and extent of the general fire precautions that need to be taken including, where necessary, capacity limits.

2.24    The local fire and rescue authority will enforce the Order in most premises and have the power to inspect the premises to check the responsible person is complying with their duties under the Order. They will look for evidence that the responsible person has carried out a suitable fire risk assessment and acted upon the significant findings of that assessment. If the enforcing authority is dissatisfied with the outcome of a fire risk assessment or the action taken, they may issue an enforcement notice that requires the responsible person to make certain improvements or, in extreme cases, issue a prohibition notice that restricts the use of all or part of the premises until improvements are made.

2.25    Further information and guidance about the Order and fire safety legislation is available from the Communities and Local Government website www.communities.gov.uk/fire.

2.26    Where there is a requirement in other legislation for premises open to the public or for employers to possess certificates attesting to the safety or satisfactory nature of certain equipment or fixtures on the premises, it would be unnecessary for a licensing condition to require possession of such a certificate. However, it would be permissible to require as a condition of a licence or certificate, if necessary, checks on this equipment to be conducted at specified intervals and for evidence of these checks to be retained by the premises licence holder or club provided this does not duplicate or gold-plate a requirement in other legislation. Similarly, it would be permissible for licensing authorities, if they receive relevant representations from responsible authorities or interested parties, to attach conditions which require equipment of particular standards to be maintained on the premises. Responsible authorities – such as health and safety authorities – should therefore make clear their expectations in this respect to enable prospective licence holders or clubs to prepare effective operating schedules and club operating schedules.

2.27    "Safe capacities" should only be imposed where necessary for the promotion of public safety or the prevention of disorder on the relevant premises. For example, if a capacity has been imposed through other legislation, it would be unnecessary to reproduce it in a premises licence. Indeed, it would also be wrong to lay down conditions which conflict with other legal requirements. However, if no safe capacity has been imposed through other legislation, a responsible authority may consider it necessary for a new capacity to be attached to the premises which would apply at any material time when the licensable activities are taking place and make representations to that effect. For example, in certain circumstances, capacity limits may be necessary in preventing disorder, as overcrowded venues can increase the risks of crowds becoming frustrated and hostile.

2.28    As noted above, a capacity limit should not be imposed as a condition of the licence on fire safety grounds (unless the licensing authority and the enforcing authority for fire safety purposes are the same) since, under article 43 of the Fire Safety Order, it would have no effect and so would not be enforceable.

2.29    The special provisions made for dancing, amplified and unamplified music in section 177 of the 2003 Act apply only to premises with a "permitted capacity" of not more than 200 persons. In this context, the capacity must be where the fire and rescue authority has made a recommendation on the capacity of the premises under the Fire Safety Order. For any application for a premises licence or club premises certificate for premises without an existing permitted capacity where the applicant wishes to take advantage of the special provisions set out in section 177 of the 2003 Act, the applicant should conduct their own risk assessment as to the appropriate capacity of the premises. They should send their recommendation to the fire and rescue authority who will consider it and then decide what the "permitted capacity" of those premises should be.

2.30    Whilst the Cinematograph (Safety) Regulations 1955 (S.I 1995/1129) which contained a significant number of regulations in respect of fire safety provision at cinemas, no longer apply, applicants taking advantage of the "grandfather rights" pursuant to Schedule 8 to the 2003 Act will have been subject to conditions which re-state those regulations in their new premises licence or club premises certificate. Any holders of a converted licence seeking to remove these conditions and reduce the regulatory burden on them (to the extent to which that can be done while still promoting the licensing objectives), would need to apply to vary their converted licences or certificates. When considering variation applications or applications for new licences, licensing authorities and responsible authorities should recognise the need for steps to be taken to assure public safety at these premises in the absence of the 1995 Regulations.

2.31    Public safety includes the safety of performers appearing at any premises.

## PUBLIC NUISANCE

2.32  The 2003 Act requires licensing authorities (following receipt of relevant representations) and responsible authorities, through representations, to make judgements about what constitutes public nuisance and what is necessary to prevent it in terms of conditions attached to specific premises licences and club premises certificates. It is therefore important that in considering the promotion of this licensing objective, licensing authorities and responsible authorities focus on impacts of the licensable activities at the specific premises on persons living and working (including doing business) in the vicinity that are disproportionate and unreasonable. The issues will mainly concern noise nuisance, light pollution, noxious smells and litter.

2.33  Public nuisance is given a statutory meaning in many pieces of legislation. It is however not narrowly defined in the 2003 Act and retains its broad common law meaning. It is important to remember that the prevention of public nuisance could therefore include low-level nuisance perhaps affecting a few people living locally as well as major disturbance affecting the whole community. It may also include in appropriate circumstances the reduction of the living and working amenity and environment of interested parties (as defined in the 2003 Act) in the vicinity of licensed premises.[2]

2.34  Conditions relating to noise nuisance will normally concern steps necessary to control the levels of noise emanating from premises. This might be achieved by a simple measure such as ensuring that doors and windows are kept closed after a particular time in the evening to more sophisticated measures like the installation of acoustic curtains or rubber speaker mounts. Any conditions necessary to promote the prevention of public nuisance should be tailored to the style and characteristics of the specific premises. Licensing authorities should be aware of the need to avoid unnecessary or disproportionate measures that could deter events that are valuable to the community, such as live music. Noise limiters, for example, are very expensive to purchase and install and are likely to be a considerable burden for smaller venues.

2.35  As with all conditions, it will be clear that conditions relating to noise nuisance may not be necessary in certain circumstances where the provisions of the Environmental Protection Act 1990, the Noise Act 1996, or the Clean Neighbourhoods and Environment Act 2005 adequately protect those living in the vicinity of the premises. But as stated earlier in this Guidance, the approach of licensing authorities and responsible authorities should be one of prevention and when their powers are engaged, licensing authorities should be aware of the fact that other legislation may not adequately cover concerns raised in relevant representations and additional conditions may be necessary.

2.36  Where applications have given rise to representations, any necessary and appropriate conditions should normally focus on the most sensitive periods. For example, music noise from premises usually occurs from mid-evening until either late evening or early morning when residents in adjacent properties may be attempting to go to sleep or are sleeping. In certain circumstances, conditions relating to noise in the immediate vicinity of the premises may also prove necessary to address any disturbance anticipated as customers enter and leave.

2.37  Measures to control light pollution will also require careful thought. Bright lighting outside premises considered necessary to prevent crime and disorder may itself give rise to light pollution for some

---

2  It should also be noted in this context that it remains an offence under the 2003 Act to sell or supply alcohol to a person who is drunk. This is particularly important because of the nuisance and anti-social behaviour which can be provoked after leaving licensed premises.

neighbours. Applicants, licensing authorities and responsible authorities will need to balance these issues.

2.38    In the context of preventing public nuisance, it is again essential that conditions are focused on measures within the direct control of the licence holder or club. Conditions relating to public nuisance caused by the anti-social behaviour of customers once they are beyond the control of the licence holder, club or premises management cannot be justified and will not serve to promote the licensing objectives.

2.39    Beyond the vicinity of the premises, these are matters for personal responsibility of individuals under the law. An individual who engages in anti-social behaviour is accountable in their own right. However, it would be perfectly reasonable for a licensing authority to impose a condition, following relevant representations, that requires the licence holder or club to place signs at the exits from the building encouraging patrons to be quiet until they leave the area and to respect the rights of people living nearby to a peaceful night.

2.40    The cumulative effects of litter in the vicinity of premises carrying on licensable activities can cause public nuisance. For example, it may be appropriate and necessary for a condition of a licence to require premises serving customers from take-aways and fast food outlets from 11.00pm to provide litter bins in the vicinity of the premises in order to prevent the accumulation of litter. Such conditions may be necessary and appropriate in circumstances where customers late at night may have been consuming alcohol and be inclined to carelessness and anti-social behaviour.

## PROTECTION OF CHILDREN FROM HARM

2.41    The protection of children from harm includes the protection of children from moral, psychological and physical harm, and this would include the protection of children from too early an exposure to strong language and sexual expletives, for example, in the context of film exhibitions or where adult entertainment is provided.

2.42    However, in the context of many licensed premises such as pubs, restaurants, café bars and hotels, it should be noted that the Secretary of State recommends that the development of family-friendly environments should not be frustrated by overly restrictive conditions in relation to children.

2.43    The Secretary of State intends that the admission of children to premises holding a premises licence or club premises certificate should normally be freely allowed without restricting conditions unless the 2003 Act itself imposes such a restriction or there are good reasons to restrict entry or to exclude children completely. Licensing authorities, the police and other authorised persons should focus on enforcing the law concerning the consumption of alcohol by minors.

2.44    Conditions relating to the access of children which are necessary to protect them from harm are self evidently of great importance. As mentioned in connection with statements of licensing policy in Chapter 13 of this Guidance, issues will arise about the access of children in connection with premises:

- where adult entertainment is provided;
- where there have been convictions of the current management for serving alcohol to minors or with a reputation for allowing underage drinking (other than in the context of the exemption in the 2003 Act relating to 16 and 17 year olds consuming beer, wine and cider in the company of adults during a table meal);
- where requirements for proof of age cards or other age identification to combat the purchase of alcohol by minors is not the norm;
- with a known association with drug taking or dealing;

App 11

- where there is a strong element of gambling on the premises (but not small numbers of cash prize machines);
- where the supply of alcohol for consumption on the premises is the exclusive or primary purpose of the services provided at the premises.

2.45   It is also possible that activities, such as adult entertainment, may take place at certain times on premises but not at other times. For example, premises may operate as a café bar during the day providing meals for families but also provide entertainment with a sexual content after 8.00pm. Such trading practices should be obvious from the operating schedule or club operating schedule provided with the relevant application allowing the framing of an appropriate, time-limited condition.

2.46   Similarly, gambling may take place in part of a leisure centre but not in other parts of those premises. This means that the access of children will need to be carefully considered by applicants, licensing authorities and responsible authorities. In many respects, it should be possible to rely on the discretion and common sense of licence and certificate holders. However, licensing authorities and responsible authorities should still expect applicants when preparing an operating schedule or club operating schedule to state their intention to exercise discretion and where they are necessary, to set out the steps to be taken to protect children from harm when on the premises.

2.47   Conditions, where they are necessary, should reflect the licensable activities taking place on the premises and can include:

- where alcohol is sold, requirements for the production of proof of age cards or other age identification before sales are made, to ensure that sales are not made to individuals under 18 years (whether the age limit is 18 or 16 as in the case of the consumption of beer, wine and cider in the company of adults during a table meal);
- limitations on the hours when children may be present;
- limitations on the presence of children under certain ages when particular specified activities are taking place;
- limitations on the parts of the premises to which children may have access;
- age limitations (below 18);
- limitations or exclusions when certain activities are taking place;
- requirements for accompanying adult (including for example, a combination of requirements which provide that children under a particular age must be accompanied by an adult); and
- full exclusion of people under 18 from the premises when any licensable activities are taking place

2.48   The Secretary of State considers that representations made by the child protection bodies and the police in respect of individual applications should be given considerable weight when they address necessary issues regarding the admission of children.

2.49   The 2003 Act provides that where a premises licence or club premises certificate authorises the exhibition of a film, it must include a condition requiring the admission of children to films to be restricted in accordance with recommendations given either by a body designated under section 4 of the Video Recordings Act 1984 specified in the licence (the British Board of Film Classification is currently the only body which has been so designated) or by the licensing authority itself. Further details are given in Chapter 10.

2.50   The admission of children to theatres, as with other licensed premises, should not normally be restricted. However, theatres may present a range of diverse activities. The admission of children to the performance of a play should normally be at the discretion of the licence holder and no condition restricting their access to plays should be attached. However, theatres may also present a wide range of entertainment including, for example, variety shows incorporating adult entertainment. A condition restricting the admission of children in such circumstances may be necessary. Entertainments may also be presented at theatres specifically for children. It may be necessary to consider whether a condition should be attached to a premises licence or club premises certificate which requires the presence of a sufficient number of adult staff on the premises to ensure the well being of the children during any emergency.

## Offences relating to the sale and supply of alcohol to children

2.51 Licensing authorities are expected to maintain close contact with the police, young offenders' teams and trading standards officers (who can carry out test purchases under s.154 of the Act) about the extent of unlawful sales and consumption of alcohol by minors and to be involved in the development of any strategies to control or prevent these unlawful activities and to pursue prosecutions. For example, where as a matter of policy, warnings are given to retailers prior to any decision to prosecute in respect of an offence, it is important that each of the enforcement arms should be aware of the warnings each of them has given.

## Table of relevant offences under the 2003 Act

| Section | Offence |
| --- | --- |
| Section 145 | Unaccompanied children prohibited from certain premises |
| Section 146 | Sale of alcohol to children |
| Section 147 | Allowing the sale of alcohol to children |
| Section 147A | Persistently selling alcohol to children |
| Section 148 | Sale of liqueur confectionery to children under 16 |
| Section 149 | Purchase of alcohol by or on behalf of children |
| Section 150 | Consumption of alcohol by children |
| Section 151 | Delivering alcohol to children |
| Section 152 | Sending a child to obtain alcohol |
| Section 153 | Prohibition of unsupervised sales by children |

App 11

# 3. Licensable activities

## SUMMARY

3.1     A premises licence authorises the use of any premises (which is defined in the Act as a vehicle, vessel or moveable structure or any place or a part of any premises) for licensable activities described and defined in section 1 (1) of and Schedules 1 and 2 to the 2003 Act.

The licensable activities are:

- the sale by retail of alcohol;

- the supply of alcohol by or on behalf of a club to, or to the order of, a member of the club;

- the provision of regulated entertainment; and

- the provision of late night refreshment.

## WHOLESALE OF ALCOHOL

3.2     The wholesale of alcohol to the general public was not licensable prior to the coming into force of the 2003 Act. Licensing authorities will want to have particular regard to the definition of "sale by retail" given in section 192 of the 2003 Act. This section makes clear that to be excluded from the meaning of "sale by retail" a sale must be:

- made from premises owned by the person making the sale, or occupied under a lease with security of tenure, and

- for consumption off the premises.

3.3     In addition, to be excluded, they must be sales which are made to:

- traders for the purpose of their trade (including, for example, another wholesaler);

- holders of club premises certificates, premises licences, or personal licences; or

- premises users who have given temporary event notices in order to make sales.

3.4     However, any other sale made to a member of the public in wholesale quantities is a licensable activity and subject to the provisions of the 2003 Act. This affects many wholesale businesses, cash and carries and bonded warehouses across England and Wales.

3.5     If an employee were buying alcohol as an "agent" for their employer and for the purposes of their employer's trade (i.e. selling alcohol), this could be treated as a sale to a trader. If, however, an employee were buying for their own consumption, this would be a retail sale, and would require a licence.

## INTERNET AND MAIL ORDER SALES

3.6     The place where the sale of alcohol takes place may be different to the place from which it is appropriated to the contract, i.e. specifically and physically selected for the particular purchaser. Section 190 provides that the sale of alcohol is to be treated as taking place where the alcohol is appropriated to the contract and this will be the premises that needs to be licensed. So, for example, a call centre receiving orders for alcohol would not need a licence, but the warehouse where the alcohol is stored and specifically selected for, and despatched to, the purchaser would need to be licensed.

3.7     In such circumstances a licensing authority will wish to carefully consider the distance selling supply chain in deciding where the alcohol is appropriated to the contract. Any premises where alcohol is supplied under a premises licence must have a designated premises supervisor. This will normally be the person in charge of the day to day running of the premises, and they will need to hold a 'personal licence'. In addition to this, all sales of alcohol must be made or authorised by a personal licence holder (see paragraphs 10.48 – 10.53 of this Guidance).

## REGULATED ENTERTAINMENT

3.8    Schedule 1 to the 2003 Act (Annex A), sets out what activities are regarded as the provision of regulated entertainment (entertainment and entertainment facilities) and those which are not and are therefore exempt from the regulated entertainment aspects of the licensing regime (including incidental music – see 3.20-3.23 below).

## ENTERTAINMENT

3.9    Subject to the conditions, definitions and the exemptions in Schedule 1, the types of entertainment regulated by the 2003 Act are:

- a performance of a play;
- an exhibition of a film;
- an indoor sporting event;
- a boxing or wrestling entertainment; (indoor and outdoor)
- a performance of live music;
- any playing of recorded music;
- a performance of dance;
- entertainment of a similar description to that falling within the performance of live music, the playing of recorded music and the performance of dance.

but only where the entertainment takes place in the presence of an audience and is provided at least partly to entertain that audience.

## ENTERTAINMENT FACILITIES

3.10   Subject to the conditions, definitions and the exemptions in Schedule 1, entertainment facilities means facilities for enabling persons to take part in entertainment consisting of:

- making music;
- dancing;
- entertainment of a similar description to making music or for dancing.

3.11   These facilities must be provided for the use of and to entertain customers. Entertainment facilities include, for example:

- a karaoke machine provided for the use of and entertainment of customers in a public house;

- a dance floor provided for use by the public in a nightclub;
- musical instruments made available for use by the public to entertain others at licensed premises.

3.12   In carrying out their functions, licensing authorities will need to consider whether an activity constitutes the provision of regulated entertainment. The following activities, for example, are not regulated entertainment:

- education – teaching students to perform music or to dance;
- activities which involve participation as acts of worship in a religious context;
- the demonstration of a product – for example, a guitar – in a music shop; or
- the rehearsal of a play or rehearsal of a performance of music to which the public are not admitted.

3.13   Much of this involves the simple application of common sense and this Guidance cannot give examples of every eventuality or possible activity. It is only when a licensing authority is satisfied that activities are entertainment or the provision of entertainment facilities that it should go on to consider the qualifying conditions, definitions and exemptions in Schedule 1 to see if a provision of regulated entertainment is involved and, as a result, if there is a licensable activity to be governed by the provisions of the 2003 Act.

3.14   There are a number of other entertainments, which are not themselves licensable activities, for which live or recorded music may be incidental to the main attraction or performance and therefore not licensable (see below). For example, stand-up comedy is not a licensable activity and musical accompaniment incidental to the main performance would not make it a licensable activity.

## PUB GAMES

3.15   Games commonly played in pubs and social and youth clubs like pool, darts, table tennis and billiards may fall within the definition of indoor sports in Schedule 1, but normally they would not be played for the entertainment of spectators but for the private enjoyment of the participants. As such, they would not normally constitute the provision of regulated entertainment, and the facilities provided (even if a pub provides them with a view to profit) do not fall within the limited list of entertainment facilities in that Schedule (see paragraph 3.10 above). It is only when games take place in the presence of an audience and are provided to, at least in part, entertain that audience, for example, a darts championship competition, that the activity would become licensable.

## PRIVATE EVENTS

3.16 Entertainment at a private event to which the public are not admitted becomes regulated entertainment and therefore licensable, only if it is provided for consideration and with a view to profit. So, for instance, a charge made to people attending a private event to cover the costs of the entertainment, and for no other purpose, would not make the entertainment licensable. The fact that a profit might inadvertently be made would be irrelevant as long as there had not been an intention to make a profit.

3.17 Schedule 1 to the 2003 Act also makes it clear that before entertainment or entertainment facilities are regarded as being provided for consideration, a charge has to be made by, or on behalf of, a person concerned with:

- the organisation or management of the entertainment; or
- the organisation or management of the facilities who is also concerned with the entertainment;

and paid by or on behalf of some or all of the persons for whom the entertainment/facilities are, provided.

3.18 This means that a private event for invited guests held in a hired private

room with a live band and dancing and no charge for admission intended to make a profit is not a regulated entertainment unless the person who hires out the room (for example, the owner of the house in which the room is situated) is also involved in the organisation or management of the entertainment. An owner may become so involved by, for example, hiring a dancefloor, sound equipment and/or smoke machine along with the room, or by arranging for a DJ or band to play at the event. In this case, the provision by the owner of the room (and any other entertainment facilities they provide) for a charge and with a view to profit will itself be a provision of regulated entertainment. By contrast, if the owner simply hires out the room for an event and is not further involved with the entertainment at the event, they will not be providing a regulated entertainment, and the event would need to be looked at separately from the hire of the room in order to determine whether it was itself an instance of regulated entertainment.

3.19 Similarly, a party organised in a private house by and for friends (and not open to the public) with music and dancing, and where a charge or contribution is made solely to cover the costs of the entertainment and not with a view to profit would not be an instance of regulated entertainment. In the same vein, any charge made by musicians or other performers or their agents to the organiser of a private event does not of itself make that entertainment licensable unless the guests attending are themselves charged for the entertainment with a view to achieving a profit.[3]

## INCIDENTAL MUSIC

3.20 The incidental performance of live music and incidental playing of recorded music may not be regarded as the provision of regulated entertainment activities under the 2003 Act in certain circumstances.

---

3 Entertainment facilities falling within paragraph 1(2)(b) of Schedule 1 of the Act (club premises) are not covered by this section of the Guidance.

This is where they are incidental to another activity which is not itself entertainment or the provision of entertainment facilities. This exemption does not extend to the provision of other forms of regulated entertainment.

3.21   Whether or not music of this kind is "incidental" to other activities is expected to be judged on a case by case basis and there is no definition in the 2003 Act. It will ultimately be for the courts to decide whether music is "incidental" in the individual circumstances of any case.

3.22   The operator of the premises concerned must first decide whether or not they need a premises licence. In considering whether or not music is incidental, one factor will be whether or not, against a background of the other activities already taking place, the addition of music will create the potential to undermine the four licensing objectives of the Act. Other factors might include some or all of the following:

- Is the music the main, or one of the main, reasons for people attending the premises?
- Is the music advertised as the main attraction?
- Does the volume of the music disrupt or predominate over other activities or could it be described as 'background' music?

Conversely, factors which would not normally be relevant include:

- Number of musicians, e.g. an orchestra may provide incidental music at a large exhibition.
- Whether musicians are paid.
- Whether the performance is pre-arranged.
- Whether a charge is made for admission to a premises.

3.23   Stand-up comedy is not regulated entertainment and musical accompaniment incidental to the main performance would not make it a licensable activity. But there are likely to be some circumstances which occupy a greyer area. In cases of doubt, operators should seek the advice of the licensing authority,

particularly with regard to their policy on enforcement.

## SPONTANEOUS MUSIC, SINGING AND DANCING

3.24   The spontaneous performance of music, singing or dancing does not amount to the provision of regulated entertainment and is not a licensable activity. The relevant part of the 2003 Act to consider in this context is paragraph 1(3) of Schedule 1 to the Act. This states that the second condition which must apply before an activity constitutes the provision of regulated entertainment is that the premises (meaning "any place") at which the entertainment is, or entertainment facilities are, provided are made available for the purpose, or purposes which include the purpose, of enabling the entertainment concerned to take place. In the case of genuinely spontaneous music (including singing) and dancing, the place where the entertainment takes place will not have been made available to those taking part for that purpose.

## SMALL VENUES PROVIDING DANCING AND AMPLIFIED OR UNAMPLIFIED MUSIC

3.25   In addition, section 177 of the 2003 Act applies to suspend most licensing conditions relating to music entertainment in certain small venues when the conditions specified in the licence are met. The section is directed at premises with a capacity of 200 or less and which are licensed for the provision of music entertainment such as, for example, some pubs with entertainment licences. A detailed description of section 177 follows below.

3.26   Subsections (1) and (2) of section 177 of the 2003 Act provide that where,

- a premises licence or club premises certificate authorises the supply of alcohol for consumption on the premises and the provision of "music entertainment" (live music or dancing or facilities enabling people to take part in those activities),

- the relevant premises are used primarily for the supply of alcohol for consumption on the premises, and

- the premises have a permitted capacity limit of not more than 200 persons (see paragraph 2.29).

any conditions relating to the provision of the music entertainment imposed on the premises licence or club premises certificate by the licensing authority, other than those set out by the licence or certificate which are consistent with the operating schedule, will be suspended except where, under subsection (5), they were imposed as being necessary for public safety or the prevention of crime and disorder or both.

3.27   Examples of premises used "primarily" for the supply of alcohol for consumption on the premises would include some public houses and some qualifying club premises, but would not normally include, for example, a restaurant.

3.28   In addition, subsection (4) of section 177 provides that where

- a premises licence or club premises certificate authorises the provision of music entertainment, and

- the premises have a permitted capacity limit of not more than 200 persons

then, during the hours of 8am and midnight, if the premises are being used for the provision of unamplified live music or facilities enabling people to take part in such entertainment, but no other type of regulated entertainment, any conditions imposed on the licence by the licensing authority, again other than those which are consistent with the operating schedule, which relate to the provision of that music entertainment will be suspended.

3.29   The "unamplified" music exemption covers any premises appropriately licensed, including, for example restaurants.

3.30   The area to which the 200 "permitted

capacity limit" applies concerns the area covered by the terms of the premises licence or club premises certificate. In this context, the capacity must be where the fire and rescue authority has made a recommendation on the capacity of the premises under the Fire Safety Order (see paragraph 2.29). The permitted capacity limit is only applicable to part of the premises where that part has been separately and accordingly licensed.

3.31   Section 177 can be disapplied in relation to any condition of a premises licence or club premises certificate following a review of the licence or certificate. This means that conditions attached to the existing premises licence relating to the provision of music entertainment can be given effect at the relevant times or that new conditions may also be imposed as an outcome of the review process.

## LATE NIGHT REFRESHMENT

3.32   Schedule 2 (Annex B) sets out what activities are regarded as the provision of late night refreshment and those which are not and are therefore exempt from the late night refreshment aspects of the licensing regime.

3.33   Schedule 2 to the 2003 Act provides a definition of what constitutes the provision of late night refreshment. It involves only the supply of 'hot food and hot drink'. For example, shops, stores and supermarkets selling cold food and cold drink that is immediately consumable from 11.00pm are not licensable as providing late night refreshment. The legislation impacts on those premises such as night cafés and take away food outlets where people may gather at any time from 11.00pm and until 5.00am with the possibility of disorder and disturbance. In this case, supply takes place when the hot food or hot drink is given to the customer, not when it is paid for. For example, when a table meal is served in a restaurant or when a takeaway is handed to a customer over the counter.

3.34  Some premises provide hot food or hot drink between 11.00pm and 5.00am by means of vending machines established on the premises for that purpose. The supply of hot drink by a vending machine is not a licensable activity and is exempt under the 2003 Act so long as the public have access to and can operate the machine without any involvement of the staff.

3.35  However, this exemption does not apply to hot food. Premises supplying hot food for a charge by vending machine are licensable if the food has been heated on the premises, even though no staff on the premises may have been involved in the transaction.

3.36  It is not expected that the provision of late night refreshment as a secondary activity in licensed premises open for other purposes such as public houses, cinemas or nightclubs or casinos should give rise to a need for significant additional conditions. The Secretary of State considers that the key licensing objectives in connection with late night refreshment are the prevention of crime and disorder and public nuisance, and it is expected that both will normally have been adequately covered in the conditions relating to the other licensable activities on such premises.

3.37  The supply of hot drink which consists of or contains alcohol is exempt under the 2003 Act as late night refreshment because it is caught by the provisions relating to the sale or supply of alcohol.

3.38  The supply of hot food or hot drink free of charge is not a licensable activity. However, where any charge is made for either admission to the premises or for some other item in order to obtain the hot food or hot drink, this will not be regarded as "free of charge". Supplies by a registered charity or anyone authorised by a registered charity are also exempt. Similarly, supplies made on vehicles – other than when they are permanently or temporarily parked – are also exempt.

3.39  Supplies of hot food or hot drink from 11.00pm are exempt from the provisions of the 2003 Act if there is no admission to the public to the premises involved and they are supplies to:

- a member of a recognised club supplied by the club;
- persons staying overnight in a hotel, guest house, lodging house, hostel, a caravan or camping site or any other premises whose main purpose is providing overnight accommodation;
- an employee supplied by a particular employer (eg. a staff canteen);
- a person who is engaged in a particular profession or who follows a particular vocation (eg. a tradesman carrying out work at particular premises);
- a guest of any of the above.

App 11

# 4. Personal licences

4.1    This Chapter provides advice about
       best practice in administering the
       process for issuing personal licences
       to sell or supply alcohol.

## REQUIREMENTS FOR A
## PERSONAL LICENCE

4.2    The sale and supply of alcohol,
       because of its impact on the wider
       community and on crime and anti-
       social behaviour, carries with it
       greater responsibility than the
       provision of regulated entertainment
       and late night refreshment. This is
       why individuals who may be
       engaged in making and authorising
       the sale and supply of alcohol
       require a personal licence. Not every
       person retailing alcohol at premises
       licensed for that purpose needs to
       hold a personal licence, but every
       sale or supply of alcohol must be at
       least authorised by such a licence
       holder (see paragraphs 10.48 –
       10.53 of this Guidance). Any
       premises at which alcohol is sold or
       supplied may employ one or more
       personal licence holders. For
       example, there may be one owner or
       senior manager and several junior
       managers holding a personal
       licence.

## WHO CAN APPLY?

4.3    In the case of an application for a
       personal licence under Part 6 of the
       2003 Act, the requirements are that
       the applicant:

- must be aged 18 or over;
- possesses a licensing qualification
  accredited by the Secretary of
  State (or one which is certified as if
  it is such a qualification or is
  considered equivalent) or is a
  person as prescribed by the
  Secretary of State by regulations;
- must not have forfeited a personal
  licence within five years of their
  application;

- has paid the appropriate fee to the
  licensing authority;

and that the police:

- have not given an objection notice
  about the grant of a personal
  licence following notification of
  any unspent relevant offence or
  foreign offence; or
- have given an objection notice
  because of a conviction for an
  unspent relevant offence or a
  foreign offence, but the licensing
  authority has not considered it
  necessary to reject the application
  on crime prevention grounds.

4.4    Any individual may apply for a
       personal licence whether or not they
       are currently employed or have
       business interests associated with
       the use of the licence. The issues
       which arise when the holder of a
       personal licence becomes
       associated with particular licensed
       premises and the personal licence
       holder is specified as the
       "designated premises supervisor"
       for those premises are dealt with in
       paragraphs 4.19 – 4.28 below.
       Licensing authorities may not
       therefore take these matters into
       account when considering an
       application for a personal licence.

## CRIMINAL RECORD

4.5    In the context of applications made
       under Part 6 of the 2003 Act, the Act
       itself does not prescribe how any
       individual should establish whether
       or not they have unspent convictions
       for a relevant offence or foreign
       offence. Regulations require that, in
       order to substantiate whether or not
       an applicant has a conviction for an
       unspent relevant offence, an
       applicant must produce a criminal
       conviction certificate or a criminal
       record certificate or the results of a
       subject access search of the police
       national computer by the National
       Identification Service to the licensing
       authority. This applies whether or not

the individual has been living for a length of time in a foreign jurisdiction.

4.6     It does not follow that such individuals will not have recorded offences in this country. All applicants are also required to make a clear statement as to whether or not they have been convicted outside England and Wales of a relevant offence or an equivalent foreign offence. This applies both to applicants ordinarily resident in England and Wales and any person from a foreign jurisdiction. Details of relevant offences as set out in the 2003 Act should be appended to application forms for the information of applicants, together with a clear warning that making any false statement is a criminal offence liable to prosecution. Relevant offences are listed in Annex C to this Guidance.

4.7     Licensing authorities are required to notify the police when an applicant is found to have an unspent conviction for a relevant offence defined in the 2003 Act or for a foreign offence. The police have no involvement or locus in such applications until notified by the licensing authority.

4.8     Where an applicant has an unspent conviction for a relevant or foreign offence, and the police object to the application on crime prevention grounds, the applicant is entitled to a hearing before the licensing authority. If the police do not issue an objection notice and the application otherwise meets the requirements of the 2003 Act, the licensing authority must grant it.

4.9     The Secretary of State recommends that, where the police have issued an objection notice, the licensing authority should normally refuse the application unless there are exceptional and compelling circumstances which justify granting it. For example, certain offences can never become spent. However, where an applicant is able to demonstrate that the offence in question took place so long ago and that they no longer have any propensity to re-offend, a licensing authority may consider that the

individual circumstances of the case are so exceptional and compelling and any risk to the community so diminished that it is right to grant the application.

4.10    If an application is refused, the applicant will be entitled to appeal against the decision. Similarly, if the application is granted despite a police objection notice, the chief officer of police is entitled to appeal against the licensing authority's determination. Licensing authorities are therefore expected to record in full the reasons for any decision that they make.

## ISSUING OF PERSONAL LICENCES BY WELSH LICENSING AUTHORITIES

4.11    Licensing authorities in Wales should consider issuing personal licences in bilingual format, in line with their own Welsh language schemes.

## LICENSING QUALIFICATIONS

4.12    Details of licensing qualifications currently accredited by the Secretary of State will be notified to licensing authorities and the details may be viewed on the DCMS website.

4.13    From time to time, licensing authorities may also be concerned that documents and certificates produced as evidence of the possession of a licensing qualification may be forged or improperly amended. Contact points for issuing authorities regarding the possible forgery of qualifications are also given on the DCMS website. It also provides information about the core content of licensing qualification courses.

## RELEVANT LICENSING AUTHORITY

4.14    Personal licences are valid for ten years unless surrendered or suspended or revoked or declared forfeit by the courts. Once granted, the licensing authority which issued the licence remains the "relevant licensing authority" for it and its holder, even though the individual

App 11

may move out of the area or take employment elsewhere. The personal licence itself will give details of the issuing licensing authority.

## CHANGES IN NAME OR ADDRESS

4.15    The holder of the licence is required by the 2003 Act to notify the licensing authority of any changes of name or address. These changes should be recorded by the licensing authority. The holder is also under a duty to notify any convictions for relevant offences to the licensing authority and the courts are similarly required to inform the licensing authority of such convictions, whether or not they have ordered the suspension or forfeiture of the licence. The holder must also notify the licensing authority of any conviction for a foreign offence. These measures ensure that a single record will be held of the holder's history in terms of licensing matters.

4.16    Licensing authorities should maintain easily accessible records and a service which can advise the police in any area and other licensing authorities promptly of any details they require about the holder of the personal licence in relation to their licensing functions. The 2003 Act authorises the provision and receipt of such personal information to such agencies for the purposes of the Act.

## CENTRAL LICENSING REGISTER

4.17    The Government, supported by licensing authorities, aims to develop a central licensing register which will, among other things, include details of all personal licence holders. Future developments relating to the creation of a central licensing register will be reported on the DCMS website.

## RENEWAL

4.18    Renewal of the personal licence every ten years provides an opportunity to ensure that the arrangements ensuring that all

convictions for relevant and foreign offences have been properly notified to the relevant licensing authority have been effective, and that all convictions have been properly endorsed upon the licence. It also provides an opportunity to ensure that the photograph of the holder on the personal licence is updated to aid identification.

## SPECIFICATION OF NEW DESIGNATED PREMISES SUPERVISORS

4.19    In every premises licensed for the supply of alcohol, a personal licence holder must be specified as the 'designated premises supervisor', as defined in the 2003 Act. This will normally be the person who has been given day to day responsibility for running the premises by the premises licence holder.

4.20    The Government considers it essential that police officers, fire officers or officers of the licensing authority can identify immediately the designated premises supervisor so that any problems can be dealt with swiftly. For this reason, the name of the designated premises supervisor and contact details must be specified on the premises licence and this must be held at the premises and displayed in summary form.

4.21    To specify a new designated premises supervisor, the premises licence holder – perhaps a supermarket chain or a pub operating company – should normally submit an application to the licensing authority (including an application for immediate interim effect) with:

•    a form of consent by the individual concerned to show that they consent to taking on this responsible role, and

•    the relevant part (Part A) of the licence.

4.22    They must also notify the police of the application.

4.23    Only one designated premises supervisor may be specified in a single premises licence, but a designated premises supervisor may supervise more than one premises as long as they are able to ensure that the four licensing objectives are properly promoted and the premises complies with licensing law and licence conditions.

4.24  Where there are frequent changes of supervisor, the premises licence holder may submit the form in advance specifying the date when the new individual will be in post and the change will take effect.

## POLICE OBJECTIONS TO NEW SUPERVISORS

4.25  The police may object to the designation of a new premises supervisor where, in exceptional circumstances, they believe that the appointment would undermine the crime prevention objective. The police can object where, for example, a particular designated premises supervisor is first appointed or transfers into particular premises and their presence in combination with particular premises gives rise to exceptional concerns. For example, where a personal licence holder has been allowed by the courts to retain their licence despite convictions for selling alcohol to minors (a relevant offence) and then transfers into premises known for underage drinking.

4.26  Where the police do object, the licensing authority must arrange for a hearing at which the issue can be considered and both parties can put their arguments. The 2003 Act provides that the applicant may apply for the individual to take up post as designated premises supervisor immediately and, in such cases, the issue would be whether the individual should be removed from this post. The licensing authority considering the matter must restrict its consideration to the issue of crime and disorder and give comprehensive reasons for its decision. Either party would be entitled to appeal if their argument is rejected.

4.27  The portability of personal licences

from one premises to another is an important concept within the 2003 Act. The Secretary of State expects that police objections would arise in only genuinely exceptional circumstances. If a licensing authority believes that the police are routinely objecting to the designation of new premises supervisors on un-exceptional grounds, they should raise the matter with the chief officer of police as a matter of urgency.

## POLICE OBJECTIONS TO EXISTING SUPERVISORS

4.28  The 2003 Act also provides for the suspension and forfeiture of personal licences by the courts following convictions for relevant offences, including breaches of licensing law. The police can at any stage after the appointment of a designated premises supervisor seek a review of a premises licence on any grounds relating to the licensing objectives if anxieties arise about the performance of a supervisor. The portability of personal licences is also important to industry because of the frequency with which some businesses move managers from premises to premises. It is not expected that licensing authorities or the police should seek to use the power of intervention as a routine mechanism for hindering the portability of a licence or use hearings of this kind as a fishing expedition to test out the individual's background and character. The Secretary of State therefore expects that such hearings should be rare and genuinely exceptional.

## CONVICTIONS AND LIAISON WITH THE COURTS

4.29  Where a personal licence holder is convicted by a court for a relevant offence, the court is under a duty to notify the relevant licensing authority of the conviction and of any decision to order that the personal licence is suspended or declared forfeit. The sentence of the court has immediate effect despite the fact that an appeal may be lodged against conviction or sentence (although the court may suspend the forfeiture or suspension of the licence pending the outcome of any appeal).

4.30    When the licensing authority receives such a notification, it should contact the holder and request the licence so that the necessary action can be taken. The holder must then produce their licence to the authority within 14 days. It is expected that the chief officer of police for the area in which the holder resides would be advised if they do not respond promptly. The licensing authority should record the details of the conviction, endorse them on the licence, together with any period of suspension and then return the licence to the holder. If the licence is declared forfeit, it should be retained by the licensing authority.

## RELEVANT OFFENCES

4.31    Relevant offences are set out in Schedule 4 to the 2003 Act (see Annex C of this Guidance).

# 5. Who needs a premises licence?

5.1  A premises licence authorises the use of any premises (which is defined in the 2003 Act as a vehicle, vessel or moveable structure or any place or a part of any premises), for licensable activities described and defined in section 1(1) of and Schedules 1 and 2 to the 2003 Act.

## RELEVANT PARTS OF ACT

5.2  In determining whether any premises should be licensed, the following parts of the 2003 Act are relevant:

5.3  Section 191 provides the meaning of "alcohol" for the purposes of the 2003 Act. It should be noted that a wide variety of foodstuffs contain alcohol but generally in a highly diluted form when measured against the volume of the product. For the purposes of the Act, the sale or supply of alcohol which is of a strength not exceeding 0.5 per cent ABV (alcohol by volume) at the time of the sale or supply in question is not a licensable activity. However, where the foodstuff contains alcohol

| Relevant part of Act | Description |
| --- | --- |
| Section 1 | Outlines the licensable activities |
| Part 3 | Provisions relating to premises licences |
| Part 4 | Provisions for qualifying clubs |
| Section 173 | Activities in certain locations which are not licensable |
| Section 174 | Premises that may be exempted on grounds of national security |
| Section 175 | Minor raffles and tombolas |
| Section 175 | Prizes of alcohol not to be treated as licensable if certain conditions are fulfilled |
| Section 176 | Prohibits the sale of alcohol at motorway service areas; and restricts the circumstances in which alcohol may be sold at garages |
| Section 189 | Special provision regarding the licensing of vessels, vehicles and moveable structures |
| Section 190 | Where the place where a contract for the sale of alcohol is made is different from the place where the alcohol is appropriated to the contract, the sale of alcohol is to be treated as taking place where the alcohol is appropriated to the contract. |
| Section 191 | Defines "alcohol" for the purposes of the Act |
| Section 192 | Defines the meaning of "sale by retail" |
| Section 193 | Defines among other things "premises", "vehicle", "vessel" and "wine" |
| Schedules 1 and 2 | Provision of regulated entertainment and Provision of late night refreshment |

at greater strengths, for example, as with some alcoholic jellies, the sale would be a licensable activity.

## PREMISES LICENSED FOR GAMBLING

5.4    Gambling is the subject of separate legislation. The Gambling Act 2005 will come into force in September 2007, when the current law (the Betting Gaming and Lotteries Act 1963, the Gaming Act 1968 and the Lotteries and Amusements Act 1976) will be repealed. Licensing authorities should not duplicate any conditions imposed by such legislation when granting, varying or reviewing licences that authorise licensable activities under the Licensing Act 2003. When making a licence application, the applicant may, in detailing the steps to be taken in promoting the licensing objectives, refer to the statutory conditions in respect of their gaming licence where relevant. In addition, any conditions which are attached to premises licences should not prevent the holder from complying with the requirements of gambling legislation or supporting regulations. Further information about the Gambling Act 2005 can be found on the DCMS website at www.culture.gov.uk.

## DESIGNATED SPORTS GROUNDS, DESIGNATED SPORTS EVENTS AND MAJOR OUTDOOR SPORTS STADIA

5.5    Outdoor sports stadia are regulated by separate legislation in relation to health and safety and fire safety, so licensing authorities should avoid any duplication when granting, varying or reviewing premises licences.

5.6    The sports events taking place at outdoor stadia do not fall within the definition of the provision of regulated entertainment under the 2003 Act; with the exception of boxing and wrestling matches. Licensing authorities should therefore limit their consideration of applications for premises licences to

activities that are licensable under the 2003 Act.

5.7    Major stadia will often have several bars and restaurants, including bars generally open to all spectators as well as bars and restaurants to which members of the public do not have free access. Alcohol will also be supplied in private boxes and viewing areas. A premises licence may make separate arrangements for public and private areas or for restaurant areas on the same premises. It may also designate areas where alcohol may not be consumed at all or at particular times.

5.8    History demonstrates that certain sports events are more likely than others to give rise to concerns about the safety of, and disorder among, spectators. Licensing authorities should take this into account in determining premises licence conditions. Because of the issues of crowd control that arise in and around sports grounds, licensing authorities are expected to give considerable weight to the views of the local chief officer of police when representations are made concerning licensable activities.

5.9    Licensing authorities should be aware that paragraphs 98 and 99(c) of Schedule 6 to the Act and the repeals of section 2(1A) and section 5A of the Sporting Events (Control of alcohol etc.) Act 1985 have not been commenced with the remaining provisions of the 2003 Act, since the effect would have been different from that which Parliament had intended. The Government is likely to seek to introduce the intended policy by alternative means and any future developments on this will be available on the DCMS website.

## SPORTS STADIA WITH ROOFS THAT OPEN AND CLOSE

5.10    Major sports grounds with roofs that open and close, such as the Millennium Stadium in Cardiff, do not fall within the definition of an "indoor sporting event" under the 2003 Act. As a result events taking place in these stadia are not 'regulated entertainment' as defined and are not licensable under the 2003 Act.

## VESSELS

5.11    The 2003 Act applies to vessels (including ships and boats) as if they were premises. A vessel which is not permanently moored or berthed is treated as if it were premises situated in a place where it is usually moored or berthed. The relevant licensing authority for considering an application for a premises licence for a vessel is therefore the licensing authority for the area in which it is usually moored or berthed.

5.12    However, an activity is not a licensable activity if it takes place aboard a vessel engaged on an international journey. An "international journey" means a journey from a place in the United Kingdom to an immediate destination outside the United Kingdom or a journey from outside the United Kingdom to an immediate destination in the United Kingdom.

5.13    If a vessel is not permanently moored and carries more than 12 passengers it is a passenger ship and will be subject to safety regulation by the Maritime and Coastguard Agency (MCA).

5.14    When a licensing authority receives an application for a premises licence in relation to a vessel, it should consider the promotion of the licensing objectives, but should not focus on matters relating to safe navigation or operation of the vessel, the general safety of passengers or emergency provision, all of which are subject to regulations which must be met before the vessel is issued with its Passenger Certificate and Safety Management Certificate.

5.15    If the MCA is satisfied that the vessel complies with Merchant Shipping standards for a passenger ship, the premises should normally be accepted as meeting the public safety objective. In relation to other public safety aspects of the application, representations made by the MCA on behalf of the Secretary of State should be given particular weight.

5.16    If a vessel, which is not permanently moored and carries no more than 12 passengers, goes to sea, it will be subject to the code for the safety of Small Commercial Vessels. This code sets the standards for construction, safety equipment and manning for these vessels and MCA will be able to confirm that it has a valid safety certificate.

5.17    If a vessel carries no more than 12 passengers and does not go to sea, it may be regulated or licensed by the competent harbour authority, navigation authority or local authority. The recommended standards for these vessels are set out in the (non-statutory) Inland Waters Small Passenger Boat Code, which provides best-practice guidance on the standards for construction, safety equipment and manning. Some authorities may use their own local rules. MCA has no direct responsibility for these vessels and will not normally comment on a premises licence application.

## INTERNATIONAL AIRPORTS AND PORTS

5.18    Under the 2003 Act, the Secretary of State may 'designate' a port, hoverport or airport with a substantial amount of international traffic so that an activity carried on there is not licensable. The Secretary of State may also preserve existing designations made under earlier legislation. Details of designated ports, hoverports and airports can be viewed on the DCMS website.

5.19    Areas at designated ports which are "airside" or "wharfside" are included in the exemption in the 2003 Act from the licensing regime. The non-travelling public does not have access to these areas and they are subject to stringent bye-laws. The exemption allows refreshments to be provided to travellers at all times of the day and night. Other parts of designated ports, hoverports and airports are subject to the normal licensing controls.

App 11

## VEHICLES

5.20 Under the 2003 Act, alcohol may not be sold on a moving vehicle and the vehicle may not be licensed for that purpose. However, licensing authorities may consider applications for the sale of alcohol from a parked or stationary vehicle. For example, mobile bars could sell alcohol at special events as long as they were parked. Any permission granted would relate solely to the place where the vehicle is parked and where sales are to take place.

5.21 The provision of any entertainment or entertainment facilities on premises consisting of or forming part of any vehicle while it is in motion and not permanently or temporarily parked is not regulated entertainment for the purposes of the 2003 Act. For example, a band performing on a moving float in a parade would not require a premises licence if performances only take place while the vehicle is in motion.

## TRAINS AND AIRCRAFT

5.22 Railway vehicles and aircraft engaged on journeys are exempted from the licensing regime. However, licensing authorities should note that some defunct aircraft and railway carriages remain in a fixed position and are used as restaurants and bars. These premises are subject to the provisions of the 2003 Act.

## GARAGES

5.23 Section 176 of the 2003 Act prohibits the sale or supply of alcohol from premises that are used primarily as a garage, or are part of premises used primarily as a garage. Premises are used as a garage if they are used for one or more of the following:
- the retailing of petrol;
- the retailing of derv;
- the sale of motor vehicles; and
- the maintenance of motor vehicles.

5.24 The licensing authority must decide whether or not any premises is used primarily as a garage. The approach endorsed so far by the courts is

based on intensity of use to establish primary use. For example, if a garage shop in any rural area is used more intensely by customers purchasing other products than by customers purchasing the products or services listed above, it may be eligible to seek authority to sell or supply alcohol.

5.25 Where there is insufficient evidence to establish primary use, it is for the licensing authority to decide whether to grant the licence and deal with any issues through enforcement action or to defer granting the licence until the primary use issue can be resolved to their satisfaction.

## LARGE SCALE TIME-LIMITED EVENTS REQUIRING PREMISES LICENCES

5.26 Licensing authorities should note that a premises licence may be sought for a short, discrete period. The 2003 Act provides for the giving of temporary event notices which are subject to various limitations (see Chapter 7 of this Guidance). Any temporary event which is not within these limits, would require the authority of a premises licence if the premises or place is currently unlicensed for the activities involved. For example, this would arise if the event would involve more than 499 attending or if a temporary event notice were given and would result in the limit for individual premises of 12 notices in a calendar year being exceeded.

5.27 The procedures for applying for and granting such a licence are identical to those for an unlimited duration premises licence except that it should be stated on the application that the applicant's intention is that the period of the licence should be limited. Licensing authorities should clearly specify on such a licence when it comes into force and when it ceases to have effect. If the sale of alcohol is involved, a personal licence holder must be specified as the designated premises supervisor.

5.28 Temporary events may range from relatively small local events, like traditional performances of a play, which may last for five days, to major pop festivals lasting only one day. The largest temporary events may attract huge crowds of over 100,000 people and the risks to public safety and to crime and disorder as well as public nuisance may be considerable.

Licensing authorities are expected to make clear in local publicity that they should be given very early notice of such major events to allow responsible authorities to discuss operating schedules with the organisers well before a formal application is submitted. Many of these events will give rise to special considerations in respect of public safety. Operating schedules should therefore reflect an awareness of these matters and in particular, advice given in the following documents will be relevant:

- The Event Safety Guide – A guide to health, safety and welfare at music and similar events (HSE 1999) ("The Purple Book") ISBN 0 7176 2453 6
- Managing Crowds Safely (HSE 2000) ISBN 0 7176 1834 X
- 5 Steps to Risk Assessment: Case Studies (HSE 1998) ISBN 07176 15804
- The Guide to Safety at Sports Grounds (The Stationery Office, 1997) ("The Green Guide") ISBN 0 11 300095 2
- Safety Guidance for Street Arts, Carnival, Processions and Large Scale Performances published by the Independent Street Arts Network, copies of which may be obtained through www.streetartsnetwork.org.uk/ pages/ publications.htm
- Fire Safety Risk Assessment – Open Air Events and Venues (ISBN 978 1 85112 823 5) is available from the Communities and Local Government website www.communities.gov.uk/fire

## ADDITIONAL FEES FOR LARGE SCALE EVENTS

5.29 It should be noted that premises licences for large scale temporary events do not automatically attract the higher fee levels set out in the relevant fee Regulations, which must be paid in addition to the standard application or variation fees when the premises licence relates to activities attracting the attendance of 5,000 or more.

5.30 Venues that are permanent or purpose built or structurally altered for the activity are exempt from the additional fee.

5.31 Regulations prescribe that the additional fee for large scale events would not be payable where the premises is a structure which is not a vehicle, vessel or moveable structure, and has been constructed or structurally altered to allow:

- the proposed licensable activities to take place;
- the premises to be modified temporarily, from time to time, if relevant for the proposed licensable activities;
- the proposed number of people on the premises at any one time;
- the premises to be used in a manner which complies with the operating schedule.

The full details of where the additional fee is applicable can be found in Regulation 4(5) of The Licensing Act 2003 (Fees) Regulations 2005 which may be viewed on the DCMS website.

App 11

# 6. Club premises certificates

6.1    This Chapter provides advice about best practice for the administration of the processes for issuing, varying, and reviewing club premises certificates and other associated procedures.

## GENERAL

6.2    Clubs are organisations where members have joined together for particular social, sporting or political purposes and then combined to buy alcohol in bulk as members of the organisation to supply in the club. They commonly include Labour, Conservative and Liberal Clubs, the Royal British Legion, other ex-services clubs, working men's clubs, miners welfare institutions, social and sports clubs.

6.3    Technically the club only sells alcohol by retail at such premises to guests. Where members purchase alcohol, there is no sale (as the member owns part of the alcohol stock) and the money passing across the bar is merely a mechanism to preserve equity between members where one may consume more than another. This explains why the 2003 Act often refers to the supply of alcohol in the context of clubs and not just to the sale by retail.

6.4    Only 'qualifying' clubs may hold club premises certificates. In order to be a qualifying club, a club must have at least 25 members and meet the conditions set out in paragraph 6.9 below. The grant of a club premises certificate means that a qualifying club is entitled to certain benefits. These include:

- the authority to supply alcohol to members and sell it to guests on the premises to which the certificate relates without the need for any member or employee to hold a personal licence;

- the absence of a requirement to specify a designated premises supervisor (see paragraphs 4.19 and 4.20 of this Guidance);

- more limited rights of entry for the police and authorised persons because the premises are considered private and not generally open to the public;

- exemption from police powers of instant closure on grounds of disorder and noise nuisance (except when being used under the authority of a temporary event notice or premises licence) because they operate under their codes of discipline and rules which are rigorously enforced; and

- exemption from orders of the magistrates' court for the closure of all licensed premises in an area when disorder is happening or expected.

6.5    Qualifying clubs should not be confused with proprietary clubs, which are clubs run commercially by individuals, partnerships or businesses for profit. These require a premises licence and are not qualifying clubs.

6.6    A qualifying club will be permitted under the terms of a club premises certificate to sell and supply alcohol to its members and their guests only. Instant membership is not permitted and members must wait at least two days between their application and their admission to the club. Any qualifying club may choose to obtain a premises licence if it decides that it wishes to offer its facilities commercially for use by the general public, including the sale of alcohol to them. However, an individual on behalf of a club may give temporary event notices in respect of the premises to cover a period of up to 96 hours on up to 12 occasions each calendar year, so long as no more than 499 people attend the event and subject to an overall maximum duration in the year of 15 days, and on such occasions may sell alcohol to the public or hire out their premises for use by the public.

6.7     The 2003 Act does not prevent visitors to a qualifying club being supplied with alcohol as long as they are 'guests' of any member of the club or the club collectively, and nothing in the 2003 Act prevents the admission of such people as guests without prior notice. For the sake of flexibility, the Act does not define "guest" and whether or not somebody is a genuine guest would in all cases be a question of fact. The term can include a wide variety of people who are invited by the qualifying club or any individual member to use the club facilities. The manner in which they are admitted as 'guests' would be for the club to determine and to consider setting out in their own club rules.

6.8     There is no mandatory requirement under the 2003 Act for guests to be signed in by a member of the club. However, a point may be reached where a club is providing commercial services to the general public in a way that is contrary to its qualifying club status. It is at this point that the club would no longer be conducted in "good faith" and would no longer meet "general condition 3" for qualifying clubs in section 62 of the 2003 Act. Under the 2003 Act the licensing authority must decide when a club has ceased to operate in "good faith" and give the club a notice withdrawing the club premises certificate. The club is entitled to appeal against such a decision to the magistrates' courts. Unless the appeal is successful, the club would need to apply for a full premises licence to cover any licensable activities taking place there.

## QUALIFYING CONDITIONS

6.9     Section 62 of the 2003 Act sets out five general conditions which a relevant club must meet to be a qualifying club. Section 63 also sets out specified matters for licensing authorities to enable them to determine whether a club is established and conducted in good faith – the third qualifying condition.

Section 64 sets out additional conditions which only need to be met by clubs intending to supply alcohol to members and guests. Section 90 of the 2003 Act gives powers to the licensing authority to issue a notice to a club withdrawing its certificate where it appears that it has ceased to meet the qualifying conditions. There is a right of appeal against such a decision.

## ASSOCIATE MEMBERS AND GUESTS

6.10    As well as their own members and guests, qualifying clubs are also able to admit associate members and their guests (i.e. members and guests from another 'recognised club' as defined by section 193 of the 2003 Act) to the club premises when qualifying club activities are being carried on without compromising the use of their club premises certificate. This reflects traditional arrangements where such clubs make their facilities open to members of other clubs which operate reciprocal arrangements.

## APPLICATIONS FOR THE GRANT OR VARIATION OF CLUB PREMISES CERTIFICATES

6.11    The arrangements for applying for or seeking to vary club premises certificates are extremely similar to those for a premises licence. Licensing authorities should therefore look to Chapter 8 of this Guidance on the handling of such applications. In that Chapter most of the references to the premises licence, premises licence holders and applicants can be read for the purposes of this Chapter as club premises certificates, qualifying clubs and club applicants.

6.12    In addition to a plan of the premises and a club operating schedule, clubs must also include the rules of the club with their application. On notifying any alteration to these rules to the licensing authority, the club is required to pay a fee set down in regulations. Licensing authorities may wish to consider returning a certified copy of the rules to the applicant with the certificate. Licensing authorities should bear in mind that they cannot require any changes to the rules to be made as a condition of receiving a certificate unless relevant representations have been made. However, if a licensing authority is satisfied that the rules of a club indicate that it does not meet the qualifying conditions in the Act, a club premises certificate should not be granted.

## STEPS NEEDED TO PROMOTE THE LICENSING OBJECTIVES

6.13 Club operating schedules prepared by clubs, as with operating schedules for premises licences, must include the steps the club intends to take to promote the licensing objectives. These will be translated into conditions included in the certificate, unless the conditions have been modified by the licensing authority following consideration of relevant representations. Guidance on these conditions is given in Chapter 10 of this Guidance.

6.14 The Secretary of State wishes to emphasise that non-profit making clubs make an important and traditional contribution to the life of many communities in England and Wales and bring significant benefits. Their activities also take place on premises to which the public do not generally have access and they operate under codes of discipline applying to members and their guests.

6.15 Licensing authorities should bear these matters in mind when considering representations and should not attach conditions to certificates unless they can be demonstrated to be strictly necessary. The indirect costs of conditions will be borne by individual members of the club and cannot be recovered by passing on these costs to the general public.

## SEX EQUALITY

6.16 The Secretary of State believes that all qualifying clubs should adopt fair and equal procedures for admitting people to membership, electing club officials and on voting rights. However, although equal treatment on the grounds of gender is important to society generally, it is not a licensing objective. Conditions should not therefore be imposed which interfere with the arrangements for granting membership or voting within the club. It would also be inappropriate to apply one set of rules to qualifying clubs and another set of rules to clubs that do not engage in qualifying club activities and do not therefore require club premises certificates. Licensing authorities should not therefore seek to challenge the bona fides of any qualifying club on these grounds.

## TEMPORARY EVENT NOTICES

6.17 Licensing authorities should note paragraph 7.13 of this Guidance in connection with permitted temporary activities in club premises.

# 7. Temporary event notices

7.1   This Chapter describes best practice in administering the arrangements in the 2003 Act for the temporary carrying on of licensed activities at premises which are not authorised by a premises licence or club premises certificate.

## GENERAL

7.2   The most important aspect of the system of permitted temporary activities is that events do not have to be authorised as such by the licensing authority. Instead the premises user notifies the event to the licensing authority and the police, subject to fulfilling certain conditions.

7.3   In general, only the police may intervene to prevent such an event taking place or to agree a modification of the arrangements; and it is characterised by an exceptionally light touch bureaucracy. The licensing authority may only ever intervene of its own volition if the statutory limits on the number of temporary event notices that may be given in various circumstances would be exceeded. Otherwise, the licensing authority is only required to issue a timely acknowledgement.

7.4   It should be noted that giving a temporary event notice does not relieve the premises user from any requirements under planning law for appropriate planning permission where it is required.

## LIMITATIONS

7.5   Such a light touch is possible because of the limitations directly imposed on the use of the system by the 2003 Act. The limitations apply to:

- the number of times a person (the "premises user") may give a temporary event notice (50 times per year for a personal licence holder and 5 times per year for other people);
- the number of times a temporary event notice may be given for any particular premises (12 times in a calendar year);
- the length of time a temporary event may last (96 hours);
- the maximum total duration of the periods covered by temporary event notices at any individual premises (15 days); and
- the scale of the event in terms of the maximum number of people attending at any one time (less than 500).

7.6   In any other circumstances, a full premises licence or club premises certificate would be required for the period of the event involved. A person may also choose to apply for a premises licence or club premises certificate if they do not wish to take advantage of the light touch arrangements.

7.7   In determining whether the maximum total duration of the periods covered by temporary event notices at any individual premises has exceeded 15 days, licensing authorities should be aware that any event beginning before midnight and continuing into the next day would count as two days towards the 15 day limitation.

7.8   Many premises users giving temporary event notices will not have commercial backgrounds or ready access to legal advice, including for example, people acting on behalf of charities, community and voluntary groups, etc who may hold public events involving licensable activities to raise funding. Licensing authorities should therefore ensure that local publicity about the system of permitted temporary activities is clear and understandable and should strive to keep the arrangements manageable and user-friendly for these groups.

App 11

## WHO CAN GIVE A TEMPORARY EVENT NOTICE?

### Personal licence holders

7.9     A personal licence holder can give a temporary event notice for licensable activities, at any premises on up to 50 occasions in each year for up to four days on each occasion (subject to the limitations for each premises – see paragraph 7.11 below), subject to informing the licensing authority and the police for the area in which the event is to take place of relevant details. The relevant information is itemised in the prescribed notice contained in regulations made by the Secretary of State, which may be viewed on the DCMS website.

7.10    A personal licence holder may also use their allocation of 50 temporary event notices at premises which have a premises licence or club premises certificate. This might be, for example, to hold an event involving live music, to extend the hours when alcohol may be sold for an ad hoc occasion or to provide late night refreshment after a quiz night. However, if the ad hoc event is something that is predictable and anticipated to occur on a number of occasions it is expected that the licensable activities would form part of the application for a premises licence.

7.11    Only 12 notices may be granted for the same premises up to an overriding maximum total duration of 15 days.

### Non-personal licence holders

7.12    The 2003 Act provides that any individual person aged 18 or over may give a temporary event notice whether or not they hold a personal licence. They will not therefore have met the tests and qualifications described in Part 6 of the Act. Where alcohol is not to be sold, this should not matter. However, many events will involve combinations of licensable activities. In the absence of a premises user holding a personal licence, the Act limits the number of notices that may be given by any non-personal licence holder to 5 occasions per year. In every other respect, the Guidance and information set out in the paragraphs above applies.

7.13    Temporary event notices may also be given by non-personal licence holders for club premises covered by club premises certificates. This means, for example, that a club which under its certificate is normally only permitted to supply alcohol to its members and their guests may during the period covered by a temporary event notice (subject to the limitation on numbers and occasions) under the authority of the notice and the responsibility of the individual giving the notice (the premises user) admit members of the public and sell alcohol to them as well as provide regulated entertainment. Only 12 notices may be given for the same club premises in any calendar year and the maximum total duration of 15 days will also apply.

## NOTIFIED PREMISES

7.14    A temporary event notice may be given for part of a building such as a single room within a village hall, a plot within a larger area of land, or a discrete area within a marquee as long as it includes a clear description of the area where the licensable activities will take place and the premises user intends to restrict the number of people present in the notified area at any one time to less than 500. If the premises user fails to restrict the numbers to a maximum of 499, they would be liable to prosecution for carrying on unauthorised licensable activities.

## NOTIFICATION ARRANGEMENTS

7.15    Premises users are required to send a temporary event notice, in the form prescribed in the regulations, to the licensing authority and the police at least 10 working days before an event. The Government recommends that notices should not be returned if they contain obvious and minor factual errors that can easily be amended.

7.16   There is nothing to prevent notification of multiple events at the same time so long as the first event is at least ten days away. For example, an individual personal licence holder wishing to exhibit and sell beer at a series of country shows may wish to give several notices simultaneously. However, this would only be possible where the events are to take place in the same licensing authority (and police area) and the premises to be used at the show would be occupied by no more than 499 people at any one time.

7.17   Although 10 working days is the minimum possible notice that may be given, licensing authorities should publicise locally their preferences in terms of forward notice and encourage notice givers to provide the earliest possible notice of events likely to take place. Licensing authorities should also consider publicising a preferred maximum time in advance of an event that applications should be made. For example, if an application is made too far in advance of an event, it may be difficult for the police to make a sensible assessment and could lead to objections that could be otherwise avoided.

7.18   Section 193 of the Act defines "working day" as any day other than a Saturday, a Sunday, Christmas Day, Good Friday, or a day which is a bank holiday under the Banking and Financial Dealings Act 1971 in England and Wales. "Ten working days" notice means ten working days exclusive of the day on which the event is to start, and exclusive of the day on which the notice is given.

## ROLE OF THE LICENSING AUTHORITY

7.19   One reason for the notification requirement is to enable the licensing authority to check that the limitations set down in Part 5 of the 2003 Act are being observed and to intervene if they are not. For example, a temporary event notice would be void unless there is a minimum of 24 hours between events notified by the same premises user, or an associate, or someone who is in business with the relevant premises user, in respect of the same premises. This is to prevent evasion of the 96 hour limit on such events and the need to obtain a full premises licence or club premises certificate for more major or permanent events. In addition, for these purposes, a notice is treated as being from the same premises user if it is given by an associate. The 2003 Act defines an associate as being:

• the spouse or civil partner of that person;

• child, parent, grandchild, grandparent, brother or sister of that person;

• an agent or employee of that person;

• the spouse or civil partner of a person listed in either of the two previous bullet points.

7.20   A person living with another person as their husband or wife is treated for these purposes as their spouse. 'Civil partner' is defined by the Civil Partnership Act 2004.

7.21   Where the application is not within the statutory parameters described earlier, the licensing authority will issue a counter notice to the person giving the notice – the premises user. Where the temporary event notice is in order, the fee prescribed by the Secretary of State paid, the event falls within the limitations in the Act, and there has been no police intervention on crime prevention grounds, the licensing authority will record the notice in its register and send an acknowledgement to the premises user.

7.22   Licensing authorities may not seek to attach any terms, conditions, limitations or restrictions on the carrying on of licensable activities at such events under the authority of a temporary event notice. It is however desirable for licensing authorities to provide local advice about proper respect for the concerns of local residents; of other legislative requirements regarding health and safety, noise pollution or the building of temporary structures; of other

App 11

necessary permissions, for example, with regard to road closures or the use of pyrotechnics in public places; with regard to local bye-laws; and the need to prevent anti-social behaviour by those attending. Premises users are not required to be on the premises for the entire duration of the event, but they will remain liable to prosecution for certain offences that may be committed at the premises during the temporary event if the event is not adequately managed/supervised including the laws governing sales of alcohol to minors. These matters may be covered in the licensing authority's statement of licensing policy.

7.23    In the case of an event proceeding under the authority of a temporary event notice, failure to adhere to the requirements of the 2003 Act, such as the limitation of no more than 499 being present at any one time, would mean that the event was unauthorised. In such circumstances, the premises user would be liable to prosecution.

7.24    Section 8 of the Act requires licensing authorities to keep a register containing certain matters, including a record of temporary notices received. Licensing authorities should be aware that there is no requirement to record all the personal information given on a temporary event notice, and should avoid recording certain details, such as national insurance numbers, which may give rise to identity fraud.

## POLICE INTERVENTION

7.25    The second and more important reason for the notification requirement is to give the police the opportunity to consider whether they should object to the event taking place on the grounds that it would undermine the crime prevention objective.

7.26    Such cases might arise because of concerns about the scale, location or timing of the event. However, in most cases, where alcohol is supplied away from licensed premises at a temporary bar under the control of a personal licence holder (e.g. at weddings or small social, community, charitable or sporting events) this should not give rise to the use of these police powers. If the police do not intervene, they will still be able to rely on their powers of closure under Part 8 of the 2003 Act should disorder or noise nuisance arise subsequently.

7.27    The police may issue an objection notice within 48 hours of being notified. This 48 hour period includes weekends and other non "working days" such as bank holidays. The licensing authority must consider the objection at a hearing before a counter notice can be issued, but it must restrict its consideration to the crime prevention objective. It may not, for example, uphold a police objection notice on grounds of public nuisance or an objection notice given more than 48 hours after the temporary event notice is given. At the hearing, the police and the premises user may be heard by the relevant licensing committee. A hearing would not be necessary if the objection notice is withdrawn by the police.

7.28    The possibility of police intervention is another reason why event organisers should be encouraged by local publicity not to rely on giving the minimum amount of notice and to contact local police licensing officers at the earliest possible opportunity about their proposals.

7.29    The police may withdraw their objection notice at any stage if the proposed premises user agrees to modify the proposal to meet their concerns. For example, if the premises user agrees to modify the period during which alcohol may be sold. The licensing authority will then be sent or delivered a copy of the modified notice by the police as proof of their agreement, but they can subsequently withdraw it.

# 8. APPLICATIONS FOR PREMISES LICENCES

## RELEVANT LICENSING AUTHORITY

8.1    Premises licences are issued by the licensing authority in which the premises are situated or in the case of premises straddling an area boundary, the licensing authority where the greater part of the premises is situated. Where the premises is located equally in two or more areas, the applicant may choose but, in these rare cases, it is important that the licensing authorities involved maintain close contact.

8.2    In section 13, the 2003 Act defines three key groups that have important roles in the context of applications, inspection, enforcement and reviews of premises licences.

## AUTHORISED PERSONS

8.3    The first group – "authorised persons" – are bodies empowered by the Act to carry out inspection and enforcement roles. The police are not included because they are separately empowered by the Act to carry out their duties. For all premises, the authorised persons include:

- officers of the licensing authority;
- fire inspectors;
- inspectors locally responsible for the enforcement of the Health and Safety at Work etc Act 1974; and
- environmental health officers.

8.4    Local authority officers will most commonly have responsibility for the enforcement of health and safety legislation, but the Health and Safety Executive is responsible for certain premises. In relation to vessels, authorised persons also include an inspector or a surveyor of ships appointed under section 256 of the Merchant Shipping Act 1995. These would normally be officers acting on behalf of the Maritime and Coastguard Agency.

The Secretary of State may also prescribe other authorised persons by means of regulations, but has not currently prescribed any additional bodies. If any are prescribed, details will be made available on the DCMS website.

## INTERESTED PARTIES

8.5    The second group – "interested parties" – are the bodies or individuals who are entitled to make representations to licensing authorities on applications for the grant, variation or review of premises licences. In addition, interested parties may themselves seek a review of a premises licence. This group includes:

- a person living in the vicinity of the premises in question;
- a body representing persons living in that vicinity, for example, a residents' association, or a parish or town council;
- a person involved in a business in the vicinity of the premises in question; and
- a body representing persons involved in such businesses, for example, a trade association.

8.6    It is expected that "a person involved in business" will be given its widest possible interpretation, including partnerships, and need not be confined to those engaged in trade and commerce. It is also expected that the expression can be held to embrace the functions of charities, churches and medical practices.

8.7    Any of these individuals or groups may specifically request a representative to make a representation on their behalf. For example, a legal representative, a

App 11

friend, a Member of Parliament, a Member of the National Assembly for Wales, or a local ward or parish councillor could all act in such a capacity.

8.8     Local councillors play an important role in their local communities. They can make representations in writing and at a hearing on behalf of an interested party such as a resident or local business if specifically requested to do so. They can also make representations as an interested party in their own right if they live, or are involved in a business, in the vicinity of the premises in question.

8.9     However, local councillors are subject to the Local Authorities (Model Code of Conduct) Order 2007 which restricts their involvement in matters, and participation in meetings to discuss matters, in which they have a 'prejudicial' interest (i.e. an interest that a member of the public would reasonably regard as so significant that it is likely to prejudice the member's judgement of the public interest). However, the latest version of the Code, which came into force on 3 May 2007, has relaxed the rules on prejudicial interest. In terms of licensing, this has the effect of allowing councillors with a prejudicial interest in an application to attend relevant meetings to make representations, answer questions or give evidence, provided that the public are also allowed to attend for the same purpose, whether under the licensing legislation or otherwise and as long as they withdraw from the meeting immediately afterwards. It must be emphasised that councillors have a duty to act in the interests of all of their constituents. Their role as a community advocate must therefore be balanced with their ability to represent specific interests.

8.10    The Code applies to any council member whether or not they are a member of the licensing committee. A member of a licensing committee, representing others or acting in their own right, would need to consider carefully at a committee meeting

whether they had a prejudicial interest in any matter affecting the licence of the premises in question which would require them to withdraw from the meeting when that matter is considered. In addition, a member with a prejudicial interest in a matter should not seek to influence improperly a decision on the licence in any other way.

8.11    In addition, councillors who are not themselves interested parties or representing interesting parties may wish to be kept informed of licensing related matters within the area, such as applications and reviews. The Act does not prevent licensing authorities from providing this information to councillors, for instance by way of regular updates, as long as it is done in a neutral way that could not be seen as 'soliciting' representations. It should be remembered that the 'licensing authority' in most cases is the full council, including all ward councillors, and each is therefore entitled to information required to inform that role.

## RESPONSIBLE AUTHORITIES

8.12    The third group – "responsible authorities" – are public bodies that must be fully notified of applications and that are entitled to make representations to the licensing authority in relation to the application for the grant, variation or review of a premises licence. All representations made by responsible authorities are relevant representations if they concern the effect of the application on the licensing objectives. For all premises, these include:
 • the chief officer of police;
 • the local fire and rescue authority;
 • the local enforcement agency for the Health and Safety at Work etc Act 1974 (see paragraph 8.4 above);
 • the local authority with responsibility for environmental health;
 • the local planning authority;
 • a body that represents those who are responsible for, or interested

in, matters relating to the protection of children from harm;

- the local weights and measures authority (trading standards); and
- any licensing authority, other than the relevant licensing authority, in whose area part of the premises are situated.

8.13   The licensing authority should indicate in its licensing policy which body it has recognised to be competent to advise it on the protection of children from harm. This may be the local authority social services department, the Area Child Protection Committee, or another competent body. This is important as applications for premises licences have to be copied to the responsible authorities by the applicant in order for them to make any representations they think are relevant.

8.14   In relation to a vessel, responsible authorities also include navigation authorities within the meaning of section 221(1) of the Water Resources Act 1991 that have statutory functions in relation to the waters where the vessel is usually moored or berthed or any waters where it is proposed to be navigated when being used for licensable activities; the Environment Agency; the British Waterways Board; and the Secretary of State. The Secretary of State in this case means the Secretary of State for Transport who in practice acts through the Maritime and Coastguard Agency (MCA). In practice, the Environment Agency and British Waterways only have responsibility in relation to vessels on waters for which they are the navigation statutory authority.

8.15   The Maritime and Coastguard Agency (MCA) is the lead responsible authority for public safety, including fire safety, issues affecting passenger ships (those carrying more than 12 passengers) wherever they operate and small commercial vessels (carrying no more than 12 passengers) which go to sea. The safety regime for passenger ships is enforced under the Merchant Shipping Acts by the Maritime and Coastguard Agency

which operates certification schemes for these vessels. Fire and rescue authorities, the Health and Safety Executive and local authority health and safety inspectors should normally be able to make "nil" returns in relation to such vessels and rely on the MCA to make any necessary representations in respect of this licensing objective.

8.16   Merchant Shipping legislation does not, however, apply to permanently moored vessels. So, for example, restaurant ships moored on the Thames Embankment, with permanent shore connections should be considered by the other responsible authorities concerned with public safety, including fire safety. Vessels carrying no more than 12 passengers which do not go to sea are not subject to MCA survey and certification, but may be licensed by the local, port or navigation authority.

8.17   The Secretary of State for Culture, Media and Sport may prescribe other responsible authorities by means of regulations. Any such secondary legislation may be viewed at the DCMS website.

## WHO CAN APPLY FOR A PREMISES LICENCE?

8.18   Any person (if an individual aged 18 or over) who is carrying on or who proposes to carry on a business which involves the use of premises (any place including one in the open air) for licensable activities may apply for a premises licence either on a permanent basis or for a time-limited period.

8.19   "A person" in this context includes, for example, a business or a partnership. Licensing authorities should not require the nomination of an individual to hold the licence or decide who is the most appropriate person to hold the licence. For example, for most leased public houses, a tenant may run or propose to run the business at the premises in agreement with a pub owning company. Both would be eligible to apply for the appropriate licence and it is for these businesses or individuals to agree contractually amongst themselves who should do so. However, in the case of a managed public house, the pub operating company should apply for the licence as the manager (an employee) would not be entitled to do so. Similarly, with cinema chains, the normal holder of the premises licence would be the company owning the cinema and not the cinema manager (an employee of the main company).

8.20    In considering joint applications (which is likely to be a rare occurrence), it must be stressed that under section 16(a) of the 2003 Act each applicant must be carrying on a business which involves the use of the premises for licensable activities. In the case of public houses, this would be easier for a tenant to demonstrate than for a pub owning company that is not itself carrying on licensable activities. The Secretary of State recommends that where licences are to be held by businesses, it is desirable that this should be a single business to avoid any lack of clarity in terms of accountability.

8.21    A public house may be owned or a tenancy held, jointly by a husband and wife or other partnerships of a similar nature, both actively involved in carrying on the licensable activities. In these cases, it is entirely possible for the husband and wife or the partners to apply jointly as applicant for the premises licence, even if they are not formally partners in business terms. This is unlikely to lead to the same issues of clouded accountability that could arise where two separate businesses apply jointly for the licence. If the application is granted, the premises licence would identify the holder as comprising both names and any subsequent applications, for example for a variation of the licence, would need to be made jointly.

8.22    A wide range of other individuals and bodies set out in section 16 of the 2003 Act may apply for premises licences. They include, for example, Government Departments, local

authorities, hospitals, schools, charities or police forces. In addition to the bodies listed in section 16, the Secretary of State may prescribe by regulations other bodies that may apply and any such secondary legislation may be viewed on the DCMS website.

8.23    There is nothing in the 2003 Act which prevents an application being made for a premises licence at premises where a premises licence is already held. For example, one individual may hold a premises licence authorising the sale of alcohol and another individual could apply for a premises licence for the same premises or part of those premises to authorise regulated entertainment. This also ensures that one business could not seek premises licences, for example, for all potential circus sites in England and Wales, and prevent other circuses from using those sites even though they had the permission of the landowner.

## APPLICATION FORMS

8.24    An application for a premises licence must be made in the prescribed form to the relevant licensing authority and be copied to each of the appropriate responsible authorities. For example, applications for premises which are not vessels should not be sent to the Maritime and Coastguard Agency. The application must be accompanied by:

- the required fee (details of fees may be viewed on the DCMS website);
- an operating schedule (see below);
- a plan of the premises in a prescribed form; and
- if the application involves the supply of alcohol, a form of consent from the individual who is to be specified in the licence as the designated premises supervisor.

8.25    The Government recommends that forms should not be returned if they contain obvious and minor factual errors that can easily be amended. Regulations containing provisions on fees and the prescribed form of applications, operating schedules and plans may be viewed on the DCMS website.

8.26 The regulations allow applications, notices or representations to be made by electronic means. However, this is subject to certain restrictions (see the regulations for further details) including that it must also be sent promptly to the recipient in writing, along with any fee, plan or other document or information if appropriate.

## PLANS

8.27 Plans should normally be drawn in standard scale (1:100), but an alternative scale may be used if the licensing authority has agreed. It would be sensible for licensing authorities to give their agreement in written form to avoid future dispute. There is no requirement for plans to be professionally drawn as long as they clearly show all the prescribed information.

## STEPS TO PROMOTE THE LICENSING OBJECTIVES

8.28 In preparing an operating schedule, the Secretary of State expects applicants to have had regard to the statement of licensing policy for their area. They should also be aware of the expectations of the licensing authority and the responsible authorities about the steps that are necessary for the promotion of the licensing objectives. Licensing authorities and responsible authorities are therefore expected so far as possible to publish material about the promotion of the licensing objectives and to ensure that applicants can readily access advice about these matters.

8.29 All parties are expected to work together in partnership to ensure that the licensing objectives are promoted collectively. Applicants are not required to seek the views of the key responsible authorities before formally submitting applications, but may find them a useful source of expert advice. Licensing authorities should encourage co-operation in order to

minimise the number of disputes which arise. Where there are no disputes, the steps that applicants propose to take to promote the licensing objectives, as set out in the operating schedule, will very often translate directly into conditions that will be attached to premises licences with the minimum of fuss.

8.30 Where permission is to be sought for regulated entertainment involving the provision of live music or other cultural activity, licensing authorities may wish to advise applicants to consider consulting the local authority arts officer or local representatives of the Musicians' Union before completing their operating schedule.

8.31 The steps to be taken should be both realistic and within the control of the applicant and management of the premises. If a licence is granted with conditions attached requiring the implementation of such steps, the conditions will be enforceable in law and it will be a criminal offence to fail to comply with them (under section 136 of the 2003 Act). As such, it would be wholly inappropriate to impose conditions outside the control of those responsible for the running of the premises.

8.32 For some premises, it is entirely possible that no measures will be needed to promote one or more of the licensing objectives, for example, because they are adequately dealt with by other existing legislation. It is however important that all operating schedules should be precise and clear about the measures that it is proposed to take to promote each of the licensing objectives and in particular, the protection of children from harm.

## VARIATIONS

8.33 Where a premises licence holder wishes to amend the licence the Act allows, in most cases, for an application to vary to be made rather than requiring an application for a new premises licence.

8.34 In the cases of a change of the name or address of someone named in the licence (section 33) or an application to vary the licence to specify a new individual as the designated premises supervisor (section 37) there are simplified processes for making such applications.

8.35    Any other changes to the licence require an application to vary under section 34 of the Act, including:

- varying the hours during which a licensable activity is permitted;
- adding or removing licensable activities;
- amending, adding or removing conditions within a licence; and
- altering any aspect of the layout of the premises which is shown on the plan.

8.36    Licensing authorities will wish to consider whether there is any likely impact on the promotion of the licensing objectives in deciding whether there is a need for an application to vary in relation to features which are not required to be shown on the plan under section 17 of the Act, but have nevertheless been included, for example, moveable furniture (altering the position of tables and chairs) or beer gardens (installation of a smoking shelter that will not affect the use of exits or escape routes).

8.37    However, it should be noted that a section 34 application cannot be used to vary a licence so as to:

- extend a time limited licence; or to
- transfer the licence from one premises to another.

8.38    If an applicant wishes to make these types of changes to the premises licence they should make a new premises licence application under section 17 of the Licensing Act 2003.

## RELAXATION OF OPENING HOURS FOR LOCAL, NATIONAL AND INTERNATIONAL OCCASIONS

8.39    It should normally be possible for applicants for premises licences and club premises certificates to anticipate special occasions which occur regularly each year – such as bank holidays and St George's or St Patrick's Day – and to include appropriate opening hours in their operating schedules. Similarly temporary event notices should be sufficient to cover other events which take place at premises that do not have a premises licence or club certificate.

8.40    However, exceptional events of local, national or international significance may arise which could not have been anticipated when the application was first made. In these circumstances, the Secretary of State may make a licensing hours order to allow premises to open for specified, generally extended, hours on these special occasions. This avoids the need for large numbers of applications to vary premises licences and club certificates. Typical events might include a one-off local festival, a Royal Jubilee, a World Cup or an Olympic Games.

8.41    Such events should be genuinely exceptional and the Secretary of State will not consider making such an order lightly. Licensing authorities (or any other persons) are advised that they should approach the Secretary of State about making an order at least six months before the celebration. Before making an order, the Secretary of State is required to consult as appropriate and this would generally enable a wide range of bodies to make representations to her for consideration. In addition, an order must be approved by both Houses of Parliament. Nine months would be the minimum period in which such a process could be satisfactorily completed.

8.42    Licensing authorities should note that the Secretary of State has not made a licensing hours order in relation to New Year's Eve. As such applicants for new licences or certificates would need to include in their applications the hours that they propose for New Year's Eve, if these are different from the standard hours applied for.

## ADVERTISING APPLICATIONS

8.43    Regulations governing the advertising of applications for the grant or variation or review of premises licences are contained in secondary legislation made by the Secretary of State and can be viewed on the DCMS website.

8.44    Applicants are required to:

- publish a notice in a local newspaper or, if there is none, in a local newsletter, circular or similar document circulating in the vicinity of the premises; and

- display a brief summary of the application on an A4 size notice immediately on or outside the premises.

8.45    The summary of the application should set out matters such as the proposed licensable activities and the proposed hours of opening and should be clearly displayed for the period during which representations may be made, together with information about where the details of the application may be viewed.

8.46    Licensing authorities in Wales should consider encouraging applicants to provide details in the alternative language (Welsh or English) to that of the main advertisement itself where the application may be viewed. Therefore, if an applicant publishes a notice in English they should be encouraged to provide a statement in Welsh as to where the application may be viewed, and vice versa. This would allow the reader of the notice to make enquiries to the licensing authority and find out the nature of the application.

8.47    Notices of applications to vary a premises licence should include a brief description of the proposed variation, e.g. details of extra hours applied for, hours varied from/to.

8.48    In the case of applications for premises licences involving internet or mail order sales, notices should be conspicuously displayed at the place where the alcohol is appropriated to the contract in accordance with the relevant regulations (see paragraph 3.6).

8.49    A vessel which is not permanently moored or berthed is treated as if it were a premises situated in a place where it is usually moored or berthed. The newspaper advertisement notice for such a vessel would need to be in relation to

this place (where it is usually moored or berthed) and there is no provision requiring such advertising in other areas, for instance, if the vessel journeys through other licensing authority areas.

8.50    So far as possible, as well as putting in place arrangements for interested parties to view a record of the application in the licensing register as described in Schedule 3 to the 2003 Act, it is expected that licensing authorities will also include these details on their websites. Charges made for copies of the register should not exceed the cost of preparing such copies.

8.51    Licensing authorities may wish to conduct random and unannounced visits to premises to confirm that notices have been clearly displayed and include relevant and accurate information.

8.52    It is open to licensing authorities to notify residents living in the vicinity of premises by circular of premises making an application, but this is not a statutory requirement.

## APPLICATIONS TO CHANGE THE DESIGNATED PREMISES SUPERVISORS

8.53    Paragraphs 4.19–4.28 above cover designated premises supervisors and applications to vary a premises licence covering sales of alcohol by specifying a new designated premises supervisor.

## PROVISIONAL STATEMENTS

8.54    Where premises are being or are about to be constructed, extended or otherwise altered for the purpose of being used for one or more licensable activities, investors may be unwilling to commit funds unless they have some assurance that a premises licence covering the desired licensable activities would be granted for the premises when the building work is completed.

8.55    The 2003 Act does not define the words "otherwise altered", but the alteration must relate to the purpose of being used for one or more licensable activities. For example, a premises licence should indicate the whole of or part of the premises which are licensed for one or more licensable activity. If the building is to be altered to allow a previously unlicensed area to be used for a licensable activity, a provisional statement may be sought for the additional area.

8.56   Any person falling within section 16 of the 2003 Act can apply for a premises licence before new premises are constructed, extended or changed. This would be possible where clear plans of the proposed structure exist and the applicant is in a position to complete an operating schedule including details of:

- the activities to take place there;
- the time at which such activities will take place;
- the proposed hours of opening;
- where the applicant wishes the licence to have effect for a limited period, that period;
- the steps to be taken to promote the licensing objectives; and
- where the sale of alcohol is involved, whether supplies are proposed to be for consumption on or off the premises (or both) and the name of the designated premises supervisor the applicant wishes to specify.

8.57   In such cases, the licensing authority would include in the licence the date upon which it would come into effect. A provisional statement will normally only be required when the information described above is not available.

8.58   The 2003 Act therefore provides for a person, if an individual aged 18 or over, who has an interest in the premises to apply for a "provisional statement". This will not be time limited, but the longer there is a delay before a premises licence is applied for, the more likely it is that there will be material changes and that the licensing authority will accept representations.

8.59   "Person" in this context includes a business. The applicant could be a firm of architects, a construction company or a financier. The application would include the particulars and plans of the premises, describe the work to be done and the licensable activities planned to take place at the premises. The application must be advertised and notified to responsible authorities in a similar way to the arrangements for applications for premises licences and as set out in regulations. Responsible authorities and interested parties may make representations. Where no representations are made, a provisional statement must be issued. Where relevant representations are made, the licensing authority must arrange a hearing to consider them. The need for a hearing can be dispensed with only by agreement of the licensing authority, the applicant for the provisional statement and all the parties who made relevant representations.

8.60   When a hearing is held, the licensing authority must decide whether, if the premises were constructed or altered in the way proposed in the schedule of works and if a premises licence was sought for those premises, it would consider it necessary for the promotion of the licensing objectives to:

- attach conditions to the licence;
- rule out any of the licensable activities applied for;
- refuse to specify the person nominated as premises supervisor; or
- reject the application.

8.61   It will then issue the applicant with a provisional statement setting out the details of that decision together with its reasons. The licensing authority must copy the provisional statement to each person who made relevant representations and the chief officer of police for the area in which the premises is situated. The licensing authority should give full and comprehensive reasons for its decision. This is important in anticipation of an appeal by any aggrieved party.

8.62   When a person applies for a premises licence in respect of premises (or part of the premises or premises which are substantially the same) for which a provisional statement has been made, representations by responsible authorities and interested parties will be excluded in certain circumstances. These are where:

- the application for a licence is in the same form as the licence described in the provisional statement;
- the work in the schedule of works has been satisfactorily completed; and
- given the information provided in the application for a provisional statement, the responsible authority or interested party could have made the same, or substantially the same, representations about the application then but failed to do so without reasonable excuse; and there has been no material change in the circumstances relating either to the premises or to the area in the vicinity of those premises since the provisional statement was made.

8.63   Licensing authorities should exclude representations in these circumstances. It will be important for investment and employment opportunities in their areas for provisional statements to function properly by providing a limited assurance. But it should be recognised that a great deal of time may pass between the issue of a provisional statement and the completion of a premises in accordance with a schedule of works. Genuine and material changes in circumstances may arise during the intervening years.

8.64   It should be noted that any decision of the licensing authority on an application for a provisional statement would not relieve an applicant of the need to apply for building control.

8.65   A provisional statement may not be sought or given for a vessel, a vehicle or a moveable structure (see section 189 of the 2003 Act).

## TRANSFERS OF PREMISES LICENCES

8.66   The 2003 Act provides for any person who may apply for a premises licence, which includes a business, to apply for a premises licence to be transferred to them. Notice of the application has to be given to the chief officer of police. Where an applicant is an individual they must be 18 years old or over. A transfer of a premises licence would often arise when a business involving licensable activities is sold to a new owner. A transfer of the licence only changes the identity of the holder of the licence and does not alter the licence in any other way.

8.67   In the vast majority of cases, it is expected that a transfer will be a very simple administrative process. Section 43 of the 2003 Act provides a mechanism which allows the transfer to come into immediate interim effect as soon as the licensing authority receives it, until it is formally determined or withdrawn. This is to ensure that there should be no interruption to normal business at the premises. If the police raise no objection about the application, the licensing authority must transfer the licence in accordance with the application, amend the licence accordingly and return it to the new holder.

8.68   In exceptional circumstances where the chief officer of police believes the transfer may undermine the crime prevention objective, the police may object to the transfer. Such objections are expected to be rare and arise because the police have evidence that the business or individuals seeking to hold the licence or business or individuals linked to such persons are involved in crime (or disorder). For example, the police would rightly seek to prevent a company having a licence transferred to it if they had evidence that the premises might be used to launder money obtained from drugs crime. Where an objection is made, the licensing authority must hold a hearing at which the authority will consider the objection. The authority's consideration would be confined to the issue of the crime prevention objective and the hearing should not be permitted to stray into other extraneous matters. The burden would be on the police to demonstrate to the authority that there were good grounds for believing that the transfer of the licence would undermine the crime prevention objective. The licensing authority must give clear and comprehensive reasons for its eventual determination in anticipation of a possible appeal by either party.

8.69    It is stressed that such objections (and therefore such hearings) should only arise in truly exceptional circumstances. If the licensing authority believes that the police are using this mechanism to vet transfer applicants routinely and to seek hearings as a fishing expedition to inquire into applicants' backgrounds, it is expected that it would raise the matter immediately with the chief officer of police.

## INTERIM AUTHORITIES

8.70    The 2003 Act provides special arrangements for the continuation of permissions under a premises licence when the holder of a licence dies suddenly or becomes bankrupt or mentally incapable. In the normal course of events, the licence would lapse in such circumstances. However, there may also be some time before, for example, the deceased person's estate can be dealt with or an administrative receiver appointed. This could have a damaging effect on those with interests in the premises, such as an owner, lessor or employees working at the premises in question; and could bring unnecessary disruption to customers' plans. The Act therefore provides for the licence to be capable of being reinstated in a discrete period of time in certain circumstances.

8.71    These circumstances arise only where a premises licence has lapsed owing to the death, incapacity or insolvency of the holder. In such circumstances, an "interim

authority" notice may be given to the licensing authority within seven days beginning the day after the licence lapsed. It should also be copied to the chief officer of police. The premises licence would lapse until such a notice is given and carrying on licensable activities in that time would be unlawful. Such activity will be an offence as an unauthorised licensable activity under section 136(1)(a) of the 2003 Act, to which there is a "defence of due diligence" provided in section 139. This may be relevant where, for example, the manager of particular premises is wholly unaware for a period of time that the premises licence holder has died. As soon as an interim authority notice is given within the seven day period, the business may continue to carry on any licensable activities permitted by the premises licence.

8.72    An interim notice may only be given either by a person with a prescribed interest in the premises as set out by the Secretary of State in regulations which may be viewed on the DCMS website; or by a person connected to the former holder of the licence (normally a personal representative of the former holder or a person with power of attorney or where someone has become insolvent that person's insolvency practitioner).

8.73    The effect of giving the notice is to reinstate the premises licence as if the person giving the notice is the holder of the licence and thereby allow licensable activities to continue to take place pending a formal application for transfer. The maximum period for which an interim authority notice may have effect is two months.

8.74    The interim authority notice ceases to have effect unless by the end of the initial 7 day period a copy of the notice has been given to the chief officer of police. Within 48 hours of receiving the copy, and if satisfied that in the exceptional circumstances of the case failure to cancel the interim authority would undermine the crime prevention objective, the police may give a notice to that effect to the licensing authority. In such circumstances, the licensing authority must hold a hearing to consider the objection notice and cancel the interim authority notice if it decides that it is necessary to do so for the promotion of the crime prevention objective.

8.75    It is expected that licensing authorities will be alert to the urgency of the circumstances and the need to consider the objection quickly.

8.76    It should also be noted that, under section 50 of the 2003 Act, where the premises licence lapses (because of death, incapacity or insolvency of the holder etc) or by its surrender, but no interim authority notice has effect, a person who may apply for the grant of a premises licence under section 16(1) may apply within 7 days of the lapse for the transfer of the licence to them with immediate effect pending the determination of the application. This will result in the licence being reinstated from the point at which the transfer application was received by the licensing authority. The person applying for the transfer must copy their application to the chief officer of police.

## RIGHT OF FREEHOLDERS ETC TO BE NOTIFIED OF LICENSING MATTERS

8.77    A person (which will include a business or company) with a property interest in any premises situated in the licensing authority's area may give notice of their interest to the authority using a prescribed form and on payment of a fee prescribed by the Secretary of State. Details of fees and forms are available on the DCMS website. It is entirely at the discretion of such persons whether they choose to register or not. It is not a legal requirement. Those who may take advantage of this arrangement include the freeholder or leaseholder, a legal mortgagee in respect of the premises, a person in occupation of the premises or any other person prescribed by the Secretary of State.

8.78    The notice will have effect for 12 months but a new notice can be given every year. Whilst the notice has effect, if any change relating to the premises concerned has been made to the licensing register (which the licensing authority has a duty to keep under section 8 of the 2003 Act), the licensing authority must notify the person who registered an interest of the matter to which the change relates. The person will also be notified of their right under section 8 to request a copy of the information contained in any entry in the register. In cases relating to interim authority notices (see above), it is important that such communications are dealt with promptly.

App 11

# 9. Determining applications

## GENERAL

9.1    When a licensing authority receives an application for a new premises licence or an application to vary an existing premises licence, it must determine whether the application has been made properly in accordance with section 17 of the 2003 Act, and in accordance with regulations made by the Secretary of State under sections 17(4), 17(5), 54 and 55 of the Act. This means that the licensing authority must consider among other things whether the application has been properly advertised in accordance with the regulations.

## WHERE NO REPRESENTATIONS ARE MADE

9.2    A hearing is not required where an application has been lawfully made and no responsible authority or interested party has made a representation. In these cases, the licensing authority must grant the application in the terms sought, subject only to conditions which are consistent with the operating schedule and relevant mandatory conditions in the Act. This should be undertaken as a simple administrative process by the licensing authority's officials who should translate the proposals contained in the operating schedule to promote the licensing objectives into clear and understandable conditions.

## WHERE REPRESENTATIONS ARE MADE

9.3    Where a representation concerning the licensing objectives is lodged by a responsible authority about a proposed operating schedule it is relevant and the licensing authority's discretion will be engaged. It will also be engaged if an interested party makes relevant representations to the licensing authority, i.e. those which are not frivolous or vexatious and which relate to the licensing objectives (see paragraphs 9.8–9.13 below). Representations can be made in opposition to, or in support of, an application.

9.4    It is for the licensing authority to decide in the first instance whether or not representations are relevant. This may involve determining whether they have been made by an interested party and whether or not, for example, an individual making a representation resides or is involved in business "in the vicinity" of the premises concerned. However, licensing authorities should be aware that their initial decision on this issue could be subject to legal challenge in the courts.

9.5    In making their initial decision on the question of vicinity, licensing authorities should consider whether the individual's residence or business is likely to be directly affected by disorder and disturbance occurring or potentially occurring on those premises or immediately outside the premises. In other words, it is the impact of issues relating to the four licensing objectives that is the key consideration.

9.6    The Government recommends that, where local authorities have chosen to define vicinity as a fixed distance from a premises, they should only ever use this as a guideline and should indicate in their policy statements that they will consider representations from those who live or work outside that distance if they can demonstrate that they are (or, in the case of new premises, are likely to be), affected by disorder and disturbance occurring (or potentially occurring) on those premises.

9.7    Where a representation concerns "cumulative impact", the licensing authority may be unable to consider this factor and would probably need to examine issues such as the proximity of the residence or business. In essence, it is expected that the decision will be approached with common sense and individuals living and working in the neighbourhood or area immediately surrounding the premises will be able to make representations.

## RELEVANT, VEXATIOUS AND FRIVOLOUS REPRESENTATIONS

9.8     A representation would only be "relevant" if it relates to the likely effect of the grant of the licence on the promotion of at least one of the licensing objectives. For example, a representation from a local businessman which argued that his business would be commercially damaged by a new licensed premises would not be relevant. On the other hand, a representation that nuisance caused by the new premises would deter customers from entering the local area and the steps proposed by the applicant to control that nuisance were inadequate would be relevant. There is no requirement for an interested party or responsible authority to produce a recorded history of problems at a premises to support their representations, and in fact this would not be possible for new premises. Further information for interested parties about the process for making representations is available in "Guidance for interested parties: Making representations" which can be found on the DCMS website.

9.9     The "cumulative impact" on the licensing objectives of a concentration of multiple licensed premises may also give rise to a relevant representation when an application for the grant or variation of a premises licence is being considered, but not in relation to an application for review which must relate to an individual premises.

9.10     It is for the licensing authority to determine whether any representation by an interested party is frivolous or vexatious on the basis of what might ordinarily be considered to be vexatious or frivolous. Vexation may arise because of disputes between rival businesses and local knowledge will therefore be invaluable in considering such matters. Frivolous representations would be essentially categorised by a lack of seriousness. An interested party who is aggrieved by a rejection of their representations on these grounds may challenge the authority's decision by way of judicial review.

9.11     Licensing authorities should not take decisions on whether representations are relevant on the basis of any political judgement. This may be difficult for ward councillors receiving complaints from residents within their own wards. If consideration is not to be delegated, contrary to the recommendation in this Guidance, an assessment should be prepared by officials for consideration by the subcommittee before any decision is taken that necessitates a hearing. Any ward councillor who considers that their own interests are such that they are unable to consider the matter independently should disqualify themselves.

9.12     The Secretary of State recommends that in borderline cases, the benefit of the doubt should be given to the interested party making the representation. The subsequent hearing would then provide an opportunity for the person or body making the representation to amplify and clarify it. If it then emerged, for example, that the representation should not be supported, the licensing authority could decide not to take any action in respect of the application.

9.13     Licensing authorities should consider providing advice on their websites about how any interested party can make representations to them.

App 11

## DISCLOSURE OF PERSONAL DETAILS OF INTERESTED PARTIES

9.14    Where a notice of a hearing is given to an applicant, the licensing authority is required under the Licensing Act 2003 (Hearings) Regulations 2005 to provide to the applicant with the notice and copies of the relevant representations that have been made.

9.15    In some exceptional and isolated circumstances interested parties may be reluctant to make representations because of fears of intimidation or violence if their personal details, such as name and address, are divulged to the applicant.

9.16    Where licensing authorities consider that the interested party has a genuine and well-founded fear of intimidation and may be deterred from making a representation because of this, they may wish to consider alternative approaches.

9.17    For instance, they could advise interested parties to provide the relevant responsible authority with details of how they consider that the licensing objectives are being undermined so that the responsible authority can make representations if appropriate and justified.

9.18    The licensing authority may also decide to withhold some or all of the interested party's personal details from the applicant, giving only enough details (such as street name or general location within a street) which would allow an applicant to be satisfied that the interested party is within the vicinity of the premises. However, withholding such detail should only be considered where the circumstances justify such action and the licensing authority is satisfied that the complaints are not frivolous or vexatious.

## HEARINGS

9.19    Regulations governing hearings may be viewed on the DCMS website. If the licensing authority decides that representations are relevant, it must hold a hearing to consider them. The need for a hearing can only be dispensed with by the agreement of the licensing authority, the applicant and all of the parties who made relevant representations. In cases where only 'positive' representations are received, without qualifications, the licensing authority should consider whether a hearing is necessary. To this end it may wish to notify the interested parties concerned and give them the opportunity to withdraw their representations. This would need to be done in sufficient time before the hearing to ensure that parties were not put to unnecessary inconvenience.

9.20    Responsible authorities should try to conclude any discussions with the applicant in good time before the hearing. If the application is amended at the last moment, the licensing committee should consider giving interested parties time to address the revised application before the hearing commences.

9.21    The Regulations require that representations must be withdrawn 24 hours before the first day of any hearing. If they are withdrawn after this time, the hearing must proceed. However, where discussions between an applicant and those making representations are taking place and it is likely that all parties are on the point of reaching agreement, the licensing authority may wish to use the power given within the hearings regulations to extend time limits, if it considers this to be in the public interest.

9.22    Applicants should be encouraged to contact responsible authorities before formulating their applications so that the mediation process may begin before the statutory time limits come into effect after submission of an application. The hearing process must meet the requirements of Regulations made by the Secretary of State. Where matters arise which are not covered by the Regulations, licensing authorities may make arrangements as they see fit as long as they are lawful.

9.23    There is no requirement in the Act for responsible authorities that have made representations to attend, but it is generally good practice and assists committees to reach more informed decisions. Where several responsible authorities within a local authority have made representations on an application, a single local authority officer may represent them at the hearing if the responsible authorities and the licensing authority agree. However, an officer of the licensing authority may not perform this role which would compromise the licensing authority's independence.

9.24 As a matter of practice, licensing authorities should seek to focus the hearing on the steps needed to promote the particular licensing objective which has given rise to the specific representation and avoid straying into undisputed areas. A responsible authority or interested party may choose to rely on their written representation. They may not add further representations to those disclosed to the applicant prior to the hearing, but they may expand on their existing representation.

9.25 In determining the application with a view to promoting the licensing objectives in the overall interests of the local community, the licensing authority must give appropriate weight to:

- the steps that are necessary to promote the licensing objectives;
- the representations (including supporting information) presented by all the parties;
- this Guidance;
- its own statement of licensing policy.

9.26 The licensing authority should give its decision at once, unless the Act itself states otherwise and provide reasons to support it. This will be important if there is an appeal by any of the parties. Notification of a decision must be accompanied by information on the right of the party to appeal. After considering all the relevant issues, the licensing authority may grant the application subject to such conditions that are consistent with the operating schedule. Any conditions imposed must be necessary for the promotion of the licensing objectives; there is no power for the licensing authority to attach a condition which is merely aspirational. For example, conditions may not be attached which relate solely to the health of customers rather than their direct physical safety.

9.27 Alternatively, the licensing authority may refuse the application on the grounds that this is necessary for the promotion of the licensing objectives. It may also refuse to specify a designated premises supervisor and/or only allow certain requested licensable activities. In the interests of transparency, the licensing authority should publish hearings procedures in full on its website to ensure that interested parties and others have the most current information.

9.28 In the context of variations, which may involve structural alteration to or change of use of the building, the decision of the licensing authority will not exempt an applicant from the need to apply for building control or planning consent where appropriate.

# 10. Conditions attached to premises licences and club premises certificates

## GENERAL

10.1    This chapter provides advice and recommendations concerning best practice in relation to conditions attached to premises licences and club premises certificates.

10.2    Conditions include any limitations or restrictions attached to a licence or certificate and essentially are the steps or actions the holder of the premises licence or the club premises certificate will be required to take or refrain from taking at all times when licensable activities are taking place at the premises in question.

10.3    All interests – licensing authorities, licence and certificate holders, authorised persons, the police, other responsible authorities and local residents and businesses – should be working together in partnership to ensure collectively that the licensing objectives are promoted.

10.4    Under former licensing regimes, the courts have made clear that it is particularly important that conditions which are imprecise or difficult for a licence holder to observe should be avoided. Failure to comply with any conditions attached to a licence or certificate is a criminal offence, which on conviction would be punishable by a fine of up to £20,000 or up to six months imprisonment or both.

10.5    Annex D provides pools of conditions (although not an exhaustive list) which relate to the four licensing objectives and could be used where necessary and appropriate to the particular circumstances of an individual licensed premises. It is important that they should not be applied universally and treated as standard conditions irrespective of circumstances.

10.6    There are three types of condition that may be attached to a licence or certificate: proposed, imposed and mandatory. Each of these categories is described in more detail below.

## PROPOSED CONDITIONS

10.7    The conditions that are necessary for the promotion of the licensing objectives should emerge initially from a prospective licensee's or certificate holder's risk assessment which applicants and clubs should carry out before making their application for a premises licence or club premises certificate. This would be translated into the steps recorded in the operating schedule or club operating schedule which must also set out the proposed hours of opening.

10.8    In order to minimise problems and the necessity for hearings, it would be sensible for applicants and clubs to consult with responsible authorities when schedules are being prepared. This would allow for proper liaison before representations prove necessary.

## CONSISTENCY WITH STEPS DESCRIBED IN OPERATING SCHEDULE

10.9    The 2003 Act provides that where an operating schedule or club operating schedule has been submitted with an application and there have been no relevant representations made by responsible authorities or interested parties, the licence or certificate must be granted subject only to such conditions as are consistent with the schedule accompanying the application and any mandatory conditions required by the Act itself.

10.10   Consistency means that the effect of the condition should be substantially the same as that intended by the terms of the operating schedule or club operating schedule. Some applicants for licences or certificates supported by legal representatives or trade associations can be expected to express steps necessary to promote the licensing objectives in clear and readily translatable terms. However, some applicants will express the terms of their operating schedules less precisely or concisely. Ensuring that conditions are consistent with the operating schedule will then be more difficult. If conditions are broken this may lead to a criminal prosecution or an application for a review and it is extremely important therefore that they should be expressed on the licence or certificate in unequivocal and unambiguous terms. It must be clear to the holder of the licence or club, to enforcement officers and to the courts what duty has been placed on the holder or club in terms of compliance.

## IMPOSED CONDITIONS

10.11  The licensing authority may not impose any conditions unless its discretion has been engaged following receipt of relevant representations and it has been satisfied at a hearing of the necessity to impose conditions. It may then only impose conditions that are necessary to promote one or more of the four licensing objectives. Such conditions must also be expressed in unequivocal and unambiguous terms to avoid legal dispute.

10.12  It is perfectly possible that in certain cases, because the test is one of necessity, where there are other legislative provisions which are relevant and must be observed by the applicant, no additional conditions at all are needed to promote the licensing objectives.

### Proportionality

10.13  The Act requires that licensing conditions should be tailored to the size, style, characteristics and activities taking place at the premises concerned. This rules out standardised conditions which ignore these individual aspects. It is

important that conditions are proportionate and properly recognise significant differences between venues. For example, charities, community groups, voluntary groups, churches, schools and hospitals which host smaller events and festivals will not usually be pursuing these events commercially with a view to profit and will inevitably operate within limited resources.

10.14  While the Secretary of State has set fees centrally for licences and certificates, licensing authorities and responsible authorities should be alive to the indirect costs that can arise because of conditions attached to licences. These could be a deterrent to holding events that are valuable to the community or for the funding of good and important causes. Such bodies may be loath to pursue appeals against any unnecessary conditions because of the costs involved. Licensing authorities should therefore ensure that any conditions they impose are only those which are necessary for the promotion of the licensing objectives, which means that they must not go further than what is needed for that purpose. Public safety concerns (and the concerns identified in the other objectives) should not of course be ignored and in considering a proportionate response to the licensing needs for such events, the physical safety of those attending such events should remain a primary objective.

### Duplication with other statutory provisions

10.15  Licensing authorities should only impose conditions which are necessary and proportionate for the promotion for the licensing objectives. If other existing law already places certain statutory responsibilities on an employer or operator of premises, it cannot be necessary to impose the same or similar duties. For example, employers and self-employed people are required by the Management of Health and Safety at Work Regulations 1999 (SI 1999/ 3242) to assess the risks to their workers and any others (including members of the public visiting the premises) who may be affected by their business and identify measures needed to avoid or control risks. Conditions enforcing these requirements are therefore unnecessary.

10.16  Similarly, licensing authorities should not seek to impose fire safety conditions that may duplicate any requirements or prohibitions that could be imposed under the Regulatory Reform (Fire Safety) Order 2005 (see paragraphs 2.20–2.29).

10.17  Further, the Act does not affect the continued use of inspection and enforcement powers conferred by other legislation; for example, the powers of an environmental health officer in relation to statutory nuisance under the Environmental Protection Act 1990.

10.18  However, these general duties will not always adequately address specific issues that arise on the premises in connection with, for example, certain types of entertainment. It is only where additional and supplementary measures are necessary to promote the licensing objectives that conditions will need to be attached to a licence.

## Hours of trading

10.19  In some town and city centre areas where the number, type and density of premises selling alcohol for consumption on the premises are unusual, serious problems of nuisance and disorder may arise outside or some distance from licensed premises. For example, concentrations of young drinkers can result in queues at fast food outlets and for public transport, which may in turn lead to conflict, disorder and anti-social behaviour. In some circumstances, flexible licensing hours may reduce this impact by allowing a more gradual dispersal of customers from premises.

10.20  However, there is no general presumption in favour of lengthening licensing hours and the four

licensing objectives should be paramount considerations at all times. Where there are objections to an application and the committee believes that changing the licensing hours would undermine the licensing objectives, they may reject the application or grant it with appropriate conditions and/or different hours from those requested.

10.21  Shops, stores and supermarkets should normally be free to provide sales of alcohol for consumption off the premises at any times when the retail outlet is open for shopping unless there are good reasons, based on the licensing objectives, for restricting those hours. For example, a limitation may be appropriate following police representations in the case of some shops known to be a focus of disorder and disturbance because youths gather there.

## Workers rights

10.22  It is not for the licensing authority to consider such matters as the rights of the workers employed on the premises who may be asked to work longer hours. There are existing protections under the Working Time Regulations 1998 (SI 1998/1833), the Employment Rights Act 1996 (as amended) and under the general employment law and laws of contract.

## Disabled people

10.23  It is important that proper steps should be taken to provide for the safety of people and performers with disabilities. However, licensing authorities and responsible authorities should avoid well meaning conditions which are intended to provide for the safety of people or performers with disabilities, but which may actively deter operators from admitting or employing them.

10.24  It is Government policy that facilities for people and performers with disabilities should be provided at places of entertainment. The Secretary of State encourages licence holders and clubs to provide facilities enabling their admission and reminds them of the duties imposed by the Disability Discrimination Act 1995. The law provides that any person providing a service to the public must make reasonable adjustments to enable disabled people to access the service. No licensing condition should therefore be attached to a licence or certificate which conflicts with or duplicates this requirement.

10.25 Service providers also have a duty to make reasonable adjustments to any physical features which make it impossible or unreasonably difficult for disabled persons to access a service, or they have to provide the service by a reasonable alternative means. Access to buildings and their facilities is also a matter addressed in Building Regulations and planned alterations affecting access may involve the need to apply for building control.

10.26 Licensing authorities should therefore be ready to offer advice to applicants for licences and certificates about how to achieve this. Conditions which state that "wheelchairs and similar equipment shall not be allowed on the premises except in accordance with the terms of any consent issued by the licensing authority" can be ambiguous and be used to justify exclusion and may be ultra vires. Conditions should be positively worded and assume the presence of people with disabilities on licensed premises.

10.27 In addition, Government guidelines exempting guide and assistance dogs from health and safety requirements have been in place since 1995. Any condition of a licence or certificate which states that "pets" may not be present on licensed premises for public safety reasons, must include a clear indication that the condition does not apply to guide or assistance dogs. Further advice can be obtained from the Disability Rights Commission's website www.drc-gb.org.

10.28 The Disability Discrimination Act 1995 does not apply to ships. However the European Council

Directive 2003/24/EC requires appropriate measures to be taken for 'persons of reduced mobility' (this means anyone who has a particular difficulty when using public transport; including elderly persons, disabled persons, persons with sensory impairments and wheelchair users, pregnant women and persons accompanying small children) on certain passenger ships engaged on domestic voyages. Further advice and guidance is contained in Merchant Shipping Notice 1789 (M) and Marine Guidance Note 306 (M) both of which are available in the Guidance and Regulations section of the Maritime and Coastguard Agency's website www.mcga.gov.uk. These documents complement the existing guidance 'The design of large passenger ships and passenger infrastructure: Guidance on meeting the needs of disabled people' which is available on the website of the Disabled Persons Transport Advisory Committee at www.dptac.gov.uk in the maritime section.

## Race equality

10.29 Licensing authorities should also avoid imposing any condition on a licence or certificate which appears to apply to a wide group of people, but in fact would have an indirect discriminatory impact on particular ethnic groups. For example, a representation requesting that "No Travellers" or "No Caravan-Dwellers" be displayed inside or on premises purportedly to prevent crime or disorder should not be accepted not least because it would conflict with the authority's race equality scheme.

## The performance of plays

10.30 The 2003 Act provides that other than for the purposes of public safety, conditions must not be attached to premises licences or club premises certificates authorising the performance of a play which attempt to censor or modify the content of plays in any way. Any such condition would be ultra vires the Act.

App 11

## Censorship

10.31   In general, other than in the context of film classification for film exhibitions, licensing authorities should not use their powers under the 2003 Act to seek to impose conditions which censor the content of any form of regulated entertainment. This is not a proper function of licensing law and cannot be properly related to the licensing objectives. The content of regulated entertainment is a matter which is addressed by existing laws governing indecency and obscenity. Where the concern is about protecting children, their access should be restricted where necessary. But no other limitation should normally be imposed.

## Copyright and royalties

10.32   Copyright law is intended to safeguard the livelihood of authors, composers, arrangers, playwrights, film-makers, publishers and makers of recordings and is extremely important and offences relating to copyright are made "relevant offences" by the 2003 Act. Conditions attached to premises licences should not require adherence to requirements in the general law that the use of copyright material must be authorised. Licensing authorities should however strongly remind applicants of the need to obtain Performing Right Society (PRS) licences and Phonographic Performance Ltd (PPL) licences and to observe other copyright arrangements; and that failure to observe the law in this area could lead to an application for the review of the premises licence or the club premises certificate on grounds of the crime prevention objective.

## Major art and pop festivals, carnivals, fairs and circuses

10.33   Licensing authorities should publicise the need for the organisers of major festivals and carnivals to approach them at the earliest opportunity to discuss arrangements for licensing activities falling under the 2003 Act. For some events, the organisers may seek a single premises licence to cover a wide range of activities at varied locations within the premises. This would involve the preparation of a substantial operating schedule, and licensing authorities should offer advice and assistance about its preparation. In particular, the licensing authority should act as a coordinating body for the input from the responsible authorities.

10.34   For other events, applications for many connected premises licences may be made which in combination will represent a single festival. It is important that licensing authorities should publicise the need for proper co-ordination of such arrangements and will need to ensure that responsible authorities are aware of the connected nature of the individual applications. Licensing authorities should encourage applicants to establish a coordinating committee to ensure a strategic approach to the development of operating schedules. The purpose would be to ensure that conditions are not included in licences which conflict with each other, make compliance uncertain or would be difficult to enforce.

10.35   In the case of circuses and fairgrounds, much will depend on the content of any entertainment presented. For example, at fairgrounds, a good deal of the musical entertainment may be incidental to the main attractions and rides at the fair which are not themselves regulated entertainment. However, in the case of a circus, music and dancing are likely to be main attractions themselves (and would be regulated entertainment) amidst a range of other activities which are not all regulated entertainment.

10.36   Particular regard should be paid to the relevant guidance provided in the publications listed at Annex E of this Guidance under 'Public Safety'.

10.37   In addition, in the context of festivals and carnivals, local authorities should bear in mind their ability to seek premises licences from the licensing authority for land or buildings under public ownership within the community in their own name. This could include, for example, village greens, market squares, promenades, community halls, local authority owned art centres and similar public areas where festivals and carnivals might take place. Performers and entertainers would then have no need to obtain a licence or give a temporary event notice themselves to enable them to give performances in these places, although they would need the permission of the local authority to put on the event. Care should be exercised to ensure that there is no confusion between the role of enforcing licensing legislation, which falls to the licensing authority, and the role of providing advice and assistance to festival and carnival organisers from other parts of the local authority.

## Discounting and sales promotions

10.38 Licensing authorities should not attach standardised blanket conditions promoting fixed prices for alcoholic drinks to premises licences or club licences or club premises certificates in an area as this is likely to breach competition law. It is also likely to be unlawful for licensing authorities or the police to promote generalised voluntary schemes or codes of practice in relation to price discounts on alcoholic drinks, 'happy hours' or drinks promotions.

10.39 However, it is acceptable for licensing authorities to encourage adoption locally of voluntary industry codes of practice which cover irresponsible drinks promotions such as that produced by the British Beer and Pub Association (the BBPA's Guidelines on On-Trade Promotions).

10.40 In general, licensing authorities should consider each application on its individual merits, tailoring any conditions carefully to cover only irresponsible promotions in the particular and individual circumstances of any premises where these are necessary for the promotion of the licensing objectives. In addition, when considering any relevant

representations which demonstrate a clear causal link between sales promotions or price discounting and levels of crime and disorder on or in the vicinity of the premises, it would be appropriate for the licensing authority to consider the imposition of a new condition prohibiting irresponsible sales promotions or the discounting of prices of alcoholic beverages at those premises. However, before pursuing any form of restrictions at all, licensing authorities should take their own legal advice. There will often be very fine lines between what is and is not lawful within the scope of their power under the 2003 Act.

## Large capacity venues used exclusively or primarily for the "vertical" consumption of alcohol (HVVDs)

10.41 Large capacity "vertical drinking" premises, sometimes called High Volume Vertical Drinking establishments (HVVDs), are premises with exceptionally high capacities, which are used primarily or exclusively for the sale and consumption of alcohol, and have little or no seating for patrons.

10.42 A comprehensive review of the research conducted in the last twenty-five years into alcohol and crime and its relationship to licensed premises, "Alcohol and Crime: Taking Stock" by Ann Deehan, Home Office Crime Reduction Research Series No.3 (1999) can be viewed on www.crimereduction.gov.uk/drugsalcohol8.htm. It shows that the environment within such establishments can have a significant bearing on the likelihood of crime and disorder arising on the premises. Key points on preventing crime and disorder include:

- controlling the capacity to prevent overcrowding and frustration to customers;
- ensuring adequate seating for customers; and
- ensuring the provision of door security teams at the premises to control capacity and ensure already drunk or disorderly individuals are not admitted.

App 11

10.43 Where necessary and appropriate, conditions can be attached to premises licences for the promotion of the prevention of crime and disorder at such premises (if not volunteered by the venue operator and following representations made on such grounds) which require adherence to:

- a prescribed capacity;
- an appropriate ratio of tables and chairs to customers based on the capacity; and
- the presence of security staff holding the appropriate SIA licence or exemption (see paragraphs 10.58–10.64) to control entry for the purpose of compliance with the capacity limit and to deny entry to individuals who appear drunk or disorderly or both.

## MANDATORY CONDITIONS

10.44 Where the 2003 Act provides for a mandatory condition to be included in a premises licence, it is the duty of the licensing authority issuing the licence to include that condition on the premises licence.

### Designated Premises Supervisor

10.45 Any premises at which alcohol is sold or supplied may employ one or more personal licence holders. The main purpose of the 'designated premises supervisor' as defined in the 2003 Act is to ensure that there is always one specified individual among these personal licence holders who can be readily identified for the premises where a premises licence is in force. That person will normally have been given day to day responsibility for running the premises by the premises licence holder.

10.46 The 2003 Act provides that, where a premises licence authorises the supply of alcohol, it must include a condition that no supply of alcohol may be made at a time when no designated premises supervisor has been specified in the licence or at a time when the designated premises supervisor does not hold a personal licence or their licence has been suspended.

10.47 The Act does not require a designated premises supervisor or any other personal licence holder to be present on the premises at all times when alcohol is sold. However, the designated premises supervisor and the premises licence holder remain responsible for the premises at all times including compliance with the terms of the Licensing Act and conditions attached to the premises licence to promote the licensing objectives.

### Authorisation by personal licence holders

10.48 In addition, the licence must require that every supply of alcohol under the premises licence must be made or authorised by a person who holds a personal licence. This in most instances will be the designated premises supervisor who must hold a valid personal licence. This does not mean that the condition should require the presence of the designated premises supervisor or any other personal licence holder on the premises at all material times.

10.49 Similarly, the fact that every supply of alcohol must be made under the authority of a personal licence holder does not mean that only personal licence holders can make sales or that they must be personally present at every transaction. A personal licence holder may authorise members of staff to make sales of alcohol but may be absent at times from the premises when a transaction takes place. However, the responsible personal licence holder will not be able to escape responsibility for the actions of anyone authorised to make sales.

10.50 "Authorisation" does not imply direct supervision by a personal licence holder of each sale of alcohol. The question arises as to how sales can be authorised. Ultimately, whether an authorisation has been given is a question of fact that would have to be decided by the courts on the evidence before it in the course of a criminal prosecution.

10.51 Nevertheless, it is important that licensing authorities, the police, employers and employees in the alcohol retail industry are given advice which promotes greater clarity and consistency. The Secretary of State considers that the following factors should be relevant in considering whether or not an authorisation has been given:

- the person(s) authorised to sell alcohol at any particular premises should be clearly identified;
- the authorisation should have specified the acts which may be carried out by the person being authorised;
- there should be an overt act of authorisation, for example, a specific written statement given to the individual being authorised; and
- there should be in place sensible arrangements for the personal licence holder to monitor the activity that they have authorised on a reasonably regular basis.

10.52 The Secretary of State strongly recommends that personal licence holders give specific written authorisations to individuals that they are authorising to retail alcohol. A single written authorisation would be sufficient to cover multiple sales over an unlimited period. This would assist personal licence holders in demonstrating due diligence should issues arise with enforcement authorities; and would protect employees if they themselves are challenged in respect of their authority to sell alcohol. The form of written authorisation is a matter for the personal licence holder, but the Secretary of State recommends that it should satisfy the criteria listed in the paragraph above. Written authorisation is not a requirement of the Act and its absence alone could not give rise to enforcement action.

10.53 It must be remembered that whilst the designated premises supervisor or a personal licence holder may authorise other individuals to sell alcohol in their absence, they are responsible for any sales that may be made. Similarly, the premises licence holder remains responsible for ensuring that licensing law and licence conditions are observed at the premises.

## Exhibition of films

10.54 The 2003 Act provides that where a premises licence or club premises certificate authorises the exhibition of a film, it must include a condition requiring the admission of children to films to be restricted in accordance with recommendations given either by a body designated under section 4 of the Video Recordings Act 1984 specified in the licence (currently only the British Board of Film Classification – BBFC) or by the licensing authority itself.

10.55 The BBFC classifies films in accordance with its published Guidelines which are based on extensive research into public opinion and professional advice. The Secretary of State therefore recommends that licensing authorities should not duplicate this effort by choosing to classify films themselves. The classifications recommended by the Board should be those normally applied unless there are very good local reasons for a licensing authority to adopt this role. Licensing authorities should note that the provisions of the 2003 Act enable them to specify the Board in the licence or certificate and, in relation to individual films, to notify the holder or club that it will make a recommendation for that particular film.

10.56 It should be noted that the effect of paragraph 5 of Schedule 1 of the Act is to exempt adverts from the definition of regulated entertainment, but not to exempt them from the definition of exhibition of a film. Since the above mandatory condition applies to 'any film' it is therefore applicable to the exhibition of adverts.

10.57 See Annex D, Part 5 for further Guidance on current BBFC classifications and other conditions relating to the exhibition of films.

## Door supervision

10.58 Under section 21 of the 2003 Act when a condition is included in a premises licence that at specified times an individual must be present at the premises to carry out a security activity (as defined in

App 11

section 21(3)(a) by reference to the Private Security Industry Act 2001 ("the 2001 Act")), the licence must include a condition requiring that individual to be licensed by the Security Industry Authority ("the SIA") under that Act, or be entitled to carry out that activity by virtue of section 4 of that Act.

10.59 Section 21 of the 2003 Act has been amended by section 25 of the Violent Crime Reduction Act 2006 to remove an anomaly whereby premises licences could require persons to be licensed by the SIA in circumstances where they were not required to be licensed under the 2001 Act. In particular, the amendment ensures that a premises licence need not require a person to hold a Security Industry Authority licence if they benefit from an exemption under section 4 of the 2001 Act. By way of example, certain employees benefit from an exemption when carrying out conduct in connection with a certified sports grounds (s.4(6 to 12)). Furthermore, in certain circumstances persons benefit from an exemption where they operate under the SIA's Approved Contractor Scheme (s4(4)).

10.60 Conditions under section 21 of the 2003 Act (as amended by the Violent Crime Reduction Act 2006) should only relate to individuals carrying out security activities defined by section 21(3)(a) of the 2003 Act. Therefore they should only relate to an activity to which paragraph 2(1)(a) of Schedule 2 to the 2001 Act applies (certain manned guarding activities) and which is licensable conduct within the meaning of section 3(2) of that Act. The requirement does not relate to individuals performing non-security related activities, and section 21 should not be used in relation to any such activities.

10.61 Section 21 of the 2003 Act continues to ensure that a premises licence need not impose such a requirement in relation to those licensed premises which the 2001 Act treats as unlicensed premises. Those are:

– premises staging plays or exhibiting films;

– casinos or bingo halls licensed under the Gaming Act 1968;

– premises where a club certificate is in force when activities are being carried on under the authority of that certificate;

See paragraph 8(3) of Schedule 2 to the 2001 Act for full details.

10.62 It should be noted, however, that the 2001 Act will require contractors and a small number of employees (those managing/supervising and those supplied under contract) to be licensed as manned guards (rather than door supervisors) when undertaking licensable conduct on premises to which paragraph 8(3) of Schedule 2 to the 2001 Act applies.

10.63 It is therefore important that if a licensing authority intends that individuals must be present to carry out security activities (as defined by section 21(3)(a) of the 2003 Act) this should be explicit, as should the mandatory condition for those individuals to hold an SIA licence or be entitled to carry out that activity by virtue of section 4 of that Act. On the other hand, where a licensing authority intends that individuals must be present to carry out other activities (for example, activities related to safety or steward activities to organise, advise and direct members of the public) no mandatory condition should be imposed under section 21 of the 2003 Act. In all cases it is important when determining whether or not a condition is to be imposed under section 21 of the 2003 Act to consider whether the activities of any individual working in licensed premises fall within the definition of security activities in section 21(3)(a) of the 2003 Act. (Regardless of whether a condition is imposed under section 21, under the 2001 Act the appropriate SIA licence must be held by any individual performing an activity for which they are licensable under that Act).

10.64 Holders of premises licences should note that the amendment under the Violent Crime Reduction Act 2006 will not affect the requirements in existing licences regarding security provision. Anyone wishing to deploy staff under the terms of the amended legislation and whose licence does not permit them to do so will need to apply to have their licence varied. The Government recommends that where an application is made to vary a licence solely in order to remove the anomaly referred to in paragraph 10.59 the licensing authority should treat the matter as expeditiously as possible, in recognition of the fact that the variation sought will almost always be purely technical in nature.

# 11.  Reviews

## THE REVIEW PROCESS

11.1   The proceedings set out in the 2003 Act for reviewing premises licences represent a key protection for the community where problems associated with the licensing objectives are occurring after the grant or variation of a premises licence.

11.2   At any stage, following the grant of a premises licence, a responsible authority, or an interested party, may ask the licensing authority to review the licence because of a matter arising at the premises in connection with any of the four licensing objectives.

11.3   In addition, a review of the licence will normally follow any action by the police to close down the premises for up to 24 hours on grounds of disorder or noise nuisance as a result of a notice of magistrates' court's determination sent to the licensing authority.

11.4   Licensing authorities may not initiate their own reviews of premises licences. Officers of the local authority who are specified as responsible authorities under the 2003 Act, such as environmental health officers, may however request reviews on any matter which relates to the promotion of one or more of the licensing objectives.

11.5   Representations made by a department of the local authority which is a responsible authority should be treated by the licensing authority in precisely the same way that they would treat representations made by any other body or individual.

11.6   In every case, the representation must relate to particular premises for which a premises licence is in existence and must be relevant to the promotion of the licensing objectives. After a licence or certificate has been granted or varied, a complaint relating to a general (crime and disorder) situation in a town centre should generally not be regarded as a relevant representation unless it can be positively tied or linked by a causal connection to particular premises, which would allow for a proper review of the licence or certificate. For instance, a geographic cluster of complaints, including along transport routes related to an individual public house and its closing time could give grounds for a review of an existing licence as well as direct incidents of crime and disorder around a particular public house.

11.7   Representations must be in writing and may be amplified at the subsequent hearing or may stand in their own right. Additional representations which do not amount to an amplification of the original representation may not be made at the hearing.

11.8   It is important to recognise that the promotion of the licensing objectives relies heavily on a partnership between licence holders, authorised persons, interested parties and responsible authorities in pursuit of common aims. It is therefore equally important that reviews are not used to drive a wedge between these groups in a way that would undermine the benefits of co-operation. It is good practice for authorised persons and responsible authorities to give licence holders early warning of their concerns about problems identified at the premises concerned and of the need for improvement. A failure to respond to such warnings is expected to lead to a decision to request a review.

11.9   Where the request originates with an interested party – e.g. a local resident, residents' association, local business or trade association – the licensing authority must first consider whether the complaint made is relevant, vexatious, frivolous or repetitious.

11.10 Further information for interested parties about the review process is available in "Guidance for interested parties: applying for a review" which can be found on the DCMS website.

## REPETITIOUS REPRESENTATIONS

11.11 Relevance, vexation and frivolousness were dealt with in paragraphs 9.8–9.13 above. A repetitious representation is one that is identical or substantially similar to:

- a ground for review specified in an earlier application for review made in relation to the same premises licence which has already been determined; or
- representations considered by the licensing authority when the premises licence was first granted; or
- representations which would have been made when the application for the premises licence was first made and which were excluded then by reason of the prior issue of a provisional statement;

and, in addition to the above grounds, a reasonable interval has not elapsed since that earlier review or the grant of the licence.

11.12 Licensing authorities are expected to be aware of the need to prevent attempts to review licences merely as a second bite of the cherry following the failure of representations to persuade the licensing authority on earlier occasions. It is for licensing authorities themselves to judge what should be regarded as a reasonable interval in these circumstances. However, the Secretary of State recommends that more than one review originating from an interested party should not be permitted within a period of twelve months on similar grounds save in compelling circumstances or where it arises following a closure order.

11.13 The exclusion of a complaint on the grounds that it is repetitious does not apply to responsible authorities which may make more than one request for a review of a premises within a 12 month period.

11.14 When a licensing authority receives a request for a review from a responsible authority or an interested party or in accordance with the closure procedures described in Part 8 of the 2003 Act, it must arrange a hearing. The arrangements for the hearing must follow the provisions set out by the Secretary of State in regulations. The details may be viewed on the DCMS website. The Secretary of State considers it particularly important that the premises licence holder is fully aware of the representations made in respect of the premises, any evidence supporting the representations and that they or their legal representatives have therefore been able to prepare a response.

## POWERS OF A LICENSING AUTHORITY ON THE DETERMINATION OF A REVIEW

11.15 The 2003 Act provides a range of powers for the licensing authority on determining a review that it may exercise where it considers them necessary for the promotion of the licensing objectives.

11.16 The licensing authority may decide that no action is necessary if it finds that the review does not require it to take any steps necessary to promote the licensing objectives. In addition, there is nothing to prevent a licensing authority issuing an informal warning to the licence holder and/or to recommend improvement within a particular period of time. It is expected that licensing authorities will regard such warnings as an important mechanism for ensuring that the licensing objectives are effectively promoted and that warnings be issued in writing to the holder of the licence. However, where responsible authorities like the police or environmental health officers have already issued warnings requiring improvement –

either orally or in writing – that have failed as part of their own stepped approach to concerns, licensing authorities should not merely repeat that approach.

11.17 Where the licensing authority considers that action under its statutory powers are necessary, it may take any of the following steps:

- to modify the conditions of the premises licence (which includes adding new conditions or any alteration or omission of an existing condition), for example, by reducing the hours of opening or by requiring door supervisors at particular times;

- to exclude a licensable activity from the scope of the licence, for example, to exclude the performance of live music or playing of recorded music (where it is not within the incidental live and recorded music exemption);

- to remove the designated premises supervisor, for example, because they consider that the problems are the result of poor management;

- to suspend the licence for a period not exceeding three months;

- to revoke the licence.

11.18 In deciding which of these powers to invoke, it is expected that licensing authorities should so far as possible seek to establish the cause or causes of the concerns which the representations identify. The remedial action taken should generally be directed at these causes and should always be no more than a necessary and proportionate response.

11.19 For example, licensing authorities should be alive to the possibility that the removal and replacement of the designated premises supervisor may be sufficient to remedy a problem where the cause of the identified problem directly relates to poor management decisions made by that individual.

11.20 Equally, it may emerge that poor management is a direct reflection of poor company practice or policy and the mere removal of the designated premises supervisor may be an inadequate response to the problems presented. Indeed, where subsequent review hearings are generated by representations, it should be rare merely to remove a succession of designated premises supervisors as this would be a clear indication of deeper problems which impact upon the licensing objectives.

11.21 Licensing authorities should also note that modifications of conditions and exclusions of licensable activities may be imposed either permanently or for a temporary period of up to three months. Temporary changes or suspension of the licence for up to three months could impact on the business holding the licence financially and would only be expected to be pursued as a necessary means of promoting the licensing objectives. So, for instance, a licence could be suspended for a weekend as a means of deterring the holder from allowing the problems that gave rise to the review to happen again. However, it will always be important that any detrimental financial impact that may result from a licensing authority's decision is necessary and proportionate to the promotion of the licensing objectives.

## REVIEWS ARISING IN CONNECTION WITH CRIME

11.22 A number of reviews may arise in connection with crime that is not directly connected with licensable activities. For example, reviews may arise because of drugs problems at the premises or money laundering by criminal gangs or the sale of contraband or stolen goods there or the sale of firearms. Licensing authorities do not have the power to judge the criminality or otherwise of any issue. This is a matter for the courts of law. The role of the licensing authority when determining such a review is not therefore to establish the guilt or innocence of any individual but to ensure that the crime prevention objective is promoted. Reviews are part of the regulatory process introduced by the 2003 Act and they are not part of criminal law and procedure. Some reviews will arise after the conviction in the criminal courts of certain individuals but not all. In any case, it is for the licensing authority to determine whether the problems associated with the alleged crimes are taking place on the premises and affecting the promotion of the licensing objectives. Where a review follows a conviction, it would also not be for the licensing authority to attempt to go behind any finding of the courts, which should be treated as a matter of undisputed evidence before them.

11.23 Where the licensing authority is conducting a review on the ground that the premises have been used for criminal purposes, its role is solely to determine what steps should be taken in connection with the premises licence, for the promotion of the crime prevention objective. It is important to recognise that certain criminal activity or associated problems may be taking place or have taken place despite the best efforts of the licensee and the staff working at the premises and despite full compliance with the conditions attached to the licence. In such circumstances, the licensing authority is still empowered to take any necessary steps to remedy the problems. The licensing authority's duty is to take steps with a view to the promotion of the licensing objectives in the interests of the wider community and not those of the individual holder of the premises licence.

11.24 As explained above, it is not the role of a licensing authority to determine the guilt or innocence of individuals charged with licensing or other offences committed on licensed premises. There is therefore no reason why representations giving rise to a review of a premises licence need be delayed pending the outcome of any criminal proceedings. As stated above, at the conclusion of a review, it will be for the licensing authority to determine on the basis of the application for the review and any relevant representations made, what action needs to be taken for the promotion

of the licensing objectives in respect of the licence in question, regardless of any subsequent judgment in the courts about the behaviour of individuals.

11.25 There is certain criminal activity that may arise in connection with licensed premises, which the Secretary of State considers should be treated particularly seriously. These are the use of the licensed premises:

- for the sale and distribution of Class A drugs and the laundering of the proceeds of drugs crime;
- for the sale and distribution of illegal firearms;
- for the evasion of copyright in respect of pirated or unlicensed films and music, which does considerable damage to the industries affected;
- for the purchase and consumption of alcohol by minors which impacts on the health, educational attainment, employment prospects and propensity for crime of young people;
- for prostitution or the sale of unlawful pornography;
- by organised groups of paedophiles to groom children;
- as the base for the organisation of criminal activity, particularly by gangs;
- for the organisation of racist activity or the promotion of racist attacks;
- for unlawful gaming and gambling; and
- for the sale of smuggled tobacco and alcohol.

11.26 It is envisaged that licensing authorities, the police and other law enforcement agencies, which are responsible authorities, will use the review procedures effectively to deter such activities and crime. Where reviews arise and the licensing authority determines that the crime prevention objective is being undermined through the premises being used to further crimes, it is expected that revocation of the licence – even in the first instance – should be seriously considered. We would also

App 11

encourage liaison with the local Crime and Disorder Reduction Partnership.

11.27 It should be noted that it is unlawful to discriminate or to refuse service on grounds of race or by displaying racially discriminatory signs on the premises. Representations made about such activity from responsible authorities or interested parties would be relevant to the promotion of the crime prevention objective and justifiably give rise to a review.

# REVIEW OF A PREMISES LICENCE FOLLOWING CLOSURE ORDER

11.28 Licensing authorities are subject to certain timescales, set out in the legislation, for the review of a premises licence following a closure order. The relevant time periods run concurrently and are as follows:

- when the licensing authority receives notice that a magistrates' court has made a closure order it has 28 days to determine the licence review: The determination must be made before the expiry of the 28th day after the day on which the notice is received;

- the hearing must be held within 10 working days, the first of which is the day after the day the notice from the magistrates' court is received;

- notice of the hearing must be given no later than 5 working days before the first hearing day. There must be five clear working days between the giving of the notice and the start of the hearing.

# 12. Appeals

12.1   This Chapter provides advice about entitlements to appeal in connection with various decisions made by a licensing authority under the provisions of the 2003 Act. Entitlements to appeal for parties aggrieved by decisions of the licensing authority are set out in Schedule 5 to the 2003 Act.

## GENERAL

12.2   Other than in the case of personal licences, an appeal has to be made to the magistrates' court for the petty sessions area (or any such area) in which the premises concerned are situated. In the case of personal licences, the appeal must be made to the magistrates' court for the petty sessions area in which the licensing authority (or any part of it) which made the decision is situated.

12.3   An appeal has to be commenced by the giving of a notice of appeal by the appellant to the justices' chief executive for the magistrates' court within a period of 21 days beginning with the day on which the appellant was notified by the licensing authority of the decision to be appealed against.

12.4   The licensing authority will always be a respondent to the appeal, but in cases where a favourable decision has been made for an applicant licence holder, club or premises user against the representations of a responsible authority or an interested party or the objections of the chief officer of police, the holder of the premises or personal licence or club premises certificate or the person who gave an interim authority notice or the premises user will also be a respondent to the appeal and the person who made the relevant representation or the chief officer of police will be the appellants.

12.5   Where an appeal has been made against a decision of the licensing authority, the licensing authority will

in all cases be the respondent to the appeal and may call as witnesses interested parties or responsible authorities who made representations against the application, if it chooses to do so. For this reason, the licensing authority may wish to keep responsible authorities and interested parties informed of developments in relation to appeals to allow them to consider their position. Provided the court considers it appropriate, the licensing authority may also call as witnesses any individual or body that they feel might assist their response to an appeal.

12.6   The court, on hearing any appeal, may review the merits of the decision on the facts and consider points of law or address both. On determining an appeal, the court may:

- dismiss the appeal;
- substitute for the decision appealed against any other decision which could have been made by the licensing authority; or
- remit the case to the licensing authority to dispose of it in accordance with the direction of the court and make such order as to costs as it thinks fit.

## LICENSING POLICY STATEMENTS AND SECTION 182 GUIDANCE

12.7   In hearing an appeal against any decision made by a licensing authority, the magistrates' court concerned will have regard to that licensing authority's statement of licensing policy and this Guidance. However, the court would be entitled to depart from either the statement of licensing policy or this Guidance if it considered it was justified to do so because of the individual circumstances of any case. In other words, while the appellate court will normally consider the matter as if it was "standing in the shoes" of the licensing authority, it would be entitled to find that the licensing authority should have departed from its own policy or the Guidance because the particular circumstances would have justified such a decision.

12.8　In addition, the appellate court is entitled to disregard any part of a licensing policy statement or this Guidance that it holds to be ultra vires the 2003 Act and therefore unlawful. The normal course for challenging a statement of licensing policy or this Guidance should be by way of judicial review, but where it is submitted to an appellate court that a statement of policy is itself ultra vires the 2003 Act and this has a direct bearing on the case before it, it would be inappropriate for the court, on accepting such a submission, to compound the original error by relying on that part of the statement of licensing policy affected.

## GIVING REASONS FOR DECISIONS

12.9　It is important that licensing authorities should give comprehensive reasons for its decisions in anticipation of any appeals. Failure to give adequate reasons could itself give rise to grounds for an appeal. It is particularly important that reasons should also address the extent to which the decision has been made with regard to the licensing authority's statement of policy and this Guidance. Reasons should be promulgated to all the parties of any process which might give rise to an appeal under the terms of the 2003 Act.

## IMPLEMENTING THE DETERMINATION OF THE MAGISTRATES' COURTS

12.10　As soon as the decision of the magistrates' courts has been promulgated, licensing authorities should implement it without delay. Any attempt to delay implementation will only bring the appeal system into disrepute. Standing orders should therefore be in place that on receipt of the decision, necessary action should be taken immediately unless ordered by the magistrates' court or a higher court to suspend such action (for example, as a result of an on-going judicial review). Except in the case of closure orders, the 2003 Act does not provide for a further appeal against the decision of the magistrates' courts and normal rules of challenging decisions of magistrates' courts will apply.

## PROVISIONAL STATEMENTS

12.11　To avoid confusion, it should be noted that a right of appeal only exists in respect of the terms of a provisional statement that is issued rather than one that is refused. This is because the 2003 Act does not empower a licensing authority to refuse to issue a provisional statement. After receiving and considering relevant representations, the licensing authority may only indicate, as part of the statement, that it would consider certain steps to be necessary for the promotion of the licensing objectives when, and if, an application was made for a premises licence following the issuing of the provisional statement. Accordingly, the applicant or any person who has made relevant representations may appeal against the terms of the statement issued.

# 13. Statements of licensing policy

13.1  This Chapter provides guidance on the development and preparation of local statements of licensing policy for publication by licensing authorities, the general principles that the Secretary of State recommends should underpin them, and core content to which licensing authorities are free to add.

## GENERAL

13.2  Section 5 of the 2003 Act requires a licensing authority to prepare and publish a statement of its licensing policy every three years. Such a policy must be published before the authority carries out any function in respect of individual applications made under the terms of the 2003 Act. During the three year period, the policy must be kept under review and the licensing authority may make any revisions to it as it considers appropriate, for instance in the light of feedback from the local community on whether the statutory objectives are being met. The first, statutory three year period began on 7 January 2005.[4] Subsequent three year periods, eg. beginning 7 January 2008 etc, are fixed and would not be altered by any other revisions that a licensing authority may choose to make within a period, or by any determination of a new policy.

13.3  Where revisions to this section 182 Guidance are made by the Secretary of State it will be for the licensing authority to determine whether revisions to its own licensing policy statement are appropriate.

13.4  Where the licensing authority determines a new policy that will apply from the beginning of the next three year period it may also decide that any changes should also apply immediately as a revision to the current policy. However, to do so the licensing authority would have to be very clear at the time of consultation that the proposed changes were intended to constitute both the new policy for the next three year period and apply in the interim as a revision to the existing policy.

13.5  The longer the time between the consultation and the start of the next three year period, the less likely it is that the licensing authority could rely on it for that purpose without consulting again.

## CONSULTATION ON POLICIES

13.6  Before determining its policy for any three year period or if revising a policy within a period, the licensing authority must consult the persons listed in section 5(3) of the 2003 Act. These are:

- the chief officer of police for the area;
- the fire and rescue authority for the area;
- persons/bodies representative of local holders of premises licences;
- persons/bodies representative of local holders of club premises certificates;
- persons/bodies representative of local holders of personal licences; and
- persons/bodies representative of businesses and residents in its area.

13.7  The views of all these persons/bodies listed should be given appropriate weight when the policy is determined. It is recognised that in some areas, it may be difficult to identify persons or bodies that represent all parts of industry affected by the provisions of the 2003 Act, but licensing authorities must make reasonable efforts to do so.

---

4  Licensing Act 2003 (Licensing statement period) Order 2004

13.8   Licensing authorities should note that the terms of the 2003 Act do not prevent them consulting other bodies or persons before determining their policies. For example, certain authorities may consider it essential to consult the Crime and Disorder Reduction Partnerships (CDRPs), British Transport Police, local Accident and Emergency Departments, bodies representing consumers, local police consultative groups or those charged locally with the promotion of tourism. They may also consider it valuable to consult local performers, performers' unions (such as the Musicians' Union and Equity) and entertainers involved in the cultural life of the local community. In London, boroughs should consider consulting the Mayor and the Greater London Authority.

13.9   Beyond the statutory requirements, it is for each licensing authority to decide the full extent of its consultation and whether any particular person or body is representative of the group described in the statute. Whilst it is clearly good practice to consult widely and to follow the Consultation Guidance published by the Cabinet Office, this may not always be necessary or appropriate. For instance, where a revision is proposed that merely updates contact details for the licensing authority or responsible authorities a simpler consultation may suffice.

13.10  Similarly, where a licensing authority has recently revised its policy within a three year period following a full consultation exercise it may not consider that further changes are necessary when determining the policy for the next three year period. As such, it may decide on a simple consultation with those persons listed in section 5(3) of the 2003 Act.

13.11  However, licensing authorities should consider very carefully whether a full consultation is appropriate as a limited consultation may not allow all persons sufficient opportunity to comment on and influence local policy. For instance, where an earlier consultation was limited to a particular part of the policy, such as a proposal to introduce a cumulative impact policy.

13.12  When undertaking consultation exercises, licensing authorities should have regard to cost and time. The Secretary of State has established fee levels to provide full cost recovery of all licensing functions including the preparation and publication of a statement of licensing policy, but this will be based on the statutory requirements. Where licensing authorities exceed these requirements, they will have to absorb those costs themselves.

## FUNDAMENTAL PRINCIPLES

13.13  All statements of policy should also begin by stating the four licensing objectives, which the licensing policy should promote. In determining its policy, a licensing authority must have regard to this Guidance and give appropriate weight to the views of consultees. The Guidance is important for consistency, particularly where licensing authority boundaries meet.

13.14  While statements of policy may set out a general approach to making licensing decisions, they must not ignore or be inconsistent with provisions in the 2003 Act. For example, a statement of policy must not undermine the right of any individual to apply under the terms of the 2003 Act for a variety of permissions and to have any such application considered on its individual merits.

13.15  Similarly, no statement of policy should override the right of any person to make representations on an application or to seek a review of a licence or certificate where provision has been made for them to do so in the 2003 Act.

13.16  Statements of policies should make clear that:

- licensing is about regulating licensable activities on licensed premises, by qualifying clubs and at temporary events within the terms of the 2003 Act; and

- the conditions attached to various authorisations will be focused on matters which are within the control of individual licensees and others with relevant authorisations, i.e. the premises and its vicinity.

13.17 Whether or not incidents can be regarded as being "in the vicinity" of licensed premises is a question of fact and will depend on the particular circumstances of the case. In cases of dispute, the question will ultimately be decided by the courts. But statements of licensing policy should make it clear that in addressing this matter, the licensing authority will primarily focus on the direct impact of the activities taking place at the licensed premises on members of the public living, working or engaged in normal activity in the area concerned.

13.18 A statement of policy should also make clear that licensing law is not the primary mechanism for the general control of nuisance and anti-social behaviour by individuals once they are away from the licensed premises and, therefore, beyond the direct control of the individual, club or business holding the licence, certificate or authorisation concerned. Nonetheless, it is a key aspect of such control and licensing law will always be part of a holistic approach to the management of the evening and night-time economy in town and city centres.

## DUPLICATION

13.19 Statements of licensing policy should include a firm commitment to avoid attaching conditions that duplicate other regulatory regimes as far as possible. Chapter 10 provides further detail on this issue.

## STANDARDISED CONDITIONS

13.20 Statements of policy should also make it clear that a key concept underscoring the 2003 Act is for conditions to be tailored to the specific premises concerned. This effectively rules out standardised conditions, as explained in paragraph 10.13 of this Guidance.

However, it is acceptable for licensing authorities to draw attention in their statements of policy to pools of conditions which applicants and others may draw on as appropriate.

## ENFORCEMENT

13.21 As part of their statement of policy, the Government strongly recommends that licensing authorities should express the intention to establish protocols with the local police and the other enforcing authorities as appropriate on enforcement issues. This would provide for a more efficient deployment of licensing authority staff, police officers environmental health officers, and others who are commonly engaged in enforcing licensing law and the inspection of licensed premises.

13.22 In particular, these protocols should also provide for the targeting of agreed problem and high risk premises which require greater attention, while providing a lighter touch for low risk premises which are well run. In some local authority areas, the limited validity of public entertainment, theatre, cinema, night café and late night refreshment house licences has in the past led to a culture of annual inspections regardless of whether the assessed risks make such inspections necessary. The 2003 Act does not require inspections to take place save at the discretion of those charged with this role. The principle of risk assessment and targeting should prevail and inspections should not be undertaken routinely but when and if they are judged necessary. This should ensure that resources are more effectively concentrated on problem premises.

## THE NEED FOR LICENSED PREMISES

13.23 There can be confusion about the difference between "need" and the "cumulative impact" of premises on the licensing objectives, for example, on crime and disorder.

"Need" concerns the commercial demand for another pub or restaurant. This is not a matter for a licensing authority in discharging its licensing functions or for its statement of licensing policy. "Need" is a matter for planning committees and for the market.

## THE CUMULATIVE IMPACT OF A CONCENTRATION OF LICENSED PREMISES

### What is cumulative impact?

13.24  "Cumulative impact" is not mentioned specifically in the 2003 Act but means in this Guidance the potential impact on the promotion of the licensing objectives of a significant number of licensed premises concentrated in one area. The cumulative impact of licensed premises on the promotion of the licensing objectives is a proper matter for a licensing authority to consider in developing its licensing policy statement.

13.25  In some areas, where the number, type and density of premises selling alcohol for consumption on the premises are unusual, serious problems of nuisance and disorder may be arising or have begun to arise outside or some distance from licensed premises. For example, concentrations of young drinkers can result in queues at fast food outlets and for public transport. Queuing in turn may be leading to conflict, disorder and anti-social behaviour. While more flexible licensing hours may reduce this impact by allowing a more gradual dispersal of customers from premises, it is possible that the impact on surrounding areas of the behaviour of the customers of all premises taken together will still be greater in these cases than the impact of customers of individual premises. These conditions are more likely to occur in town and city centres, but may also arise in other urban centres and the suburbs.

### Evidence of cumulative impact

13.26  There should be an evidential basis for the decision to include a special

policy within the statement of licensing policy. For example, Crime and Disorder Reduction Partnerships will often have collated information which demonstrates cumulative impact as part of their general role on anti-social behaviour; and crime prevention strategies may have already identified cumulative impact as a local problem. Similarly, environmental health officers may be able to demonstrate concentrations of valid complaints relating to noise disturbance. The open meetings recommended at paragraph 1.22 of this Guidance should also assist licensing authorities in keeping the situation as to whether an area is nearing this point under review.

13.27  After considering the available evidence and consulting those individuals and organisations listed in section 5(3) of the 2003 Act and any others, a licensing authority may be satisfied that it is appropriate and necessary to include an approach to cumulative impact in the licensing policy statement. In this case, it should indicate in the statement that it is adopting a special policy of refusing new licences whenever it receives relevant representations about the cumulative impact on the licensing objectives which it concludes after hearing those representations should lead to refusal (see paragraphs 13.29–13.32 below).

13.28  The steps to be followed in considering whether to adopt a special policy within the statement of licensing policy are summarised below.

## STEPS TO A SPECIAL POLICY

- Identify concern about crime and disorder or public nuisance
- Consider whether there is good evidence that crime and disorder or nuisance are happening and are caused by the customers of licensed premises, or that the risk of cumulative impact is imminent
- Identify the boundaries of the area where problems are occurring
- Consult with those specified in section 5(3) of the 2003 Act, and subject to the outcome of the consultation

- Include and publish details of special policy in licensing policy statement

### Effect of special policies

13.29 The effect of adopting a special policy of this kind is to create a rebuttable presumption that applications for new premises licences or club premises certificates or variations that are likely to add to the existing cumulative impact will normally be refused, following relevant representations, unless the applicant can demonstrate in their operating schedule that there will be no negative cumulative impact on one or more of the licensing objectives.

13.30 However, a special policy must stress that this presumption does not relieve responsible authorities or interested parties of the need to make a relevant representation, referring to information which had been before the licensing authority when it developed its statement of licensing policy, before a licensing authority may lawfully consider giving effect to its special policy. If there are no representations, the licensing authority must grant the application in terms that are consistent with the operating schedule submitted.

13.31 Once adopted, special policies should be reviewed regularly to assess whether they are needed any longer or need expanding.

13.32 The absence of a special policy does not prevent any responsible authority or interested party making representations on a new application for the grant, or variation, of a licence on the grounds that the premises will give rise to a negative cumulative impact on one or more of the licensing objectives.

## LIMITATIONS ON SPECIAL POLICIES RELATING TO CUMULATIVE IMPACT

13.33 It would normally not be justifiable to adopt a special policy on the basis of a concentration of shops, stores or supermarkets selling alcohol for consumption off the premises. Special policies will usually address the impact of a concentration of licensed premises selling alcohol for consumption on the premises.

13.34 A special policy should never be absolute. Statements of licensing policy should always allow for the circumstances of each application to be considered properly and for licences and certificates that are unlikely to add to the cumulative impact on the licensing objectives to be granted. After receiving representations in relation to a new application for or a variation of a licence or certificate, the licensing authority must consider whether it would be justified in departing from its special policy in the light of the individual circumstances of the case. The impact can be expected to be different for premises with different styles and characteristics. For example, while a large nightclub or high capacity public house might add to problems of cumulative impact, a small restaurant or a theatre may not. If the licensing authority decides that an application should be refused, it will still need to show that the grant of the application would undermine the promotion of one of the licensing objectives and that necessary conditions would be ineffective in preventing the problems involved

13.35 Special policies should never be used as a ground for revoking an existing licence or certificate when representations are received about problems with those premises. The "cumulative impact" on the promotion of the licensing objectives of a concentration of multiple licensed premises should only give rise to a relevant representation when an application for the grant or variation of a licence or certificate is being considered. A review must relate specifically to individual premises, and by its nature, "cumulative impact" relates to the effect of a concentration of many premises. Identifying individual premises in the context of a review would inevitably be arbitrary.

13.36 Special policies can also not be used to justify rejecting applications to vary an existing licence or certificate except where those modifications are directly relevant to the policy (as would be the case with an application to vary a licence with a view to increasing the capacity limits of the premises) and are strictly necessary for the promotion of the licensing objectives.

13.37 A special policy relating to cumulative impact cannot justify and should not include provisions for a terminal hour in a particular area. For example, it would be wrong not to apply the special policy to applications that include provision to open no later than, for example, midnight, but to apply the policy to any other premises that propose opening later.

13.38 Special policies must not impose quotas – based on either the number of premises or the capacity of those premises – that restrict the consideration of any application on its individual merits or which seek to impose limitations on trading hours in particular areas. Quotas that indirectly have the effect of predetermining the outcome of any application should not be used because they have no regard to the individual characteristics of the premises concerned. Public houses, nightclubs, restaurants, hotels, theatres, concert halls and cinemas all could sell alcohol, serve food and provide entertainment but with contrasting styles and characteristics. Proper regard should be given to those differences and the differing impact they will have on the promotion of the licensing objectives.

## OTHER MECHANISMS FOR CONTROLLING CUMULATIVE IMPACT

13.39 Once away from the licensed premises, a minority of consumers will behave badly and unlawfully. To enable the general public to appreciate the breadth of the strategy for addressing these problems, statements of policy should also indicate the other mechanisms both within and outside the licensing regime that are

available for addressing such issues. For example:

## OTHER MEASURES TO CONTROL CUMULATIVE IMPACT

- Planning controls.
- Positive measures to create a safe and clean town centre environment in partnership with local businesses, transport operators and other departments of the local authority.
- The provision of CCTV surveillance in town centres, ample taxi ranks, provision of public conveniences open late at night, street cleaning and litter patrols.
- Powers of local authorities to designate parts of the local authority area as places where alcohol may not be consumed publicly.
- Police enforcement of the general law concerning disorder and anti-social behaviour, including the issuing of fixed penalty notices.
- The prosecution of any personal licence holder or member of staff at such premises who is selling alcohol to people who are drunk.
- The confiscation of alcohol from adults and children in designated areas.
- Police powers to close down instantly for up to 24 hours any licensed premises or temporary event on grounds of disorder, the likelihood of disorder or noise emanating from the premises causing a nuisance.
- The power of the police, other responsible authorities or a local resident or business to seek a review of the licence or certificate in question.
- Other local initiatives that similarly address these problems.

## LICENSING HOURS

13.40 With regard to licensing hours, the statement of policy should generally emphasise the consideration which will be given to the individual merits of an application. The Government recommends that statements of policy should recognise that, in some circumstances, flexible licensing hours for the sale of alcohol can help to ensure that the concentrations of customers leaving premises simultaneously are avoided. This can help to reduce the friction at late night fast food outlets, taxi ranks and other sources of transport which lead to disorder and disturbance.

13.41 The Government also wants to ensure that licensing hours should not inhibit the development of thriving and safe evening and night-time local economies which are important for investment and employment locally and attractive to domestic and international tourists. Providing consumers with greater choice and flexibility is an important consideration, but should always be balanced carefully against the duty to promote the four licensing objectives and the rights of local residents to peace and quiet.

13.42 Statements of licensing policy should indicate that shops, stores and supermarkets, are free to provide sales of alcohol for consumption off the premises at any times when the retail outlet is open for shopping unless there are good reasons, based on the licensing objectives, for restricting those hours. For example, a limitation may be appropriate following police representations in the case of some shops known to be a focus of disorder and disturbance because youths gather there. Statements of licensing policy should therefore reflect this general approach.

## CHILDREN

13.43 The 2003 Act made it an offence to permit children under the age of 16 who are not accompanied by an adult to be present on premises being used exclusively or primarily for supply of alcohol for consumption on those premises under the authorisation of a premises licence, club premises certificate or where that activity is carried on under the authority of a temporary event notice.

13.44 In addition, it is an offence to permit the presence of children under 16 who are not accompanied by an adult between midnight and 5am at other premises supplying alcohol for consumption on the premises under

the authority of any premises licence, club premises certificate or temporary event notice. Outside of these hours, the offence does not prevent the admission of unaccompanied children under 16 to the wide variety of premises where the consumption of alcohol is not the exclusive or primary activity. Between 5am and midnight the offence would not necessarily apply to many restaurants, hotels, cinemas and even many pubs where the main business activity is the consumption of both food and drink. This does not mean that children should automatically be admitted to such premises and the following paragraphs are therefore of great importance notwithstanding the new offences created by the 2003 Act.

13.45 It is not intended that the definition "exclusively or primarily" in relation to the consumption of alcohol should be applied in a particular way by reference to turnover, floor space or any similar measure. The expression should be given its ordinary and natural meaning in the context of the particular circumstances. It will normally be quite clear that the business being operated at the premises is predominantly the sale and consumption of alcohol. Mixed businesses may be harder to pigeonhole and it would be sensible for both operators and enforcement agencies to consult where necessary about their respective interpretations of the activities taking place on the premises before any moves are taken which might lead to prosecution.

13.46 The fact that the new offence may effectively bar children under 16 unaccompanied by an adult from premises where the consumption of alcohol is the exclusive or primary activity does not mean that the 2003 Act automatically permits unaccompanied children under the age of 18 to have free access to other premises or to the same premises even if they are accompanied or to premises where the consumption of alcohol is not involved. Subject only to the provisions of the 2003 Act and any licence or certificate conditions, admission will always be at the discretion of those managing the premises. The 2003 Act includes on the one hand, no presumption of giving children access or on the other hand, no presumption of preventing their access to licensed premises. Each application and the circumstances obtaining at each premises must be considered on its own merits.

13.47 A statement of licensing policy must not therefore seek to limit the access of children to any premises unless it is necessary for the prevention of physical, moral or psychological harm to them. Licensing policy statements should not attempt to anticipate every issue of concern that could arise in respect of children in relation to individual premises and as such, general rules should be avoided. Consideration of the individual merits of each application remains the best mechanism for judging such matters.

13.48 A statement of policy should highlight areas that will give rise to particular concern in respect of children. For example, these should include premises:

- where entertainment or services of an adult or sexual nature are commonly provided;
- where there have been convictions of members of the current staff at the premises for serving alcohol to minors or with a reputation for underage drinking;
- with a known association with drug taking or dealing[5];
- where there is a strong element of gambling on the premises (but not, for example, the simple presence of a small number of cash prize gaming machines); and
- where the supply of alcohol for

consumption on the premises is the exclusive or primary purpose of the services provided at the premises.

13.49 In the context of paragraph 13.48 above, it is not possible to give an exhaustive list of what amounts to entertainment or services of an adult or sexual nature. Applicants, responsible authorities and licensing authorities will need to apply common sense to this matter. However, such entertainment or services, for example, would generally include topless bar staff, striptease, lap-, table- or pole-dancing, performances involving feigned violence or horrific incidents, feigned or actual sexual acts or fetishism, or entertainment involving strong and offensive language.

13.50 A statement of policy should make clear the range of alternatives which may be considered for limiting the access of children where that is necessary for the prevention of harm to children. These, which can be adopted in combination, include:

- limitations on the hours when children may be present;
- limitations excluding the presence of children under certain ages when particular specified activities are taking place;
- limitations on the parts of premises to which children might be given access;
- age limitations (below 18);
- requirements for accompanying adults (including for example, a combination of requirements which provide that children under a particular age must be accompanied by an adult); and
- full exclusion of those people under 18 from the premises when any licensable activities are taking place.

---

5   Police, licensing authorities and licensees need to be aware that following its commencement on the 20th January 2004, a new power is available under the Anti-Social Behaviour Act 2003 to close premises where there is the production supply or use of class A drugs and serious nuisance or disorder. This power provides an extra tool to the police to enable rapid action against a premises where there is a Class A drug problem, enabling its closure in as little as 48 hours should this be necessary. Police authorities are advised to consult the Notes of Guidance on the use of this power (Home Office, 2004) available on the Home Office website. These powers will also be covered in brief in the update to Safer Clubbing available in 2004.

13.51 Statements of policy should also make clear that conditions requiring the admission of children to any premises cannot be attached to licences or certificates. Where no licensing restriction is necessary, this should remain a matter for the discretion of the individual licensee or club or person who has given a temporary event notice. Venue operators seeking premises licences and club premises certificates may also volunteer such prohibitions and restrictions in their operating schedules because their own risk assessments have determined that the presence of children is undesirable or inappropriate. Where no relevant representations are made to the licensing authority concerned, these volunteered prohibitions and restrictions will become conditions attached to the licence or certificate and will be enforceable as such. No other conditions concerning the presence of children on premises may be imposed by the licensing authority in these circumstances.

## RESPONSIBLE AUTHORITY AND CHILDREN

13.52 A statement of licensing policy should indicate which body the licensing authority judges to be competent to act as the responsible authority in relation to the protection of children from harm. This may be the local authority social services department, the Area Child Protection Committee, or another competent body. It would be practical and useful for statements of licensing policy to include the correct descriptions of the responsible authorities in any area and appropriate contact details.

## CHILDREN AND CINEMAS

13.53 The statement of policy should make clear that in the case of premises giving film exhibitions, the licensing authority will expect licensees or clubs to include in their operating schedules arrangements for restricting children from viewing age-restricted films classified according to the recommendations of the British Board of Film Classification or the licensing authority itself. Where a licensing authority intends to adopt its own system of classification, its statement of policy should indicate where the information regarding such classifications will be published and made available to licensees, clubs and the general public.

13.54 The 2003 Act also provides that it is mandatory for a condition to be included in all premises licences and club premises certificates authorising the exhibition of films for the admission of children to the exhibition of any film to be restricted in accordance with the recommendations given to films either by a body designated under section 4 of the Video Recordings Act 1984 – the British Board of Film Classification is the only body which has been so designated – or by the licensing authority itself.

## INTEGRATING STRATEGIES

13.55 The Secretary of State recommends that statements of policy should provide clear indications of how the licensing authority will secure the proper integration of its licensing policy with local crime prevention, planning, transport, tourism, race equality schemes, and cultural strategies and any other plans introduced for the management of town centres and the night-time economy. Many of these strategies are not directly related to the promotion of the four licensing objectives, but, indirectly, impact upon them. Co-ordination and integration of such policies, strategies and initiatives are therefore important.

## CRIME PREVENTION

13.56 Licensing policy statements should indicate that conditions attached to premises licences and club premises certificates will, so far as possible, reflect local crime prevention strategies. For example, the provision of closed circuit television cameras in certain premises. Where appropriate it should reflect the input of the local Crime and Disorder Reduction Partnership.

## CULTURAL STRATEGIES

13.57   In connection with cultural strategies, licensing policy statements should include clearly worded statements indicating that they will monitor the impact of licensing on the provision of regulated entertainment, and particularly live music and dancing, for example, by considering whether premises that provide live music or culture are represented on licensing stakeholder forums, and ensuring that local cultural officers are regularly consulted about the impact on local culture. Where appropriate, town centre managers have an important role in coordinating live music events in town centres and can be an important source of information.

13.58   Care will be needed to ensure that only necessary, proportionate and reasonable licensing conditions impose any restrictions on these events. Where there is any indication that events are being deterred by licensing requirements, statements of licensing policy should be re-visited with a view to investigating how the situation might be reversed. Broader cultural activities and entertainment may also be affected. In developing their statements of licensing policy, licensing authorities should also consider any views of the local authority's arts committee, where one exists.

13.59   Over 325 local authorities from all over England and Wales are members of the National Association of Local Government Arts Officers (NALGAO), which is the largest organisation in the country representing local government art interests. Some local authorities do not yet have arts specialists or arts development officers and in such circumstances, a licensing authority may wish to consult NALGAO for practical help and advice.

13.60   The United Kingdom ratified the International Covenant on Economic, Social and Cultural Rights (ICESCR) in 1976. Article 15 of the Covenant requires that progressive measures be taken to ensure that everyone can participate in the cultural life of the community and enjoy the arts. It is therefore important that the principles underpinning ICESCR are integrated, where possible, with the licensing authority's approach to the licensing of regulated entertainment.

## TRANSPORT

13.61   A statement should describe any protocols agreed between the local police and other licensing enforcement officers and indicate that arrangements will be made for them to report to local authority transport committees so that those committees may have regard to the need to disperse people from town and city centres swiftly and safely when developing their policies. When developing the statement licensing authorities should have regard to the existing policies and strategies of the relevant local transport authority, as set out in their Local Transport Plan. They may also wish to consult licensees who are likely to have a good knowledge of customer expectation and behavioural patterns in relation to transport options.

## TOURISM AND EMPLOYMENT

13.62   A statement should indicate that arrangements have been made for licensing committees to receive, when appropriate, reports on the needs of the local tourist economy for the area to ensure that these are reflected in their considerations.

13.63   It should also state the licensing authority's intention to keep their licensing committee apprised of the employment situation in the area and the need for new investment and employment where appropriate.

## PLANNING AND BUILDING CONTROL

13.64   The statement of licensing policy should indicate that planning, building control and licensing regimes will be properly separated to avoid duplication and inefficiency. Applications for premises licences for permanent commercial premises should normally be from businesses with planning consent for the property concerned. However, applications for licences may be made before any relevant planning permission has been sought or granted by the planning authority.

13.65   The planning and licensing regimes involve consideration of different (albeit related) matters. For instance, licensing considers public nuisance whereas planning considers amenity. As such licensing applications should not be a re-run of the planning application and should not cut across decisions taken by the local authority planning committee or following appeals against decisions taken by that committee. Licensing committees are not bound by decisions made by a planning committee, and vice versa.

13.66   The granting by the licensing committee of any variation of a licence which involves a material alteration to a building would not relieve the applicant of the need to apply for planning permission or building control where appropriate.

13.67   There are also circumstances when as a condition of planning permission, a terminal hour has been set for the use of premises for commercial purposes. Where these hours are different to the licensing hours, the applicant must observe the earlier closing time. Premises operating in breach of their planning permission would be liable to prosecution under planning law.

13.68   Proper integration should be assured by licensing committees, where appropriate, providing regular reports to the planning committee on the situation regarding licensed premises in the area, including the general impact of alcohol related crime and disorder. This would enable the planning committee to have regard to such matters when taking its decisions and avoid any unnecessary overlap. A planning authority may also make representations as a responsible authority as long as they relate to the licensing objectives.

## PROMOTION OF RACIAL EQUALITY

13.69   A statement of licensing policy should also recognise that:

* the Race Relations Act 1976, as amended by the Race Relations (Amendment) Act 2000, places a legal obligation on public authorities to have due regard to the need to eliminate unlawful discrimination; and to promote equality of opportunity and good relations between persons of different racial groups;

* local authorities are also required under the 1976 Act, as amended, to produce a race equality scheme, assess and consult on the likely impact of proposed policies on race equality, monitor policies for any adverse impact on the promotion of race equality, and publish the results of such consultations, assessments and monitoring;

* guidance on how to prepare race impact assessments has been produced by the Commission for Racial Equality (CRE) in consultation with a Home Office cross-Whitehall user group and a CRE-led public authority advisory group. This guidance is available on www.cre.gov.uk/duty/reia/index.html;

* the statement of licensing policy should therefore refer to this legislation and in turn, the statement of policy should be referenced in the race equality scheme.

## LIVE MUSIC, DANCING AND THEATRE

13.70   Statements of licensing policy should also recognise that as part of implementing local authority cultural strategies, proper account should be taken of the need to encourage and promote a broad range of entertainment, particularly live music, dancing and theatre, including the performance of a wide range of traditional and historic plays, for the wider cultural benefit of communities. A natural concern to prevent disturbance in neighbourhoods should always be carefully balanced with these wider cultural benefits, particularly those for children.

13.71 In determining what conditions should be attached to licences and certificates as a matter of necessity for the promotion of the licensing objectives, licensing authorities should be aware of the need to avoid measures which deter live music, dancing and theatre by imposing indirect costs of a disproportionate nature. Performances of live music and dancing are central to the development of cultural diversity and vibrant and exciting communities where artistic freedom of expression is a fundamental right and greatly valued. Traditional music and dancing are parts of the cultural heritage of England and Wales. Music and dancing also help to unite communities and particularly in ethnically diverse communities, new and emerging musical and dance forms can assist the development of a fully integrated society. It should also be noted that the absence of cultural provision in any area can itself lead to the young people being diverted into anti-social activities that damage communities and the young people involved themselves.

13.72 To ensure that cultural diversity thrives, local authorities should consider establishing a policy of seeking premises licences from the licensing authority for public spaces within the community in their own name. This could include, for example, village greens, market squares, promenades, community halls, local authority owned art centres and similar public areas. Performers and entertainers would then have no need to obtain a licence or give a temporary event notice themselves to enable them to give a performance in these places. They would still require the permission of the local authority as the premises licence holder for any regulated entertainment that it was

proposed should take place in these areas. DCMS has established a Register of Local Authority Licensed Public Spaces in England in Wales. This is to help event organisers and touring entertainment providers determine whether their event could take place in a particular local authority area without the need for a separate authorisation. It also directs them to the appropriate person to find out more information and to obtain permission to use the space. The Register and further details are available on the DCMS website.

13.73 The Violent Crime Reduction Act 2006 amends the Criminal Justice and Police Act 2001 to clarify when and where a Designated Public Places Order (DPPO) would apply. The effect of the amendment is that where a local authority occupies or manages premises, or where premises are managed on its behalf, and it licences that place for alcohol sales, the DPPO will not apply when the licence is being used for alcohol sales (or 30 minutes after), but the place will be the subject to the DPPO at all other times. This will allow local authorities to promote community events whilst still using DPPOs to tackle the problems of anti-social drinking. Further guidance about DPPOs is available from the Home Office.

13.74 It should be noted that when one part of a local authority seeks a premises licence of this kind from the licensing authority, the licensing committee and its officers must consider the matter from an entirely neutral standpoint. If relevant representations are made, for example, by local residents or the police, they must be considered fairly by the committee. Anyone making a representation who is genuinely aggrieved by a positive decision in favour of a local authority application by the licensing authority would be entitled to appeal to the magistrates' court and thereby receive an independent review of any decision.

13.75 The Secretary of State recommends that licensing authorities should publish contact points in their statements of licensing policy where members of public can obtain advice about whether or not activities fall to be licensed.

## ADMINISTRATION, EXERCISE AND DELEGATION OF FUNCTIONS

13.76 The 2003 Act provides that the functions of the licensing authority (including its determinations) are to be taken or carried out by its licensing committee (except those relating to the making of a statement of licensing policy or where another of its committees has the matter referred to it). The licensing committee may delegate these functions to sub-committees or in appropriate cases, to officials supporting the licensing authority. Where licensing functions are not automatically transferred to licensing committees, the functions must be carried out by the licensing authority as a whole and not by its executive. Statements of licensing policy should indicate how the licensing authority intends to approach its various functions. Many of the decisions and functions will be purely administrative in nature and statements of licensing policy should underline the principle of delegation in the interests of speed, efficiency and cost-effectiveness.

13.77 The 2003 Act does not prevent the development by a licensing authority of collective working practices with other parts of the local authority or other licensing authorities for work of a purely administrative nature, e.g. mail-outs. In addition, such administrative tasks may be contracted out to private businesses. But any matters regarding licensing decisions must be carried out by the licensing committee, its sub-committees or officers.

13.78 Where under the provisions of the 2003 Act, there are no relevant representations on an application for the grant of a premises licence or club premises certificate or police objection to an application for a personal licence or to an activity taking place under the authority of a temporary event notice, these matters should be dealt with by officers in order to speed matters through the system. Licensing committees should receive regular reports on decisions made by officers so that they maintain an overview of the general situation. Although essentially a matter for licensing authorities to determine themselves, the Secretary of State recommends that delegation should be approached in the following way:

## 13.79  RECOMMENDED DELEGATION OF FUNCTIONS

| Matter to be dealt with | Full Committee | Sub Commmittee | Officers |
|---|---|---|---|
| Application for personal licence | | If a police objection | If no objection made |
| Application for personal licence with unspent convictions | | All cases | |
| Application for premises licence/ club premises certificate | | If a relevant representation made | If no relevant representation made |
| Application for provisional statement | | If a relevant representation made | If no relevant representation made |
| Application to vary premises licence/ club premises certificate | | If a relevant representation made | If no relevant representation made |
| Application to vary designated premises supervisor | | If a police objection | All other cases |
| Request to be removed as designated premises supervisor | | | All cases |
| Application for transfer of premises licence | | If a police objection | All other cases |
| Applications for interim authorities | | If a police objection | All other cases |
| Application to review premises licence/ club premises certificate | | All cases | |
| Decision on whether a complaint is irrelevant frivolous vexatious etc | | | All cases |
| Decision to object when local authority is a consultee and not the relevant authority considering the application | | All cases | |
| Determination of a police objection to a temporary event notice | | All cases | |

# Annex A

**Extract from the Licensing Act 2003: Regulated Entertainment**

**SCHEDULE 1**

Section 1

PROVISION OF REGULATED ENTERTAINMENT

PART 1

GENERAL DEFINITIONS

*The provision of regulated entertainment*

1  (1)  For the purposes of this Act the "provision of regulated entertainment" means the provision of–

    (a)  entertainment of a description falling within paragraph 2, or

    (b)  entertainment facilities falling within paragraph 3, where the conditions in sub-paragraphs (2) and (3) are satisfied.

  (2)  The first condition is that the entertainment is, or entertainment facilities are, provided–

    (a)  to any extent for members of the public or a section of the public,

    (b)  exclusively for members of a club which is a qualifying club in relation to the provision of regulated entertainment, or for members of such a club and their guests, or

    (c)  in any case not falling within paragraph (a) or (b), for consideration and with a view to profit.

  (3)  The second condition is that the premises on which the entertainment is, or entertainment facilities are, provided are made available for the purpose, or for purposes which include the purpose, of enabling the entertainment concerned (whether of a description falling within paragraph 2(1) or paragraph 3(2)) to take place.

    To the extent that the provision of entertainment facilities consists of making premises available, the premises are to be regarded for the purposes of this sub paragraph as premises "on which" entertainment facilities are provided.

  (4)  For the purposes of sub-paragraph (2)(c), entertainment is, or entertainment facilities are, to be regarded as provided for consideration only if any charge–

    (a)  is made by or on behalf of–

      (i)  any person concerned in the organisation or management of that entertainment, or

      (ii)  any person concerned in the organisation or management of those facilities who is also concerned in the organisation or management of the entertainment within paragraph 3(2) in which those facilities enable persons to take part, and

    b)  is paid by or on behalf of some or all of the persons for whom that (entertainment is, or those facilities are, provided.

  (5)  In sub-paragraph (4), "charge" includes any charge for the provision of goods or services.

  (6)  For the purposes of sub-paragraph (4)(a), where the entertainment consists of the performance of live music or the playing of recorded music, a person performing or playing the music is not concerned in the organisation or management of the entertainment by reason only that he does one or more of the following–

    (a)  chooses the music to be performed or played,

    (b)  determines the manner in which he performs or plays it,

    (c)  provides any facilities for the purposes of his performance or playing of the music.

(7)  This paragraph is subject to Part 2 of this Schedule (exemptions).

*Entertainment*

2    (1)  The descriptions of entertainment are–

(a)  a performance of a play,

(b)  an exhibition of a film,

(c)  an indoor sporting event,

(d)  a boxing or wrestling entertainment,

(e)  a performance of live music,

(f)  any playing of recorded music,

(g)  a performance of dance,

(h)  entertainment of a similar description to that falling within paragraph (e), (f) or (g),

where the entertainment takes place in the presence of an audience and is provided for the purpose, or for purposes which include the purpose, of entertaining that audience.

(2)  Any reference in sub-paragraph (1) to an audience includes a reference to spectators.

(3)  This paragraph is subject to Part 3 of this Schedule (interpretation).

*Entertainment facilities*

3    (1)  In this Schedule, "entertainment facilities" means facilities for enabling persons to take part in entertainment of a description falling within sub-paragraph (2) for the purpose, or for purposes which include the purpose, of being entertained.

(2)  The descriptions of entertainment are–

(a)  making music,

(b)  dancing,

(c)  entertainment of a similar description to that falling within paragraph (a) or (b).

(3)  This paragraph is subject to Part 3 of this Schedule (interpretation).

*Power to amend Schedule*

4    The Secretary of State may by order amend this Schedule for the purpose of modifying–

(a)  the descriptions of entertainment specified in paragraph 2, or

(b)  the descriptions of entertainment specified in paragraph 3,

and for this purpose "modify" includes adding, varying or removing any description.

PART 2

EXEMPTIONS

*Film exhibitions for the purposes of advertisement, information, education, etc.*

5    The provision of entertainment consisting of the exhibition of a film is not to be regarded as the provision of regulated entertainment for the purposes of this Act if its sole or main purpose is to–

(a)  demonstrate any product,

(b)  advertise any goods or services, or

(c)  provide information, education or instruction.

*Film exhibitions: museums and art galleries*

6    The provision of entertainment consisting of the exhibition of a film is not to be regarded as the provision of regulated entertainment for the purposes of this Act if it consists of or forms part of an exhibit put on show for any purposes of a museum or art gallery.

*Music incidental to certain other activities*

7    The provision of entertainment consisting of the performance of live music or the playing of recorded music is not to be regarded as the provision of regulated entertainment for the purposes of this Act to the extent that it is incidental to some other activity which is not itself–

(a)  a description of entertainment falling within paragraph 2, or

(b)  the provision of entertainment facilities.

*Use of television or radio receivers*

8    The provision of any entertainment or entertainment facilities is not to be regarded as the provision of regulated entertainment for the purposes of this Act to the extent that it consists of the simultaneous reception and playing of a programme included in a programme service within the meaning of the Broadcasting Act 1990 (c. 42).

*Religious services, places of worship etc.*

9        The provision of any entertainment or entertainment facilities–

(a)  for the purposes of, or for purposes incidental to, a religious meeting or service, or

(b)  at a place of public religious worship,

     is not to be regarded as the provision of regulated entertainment for the purposes of this Act.

*Garden fêtes, etc.*

10  (1)  The provision of any entertainment or entertainment facilities at a garden fête, or at a function or event of a similar character, is not to be regarded as the provision of regulated entertainment for the purposes of this Act.

    (2)  But sub-paragraph (1) does not apply if the fête, function or event is promoted with a view to applying the whole or part of its proceeds for purposes of private gain.

    (3)  In sub-paragraph (2) "private gain", in relation to the proceeds of a fête, function or event, is to be construed in accordance with section 22 of the Lotteries and Amusements Act 1976 (c. 32).

*Morris dancing etc.*

11  The provision of any entertainment or entertainment facilities is not to be regarded as the provision of regulated entertainment for the purposes of this Act to the extent that it consists of the provision of–

(a)  a performance of morris dancing or any dancing of a similar nature or a performance of unamplified, live music as an integral part of such a performance, or

(b)  facilities for enabling persons to take part in entertainment of a description falling within paragraph (a).

*Vehicles in motion*

12  The provision of any entertainment or entertainment facilities–

(a)  on premises consisting of or forming part of a vehicle, and

(b)  at a time when the vehicle is not permanently or temporarily parked,

     is not to be regarded as the provision of regulated entertainment for the purposes of this Act.

PART 3

INTERPRETATION

*General*

13  This Part has effect for the purposes of this Schedule.

*Plays*

14  (1)  A "performance of a play" means a performance of any dramatic piece, whether involving improvisation or not,–

(a)  which is given wholly or in part by one or more persons actually present and performing, and

(b)  in which the whole or a major proportion of what is done by the person or persons performing, whether by way of speech, singing or action, involves the playing of a role.

    (2)  In this paragraph, "performance" includes rehearsal (and "performing" is to be construed accordingly).

*Film exhibitions*

15   An *"exhibition of a film"* means any exhibition of moving pictures.

*Indoor sporting events*

16   (1)   An "indoor sporting event" is a sporting event–
   (a)   which takes place wholly inside a building, and
   (b)   at which the spectators present at the event are accommodated wholly inside that building.

   (2)   In this paragraph–
   "building" means any roofed structure (other than a structure with a roof which may be opened or closed) and includes a vehicle, vessel or moveable structure,
   "sporting event" means any contest, exhibition or display of any sport, and
   "sport" includes–
   (a)   any game in which physical skill is the predominant factor, and
   (b)   any form of physical recreation which is also engaged in for purposes of competition or display.

*Boxing or wrestling entertainments*

17   A "boxing or wrestling entertainment" is any contest, exhibition or display of boxing or wrestling.

*Music*

18   "Music" includes vocal or instrumental music or any combination of the two.

# Annex B

**Extract from the Licensing Act 2003: Late Night Refreshment**

## SCHEDULE 2

Section 1

### PROVISION OF LATE NIGHT REFRESHMENT

*The provision of late night refreshment*

1   (1)   For the purposes of this Act, a person "provides late night refreshment" if–

    (a)   at any time between the hours of 11.00 p.m. and 5.00 a.m., he supplies hot food or hot drink to members of the public, or a section of the public, on or from any premises, whether for consumption on or off the premises, or

    (b)   at any time between those hours when members of the public, or a section of the public, are admitted to any premises, he supplies, or holds himself out as willing to supply, hot food or hot drink to any persons, or to persons of a particular description, on or from those premises, whether for consumption on or off the premises,

    unless the supply is an exempt supply by virtue of paragraph 3, 4 or 5.

    (2)   References in this Act to the "provision of late night refreshment" are to be construed in accordance with sub-paragraph (1).

    (3)   This paragraph is subject to the following provisions of this Schedule.

*Hot food or hot drink*

2   Food or drink supplied on or from any premises is "hot" for the purposes of this Schedule if the food or drink, or any part of it,–

    (a)   before it is supplied, is heated on the premises or elsewhere for the purpose of enabling it to be consumed at a temperature above the ambient air temperature and, at the time of supply, is above that temperature, or

    (b)   after it is supplied, may be heated on the premises for the purpose of enabling it to be consumed at a temperature above the ambient air temperature.

*Exempt supplies: clubs, hotels etc. and employees*

3   (1)   The supply of hot food or hot drink on or from any premises at any time is an exempt supply for the purposes of paragraph 1(1) if, at that time, a person will neither–

    (a)   be admitted to the premises, nor

    (b)   be supplied with hot food or hot drink on or from the premises,

    except by virtue of being a person of a description falling within sub-paragraph (2).

    (2)   The descriptions are that–

    (a)   he is a member of a recognised club,

    (b)   he is a person staying at a particular hotel, or at particular comparable premises, for the night in question,

    (c)   he is an employee of a particular employer,

    (d)   he is engaged in a particular trade, he is a member of a particular profession or he follows a particular vocation,

    (e)   he is a guest of a person falling within any of paragraphs (a) to (d).

    (3)   The premises which, for the purposes of sub-paragraph (2)(b), are comparable to a hotel are–

    (a)   a guest house, lodging house or hostel,

    (b)   a caravan site or camping site, or

    (c)   any other premises the main purpose of maintaining which is the provision of facilities for overnight accommodation.

**App 11**

*Exempt supplies: premises licensed under certain other Acts*

4     The supply of hot food or hot drink on or from any premises is an exempt supply for the purposes of paragraph 1(1) if it takes place during a period for which–

   (a)  the premises may be used for a public exhibition of a kind described in section 21(1) of the Greater London Council (General Powers) Act 1966

        (c. xxviii) by virtue of a licence under that section, or

   (b)  the premises may be used as near beer premises within the meaning of section 14 of the London Local Authorities Act 1995 (c. x) by virtue of a licence under section 16 of that Act.

*Miscellaneous exempt supplies*

5     (1)  The following supplies of hot food or hot drink are exempt supplies for the purposes of paragraph 1(1)–

   (a)  the supply of hot drink which consists of or contains alcohol,

   (b)  the supply of hot drink by means of a vending machine,

   (c)  the supply of hot food or hot drink free of charge,

   (d)  the supply of hot food or hot drink by a registered charity or a person authorised by a registered charity,

   (e)  the supply of hot food or hot drink on a vehicle at a time when the vehicle is not permanently or temporarily parked.

   (2)  Hot drink is supplied by means of a vending machine for the purposes of sub paragraph (1)(b) only if–

   (a)  the payment for the hot drink is inserted into the machine by a member of the public, and

   (b)  the hot drink is supplied directly by the machine to a member of the public.

   (3)  Hot food or hot drink is not to be regarded as supplied free of charge for the purposes of sub-paragraph (1)(c) if, in order to obtain the hot food or hot drink, a charge must be paid–

   (a)  for admission to any premises, or

   (b)  for some other item.

   (4)  In sub-paragraph (1)(d) "registered charity" means–

   (a)  a charity which is registered under section 3 of the Charities Act 1993

        (c. 10), or

   (b)  a charity which by virtue of subsection (5) of that section is not required to be so registered.

*Clubs which are not recognised clubs: members and guests*

6     For the purposes of this Schedule–

   (a)  the supply of hot food or hot drink to a person as being a member, or the guest of a member, of a club which is not a recognised club is to be taken to be a supply to a member of the public, and

   (b)  the admission of any person to any premises as being such a member or guest is to be taken to be the admission of a member of the public.

# Annex C

**Extract from the Licensing Act 2003: Relevant Offences**

This reproduces Schedule 4 of the Licensing Act 2003 as amended by SI 2005/2366 The Licensing Act 2003 (Personal licence: relevant offences) (Amendment) Order 2005. NB. A violent offence under paragraph 19 is 'any offence which leads, or is intended or likely to lead to a person's death or to physical injury to a person'. This would include Actual Bodily Harm and, common assault where it leads to physical injury.

## SCHEDULE 4

Section 113

### PERSONAL LICENCE: RELEVANT OFFENCES

1   An offence under this Act.
2   An offence under any of the following enactments–
   (a) Schedule 12 to the London Government Act 1963 (c. 33) (public entertainment licensing);
   (b) the Licensing Act 1964 (c. 26);
   (c) the Private Places of Entertainment (Licensing) Act 1967 (c. 19);
   (d) section 13 of the Theatres Act 1968 (c. 54);
   (e) the Late Night Refreshment Houses Act 1969 (c. 53);
   (f) section 6 of, or Schedule 1 to, the Local Government (Miscellaneous Provisions) Act 1982 (c. 30);
   (g) the Licensing (Occasional Permissions) Act 1983 (c. 24);
   (h) the Cinemas Act 1985 (c. 13);
   (i) the London Local Authorities Act 1990 (c. vii).
3   An offence under the Firearms Act 1968 (c. 27).
4   An offence under section 1 of the Trade Descriptions Act 1968 (c. 29) (false trade description of goods) in circumstances where the goods in question are or include alcohol.
5   An offence under any of the following provisions of the Theft Act 1968 (c. 60)–
   (a) section 1 (theft);
   (b) section 8 (robbery);
   (c) section 9 (burglary);
   (d) section 10 (aggravated burglary);
   (e) section 11 (removal of articles from places open to the public);
   (f) section 12A (aggravated vehicle-taking), in circumstances where subsection (2)(b) of that section applies and the accident caused the death of any person;
   (g) section 13 (abstracting of electricity);
   (h) section 15 (obtaining property by deception);
   (i) section 15A (obtaining a money transfer by deception);
   (j) section 16 (obtaining pecuniary advantage by deception);
   (k) section 17 (false accounting);
   (l) section 19 (false statements by company directors etc.);
   (m) section 20 (suppression, etc. of documents);
   (n) section 21 (blackmail);
   (o) section 22 (handling stolen goods);
   (p) section 24A (dishonestly retaining a wrongful credit);
   (q) section 25 (going equipped for stealing etc.).

App 11

6   An offence under section 7(2) of the Gaming Act 1968 (c. 65) (allowing child to take part in gaming on premises licensed for the sale of alcohol).
7   An offence under any of the following provisions of the Misuse of Drugs Act 1971 (c. 38)–
    (a)  section 4(2) (production of a controlled drug);
    (b)  section 4(3) (supply of a controlled drug);
    (c)  section 5(3) (possession of a controlled drug with intent to supply);
    (d)  section 8 (permitting activities to take place on premises).
8   An offence under either of the following provisions of the Theft Act 1978 (c. 31)–
    (a)  section 1 (obtaining services by deception);
    (b)  section 2 (evasion of liability by deception).
9   An offence under either of the following provisions of the Customs and Excise Management Act 1979 (c. 2)–
    (a)  section 170 (disregarding subsection (1)(a)) (fraudulent evasion of duty etc.);
    (b)  section 170B (taking preparatory steps for evasion of duty).
10  An offence under either of the following provisions of the Tobacco Products Duty Act 1979 (c. 7)–
    (a)  section 8G (possession and sale of unmarked tobacco);
    (b)  section 8H (use of premises for sale of unmarked tobacco).
11  An offence under the Forgery and Counterfeiting Act 1981 (c. 45) (other than an offence under section 18 or 19 of that Act).
12  An offence under the Firearms (Amendment) Act 1988 (c. 45).
13  An offence under any of the following provisions of the Copyright, Designs and Patents Act 1988 (c. 48)–
    (a)  section 107(1)(d)(iii) (public exhibition in the course of a business of article infringing copyright);
    (b)  section 107(3) (infringement of copyright by public performance of work etc.);
    (c)  section 198(2) (broadcast etc. of recording of performance made without sufficient consent);
    (d)  section 297(1) (fraudulent reception of transmission);
    (e)  section 297A(1) (supply etc. of unauthorised decoder).
14  An offence under any of the following provisions of the Road Traffic Act 1988 (c. 52)–
    (a)  section 3A (causing death by careless driving while under the influence of drink or drugs);
    (b)  section 4 (driving etc. a vehicle when under the influence of drink or drugs);
    (c)  section 5 (driving etc. a vehicle with alcohol concentration above prescribed limit).
15  An offence under either of the following provisions of the Food Safety Act 1990 (c. 16) in circumstances where the food in question is or includes alcohol–
    (a)  section 14 (selling food or drink not of the nature, substance or quality demanded);
    (b)  section 15 (falsely describing or presenting food or drink).
16  An offence under section 92(1) or (2) of the Trade Marks Act 1994 (c. 26) (unauthorised use of trade mark, etc. in relation to goods) in circumstances where the goods in question are or include alcohol.
17  An offence under the Firearms (Amendment) Act 1997 (c. 5).
18  A sexual offence, being an offence
    (a)  listed in Part 2 of Schedule 15 to the Criminal Justice Act 2003[2], other than the offence mentioned in paragraph 95 (an offence under section 4 of the Sexual Offences Act 1967 (procuring others to commit homosexual acts));
    (b)  an offence under section 8 of the Sexual Offences Act 1956 (intercourse with a defective);
    (c)  an offence under section 18 of the Sexual Offences Act 1956 (fraudulent abduction of an heiress).

19   A violent offence, being any offence which leads, or is intended or likely to lead, to a person's death or to physical injury to a person, including an offence which is required to be charged as arson (whether or not it would otherwise fall within this definition).

20   An offence under section 3 of the Private Security Industry Act 2001 (c. 12) (engaging in certain activities relating to security without a licence).

# Annex D
# Pools of conditions

## CORE PRINCIPLES

1. When applicants are preparing their operating schedules or club operating schedules, responsible authorities are considering applications and licensing authorities are considering applications following the receipt of relevant representations, they should consider whether the measures set out below are necessary to promote the licensing objectives.

2. Any risk assessment to identify necessary measures should consider the individual circumstances of the premises (including local knowledge) and take into account a range of factors including:

   • the nature and style of the venue;
   • the activities being conducted there;
   • the location; and
   • the anticipated clientele.

**Under no circumstances should licensing authorities regard these conditions as standard conditions to be automatically imposed in all cases.**

3. Any individual preparing an operating schedule or club operating schedule is at liberty to volunteer any measure, such as those below, as a step they intend to take to promote the licensing objectives. When measures are incorporated into the licence or certificate as conditions, they become enforceable under the law and any breach could give rise to prosecution.

4. Licensing authorities should carefully consider conditions to ensure that they are not only necessary but realistic, practical and achievable, so that they are capable of being met. Failure to comply with any conditions attached to a licence or certificate is a criminal offence, which on conviction would be punishable by a fine of up to £20,000 or up to six months imprisonment or both. As such, it would be wholly inappropriate to impose conditions outside the control of those responsible for the running of the premises. It is also important that conditions which are imprecise or difficult to enforce should be avoided.

5. It should be borne in mind that club premises operate under codes of discipline to ensure the good order and behaviour of members and that conditions enforcing offences under the Act are unnecessary.

## PART 1. CONDITIONS RELATING TO THE PREVENTION OF CRIME AND DISORDER

### Text/Radio pagers

Text and radio pagers connecting premises licence holders, designated premises supervisors, managers of premises and clubs to the local police can provide for rapid response by the police to situations of disorder which may be endangering the customers and staff on the premises.

Pagers provide two-way communication, allowing licence holders, managers, designated premises supervisors and clubs to report incidents to the police, and the police to warn those operating a large number of other premises of potential trouble-makers or individuals suspected of criminal behaviour who are about in a particular area. Pager systems can also be used by licence holders, door supervisors, managers, designated premises supervisors and clubs to warn each other of the presence in an area of such people.

The Secretary of State recommends that text or radio pagers should be considered for public houses, bars and nightclubs operating in city and town centre leisure areas with a high density of licensed premises. These conditions may also be appropriate and necessary in other areas.

It is recommended that a condition requiring the text/radio pager links to the police should include the following requirements:

- the text/pager equipment is kept in working order at all times;
- the pager link is activated, made available to and monitored by the designated premises supervisor or a responsible member of staff at all times that the premises are open to the public;
- any police instructions/directions are complied with whenever given; and
- all instances of crime or disorder are reported via the text/radio pager link by the designated premises supervisor or a responsible member of staff to an agreed police contact point.

## Door supervisors

Conditions relating to the provision of door supervisors and security teams may be valuable in:

- preventing the admission and ensuring the departure from the premises of the drunk and disorderly, without causing further disorder;
- keeping out individuals excluded by court bans or by the licence holder;
- searching and excluding those suspected of carrying illegal drugs, or carrying offensive weapons; and
- maintaining orderly queuing outside venues.

Where the presence of door supervisors conducting security activities is to be a condition of a licence, which means that they would have to be registered with the Security Industry Authority, conditions may also need to deal with:

- the number of supervisors;
- the displaying of name badges;
- the carrying of proof of registration;
- where, and at what times, they should be stationed on the premises; and
- whether at least one female supervisor should be available (for example, if female customers are to be given body searches).

Door supervisors also have a role to play in ensuring public safety (see Part 2) and the prevention of public nuisance (see Part 4).

## Bottle bans

Glass bottles may be used as weapons to inflict serious harm during incidents of disorder. A condition can prevent sales of drinks in glass bottles for consumption on the premises. This should be expressed in clear terms and include the following elements:

- no bottles containing beverages of any kind, whether open or sealed, shall be given to customers on the premises whether at the bar or by staff service away from the bar;
- no customers carrying open or sealed bottles shall be admitted to the premises at any time that the premises are open to the public (note: this needs to be carefully worded where off-sales also take place);

In appropriate circumstances, the condition could include exceptions, for example, as follows:

- but bottles containing wine may be sold for consumption with a table meal by customers who are seated in an area set aside from the main bar area for the consumption of food.

Bottle bans may also be a relevant necessary measure to promote public safety (see Part 2).

## Plastic containers and toughened glass

Glasses containing drinks may be used as weapons and in untoughened form, can cause very serious injuries. Where necessary, consideration should therefore be given to conditions requiring the use of safer alternatives which inflict less severe injuries. Location and style of the venue and the activities carried on there are particularly important in assessing whether a condition is necessary. For example, the use of glass containers on the terraces of some outdoor sports grounds may obviously be of concern, and similar concerns may also apply to indoor sports events such as boxing matches. Similarly, the use of plastic containers or toughened glass may be a necessary condition during the televising of live sporting events, such as international football matches, when there may be high states of excitement and emotion fuelled by alcohol.

The use of plastic or paper drinks containers and toughened glass may also be relevant as measures necessary to promote public safety (see Part 2).

## Open containers not to be taken from the premises

Drinks purchased in licensed premises or clubs may be taken from those premises for consumption elsewhere. This is lawful where premises are licensed for the sale of alcohol for consumption off the premises. However, consideration should be given to a condition preventing customers from taking alcoholic and other drinks from the premises in open containers (eg glasses and opened bottles) for example, by requiring the use of bottle bins on the premises. This may again be necessary to prevent the use of these containers as offensive weapons in surrounding streets after individuals have left the premises.

Restrictions on taking open containers from the premises may also be relevant necessary measures to prevent public nuisance (see Part 4).

## CCTV

The presence of CCTV cameras can be an important means of deterring and detecting crime at and immediately outside licensed premises. Conditions should not just consider a requirement to have CCTV on the premises, but also the precise siting of each camera, the requirement to maintain cameras in working order, and to retain recordings for an appropriate period of time.

The police should provide individuals conducting risk assessments when preparing operating schedules with advice on the use of CCTV to prevent crime.

## Restrictions on drinking areas

It may be necessary to restrict the areas where alcoholic drinks may be consumed in premises after they have been purchased from the bar. An example would be at a sports ground where the police consider it necessary to prevent the consumption of alcohol on the terracing during particular sports events. Conditions should not only specify these areas, but indicate the circumstances in which the ban would apply and times at which it should be enforced.

Restrictions on drinking areas may also be relevant necessary measures to prevent public nuisance (see Part 4).

## Capacity limits

Capacity limits are most commonly made a condition of a licence on public safety grounds (see Part 2), but should also be considered for licensed premises or clubs where overcrowding may lead to disorder and violence. If such a condition is considered necessary, door supervisors may be needed to ensure that the numbers are appropriately controlled (see above).

## Proof of age cards

It is unlawful for children under 18 to attempt to buy alcohol just as it is unlawful to sell or supply alcohol to them. To prevent these crimes, it may be necessary for certain licensed premises to require the production of "proof of age" before sales are made. The Secretary of State strongly supports the PASS accreditation system which aims to approve and accredit various proof of age schemes that are in existence. This ensures that such schemes maintain high standards, particularly in the area of integrity and security. While conditions may refer directly to PASS accredited proof of age cards, they should also allow for the production of other proof, such as photo-driving licences, student cards and passports.

Since many adults in England and Wales do not currently carry any proof of age, the wording of any condition will require careful thought. For example, many premises have adopted the "Challenge 21" or other similar initiatives. Under the "Challenge 21" initiative those premises selling or supplying alcohol require sight of evidence of age from any person appearing to be under the age of 21 and who is attempting to buy alcohol. Making this a licensing condition would ensure that most minors – even those looking older – would need to produce appropriate proof of age before making a purchase.

Proof of age may also be relevant and necessary to protect children from harm (see Part 5).

## Crime prevention notices

It may be necessary at some premises for notices to be displayed which warn customers of the prevalence of crime which may target them. Some premises may be reluctant to volunteer the display of such notices for commercial reasons. For example, in certain areas, a condition attached to a premises licence or club premises certificate might require the display of notices at the premises which warn customers about the need to be aware of pickpockets or bag snatchers, and to guard their property. Similarly, it may be necessary for notices to be displayed which advise customers not to leave bags unattended because of concerns about terrorism. Consideration could be given to a condition requiring a notice to display the name of a contact for customers if they wish to report concerns.

## Drinks promotions

Licensing authorities should not attach standardised blanket conditions promoting fixed prices for alcoholic drinks to premises licences or club premises certificates in an area as this is likely to breach competition law. It is also likely to be unlawful for licensing authorities or police officers to promote voluntary arrangements of this kind as this can risk creating cartels.

However, conditions specifically designed to address irresponsible drinks promotions or discounting at individual premises may be permissible provided they are necessary for the promotion of the licensing objectives. Licensing authorities should be aware that there may often be a very fine line between responsible and irresponsible promotions. It is therefore vital that they consider these matters objectively in the context of the licensing objectives and before pursuing any form of restrictions at all, take their own legal advice.

## Signage

It may be necessary for the normal hours at which licensable activities are permitted to take place under the terms of the premises licence or club premises certificate to be displayed on or immediately outside the premises so that it is clear if breaches of these terms are taking place.

Similarly, it may be necessary for any restrictions on the admission of children to be displayed on or immediately outside the premises to deter those who might seek admission in breach of those conditions.

## Large capacity venues used exclusively or primarily for the "vertical" consumption of alcohol (HVVDs)

Large capacity "vertical drinking" premises, sometimes called High Volume Vertical Drinking establishments (HVVDs), are premises which have exceptionally high capacities, used primarily or exclusively for the sale and consumption of alcohol, and little or no seating for patrons.

Where necessary and appropriate, conditions can be attached to licences for these premises which require adherence to:

- a prescribed capacity;
- an appropriate ratio of tables and chairs to customers based on the capacity; and
- the presence of security staff holding the appropriate SIA licence or exemption (see paragraphs 10.58–10.64) to control entry

for the purpose of compliance with the capacity limit.

## PART 2. CONDITIONS RELATING TO PUBLIC SAFETY

The attachment of conditions to a premises licence or club premises certificate will not in any way relieve employers of the statutory duty to comply with the requirements of other legislation including the Health and Safety at Work etc Act 1974, associated regulations and especially the requirements under the Management of Health and Safety at Work Regulations 1999, and the Regulatory Reform (Fire Safety) Order 2005 to undertake risk assessments. Employers should assess the risks, including risks from fire, and take measures necessary to avoid and control them. Conditions enforcing these requirements are therefore unnecessary.

From 1 October 2006 the Regulatory Reform (Fire Safety) Order 2005 replaced previous fire safety legislation. Licensing authorities should note that under article 43 of the Regulatory Reform (Fire Safety) Order 2005 any conditions imposed by the licensing authority that relate to any requirements or prohibitions that are or could be imposed by the Order have no effect. This means that licensing authorities should not seek to impose fire safety conditions where the Order applies. See Chapter 2 for more detail about the Order.

## General

Additional matters relating to cinemas and theatres are considered in Part 3. It should also be recognised that special issues may arise in connection with outdoor and large scale events.

In addition, to considering the points made in this Part, those preparing operating schedules or club operating schedules, licensing authorities and responsible authorities should consider:

- Model National and Standard Conditions for Places of Public Entertainment and Associated Guidance ISBN 1 904031 11 0 (Entertainment Technology Press – ABTT Publications)
- The Event Safety Guide – A guide to health, safety and welfare at music and similar events (HSE 1999) ("The Purple Book") ISBN 0 7176 2453 6
- Managing Crowds Safely (HSE 2000) ISBN 0 7176 1834 X

App 11

- 5 Steps to Risk Assessment: Case Studies (HSE 1998) ISBN 07176 15804
- The Guide to Safety at Sports Grounds (The Stationery Office, 1997) ("The Green Guide") ISBN 0 11 300095 2
- Safety Guidance for Street Arts, Carnival, Processions and Large Scale Performances published by the Independent Street Arts Network, copies of which may be obtained through: www.streetartsnetwork.org.uk/pages/publications.htm
- The London District Surveyors Association's "Technical Standards for Places of Public Entertainment" ISBN 0 9531229 2 1

The following British Standards should also be considered:

- BS 5588 Part 6 (regarding places of assembly)
- BS 5588 Part 9 (regarding ventilation and air conditioning systems)
- BS 5588 Part 9 (regarding means of escape for disabled people)
- BS 5839 (fire detection, fire alarm systems and buildings)
- BS 5266 (emergency lighting systems)

**In most premises existing legislation will provide adequately for the safety of the public or club members and guests. However, where this is not the case, consideration might be given to the following conditions.**

### Safety checks

- Safety checks are carried out before the admission of the public.
- Details of such checks are kept in a Log-book.

### Escape routes

- Exits are kept unobstructed, with non-slippery and even surfaces, free of trip hazards and clearly identified.
- Where chairs and tables are provided in restaurants and other premises, internal gangways are kept unobstructed.
- All exits doors are easily openable without the use of a key, card, code or similar means.
- Doors at such exits are regularly checked to ensure that they function satisfactorily and a record of the check kept.
- Any removable security fastenings are removed whenever the premises are open to the public or occupied by staff.

- The edges of the treads of steps and stairways are maintained so as to be conspicuous.

### Disabled people

- When disabled people are present, adequate arrangements exist to enable their safe evacuation in the event of an emergency; and disabled people on the premises are made aware of those arrangements.

### Lighting

- In the absence of adequate daylight, the lighting in any area accessible to the public, members or guests shall be fully in operation when they are present.
- Emergency lighting is not altered.
- Emergency lighting batteries are fully charged before the admission of the public, members or guests.
- In the event of the failure of normal lighting, where the emergency lighting battery has a capacity of one hour, arrangements are in place to ensure that the public, members or guests leave the premises within 20 minutes unless within that time normal lighting has been restored and the battery is being re-charged; and, if the emergency lighting battery has a capacity of three hours, the appropriate period by the end of which the public should have left the premises is one hour.

### Curtains, hangings, decorations and upholstery

- Curtains, hangings and temporary decorations are arranged so as not to obstruct exits
- temporary decorations are not used without prior notification to the licensing authority/relevant responsible authority.

### Capacity limits

- Arrangements are made to ensure that any capacity limit imposed under the premises licence or club premises certificate is not exceeded.
- The licence holder, a club official, manager or designated premises supervisor should be aware of the number of people on the premises and required to inform any authorised person on request.

### Access for emergency vehicles

- Access for emergency vehicles is kept clear and free from obstruction.

## First aid

- Adequate and appropriate supply of first aid equipment and materials is available on the premises.
- If necessary, at least one suitably trained first-aider shall be on duty when the public are present; and if more than one suitably trained first-aider that their respective duties are clearly defined.

## Temporary electrical installations

- Temporary electrical wiring and distribution systems are not provided without notification to the licensing authority at least ten days before commencement of the work and/or prior inspection by a suitable qualified electrician.
- Temporary electrical wiring and distribution systems shall comply with the recommendations of BS 7671 or where applicable BS 7909.
- Where they have not been installed by a competent person, temporary electrical wiring and distribution systems are inspected and certified by a competent person before they are put to use.

With regard to the first bullet above, it should be recognised that ten days notice may not be possible where performances are supported by outside technical teams. For example, where temporary electrical installations are made in theatres for television show performances. In such circumstances, the key requirement is that conditions should ensure that temporary electrical installations are only undertaken by competent qualified persons, for example, employed by the television company.

## Indoor sports entertainments

- If necessary, an appropriately qualified medical practitioner is present throughout a sports entertainment involving boxing, wrestling, judo, karate or other sports entertainment of a similar nature.
- Any ring is constructed and supported by a competent person and inspected by a competent authority.
- At any wrestling or other entertainments of a similar nature members of the public do not occupy any seat within 2.5 metres of the ring.
- At water sports entertainments, staff adequately trained in rescue and life safety procedures are stationed and remain within the vicinity of the water at all

material times (see also Managing Health and Safety in Swimming Pools issued jointly by the Health and Safety Commission and Sport England).

## Special effects

The use of special effects in venues of all kinds being used for regulated entertainment is increasingly common and can present significant risks. Any special effects or mechanical installation should be arranged and stored so as to minimise any risk to the safety of the audience, the performers and staff. Further details and guidance are given in Part 3.

## Alterations to the premises

Premises should not be altered in such a way as to make it impossible to comply with an existing licence condition without first seeking a variation of the premises licence to delete the relevant public safety condition. The applicant will need to propose how they intend to take alternative steps to promote the public safety objective in a new operating schedule reflecting the proposed alteration to the premises. The application for variation will enable the responsible authorities with expertise in safety matters to consider whether the proposal is acceptable.

## Other measures

Other measures previously mentioned in relation to the Prevention of Crime and Disorder may also be relevant as necessary to promote public safety. These might include the provision of door supervisors, bottle bans, and requirements to use plastic or toughened glass containers (see Part 1 for further detail).

## PART 3. THEATRES, CINEMAS, CONCERT HALLS AND SIMILAR PLACES (PROMOTION OF PUBLIC SAFETY)

In addition to the points in Part 2, there are particular public safety matters which should be considered in connection with theatres and cinemas.

## PREMISES USED FOR CLOSELY SEATED AUDIENCES

### Attendants

(a) The number of attendants on each floor in a closely seated auditorium should be as set out on the table below:

App 11

| Number of members of the audience present on a floor | Minimum number of attendants required to be present on that floor |
|---|---|
| 1–100 | One |
| 101–250 | Two |
| 251–500 | Three |
| 501–750 | Four |
| 751–1000 | Five |

**And one additional attendant for each additional 250 persons (or part thereof)**

(b) Attendants shall not be engaged in any duties that would prevent them from promptly discharging their duties in the event of an emergency or require their absence from that floor or auditorium where they are on duty.

(c) Any attendant shall be readily identifiable to the audience (but this need not entail the wearing of a uniform).

(d) The premises shall not be used for a closely seated audience except in accordance with seating plan(s), a copy of which is available at the premises and shall be shown to any authorised person on request.

(e) No article shall be attached to the back of any seat which would reduce the clear width of seatways or cause a tripping hazard or obstruction.

(f) A copy of any certificate relating to the design, construction and loading of any temporary seating shall be kept available at the premises and shall be shown to any authorised person on request.

## Seating

Where the potential audience exceeds 250 all seats in the auditorium should, except in boxes accommodating not more than 8 persons, be either securely fixed to the floor or battened together in lengths of not fewer than four or more than twelve.

## Standing and sitting in gangways etc

(a) Sitting on floors shall not be permitted except where authorised in the premises licence or club premises certificate.

(b) Waiting or standing shall not be permitted except in areas designated in the premises licence or club premises certificate.

(c) In no circumstances shall anyone be permitted to
(i) sit in any gangway;
(ii) stand or sit in front of any exit; or
(iii) stand or sit on any staircase including any landings.

## Drinks

Except as authorised by the premises licence or club premises certificate, no drinks shall be sold to or be consumed by a closely seated audience except in plastic and paper containers.

## Balcony Fronts

Clothing or other objects shall not be placed over balcony rails or upon balcony fronts.

## Special effects

Any special effects or mechanical installation should be arranged and stored so as to minimise any risk to the safety of the audience, the performers and staff.

Specials effects include:

- dry ice machines and cryogenic fog;
- smoke machines and fog generators;
- pyrotechnics, including fireworks;
- real flame;
- firearms;
- motor vehicles;
- strobe lighting;
- lasers;
- explosives and highly flammable substances.

In certain circumstances, it may be necessary to require that certain special effects are only used with the prior notification of the licensing authority. In these cases, the licensing authority should notify the fire and rescue authority, who will exercise their inspection and enforcement powers under the Regulatory Reform (Fire Safety) Order 2005.

Further guidance can be found in the following publications:

- HSE Guide 'The radiation safety of lasers used for display purposes' (HS(G)95;
- 'Smoke and vapour effects used in entertainment' (HSE Entertainment Sheet No 3);
- 'Special or visual effects involving explosives or pyrotechnics used in film and television production' (HSE Entertainment Sheet No 16);
- 'Electrical safety for entertainers' (HSE INDG 247);

- 'Theatre Essentials' – Guidance booklet produced by the Association of British Theatre Technicians 8.

## Ceilings

All ceilings in those parts of the premises to which the audience are admitted should be inspected by a suitably qualified person who will decide when a further inspection is necessary and a certificate concerning the condition of the ceilings forwarded to the licensing authority.

## PREMISES USED FOR FILM EXHIBITIONS

### Attendants – premises without a staff alerting system

Where the premises are not equipped with a staff alerting system the number of attendants present should be as set out in the table below:

(b) Staff shall not be considered as being available to assist in the event of an emergency if they are:

(i) the holder of the premises licence or the manager on duty at the premises; or

(ii) a member of staff whose normal duties or responsibilities are likely to significantly affect or delay their response in an emergency situation; or

(iii) a member of staff whose usual location when on duty is more than 60 metres from the location to which they are required to go on being alerted to an emergency situation.

(c) Attendants shall as far as reasonably practicable be evenly distributed throughout all parts of the premises to which the public have access and keep under observation all parts of the premises to which the audience have access.

| Number of members of the audience present | Minimum number of attendants required on the premises to be on duty |
| --- | --- |
| 1–250 | Two |
| And one additional attendant for each additional 250 | members of the audience present (or part thereof) |
| Where there are more than 150 members of audience in any auditorium or on any floor | At least one attendant shall be present audience in any auditorium or on any floor |

### Attendants – premises with a staff alerting system

(a) Where premises are equipped with a staff alerting system the number of attendants present should be as set out in the table below:

(d) The staff alerting system shall be maintained in working order.

### Minimum lighting

The level of lighting in the auditorium should be as great as possible consistent with the

| Number of members of the audience present on the premises | Minimum number of attendants required to be on duty | Minimum number of other staff on the premises who are available to assist in the event of an emergency |
| --- | --- | --- |
| 1–500 | Two | One |
| 501–1000 | Three | Two |
| 1001–1500 | Four | Four |
| 1501 or more | Five plus one for every 500 (or part thereof) persons over 2000 on the premises | Five plus one for every 500 (or part thereof) persons over 2000 on the premises |

effective presentation of the film; and the level of illumination maintained in the auditorium during the showing of films would normally be regarded as satisfactory if it complies with the standards specified in BS CP 1007 (Maintained Lighting for Cinemas).

# PART 4. CONDITIONS RELATING TO THE PREVENTION OF PUBLIC NUISANCE

It should be noted that provisions of the Environmental Protection Act 1990, the Noise Act 1996 and the Clean Neighbourhoods and Environment Act 2005 provide some protection to the general public from the effects of noise nuisance. In addition, the provisions in Part 8 of the Licensing Act 2003 enable a senior police officer to close down instantly for up to 24 hours licensed premises and premises carrying on temporary permitted activities that are causing nuisance resulting from noise emanating from the premises. These matters should be considered before deciding whether or not conditions are necessary for the prevention of public nuisance.

## Hours

The hours during which the premises are permitted to be open to the public or to members and their guests can be restricted by the conditions of a premises licence or a club premises certificate for the prevention of public nuisance. But this must be balanced by the potential impact on disorder which may result from arbitrarily fixed closing times. However, there is no general presumption in favour of lengthening licensing hours and the four licensing objectives should be paramount considerations at all times.

Restrictions could be necessary on the times when certain licensable activities take place even though the premises may be open to the public as such times. For example, the playing of recorded music after a certain time might be prohibited, even though other licensable activities are permitted to continue. Or the playing of recorded music might only be permitted after a certain time where conditions have been attached to the licence or certificate to ensure that any potential nuisance is satisfactorily prevented.

Restrictions might also be necessary on the parts of premises that might be used for certain licensable activities at certain times. For example, while the provision of regulated entertainment might be permitted while the

premises is open to the public or members and their guests, regulated entertainment might not be permitted in garden areas of the premises after a certain time.

In premises where existing legislation does not provide adequately for the prevention of public nuisance, consideration might be given to the following conditions.

## Noise and vibration

In determining which conditions are necessary and appropriate, licensing authorities should be aware of the need to avoid unnecessary or disproportionate measures that could deter the holding of events that are valuable to the community, such as live music. Noise limiters, for example, are very expensive to purchase and install and are likely to be a considerable burden for smaller venues. The following conditions may be considered:

- Noise or vibration does not emanate from the premises so as to cause a nuisance to nearby properties. This might be achieved by one or more of the following conditions:
  - a simple requirement to keep doors and windows at the premises closed;
  - limiting live music to a particular area of the building;
  - moving the location and direction of speakers away from external walls or walls that abut private premises;
  - installation of acoustic curtains;
  - fitting of rubber seals to doorways;
  - installation of rubber speaker mounts;
  - requiring the licensee to take measure to ensure that music will not be audible above background level at the nearest noise sensitive location;
  - require licensee to undertake routine monitoring to ensure external levels of music are not excessive and take appropriate action where necessary;
  - noise limiters on amplification equipment used at the premises (if other measures have been unsuccessful).
- Prominent, clear and legible notices are displayed at all exits requesting the public to respect the needs of local residents and to leave the premises and the area quietly.
- The use of explosives, pyrotechnics and fireworks of a similar nature which could cause disturbance in surrounding areas are restricted.

- The placing of refuse – such as bottles – into receptacles outside the premises takes place at times that will minimise the disturbance to nearby properties.

## Noxious smells

- Noxious smells from licensed premises are not permitted so as to cause a nuisance to nearby properties and the premises are properly vented.

## Light pollution

- Flashing or particularly bright lights on or outside licensed premises do not cause a nuisance to nearby properties. Any such condition needs to be balanced against the benefits to the prevention of crime and disorder of bright lighting in certain places.

## Other measures

Other measures previously mentioned in relation to the Prevention of Crime and Disorder may also be relevant as necessary to prevent public nuisance. These might include the provision of door supervisors, open containers not to be taken from the premises, and restrictions on drinking areas (see Part 1 for further detail).

## PART 5. CONDITIONS RELATING TO THE PROTECTION OF CHILDREN FROM HARM

An operating schedule or club operating schedule should indicate any decision for the premises to exclude children completely. This would mean there would be no need to detail in the operating schedule steps that the applicant proposes to take to promote the protection of children from harm. Otherwise, where entry is to be permitted, the operating schedule should outline the steps to be taken to promote the protection of children from harm while on the premises.

## Access for children to licensed premises – in general

Restrictions on the access of children under 18 to premises where licensable activities are being carried on should be made where it is necessary to protect children from harm. Precise policy and details will be a matter for individual licensing authorities.

The Secretary of State recommends (unless there are circumstances justifying the contrary) that:

- for any premises with known associations (having been presented with evidence) with or likely to give rise to:

- heavy or binge or underage drinking;
- drugs;
- significant gambling; or
- any activity or entertainment (whether regulated entertainment or not) of a clearly adult or sexual nature, there should be a strong presumption against permitting any access at all for children under 18 years.
- for any premises, not serving alcohol for consumption on the premises, but where the public are allowed on the premises after 11.00pm in the evening, there should be a presumption against the presence of children under the age of 12 unaccompanied by adults after that time.

Applicants wishing to allow access under the above circumstances, should when preparing new operating schedules or club operating schedules or variations of those schedules:

- explain their reasons; and
- outline in detail the steps that they intend to take to protect children from harm on such premises.

In any other case the Secretary of State recommends that, subject to the premises licence holder's or club's discretion, the expectation would be for unrestricted access for children subject to the terms of the 2003 Act.

## Age Restrictions – specific

Whilst it may be appropriate to allow children unrestricted access at particular times and when certain activities are not taking place, licensing authorities will need to consider:

- the hours of day during which age restrictions should and should not apply. For example, the fact that adult entertainment may be presented at premises after 8.00pm does not mean that it would be necessary to impose age restrictions for earlier parts of the day;
- types of event or activity that are unlikely to require age restrictions, for example:
  - family entertainment; or
  - non-alcohol events for young age groups, such as under 18s dances,
- types of event or activity which give rise to a more acute need for age restrictions than normal, for example:
- during "Happy Hours" or on drinks promotion nights;
- during activities outlined in the first bullet point in the first paragraph above.

App 11

## Age restrictions – cinemas

The British Board of Film Classification classifies films in accordance with its published Guidelines which are based on extensive research into public opinion and professional advice. The Secretary of State therefore recommends that licensing authorities should not duplicate this effort by choosing to classify films themselves. The classifications recommended by the Board should be those normally applied unless there are very good local reasons for a licensing authority to adopt this role. Licensing authorities should note that the provisions of the 2003 Act enable them to specify the Board in the licence or certificate and, in relation to individual films, to notify the holder or club that it will make a recommendation for that particular film.

Licensing authorities should be aware that the BBFC currently classifies films in the following way:

- U Universal – suitable for audiences aged four years and over
- PG – Parental Guidance. Some scenes may be unsuitable for young children.
- 12A – Passed only for viewing by persons aged 12 years or older or persons younger than 12 when accompanied by an adult.
- 15 – Passed only for viewing by persons aged 15 years and over.
- 18 – Passed only for viewing by persons aged 18 years and over.

Licensing authorities should note that these classifications may be subject to occasional change and consult the BBFC's website at www.bbfc.co.uk before applying relevant conditions.

The Secretary of State considers that, in addition to the mandatory condition imposed by section 20, conditions restricting the admission of children to film exhibitions should include that:

- where the licensing authority itself is to make recommendations on the admission of children to films, the cinema or venue operator must submit any film to the authority that it intends to exhibit 28 days before it is proposed to show it. This is to allow the authority time to classify it so that the premises licence holder is able to adhere to any age restrictions then imposed;
- immediately before each exhibition at the premises of a film passed by the British Board of Film Classification there shall be exhibited on screen for at least five

seconds in such a manner as to be easily read by all persons in the auditorium a reproduction of the certificate of the Board or, as regards a trailer advertising a film, of the statement approved by the Board indicating the classification of the film;

- when a licensing authority has made a recommendation on the restriction of admission of children to a film, notices are required to be displayed both inside and outside the premises so that persons entering can readily be made aware of the classification attached to any film or trailer. Such a condition might be expressed in the following terms:

"Where a programme includes a film recommended by the licensing authority as falling into an age restrictive category no person appearing to be under the age specified shall be admitted to any part of the programme; where a programme includes a film recommended by the licensing authority as falling into a category requiring any persons under a specified age to be accompanied by an adult no person appearing to be under the age specified shall be admitted to any part of the programme unaccompanied by an adult, and the licence holder shall display in a conspicuous position a notice clearly stating the relevant age restrictions and requirements. For example:

## PERSONS UNDER THE AGE OF [INSERT APPROPRIATE AGE] CANNOT BE ADMITTED TO ANY PART OF THE PROGRAMME

Where films of different categories form part of the same programme, the notice shall refer to the oldest age restriction.

This condition does not apply to members of staff under the relevant age while on-duty provided that the prior written consent of the person's parent or legal guardian has first been obtained."

## Theatres

The admission of children to theatres, as with other licensed premises, is not expected to be restricted normally unless it is necessary to promote the protection of children from harm. However, theatres may be the venue for a wide range of activities. The admission of children to the performance of a play should normally be left to the discretion of the licence holder and no condition restricting the access of children to plays should be attached. However, theatres may also present entertainment including, for example, variety shows, incorporating adult entertainment. A condition restricting the admission of children in such circumstances may be necessary. Entertainment may also be presented at theatres specifically for children (see below).

Licensing authorities are also expected to consider whether a condition should be attached to a premises licence which requires the presence of a sufficient number of adult staff on the premises to ensure the well being of children during any emergency (See Part 3).

## Performances especially for children

Where performances are presented especially for unaccompanied children in theatres and cinemas, licensing authorities will also wish to consider conditions to specify that:

• an attendant to be stationed in the area(s) occupied by the children, in the vicinity of each exit, provided that on each level occupied by children the minimum number of attendants on duty should be one attendant per 50 children or part thereof.

Licensing authorities should also consider whether or not standing should be allowed. For example, there may be reduced risk for children in the stalls than at other levels or areas in the building.

## Children in performances

There are many productions each year that are one-off shows where the cast is made up almost entirely of children. They may be taking part as individuals or as part of a drama club, stage school or school group. The age of those involved may range from 5 to 18. The Children (Performances) Regulations 1968 as amended set out requirements for children performing in a show. Licensing authorities should familiarise themselves with these Regulations and not duplicate any of these requirements. However, if it is necessary to consider imposing conditions, in addition to these requirements, for the promotion of the protection of children from harm then the licensing authority should consider the matters outlined below.

• **Venue** – the backstage facilities should be large enough to accommodate safely the number of children taking part in any performance.

• **Special effects** – it may be inappropriate to use certain special effects, including smoke, dry ice, rapid pulsating or flashing lights, which may trigger adverse reactions especially with regard to children.

• **Care of children** – theatres, concert halls

and similar places are places of work and may contain a lot of potentially dangerous equipment. It is therefore important that children performing at such premises are kept under adult supervision at all times including transfer from stage to dressing room and anywhere else on the premises. It is also important that the children can be accounted for at all times in case of an evacuation or emergency.

## The Portman Group Code of Practice on the Naming, Packaging and Promotion of Alcoholic Drinks

The Portman Group operates, on behalf of the alcohol industry, a Code of Practice on the Naming, Packaging and Promotion of Alcoholic Drinks. The Code seeks to ensure that drinks are packaged and promoted in a socially responsible manner and only to those who are 18 years old or older. Complaints about products under the Code are considered by an Independent Complaints Panel and the Panel's decisions are published on the Portman Group's website, in the trade press and in an annual report. If a product's packaging or point-of-sale advertising is found to be in breach of the Code, the Portman Group may issue a Retailer Alert Bulletin to notify retailers of the decision and ask them not to replenish stocks of any such product or to display such point-of-sale material, until the decision has been complied with. The Code is an important mechanism in protecting children from harm because it addresses the naming, marketing and promotion of alcohol products sold in licensed premises in a manner which may appeal to or attract minors. Consideration can be given to attaching conditions to premises licences and club premises certificates that require compliance with the Portman Group's Retailer Alert Bulletins.

## Proof of Age cards

Proof of age cards are discussed under Part 1 in connection with the prevention of crime and disorder. However, a requirement for the production of proof of age cards before any sale or supply of alcohol is made could be attached to any premises licence or club premises certificate for the protection of children from harm.

Proof of age cards can also ensure that appropriate checks are made where the presence of children is restricted by age at certain times, such as 16.

Since many adults in England and Wales do not currently carry any proof of age, the wording of any condition will require careful thought. For example, many premises have adopted the "Challenge 21" or other similar initiatives. Under the "Challenge 21" initiative those premises selling or supplying alcohol require sight of evidence of age from any person appearing to be under the age of 21 and who is attempting to buy alcohol. Making this a licensing condition would ensure that most minors – even those looking older – would need to produce appropriate proof of age before making such a purchase.

# Annex E
# Useful information and contacts

## BRITISH BEER AND PUB ASSOCIATION PARTNERSHIPS INITIATIVE

The Government and the British Beer and Pub Association (BBPA) are committed to encouraging the voluntary participation of licensees' groups in their local Crime and Disorder Reduction Partnerships; and encouraging CDRPs and local representatives of the hospitality industry to work together in partnership. Since March 2000, 240 CDRPs have sought industry involvement in the work of their partnership. The Government and the BBPA continue to work to encourage further participation.

## NATIONAL PUBWATCH AND LOCAL PUBWATCH SCHEMES

Pubwatch schemes have been in existence throughout the United Kingdom for over 20 years and range in size from over 200 premises in cities to small rural schemes with as few as 5 premises involved. The basic working principle underpinning a Pubwatch scheme is that the licensees of the premises involved agree on a number of policies to counter individuals who threaten damage, disorder, and violence or use or deal in drugs in their premises. Normally, action consists of agreeing to refuse to serve individuals that cause, or are known to have caused, these sorts of problems. Refusal of admission and service to those that cause trouble has proved to be effective in reducing anti-social behaviour. To work effectively any Pubwatch scheme must work closely with the police, licensing authorities and other agencies. National Pubwatch is an entirely voluntary organisation set up to support existing pubwatches and encourage the creation of new pubwatch schemes with the key aim of achieving a safe, secure social drinking environment in all licensed premises throughout the UK helping to reduce drink-related crime.

The National Pubwatch Good Practice Guide provides advice on how such schemes can be established locally and includes Codes of Practice on sharing information, photographs and banning policies with regard to responsibilities under the Data Protection Act 1998. Licensing authorities should familiarise themselves with Pubwatch schemes operating in their areas and support their aims. Information about Pubwatch can be obtained through their website: www.nationalpubwatch.org.uk

## BEST BAR NONE

The Best Bar None Awards scheme was developed by the Manchester City Centre Safe project in late 2001 as part of its overall remit to address alcohol related crime. The scheme provides an incentive for operators to raise management standards and complements targeted enforcement action.

The key elements of Best Bar None are:

- the promotion of responsible licensed trade management;
- promotion of socially responsible drinking;
- commitment to caring for and protecting customers;
- commitment to reducing the potential for disorder in town centres and public places arising from alcohol abuse.

Assessment involves examination of policy and practice in a wide range of areas, including, for example:

- door and security policies and practice;
- first aid provision;
- health and safety provision;
- policy and practice in dealing with customers;
- handling instances of alcohol abuse;
- pastoral care of customers, including provision of advice and information;
- policy and practice in dealing with drugs;
- managing customer behaviour;
- attention to detail in licensing standards compliance;

App 11

- engagement with all relevant stakeholders in tackling the issues.

Information about Best Bar None and further contact details can be obtained through their website: www.bestbarnone.com.

## SAFER CLUBBING – DRUGS IN CLUBS

The Government outlined its commitment to addressing drugs in clubs in 1998 in its strategy 'Tackling Drugs to Build a Better Britain'. In 2001 the Home Office and the London Drug Policy Forum produced guidance entitled "Safer Clubbing" which, building on the earlier success of 'Dance Till Dawn Safely', was nationally welcomed and proved an extremely useful document for licensing officers, club managers and promoters. The aim of reducing the potential for harm through better management of dance venues was affirmed in the 2003 "Updated Drug Strategy" which may be viewed with "Safer Clubbing" at www.drugs.gov.uk

A key element of the strategy described in "Safer Clubbing" is the use of necessary and appropriate licensing conditions to control the environment at relevant premises. The Secretary of State commends this document for use by the police, all licensing authorities, all responsible authorities and all authorised persons under the 2003 Act.

"Safer Clubbing" recommends that every Drug Action Team which has clubs in its area, should take the lead in getting the police, club owners and promoters, local authorities and local drug agencies to sit down together and plan a strategy which ensures that dance events take place in as safe an environment as possible. There may also be the need to involve existing multi-agency partnerships, such as Crime and Disorder Reduction Partnerships, or town centre management groups, in developing a strategy.

"Safer Clubbing" also shows that clubs themselves have a responsibility to develop a drugs policy and in many cases will wish to contact the Drug Action Team (DAT) in order to pursue this. Clubs and their owners will need to work with the police, local and licensing authorities and drug services, as represented on the DAT, to develop a drug policy combating drugs dealing and use and ensuring the safety of their venue. Certain factors exacerbate the risks to the safety of those taking drugs. These include taking combinations of controlled drugs and/or mixing these with alcohol and becoming overheated and exercising to exhaustion. All these factors are commonly found at dance events. Many drugs, and combinations of drugs, are used in the club setting and staff should be trained to recognise symptoms and there should be appropriate provision of trained first aiders. Recreational drug misuse frequently involves Ecstasy, from which approximately 80-100 people have died in the last ten years. The majority of these deaths have been due to acute heat stroke. In most cases the heat stroke has been caused by a combination of factors:

- Ecstasy causes body temperature to rise significantly;
- non-stop dancing increases this already elevated temperature;
- poor ventilation, over-heated venues and overcrowding, increase temperature further;
- inadequate intake of water (or other non-alcoholic drinks) exacerbates dehydration and impairs the body's ability to cool itself; and
- taking alcohol or other drugs with Ecstasy can further cause the body to overheat.

Licensing conditions can impact on all these factors. In addition, licensing authorities are encouraged to ensure that their officers engage in the following key activities:

- providing clear information on the licensing authority's policy on safer clubbing in its local statement of policy;
- providing clear information on how to prepare operating schedules or club operating schedules in support of applications for premises licences or club premises certificates;
- providing induction training to councillors serving on licensing committees;
- advising venue owners on how to establish and maintain a safe environment;
- advising venue owners, in partnership with police licensing officers, on developing a venue drug policy;
- advising venue operators what to do in the event of an emergency where drugs are known or suspected to be involved;
- ensuring that sufficient first aiders are always present at a venue and are trained to a high standard;
- informing clubbers of their rights;
- liaising with police licensing and other officers to ensure good communication about potentially dangerous venues;

- encouraging venues to use outreach services;
- encouraging venues to provide safe and accessible transport home;
- surveying clubbers on their views of the safety aspects of different local venues;
- monitoring the operation of clubs at times of peak occupancy;
- ensuring that door supervisors are properly registered with the Security Industry Authority;
- ensuring that door supervisors have been properly trained; and
- encouraging the provision of free cool water and "chill out areas" so that clubbers do not become overly exhausted or dehydrated.

Safer Clubbing has been directly aimed at late night club type venues which have been associated with drug misuse. It will be updated in 2004 to take account of the need to ensure the safety of people attending events at all licensed premises which can now operate the type of music events at which people are more likely to take drugs.

"Safer Clubbing" concerns drugs and nightclubs. The Home Office, in conjunction with the Department of Health, the DCMS and key stakeholders, has also produced the Safer Clubbing Guide that provides comprehensive new advice for nightclub owners, dance event promoters and existing local authority licensing departments on how to ensure the health and safety of anyone attending dance events in England. The Guide can be viewed in full on www.drugs.gov.uk.

## RESEARCH

For information on potential alcohol-related harms generally, and the relationship between alcohol and crime specifically, licensing authorities are invited to look at the Prime Minister's Strategy Unit's interim analysis paper which was produced to summarise the evidence based on all forms of alcohol-related harm www.strategy.gov.uk/work_areas/alcohol_misuse/inte rim.asp. Up-to-date information on alcohol-related crime research can be found on the Home Office's alcohol and crime research page http://www.homeoffice.gov.uk/rds/alcohol1.html. It is also important for local areas to understand their local alcohol-related crime problems. The Home Office has produced guidance for local agencies into the different sources of data available and how to collect it in order to adequately audit local problems http://www.homeoffice.gov.uk/rds/dprpubs1.html. Some key findings from the British Crime Survey in relation to alcohol and crime are:

- Almost half of all violence is alcohol-related (47%) Stranger violence and acquaintance violence are the most likely to be committed by someone under the influence of alcohol (58% and 51% respectively)
- One in 5 violent incidents occur in or around a pub or clubs (21%)
- A quarter of the population consider drunk and rowdy behaviour a 'very' or 'fairly' big problem in their local area.

## PUBLIC SAFETY

There are a number of key safety publications in the context of regulated entertainment with which licensing authorities should be familiar. They include:

- The Event Safety Guide – A guide to health, safety and welfare at music and similar events (HSE 1999) ("The Purple Book") ISBN 0 7176 2453 6
- Managing Crowds Safely (HSE 2000) ISBN 0 7176 1834 X
- 5 Steps to Risk Assessment: Case Studies (HSE 1998) ISBN 07176 15804
- The Guide to Safety at Sports Grounds (The Stationery Office, 1997) ("The Green Guide") ISBN 0 11 300095 2
- Safety Guidance for Street Arts, Carnival, Processions and Large Scale Performances published by the Independent Street Arts Network, copies of which may be obtained through www.streetartsnetwork.org.uk/pages/publications.htm.

## QUALIFICATIONS SUPPORTING THE LICENSING OBJECTIVES

A range of qualifications, designed to support the licensing objectives, are available from the British Institute of Innkeeping (BII), in addition to the statutory requirement for personal licence holders to have an accredited licensing qualification. These include the National Certificate for Entertainment Licensees, the National Certificate for Licensees (Drugs Awareness), the National Certificate for Door Supervisors and the Barperson's National Certificate. The BII is also developing a further range of courses and qualifications covering issues such as risk assessment, conflict management, retail operations and the sale of age-restricted products. Further information is available by contacting the BII by e-mail at the following address: info@bii.org.

## THE PORTMAN GROUP CODE OF PRACTICE ON THE NAMING, PACKAGING AND PROMOTION OF ALCOHOLIC DRINKS

The Portman Group operates, on behalf of the alcohol industry, a Code of Practice on the Naming, Packaging and Promotion of Alcoholic Drinks. The Code seeks to ensure that drinks are packaged and promoted in a socially responsible manner and only to those who are 18 years old or older. Complaints about products under the Code are considered by an Independent Complaints Panel and the Panel's decisions are published on the Portman Group's website, in the trade press and in an annual report. If a product's packaging or point-of-sale advertising is found to be in breach of the Code, the Portman Group may issue a Retailer Alert Bulletin to notify retailers of the decision and ask them not to replenish stocks of any such product or to display such point-of-sale material, until the decision has been complied with. The Code is an important weapon in protecting children from harm because it addresses the naming, marketing and promotion of alcohol products sold in licensed premises in a manner which may appeal to or attract minors. The Secretary of State commends the Code to licensing authorities and recommends that they should commend it in their statements of licensing policy.

## RESPONSIBLE RETAILING OF ALCOHOL: GUIDANCE FOR THE OFF TRADE

The Association of Convenience Stores, the British Retail Consortium and the Wine and Spirits Trade Association have jointly produced a guide to responsible alcohol retailing. The Guide covers the key areas of underage sales, proof of age cards, staff training and alcohol promotions. The Guide is available online at: www.thelocalshop.com/responsibleretailing.

For more information on alcohol retailing in off licences contact:

Association of Convenience Stores www.thelocalshop.com or ring 01252515001

British Retail Consortium www.brc.org.uk or ring 020 7854 8900

Wine and Spirit Trade Association www.wsta.org.uk or ring 020 7089 3877

## ENQUIRIES

Any enquires about the content of this Guidance should be made to:

**Licensing Policy Team**
**Department for Culture, Media and Sport**
**Tourism, Licensing and Economic Impact**
**Division 6th Floor**
**2–4 Cockspur Street**
**London SW1Y 5DH**
**Telephone: 020 7211 6380**
**e.mail: enquiries@culture.gov.uk**

# Index

App 11

App 11

# APPENDIX 12: GUIDANCE ISSUED BY DCMS ON POLICE POWERS TO CLOSE PREMISES UNDER THE LICENSING ACT 2003 (JUNE 2007)

## Police Powers to Close Premises under the Licensing Act 2003

1. Part 8 of the Licensing Act 2003 ('the 2003 Act') significantly extended the existing powers of the police (a) to seek court orders to close licensed premises in a geographical area that is experiencing or likely to experience disorder; and (b) to close down instantly individual licensed premises that are:
- disorderly;
- likely to become disorderly; or
- are causing nuisance as a result of noise from the premises.

These powers are available in relation to:
- premises licensed for the provision of regulated entertainment; and late night refreshment; and to
- premises for which a temporary event notice has effect.

2. On 6 April 2007, the Violent Crime Reduction Act 2006 amended Part 8 of the 2003 Act to insert a new offence of persistently selling alcohol to children (new sections 147A and B) and related closure powers (new sections 169A and B) where there is good evidence that a premises licence holder has committed this offence.

### Status of the Guidance

3. This guidance has no binding effect on police officers who, within the terms of their force, orders and the law, remain operationally independent. The guidance is provided to support and assist them in interpreting and implementing Part 8 of the 2003 Act in the interests of public safety, the prevention of disorder and the reduction of anti-social behaviour. Part 8 of the 2003 Act can assist in the overall Government strategy to reduce anti-social behaviour.

4. It is recognised that this guidance cannot cater for every circumstance and that instances may arise where officers will determine the need to operate in ways which will not wholly conform to it. However, at all times, senior police officers deploying the powers in question should seek to ensure that their actions are appropriate, proportionate and necessary.

5. Police officers reading this guidance may also find it beneficial to familiarise themselves with the terms of:
- the explanatory notes accompanying the 2003 Act;
- Part 3 of the Environmental Protection Act 1990;
- The Noise Act 1996;
- The Clean Neighbourhoods and Environment Act 2005
- The Violent Crime Reduction Act 2006
- section 19 of the Criminal Justice and Police Act 2001
- section 1 of the Anti-Social Behaviour Act 2003

### General

6. Part 7 of the 2003 Act provides that licensees, designated premises supervisors, members or officers of clubs, premises users who have given a temporary event notice under Part 5 and certain staff of licensed premises commit offences if they:
- allow disorderly conduct on licensed premises; or
- sell alcohol to someone who is drunk;

7. These offences may also be committed by persons not necessarily selling alcohol themselves but allowing sales or supplies to take place. Running alongside these offences are powers afforded to licence holders and others to expel drunk and disorderly customers from premises.

8. The extended police powers in Part 8 of the 2003 Act underline the social responsibilities of those in the hospitality, leisure and entertainment industry and the requirement that they maintain order at their premises. The need to enforce these provisions will usually arise where there has been a failure to comply with the duties referred to above.

9. However, police officers should bear in mind that decisions to close licensed premises, or premises where a temporary event notice has effect, will almost always have a seriously damaging commercial impact on the business involved, and possibly on the livelihoods of licence holders and others or disrupt a community or charitable event that has been planned for a considerable period of time. It is therefore essential that orders are sought only where necessary to prevent disorder.

### Orders to close premises in an area experiencing disorder

10. Under section 160 of the 2003 Act a police officer of the rank of superintendent or above may ask a magistrates' court to make an order requiring all premises holding premises licences or subject to a temporary event notice which are situated at or near the place of the disorder or anticipated disorder to be closed for a period up to 24 hours. The court may not make such an order unless it is satisfied that it is necessary to prevent disorder. A constable may use necessary force to close any premises covered by such an order.

11. These orders should normally be sought where the police anticipate public order problems (very often fuelled by the ready availability of alcohol) as a result of intelligence or publicly available information, but may also be used in an emergency.

12. Events which might justify action under section 160 could include football fixtures with a history of public order problems; and demonstrations which are thought likely to be hijacked by extreme or violent groups. Where it is possible to anticipate disorder in this way, the courts should be involved and make the decision on the application of a police officer of the rank of superintendent or above as to whether widespread closure is justified.

13. When seeking an order under section 160 of the 2003 Act, the burden of proof will fall on the police to satisfy the court that their intelligence or evidence is sufficient to demonstrate that such action is necessary. Where serious disorder is anticipated, many holders of premises licences and premises users who have given temporary event notices will want to co-operate with the police, not least for the protection of their premises and customers. So far as possible, and where time is available, police officers should initially seek voluntary agreement to closure in an area for a particular period of time. The courts should therefore only be involved where other alternatives are not available.

### Closure orders for identified premises

14. Disorder and noise nuisance will more commonly arise in circumstances that cannot readily be anticipated. Section 161 of the 2003 Act provides that a senior police officer of the rank of inspector or above may make an order closing individual premises covered by premises licences or a temporary event notice for up to 24 hours where disorder is taking place, or is likely to take place imminently or a nuisance is being caused by noise emanating from the premises. These orders may only be made where it is necessary in the interests of public safety or to prevent the nuisance caused by noise coming from the premises. They should not be used where it has been possible to anticipate the disorder arising, as described above. The appropriate course then is to seek a court order in respect of an application under section 160 of the 2003 Act.

### Conduct of the premises licence holder

15. Section 161 of the 2003 Act also provides that the senior police officer must consider the conduct of the premises licence holder, manager, designated premises supervisor or premises user who has given a temporary event notice, before making a closure order. If they have acted incompetently, inadequately or actually provoked or caused the problems or, alternatively, have called the police in promptly and acted sensibly to try to prevent disorder or noise nuisance, the officer may take these factors into account.

16. In this context, it must be understood that the powers to close licensed premises are not a penalty to be imposed on the licence holder. Part 7 of the 2003 Act contains offences of allowing disorderly conduct on licensed premises for which, on conviction, a court may impose an appropriate penalty on a licence holder. Similarly, the Environmental Protection Act 1990, the Noise Act 1996 and the Clean Neighbourhoods and Environment Act 2005 provide for penalties to be imposed by the courts on those who are convicted of causing a statutory noise nuisance.

17. The powers in sections 161–170 of the 2003 Act are, first and foremost, designed to protect the public whether a licensee or manager or any other person is at fault or not. This means that even if the licence holder, managers or other persons have done all they can to prevent the disorder or noise nuisance, a senior police officer may on occasions, still believe that closure is necessary to safeguard the public or to prevent the public nuisance. These will be fine judgements, appropriately pitched at a senior police rank. But the police's overriding consideration should always be the public interest. On many occasions, other options will be available to the police, some of which are discussed below.

**Voluntary co-operation**

18. The police should, whenever possible, seek the voluntary co-operation of licensees, managers and others in resolving incidents of disorder, potential disorder and noise nuisance rather than move directly to a decision to use a closure order. Police officers should be aware that any decision to deploy the powers available to them to make a closure order under section 161 of the 2003 Act will almost inevitably lead, after an initial hearing before the courts, to a review of the licence by the licensing authority. This will involve determining whether or not it is necessary for the promotion of the licensing objectives to take any steps in relation to the licence, including revocation. A decision by the licensing authority to proceed on that basis will therefore involve police attendance at the hearing and the preparation of material relating to the review. Senior police officers will only want to commit such resources if necessary and justified in the public interest.

19. If police officers are aware that any premises are showing signs of problematic behaviour relating to disorder, excessive drunkenness or noise which is disturbing local residents, it is sensible to provide early warnings and reminders to licensees, managers and designated premises supervisors of their responsibilities and duties under licensing law; and of the police powers of closure. Similarly, where despite warnings, licensed premises exhibit problems over a period of time, but no single instance is sufficient in itself to justify closure action, it is open to the police to seek a review of the premises licence under Part 3 of the 2003 Act in the normal way.

20. Where a senior police officer of inspector rank or above reasonably believes that closure of a premises is necessary under the terms of the 2003 Act, police officers should advise either the licence holder, or designated premises supervisor, or premises user or manager of the premises immediately and, wherever possible, give them an opportunity to close the premises voluntarily, on police advice, until the following day. A closure order will normally only have to be made if police advice is disputed or rejected and it becomes necessary to take action to impose closure. When giving advice to close voluntarily, police officers should make clear that they are not engaging in a negotiation. The view of the senior police officer will be final until a court decides otherwise.

21. However, even if the licensee, designated premises supervisor, manager or premises user is willing to close voluntarily, it will remain open to the senior police officer to decide to serve a closure order, if they judge that to be the right course of action in all the circumstances. It is recognised that circumstances could arise which necessitate such action.

22. Against this background, police officers should also note that a decision not to make a closure order or to agree to voluntary closure will not prevent a later decision by the police to seek a review of the premises licence by a licensing authority, if that course of action is judged appropriate.

App 12

### "In the vicinity" of licensed premises

23. A closure order may be made on grounds of disorder on or 'in the vicinity' of and related to the premises. Whether or not an incident is "in the vicinity of" and "related to" the licensed premises are ultimately matters of fact to be decided by the courts. However, it is important to note the senior police officer making the closure order must have a reasonable belief that disorder in the vicinity of the premises is related to the premises and that closure must be "necessary in the interests of public safety". This issue also arises in the context of any extension of a closure order.

24. Some licensees and others may consider it unfair that they should be held accountable for incidents taking place outside their immediate control. However, as explained elsewhere, closure orders were not designed as penalties but as a means of ensuring public safety and the prevention of public nuisance.

25. It should also be noted that the interpretation of "in the vicinity" does not arise in the context of "nuisance caused by noise coming from premises" because section 161 of the 2003 Act requires that the noise is emanating from the premises rather than any other source. In other words, noise from the premises itself is relevant: noise from customers in the street beyond the premises cannot be taken into account.

### "Likely" disorder

26. A further question arises as to when any future disorder is likely to take place to justify a closure order being made. The 2003 Act requires that the disorder should be likely to be imminent. There also has to be a reasonable belief related to the particular licensed premises involved, which makes closure of those particular premises under this provision *necessary* in the interests of public safety. This means that the expected incident must be happening or be imminent, in which case closure of the licensed premises should actively diminish the probability that disorder will take place in the immediate future.

### "Public nuisance caused by noise coming from the premises"

27. The 2003 Act does not define the term "public nuisance". Parliament has decided not to constrain the interpretation of the term by providing a more restrictive definition. Whether or not there is "public nuisance" will depend upon the circumstances of the particular case. Ultimately any questions of interpretation will be decided by the courts. However, this means that senior police officers are required to judge reasonably whether the noise is causing a nuisance. Such judgements will inevitably have a subjective quality and officers will need to bring their experience to bear in making them.

28. It is important to note that the "noise" in question must be emitted from the licensed premises as defined, i.e. any area designated as such on the plan of the premises. This may include, in some (but not all) cases, a beer garden, courtyard or street terrace. Noise nuisance arising solely from people in the street outside the perimeter of the licensed premises would not be sufficient to justify the use of these powers, even if those making the noise occasionally enter the licensed premises to purchase alcohol, etc.

29. In addition, the power should only be used where the senior police officer reasonably believes that a nuisance is being caused to the public. Accordingly, the senior police officer should normally have cause to believe that particular individuals in the vicinity are being annoyed by the noise from the licensed premises. Liaison with local government enforcement officers with existing powers for controlling noise nuisance would therefore be beneficial.

30. It will ultimately be for senior police officers to decide, in the circumstances of any case, whether it is appropriate for them to deploy these powers, which are likely ultimately to lead to the review of the premises licence for the premises affected with the possibility of a licensing authority determining that it is necessary for the promotion of the licensing objectives to take steps in relation to that licence, which may include its revocation.

**Enforcing a closure order**

31. The 2003 Act does not require the licence holder or the police to clear the premises of customers following the service of a closure order. It is assumed that normally premises would empty, there being no purpose to the presence of customers if relevant items, licensable activities or facilities may no longer be sold, supplied or provided. However, a customer commits no offence if they are *not* asked to leave and remain on the premises. The closure relates to the carrying on of the licensable activities. The licence holder, premises user, designated premises supervisor or manager of the premises similarly commit no offence arising from the mere presence of such an individual. However, if an individual who is drunk or disorderly is asked to leave by a constable, a licence holder or others and then refuses to leave, they become liable to prosecution. Where a police officer is asked for assistance to remove such a customer, the officer is under a statutory duty to afford that assistance.

32. The lack of any duty on customers to leave the premises automatically following the service of a closure order is important. However, it would be open to the police to propose a phased emptying of premises for the purpose of dispersing, for example, disorderly gangs separately or because it is in the interests of public safety to keep law-abiding customers inside for a temporary period while troublemakers outside are dispersed by the police.

33. It should also be noted that "premises" for the purposes of the Act includes any place. Some premises licences and temporary event notices relate to places wholly or mainly in the open air, like a park or recreation ground. If the police consider it necessary to clear such an area, they will need to consider carefully the resource implications of enforcement, particularly where there are a large number of ways of accessing the area.

34. The police officers involved should also recognise that closing premises will sometimes involve putting a potentially volatile and disgruntled group of customers onto the streets. In this context, where possible, it is good practice to ensure that other licensed premises nearby are warned of the action being taken and of licence holders' and others' obligations not to allow disorderly conduct on their premises. As stated above, under the 2003 Act, police officers are under a duty, when requested by a licence holder or other person as referred to above, to assist in ensuring that drunken or disorderly persons are expelled from licensed premises, and police officers should therefore offer assistance when necessary in preventing the entry of troublemakers to other licensed premises who might be seeking to cause new problems elsewhere.

35. Police officers are also reminded that, particularly where large capacity venues are involved, they may need additional police assistance to clear the resulting crowd and the availability of that assistance should be considered before any decision is made to make a closure order.

**Length of police closure order**

36. Subject to very limited exceptions, the duration of the order under section 161 of the 2003 Act cannot exceed 24 hours. However, it is important to note that this does not mean that the length of the closure should automatically be set for 24 hours on every occasion. The criteria for making a closure order places an obligation on the senior police officer to close the premises for the period they estimate it would take to end the threat to public safety, or as the case may be, the nuisance to the public. In practice, therefore, closure orders could last between 30 minutes and 24 hours depending on the circumstances of each case. An extension to that closure period can be made only if the senior police officer reasonably believes that the court would not have determined its consideration by the end of that period and certain conditions are met. Those conditions are the same as the circumstances which gave rise to the closure order. The extension may be for a further period of up to 24 hours from the end of the closure period.

37. If, for example, a closure is made at 9pm on a Monday evening because of disorder caused by gangs fighting in a public house, closure might only be appropriate for up to the time when the premises licence requires the premises to close, perhaps midnight. This could be because the senior police officer reasonably believes that there is a threat of gang members (those not arrested) returning to the premises before closing time but after the police have left. However, if the threat is not expected to have subsided by closing time, it may be appropriate to impose a closure for a period extending into the following day.

### The "manager" of the premises

38. The 2003 Act refers to the "manager of the premises" who is defined as any person who works in the relevant premises in a capacity, whether paid or unpaid, which gives them authority to close the premises. This is particularly relevant to the arrangements for serving a closure order. It is not therefore relevant whether or not the individual has the expression "manager" in their job title or description. If the holder of a premises licence or the designated premises supervisor or premises user has left any member of staff in charge of the premises, with responsibility at that time for compliance with the licensing laws, that person will normally have been given delegated authority to close the premises. Accordingly, the individual could therefore be served with notice of a closure order.

### Service of closure orders when a decision has been made remotely

39. Where a senior police officer makes a decision to close licensed premises in accordance with the 2003 Act, notice of the closure order, providing the required written details, may be served by *any constable* on the holder of the premises licence, the designated premises supervisor, premises user or the manager of the relevant premises. The senior police officer does not have to be present at the premises to authorise service of an order, but may make a decision on the basis of information supplied by other police officers. In this case, the senior police officer remains accountable for the decision. This is particularly important in rural areas where an inspector might otherwise need to make a seventy mile round trip to consider making an order allowing an unreasonable period to pass during which public safety might be at risk. A specimen of a closure order is attached to this guidance.

40. Senior police officers should, as a matter of good practice, attempt to attend wherever possible in order to make a full and personal assessment. Parliament considered that only officers of these ranks and experience should make these decisions because of the serious potential consequences of the decision made. As explained above, it is of course recognised that it will be difficult for officers, particularly in rural force areas, to attend on every occasion. Where the relevant senior officer cannot attend, it will be important that the information passed to the relevant senior officer is comprehensive and contemporaneously recorded, so that they can be clear about the reasons for closure when or if required to present them to the relevant magistrates' court.

### Service of closure orders generally

41. Notice of a closure order must always be given in writing. "Given", in this context, is the delivery of the notice to the individual. This should normally involve personal service and means therefore that the notice should normally be handed by a police constable to the holder of the premises licence, designated premises supervisor, premises user or the manager of the premises. If any of these persons refuses to accept the written notice of a closure order, the fact should be noted so that it might be made known to the relevant magistrates' court at the hearing that will follow. The written notice should then be left in plain sight of the relevant person on whom it is being served. They should also be advised orally that the notice contains details of their rights and duties under the 2003 Act.

### Relationship with local licensees and managers

42. It is important that the closure powers should not in any way be allowed to drive a wedge between the police and local licence holders, designated premises supervisors and managers. It would be damaging to the police's capacity to control public order and drunkenness, if any of these persons were reluctant to call the police to attend when incidents are taking place because they feared that the police would close their premises. Licence holders and others should be encouraged to give the police early warning of developing problems, where appropriate allowing police intervention before an incident is allowed to get out of hand. The Government fully supports local initiatives like Pubwatch and wishes to see them develop and thrive.

43. It is recognised that the role of the police in enforcing licensing law will vary between force areas. For all police forces, resources will be a key issue and senior officers will have to make difficult decisions about prioritisation according to the prevailing circumstances in any

area. Licensees should know what is expected of them by local police officers in terms of clear standards with regard to the prevention of crime and disorder, particularly alcohol-related crime and disorder and anti-social behaviour. Police officers should therefore always be willing to offer advice to licensees and others on problems associated with these matters.

### Nearby licensed premises

44. Where disorder is taking place or is expected to take place imminently in the vicinity of several adjacent or closely situated premises, there are likely to be occasions when the responsible senior police officer reasonably concludes that the closure of all the closely situated licensed premises is necessary in the interests of public safety. However, the same course of action in the case of each of the premises should not necessarily be automatic. For example, if one of the designated premises supervisors is prepared to close their premises voluntarily or has been more proactive than another in seeking to prevent disorder, the senior police officer may reasonably decide not to make a closure order for those premises, while deciding to impose the closure of others. Where several closures are pursued simultaneously, a separate closure order must be made for each of the licensed premises.

### Noise nuisance and liaison with the local authority

45. The powers include the capacity to close licensed premises to prevent nuisance to the public which is the result of noise coming from the premises. The 2003 Act does not define what constitutes nuisance and it will bear its common law meaning. Ultimately, nuisance will be a matter of fact to be decided by the courts in any case. However, senior police officers will need to use their own experience and common sense to decide when noise levels reaching outside the premises have become unacceptable.

46. The enforcement of the law relating to statutory noise nuisance legislation is primarily a matter for local authority officers, sometimes working in tandem with police officers. Their powers to take quick action to resolve noise nuisance are however limited, particularly where the noise from commercial premises is caused by people rather than amplified electronic equipment. The powers in the 2003 Act offer a means of resolving noise nuisance problems from licensed premises quickly.

47. The 2003 Act anticipates that any noise coming from the premises should be disturbing members of public, for example, in the street or residing locally – otherwise it could not constitute a nuisance. In practice therefore, it is likely to be that the police will usually take action under their powers following complaints made by the general public. Such complaints may, in certain circumstances, be channelled to the police by local authority officers who may initially be the natural point of contact for a complainant. However, the decision as to whether the noise constitutes a nuisance for the purposes of the exercise of the powers in the 2003 Act is a matter for the senior police officer to decide, and no formal complaint from any individual is necessary before the powers may be exercised. Given their experience of noise problems, the officer may find it helpful to consult local authority enforcement officers, if available, before making a decision about the level of noise involved. In addition, under the Environmental Protection Act 1990, local authority enforcement officers have powers to confiscate, for example, noisy equipment which may be causing the problem and avoid the need to close the premises. On occasions, such consultation in respect of an incident which is ongoing may prove impossible without an unacceptable delay.

48. There is therefore some advantage in police forces discussing these matters generally with the local authority to draw on their experience and establish guidelines for officers about noise issues. Chief officers of police may find it valuable and helpful to agree a protocol with the local authority for the handling of noise nuisance issues associated with premises licensed under the 2003 Act or in respect of premises operating under temporary event notices. This would enable a consistent approach to be taken by the police and other local authority enforcement officers.

49. Where problems are noise related, there should often be scope for resolving the problem without the need to impose a closure order. In this context, police officers should consider voluntary co-operation. For example, noise problems can arise during summer months because of doors or windows left open or customers drinking or enjoying entertainment in the garden

area of the premises. It would be open to the police to request the licensee, designated premises supervisor, premises user or manager of the premises to close the doors and windows, or to require customers to remain inside. If they comply and the officer is then satisfied that these actions would prevent further nuisance to the public, there may be no need to make a closure order.

### Stating the effects of sections 162 to 168 of the 2003 Act

50. A closure order must contain:
- details of the premises which are to be closed;
- the period for which the order is requiring them to be closed for up to 24 hours;
- the grounds or reasons for the decision; and
- the effect of sections 162 to 168 of the 2003 Act.

51. The Annex to this guidance provides a specimen of what a closure order should look like, and provides a statement of the effect of sections 162 to 168 of the 2003 Act. It is open to the police forces to take their own legal advice as to what the statement should include. However, it is important that it covers the crucial areas shown in the Annex and in particular, that licence holders and others fully understand the consequences of committing the offences associated with failure to comply with a closure order made by the police and extended by the police or the courts.

### Anti-Social Behaviour Act 2003

52. Police, licensing authorities and licensees should also be aware of the power available under the Anti-Social Behaviour Act 2003 to close premises where there is the production, supply or use of class A drugs and serious nuisance or disorder. This power provides an extra tool to the police to enable rapid action against a premises where there is a Class A drug problem, enabling its closure in as little as 48 hours should this be necessary. Police authorities are advised to consult the Notes of Guidance on the use of this power (Home Office, 2004) available on the Home Office website. These powers are also be covered in brief in 'Safer Clubbing' produced by the Home Office and the London Drug Policy Forum (www.drugs.gov.uk).

# ANNEX

## [SPECIMEN]

## CLOSURE ORDER MADE UNDER SECTION 161 OF THE LICENSING ACT 2003

Date and Time:_____

**Police Force:**_____

**Name and rank of Senior Police Officer making the order:**

_____

**Premises to be closed:**

_____

_____

**Period of closure (until – time and date):**

_____

**Reason (grounds) for Closure:**

_____

_____

_____

**Attention is drawn to the attached Notes which form part of this order.**

**1 Name of person to whom notice of the order has been given and his or her capacity in relation to the premises:**

_____

**Signature of Person to whom notice of the order has been given:**_____

**Notes to be served with specimen closure order:**

A senior police officer has decided to make this closure order under the terms of section 161 of the Licensing Act 2003, requiring the relevant premises specified in the order to be closed for the period of time specified in the order.

Your attention is drawn to section 161(6) of the 2003 Act. This makes it an offence for a person, without reasonable excuse, to permit relevant premises to be open in contravention of this closure order or any extension of it, and any person found guilty of such an offence shall be liable to a fine not exceeding £20,000 or to imprisonment for a term not exceeding three months or to both.

By virtue of section 171(2) and (3) of the 2003 Act, relevant premises are to be regarded as open, for the purposes of this order, if any person other than the holder of the premises licence for the premises, any designated premises supervisor, the premises user in connection with a temporary event notice, a manager of the premises, any person who usually lives at the premises or any member of the family of any of the former, enters the premises and buys, or is otherwise supplied with food or drink or any item usually sold on the premises or, while he is on the premises, they are used for the provision of regulated entertainment.

**Sections 162–168 of the Licensing Act 2003**

This part of the closure order now explains the effects of sections 162–168 of the 2003 Act as required by section 161(4)(d) of that Act.

**Initial hearing**

- The senior police officer who made the closure order is under a statutory duty to apply to the magistrates' court for it to consider the order, or any extension of it, as soon as reasonably practicable after it comes into force.
- The magistrate's court must consider the closure order made by a senior police officer as soon as practicable after receiving the application, by holding a hearing and determining whether to exercise its powers under section 165 of the 2003 Act.
- Under law on human rights, you are entitled to attend the hearing, to be legally represented, and to make representations to the court before any decision is taken. The chief executive to the magistrates' court will be able to advise you about the details of the procedures which apply in your area.
- A discretion is provided for the magistrates to revoke the order and any extension of it, if it is still in force; or to order that the premises remain closed or be closed until a review of the licence has taken place; or to order that the premises remain closed until a review of the licence has taken place but subject to such exceptions or conditions that they may specify. The last of these powers would enable the court to allow premises to re-open but subject to certain new terms and conditions which they may decide to impose.
- When deciding whether the premises should be allowed to re-open or remain closed, the court must consider whether closure of the premises is necessary in the interests of public safety to prevent disorder or likely disorder (where the closure order was made for this reason) or to prevent further public nuisance caused by noise (where the closure order was made for this reason).
- It is an offence for any person who permits the premises to open in contravention of an order made by the magistrates for the closure of the premises, and the 2003 Act provides for an offender on conviction to be liable to a fine not exceeding £20,000 or to three months imprisonment or to both.
- It is an offence for any person who fails to comply with or does an act in contravention of any order made by the magistrates in relation to the premises in these proceedings, and provides for an offender on conviction to be liable to a fine not exceeding £20,000 or to three months imprisonment or to both.
- Where, for whatever reason, the courts are unable to consider a closure order before it expires, the senior police officer concerned may extend the order for up to another period of 24 hours if certain circumstances obtain. These are that the officer reasonably believes that the closure of the premises continues to be necessary in the interests of public safety to prevent disorder, or likely disorder or to prevent further public nuisance caused by noise. Such extensions can be made on an indefinite number of occasions.
- The senior police officer is required to give notice to the holder of the premises licence for the premises, or any designated premises supervisor, or the premises user in connection with a temporary event notice, or a manager of the premises of such extensions of the closure order.
- The senior police officer may cancel the closure order or any extension of it at any time after it has been issued, but before it has been considered by the court. In this case, the court must still consider the closure order originally served, and the licensing authority will still be obliged to review the premises licence.
- The senior police officer is required to cancel the order if they reasonably believe that closure of the premises is no longer necessary in the interests of public safety to prevent disorder or to prevent further public nuisance; and to notify the holder of the premises licence for the premises, or any designated premises supervisor, or the premises user in connection with a temporary event notice, or a manager of the premises.

**Review hearing**

- The licensing authority must review the premises licence in respect of the premises no later than 28 days after it is notified of the magistrates' courts' determination. The authority is empowered, if necessary to promote the licensing objectives, to modify the conditions of the premises licence, exclude a licensable activity from the scope of the licence, remove the designated premises supervisor from the licence, suspend the licence for a period not exceeding three months or revoke the licence. Their consideration is not confined solely to the incident which gave rise to the service of the closure order. They may examine any issues which are relevant to the promotion of the licensing objectives.

- Where a decision has been made to revoke the premises licence, the decision has no effect until the expiry of the time permitted for appealing against the decision; and if an appeal is made until the appeal is disposed of.

# APPENDIX 13: GUIDANCE ISSUED BY DCMS ON EXPEDITED/SUMMARY LICENCE REVIEWS UNDER THE LICENSING ACT 2003 (OCTOBER 2007)

## INTRODUCTION

1.1 This Guidance explains how to use new provisions in the Licensing Act 2003 (the 2003 Act) which allow a quick process for attaching interim conditions to a licence and a fast track licence review when the police consider that the premises concerned is associated with serious crime or serious disorder (or both). These provisions were inserted at section 53A of the 2003 Act by the Violent Crime Reduction Act 2006 and came into force on 1 October 2007. This guidance has no statutory basis but is intended to assist police forces and licensing authorities when considering using the new procedures.

1.2 The new powers apply only where a premises licence authorises the sale of alcohol. They do not apply in respect of other premises licences, nor to those operating under a club premises certificate. The purpose of the new powers is to complement existing procedures in the Licensing Act 2003 for tackling crime and disorder associated with licensed premises. The existing powers, in Part 8 of the 2003 Act, provide for the instant closure of premises by the police in some circumstances, and the review of premises' licences by the licensing authority. The new powers, which are in Part 3, are aimed at tackling serious crime and serious disorder, in particular (but not exclusively) the use of guns and knives.

1.3 The new powers will allow:

- the police to trigger a fast track process to review a premises licence where the police consider that the premises are associated with **serious** crime or **serious** disorder (or both); and
- the licensing authority to respond by taking interim steps quickly, **where appropriate**, pending a full review.

1.4 In summary, the process is:

- a local chief officer of police may apply to the licensing authority for an expedited review of a premises licence where a senior police officer has issued a certificate stating that in his/her opinion the premises are associated with serious crime or serious disorder (or both);
- on receipt of the application and the certificate the licensing authority must within 48 hours consider whether it is necessary to take interim steps pending determination of the review of the premises licence – the authority must in any event undertake a review within 28 days of receipt of the application.

1.5 The range of options open to the licensing authority at the interim steps stage are:

- modification of the conditions of the premises licence;
- the exclusion of the sale of alcohol by retail (or other licensable activities) from the scope of the licence;
- removal of the designated premises supervisor from the licence; and
- suspension of the licence.

1.6 Following the full licence review the Licensing Authority may do any of the above or may revoke the licence.

1.7 The purpose of this guidance is to:

- set out the circumstances where the power might be used; and
- outline the process and the steps at each stage.

1.8 The process is set out in the diagram at Annex A.

## THE STEPS

### 2. Triggering the expedited review

2.1 Section 53A of the Licensing Act 2003 determines who may apply for an expedited review and the circumstances where it might be used.

**Application for expedited review**

2.2   The chief officer of police for the local area may apply to the relevant licensing authority for
      an expedited licence review if a **senior member** of the force has issued a **certificate** that in
      his/her opinion a licensed premises is associated with **serious crime or serious disorder
      (or both).**

2.3   The key definitions used above are:

   • **Senior member of the force:** this must be an officer of the rank of superintendent or
     above.

   • **Certificate:** this is a formal note which identifies the licensed premises and includes a
     signed statement by a senior officer that he believes the premises is associated with
     serious crime, serious disorder or both. **This form is not prescribed in legislation.
     However, a sample form which forces may wish to adopt is attached at annex B to
     this guidance.**

   • **Serious crime:** The tests to determine the kinds of conduct that amount to serious crime
     are set out in Section 81(3)(a) and (b) of the Regulation of Investigatory Powers Act
     (2000). Those tests are: (a) that the conduct constitutes an offence for which a person 21
     years of age or over with no previous convictions could reasonably be expected to be
     sentenced to imprisonment for 3 or more years or (b) that the conduct involves the use
     of violence, results in substantial financial gain or is conduct by a large number of
     persons in pursuit of a common purpose.

   • **Serious Disorder:** There is no definitive list of behaviours that constitute serious dis-
     order, and the matter is one for judgment by the local police. The phrase should be
     understood in its ordinary English sense, as is the case under section 12 of the Public
     Order Act 1986, where it is also used.

   • **The Application for a summary or expedited review:** this is an application made by,
     or on behalf of, the Chief Officer of Police under s.53A of the Licensing Act 2003. The
     application must be made on a form prescribed by Schedule 8A to the Licensing Act
     2003 (Premises licences and club premises certificates) Regulations 2005 (SI 2005/42).
     Schedule 8A was inserted by the Licensing Act 2003 (Summary Review of Premises
     Licences) Regulations 2007 (SI 2007/2502), and must be accompanied by the certificate
     issued by a senior officer. The form which must be used is reproduced in annex C of this
     guidance.

2.4   In deciding whether to sign a certificate the senior officer will want to consider the follow-
      ing (as applicable):

   • the track record of the licensed premises concerned and whether the police have
     previously had cause to give advice about serious criminal or disorderly conduct (or
     the likelihood of such conduct) attributable to activities taking place on the premises –
     it is not expected that this power will be used as a first response to a problem;

   • the nature of the likely crime and/or disorder – is the potential incident sufficiently
     serious to warrant using this power?

   • should an alternative power be deployed? Is the incident sufficiently serious to warrant
     use of the powers in Sections 161–165 in Part 8 of the Licensing Act 2003 to close the
     premises? Or could the police trigger a standard licence review to address the problem?
     Alternatively, could expedited reviews be used in conjunction with other powers? For
     example modifying licence conditions following the use of a closure power.

   • what added value will use of the expedited process bring? How would any interim
     steps that the licensing authority might take effectively address the problem?

2.5   It is recommended that these points are addressed in the Chief Officer's application to the
      licensing authority. In particular, it is important to explain why other powers or actions are
      not felt to be appropriate. It is up to the police to decide whether to include this information
      in the certificate or in section 4 of the application for summary review. The police will also
      have an opportunity later to make representations in relation to the full review.

2.6   In triggering the process, the police will wish to take into account the fact that an intended
      use of the power is to tackle the use of dangerous weapons and the violence they fuel. For
      example, in appropriate circumstances the police might wish to make representations to the
      licensing authority suggesting that they modify the conditions of premises' licence to

require searches of customers for offensive weapons upon entry. Under the new power this could be done on an interim basis, pending a full hearing of the issues within the prescribed 28-day timeframe.

2.7 Similarly, the power could, **where appropriate**, be used to reduce the risk of injury caused by glass by requiring the adoption of a safer alternative (but see paras 3.6 and 3.7 below).

2.8 However, as the explanatory notes that accompanied the Violent Crime Reduction Act state: 'These are selective measures. It is not the aim to require all licensed premises to undertake these searches or use toughened glass. Rather, the policy aim is to provide a selective tool, to be used proportionately, to limit this condition to those pubs that are at risk either because police intelligence shows there is a risk of knives/guns being carried or because crime and disorder has occurred on the premises'.

### 3. The Licensing Authority and the interim steps

3.1 Within 48 hours of receipt of the chief officer's application, the Licensing Authority must give the premises licence holder and responsible authorities a copy of the application for review and a copy of the certificate, and must also consider whether it is necessary to take interim steps. When calculating the 48 hour period any non-working day can be disregarded.[1]

3.2 The licensing authority may wish to consult the police about the steps that it thinks necessary, pending the determination of the review, to address the immediate problems with the premises, in particular the likelihood of serious crime and/or serious disorder. The licensing authority may consider the interim steps without the holder of the premises licence having been given an opportunity to make representations. (This does not, of course mean that the authority *cannot* afford such an opportunity if it thinks it appropriate and feasible to do so in all the circumstances).

3.3 The determination of interim steps is not a matter that may be delegated to an officer of the licensing authority. The relevant decisions must be taken by the relevant licensing sub-committee, or by the authority acting as a whole (see new section 10(4)(via) of the 2003 Act). It should also be noted that there is no requirement for a formal hearing in order to take interim steps. This means that the relevant sub committee members can communicate by telephone or other remote means in order to reach a decision. A written record should always be produced as soon as possible after a decision is reached.

3.4 The interim steps that the licensing authority must consider taking are:
- the modification of the conditions of the premises licence;
- the exclusion of the sale of alcohol by retail (or other licensable activities) from the scope of the licence;
- the removal of the designated premises supervisor from the licence; and
- the suspension of the licence.

Modification of the conditions of the premises licence can include altering or modifying existing conditions or adding any new conditions, including those that restrict the times at which licensable activities authorised by the licence can take place. Further examples of possible licensing conditions, including those aimed at tackling crime and disorder, can be found in the Guidance to Licensing Authorities issued by the Secretary of State under section 182 of the Licensing Act 2003.

3.5 If the licensing authority decides to take steps at the interim stage then:
- the decision takes effect immediately, or as soon after then as the licensing authority directs; but
- the licensing authority must give immediate notice of its decision and its reasons for doing so to the holder of the premises licence and the chief officer of police who made the application. The Act does not specify that the immediate notice has to be in writing.

---

1   This means that, for example, if the application was received at 3pm on a Friday, the 48 hour period would cover the remaining 9 hours on that Friday and the remaining 39 hours starting on the Monday morning (provided it was not a bank holiday). In this case the licensing authority would have to decide on interim steps by 3pm on the Tuesday.

However, in an individual case the licensing authority may consider that the need for immediate communication at least initially requires a non-written approach, such as a telephone call. This may happen when, for example, the authority decides that the decision should have immediate effect. In such a case, the decision and the reasons for it should be explained clearly and in full to the licence-holder (or someone who is empowered to act for the licence-holder), and the call followed up as soon as possible with a written version of the decision and the reasons (for example by email or fax) which is identical, or not significantly different from the version given by phone.

3.6   The licensing authority in deciding when its decision on interim steps should take effect should consider the practical implications of compliance in relation to the premises. For example to comply with a modification of the conditions of a licence that requires employment of door supervisors, those running the premises may need some time to recruit appropriately qualified and accredited staff.

3.7   In addition, very careful consideration needs to be given to interim steps which would require significant cost or permanent or semi-permanent adjustments to a premises which would be difficult to remove if the outcome of the subsequent full review was to withdraw or modify those steps. For example, making structural changes, installing additional CCTV or replacing all glassware with safer alternatives may be valid steps, but might be disproportionate if they are not likely to be deemed necessary following the full review (or any subsequent appeal). The focus for interim steps should be on the immediate measures that are necessary to prevent serious crime or serious disorder occurring. In some circumstances, it might be better to seek suspension of the licence pending the full review, rather than imposing a range of costly conditions or permanent adjustments.

## 4. Making representations against the interim steps

4.1   The premises licence holder may make representations against the interim steps taken by the licensing authority. There is no time limit for the premises licence holder to make representations on the interim steps, although in practice this would at some point be superseded by the full review which would have to be completed within 28 days of the application being received by the licensing authority. On receipt of the representations the licensing authority must (if the representations are not withdrawn) hold a hearing within 48 hours of receipt. When calculating the 48 hour period any non-working day can be disregarded.

4.2   The licensing authority must give advance notice of the hearing to the premises licence holder and the chief officer of police. Given that these measures are designed to deal with serious crime and serious disorder on an interim basis only, the process is designed to avoid delay and, as such, significant portions of the Licensing Act 2003 (Hearings) Regulations 2005 (SI 2005/44) are disapplied in order to streamline the hearing process. One result of this is that licensing authority cannot adjourn the hearing to a later date if the licence holder fails to attend at the scheduled time, as is the case under the normal review procedure. And as is the case with that procedure, the licence holder does not have to be present for the hearing to take place. In addition, there is no timescale for notifying the licence holder of the hearing under the modified Hearings regulations, providing the notification takes place before the hearing is held. However, it is imperative that the licence holder be given as much notice as is possible in the circumstances to afford him or her the maximum practicable opportunity to attend the hearing. Licensing authorities should bear in mind that the usual principles of public law decision-making will apply to interim determinations, in a form that has regard to the statutory context of an expedited process.

4.3   At the hearing the licensing authority must:

- consider whether the interim steps are necessary for the promotion of the licensing objectives; and
- determine whether to withdraw or modify the steps taken.

4.4   When considering the case the licensing authority must take into account:

- the senior officer's certificate that accompanied the application;
- the chief officer's representations (if any); and
- any representations made by the premises licence holder.

4.5 There is no right of appeal to a magistrates' court against the licensing authority's decision at this stage.

## 5. The review of the premises licence

5.1 The licensing authority must hold a review of the premises licence within 28 days of receipt of the chief officer's application. This must take place even if the chief officer asks to withdraw his application or representations. At the hearing, the licensing authority must consider:

- what steps it considers necessary for the promotion of the licensing objectives; and
- consider what steps should be taken to secure the promotion of the licensing objectives including whether the interim steps should be made permanent.

5.2 The steps the licensing authority can take are:

- the modification of the conditions of the premises licence;
- the exclusion of the sale of alcohol by retail (or other licensable activities) from the scope of the licence;
- the removal of the designated premises supervisor from the licence;
- the suspension of the licence for a period not exceeding 3 months; and
- the revocation of the licence.

Modification of the conditions of the premises licence can include altering or modifying existing conditions or adding any new conditions, including those that restrict the times at which licensable activities authorised by the licence can take place. Further examples of possible licensing conditions, including those aimed at tackling crime and disorder, can be found in the Guidance to Licensing Authorities issued by the Secretary of State under section 182 of the Licensing Act 2003.

5.3 The licensing authority must:

- advertise the review inviting representations from interested parties[2] for no less than seven consecutive days, by notice as described in regulation 38 of the Licensing Act 2003 (Premises licences and club premises certificates) Regulations 2005 (SI 2005/42), and, if applicable, on the authority's website (see regulation 38(1)(b) of the above Regulations). The relevant notices should be published on the day after the day of receipt of the chief officer's application.
- advertise that any representations made by the premises licence holder, responsible authority and interested parties should be submitted to the licensing authority within 10 working days of the advertisement of the review appearing.
- give formal notice of the hearing no later than five working days before the day or first day on which the hearing is to be held to the premises licence holder and to every responsible authority[3].

5.4 A party shall give to the authority a notice no later than two working days before the day or the first day on which the hearing is to be held stating –

- whether he intends to attend or be represented at the hearing;
- whether he considers a hearing to be unnecessary.
- whether he would like permission for any other person (other than the person he intends to represent him at the hearing) to appear at the hearing and, if so, explain on which points that person will be able to contribute.

5.5 The regulations relating to hearings are set out in the Licensing Act 2003 (Hearings) Regulations 2005 (S.I. 2005/44). These Regulations apply to final hearings under the new power in a similar way to hearings following closure orders under section 167 of the Licensing Act (it should be emphasised that the truncated version of the Regulations described in paragraph 4.2 above applies to interim hearings only). The issues dealt with by the Regulations include who can make representations and what those representations can be about. It is therefore possible for interested parties or responsible authorities to make representations in relation

---

2   Interested parties are defined under section 13 (3) of the Licensing Act 2003.
3   Responsible authorities are defined under section 13(4) of the Licensing Act 2003.

to any of the licensing objectives, not just crime and disorder. Similarly, where it is in the public interest, the regulations relating to the exclusion of individuals from hearings, or conducting the hearing in private, will apply.

5.6 The licensing authority must take into account any relevant representations made. Relevant representations are those that:

- relate to one or more of the licensing objectives;
- have not been withdrawn; and
- are made by the premises licence holder, a responsible authority or an interested party (who is not also a responsible authority).

5.7 The licensing authority must notify its decision and the reasons for making it to:

- the holder of the premises licence;
- any person who made relevant representations; and
- the chief officer of police who made the original application.

## 6. Right of Appeal

6.1 An appeal may be made within 21 days of the licence holder being notified of the licensing authority's decision to a magistrates' court. An appeal may be made by the premises licence holder, the chief officer of police and/or any other person who made relevant representations.

6.2 The decision of the licensing authority, following the review hearing, will not have effect until the end of the period allowed for appeal, or until the appeal is disposed of. Any interim steps taken will remain in force over these periods.

## EXPEDITED LICENCE REVIEWS: MAIN STEPS

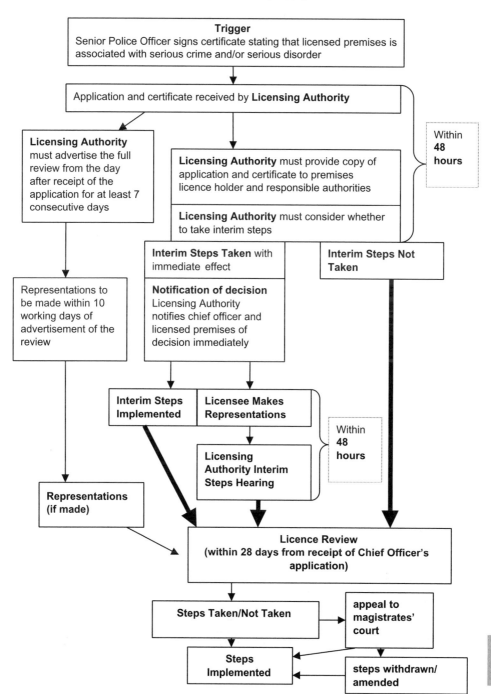

**[insert name and address of police force]**

**CERTIFICATE UNDER SECTION 53A(1)(b) OF THE LICENSING ACT 2003**

I hereby certify that in my opinion the premises described below are associated with serious crime / serious disorder / both serious crime and serious disorder[4].

*Premises*[5]:

Premises licence number (if known):

Name of premises supervisor (if known):

I am a ...........................................[6] in the ................................................ police force.

I am giving this certificate because I am of the opinion that other procedures under the Licensing Act are inappropriate in this case, because[7]:

......................................................................................................................
(Signed)                            (Date)

---

[4] Delete as applicable.
[5] Include business name and address and any other relevant identifying details.
[6] Insert rank of officer giving the certificate, which must be superintendent or above.
[7] Give a brief description of why other procedures such as a standard review process are thought to be inappropriate, e.g. the degree of seriousness of the crime and/or disorder, the past history of compliance in relation to the premises concerned.

ANNEX C

FORM FOR APPLYING FOR A SUMMARY LICENCE REVIEW

*[Insert name and address of relevant licensing authority and its reference number (optional)]*

**Application for the review of a premises licence under section 53A of the Licensing Act 2003 (premises associated with serious crime or disorder)**

---

PLEASE READ THE FOLLOWING INSTRUCTIONS FIRST

Before completing this form please read the guidance notes at the end of the form. If you are completing the form by hand please write legibly in block capitals. In all cases ensure that your answers are inside the boxes and written in black ink. **Use additional sheets if necessary.**

I.................................................................... **[on behalf of] the chief officer of police for the** .................................................................... **police area apply for the review of a premises licence under section 53A of the Licensing Act 2003.**

**1. *Premises details:***

| |
|---|
| Postal address of premises, or if none or not known, ordnance survey map reference or description: <br><br> Post town: <br><br> Post code (if known): |

**2. *Premises licence details:***

| |
|---|
| Name of premises licence holder (if known): <br><br> Number of premises licence (if known): |

**3. *Certificate under section 53A(1)(b) of the Licensing Act 2003* [*Please read guidance note 1*]:**

| |
|---|
| I confirm that a certificate has been given by a senior member of the police force for the police area above that in his opinion the above premises are associated with serious crime or disorder or both, and the certificate accompanies this application. *(Please tick the box to confirm)*     ☐ |

**4. *Details of association of the above premises with serious crime, serious disorder or both:***
[Please read guidance note 2]

| |
|---|
| |

App 13

**Signature of applicant:**
**Date:**
**Capacity:**

**Contact details for matters concerning this application:**

**Address:**
**Telephone number(s):**
**email:**

Notes for guidance:

1. A certificate of the kind mentioned in the form must accompany the application in order for it to be valid under the terms of the Licensing Act 2003. The certificate must explicitly state the senior officer's opinion that the premises in question are associated with serious crime, serious disorder or both.
Serious crime is defined by reference to section 81 of the Regulation of Investigatory Powers Act 2000. In summary, it means:
– conduct that amounts to one or more criminal offences for which a person who has attained the age of eighteen and has no previous convictions could reasonably be expected to be sentenced to imprisonment for a term of three years or more; or
– conduct that amounts to one or more criminal offences and involves the use of violence, results in substantial financial gain or is conduct by a large number of persons in pursuit of a common purpose.
Serious disorder is not defined in legislation, and so bears its ordinary English meaning.

2. Briefly describe the circumstances giving rise to the opinion that the above premises are associated with serious crime, serious disorder, or both.

# INDEX